HANDBOOK
of
COGNITION

HANDBOOK
of
COGNITION

Edited by
KOEN LAMBERTS
and ROBERT L. GOLDSTONE

LEARNING
RESOURCES
CENTRE

**SAGE** Publications
London • Thousand Oaks • New Delhi

153

6382

First published 2005

Reprinted 2006

Apart from any fair dealing for the purposes of research or
private study, or criticism or review, as permitted under the
Copyright, Designs and Patents Act, 1988, this publication may
be reproduced, stored or transmitted in any form, or by any means,
only with the prior permission in writing of the publishers, or in
the case of reprographic reproduction, in accordance with the
terms of licences issued by the Copyright Licensing Agency.
Inquiries concerning reproduction outside those terms should be
sent to the publishers.

SAGE Publications Ltd
1 Oliver's Yard
55 City Road
London EC1Y 1SP

SAGE Publications Inc.
2455 Teller Road
Thousand Oaks, California 91320

SAGE Publications India Pvt Ltd
B-42, Panchsheel Enclave
Post Box 4109
New Delhi 110 017

British Library Cataloguing in Publication data
A catalogue record for this book is available from
the British Library

ISBN-10 0-7619-7277-3 (hbk)   ISBN-13 978-0-7619-7277-8 (hbk)

Library of Congress Control Number available

Typeset by C&M Digitals (P) Ltd., Chennai, India
Printed in Great Britain by The Cromwell Press Ltd., Trowbridge, Wiltshire

Contents

List of Contributors

Claus Bundesen is Professor of Cognitive Psychology at the University of Copenhagen, Director of the Centre for Visual Cognition in Copenhagen, and Director of the Danish Graduate School of Psychology. He is a member of the executive committees of the International Association for the Study of Attention and Performance and the European Society for Cognitive Psychology, Editor in Chief of the *European Journal of Cognitive Psychology*, and member of the editorial boards of *Psychological Review*, *Psychological Research* and *Visual Cognition*. His achievements include measurement of effects of visual size in pattern recognition and apparent movement and development of mathematical models of selective attention in vision.

Nick Chater is Professor of Psychology and Director of the Institute for Applied Cognitive Science at the University of Warwick. His research focuses on building mathematical and computational models of cognitive processes, including reasoning, decision making, language processing and acquisition, and perception and categorization. He is particularly interested in 'rational' models of cognition. He is also interested in the application of cognitive science to the private and public sectors.

Yvonne Delevoye-Turrell is a postdoctorate fellow in the Neuroscience Laboratory (CNRS) located within the psychiatric unit of the University Hospitals of Lille, France. After completing a PhD on the predictive adjustments of motor parameters in collisions (University of Birmingham, UK, September 2000), she initiated a research project on the systematic investigation of the motor deficits characterizing the psychiatric illness of schizophrenia. Overall, the topic of her research centres on the problem of motor prediction: how does the brain adapt motor actions to the continuously changing dynamics of the environment? Using schizophrenia as a pathological model, her research now aims at the development of a cognitive model of the motor systems that incorporates three types of predictive mechanisms: automatic, controlled and voluntary. The fine integration of these different functions would achieve efficient and optimized adjustments of motor behaviour.

Alan Garnham is Professor of Experimental Psychology at the University of Sussex, Brighton, UK. He has been a member of faculty at Sussex since 1985. Before that he spent two years at the University of Reading. His main research interests are in psycholinguistics, in particular the comprehension of anaphoric expressions, the role of inference in comprehension, and the role of non-syntactic information in parsing. His work in psycholinguistics is carried out in the mental models framework. He is also interested in the application of mental models theory to reasoning, and in particular in the role of prior beliefs on reasoning.

Thomas Habekost is a PhD student at the Centre for Visual Cognition, University of Copenhagen. He has also been visiting scholar at the Cognition and Brain Sciences Unit in Cambridge. His research focuses on the neural basis of visual attention, especially through studies of brain damage. His work includes mathematical modelling of attentional deficits and development of bootstrap methods in neuropsychological testing. He has also contributed to the NTVA model of attentional effects in single cells.

William G. Hayward is an Associate Professor in the Department of Psychology at the Chinese University of Hong Kong. He received a BA and MA from the University of Canterbury, New Zealand, and a PhD from Yale University. After spending four years as a lecturer at the University of Wollongong in Australia, he has been at CUHK since 1999. His research focuses on the information that subserves object recognition processes, examining such issues as the debate between view-based and structural description theories, the role of outline shape information in recognition judgements, and the relationship between mental rotation and object recognition. In addition, he currently has research projects investigating visual attention (particularly visual search) and human factors of the World Wide Web.

Evan Heit is on the faculty of the Psychology Department at the University of Warwick. Since obtaining his PhD from Stanford University in 1990, he has worked in three related areas of cognitive psychology: categorization, inductive reasoning and recognition memory. He is especially interested in issues that are relevant to two or more of these areas, such as the effects of prior knowledge, and psychological accounts that can be applied to two or more of these, such as Bayesian models.

Glyn W. Humphreys is Professor of Cognitive Psychology at the University of Birmingham. He has long-standing interests in high-level visual cognition, using converging data from experimental psychology, neuropsychology, computational modelling and functional brain imaging. He is the editor of the journal *Visual Cognition* and has received the British Psychological Society's Spearman and President Awards for research, along with the Cognitive Psychology Prize.

Woojae Kim is a graduate student in the Department of Psychology at the Ohio State University, Columbus, Ohio. His research interests include connectionist modelling of language learning, model selection methods, and Bayesian statistics.

Barbara J. Knowlton is an Associate Professor of Psychology at UCLA. Her research focuses on the neural substrates of memory and executive function. One of her main interests is the study of multiple forms of implicit learning, both in terms of psychological properties and supporting brain structures. Another interest is the role of the medial temporal lobe in the formation and retrieval of episodic memory.

John K. Kruschke is Professor of Psychology at Indiana University, Bloomington, where he has been employed since earning his PhD from the University of California at Berkeley in 1990. He studies how people allocate attention during simple learning tasks, and he creates mathematical models and computer simulations to rigorously test theories of attention in learning. He was a recipient of the Troland Research Award from the United States National Academy of Sciences in 2002, and has received teaching excellence awards from Indiana University.

Koen Lamberts is Professor of Psychology at the University of Warwick. Following his PhD at the University of Leuven (Belgium) in 1992, he was a post-doctoral research associate at the University of Chicago, and then moved to a lectureship at the University of Birmingham. He moved to Warwick in 1998, where he has been head of the Psychology Department since 2000. He has won the British Psychological Society's Cognitive Award (1996) and the Experimental Psychology Society Prize (1997). His research interests include mathematical models of cognitive processes in perceptual categorization and recognition memory.

Randi C. Martin is the Elma Schneider Professor of Psychology and Department Chair at Rice University where she has been a faculty member since 1982. Her research interests are in cognition and cognitive neuroscience, with a particular interest in language processing. Much of her research has been concerned with the nature of verbal short-term memory and its role in the comprehension, production and learning of language. She has also carried out studies on reading and spelling, semantic representation and executive function. In addition to behavioural studies with normal and brain-damaged populations, her recent work has included functional neuroimaging studies of language processing.

Craig R. M. McKenzie is Associate Professor of Psychology at the University of California, San Diego, where he has been since receiving his PhD from the University of Chicago in 1994. His research interests include inference, uncertainty and choice. Most of his recent research centres on how higher-order cognition is influenced by the predictable structure of our natural environment.

James M. McQueen is a member of the scientific staff at the Max Planck Institute for Psycholinguistics, Nijmegen, The Netherlands, where he has been since 1993. Prior to that appointment, he held a postdoctoral position at the MRC Applied Psychology Unit, Cambridge, UK. He studies spoken language processing, especially spoken word recognition. His research focuses on the way in which the information in the speech signal makes contact with stored lexical knowledge as we process spoken language, on how we perceive speech sounds, and on how we segment the acoustically continuous speech signal into discrete words during speech comprehension.

Jae I. Myung is Professor of Psychology at the Ohio State University, Columbus, Ohio. After completing his graduate study at Purdue University in 1990 and one-year postdoctoral work at the University of Virginia, he moved to Ohio State in 1991 and has been there since. The focus of his recent research efforts has been on the development of statistical methods for testing and selecting among mathematical models of cognition, especially Bayesian inference methods and minimum description length.

Ian Neath   is Professor of Psychology at Purdue University in West Lafayette, Indiana, where he has been on the faculty since receiving his PhD in 1991. His research interests focus on human memory as a discrimination problem, with remembering and forgetting reflecting the outcome of the discrimination decision. He is especially interested in distinctiveness models of memory as well as models of immediate memory. Both types of models account for memory performance without the concept of decay and both emphasize the functional importance of the type of processing.

Mike Oaksford   is Professor of Experimental Psychology at Cardiff University, Wales, UK. He was a postdoctoral research fellow at the Centre for Cognitive Science, University of Edinburgh, and was then lecturer at the University of Wales, Bangor, and senior lecturer at the University of Warwick, before moving to Cardiff University in 1996. His research interests are in the area of human reasoning and decision making. In particular, with his colleague Nick Chater, he has been developing a Bayesian probabilistic approach to deductive reasoning tasks. According to this approach, reasoning 'biases' are the result of applying the wrong normative model and failing to take account of people's normal environment. He also studies the way the emotions affect and interact with reasoning and decision making processes.

Hans Op de Beeck   is a postdoctoral associate in the Department of Brain and Cognitive Sciences at the Massachusetts Institute of Technology. He obtained his PhD at the University of Leuven (Belgium) in April 2003. His research focuses on the cognitive neuroscience of object recognition and categorization. Research topics include the effect of visual learning on object representations and the relation between object similarity and categorization. His work involves human and monkey subjects, and a range of methodologies (psychophysics, single-cell recordings and fMRI).

Mark A. Pitt   is Professor of Psychology at Ohio State University. He began his academic career at OSU studying the age-old question of how memory influences perception. In particular, he sought to understand how knowledge of one's language (e.g. its words and linguistic structure) affects its perception. In 1995 this work led him to become interested in how to compare computational models of these and other psychological processes. Done in collaboration with his buddy down the hall, In Jae Myung, the early work has a Bayesian flavour and focused on quantifying the complexity of statistical models. Subsequent research probes the concept of complexity more deeply to obtain a richer understanding of model behaviour, the goal being to clarify the relationship between a model, the theory from which it was derived, and the experimental data being modelled. He cannot seem to make up his mind which topics he likes more, maths modelling or psycholinguistics, so he continues to study both.

Christopher J. Plack   is Professor of Psychology at the University of Essex, Colchester, UK. He studied at the University of Cambridge before taking post-doctoral positions at the University of Minnesota in 1990 and at the University of Sussex in 1992. In 1994 he was awarded a Royal Society University Research Fellowship. He has been at Essex since 1998. In his research he uses psychophysical techniques to measure basic auditory processes, particularly those underlying the sensations of pitch and loudness, and the integration of information over time. He has also helped develop techniques for measuring the response of the basilar membrane in the human cochlea, the structure responsible for separating out the different frequency components of sounds.

Alexander Pollatsek   is Professor of Psychology at the University of Massachusetts. His research interests are varied, including mathematical and statistical reasoning, visual perception and cognition, and applied areas such as driving safety. However, his major research interest is in language, and specifically, the process of reading. Most of this work is in collaboration with Keith Rayner and examines the process of reading using the pattern of eye movements while people read text, and many studies also involve making changes in the text when the reader's eyes are moving. This research has established that the area of text from which readers extract information is quite small, and also that phonological processing is routinely used – even by skilled readers. His recent research has explored the role of morphemes in word identification in English, Finnish and Hebrew.

Keith Rayner   is Distinguished University Professor in the Psychology Department at the University of Massachusetts, Amherst. He was on the faculty at the University of Rochester from 1973 to 1978 prior to moving to the University of Massachusetts. He was Visiting Professor at the University of Oxford (1984–1985), an Invited Fellow at the Netherlands Institute for Advanced Study (1987–1988) and Leverhulme Visiting Professor at the University of Durham (2001–2002). His research interests are primarily in the area of skilled reading and language processing. With Alexander Pollatsek and other colleagues, he has used the eye-movement methodology to study various issues related to moment-to-moment processing. He was editor of the *Journal of Experimental Psychology: Learning, Memory, and Cognition* from 1990 to 1995, and is currently editor of *Psychological Review*.

M. Jane Riddoch   is a Professor in Cognitive Neuropsychology at the University of Birmingham. She has been a member of the faculty in the School of Psychology, University of Birmingham, since 1989. Her research interests focus on visual attention (grouping processes in perceptual organization and their interaction with visual attention), space processing (investigation of the neural mechanisms involved in space perception and cognition), mental imagery (investigations into the equivalence of mental imagery and visual perception), shape and object recognition (investigations into the nature of processing underlying object recognition) and vision and action (investigations into how visual information is used in the selection of actions to objects).

David R. Shanks is Professor of Experimental Psychology and Head of the Psychology Department at University College London, and is also Scientific Director of the ESRC Centre for Economic Learning and Social Evolution, UCL. His research interests cover human learning, memory and decision making. He is particularly interested in the use of broad computational models that deploy a small set of fundamental principles such as error correction to elucidate a range of mental processes. An example is the use of connectionist models to simulate category learning, amnesia, probability judgement and choice behaviour. He is the author of *The Psychology of Associative Learning* (Cambridge University Press, 1995).

Aimée M. Surprenant is an Associate Professor in the Department of Psychological Sciences at Purdue University, in West Lafayette, Indiana. She received a BA in psychology from New York University in 1988 and a PhD in cognitive psychology from Yale University in 1992. She received a National Research Service Award from the National Institutes of Health for postdoctoral work at Indiana University in the Department of Speech and Hearing Sciences. Her research focuses on the effects of noise on the perception of and memory for auditorily presented information.

Michael J. Tarr is the Fox Professor of Ophthalmology and Visual Sciences in the Department of Cognitive and Linguistic Sciences at Brown University (Providence, Rhode Island). Prior to that he was a professor at Yale University. His research focuses on mid- and high-level visual processing in the primate brain. The basic question he would like to answer is 'How does vision make sense of the world around us?' Current interests aimed at answering this question include the types of visual inferences made about lighting in the environment, the role of surface properties in object recognition, and the nature of processing in domains of perceptual expertise (including face recognition). When not pondering such problems, he is often riding his bike or playing in his wood shop.

Johan Wagemans is Professor in Psychology at the University of Leuven, Belgium. He has been visiting professor at the University of Nijmegen, The Netherlands, and at the University of Virginia. His research interests are all in visual perception, mainly in perceptual organization (e.g. grouping, symmetry, subjective contours), shape perception (e.g. picture identification, categorization, 3-D objects) and depth perception (e.g. texture, motion, stereo). He has interdisciplinary research projects with neuroscientists and computer vision engineers. He has published about 70 papers in international research journals and is currently editor of *Acta Psychologica*.

Edward A. Wasserman is the Stuit Professor of Experimental Psychology at the University of Iowa. He received his PhD from Indiana University in 1972 and was a postdoctoral associate at the University of Sussex. His research programme includes the comparative analysis of learning, memory and cognition, with special interests in causation, conceptualization and visual perception. His most recent work has studied the recognition of objects by pigeons, and the discrimination of variability by pigeons, baboons and humans.

Felix A. Wichmann   is a research scientist and head of the Computational Vision Laboratory in the Empirical Inference Department of the Max Planck Institute for Biological Cybernetics in Tübingen, Germany. He did his undergraduate studies and received his doctorate from the University of Oxford, UK, and was a Junior Research Fellow at Magdalen College. Prior to moving to the MPI in Tübingen he was a postdoctoral visiting fellow at the University of Leuven, Belgium. His main interests are quantitative models of spatial vision and the implications of natural image statistics for models of human vision. Recently, he has begun to explore the application of machine learning methods to problems of human categorization.

Alan M. Wing   is Professor of Human Movement in the School of Psychology at the University of Birmingham. He heads the Sensory Motor Neuroscience group in the interdisciplinary Brain Behavioural Science Centre. Previously he was Assistant Director at the MRC Applied Psychology Unit in Cambridge. He has published widely on motor psychophysics of normal and impaired control of movement and balance, including three edited volumes. His current research includes reactive and predictive control of movement of the upper and lower limbs, active touch, rhythm and timing.

Denise H. Wu   is a postdoctoral research fellow at the Center for Cognitive Neuroscience, University of Pennsylvania. She studied in the Psychology Department at Rice University and received her PhD in January 2003. Her research mainly concentrates on long-term linguistic representation, verbal short-term memory and the interaction between the two. She has studied reading mechanisms with brain-damaged patients. She has also employed the functional neuroimaging technique to examine the neural substrates of semantic and phonological short-term memory. Her current research focuses on processing of action and verbs.

Michael E. Young   is an Assistant Professor of Psychology and Director of the Brain and Cognitive Sciences programme at Southern Illinois University at Carbondale. He received his PhD from the University of Minnesota and was a postdoctoral associate at the University of Iowa. His research interests include the perception of stimulus variability and the psychology of causal learning and perception. His most recent work incorporates models of visual search into models of variability discrimination and explores the impact of temporal predictability on causal judgements.

Acknowledgements

The author and publishers wish to thank the following for permission to use copyright material:

CHAPTER 1

Figure 1.1

Wandell, 1995, *Foundations of Vision*, Fig 7.16, p. 222. Sunderland MA: Sinauer

Figure 1.2

Adelson, E. H., & Bergen, J. R. (1991). 'The plenoptic function and the elements of early vision', Fig 1.8, in, Landy, M. S., & Movshon A. (Eds.), *Computational Models of Visual Processing*. Cambridge MA: MIT Press

Figure 1.3

Adelson, E. H., & Bergen, J. R. (1991). 'The plenoptic function and the elements of early vision', Fig 1.14, in, Landy, M. S., & Movshon A. (Eds.), *Computational Models of Visual Processing*. Cambridge MA: MIT Press

Figure 1.4

Adelson, E. H., & Bergen, J. R. (1991). 'The plenoptic function and the elements of early vision', Fig 1.15, in, Landy, M. S., & Movshon A. (Eds.), *Computational Models of Visual Processing*. Cambridge MA: MIT Press

CHAPTER 2

Figure 2.1

Farah, Martha (1990), *Visual Agnosia: Disorders of Object Recognition*, Figs 16 & 17, p. 61. Cambridge MA: MIT Press

Figure 2.3

Reprinted from *Cognitive Psychology, Vol 21(2)*. Tarr, M. J., & Pinker 'Mental Rotation and Orientation-Depdence in Shape', Fig 1, p. 243, and Fig 6, p. 255, 1989, with permission from Elsevier.

Figure 2.5

Biederman, I., & Cooper (1991), 'Priming Counter-Deleted Images: Evidence for Intermediate Representations in Visual Object Recognition', Fig 1, *Cognitive Psychology, 23(3)*. Elsevier

Every effort has been made to trace all the copyright holders, but if any have been overlooked or if any additional information can be given the publishers will make the necessary amendments at the first opportunity.

Preface

This book aims to provide an overview of current theory and research in cognitive psychology. Of course, it is quite a challenge to capture the essence of such a large and active research area in a single volume. There is so much to be said about cognition and cognitive psychology that any overview must be selective. Nevertheless, we have tried to produce a text that is as comprehensive as possible, and yet provides sufficient depth to satisfy a more specialist audience.

This Handbook is not an introduction to cognitive psychology. We presume that the reader already has a background in cognitive psychology or cognitive science. The chapters are intended to introduce specialist areas of the field to advanced students and researchers. The advanced level of the text also implies that difficult or controversial topics have not been avoided, as is so often the case in introductory textbooks. In addition, the authors have often presented a personal view on what they see as the most important issues in their field. We hope that this approach will benefit the reader who wants to get a thorough update on the true state-of-the-art in perhaps less familiar areas of cognitive psychology.

Although the following nineteen chapters cover a wide range of topics, they are unified in teaching us not to take ourselves for granted. Each one of us is cognitively more impressive than it would seem when we are struggling to recollect our best friend's sister's name. Even in an age of unprecedented technological advances, most of us would be sceptical if we were told of a single machine that was able to speak English fluently, learn to understand a new language within three years, efficiently store any number of different data structures (e.g. images, songs, facial expressions, words, odours, etc.), recognize familiar faces within a half a second, play a reasonable game of chess, learn how to play new games, fix a bicycle, and answer various posed questions in mathematics and poetry interpretation. Yet we are all existent proofs of the possibility of such machines. We do it all, and in most cases do it better than special-purpose machines designed to perform only one of the above tasks. People tend to focus on individual differences. We may wonder why we are so poor at spatial navigation compared to others, and be impressed at an acquaintance's memory span. Upon further reflection, the sophisticated cognitive equipment shared by all people is even more striking. Understanding the nature of this shared equipment is a worthy enterprise, and one that is adroitly undertaken by the chapters here.

The Handbook is divided into six parts. The division is thematic and methodological. The first four parts each cover a broad aspect of cognition, whereas the final two sections group together chapters that have a common methodological focus.

Part I (Perception, Attention and Action) contains five chapters. Wagemans, Wichmann and Op de Beeck give a broad introduction to visual perception. They review a number of classic studies that fit within the 'measurement approach' to low-level vision, which is concerned with finding systematic laws that relate objective stimulus characteristics to subjective impressions. They also discuss the natural image statistics approach, and indicate how this complements the measurement approach. Their overview then proceeds to mid-level vision, focusing on how vision creates psychologically meaningful internal representations. Finally, they examine the offerings of two radically different viewpoints on perception, Gestalt psychology and Gibson's ecological approach.

The chapter by Hayward and Tarr focuses on high-level vision, addressing the question of how we see *objects*. The low- and mid-level processes discussed by Wagemans et al. ultimately serve the main purpose of vision, which is to create an adequate representation of the environment and the objects it contains. Hayward and Tarr discuss the processes that underlie our ability to recognize objects, despite variations in viewing conditions (such as luminance, viewpoint, etc.) or object features. They discuss the merits of multiple-view theories of object recognition (in which it is assumed that recognition is achieved through combination of information from specific object views stored in memory) and structural description theories (which assume that recognition proceeds on the basis of viewpoint-independent structural object models in memory). Together, the first two chapters provide a comprehensive overview of some of the most important and challenging issues in current research on visual perception.

In the third chapter, Plack takes us on an extensive tour of auditory perception. He introduces the physiology of the auditory system, followed by a detailed discussion of the processes involved in loudness perception, pitch perception, temporal resolution (which is the ability to follow changes in a sound over time), sound localization, auditory scene analysis and auditory object identification. The chapter highlights the challenges posed by each of these tasks, and thereby conveys just how sophisticated and complex auditory perception really is.

Bundesen and Habekost's chapter on attention deals with the selectivity of perception. At any time, the perceiver focuses only on certain aspects of the environment, thereby excluding other aspects. The question is how such selectivity can be achieved. Bundesen and Habekost explore a wide range of theories that aim to address this problem, from the early filter models of the 1950s to recent mathematical and computational theories of attention. They also review the experimental results that have supported different theoretical proposals. Attention research is an area of cognitive psychology that has witnessed remarkable cumulative theory development in a relatively short time. The chapter gives an insight into the empirical and conceptual underpinnings of this development.

In the fifth chapter in Part I, Delevoye-Turrell and Wing present an overview of the mechanisms that control actions and motor behaviour. They demonstrate how motor actions depend on goals, environmental constraints and knowledge of effector limits. Motor control involves the integration of these different sources of information. Delevoye-Turrell and Wing discuss in great depth how the notions of control and feedback are essential for understanding motor actions. For example, they analyse reactions to unpredictable events, showing that the central nervous system can rapidly use incoming sensorimotor and visual information to adjust ongoing movements. Perceptual information constantly feeds into motor processes, providing information about the context for movement, about errors in attaining movement targets, and about the effects of movements on the environment.

Part II (Learning and Memory) contains four chapters. The distinction between learning and memory as areas of research is somewhat artificial (learning clearly involves memory, and all memory tasks require initial learning), but because they have each generated distinctive research programmes, it seemed appropriate to maintain the division in the Handbook. At the same time, the four chapters in this section show the close links that exist between research on learning and memory. In their chapter on theories of learning, Young and Wasserman start with an overview of the major empirical findings that must be explained by theories of learning. They discuss the role of time (including the notions of contiguity and contingency), competition among predictors (which occurs in blocking and the relative validity effect), configural learning (which involves acquisition of information about entire sets of features, events or cues), generalization and similarity, and unlearning. In the second part of their chapter, Young and Wasserman introduce a number of theories of learning. They make a distinction between theories of supervised learning (in which feedback leads to a reduction of the discrepancy between actual and ideal responses) and unsupervised learning (in which statistical regularities in the environment are detected and represented, without being driven by the aim to reach some explicit performance target). They end with a plea for greater integration between different fields of cognitive psychology that all address issues related to learning.

Kruschke's chapter on category learning addresses the question of how we learn to group things together in categories. Categorization lends structure, simplicity and predictability to the mental representation of our environment. Kruschke shows that contemporary theories of categorization vary on how categories are assumed to be represented, on how abstract the representations of categories are supposed to be, and on how they assume that stored category information is used to categorize new stimuli. He reviews instances of each type of theory, discusses the roles of rules and similarity, investigates the relation between categorization and induction, and emphasizes the importance of attention for a comprehensive theory of category learning.

In the chapter on implicit learning, Shanks reviews empirical and theoretical research into learning that proceeds both unintentionally and unconsciously. He investigates the empirical and conceptual basis of claims for implicit learning, and asks whether implicit learning should be seen as independent from explicit learning. He also presents a critical review of a common technique for the study of implicit learning (the dissociation technique). Shanks concludes that it has not yet been proved that truly unintentional and unconscious learning exists, although the empirical studies that have given rise to claims about implicit learning have raised many important questions.

In their chapter on the mechanisms of memory, Neath and Surprenant discuss a number of general principles that apply to all memory tasks. They discuss the importance of interactions between encoding and retrieval, task purity, forgetting and interference, retrieval cues, constructive and reconstructive processes, and false memory. They outline and review the principles of three basic conceptions of memory: the systems view, the processing view and the functional view.

Part III (Language) contains three chapters on different aspects of language processing. Garnham reviews language comprehension. Language comprehension can be studied at different levels. The chapter starts with a discussion of (written) word recognition, showing that word recognition is sensitive to a large number of variables (such as frequency, regularity, etc.). Garnham then moves on to how we understand groups of words (syntactic processing), discussing various issues related to the derivation of meaning from sentences. Finally, he provides an extensive discussion of how we understand discourse and text, presenting mental models theory and its alternatives.

Speech perception is the focus of the chapter by McQueen. He explains how spoken word recognition involves a complex decoding problem, and argues that spoken word perception involves the simultaneous evaluation of multiple, competing lexical hypotheses. He also presents evidence for phonetic analysis of speech prior to lexical processing, and he discusses several models of speech perception.

Pollatsek and Rayner's chapter is devoted to reading, focusing primarily on the processes involved in word identification. They present an overview of the methods that are used to study reading, including brief presentation of stimuli, speeded naming and examination of eye movements. Pollatsek and Rayner further discuss the relation between encoding of letters and encoding of words, the role of auditory coding in word identification, and the speed and automaticity of identifying words. A large part of the chapter addresses eye movements in reading, with discussion of topics such as perceptual span, parafoveal preview and computational modelling of eye movements.

Part IV (Reasoning and Decision Making) contains two chapters on reasoning and decision making. Chater, Heit and Oaksford review the reasoning literature. Reasoning refers to inferential processing that derives verbally stated conclusions from premises. The chapter first introduces a number of issues related to form and content of arguments. The authors then describe Wason's classical studies with the selection task, which were among the first to cast doubt on the assumption that humans are generally rational. They present four approaches to explaining deductive reasoning, and provide an overview of data and theories of inductive reasoning.

McKenzie gives an overview of research on decision making. In the 1960s, it was widely assumed that normative statistical models provided a good basis for understanding human choice. This view was challenged in the 1970s, mainly under the impulse of Kahneman and Tversky's groundbreaking work on heuristics and biases in decision making. Since the 1990s, it has become increasingly clear that studying decision making independent of environmental considerations can lead to misleading conclusions. Much of the chapter is devoted to the context or environment in which decisions are made. McKenzie shows that seemingly irrational decisions turn out to be adaptive when their environmental context is taken into account.

The three chapters in Part V (Cognitive Neuropsychology) have a common methodological focus. Each chapter in this section gives an overview of an area of cognitive neuropsychology. The chapters revisit many issues that have also been addressed in the previous sections, but they do so from a different perspective. The chapters demonstrate just how much can be learned from the study of patients with selective disturbances of a cognitive ability, and how data from such patients can lead to surprising new insights about normal cognition. The three chapters complement the first three parts of the Handbook (focusing on perception, memory and language, respectively – the neuropsychology of reasoning and decision making is far less established than these three areas).

Humphreys and Riddoch review the cognitive neuropsychology of object recognition and action. They discuss the implications of impairments in object recognition for our understanding of high-level vision. Patient data have challenged traditional views of object recognition, and opened up new avenues of investigation. Humphreys and Riddoch also discuss differences between recognition of objects, faces and words, the links between objects and actions, and computational models of object recognition and action.

Knowlton discusses the cognitive neuropsychology of learning and memory. She reviews how studies of patients with amnesia supports a distinction between implicit and explicit memory, and touches upon a number of issues related to this fundamental distinction. She also discusses the logic of double dissociations, Alzheimer's disease and dementia, frontotemporal dementia, the role of the frontal lobes in memory, memory and ageing, and the relation between neuropsychology and functional neuroimaging.

Martin and Wu review the cognitive neuropsychology of language. They discuss neuropsychological data and theoretical issues with regard to the comprehension and production of single words and sentences. They also review the neuropsychology of reading and spelling and the interaction between syntactic and semantic processing.

Part VI (Modelling Cognition) contains two chapters that discuss various aspects of formal modelling of cognitive processes. Formal modelling has become firmly established as a standard technique in cognitive psychology. Lamberts provides a basic introduction to mathematical models of cognition. He discusses the different types of models that can be constructed, and explains what model parameters are and how their values can be estimated using goodness-of-fit criteria. The chapter ends with a discussion of formal modelling as a tool for data analysis. Myung, Pitt and Kim's chapter offers a more advanced discussion of several central issues in formal modelling of cognition. They review model specification and parameter estimation, and focus extensively on model evaluation and model testing. They introduce the concepts of model complexity and model generalizability. Model selection is also treated in considerable depth. Together, the two chapters on modelling cognition offer an accessible and yet advanced overview of the principles of formal modelling.

As will be clear from this overview, this Handbook is the result of the joint efforts of a large number of people. We thank all of the contributors to the volume, as well as the referees who provided invaluable feedback and advice. We are deeply grateful for the enthusiasm and dedication of everyone who was involved in the project.

Koen Lamberts

Robert L. Goldstone

PART ONE

Perception, Attention and Action

1

Visual Perception I: Basic Principles

JOHAN WAGEMANS, FELIX A. WICHMANN
AND HANS OP DE BEECK

Human visual perception starts with two-dimensional (2-D) arrays of light falling on our retinae. The task of the visual perception is to enable us to use the information provided in the array of light in order to react appropriately to the objects surrounding us. One way to try and view the process of vision is to divide the problem into three parts: first, how the visual information falling on the retinae is encoded; second, how it is represented; and finally, how it is interpreted. The next chapter, 'Visual Perception II: High-Level Vision', speaks more directly to the third issue; that is, how visual signals of objects are interpreted and represented (the two are obviously connected). In the first half of this chapter we are mainly concerned with the early stages of visual processing: How is information encoded and extracted in the first place? Can we find general, basic principles according to which our visual system appears to function, both in how it encodes and represents visual information? And, if so, can we find, from an engineering or information-theoretic point of view, reasons why the visual system may be organized the way we think it is? The second half of this chapter looks at ways of going beyond the first encoding of visual information. What additional processing is required? What experimental findings do we need to accommodate? Both the latest insights from neurophysiological research as well as classic findings from psychophysics will be reviewed that speak to issues going beyond early vision.

With half our brain devoted to visual areas, vision is clearly our most important sense. We usually know about the world, where objects are, what they are, how they move, and how we can manipulate them, through vision. Because we are so incredibly good at perceiving the world through vision, and because vision usually feels effortless, the visual world is often almost treated as a 'given'. So much so that many of our words to describe important mental events are metaphors borrowed straight from vision. We tend to 'see' solutions, have 'bright' ideas, 'look' at them from a different 'viewpoint' as if the visual world was objectively there and directly accessible through our eyes. Thus, it is perhaps not surprising that many non-experts are often initially puzzled as to what there is to study (other than prescribing glasses as an optician or studying anatomy) when vision scientists say they are studying the visual system and the mechanisms enabling us to see. But in reality the problem of understanding vision is a formidable task and has attracted generations of thinkers from philosophy, mathematics, physics, biology, psychology and, more recently, computer science, to ponder over often deceptively simple-sounding central questions such as 'Why do things look as they do?' (Koffka, 1935: 76).

The emphasis in this chapter is on 'basic principles' of vision. The starting point of the chapter is the initial encoding of light on the retinae and the translation of the retinal images into neural representations of the visual world. This field of research is often referred to as 'early vision' or 'low-level vision'. First, we review a small number of papers that are classics in the field of early vision, or that have illuminated the basic principles of a certain aspect of early visual perception. Second, we argue that virtually all of the current research on early vision follows what we call the (physical) 'measurement approach' to early vision. We make this hypothesis explicit and show how much of the work (both current and classic) fits into this framework. We also offer a basic principle under which much of the work can be summarized. Third, we look at a comparatively recent field of research, namely natural image statistics, and show how some of the major results of this field are in good agreement with, and provide a complementary viewpoint on, those obtained within the measurement approach. Fourth, we want to look beyond early vision and consider mid-level vision, concerned with perhaps the most crucial step in visual processing: how to transform the measured physical variables into a representational system for seeing as active observers and actors in the world.

Early vision as measurement successfully fits or 'explains' a large number of psychophysical and neurophysiological studies (with reduced stimuli) and to most scientists it appears a 'natural' or 'obvious' first step in visual processing. However, thus far, its primitives have not proved to be particularly successful in going beyond the detection and discrimination of simple gratings or noise patterns. In the fourth section we shall look at approaches trying to find psychologically meaningful internal representations and look at, for example, primitive features versus shape features, and at neurophysiological examinations of interactions outside the classical receptive fields. In the fifth and sixth sections we go one step even further and examine the offerings of two radically different viewpoints on perception, Gestalt psychology and Gibson's ecological approach. We evaluate whether they represent alternatives to the traditional way of thinking about visual perception, or rather offer complementary angles on the subject. In doing so, we cover a large number of classic and recent studies on topics such as visual illusions, ambiguous figures, 'biological motion' perception, etc. These clearly do not belong to 'early vision' but they might help to clarify why things look the way they do.

Early Visual Processing

Mimicking the experimental approach that is so very successful in physics, the study of visual processes traditionally has been directed at isolated physical dimensions of visual information such as luminance, colour or motion. Many classic and often exceptionally ingenious and elegant experiments have been carried out in these domains. In the following paragraphs we review some of them in very condensed form, concentrating on the psychophysics and neurophysiology of spatial vision and motion perception. We feel it is worth starting with a few of the original classic papers both to give credit where it is due and to provide the historical background for some of the ideas currently taken almost for granted. Obviously, given the severe constraints on the length of our chapter, this selection has to be both small and somewhat idiosyncratic. Different authors might have picked a different set of papers, but we do hope that at least some of those we have picked are universally accepted as classics.

Optical resolution limits of the eye

In the case of the optics of the eye, perhaps the first very influential measurements were carried out by Campbell and Gubitsch (1966) using a modified ophthalmoscope. A bright light was shone through a narrow slit into the subject's eye. Some of the light is reflected off the retina, passes back out of the eye through the pupil, and is measured as a function of spatial position using a photodetector. Using this method, sometimes called the double-pass method, as the light passes both in and out of the eye again, Campbell and Gubitsch determined the human linespread function (LSF) of the optics. The LSF is a one-dimensional (1-D) function, characterizing an optical apparatus along one spatial dimension only. Had Campbell and Gubitsch used a point of light rather than a narrow line, that would have enabled them, in theory, to measure the pointspread function (PSF) of the optics, characterizing its optical properties in 2-D space. Thus, the PSF is in general much more informative than the LSF. However, estimating the PSF is technically much more difficult using a modified ophthalmoscope and a photodetector. Furthermore, the human eye is nearly equal in all directions (i.e. isotropic) and because of this the PSF can be deduced from the LSF – in anisotropic systems this is generally not the case, however. The LSF, on the other hand, can always be obtained from the PSF. The Fourier domain equivalent of the LSF is the (complex-valued) optical transfer function (OTF). However, because the LSF is even-symmetric, no phase shifts are introduced and the (real-valued) modulation transfer function (MTF) is sufficient to characterize the human optics. (The pure MTF characterization of the human optics holds at least to a very good approximation for smaller pupil diameters; see Liang & Williams, 1997.) The initial double-pass measurements are in reasonably good agreement with later methods such as interferometry (Williams, Brainard, McMahon, & Navarro, 1994) or wave-front sensor methods (Liang & Williams, 1997), showing just how good and careful Campbell and Gubitsch had been.

All measurements of the human MTF indicate that, under optimal conditions, retinal contrast is already halved at approximately 10–12 cycles per visual degree (cpd), and down to 25% by about 25 cpd. This implies that if you take a square-wave grating of 10 cpd, i.e. 10 thin black and white lines subtending one degree of visual angle on the retina, the image on the retina will be that of a square wave with 10 thin dark and light grey stripes with only half the original contrast. In addition, the lines will not be clear but have fuzzy edges and tend to blur together. The maximal spatial frequency resolvable is in the region of 60 cpd. Clearly, the optical limits constitute boundary conditions for what humans could possibly resolve and perceive. Indeed, the human contrast sensitivity function (CSF) – the human analogue of the optical MTF – shows that the shape of the high-frequency fall-off of the human CSF for static patterns is in large part of an optical nature: the neural machinery coming after the optics makes near-perfect use of all the information actually falling on the retina. The fall-off in human sensitivity for low-frequency gratings, on the other hand, is not present in the (monotonically decreasing) optical MTF and, hence, must be neuronal in origin.

Spatial vision

In one of the most influential papers in spatial vision, Campbell and Robson (1968) argued that (at least some) visual stimuli may be best represented in the Fourier domain in order to predict detection and discrimination performance of human observers. This seemingly counter-intuitive claim implies that the representational format for visual stimuli may not always resemble our phenomenology, and that, to a first approximation, the early visual system's essential properties could be captured in a linear system (linear spatial frequency 'channels'). Particularly during the 70s and 80s of the last century, a multitude of psychophysical experiments explored the response of the visual system to gratings of various sorts alone or in combination, hoping to find the (linear) transfer function equivalent of the early visual system. Graham and Nachmias (1971) studied the detectability of single versus compound gratings and found conclusive evidence for the multiple channel model. Their results for the detectability of compound gratings agreed with the predictions from probability summation between independent detectors. Thus, it appeared that the overall sensitivity to sine-wave gratings of various spatial frequencies (CSF) is brought about by several independent channels of smaller bandwidth. However, over the last decades it has become clear that the visual system does not perform a global Fourier transform over the whole visual field (Westheimer, 2001) but rather an analysis akin to subband transforms (Koenderink, 1984; Simoncelli & Adelson, 1990) or wavelets (Mallat, 1987), jointly encoding information about space and spatial frequency (Daugman, 1984, 1985). The amplitude spectrum of a global Fourier analysis in vision maximizes resolution in terms of spatial-frequency content but sacrifices resolution in space. Conversely, a pixel-by-pixel analysis of an image is maximally precise in spatial resolution but provides little information about spatial-frequency content. Subband or wavelet transforms, on the other hand, are a compromise between the two extremes.

In the neurophysiology of spatial vision, one of the first major breakthroughs came with Kuffler's (1953) discovery that ganglion cells in the mammalian retina predominantly respond to isolated spots of light and that their receptive fields have a clear centre–surround structure with an excitatory (inhibitory) centre and an inhibitory (excitatory) surround, termed on- (off-) centre ganglion cells (see also Barlow, 1953). This initial success was followed by the discovery of the receptive-field structure of cells in the first visual cortical area (area 17 in cats, V1 in monkeys) by Hubel and Wiesel (1959, 1962 in the cat, 1968 in the monkey). Unlike those in the retina, cells in the visual cortex respond best to simple line-like stimuli of different lengths and orientations, and those cells were termed 'bar-detectors' by Hubel and Wiesel. Again, at least in simple cells, the receptive fields have clearly demarcated excitatory and inhibitory subregions.

The connection between the neurophysiological findings in early visual cortex and the previously mentioned psychophysically afforded joint consideration of space and the Fourier domain was brought about by two important papers in the late 1960s. First, Enroth-Cugell and Robson (1966) showed that a large number of cat ganglion cells, mainly the so-called X-cells, sum stimuli linearly over their receptive fields across excitatory and inhibitory subregions. This linear summation, later also found to hold for monkey V1 simple cells by Hubel and Wiesel, is a prerequisite for any model of early vision performing a subband or wavelet decomposition. Second, Blakemore and Campbell (1969) extended the description of simple cells responding to 'bars' of various widths, orientations and lengths, and described them as jointly selective to orientation and size; that is, to small subspaces of the 2-D Fourier domain. Hence, one way of looking at simple cells is to view them as the (approximately) linear kernels of a wavelet decomposition. With a subsequent static nonlinearity and a decision mechanism, this still forms the basis for most models of early spatial vision, such as that shown in Figure 1.1.

The seminal study of Campbell and Robson (1968) suggested that the visual system is comprised of spatial-frequency selective channels.

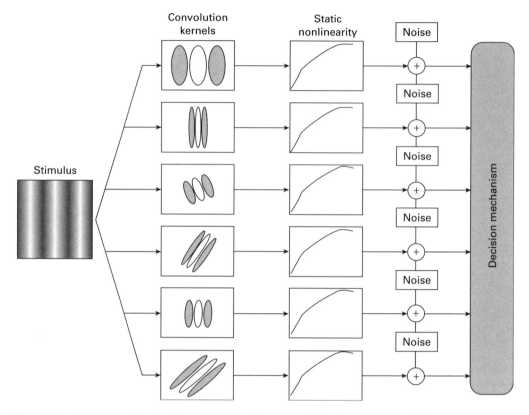

Figure 1.1   *Standard model of early spatial vision: linear convolution kernels, followed by a nonlinearity and a decision mechanism (adapted from Wandell, 1995, p. 222, Fig. 7.16).*

Subsequent psychophysical research has cast doubt on the notion of linear and independent channels (Derrington & Henning, 1989; Henning, Hertz, & Broadbent, 1975) but the multi-channel model still captures many aspects of early spatial vision and, even in nonlinear systems, determination of the linear component of the system usually remains important (Henning, Bird, & Wichmann, 2002).

Motion

The study of the perception of motion has a very long tradition in vision and was one of the main areas of research of Gestalt psychology in the 1920s and 1930s when many effects such as apparent motion were already well described (e.g. Wertheimer, 1912). However, Hassenstein and Reichardt's (1956) experiments and subsequent analysis on the optokinetic response of the beetle *Chlorophanus* to moving drums with regular and irregular stripes of various luminance levels and widths stand out as perhaps the first study driven by quantitative predictions from a formal mathematical model. Hassenstein and Reichardt hypothesized that the

mathematical operation of autocorrelation was implemented in the insect brain. Later expanded by Reichardt (1961), this model of insect motion sensing forms the basis of virtually all models of early motion perception, whether in insects, mammals or man. The 'Reichardt detector' works by correlating the responses from different ommatidia (light-sensitive cells) separated in space and time to find coincident activity. Assume two ommatidia, o_1 and o_2, with distance Δx between them, and a response delay $\Delta \tau$ in the neuronal circuitry connecting them to a cell further down the processing stream. Assume further that the cell further down the processing stream, c, is only activated if it receives a spike from both o_1 and o_2 within a very narrow time window ('at the same time' within biological precision). Hence, c itself will only become active if and only if an object moves across o_1 and o_2 with velocity $v = \Delta x / \Delta \tau$ to produce coincident spikes at c. The three cells, o_1, o_2 and c, form a velocity- (and direction-) tuned motion sensor, the Reichardt detector. For models of human motion perception, the point samples of the insect eye, o_1 and o_2, are replaced by the spatially extended receptive fields of V1 cells, and the design principle is typically phrased as a 'delay-and-compare-principle' rather than in terms of correlation. At least in spirit, all current motion detectors (e.g. Adelson & Bergen, 1985) still follow Reichardt's lead and hence they are called 'elaborated Reichardt detectors' (van Santen & Sperling, 1985).

Other classic contributions

The studies we mentioned are but a few of the many important contributions to early vision. In passing, we should note that the quantitative analysis of visual perception would not be possible without Tanner and Swets' (1954) application of statistical decision theory to psychology. The absolute limits of visual detection in terms of the number of quanta absorbed by the photoreceptors were first explored by Hecht, Shlaer, and Pirenne (1942). Likewise, no account of colour vision can be complete without mentioning at least Young (1802) and von Helmholtz (1852) for their work and theorizing about trichromacy and their realization that it is a property of the visual system and not of physics, as well as Hurvich and Jameson (1957) for their theory of colour-opponency. Finally, accounts of stereo vision must include Wheatstone (1838), who invented the stereogram; Julesz's (1964, 1971) random-dot stereograms which first demonstrated that binocular disparity alone, in the absence of any other cues to depth, can lead to vivid depth percepts; and Barlow, Blakemore, and Pettigrew's (1967) study on the neurophysiology of binocular cells in the visual cortex, the neurophysiological basis of stereo vision. Encouraged by his own work on the properties of cells in the frog's retina (and the suggestion of their important functional significance as signals for bugs to eat or predators to avoid; see Lettvin, Maturana, McCulloch, & Pitts, 1959) and by subsequent work in cat and monkey cortex, Barlow (1972) suggested the possibility of 'a neuron doctrine for perceptual psychology'; that is, a set of principles to link the activities of single cells to meaningful perceptions. Despite occasional criticisms of this doctrine, no alternative has had the force to replace the status of the single neuron as the basic unit of vision (see also Lennie, 1998). The legacy of single-unit recording is still very strong, even in the present days of cognitive neuroscience, with the advent of a whole battery of other measurement techniques at more microscopic or more macroscopic levels. In Barlow's words, 'action potentials are the fire, all else is … smoke' (quoted in Nakayama, 1998: 313).

As we indicated, our list of classic papers is by no means exhaustive. Still, often the vast number of beautiful experiments and their results almost obscure the question we most want an answer to: What is vision for? Can we find general basic principles? Can the research on the early stages of information processing in the brain be subsumed under a more general heading, so as to help us connect the seemingly isolated pieces of knowledge into a coherent picture?

Early Vision as Measurement

The previous section enumerated some of the classic findings in early vision and, at first sight, they may appear rather heterogeneous. In spatial vision or pattern perception, it is often fruitful to consider the stimuli in the Fourier domain, as the visual system appears to initially code the world via bandpass filters. Motion detection is probably accomplished by local 'delay-and-compare' operators, colour perception is based on colour-opponent channels, and the disparity between images falling on the retinae of our two eyes can be used to recover information about depth. However, we argue that all of the above can be concisely and elegantly subsumed under a common framework: taking measurements via blurred derivates. This point is very clearly put forward in a chapter by Adelson and Bergen (1991). The first or most basic task of vision is to measure what is out in the world. The more information is measured directly the less the visual system has to make hypothetical inferences that go beyond the available data.

Adelson and Bergen start by asking what any visual system could potentially see – what information is contained in the distribution of light filling a region of space? They parameterize a function containing all that could potentially be seen in a volume of space and term this function the plenoptic function P ('plenoptic' being composed of 'plenus', meaning complete, and 'optic'). The plenoptic function is independent of any organism or the anatomy of any specific sensitivities of a particular organism. It contains, for example, the polarization direction of light which we, as human observers, are unable to perceive. If, instead of focusing on all that could potentially be seen within a volume of space, we consider what a human observer can see, the intensity distribution F sampled by our eyes is a function of five parameters or dimensions only:

$$F = P(x, y, t, \lambda, V_x)$$

Each ray of light passing through the pupil of the eye is registered by the 2-D retina, providing us with information about a (small) range of the coordinates x and y of P, and its intensity is a function of time t measured by temporal filters in the retina. However, the intensity of F will in addition depend on the wavelength λ of light sampled by the three

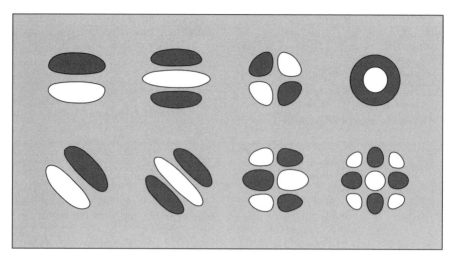

Figure 1.2   *An ensemble of blurred low-order derivative operators (adapted from Adelson & Bergen, 1991, p. 10, Fig. 1.8).*

cone types. Finally, V_x indicates that we have two eyes that, to a first approximation, are only offset along one dimension of space, which we term x. The task of early vision can thus be formalized as that of adequately measuring the plenoptic function – our internal representation F of P out in the world. If measured and internally represented in sufficient detail, all the potential visual information is available for subsequent analysis (Koenderink & van Doorn, 1987). From a mathematical point of view, function characterisation is well accomplished by taking local derivatives. In mathematics, the derivative is taken at a point, but for smoothly varying functions with noise (both external and internal to the organism), we gain more robust information if we take the derivative within a small neighbourhood; that is, we first take a local average (blur) and then the derivative. Since both blurring and taking the derivative are linear operators, we can fuse both operations into a single blurred derivative operator, which we apply to the image. Figure 1.2 shows an ensemble of blurred low-order derivative operators.

It is important to note that we can take directional derivatives too. Instead of just taking one along x, we can take a 'tilted' one along $x + y$, or one oriented in space-time along $x + t$. Figure 1.2 shows oriented derivative operators in row 2, columns 1 and 2. Depending on which dimensions of the plenoptic function the derivatives are applied to, the measurements correspond to very different visual events – not all necessarily easily described in, or meaningful in, language. As an example, take the operator from the top left corner of Figure 1.2. If the x- and y-axes correspond to space (x, y), then such an operator responds well to a horizontally oriented edge-like structure. If the axes correspond to t and x, however, it corresponds to a 'full-field-brightening'

detector. Figure 1.3 shows the labels of all 1-D first- and second-derivative operators. Figure 1.4 shows a table of the different measurements a 2-D, tilted second-order derivative can provide if we just apply it to different dimensions of the plenoptic function.

To a first approximation, these blurred derivative operators very much resemble simple cell receptive fields. There are, of course, different ways to formalize receptive fields as either Gabor functions, difference of Gaussians (DoGs) or derivatives of Gaussian, among others. However, all of them can be viewed as blurred derivative operators as long as they look roughly similar with inhibitory and excitatory subregions. Whichever formal mathematical receptive field model is chosen, we can integrate the function the appropriate number of times and this yields the spatial weighting or blurring function. In case of Gabor functions or DoGs, the resulting blurring function will not be a perfect Gaussian but in the light of the large variability in measured receptive field profiles of actual cells, it will be fairly close.

From the previously mentioned psychophysical studies, we know about the existence of channels with different spatial frequency tuning. Furthermore, the channels' likely neuronal implementation is in the spatial receptive fields of simple cells in primary visual cortex. The receptive fields can be interpreted as taking local blurred measurements along the spatial dimensions. Note further that the Fourier domain description of a blurred derivative operator is a band-pass filter; that is, a spatial frequency channel. Similarly, a Reichardt detector is nothing but a blurred derivative operator in space-time followed by a non-linearity, and colour-opponency is the result of taking blurred derivatives along the wavelength dimension. What previously appeared as a disparate set of

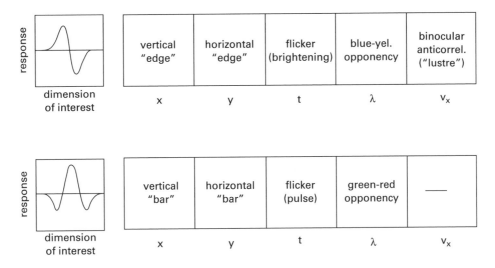

Figure 1.3   *Labels of all 1-D first- and second-derivative operators (adapted from Adelson & Bergen, 1991, p. 15, Fig. 1.14).*

operations in different domains (space, motion, colour) is nicely subsumed under a single functional description, namely that of taking local, blurred derivatives (measurements) of the plenoptic function in order to make them available for subsequent analysis.

This may be the place to stress that in vision science it often pays to think about the same thing in different ways: spatial receptive fields of simple cells can beneficially be seen as local change detectors, as bandpass filters in the Fourier domain, or as kernels of a wavelet decomposition. These are not mutually exclusive ways of thinking about them. Sometimes they are best thought of in space (blurred derivative operators), for example when considering line drawings; sometimes the Fourier domain is the most helpful perspective (bandpass filters), for example when considering periodic patterns. Frequently, the joint consideration of space and Fourier domain is required (wavelet decomposition), typically when considering complex stimuli such as natural images.

NATURAL IMAGE STATISTICS

In the previous section we argued that it is beneficial to view the first task of any visual system as measurement of what could possibly be seen; that is, to obtain information about the plenoptic function via (blurred) derivatives. However, each firing of a neuron is expensive in metabolic terms. Hence, it would be 'sensible' if only a limited number of cells were active for a given stimulus. In addition, the frequency of stimuli, or signals, should

be taken into account too: very frequent signals should be coded with fewer active cells than rare signals. Furthermore, we have only a limited number of neurons devoted to vision; that is, neurons should be well distributed to sample the plenoptic function in all behaviourally relevant parts.

Attneave (1954) and Barlow (1961) were the first to hypothesize that there should be a connection between the statistical regularities of the visual world we inhabit and the structure and functioning of our visual system. Our visual system should be adapted to the statistics of 'natural images' through evolution and developmental processes. Recently, with the advent of sufficiently powerful desktop computers, the study of the general statistics of natural images has become a topic of growing interest, with research attempting to relate the statistical properties of natural scenes to the processing in the early stages of the mammalian visual system (Atick, 1992; Bell & Sejnowski, 1997; Field, 1987, 1994; Kersten, 1987; Olshausen & Field, 1996; for a review, see Simoncelli & Olshausen, 2001). The hypothesized connection between the statistics of natural images and the properties of sensory neurons in the visual system comes from a concept from information theory, called efficient coding. Coding efficiency offers a formalization of what the previous paragraph alluded to in everyday language: the limited number of neurons should code all that is relevant to the animal using the smallest possible number of active neurons (i.e. sparse coding). The requirement to code everything of relevance will be reflected in the distribution of the individual neural responses (i.e. in the distribution of what they code). The requirement to minimize the number of active neurons leads to the need to

	x	y	t	λ	v_x
x	—				
y	diag. "bar" static achromatic no dispar.	—			
t	vert. "bar" **leftward** achromatic no dispar.	hor. "bar" **downward** achromatic no dispar.	—		
λ	**vertical** static **hue-sweep** no dispar.	**horiz.** static **hue-sweep** no dispar.	full-field **sequential** **hue-sweep** no dispar.	—	
v_x	vert. "bar" static achromatic **hor. dispar.**	hor. "bar" static achromatic **vert. dispar.**	full-field **sequential** achromatic **eye-order**	full-field static **hue-shift** **lustre**	—

Figure 1.4   Different measurements are obtained when applying a 2-D tilted second-order derivative operator to the different dimensions of the plenoptic function (adapted from Adelson & Bergen, 1991, p. 15, Fig. 1.15).

reduce redundancy between neurons; that is, to avoid having too many neurons code the same information. This will be reflected in the distribution of statistical dependences between neurons (i.e. one attempts to enforce, as much as possible, response independence between neurons).

Perhaps the best-known statistical regularity of natural images is that they are (nearly) scale-invariant; that is, their amplitude spectra fall (nearly) inversely with frequency (i.e. the often cited $1/f$ amplitude spectrum or $1/f^2$ power spectrum of natural images, e.g. Field, 1987; for an overview, see Ruderman & Bialek, 1994). A well-known finding

from neurophysiology is that the bandwidths of cells in the early stages of visual processing *increase* linearly with spatial frequency, with a typical bandwidth of 1.0 to 3.0 octaves (e.g. De Valois, Albrecht, & Thorell, 1982; Tolhurst & Thompson, 1982). This implies that receptive fields are self-similar in *shape*; that is, they are just size-scaled versions of each other and are thus modelled well, at the level of V1, by wavelets that exhibit precisely this property. However, the important implication for the current purpose is that this bandwidth increase with spatial frequency more or less compensates for the amplitude spectrum decrease in natural images: on average, cells in V1 are equally active when presented with natural images, independent of their preferred spatial frequency. This is, of course, most welcome, as it makes efficient use of the neuronal resources by effectively 'whitening' the input.

A related issue is that natural images are highly redundant; that is, they exhibit large correlations between neighbouring pixels. The world consists of (partially occluded) objects, and nearby regions of the same object or surface are likely to share the same brightness (luminance) and colour. Coding natural images point by point (or pixel by pixel) is thus a very ineffective representational format. However, at the level of the photoreceptors this is how the visual system represents its input. On information-theoretical grounds one of the major goals of early vision should thus be to represent the input in a different, more efficient, form. What we want is to represent the (natural) input image x (the random variable) as the (linear) weighted sum of a number of basis functions b_i (the spatial receptive fields of cells) with associated hidden (latent) random variables y_i (the responses of the cells), or $x = \sum_N b_i y_i$. For each different image x the y_i's will be different, effectively determining which of the b_i's are needed to represent the image. Truncated principal component analysis (PCA) achieves this for a set of images $\mathbf{x}$ by finding a small set of (orthogonal) b_i's, resulting in a very compact code – effectively the constraint is to minimize N. However, for biological systems, a sparse coding model is preferable in which we do not enforce that we have few b_i's, as in truncated PCA, but that, for any given x from $\mathbf{x}$, only a few of the b_i's are active; that is, y_i is zero for most i but N can be very large. There may well be very many b_i's as very different basis functions are needed to code the different images and the set of active basis functions differs for each image (and there are indeed many more V1 simple cells than retinal ganglion and LGN cells). Looking at the response of an individual basis function as a function of the input images $\mathbf{x}$, the sparse coding scheme results in a highly kurtotic distribution: for most images our basis function is silent (associated y_i is zero), but for a small number it is highly active.

In an influential study, Olshausen and Field (1996) trained a neural network to perform a sparse coding of natural images and found that the resulting basis functions b_i needed to represent natural images were localized in space and resembled V1 simple cells in their spatial response profiles. Furthermore, Olshausen and Field showed that the responses of the individual b_i's were fairly independent. More recently, several researchers have applied variants of independent component analysis (ICA) to natural images (Bell & Sejnowski, 1997; Hoyer & Hyvärinen, 2002; Hyvärinen & Hoyer, 2000; van Hateren & Ruderman, 1998). ICA is a statistical technique for decomposing a complex data set into independent subparts, often used for what is termed Blind Source Separation problems (for an introduction, see Stone, 2002). ICA, like PCA, is a linear transformation of the original data in which the desired representation is the one that minimizes the statistical dependence of the components of the representation (here, the responses of the b_i's are as independent of each other as possible). Applied to natural images, ICA too results in a sparse, distributed code with basis functions very much like those of V1 simple cells. Thus, it appears that maximizing response independence, together with the highly correlated statistical structure inherent in natural images, is sufficient to obtain a sparse code.

In summary, given the statistical structure of natural images, techniques for redundancy reduction and efficient coding result in simple-cell-like receptive fields. In the framework of this chapter, efficient coding results in blurred derivative operators – an amazing finding. This offers a third perspective on early vision. First, in the space domain, we require local plenoptic function estimators. Second, in the Fourier domain, we require bandpass filters. Third, from an information-theoretic viewpoint, we require redundancy reduction, sparse coding and whitening of the input signals. All three requirements are met by the same, self-similar local blurred first- and second-derivative operators taking measurements of the plenoptic function. (In addition, this helps to explain why most simple cells resemble first and second-derivatives of a blurring function, and not also the fourth or seventh derivatives, or why no local Taylor expansions around some points of the plenoptic function have been reported, which could equally well be used to represent the image: they would not lead to a code that is as sparse and independent.)

BEYOND EARLY VISION: HIGHER-LEVEL VISUAL DESCRIPTIONS

Using local blurred derivative operators to measure the visual input is a first starting point in visual perception. Furthermore, the local derivative operators look very much like the independent components of natural images. Thus, these measurements are an efficient way to represent the visual input (reducing redundancy). However, the information contained in the measurements may not be expressed in a format that allows the organism to grasp the meaning of the visual input and to choose appropriate actions at a glance. Measuring local physical dimensions is obviously not the ultimate goal of vision; these measurements need to be transformed into a description of visual images in terms of meaningful units such as objects. This derivation of a higher-level description of the

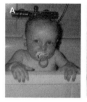

Figure 1.5   Limitations of Fourier analysis of natural images. (A) A scene with a number of solid objects. (B) Another image with the same Fourier spectrum and a random phase spectrum. (C) Another image with the same Fourier spectrum and phase spectrum resulting in local oriented edges.

Figure 1.6   Limitations of local blurred derivatives. (A) A simple stimulus consisting of three shapes. (B) A transformed version with a change of one of the salient properties of one of the shapes (i.e. main axis is straight or bent). (C) A transformed version with a position change of one of the shapes. The output of local blurred derivatives will change more dramatically by the position change (A–C) than by the curvature change (A–B), while the perceived dissimilarity is smaller for the position change than for the curvature change.

visual input will likely involve interactions between local units and the creation of higher-level units. Two general principles guide this transformation.

First, the local blurred derivatives are not sensitive to long-range statistical dependences that are very common in natural images (Brunswik & Kamiya, 1953; Elder & Goldberg, 2002; Geisler, Perry, Super, & Gallogly, 2001; Sigman, Cecchi, Gilbert, & Magnasco, 2001). These dependences are not captured by techniques such as ICA, partly because these are limited to a description of images in terms of linear superposition (Schwartz & Simoncelli, 2001; Simoncelli & Olshausen, 2001). Figure 1.5 provides a simple illustration in the case of spatial vision. The natural image in Figure 1.5A represents a scene containing several solid objects. It is possible to create images with the same Fourier spectrum and either a random phase spectrum (Figure 1.5B) or a phase spectrum resulting in local oriented edges (Figure 1.5C). As discussed before, the measurement by local blurred derivatives is adapted to the properties of a natural image that are also present in Figure 1.5C. It is clear that many of the regularities occurring in a natural image are not present in Figure 1.5C, and likewise the local blurred derivatives do not capture these regularities. Here we will focus on spatial dependences. Another approach would be to model the dependences in sequences of images (see Simoncelli & Olshausen, 2001).

Second, the output of the local blurred derivatives is too sensitive to physical image changes that are irrelevant for important functions like object recognition. Figures 1.6B and 1.6C show two transformations of the object image in Figure 1.6A. A basic property of the object, whether its main axis is straight or curved, is changed in Figure 1.6B, while the difference between 1.6A and 1.6C is a position change of the object. The output of local blurred derivatives will change more dramatically by the position change than by the curvature change. It is

clear that in order to recognize an object, a system needs to be very sensitive to object changes but not to position changes. It is a desirable property of the first measurement that it is as sensitive as possible to all aspects of the visual input, but behavioural tasks require this measurement to be transformed into another representation format. And, to the extent that other behavioural tasks pose different restrictions, it would be preferable to segregate processing in order to construct different representation formats. In line with this idea, several divisions of the visual system into parallel processing streams have been proposed (e.g. Creem & Proffitt, 2001a; Goodale & Milner, 1992; Livingstone & Hubel, 1984; Ungerleider & Mishkin, 1982).

Changing the representation format by introducing sensitivity to long-range dependences is not only relevant for pattern perception; it is a general principle applicable to the same variety of domains for which the first processing steps could be characterized by local blurred derivatives. Indeed, local 'delay-and-compare' operators are integrated in order to have a global percept of motion and optic flow (Adelson & Bergen, 1985; Adelson & Movshon, 1982; Hildreth & Koch, 1987); the colour-opponent channels interact in order to create true colour perception with properties such as colour constancy (e.g. Land, 1983; Maloney & Wandell, 1986); and the disparity of local image patches is integrated to recover the absolute and relative depth of image regions (Cumming & DeAngelis, 2001; Janssen, Vogels, & Orban, 2000). Note, however, that the specific way in which the local filters are integrated will vary. Furthermore, the construction of useful representation formats will often require an integration of information from different kinds of filters. For example, luminance information and disparity can both signal the presence of a particular shape, either alone or in combination with the other cue. It has been shown that the responses of most neurons in the cortical areas V1 and V2 are influenced by changes in different submodalities (Gegenfurtner, Kiper, & Fenstemaker, 1996; Lennie, 1998; van Ee & Anderson, 2001). This observation has prompted the formulation of the 'multiplex theory', which states that neurons signal the occurrence of a specific combination of a spatial pattern with a particular motion, colour or disparity. The strong version of this theory is controversial in light of the many findings that at least some specialization occurs at many levels of the processing hierarchy (e.g. Felleman & Van Essen, 1991; Livingstone & Hubel, 1984; Zeki, 1993). Moreover, even if one adheres to the multiplex theory, it could still be useful to analyse the processing of each submodality separately.

Interactions between local derivatives

The remaining part of this section will review approaches to finding higher-order representational formats in the domain of pattern perception. As noted before, psychophysical work with simple sinusoidal gratings containing one orientation has revealed that visual processing starts with oriented local bandpass filters similar to the properties of simple cells in V1 (Hubel & Wiesel, 1968). These cells respond to an oriented grating or bar within a range of spatial frequency/thickness in a phase-dependent way. The classical receptive field (CRF) of these neurons (i.e. the part of the visual field in which stimuli evoke excitatory or inhibitory responses) is composed of excitatory and inhibitory subregions, and the responses of the neurons is determined by a linear summation of these subregions. A controversial issue is how these oriented receptive fields with excitatory and inhibitory subregions are constructed. Hubel and Wiesel (1968) originally suggested that a specific combination of concentric receptive fields could account for oriented receptive field properties, but recurrent connections between simple cells and even feedback connections also contribute (Ferster & Miller, 2000). Thus, even the construction of local blurred derivatives could already involve some local interactions between units and top-down influences (see also Bullier, Hupé, James, & Girard, 2001).

The investigations with simple stimuli, as illustrated in the first section, reveal the initial building blocks of the visual system, but more complex interactions will not be visible simply because the stimuli do not activate these interactions. A simple extension of the previously described studies is to present several small patches of sinusoidal gratings (usually convolved with a Gaussian filter, effectively creating so-called 'Gabor patches') simultaneously

at different locations in the visual field (e.g. Polat & Sagi, 1994; for a review, see Polat, 1999). This paradigm revealed that the detection of a target patch is influenced by the presence of other patches. Sensitivity is increased maximally when the orientation of these 'flankers' is collinear with the orientation of the target patch. Likewise, the responses of simple cells to a grating in their receptive field is influenced by the presence and orientation of gratings outside the receptive field, including effects such as collinear facilitation and side-inhibition (Allman, Miezin, & McGuinness, 1985; Knierim & Van Essen, 1992; Sillito, Grieve, Jones, Cudeiro, & Davis, 1995). The part of the visual field at which stimuli evoke no responses by themselves but influence the responses to stimuli within the CRF is called the surround, or the non-classical receptive field. The flanker effects are a simple demonstration of surround influences that could play a substantial role in processing the long-range dependences found between image patches in natural images. In general, neighbouring image patches tend to contain collinear orientations (Sigman et al., 2001), so the presence of collinear flankers in a natural image increases the probability that the image patch between those flankers contains that particular orientation. It has been suggested that the surrounds of V1 neurons are based upon lateral connections that are related closely to image statistics (Gilbert, Sigman, & Crist, 2001). Sigman et al. (2001) note two important consequences of this correspondence between intracortical interactions and image statistics. First, the responses of neurons to natural images will be more statistically independent than could be achieved by local blurred derivatives, as has indeed been verified empirically (Vinje & Gallant, 2000). Second, the stimulus configurations that will be coded best will be the most probable ones given the statistics.

A consequence of interactions between the processing of local image patches is that the perception of a global image is not simply the sum of the independent processing of local image elements. This general hypothesis was central to Gestalt psychology and will be discussed in more detail later in this chapter. Although the theoretical ideas of Gestalt psychology are not consistent with current thinking in terms of interactions between local measurements, we shall suggest that the Gestalt phenomena themselves are.

Creation of 'higher-level' units

Allowing for interactions between local filters is just only one way to make the visual system sensitive to higher-order and long-range dependences. Alternatively, new units could be created that are tuned to more complex image features. A well-known example are 'complex cells', exhibiting similar response properties to simple cells but with phase-independent responses to oriented gratings. Thus, they respond to a grating with a particular orientation and spatial frequency no matter how it is positioned relative to the receptive field. For complex cells, it is impossible to delineate subregions in the receptive field whose responses are combined linearly. Complex cells are the first example of creating invariances (in this case for position). Shams and von der Malsburg (2002) showed that the position information in a population of complex cells is still sufficiently detailed for object identification, but at the same time – due to its inherent ambiguities – also robust to changes in background, lighting and small deformations. A variety of specific cortical wiring patterns have been proposed to account for more complex tuning properties such as complex cells showing end-inhibition ('hypercomplex cells', see Hubel & Wiesel, 1968), cells tuned to local curvature (Dobbins, Zucker, & Cynader, 1987), and contour cells responding to both 'real' and 'illusory' contours (von der Heydt, 1994), to name only a few examples. Riesenhuber and Poggio (1999) proposed a general distinction between a mechanism for the creation of neurons tuned to more complex features and a mechanism for the creation of more invariance. In their model, a neuron tuned to a more complex feature is created by computing a linear summation of all its afferents. In this way, they extend the basic principle used to create orientation selectivity in simple cells to more complex cases. Invariance is achieved by a nonlinear maximum operation, where the strongest afferent determines the response. This is consistent with the proposal that the phase-independence of complex cells is created by nonlinearly pooling the responses of simple cells. Note that these two mechanisms are formulated in a very general way, and that the properties of the actual afferents that are combined determine the properties of the postsynaptic neuron.

Most investigations of the processing of complex spatial features like corners, curvature and (at higher stages) complete objects were not performed with gratings, nor with natural images (the other extreme), but with isolated shapes (uniformly filled silhouettes, line drawing or shaded objects). Neurons in intermediate stages of the cortical processing hierarchy are tuned to specific local shape features like corners and curved lines (in V2, see Hegde & Van Essen, 2000), or for the occurrence of a particular type of curvature in specific parts of a shape (in V4, see Pasupathy & Connor, 2001, 2002). The lattter type of tuning is an example of the encoding of a particular combination of a local shape feature within a global shape. The tuning functions of these neurons are still spatially restricted, but they exhibit more invariance for position changes compared to V1 neurons. Several studies suggest that neurons in the final stages of the visual system (in

inferotemporal [IT] cortex) are directly involved in shape perception, are tuned for complex shapes, and exhibit an even larger, but not absolute, invariance for position and size changes (Gross, 1994; Logothetis, Pauls, & Poggio, 1995; Logothetis & Sheinberg, 1996; Op de Beeck & Vogels, 2000; Tanaka, 1996).

Until now, we have presented a bottom-up view of visual perception in which processing proceeds unidirectionally from simple to more complex tuning properties. However, anatomical studies have revealed the existence of massive feedback connections in the reverse direction, and many neurophysiological studies have indicated a role of these connections in the response properties of neurons, even in V1 (for reviews, see Bullier et al., 2001; Lamme & Roelfsema, 2000). The Gestalt phenomena discussed later indicate that a coherent model of visual perception should incorporate a bidirectional view of visual processing.

The final stage of visual processing

The gradual construction of a shape representation in several steps starting from local blurred derivatives is incorporated in all current models of shape perception (e.g. Biederman, 1987; Edelman, 1999; Riesenhuber & Poggio, 1999). Poggio, Edelman and colleagues proposed a general framework for the transition from the representation of local physical image properties to the representation of complex objects (e.g. Edelman, 1999; Poggio & Edelman, 1990; Poggio & Girosi, 1990). Local blurred derivatives represent a specific tuning for physical dimensions such as position, spatial frequency, orientation and temporal frequency. The tuning of higher-level neurons is defined in a representational space determined by psychologically meaningful dimensions (Shepard, 2001). Edelman (1999), among others, proposed a specific class of mathematical functions, radial basis functions (RBFs), to characterize the tuning of high-level neurons. RBFs have a maximum response for an optimal stimulus. Their responses to other stimuli is determined by their distance of these stimuli from the optimal stimulus in the psychological space. Each function is characterized by only one parameter that determines the position of its optimal stimulus. Neurophysiological recordings in high-level visual cortex of the macaque monkey (IT cortex) confirmed that a strong relationship exists between psychological distance and the response profiles of individual neurons (Op de Beeck, Wagemans, & Vogels, 2001).

The RBF model is an elaborated version of a template theory. Template theories (Tarr & Bülthoff, 1998) conceptualize the recognition of a shape as a matching process between global templates that are stored in memory (or interpolations of these templates) and the representation of the input (which can be normalized or transformed to account for parameters such as size and viewpoint). Without the gradual construction of the high-level RBF units, the RBF model would be just another example of a template theory. The next chapter will discuss in more detail how template theories relate to more symbolic theories of shape representation (e.g. Biederman, 1987; Marr & Nishihara, 1978). These theories propose a limited alphabet of simple shapes (parts). Each complex shape is represented by a structural description that describes the parts of the complex shape and how they relate to each other. Although these theories capture important aspects of how human subjects *understand* the shape of an object, their status as a model for shape *perception* is not that clear. Most importantly, it is doubtful whether shape perception by non-human primates and even human subjects involves the construction of a structural description except in some specific tasks (Edelman & Intrator, 2003).

Nevertheless, several behavioural and neurophysiological experiments suggest that some assumptions behind these symbolic theories need to be incorporated in the RBF model, which can be done without leaving the template theory framework. First, human subjects, as well as macaque IT neurons, show a remarkable sensitivity for those shape features that were used to define the shape alphabet (Biederman & Bar, 1999; Vogels, Biederman, Bar, & Lorincz, 2001). As discussed in the next chapter, this increased sensitivity can be incorporated in models without adhering to a symbolic part-based shape description.

Second, at least part of the representation of shapes involves an independent coding of some shape dimensions (Arguin & Saumier, 2000; Op de Beeck, Wagemans, & Vogels, 2003; Stankiewicz, 2002). For example, subjects can selectively attend to the curvature of a stimulus while ignoring its aspect ratio. Garner (1974) introduced the concept of 'separable dimensions' to refer to dimensions that can be processed independently from each other and 'integral dimensions' to refer to dimensions that cannot be processed independently, even when they are redundant or would interfere with each other. Behavioural and neurophysiological studies with several combinations of dimensions (e.g. spatial frequency and orientation, see Jones, Stepnoski, & Palmer, 1987; Mazer, Vinje, McDermott, Schiller, & Gallant, 2002; Vogels, Eeckhout, & Orban, 1988; or colour and shape, see Komatsu & Ideura, 1993) suggested that behavioural evidence for the independent processing of two dimensions is reflected at the level of single neurons by tuning curves that tend to separate the two dimensions (the 2-D tuning curve being equal to the product of the two 1-D tuning curves). An extension of this mechanism to shape representation predicts that IT neurons are not simply tuned for the global similarity to their optimal stimulus (as

RBF units would be), but that these tuning curves will be oriented in a specific way with respect to a set of independent shape dimensions.

Third, it can be doubted whether the complete lack of sensitivity to object structure in the original RBF model is a good model for macaque object perception (Hummel, 2000). Confronted with two stimuli, one representing a circle on top of a square and the other a square on top of a circle, human subjects immediately note that these configurations are different but also that they consist of the same parts. As noted by Biederman (1987), it is an important and still unanswered question whether this understanding of object structure is still part of the visual representation that humans share with other animals, or whether it merely illustrates how human subjects extend their capability of using symbolic systems with specific rules/grammar to other domains such as vision. Edelman and Intrator (2003) suggest that networks with units that are coarsely tuned to object fragments (instead of whole objects) as well as position could provide information on both global similarity and constituent parts at the same time. This proposal is consistent with the idea of models containing units with a mixed complexity and without absolute position invariance. Furthermore, it is consistent with the neurophysiological findings that IT neurons display a variety in tuning complexity (Tanaka, 1996) and in selectivity for shape and position (Op de Beeck & Vogels, 2000; Op de Beeck et al., 2001).

Flexibility of visual processing

We suggested that the specific way in which the attributes of visual images are encoded is a function of a sensitivity to the statistics of these images, with a gradual shift from local to more global regularities, together with a sensitivity for task demands. These two factors can work on an evolutionary as well as a developmental time scale. Evolution could have shaped the primate visual system to become adapted to the aspects of the input that are invariant across generations, as well as to the tasks that primates face in their natural environment. However, it is conceivable that many properties of visual processing could be adapted to the situations that an individual has encountered during its lifetime. There is evidence that a complete disruption of the input to the visual system early in life reduces orientation selectivity and its columnar organization but does not abolish it (Hubel & Wiesel, 1963; see also Sengpiel, Stawinski, & Bonhöffer, 1999). Furthermore, the structure in visual images without a predisposition of a cortical area towards orientation selectivity and columns is also a sufficient factor to induce orientation selectivity and at least some columnar organization. Sharma, Angelucci, and Sur (2000) rewired the brain and provided primary auditory cortex (A1) with visual input. This manipulation resulted in the appearance of orientation selectivity and some (but no perfect) columnar organization in A1. So, evolution made some properties of visual processing quite robust against dramatic changes in visual input, but a normal visual input is sufficient to induce some of these properties in 'unprepared' cortical tissue.

Many learning phenomena involve less drastic manipulations that appear later in life. The basic features of processing throughout visual cortex are established a few months after birth (at least in monkeys, see Rodman, Scalaidhe, & Gross, 1993; the maturation of high-level visual cortex in humans takes longer, Alvarado & Bachevalier, 2000). After this early period, all-or-none manipulations of visual input (e.g. by lesioning part of the retina) can still result in dramatic changes of tuning properties (Kaas, 2000), but most manipulations are less extreme (e.g. performing a particular task or seeing particular stimuli for a few hours each day). These manipulations are still associated with changes in behaviour and neurophysiology but they do not alter the basic organization of visual cortex. Even to the contrary, this basic organization will determine the actual changes induced by learning ('bounded' flexibility). One example is the variety of after-effects following adaptation. In general, adaptation refers to the reduction in responsiveness of neurons to stimuli that are presented for a long time. This reduction is strongest for those neurons that initially respond strongest, and as a consequence this mechanism can alter the perception of and responsiveness to new stimuli because the adapted neurons will respond less than normal to the new stimuli (e.g. Saul & Cynader, 1989). As a consequence, the new stimulus will be perceived as more dissimilar from the adapted stimulus than it actually is. This effect was revealed at the various levels of the cortical processing hierarchy. For example, adaptation to a grating oriented obliquely clockwise from vertical causes a subsequently presented vertical grating to be perceived as being oriented obliquely anti-clockwise (Blakemore & Campbell, 1969); adaptation to single-part shapes causes subsequently presented shapes that differ on a particular shape dimension (aspect ratio, tapering or curvature) to be perceived as being more different on that dimension than the actual difference (Suzuki & Cavanagh, 1998); and adaptation to a non-prototypical face causes a prototypical face to be perceived as being non-prototypical in the opposite direction in a parametric face space (Leopold, O'Toole, Vetter, & Blanz, 2001).

Another example of bounded flexibility is the effect of the repeated presentation of complex stimuli on neuronal responses. First, it was suggested that increased stimulus familiarity results in a sparser representation: a better selectivity overall with only a few neurons that respond strongly to familiar stimuli (Kobatake, Wang, & Tanaka, 1998; Rainer & Miller, 2000). Second, a Hebbian learning mechanism was proposed that would decrease the selectivity for stimuli that are contingent in time (Oram & Foldiak, 1996; Sakai & Miyashita, 1991). This mechanism could contribute to the construction of position invariance in higher-order visual areas, as well as to the construction of invariance for the viewpoint of very familiar objects because these objects are seen in a series of viewpoints when they are manipulated (Booth & Rolls, 1998; Wallis & Rolls, 1997). These two unsupervised learning mechanisms can alter the degree of selectivity for familiar objects, but it can be doubted whether radically different models (e.g. Biederman & Kalocsai, 1997) are needed to account for the representation of familiar versus unfamiliar objects. This issue can be illustrated with the most typical example of highly familiar objects: faces. Many studies have revealed that faces (as well as other classes of familiar objects, see Diamond & Carey, 1986) are processed in a more 'wholistic' way compared to other objects (e.g. Carey & Diamond, 1977; Farah, Wilson, Drain, & Tanaka, 1998). This result can be incorporated in the RBF model by assuming that the consistent way in which face features come together in the same configuration in evolution and development will result in the creation of units preferring stimuli that contain a complex combination of these face features. Recent single-cell recordings in IT cortex have provided evidence for such a mechanism (Baker, Behrmann, & Olson, 2002). Suggestions for similar learning mechanisms were made during the analysis of the superior ability of chess experts to recall chess positions (e.g. Gobet, 1998).

A final example of bounded flexibility in the visual system is the effect of attentional modulation. Behavioural paradigms have shown that it is possible to attend to some features while ignoring others, and these effects are accompanied by changes in neuronal responsiveness and maybe even selectivity (Desimone & Duncan, 1995; Treue, 2001). Other studies have suggested more long-term changes in visual processing as a consequence of task relevance (e.g. Schoups, Vogels, Qian, & Orban, 2001). This evidence clearly suggests that attention and task relevance can change profoundly how well particular stimulus features are encoded, but it is still controversial whether these modulations involve more than a shifting of priorities. For example, Op de Beeck et al. (2003) found that selective attention can selectively enhance the processing of one of two shape dimensions provided that these dimensions are encoded independently in the visual system (e.g. aspect ratio and curvature). However, whether shape dimensions are encoded independently or not seems to be an aspect of visual processing that cannot be altered.

Beyond Early Vision: Gestalt Psychology

In the preceding section, the 'early-vision-as-measurement' approach was extended to deal with phenomena beyond the level of local blurred derivatives. Sensitivity to long-range dependences in natural images could be achieved by interactions between local filters or by the creation of new units that are tuned to more complex image features. Phenomena such as stimulus adaptation, perceptual learning and attentional modulation were taken as evidence that the neural architecture is flexible to a certain extent. In the current section, we review a series of phenomena that were discovered one by one over an extended period of more than a century, and that have sometimes been used to challenge the measurement approach. For the sake of convenience, we list these phenomena under the umbrella of 'Gestalt' (because they argue for the primacy of the whole configuration), but not all of these have been discovered by Gestalt psychologists in the strict sense. We shall also present the basic theoretical principles proposed by Gestalt psychology to explain the Gestalt phenomena. Throughout this section, however, we shall argue that all of the phenomena can be explained on the basis of the extended measurement approach. In fact, even the Gestalt-theoretical principles will be shown to be compatible with theories and models that start from early-vision principles.

Gestalt laws of perceptual organization

In the projection of light on the retina, no distinction is made between the light reflected by figures and the light reflected by the background. So, the visual system is confronted with the formidable task of grouping the sensations arising from single coherent objects together and separating these from sensations caused by visible elements from the background. Gestalt psychology is perhaps best known for its discovery of the factors that determine this unit formation and figure–ground segregation, the so-called *Gestalt laws of perceptual organization*. Although many of the phenomena were already well established by quite imaginative empirical studies in the early days of visual science (e.g. Exner, 1875; Mach, 1896/1959; Schumann, 1900; von Ehrenfels, 1890), they became integrated into a new theoretical framework only with the work of Koffka (e.g. 1935), Köhler (e.g. 1929) and Wertheimer (e.g. 1923).

It is within this so-called 'Berlin school' that the diverse grouping principles (e.g. area, proximity, similarity, good continuation, symmetry, convexity, closure, common fate, etc.) were considered as different instantiations of the same basic principle, namely the *minimum* or *simplicity principle*. The visual system has a tendency to organize the visual input as simply as possible. This principle has sometimes been formulated as the law of *Prägnanz* ('goodness') – the overarching Gestalt law stating that the organization that we perceive will be as good as the incoming information allows it to be. For example, in the absence of other influences, we will group similar elements that are close together or move together, and we will perceive closed figures with minimal area, smooth contours, maximal symmetry and maximal convexity. The tendency towards simplicity, as Gestalt psychologists saw it, is an intrinsic (innate) force towards equilibrium within the visual system, not based on experience with regular shapes in the real world (i.e. not based on likelihood judgements). They formulated their own position in contrast with the then dominant elementalist/structuralist (Wundt) and empiricist/inferential (von Helmholtz) views, and they were inspired by the discovery in physics of universal laws of dynamics specifying what is simple and natural in the physical universe (for historical perspective, see Asch, 1995; Hochberg, 1998). (Because the minimum principle is a key notion within Gestalt theories, we shall return to it briefly in the evaluation section below.)

Despite the power of these early demonstrations, the popularity of Gestalt psychology declined gradually in the middle of the last century, especially in the United States (for exceptions, see e.g. Hochberg & McAlister, 1953; Hochberg & Silverstein, 1956). Interesting empirical work continued in Germany (e.g. Metzger, 1936/1975), Italy (e.g. Kanizsa, 1979), Belgium (e.g. Michotte, 1946) and other European countries, as well as in Japan (e.g. Oyama, 1961). However, the dissatisfaction with the lack of explanatory power of the minimum principle grew. Interactions between the different principles when multiple factors co-occur in richer displays were difficult to predict. Moreover, it was virtually impossible to translate the descriptive laws into neural mechanisms, except for the vague idea of electrical field forces in the brain, which was especially prominent in the works by Köhler (1929, 1940). This situation has changed gradually in the late 80s and 90s of the last century when more modern experimental methods were applied to measure the grouping principles more quantitatively and when enough was known about the neural level of the visual system. As a result, there is now a flourishing neo-Gestalt literature (for reviews, see Kovács, 1996; Palmer, 2002; Spillman, 1999). We shall briefly mention some of this more recent work here and focus on its possible potential implications for the measurement approach.

Each of the well-known Gestalt principles has now been studied further by more advanced psychophysical paradigms, for example grouping by proximity and similarity (e.g. Ben-Av & Sagi, 1995;

Compton & Logan, 1993; Kubovy & Wagemans, 1995; Kubovy, Holcombe, & Wagemans, 1998; Quinlan & Wilton, 1998; van Oeffelen & Vos, 1983), good continuation (e.g. Feldman, 1997; Field, Hayes, & Hess, 1993; Kellman & Shipley, 1991), symmetry (for reviews, see Wagemans, 1995, 1997), convexity (e.g. Bertamini, 2001; Elder & Zucker, 1998), closure (e.g. Elder & Zucker, 1994; Kovács & Julesz, 1993) and common fate (e.g. Uttal, Spillman, Sturzel, & Sekuler, 2000). In many of these cases, the Gestalt principles interact and appear to work synergistically. For example, when two weak parametric variations of good continuation and common fate are combined, grouping strength is higher than predicted by probability summation (e.g. Lee & Blake, 2001); symmetry interacts with proximity (e.g. Wenderoth, 1996), good continuation (e.g. Wenderoth, 1995) and convexity (e.g. Kanizsa & Gerbino, 1976); closure is more than just good continuation of a contour grouping until it meets its starting point again (e.g. Kovács & Julesz, 1993); connectedness is more than just very close proximity (e.g. van Lier & Wagemans, 1998); and so on.

These effects are sometimes considered as the hallmark of 'Gestalt' in the true sense of a 'structured whole' being more than the sum of the parts (see below). However, nonlinear interactions between simpler mechanisms can produce these effects and they are thus not incompatible with the account outlined in the earlier sections. For example, many of the striking aspects of symmetry detection can be explained by a 'bootstrap' mechanism in which local groupings initiate the formation of larger units that then suggest a local axis of symmetry. This higher level then facilitates additional local groupings when they are all consistent with the same global structure (e.g. Wagemans, Van Gool, Swinnen, & Van Horebeek, 1993). In such an account, local grouping mechanisms cooperate in the sense that they facilitate each other interactively and synergistically (for other applications of these notions, see e.g. Lee & Blake, 2001; Yen & Finkel, 1998).

More important as a step towards further understanding are recent attempts to relate the validity of the grouping principles to natural image statistics (e.g. Elder & Goldberg, 2002; Geisler et al., 2001; Sigman et al., 2001). This line of work is based on earlier attempts (e.g. Brunswik & Kamiya, 1953) that were doomed to fail because of a lack of image-processing tools and computer power. The nice aspect of this congruency between traditional Gestalt laws and their reliability in natural images is that it might help to solve the age-old controversy between simplicity as defended in the Gestalt school of thought and likelihood as defended in the more cognitive tradition (e.g. Chater, 1996; Hatfield & Epstein, 1985; Leeuwenberg & Boselie, 1988; Pomerantz & Kubovy, 1986; van der Helm, 2000).

In addition to the classic Gestalt laws of perceptual organization, a number of new laws have been proposed in recent studies. For example, Palmer and Rock (1994) have proposed 'uniform connectedness' as a new, even more fundamental principle of perceptual organization because it defines the regions or blobs that then become grouped by the other principles. In this sense, uniform connectedness is supposed to create the entry-level units of perceptual organization. However, whether this is really a new principle is uncertain (Peterson, 1994) and the empirical support seems rather mixed at best (e.g. Beck & Palmer, 2002; Han, Humphreys, & Chen, 1999; Kimchi, 1998). Another proposed new principle of perceptual grouping is temporal coherence or temporal synchrony (e.g. Lee & Blake, 1999; Usher & Donnelly, 1998). This principle appears quite important in the light of the speculations about the role of synchronicity of neuronal firing rates as a neural binding mechanism (e.g. Engel & Singer, 2001; Singer & Gray, 1995; but, for a critical evaluation of this hypothesis, see Shadlen & Movshon, 1999). However, again the empirical support is still quite controversial (for a review, see Farid, 2002) and one might argue that temporal grouping is just a generalization of the well-known 'common fate' principle. Coherence or synchrony can be defined as a simultaneous change in some property, not just speed or direction of motion as in the original formulation.

Returning to the issue of *figure–ground segregation* itself, which is part of the problem addressed by the Gestalt laws, there is interesting neurophysiological work that can help to clarify possible underlying mechanisms. Lamme (1995) was one of the first to suggest that activity in V1 neurons is involved in figure–ground segregation of textured displays with local orientation differences. Whereas the early responses (~55 ms) are selective to the orientation of the elements as such, the responses of V1 neurons at longer latencies (~100 ms) signal the orientation difference between the textured figures and their backgrounds (Lamme, Rodriguez, & Spekreijse, 1999). Their activity is clearly influenced by contextual modulations outside their classical receptive fields, a modulation that is most likely a manifestation of recurrent processing, involving horizontal connections and extrastriate areas (Lamme, Supèr, & Spekreijse, 1998). This idea seems supported by masking studies (Lamme, Zipser, & Spekreijse, 2002) and an implementation in a recurrent network (Roelfsema, Lamme, Spekreijse, & Bosch, 2002). However, some caution is needed because failures to replicate the original results (Rossi, Desimone, & Ungerleider, 2001) as well as direct supportive evidence (Bullier et al., 2001; Hupé, James, Payne, Lomber, Girard, & Bullier, 1998) have been reported since. In any event, this line of research clearly suggests that seemingly complex processes that depend on contextual interactions and feedback from higher levels are within the reach of the neuron doctrine (for a review, see Albright & Stoner, 2002).

Other Gestalt phenomena

In this section, we briefly review some other phenomena that have often received Gestaltist interpretations. As before, we shall argue that they are now often explained in terms of the extended measurement approach.

Many of the well-known *geometrical-optical illusions* are actually demonstrations of the fact that the perceptual units are not necessarily direct replicas of the corresponding physical units. Simple metric properties such as length and orientation are often misperceived because the elements are embedded in larger structures that influence the low-level processing of the smaller primitives. Examples of this are the incorrect perception of line length in the Müller–Lyer illusion (Figure 1.7A) because of the inward or outward wings (inducing shrinkage or expansion, respectively); the perception of long (vertical and horizontal) parrallel lines as converging or diverging, depending on the superposition of short (left and right) line segments in the case of the Zöllner illusion (Figure 1.7B); the perception of parallel straight lines as curved positively (convex) or negatively (concave), depending on the superposition of converging or diverging oblique lines, respectively, in the case of the Wundt illusion (Figure 1.7C); the café-wall illusion (Figure 1.7D); etc. (for reviews, see Coren & Girgus, 1980; Gillam, 1998).

These illusions are now explained within the (extended) measurement approach. For example, Ginsburg (1986) has argued that they depend upon a resolution failure arising from low-pass spatial filtering. Morgan and his colleagues have argued for the role of second-stage filters or higher-order 'eclectic' or 'collector' units (collecting information from different lower-order units) for the spatial pooling of position and orientation information (e.g. Morgan, 1999; Morgan & Casco, 1990; Morgan, Hole, & Glennerster, 1990). The general principle seems to be one of *local contrast enhancement*. This principle operates in the domain of many visual attributes, be it length, orientation or curvature of primitive features as in the cases above, or more complex properties such as the size of closed shapes (as in the Ebbinghaus circles; see Figure 1.7E). It also operates on unidimensional properties such as the brightness of a luminance ramp (as in the Mach bands; see Figure 1.7F) or the illusory spots with brightness differences in an array of discrete elements (as in the Hermann grid; see Figure 1.7G). Despite the diversity of these visual illusions, there is hope that it will be possible to describe all of them in a unified theoretical framework, perhaps in terms of a nonlinear diffusion process yielding smooth surfaces whose global shape properties (e.g. curvature) determine their perception (Verstraelen, 2002, 2003). Such a framework has already been applied successfully in computer vision, both for early-vision tasks (e.g. Proesmans, Pauwels, & Van Gool, 1994) and for perceptual grouping (e.g. Proesmans & Van Gool, 1999).

A typical Gestalt phenomenon, which was made famous by the Italian Gestalt psychologist Kanizsa (1976), is the perception of illusory or *subjective contours* in displays like Figure 1.8 (for a review, see Peterhans & von der Heydt, 1991). A contour is seen where no physical luminance difference exists (hence, illusory or subjective contour) and usually this is accompanied by a subjective brightness enhancement of the central figure. Direct neurophysiological correlates have been observed in macaque area V2 (von der Heydt, Peterhans, & Baumgartner, 1984) and in later studies even as early as V1 (Grosof, Shapley, & Hawken, 1993). The fact that the response latencies of these V1 neurons are longer than those reported for the V2 neurons suggests that the brain fills in the subjective contours on the basis of feedback from higher areas with specific dynamic properties (Lee & Nguyen, 2001). Neural correlates of illusory contours have now also been examined in humans, using ERPs (e.g. Proverbio & Zani, 2002) or fMRI (e.g. Hirsch et al., 1995). Subjective contour formation has also been simulated in neurocomputational models (e.g. Grossberg & Mingolla, 1985; Heitger, von der Heydt, Peterhans, Rosenthaler, & Kubler, 1998; Kelly & Grossberg, 2000; Peterhans & Heitger, 2001). More recent work has attempted to address the interaction between bottom-up grouping of the local edge elements and the top-down effects from surface formation and depth segregation in terms of nonlinear diffusion processes with even higher biological and psychological plausibility (Kogo, Strecha, Caenen, Wagemans, & Van Gool, 2002).

Related to illusory contours is the phenomenon of *amodal completion*; that is, the process of 'seeing' what is behind an occluder (e.g. Kanizsa, 1979; Michotte, Thinès, & Crabbé, 1964). The 'filling-in' of the hidden part clearly depends on an interplay between local factors (such as good continuation) and global factors (such as symmetry), which can be shown to interact (e.g. Boselie, 1994; van Lier, van der Helm, & Leeuwenberg, 1995; van Lier & Wagemans, 1999). Whether or not the processes that are involved are the same as those in illusory contour formation remains uncertain (e.g. Gold, Murray, Bennett, & Sekuler, 2000; Pillow & Rubin, 2002; Shipley & Kellman, 1992).

Another typical Gestalt phenomenon is the perception of *multistable stimuli*, stimuli that can be perceived in different ways. This often follows from the fact that the input does not allow a unique perceptual grouping or figure–ground segregation to emerge. Well-known examples are the regular

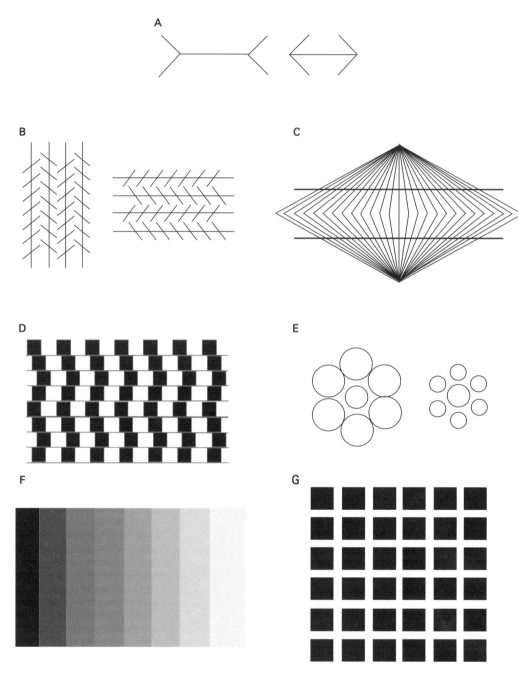

Figure 1.7   *Some well-known geometrical-optical illusions. (A) Müller–Lyer illusion.*
(B) Zöllner illusion. (C) Wundt illusion. (D) Café-wall illusion. (E) Ebbinghaus circles.
(F) Mach bands. (G) Hermann grid.

arrays of dots (Figure 1.9A), which can be organized in rows or columns (Kubovy & Wagemans,
1995; Schumann, 1904); arrays of equilateral triangles (Figure 1.9B), which can be seen as pointing
in one of three directions (Attneave, 1971); bistable

motion quartets (Figure 1.9C), which can be
seen to move either horizontally or vertically
(Ramachandran & Anstis, 1983); the Necker cube
(Figure 1.9D), which can be seen in two different
3-D orientations; the young or old woman in the

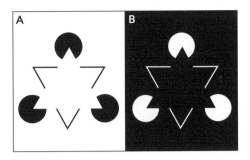

Figure 1.8 *Kanizsa triangles, with two components of the illusion: illusory contours and perceived brightness differences. In (A) the central triangle is perceived as whiter than the background; in (B) as darker.*

Boring figure (Figure 1.9E); Rubin's vase-faces (Figure 1.9F); etc. (for a review, see Leopold & Logothetis, 1999).

These multistable perceptions share two interesting characteristics. First, the alternative interpretations are never seen together. What is seen is always a coherent percept based on the global features of one alternative, never an incoherent percept in which local fragments of the different alternatives are combined. (In this sense, this phenomenon resembles the perception of impossible figures in which globally conflicting aspects of a stimulus are integrated without noticing the conflicts, e.g. Penrose's impossible triangle in Figure 1.9G.) It is as if the brain settles into one quasi-stable interpretation at a time and actively suppresses the other one(s). The same is believed to occur in so-called 'binocular rivalry' (i.e. switching between two alternative percepts when rivalry stimuli are presented to the two eyes). Recent studies have examined this competition (Blake & Logothetis, 2002) or have used it to investigate the neural basis of consciousness (e.g. Crick & Koch, 1998; Kanwisher, 2001; Logothetis, 1998) using either single-cell recordings in awake monkeys (e.g. Leopold & Logothetis, 1996; Logothetis & Schall, 1989) or fMRI in humans (e.g. Lumer, Friston, & Rees, 1998; Tong, Nakayama, Vaughan, & Kanwisher, 1998). Models of perceptual multistability usually postulate that the alternations are due to adaptive nonlinear inhibitory interactions between 'channels', each responding to one of the competing percepts, with some random noise (in the channels or in their interactions) to account for the stochastic component (e.g. Blake, 1989). This type of model may also account for specific dynamical aspects of multistable organization such as adaptation and perceptual 'trapping' (e.g. Suzuki & Grabowecky, 2002). The notion that different percepts are in competition for access to awareness has recently been generalized to the processing of rapidly presented sequences of stimuli and backward masking (e.g. Keysers & Perrett, 2002).

Second, in cases of arrays of multiple discrete elements (dots or triangles), the perception switches for the whole display simultaneously. This clearly shows that this switching is a global, collective phenomenon that has some of the properties of non-linear dynamical systems, such as *cooperativity and hysteresis* (e.g. Hock, Kelso, & Schöner, 1993; Hock, Schöner, & Hochstein, 1996; Ploeger, van der Maas, & Hartelman, 2002). These dynamical aspects had been noticed previously regarding other cases of self-organization or perceptual grouping processes to establish global coherence in individual static patterns such as vector graphs (e.g. Caelli & Dodwell, 1982), Glass patterns (e.g. Dakin, 1997; Glass & Perez, 1973) and symmetric patterns (e.g. Wagemans et al., 1993); two static patterns in the case of random-dot stereograms (e.g. Anderson, 1992; Anderson & Nakayama, 1994); or multiple frames in the case of kinematograms (e.g. Chang & Julesz, 1984; Gepshtein & Kubovy, 2000; Williams, Phillips, & Sekuler, 1994). (Because these dynamical-systems notions are central within Gestalt theorizing, we shall return to them briefly in the evaluation section below.)

The apparent primacy of the Gestalt

A basic tenet of Gestalt psychology is that the whole is different from the sum of the parts. This means that what we perceive cannot be explained as the simple linear addition of features delivered by early vision; nonlinear interactions between the low-level features or with high-level processes are required. Two characteristics of these true Gestalt phenomena have been highlighted: first, that the whole may be perceived prior to its parts; and second, that the parts may be altered by the whole within which they are embedded.

The best example of the first characteristic of Gestalt perception – that the whole may be perceived prior to its parts – is Navon's (1977, 1981) evidence for *global precedence* or, in his own words, the perception of 'the forest before the trees' in the case of hierarchical letters. A large letter presented as an organized array of small letters, for example a big S made of small H's, is more likely to interfere with an auditorily presented target letter than the small letters constituting the large letter. This demonstrates that the whole (i.e. the large letter) is perceived prior to the parts (i.e. the small letters) and thus that the whole cannot be perceived by aggregating the information about the parts. Subsequent research has shown that the global precedence effect might depend on the size scale or spatial frequency to which observers initially direct their attention, on the visual angle, or

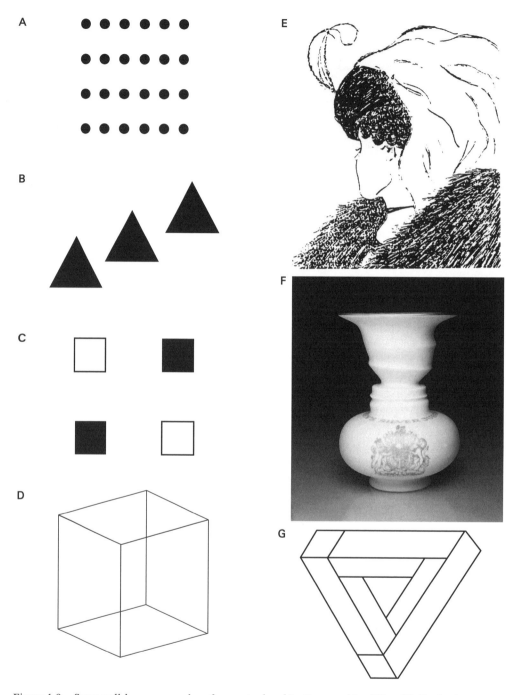

Figure 1.9 *Some well-known examples of perceptual ambiguity or multistability. (A) Dot lattice with columns and rows. (B) Equilateral triangles. (C) Bistable motion quartets. (D) Necker cube. (E) Boring figure (wife/mother-in-law). (F) Rubin's vase-faces. (G) Penrose's impossible triangle.*

on the limited resolution of the small-scale letters (for a review, see Kimchi, 1992).

The priority of the wholistic level of processing has also been shown for other types of hierarchical patterns (e.g. large squares consisting of small triangles) by Kimchi and her colleagues. In a review of this line of work, Kimchi (1992) has made a useful distinction between the geometrically defined stimulus levels of global configuration and local elements and the perceptual levels of processing of form, texture and figural parts. The perceptual effects in hierarchical patterns depend strongly on the number and size of the elements: when many small elements (e.g. triangles) constitute a pattern or configuration (e.g. a square), the local elements are processed as texture (i.e. a surface quality) and the global configuration as form. The global configuration and local elements are then separable in the sense that the local elements can be replaced by other local elements without affecting the perception of the global form (hence, surface quality). In contrast, when few large elements constitute a pattern or configuration, both the local and global stimulus levels are processed as form, and the elements in such patterns are perceived as figural parts of the overall form. The global configuration and local elements are then no longer separable. Working with Garner's (1974) operationalization of separable and integral dimensions, Kimchi and her colleagues have found corroborating evidence for this account using simple features such as line orientation and curvature as component properties and typical Gestalt features such as closure, intersection and parallelism as configural properties (e.g. Kimchi, 1994; Kimchi & Bloch, 1998).

The second characteristic of Gestalt perception – that the parts may be altered by the whole within which they are embedded – can work in two directions, either negatively or positively. The best-known example of a negative influence is the case of so-called *embedded figures* (Gottschaldt, 1926). Some simple shapes disappear from experience when they are incorporated in a context that is organized differently (see Figure 1.10). Pomerantz and his colleagues have reduced this classic Gestalt phenomenon to its essentials in their work on so-called *configural effects* and showed its potential benefits (e.g. Pomerantz & Garner, 1973; Pomerantz & Pristach, 1989; Pomerantz, Sager, & Stoever, 1977). One way to demonstrate these effects is by adding redundant contexts that create emergent features. For example, when looking for a left-oblique line element '\' in a simple array of right-oblique line elements '/', response times might decrease dramatically when a redundant array of 'L'-shapes is added (e.g. from 1885 ms in the simple feature search to 750 ms when the context is added). Likewise, a simple curved line '(' is much easier to find amongst ')' distractors when a redundant array of additional curved lines ')' is added (e.g. from 2400 ms to 1450 ms). The reason is that grouping produces emergent features that are much stronger perceptual units than their component 'simple' features: triangles versus arrows in the case of '\' versus '/' with redundant 'L' context, and circles '()' versus pairs '))' in the case of '(' versus ')' with redundant ')' context. In other words, adding 'noise' to a stimulus might actually improve performance when the stimulus is then organized differently, creating perceptual units with emergent properties that are perceptually more salient. They create better shapes with higher Gestalt qualities, which are in a sense more basic for to the visual system than the primitive features of which they are made. Typical emergent features have Gestalt properties such as closure, symmetry and parallelism, all attributes known to constitute perceptual 'goodness' or 'Prägnanz'. Many of these configural effects also occur in unexpected situations, for example with apparently simple stimuli in standard experimental paradigms (e.g. visual search, dual-task paradigms). If perceptual organization is not taken into account, some odd-looking results might be obtained (e.g. steeply negative search slopes, better dual- than single-task performance) that stem from a mismatch between how the experimenter defines the stimulus and how the perceiver organizes the stimulus (Pomerantz, 2002).

Another variant of the same principle – that a particular feature of an object may be seen better when it is embedded into a larger whole than when presented in isolation – is the so-called *object superiority effect*. An early example of this phenomenon is the word 'superiority effect', showing that letters were better recognized when presented in a meaningful word than when presented alone or in a non-word (e.g. Johnston & McClelland, 1974; Reicher, 1969; Wheeler, 1970). Soon afterwards, similar results were obtained for the perception of 2-D straight-line fragments when part of a Necker cube (Weisstein & Harris, 1974), the perception of parts of a face like eyes, noses and mouths (Homa, Haver, & Schwartz, 1976), and the perception of objects in scenes (Biederman, Rabinowitz, Glass, & Stacy, 1974). The seemingly paradoxical nature of these phenomena is that the whole must be perceived after the processing of the parts and yet the processing of the parts benefits from the perception of the whole. Research in nonlinear neural network dynamics has shown that these effects result from cooperative and competitive feedback interactions between layers and units coding the whole and the parts, respectively (e.g. McClelland & Rumelhart, 1986; Rumelhart & McClelland, 1986).

All these phenomena seem to indicate that global attributes of a stimulus may be perceived first and that these global attributes may determine our percepts so strongly as to suppress the processing of the individual features that constituted the whole percept in the first place. However, what is presented at the level of phenomenal awareness or conscious perception may only be the end product of a series of unconscious processing steps that are implemented in different visual areas in the brain. What appear to be puzzling paradoxes may just be the side effects of our 'theatre of consciousness' masking what goes on 'behind the

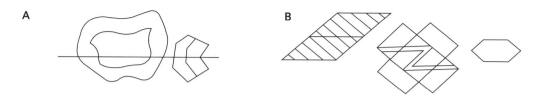

Figure 1.10   *Embedded figures. The number 4 is hidden in (A). (B) The smaller six-sided shape at the right is hidden in both of the larger, more complex patterns at the left and in the middle.*

curtains'. The fact that one cannot report the parts is no proof that they are not processed first, and even in those cases where feedback mechanisms have suppressed the lower-level features, these effects will occur relatively late. The initial stages of processing may still have worked with the standard low-level features.

In this respect, it may be useful to distinguish between two quite different aspects of 'early vision' or 'low-level vision' that are usually not disentangled, namely their spatial location in the 'low' range of brain areas and their temporal location 'early' in the stream of processing. Many of the phenomena reviewed above are consistent with a so-called *reverse hierarchy theory* of visual perception (Hochstein & Ahissar, 2002) in which either the site or the time of processing are opposed to a simple reading of 'early vision' implying low-level brain areas, processing and representing low-level features (i.e. simple lines, edges and spots of light). In this view, it comes as no surprise that even primary visual cortex may be involved in figure–ground perception (Lamme, 1995), in object-based attention (Roelfsema, Lamme, & Spekreijse, 1998), and in higher-level vision in general (Lee, Mumford, Romero, & Lamme, 1998; Lee, Yang, Romero, & Mumford, 2002). Moreover, this view is consistent with general theories about the role of massive feedback pathways and so-called *re-entrant processing* (Edelman, 1989; Ullman, 1995), which have also been applied to specific phenomena such as backward masking (DiLollo, Enns, & Rensink, 2000; DiLollo, Kawahara, Zuvic, & Visser, 2001). In line with these notions are recent speculations about an alternative neural theory of consciousness based on work with blindsight patients (e.g. Stoerig & Cowey, 1997) and studies with transcranial magnetic stimulation (e.g. Pascual-Leone & Walsh, 2001), suggesting that visual awareness may depend on the completion of a feedback sweep from higher visual areas down to the earliest visual area, V1 (e.g. Lamme, 2000, 2001).

These results point to the fact that early-vision-as measurement is only a first step in visual processing, and that the units used to do local, blurred derivative measurements are thereafter perhaps re-used for more complex signalling. Note that this would imply that it may be impossible to map visual tasks in any simple way on to brain areas. Watt and Phillips (2000) have recently proposed a visual processing model akin to this notion. They distinguish between two types of visual grouping. In the first type, V1 simple cells combine activity from a pre-specified set of inputs (corresponding to the classical receptive field) according to the pre-specified pattern of excitation and inhibition, to compute whatever feature they signal. When cascaded, this form of grouping produces feature hierarchies that have the ability to classify input into pre-specified output categories. In the second type, called *dynamic grouping*, the manner of combination of the features is not pre-specified and the nature of the output is determined by the interaction of its organizational processes and the current input rather than being limited to a restricted set of categories. Furthermore, both types of grouping interact and can be combined flexibly to produce a coherent system with richly structured visual descriptions (e.g. Hummel & Biederman, 1992; Phillips & Singer, 1997; Watt, 1991). This framework is remarkably consistent, if not isomorphic, with the three-step extension of the early-vision-as-measurement approach that we have outlined above. Indeed, we have distinguished between interactions between local derivatives (level 1), creation of 'higher-level' units (level 2) and a final stage of visual processing (level 3), in which we included additional generalizations and further modulations to enhance its flexibility.

Gestalt-theoretic notions: further discussion and evaluation

Although we have argued that there is nothing special about the Gestalt phenomena reviewed above that forces us to step away from the (extended) measurement approach, two (related) Gestalt-theoretic notions – the minimum principle and the field dynamics of the processes in the brain – require a short additional comment. Because of the global and dynamic nature of these principles, they may appear out of reach of the (extended) measurement approach.

First, without further specification, the *minimum principle* looks circular: the visual system organizes the visual input as simply as possible, but what does this mean? If it means 'looking simple to us', we are faced with explanatory circularity. Based on earlier attempts to quantify simplicity in information-theoretic terms (e.g. Attneave, 1954; Hochberg & McAlister, 1953), Leeuwenberg (1969, 1971) has invented a coding theory to describe all possible percepts, to quantify their information load (i.e. how 'costly' they are) and to predict the perceptual outcome (i.e. the percept with the smallest information load). This theory has been applied successfully to phenomena such as amodal completion where it can deal with local as well as global factors (e.g. van Lier et al., 1995). In a later development (e.g. van der Helm & Leeuwenberg, 1996), the primitives of the coding theory and the specific rules used to express the complexity of the code have been mathematically justified. This so-called 'holographic approach' (reflecting the nested structure of regularities in the coding sequences) has been used to 'explain' perceptual goodness of visual regularities (e.g. the saliency of different symmetries as reviewed by Wagemans, 1995). However, one should be aware that this theory addresses only the representation level: it only describes the structure of regularities in the representations of visual patterns, and it does not specify how these representations come about (i.e. the processes leading to these representations, let alone the underlying mechanisms). Fortunately, this representational approach can be supplemented with a processing approach such as the bootstrap account mentioned earlier to explain visual detection of symmetry (e.g. Wagemans et al., 1993; Wagemans, 1997). As a result of an exchange of ideas between van der Helm and Leeuwenberg (1999) and Wagemans (1999), a hybrid 'holographic bootstrap' approach now seems possible. This illustrates one of the claims we make in this chapter, namely that Gestalt ideas are not incompatible with a standard vision-as-measurement approach. Other process models of symmetry detection, making use of filters derived more directly from early-vision work (e.g. Dakin & Hess, 1997; Dakin & Watt, 1994; Rainville & Kingdom, 2000), testify to the same point.

Compatibility with the standard approach may appear less obvious for the second Gestalt-theoretical notion. Köhler (e.g. 1929, 1940) was the proponent of Gestalt psychology who argued most vehemently that perceptual organization must result from the intrinsic dynamics of electrical field forces in the cortex. More than half a century ago, Lashley, Chow, and Semmes (1951) had already demonstrated the limited empirical validity of this theoretical claim in experiments preventing the flow of electrical currents with cortically implanted metallic plates. Modern neuroimaging techniques (such as EEG and MEG) can now map local field potentials with some precision (both on and within the cortex), and it is generally agreed that the field potentials are the result rather than the cause of neuronal activity (e.g. Nunez, 2000).

Some neural network theorists have continued to study dynamical aspects. For example, perceptual dynamics can be described as seeking stable minima in some suitably characterized 'energy landscape' (Hopfield, 1982). This notion of energy minimization is not only an interesting metaphor to describe the Gestaltist minimum principle underlying the laws of perceptual organization, duplicating the universal laws of dynamics as in the formation of a soap bubble (Attneave, 1982; van der Helm, 1994; van Leeuwen & van den Hof, 1991). It has also inspired useful practical applications in computer vision based on techniques such as stochastic relaxation (e.g. Geman & Geman, 1984), simulated annealing (e.g. Kirkpatrick, Gelatt, & Vecchi, 1983) and Markov random fields (e.g. Zhu, 1999). Furthermore, theoretical neuroscientists have shown that the constraints imposed by highly specific patterns of connections within a neural network are not incompatible with a rich dynamic response. Traditional linear feedforward networks have severe limitations in this respect, but it is now well established that nonlinear recurrent networks have much more interesting dynamic properties (Amit, 1989; Haken, 1983; von der Malsburg, 1999). Finally, dynamic neural field theory has been applied successfully, for instance to motion perception (Giese, 1999), in a way that clearly goes beyond (elaborated) Reichardt detectors but that is still compatible with the extended measurement approach. All of these recent developments relate somehow to the currently popular dynamical system approaches in physics, with their emphasis on nonlinear complex systems and chaos theory (e.g. Gleick, 1987; Kauffman, 1995; Lewin, 1992). They continue to provide fuel to the original Gestalt dream of self-organization as an emergent property of the intrinsic dynamics of the brain as a complex system. (For accessible introductions to these approaches, techniques and applications for psychologists, neuroscientists and cognitive scientists, see Heath, 2000, Wilson, 1999, and Ward, 2002, respectively. Credit must also be given to Kelso, 1995, who has been one of the advocates of the role of dynamic patterns in brain and behaviour.)

Although the dynamics require a different level of description, they are, of course, not incompatible with the extended measurement approach and the neuron doctrine. A good example to illustrate this is the case of multistability, more specifically binocular rivalry, which we introduced earlier. Wilson, Blake, and Lee (2001) have developed a model that is able

A

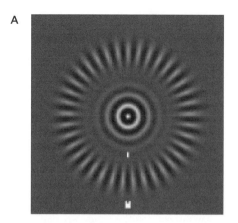

B

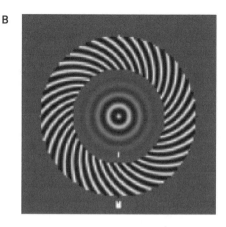

C

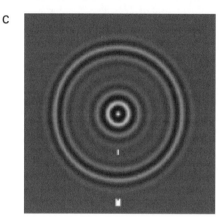

Figure 1.11 *Stimuli from the study by Wilson et al. (2001) of the dynamics of switching and dominance waves in multistable perceptual organization. (B) High-contrast spiral grating presented to one eye in rivalry with either a low-contrast radial (A) or concentric (C) grating presented to the other eye. When switching from one percept to the other, the locally dominant percept usually spreads around the annulus.*

to simulate the dynamics of switching and the systematic transitions in dominance as one stimulus sweeps the other out of conscious awareness (i.e. 'dominance waves'). In their experiments, one eye received a high-contrast spiral grating and the other eye received a lower-contrast radial or concentric grating, all presented on an annulus (see Figure 1.11). When the stimulus in the other eye starts to dominate the percept, it usually achieves local dominance first and then propagates around the annulus. In their model, there are two layers of cortical neurons, one sensitive to the spiral pattern and one sensitive to the monocular target pattern (radial, concentric or spiral). Through interneurons, each neuron in each layer inhibits a range of neurons in the opposing layer. To simulate collinear facilitation, neighbouring neurons within a layer have weak reciprocal excitatory connections. The excitatory neurons in both layers (but not the inhibitory interneurons) incorporate slow, hyperpolarized currents to produce spike-rate adaptation. With the appropriate parameters for the spatial range of inhibition and excitation and for the temporal properties for adaptation, all derived from neurophysiological and psychophysical experiments,

the dynamics of dominance wave propagation could be simulated with reasonable precision.

BEYOND EARLY VISION: GIBSON'S ECOLOGICAL APPROACH

During the first half of his career, Gibson (e.g. 1950a) developed something akin to 'higher-order' psychophysics, focusing on the visual system's measurement of higher-order variables (e.g. invariant ratios, texture gradients) in the ordinal stimulation of the optic array – the structured pattern of light rays reaching the eye. Like Gestalt psychology, he held elementarist bottom-up notions in contempt, and shared their enthusiasm for holistic alternatives without much concern about intermediate processing mechanisms. In the second half of his career, however, he distanced himself from his earlier work because it was still based on classic distinctions between sensation and perception, between stimuli and responses, and between observer and environment. He gradually developed the 'ecological approach' to visual perception (e.g. Gibson, 1979), a radically different approach, that could no longer be compared to anything before (e.g. Fodor & Pylyshyn, 1981; Turvey, Shaw, Reed, & Mace, 1981). Because of the far-reaching consequences of his approach for the whole field of vision science and its underlying assumptions, we need to address it in this chapter too. We shall explain its most central tenets, illustrate the kind of research inspired by it, and conclude that, actually, and in contrast to Gibson's own view, its most interesting aspects can also be accommodated within the extended measurement approach.

Ecological approach: central ideas and concepts

The central tenet of Gibson's (1979) ecological approach to perception is that an actively perceiving and behaving organism in its natural environment has much more information available than traditionally assumed for the case of a passive observer in a typical laboratory experiment (see also Michaels & Carello, 1981). If sensory information is sufficiently specific about the objects, spatial layout and events in our environment, then accurate perception does not require additional information that is not immediately available in the stimulation. No intermediate processes are then needed, according to Gibson, and perception is just the *direct pick-up* of this available information. It requires only that perceiving organisms are tuned to, or resonate to, the appropriate information in the optic array or optic flow field. Of course, from the traditional point of view of vision science, this is nonsense: a complete theory about perception must specify how the information is encoded in the visual system and how it is processed and represented to yield the information that is needed to guide our actions (e.g. Marr, 1982; Ramachandran, 1985). However, the central issue in the discussion about direct versus indirect (mediated or inferential) perception is, in fact, the question of the appropriateness of standard physical terms to describe the incoming information (i.e. the way this chapter started). Gibson (1960) and his followers have argued that the low-level physical variables to describe light (i.e. wavelength and amplitude, corresponding to hue and intensity) are inappropriate. Instead, one needs higher-order variables that correspond to the characteristics of the objects, scenes and events of interest much more directly (Michaels & Carello, 1981).

To study the available stimulus information in natural organism–environment ecosystems, Gibson (1961) started a new discipline, which he called *ecological optics*. The possibility of direct perception is quite controversial (e.g. Stoffregen & Bardy,

2001; Ullman, 1980), to say the very least, but ecological optics has yielded important discoveries for other vision scientists who are not committed to the idea of direct perception (e.g. also for the computational approach defined by Marr, 1982 – see the next chapter). Rather than addressing the historical and philosophical aspects of the ecological approach (e.g. Reed, 1988), or entering the debate about direct or indirect perception, we shall briefly introduce two central notions in Gibson's work, invariants and affordances, and then illustrate the major characteristics of the ecological approach to visual perception with two exemplary lines of research.

One of the key concepts in Gibson's ecological approach is the notion of *invariants*, defined as properties in the visible information that are constant or unchanged despite local changes in the optic array due to object motion or global changes in the optic flow field due to observer movement. It is useful to distinguish between topographic or structural invariants (structural properties in visual space that hold over the course of an event), and dynamic or transformational invariants (rules that govern the nature of change over the course of an event; Cutting, 1981a; Michaels & Carello, 1981). A prime example of a topographic invariant is the horizon-ratio, which provides good information about object size, regardless of viewing distance, when taken relative to eye-height (e.g. Bingham, 1993a, 1993b; Wraga, 1999a, 1999b). Based on a well-known theorem from projective geometry, a number of studies have addressed the role of cross-ratios in shape and motion perception (e.g. Cutting, 1986; Niall, 1992; Niall & McNamara, 1990). Dynamic invariants play a role in the perception of rolling wheels (e.g. Proffitt & Cutting, 1980), the perception of changing age in the profile of a human head (e.g. Mark & Todd, 1985; Pittenger, Shaw, & Mark, 1979) and the perception of biological motion (see below).

Another central notion in Gibson's theoretical framework is that of *affordances*, a term that Gibson (1979, 1982) has invented to express the idea that observers may be attuned to the properties of objects in relation to the actions that can be performed on them. Affordances are opportunities for action. For example, when looking at a chair, the first thing that comes to mind is not, according to Gibson, a pictorial representation of a particular chair or a structural description of a somewhat more abstract version of it. Instead, observers notice the higher-order relations between surfaces that define the sit-on-ability of a chair in relation to their own body proportions. This line of reasoning has been applied in studies of sitting and stair climbing (Mark, 1987), traversability of surfaces (Gibson, Riccio, Schmuckler, Stoffregen, Rosenberg, & Taormina, 1987), pulling (Michaels & de Vries, 1998), perceived heaviness of objects (Turvey,

Shockley, & Carello, 1999), tool use (van Leeuwen, Smitsman, & van Leeuwen, 1994), S-R compatibility effects in apparent motion perception (Michaels, 1988, 1993; Proctor, Van Zandt, Lu, & Weeks, 1993) and beyond visual perception in social and educational psychology (Greeno, 1994).

Ecological approach: two exemplary lines of research

We shall briefly discuss some classic and recent work on visual timing of approaching objects and on biological motion. We have chosen these two lines of research because they constitute excellent examples to illustrate the major characteristics of the ecological approach. Moreover, these phenomena have also been studied by vision scientists who would not call themselves Gibsonians (thereby demonstrating Gibson's impact on those who do not share the same theoretical commitments).

The first example is the study of *visual timing of approaching objects* (for a review, see Tresilian, 1999). To be able to make interceptions (e.g. to hit or catch an approaching ball) or to avoid collisions, we need to be able to estimate the time remaining before collision occurs (i.e. time-to-collision, or TTC for short). It can be shown that TTC is specified in the ratio of the approaching object's image relative to the rate of change in size; that is, the relative rate of image dilation, known as *tau* (τ). Because τ does not involve measurements of speeds, distances or accelerations, it requires no complex computations. This is especially attractive to Gibson: an ecologically relevant action can be coupled directly to a higher-order relation available in the optic flow field. What appears to be a complex information-processing situation may turn out to be based on a very simple mechanism. Moreover, it is a generally available type of information, independent of the specific eye of the perceiving organism. It comes as no surprise then that τ has been shown to be the basis of many cases of interceptive actions in many species: for instance, for the timing of wing retraction in plummeting gannets (Lee & Reddish, 1981), leg extension in landing house flies (Wagner, 1982), ball hitting (Bootsma & van Wieringen, 1990) and catching (Savelsbergh, Whiting, & Bootsma, 1991).

Perhaps more surprising is the finding that single neurons are sensitive to the optical expansion pattern of an approaching object, called 'looming'. Rind and Simmons (1999) have reviewed evidence for neurons that are tightly tuned to detect objects that are approaching on a direct collision course. At least in the optic tectum of pigeons, these collision-sensitive neurons signal the time remaining before collision (Sun & Frost, 1998). In the brain of the locust, wide-field, movement-sensitive visual neurons have been found whose responses could be described simply by multiplying the velocity of the image edge with an exponential function of the size of the object's image on the retina (Hatsopoulus, Gabbiani, & Laurent, 1995). The activity of these neurons peaks when the approaching object reaches a certain angular size and thus these neurons can anticipate collision. Because these neurons receive distinct inputs about image size and velocity, they could be considered as the ideal implementation of a specialized mechanism for collision anticipation, which is perfectly compatible with the extended measurement approach (outlined in the first half of this chapter), in which higher-level descriptions are derived from lower-order building blocks, tailored to serve a specific purpose.

The second example is the study of *biological motion perception*. Johansson (1973) created so-called 'point-light walker displays' by filming human actors in the 'dark', wearing black clothing with a dozen light patches on their head, hip and joints (shoulders, elbows, wrists, knees and ankles). When stationary, only a random collection of dots is seen. When put into motion, however, a vivid impression of a human body performing a particular action (walking, cycling, climbing stairs, doing push-ups, hugging, etc.) immediately arises, after only 200 ms or so (Johansson, 1975). Subsequent research has shown that these biological motion displays can be used to recognize the identity of a familiar person or the gender of an unfamiliar person (Cutting, Proffitt, & Kozlowski, 1978) and even to estimate the weight of a lifted box (Runeson & Frykholm, 1981). Even infants as young as three months (Fox & McDaniel, 1982) and cats (Blake, 1993) perceive biological motion.

The striking aspect here, which Gibson (1977) immediately liked very much, is that motion can turn a random array of dots into a meaningful event. He argued that the appropriate information for this event perception is thus the higher-order spatio-temporal movement pattern instead of the lower-order individual dot positions. The fact that this perception is so immediate and vivid, and that infants and cats are capable of it, could be interpreted to suggest that no complex processing mechanisms are involved. Furthermore, Cutting et al. (1978) were able to identify a simple invariant property that can be used for gender classification: when taking the hips and shoulders as corner points defining a virtual quadrangle, the centre of movement at the crossing of the two diagonals is located higher in female than in male walkers.

Two caveats must be made, however. First, the spatio-temporal movement pattern is defined by the specific combinations of spatial relations between the dots and how they change over time. There is nothing in this stimulus that is incompatible with a description in terms of the well-known variables of the measurement approach. Second, the apparent immediacy of the percept is no evidence that there is no processing involved. Indeed, even Johansson (1973) used a specific process model, which he called 'vector analysis', to describe what is going on. Likewise, Cutting (1981b) has developed a coding theory of gait perception, which is very similar in spirit to Leeuwenberg's (1969, 1971) coding theory for perceptual organization of static patterns (see above). Restle (1979) had already extended Leeuwenberg's coding theory for simpler cases of event perception from Johansson's (1950) earlier work.

Cutting and Proffitt (1982) have used vector analysis to describe the visual perception of Johansson's (1950) event configurations. Imagine a display consisting of seven light points, two parallel horizontal rows of three points, one on top and one below, and one central point in the middle between the two rows. Imagine further that this display is put into motion in such a way that the two groups of three points translate horizontally across the screen and the central point follows a diagonal trajectory from the lower left corner (close to the left-most point of the lower row) to the upper right corner (close to the right-most point of the upper row). What is then seen is that the central point moves up and down within a vertically grouped column of three points, while this group is nested in a larger group translating across the screen. In other words, the absolute diagonal motion of the central point is decomposed into a vertical component of relative motion and a horizontal component of common motion. A similar analysis can be applied to the absolute cycloid motions of two points on the rim of a rolling wheel, being decomposed into a pair of points rotating relative to one another and tracing a sinusoidal path of common motion. These displays had already been used by the Gestalt psychologists Rubin (1927) and Duncker (1929) to argue for the role of grouping and organization in motion perception (against just seeing the absolute motions). It now turned out to be relatively straightforward to extend such a vector analysis to the case of hierarchically nested groups in point-light walker displays performing different biological motions (Cutting, 1981b). Similar ideas have been used in computational models developed to extract the connectivity pattern inherent in such displays (Hoffman & Flinchbaugh, 1982; Webb & Aggarwal, 1982) and, in combination with the notion of structural invariants, to explain hierarchical organization in motion perception (Bertamini & Proffitt, 2000).

Furthermore, later research has clearly demonstrated the role of global processing. For example, Sumi (1984) showed that a human walker is much harder to see when turned upside-down (very much like the inversion effect arguing for configural processing in faces). A point-light walker can be detected in a background of masking elements performing the same local motions (Cutting, Moore, & Morrison, 1988), a result which has been taken to support the notion that the walker's global form, specified by the overall motion pattern, precedes the perception of the individual light-points or their local relations (Bertenthal & Pinto, 1994). Likewise, the global motion of a point-light walker can still be seen across apertures, while only the local motions remain visible when non-biological motions (e.g. cutting scissors) are shown (Shiffrar, Lichtey, & Heptulla-Chatterjee, 1997). In other words, in addition to the low-level mechanisms (Mather, Radford, & West, 1992), some top-down component seems to be involved as well (see also Bülthoff, Bülthoff, & Sinha, 1998).

Recent neurophysiological research also indicates that relatively high-level, integrative mechanisms play a role in biological motion perception. For example, neurons that are sensitive to point-light walkers have been found in the anterior superior temporal polysensory area (STPa) in the superior temporal sulcus (STS) of the macaque cortex (Oram & Perrett, 1994). Single-case studies with brain-damaged patients have revealed an interesting pattern of double dissociations. Patients with normal sensitivity to low-level motion parameters such as direction and speed were impaired on biological motion (Schenk & Zihl, 1997a, 1997b), while some dorsal patients who were severely impaired on low-level motion perception tasks (to the extent that they were called 'motion-blind') could still see biological motion (McLeod, Dittrich, Driver, Perrett, & Zihl, 1996; Vaina, LeMay, Bienfang, Choi, & Nakayama, 1990). Some ventral patients who were unable to recognize objects or faces (suffering from agnosia or prosopagnosia, respectively) could still perceive biological motion correctly, while patients with lesions to some portions in the STS failed on biological motion with intact low-level motion perception and object/face recognition (Vaina, 1994). This set of results suggests that biological motion perception depends on an interplay between low-level and high-level motion systems, in interaction with a high-level form, perception system. This hypothesis has recently been confirmed in neuroimaging studies (e.g. Grossman & Blake, 2002; Vaina, Solomon, Chowdhury, Sinha, & Belliveau, 2001).

All of this illustrates one of the major claims in this chapter – that what looks simple may be complex and vice versa. In this case, a deceptively simple-looking visual phenomenon may involve a wealth of visual processes. The other way around, the effective stimulus may appear complex to be described completely in mathematical terms, but that need not rule out that its processing is still based on the building blocks of the (extended) measurement approach. These points receive strong support from recent work by Giese and his colleagues. Giese and Lappe (2002) have generated a new stimulus set by pairwise spatio-temporal morphing between four different biological motions (i.e. walking, running, limping and marching). This technique (which was developed earlier in the context of computer vision work by Giese & Poggio, 2000) uses linear combinations of prototypical example movements by computing the spatio-temporal correspondences between the two trajectories of the feature points (i.e. the 2-D coordinates of the joints of the point-light walker). The trajectories can be characterized by time-dependent vectors and the correspondence field between two trajectories can be defined by the spatial shifts and the temporal shifts that transform the first trajectory into the second. The correspondence problem can then be formulated as an optimization problem minimizing the spatial and temporal shifts (for more details, see Giese & Poggio, 2000). The weights of the linear combinations of the biological motion prototypes define a metric linear space over the class of mixed biological motions.

Stimuli sampled from this space were shown to observers and their classification probabilities followed the metric space properties quite nicely (duplicating previous results with static shapes, see Op de Beeck et al., 2001). This property makes it possible to derive so-called 'generalization fields' for biological motions (very similar to the notion of RBF for higher-level descriptors, as explained above). The experimental results point out, for instance, that 'walking' was characterized by larger generalization fields than the other prototypes, probably because of its larger familiarity. Naturalness ratings of hybrid stimuli could be predicted quite well from the naturalness ratings of the prototypes and their weights in the linear combination.

In a related line of research, Giese and Poggio (2002, 2003) have developed a neural network model with two pathways, one for form and one for motion. Each pathway consists of a hierarchy of neural units with increasing receptive field size, corresponding to what is known neurophysiologically. For the (ventral) form pathway, this hierarchy includes (1) 'simple cells' modelled by Gabor filters (V1), (2) 'complex cells' that respond maximally to oriented bars, irrespective of position (V2, V4), (3) view-tuned units selective to different body poses (IT and STS), and (4) motion-pattern selective units (STS). Similarly, the (dorsal) motion pathway consists of (1) local motion detectors (V1, V2), (2) local components of the optic flow field such as translation, expansion and contraction (MT, MST), (3) complex instantaneous optic flow fields (STS), and (4) the same motion-pattern selective units as in the form pathway (also STS). The different layers in these pathways are highly consistent with the hierarchical representations previously proposed by Riesenhuber and Poggio (1999) for object coding (as outlined above).

Selectivity for temporal order in biological motion was achieved by asymmetric lateral connections between the different layers within each pathway, with facilitation of the subsequent level and inhibition of the preceding level. As a result, a travelling pulse of activity in the output representation of the recurrent neural network was stabilized only when the stimulus frames were presented in the right temporal order, not when they were presented in inverse or random temporal order (corresponding to human perception, see Verfaillie, 2000). Other simulations with this neural network have shown its capabilities of mimicking a large number of well-known experimental results, such as graceful degradation of activity in the recognition layer of the form pathway when the 3-D view was turned away from the learned prototype (as in Verfaillie, 1993) and graceful degradation of activity in the recognition layer of the motion pathway when more and more masking dots were added (as in Cutting et al., 1988). Likewise, the generalization fields of the motion-pattern selective units in the form pathway when the model – which was trained on three prototypical biological motions (walking, running and limping) – was then tested on the morphs (using the technique of Giese & Poggio, 2000) agreed very well with the generalization fields of human observers (as found by Giese & Lappe, 2002). All of this constitutes a quite convincing plausibility proof that the recognition of complex biological motion patterns might be based on relatively simple and well-established neural mechanisms using the building blocks of the extended measurement approach.

Ecological approach: impact and evaluation

The ecological approach has made one undoubtedly major contribution to vision science and that is the discovery of many useful sources of information (e.g. texture gradients, motion parallax, optic flow). Gibson's contribution would have been considerable already on the basis of his focus on the importance of surfaces and spatial layout in our visual world (e.g. Gibson, 1950a, 1950b; see also Cutting & Vishton, 1995; Nakayama, He, & Shimojo, 1995) and on the role of object motion and observer movement (e.g. Gibson, 1954/1994; see also Blake, 1994; Koenderink, 1986; Nakayama, 1985, 1994). *Ecological optics* continues to be quite interesting and challenging. For example, how material properties of objects are specified in the light appears to be poorly understood (e.g. Pont & Koenderink, 2002).

The theory of *direct pick-up* of higher-order invariants, which Gibson considered as the other side of the coin of identifying sources of information, we find much less interesting. Suppose that it is possible to demonstrate that higher-order invariants exist that uniquely specify an interesting property of objects, scenes or events. As vision scientists (not ecological opticians), we need to know how this information is picked up, extracted, represented and used by the visual system. By introducing the notion of a 'smart mechanism', Runeson (1977) does little more than creating a black box for each direct-perceptual competence that one is able to postulate. Consider Runeson's metaphor of a polar planimeter. This instrument allows one to measure the area (i.e. a higher-order variable) of any randomly shaped planar figure directly – without calculations or inferences based on lower-order variables such as length or angle. Runeson calls this planimeter a smart mechanism. He contrasts this with rote mechanisms consisting of large numbers of a few types of basic components, each of which performing a rather simple task (just like neurons). Complex tasks (like most visual tasks) are possible only through intelligent and flexible interconnections between the components (very much like programming a computer). In contrast, smart mechanisms consist of a small number of specialized components that capitalize on the peculiarities of the situation and the task.

So, in essence, the relevant questions are empirical: What are the building blocks of the mechanisms – general-purpose or specialized? And how are they combined – flexibly for each new situation, or compiled into some fixed visual routines (Ullman, 1984)? And finally, if compiled, is this compilation wired-in during evolution (phylogenetically) or learned during an individual's lifetime (developmentally) or in the course of some extensive perceptual training? Ramachandran (1990) has proposed a so-called 'utilitarian theory of perception', rooted in his earlier idea (Ramachandran, 1985) that the visual system might consist of a 'bag of tricks', a series of short-cuts and make-do devices specifically tailored to one's needs. This idea is rather similar to the ecological notion of 'smart mechanisms', but Ramachandran is clearly not a Gibsonian. His work is rooted in the same tradition of the (extended) measurement approach that we have outlined in the first half of this chapter. We see no alternative for vision scientists who want to understand vision at the level of mechanisms (psychophysically) and their implementation (neurophysiologically). The discussion about direct-perceptual 'smart mechanisms' or inferential-cognitive 'cue heuristics' (e.g. Hecht, 1996; Runeson, Juslin, & Olsson, 2000) is not very fruitful. We shall therefore leave it and turn to Gibson's impact on recent empirical work regarding two of his key concepts, invariants and affordances, and at the end also briefly to some more general developments in vision science at large.

Let us start with the very important notion of *invariants*. Cassirer (1944) was one of the first to stress the relevance of group theory and the systematization of geometries in Klein's famous Erlanger Programme (Klein, 1893; see also Klein, 1908) to perception. In the United States, however, it was Gibson (1950a, 1960) who argued forcefully for the role of invariants as revealed through transformations, but he actually never seriously considered its mathematical foundations. It was the mathematician Hoffman (1966) who developed a group-theoretic account of visual perception (Lie algebra), but this was picked up by psychologists only when Dodwell (1983) made it more accessible to them (see also Hoffman, 1985, 1994). Four lines of research can be distinguished that all make use of this conglomerate of group theory, invariants under transformations, and Klein's classification of geometries. Not all of these necessarily fit into an ecological approach but they might be perceived like that, so it is useful to clarify this a bit further.

First, and most closely related to Gibson's own work, is research that was directly addressed at identifying a particular invariant and testing its usefulness in a specific perceptual task. Good examples here are the above-mentioned studies on cross-ratios (e.g. Cutting, 1986; Niall, 1992), rolling wheels (e.g. Proffitt & Cutting, 1980) and biological motion (e.g. Cutting et al., 1978). Second are group-theoretic applications to the perception of pairs of static patterns related by specific geometrically well-controlled transformations, using impoverished (and thus, in a sense, unecological) stimuli. We have investigated the role of a specific affine invariant for judgements of 2-D shape equivalence under affine transformations (Tibau, Willems, & Wagemans, 2000; Wagemans, Van Gool, & Lamote, 1996). We have tested predictions about minimal information conditions derived from a group-theoretic account of affine versus projective transformations (Wagemans, Van Gool, Lamote, & Foster, 2000). Wagemans and Tibau (1999) have introduced affine and projective variations on a simple stimulus (three collinear points rotating in a slanted plane), in an attempt to discover the critical information in a situation that had been taken as evidence for the use of projective invariants before (Lappin & Fuqua, 1983). And we have compared perspective with more general projective shape equivalence (Wagemans, Lamote, & Van Gool, 1997). Third, outside of Gibson's direct influence, are transformational accounts of 'goodness' of structure and regularity in simple dot patterns (Garner, 1974; Palmer, 1982, 1983), also applied in specific studies of symmetry detection (Wagemans, 1993, 1995, 1997, 1999; Wagemans et al., 1993). This account shares with Gibson the assumption that the visual system's sensitivity to structure and regularity derives from its experience with specific groups of transformations (see below).

In all of these cases, it is useful to point out that it is possible to derive different invariants for different stimulus conditions and visual tasks, and that a limited set of general 'building blocks' for these invariants can be identified (Van Gool, Moons, Pauwels, & Wagemans, 1994). Useful properties are, for instance, bisection, parallelism, tangents, inflections, equality of angles, of lengths, of areas, etc., all of which are properties that are not too difficult to imagine being extracted by the higher-level visual descriptors derived from early-vision primitives (as outlined in the first half of this chapter). Furthermore, the fact that the same invariants and their building blocks have been used in fast, robust and reliable computer vision applications, even in realistic environments (e.g. Van Gool, 1998; Van Gool, Moons, Pauwels, & Oosterlinck, 1995), can be taken as a plausibility proof for their usefulness. Nothing mysterious happens in the case of these invariants that cannot be incorporated into our standard measurement approach.

A fourth line of research, worth mentioning separately because it is quite relevant to our discussion of basic principles, is a fruitful series of studies by Koenderink, Lappin, Todd and co-workers on the geometry of surface perception, 3-D shape perception and 3-D space perception. These authors are clearly influenced by Gibson's work but they certainly do not share all of his ideas. Koenderink, van Doorn and co-workers have developed an extensive research programme asking observers to look at 2-D pictures of 3-D objects with a moderately complex, smooth surface structure (e.g. female torsos, Brancusi sculptures) and to perform simple tasks regarding the perceived local surface structure (e.g. local slant or curvature judgements, depth order). They have called this topic of research 'pictorial relief' to indicate the shape of surfaces in 'pictorial space' – the 3-D spatial impression obtained when looking at 2-D pictures (for a review, see Koenderink & van Doorn, 2003). They have been mainly interested in the geometric properties of this pictorial space, in comparison to the 3-D Euclidean properties of physical space. It would lead us too far to review this work here, but one of the major findings deserves mentioning in the context of the measurement approach. The local surface measurements always allow for the reconstruction of a consistent, smooth overall shape with two interesting characteristics. On the one hand, large inaccuracies and inconsistencies are found that vary with objects, observers and viewing conditions, and that usually involve the global depth scale for the surface as a whole (i.e. how far extended in depth the surface is perceived to be along the line of sight). On the other hand, perception of the qualitative shape of the surface is always remarkably reliable and accurate.

Similar results have been found in studies of shape perception using other than pictorial depth cues,

for instance using stereo or structure-from-motion (e.g. Koenderink, Kappers, Todd, Norman, & Phillips, 1996; Perotti, Todd, Lappin, & Phillips, 1998; Todd, Norman, Koenderink, & Kappers, 1997). The overall conclusion of this line of research is that the structure of perceived shape need not be Euclidean but can be affine or even ordinal (e.g. Todd, Chen, & Norman, 1998; Todd & Reichel, 1989). This should be seen as a warning not to take the properties of physical space for granted as the building blocks for visual measurements. A similar conclusion applies to the geometrical structure of the overall optical space as derived from simple spatial judgements (such as intersections of lines connecting visible objects) in full-cue, open-field conditions, a truly ecological type of research with respect to the stimulus situation (e.g. Koenderink, van Doorn, & Kappers, 2002; Koenderink, van Doorn, & Lappin, 2000; Todd, Oomes, Koenderink, & Kappers, 2001).

The issue of visual primitives has been addressed quite explicitly in a recent review paper on the foundations of spatial vision by Lappin and Craft (2000). They were interested in the spatial properties that are preserved in the mapping of the spatio-temporal environmental structure (objects, spatial layout and events) into the spatio-temporal structure in retinal images, neural representations, perceptual experiences and behavioural actions. They examined spatial structures composed of one, two, three or five points, involving space differentials of zeroth, first and second order, in one and two spatial dimensions. On the basis of experimental results regarding acuity thresholds for lower-order relations and higher-order structure, with noise added at different levels, they concluded that second-order differential structure of the 2-D neighbourhood of a point is the effective primitive of human spatial vision. Although this effectively fourth order might seem too high an order to be a primitive building block, earlier work by Koenderink (e.g. 1984, 1988, 1990) and Koenderink and van Doorn (e.g. 1987, 1990, 1992) has shown that this type of primitive spatial structure can be detected by simple local receptive-field operators, constructed from derivatives of Gaussian kernels. Based on their own empirical findings, Lappin and Craft concluded further that visual information about the fourth-order structure was not derived from lower-order primitives. The acuity thresholds for the higher-order structure would then necessarily have been greater than those for the lower-order structure (with noise being accumulated or even multiplied). Again, this indicates the critical importance of thinking about measurements and primitives in the right terms (i.e. mathematically sound and psychophysically and neurophysiologically plausible).

The discussion of the impact of Gibson's second key notion of *affordances* can be much shorter. The idea that observers (usually) see what (at least some) objects afford us to do with them is now generally accepted. Although it is virtually impossible to test any more specific hypotheses derived from this concept, two lines of research can be identified that seem to be somewhat related to Gibson's theorizing about affordances. The fact that this research has gone much beyond Gibson's original ideas about affordances can be interpreted as evidence for its generality as well as its vagueness. One line of research addresses the notion that the perceptual and motor systems must interact to see the behavioural potential of objects, a notion that has received a good deal of support in cognitive neuroscience studies. For example, Arbib (1997) has developed models of various subregions of the posterior parietal cortex and how they process visual information to support actions such as saccading (in lateral intraparietal area or LIP) and grasping (in anterior intraparietal area or AIP). In addition, he has shown how these areas interact with IT and with premotor areas (such as F5) to augment the affordance information and to resolve the action opportunities provided by multiple affordances. Likewise, a recent PET study (Grezes & Decety, 2002) has shown activation of motor areas in object perception tasks, which is consistent with the idea that the perception of objects automatically activates certain action patterns that can be made towards them.

In a second line of research, Proffitt and his co-workers have further developed the idea of behavioural potential in the context of slant estimation. It is well known that slant is usually *under*estimated when textured displays are presented on a flat (computer) screen (Flock, 1965; Freeman, 1965; Gibson, 1950b). Geographical slant of a real hill, in contrast, was greatly *over*estimated when observers had to report their visual perception (verbal estimate or visible disc-sector adjustment) but not when they were asked to provide a more direct, non-visual, haptic estimate (invisible palm-board adjustment), both when observers faced directly towards the incline of a hill (Bhalla & Proffitt, 1999) and when observers were allowed to view the hill from aside (Proffitt, Creem, & Zosh, 2001). Furthermore, slant overestimation of hills viewed from the top was greater than that of hills viewed from the base, consistent with the idea that slant overestimation reflects the potential behavioural effort – walking carefully down a grass-covered incline without slipping is a more demanding motor task than walking up a hill (e.g. Proffitt, Bhalla, Gossweiler, & Midgett, 1995). This hypothesis was tested directly by manipulating fatigue: after subjects had been running until they were tired (for half an hour or so), the slant estimates went up by an average of 30%.

The finding of a dissociation between conscious reports of perceptual judgements and more automatic (unconscious?) behavioural measures has suggested the possibility of two different types of representations in slant estimation (Creem &

Proffitt, 1998) and in many other situations. Indeed, Goodale and Milner (1992; see also Milner & Goodale, 1995) have used this dissociation found in brain-damaged patients to reinterpret the well-known anatomical segregation of a ventral and dorsal pathway, not as a what- and a where-stream, but as a pathway for conscious perception of object identity and meaning and an unconscious perception-for-action pathway. Similarly, in healthy observers, some of the well-known visual illusions such as the Müller–Lyer and the Ebbinghaus circles tend to be greatly reduced when an action measure such as grasping is used (Aglioti, DeSouza, & Goodale, 1995; Haffenden & Goodale, 1998). More recent research, however, has shown that this perception–action dissociation interacts with the perceptual encoding situation (see also Franz, Gegenfurtner, Bülthoff, & Fahle, 2000). For example, Wraga, Creem, and Proffitt (2000) have disentangled viewer- and object-centred encoding. When object-centred encoding of a Müller–Lyer configuration was induced, both verbal and motor tasks showed evidence for an illusion. In contrast, when viewer-centred (or egocentric) encoding was induced, a significant perception–action dissociation was obtained in the sense that verbal judgements continued to exhibit the illusion bias, whereas blind-walking judgements did not. Bruno (2001) has reviewed this recent literature and concluded that the issue of visuomotor dissociations in healthy individuals is far from settled.

What is clear, however, is that there seems to be a complex interplay between different types of representations depending on the task requirements. In that sense, we have progressed far from Gibson's original (and rather vague) idea that people detect affordances and that the perceptual and motor systems are intricate parts of a larger perceptuo-motor system (Gibson, 1966, 1979). For example, using an interference paradigm, Creem and Proffitt (2001b) have shown that mere object grasping was possible on the basis of visuomotor information only. However, when a semantically appropriate action had to be performed (e.g. grasping the handle of a toothbrush appropriately to start brushing), the retrieval of semantic information was required and thus the cognitive system and the action had to interact. This seems no longer compatible with a direct-perception explanation of affordances. Apparently, some large-scale object-related actions can be processed in a purely visuomotor way, whereas guidance of more fine-scaled, semantically specific object-related actions depends on top-down, semantic influences. Again, the overall conclusion is that detailed knowledge of the processing mechanisms is required for a better understanding of what is going on in vision and its relation to action.

To conclude our discussion of the impact of Gibson's ecological approach, we should like to mention two *more general* characteristics of his work that have fostered two new theoretical perspectives with great potential. First, Gibson (1966, 1979) has been one of the advocates of taking an evolutionary view on perception: What is vision for? And how could the visual mechanisms of vertebrates (eye and brain) have evolved from the available light sensors and nerve cells of more primitive organisms? This focus may have inspired other theoreticians who have discovered important principles of perception with an evolutionary grounding. For example, Shepard (2001) has argued that the basic principles or fundamental laws governing perception and cognition are the evolutionary imprint of the structures and transformations of objects in the world. If the internal representations and transformations follow the rules of kinematic geometry, that is because we have internalized these through our interactions with the objects in the world. Likewise, it is through evolution that our neural mechanisms exploit the statistical regularities of natural images and rely on redundancy reduction or exploitation as a fundamental principle of sensory coding, underlying diverse phenomena such as lateral inhibition, after-effects, adaptation and sparse coding (Barlow, 2001). We refer to Proffitt and Kaiser (1998) for an excellent discussion of the different internalization proposals in theories of perception (including statistical regularities, geometries, group concepts and the universal laws of organization).

A second new development certainly builds on Gibson's (meta)theoretical framework. In line with his direct perception theory, Gibson (1979) is famous (if not infamous) for his eschewing (if not detesting) of internal representations as necessary components of our understanding of perception (or even cognition). This aspect of his theorizing – which he shares with behaviourism (despite his strong reaction against their S-R approach) – has been taken up again by recent attempts to minimize the role of representations for understanding natural or producing artificial intelligence. In cognitive science, these trends are referred to as 'situated' (Pylyshyn, 2000) or 'embodied' cognition (Clark, 1999). Similar ideas are becoming increasingly popular in robotics (e.g. 'intelligence without representation', Brooks, 1991; 'autonomous agents', Maes, 1991; 'evolutionary robotics', Nolfi & Floreano, 2002) and computer vision (e.g. 'animate vision', Ballard, 1991; 'active vision', Blake & Yuille, 1992). Even 'artificially evolved simple vision systems', very much like Gibsonian 'smart mechanisms', have been proposed in opposition to more traditional knowledge-based vision systems (e.g. Cliff & Noble, 1997). We shall have to await further progress within these newly emerging paradigms to judge whether this is just the typical waxing and waning of theoretical vogues (from behaviourist to cognitivist, and back again), or whether this turns out to be a truly fruitful alternative to more standard approaches.

Building on these new developments in cognitive science and artificial intelligence, and connecting them to the new developments in large-scale neural networks, Thompson and Varela (2001) have proposed to expand the standard one-way causal-explanatory relationship from internal neural events to conscious experience (e.g. Crick & Koch, 1998; Kanwisher, 2001; Logothetis, 1998) into a more radically embodied view on neural dynamics and consciousness with two challenging propositions. First, because of emergent processes in a nonlinear, complex, dynamic system like the brain, with large-scale networks of nonlinear oscillators (for a review, see Varela, Lachaux, Rodriguez, & Martinerie, 2001), two-way, reciprocal relationships exist between neural events and conscious experience, with local-to-global or upward causation as well as global-to-local or downward causation. Second, the processes that are crucial for consciousness cut across brain–body–world divisions rather than being brain-bound neural events. The nervous system, the body and the environment are highly structured dynamical systems that are coupled to each other on multiple levels (for a review, see Chiel & Beer, 1997). It is thus most unlikely that one can just 'peel away' the body and the environment as being external to the internal brain processes that are crucial to consciousness. The philosophical thought experiment of a 'brain-in-a-vat' must be exposed as an infertile fiction.

All of this has taken us far from Gibson's ecological approach to visual perception. However, it should be clear from the final paragraphs above that Gibson has definitely been a very influential perceptual psychologist (and thinker). The empirically useful bits in his own work and in the work of those who have been inspired by him (directly or indirectly – pun intended) are not incompatible with the (extended) measurement approach. Indeed, the importance of a good description of the incoming information, the role of higher-level invariants (when taken as higher-level descriptions), and the strong coupling to functional needs in interaction with the environment (through evolutionary mechanisms and perceptual learning) all receive further support from a properly understood ecological approach to perception.

CONCLUSION

As Koffka (1935) himself recognized, the fundamental question of why things look the way they do can be understood in two different ways: first, as a phenomenological question of why it is that our conscious visual experience possesses certain qualities (e.g. the roundness of a circle, the redness of an apple), and second, as a functional and adaptive question of how these percepts can be veridical in the sense of corresponding to the object properties themselves. At first sight, the 'early-vision-as-measurement' approach (outlined in the first three sections of this chapter) may appear incapable of answering these questions because 'blurred derivatives' just seem too far away from conscious and veridical perception. However, we hope to have illustrated in the remaining sections that this approach provides the proper primitives to start building detailed theoretical explanations of the underlying visual mechanisms.

In a purely bottom-up account, the consciousness of Gestalt qualities referred to in the first version of Koffka's question appears as a mysterious ingredient added on to the final, high-level representation delivered by early- and mid-level vision. More recent accounts have stressed the complicated interplay between feedforward, bottom-up processes and recurrent, feedback processes, but even in these models the information coming into the visual system is first represented by blurred derivatives. The primitives of conscious vision may not be those of early vision, but understanding all the mechanisms at all the levels that are involved in the processing of visual information leading to conscious vision will have to include the psychophysically and neurophysiologically recorded primitives from the measurement approach. In a rigidly understood version of the measurement approach, as perhaps suggested by the original filter or channel models, the number and type of primitives may have seemed too limited to be able to explain the richness and flexibility of visual perception revealed by all of the well-known perceptual phenomena (reviewed in the final sections of this chapter). As argued earlier, however, the extended measurement approach is indeed capable of producing much more flexible higher-level units, and nothing in these phenomena is thus incompatible with this approach.

Regarding the second version of Koffka's question, the functional and adaptive question about veridicality, there is no reason to resort to the far-reaching claims of Gibson's ecological approach about direct pick-up of higher-order invariants that are in a one-to-one correspondence to the affordances of the objects and events around us. The ecological validity of the visual primitives discovered by the measurement approach and of specific properties of certain grouping principles has received considerable empirical support from recent studies with natural images. The extent to which evolution has produced hard-wired 'smart mechanisms' devoted to the appropriate type of information, or leaves room for more general building blocks ('modules') that can be combined more flexibly according to the requirements of the task at hand or to the specific regime of visual stimulation, is an open empirical question, not a matter of dogma imposed by an overarching framework with metaphysical presumptions.

In sum, using a wide variety of techniques and methods, considerable progress has been made towards understanding an ever wider variety of visual phenomena. However, most of this work can be captured under the umbrella of standard vision science, which is based on the foundations of the measurement approach. Even those studies performed by Gestalt and Gibsonian psychologists, who have vehemently opposed themselves against his framework, have yielded empirical results that are generally perfectly compatible with the measurement approach. To determine how exactly all these bits and pieces discovered so far fit in as parts of a complete explanation of why things look the way they do constitutes a series of interesting challenges. They are the source of great fun to a large number of vision scientists.

REFERENCES

Adelson, E. H., & Bergen, J. R. (1985). Spatiotemporal energy models for the perception of motion. *Journal of the Optical Society of America A, 2*, 284–299.

Adelson, E. H., & Bergen, J. R. (1991). The plenoptic function and the elements of early vision. In M. S. Landy & J. A. Movshon (Eds.), *Computational models of visual processing* (pp. 3–20). Cambridge, MA: MIT Press.

Adelson, E. H., & Movshon, J. A. (1982). Phenomenological coherence of moving visual patterns. *Nature, 300*, 523–525.

Aglioti, S., DeSouza, J. F. X., & Goodale, M. A. (1995). Size-contrast illusions deceive the eye but not the hand. *Current Biology, 5*, 679–685.

Albright, T. D., & Stoner, G. R. (2002). Contextual influences on visual processing. *Annual Review of Neuroscience, 25*, 339–379.

Allman, J., Miezin, F., & McGuinness, E. (1985). Stimulus specific responses from beyond the classical receptive field: neurophysiological mechanisms for local-global comparisons in visual neurons. *Annual Review of Neuroscience, 8*, 407–430.

Alvarado, M. C., & Bachevalier, J. (2000). Revisiting the maturation of medial temporal lobe memory functions in primates. *Learning and Memory, 7*, 244–256.

Amit, D. J. (1989). *Modelling brain function: the world of attractor neural networks*. Cambridge: Cambridge University Press.

Anderson, B. L. (1992). Hysteresis, cooperativity, and depth averaging in dynamic random-dot stereograms. *Perception and Psychophysics, 51*, 511–528.

Anderson, B. L., & Nakayama, K. (1994). Toward a general theory of stereopsis: binocular matching, occluding contours, and fusion. *Psychological Review, 101*, 414–445.

Arbib, M. A. (1997). From visual affordances in monkey parietal cortex to hippocampo-parietal interactions underlying rat navigation. *Philosophical Transactions of the Royal Society of London B, 352*, 1429–1436.

Arguin, M., & Saumier, D. (2000). Conjunction and linear non-separability effects in shape encoding. *Vision Research, 40*, 3099–3115.

Asch, M. G. (1995). *Gestalt psychology in German culture, 1890–1967: Holism and the quest for objectivity*. New York: Cambridge University Press.

Atick, J. J. (1992). Could information theory provide an ecological theory of sensory processing? *Network: Computation in Neural Systems, 3*, 213–251.

Attneave, F. (1954). Some informational aspects of visual perception. *Psychological Review, 61*, 183–193.

Attneave, F. (1971). Multistability in perception. *Scientific American, 225*, 62–71.

Attneave, F. (1982). Prägnanz and soap bubble systems: a theoretical exploration. In J. Beck (ed.), *Organization and representation in perception* (pp. 11–29). Hillsdale, NJ: Erlbaum.

Baker, C. I., Behrmann, M., & Olson, C. R. (2002). Impact of learning on representation of parts and wholes in monkey inferotemporal cortex. *Nature Neuroscience, 5*, 1210–1216.

Ballard, D. (1991). Animate vision. *Artificial Intelligence, 48*, 57–86.

Barlow, H. B. (1953). Summation and inhibition in the frog's retina. *Journal of Physiology, 119*, 69–88.

Barlow, H. B. (1961). Possible principles underlying the transformation of sensory messages. In W. A. Rosenblith (ed.), *Sensory communication* (pp. 217–234). Cambridge, MA: MIT Press.

Barlow, H. B. (1972). Single units and sensation: a neuron doctrine for perceptual psychology? *Perception, 1*, 371–394.

Barlow, H. B. (2001). The exploitation of regularities in the environment by the brain. *Behavioral and Brain Sciences, 24*, 602–607.

Barlow, H. B., Blakemore, C., & Pettigrew, J. D. (1967). The neural mechanisms of binocular depth discrimination. *Journal of Physiology, 193*, 327–342.

Beck, D. M., & Palmer, S. E. (2002). Top-down influences on perceptual grouping. *Journal of Experimental Psychology: Human Perception and Performance, 28*, 1071–1084.

Bell, A. J., & Sejnowski, T. J. (1997). The 'independent components' of natural scenes are edge filters. *Vision Research, 37*, 3327–3338.

Ben-Av, M. B., & Sagi, D. (1995). Perceptual grouping by similarity and proximity: experimental results can be predicted by intensity autocorrelations. *Vision Research, 35*, 853–866.

Bertamini, M. (2001). The importance of being convex: an advantage for convexity when judging position. *Perception, 30*, 1295–1310.

Bertamini, M., & Proffitt, D. R. (2000). Hierarchical motion organization in random dot configurations. *Journal of Experimental Psychology: Human Perception and Performance, 26*, 1371–1386.

Bertenthal, B., & Pinto, J. (1994). Global processing of biological motion. *Psychological Science, 5*, 221–225.

Bhalla, M., & Proffitt, D. R. (1999). Visuo-motor recalibration in geographical slant perception. *Journal of Experimental Psychology: Human Perception and Performance, 25*, 1076–1096.

Biederman, I. (1987). Recognition-by-components: a theory of human image understanding. *Psychological Review, 94*, 115–147.

Biederman, I., & Bar, M. (1999). One-shot viewpoint invariance in matching novel objects. *Vision Research, 39*, 2885–2899.

Biederman, I., & Kalocsai, P. (1997). Neurocomputational bases of object and face recognition. *Philosophical Transactions of the Royal Society of London B, 352*, 1203–1219.

Biederman, I., Rabinowitz, J. C., Glass, A. L., & Stacy, E. W., Jr. (1974). On the information extracted from a glance at a scene. *Journal of Experimental Psychology, 103*, 597–600.

Bingham, G. P. (1993a). Perceiving the size of trees: biological form and the horizon ratio. *Perception and Psychophysics, 54*, 485–495.

Bingham, G. P. (1993b). Perceiving the size of trees: form as information about scale. *Journal of Experimental Psychology: Human Perception and Performance, 19*, 1139–1161.

Blake, A., & Yuille, A. (Eds.) (1992). *Active vision*. Cambridge, MA: MIT Press.

Blake, R. (1989). A neural theory of binocular rivalry. *Psychological Review, 96*, 145–167.

Blake, R. (1993). Cats perceive biological motion. *Psychological Science, 4*, 54–57.

Blake, R. (1994). Gibson's inspired but latent prelude to visual motion perception. *Psychological Review, 101*, 324–328.

Blake, R., & Logothetis, N. K. (2002). Visual competition. *Nature Reviews Neuroscience, 3*, 1–11.

Blakemore, C., & Campbell, F. W. (1969). On the existence of neurons in the human visual system selectively sensitive to the orientation and size of retinal images. *Journal of Physiology, 203*, 237–260.

Booth, M. C. A., & Rolls, E. T. (1998). View-invariant representations of familiar objects by neurons in the inferior temporal visual cortex. *Cerebral Cortex, 8*, 510–523.

Bootsma, R. J., & van Wieringen, P. C. W. (1990). Timing an attacking forehand drive in table tennis. *Journal of Experimental Psychology: Human Perception and Performance, 16*, 21–29.

Boselie, F. (1994). Local and global factors in visual occlusion. *Perception, 23*, 517–528.

Brooks, R. A. (1991). Intelligence without representation. *Artificial Intelligence, 47*, 139–159.

Bruno, N. (2001). When does action resist visual illusions? *Trends in Cognitive Sciences, 5*, 379–382.

Brunswik, E., & Kamiya, J. (1953). Ecological cue-validity of 'proximity' and of other Gestalt factors. *American Journal of Psychology, 66*, 20–32.

Bullier, J., Hupé, J.-M., James, A. C., & Girard, P. (2001). The role of feedback connections in shaping the responses of visual cortical neurons. *Progress in Brain Research, 134*, 193–204.

Bülthoff, I., Bülthoff, H. H., & Sinha, P. (1998). Top-down influences on stereoscopic depth-perception. *Nature Neuroscience, 1*, 254–257.

Caelli, T., & Dodwell, P. (1982). The discrimination of structure in vector-graphs: local and global effects. *Perception and Psychophysics, 32*, 314–326.

Campbell, F. W., & Gubitsch, R. W. (1966). Optical quality of the human eye. *Journal of Physiology, 186*, 558–578.

Campbell, F. W., & Robson, J. G. (1968). Application of Fourier analysis to the visibility of gratings. *Journal of Physiology, 197*, 551–566.

Carey, S., & Diamond, R. (1977). From piecemeal to configurational representation of faces. *Science, 195*, 312–314.

Cassirer, E. (1944). The concept of group and the theory of perception. *Philosophy and Phenomenological Research, 5*, 1–35.

Chang, J. J., & Julesz, B. (1984). Cooperative phenomena in apparent movement perception of random-dot cinematograms. *Vision Research, 24*, 1781–1788.

Chater, N. (1996). Reconciling simplicity and likelihood principles in perceptual organization. *Psychological Review, 103*, 566–591.

Chiel, H., & Beer, R. (1997). The brain has a body: adaptive behavior emerges from interactions of nervous system, body and environment. *Trends in Neurosciences, 20*, 553–557.

Clark, A. (1999). An embodied cognitive science? *Trends in Cognitive Sciences, 3*, 345–351.

Cliff, D., & Noble, J. (1997). Knowledge-based vision and simple visual machines. *Philosophical Transactions of the Royal Society of London B, 352*, 1165–1175.

Compton, B. J., & Logan, G. D. (1993). Evaluating a computational model of perceptual grouping. *Perception and Psychophysics, 53*, 403–421.

Coren, S., & Girgus, J. S. (1980). Principles of perceptual organization and spatial distortion: the Gestalt illusions. *Journal of Experimental Psychology: Human Perception and Performance, 6*, 404–412.

Creem, S. H., & Proffitt, D. R. (1998). Two memories for geographical slant: separation and interdependence of action and awareness. *Psychonomic Bulletin and Review, 5*, 22–36.

Creem, S. H., & Proffitt, D. R. (2001a). Defining the cortical visual systems: 'what', 'where', and 'how'. *Acta Psychologica, 107*, 43–68.

Creem, S. H., & Proffitt, D. R. (2001b). Grasping objects by their handles: a necessary interaction between cognition and action. *Journal of Experimental Psychology: Human Perception and Performance, 27*, 218–228.

Crick, F., & Koch, C. (1998). Consciousness and neuroscience. *Cerebral Cortex, 8*, 97–107.

Cumming, B. G., & DeAngelis, G. C. (2001). The physiology of stereopsis. *Annual Review of Neuroscience, 24*, 203–238.

Cutting, J. E. (1981a). Six tenets for event perception. *Cognition, 10*, 71–78.

Cutting, J. E. (1981b). Coding theory adapted to gait perception. *Journal of Experimental Psychology: Human Perception and Performance, 7*, 71–87.

Cutting, J. E. (1986). *Perception with an eye for motion.* Cambridge, MA: MIT Press/Bradford Books.

Cutting, J. E., Moore, C., & Morrison, R. (1988). Masking the motions of human gait. *Perception and Psychophysics, 44*, 339–347.

Cutting, J. E., & Proffitt, D. R. (1982). The minimum principle and the perception of absolute, common, and relative motion. *Cognitive Psychology, 14*, 211–246.

Cutting, J. E., Proffitt, D. R., & Kozlowski, L. T. (1978). A biomechanical invariant for gait perception. *Journal of Experimental Psychology: Human Perception and Performance, 4*, 357–372.

Cutting, J. E., & Vishton, P. M. (1995). Perceiving layout and knowing distances: the integration, relative potency, and contextual use of different information about depth. In W. Epstein & S. Rogers (Eds.), *Perception of space and motion* (pp. 69–117). San Diego, CA: Academic Press.

Dakin, S. C. (1997). The detection of structure in Glass patterns: psychophysics and computational models. *Vision Research, 37*, 2227–2246.

Dakin, S. C., & Hess, R. F. (1997). The spatial mechanisms mediating symmetry perception. *Vision Research, 37*, 2915–2930.

Dakin, S. C., & Watt, R. J. (1994). Detection of bilateral symmetry using spatial filters. *Spatial Vision, 8*, 393–413.

Daugman, J. G. (1984). Spatial visual channels in the Fourier plane. *Vision Research, 24*, 891–910.

Daugman, J. G. (1985). Uncertainty relation for resolution in space, spatial frequency, and orientation optimized by two-dimensional visual cortical filters. *Journal of the Optical Society of America A, 2*, 1160–1169.

Derrington, A. M., & Henning, G. B. (1989). Some observations on the masking effects of two-dimensional stimuli. *Vision Research, 29*, 241–246.

Desimone, R., & Duncan, J. (1995). Neural mechanisms of selective visual attention. *Annual Review of Neuroscience, 18*, 193–222.

De Valois, D. L., Albrecht, D. G., & Thorell, L. G. (1982). Spatial frequency selectivity of cells in macaque visual cortex. *Vision Research, 22*, 545–559.

Diamond, R., & Carey, S. (1986). Why faces are and are not special: an effect of expertise. *Journal of Experimental Psychology: General, 115*, 107–117.

DiLollo, V., Enns, J. T., & Rensink, R. (2000). Competition for consciousness among visual events: the psychophysics of re-entrant visual processes. *Journal of Experimental Psychology: General, 129*, 481–507.

DiLollo, V., Kawahara, J., Zuvic, S. M., & Visser, T. A. W. (2001). The preattentive emperor has no clothes: a dynamic redressing. *Journal of Experimental Psychology: General, 130*, 479–492.

Dobbins, A., Zucker, S. W., & Cynader, M. S. (1987). End-stopped neurons in the visual cortex as a substrate for calculating curvature. *Nature, 329*, 438–441.

Dodwell, P. C. (1983). The Lie transformation group model of visual perception. *Perception and Psychophysics, 34*, 1–16.

Duncker, K. (1929). Über induzierte Bewegung. *Psychologische Forschung, 12*, 180–259.

Edelman, G. (1989). *The remembered present.* New York: Basic Books.

Edelman, S. (1999). *Representation and recognition in vision.* Cambridge, MA: MIT Press.

Edelman, S., & Intrator, N. (2003). Towards structural systematicity in distributed, statically bound visual representations. *Cognitive Science, 27*, 73–109.

Elder, J. H., & Goldberg, R. M. (2002). Ecological statistics of Gestalt laws for the perceptual organization of contours. *Journal of Vision*, *2*, 324–353, http:// journalofvision. org/2/4/5/, DOI 10.1167/2.4.5.

Elder, J. H., & Zucker, S. W. (1994). A measure of closure. *Vision Research*, *34*, 3361–3369.

Elder, J. H., & Zucker, S. W. (1998). Evidence for boundary-specific grouping. *Vision Research*, *38*, 143–152.

Engel, A. K., & Singer, W. (2001). Temporal binding and the neural correlates of sensory awareness. *Trends in Cognitive Sciences*, *5*, 16–25.

Enroth-Cugell, C., & Robson, J. G. (1966). The contrast sensitivity of retinal ganglion cells of the cat. *Journal of Physiology*, *187*, 517–522.

Exner, S. (1875). Experimentelle Untersuchung der einfachsten psychischen Processe. *Pflügers Archiv für die Gesammte Physiologie des Menschen und der Tiere*, *11*, 403–432.

Farah, M. J., Wilson, K. D., Drain, M., & Tanaka, J. N. (1998). What is 'special' about face perception? *Psychological Review*, *105*, 482–498.

Farid, H. (2002). Temporal synchrony in perceptual grouping: a critique. *Trends in Cognitive Sciences*, *6*, 284–288.

Feldman, J. (1997). Curvilinearity, covariance, and regularity in perceptual groups. *Vision Research*, *37*, 2835–2848.

Felleman, D. J., & Van Essen, D. C. (1991). Distributed hierarchical processing in the primate cerebral cortex. *Cerebral Cortex*, *1*, 1–47.

Ferster, D., & Miller, K. D. (2000). Neural mechanisms of orientation selectivity in the visual cortex. *Annual Review of Neuroscience*, *23*, 441–471.

Field, D. J. (1987). Relations between the statistics of natural images and the response properties of cortical cells. *Journal of the Optical Society of America A*, *4*, 2379–2394.

Field, D. J. (1994). What is the goal of sensory coding? *Neural Computation*, *6*, 559–601.

Field, D. J., Hayes, A., & Hess, R. F. (1993). Contour integration by the human visual system: evidence for a local 'association field'. *Vision Research*, *33*, 173–193.

Flock, H. R. (1965). Optical texture and linear perspective as stimuli for slant perception. *Psychological Review*, *72*, 505–514.

Fodor, J. A., & Pylyshyn, Z. W. (1981). How direct is visual perception? Some reflections on Gibson's 'Ecological Approach'. *Cognition, 9*, 139–196.

Fox, R., & McDaniel, C. (1982). The perception of biological motion by human infants. *Science*, *218*, 486–487.

Franz, V. H., Gegenfurtner, K. R., Bülthoff, H. H., & Fahle, M. (2000). Grasping visual illusions: no evidence for a dissociation between perception and action. *Psychological Science*, *11*, 20–25.

Freeman, R. B. (1965). Ecological optics and visual slant. *Psychological Review*, *72*, 501–504.

Garner, W. R. (1974). *The processing of information and structure*. Hillsdale, NJ: Erlbaum.

Gegenfurtner, K. R., Kiper, D. C., & Fenstemaker, S. B. (1996). Processing of color, form, and motion in macaque area V2. *Visual Neuroscience*, *13*, 161–172.

Geisler, W. S., Perry, J. S., Super, B. J., & Gallogly, D. P. (2001). Edge co-occurence in natural images predicts contour grouping performance. *Vision Research*, *41*, 711–724.

Geman, S., & Geman, D. (1984). Stochastic relaxation, Gibbs distribution, and the Bayesian restoration of images. *IEEE Transactions on Pattern Analysis and Machine Intelligence*, *PAMI-6*, 721–742.

Gepshtein, S., & Kubovy, M. (2000). The emergence of visual objects in space-time. *Proceedings of the National Academy of Sciences of the USA*, *97*, 8186–8191.

Gibson, E. J., Riccio, G., Schmuckler, M. A., Stoffregen, T. A., Rosenberg, D., & Taormina, J. (1987). Detection of the traversability of surfaces by crawling and walking infants. *Journal of Experimental Psychology: Human Perception and Performance*, *13*, 533–544.

Gibson, J. J. (1950a). *The perception of the visual world*. Boston, MA: Houghton Mifflin.

Gibson, J. J. (1950b). The perception of visual surfaces. *American Journal of Psychology*, *63*, 367–384.

Gibson, J. J. (1954). The visual perception of objective motion and subjective movement. *Psychological Review, 61*, 304–314. (Reprinted in 1994, *Psychological Review*, *101*, 318–323.)

Gibson, J. J. (1960). Information contained in light. *Acta Psychologica*, *17*, 23–30.

Gibson, J. J. (1961). Ecological optics. *Vision Research*, *1*, 253–262.

Gibson, J. J. (1966). *The senses considered as perceptual systems*. Boston, MA: Houghton Mifflin.

Gibson, J. J. (1977). On the analysis of change in the optic array. *Scandinavian Journal of Psychology*, *18*, 161–163.

Gibson, J. J. (1979). *The ecological approach to visual perception*. Boston, MA: Houghton Mifflin.

Gibson, J. J. (1982). Notes on affordances. In E. Reed & R. Jones (Eds.), *Reasons for realism: selected essays of James J. Gibson* (pp. 401–418). Hillsdale, NJ: Erlbaum.

Giese, M. A. (1999). *Dynamic neural field theory for motion perception*. Boston, MA: Kluwer.

Giese, M. A., & Lappe, M. (2002). Measurement of generalization fields for the recognition of biological motion. *Vision Research*, *42*, 1847–1858.

Giese, M. A., & Poggio, T. (2000). Morphable models for the analysis and synthesis of complex motion patterns. *International Journal of Computer Vision*, *38*, 59–73.

Giese, M. A., & Poggio, T. (2002). Biologically plausible neural model for the recognition of biological motion and actions (AI Memo 2002–012). Cambridge, MA: MIT AI Lab.

Giese, M. A., & Poggio, T. (2003). Neural mechanisms for the recognition of biological movements. *Nature Reviews Neuroscience*, *4*, 179–192.

Gilbert, C. D., Sigman, M., & Crist, R. E. (2001). The neural basis of perceptual learning. *Neuron*, *31*, 681–697.

Gillam, B. (1998). Illusions at century's end. In J. Hochberg (ed.), *Perception and cognition at century's end* (pp. 95–136). San Diego, CA: Academic Press.

Ginsburg, A. P. (1986). Spatial filtering and visual form perception. In K. R. Boff, L. Kaufman, & J. R. Thomas (Eds.), *Handbook of perception and human performance* (Vol. 2, pp. 34–1–34–41). New York: Wiley.

Glass, L., & Perez, R. (1973). Perception of random dot interference patterns. *Nature*, *246*, 360–362.

Gleick, J. (1987). *Chaos*. London: Penguin Books.

Gobet, F. (1998). Expert memory: a comparison of four theories. *Cognition, 66,* 115–152.

Gold, J. M., Murray, R. F., Bennett, P. J., & Sekuler, A. B. (2000). Deriving behavioural receptive fields for visually completed contours. *Current Biology, 10,* 663–666.

Goodale, M. A., & Milner, A. D. (1992). Separate visual pathways for perception and action. *Trends in Neurosciences, 15,* 22–25.

Gottschaldt, K. (1926). Über den Einfluss der Ehrfahrung auf die Wahrnehmung von Figuren, I. *Psychologische Forschung, 8,* 261–317.

Graham, N., & Nachmias, J. (1971). Detection of grating patterns containing two spatial frequencies: a comparison of single-channel and multiple-channel models. *Vision Research, 11,* 251–259.

Greeno, J. G. (1994). Gibson's affordances. *Psychological Review, 101,* 336–342.

Grezes, J., & Decety, J. (2002). Does visual perception of object afford action? Evidence from a neuroimaging study. *Neuropsychologia, 40,* 212–222.

Grosof, D. H., Shapley, R. M., & Hawken, M. J. (1993). Macaque V1 neurons can signal 'illusory' contours. *Nature, 365,* 550–552.

Gross, C. G. (1994). How inferior temporal cortex became a visual area. *Cerebral Cortex, 4,* 455–469.

Grossberg, S., & Mingolla, E. (1985). Neural dynamics of form perception: boundary completion, illusory figures, and neon color spreading. *Psychological Review, 92,* 173–211.

Grossman, E. D., & Blake, R. (2002). Brain areas active during visual perception of biological motion. *Neuron, 35,* 1167–1175.

Haffenden, A. M., & Goodale, M. A. (1998). The effect of pictorial illusion on prehension and perception. *Journal of Cognitive Neuroscience, 10,* 122–136.

Haken, H. (1983). *Synergetics.* Berlin: Springer.

Han, S., Humphreys, G. W., & Chen, L. (1999). Uniform connectedness and classical Gestalt principles of perceptual grouping. *Perception and Psychophysics, 61,* 661–674.

Hassenstein, B., & Reichardt, W. (1956). Systemtheoretische Analyse der Zeit, Reihenfolgen und Vorzeichenauswertung bei der Bewegungsrezeption des Rüsselkäfers *Chlorophanus. Zeitschrift für Naturforschung, Teil B, 11,* 513–524.

Hatfield, G., & Epstein, W. (1985). The status of the minimum principle in the theoretical analysis of visual perception. *Psychological Bulletin, 97,* 155–186.

Hatsopoulus, N., Gabbiani, F., & Laurent, G. (1995). Elementary computation of object approach by a wide-field visual neuron. *Science, 270,* 1000–1003.

Heath, R. A. (2000). *Nonlinear dynamics: techniques and applications in psychology.* Mahwah, NJ: Erlbaum.

Hecht, H. (1996). Heuristics and invariants in dynamic event perception: immunized concepts or non-statements? *Psychonomic Bulletin and Review, 3,* 61–70.

Hecht, S., Shlaer, S., & Pirenne, M. H. (1942). Energy, quanta, and vision. *Journal of General Physiology, 25,* 819–840.

Hegde, J., & Van Essen, D. C. (2000). Selectivity for complex shapes in primate visual area V2. *Journal of Neuroscience, 20,* RC61.

Heitger, F., von der Heydt, R., Peterhans, E., Rosenthaler, L., & Kubler, O. (1998). Simulation of neural contour mechanisms: representing anomalous contours. *Image and Vision Computing, 16,* 407–421.

Henning, G. B., Bird, C. M., & Wichmann, F. A. (2002). Contrast discrimination with pulse-trains in pink noise. *Journal of the Optical Society of America A, 19,* 1259–1266.

Henning, G. B., Hertz, B. G., & Broadbent, D. E. (1975). Some experiments bearing on the hypothesis that the visual system analyzes patterns in independent bands of spatial frequency. *Vision Research, 15,* 887–899.

Hildreth, E. C., & Koch, C. (1987). The analysis of visual motion: from computational theory to neuronal mechanisms. *Annual Review of Neuroscience, 10,* 477–533.

Hirsch, J., DeLaPaz, R. L., Relkin, N. R., Victor, J., Kim, K., Li, T., Borden, P., Rubin, N., & Shapley, R. (1995). Illusory contours activate specific regions in human visual cortex: evidence from functional magnetic resonance imaging. *Proceedings of the National Academy of Sciences of the USA, 92,* 6469–6473.

Hochberg, J. (1998). Gestalt theory and its legacy: organization in eye and brain, in attention and mental representation. In J. Hochberg (ed.), *Perception and cognition at century's end* (pp. 253–306). San Diego, CA: Academic Press.

Hochberg, J., & McAlister, E. (1953). A quantitative approach to figural goodness. *Journal of Experimental Psychology, 46,* 361–364.

Hochberg, J., & Silverstein, A. (1956). A quantitative index of stimulus-similarity: proximity versus differences in brightness. *American Journal of Psychology, 69,* 456–458.

Hochstein, S., & Ahissar, M. (2002). View from the top: hierarchies and reverse hierarchies in the visual system. *Neuron, 36,* 791–804.

Hock, H. S., Kelso, J. A. S., & Schöner, G. (1993). Bistability and hysteresis in the organization of apparent motion patterns. *Journal of Experimental Psychology: Human Perception and Performance, 19,* 63–80.

Hock, H. S., Schöner, G., & Hochstein, S. (1996). Perceptual stability and the selective adaptation of perceived and unperceived motion directions. *Vision Research, 36,* 3311–3323.

Hoffman, D. D., & Flinchbaugh, B. E. (1982). The interpretation of biological motion. *Biological Cybernetics, 42,* 195–204.

Hoffman, W. C. (1966). The Lie algebra of visual perception. *Journal of Mathematical Psychology, 3,* 65–98.

Hoffman, W. C. (1985). Geometric psychology generates the visual Gestalt. *Canadian Journal of Psychology, 39,* 491–528.

Hoffman, W. C. (1994). Conformal structures in perceptual psychology. *Spatial Vision, 8,* 19–31.

Homa, D., Haver, B., & Schwartz, T. (1976). Perceptibility of schematic face stimuli: evidence for a perceptual Gestalt. *Memory and Cognition, 4,* 176–185.

Hopfield, J. J. (1982). Neural networks and physical systems with emergent collective computational abilities.

Proceedings of the National Academy of Sciences of the USA, 79, 2554–2558.

Hoyer, P., & Hyvärinen, A. (2002). A two-layer sparse coding model learns simple and complex cell receptive fields and topography from natural images. *Vision Research, 42*, 1593–1605.

Hubel, D. H., & Wiesel, T. N. (1959). Receptive fields of single neurons in the cat's striate cortex. *Journal of Physiology, 148*, 574–591.

Hubel, D. H., & Wiesel, T. N. (1962). Receptive fields, binocular interaction and functional architecture in the cat's visual cortex. *Journal of Physiology, 148*, 574–591.

Hubel, D. H., & Wiesel, T. N. (1963). Receptive fields of cells in striate cortex of very young, visually inexperienced kittens. *Journal of Neurophysiology, 26*, 994–1002.

Hubel, D. H., & Wiesel, T. N. (1968). Receptive fields and functional architecture of monkey striate cortex. *Journal of Physiology, 195*, 215–243.

Hummel, J. E. (2000). Where view-based theories break down: the role of structure in shape perception and object recognition. In E. Dietrich & A. Markman (Eds.), *Cognitive dynamics: conceptual change in humans and machines* (pp. 157–185). Hillsdale, NJ: Erlbaum.

Hummel, J. E., & Biederman, I. (1992). Dynamic binding in a neural network for shape recognition. *Psychological Review, 99*, 480–517.

Hupé, J. M., James, A. C., Payne, B. R., Lomber, S. G., Girard, P., & Bullier, J. (1998). Cortical feedback improves discrimination between figure and background by V1, V2 and V3 neurons. *Nature, 394*, 784–787.

Hurvich, L. M., & Jameson, D. (1957). An opponent-process theory of color vision. *Psychological Review, 64*, 384–404.

Hyvärinen, A., & Hoyer, P. (2000). Emergence of phase and shift invariant features by decomposition of natural images into independent feature subspaces. *Neural Computation, 12*, 1705–1720.

Janssen, P., Vogels, R., & Orban, G. A. (2000). Three-dimensional shape coding in inferior temporal cortex. *Neuron, 27*, 385–397.

Johansson, G. (1950). *Configurations in event perception.* Uppsala: Almqvist & Wiksell.

Johansson, G. (1973). Visual perception of biological motion and a model for its analysis. *Perception and Psychophysics, 14*, 201–211.

Johansson, G. (1975). Visual motion perception. *Scientific American, 232*, 76–88.

Johnston, J. C., & McClelland, J. L. (1974). Perception of letters in words: seek not and ye shall find. *Science, 184*, 1192–1194.

Jones, J. P., Stepnoski, A., & Palmer, L. A. (1987). The two-dimensional spectral structure of simple receptive fields in cat striate cortex. *Journal of Neurophysiology, 58*, 1212–1232.

Julesz, B. (1964). Binocular depth perception without familiarity cues. *Science, 145*, 356–362.

Julesz, B. (1971). *Foundations of cyclopean perception.* Chicago: University of Chicago Press.

Kaas, J. H. (2000). The reorganization of sensory and motor maps after injury in adult mammals. In M. S. Gazzaniga (ed.), *The new cognitive neurosciences* (pp. 223–236). Cambridge, MA: MIT Press.

Kanizsa, G. (1976). Subjective contours. *Scientific American, 234*, 48–52.

Kanizsa, G. (1979). *Organization in vision: essays on Gestalt perception.* New York: Praeger.

Kanizsa, G., & Gerbino, W. (1976). Convexity and symmetry in figure-ground organization. In M. Henle (ed.), *Art and artefacts* (pp. 25–32). New York: Springer.

Kanwisher, N. (2001). Neural events and perceptual awareness. *Cognition, 79*, 83–113.

Kauffman, S. (1995). *At home in the universe: the search for the laws of self-organization and complexity.* New York: Oxford University Press.

Kellman, P. J., & Shipley, T. F. (1991). A theory of visual interpolation in object perception. *Cognitive Psychology, 23*, 141–221.

Kelly, F., & Grossberg, S. (2000). Neural dynamics of 3-D surface perception: figure-ground separation and lightness perception. *Perception and Psychophysics, 62*, 1596–1618.

Kelso, J. A. S. (1995). *Dynamic patterns: the self-organization of brain and behavior.* Cambridge, MA: MIT Press.

Kersten, D. (1987). Predictability and redundancy of natural images. *Journal of the Optical Society of America A, 4*, 2395–2400.

Keysers, C., & Perrett, D. I. (2002). Visual masking and RSVP reveal neural competition. *Trends in Cognitive Sciences, 6*, 120–125.

Kimchi, R. (1992). Primacy of wholistic processing and global/local paradigm: a critical review. *Psychological Bulletin, 112*, 24–38.

Kimchi, R. (1994). The role of wholistic configural properties versus global properties in visual form perception. *Perception, 23*, 489–504.

Kimchi, R. (1998). Uniform connectedness and grouping in the perceptual organization of hierarchical patterns. *Journal of Experimental Psychology: Human Perception and Performance, 24*, 1105–1118.

Kimchi, R., & Bloch, B. (1998). The importance of configural properties in visual form perception. *Psychonomic Bulletin and Review, 5*, 135–139.

Kirkpatrick, S., Gelatt, C. D., Jr., & Vecchi, M. P. (1983). Optimization by simulated annealing. *Science, 220*, 671–680.

Klein, F. (1893). Vergleichende Betrachtungen über neuere geometrische Forschungen ('Erlanger Programm'). *Mathematische Annalen, 43*, 63–100.

Klein, F. (1908). *Elementary mathematics from an advanced standpoint.* New York: Macmillan.

Knierim, J. J., & Van Essen, D. C. (1992). Neuronal responses to static texture patterns in area V1 of the alert macaque monkey. *Journal of Neurophysiology, 67*, 961–980.

Kobatake, E., Wang, G., & Tanaka, K. (1998). Effects of shape-discrimination training on the selectivity of inferotemporal cells in adult monkeys. *Journal of Neurophysiology, 80*, 324–330.

Koenderink, J. J. (1984). The structure of images. *Biological Cybernetics, 50*, 363–370.

Koenderink, J. J. (1986). Optic flow. *Vision Research, 26,* 161–180.

Koenderink, J. J. (1988). Operational significance of receptive field assemblies. *Biological Cybernetics, 58,* 163–171.

Koenderink, J. J. (1990). The brain a geometry engine. *Psychological Research, 52,* 122–127.

Koenderink, J. J., Kappers, A. M. L., Todd, J. T., Norman, J. F., & Phillips, F. (1996). Surface range and attitude probing in stereoscopically presented dynamic scenes. *Journal of Experimental Psychology: Human Perception and Performance, 22,* 869–878.

Koenderink, J. J., & van Doorn, A. J. (1987). Representation of local geometry in the visual system. *Biological Cybernetics, 55,* 367–375.

Koenderink, J. J., & van Doorn, A. J. (1990). Receptive field families. *Biological Cybernetics, 63,* 291–297.

Koenderink, J. J., & van Doorn, A. J. (1992). Generic neighborhood operators. *IEEE Transactions on Pattern Analysis and Machine Intelligence, PAMI-14,* 597–605.

Koenderink, J. J., & van Doorn, A. J. (2003). Pictorial space. In H. Hecht, R. Schwartz, & M. Atherton (Eds.), *Looking into pictures: an interdisciplinary approach to pictorial space* (pp. 239–299). Cambridge, MA: MIT Press.

Koenderink, J. J., van Doorn, A. J., & Kappers, A. M. L. (2002). Pappus in optical space. *Perception and Psychophysics, 64,* 380–391.

Koenderink, J. J., van Doorn, A. J., & Lappin, J. S. (2000). Direct measurement of the curvature of visual space. *Perception, 29,* 69–79.

Koffka, K. (1935). *Principles of Gestalt psychology.* New York: Harcourt, Brace & World.

Kogo, N., Strecha, C., Caenen, G., Wagemans, J., & Van Gool, L. (2002). Reconstruction of subjective surfaces from occlusion cues. In H. H. Bulthoff, S.-W. Lee, T. A. Poggio, & C. Wallraven (Eds.), *Lecture Notes in Computer Science: Proceedings BMCV 2002* (pp. 311–321). Heidelberg: Springer.

Köhler, W. (1929). *Gestalt psychology.* New York: Liveright.

Köhler, W. (1940). *Dynamics in psychology.* New York: Liveright.

Komatsu, H., & Ideura, Y. (1993). Relationships between color, shape, and pattern selectivities of neurons in the inferior temporal cortex of the monkey. *Journal of Neurophysiology, 70,* 677–694.

Kovács, I. (1996). Gestalten of today: early processing of visual contours and surfaces. *Behavioural Brain Research, 82,* 1–11.

Kovács, I., & Julesz, B. (1993). A closed curve is much more than an incomplete one: effect of closure in figure-ground segmentation. *Proceedings of the National Academy of Sciences of the USA, 90,* 7495–7497.

Kubovy, M., Holcombe, A. O., & Wagemans, J. (1998). On the lawfulness of grouping by proximity. *Cognitive Psychology, 35,* 71–98.

Kubovy, M., & Wagemans, J. (1995). Grouping by proximity and multistability in dot lattices: a quantitative Gestalt theory. *Psychological Science, 6,* 225–234.

Kuffler, S. W. (1953). Discharge patterns and functional organization of mammalian retina. *Journal of Neurophysiology, 16,* 37–68.

Lamme, V. A. F. (1995). The neurophysiology of figure-ground segregation in primary visual cortex. *Journal of Neuroscience, 15,* 1605–1615.

Lamme, V. A. F. (2000). Neural mechanisms of visual awareness: a linking proposition. *Brain and Mind, 1,* 385–406.

Lamme, V. A. F. (2001). Blindsight: the role of feedforward and feedback corticocortical connections. *Acta Psychologica, 107,* 209–228.

Lamme, V. A. F., Rodriguez, V., & Spekreijse, H. (1999). Separate processing dynamics for texture elements, boundaries and surfaces in primary visual cortex. *Cerebral Cortex, 9,* 406–413.

Lamme, V. A. F., & Roelfsema, P. R. (2000). The distinct modes of vision offered by feedforward and recurrent processing. *Trends in Neurosciences, 23,* 571–579.

Lamme, V. A. F., Supèr, H., & Spekreijse, H. (1998). Feedforward, horizontal, and feedback processing in the visual cortex. *Current Opinion in Neurobiology, 8,* 529–535.

Lamme, V. A. F., Zipser, K., & Spekreijse, H. (2002). Masking interrupts figure-ground signals in V1. *Journal of Cognitive Neuroscience, 14,* 1044–1053.

Land, E. H. (1983). Recent advances in retinex theory and some implications for cortical computations: color vision and the natural image. *Proceedings of the National Academy of Sciences of the USA, 80,* 5163–5169.

Lappin, J. S., & Craft, W. D. (2000). Foundations of spatial vision: from retinal images to perceived shapes. *Psychological Review, 107,* 6–38.

Lappin, J. S., & Fuqua, M. A. (1983). Accurate visual measurement of three-dimensional moving patterns. *Science, 221,* 480–482.

Lashley, K. S., Chow, K. L., & Semmes, J. (1951). An examination of the electrical field theory of cerebral integration. *Psychological Review, 58,* 123–136.

Lee, D. N., & Reddish, P. E. (1981). Plummeting gannets: a paradigm of ecological optics. *Nature, 293,* 293–294.

Lee, S.-H., & Blake, R. (1999). Visual form created solely from temporal structure. *Science, 284,* 1165–1168.

Lee, S.-H., & Blake, R. (2001). Neural synergy in visual grouping: when good continuation meets common fate. *Vision Research, 41,* 2057–2064.

Lee, T. S., Mumford, D., Romero, R., & Lamme, V. A. F. (1998). The role of the primary visual cortex in higher level vision. *Vision Research, 38,* 2429–2454.

Lee, T. S., & Nguyen, M. (2001). Dynamics of subjective contour formation in the early visual cortex. *Proceedings of the National Academy of Sciences of the USA, 98,* 1907–1911.

Lee, T. S., Yang, C. F., Romero, R., & Mumford, D. (2002). Neural activity in early visual cortex reflects behavioral experience and higher-order perceptual saliency. *Nature Neuroscience, 5,* 589–597.

Leeuwenberg, E. L. J. (1969). Quantitative specification of information in sequential patterns. *Psychological Review, 76,* 216–220.

Leeuwenberg, E. L. J. (1971). A perceptual coding language for visual and auditory patterns. *American Journal of Psychology, 84,* 307–349.

Leeuwenberg, E., & Boselie, F. (1988). Against the likelihood principle in visual perception. *Psychological Review*, *95*, 485–491.

Lennie, P. (1998). Single units and visual cortical organization. *Perception*, *27*, 889–935.

Leopold, D. A., & Logothetis, N. K. (1996). Activity changes in early visual cortex reflect monkeys' percepts during binocular rivalry. *Nature*, *379*, 549–553.

Leopold, D. A., & Logothetis, N. K. (1999). Multistable phenomena: changing views in perception. *Trends in Cognitive Sciences*, *3*, 254–264.

Leopold, D. A., O'Toole, A. J., Vetter, T., & Blanz, V. (2001). Prototype-referenced shape encoding revealed by high-level after effects. *Nature Neuroscience*, *4*, 89–94.

Lettvin, J. Y., Maturana, H. R., McCulloch, W. S., & Pitts, W. H. (1959). What the frog's eye tells the frog's brain. *Proceedings of the Institute of Radio Engineers*, *47*, 1940–1951.

Lewin, R. (1992). *Complexity: life at the edge of chaos*. New York: Macmillan.

Liang, J., & Williams, D. R. (1997). Aberrations and retinal image quality of the normal human eye. *Journal of the Optical Society of America A*, *14*, 2873–2883.

Livingstone, M. S., & Hubel, D. H. (1984). Anatomy and physiology of a color system in the primate visual cortex. *Journal of Neuroscience*, *4*, 309–356.

Logothetis, N. K. (1998). Single units and conscious vision. *Philosophical Transactions of the Royal Society of London B*, *353*, 1801–1818.

Logothetis, N. K., Pauls, J., & Poggio, T. (1995). Shape representation in the inferior temporal cortex of monkeys. *Current Biology*, *5*, 552–563.

Logothetis, N. K., & Schall, J. D. (1989). Neuronal correlates of subjective visual perception. *Science*, *245*, 761–763.

Logothetis, N. K., & Sheinberg, D. L. (1996). Visual object recognition. *Annual Review of Neuroscience*, *19*, 577–621.

Lumer, E. D., Friston, E. J., & Rees, G. (1998). Neural correlates of perceptual rivalry in the human brain. *Science*, *280*, 1930–1934.

Mach, E. (1959). *The analysis of sensations*. New York: Dover. (Original work published 1896.)

Maes, P. (ed.) (1991). *Designing autonomous agents: theory and practice from biology to engineering and back*. Cambridge, MA: MIT Press.

Mallat, S. G. (1987). A theory of multiresolution signal decomposition: the wavelet representation. GRASP Lab Technical Memo. University of Pennsylvania, Department of Computer and Information Science, MS-CIS-87-22.

Maloney, L. T., & Wandell, B. A. (1986). Color constancy: a method for recovering surface spectral reflectance. *Journal of the Optical Society of America*, *3*, 29–33.

Mark, L. S. (1987). Eye-height-scaled information about affordances: a study of sitting and stair climbing. *Journal of Experimental Psychology: Human Perception and Performance*, *13*, 361–370.

Mark, L. S., & Todd, J. T. (1985). Describing perceptual information about human growth in terms of geometric invariants. *Perception and Psychophysics*, *37*, 249–256.

Marr, D. (1982). *Vision: a computational investigation into the human representation and processing of visual information*. San Francisco, CA: Freeman.

Marr, D., & Nishihara, H. K. (1978). Representation and recognition of three-dimensional shapes. *Proceedings of the Royal Society of London B*, *200*, 269–294.

Mather, G., Radford, K., & West, S. (1992). Low-level visual processing of biological motion. *Proceedings of the Royal Society of London B*, *249*, 149–155.

Mazer, J. A., Vinje, W. E., McDermott, J., Schiller, P. H., & Gallant, J. L. (2002). Spatial frequency and orientation tuning dynamics in area V1. *Proceedings of the National Academy of Sciences of the USA*, *99*, 1645–1650.

McClelland, J. L., Rumelhart, D. E., and the PDP Research Group (1986). *Parallel distributed processing: explorations in the microstructure of cognition. Vol. 2: Psychological and biological models*. Cambridge, MA: MIT Press.

McLeod, P., Dittrich, W., Driver, J., Perrett, D., & Zihl, J. (1996). Preserved and impaired detection of structure from motion by a 'motion-blind' patient. *Visual Cognition*, *3*, 363–391.

Metzger, W. (1975). *Gesetze des Sehens* (3rd ed.). Frankfurt: Kramer. (First edition published 1936.)

Michaels, C. F. (1988). Apparent motion: evidence for the detection of affordances. *Journal of Experimental Psychology: Human Perception and Performance*, *14*, 231–240.

Michaels, C. F. (1993). Destination compatibility, affordances, and coding rules: a reply to Proctor, Van Zandt, Lu, and Weeks. *Journal of Experimental Psychology: Human Perception and Performance*, *19*, 1121–1127.

Michaels, C. F., & Carello, C. (1981). *Direct perception*. Englewood Cliffs, NJ: Prentice-Hall.

Michaels, C. F., & de Vries, M. M. (1998). Higher order and lower order variables in the visual perception of relative pulling force. *Journal of Experimental Psychology: Human Perception and Performance*, *24*, 526–546.

Michotte, A. (1946). *La perception de la causalité*. Leuven: Institut Supérieur de Philosophie.

Michotte, A., Thinès, G., & Crabbé, G. (1964). *Les compléments amodaux des structures perceptives*. Leuven: Studia Psychologica.

Milner, A. D., & Goodale, M. A. (1995). *The visual brain in action*. Oxford: Oxford University Press.

Morgan, M. J. (1999). The Poggendorff illusion: a bias in the estimation of the orientation of virtual lines by second-stage filters. *Vision Research*, *39*, 2361–2380.

Morgan, M. J., & Casco, C. (1990). Spatial filtering and spatial primitives in early vision: an explanation of the Zöllner-Judd class of geometrical illusion. *Proceedings of the Royal Society of London B*, *242*, 1–10.

Morgan, M. J., Hole, G. J., & Glennerster, A. (1990). Biases and sensitivities in geometrical illusions. *Vision Research*, *30*, 1793–1810.

Nakayama, K. (1985). Biological image motion processing: a review. *Vision Research*, *25*, 625–660.

Nakayama, K. (1994). James J. Gibson – an appreciation. *Psychological Review*, *101*, 329–335.

Nakayama, K. (1998). Vision fin de siècle: a reductionist explanation of perception for the 21st century? In

J. Hochberg (ed.), *Perception and cognition at century's end* (pp. 307–331). San Diego, CA: Academic Press.

Nakayama, K., He, Z. J., & Shimojo, S. (1995). Visual surface representation: a critical link between lower-level and higher-level vision. In S. M. Kosslyn & D. N. Osherson (Eds.), *Visual cognition* (pp. 1–70). Cambridge, MA: MIT Press.

Navon, D. (1977). Forest before trees: the precedence of global features in visual perception. *Cognitive Psychology, 9*, 353–383.

Navon, D. (1981). The forest revisited: more on global precedence. *Psychological Research, 43*, 1–32.

Niall, K. (1992). Projective invariance and the kinetic depth effect. *Acta Psychologica, 81*, 127–168.

Niall, K., & McNamara, J. (1990). Projective invariance and picture perception. *Perception, 19*, 637–660.

Nolfi, S., & Floreano, D. (2002). Synthesis of autonomous robots through evolution. *Trends in Cognitive Sciences, 6*, 31–36.

Nunez, P. L. (2000). Toward a quantitative description of large-scale neocortical dynamic function and EEG. *Behavioral and Brain Sciences, 23*, 371–437.

Olshausen, B. A., & Field, D. J. (1996). Emergence of simple-cell receptive field properties by learning a sparse code for natural images. *Nature, 381*, 607–609.

Op de Beeck, H., & Vogels, R. (2000). Spatial sensitivity of macaque inferior temporal neurons. *Journal of Comparative Neurology, 426*, 505–518.

Op de Beeck, H., Wagemans, J., & Vogels, R. (2001). Inferotemporal neurons represent low-dimensional configurations of parameterized shapes. *Nature Neuroscience, 4*, 1244–1252.

Op de Beeck, H., Wagemans, J., & Vogels, R. (2003). The effect of category learning on the representation of shape: dimensions can be biased, but not differentiated. *Journal of Experimental Psychology: General, 132*, 491–511.

Oram, M. W., & Foldiak, P. (1996). Learning generalisation and localisation: competition for stimulus type and receptive field. *Neurocomputing, 11*, 297–321.

Oram, M. W., & Perrett, D. I. (1994). Responses of anterior superior temporal polysensory (STPa) neurons to biological motion stimuli. *Journal of Cognitive Neuroscience, 6*, 99–116.

Oyama, T. (1961). Perceptual grouping as a function of proximity. *Perceptual and Motor Skills, 3*, 305–306.

Palmer, S. E. (1982). Symmetry, transformation, and the structure of perceptual systems. In J. Beck (ed.), *Organization and representation in perception* (pp. 95–144). Hillsdale, NJ: Erlbaum.

Palmer, S. E. (1983). The psychology of perceptual organization: a transformational approach. In J. Beck, B. Hope, & A. Rosenfeld (Eds.), *Human and machine vision* (Vol. 1, pp. 269–339). New York: Academic Press.

Palmer, S. E. (2002). Perceptual organization in vision. In S. Yantis (ed.), *Stevens' handbook of experimental psychology* (3rd ed.). *Vol. 1: Sensation and perception* (pp. 177–234). New York: Wiley.

Palmer, S. E., & Rock, I. (1994). Rethinking perceptual organization: the role of uniform connectedness. *Psychonomic Bulletin and Review, 1*, 29–55.

Pascual-Leone, A., & Walsh, V. (2001). Fast backprojections from the motion to the primary visual area necessary for visual awareness. *Science, 292*, 510–512.

Pasupathy, A., & Connor, C. E. (2001). Shape representation in area V4: position-specific tuning for boundary conformation. *Journal of Neurophysiology, 86*, 2505–2519.

Pasupathy, A., & Connor, C. E. (2002). Population coding of shape in V4. *Nature Neuroscience, 5*, 1332–1338.

Perotti, V. J., Todd, J. T., Lappin, J. S., & Phillips, F. (1998). The perception of surface curvature from optical motion. *Perception and Psychophysics, 60*, 377–388.

Peterhans, E., & Heitger, F. (2001). Simulation of neuronal responses defining depth order and contrast polarity at illusory contours in monkey area V2. *Journal of Computational Neuroscience, 10*, 195–211.

Peterhans, E., & von der Heydt, R. (1991). Subjective contours: bridging the gap between psychophysics and physiology. *Trends in Neurosciences, 14*, 112–119.

Peterson, M. A. (1994). The proper treatment of uniform connectedness. *Psychonomic Bulletin and Review, 1*, 509–514.

Phillips, W. A., & Singer, W. (1997). In search of common foundations for cortical computation. *Behavioral and Brain Sciences, 20*, 657–722.

Pillow, J., & Rubin, N. (2002). Perceptual completion across the vertical meridian and the role of early visual cortex. *Neuron, 33*, 805–813.

Pittenger, J. B., Shaw, R. E., & Mark, L. S. (1979). Perceptual information for the age-level of faces as a higher-order invariant of growth. *Journal of Experimental Psychology: Human Perception and Performance, 5*, 478–493.

Ploeger, A., van der Maas, H. L. J., & Hartelman, P. A. I. (2002). Stochastic catastrophe analysis of switches in the perception of apparent motion. *Psychonomic Bulletin and Review, 9*, 26–42.

Poggio, T., & Edelman, S. (1990). A network that learns to recognize three-dimensional objects. *Nature, 343*, 263–266.

Poggio, T., & Girosi, F. (1990). Regularization algorithms for learning that are equivalent to multilayer networks. *Science, 247*, 978–982.

Polat, U. (1999). Functional architecture of long-range perceptual interactions. *Spatial Vision, 12*, 143–162.

Polat, U., & Sagi, D. (1994). The architecture of perceptual spatial interactions. *Vision Research, 34*, 73–78.

Pomerantz, J. R. (2002). Several strange effects arising from perceptual grouping in vision. *Abstracts of the Annual Meeting of the Psychonomic Society, 6*, No. 564, p. 83.

Pomerantz, J. R., & Garner, W. R. (1973). Stimulus configuration in selective attention tasks. *Perception and Psychophysics, 14*, 565–569.

Pomerantz, J. R., & Kubovy, M. (1986). Theoretical approaches to perceptual organization: simplicity and likelihood principles. In K. R. Boff, L. Kaufman, & J. P. Thomas (Eds.), *Handbook of perception and human performance* (Vol. 2, pp. 36–46). New York: Wiley.

Pomerantz, J. R., & Pristach, E. (1989). Emergent features, attention, and the perceptual glue in visual form perception. *Journal of Experimental Psychology: Human Perception and Performance, 15*, 635–649.

Pomerantz, J. R., Sager, L. C., & Stoever, R. J. (1977). Perception of wholes and of their component parts: some configural superiority effects. *Journal of Experimental Psychology: Human Perception and Performance, 3*, 422–435.

Pont, S. C., & Koenderink, J. J. (2002). Bidirectional texture contrast function. In A. Heyden, G. Sparr, M. Nielsen, & P. Johansen (Eds.), *Proceedings of the European Conference on Computer Vision – ECCV2002*, (Vol. 4, pp. 808–822). Heidelberg: Springer.

Proctor, R. W., Van Zandt, T., Lu, C.-H., & Weeks, D. J. (1993). Stimulus-response compatibility for moving stimuli: perception of affordances or directional coding? *Journal of Experimental Psychology: Human Perception and Performance, 19*, 81–91.

Proesmans, M., Pauwels, E., & Van Gool, L. (1994). Coupled geometry-driven diffusion equations for low-level vision. In B. M. ter Haar Romeny (ed.), *Geometry-driven diffusion in computer vision* (pp. 191–228). Dordrecht: Kluwer.

Proesmans, M., & Van Gool, L. (1999). Grouping based on coupled diffusion maps. In D. A. Forsyth, J. L. Mundy, V. di Gesú, & R. Cipolla (Eds.), *Shape, contour and grouping in computer vision* (pp. 196–213). Berlin: Springer.

Proffitt, D. R., Bhalla, M., Gossweiler, R., & Midgett, J. (1995). Perceiving geographical slant. *Psychonomic Bulletin and Review, 2*, 409–428.

Proffitt, D. R., Creem, S. H., & Zosh, W. D. (2001). Seeing mountains in mole hills: geographical slant perception. *Psychological Science, 12*, 418–423.

Proffitt, D. R., & Cutting, J. E. (1980). An invariant for wheel-generated motions and the logic of its determination. *Perception, 9*, 435–449.

Proffitt, D. R., & Kaiser, M. K. (1998). The internalization of perceptual processing constraints. In J. Hochberg (ed.), *Perception and cognition at century's end* (pp. 169–197). San Diego, CA: Academic Press.

Proverbio, A. M., & Zani, A. (2002). Electrophysiological indexes of illusory contours perception in humans. *Neuropsychologia, 40*, 479–491.

Pylyshyn, Z. W. (2000). Situating vision in the world. *Trends in Cognitive Sciences, 4*, 197–207.

Quinlan, P. T., & Wilton, R. N. (1998). Grouping by proximity or similarity? Competition between the Gestalt principles in vision. *Perception, 27*, 417–430.

Rainer, G., & Miller, E. K. (2000). Effects of visual experience on the representation of objects in the prefrontal cortex. *Neuron, 27*, 179–189.

Rainville, S. J. M., & Kingdom, F. A. A. (2000). The functional role of oriented spatial filters in the perception of mirror symmetry: psychophysics and modeling. *Vision Research, 40*, 2621–2644.

Ramachandran, V. S. (1985). The neurobiology of perception. *Perception, 14*, 97–103.

Ramachandran, V. S. (1990). Interactions between motion, depth, color, and form: the utilitarian theory of perception. In C. Blakemore (ed.), *Vision: coding and efficiency* (pp. 346–360). Cambridge: Cambridge University Press.

Ramachandran, V. S., & Anstis, S. M. (1983). Perceptual organization in moving patterns. *Nature, 304*, 529–531.

Reed, E. S. (1988). *James J. Gibson and the psychology of perception*. New Haven, CT: Yale University Press.

Reichardt, W. (1961). Autocorrelation: a principle for the evaluation of sensory information by the central nervous system. In W. A. Rosenblith (ed.), *Sensory communication* (pp. 303–317). Cambridge, MA: MIT Press.

Reicher, G. M. (1969). Perceptual recognition as a function of meaningfulness of stimulus materials. *Journal of Experimental Psychology, 81*, 275–280.

Restle, F. (1979). Coding theory of the perception of motion configurations. *Psychological Review, 86*, 1–24.

Riesenhuber, M., & Poggio, T. (1999). Hierarchical models of object recognition in cortex. *Nature Neuroscience, 2*, 1019–1025.

Rind, E. C., & Simmons, P. J. (1999). Seeing what is coming: building collision sensitive neurons. *Trends in Neurosciences, 22*, 215–220.

Rodman, H. R., Scalaidhe, S. P. O., & Gross, C. G. (1993). Response properties of neurons in temporal cortical visual areas of infant monkeys. *Journal of Neurophysiology, 70*, 1115–1136.

Roelfsema, P. R., Lamme, V. A. F., & Spekreijse, H. (1998). Object-based attention in the primary visual cortex of the macaque monkey. *Nature, 395*, 376–381.

Roelfsema, P. R., Lamme, V. A., Spekreijse, H., & Bosch, H. (2002). Figure-ground segregation in a recurrent network architecture. *Journal of Cognitive Neuroscience, 14*, 525–537.

Rossi, A. F., Desimone, R., & Ungerleider, L. G. (2001). Contextual modulation in primary visual cortex of macaques. *Journal of Neuroscience, 21*, 1698–1709.

Rubin, E. (1927). Visuell wahrgenommene wirkliche Bewegungen. *Zeitschrift für Psychologie, 103*, 384–392.

Ruderman, D. L., & Bialek, W. (1994). Statistics of natural images: scaling in the woods. *Physical Review, 73*, 814–817.

Rumelhart, D. E., McClelland, J. L., and the PDP Research Group (1986). *Parallel distributed processing: explorations in the microstructure of cognition. Vol. 1: Foundations.* Cambridge, MA: MIT Press.

Runeson, S. (1977). On the possibility of 'smart' perceptual mechanisms. *Scandinavian Journal of Psychology, 18*, 172–179.

Runeson, S., & Frykholm, G. (1981). Visual perception of lifted weight. *Journal of Experimental Psychology: Human Perception and Performance, 7*, 733–740.

Runeson, S., Juslin, P., & Olsson, H. (2000). Visual perception of dynamic properties: cue heuristics versus direct-perceptual competence. *Psychological Review, 107*, 525–555.

Sakai, K., & Miyashita, Y. (1991). Neural organization for the long-term memory of paired associates. *Nature, 354*, 152–155.

Saul, A. B., & Cynader, M. S. (1989). Adaptation in single units in visual cortex: the tuning of aftereffects in the spatial domain. *Visual Neuroscience, 2*, 593–607.

Savelsbergh, G. J. P., Whiting, T. H. A., & Bootsma, R. J. (1991). Grasping tau. *Journal of Experimental*

Psychology: Human Perception and Performance, *17*, 315–322.

Schenk, T., & Zihl, J. (1997a). Visual motion perception after brain damage. Part 1: Deficits in global motion perception. *Neuropsychologia*, *35*, 1289–1297.

Schenk, T., & Zihl, J. (1997b). Visual motion perception after brain damage. Part 2: Deficits in form-from-motion perception. *Neuropsychologia*, *35*, 1299–1310.

Schoups, A., Vogels, R., Qian, N., & Orban, G. A. (2001). Practising orientation identification improves orientation coding in V1 neurons. *Nature*, *412*, 549–553.

Schumann, F. (1900). Einige Beobachtungen über die Zusammenfassung von Gesichtseindrucken zu Einheiten. *Zeitschrift für Psychologie*, *23*, 1–23.

Schumann, F. (1904). Beiträge zur Analyse der Gesichtswahrnehmungen. IV. Die Schätzung der Richtung. *Zeitschrift für Psychologie*, *36*, 161–185.

Schwartz, O., & Simoncelli, E. P. (2001). Natural signal statistics and sensory gain control. *Nature Neuroscience*, *4*, 819–825.

Sengpiel, F., Stawinski, P., & Bonhöffer, T. (1999). Influence of experience on orientation maps in cat visual cortex. *Nature Neuroscience*, *2*, 727–732.

Shadlen, M., & Movshon, J. (1999). Synchrony unbound: a critical evaluation of the temporal binding hypothesis. *Neuron*, *24*, 67–77.

Shams, L., & von der Malsburg, C. (2002). The role of complex cells in object recognition. *Vision Research*, *42*, 2547–2554.

Sharma, J., Angelucci, A., & Sur, M. (2000). Induction of visual orientation modules in auditory cortex. *Nature*, *404*, 841–847.

Shepard, R. N. (2001). Perceptual-cognitive universals as reflections of the world. *Behavioral and Brain Sciences*, *24*, 581–601.

Shiffrar, M., Lichtey, L., & Heptulla-Chatterjee, S. (1997). The perception of biological motion across apertures. *Perception and Psychophysics*, *59*, 51–59.

Shipley, T. F., & Kellman, P. J. (1992). Perception of partly occluded objects and illusory figures: evidence for an identity hypothesis. *Journal of Experimental Psychology: Human Perception and Performance*, *18*, 106–120.

Sigman, M., Cecchi, G. A., Gilbert, C. D., & Magnasco, M. O. (2001). On a common circle: natural scenes and Gestalt rules. *Proceedings of the National Academy of Sciences of the USA*, *98*, 1935–1940.

Sillito, A. M., Grieve, K. L., Jones, H. E., Cudeiro, J., & Davis, J. (1995). Visual cortical mechanisms detecting focal orientation discontinuities. *Nature*, *378*, 492–496.

Simoncelli, E. P., & Adelson, E. H. (1990). Non-separable extensions of quadrature mirror filters to multiple dimensions. *Proceedings of the IEEE*, *78*, 652–664.

Simoncelli, E. P., & Olshausen, B. A. (2001). Natural image statistics and neural representation. *Annual Review of Neuroscience*, *24*, 1193–1216.

Singer, W., & Gray, C. (1995). Visual feature integration and the temporal correlation hypothesis. *Annual Review of Neuroscience*, *18*, 555–586.

Spillman, L. (1999). From elements to perception: local and global processing in visual neurons. *Perception*, *28*, 1461–1492.

Stankiewicz, B. J. (2002). Empirical evidence for independent dimensions in the visual representation of three-dimensional shape. *Journal of Experimental Psychology: Human Perception and Performance*, *28*, 913–932.

Stoerig, P., & Cowey, A. (1997). Blindsight in man and monkey. *Brain*, *120*, 535–559.

Stoffregen, T. A., & Bardy, B. G. (2001). On specification and the senses. *Behavioral and Brain Sciences*, *24*, 195–261.

Stone, J. V. (2002). Independent component analysis: an introduction. *Trends in Cognitive Sciences*, *6*, 59–64.

Sumi, S. (1984). Upside-down presentation of the Johansson moving light-spot pattern. *Perception*, *13*, 283–286.

Sun, H. J., & Frost, B. J. (1998). Computation of different optical variables of looming objects in pigeon nucleus rotundus neurons. *Nature Neuroscience*, *1*, 296–303.

Suzuki, S., & Cavanagh, P. (1998). A shape-contrast effect for briefly presented stimuli. *Journal of Experimental Psychology: Human Perception and Performance*, *24*, 1315–1341.

Suzuki, S., & Grabowecky, M. (2002). Evidence for perceptual 'trapping' and adaptation in multistable binocular rivalry. *Neuron*, *36*, 143–157.

Tanaka, K. (1996). Inferotemporal cortex and object vision. *Annual Review of Neuroscience*, *19*, 109–139.

Tanner, W. P., & Swets, J. A. (1954). A decision-making theory of visual detection. *Psychological Review*, *61*, 401–409.

Tarr, M. J., & Bülthoff, H. H. (1998). Image-based object recognition in man, monkey, and machine. *Cognition*, *67*, 1–20.

Thompson, E., & Varela, F. J. (2001). Radical embodiment: neural dynamics and consciousness. *Trends in Cognitive Sciences*, *5*, 418–425.

Tibau, S., Willems, B., & Wagemans, J. (2000). The influence of two-dimensional stimulus properties in a reproduction-from-depth task with minimal information stimuli. *Spatial Vision*, *13*, 359–376.

Todd, J. T., Chen, L., & Norman, J. F. (1998). On the relative salience of euclidean, affine, and topological structure for 3-D form discrimination. *Perception*, *27*, 273–282.

Todd, J. T., Norman, J. F., Koenderink, J. J., & Kappers, A. M. L. (1997). Effects of texture, illumination, and surface reflectance on stereoscopic shape perception. *Perception*, *26*, 807–822.

Todd, J. T., Oomes, A. H. J., Koenderink, J. J., & Kappers, A. M. L. (2001). On the affine structure of perceptual space. *Psychological Science*, *12*, 191–196.

Todd, J. T., & Reichel, F. D. (1989). Ordinal structure in the visual perception and cognition of smoothly curved surfaces. *Psychological Review*, *96*, 643–657.

Tolhurst, D. J., & Thompson, I. D. (1982). On the variety of spatial frequency selectivities shown by neurons in area 17 of the cat. *Proceedings of the Royal Society of London B*, *213*, 183–199.

Tong, F., Nakayama, K., Vaughan, J. T., & Kanwisher, N. (1998). Binocular rivalry and visual awareness in human extrastriate cortex. *Neuron*, *21*, 753–759.

Tresilian, J. R. (1999). Visually timed action: time-out for 'tau'? *Trends in Cognitive Sciences*, *3*, 301–310.

Treue, S. (2001). Neural correlates of attention in primate visual cortex. *Trends in Neurosciences*, *24*, 295–300.

Turvey, M. T., Shaw, R. E., Reed, E. S., & Mace, W. M. (1981). Ecological laws of perceiving and acting: in reply to Fodor and Pylyshyn. *Cognition*, *9*, 237–304.

Turvey, M. T., Shockley, K., & Carello, C. (1999). Affordance, proper function, and the physical basis of perceived heaviness. *Cognition*, *73*, B17–B26.

Ullman, S. (1980). Against direct perception. *Behavioral and Brain Sciences*, *3*, 373–415.

Ullman, S. (1984). Visual routines. *Cognition*, *18*, 97–159.

Ullman, S. (1995). Sequence seeking and counter-streams: a computational model for bidirectional information flow in the visual cortex. *Cerebral Cortex*, *5*, 1–11.

Ungerleider, L. G., & Mishkin, M. (1982). Two cortical visual systems. In D. J. Eagle, M. A. Goodale, & R. J. Mansfield (Eds.), *Analysis of visual behavior* (pp. 549–586). Cambridge, MA: MIT Press.

Usher, M., & Donnelly, N. (1998). Visual synchrony affects binding and segmentation in perception. *Nature*, *394*, 179–182.

Uttal, W. R., Spillman, L., Sturzel, F., & Sekuler, A. (2000). Motion and shape in common fate. *Vision Research*, *40*, 301–310.

Vaina, L. M. (1994). Functional segregation of color and motion processing in the human visual-cortex: clinical evidence. *Cerebral Cortex*, *4*, 555–572.

Vaina, L. M., LeMay, M., Bienfang, D. C., Choi, A. Y., & Nakayama, K. (1990). Intact biological motion and structure from motion perception in a patient with impaired motion mechanisms: a case-study. *Visual Neurosciences*, *5*, 353–369.

Vaina, L. M., Solomon, J., Chowdhury, S., Sinha, P., & Belliveau, J. W. (2001). Functional neuroanatomy of biological motion perception in humans. *Proceedings of the National Academy of Sciences of the USA*, *98*, 11656–11661.

van der Helm, P. A. (1994). The dynamics of Prägnanz. *Psychological Research*, *56*, 224–236.

van der Helm, P. A. (2000). Simplicity versus likelihood in visual perception: from surprisals to precisals. *Psychological Bulletin*, *126*, 770–800.

van der Helm, P. A., & Leeuwenberg, E. L. J. (1996). Goodness of visual regularities: a nontransformational approach. *Psychological Review*, *103*, 429–456.

van der Helm, P. A., & Leeuwenberg, E. L. J. (1999). A better approach to goodness: reply to Wagemans (1999). *Psychological Review*, *106*, 622–630.

van Ee, R., & Anderson, B. L. (2001). Motion direction, speed and orientation in binocular matching. *Nature*, *410*, 690–694.

Van Gool, L. (1998). Projective subgroups for grouping. *Philosophical Transactions of the Royal Society of London A*, *356*, 1251–1266.

Van Gool, L., Moons, T., Pauwels, E., & Oosterlinck, A. (1995). Vision and Lie's approach to invariance. *Image and Vision Computing*, *13*, 259–277.

Van Gool, L., Moons, T., Pauwels, E., & Wagemans, J. (1994). Invariance from the Euclidean geometer's perspective. *Perception*, *23*, 547–561.

van Hateren, J. H., & Ruderman, D. L. (1998). Independent component analysis of natural image sequences yields spatio-temporal filters similar to simple cells in primary visual cortex. *Proceedings of the Royal Society of London B*, *265*, 2315–2320.

van Leeuwen, C., & van den Hof, M. (1991). What has happened to Prägnanz? Coding, stability, or resonance. *Perception and Psychophysics*, *50*, 435–448.

van Leeuwen, L., Smitsman, A., & van Leeuwen, C. (1994). Affordances, perceptual complexity, and the development of tool use. *Journal of Experimental Psychology: Human Perception and Performance*, *20*, 174–191.

van Lier, R. J., van der Helm, P. A., & Leeuwenberg, E. L. J. (1995). Competing global and local completions in visual occlusions. *Journal of Experimental Psychology: Human Perception and Performance*, *21*, 571–583.

van Lier, R. J., & Wagemans, J. (1998). Effects of physical connectivity on the representational unity of multipart configurations. *Cognition*, *69*, B1–B9.

van Lier, R., & Wagemans, J. (1999). From images to objects: global and local completions of self-occluded parts. *Journal of Experimental Psychology: Human Perception and Performance*, *25*, 1721–1741.

van Oeffelen, M. P., & Vos, P. G. (1983). An algorithm for pattern description on the level of relative proximity. *Pattern Recognition*, *16*, 341–348.

van Santen, J. P. H., & Sperling, G. (1985). Elaborated Reichardt detectors. *Journal of the Optical Society of America A*, *1*, 451–473.

Varela, F., Lachaux, J.-P., Rodriguez, E., & Martinerie, J. (2001). The brainweb: phase synchronization and large-scale integration. *Nature Reviews Neuroscience*, *2*, 229–239.

Verfaillie, K. (1993). Orientation-dependent priming effects in the perception of biological motion. *Journal of Experimental Psychology: Human Perception and Performance*, *19*, 992–1023.

Verfaillie, K. (2000). Perceiving human locomotion: priming effects in direction discrimination. *Brain and Cognition*, *44*, 192–213.

Verstraelen, L. (2002, December). Some remarks on geometry and vision. Talk presented at the UNESCO Conference for Mathematics and the Development of Human Sciences, Bucharest, Romania.

Verstraelen, L. (2003). A remark on visual illusions and neuroscience: 'Basically, we only see what there is to be seen.' *Psychological Reports* (April 2003). Leuven, Belgium: University of Leuven, Laboratory of Experimental Psychology.

Vinje, W. E., & Gallant, J. L. (2000). Sparse coding and decorrelation in primary visual cortex during natural vision. *Science*, *287*, 1273–1276.

Vogels, R., Biederman, I., Bar, M., & Lorincz, A. (2001). Inferior temporal neurons show greater sensitivity to nonaccidental than to metric shape differences. *Journal of Cognitive Neuroscience*, *13*, 444–453.

Vogels, R., Eeckhout, H., & Orban, G. A. (1988). The effect of feature uncertainty on spatial discriminations. *Perception, 17*, 565–577.

von der Heydt, R. (1994). Form analysis in visual cortex. In M. S. Gazzaniga (ed.), *The cognitive neurosciences* (pp. 365–382). Cambridge, MA: MIT Press.

von der Heydt, R., Peterhans, E., & Baumgartner, G. (1984). Illusory contours and cortical neuron responses. *Science, 224*, 1260–1262.

von der Malsburg, C. (1999). The what and where of visual binding: the modeler's perspective. *Neuron, 24*, 95–104.

von Ehrenfels, C. F. (1890). Über Gestaltqualitäten. *Vierteljahrsschrift für wissenschaftliche Philosophie, 14*, 249–292.

von Helmholtz, H. (1852). Über die Theorie der zusammengesetzten Farben. *Annalen der Physik, Leipzig, 887*, 45–66.

Wagemans, J. (1993). Skewed symmetry: a nonaccidental property used to perceive visual forms. *Journal of Experimental Psychology: Human Perception and Performance, 19*, 364–380.

Wagemans, J. (1995). Detection of visual symmetries. *Spatial Vision, 9*, 9–32.

Wagemans, J. (1997). Characteristics and models of human symmetry detection. *Trends in Cognitive Sciences, 1*, 346–352.

Wagemans, J. (1999). Toward a better approach to goodness: comments on van der Helm and Leeuwenberg (1996). *Psychological Review, 106*, 610–621.

Wagemans, J., Lamote, C., & Van Gool, L. (1997). Shape equivalence under perspective and projective transformations. *Psychonomic Bulletin and Review, 4*, 248–253.

Wagemans, J., & Tibau, S. (1999). Visual measurement of relative distances between three collinear dots rotating in a slanted plane. *Perception, 28*, 267–282.

Wagemans, J., Van Gool, L., & Lamote, C. (1996). The visual system's measurement of invariants need not itself be invariant. *Psychological Science, 7*, 232–236.

Wagemans, J., Van Gool, L., Lamote, C., & Foster, D. H. (2000). Minimal information to determine affine shape equivalence. *Journal of Experimental Psychology: Human Perception and Performance, 26*, 443–468.

Wagemans, J., Van Gool, L., Swinnen, V., & Van Horebeek, J. (1993). Higher-order structure in regularity detection. *Vision Research, 33*, 1067–1088.

Wagner, H. (1982). Flow field variables trigger landing in flies. *Nature, 297*, 147–148.

Wallis, G., & Rolls, E. T. (1997). Invariant face and object recognition in the visual system. *Progress in Neurobiology, 51*, 167–194.

Wandell, B. A. (1995). *Foundations of vision.* Sunderland, MA: Sinauer.

Ward, L. M. (2002). *Dynamical cognitive science.* Cambridge, MA: MIT Press.

Watt, R. J. (1991). *Understanding vision.* New York: Academic Press.

Watt, R. J., & Phillips, W. A. (2000). The function of dynamic grouping in vision. *Trends in Cognitive Sciences, 4*, 447–454.

Webb, J. A., & Aggarwal, J. K. (1982). Structure from motion of rigid and jointed objects. *Artificial Intelligence, 19*, 107–130.

Weisstein, N., & Harris, C. S. (1974). Visual detection of line segments: an object superiority effect. *Science, 186*, 752–755.

Wenderoth, P. (1995). The role of pattern outline in bilateral symmetry detection with briefly flashed dot patterns. *Spatial Vision, 9*, 57–77.

Wenderoth, P. (1996). The effects of dot pattern parameters and constraints on the relative salience of vertical bilateral symmetry. *Vision Research, 36*, 2311–2320.

Wertheimer, M. (1912). Experimentelle Studien über das Sehen von Bewegung. *Zeitschrift für Psychologie, 71*, 161–265.

Wertheimer, M. (1923). Untersuchungen zur Lehre von der Gestalt. *Psychologische Forschung, 4*, 301–350.

Westheimer, G. (2001). The Fourier theory of vision. *Perception, 30*, 531–541.

Wheatstone, C. (1838). Contributions to the physiology of vision. Part I: On some remarkable, and hitherto unobserved, phenomena of binocular vision. *Philosophical Transactions of the Royal Society of London, 128*, 371–394.

Wheeler, D. D. (1970). Processes in word recognition. *Cognitive Psychology, 1*, 59–85.

Williams, D. R., Brainard, D. H., McMahon, M. J., & Navarro, R. (1994). Double-pass and interferometric measures of the optical quality of the eye. *Journal of the Optical Society of America A, 11*, 3123–3135.

Williams, D., Phillips, G., & Sekuler, R. (1994). Hysteresis in the perception of motion direction as evidence for neural cooperativity. *Nature, 324*, 253–255.

Wilson, H. R. (1999). *Spikes, decision, and actions: dynamical foundations of neuroscience.* New York: Oxford University Press.

Wilson, H. R., Blake, R., & Lee, S.-H. (2001). Dynamics of travelling waves in visual perception. *Nature, 412*, 907–910.

Wraga, M. (1999a). The role of eye height in perceiving affordances and object dimensions. *Perception and Psychophysics, 61*, 490–507.

Wraga, M. (1999b). Using eye height in different postures to scale the heights of objects. *Journal of Experimental Psychology: Human Perception and Performance, 25*, 518–530.

Wraga, M., Creem, S. H., & Proffitt, D. R. (2000). Perception-action dissociations of a walkable Müller-Lyer configuration. *Psychological Science, 11*, 239–243.

Yen, S.-C., & Finkel, L. H. (1998). Extraction of perceptually salient contours by striate cortical networks. *Vision Research, 38*, 719–741.

Young, T. (1802). The Bakerian lecture: on the theory of light and colours. *Philosophical Transactions of the Royal Society of London, 92*, 12–48.

Zeki, S. (1993). *A vision of the brain.* Oxford: Blackwell Scientific.

Zhu, S.-C. (1999). Embedding Gestalt laws in Markov random fields. *IEEE Transactions on Pattern Analysis and Machine Intelligence, PAMI-21*, 1170–1187.

2

Visual Perception II: High-Level Vision

WILLIAM G. HAYWARD AND MICHAEL J. TARR

While cognition is possible without perception (e.g. the proverbial 'brain in a vat'), it is through our perceptual abilities that we can interact with the world. Although we sense our environment through two-dimensional (2-D) arrays of light (or continuous streams of sound energy), what we perceive and think about are three-dimensional (3-D) *objects*. Consequently, human perception and cognition requires that we explain how humans learn, remember, recognize, manipulate, act on and react to such objects. Perception is the process that allows us to interact with objects in the world, providing both a way to gather information about them and a way of acting upon them.

In humans and other primates, the most salient perceptual system is vision. Traditionally, the study of visual processes has been directed at discrete dimensions of visual information, such as thresholds of luminance (e.g. König & Brodhun, 1889; Hecht, Shlaer, & Pirenne, 1942), mechanisms of stereopsis (e.g. Wheatstone, 1838), or color (e.g. Gregory, 1977). Hubel and Wiesel's (1959, 1962) Nobel prize-winning discovery of orientation-selective cells in the cat brain saw a broadening of such dimensions to include orientation of edges, length, spatial frequency and many other more complex visual attributes. Contemporary developments in these fields have been covered in depth in the previous chapter. In this chapter, however, we discuss a growing body of work that has addressed a different question: how do we see *objects*? That is, rather than examining the kinds of information gained through our sensory systems, how is this information used to derive knowledge about objects

in the world around us? As we shall see, answering this question has proved very difficult. Consider that in low-level vision, a theorist can point to cells in the retina that respond selectively to different wavelengths of light, or neurons in primary visual cortex that spike most actively when lines of a particular orientation or disparity are presented within their receptive fields; said theorist can then build an account of the manner in which this information (wavelengths, orientations, disparities) is organized by perceptual processes. When thinking about objects, however, there is no simple mapping between neural codes and our phenomenology. Rather, single objects contain vast amounts of information that is somehow organized and recruited in a task-appropriate fashion according to higher-order functional considerations.

THE APPROACH OF DAVID MARR

One of the most important and oft-studied elements of high-level vision is object recognition. That is, how do we learn and recognize 3-D objects despite variations in input due to changes in lighting, position, pose and structure? The study of object recognition is typically characterized as making a major leap forward with the seminal work of David Marr and his collaborators at MIT in the 1970s. Marr's work was ground-breaking in its synthesis of many different strands of perceptual, neurophysiological and computational work, but in turn was built upon a variety of earlier work. Of particular influence on Marr's thinking were the ecological approach of James J. Gibson, the literature on how brain injury affects object perception within the field of neuropsychology, and early attempts to build computers that could 'see' in the field of artificial intelligence (AI). Each of these antecedents will be reviewed briefly.

Influences on Marr

James J. Gibson's theory of direct perception

Gibson's (1950, 1966, 1979) theory of direct perception is well known and covered by many other authors (e.g. Shepard, 1984). It eschews the idea that ambiguous sensory input must be interpreted by higher-order perceptual mechanisms and is used as the basis for further computation. Instead Gibson proposed that the visual environment is well ordered and contains 'invariants' that *directly* specify the physical structure of the world. Thus, visual input is already structured at the earliest levels of perception and the role of sensory systems is simply to 'pick up' the information inherent in this input. Gibson hypothesized that the mechanisms of vision were simple once understood, because objects in the world provide structured excitation of receptors such that no computation by higher mechanisms is needed. Although Marr was strongly influenced by Gibson's thinking, it is clear that Marr did not share the view that computation was unnecessary; Marr's approach to vision posits a hierarchy of progressively more complex computations in order to make inferences based on visual input. It was Gibson's emphasis on the *function* of vision rather than its mechanisms that had perhaps the strongest impact on Marr. This focus on the functional nature of perception was reflected in Marr's highest level of psychological explanation, the computational level, which asks 'what is the goal of the computation?' (Marr, 1982: 25). In Marr's view, an account of low-level perceptual processes (such as oriented edges as coded by orientation-selective neurons) was not complete without asking how those neural networks participate in higher-order processes such as object recognition.

Cognitive neuropsychology

During the nineteenth and twentieth centuries when most vision researchers were concentrating on fundamental aspects of vision such as intensity thresholds or wavelength discriminations, one set of researchers addressed issues that are reflected in the representational aspects of Marr's theory. Neuropsychologists who worked with patients with lesions to parietal or ventral regions of visual cortex had been drawing on Lissauer's (1890) distinction between *apperceptive* and *associative* agnosia. Patients with each type of agnosia were judged to have relatively intact low-level vision; however, apperceptive agnosics were judged to have an inability to encode shape information about objects, whereas associative agnosics appeared to retain their ability to perceive shape (e.g. they could draw many named objects), but were unable to use that information to recognize the objects depicted (which results in the oft-cited paradox that an associative agnosic patient can draw an image of an object that he or she cannot recognize; see Figure 2.1). This taxonomy rested on a hierarchy of processes for recognizing objects: low-level processes encoded primitive object features, mid-level processes organized the features in coherent object representations, and high-level processes used such representations in the process of recognition/identification. Marr's model adopts a similar structure, assuming that there is a progression from low- to mid- to high-level vision, this last stage capturing how objects are represented and recognized.

More recent work on cognitive neuropsychology also had an impact on Marr's thinking. Marr was particularly taken with the ideas of Elizabeth Warrington, who studied a range of patients with parietal lesions. Those with damage to the right parietal lobe were able to recognize objects from conventional (or *canonical*) views, but were unable to recognize the objects from unconventional views, such as from directly above. Patients with left parietal lobe damage were unable to name, identify or state the purpose of objects, but they could correctly perceive an object's shape, even from unconventional views. Marr (1982) notes that he drew two conclusions from a 1973 talk by Warrington:

> First, the representation of the shape of an object is stored in a different place and is therefore a quite different type of thing from the representation of its use and purpose. And second, vision alone can deliver an internal description of the shape of a viewed object, even when the object was not recognized in the conventional sense of understanding its use and purpose. (p. 35)

AI models of vision

An early and continuing sub-goal of AI has been to develop robust machine vision systems that are capable of inferring the spatial structure of their physical environment via cameras or other artificial sensory devices. Attempts to build such systems serve to illuminate the sophistication of human vision – even the most recent and most sophisticated artificial vision systems fall far short of human capabilities. Despite the lack of success in

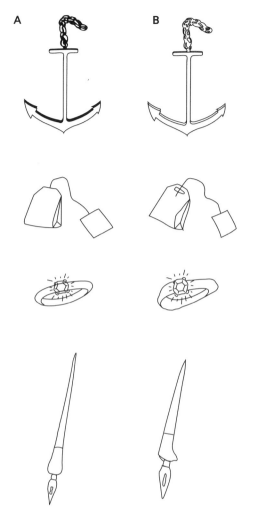

Hubel and Wiesel's (1959, 1962) findings regarding shape selectivity in mammalian visual cortex. The common interpretation of this finding was that early vision recoded images in terms of oriented *edges*. Based on this result, AI researchers adopted approaches in which an edge-map or line drawing formed the representation of the scene at an initial stage of visual processing and that edge inter-pretation was a critical antecedent to object recog-nition (Horn, 1986; Waltz, 1975). Marr made a similar assumption and placed a heavy emphasis on computational mechanisms for edge extraction (Marr & Hildreth, 1980).

Given edges as an intermediate form of visual representation, Marr followed a second tenet adopted by AI researchers – recovering 3-D models of objects. The notion of 3-D object models arose from computer-aided design and computer graphics where images of 3-D objects were synthesized by generating 3-D volumes as component parts of objects and then projecting them into the image ('rendering' them; Foley, Van Dam, Feiner, & Hughes, 1990). Computer vision systems adopted the opposite approach of positing mechanisms for inferring 3-D volumes from images (usually described as edge-maps; Binford, 1971; Brooks, 1983). Such systems inspired Marr; primate vision might solve the problem of recognizing objects across changes in viewpoint, lighting and configura-tion using a similar strategy, one that replaced con-figurations of edges with 3-D volumes for each part of a visual object. Hence, Marr took the 'standard' approach that was popular within the machine vision community in the early 1970s and extended it to human object recognition.

Marr's model of object representation

Consider some of the most important aspects of human object recognition that Marr felt required an explanation. First and foremost is the paradox of all biological vision systems: we perceive and function in a 3-D world, yet the patterning of light that falls on our retinae is 2-D. This mismatch in dimension-ality between the world and the sensory transducers we use to gain information about the world presents the visual system (and perceptual theorists!) with an immense problem. Marr's assumption was that the visual system converts 2-D retinal stimulation into 3-D representations of objects – that is, *recovering* a mental representation that reproduces the physical nature of the real world (something posited by Shepard and colleagues as well; Shepard & Metzler, 1971).

Marr identified another crucial aspect of the recognition behavior of humans: the fact that we are able to apply different names to the same thing. Specifically, we classify objects at multiple levels (Rosch, Mervis, Gray, Johnson, & Boyes-Braem,

Figure 2.1 *Examples of associative agnosic patients' picture-copying ability without concurrent visual object recognition. The picture of the left is the original, and on the right is the patient's copy. Despite the close similarity between the target and copy, patients were unable to name either the original picture or the copy (from Farah, 1990, Fig. 16 and 17, p. 61).*

building artificial vision systems, ideas drawn from AI models of vision have had enormous influence on how we study human vision. In particular, they have provided some of the key ideas adopted by Marr in his model of vision and recognition. Two concepts in particular, edge-based processing and three-dimensional (3-D) object models, were central to Marr's thinking. Some of the first com-puter vision models were strongly influenced by

1976) – a process that has a visual, as well as semantic, basis. That is, when a human observer sees an object, he or she does not simply recognize the object in isolation; he or she is able to judge its categorical relationship relative to other objects. Thus, a cow can be identified as a cow, but also as a four-legged mammal similar to a horse, less similar to a human, and very dissimilar from a rock (at least visually, if not in terms of behavior). Marr held that the multi-level categorical structure of object recognition was not an artifactual aspect of the task; but rather, in a very real sense, object recognition *is* object classification at a given level. Objects are identified as being certain things because they are not other things. Thus, any theory of object representation should be able to account for object classification at multiple levels, as well as the 2-D/3-D paradox discussed above.

Marr's approach (developed with his students Ellen Hildreth, Keith Nishihara and Shimon Ullman) attempted to explain both of these phenomena. As noted above, his solution to the first problem (2-D to 3-D) was to propose a bottom-up sequence of processing stages that transform or *reconstruct* noisy retinal input (2-D) into highly structured, volumetric object (3-D) representations. The first two stages of Marr's model rely on representations of the retinal image that is presented to the visual system, rather than representations of objects or the scene. The initial stage, inspired by the response properties of neurons in early vision, is referred to as the *primal sketch*. This viewer-centered representation captures intensity changes across an image, producing a rough representation of the contours present in the scene. The primal sketch in turn provides the input for the *2 ½-D sketch*, which represents both the shape and orientation of visible surfaces in a scene, again from the perspective of the viewer (the term 'sketch' was applied by Marr to any viewer-centered representation). Unlike the primal sketch, the $2\frac{1}{2}$-D sketch is actually a composite of many separable processes in early vision. That is, a coherent description of a given surface is determined by a variety of perceptual processes, including stereopsis, structure-from-motion, shape-from-shading, texture processing, and so on.

The primal and $2\frac{1}{2}$-D sketches constitute Marr's conceptualization of low- and mid-level vision. In particular, Marr based his ideas on an extensive body of knowledge regarding visual physiology and theoretical neuroscience. As such, Marr's thoughts about these levels of visual processing were influential in codifying a particular approach, but were not ground-breaking. Nearly all theories of vision assume that retinotopic information is simply a starting point for a series of transformations leading to more complex representations such as edges and surfaces. Where theories diverge is in what is done with such mid-level information. With his focus on the functional nature of vision, Marr argued (largely in collaboration with Keith Nishihara; Marr & Nishihara, 1978) that the later stages of visual processing must involve a shift from viewer-centered (arising from the initial retinotopic frame of reference) to *object-centered* coordinates.

Consider that early- and mid-level visual representations are thought to capture visual information as it originally appeared in the scene; that is, relative to the observer. This means that every shift in the position of the observer or the orientation of an object will change the scene description; a surface or edge located at a given set of coordinates at one moment will be at a different set of coordinates at the next moment. In contrast, consider an object described in object-centered coordinates; that is, a frame-of-reference based on the object itself. Moving the observer or the object will *not* change the representation of the object *so long as the same object-centered frame maintains* from one moment to the next. It is this last point that is critical to the distinction between viewer- and object-centered representations: the coordinates of a given object feature or part will remain the same in an object-centered description if a method for consistently deriving the same object-centered coordinate system can be performed across a varying image; in a viewer-centered description the coordinates of a given object feature or part will not remain constant as the image varies.

Another innovation of Marr and Nishihara's model was the explicit assumption that high-level object representations were *visual* entities. Although other models of object identification had posited viewpoint-independent representations, they had done so based on objects being recoded in terms of feature lists or semantic information that was not visual. In contrast, Marr and Nishihara's theory included high-level visual representations derived in bottom-up fashion from the outputs of earlier stages of visual processing.[1] Their critical insight was that visual components of objects – parts – could be *recovered* from intermediate visual representations. They proposed that primary axes (defined by properties such as elongation, symmetry or motion) are determined for each visible surface identified in the $2\frac{1}{2}$-D sketch. These axes are then used to derive *generalized cylinders* (created by sweeping a closed cross-section along an axis). In combination with inter-part spatial relations, the recovered generalized cylinders representing the parts of an object form a *structural-description*. Importantly, because the derivation of generalized cylinders encompasses a transformation from viewer-centered to object-centered coordinates, the structural description is itself object-centered or viewpoint-invariant. This is possible because nearly all views of the object show the same primary axes and consequently give rise to the same part-based structural-description in the same coordinate system regardless of initial viewing parameters. Marr and Nishihara also theorized that views of an object that do not clearly show its major axes will be difficult to recognize because no consistent recovery of an object-centered coordinate system will be possible – a point inspired by the neuropsychological observations mentioned earlier (Warrington & Taylor, 1973).

A final important aspect of Marr and Nishihara's theory is that it provides a representation that can support the classification of objects at multiple levels. This is accomplished through the hierarchical, coarse-to-fine nature of the structural-description encoded for each object. That is, an object is not simply represented at one scale. Rather, the rough configuration of parts is captured at the coarsest levels of the representation and then the details of each part are encoded at progressively finer levels (Figure 2.2). Because object categories are often based on visual similarity (Rosch et al., 1976), different levels of specificity within the representation will support different levels of visual categorization. Within this framework, superordinate classification is accomplished by common axis descriptions at the coarsest levels of the part hierarchy, particularly animals and plants that develop their eventual shape through maturation. For example, the axis descriptions of dogs, cats and other medium-sized quadrupeds will be relatively similar. To categorize an object as a 'quadruped' or 'mammal', a perceiver could simply analyze the coarse axis structure of the object. At the same time, additional information about the specific parts that form the structural-description of each object will help to differentiate between basic-level categories (Rosch et al., 1976). For example, distinguishing between dogs and cats might involve analysis of the other parameters (e.g. length, width) of the parts. Finally, telling apart individuals within a basic-level class requires information about an object's parts at all levels as well as the spatial relations between the parts.

The impact of Marr and Nishihara's model cannot be overstated; prior to this point the problem of object recognition was essentially an ignored problem (see Pinker, 1984). Following the introduction of their theory, many psychologists for the first time began to study the visual recognition problem and the idea of using an object's axes to derive an object-centered description became the 'standard' theory. The consensus was that if it were possible to recover an object-centered 3-D part-based object representation from the retinal array, the goal of object *constancy* could be explained in a heretofore unanticipated manner. What was left open was the question of whether such a representation was actually derivable from the image. As fundamental as this concern was to Marr and Nishihara's theory, they provided essentially no psychophysical or computational evidence to indicate how the recovery process might proceed.

THEORIES OF OBJECT RECOGNITION AFTER MARR

Marr's death at a young age meant that his theory was never pursued as it might have been otherwise. As an extant theory, it had two problems. First, exact methods for deriving an object-centered description from viewer-centered input were not available and computational implementations of this process were not particularly successful. Second, Marr and Nishihara offered no specific behavioral or neural evidence to support their theory and, in particular, the claim that high-level object representations were object-centered. In response to these unresolved issues, several different research programs emerged. Some psychologists, for instance Pinker (1984) and Jolicoeur (1985), questioned the idea that objects were represented as viewpoint-invariant part-based models. Other psychologists, most notably Biederman (1985), proposed a modified version of Marr and Nishihara's model that addressed both the nature of the recovery mechanisms and the lack of empirical support.

Object recognition through mental transformations?

The school of thought represented by Pinker and Jolicoeur proposed that Marr had made an error in assuming that representations subserving object recognition would necessarily have to be object-centered. They noted the findings of Shepard (Shepard & Cooper, 1982; Shepard & Metzler, 1971), who observed that some extremely difficult visual judgments with misoriented shapes could be solved using a mental transformation process referred to as 'mental rotation'. Shepard and colleagues expended a great deal of effort to demonstrate that the mental rotation process was the analog of a physical rotation in the 3-D world. Thus, upon viewing an object from one viewpoint, it could be mentally rotated into correspondence with one's memory for the same object in a different viewpoint. The critical point is that both the input shape and the object in memory are described in viewer-centered coordinates; that is, as they originally appeared to the viewer. In and of themselves such representations could not be matched, but they could be manipulated by an internal cognitive process which transformed the orientation of one of the representations to the orientation of the other representation – much as one might rotate an object in the physical world to align it with a second object. The behavioral signature of the mental rotation process was a roughly linear function of increasing response times (and error rates) with

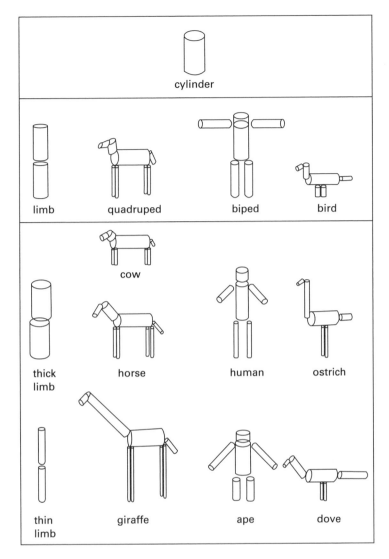

cylinder

| limb | quadruped | biped | bird |

cow

| thick limb | horse | human | ostrich |

| thin limb | giraffe | ape | dove |

Figure 2.2 *Marr and Nishihara's (1978) approach for representing objects as 3-D models, using generalized cylinders and spatial relations as features. One important property is the coding of objects along a continuum of generality/specificity. For example, a superordinate category might be encoded as a very simple set of relations among coarse-described volumes, basic-level visual categories as more precise relations and generalized cylinders of a more specific shape, and individual exemplars as specific spatial relations between a large number of shape-specific generalized cylinders at many different scales (from Marr 1982, Fig. 5–10, p. 319).*

increasing rotation magnitudes. That is, the larger the rotation, the longer it took.

Although Shepard viewed mental rotation as a property of an imagery system,[2] theorists in the post-Marr era speculated that it might be a generic property of high-level vision. For example, Palmer, Rosch, and Chase (1981) had expanded upon the observation that *canonical* views of an object support faster and more accurate object recognition relative to other views of the same object. Palmer et al. observed that there was a graded structure to view quality; views could be organized in a hierarchy ranging from best to worst along a range of dependent variables including subjective (ratings) and objective (recognition latency) measures. Similarly, Corballis (1988) speculated that at least part of this cost might be due to a mental rotation-like process, where only some views of the object were mentally represented (e.g. those that provided the highest-quality visual information); if such views were encountered at a later time they would be recognized very easily. Other views, however, would not be instantiated (at least partially to reduce the memory requirements of the system, a problem that had led Marr and Nishihara to propose the use of a 3-D model in the first place); if such views were encountered at a point in the future, mental rotation would be necessary to align them with stored views. This proposal helps explain the results of Palmer et al. Given mental representations of canonical views of objects, views progressively further from such views would be recognized more slowly and with lower accuracy, thereby producing the graded hierarchy of views reported by Palmer et al.

A similar argument, with empirical support, had been made by Jolicoeur (1985). In one experiment he simply had subjects name common mono-oriented objects (e.g. a cow) at upright or at one of several orientations generated by rotations in the picture plane. Jolicoeur observed that on the first block of trials, naming times were progressively slower as objects were rotated further from the upright (apart from a small 'dip' at 180°). However, if subjects were shown the same objects in the same orientations on a second block of trials, he found that naming times and the overall effect of orientation diminished considerably. Jolicoeur's conjecture was that his subjects had employed mental rotation in order to recognize objects seen for the first time from unfamiliar viewpoints, but that by the second encounter they had learned *either* viewpoint-invariant features that bypassed mental rotation or they had encoded representations of each object at each orientation shown during the initial block of trials. Unfortunately, nothing in Jolicoeur's study differentiated between these two possibilities.

Tarr and Pinker (1989) developed a methodology for determining whether viewpoint invariance is conferred through the extraction of viewpoint-invariant features or through multiple viewpoint-specific representations. They created a set of novel 2-D shapes that consisted of vertical and horizontal line segments connected in different configurations (Figure 2.3). During the initial phase of the experiment, Tarr and Pinker's subjects learned to name each of the shapes from a single orientation. In a second phase, their subjects practiced naming the shapes shown at a small number of orientations generated by rotations in the picture plane. This portion of the experiment replicated Jolicoeur's study in that subjects were encountering now-familiar mono-oriented objects in new, unfamiliar orientations. As in Jolicoeur's study, naming times at new orientations were initially dependent on the distance from the 'upright' orientation, but became less and less so with repeated exposures. At this point it is unclear what subjects have learned to circumvent the effects of orientation. To address this question,

Tarr and Pinker included a third phase in which the same shapes were now shown to subjects at new orientations interspersed between the orientations shown during the second phase. Naming times were found to be once again dependent on orientation, but now systematically related to the distance from the nearest of *several* familiar orientations. Critically, the magnitude of this effect was comparable to that observed at the beginning of the study when subjects were naming the shapes in new orientations for the first time. Tarr and Pinker concluded that the reason for their subjects' viewpoint-independent behavior during the second phase of the experiment was that they had learned *multiple views* of each shape and that a mental transformation process, possibly mental rotation, was used to align the same shapes in novel orientations with familiar orientations encoded in visual memory.[3] The critical point is that they posited an object representation that was *view-based* (sometimes also referred to as *image-based*) in that it encoded the appearance of an object in terms of one or more specific viewpoints.

Revisiting structural-descriptions

At about the same time some researchers were proposing alternatives to Marr and Nishihara's model, Biederman (1985; Hummel & Biederman, 1992) presented an amended version of the structural-description approach that addressed some of its most significant problems. Viewpoint-invariant structural-descriptions appealed to Biederman because they seemingly reduce both the memory and computational burdens placed on the visual system. Such descriptions necessitate only a few representations per object, whereas view-based representations potentially consist of hundreds if not thousands of specific views per object. Moreover, structural-descriptions are abstracted away from an object's specific appearance, therefore many objects might be represented by a single, more abstract, structural-description. In contrast, view-based models seemed to posit representations that were tied closely to the appearance of a particular object, therefore individual objects would be distinct in visual memory, taxing both memory capacity and one's ability to identify an object if its appearance changed only slightly.

Biederman relied on a *compositional* model in which a restricted set of 'building blocks' or *qualitative* primitives might be used in combination to represent all objects. The key idea is that even though a small number of primitives might each alone be very simple, configurations of several of them could capture the coarse shape of most objects. In many ways Biederman's theory, called *recognition-by-components* (RBC), is analogous to phonemes or letters: a small set of basic units can be

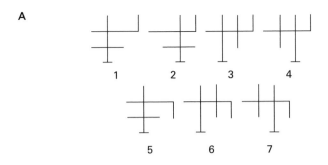

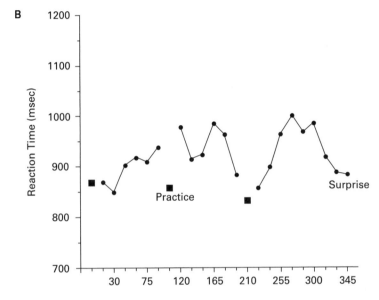

Figure 2.3   *(a) The simple 2-D shapes used in Tarr and Pinker (1989). (b) Response latencies to these learned shapes in the final 'surprise' test phase. Notice that recognition performance at familiar orientations is very good, but that response times at unfamiliar orientations generally increase with distance from the nearest familiar orientation (from Tarr & Pinker, 1989, Fig. 1, p. 243, and Fig. 6, p. 255).*

combined to form a huge range of complex structures (words, sentences, etc.). Biederman proposed that the basic units of object representation are 3-D volumes known as *geons* (for *geometric ions*), two or three of which are assembled to form a structural-description of an object.

Another important idea in Biederman's theory was the method by which geons were recovered from the image. Instead of relying on the primary axes and overall shape of the parts of an object, RBC derives geons from configurations of contours that are likely to arise during mid-level vision and, in particular, from perceptual organization. Specifically, each geon is defined by the presence of a particular set of *non-accidental properties* (Lowe, 1985). These properties are contour configurations that are so unlikely to have arisen in an image by chance that they almost certainly denote a specific structure in the distal object. Examples of such properties include co-terminating lines, collinear points, symmetry and parallelism. According to Biederman, an image of an object is first segmented into its constituent parts (using a process such as that proposed by Hoffman and Richards, 1984), and then each part is recoded as a given geon according to the particular set of non-accidental properties seen for that part. For example, a 'brick' (a box-like geon) would be recovered on the basis of several Y-junctions, parallel lines, and a rectangular, symmetric, constant cross-section. On a similar basis, geons were assigned for each part of an object and these geons along with their qualitative spatial arrangement formed the object representation. Not only is this recovery method better specified than that proposed by Marr and Nishihara, but it changes the task of object classification from a quantitative process in the original model to a qualitative process in which many different configurations of features in the image give rise to the same object representation. For example, many different views of a single object part and the parts of many different objects will show the particular Y-junctions, parallel lines, and rectangular, symmetric, constant cross-section consistent with a brick.

It is noteworthy that RBC's reliance on qualitative descriptions of object parts moves away from the idea that structural-descriptions are represented in an object-centered frame of reference. In RBC, structural-descriptions are viewpoint-invariant, but they are not object-centered. That is, many different views of an object will give rise to the same configuration of geons, hence over a wide range of viewpoints object recognition depends on the same object representation. At the same time, geon-based structural-descriptions are dependent on viewing conditions in that a given representation holds only for views that show the same visible parts and consequently the same geons. If an observer's viewpoint or an object orientation changes in a manner that changes the visible parts, a new and distinct geon structural-description must be recovered. This property of the model implies that a single object or object class will be coded in visual memory as multiple geon configurations, one for each distinct view of the object. In contrast, in Marr and Nishihara's model, one representation per object was sufficient. Thus, as Biederman (2000) has noted, RBC is, to some extent, 'view-based'; the real question is the specificity of the encoded views.

Multiple-views or structural-descriptions?

Despite some similarities, there are significant differences between view-based models and structural-description models as articulated above and in the field. This has been made clear in a series of exchanges that have been published in recent years (Tarr & Bülthoff, 1995; Biederman & Gerhardstein, 1995). Perhaps the most basic difference concerns the format of the representation underlying recognition; Bülthoff, Jolicoeur, Tarr and others propose that view-based representations capture the appearance of the surfaces of an object, including their shape, color, texture and shading, whereas Biederman holds that geon structural-descriptions are qualitative entities that capture the rough shape of an object's parts and little else. One important consequence of this difference is that view-based representations are predicted to be relatively unstable over changes in viewing conditions while, in contrast, geon structural-descriptions are predicted

to be relatively stable over the same changes in viewing conditions. Thus, the two approaches present two clear alternatives regarding object recognition performance over changes in viewpoint. Specifically, in view-based models even small changes to an object's orientation should detrimentally affect recognition, as the encoded and perceived representations will be different, and a time-consuming normalization process will be required to match them. In the geon structural-description model even large changes to an object's orientation will not be detrimental to recognition so long as the orientation change does not alter which geons are visible or the spatial relations between them.

These straightforward predictions led to a series of increasingly complex psychophysical studies of visual object recognition during the 1990s. Although each side of the debate has interpreted various results in their favor, a definitive answer has yet to be achieved. Below we consider some of the most compelling evidence (albeit with our own biases). At the same time, we argue that this body of evidence might be more usefully considered as something other than simply evidence for one theory or the other. As noted earlier, there is an essential similarity between the two schools of thought, which is that both approaches posit that *some* changes in appearance of an object will affect object recognition performance. The real question concerns the conditions under which recognition is affected and what this tells us about the underlying representation. View-based theories hold that most changes in appearance will affect performance, whereas RBC predicts performance costs only following changes that alter which parts are visible. The situation gets even murkier when one considers recent claims by Biederman that even in cases where no parts change between two views, there may still be small recognition costs due to factors such as difficulty in resolving the image and transient system activity (Biederman, 2000; Biederman & Bar, 1999, 2000). As such, it is difficult to know how to interpret apparent tests of one approach versus another. Nevertheless, we shall consider the effects of changes to different stimulus properties in turn, and conclude by considering what this evidence says about competing models of object recognition.

Changes in viewpoint

Of the many transformations that a 3-D object can undergo, by far the most studied is a change in viewpoint (generated by either observer movement or object rotation). Experiments manipulating viewpoint are so pervasive for two reasons: (1) such changes are common in the 'real world'; and (2) such changes can produce dramatic changes in the visible geometry of an object, particularly in terms of a 3-D object's 2-D projection. Indeed, more than changes in scale, illumination or position, viewpoint was the source of variability identified by Marr as requiring a specific solution, and it was this transformation that is addressed most directly by both view-based and structural-description models.

The most simple question that can be asked about changes in viewpoint is whether they affect recognition performance. The answer is, unfortunately, not as straightforward. Consider that almost any change in viewpoint results in some, albeit often minor, recognition costs (Tarr, Williams, Hayward, & Gauthier, 1998). More importantly, these recognition costs are typically systematically related to the magnitude of transformation; that is, small rotations yield small costs while large rotations yield large costs (Tarr, 1995; although this systematicity begins to break down past 90°). At the same time, relatively large recognition costs are observed whenever there is a change in the visible features or parts between two views of an object as compared to view changes of an equivalent magnitude that do not change feature and part visibility (Biederman & Gerhardstein, 1993; Hayward, 1998). Not surprisingly, the general fact that there are often effects of viewpoint, particularly effects proportional to the degree of viewpoint change, has been cited as supporting evidence for the view-based approach. However, the fact that these effects are modulated by feature and part visibility provides evidence for RBC.

Evaluating these conflicting interpretations is a useful exercise that helps to illuminate current thinking on the process of object recognition. Following Jolicoeur's (1985) and Tarr and Pinker's (1989) observations of viewpoint dependences in object recognition, numerous studies have run variations on their basic paradigm – naming objects from unfamiliar views – and have obtained similar results under a variety of conditions. For example, Tarr (1995) created novel 3-D objects with properties similar to the 2-D shapes used by Tarr and Pinker (1989) and ran a study using the same three phases. However, unlike earlier studies, the objects were rotated in depth around either the *x, y* or *z* axis. Consistent with the results of his earlier study, Tarr observed that naming times increased in a roughly linear fashion as a function of distance from the nearest familiar viewpoint. This result was important for demonstrating (1) that the previous viewpoint-dependent patterns of recognition performance did not arise simply because top–bottom spatial relations were disrupted by rotations exclusively in the picture-plane; and (2) that mechanisms of viewpoint-dependent recognition are not restricted to transformations that preserve feature visibility – with rotations in depth, the visible surfaces of the object changed from one view to another, yet viewpoint normalization was still possible.

Many other studies have found results similar to those of Tarr (1995), including Srinivas (1993, 1995), Humphrey and Khan (1992), Perrett et al. (1989), and Rock and DiVita (1987). The majority of these studies have simply examined recognition latencies as a function of viewpoint difference between study and test views. As such, they do not provide strong evidence for any specific view-based theory. However, they are useful in that they have demonstrated that viewpoint-dependent mechanisms are recruited over a wide range of conditions and object types. Moreover, there is the consistent finding of a recognition process that is specifically sensitive to the distance between known and novel views of objects. That is, recognition becomes progressively more difficult as viewpoint differences increase. What sorts of mechanisms might be consistent with this basic prediction? One notable possibility was set forth by Poggio and Edelman (1990). They proposed a view *interpolation* process in which the features of known views of a given object are used in combination to support the recognition of that same object in unknown views *without* the use of a mental transformation.

In order to more directly investigate whether an interpolation mechanism might account for viewpoint-dependent patterns of recognition performance, Bülthoff and Edelman (1992) conducted a study in which they manipulated the locations of new, unknown views relative to the locations of known views. To increase generality, they employed two distinct sets of objects where members of each set were very similar to one another. One set consisted of objects that appeared to be sections of wire connected together (*wireclips* or *paperclips*), and the other set consisted of objects that were spheroid in shape with extrusions protruding from the surface at various points (*amoeboids*). Subjects studied each object from two different views separated by 75° (in order to facilitate the perception of 3-D structure, each view showed the object rotating slightly, and was presented stereoscopically). Following this training, a series of objects from the same set were shown, and subjects judged whether each test object was the same as the studied object or not. Three different spatial relationships between each test view and the two studied views were included: (1) in INTER trials, the test view occurred between the two studied views; (2) in EXTRA trials, the test view occurred outside the studied views, but along the same axis that separated with studied views; (3) in ORTHO trials, the test view occurred along an axis that was orthogonal to the studied views.

Bülthoff and Edelman observed that across all three conditions there was a characteristic decrease in recognition performance with increasing separation between the closest familiar view and the test view (Figure 2.4). However, critical to evaluating the interpolation model, the magnitude of the

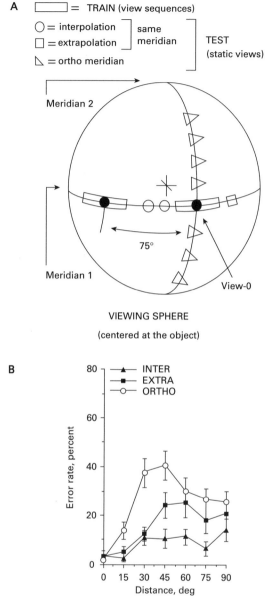

Figure 2.4   *(a) Schematic of the object views used in Bülthoff and Edelman (1992). Imagine an object sits at the center of the sphere, and points on the surface represent specific views of the object. Training views are shown as the rectangles along Meridian 1; test views are either between the two sets of training views (interpolation), outside the training views but along the same meridian (extrapolation), or along Meridian 2 (orthogonal). (b) Recognition error rates, showing better performance for interpolated than extrapolated or orthogonal views (from Bülthoff & Edelman, 1992, Fig. 2 and 3, p. 62).*

viewpoint effect (e.g. the cost relative to the degree of rotation) varied according to condition. Specifically, costs were largest in the ORTHO condition, intermediate in the EXTRA condition, and smallest in the INTER condition. Thus, recognition performance was not simply a function of the distance from the single nearest studied view (per Tarr and Pinker, 1989), but rather was related to the position of a given test view relative to the *set* of known views. Bülthoff and Edelman (1992) interpreted these results as evidence for the use of an interpolation mechanism in matching unfamiliar views to familiar views. That is, the appearance of views falling between known views can be predicted much more accurately than can the appearance of views falling outside of known views. The concept of view interpolation has been elaborated in a series of computational models, the most notable of which is detailed in Edelman (1999), as well as several more recent psychophysical studies (Williams & Tarr, 1999; Wong & Hayward, 2002).

Whereas most of the studies cited above were primarily concerned with recognition performance as test views are rotated further and further from studied views, Biederman and colleagues conducted several studies in the 1990s that examined recognition for a variety of geometric changes across constant changes in viewpoint. For example, Biederman and Gerhardstein (1993) created a set of objects that were each composed of several different geons in different spatial arrangements. Across constant rotation of 45°, subjects judged whether an image presented immediately following a study object was the same object (albeit in a different view) or a different object (e.g. composed of different geons). When the object was the same object but rotated, the second view could either show the same configuration of parts as the first view or show a different configuration of parts (in this latter condition at least one part was occluded and/or another part became visible).

Biederman and Gerhardstein reasoned that if objects in these two conditions were matched via a mental transformation, recognition costs should be relatively similar in both cases. In fact, the same-parts condition showed a minimal effect of viewpoint, whereas the different-parts condition showed large effects of viewpoint on recognition performance. The authors argued that such results demonstrate that configurations of geons determine recognition performance across changes in viewpoint. That is, observers are sensitive to the visible parts of an object, but not to the specific viewpoint from which those parts were seen.

Of course, changing the visible parts of an object also changes the visible features of an object, including local contours, bounding contours and visible surfaces. For instance, Hayward (1998) found that similar results could be obtained when an image of an object was shown initially and then matched to a silhouette (where the recovery of 3-D volumes was much more difficult). As the bounding contour is one of the most salient properties of an object from any particular viewpoint, it is not surprising to find it implicated in recognition tasks. More generally, it is worth noting that finding a correlation between a subject's ability to recognize an object and a change in visible parts or any of the accompanying featural changes does not constitute direct evidence for geons forming the representation of said parts.

In part to address this concern and uncover more specific evidence about the shape representations underlying recognition, Biederman and Bar (1999) examined recognition performance costs following different transformations of object shape. Subjects made same/different judgments to two sequentially presented objects, which were either identical two-part objects, or differed on the basis of one part. If one part differed between the objects, the difference was either *metric*, such as a change in length, width, or the angle of connection to another part, or *qualitative*, such as whether the part had a straight or curved axis, or whether it was tapered at one end. To ensure that any differences obtained between these conditions were due to the type of change and not the magnitude of the change independent of its type, stimuli at one viewpoint were independently verified to be equally discriminable; that is, when there was no change in viewpoint, subjects made errors of a similar magnitude to the metric and qualitative changes. In contrast, following object rotation, subjects made few errors with the qualitative changes but many errors with the metric changes. Biederman and Bar argue that this result constitutes evidence for geons, as they are based upon properties of contours similar to those that changed in the qualitative condition. On the other hand, they argue that differences in metric properties do not provide useful information for generalizing across changes in viewpoint.

Although Biederman and Bar's results do indicate the heavy weight placed on qualitative properties of shape by the visual recognition system, they, again, do not speak directly to the issue of whether local qualitative features are combined to form geons. Indeed, many other models of shape representation place a similar emphasis on qualitative features, yet do not assume that they are combined into geons or other primitives (Koenderink, 1987; Wagemans, Van Gool, & Lamote, 1996). Among others, Tarr and Kriegman (2001) have tested the basic assumptions of such models and found support for the notion that observers are more sensitive to changes in viewpoint when there is a concurrent qualitative change in the visible features of the object. Hayward and Tarr (1997) specifically pitted this assumption against the idea that qualitative features were not processed independently, but rather were combined into geons or other 3-D parts. Using a same/different sequentially matching task, they compared object rotations for single 3-D parts (geons). Rotations of equal magnitude could either qualitatively or metrically change the configuration of visible features for a given part. However, since each object was made up of only a single geon (e.g. a 'brick'), the particular geon or part specified was unchanged regardless of object rotation. Thus, a model relying on a geon-based representation would predict no difference between metric and qualitative changes in this experiment. In contrast, a model

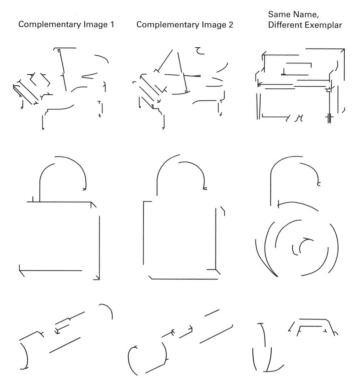

Figure 2.5   *Stimuli used in Biederman and Cooper (1991b). Despite the images in the left and center columns sharing no common contours, priming of object naming times was equivalent for identical images and images to their complements. Naming priming to a different-shaped but same-named exemplar (right column), however, was impaired (from Biederman & Cooper, 1991b, Fig. 1, p. 397).*

relying only on local qualitative features would predict differences between the qualitative and metric object rotation conditions. Hayward and Tarr found clear differences in performance depending on condition: much larger costs of viewpoint change were obtained for the qualitative change condition despite the fact that the part specified by the local features never changed. They conclude that, taken with other results, their findings indicate that object representations do seem to place an emphasis on qualitative features, but that such features are not combined to form geons.

Changes in object features

A second way to assess the nature of the representations underlying object recognition is to vary geometric aspects of an object (without manipulating viewpoint). For example, Biederman and Cooper (1991b) conducted a priming study in which subjects named line drawings of common everyday objects in two different blocks of trials. For each object, two different, complementary line drawings were created

such that each member of a pair showed contours that did not overlap with the contours shown in the other member of the pair (Figure 2.5). Biederman and Cooper found that if both members of the stimulus pair showed all the parts of the object (though different contours for each part), the degree of priming in the second block of trials was equal regardless of whether the same line drawing or its complement was presented. Thus, although the two images were completely different at the pixel level, there was no effect of this manipulation on facilitating object naming. This result suggests that the representation mediating priming is not based on the image itself, but rather is based on a representation that codes higher-order features of the object.

Illumination

An oft-overlooked, but important change that can occur to an image of an object is a change in lighting direction. If a light is moved or an object is moved relative to a light, there will be changes in both cast and attached shadows (and consequently shadow edges), in shading gradients, and in specularities. As well as directly changing the appearance of the image, all of these changes could potentially change the perceived shape and, hence, affect visual recognition performance. Although there have been few studies specifically examining the question of how a change in lighting direction impacts recognition (apart from how it affects face recognition; see Johnston, Hill, & Carman, 1992), it has often been observed that shape-selective neurons in visual cortex are also sometimes selective for lighting direction (Hietanen, Perrett, Oram, Benson, & Dittrich, 1992). Tarr, Kersten, and Bülthoff (1998) built on this fact and the finding that cast shadows are extremely useful in disambiguating the 3-D scene (Kersten, Mamassian, & Knill, 1997). They investigated the recognition of novel objects across changes in lighting direction that also changed the shadows cast by one part of an object onto another part of the same object. Such changes were found to hurt recognition performance; however, the same magnitude change in lighting direction in the absence of cast shadows (thus only changing the shading gradients on an object's surfaces) did not impair recognition. Tarr et al. conclude that the visual system represents information about lighting direction because it is useful for telling the observer something about the 3-D layout of objects and the scene. However, unlike information about viewpoint, they hypothesize that the visual system builds a model of illumination that is abstracted away from the original image (albeit still tied to a particular lighting direction). As evidence for this claim, they ran an additional experiment in which subjects learned to name objects under a given illumination direction and viewpoint. Recognition performance was affected by a change in the direction of the illumination independent of whether the viewpoint was familiar or not. Thus, whatever was represented about illumination apparently was not tied to the appearance of the object as it was originally encountered. In contrast, as reviewed above, information about viewpoint is often tied to initial viewing conditions.

Other stimulus properties

Of course, there are a great many other image properties that can be manipulated to examine the effect of such changes on recognition performance. Many such variables have been investigated by Biederman and colleagues. For example, they have investigated alterations of objects in terms of scale (Biederman & Cooper, 1992; Fiser & Biederman, 2001), translation and reflection (Biederman & Cooper, 1991a; Fiser & Biederman, 2001). In almost every case they report essentially no decrement in recognition performance across such changes.

Such a finding of invariance can be useful in postulating the neural locus of object recognition because of what is known about the receptive field size and response properties of neurons in different points on the ventral visual pathway, the stream that is thought to be primarily responsible for conscious object recognition (Milner & Goodale, 1995; Ungerleider & Mishkin, 1982). For example, cells in area V1 (primary visual cortex in the occipital lobe) typically have a receptive field no larger than 2° of visual angle. Thus, if a stimulus is translated by 2°, a neuron that was fully activated by the original stimulus will no longer remain active. At higher levels of the ventral pathway, however, receptive fields become larger and larger, and thus patterns of recognition performance that remain invariant over changes in certain stimulus properties can be attributed to visual areas with cells whose receptive fields would cover that area. Fiser and Biederman (2001), for example, argue that their finding of recognition invariance with an 8° translation across hemifields necessarily implicates the human homologue of area TEO in the monkey, thought to be the anterior portion of the inferior temporal lobe.

Of course, one difficulty with evaluating such studies is that the finding of invariance is a null result. As such, it may be that the property being investigated is not relevant to the task at hand or that other properties provide sufficient information to perform the task accurately (and allowing subjects to ignore the change in the manipulated property). Moreover, other researchers have reported studies using similar designs in which changes to particular properties *did* impact recognition performance (e.g. Srinivas, 1993; Jolicoeur, 1987; Wurm, Legge, Isenberg, & Luebker, 1993; Tanaka & Presnell, 1999). In the end the jury is still out; clearly subjects *can* learn to encode many different aspects of an object, but the question is whether they do so automatically and as part and parcel of their default visual recognition strategy.

Integrating experiments on object constancy

At the start of this section we contrasted two different approaches to object recognition. Does either approach provide a coherent explanation of the evidence we have just examined?[4] First, let us consider Biederman's approach. In the face of numerous studies (including those described above) showing recognition performance that was sensitive to viewpoint, Biederman and Gerhardstein (1993) proposed three conditions that were necessary for the RBC model to apply. The conditions were: (i) the object should be decomposable into geons, (ii) different objects should have different geon descriptions, and (iii) all tested views should show the same geons in the same spatial relationship. Their logic was that experiments using highly confusable stimuli were not applicable to 'everyday' object recognition, in that they demanded a level of precision in recognition that was unlike 'the vast majority' of recognition tasks (with the possible exception of face recognition). The experiments presented in light of these arguments then demonstrated that when the three conditions were met, object recognition was viewpoint-invariant.

Many researchers were quick to argue with the validity of Biederman and Gerhardstein's conditions. For example, Tarr and Bülthoff (1995) noted that the conditions did not define what observers do in the world, but what would observers *have to do* in order for RBC to explain their behavior. Thus, they argued, there was no ecological validation of Biederman and Gerhardstein's claims. In addition, Tarr and Bülthoff pointed out that the actual experiments often involved placing a single perceptually salient and diagnostic component on each object in a stimulus set. A similar result could be achieved, argued Tarr and Bülthoff, by painting the objects different colors.

Perhaps more persuasively, recent studies have found that observers often exhibit viewpoint-dependent patterns of performance under conditions that conform to those spelled out by Biederman and Gerhardstein. Tarr, Williams, Hayward, and Gauthier (1998) found viewpoint-dependent naming and sequential matching performance using single geons. Hayward and Tarr (1997) found viewpoint-dependent performance with simple two-part objects that also fulfilled the three conditions. Finally, Tarr, Bülthoff, Zabinski, and Blanz (1997) showed that the addition of geons to an object does not necessarily lead to viewpoint-invariant performance; if an object contains more than one geon, it can become confusable with other objects that contain the same geons in different configurations, particularly if the spatial relations between components are very similar (see also Johnston & Hayes, 2000). In turn, Biederman has criticized these studies, and continues to push for a model based on geons. He notes that the viewpoint costs in the studies that fulfill his conditions are typically much smaller than the costs in studies using paperclips (e.g. Bülthoff & Edelman, 1992) or objects composed of cubes (Tarr, 1995). He explains these costs as being due to several different possible artifacts, such as an episodic memory representation (Biederman & Cooper, 1992), a difficulty in seeing qualitative features in shaded images (Biederman & Bar, 1999), or a change signal from a neural system independent of recognition (Biederman, 2000; Biederman & Bar, 1999). In our view, these criticisms are not particularly compelling. With every new result, the scope of RBC appears smaller and smaller; first, specific conditions are set for the validity of its predictions, and then results from tests that fulfill the conditions are dismissed on the basis of ad hoc, extra-theory conjectures.

If geons do not provide a coherent basis for the many studies discussed to this point, do view-based theories provide a better account? At this stage, the answer must also be no. The main difficulty with current view-based models is their lack of specificity. While they have in common a general prediction of increasing viewpoint costs with larger rotations between views, the mechanism proposed as underlying such performance has varied from mental rotation (Tarr & Pinker, 1989) to relatively unspecified 'image features' (Hayward & Tarr, 1997) to ad hoc collections of vertices (Bricolo, Poggio, & Logothetis, 1997) or image features (Mel, 1997). When the mechanism is vague enough, almost any pattern of performance that falls within the rubric of increasing costs following viewpoint difference might be counted as support for the position (which is problematic, as one pattern of behavioral responding may be derived from multiple cortical circuits; Gauthier, Hayward, Tarr, Anderson, Skudlarski, & Gore, 2002). On the other hand, the position becomes difficult to test. For example, it is entirely possible that a view-based model could be proposed that would be sensitive to qualitative features (see Riesenhuber & Poggio, 1999), and therefore might predict the results of Biederman and Bar's experiment. With such a wide variety of possibilities, view-based theories are not particularly compelling theoretically.

Why have view-based theories been relatively successful over the last ten years, if they are so theoretically underspecified? One can point to a number of reasons. First, it is clear from a great many studies that view-specific patterns of performance are the norm (even many of Biederman's studies find this result, although the pattern may be more or less severe). Second, the only real alternative, Biederman's RBC, has been relatively unsuccessful at accounting for many results. Third, specifying the information used in recognition decisions, and the mechanism that processes that information, is an extraordinarily difficult task. Indeed, we know that object categories do not have fixed boundaries (e.g. Rosch et al., 1976), and therefore finding visual features that accurately specify the identity of the objects is a daunting task. Given this difficulty, the failure of view-based theories to more clearly specify their mechanisms has been tolerated.

Of course, one possible resolution to the debate over models of object recognition is to propose a dichotomous model in which a structural-description process coexists with a view-based process. This solution has been favored by several protagonists (e.g. Jolicoeur, 1990; Farah, 1992; Tarr & Bülthoff, 1995), who suggest that a primarily view-based strategy may be used with object sets that are more similar to one another (such as faces) whereas a structural-description approach might be used for more dissimilar objects. Most objects will fall between these extremes, and thus might show influences of both processes, resulting in small viewpoint costs. Such an explanation would therefore help explain differences in the size of viewpoint costs between different studies.

Although attractive, such a resolution should be handled with caution for two reasons. The first point is based on the logic of Occam's razor; adding complexity to the theory makes it less attractive, and also makes it much more difficult to falsify, as we would now predict that the results of any experiment should show *either* view-specific *or* viewpoint-invariant performance! Second, Hayward and Williams (2000) have shown that the relationship between object discriminability and viewpoint cost functions may not be as strong as intuitively thought. The authors used objects that could be categorized in different ways so that a given object discrimination could be between objects that were either very similar to each other, very distinct from each other, or intermediate in similarity. It was reasoned that if viewpoint costs were due to similarity, they should be most severe when the objects were similar and much smaller when the objects were distinct. In fact, across two experiments, the viewpoint cost functions were identical in all conditions except when a color cue was able to distinguish the objects from each other. On the basis of these results, Hayward and Williams argue that object similarity may not be the most crucial factor in determining viewpoint cost functions; instead, object geometry (whether objects contain geometric features, such as qualitative features, that allow for robust generalization across viewpoint) may be particularly important. At this stage it is too early to draw conclusions about the basis of such differences. However, drawing on results such as those obtained by Hayward and Williams, Tarr (2003) has shifted to arguments in favor of a single system to support the recognition of objects at all levels.

Levels of Object Classification

Until now, we have treated the process of object recognition as leading to a single outcome – recognition. We have noted that in some situations (e.g. the qualitative change condition of Biederman & Bar, 1999) this task may be relatively easier than in other situations (e.g. Bülthoff & Edelman, 1992), but the difficulty has been considered as simply difficulty in differentiating a given object from other objects in the recognition set. However, consider that objects can be identified with an infinite number of terms, because, as Marr noted, object recognition is really the task of object *classification*. Consider an office chair. If you are shown a picture of the object, and asked to name it, you will likely say 'chair'. However, you might also say 'office chair'. Clearly, both answers are correct, but they identify the object with differing amounts of specificity. The former term identifies the object as being a different kind of object from a desk, but identifies it as being the same kind of thing as a dining-room chair. The latter term, on the other hand, identifies it as being distinct from both these objects. This process can be extended to infinity; the chair may be identified as a 'Herman Miller Aeron office chair' or as a 'piece of furniture' or as an 'object smaller than a car'. We may be loath to accept some of these as names of the object, but the distinction between names and classifications, such as it is, is fuzzy at best.

Of course, in general we agree about the appropriate classification for a given object. Most of us will say 'chair' when shown a particular picture because we take this to be a classification that distinguishes the object from others that are dissimilar (e.g. tables) and places within the classification other objects that are similar (e.g. office chairs and dining-room chairs). There is flexibility, though, in determining such levels, and the appropriate level can be altered by factors such as expertise. For example, most people, when shown different species of fish, will use that term as the common label. However, expert scuba divers, when shown a picture, will likely name the object as 'angelfish' or 'butterfly-fish' or 'garoupa'. In essence, this behavior shows that the divers now consider each type of fish as distinctive enough to warrant its own category. Note that this change in level is not simply a function of knowing the verbal label for the more specific level, as the same scuba divers will call their office chair a 'chair' even though they know it is different from a dining-room chair; despite the differences, they consider both types of objects as having greater similarities than distinctive attributes.

Differences in levels of classification were extensively studied by Rosch et al. (1976). They argued that the level of classification at which objects are usually named is psychologically important for a number of reasons. For example, it is typically also the first concept (relative to other possible classifications of the object) to be learned, it is the level at which classification is verified most quickly, and it is the highest level at which parts and functions of an object are shared by all exemplars. To mark its psychological significance, Rosch et al. termed it the *basic* level of categorization, whereas levels of classification that are more specific are termed *subordinate* and levels more general are termed *superordinate*. As we have already noted, one person's basic level may be another's superordinate level, and thus these levels will vary, to some extent, across people. In part because of this possibility for confusion, Jolicoeur, Gluck, and Kosslyn (1984) created an alternative term, the *entry* level of classification, which refers specifically to the level that is most quickly verified. In general the entry level and basic level will be identical, but the new term makes some cases easier to deal with (e.g. penguins, which are subordinate members of a basic level, *birds*, yet are named more quickly as *penguins*).

Biederman's RBC model was specifically designed to be a model of entry-level recognition. Thus, he acknowledged that other, more specific identifications were possible, but that these would be beyond the scope of his theory (to be fair, it was this a priori concern that partially motivated the three conditions for viewpoint invariance of Biederman & Gerhardstein, 1993). On the other hand, many authors have suggested that the objects used in studies such as those by Tarr (1995; Tarr & Pinker, 1989) and Bülthoff and Edelman (1992) might be considered as members of single entry-level categories ('paperclip'). Discriminating one from another would thus be a task of subordinate-level categorization. On this basis, the previous discussion relating viewpoint costs to the specificity of discrimination can also be considered as one of differing levels of classification, where RBC might explain entry-level recognition and view-based theories might explain subordinate-level performance. For the same reasons identified earlier, however, this distinction is problematic. Most experiments show some amount of viewpoint dependence, regardless of whether the objects are considered as requiring entry-level or subordinate-level categorization (e.g. Hayward, 1998; Tarr, Williams, Hayward, & Gauthier, 1998). Hayward and Williams' (2000) finding of similar viewpoint costs for object sets of differing discriminability can be interpreted as showing no effect of differing levels of categorization. Finally, in an alternative argument, Biederman, Subramaniam, Bar, Kaloscai, and Fiser (1999) have argued that *all* classification, even at the subordinate level, is performed on the basis of qualitative features (and thus that the recognition process in subordinate-level classification should be viewpoint-invariant, although there may be costs involved with identifying the location within the object at which a useful feature occurs).

Whether one takes the view that all levels of categorization are performed on the basis of either view-specific or qualitative information, or alternatively that different information is used at different levels, one still makes the assumption that recognition is driven primarily by the available information. But what happens as the perceiver becomes more expert with a stimulus class? We have already discussed evidence suggesting that the entry level changes as one gains expertise, as experts use a level for identification that for non-experts is subordinate. Can this flexibility also result in experts using different *kinds* of information?

Research from a different domain within object recognition can illuminate this question. Theorists have long identified faces as an object category that seems to require a different sort of explanation than that required for the recognition of other objects. On

the one hand, the entry level for faces seems to be an individual name. On the other hand, all faces are very similar to one another; they share the same parts in the same spatial configuration, and thus to identify a particular face a perceiver needs a much more specific identification than for other objects. It seems that, in terms of the similarities among object classes, recognizing individual faces *should* be an example of subordinate-level classification, and yet because of our expertise with the stimulus class we are able to identify them at the entry level.

Given the peculiar nature of faces, is the information used to recognize them the same as the information used for other object classes? Many studies suggest not. In an early investigation, Yin (1969) showed that inverted faces were much more difficult to recognize than other inverted objects. Introspective accounts of inverted face recognition suggest that although one can identify that it is an inverted face, and that it has all requisite face components (that is, one knows immediately if the inverted face is missing an eye or the mouth), one is unable to 'put the components together'. This sense of a disruption to spatial processing of the face configuration is supported by empirical data. For example, Tanaka and Farah (1993) trained subjects to name individual faces and then had them discriminate between an individual part of each face and a distractor part (Figure 2.6). The part ('Larry's nose') and the distractor (a different nose) both appeared either in the learned face ('Larry's face') or in a scrambled version of the face ('Larry's face with all the features moved about'). Although in both discriminations the relevant facial feature was the only source of variation between the images, discrimination of the parts was more accurate when in the context of the learned face rather than the altered face. Such results suggest that, unlike with other objects, the sensitivity of the perceiver is to the face as a whole, including parts not relevant to the task at hand, rather than to the individual components in isolation.

Additional studies suggest that the sensitivity to configural information in the face is not computed in isolation, but rather in relation to other, known faces. Rhodes, Brennan, and Carey (1987) investigated the relationship between recognition of a face and pre-existing knowledge of other faces. They produced line drawings of faces, and marked the positions of landmarks on each face. They then compared the positions of each landmark across the entire set of faces, which allowed them to compute the average position for each landmark. The derivation of the average set of landmarks allowed them to compute the extent, for each face, that each landmark differed from the average landmark. These differences could be used in one of two ways: faces could be altered so that each landmark was moved toward the average, or each landmark would be moved away from the average. The former created faces that were more similar to the other faces in the

A

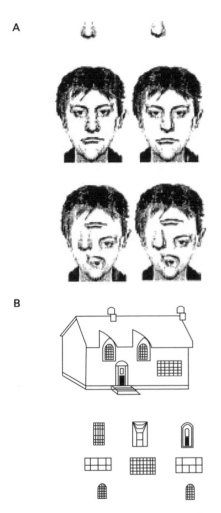

B

Figure 2.6 *Stimuli used in Tanaka and Farah (1993). (a) Subjects learned a set of faces and then had to identify components of each individual. In the comparisons shown here, the nose is the* only *difference between the pair of images, yet part identification performance was better when the noses were shown in the familiar, learned facial configuration as compared to when they were shown in isolation or in the context of transformed or scrambled features. (b) When subjects performed a similar task with houses, no advantage for the familiar, learned configuration was observed (from Tanaka & Farah, 1993, Fig. 1, p. 231, and Fig. 5, p. 239).*

stimulus set (*anti-caricatures*) whereas the latter manipulation created faces that were more distinct from the others (*caricatures*). Subjects were then asked to recognize the original line drawings, the

anti-caricatures or the caricatures. Although the line drawings were the most accurate depiction of the face, subjects found the caricatures easiest to identify (and the anti-caricatures most difficult). Thus, recognition was easier when a target face was more distinct from other faces in the set.

On the basis of such results, many theorists have proposed that the processes mediating face recognition might be *special*, in that they are used only for the recognition of faces. Rationale for this view includes the findings of extreme viewpoint dependence by Yin (1969); the fact that, as a social species, face recognition in humans is important for survival; and the previously discussed fact that faces are more similar to each other than are most other objects that we recognize. More recent evidence comes from studies of the neural substrate underlying face recognition, by using functional magnetic resonance imaging (fMRI). Kanwisher, McDermott, and Chun (1997) had subjects view intact faces or control stimuli such as scrambled faces, hands, houses or other objects. They found that portions of the fusiform gyrus within visual cortex produced more activation to intact faces than to any other stimulus, and concluded that this region is involved in the perception of faces but not other objects.

Simply finding differences in the recognition of faces and other objects may not be strong evidence for face recognition being a 'special' process. In particular, it is important to consider both the stimulus parameters (faces are similar to each other) and expertise of observers. Studies that have controlled these factors carefully have generally found face-like patterns of performance for non-face objects. For example, Rhodes and McLean (1990) found a caricature effect in recognition of birds by experts, but not novices. Gauthier and Tarr (1997) trained subjects to recognize novel figures ('Greebles') until they became experts (defined as the point at which they were able to identify individual Greebles as quickly as they could classify them according to more general categorical features). Much like Tanaka and Farah's (1993) study, Greeble experts, but not Greeble novices, found it more difficult to identify Greeble parts when other Greeble parts were moved, suggesting that subjects were using configural information to perform the task.

In addition to the behavioral evidence reviewed above, there is a growing body of work using brain imaging that has come to similar conclusions. Gauthier and colleagues have shown that the so-called fusiform face area (or FFA) responds equally to other stimuli given particular characteristics of the recognition task. Gauthier, Anderson, Tarr, Skudlarski, and Gore (1997) noted that in the tasks of Kanwisher et al. (1997) and other, similar studies, control objects are typically identified at the entry level (this will likely be true unless specific instructions are given to do otherwise, given the definition of entry level as the first name that is produced), whereas faces require some degree of subordinate-level processing. Gauthier had subjects perform either entry-level or subordinate-level discrimination tasks in an fMRI paradigm, and found selective activation of the FFA in the subordinate-level task relative to the entry-level task.

In a second study Gauthier, Tarr, Anderson, Skudlarski, and Gore (1999) extended the earlier work of Gauthier and Tarr (1997) by examining the neural locus of activation in the brains of Greeble experts; they found that when subjects had attained expertise, their functionally defined FFA was selectively active for Greebles as compared to common objects. Moreover, their FFA showed selectivity for upright as compared to inverted Greebles. In contrast, Greeble novices do not show selective activity in their functionally defined FFA for Greebles versus objects or upright versus inverted Greebles. A follow-up study demonstrated similar patterns of neural activity for extant bird and car experts (but only for their domain of expertise; Gauthier, Skudlarski, Gore, & Anderson, 2000). Although the debate over specialization of the FFA and other regions of the ventral visual processing pathway continues (for example, see recent papers by Gauthier, 2000; Ishai, Ungerleider, Martin, & Haxby, 2000; Tarr & Gauthier, 2000; Kanwisher, 2000), it is clear that given certain conditions, the visual recognition of non-face objects becomes very similar to recognition of faces. Such findings cast doubt on a strong interpretation of the 'faces are special' hypothesis. At the same time it appears as though the acquisition of expertise somehow 'tunes' visual recognition mechanisms to recruit different information in processing the domain(s) of expertise. Whether such differences reflect changes to a single substrate or the functioning of multiple recognition systems is not yet established.

CONCLUSIONS

We began this review by considering Marr's theory as the first modern theory of high-level vision. In the twenty years since his death, great numbers of studies have been conducted, but what progress has been made? To put it another way, what results would surprise Marr today? Certainly advances in computational and cellular physiology and brain imaging have changed the way we assess both neural functioning and behavior, but often these techniques are used to reinforce existing positions rather than to explore new questions. In terms of ongoing debates about the most applicable model of visual recognition, a small number of general conclusions can, to our minds, be drawn:

1 Strict template theories (e.g. based on retinal coordinates) are unlikely to be successful (of course, Marr knew this).
2 Changes in viewpoint typically produce costs in recognition performance, albeit small costs in some circumstances.
3 Despite great increases in computational power, the derivation of a 3-D structural-description, even as prescribed by RBC, remains elusive.

Based on the latter two points, we believe that it is reasonable to conclude that Marr would no longer put his faith in a model that jumps from a $2\frac{1}{2}D$ sketch to a 3-D model. This is not to say that 3-D models have no place in visual processing; we know from simple demonstrations of visual imagery and mental rotation that perceivers have access to something akin to a 3-D representation of objects. But such representations may have little role in everyday object recognition (Gauthier et al., 2002).

4 Face recognition places different demands on visual processing as compared to most other object recognition tasks. However, mechanisms to satisfy such demands can be flexibly deployed to other visual stimuli under certain conditions, particularly following the acquisition of expertise or when a fine-level discrimination amongst members of a homogeneous object class must be made.

Point 4 suggests the need for specific explanation of the information and processes recruited in the recognition of faces as compared to generic object recognition, but without the dogma of whether such processes are *special*.

5 The core representation underlying general object recognition remains unknown.

The final point would, we are sure, disappoint Marr. Even to the extent that qualitative features are useful, our interpretation of current evidence is that there is no compelling reason to assume that the representations underlying object recognition are composed of volumetric primitives. At the same time, little progress has been made on this topic by view-based theorists. These problems suggest that alternative approaches to the problem may be needed. One difficulty concerns the deterministic use of features. It is assumed by many researchers that, at some time, a canonical set of features that define cars, computers and cougars will be uncovered (be they geons or image features). We see no evidence that the field is successfully developing these proposals. Theories of categorization, of course, have long held that categories cannot be defined by feature lists (e.g. Rosch et al., 1976; Wittgenstein, 1953), and there is no reason to believe that such established truths will be suspended for the benefit of the vision community. Therefore, novel approaches to the problem will be required. This may involve the use of top-down information to supplement bottom-up cues, the use of attention to specify particular features on an ad hoc basis as crucial in a given recognition task (after all, you can take almost any object, put a working light-bulb on the top, and call it a *lamp*[5]), and the realization that almost *anything* in the image might constitute a feature in appropriate conditions. Given the nature of high-level vision as an investigation of the function of vision, this last point may not be too surprising, even to Marr.

NOTES

1 As alluded to earlier, one should probably credit Shepard and Metzler (1971) with introducing the notion of high-level, purely visual representations.

2 Interestingly, Shepard and Cooper (1982) were aware that mental rotation might be posited as a mechanism for dealing with viewpoint variation in object recognition. However, they believed that executing a mental rotation required *prior* knowledge of the direction and magnitude of the rotation. Their intuitions told them that the only way to obtain such information was by the recognition of the object. Therefore, they doubted that mental rotation was of much use in object recognition.

3 Tarr and Pinker (1989) cite computational methods developed by Ullman (1989) that address Shepard and Cooper's concerns regarding the need for prior knowledge of rotation direction and magnitude. Ullman and his students implemented several versions of an 'alignment' algorithm in which the direction and magnitude of the transformation necessary to align an input shape with a version of that shape in memory are pre-computed prior to recognition using only a small amount of shape information.

4 The reader should be made aware that we are certainly not impartial in this debate. We have published numerous papers arguing strongly for view-based solutions to the object constancy. The reader is referred to two exchanges of views (Tarr & Bülthoff, 1995 vs. Biederman & Gerhardstein, 1995; Hayward & Tarr, 2000 vs. Biederman & Bar, 2000) for arguments on each side.

5 Our thanks to Cassandra Moore for this example.

REFERENCES

Biederman, I. (1985). Human image understanding: recent research and a theory. *Computer Vision, Graphics, and Image Processing, 32*, 29–73.

Biederman, I. (2000). Recognizing depth-rotated objects: a review of recent research and theory. *Spatial Vision, 13*, 241–253.

Biederman, I., & Bar, M. (1999). One-shot viewpoint invariance in matching novel objects. *Vision Research, 39*, 2885–2899.

Biederman, I., & Bar, M. (2000). Differing views on views: response to Hayward and Tarr (2000). *Vision Research, 40*, 3901–3905.

Biederman, I., & Cooper, E. E. (1991a). Evidence for complete translational and reflectional invariance in visual object priming. *Perception, 20*, 585–593.

Biederman, I., & Cooper, E. E. (1991b). Priming contour-deleted images: evidence for intermediate representations in visual object recognition. *Cognitive Psychology, 23*, 393–419.

Biederman, I., & Cooper, E. E. (1992). Size invariance in visual object priming. *Journal of Experimental Psychology: Human Perception and Performance, 18*, 121–133.

Biederman, I., & Gerhardstein, P. C. (1993). Recognizing depth-rotated objects: evidence and conditions for three-dimensional viewpoint invariance. *Journal of Experimental Psychology: Human Perception and Performance, 19*, 1162–1182.

Biederman, I., & Gerhardstein, P. C. (1995). Viewpoint-dependent mechanisms in visual object recognition: reply to Tarr and Bülthoff (1995). *Journal of Experimental Psychology: Human Perception and Performance, 21*, 1506–1514.

Biederman, I., Subramaniam, S., Bar, M., Kaloscai, P., & Fiser, J. (1999). Subordinate-level object classification reexamined. *Psychological Research, 62*, 131–153.

Binford, T. O. (1971, December). Visual perception by computer. Paper presented at the IEEE Conference on Systems and Control, Miami, FL.

Bricolo, E., Poggio, T., & Logothetis, N. K. (1997). 3-D object recognition: a model of view-tuned neurons. In M. C. Mozer, M. I. Jordan, & T. Petsche (Eds.), *Advances in neural information processing systems 9* (pp. 41–47). Cambridge, MA: MIT Press.

Brooks, R. A. (1983). Model-based three-dimensional interpretations of two-dimensional images. *IEEE Transactions on Pattern Analysis and Machine Intelligence, 5*, 140–149.

Bülthoff, H. H., & Edelman, S. (1992). Psychophysical support for a two-dimensional view interpolation theory of object recognition. *Proceedings of the National Academy of Sciences of the USA, 89*, 60–64.

Corballis, M. C. (1988). Recognition of disoriented shapes. *Psychological Review, 95* (12), 115–123.

Edelman, S. (1999). *Representation and recognition in vision*. Cambridge, MA: MIT Press.

Farah, M. J. (1990). *Visual agnosia: disorders of object recognition and what they tell us about normal vision*. Cambridge, MA: MIT Press.

Farah, M. J. (1992). Is an object an object an object? Cognitive and neuropsychological investigations of domain-specificity in visual object recognition. *Current Directions in Psychological Science, 1*, 164–169.

Fiser, J., & Biederman, I. (2001). Invariance of long-term visual priming to scale, reflection, translation, and hemisphere. *Vision Research, 41*, 221–234.

Foley, J., Van Dam, A., Feiner, S., & Hughes, J. (1990). *Computer graphics principles and practice* (2nd ed.). Reading, MA: Addison-Wesley.

Gauthier, I. (2000). What constrains the organization of the ventral temporal cortex? *Trends in Cognitive Sciences*, *4*, 1–2.

Gauthier, I., Anderson, A. W., Tarr, M. J., Skudlarski, P., & Gore, J. C. (1997). Levels of categorization in visual recognition studied with functional magnetic resonance imaging. *Current Biology*, *7*, 645–651.

Gauthier, I., Hayward, W. G., Tarr, M. J., Anderson, A. W., Skudlarski, P., & Gore, J. C. (2002). BOLD activity during mental rotation and viewpoint-dependent object recognition. *Neuron*, *34*, 161–171.

Gauthier, I., Skudlarski, P., Gore, J. C., & Anderson, A. W. (2000). Expertise for cars and birds recruits brain areas involved in face recognition. *Nature Neuroscience*, *3*, 191–197.

Gauthier, I., & Tarr, M. J. (1997). Becoming a 'Greeble' expert: exploring the face recognition mechanism. *Vision Research*, *37*, 1673–1682.

Gauthier, I., Tarr, M. J., Anderson, A. W., Skudlarski, P., & Gore, J. C. (1999). Activation of the middle fusiform 'face area' increases with expertise in recognizing novel objects. *Nature Neuroscience*, *2*, 568–573.

Gibson, J. J. (1950). *The perception of the visual world*. Boston, MA: Houghton Mifflin.

Gibson, J. J. (1966). *The senses considered as perceptual systems*. Boston, MA: Houghton Mifflin.

Gibson, J. J. (1979). *The ecological approach to visual perception*. Boston, MA: Houghton Mifflin.

Gregory, R. L. (1977). Vision with isoluminant colour contrast. 1. A projection technique and observations. *Perception*, *6*, 113–119.

Hayward, W. G. (1998). Effects of outline shape in object recognition. *Journal of Experimental Psychology: Human Perception and Performance*, *24*, 427–440.

Hayward, W. G., & Tarr, M. J. (1997). Testing conditions for viewpoint invariance in object recognition. *Journal of Experimental Psychology: Human Perception and Performance*, *23*, 1511–1521.

Hayward, W. G., & Tarr, M. J. (2000). Differing views on views: reply to Biederman and Bar (1999). *Vision Research*, *40*, 3895–3899.

Hayward, W. G., & Williams, P. (2000). Viewpoint dependence and object discriminability. *Psychological Science*, *11*, 7–12.

Hecht, S., Shlaer, S., & Pirenne, M. H. (1942). Energy, quanta, and vision. *Journal of General Physiology*, *25*, 819–840.

Hietanen, J. K., Perrett, D. I., Oram, M. W., Benson, P. J., & Dittrich, W. H. (1992). The effects of lighting conditions on responses of cells selective for face views in the macaque temporal cortex. *Experimental Brain Research*, *89*, 151–171.

Hoffman, D. D., & Richards, W. (1984). Parts of recognition. *Cognition*, *18*, 65–96.

Horn, B. K. P. (1986). *Robot vision*. Cambridge, MA: MIT Press.

Hubel, D. H., & Wiesel, T. N. (1959). Receptive fields of single neurons in the cat's striate cortex. *Journal of Physiology*, *148*, 574–591.

Hubel, D. H., & Wiesel, T. N. (1962). Receptive fields, binocular interaction and functional architecture in the cat's visual cortex. *Journal of Physiology*, *160*, 106–154.

Hummel, J. E., & Biederman, I. (1992). Dynamic binding in a neural network for shape recognition. *Psychological Review*, *99*, 480–517.

Humphrey, G. K., & Khan, S. C. (1992). Recognizing novel views of three-dimensional objects. *Canadian Journal of Psychology*, *46*, 170–190.

Ishai, A., Ungerleider, L. G., Martin, A., & Haxby, J. V. (2000). The representation of objects in the human occipital and temporal cortex. *Journal of Cognitive Neuroscience*, *12* (Suppl. 2), 35–51.

Johnston, A., Hill, H., & Carman, N. (1992). Recognising faces: effects of lighting direction, inversion, and brightness reversal. *Perception*, *21*, 365–375.

Johnston, M. B., & Hayes, A. (2000). An experimental comparison of viewpoint-specific and viewpoint-independent models of object representation. *Quarterly Journal of Experimental Psychology Section A: Human Experimental Psychology*, *53*, 792–824.

Jolicoeur, P. (1985). The time to name disoriented natural objects. *Memory and Cognition*, *13*, 289–303.

Jolicoeur, P. (1987). A size-congruency effect in memory for visual shape. *Memory and Cognition*, *15*, 531–543.

Jolicoeur, P. (1990). Identification of disoriented objects: a dual-systems theory. *Mind and Language*, *5*, 387–410.

Jolicoeur, P., Gluck, M., & Kosslyn, S. M. (1984). Pictures and names: making the connection. *Cognitive Psychology*, *16*, 243–275.

Kanwisher, N. (2000). Domain specificity in face perception. *Nature Neuroscience*, *3*, 759–763.

Kanwisher, N., McDermott, J., & Chun, M. M. (1997). The fusiform face area: a module in human extrastriate cortex specialized for face perception. *Journal of Neuroscience*, *17*, 4302–4311.

Kersten, D., Mamassian, P., & Knill, D. C. (1997). Moving cast shadows induce apparent motion in depth. *Perception*, *26*, 171–192.

Koenderink, J. J. (1987). An internal representation for solid shape based on the topological properties of the apparent contour. In W. Richards & S. Ullman (Eds.), *Image understanding: 1985–86* (pp. 257–285). Norwood, NJ: Ablex.

König, A., & Brodhun, E. (1889). Experimentelle Untersuchungen über die psychophysie Fundamentalformel in Bezug auf den Gesichtssinn. *Sitzungsberichteder Preussische Akademie Wissenschaften, Berlin*, *27*, 641–644.

Lissauer, H. (1890). Ein Fall von Seelenblindheit nebst einem Beitrage zur Theory derselben. *Archiv für Psychiatrie und Nervenkrankheiten*, *21*, 222–270.

Lowe, D. G. (1985). *Perceptual organization and visual recognition*. Boston, MA: Kluwer.

Marr, D. (1982). *Vision: a computational investigation into the human representation and processing of visual information*. San Francisco: Freeman.

Marr, D., & Hildreth, E. (1980). Theory of edge detection. *Proceedings of the Royal Society of London B*, *207*, 187–217.

Marr, D., & Nishihara, H. K. (1978). Representation and recognition of the spatial organization of three-dimensional shapes. *Proceedings of the Royal Society of London B, 200*, 269–294.

Mel, B. (1997). SEEMORE: combining color, shape, and texture histogramming in a neurally inspired approach to visual object recognition. *Neural Computation, 9*, 779–804.

Milner, A. D., & Goodale, M. A. (1995). *The visual brain in action*. Oxford: Oxford University Press.

Palmer, S., Rosch, E., & Chase, P. (1981). Canonical perspective and the perception of objects. In J. Long & A. Baddeley (Eds.), *Attention and performance IX* (pp. 135–151). Hillsdale, NJ: Lawrence Erlbaum.

Perrett, D. I., Harries, M. H., Bevan, R., Thomas, S., Benson, P. J., Mistlin, A. J., Chitty, A. J., Hietanen, J. K., & Ortega, J. E. (1989). Frameworks of analysis for the neural representations of animate objects and actions. *Journal of Experimental Biology, 146*, 87–113.

Pinker, S. (1984). Visual cognition: an introduction. *Cognition, 18*, 1–63.

Poggio, T., & Edelman, S. (1990). A network that learns to recognize three-dimensional objects. *Nature, 343*, 263–266.

Rhodes, G., Brennan, S., & Carey, S. (1987). Identification and ratings of caricatures: implications for mental representations of faces. *Cognitive Psychology, 19*, 473–497.

Rhodes, G., & McLean, I. G. (1990). Distinctiveness and expertise effects with homogeneous stimuli: towards a model of configural coding. *Perception, 19*, 773–794.

Riesenhuber, M., & Poggio, T. (1999). Hierarchical models of object recognition in cortex. *Nature Neuroscience, 2*, 1019–1025.

Rock, I., & DiVita, J. (1987). A case of viewer-centered object perception. *Cognitive Psychology, 19*, 280–293.

Rosch, E., Mervis, C. B., Gray, W. D., Johnson, D. M., & Boyes-Braem, P. (1976). Basic objects in natural categories. *Cognitive Psychology, 8*, 382–439.

Shepard, R. N. (1984). Ecological constraints on internal representation: resonant kinematics of perceiving, imagining, thinking, and dreaming. *Psychological Review, 91* (44), 417–447.

Shepard, R. N., & Cooper, L. A. (1982). *Mental images and their transformations*. Cambridge, MA: MIT Press.

Shepard, R. N., & Metzler, J. (1971). Mental rotation of three-dimensional objects. *Science, 171*, 701–703.

Srinivas, K. (1993). Perceptual specificity in nonverbal priming. *Journal of Experimental Psychology: Learning, Memory, and Cognition, 19*, 582–602.

Srinivas, K. (1995). Representation of rotated objects in explicit and implicit memory. *Journal of Experimental Psychology: Learning, Memory, and Cognition, 21*, 1019–1036.

Tanaka, J. W., & Farah, M. J. (1993). Parts and wholes in face recognition. *Quarterly Journal of Experimental Psychology Section A, 46*, 225–245.

Tanaka, J. W., & Presnell, L. M. (1999). Color diagnosticity in object recognition. *Perception and Psychophysics, 61*, 1140–1153.

Tarr, M. J. (1995). Rotating objects to recognize them: a case study of the role of viewpoint dependency in the recognition of three-dimensional objects. *Psychonomic Bulletin and Review, 2*, 55–82.

Tarr, M. J. (2003). Visual object recognition: can a single mechanism suffice? In M. A. Peterson & G. Rhodes (Eds.), *Perception of faces, objects, and scenes: analytic and holistic processes* (pp.177–211). Oxford: Oxford University Press.

Tarr, M. J., & Bülthoff, H. H. (1995). Is human object recognition better described by geon-structural-descriptions or by multiple-views? *Journal of Experimental Psychology: Human Perception and Performance, 21*, 1494–1505.

Tarr, M. J., Bülthoff, H. H., Zabinski, M., & Blanz, V. (1997). To what extent do unique parts influence recognition across changes in viewpoint? *Psychological Science, 8*, 282–289.

Tarr, M. J., & Gauthier, I. (2000). FFA: a flexible fusiform area for subordinate-level visual processing automatized by expertise. *Nature Neuroscience, 3*, 764–769.

Tarr, M. J., Kersten, D., & Bülthoff, H. H. (1998). Why the visual system might encode the effects of illumination. *Vision Research, 38*, 2259–2275.

Tarr, M. J., & Kriegman, D. J. (2001). What defines a view? *Vision Research, 41*, 1981–2004.

Tarr, M. J., & Pinker, S. (1989). Mental rotation and orientation-dependence in shape recognition. *Cognitive Psychology, 21*, 233–282.

Tarr, M. J., Williams, P., Hayward, W. G., & Gauthier, I. (1998). Three-dimensional object recognition is viewpoint-dependent. *Nature Neuroscience, 1*, 275–277.

Ullman, S. (1989). Aligning pictorial descriptions: an approach to object recognition. *Cognition, 32*, 193–254.

Ungerleider, L. G., & Mishkin, M. (1982). Two cortical visual systems. In D. J. Ingle, M. A. Goodale, & R. J. W. Mansfield (Eds.), *Analysis of visual behavior* (pp. 549–586). Cambridge, MA: MIT Press.

Wagemans, J., Van Gool, L., & Lamote, C. (1996). The visual system's measurement of invariants need not itself be invariant. *Psychological Science, 7*, 232–236.

Waltz, D. L. (1975). Understanding line drawings of scenes with shadows. In P. H. Winston (ed.), *The psychology of computer vision* (pp. 19–91). New York: McGraw-Hill.

Warrington, E. K., & Taylor, A. M. (1973). The contribution of right parietal lobe to object recognition. *Cortex, 9*, 152–164.

Wheatstone, C. (1838). Contributions to the physiology of vision, Part 1: On some remarkable and hitherto unobserved phenomena of binocular vision. *Philosophical Transactions of the Royal Society of London, 128*, 371–394.

Williams, P., & Tarr, M. J. (1999). Orientation-specific possibility priming for novel three-dimensional objects. *Perception and Psychophysics*, *61*, 963–976.

Wittgenstein, L. (1953). *Philosophical investigations. Philosophische Untersuchungen*. New York: Macmillan.

Wong, C-N., & Hayward, W. G. (2002). View generalization in object recognition by pooled activation. Manuscript submitted for publication.

Wurm, L. H., Legge, G. E., Isenberg, L. M., & Luebker, A. (1993). Color improves object recognition in normal and low vision. *Journal of Experimental Psychology: Human Perception and Performance*, *19*, 899–911.

Yin, R. K. (1969). Looking at upside-down faces. *Journal of Experimental Psychology*, *81*, 141–145.

3

Auditory Perception

CHRISTOPHER J. PLACK

INTRODUCTION

The problem of hearing

Most of us live in very noisy environments. Throughout the day we are bombarded by sounds, some of which are useless, some annoying, and some of which may be vital for our survival. Although the auditory system evolved in more peaceful times than these, it still manages to perform remarkably well on the incredibly complex task that is demanded of it. In most cases we seem to hear so effortlessly that we do not appreciate the depth of the neural processing that underlies our perceptions.

Our ears receive a mixture of all the sounds in the environment at a given time. We have to be able to separate out the sounds in which we are interested, then decode the separated sounds into meaningful information. A commonly used analogy can help illustrate the difficulty of the problem. Imagine that you are paddling on the shore of a lake. Three people are swimming on the lake, producing ripples that combine to form a complex pattern of tiny waves arriving at your feet. Looking only at the pattern of waves below you, you have to calculate: (i) how many swimmers there are and where they are located on the lake; (ii) how many swimming strokes each one is making every second; and (iii) which swimming stroke each one is using. If you think that is hard, try doing the same thing with a speedboat on the water, producing huge, slow waves that crash over your legs. Although the computation sounds impossible, the auditory system can manage tasks of even greater complexity involving sound waves. The research presented in this chapter is a small representative of over a hundred years of investigation into how this is achieved.

What is psychoacoustics?

Psychoacoustics can be defined simply as the psychological study of hearing. The aim of psychoacoustic research is to find out how hearing works. In other words, the aim is to discover how sounds are processed by the ear and the brain in order to give the listener information about the world outside. Many of the problems approached by psychoacousticians have very little to do with the popular conception of psychology. For example, some of my own research has been concerned with how the intensity of a sound is represented by nerve cells in the auditory system. One might imagine that this would be a concern of neurophysiology, and indeed it is. However, whereas an auditory physiologist might approach the problem by recording from a neuron inside the brain of a guinea pig, a psychoacoustician might approach the problem by measuring the ability of human listeners to make discriminations between carefully chosen sounds presented over headphones. The fact that we measure the *behavioral* responses of human listeners is essentially why psychoacoustics is regarded as a branch of psychology. Since behavioral measurements can be used to address some very diverse problems in hearing, the field of psychoacoustics covers a broad range of hearing-related topics, of which an overview is provided here.

It is possible that the term 'psychoacoustics' was first used in the United States during the Second World War. A secret government project was set up to investigate, in part, the potential of acoustic weapons. One of the members of the team, Dr T. W. Forbes, when describing their field of activity remarked, 'This is psycho-acoustics', and the term has stuck. It should be noted that the project failed to produce anything close to an acoustic death beam, although the team was successful in developing a sound system for broadcasting propaganda from aircraft (Burris-Meyer & Mallory, 1960).

THE PHYSICS OF SOUND

The nature of sound

Sound is simply a sequence of pressure variations in some medium. For our purposes that medium is the air. An example will help to illustrate what goes on when sound is produced. A loudspeaker converts electrical voltage variations into pressure variations in the air. The loudspeaker pushes and pulls at the air. This causes a high pressure when the speaker cone is moving outwards, and a low pressure when the speaker cone is moving inwards. These pressure variations are called sound waves. Sound waves are longitudinal waves, so that the particles transmitting the wave, the molecules in the air, oscillate backwards and forwards in the direction of propagation of the wave. Sound frequency refers to the number of cycles of the sound wave that occur at a given location during a given period of time. High frequencies are popularly associated with treble and low frequencies are associated with bass. The frequency of a sound is usually measured in cycles per second or *Hertz* (abbreviated Hz; 1 kHz = 1000 Hz).

The *intensity* of a sound wave is proportional to the *square* of the pressure. Sound intensity is often expressed in logarithmic units called *decibels* (dB):

$$
\begin{aligned}
\text{Sound level in dB} &= 10 \times \log_{10}(I/I_0) \\
&= 20 \times \log_{10}(P/P_o) \quad (3.1)
\end{aligned}
$$

where I is intensity, I_0 is a reference intensity, P is pressure, and P_o is a reference pressure. Conventionally, sound level is expressed relative to a pressure of 2×10^{-5} N/m². A sound level expressed relative to this reference point is called a sound pressure level (SPL). A useful property of the dB scale is that an increase of 10 dB corresponds to a factor of 10 increase in intensity (hence 20 dB is a factor of 100, 30 dB a factor of 1000, and so on) and 3 dB is approximately a doubling of intensity.

The pressure variations produced by a sound source travel through the air in much the same way as the ripples produced by dropping a stone in a pond travel through water. However, whereas water waves on a flat pond propagate only in two dimensions, along the surface of the pond, sound waves can propagate in all directions in three-dimensional space. Although sources such as a loudspeaker or a human voice are directional to a certain extent, in that a large proportion of the sound energy travels in

one direction away from the source, sound will tend to bend or *diffract* around any obstacle. The amount of diffraction depends on the frequency of the sound wave: low frequencies diffract more than high frequencies. Low frequencies are also less easily absorbed by intervening materials such as walls and floors, so that neighbors often complain of the bass sound from late-night parties disrupting their sleeping habits. It is quite difficult to insulate rooms from very low frequencies. At my laboratory in the University of Essex, we have been made well aware recently that even professional soundproof booths can be breached by low rumbles from building work.

Sound waves travel from their source through the air at the speed of sound. Although the value depends on the density of the air, at atmospheric pressure the speed of sound is about 330 meters per second (m/s), 740 miles per hour, or Mach 1.

Fourier analysis and the spectrum

A sound whose pressure varies according to a sine wave is called a *pure tone*. For immediate reference, the sound made by someone whistling is almost a pure tone. A pure tone is characterized by having only one *frequency component*, the rate of pressure variations of the pure tone itself. This makes the pure tone a special type of tone. (A tone can be regarded generally as any sound wave that repeats itself over time.) A pure tone can be characterized in terms of its magnitude (the size of the pressure variation), its frequency (the rate at which the pressure varies), and its *phase*, which refers to the point reached on the pressure cycle at a particular time and place. So for a pure tone:

$$
x(t) = A \sin(2\pi f_0 t + \phi) \quad (3.2)
$$

where $x(t)$ is the pressure variation over time t, A is the peak amplitude (or pressure), f_0 is the frequency of the pure tone, and ϕ is the phase.

The pure tone is regarded mathematically as the basic building block of sounds. *Any* sound wave can be produced by adding together pure tones of different magnitudes, frequencies and phases. The whole concept of frequency is linked to the idea of the pure tone. A warm, bass sound contains low-frequency pure tones. A bright, treble sound contains high-frequency pure tones. Fourier analysis is the mathematical technique for separating a complex sound into its pure-tone frequency components. The pure tones that make up a given sound determine the *spectrum* of that sound. A spectrum is often plotted on a graph showing the variation in the magnitude of the pure-tone components that make up a sound as a function of their frequencies. Low-frequency components appear on the left-hand side of the graph and high-frequency components on the right-hand side of the graph. The height of the line corresponding to each frequency component illustrates its magnitude or intensity.

Periodic sounds (such as musical tones) have pressure variations that repeat over time, and are often perceived as having a distinct *pitch*. The repetition rate (or *fundamental frequency*, F0) determines the pitch that is heard. These sounds have spectra composed of a series of discrete sinusoidal components (*harmonics*) spaced at regular intervals. The spacing (in Hz) is equal to the overall repetition rate of the waveform (in Hz). Non-periodic sounds, such as noises, have spectra consisting of a continuous distribution of frequency components.

Amplitude and frequency modulation

Amplitude modulation (AM) refers to a variation in the overall level of a sound over time. Frequency modulation (FM) refers to a variation in the frequency of a sound over time. Both types of modulation can be characterized by the depth of the modulation (the magnitude of the level or frequency excursions) and the frequency of the modulation. It is common in hearing experiments to modulate the original *carrier* sound sinusoidally. For pure-tone carriers, the equations for sinusoidal AM and FM respectively are as follows:

$$x_{AM}(t) = A(1 + m \sin 2\pi f_m t) \sin(2\pi f_0 t + \phi) \ (3.3)$$
$$x_{FM}(t) = A \sin\{2\pi f_0 t + \beta \sin(2\pi f_m t + \phi)\} \quad (3.4)$$

where m is the modulation depth for AM, β is the modulation index ($\Delta f/f_m$ where Δf is the frequency excursion) for FM, and f_m is the modulation frequency. Modulating a waveform introduces changes to the spectrum, specifically *spectral side bands*. For a sinusoidally amplitude modulated pure tone, there are three components in the spectrum with frequencies equal to $f_0 - f_m$, f_0, and $f_0 + f_m$ ($f_0 - f_m$ and $f_0 + f_m$ are the side bands). Sinusoidal FM consists of more frequency components, spaced at f_m, but if β is small the same three components found in AM dominate, albeit with different *phases*. See Hartmann (1997) for an excellent overview of the mathematics of these and other sound waves.

In the case of AM, it is often convenient to distinguish the rapid pressure variations of the carrier from the slower changes in the overall amplitude of these fluctuations caused by the modulator. These two aspects of a signal are sometimes referred to as 'fine structure' and 'envelope' respectively (Viemeister & Plack, 1993).

Figure 3.1 illustrates the waveforms and spectra of some artificial stimuli of the kind often used by psychoacousticians.

Sounds in the real world

Now that we have considered some of the physical characteristics of sounds, we can examine which of these characteristics carry the crucial information for sounds in our environment. For most of us, speech is probably the most important (and common) type of sound we encounter. Speech is characterized by variations in: spectral pattern (which helps identify both vowels and consonants), repetition rate (which determines the intonation contour of voiced sounds), and intensity (for example, stop consonants such as /p/ or /t/ can be characterized by a very brief period of silence). In other words, information is carried by a temporal sequence of features. The same is true of music, where the variation in repetition rate, or melody, is clearly of prime importance. Different musical instruments, like vowels, are characterized in part by their spectral pattern: bright instruments such as the trumpet contain more high-frequency components than warm instruments such as the French horn, even when playing the same note. Regular modulations such as vibrato (FM) and tremolo (AM) are commonly employed in music.

For the auditory system to be able to interpret these sounds, it has to be sensitive to *spectral features* (frequency composition) and *repetition rate*. Importantly, it also has to be able to follow *rapid changes* in these characteristics over time, as it is the *sequence of features* that carry the meaning.

As described in the Introduction, being able to identify individual sounds and extract their meaning is not the only problem faced by the auditory system. Separating out sounds originating from different sources, and grouping together sounds originating from the same source, is also very important in many situations (for example, following a single conversation at a party or in a noisy office). We shall see later on how spectral features, repetition rate and temporal cues are used by the auditory system to deconstruct the 'auditory scene'.

THE ANATOMY AND PHYSIOLOGY OF THE EAR

Anatomy

Figure 3.2 illustrates the main anatomical features of the peripheral auditory system. The *pinna* is the external part of the ear, the cartilaginous flap onto which you hook your sunglasses. The pinna is the part that gets cut off when someone has his ear cut off, although the hearing sense is affected very little by this amputation. The pinnae are more important in other animals (bats, dogs, etc.) than they are in man, where they are a bit too small and inflexible to

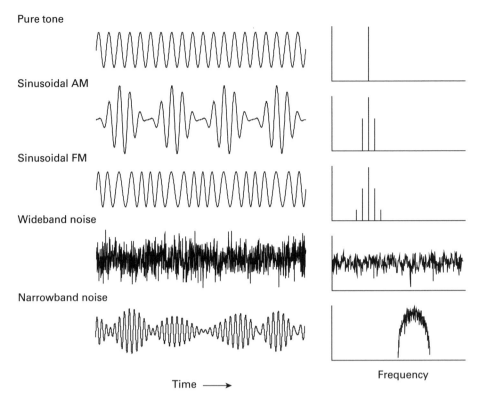

Figure 3.1   *The waveforms and spectra of some frequently used psychoacoustic stimuli.*

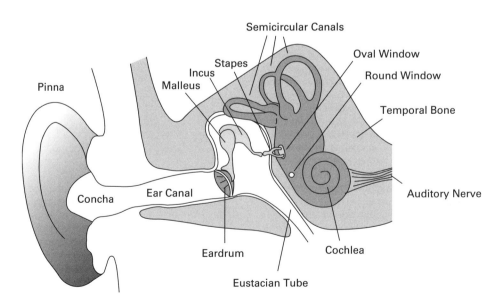

Figure 3.2   *The major parts of the peripheral anditory system. (Illustration © C. Plack).*

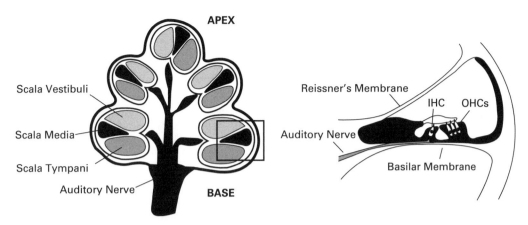

APEX

Scala Vestibuli

Scala Media

Scala Tympani

Auditory Nerve

BASE

Reissner's Membrane

IHC   OHCs

Auditory Nerve

Basilar Membrane

Figure 3.3   *A cross-section of the cochlea (left) looking at the spiral from the side (in contrast to the view from the top in Figure 3.2). The boxed section is magnified further (right) to reveal the basilar membrane, an inner hair cell (IHC) and three outer hair cells (OHCs). (Illustration © C. Plack.)*

be very useful. They do, however, help the auditory system determine the location of a sound source. The *ear canal* is the short, and crooked, tube that joins the outside world to the *eardrum* (a thin membrane). The tube has a resonance, just like an organ pipe, and this resonance makes us more sensitive to sound frequencies between about 500 Hz and 4000 Hz. The pinna and the ear canal make up the *outer ear*. This is the last stage in hearing where sound waves are carried by the air.

Vibrations at the eardrum are transmitted through the middle ear by three tiny bones, the malleus, incus and stapes. Their job is to transmit the pressure variations in an air-filled compartment (the ear canal) into pressure variations in a fluid-filled compartment (the *cochlea*) as efficiently as possible. This is not as trivial as it might seem. If you shout at someone underwater in a swimming pool, most of the sound is reflected back from the surface of the pool. Water has a much higher *impedance* than air, which means the energy is reflected back in the same way as a table tennis ball will bounce back off a football rather than donating all its energy to the forward motion of the football. The bones in the middle ear solve this problem by concentrating the vibrational energy of the air onto a smaller area (the *oval window* in the cochlea) than the collection area (the eardrum). They also act as a lever system so that large, weak vibrations at the eardrum are converted into small, strong vibrations at the oval window. In electrical terms, these bones can be regarded as an impedance-matching transformer.

Attached to the malleus and stapes are tiny muscles that contract at high sound levels, reducing the magnitude of the vibrations transmitted to the cochlea and hence effectively turning down the volume of the sound. This mechanism is most effective at reducing the level of low-frequency sounds and does not do much to protect the cochlea against high-frequency sounds, which are often the most damaging.

The cochlea and the basilar membrane

The cochlea is a thin, fluid-filled tube, coiled round into a snail-shape in order to save space. In humans, the whole cochlea, if stretched out into a straight tube, would be about 4 cm long. The cochlea is filled with an ionic solution. Connected to the same fluid-filled compartment are the *semicircular canals* that are involved in balance. As described above, vibrations enter the cochlea via the stapes, which is connected to the oval window, a flexible membrane in the wall of the cochlea.

Running along the whole length of the cochlea, and dividing it in two, is the *basilar membrane* (see Figure 3.3). The basilar membrane vibrates in response to the incoming sound, but in a very particular way. The basilar membrane can separate out the different frequency components of a sound mechanically. Each place along the basilar membrane is sensitive to a narrow range of frequencies. The basilar membrane at the *base* of the cochlea, near the oval window, is thin and stiff. This area is most sensitive to high frequencies. The other end of the basilar membrane, at the tip or the *apex* of the cochlea, is comparatively thick and compliant and is most sensitive to low frequencies. The properties of the basilar membrane vary continuously between these extremes along its length, so that each place on the basilar membrane has its own particular frequency of sound, or *characteristic frequency*, to which it is maximally sensitive.

This is absolutely crucial to human hearing. Let us consider what this means. Imagine a double bass and a piccolo playing simultaneously. Most of the energy of the double bass is concentrated in low-frequency (or bass) regions. Most of the energy of the piccolo is concentrated in high-frequency (or treble) regions. The two instruments are playing simultaneously, so the sound waves are mixed together in the air to produce a sound wave that is a combination of the waves from the two sources. Because these two waves cover different frequency ranges, however, the basilar membrane can separate out the sound originating from each instrument so that we can clearly hear the two sounds as distinct entities. The detailed spectral decomposition carried out by the basilar membrane also helps us to *identify* the two sounds in terms of their spectral features. Human sensitivity to frequency extends from around 20 Hz to around 20 kHz, although most of the acoustic information that is important to us (for example, speech and music) is carried by frequency components below 4 kHz.

Arranged along the whole length of the basilar membrane are rows of *hair cells*. Hair cells, as their name suggests, have minute hairs, or more correctly *stereocilia*, extruding from their tops. In the cochlea there is one row of *inner hair cells* and three rows of *outer hair cells*. The outer hair cells are now thought to change the mechanical properties of the basilar membrane. They improve the sensitivity of the ear by effectively amplifying the vibration of the membrane in response to low and medium sound levels (perhaps 0–80 dB SPL), but only for sound frequencies close to the characteristic frequency of each place on the membrane. (Whether this is a 'true' amplification in the sense of metabolic energy being fed into the motion of the basilar membrane is still a matter of debate.) As well as improving sensitivity, this process greatly enhances the basilar membrane's ability to separate out the frequency components in a sound. A healthy ear can individually hear out frequency components separated by around 15–20% in frequency (Moore, 2003; Plomp, 1964a).

The outer hair cells are very sensitive to damage from loud noise, which can cause permanent loss of sensitivity and frequency selectivity. Damage to the outer hair cells is the principal cause of hearing loss. Outer hair cells can also be inactivated reversibly by drugs such as aspirin.

Transduction

The inner hair cells are responsible for transducing the vibrations of the basilar membrane into electrical activity in the auditory nerve. Vibrations on the membrane cause the hairs on a cell to sway from side to side, which causes an electrical change (depolarization) in the cell. The inner hair cells synapse onto auditory nerve fibers. Each nerve fiber is connected to a particular place in the cochlea and therefore has a particular characteristic frequency.

The *tonotopic* organization of the auditory system (different nerve fibers in an area of tissue being sensitive to different frequencies in an orderly spatial arrangement) continues up to the auditory cortex.

Auditory nerve fibers transmit information as a sequence of electrical impulses (*action potentials*). In general, the higher the magnitude of a sound, the more impulses travel down the axon of the nerve fiber every second. In addition, for frequencies below about 5000 Hz, auditory nerve fibers will tend to produce impulses that are synchronized with the period of the incoming sound waveform. This is called *phase locking*, because neurons tend to produce impulses at a particular time, or phase, in the cycle of the sound wave (see Figure 3.4). Phase locking is a result of the properties of the inner hair cells, which depolarize only when the hairs are bent in one direction (away from the center of the cochlea). Although neurons do not normally produce impulses at rates of greater than a few hundred per second, information may be combined across neurons to represent the repetition rate of high-frequency tones. So if one neuron produces impulses on the first, third, fifth, etc., cycle of the incoming sound wave, another might produce impulses on the second, fourth, sixth, etc., cycle of the sound wave and the combined firing rate of the two would be equal to the repetition frequency. In reality, neurons are not nearly as regular as this simplistic example might suggest, but the principle is basically the same. It is thought that neural phase locking could be used by higher auditory centers to determine the pitch of tones.

The auditory nerve connects to the cochlear nucleus in the brainstem. Unlike the visual system in which the retina is connected almost directly (via the thalamus) to the visual cortex, in the auditory system there are several important subcortical nuclei (the cochlear nucleus, the superior olive, the lateral lemniscus, the inferior colliculus and the medial geniculate nucleus of the thalamus) that process the neural information before it is delivered to the auditory cortex, located on the temporal lobe.

FREQUENCY SELECTIVITY

The importance of frequency selectivity

In the visual system, a spatial arrangement of light sources or reflective surfaces (the visual scene) is mapped onto a spatial arrangement of photoreceptors in the retina and subsequently onto a spatial arrangement of neurons in the visual cortex. The visual system performs a *place-to-place* mapping of the visual world. In contrast, in the auditory system the different *frequency components* of a sound are mapped onto a spatial arrangement of hair cells in the cochlea, and this tonotopic organization is

Input waveform

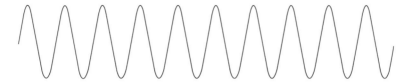

Simulated auditory nerve activity

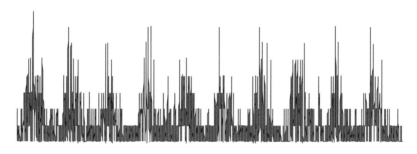

Time ⟶

Figure 3.4 *A simulation of the auditory nerve activity in response to a 250 Hz pure tone. The activity pattern represents the summed action potentials produced by 500 nerve fibers. The nerve fibers show clear phase locking, with a peak of activity on every cycle of the incoming waveform.*

maintained up to higher neural centers. In other words, the auditory system performs a *frequency-to-place* mapping of the auditory world. Whereas the visual system has only three different spectral sensitivities (the three cones), the auditory system has, arguably, several hundred. Visual objects are characterized mainly by their shapes. Auditory objects are characterized mainly by their spectra, and by the way their spectra change over time. For example, different vowel sounds in speech can be identified by characteristic spectral peaks called 'formants'. The way in which the frequencies of the formants change over time helps identify preceding consonants.

Our ability to identify sounds, and to separate out sounds occurring simultaneously, depends on the frequency selectivity of the cochlea. In this section the psychophysics of frequency selectivity will be described.

Masking and the critical band

Masking refers to the process by which one sound (the masker) renders another sound (the signal) less detectable. Masking is one of the main tools used by psychoacousticians to investigate the basic mechanisms of hearing. Fletcher (1940) presented a pure tone in a band of noise that contained a narrow range of frequency components centered on the frequency of the tone. He varied the level of the tone to find the masked threshold, the level at which the tone was just detectable. He then increased the range of frequencies (the *bandwidth*) of the noise, while keeping the spectral density (the power per unit frequency) constant. For narrow noise bands, threshold increased (more masking) as the noise band was widened. Beyond a particular bandwidth, however, further increases in bandwidth did not affect the threshold. Fletcher termed this bandwidth the 'critical bandwidth'.

Fletcher's experiment demonstrates the frequency selectivity of the auditory system. Noise components close to the frequency of the tone contribute to masking, but noise components away from the frequency of the tone are separated from the tone perceptually and therefore do not contribute to masking. Using this and similar techniques, Fletcher was able to estimate the frequency selectivity of the auditory system.

Auditory filters and excitation patterns

Modern masking techniques have enabled researchers to determine more accurately the frequency-selective properties of the auditory system. For any given pure-tone signal, masker frequency components will produce more masking the closer they are in frequency to the signal. It is possible to describe this effect in terms of an *auditory filter*. An auditory filter

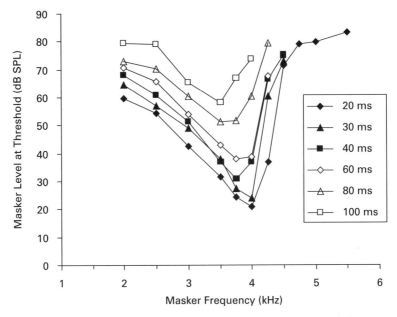

Figure 3.5 *Psychophysical tuning curves at 4 kHz, showing the masker level needed to
mask a 4 kHz signal as a function of masker frequency. The signal had a fixed level
10-dB above absolute threshold, and was presented after the masker (forward masking).
The masker–signal interval was varied to produce a set of PTCs for a range of masker
levels. As level increases the tuning curve becomes broader (less frequency selectivity,
larger ERB) and the tip of the tuning curve shifts down in frequency. This implies that
the place on the basilar membrane tuned to 4 kHz at low levels becomes most sensitive
to* lower *frequencies at high levels. Data are from Yasin and Plack (2003).*

is a weighting function describing the amount of
reduction (or attenuation) of a frequency component as a function of its distance from the center frequency of the filter. The center frequency of the
filter is the frequency to which it is most sensitive.
This frequency is often assumed (as a convention
only) to receive no attenuation. The sharpness of
tuning of an auditory filter can be characterized by
the *equivalent rectangular bandwidth* (ERB). The
ERB is the bandwidth of a rectangular filter with
the same peak output and the same area (in units of
intensity) as the auditory filter. In short, the smaller
the ERB, the sharper the tuning.

Patterson, Moore and colleagues (Glasberg &
Moore, 1990; Patterson, 1976; Patterson & Nimmo-
Smith, 1980) developed a technique in which a pure
tone is presented in the spectral notch between two
bands of noise. As the noise bands are moved closer
to the tone in frequency, the threshold for the tone
increases (more masking). By measuring the way in
which threshold changes as the noise bands are
moved, it is possible to derive the shape of the auditory filter. This technique has been called the
'notched noise method'.

The shape of the auditory filter can also be estimated by measuring a *psychophysical tuning curve*
or PTC (see Figure 3.5). For example, a pure tone

signal is presented at a low level. A pure-tone
masker with a variable frequency is then presented
and its level adjusted until it just renders the signal
undetectable (Vogten, 1974). Maskers close to the
signal in frequency require a lower level than
maskers remote from the signal in frequency. The
entire tuning curve is a plot of the masker level
needed as a function of frequency. The curve can be
regarded as an upside-down auditory filter.

Using these techniques it has been possible to
determine how the ERB of the auditory filter varies
with center frequency. Glasberg and Moore (1990)
estimated that the ERB follows the relation:

$$ERB = 24.7(0.00437F + 1) \qquad (3.5)$$

where F is the center frequency of the filter. For frequencies above about 1 kHz, the ERB is approximately proportional to the center frequency.

It is probable that each auditory filter has a direct
physiological locus. An auditory filter with a given
center frequency is thought to reflect the tuning
properties of the place on the basilar membrane
tuned to that frequency. Physiological tuning curves
can be measured by estimating the level of a tone of

varying frequency required to produce either a criterion increase in vibration of the basilar membrane at a particular place (Murugasu & Russell, 1996; Ruggero, Rich, Recio, Narayan, & Robles, 1997; Sellick, Patuzzi, & Johnstone, 1982) or a criterion increase in the firing rate of a particular auditory nerve fiber (Evans, 1975; Evans, Pratt, Spenner, & Cooper, 1992; Liberman & Kiang, 1978). Tones closer to characteristic frequency require a lower level to produce the change in response. These tuning curves compare well with those measured psychophysically in humans. Indeed, it has been shown that ERBs estimated behaviorally in guinea pigs correspond well to auditory nerve tuning curves measured in the same species (Evans et al., 1992). In other words, *the frequency selectivity of the entire auditory system is determined by the frequency selectivity of the cochlea.*

Just as the basilar membrane can be regarded as a continuous array of characteristic frequencies, varying from high frequencies at the base to low frequencies at the apex, so behavioral frequency selectivity can be modeled as a continuous array of overlapping auditory filters, each with a slightly different center frequency. It is possible to estimate the output of this bank of filters (level as a function of center frequency) in response to any sound. Such a plot is called an *excitation pattern* (Moore & Glasberg, 1983b). The excitation pattern is assumed to be equivalent to the overall pattern of vibration on the basilar membrane. Figure 3.6 shows the excitation pattern for the vowel /i/.

Nonlinearity

It was described earlier how the outer hair cells at a given place on the basilar membrane might effectively amplify low- and medium-level sounds with frequencies close to the characteristic frequency of that place. This level- and frequency-dependent amplification has two important consequences. First, the response of a place on the basilar membrane to a pure tone near characteristic frequency is linear at low levels (below about 35 dB SPL), but highly *nonlinear* and *compressive* at medium to high levels (Robles, Ruggero, & Rich, 1986; Ruggero et al., 1997). (Figure 3.7 shows the response at a single place on the basilar membrane to pure tones of different frequencies.) At medium levels, a given change in the level of the tone will not produce an equivalent change in the response of the basilar membrane. The compression at high characteristic frequencies may be as great as 5:1 (Oxenham & Plack, 1997; Yates, Winter, & Robertson, 1990) so that a 5 dB increase in the level of the input tone may result in only a 1 dB increase in the level of vibration on the basilar membrane. Another way of expressing this is as follows:

$$A = kP^{0.2} \qquad (3.6)$$

where A is the amplitude of vibration on the basilar membrane, P is the pressure of the sound wave, and k is a constant. If the growth were linear, the exponent would be 1. The compression means that a large range of input levels (120 dB, or a factor of a million million in intensity, at 1 kHz) can be represented by a much smaller range of levels of vibration on the basilar membrane (perhaps 60 dB or less). There is some evidence that the basilar membrane may become more linear (less compressive) for characteristic frequencies below about 1 kHz (Rhode & Cooper, 1996).

The second consequence of the action of the outer hair cells is that the auditory filter shape changes with level (see Figure 3.5). The ERB increases with level, due mainly to a flattening of the slope on the low-frequency side of the auditory filter, and the center frequency of the filter decreases. It is possible to understand this effect by imagining the tuning curve of a place on the basilar membrane without the action of the outer hair cells (similar to the high-level PTC in Figure 3.5). The tuning curve is linear (i.e. it does not change shape with input level) but broadly tuned. The outer hair cells (effectively) amplify components with frequencies *above* the tuning of the linear, passive, response. This produces the sharply tuned tip response seen in Figure 3.5. Because this amplification is greatest for low input levels, at high input levels the linear response dominates, and the auditory filter has broader tuning and a lower center frequency.

This process can be modeled using a filter with two resonances, one linear and one nonlinear. The response to low/medium-level sounds close to the characteristic frequency is determined by the nonlinear pathway, whereas the response to high-level sounds, and sounds lower than the characteristic frequency, is determined by the linear pathway. The DRNL (dual resonance nonlinear) model of Meddis and colleagues uses this approach (Meddis, O'Mard, & Lopez-Poveda, 2001).

In a linear system, no frequency components can be produced that were not in the original signal. The nonlinearity on the basilar membrane creates distortion products, *combination tones*, that are sometimes clearly audible. When two pure tones with frequencies f_1 and f_2 are presented, extra frequency components with frequencies given by $f_2 - f_1$ and $2f_1 - f_2$ may be generated on the basilar membrane.

A final consequence of the nonlinearity of the basilar membrane that has perceptual consequences is *suppression*. The response to one tone at a given place on the basilar membrane can be reduced by the addition of another tone higher or lower in frequency than the suppressed tone (Arthur, Pfeiffer, & Suga, 1971; Ruggero, Robles, & Rich, 1992). Suppression is not due to a neural lateral inhibition system as found in the visual

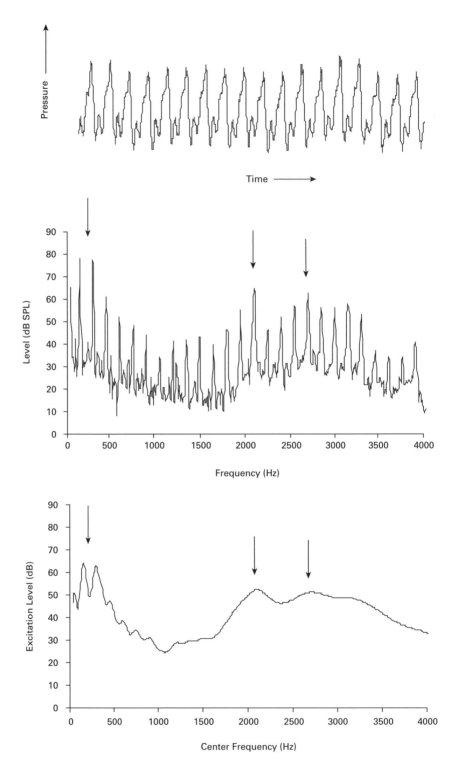

Figure 3.6 *The waveform (top), spectrum (middle) and excitation pattern (the spectral representation in the cochlea, bottom) for the vowel sound /i/. The spectrum contains a regular pattern of harmonics, with equal spacing along the frequency axis. The broad spectral peaks (formants) are indicated by arrows. The excitation pattern shows that the auditory system can resolve the harmonics around the first formant, but that higher harmonics are not resolved.*

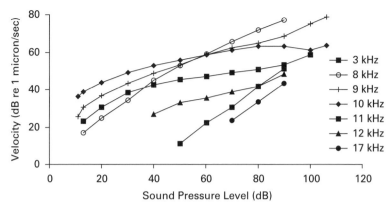

Figure 3.7 *Basilar membrane velocity–intensity functions for a chinchilla, showing BM velocity (in dB) as a function of input level (in dB SPL) for pure tones of different frequencies. Velocities were measured at a single place on the BM with a characteristic frequency of 10 kHz. Notice that the response to a tone near characteristic frequency is highly compressive (linear growth has a slope of 1 on these coordinates, as exemplified by the response curves for 3 kHz and 17 kHz pure tones). The data are replotted from Ruggero et al. (1997).*

system, but is the result of the complex mechanical properties of the basilar membrane. Suppression can be observed psychophysically. Houtgast (1974) used *pulsation threshold* to demonstrate suppression. Pulsation threshold is a measurement technique in which one sound is alternated with a second sound. If the first ('masker') sound is high enough in level, then the second ('test') sound may appear to be continuous, rather than pulsing. This is a version of the continuity illusion (Miller & Licklider, 1950). Houtgast argued that the continuity effect occurs when the neural response to the masker across center frequency overlaps with the neural response to the test sound, such that there is no reduction in response at the transition between the test sound and the masker. In other words, if two tones are being alternated, the level of the test tone at which the perception changes from pulsing to continuous (the pulsation threshold) provides an estimate of the effective level of the masker at the test-tone frequency.

If the masker is presented simultaneously with another tone (the 'suppressor'), then the effective level of the masker may be reduced, so that the threshold (or pulsation threshold) for the subsequent test tone is also reduced. On the basis of analogous physiological measurements (Arthur et al., 1971), suppression is assumed to occur only when the suppressor and the suppressee are simultaneous. Houtgast showed that the reduction in threshold occurs when the suppressor is in particular frequency regions higher and lower in frequency than the masker, and (generally) at a higher level than the masker (see Figure 3.8).

LOUDNESS AND INTENSITY CODING

Loudness

Loudness may be regarded as the *perceptual correlate* of sound intensity. Loudness refers to the subjective magnitude of a sound, as opposed to pressure, intensity, power or level, which refer to the physical magnitude of a sound. There are three basic techniques for measuring loudness: *magnitude estimation, magnitude production* and *loudness matching*. In magnitude estimation, listeners are required to give a number corresponding to the loudness of a given sound, or to indicate how much louder one sound appeared than another. In magnitude production, listeners are given a number and asked to adjust the level of a sound until its loudness matches that number. Alternatively, they may be presented with a standard sound and be required to adjust the level of a second sound so that the ratio between the loudnesses of the two corresponds to a number given by the experimenter. In loudness matching, listeners are required to adjust the level of one sound until it appears to be *identical* in loudness to a reference sound.

The absolute threshold of a given sound refers to the lowest level of that sound that can just be detected. The *audiogram* is a measure of the absolute threshold for a given individual/ear as a function of frequency. A typical audiogram for a normally hearing listener is given by the lower curve on Figure 3.9. Above absolute threshold, as the intensity of a sound is increased, the loudness of the sound will also increase. Magnitude estimation

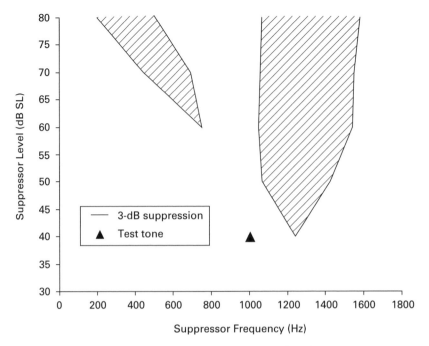

Figure 3.8   *Suppression regions for a 1 kHz test tone from Houtgast (1974). A suppressor tone within the solid lines produced at least 3 dB of suppression, i.e. a 3 dB reduction in the effective level of a 40 dB SL masker. 'SL' refers to sensation level, or level above absolute threshold.*

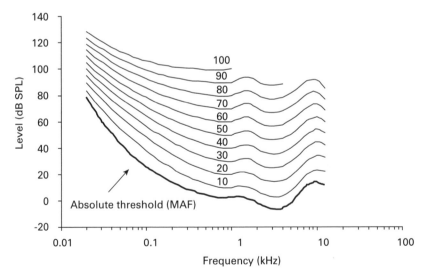

Figure 3.9   *Equal loudness contours from the latest draft ISO standard (ISO/DIS 226). Each contour represents the levels and frequencies of tones of equal loudness, measured relative to a 1 kHz tone. The level of the 1 kHz tone for each curve in dB SPL is shown on the figure above each loudness contour. Also shown is the lowest detectable level at each frequency. Stimuli were presented in the free field, with a sound source directly in front of the listener.*

and magnitude production can be used to determine how loudness is related to sound intensity. Stevens' power law (Stevens, 1957) is based on the observation that for many sensory quantities, the perceptual magnitude of a quantity scales with the power of the physical magnitude of that quantity. For loudness the exponent appears to be somewhere between 0.2 and 0.3 for levels above about 40 dB SPL (Buus, Musch, & Florentine, 1998; Stevens, 1957; Zwicker & Fastl, 1990) so that:

$$L \approx kI^{0.25} \qquad (3.7)$$

where L is loudness, I is intensity, and k is a constant. For levels below 40 dB SPL, loudness grows more rapidly with intensity. The unit of loudness is the sone. One sone is defined (arbitrarily) to be the loudness of a 1 kHz pure tone at a level of 40 dB SPL. It is interesting that the loudness exponent is similar to the compression exponent of the basilar membrane. For a pure tone at least, loudness is approximately proportional to the *intensity* of vibration (the square of the amplitude of vibration) on the basilar membrane (Buus et al., 1998; Schlauch, DiGiovanni, & Reis, 1998).

Loudness matching can be used to compare the loudnesses of two sounds with different characteristics, for example different frequencies or bandwidths. In this way it is possible to measure how loudness varies with frequency. The relation can be expressed as an *equal-loudness contour*, a line joining the levels of pure tones with different frequencies that have the same loudness (see Figure 3.9).

Intensity discrimination

Intensity discrimination refers to our ability to detect a change in the level of a sound. The *just noticeable difference* (JND) in intensity can be expressed in many ways. Two of the most often used are the Weber fraction (expressed as a logarithm) and ΔL:

$$\text{Weber fraction (in dB)} = 10 \times \log_{10}(\Delta I/I) \quad (3.8)$$
$$\Delta L = 10 \times \log_{10}\{(I + \Delta I)/I\} \qquad (3.9)$$

where I is the baseline, *pedestal*, intensity and ΔI is the smallest detectable change in that intensity.

For wideband noise (a stimulus containing a broad spread of frequency components) the Weber fraction is roughly constant as a function of level for levels above about 20 dB SPL (Miller, 1947), having a value of around -10 dB (corresponding to a ΔL of around 0.4 dB). This means that the smallest detectable increment in intensity is proportional to the pedestal intensity, a property called *Weber's Law* that is common across sensory systems.

For pure tones it has been found that the Weber fraction decreases slightly with intensity (sensitivity improves), so that a plot of log10(ΔI) against log10(I) has a slope of about 0.9. The 'near miss' to Weber's Law (McGill & Goldberg, 1968) is thought to reflect the spread of excitation along the basilar membrane as the level of the tone increases (Moore & Raab, 1974; Viemeister, 1972; Zwicker, 1956). At low levels only a small region of the basilar membrane is stimulated (the region surrounding the place tuned to the pure-tone frequency), but as the level is increased a wider area is stimulated. The extra information traveling up the auditory nerve may improve discrimination, particularly for the high-frequency side of the excitation pattern, where the growth of excitation with level is linear rather than compressive. (In other words, a given change in stimulus level produces a greater change in excitation on the high-frequency side.)

The dynamic range of hearing and the coding of intensity

The dynamic range of hearing refers to the range of intensities over which we can make meaningful discriminations. For example, although we may be able to 'hear' a sound at 130 dB SPL (note: don't try this at home!), we probably cannot discriminate this from a sound of 135 dB SPL using hearing. The dynamic range of hearing extends from around 0 dB SPL (at medium frequencies, say 500 Hz to 6 kHz) to around 120 dB SPL (Viemeister & Bacon, 1988). 120 dB SPL is a very high intensity (loud rock group) and will cause serious damage if experienced for a prolonged period of time.

The wide dynamic range has provided a problem for theories of how intensity is coded in the auditory system, because if intensity is represented only in terms of the firing rate of neurons (as suggested by the physiology), then one might expect that the dynamic range would be much less. Most auditory nerve fibers cannot increase their firing rates with increases in intensity if the input level is much greater than 60 dB SPL. This is called saturation. However, there are a few fibers with larger dynamic ranges (Sachs & Abbas, 1974), and it is possible that these fibers code intensity at higher levels. Although the predominance of fibers with small dynamic ranges in the auditory nerve might suggest much finer discrimination at low levels (Viemeister, 1988), it is possible that a limitation at a higher level in the auditory pathway does not use this information optimally. It is this central limitation that may determine Weber's Law (see Plack & Carlyon, 1995b, for a more thorough discussion of this issue).

Absolute and relative intensity coding

Although we are sensitive to the absolute intensity of sounds to some extent, as reflected by the sensation of loudness, for identifying sounds it is the *relative* intensities of features within the sound that are most important. For example, the identity of the

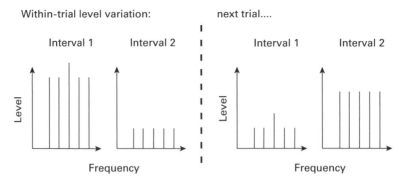

Figure 3.10   *An illustration of the spectra of stimuli used in a typical profile analysis experiment. On each trial, the listener has to judge which of two stimuli contains the incremented frequency component. The overall level of each stimulus is randomized, so that listeners are forced to make a comparison of level across frequency.*

vowel /i/ does not change with overall level. It is defined (in part) by the pattern of spectral peaks and dips associated with this sound, i.e. by the relative intensities of features across frequency.

Experiments involving spectral shape discrimination, or profile analysis (Green, 1988; Green & Kidd, 1983; Green, Kidd, & Picardi, 1983), have shown that we are very good at making relative intensity judgments across frequency. We can detect an intensity increment applied to a target pure tone relative to a background of several pure tones of different frequencies, even when the overall level of the tones is randomized (see Figure 3.10). The randomization ensures that the discrimination cannot be based on an absolute intensity judgment. Plack (1996) has drawn similar conclusions regarding relative intensity judgments across time. Furthermore, there is evidence that representations of relative intensity may form more robust memory traces than representations of absolute intensity. Comparisons of two spectral profiles can be made accurately over longer delays than comparisons of two absolute intensities (Green et al., 1983). These relative representations may be an important stage in the identification of auditory objects.

In theory, there are two ways in which the frequency of a pure tone may be represented in the auditory system. First, it may be represented by the place of maximum activity on the basilar membrane (the further towards the apex of the basilar membrane, the lower the frequency of the pure tone). Second, it may be represented by the pattern of phase locking (the time interval between spikes in the auditory nerve will tend to be an integer multiple of the period, 1/frequency, of the pure tone). While there is still some debate over which of these mechanisms is used and for which types of stimuli, it is now thought that the pitch of low-frequency pure tones (less than perhaps 4–5 kHz) is represented by the temporal neural code (phase locking), while the pitch of high-frequency pure tones is represented by the place of maximum activity on the basilar membrane (see Moore, 2003, for a review). The smallest detectable frequency difference is around 0.2% for tones less than about 4 kHz (Moore, 1973; Sek & Moore, 1995) but increases dramatically for higher frequencies. The results may reflect a change in mechanism. In addition, it is notable that pure tones with frequencies above 5 kHz cannot be used to produce a recognizable musical melody (Attneave & Olson, 1971). It is possible, therefore, that temporal coding underlies musical pitch.

PITCH

The pitch of pure tones

Just as loudness may be regarded as the perceptual correlate of sound intensity, pitch may be regarded as the perceptual correlate of the *repetition rate* of a sound waveform. This is easy to illustrate with pure tones, which have a single frequency component corresponding to the repetition rate of the sinusoidal waveform.

The pitch of complex tones

The term 'complex tone' refers to any sound waveform that repeats over time (i.e. is periodic) and is not sinusoidal (i.e. is not a pure tone). As described earlier, a periodic waveform can be described in terms of a series of harmonics: frequency components that are spaced at intervals equal to the repetition rate of the overall waveform. Examples of complex tones include the sounds produced by a (non-percussive) musical instrument, and vowel sounds in speech. As described earlier, the pitch heard is usually determined by the repetition rate (or F0) of the overall waveform. A complex tone with an F0 of 100 Hz will have the same pitch as a pure tone with a frequency of 100 Hz. In a sense a pure tone may be regarded as a complex tone in which only the first harmonic is present.

We have seen how the ERB of the auditory filter is approximately proportional to center frequency. For a given harmonic series, the ERB will be smaller for the low harmonic numbers than for the high. Because the spacing of the components is constant, the low harmonic numbers will be better resolved from each other than the high harmonic numbers. In fact, harmonic numbers up to harmonic number 10 (according to the highest estimates) are said to be *resolved*, producing separate peaks of activation on the basilar membrane, whereas higher harmonic numbers are said to be *unresolved* (see Figure 3.11). Unresolved harmonics interact on the basilar membrane to produce a pattern of vibration that repeats at the same rate as the overall repetition rate of the complex (F0).

Resolvability depends more on harmonic number than on frequency per se. For example, if the repetition rate of the complex is doubled, then the harmonics are spaced twice as far apart. However, each harmonic is doubled in frequency and therefore shifted to a place on the basilar membrane where the auditory filters are approximately twice as broad. These two effects tend to cancel out, so that the resolvability of a given harmonic number does not change substantially with the repetition rate.

Theories of pitch perception

In the past there were two main explanations for how the auditory system derives the pitch of a complex tone. These rival models of pitch perception tended to focus on the possible contributions of the resolved and unresolved harmonics. *Pattern recognition models* (Goldstein, 1973; Terhardt, 1974) suggested that pitch is derived by an analysis of the patterning of the individual resolved harmonics. For example, if the ear finds that frequencies of 400, 500 and 600 Hz are present, then it is reasonable to assume that the F0 is 100 Hz. *Temporal models* (Schouten, 1940, 1970), on the other hand, suggested that pitch is derived from an analysis of the repetition rates of the waveforms produced by the interaction of the (mainly unresolved) harmonics.

It is now known that a pitch may be heard when only resolved harmonics or only unresolved harmonics (Moore & Rosen, 1979) are presented, so that neither model can be supported as a universal model of pitch. However, the resolved harmonics (particularly harmonic numbers 3, 4 and 5) do tend to dominate pitch perception, such that a shift in the

frequency of an individual resolved harmonic has a much larger effect on the pitch of the complex than a shift in the frequency of an unresolved harmonic (Moore, Glasberg, & Peters, 1985; Ritsma, 1967).

Some modern theories of pitch perception suggest that there is a single mechanism that combines the information from the resolved and unresolved harmonics (Meddis & Hewitt, 1991; Moore, 2003). These models are based on the finding that the neural response in the auditory nerve is synchronized or phase-locked to the output of each individual auditory filter. Neurons that have low characteristic frequencies will phase-lock to the individual resolved harmonics, whereas neurons with higher characteristic frequencies will phase-lock to the interacting unresolved harmonics (see Figure 3.11). In both cases, there will be inter-spike intervals (ISIs) that correspond to the period of the original waveform. For example, a neuron responding to the second harmonic of a 100 Hz F0 may produce impulses separated by 5 ms (phase-locked to 200 Hz), but the 10 ms interval (two cycles) corresponding to the period of the complex will also be present. By picking the most prominent ISI across frequency channels, it is argued, an estimate of F0 may be obtained. Several models suggest that an effective way of extracting periodicity is a computation of the autocorrelation function (ACF) (Licklider, 1951). An ACF is produced by correlating a signal with a delayed representation of itself. At time delays equal to integer multiples of the repetition rate of a waveform, the correlation will be strong. A simple addition of the ACFs from several frequency channels produces a summary function that provides a good description of many pitch phenomena (Meddis & Hewitt, 1991).

However, it has also been suggested that there may be separate pitch mechanisms for resolved and unresolved harmonics (Carlyon & Shackleton, 1994; Plack & Carlyon, 1995a). In an experiment involving the simultaneous comparison of F0's between groups of harmonics, Carlyon and Shackleton (1994) showed that comparing a resolved with a resolved group or an unresolved with an unresolved group is easier than comparing a resolved with an unresolved group. This suggests that there may be separate pitch mechanisms for the two harmonic types and that comparing the output of the two mechanisms involves an additional 'comparison noise'. Furthermore, Grimault, Micheyl, Carlyon, & Collet (2002) showed that listeners trained on an F0-discrimination task involving resolved harmonics showed improved performance on other resolved conditions compared to unresolved conditions, and vice versa. In other words, the effect of training is specific to the resolvability of the components to some extent, again suggesting separate mechanisms.

Plack and Carlyon (1995a) and White and Plack (1998) argued that a single pitch mechanism that simply examines the ISI corresponding to F0 across channels may not be optimally processing the

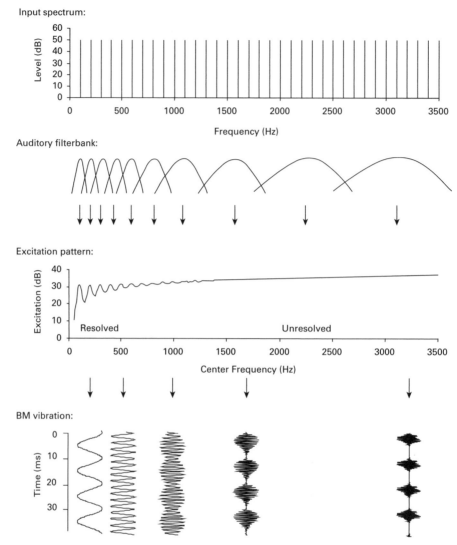

Figure 3.11 *The spectrum and excitation pattern of a pulse train: a complex tone consisting of a sequence of impulses equally spaced in time. Because the bandwidth of the auditory filter increases with center frequency, the lower harmonics are resolved (producing separate peaks of excitation) and the higher harmonics are unresolved. The bottom panel shows simulated basilar membrane vibration for places tuned to 100, 400, 800, 1600 and 3200 Hz. The resolved harmonics produce near-sinusoidal patterns of vibration, whereas the unresolved harmonics interact to produce a complex pattern of vibration that repeats at F0 (in this case 100 Hz).*

temporal information present in the auditory nerve for the resolved harmonics. For example, although the second harmonic of a 100 Hz F0 will produce ISIs of 5 ms, the ACF models ignore these intervals and process only the 10 ms ISIs. An alternative scheme would use 'all-order' ISIs to estimate the frequency of each component, and to combine these estimates via a pattern-recognition mechanism to determine pitch. This would have the advantage of exploiting the potentially faster information rate of the shorter ISIs present at high frequencies. The idea that shorter intervals provide a higher information rate is supported by the finding that a shorter duration is needed to produce an accurate estimate of the frequency of a 1000 Hz pure tone, compared either to a 200 Hz pure tone or to a group of unresolved harmonics having an F0 of 200 Hz (Plack & Carlyon, 1995a).

With regard to the pitch mechanism for unresolved harmonics, recent experiments have manipulated the individual periods within a complex tone (Kaernbach & Demany, 1998; Plack & White, 2000). For example, imagine we start with a regular pulse train then jitter every other pulse in time. Now each successive ISI is random, although there is still a strong periodicity between the alternate 'unjittered' pulses ('second-order' ISIs). This periodicity is very clear in the ACF of the waveform but it is *not* heard by listeners if the complex is filtered to contain only unresolved harmonics (Kaernbach & Demany, 1998). The results seem to suggest that, for unresolved harmonics at least, the auditory system may analyze only the periods between successive peaks in the waveform (or 'first order' ISIs), rather than use the ACF to search for *any* regularity in the waveform. However, the conclusions are not so clear-cut if the ACF analysis is performed on a simulation of neural activity, rather than on the waveforms themselves (Pressnitzer, de Cheveigné, & Winter, 2002). Because of the stochastic nature of the simulated spike generation, the second-order stimulus used by Kaernbach and Demany shows only a broad peak in correlation similar to that produced by a random comparison. (Random sequences contain broad second-order periodicity, corresponding to twice the mean of the distribution from which the random intervals are selected.) The overall conclusion from these results seems to be that a model based on the ACF of the physical waveform will not work for these stimuli, but that models based on the ACF of the neural response may have some life left.

So it remains undecided whether a single mechanism can account for all pitch phenomena. Furthermore, it is not clear where in the auditory system such a mechanism could be implemented. Mechanisms incorporating a summary ACF (produced by a simultaneous summation of the individual ACFs) could be implemented subcortically, in the brainstem nuclei. However, data from Ciocca and Darwin (1999) suggest a much more central locus for the synthesis of the information from the various frequency channels. Ciocca and Darwin found that a mistuned fourth harmonic still contributes to the pitch of the complex as a whole even when it is presented before or after the rest of the complex. Indeed, if the harmonic is presented after the complex, the mistuning is still effective when the silent gap between the complex and the harmonic is 80 ms. The work is an extension of an earlier study by Hall and Peters (1981) who showed that three successive harmonics (with a total duration of 140 ms) could be integrated together to form a unified pitch, if they were presented in a background noise at a low signal-to-noise ratio. If information from individual harmonics is being integrated over such a long duration, then this suggests that the hypothetical 'pitch processor' is located in the cortex, since no neurons with integration times as long as 100 ms have been found in the brainstem.

What is clear at the time of writing is that, after a huge amount of research (by psychoacoustics standards) into pitch, there are still considerable doubts about the actual mechanism used by the auditory system to extract F0.

TEMPORAL RESOLUTION

Measures of temporal resolution

Temporal resolution can be defined as the ability of the auditory system to follow changes in a sound over time (Viemeister & Plack, 1993). If the system is 'sluggish' (i.e. temporal resolution is poor), then rapid changes will not be followed. We can think of the internal representation of a sound being blurred in time in the same way as an out-of-focus visual image is blurred in space (and in the same way as the basilar membrane produces a 'smoothed' representation of the frequency components in a sound).

Perhaps the simplest method of measuring temporal resolution is the gap-detection task, in which the listener is required to detect the presence of a brief interruption in a sound (Buus & Florentine, 1985; Plomp, 1964b; Shailer & Moore, 1983). The shortest gap that can be detected is a measure of temporal resolution. Care must be taken in these experiments to make sure that the gap is detectable only in terms of the change in level across time. For example, when a sinusoid is interrupted, this produces a change in the *spectrum* of the sound (spectral splatter) that involves the distribution of energy to lower and higher frequencies. In this case, the gap may be detected merely by detecting the presence of off-frequency energy. If a noise is introduced to mask the off-frequency energy, then the gap threshold for a sinusoidal signal is about 4–5 ms (Shailer & Moore, 1987), and is roughly independent of frequency at least for frequencies above about 400 Hz. The gap threshold for a broadband noise is around 2–3 ms (Penner, 1977; Plomp, 1964b).

The invariance of temporal resolution with frequency is important as it suggests that resolution is not limited by 'ringing' in the auditory filters. If a signal is terminated abruptly, then the basilar membrane will continue to vibrate for a short time. The duration of this ringing response is determined by the bandwidth of the filter: in general, highly tuned filters will ring for longer than broad filters. The bandwidth of the auditory filter increases with increasing center frequency so it might be expected that the longer ringing response at low frequencies would lead to poorer temporal resolution. The finding that this is not the case suggests that temporal resolution is limited by more central (i.e. neural) mechanisms.

A more general measure of temporal resolution is the *temporal modulation transfer function* (TMTF). The TMTF can be described by a plot of the smallest detectable depth of AM as a function of modulation rate. For a broadband noise carrier, listeners show roughly equal sensitivity to modulation rates up to around 50 Hz, and then sensitivity falls off (Bacon & Viemeister, 1985; Viemeister, 1979). However, it has been argued that high-frequency 'inherent fluctuations' in the noise envelope limit performance at high modulation rates (Dau, Kollmeier, & Kohlrausch, 1997a). If sinusoidal carriers, which have flat envelopes, are used, then high sensitivity is shown for modulation rates up to 150 Hz (Kohlrausch, Fassel, & Dau, 2000). Care must be taken in these experiments to ensure that the spectral side bands (either side of the carrier frequency with a spacing equal to the modulation frequency) cannot be resolved by the auditory filters. This can be achieved by using high carrier frequencies (which excite high-frequency, broad auditory filters).

The TMTF displays a *lowpass* characteristic, showing more sensitivity to low modulation frequencies than high. However, we can still detect 100% AM (i.e. modulation that fluctuates from a peak value down to silence) at modulation rates over 1000 Hz. The equivalent maximum frequency for the detection of a flickering light by the visual system is only around 50 Hz. In other words, the auditory system can respond much more quickly than the visual system to changes in a stimulus over time. This may reflect the fact that auditory information is carried mainly by the changes in the characteristics of sound over time, whereas a static (or slowly changing) image can convey a great deal of visual information.

Non-simultaneous masking

Non-simultaneous masking refers to the decrease in the detectability of a signal presented either before (backward masking) or after (forward masking) a masking sound. For both types of masking, the threshold level at which the signal can just be detected (and therefore the amount of masking) increases as the signal is brought closer to the masker in time. Forward masking lasts for around 100 ms after the offset of the masker (Jesteadt, Bacon, & Lehman, 1982), whereas backward masking tends to be a much weaker effect, which depends on the amount of practice, and is possibly more dependent on attentional factors. Well-trained listeners may show backward masking that extends to only 10 ms or so before the onset of the masker (Oxenham & Moore, 1994).

It has been known for many years that the growth of forward masking is nonlinear (Jesteadt et al., 1982;

Moore & Glasberg, 1983a; Munson & Gardner, 1950). A given increase in masker level usually causes a much smaller increase in the signal level at threshold. That is, the signal-to-masker ratio at threshold decreases as level is increased. This produces a shallow line on a plot of signal level at threshold versus masker level. The growth of forward masking becomes shallower as the gap between the signal and masker is increased (Jesteadt et al., 1982; Moore & Glasberg, 1983a). This may be related to the finding that the growth of forward masking is dependent mainly on signal level (Plack & Oxenham, 1998). The shallowest growth is observed when the masker level is high and the signal level is low. This tends to be the case for long masker–signal intervals. Conversely, when both the signal and the masker level are high, the growth of masking is roughly linear (Munson & Gardner, 1950; Oxenham & Plack, 1997; Plack & Oxenham, 1998). Figure 3.12 illustrates the effect.

It is now thought that the nonlinearity in forward masking is a consequence of the nonlinear response of the basilar membrane. The shallow growth for low signal levels can be explained on the basis that the response of the basilar membrane to a tone at CF is linear at low levels and compressive at higher levels. If the tone is in the low-level, linear region, then a given increase in signal level (in dB) will produce the same increase in basilar membrane vibration (in dB). If the masker is at a higher level, and is therefore in the compressive region of the basilar membrane function, then a given increase in masker level will produce a smaller increase in BM vibration. It follows that if the signal-to-masker ratio in terms of basilar membrane vibration is to remain constant, physical masker level has to grow more rapidly than physical signal level, leading to a shallow slope. A prediction of this hypothesis is that if the signal level at threshold is made high enough so that it too falls within the compressive region of the basilar membrane, then both masker and signal response should grow at the same rate and the growth of masking should be *linear*. This prediction has been confirmed (Plack & Oxenham, 1998).

The demonstration that the nonlinear characteristics of forward masking may depend only upon the response of the basilar membrane has provided a fruitful avenue of research recently. It is now considered possible to measure the response of the human basilar membrane using forward masking experiments. In particular, by comparing the growth of forward masking for a masker at the same frequency as the signal (within the *compressive* portion of the tuning curve) with the growth of forward masking for a masker well below the frequency of the signal (within the *linear* portion of the tuning curve), it is possible to derive the nonlinear basilar membrane response to a tone at characteristic frequency (Moore, Vickers, Plack, & Oxenham, 1999; Nelson, Schroder, & Wojtczak, 2001; Oxenham & Plack, 1997).

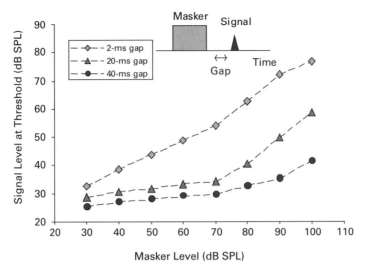

Figure 3.12   *Forward masking growth functions for three different masker–signal
intervals. The signal level at threshold is plotted as a function of masker level. The
slopes are shallow and nonlinear at low signal levels and linear at high signal levels.
Data are from Plack and Oxenham (1998).*

PTCs tend to be sharper (reflecting greater frequency selectivity) when measured using forward masking than when measured using simultaneous masking (Houtgast, 1974; Moore, 1978; Moore, Glasberg, & Roberts, 1984; Vogten, 1978). This difference may be explained in terms of suppression if it is assumed that the masking process in simultaneous masking is partly excitatory (i.e. due to masker energy falling within the auditory filter centered on the signal) and partly suppressive (Delgutte, 1990; Moore & Vickers, 1997; Oxenham & Plack, 1998). Because the suppressive region extends beyond the tuning curve either side of the test frequency (Houtgast, 1974; Shannon, 1976), the extra effect of suppression in reducing the signal level may reduce the level of the masker needed in these regions, thereby broadening the tuning curve.

The temporal window model

The observation that the response characteristics of the basilar membrane can account for nearly all the nonlinear aspects of non-simultaneous masking (Moore & Oxenham, 1998) suggests that subsequent to the cochlea the temporal mechanisms that produce forward masking are *linear* in the intensity domain (Plack & Oxenham, 1998).

Based on this approach is the temporal window model (Moore, Glasberg, Plack, & Biswas, 1988; Oxenham & Moore, 1994; Plack & Moore, 1990), which can account for both non-simultaneous masking and other aspects of temporal resolution. The model assumes that the internal representation

of a stimulus is smoothed in time by the action of a sliding intensity integrator, or temporal window. An assumption of the model is that temporal masking, both forward and backward, is a result of this integration process: the signal is masked because the temporal window centered on the time of signal presentation integrates masker energy for times before and/or after (see Figure 3.13). Forward masking is assumed to arise from a persistence of the neural activity produced by the masker, not because of the reduction in sensitivity associated with neural adaptation (Oxenham, 2001). The temporal window can be regarded as an estimate of the temporal resolution limitations of the entire auditory system central to the cochlea.

Figure 3.14 is a schematic illustration of the stages of a recent version of the model. The first stage is a nonlinear auditory filter based on the DRNL filter of Meddis et al. (2001). This exhibits a compressive response to frequency components near the characteristic frequency of the filter, and a linear response to components below characteristic frequency. This stage of the model simulates the activity at a given place on the basilar membrane. The response of the whole cochlea can be derived by computing the output of the auditory filter as a function of characteristic frequency. In the next stage, the output of the cochlea is squared to provide units of intensity, and then smoothed by the temporal window. Notice that the slope of the temporal window is shallower for times before the center. This produces more forward masking than backward masking, since more forward masker energy falls within a window centered on the time of

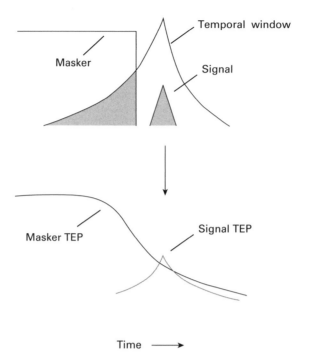

Figure 3.13 *An illustration of how the temporal window model accounts for forward masking. A temporal window centered on the time of occurrence of the signal integrates signal energy and some of the masker energy from the forward masker. This energy acts to mask the signal just as if the masker and signal were simultaneous. The bottom panel shows temporal excitation patterns (TEPs) for the signal and the masker. The TEP is the output of the temporal window as a function of the center time of the window.*

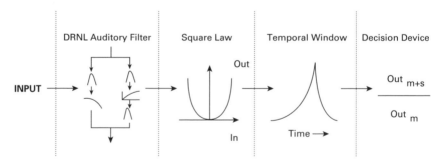

Figure 3.14 *Schematic of the temporal window model, comprising the DRNL auditory filter, a square-law rectifier, an exponentially weighted temporal window and a decision device (based on Plack, Oxenham, & Drga, 2002).*

presentation of the signal. The temporal equivalent of the ERB is the *equivalent rectangular duration* (ERD) of the window. The ERD is around 8 ms and is assumed not to vary with frequency, since measures of temporal resolution such as gap detection do not vary with frequency.

The final stage of the model is a decision device that can be used to predict masked thresholds. In this case, masked threshold is assumed to depend on the ratio of the output of the model in response to the masker plus signal, divided by the output of the model in response to the masker alone, for a window centered on the time of presentation of the signal.

A plot of the output of the model as a function of time and frequency is called a *spectro-temporal excitation pattern* or STEP (see Figure 3.15). The

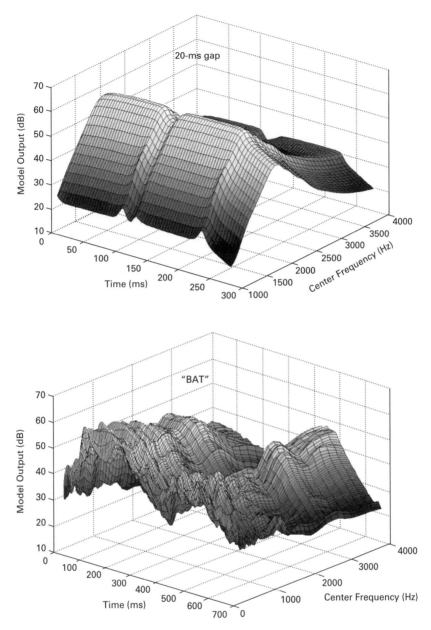

Figure 3.15   *The upper panel shows the spectro-temporal excitation pattern (STEP) for two 2 kHz pure tones separated by a 20 ms gap. The smoothing effect of the temporal window has filled in the gap to some extent. The lower panel shows the STEP for the utterance 'bat'. The low-frequency resolved harmonics and the upper formant peaks (composed of unresolved harmonics) can be seen for times up to 300 ms. The 't' sound produces excitation at high center frequencies around 500 ms after the start.*

STEP can be regarded as an estimate of the *perceptual representation* of an acoustic stimulus, with the caveat that phase locking/neural synchrony information is discarded by the present version of the model. Apart from this, to a first approximation any information that is visible in the STEP is available to the auditory system, and any information that is present in the signal but not in the STEP is masked, i.e. is unavailable to the auditory system.

Modulation

It has been argued here that acoustic information is carried mainly by the temporal pattern of auditory events. At a basic level, therefore, the perception of changes in the level (AM) and in the frequency (FM) of sounds across time is of importance to us. For example, many speech sounds are characterized by the comparatively slow (10 Hz or so) glides in the spectral peaks (formants) across time. These glides can be regarded as a type of FM.

The modulation filterbank

It was described earlier how the auditory system overall shows a lowpass characteristic in response to AM signals. Low-frequency modulations are passed and high-frequency modulations are attenuated (Bacon & Viemeister, 1985; Kohlrausch et al., 2000; Viemeister, 1979). However, this may not be the whole story. It has been observed that detecting the presence of 'signal' modulation in the presence of additional 'masker' modulation (both imposed on a broadband noise carrier) is most difficult when the signal and masker modulation frequencies are similar (Bacon & Grantham, 1989; Houtgast, 1989). By analogy with the frequency selectivity in the *audio-frequency* domain exhibited by the cochlea, Dau and colleagues have argued that the auditory system exhibits frequency selectivity in the *modulation* (or envelope) domain (Dau et al., 1997a; Dau, Kollmeier, & Kohlrausch, 1997b). As further support for their claim, Dau et al. (1997a) cite physiological evidence from Langner and Schreiner (1988) suggesting that there may be a 'modulation map' in the inferior colliculus in the brainstem, different neurons being sensitive to different modulation frequencies.

Like a bank of auditory filters, the modulation filterbank is characterized by an array of overlapping bandpass filters, each tuned to a slightly different modulation frequency (Dau et al., 1997a). A separate modulation filterbank is assumed to operate on the output of each auditory filter (Dau et al., 1997b). In the original model of Dau et al., the bandwidth of the modulation filters was fixed at around 5 Hz for modulation rates up to 10 Hz, and for higher frequencies the bandwidth was half the modulation center frequency. Recently, the estimated width of the modulation filters has increased to a value equal to the center frequency (Ewert & Dau, 2000). Detection of a signal modulation is assumed to depend on the amount of masker modulation that falls within the modulation filter centered on the signal modulation frequency. Similarly, low rates of modulation will be 'heard out' in the presence of high rates of modulation, since they fall into separate modulation filters.

The modulation filterbank can account for many aspects of modulation masking, although, being a comparatively new theory, there is controversy over the central premise. Looking at the broader picture, it seems plausible that the auditory system may use modulation rate to decompose a complex sound, perhaps as a means of separating out sounds originating from different sources.

Comodulation masking release

Recall the band-widening experiment of Fletcher (1940). Hall, Haggard, & Fernandes (1984) replicated this experiment with a crucial difference: the noise band was amplitude modulated. They discovered that as the noise band was widened up to around the critical bandwidth, the threshold of the signal increased, as observed by Fletcher (more noise energy in the auditory filter). However, as the bandwidth was increased beyond this point, instead of remaining constant as in the earlier study, the threshold of the signal decreased. This decrease is called comodulation masking release (CMR). Other studies have used a modulated noise band or sinusoid centered on the signal as the on-frequency masker, and added additional, 'flanking', noise bands or sinusoids with frequencies removed from the masker but with coherent modulation (Fantini, Moore, & Schooneveldt, 1993; Grose & Hall, 1989; Hall et al., 1984; Schooneveldt & Moore, 1987). The results have confirmed that adding extra flanking sounds in a frequency region removed from the signal can reduce threshold if the additional sound is modulated coherently (i.e. in phase) with the masker.

Some of the effects of the coherent modulation, when the flanking bands are close in frequency to the signal, may result from *within-channel cues*. The flanking components may interact with the on-frequency band within a single auditory filter, producing a pattern of envelope fluctuations that improves the detectability of the added signal (Schooneveldt & Moore, 1987; Verhey, Dau, & Kollmeier, 1999). However, CMR is still present, albeit reduced, for flankers remote from the signal frequency (Cohen, 1991), and can also be observed when the flankers are presented to the opposite ear to the signal and the on-frequency band (Cohen & Schubert, 1987; Fantini & Moore, 1994; Schooneveldt & Moore, 1987). This 'true' CMR may cause a reduction in signal threshold of only 7 dB or so, but it does indicate that the auditory system is able to use coherent modulation across frequency (and ear) to increase the detectability of the signal. One way in which this may occur is if the auditory system uses the flanking band to tell it when to listen for the signal. For example, if the flanking band is at a trough in the modulation, then this will be a good time to listen for the signal because the on-frequency masker intensity will be low at this time (Buus, 1985). This has been referred to as the *dip-listening model*. Alternatively, the auditory system may compare the pattern of modulation across frequency. When the signal is added, this will cause the pattern of modulation to differ between the signal/masker frequency and the flanker frequency, and this is a cue to the presence of the signal (Richards, 1987).

Whatever the mechanisms underlying CMR – and there may be several – the results suggest that the auditory system has the ability to separate sounds on the basis of coherent envelope fluctuations across channels. This could be useful in the environment, where the sound components from a single sound source are often highly correlated, in terms of increases and decreases in level, across frequency. For example, the components of speech increase and decrease in level together from vowels to consonants. CMR may be an aspect of one of the mechanisms that helps us to segregate sounds that arise from different sources.

FM and AM

At first glance, FM and AM appear to be quite different aspects of dynamic stimuli: in the former the frequency is varying, in the latter the amplitude is varying. However, this distinction is not so clear-cut for a system that can perform frequency analysis. Imagine a pure tone that is frequency modulated. The output of an auditory filter centered within the excitation pattern produced by the tone will increase as the frequency of the tone moves towards the center frequency of the filter, and decrease as the frequency of the tone moves away from the center of the filter. In other words, the output of the filter will be *amplitude* modulated.

For rates of FM greater than around 10 Hz, the detection of FM appears to be based on the detection of the induced AM. Models based on level changes in the excitation pattern can account for the FM detection threshold (Madden & Fire, 1996; Moore & Sek, 1994; Zwicker, 1970). For very low rates of FM, say 2 Hz, there seems to be another mechanism. It has been suggested that, when the rate is low, the auditory system can follow the change in frequency by tracking the change in phase locking over time (Sek & Moore, 1995). We saw earlier that phase locking is thought to determine the pitch of pure tones for frequencies less than 5 kHz or so. FM detection at low rates, therefore, may be based more on pitch cues than on level cues.

SOUND LOCALIZATION

Time and level differences

Having two ears rather than one helps us to localize sounds in space. A sound coming from the right will arrive at the right ear before the left ear. The sound will also have a higher level in the right ear because of the shadowing effect of the head. This means that each direction in space around the *horizontal* plane (i.e. varying in *azimuth*) will have an *interaural time difference* (ITD) and an *interaural level difference* (ILD) associated with it.

ILDs are only useful at high frequencies (greater than 500 Hz) because low-frequency sounds tend to diffract round the head, reducing the magnitude of the ILD. Conversely, for continuous pure tones, ITDs are not useful at high frequencies because the maximum time difference between the ears (when the sound source is directly to the right or left) is around 0.65 ms (Feddersen, Sandel, Teas, & Jeffress, 1957). For pure-tone frequencies higher than around 750 Hz, this difference is greater than half a cycle of the waveform, so that there is ambiguity over which ear contains the leading sound. For more complex sounds that contain envelope fluctuations, ITDs can be used at higher frequencies, because the arrival times of the envelopes (as opposed to the fine structure) can be compared between the two ears (Henning, 1974; Klump & Eady, 1956).

The binaural system is extremely sensitive to time differences between the two ears. For a 1 kHz pure tone, an ITD of around 10 μs (10 *millionths* of a second) can be discriminated from a reference ITD of 0 (Klump & Eady, 1956). An increase in time delay by 10 μs corresponds to a shift in location of about 1° in azimuth. This remarkable acuity implies that precise timing information in the auditory system (in the form of phase-locked neural spikes) is maintained up to the stage where the responses from the two ears are combined. For the processing of timing differences this is thought to be a nucleus in the brainstem called the medial superior olive (Yin & Chan, 1988).

In dramatic contrast to the auditory system's accuracy in detecting static differences in ITD, our ability to follow *changes* in the ITD over time (corresponding to an object that moves in space) is quite poor. This insensitivity has been called 'binaural sluggishness' (Grantham & Wightman, 1979). For example, sinusoidal oscillations in ITDs cannot be tracked at rates greater than around 2.4 Hz (Blauert, 1972). The binaural system seems to require a long time (perhaps several hundred milliseconds) to make an accurate estimate of location using ITDs.

A particular ITD or ILD does not specify uniquely the location of the sound source. For example, a sound from directly in front has the same ITD as a sound directly behind. In general there is a 'cone of confusion' projecting sideways from the head for each ITD (Mills, 1972). For each point on the cone the ITD is identical (see Figure 3.16). This ambiguity can be resolved by head movements (Hirsh, 1971). For example, if a sound is directly in front, a turn of the head to the right will increase the level in the left ear, whereas if a sound is directly behind, the same movement will increase the level in the right ear.

Figure 3.16   *A cone of confusion. All sound sources on the surface of the cone produce approximately the same ITD.*

It has been shown that introducing a difference in ITDs (or indeed ILDs) between a pure-tone signal and a noise masker, so that the signal and masker appear to originate from different points in space, can produce a dramatic improvement in the detectability of the signal (Hirsh, 1948; Jeffress, Blodgett, & Deatherage, 1952). The difference in threshold between the condition where the masker and the signal are identical in the two ears, and the condition where there is a binaural disparity, is called the *binaural masking level difference* (BMLD). The BMLD can be as great as 15 dB when the masker is the same in the two ears and the signal is simply inverted in one ear to produce an ITD of half a cycle. Binaural disparity can also produce an improvement in speech intelligibility in noise (Levitt & Rabiner, 1967).

Monaural cues

In addition to the binaural cues of ITDs and ILDs that require a comparison between the two ears, there are also monaural cues to sound localization. These result mainly from the modifications to the sound produced by reflections and diffractions around the pinna (Batteau, 1967; Gardner & Gardner, 1973). A particular direction in space is associated with a characteristic pattern (like a signature) of spectral peaks and notches, mainly imposed on frequency components above about 4 kHz (Hebrank & Wright, 1974). It appears that the auditory system can use these patterns to help localize sounds. The modifications can be described by a set of *head-related transfer functions* (HRTFs). Each HRTF defines the filtering effect of an individual pinna in response to a sound coming from a particular direction in space. Sounds played over headphones tend to appear as if they come from within the head, rather than being external. However, if the input to both earpieces is

processed using HRTFs that mimic the effects of the pinnae, then the sounds appear to be external, creating a much more realistic perception. Pinna cues can be used to localize sounds in the *vertical* plane (elevation), as well as in the horizontal plane. Pinna cues are, therefore, another means to resolve the cone of confusion problem.

Wightman and Kistler (1992) processed wideband noise stimuli using artificial HRTFs so that they could independently control (and trade off against each other) the ITD, ILD and pinna cues. They found that the location of wideband stimuli was dominated by the ITD cues. It was only when the noise was highpass filtered to contain only frequencies above 5 kHz that the ITDs became unimportant, and performance was dependent on ILD and pinna cues. For natural sounds, therefore, ITDs appear to provide the most important cues for sound localization.

AUDITORY SCENE ANALYSIS

At any one time we may be receiving acoustic information from a variety of sources. For example, we may be trying to listen to a conversation with a friend while music is playing on the radio and cars are passing outside. We require auditory mechanisms that can assign each component of the mixture of sounds entering our ears to a particular *sound source*, so that we may separate out the sounds we are interested in (the conversation) from the sounds we are not interested in (the music and the car noises). Bregman (1990) has termed this process *auditory scene analysis*. We can divide the overall process into *simultaneous grouping*, assigning sounds that occur simultaneously to different sources, and *sequential grouping*, assigning sequences of sounds (for example, musical melodies, or sequences of words) to different sources.

The Gestalt psychologists in the 1930s (Koffka, 1935) suggested that we organize our percepts according to certain principles. These principles can be regarded as 'rules of thumb' that take account of the ways in which sensory stimuli are produced in the environment. We can use this knowledge to help us make sense of a complex sound mixture. The most important of these principles for audition are:

1   *Similarity*: sounds that are similar in some way are likely to come from the same sound source.
2   *Good continuation*: sounds that flow naturally from one to the other (without any abrupt discontinuities) are likely to come from the same sound source.
3   *Common fate*: sounds that vary together (for example, are turned on and off at the same time) are likely to come from the same sound source.
4   *Disjoint allocation*: no single sound can originate from two different sources simultaneously.

5   *Closure*: a continuous sound obscured briefly by a second sound (e.g. speech interrupted by a door slam) is assumed to be continuous during the interruption unless there is evidence to the contrary. This is the principle behind the illusion of continuity in pulsation threshold experiments.

In practice, these principles ensure that our perception of 'natural' sounds is organized into the simplest pattern consistent with the sensory information and with our experience. Of course psychoacousticians, being devious people by training, can create artificially sounds that are decidedly *un*natural in order to test these principles to breaking point.

Simultaneous grouping

Probably the hardest task performed by the auditory system is to separate out sounds that are presented at the same time. The total sound entering the two ears is a complex mixture of all the sounds in the environment, and there may be considerable overlap both temporally and spectrally between sound components that we wish to segregate.

A strong cue to the separation of simultaneous sounds is based on the Gestalt principle of *common fate*. In particular, sound components that start together are grouped together, whereas sound components that start at different times are segregated. An example that has received some attention is the segregation of individual harmonics from vowel sounds. If a single harmonic in a vowel is started at least 32 ms before the rest of the vowel, then this can reduce the effect of the harmonic on the overall quality of the vowel, suggesting that the harmonic is segregated perceptually (Darwin, 1984; Darwin & Sutherland, 1984). The effect increases as the onset asynchrony is increased. Similarly, the contribution of a (mistuned) harmonic to the pitch of a complex tone is reduced when the harmonic starts 160 ms before the rest of the complex (Darwin & Ciocca, 1992). In profile analysis, in which listeners are required to make a discrimination of spectral shape, performance is reduced if there is an onset disparity between the target component and the other components (Green & Dai, 1992; Hill & Bailey, 1997). Presumably, if the target component is segregated from the background, it is harder to make the across-frequency comparison (Hill & Bailey, 1997). It is understandable that we do not want to allow sound components from other sources to influence our identification of the sound from the source in which we are interested. Onset disparities can be used by a musician to help emphasize her part in relation to the rest of the orchestra. By departing slightly from the notated metric positions, the notes are heard to stand out perceptually (Rasch, 1978, 1979).

More generally, there is evidence that sound components that are amplitude or frequency modulated together (i.e. coherently) will be heard out from sounds that are not modulated (McAdams, 1989; Moore & Bacon, 1993). It is less clear whether components can be segregated on the basis of incoherent AM (Summerfield & Culling, 1992), in which different components have different patterns of AM, and there seems to be little evidence that FM incoherence can be used to segregate components (Carlyon, 1994; McAdams, 1989; Summerfield & Culling, 1992).

Repetition rate or F0 is another strong cue for simultaneous segregation. The normal percept of a fused vowel can be disrupted by separating the harmonics into two groups and giving each group a different F0 (Broadbent & Ladefoged, 1957). When the F0's of two different vowels differ by 6% or more it is much easier to hear them out individually than if they have the same F0 (Assmann & Summerfield, 1990; Scheffers, 1983). Similarly, speech identification for words masked by continuous speech improves as the F0 between the target and the background is increased (Brokx & Nooteboom, 1982).

The effect of F0 can be regarded as an example of the Gestalt principle of *similarity*. Usually a vibrating sound source (such as a voice or a musical instrument) will produce a complex tone with a single F0. Only those frequency components that are harmonically related to the vibration frequency of the sound source (i.e. *similar* in that they are from the same harmonic series) can be assumed to originate from that sound source. A resolved harmonic in a complex tone that is mistuned by 3% or so from its correct harmonic position will tend to 'pop out' from the other harmonics perceptually (Moore, Peters, & Glasberg, 1985). A shift of 8% in frequency is enough to remove the contribution of a resolved harmonic to the overall quality of a vowel (Darwin & Gardner, 1986).

Despite the improvement in signal detection caused by a spatial separation of the signal and the masker in the BMLD phenomenon described earlier, differences in spatial location appear to have only a small effect on simultaneous sound segregation. Darwin and Ciocca (1992) found that presenting a mistuned harmonic to the ear opposite to the rest of the complex produced only a slight reduction in the effect of the harmonic on the overall pitch of the complex. The result implies that the mistuned harmonic was still being grouped with the others. Culling and Summerfield (1995) have demonstrated that vowels composed of synthesized formants cannot be separated when the formants for each vowel are identified only by common ITD.

Sequential grouping

Sequential grouping involves grouping *over time* the sequence of sounds that originate from the same sound source. An example is following an individual melody in a complex piece of music, or following

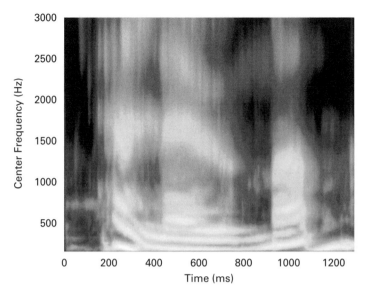

Figure 3.17   *The STEP for the utterance 'hello mum', plotted in the form of a spectrogram. Light colors indicate high levels at the output of the temporal window model. It can be seen that the main spectral features, such as formants and low-frequency resolved harmonics, appear to glide smoothly between one speech sound and the next. This helps to group the sounds sequentially.*

the speech sounds produced by one speaker in a room with many people speaking at once. The Gestalt principles of most relevance here are those of *similarity* and *good continuation*.

It has been shown, for example, that our ability to separate two melodies depends on the frequency or F0 separation between them. A melody played on a double bass or bass guitar is easily heard out from a melody played on a violin or lead guitar. Dowling (1973) showed that if two melodies were *interleaved* (i.e. notes from one melody were alternated with notes from another melody), then it was much easier to hear the two melodies separately if they occupied different frequency ranges. Melodies close in frequency tend to sound 'fused' together, forming a single melody.

Segregation is possible for wide F0 separations even when the two melodies are played using unresolved complex tones occupying the *same frequency region* (Vliegen & Oxenham, 1999). The result implies that spectral differences between the two melodies are not *necessary* for segregation if there is a difference in F0. However, spectral difference alone appears to be a very strong cue for sequential grouping. Sounds that have very different timbres, for example complex tones with harmonics occupying different spectral regions, tend to segregate (Bregman, 1990; Wessel, 1979). In music this means that melodies will tend to segregate if they are played on different instruments.

In addition to frequency and F0, differences in *intensity* and *spatial location* also promote segregation (Dowling, 1973; van Noorden, 1975). If the notes

from one of two interleaved melodies are played at a different level, or appear to come from a different point in space, to the notes from the other melody, they are more likely to be segregated. If speech sounds in a sequence are alternated between the two ears (an extreme form of spatial disparity based on ILDs), then the intelligibility of the speech is reduced (Cherry & Taylor, 1954). Similarly, listeners are able to selectively attend to a sequence of words with common ITDs (Darwin & Hukin, 1999). The strong effect of location in *sequential* grouping and attention is in contrast to the weak effect of location in *simultaneous* grouping. We can follow a sequence of sounds that originate from a particular point in space, but we do not seem to segregate simultaneous sound components on the basis of the locations of the sound sources. The importance of all these attributes – repetition rate, timbre, intensity and location – suggests that sequential grouping is based on similarity in a fairly broad sense.

Consistent with the Gestalt principle of *good continuation*, it is more likely that a sequence will appear fused if the transitions between successive elements are smooth and natural. If an abrupt jump in F0 is introduced into a recording of a single person speaking, then listeners tend to report that a new person has taken over as speaker at the point of discontinuity (Darwin & Bethell-Fox, 1977). The smooth movement of formants from one vowel to another (see Figure 3.17) helps grouping (Dorman, Cutting, & Raphael, 1975). In the same way, smooth frequency glides connecting the notes of a

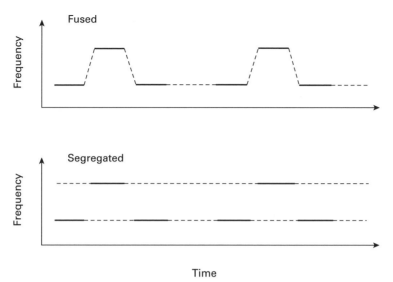

Figure 3.18 *The thick lines show the stimuli used by van Noorden (1975) to study stream segregation. The dotted lines illustrate the two possible percepts of fusion (galloping rhythm) and segregation.*

melody help it to sound fused (Bregman, 1990; Bregman & Dannenbring, 1973).

Importance of attention

The stimuli developed by van Noorden (1975) illustrate the two percepts of fusion and segregation very well (see Figure 3.18). Two tones, A and B (where B is higher in frequency than A), are played in the sequence ABA-ABA-ABA-ABA, etc. When the frequency separation between the tones is small (say 5% or so), and when the repetition rate is slow, the sequence is heard as a single galloping rhythm. When the frequency separation is larger, or the tones are played at a faster rate, the A and B tones segregate into two separate streams of notes.

The streaming effect can take some time to build up, so that the ABA sequence can sound fused initially, but after listening for several seconds the percept changes to one of segregation, and the galloping rhythm is lost. Carlyon, Cusack, Focton, & Robertson (2001) showed that this build-up of streaming did not occur when subjects were asked to attend to sounds presented in the *opposite* ear to the tone sequence. In one condition, they asked listeners to attend to this opposite-ear task for the first 10 seconds of the tone sequence, and then to start making segregation judgments. The listeners mostly responded that the sequence was fused, indicating that the build-up of streaming had not occurred when the listeners were not attending to the tones. In other words it is possible that in the *absence of attention* the notes tend to stay fused into one perceptual stream. That attention is necessary for some types of auditory stream segregation suggests that it is a relatively 'high-level' process, or at least a low-level process that receives some control from executive processes in the brain.

THE IDENTIFICATION OF AUDITORY OBJECTS

We have seen that the auditory system analyzes sounds in terms of their spectra (and possibly their *modulation* spectra), their repetition rates or F0's, and their spatial location. In addition, the auditory system appears to be very sensitive to *changes* in the characteristics of sounds over time. We saw in the previous section how the auditory system uses this information to separate out sound components that originate from different sources. Now we shall examine briefly how the information about a given sound source may be extracted; in other words, how the acoustic information is used to identify an *auditory object*.

Timbre

The loudness of a sound is the perceptual attribute that is most closely related to sound intensity. The pitch of a sound is the perceptual attribute that is most closely related to waveform repetition rate. Timbre can be defined as all the additional aspects of auditory sensation that cannot be defined as loudness or pitch. In other words, timbre is 'that attribute of auditory sensation in terms of which a listener can judge that two sounds similarly presented and having the same loudness and pitch are dissimilar' (American Standards Association, 1960; cited in Moore, 2003).

It is clear that spectral shape helps identify many sounds that are important to us. Different vowel sounds contain spectral peaks at different frequencies, corresponding to resonances in the vocal tract (see Figures 3.6, 3.15 and 3.17). The identity of an individual speaker is determined by the F0 of the vowels in their speech, but also by the individual pattern of formant frequencies (Matsumoto, Hiki, Sone, & Nimura, 1973). In music, sounds from different instruments can differ greatly in their spectra. It was mentioned earlier that bright instruments such as the trumpet contain proportionally more high-frequency components than warm instruments such as the French horn.

The primary role of the peripheral auditory system is to perform a frequency analysis of the sounds entering the ear. Listeners are good at making comparisons across the spectrum (Green et al., 1983), and at detecting changes in the spectrum over time (Madden & Fire, 1997; Sek & Moore, 1995). In the section on intensity discrimination it was argued that, for identifying sounds, it is the *relative* intensities of features within the sound that are most important. For most sounds identity does not change with overall level. It is conceivable that at some stage in the auditory system we represent sound features in terms of their relative levels (across frequency and time) rather than their absolute levels (Plack & Carlyon, 1995b). Weber's Law may be a consequence of a coding strategy based on relative intensity.

In addition to spectral shape, Handel (1995) identifies some other components of timbre that help identify auditory objects. Onset and offset transients (attack and decay) can help us to identify, for example, an instrument that is plucked or bowed, or an object that 'rings' for a long time after being struck (such as a glass or a bell) versus an object that is highly damped. Sounds are often perceived very differently when they are reversed in time, despite the fact that this operation does not affect the magnitude spectrum (Patterson, 1994a, 1994b). The identification of transients is helped by the acute temporal resolution of the auditory system that allows it to track the temporal envelope. The presence or absence of noise is another important cue. Often when an object is struck or excited a characteristic pattern of irregular acoustic energy is initiated, such as the scratch of a violin bow, or the initial blast of a trumpet. Finally, many auditory objects are associated with characteristic patterns, or rhythms, of acoustic events over time, such as footsteps, or hammering and knocking.

Variability of features

A major problem faced by the auditory system is that very often there is not a one-to-one mapping between sound features and sound identity. In free-flowing speech, a vowel sound is not a static pattern of spectral peaks but is constantly changing as the articulators in the vocal tract (tongue, lips, etc.) move between the position corresponding to one speech sound and the position corresponding to the next speech sound. This is called *co-articulation*. Co-articulation means that the acoustic waveform corresponding to a particular vowel is heavily modified by the characteristics of the speech sounds before and after the vowel. Furthermore, factors such as accent, and individual differences in the shape of the vocal tract, will also modify the spectrum of the vowel.

The fact that the features that identify auditory objects are generally *context-dependent* means that the higher auditory system must be flexible in the way in which it interprets acoustic information. If invariant cues exist for each auditory object, then they must be complex combinations of different features, rather than a simple detector that says 'I have a spectral peak here, therefore this is an /a/', for example. Furthermore, the identification of many objects is multimodal, involving both vision and hearing. What we see can influence what we hear and vice versa. A famous example of this is the McGurk effect (McGurk & McDonald, 1976), in which the perception of a speech sound is influenced by the perceived lip movements of the speaker.

SUMMARY

In this chapter, I have attempted to provide an overview of what I consider to be some of the important aspects of auditory perception. This overview has been biased, inevitably, towards those areas of research in which I have an active interest. I have tried to build up from what we know about the basic mechanisms of hearing, to more complex processes such as sound segregation. I have tried to show how these higher processes are dependent on the more fundamental analysis of sounds in terms of spectrum, repetition rate, temporal envelope and location.

The 'take-home messages' from this account are as follows:

1   The ear behaves as a *frequency analyzer*. The spectrum is as central to the way we perceive sounds as spatial information is to the way we perceive visual stimuli.
2   The ear is highly *compressive*: a large range of input intensities is mapped onto a much smaller range of basilar membrane displacements and perceived magnitudes (loudness).
3   Pitch is the perceptual correlate of the repetition rate of an acoustic waveform. The pitch of both pure tones and complex tones may be coded by neural activity synchronized (phase-locked) to the repetition rate.

4 Acoustic information is often carried by rapid changes in the characteristics of a sound over time. The ear is very sensitive to rapid temporal fluctuations.

5 Sounds can be located in space using our two ears, and by using monaural (pinna) cues. We can use this information to help us track a sequence of sounds arising from a given location.

6 Sound segregation is possibly the hardest task performed by the auditory system. A variety of cues such as harmonicity and onset differences are used to segregate simultaneous sounds originating from different sources. Sound sequences are tracked across time using similarity along a number of different dimensions.

7 Auditory objects are identified by characteristic patterns of energy across frequency and time. The features that identify a sound are *multidimensional*. These features vary from one presentation to the next and identification sometimes depends on an analysis of the auditory (and visual) context.

ACKNOWLEDGMENTS

I am very grateful to Brian Moore for a helpful review, and to Deb Fantini and Vit Drga for comments on an earlier version of this chapter. Yo-iti Suzuki and Hisashi Takeshima kindly supplied the equal loudness contours for Figure 3.9. Koen Lamberts provided support and encouragement throughout the process. Figures 3.2 and 3.3 © the author.

REFERENCES

American Standards Association (1960). *Acoustical Terminology SI*, 1–1960.

Arthur, R. M., Pfeiffer, R. R., & Suga, N. (1971). Properties of 'two tone inhibition' in primary auditory neurones. *Journal of Physiology*, *212*, 593–609.

Assmann, P. F., & Summerfield, Q. (1990). Modeling the perception of concurrent vowels: vowels with different fundamental frequencies. *Journal of the Acoustical Society of America*, *88*, 680–697.

Attneave, F., & Olson, R. K. (1971). Pitch as a medium: a new approach to psychophysical scaling. *American Journal of Psychology*, *84*, 147–166.

Bacon, S. P., & Grantham, D. W. (1989). Modulation masking: effects of modulation frequency, depth and phase. *Journal of the Acoustical Society of America*, *85*, 2575–2580.

Bacon, S. P., & Viemeister, N. F. (1985). Temporal modulation transfer functions in normal-hearing and hearing-impaired subjects. *Audiology*, *24*, 117–134.

Batteau, D. W. (1967). The role of the pinna in human localization. *Proceedings of the Royal Society of London B*, *168*, 158–180.

Blauert, J. (1972). On the lag of lateralization caused by interaural time and intensity differences. *Audiology*, *11*, 265–270.

Bregman, A. S. (1990). *Auditory scene analysis*. Cambridge, MA: MIT Press.

Bregman, A. S., & Dannenbring, G. L. (1973). The effect of continuity on auditory stream segregation. *Perception and Psychophysics*, *13*, 308–312.

Broadbent, D. E., & Ladefoged, P. (1957). On the fusion of sounds reaching different sense organs. *Journal of the Acoustical Society of America*, *29*, 708–710.

Brokx, J. P. L., & Nooteboom, S. G. (1982). Intonation and the perceptual separation of simultaneous voices. *Journal of Phonetics*, *10*, 23–36.

Burris-Meyer, H., & Mallory, V. (1960). Psycho-acoustics, applied and misapplied. *Journal of the Acoustical Society of America*, *32*, 1568–1574.

Buus, S. (1985). Release from masking caused by envelope fluctuations. *Journal of the Acoustical Society of America*, *78*, 1958–1965.

Buus, S., & Florentine, M. (1985). Gap detection in normal and impaired listeners: the effect of level and frequency. In A. Michelsen (ed.), *Time resolution in auditory systems* (pp. 159–179). New York: Springer.

Buus, S., Musch, H., & Florentine, M. (1998). On loudness at threshold. *Journal of the Acoustical Society of America*, *104*, 399–410.

Carlyon, R. P. (1994). Further evidence against an across-frequency mechanism specific to the detection of frequency modulation (FM) incoherence between resolved frequency components. *Journal of the Acoustical Society of America*, *95*, 949–961.

Carlyon, R. P., Cusack, R., Foxton, J. M., & Robertson, I. H. (2001). Effects of attention and unilateral neglect on auditory stream segregation. *Journal of Experimental Psychology: Human Perception and Performance*, *27*, 115–127.

Carlyon, R. P., & Shackleton, T. M. (1994). Comparing the fundamental frequencies of resolved and unresolved harmonics: evidence for two pitch mechanisms? *Journal of the Acoustical Society of America*, *95*, 3541–3554.

Cherry, E. C., & Taylor, W. K. (1954). Some further experiments upon the recognition of speech, with one and with two ears. *Journal of the Acoustical Society of America*, *26*, 554–559.

Ciocca, V., & Darwin, C. J. (1999). The integration of nonsimultaneous frequency components into a single virtual pitch. *Journal of the Acoustical Society of America*, *105*, 2421–2430.

Cohen, M. F. (1991). Comodulation masking release over a three octave range. *Journal of the Acoustical Society of America*, *90*, 1381–1384.

Cohen, M. F., & Schubert, E. D. (1987). Influence of place synchrony on detection of a sinusoid. *Journal of the Acoustical Society of America*, *81*, 452–458.

Culling, J. F., & Summerfield, Q. (1995). Perceptual segregation of concurrent speech sounds: absence of across-frequency grouping by common interaural delay. *Journal of the Acoustical Society of America*, *98*, 785–797.

Darwin, C. J. (1984). Perceiving vowels in the presence of another sound: constraints on formant perception. *Journal of the Acoustical Society of America*, *76*, 1636–1647.

Darwin, C. J., & Bethell-Fox, C. E. (1977). Pitch continuity and speech source attribution. *Journal of Experimental Psychology: Human Perception and Performance*, *3*, 665–672.

Darwin, C. J., & Ciocca, V. (1992). Grouping in pitch perception: effects of onset asynchrony and ear of presentation of a mistuned component. *Journal of the Acoustical Society of America*, *91*, 3381–3390.

Darwin, C. J., & Gardner, R. B. (1986). Mistuning a harmonic of a vowel: grouping and phase effects on vowel quality. *Journal of the Acoustical Society of America*, *79*, 838–845.

Darwin, C. J., & Hukin, R. (1999). Auditory objects of attention: the role of interaural time differences. *Journal of Experimental Psychology: Human Perception and Performance*, *25*, 617–629.

Darwin, C. J., & Sutherland, N. S. (1984). Grouping frequency components of vowels: when is a harmonic not a harmonic? *Quarterly Journal of Experimental Psychology*, *36A*, 193–208.

Dau, T., Kollmeier, B., & Kohlrausch, A. (1997a). Modeling auditory processing of amplitude modulation. I. Detection and masking with narrow-band carriers. *Journal of the Acoustical Society of America*, *102*, 2892–2905.

Dau, T., Kollmeier, B., & Kohlrausch, A. (1997b). Modeling auditory processing of amplitude modulation. II. Spectral and temporal integration. *Journal of the Acoustical Society of America*, *102*, 2906–2919.

Delgutte, B. (1990). Physiological mechanisms of psychophysical masking: observations from auditory-nerve fibers. *Journal of the Acoustical Society of America*, *87*, 791–809.

Dorman, M. F., Cutting, J. E., & Raphael, L. J. (1975). Perception of temporal order in vowel sequences with and without formant transitions. *Journal of Experimental Psychology: Human Perception and Performance*, *1*, 121–129.

Dowling, W. J. (1973). The perception of interleaved melodies. *Cognitive Psychology*, *5*, 332–337.

Evans, E. F. (1975). Cochlear nerve and cochlear nucleus. In W. D. Keidel & W. D. Neff (Eds.), *Handbook of sensory physiology* (Vol. 5/2, pp. 1–108). Berlin: Springer.

Evans, E. F., Pratt, S. R., Spenner, H., & Cooper, N. P. (1992). Comparisons of physiological and behavioural properties: auditory frequency selectivity. *Advances in the Biosciences*, *83*, 159–169.

Ewert, S. D., & Dau, T. (2000). Characterizing frequency selectivity for envelope fluctuations. *Journal of the Acoustical Society of America*, *108*, 1181–1196.

Fantini, D. A., & Moore, B. C. J. (1994). A comparison of the effectiveness of across-channel cues available in comodulation masking release and profile analysis tasks. *Journal of the Acoustical Society of America*, *96*, 3451–3462.

Fantini, D. A., Moore, B. C. J., & Schooneveldt, G. P. (1993). Comodulation masking release (CMR) as a function of type of signal, gated or continuous masking, monaural or dichotic presentation of flanking bands, and center frequency. *Journal of the Acoustical Society of America*, *93*, 2106–2115.

Feddersen, W. E., Sandel, T. T., Teas, D. C., & Jeffress, L. A. (1957). Localization of high-frequency tones. *Journal of the Acoustical Society of America*, *29*, 988–991.

Fletcher, H. (1940). Auditory patterns. *Review of Modern Physics*, *12*, 47–65.

Gardner, M. B., & Gardner, R. S. (1973). Problem of localization in the median plane: effect of pinnae cavity occlusion. *Journal of the Acoustical Society of America*, *53*, 400–408.

Glasberg, B. R., & Moore, B. C. J. (1990). Derivation of auditory filter shapes from notched-noise data. *Hearing Research*, *47*, 103–138.

Goldstein, J. L. (1973). An optimum processor theory for the central formation of the pitch of complex tones. *Journal of the Acoustical Society of America*, *54*, 1496–1516.

Grantham, D. W., & Wightman, F. L. (1979). Detectability of a pulsed tone in the presence of a masker with time-varying interaural correlation. *Journal of the Acoustical Society of America*, *65*, 1509–1517.

Green, D. M. (1988). *Profile analysis*. New York: Oxford University Press.

Green, D. M., & Dai, H. (1992). Temporal relations in profile comparisons. In Y. Cazals, L. Demany, & K. Horner (Eds.), *Auditory physiology and perception* (pp. 471–478). Oxford: Pergamon Press.

Green, D. M., & Kidd, G. (1983). Further studies of auditory profile analysis. *Journal of the Acoustical Society of America*, *73*, 1260–1265.

Green, D. M., Kidd, G., & Picardi, M. C. (1983). Successive versus simultaneous comparison in auditory intensity discrimination. *Journal of the Acoustical Society of America*, *73*, 639–643.

Grimault, N., Micheyl, C., Carlyon, R. P., & Collet, L. (2002). Evidence for two pitch encoding mechanisms using a selective auditory training paradigm. *Perception and Psychophysics*, *64*, 189–197.

Grose, J. H., & Hall, J. W. (1989). Comodulation masking release using SAM tonal complex maskers: effects of modulation depth and signal position. *Journal of the Acoustical Society of America*, *85*, 1276–1284.

Hall, J. W., Haggard, M. P., & Fernandes, M. A. (1984). Detection in noise by spectro-temporal pattern analysis. *Journal of the Acoustical Society of America*, *76*, 50–56.

Hall, J. W., & Peters, R. W. (1981). Pitch from nonsimultaneous successive harmonics in quiet and noise. *Journal of the Acoustical Society of America*, *69*, 509–513.

Handel, S. (1995). Timbre perception and object identification. In B. C. J. Moore (ed.), *Hearing* (pp. 425–461). New York: Academic Press.

Hartmann, W. M. (1997). *Signals, sound, and sensation*. New York: Springer.

Hebrank, J., & Wright, D. (1974). Spectral cues used in the localization of sounds on the median plane. *Journal of the Acoustical Society of America*, 56, 1829–1834.

Henning, G. B. (1974). Detectability of interaural delay in high-frequency complex waveforms. *Journal of the Acoustical Society of America*, 55, 84–90.

Hill, N. I., & Bailey, P. J. (1997). Profile analysis with an asynchronous target: evidence for auditory grouping. *Journal of the Acoustical Society of America*, 102, 477–481.

Hirsh, I. J. (1948). The influence of interaural phase on interaural summation and inhibition. *Journal of the Acoustical Society of America*, 20, 536–544.

Hirsh, I. J. (1971). Masking of speech and auditory localization. *Audiology*, 10, 110–114.

Houtgast, T. (1974). Lateral suppression in hearing. PhD thesis, Free University of Amsterdam, The Netherlands.

Houtgast, T. (1989). Frequency selectivity in amplitude modulation detection. *Journal of the Acoustical Society of America*, 85, 1676–1680.

Jeffress, L. A., Blodgett, H. C., & Deatherage, B. H. (1952). The masking of tones by white noise as a function of the interaural phases of both components. I. 500 cycles. *Journal of the Acoustical Society of America*, 24, 523–527.

Jesteadt, W., Bacon, S. P., & Lehman, J. R. (1982). Forward masking as a function of frequency, masker level, and signal delay. *Journal of the Acoustical Society of America*, 71, 950–962.

Kaernbach, C., & Demany, L. (1998). Psychophysical evidence against the autocorrelation theory of auditory temporal processing. *Journal of the Acoustical Society of America*, 104, 2298–2306.

Klump, R. G., & Eady, H. R. (1956). Some measurements of interaural time difference thresholds. *Journal of the Acoustical Society of America*, 28, 859–860.

Koffka, K. (1935). *Principles of Gestalt psychology*. New York: Harcourt & Brace.

Kohlrausch, A., Fassel, R., & Dau, T. (2000). The influence of carrier level and frequency on modulation and beat-detection thresholds for sinusoidal carriers. *Journal of the Acoustical Society of America*, 108, 723–734.

Langner, G., & Schreiner, C. (1988). Periodicity coding in the inferior colliculus of the cat. I. Neuronal mechanism. *Journal of Neurophysiology*, 60, 1799–1822.

Levitt, H., & Rabiner, L. R. (1967). Binaural release from masking for speech and gain in intelligibility. *Journal of the Acoustical Society of America*, 42, 601–608.

Liberman, M. C., & Kiang, N. Y. S. (1978). Acoustic trauma in cats: cochlear pathology and auditory-nerve activity. *Acta Otolaryngolica* (Suppl. 358), 1–63.

Licklider, J. C. R. (1951). A duplex theory of pitch perception. *Experientia*, 7, 128–133.

Madden, J. P., & Fire, K. M. (1996). Detection and discrimination of gliding tones as a function of frequency transition and center frequency. *Journal of the Acoustical Society of America*, 100, 3754–3760.

Madden, J. P., & Fire, K. M. (1997). Detection and discrimination of frequency glides as a function of direction, duration, frequency span, and center frequency. *Journal of the Acoustical Society of America*, 102, 2920–2924.

Matlin, M. W., & Foley, H. J. (1992). *Sensation and perception* (3rd ed.). Boston: Allyn & Bacon.

Matsumoto, H., Hiki, S., Sone, T., & Nimura, T. (1973). Multidimensional representation of personal quality of vowels and its acoustical correlates. *IEEE Transactions on Audio and Electroacoustics*, AU-21, 428–436.

McAdams, S. (1989). Segregation of concurrent sounds. I. Effects of frequency modulation coherence. *Journal of the Acoustical Society of America*, 86, 2148–2159.

McGill, W. J., & Goldberg, J. P. (1968). A study of the near-miss involving Weber's Law and pure-tone intensity discrimination. *Perception and Psychophysics*, 4, 105–109.

McGurk, H., & McDonald, J. (1976). Hearing lips and seeing voices. *Nature*, 264, 746–748.

Meddis, R., & Hewitt, M. (1991). Virtual pitch and phase sensitivity studied using a computer model of the auditory periphery: pitch identification. *Journal of the Acoustical Society of America*, 89, 2866–2882.

Meddis, R., O'Mard, L. P., & Lopez-Poveda, E. A. (2001). A computational algorithm for computing nonlinear auditory frequency selectivity. *Journal of the Acoustical Society of America*, 109, 2852–2861.

Miller, G. A. (1947). Sensitivity to changes in the intensity of white noise and its relation to masking and loudness. *Journal of the Acoustical Society of America*, 19, 609–619.

Miller, G. A., & Licklider, J. C. R. (1950). The intelligibility of interrupted speech. *Journal of the Acoustical Society of America*, 22, 167–173.

Mills, A. W. (1972). Auditory localization. In J. V. Tobias (ed.), *Foundations of modern auditory theory* (Vol. II, pp. 301–345). New York: Academic Press.

Moore, B. C. J. (1973). Frequency difference limens for short-duration tones. *Journal of the Acoustical Society of America*, 54, 610–619.

Moore, B. C. J. (1978). Psychophysical tuning curves measured in simultaneous and forward masking. *Journal of the Acoustical Society of America*, 63, 524–532.

Moore, B. C. J. (2003). *An introduction to the psychology of hearing* (5th ed.). New York: Academic Press.

Moore, B. C. J., & Bacon, S. P. (1993). Detection and identification of a single modulated carrier in a complex sound. *Journal of the Acoustical Society of America*, 94, 759–768.

Moore, B. C. J., & Glasberg, B. R. (1983a). Growth of forward masking for sinusoidal and noise maskers as a function of signal delay: implications for suppression in noise. *Journal of the Acoustical Society of America*, 73, 1249–1259.

Moore, B. C. J., & Glasberg, B. R. (1983b). Suggested formulae for calculating auditory-filter bandwidths and excitation patterns. *Journal of the Acoustical Society of America*, 74, 750–753.

Moore, B. C. J., Glasberg, B. R., & Peters, R. W. (1985). Relative dominance of individual partials in determining the pitch of complex tones. *Journal of the Acoustical Society of America*, 77, 1853–1860.

Moore, B. C. J., Glasberg, B. R., Plack, C. J., & Biswas, A. K. (1988). The shape of the ear's temporal window. *Journal of the Acoustical Society of America*, *83*, 1102–1116.

Moore, B. C. J., Glasberg, B. R., & Roberts, B. (1984). Refining the measurement of psychophysical tuning curves. *Journal of the Acoustical Society of America*, *76*, 1057–1066.

Moore, B. C. J., & Oxenham, A. J. (1998). Psychoacoustic consequences of compression in the peripheral auditory system. *Psychological Review*, *105*, 108–124.

Moore, B. C. J., Peters, R. W., & Glasberg, B. R. (1985). Thresholds for the detection of inharmonicity in complex tones. *Journal of the Acoustical Society of America*, *77*, 1861–1867.

Moore, B. C. J., & Raab, D. H. (1974). Pure-tone intensity discrimination: some experiments relating to the 'near miss' to Weber's Law. *Journal of the Acoustical Society of America*, *55*, 1049–1054.

Moore, B. C. J., & Rosen, S. M. (1979). Tune recognition with reduced pitch and interval information. *Journal of Experimental Psychology*, *31*, 229–240.

Moore, B. C. J., & Sek, A. (1994). Effects of carrier frequency and background noise on the detection of mixed modulation. *Journal of the Acoustical Society of America*, *96*, 741–751.

Moore, B. C. J., & Vickers, D. A. (1997). The role of spread of excitation and suppression in simultaneous masking. *Journal of the Acoustical Society of America*, *102*, 2284–2290.

Moore, B. C. J., Vickers, D. A., Plack, C. J., & Oxenham, A. J. (1999). Inter-relationship between different psychoacoustic measures assumed to be related to the cochlear active mechanism. *Journal of the Acoustical Society of America*, *106*, 2761–2778.

Munson, W. A., & Gardner, M. B. (1950). Loudness patterns – a new approach. *Journal of the Acoustical Society of America*, *22*, 177–190.

Murugasu, E., & Russell, I. J. (1996). The effect of efferent stimulation on basilar membrane displacement in the basal turn of the guinea pig cochlea. *Journal of Neuroscience*, *16*, 325–332.

Nelson, D. A., Schroder, A. C., & Wojtczak, M. (2001). A new procedure for measuring peripheral compression in normal-hearing and hearing-impaired listeners. *Journal of the Acoustical Society of America*, *110*, 2045–2064.

Oxenham, A. J. (2001). Forward masking: adaptation or integration? *Journal of the Acoustical Society of America*, *109*, 732–741.

Oxenham, A. J., & Moore, B. C. J. (1994). Modeling the additivity of nonsimultaneous masking. *Hearing Research*, *80*, 105–118.

Oxenham, A. J., & Plack, C. J. (1997). A behavioral measure of basilar-membrane nonlinearity in listeners with normal and impaired hearing. *Journal of the Acoustical Society of America*, *101*, 3666–3675.

Oxenham, A. J., & Plack, C. J. (1998). Suppression and the upward spread of masking. *Journal of the Acoustical Society of America*, *104*, 3500–3510.

Patterson, R. D. (1976). Auditory filter shapes derived with noise stimuli. *Journal of the Acoustical Society of America*, *59*, 640–654.

Patterson, R. D. (1994a). The sound of a sinusoid: spectral models. *Journal of the Acoustical Society of America*, *96*, 1409–1418.

Patterson, R. D. (1994b). The sound of a sinusoid: time-interval models. *Journal of the Acoustical Society of America*, *96*, 1419–1428.

Patterson, R. D., & Nimmo-Smith, I. (1980). Off-frequency listening and auditory-filter asymmetry. *Journal of the Acoustical Society of America*, *67*, 229–245.

Penner, M. J. (1977). Detection of temporal gaps in noise as a measure of the decay of auditory sensation. *Journal of the Acoustical Society of America*, *61*, 552–557.

Plack, C. J. (1996). Temporal factors in referential intensity coding. *Journal of the Acoustical Society of America*, *100*, 1031–1042.

Plack, C. J., & Carlyon, R. P. (1995a). Differences in fundamental frequency discrimination and frequency modulation detection between complex tones consisting of resolved and unresolved harmonics. *Journal of the Acoustical Society of America*, *98*, 1355–1364.

Plack, C. J., & Carlyon, R. P. (1995b). Loudness perception and intensity coding. In B. C. J. Moore (ed.), *Hearing* (pp. 123–160). New York: Academic Press.

Plack, C. J., & Moore, B. C. J. (1990). Temporal window shape as a function of frequency and level. *Journal of the Acoustical Society of America*, *87*, 2178–2187.

Plack, C. J., & Oxenham, A. J. (1998). Basilar membrane nonlinearity and the growth of forward masking. *Journal of the Acoustical Society of America*, *103*, 1598–1608.

Plack, C. J., Oxenham, A. J., & Drga, V. (2002). Linear and nonlinear processes in temporal masking. *Acustica*, *88*, 348–358.

Plack, C. J., & White, L. J. (2000). Pitch matches between unresolved complex tones differing by a single inter-pulse interval. *Journal of the Acoustical Society of America*, *108*, 696–705.

Plomp, R. (1964a). The ear as a frequency analyzer. *Journal of the Acoustical Society of America*, *36*, 1628–1636.

Plomp, R. (1964b). The rate of decay of auditory sensation. *Journal of the Acoustical Society of America*, *36*, 277–282.

Pressnitzer, D., de Cheveigné, A., & Winter, I. M. (2002). Perceptual pitch shifts for sounds with similar waveform autocorrelation. *Acoustic Research Letters Online*, *3*, 1–6.

Pressnitzer, D., & Patterson, R. D. (2001). Distortion products and the pitch of harmonic complex tones. In D. J. Breebaart, A. J. M. Houtsma, A. Kohlrausch, V. F. Prijs, & R. Schoonhoven (Eds.), *Physiological and psychophysical bases of auditory function* (pp. 97–104). Maastricht: Shaker.

Rasch, R. A. (1978). The perception of simultaneous notes such as in polyphonic music. *Acustica*, *40*, 21–23.

Rasch, R. A. (1979). Synchronization in performed ensemble music. *Acustica*, *43*, 121–131.

Rhode, W. S., & Cooper, N. P. (1996). Nonlinear mechanics in the apical turn of the chinchilla cochlea in vivo. *Auditory Neuroscience*, *3*, 101–121.

Richards, V. M. (1987). Monaural envelope correlation perception. *Journal of the Acoustical Society of America*, *82*, 1621–1630.

Ritsma, R. J. (1967). Frequencies dominant in the perception of the pitch of complex sounds. *Journal of the Acoustical Society of America*, *42*, 191–198.

Robles, L., Ruggero, M. A., & Rich, N. C. (1986). Basilar membrane mechanics at the base of the chinchilla cochlea. I. Input-output functions, tuning curves, and response phases. *Journal of the Acoustical Society of America*, *80*, 1364–1374.

Ruggero, M. A., Rich, N. C., Recio, A., Narayan, S. S., & Robles, L. (1997). Basilar-membrane responses to tones at the base of the chinchilla cochlea. *Journal of the Acoustical Society of America*, *101*, 2151–2163.

Ruggero, M. A., Robles, L., & Rich, N. C. (1992). Two-tone suppression in the basilar membrane of the cochlea: mechanical basis of auditory-nerve rate suppression. *Journal of Neurophysics*, *68*, 1087–1099.

Sachs, M. B., & Abbas, P. J. (1974). Rate versus level functions for auditory-nerve fibres in cats: tone burst stimuli. *Journal of the Acoustical Society of America*, *56*, 1835–1847.

Scheffers, M. T. M. (1983). Sifting vowels: auditory pitch analysis and sound segregation. PhD thesis, University of Groningen, The Netherlands.

Schlauch, R. S., DiGiovanni, J. J., & Reis, D. T. (1998). Basilar membrane nonlinearity and loudness. *Journal of the Acoustical Society of America*, *103*, 2010–2020.

Schooneveldt, G. P., & Moore, B. C. J. (1987). Comodulation masking release (CMR): effects of signal frequency, flanking-band frequency, masker bandwidth, flanking-band level, and monotic versus dichotic presentation of the flanking band. *Journal of the Acoustical Society of America*, *82*, 1944–1956.

Schouten, J. F. (1940). The residue and the mechanism of hearing. *Proceedings, Koninklijke Nederlandse Academic van Wetenschappers*, *43*, 991–999.

Schouten, J. F. (1970). The residue revisited. In R. Plomp & G. F. Smoorenburg (Eds.), *Frequency analysis and periodicity detection in hearing* (pp. 41–54). Leiden: A. W. Sijthoff.

Sek, A., & Moore, B. C. J. (1995). Frequency discrimination as a function of frequency, measured in several ways. *Journal of the Acoustical Society of America*, *97*, 2479–2486.

Sellick, P. M., Patuzzi, R., & Johnstone, B. M. (1982). Measurement of basilar membrane motion in the guinea pig using the Mössbauer technique. *Journal of the Acoustical Society of America*, *72*, 131–141.

Shailer, M. J., & Moore, B. C. J. (1983). Gap detection as a function of frequency, bandwidth, and level. *Journal of the Acoustical Society of America*, *74*, 467–473.

Shailer, M. J., & Moore, B. C. J. (1987). Gap detection and the auditory filter: phase effects with sinusoidal stimuli. *Journal of the Acoustical Society of America*, *74*, 467–473.

Shannon, R. V. (1976). Two-tone unmasking and suppression in a forward-masking situation. *Journal of the Acoustical Society of America*, *59*, 1460–1470.

Stevens, S. S. (1957). On the psychophysical law. *Psychological Review*, *64*, 153–181.

Summerfield, Q., & Culling, J. (1992). Auditory segregation of competing voices: absence of effects of FM or AM coherence. *Philosophical Transactions of the Royal Society of London B*, *336*, 357–366.

Terhardt, E. (1974). Pitch, consonance, and harmony. *Journal of the Acoustical Society of America*, *55*, 1061–1069.

van Noorden, L. P. A. S. (1975). Temporal coherence in the perception of tone sequences. PhD thesis, Eindhoven University of Technology, The Netherlands.

Verhey, J. L., Dau, T., & Kollmeier, B. (1999). Within-channel cues in comodulation masking release (CMR): experiments and model predictions using a modulation-filterbank model. *Journal of the Acoustical Society of America*, *106*, 2733–2745.

Viemeister, N. F. (1972). Intensity discrimination of pulsed sinusoids: the effects of filtered noise. *Journal of the Acoustical Society of America*, *51*, 1256–1269.

Viemeister, N. F. (1979). Temporal modulation transfer functions based upon modulation thresholds. *Journal of the Acoustical Society of America*, *66*, 1364–1380.

Viemeister, N. F. (1988). Intensity coding and the dynamic range problem. *Hearing Research*, *34*, 267–274.

Viemeister, N. F., & Bacon, S. P. (1988). Intensity discrimination, increment detection, and magnitude estimation for 1-kHz tones. *Journal of the Acoustical Society of America*, *84*, 172–178.

Viemeister, N. F., & Plack, C. J. (1993). Time analysis. In W. A. Yost, A. N. Popper, & R. R. Fay (Eds.), *Human psychophysics* (pp. 116–154). New York: Springer.

Vliegen, J., & Oxenham, A. J. (1999). Sequential stream segregation in the absence of spectral cues. *Journal of the Acoustical Society of America*, *105*, 339–346.

Vogten, L. L. M. (1974). Pure-tone masking: a new result from a new method. In E. Zwicker & E. Terhardt (Eds.), *Facts and models in hearing* (pp. 142–155). Berlin: Springer.

Vogten, L. L. M. (1978). Low-level pure-tone masking: a comparison of 'tuning curves' obtained with simultaneous and forward masking. *Journal of the Acoustical Society of America*, *63*, 1520–1527.

Wessel, D. L. (1979). Timbre space as a musical control structure. *Computer Music Journal*, *3*, 45–52.

White, L. J., & Plack, C. J. (1998). Temporal processing of the pitch of complex tones. *Journal of the Acoustical Society of America*, *103*, 2051–2063.

Wightman, F. L., & Kistler, D. J. (1992). The dominant role of low-frequency interaural time differences in sound localization. *Journal of the Acoustical Society of America*, *91*, 1648–1661.

Yasin, I., & Plack, C. J. (2003). The effects of a high frequency suppressor on derived basilar membrane response functions. *Journal of the Acoustical Society of America, 114*, 322–332.

Yates, G. K., Winter, I. M., & Robertson, D. (1990). Basilar membrane nonlinearity determines auditory nerve rate-intensity functions and cochlear dynamic range. *Hearing Research, 45*, 203–220.

Yin, T. C. T., & Chan, J. C. K. (1988). Neural mechanisms underlying interaural time sensitivity to tones and noise. In G. M. Edelman, W. E. Gall, & W. M. Cowan (Eds.), *Auditory function* (pp. 385–430). New York: Wiley.

Zwicker, E. (1956). Die Elementaren Grundlagen zur Bestimmung der Informationskapazität des Gehörs. *Acustica, 6*, 365–381.

Zwicker, E. (1970). Masking and psychological excitation as consequences of the ear's frequency analysis. In R. Plomp & G. F. Smoorenburg (Eds.), *Frequency analysis and periodicity detection in hearing* (pp. 376–396). Leiden: A. W. Sijthoff.

Zwicker, E., & Fastl, H. (1990). *Psychoacoustics: facts and models*. Berlin: Springer.

4

Attention

CLAUS BUNDESEN AND THOMAS HABEKOST

This chapter provides an overview of modern research on attention. 'Attention' is a general term for selectivity in perception. The selectivity implies that at any instant a perceiving organism focuses on certain aspects of the stimulus situation to the exclusion of other aspects. This definition encompasses a wide range of cognitive phenomena, and many different aspects of attentional function have been investigated. While covering this diversity, the present chapter also reflects a coherent field of study in which general progress has been made.

EARLY WORK

Modern research on attention was pioneered in the early 1950s by studies on selective listening. Cherry (1953) investigated the ability to attend to one speaker in the presence of others (the *cocktail party problem*) by asking his subjects to repeat a prose message while they heard it, rather than waiting until it finished. When the message to be repeated (*shadowed*) was presented to one ear while a message to be ignored was presented to the other ear (*dichotic* presentation), subjects were unable to recall the content of the unattended message. If the message to be ignored consisted of human speech, the listening subjects did not fail to identify it as such, but they were unable to report any word or phrase heard in the rejected ear. Furthermore, they were unable to make definite identification of the language as being English. Except for simple physical characteristics, the message to be ignored appeared to be 'filtered out'.

The studies on selective listening inspired the first modern theory of attention, the *filter* theory of Broadbent (1958). This theory also pioneered the use of flow-chart models in cognitive psychology (see Figure 4.1). In Broadbent's conception, information flows from the senses through many parallel input channels into a short-term memory store. The short-term store can hold the information for only a few seconds. Access to response systems depends on a *limited-capacity channel*, whose ability to transmit information is much smaller than the total capacity of the parallel input channels. Therefore, a selective filter operates between the short-term memory and the limited-capacity channel. The filter acts as an all-or-none switch, selecting information from just one of the parallel input channels at a time.

Broadbent (1958) defined an input channel as a class of sensory events that share a simple physical feature. Except for analysis of such features, stimuli on unattended channels should not be perceived. This conjecture accounted for the main results of the early studies on selective listening, but was soon challenged.

Moray (1959) and others showed that subjectively important words (e.g. the subjects' own name) tended to be recognized even if presented on the non-shadowed channel. To accommodate such findings, Treisman (1964a, 1964b) developed a variation of filter theory in which the filter operates in a graded rather than an all-or-none fashion. In Treisman's *attenuation* theory, unattended messages are weakened rather than blocked from further analyses. Both selected and attenuated messages are transmitted to a recognition system with word recognition units. Because thresholds of recognition units for important words are lowered, these words tend to be recognized even if appearing in attenuated messages.

In the filter theories of Broadbent and Treisman, attentional selection occurs at an earlier stage of

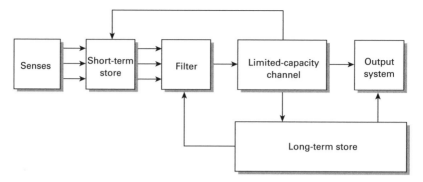

Figure 4.1   *Architecture of the filter model of Broadbent (1958). Arrows depict the flow
of information from the senses through short- and long-term memory stores towards the
output system. Multiple arrows represent parallel channels with high capacity for
information transmission. (Adapted from Perception and Communication (p. 299), by
D. E. Broadbent, 1958, Oxford: Pergamon Press. Copyright 1958 by D. E. Broadbent.)*

processing than stimulus recognition. Such theories
are called *early-selection* theories. In *late-selection*
theories, attentional selection occurs later in
processing than stimulus recognition. The first late-
selection theory was outlined by Deutsch and
Deutsch (1963), who proposed that attended and
unattended messages receive the same amount of
analysis by the recognition system. However, after
a stimulus has been recognized, the *importance* of
the stimulus is retrieved, and the stimulus with the
greatest importance is selected for further processing
including conscious awareness.

The general theories of Broadbent, Treisman, and
Deutsch and Deutsch set the stage for the development of more specific models of attention. Most of
these models were based on studies of performance
in simple visual tasks that afforded more rigorous
experimental control of temporal relations between
stimuli. Auditory studies remained an active field of
research (cf. Scharf, 1998), but became less central
in mainstream discussions.

Most studies of visual attention have concerned
our ability to *divide* attention between multiple
stimuli and our ability to *focus* attention on *targets*
(stimuli to be attended) rather than *distractors* (stimuli
to be ignored). The course of these processes over
short periods of time (fractions of a second) has
been at the center of inquiry. Our ability to
sustain attention over longer periods of time (*vigilance*) has aroused less theoretical interest (but see
Parasuraman, Warm, & See, 1998, for a discussion).

SIMPLE SERIAL MODELS OF VISUAL WHOLE REPORT AND SEARCH

A *serial* model of attention is a model in which only
one stimulus is attended at a time. A serial model is

said to be *simple* if the order in which stimuli are
attended is independent of whether they are targets
or distractors. Simple serial models have traditionally been very influential, the prime example being
the *feature integration theory* of Treisman and
Gelade (1980; see below).

Whole report

Whole report is a major experimental paradigm for
the study of divided attention. In classical visual
whole report experiments by Sperling (1960, 1963),
subjects were instructed to report as many letters as
possible from a briefly exposed array of unrelated
letters followed by a pattern mask. The number of
correctly reported letters (the score) depended on
the *stimulus-onset asynchrony* (SOA) between the
letter array and the mask. For each subject, there
seemed to be a minimal effective exposure duration, t_0, below which the score was zero (corrected
for guessing). As the SOA exceeded t_0, the mean
score initially increased at a high rate (about one
letter per 10–15 ms) and then leveled off as it
approached a value of about four letters or the
number of letters in the stimulus, whichever was
smaller. This last finding indicated a visual immediate memory span of about four items, a result
that has been generally replicated since (Vogel,
Woodman, & Luck, 2001; see also this chapter's sections
on FIRM and TVA: the *K* parameter, pp. 117 and 118).

Sperling (1963) proposed a simple serial model to
account for the initial, strong and approximately
linear increase in mean score as SOA exceeded t_0. By
this model the subject encodes one letter at a time,
requiring 10–15 ms for each. The serial encoding is
interrupted when the stimulus is terminated by the
mask or when the number of encoded letters reaches
the immediate memory span of the subject.

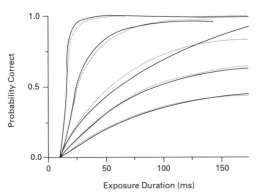

Figure 4.2   *Probability correct in whole report as a function of exposure duration for each display location in a horizontal array of five letters (Sperling, 1967). Observed data for one typical subject are represented by five solid curves. A theoretical fit by a parallel processing model is indicated by dotted curves. If display locations are numbered from left to right and observed curves or theoretical curves are numbered from top to bottom, curve 1 = location 1, curve 2 = location 2, curve 3 = location 3, curve 4 = location 5, and curve 5 = location 4. (From 'A theory of visual attention', by C. Bundesen, 1990, Psychological Review, 97, p. 531. Copyright by the American Psychological Association. Solid curves are from 'Successive approximations to a model for short-term memory', by G. Sperling, 1967, Acta Psychologica, 27, p. 289. Copyright 1967 by Elsevier.)*

The simple serial model for whole report behavior was later rejected by Sperling (1967). The rejection was based on the observation that, as exposure duration increases, all items in a display are reported with above chance accuracy before any one item can be reported with perfect accuracy. This effect is illustrated in Figure 4.2, which shows the accuracy of report for a typical subject. The score is plotted as a function of exposure duration for each location in a horizontal array of five letters terminated by a pattern mask. For this subject, the order of the successive locations that are reported correctly is generally left to right (1 to 5), except that location 5 is reported correctly at shorter exposures than location 4. The observation that all locations begin to be reported at better than chance levels even at the briefest exposures could be accommodated by a simple serial model, if the order of scanning varied from trial to trial (Sperling, 1967: footnote 1). However, Sperling preferred a parallel-processing interpretation.

Search

In a typical experiment on visual search, the subject must indicate 'as quickly as possible' whether a target is present in a display. The target either belongs to a predesignated category such as *red* or letter type T or must be determined by the subject from display to display as the 'odd one out'. The display contains either one or no occurrences of the target as well as a varying number of distractors. Positive (*present*) and negative (*absent*) reaction times are analyzed as functions of display size. Following Nickerson (1966) and Sternberg (1967), simple serial models have been used extensively in analyzing reaction times from visual search experiments. The method of analysis was spelled out by Sternberg (1966, 1969a, 1969b, 1998). The basics are as follows.

By a simple serial model, items are scanned one by one. As each item is scanned, it is classified as a target or as a distractor. A negative reaction is initiated if and when all items have been scanned and classified as distractors. Thus, the number of items processed before a negative reaction is initiated equals the display set size, N, whereas the rate of increase in mean negative reaction time as a function of N equals the mean time taken to process one item, Δt. In an *exhaustive* search process, a positive reaction is made if a target is found, but the reaction is not initiated until all display items have been processed. Therefore, the rate of increase in mean positive reaction time as a function of N also equals Δt. However, in a *self-terminating* search process, a positive reaction is initiated as soon as a target is found. As the order in which items are scanned is independent of their status as targets versus distractors, the mean number of items processed before a positive reaction is initiated equals $(1 + 2 + \cdots + N)/N = (1 + N)/2$, so the rate of increase in mean positive reaction time as a function of N equals $\Delta t/2$.

Feature and conjunction search

Treisman, Sykes, and Gelade (1977) introduced a widespread distinction between feature and conjunction search. In *feature search*, the target differs from the distractors by possessing a simple 'physical' feature (e.g. a particular color, size or curvature; see Wolfe, 1998a) not shared by any of the distractors. For example, the target can be a red X among distractors that are black X's. In such conditions, the target phenomenally may appear to pop out from the background of distractors without any need to scan the display by saccadic eye movements or shifts of attention. Behaviorally, search can be fast and little affected by display size (see Figure 4.3; but also see Bundesen, 1990: fig. 8).

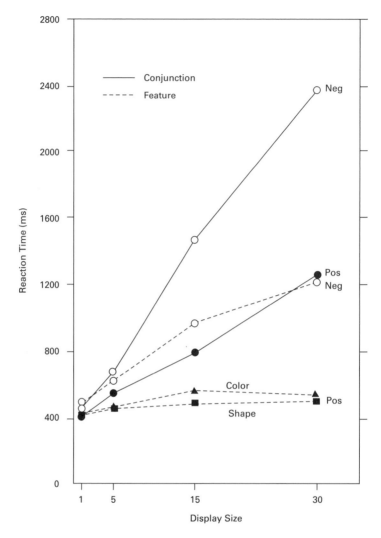

Figure 4.3   *Positive and negative mean reaction times in visual search as functions of display size in experiment 1 of Treisman and Gelade (1980). Solid lines are for conjunction search (for a green T among brown T's and green X's), dotted lines for feature search (for a blue letter or an S among brown T's and green X's). (From 'A feature-integration theory of attention', by A. M. Treisman and G. Gelade, 1980, Cognitive Psychology, 12, p. 104. Copyright 1980 by Academic Press.)*

In *conjunction search*, the target differs from the distractors by showing a predefined conjunction of physical features (e.g. both a particular color and a particular shape), but the target is not unique in any of the component features of the conjunction (i.e. in color or in shape). For example, the target can be a red X among black X's and red O's. In such conditions, the search process may be effortful and appear to consist in scrutinizing the display part by part or even item by item. Behaviorally, search times tend to be longer, and positive and negative mean reaction times tend to be approximately linear functions of display size with substantial slopes and positive-to-negative slope ratios of about 1:2 (see Figure 4.3). This response pattern is predicted by a simple self-terminating serial model.

Feature integration theory (FIT)

Treisman and her associates explained the relationship between feature and conjunction search by their feature integration theory of attention (FIT; Treisman & Gelade, 1980). According to FIT, simple stimulus features such as color, size and orientation are registered automatically, without attention, and in parallel across the visual field. The features are stored in separate *feature maps*, each of which is organized retinotopically (i.e. in such a way that features depicted side by side on the retina are represented in adjacent areas on the map; see, e.g., Zeki, 1993). Localizing a feature requires spatial attention, but merely determining whether a feature is present can be done preattentively. Thus, feature search can be done in parallel across the visual field.

The central hypothesis of FIT is that spatial attention is necessary for correct integration (*binding*) of individual features into whole object representations. This comes about when an attention *window* (or 'spotlight') moves within a *master map of locations* and selects from the feature maps whatever features are currently represented at the attended location. The selected features are conjoined to form an object, which in turn is compared to stored representations for recognition. After binding the features, the attention window moves to another location and initiates a new recognition process. This way attention proceeds serially from object to object, at a rate typically estimated at 40–60 ms per item. Thus, whereas feature search should be a fast, parallel process, conjunction search should be a relatively slow, serial process because conjunction search requires binding of features into objects.

Empirical support for FIT has come both from early studies of visual search (see Treisman, 1988) and from demonstrations of *illusory conjunctions*, in which features of one object are erroneously attributed to another (Robertson, Treisman, Friedmann-Hill, & Grabowecky, 1997; Treisman & Paterson, 1984; Treisman & Schmidt, 1982). In FIT, illusory conjunctions are explained by failures of focusing attention (Treisman, 1999; but also see Tsal, Meiran, & Lavie, 1994).

Problems with FIT

From findings of approximately linear reaction time functions of display size with positive-to-negative slope ratios of about 1:2, Treisman and her colleagues concluded that conjunction search is performed by scanning items one at a time. However, fairly similar predictions obtain if attention is shifted among small non-overlapping groups of items such that processing is parallel within groups, but serial between groups, and shifting is random with respect to the distinction between target and distractors. In this case, the total processing time should be approximately a linear function of the number of groups processed.

Furthermore, the mean number of groups processed should be approximately linearly related to display size for both positive and negative displays with a positive-to-negative slope ratio of 1:2. Pashler (1987) proposed this sort of explanation for conjunction search, whereas Treisman and Gormican (1988) proposed the same sort of explanation for feature search with low target–distractor discriminability.

Other findings have undermined the original formulation of FIT. Nakayama and Silverman (1986) and Wolfe, Cave, and Franzel (1989) found that, contrary to the predictions of FIT, some forms of conjunction search can be conducted very rapidly. Duncan and Humphreys (1989) reported that when similarity between stimuli was systematically varied, the slopes of the functions relating reaction time to display size showed no clear division between (fast, parallel) search for features and (slow, serial) search for conjunctions. Instead, for all search materials, difficulty increased with increased similarity of targets to distractors and with decreased similarity between distractors, producing a continuum of search efficiency. Likewise, in a large sample of experiments, Wolfe (1998b) found no indication of a bimodal distribution reflecting parallel versus serial search patterns. In light of such findings, FIT has been revised (Treisman & Sato, 1990) and is now more aptly characterized as a selective serial model (see the Guided Search Model section below, p. 115, for a related theory).

SIMPLE PARALLEL MODELS OF VISUAL WHOLE REPORT AND SEARCH

A *parallel* model of attention is a model in which several stimuli can be attended at the same time. If processing times for individual stimuli in a display are statistically independent (in the sense that they are mutually independent random variables), the model is called an *independent* parallel model. If the processing time distributions for the stimuli are independent of the size and constituency of the displays in which they are presented, the model is said to have *unlimited processing capacity* (cf. Bundesen, 1987; Townsend & Ashby, 1983). An independent parallel model with unlimited processing capacity is called a *simple* parallel model. The first simple parallel models of visual processing of multielement displays were the *independent channels models* developed by C. W. Eriksen and his colleagues (C. W. Eriksen, 1966; C. W. Eriksen & Lappin, 1965, 1967; C. W. Eriksen & Spencer, 1969). In these models display elements are processed in parallel at levels up to and including the level of stimulus recognition.

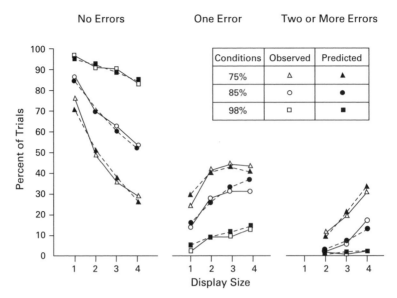

Figure 4.4   *Mean proportion of trials having 0, 1 and 2 or more errors as a function of display size and level of exposure duration in the whole-report experiment by Eriksen and Lappin (1967). Group data for 4 subjects. Exposure duration conditions were determined for each subject so as to yield about 75%, 85% and 98% correct reports, respectively, at a display size of 1. (From 'Independence in the perception of simultaneously presented forms at brief durations', by C. W. Eriksen and J. S. Lappin, 1967, Journal of Experimental Psychology, 73, p. 470. Copyright 1967 by the American Psychological Association.)*

Whole report

C. W. Eriksen and Lappin (1967) tested an independent channels model for whole report. Their stimulus displays contained 1, 2, 3 or 4 letters, which were randomly drawn from the set {A, O, U}. The letters appeared at one or more corners of an imaginary square centered on the fixation point. The probability of a particular letter occurring at a particular corner was independent of whatever other letters appeared in the display.

By the independent channels model, the probability of correct report of any given letter should be independent of display size as well as random variations in accuracy of report for other letters in the display. Thus, under a given set of viewing conditions, the number of correctly reported letters obtained with display size N should follow a binomial distribution for N Bernoulli trials with a certain probability p for success, where p is a constant independent of N (see, e.g., Ross, 2000). Equivalently, the number of errors should be binomially distributed with parameters N and $1 - p$.

Figure 4.4 shows a fit of the independent channels model to the proportion of trials having 0, 1 and 2 or more errors as a function of display size with level of exposure duration as the parameter. As

can be seen, the fit is very close for all display sizes and all three exposure-duration conditions.

Search

Simple parallel models have been used very widely to account for cases in which visual search is highly efficient (small effects of display size). As pointed out by Treisman and her associates (e.g. Treisman & Gelade, 1980), this includes cases of feature search with high target–distractor discriminability. In a theory proposed by Schneider and Shiffrin (1977) and Shiffrin and Schneider (1977), it also includes cases of search for more complex targets when subjects have been trained consistently in detecting those particular targets (also see Czerwinski, Lightfoot, & Shiffrin, 1992; Kyllingsbæk, Schneider, & Bundesen, 2001).

In the theory of Shiffrin and Schneider, slow, serial, *controlled search* for particular items can develop into fast, parallel, *automatic detection* of the same items. Automatic detection occurs without subject control and without stressing the capacity limitations of the system. The development of automatic detection presupposes that the mapping of stimuli to responses is *consistent* rather than *varied* over trials (for further discussion, see Pashler, 1998: chap. 8).

The processing of ignored information or 'the fate of the rejected stimuli' is an important question in attention research. It bears on major theoretical issues such as serial versus parallel processing and early versus late selection. For example, feature integration theory predicts that ignored items are analyzed only at the level of simple features. On the other hand, semantic processing of distractors is prima facie evidence for parallel models. Various experimental paradigms have been used to index the extent of processing of irrelevant stimulus information. Most of these methods provide measures of automatic interference from the irrelevant information.

Stroop and flanker interference

In a classical task developed by Stroop (1935), subjects are asked to name the color of the ink used to print a word. The *Stroop effect* denotes the fact that the task is more difficult when the word itself is the name of a different color (e.g. *red* printed in blue) than when the word does not refer to a color or refers to the color shown by the ink (*blue* printed in blue). The Stroop effect has been widely studied (for a review, see MacLeod, 1991) and is generally considered to result from conflict in late, response-related stages of processing. The Stroop task requires that the subject attends to a particular feature of an object (*featural attention*) while ignoring another feature of the same object, and the Stroop effect indicates semantic processing of the feature to be ignored. Other tasks have been devised to address the issue of mandatory processing of distracting *objects*.

In the *flankers task* of B. A. Eriksen and Eriksen (1974), subjects are asked to focus attention on a target presented in a known spatial location (*spatial attention*). Usually the target is a letter, and the subject is required to make a speeded binary classification (e.g. move a lever in one direction if the letter is a T or a K, but in the opposite direction if the letter is an S or a C). The target is flanked by letters that should be ignored. However, the task is more difficult when the flankers are *response-incompatible* with the target (S's or C's flanking a T) than when the flankers are *neutral* (e.g. X's flanking a T) or *response-compatible* with the target (T's or K's flanking a T). B. A. Eriksen and Eriksen tentatively concluded that the flankers are processed in parallel with the target up to and including the stage of letter recognition.

Flanker interference decreases in strength as the spatial distance of the flankers from the target is increased (B. A. Eriksen & Eriksen, 1974). The effect also decreases if the flankers appear in another color than the target, even when color is irrelevant to the task (Harms & Bundesen, 1983; also see Baylis & Driver, 1992; Kramer & Jacobson, 1991). Harms and Bundesen (1983) conjectured that the strength of flanker interference depends on the extent to which a flanker is perceptually grouped with the target (for further discussion, see Cave & Bichot, 1999).

Paquet and Lortie (1990) criticized the view that flanker interference is evidence of late selection. They found markedly reduced interference from distractors when subjects were given optimal conditions for focusing attention. These conditions were achieved by displaying a cue exactly at the target position at the start of each trial. The finding of Paquet and Lortie supports the possibility of early filtering. However, absence of flanker interference does not rule out semantic processing of distractor items. Evidence for such processing has been found by the method of negative priming (Driver & Tipper, 1989; Fox, 1995b).

Negative priming

Negative priming (NP) refers to the following phenomenon. When an object is ignored (in a *prime* trial), subsequent responses to that object (in *probe* trials) are generally slower and less accurate than responses to novel objects. In recent years NP has attracted considerable interest, in part because the effect has appeared to provide direct evidence of inhibitory mechanisms in attention.

Dalrymple-Alford and Budayr (1966) presented the first demonstration of NP, using a Stroop procedure. The effect was replicated in other experimental conditions by Tipper and Cranston (1985) and Tipper (1985). Upon discovering this generality, Tipper (1985) labeled the effect 'negative priming'. In the experiments of Tipper (1985) and Tipper and Cranston (1985), subjects were presented with outline drawings of pairs of overlapping objects: one target and one distractor. The target always appeared in a predesignated color. In the *attended repetition* condition of the experiments, the target object was the same in the probe as in the prime display. In the *ignored repetition* condition, the distractor object of the prime trial appeared as target in the probe display. In the control condition, stimulus repetitions did not occur. Response times were shortest in attended repetition, intermediate in the control condition, and longest in ignored repetition.

In the following years, NP was demonstrated in many different experimental designs (for reviews, see Fox, 1995a; May, Kane, & Hasher, 1995). The priming effect has been shown not only for identical objects, but also for objects similar in physical or even purely semantic properties. For semantic NP to occur, the ignored object must have received high-level processing in the prime trial.

Several accounts of the effect have been proposed. Tipper and Cranston's (1985) *selective inhibition* theory was motivated by findings that NP varies with the response demands of the probe display (Lowe, 1979; see also Moore, 1994). According to Tipper and Cranston, the prime display activates the representations of both the target and the distractor, but inhibits the distractor's translation into a response code. Subsequently, if the subject expects the probe display to demand a (difficult) selection among response alternatives, attentional alertness is maintained. This active *selection state* also maintains the otherwise fleeting inhibition. Thus, if the prime distractor appears as probe target, the response is delayed – NP. By contrast, if the probe task is not expected to require selection among alternatives (e.g. if single probes are consistently presented), the selection state is abandoned. In this case, the response inhibition decays, but the distractor's underlying representation remains active. The response to the same item in the probe display is therefore faster than responses to neutral items – a positive priming effect.

Neill, Valdes, Terry, and Gorfein (1992) suggested a different explanation for NP, shifting the emphasis from attention to memory. In their *episodic retrieval* account, the NP effect is generated on the probe trial: the presentation of a stimulus automatically results in retrieval of the last episode involving that stimulus (cf. Logan, 1988). The retrieval process activates the stimulus's attributes including response tags from the previous episode like 'ignore it'. Retrieval of such inhibitory response tags should generate the NP effect.

Faced with these rival accounts, some authors have favored a mixed account of NP in which some findings are explained in terms of attentional inhibition and others by memory mechanisms (Fox, 1995a; May et al., 1995; but see Milliken, Joordens, Merikle, & Seiffert, 1998, for an integration of memory and attentional explanations of NP). The empirical literature on NP is by now extensive and quite complex. The generality of the effect has been firmly established, but no theory explains all the findings. On the whole, the NP effect seems consistent with an inhibitory account (Tipper, 2001) without providing clear evidence of inhibitory mechanisms. In general, the role of inhibitory mechanisms in attention remains controversial (cf. Milliken & Tipper, 1998).

The *locus of selection*, early versus late, has been much debated in attention research. Lavie (1995) proposed a theory that accommodates findings from both flanker interference and negative priming experiments. She suggested that the extent to which distractors are processed depends on the perceptual load of the task. If perceptual load is low, distractors are processed automatically, giving rise to interference effects. This corresponds to late selection. If perceptual load is high, distractors receive little processing – early selection. In accordance with this principle, Lavie and Fox (2000) found the NP effect to decrease under conditions of high perceptual load. Thus the level of perceptual load seems to modulate effects of automatic interference.

Some researchers have argued that the question of early versus late selection is ill-posed (e.g. Allport, 1989, 1993). On the one hand, selectivity may be found at multiple levels of processing. For example, electrophysiological studies have provided strong evidence of attention effects at early stages of visual processing (see, e.g., Hillyard, Vogel, & Luck, 1999), and a large body of behavioral evidence points to selectivity at later stages. On the other hand, attentional selection and stimulus recognition may be two aspects of the same process rather than two different stages of processing. We consider this idea below in the section on TVA (p. 118).

FINDINGS ON ATTENTIONAL ORIENTING, SHIFTING AND DWELLING

The dynamics of deploying and redirecting attention is important for understanding the mechanisms of selection. For example, a typical serial model assumes that attention focuses on one object in the visual field at a time, moving about at a high speed. In contrast, a typical parallel model assumes a broad distribution of processing resources over the visual field, shifting slowly, but comprising many objects simultaneously. Orienting, shifting and dwelling of attention have been studied extensively. Central findings are presented in this section.

Set for spatial position

Classical work on spatial orienting of attention was done by C. W. Eriksen, Posner and their collaborators using a simple cuing paradigm. In this paradigm, the subject is presented with an attentional cue followed by a target that requires a speeded response. Usually, the target appears in a peripheral location, and the cue tells the subject where the target is likely to appear, but the subject must maintain fixation at a central fixation point. Thus attentional orienting is *covert* (decoupled from eye movements; cf. C. W. Eriksen & Hoffman, 1973; Posner, 1980).

Two types of attentional cues have been used: central and peripheral. *Central* cues appear at fixation and give symbolic information about the occurrence of the target. A good example is an arrow pointing at the likely location of the target, telling the subject to 'push' attention (*endogenously*, i.e. voluntarily) to the indicated location. *Peripheral* cues appear in the periphery of the visual field, 'pulling' attention (*exogenously*, i.e. automatically) to the location of the cue. As an example, the pull can be generated by a cue with an abrupt onset (cf. the Findings on Attentional Capture section p. 120 below).

In the version developed by Posner and his associates (e.g. Posner, Nissen, & Ogden, 1978; Posner, Snyder, & Davidson, 1980), the cuing paradigm provides measures of both attentional cost and attentional benefit. With central cuing, the *benefit* is measured by decrease in reaction time to a target following a *valid* cue (i.e. an informative cue that turns out to be true) compared to the reaction time to a target following a *neutral* (i.e. non-informative) cue. The *cost* is measured by increase in reaction time to a target following an *invalid* cue (an informative cue that turns out to be false) rather than a neutral cue.

Posner and Cohen (1984) reported that a non-informative peripheral cue followed by a target at the same location facilitates responses to the target if the cue–target interval (SOA) is short (e.g. 100 ms). Apparently, the cue produces an automatic orienting of attention that facilitates detection of targets in the cued area. However, if the cue–target interval is longer than a few hundred milliseconds (e.g. 300 or 500 ms), responses to the target are slower when the target appears in the cued area compared with uncued areas. Posner and Cohen proposed that in this case, attention is initially captured by the cue, but then shifted away from the cued area so that the initial facilitation is replaced by inhibition. The phenomenon is called *inhibition of return*. Posner and Cohen found the inhibition to persist for more than a second after cuing. Inhibition of return has been demonstrated in many different paradigms (see, e.g., Gibson & Egeth, 1994; Pratt & Abrams, 1999) and seems to be a pervasive phenomenon of attentional orienting. The phenomenon may reflect a 'novelty bias' ensuring that visual exploration proceeds efficiently without revisiting searched locations (Milliken & Tipper, 1998).

Spotlight and zoom lens models

Posner (1980) interpreted the findings on spatial orienting in terms of a spotlight model of attention. According to this view, attention is unitary, spatially delimited, and 'moves' about in visual space. The similarity to eye movements is not coincidental, as there are close functional links between the oculomotor system and visual attention (for an account of this complex relationship, see Hoffman, 1998). However, attention is not strictly dependent on eye movements, as witnessed by our ability to orient covertly.

C. W. Eriksen and Yeh (1985) and C. W. Eriksen and St James (1986) proposed an alternative, a zoom lens model of the visual attentional field. In this conception, the attentional field can vary in size from an area subtending less than 1° of visual angle to the size of the entire visual field. As total processing capacity is limited, the amount of processing capacity allocated to a given attended location declines as the size of the attentional field is increased. However, the attentional field cannot be split among non-contiguous locations (for a contrasting view, see Shaw, 1978). Direct tests of this assumption have been attempted, but the issue is still not settled (cf. C. W. Eriksen & Webb, 1989; for a review, see Cave & Bichot, 1999).

The spotlight and zoom lens models describe attention as an inherently *spatial* phenomenon. This conception has been very influential (cf., e.g., feature integration theory), but *object-based* theories of attention have also been proposed (Bundesen, 1990; Duncan, 1984; Kahneman, 1973). According to these theories, processing capacity is allocated to objects rather than the locations at which the objects appear. Space- and object-based accounts of attention have traditionally rivaled, but integrated accounts have recently been proposed (Humphreys, 1999; Logan, 1996).

Set for size and orientation

Attentional sets for size and orientation have also been described. For example, Larsen and Bundesen (1978; see also Cave & Kosslyn, 1989) presented subjects with a sequence of letters in various sizes such that following the presentation of a letter in a given size, the probability that the next letter appeared in the same size was high (80%). The time taken to classify a letter increased with divergence between the cued size (given by the size of the preceding letter) and the actual stimulus size. Specifically, when letters were not repeated, the increment in latency was approximately proportional to the logarithm of the ratio between the cued size and the actual size.

In a related experiment showing attentional set for orientation, Jolicoeur (1990) presented subjects with two letters in rapid succession. Each letter appeared at the center of the visual field in one of two possible orientations. The subjects' task was to name the two letters at the end of the trial. Naming responses to the second letter were more accurate when its orientation was the same as the orientation of the first letter than when it was different.

Attentional blink and dwell time

When two masked targets are presented sequentially with a separation of more than 500 ms, the presentation of the first target (T1) has little effect on the report of the second target (T2). But when T1

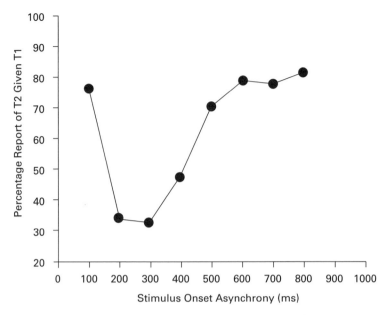

Figure 4.5   *Percentage report of the second target (T2) given report of the first target (T1) as a function of stimulus onset asynchrony in experiment 1 of Chun and Potter (1995). (Reprinted from 'A two-stage model for multiple target detection in rapid serial visual presentation', by M. M. Chun and M. C. Potter, 1995, Journal of Experimental Psychology: Human Perception and Performance, 21, p. 112. Copyright 1995 by the American Psychological Association.)*

and T2 are presented within approximately 500 ms of each other, and both targets are reported, report of T2 is impeded. This pattern of results has been labeled the *attentional blink*.

The attentional blink has been investigated by presenting subjects with a rapid sequence of stimuli (e.g. 6–20 items/s) at a fixed location (*rapid serial visual presentation*; RSVP). In an early demonstration of the phenomenon, Broadbent and Broadbent (1987) instructed subjects to report two target words embedded in an RSVP stream of words (see also Weichselgartner & Sperling, 1987). The targets were indicated by capital letters. Broadbent and Broadbent found a marked deficit in reporting both words when the temporal interval between them was less than about 400 ms. Subsequent research has established the precise time course of the effect (Chun & Potter, 1995; Shapiro, Raymond, & Arnell, 1994). The proportion of correct reports of T2 typically is a U-shaped function of the SOA between T1 and T2 (see Figure 4.5). Performance is lowest about 300 ms after onset of T1, whereas items within 100 ms of T1 onset are relatively spared.

Raymond, Shapiro, and Arnell (1992) showed that identification of T1 disturbed not only identification but also simple detection of fully prespecified T2 items. Furthermore, Raymond et al. found that T1 processing must be interrupted by another visual stimulus or the attentional blink will not occur. When the item

immediately following T1 was replaced by a blank interval, the attentional blink was substantially diminished. Finally, Raymond et al. established that detection of T2 was impaired only when a response to T1 was required. When the subject was instructed to ignore T1, T2 was readily detected, which made sensory masking an implausible explanation for the effect. Raymond et al. therefore coined the term *attentional* blink. Later studies have confirmed the non-sensory nature of the phenomenon (Shapiro, Driver, Ward, & Sorensen, 1997; Vogel, Luck, & Shapiro, 1998), although some masking effects have been reported (Brehaut, Enns, & DiLollo, 1999).

Chun and Potter (1995) proposed a *two-stage* model of the attentional blink. At the first stage, features of each RSVP item are detected in parallel. The attentional blink results from the limited capacity of the second, serial stage of processing. At this stage items detected at the first stage receive full semantic processing and are consolidated for report, but only one at a time. During the consolidation of a selected item, other items are still being detected at the parallel stage. However, representations generated at the parallel stage of processing are short-lived and vulnerable to interference from other items. Therefore, as long as T1 occupies the serial stage of processing, subsequent targets tend to be lost.

Shapiro et al. (1994) suggested an *interference* model. In this model, the attentional blink results from competition among several items for processing resources in visual short-term memory (VSTM). Initially items are compared to an attentional template (cf. Duncan & Humphreys, 1989) and good matches (i.e. targets) receive greater weight in the competition for conscious retrieval. T1 is a strong competitor, and until it can be transferred to a more durable memory store, it reduces available capacity for subsequent items including T2. This results in frequent intrusion errors, T2 being mixed up with distracting items. Like the two-stage model of Chun and Potter, the interference model assumes unlimited-capacity parallel preprocessing of all items followed by full processing in a limited-capacity system. However, the interference model assumes that the limited-capacity system works in parallel, so that several items undergo semantic processing at the same time. (See Isaak, Shapiro, & Martin, 1999, for empirical support for the interference model. See McLaughlin, Shore, & Klein, 2001, for modifications of both the interference and the two-stage models.)

The dynamics of attention can be described as a temporal series of distributions of processing resources across objects in space, linked by reallocations of processing resources from one distribution to the next one. The *attentional dwell time* is the time a particular distribution of processing resources is maintained. The attentional blink has been taken as evidence for a dwell time of several hundred milliseconds (Ward, Duncan, & Shapiro, 1996). Additional support for this estimate has been obtained from a simplified version of the RSVP task (Duncan, Ward, & Shapiro, 1994). Although it has been suggested that the dwell time estimated by Duncan et al. (1994) was inflated by masking effects (Moore, Egeth, Berglon, & Luck, 1996), the estimate seems consistent with electrophysiological results in the monkey (Chelazzi, Duncan, Miller, & Desimone, 1998; Chelazzi, Miller, Duncan, & Desimone, 1993). However, a dwell time of this order of magnitude is inconsistent with simple serial models of visual search, in which attention moves from object to object at a speed of a few dozen milliseconds per item. In the next section a more recent type of serial models is presented. Though still troublesome, the findings on attentional dwell time are more compatible with these models.

SELECTIVE SERIAL MODELS OF VISUAL SEARCH

In *selective* serial models, items in the stimulus display are attended one at a time, but the sequential order in which items are attended depends on their status as targets versus distractors. When a target and a distractor compete for attention, the target is more likely to win.

Two-stage model of Hoffman

The first selective serial model of visual search was proposed by Hoffman (1978, 1979). It was motivated by findings on the time taken to shift attention in response to a visual cue (e.g. Colegate, Hoffman, & Eriksen, 1973). These findings cast doubt on the notion that attention can be shifted from item to item at the high rates presumed in simple serial models.

In Hoffman's model, visual search is a two-stage process in which a parallel evaluation of the entire stimulus display guides a slow serial processor (cf. Neisser, 1967). The parallel evaluation is preattentive and quick, but prone to error. For each item in the display, the outcome is an overall measure of the similarity between this item and the prespecified targets. Items are transferred one by one to the second stage of processing. The serial transfer mechanism is slow (about one item per 100 ms), but it makes search efficient by transferring items in order of decreasing overall similarity to the prespecified targets. Thus, if there is a target in the display, the target is likely to be among the first items transferred to the second stage of processing.

Guided search model

Wolfe and his associates (Cave & Wolfe, 1990; Wolfe, 1994; Wolfe et al., 1989) developed a selective serial model called *guided search*. The model combines elements of the two-stage model of Hoffman with elements of the feature integration theory of Treisman and her associates. As in feature integration theory, simple stimulus features are registered automatically, without attention, and in parallel across the visual field. Registration of objects (items defined by conjunctions of features) requires a further stage of processing at which attention is directed serially to each object. As in Hoffman's model, the outcome of the first, parallel stage of processing guides the serial processing at the second stage. In Guided Search 2.0 (Wolfe, 1994), the guidance works as follows.

Initially the stimulus display is analyzed in parallel for a limited set of basic visual features. The results are represented in separate maps for each feature dimension such as color, size and orientation. For instance, the feature map for color contains the outputs from four broadly tuned 'categorical' channels: a red, a yellow, a green and a blue channel. Based on these feature maps, an array of activation values (attention values) is generated for each feature dimension. This array also forms a map of the visual field. Each activation value is a weighted sum of a bottom-up and a top-down component, with weights depending on current task demands. For a particular location within a map for a given feature dimension, the bottom-up component is a measure of differences between the value of the feature at that location and values of the same feature at neighboring loci. The top-down component for a feature dimension at a given location equals the output of a selected one of the broadly tuned categorical channels (e.g. 'red' for the color dimension, 'shallow' for orientation). The categorical channel is selected so that it differentiates the target from the distractors as well as possible. After activations have been calculated in separate maps for each feature dimension, they are summed across feature dimensions to produce a single overall activation map (cf. the *saliency map* of Koch & Ullman, 1985; see also Itti, Koch, & Niebur, 1999). In simulations, a certain level of Gaussian noise is also added at each location. The final overall activation values represent the evaluation given by the parallel stage of how likely the stimulus at each location is to be a target.

Whereas the parallel stage suggests probable targets, the serial stage classifies each item it processes as a target or as a distractor. Items are processed one by one in order of decreasing activation in the overall activation map. Rejection of an item lowers its activation value to ensure that the item is not rechecked. The serial processing stops when a target is found or when all items with activations above a certain value have been processed. In the computer simulation of Wolfe (1994), items are processed at a rate of 50 ms per item with a standard deviation of 25 ms.

The guided search model accounts for many findings from experiments on visual search. It was motivated, in particular, by demonstrations of fast conjunction search. Some demonstrations of fast conjunction search (e.g. Nakayama & Silverman, 1986) are accommodated by assuming that for some feature dimensions, top-down control is very effective. Other demonstrations (e.g. Wolfe et al., 1989) are accommodated by assuming that in some subjects, the level of Gaussian noise is very low. Further applications are found in Wolfe (1994, 1998a).

Problems with guided search

Selective serial models resolve the conflict between data suggesting that attention shifting is slow and data showing only slight effects of display size in visual search (e.g. 10 ms per item; Sperling, Budiansky, Spivak, & Johnson, 1971) by assuming that the serial processing is limited to targets and target-like items. However, a closely related problem for serial models has not been resolved: the conflict between data suggesting that attention shifting is slow and data suggesting processing rates of up to one item per 10–15 ms in whole report (e.g. Sperling, 1963); that is, in a task in which all items are targets.

The guided search model also has problems in accounting for search slopes. Wolfe (1994) and his associates examined 708 sets of positive (target

present) and negative (target absent) search slopes from subjects tested on many different search tasks. Among these 708 sets, 167 had positive slopes greater than 20 ms per item. This subset showed a (harmonic) mean positive-to-negative slope ratio of 0.50. Another 187 had positive slopes less than 5 ms per item. For this subset, the (harmonic) mean positive-to-negative slope ratio was nearly the same (0.53). The guided search model has difficulty explaining these findings. The model predicts a 1:2 slope ratio in the limiting case in which activations caused by targets and distractors are identically distributed so that search is random ('blind' with respect to the distinction between target and distractors). However, when target activations are stronger than distractor activations, targets should be more likely to be among the first items scanned. Thus, when search becomes guided, both the positive search slope and the positive-to-negative slope ratio might be expected to decrease. The results of Wolfe's (1994) study of 708 sets of search slopes went counter to this expectation. To accommodate the results, Wolfe (1994) assumed that as signal strength increases, the mean of the distribution of target activations increases, while the standard deviation decreases. However, this assumption seems implausible and in conflict with Weber's Law (cf. Bundesen, 1998a).

Horowitz and Wolfe (1998) presented evidence against a basic assumption in guided search: that items already searched are marked to prevent rescanning. Subjects searched for a rotated T among rotated L's, which yielded a search slope of 20–30 ms per item with normal, 'static' displays. In the critical condition, all letters in a display were relocated at random every 111 ms. This manipulation should make it impossible for subjects to keep track of the progress of search. Nevertheless, search slopes were unaffected. This finding goes against serial models that assume display items are sampled one by one without replacement. The finding also contradicts parallel models that assume that information about the identity of display items is gradually accumulated over time. As noted by Horowitz and Wolfe, the result is consistent with a 'memoryless' serial model in which items are sampled with replacement so that the same item may be sampled again and again. The result also agrees with a parallel model in which processing times of display items are exponentially distributed. The exponential distribution is the only distribution endowed with complete lack of memory (i.e. a constant hazard function; see Feller, 1968: 459, for a proof).

LIMITED-CAPACITY PARALLEL MODELS
OF VISUAL SEARCH

Corresponding to the development of simple serial models into selective serial models, there has been a development from simple parallel models to limited-capacity parallel models and race-based models of selection. The latter models account for a wider range of experimental findings. For example, the linear relations between mean reaction time and display size predicted by simple serial models cannot be explained by simple parallel models (see Townsend & Ashby, 1983: 92, for a proof; for a contrasting view, see Palmer, 1995; Palmer, Verghese, & Pavel, 2000). However, the linear relations can be explained by independent parallel models with limited processing capacity (Atkinson, Holmgren, & Juola, 1969; Townsend, 1969).

As an example, consider a display of N items that are processed in parallel. Let $v_i(t)$ be the amount of processing capacity devoted to item i at time t. Mathematically, $v_i(t)$ is defined as the hazard function for the processing time of item i (i.e. $v_i(t)$ is the conditional probability density that item i completes processing at time t, given that item i has not completed processing before time t). Let the total processing capacity spread across items in the display be a constant C; that is,

$$\sum_{i=1,N} v_i(t) = v_1(t) + v_2(t) + \cdots + v_N(t) = C \quad (4.1)$$

Then the time until the first item completes processing is exponentially distributed with rate parameter C. (In general, the minimum of n independent, exponentially distributed variables is itself exponentially distributed with a rate parameter equal to the sum of the rate parameters of the n variables.) Suppose that when the first completion occurs, the processing capacity is redistributed among the remaining $N-1$ items. Then the time from the first to the second completion is exponentially distributed with the same rate parameter C. If the process repeats until all N items have been completed, then the mean time taken to complete processing of the N items increases linearly with display size N.

Shaw (1978; Shaw & Shaw, 1977) proposed an *optimal capacity-allocation model*, which extended the limited-capacity model of Atkinson et al. (1969) and Townsend (1969) to situations in which the likelihood that a target occurs at a given location varies across display locations. An *allocation policy* (cf. Kahneman, 1973) is a way of allocating and reallocating the total processing capacity C across display locations. For any distribution of the probability of target occurrence across the display locations, there is an optimal allocation policy: an allocation policy that, for any time t, maximizes the probability that the target has been recognized by time t (cf. Shaw, 1978; also see Townsend & Ashby, 1983: 139–145). After considerable experience with a given probability distribution, the subject is assumed to adopt the optimal allocation policy.

Shaw (1978) fitted the optimal capacity-allocation model to differences in mean reaction time between high- and low-probability locations in a detection task. The model provided reasonable fits, but the empirical support was not overwhelming. However, the principle of optimization seems important (cf. Sperling, 1984), and goodness of fit might be improved by including time costs of reallocations of processing capacity (shifts of attention; cf. Bundesen, 1990: 537).

RACE MODELS OF SELECTION

In *race models of selection* from multielement displays, display items are processed in parallel, and attentional selection is made of those items that first finish processing (the winners of the race). Thus selection of targets rather than distractors is based on processing of targets being faster than processing of distractors (Bundesen, 1987, 1993b; Bundesen, Shibuya, & Larsen, 1985).

FIRM

Shibuya and Bundesen (1988) proposed a fixed-capacity independent race model, FIRM. The model describes the processing of a stimulus display as follows. First an *attentional weight* is computed for each item in the display. The weight is a measure of the strength of the sensory evidence that the item is a target. Then the available processing capacity (a total amount of C items/s) is distributed across the items in proportion to their weights. The amount of processing capacity that is allocated to an item determines how fast the item can be encoded into visual short-term memory (VSTM). Finally the encoding race between the items takes place. The time taken to encode an item is assumed to be exponentially distributed with a rate parameter equal to the amount of processing capacity that is allocated to the item. The items that are selected (i.e. stored in VSTM) are those items whose encoding processes complete before the stimulus presentation terminates and before VSTM has been filled up.

Detailed tests of FIRM have been made in *partial report* experiments, in which subjects report as many targets as possible from a briefly exposed display showing a mixture of targets and distractors. Shibuya and Bundesen (1988) investigated partial report performance as a function of exposure duration by using stimulus displays terminated by pattern masks. Each display was a circular array of letters and digits, centered on fixation, and the task was to report the digits. Exposure duration ranged from 10 to 200 ms. Figure 4.6 shows a fit of FIRM to data for an individual subject. As can be seen, the model predicted the entire probability distribution of the score (the number

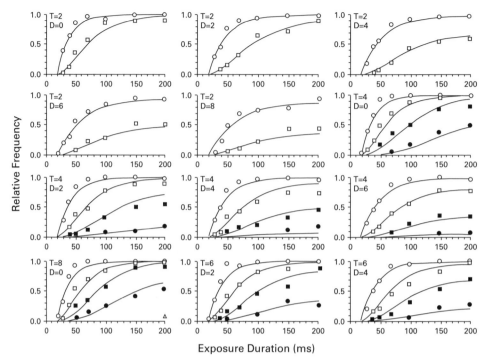

Figure 4.6   *Relative frequency of scores of j or more (correctly reported targets) as a function of exposure duration with j, number of targets T, and number of distractors D as parameters in the partial report experiment of Shibuya and Bundesen (1988). Data are shown for subject MP. Parameter j varies within panels; j is 1 (open circles), 2 (open squares), 3 (solid squares), 4 (solid circles) or 5 (triangle). T and D vary among panels. Smooth curves represent a theoretical fit to the data by the FIRM model. For clarity, observed frequencies less than 0.02 were omitted from the figure. (Adapted from 'Visual selection from multielement displays: measuring and modeling effects of exposure duration', by H. Shibuya and C. Bundesen, 1988, Journal of Experimental Psychology: Human Perception and Performance, 14, p. 595. Copyright 1988 by the American Psychological Association.)*

of correctly reported targets) as a function of both the exposure duration and the numbers of targets and distractors in the display. This complex distribution was modeled using only four parameters: C (processing capacity), α (ratio of the attentional weight of a distractor to the attentional weight of a target), K (short-term storage capacity), and t_0 (minimum effective exposure duration). The fit was obtained with parameter C at 49 items/s, α at 0.4, K at 3.7 items, and t_0 at 19 ms. (See Shibuya, 1991, for comparison of the fit provided by FIRM with fits by other serial and parallel models. Also see Shibuya, 1993, for further elaboration and testing of FIRM.)

THEORY OF VISUAL ATTENTION (TVA)

Bundesen (1990) attempted to integrate findings on single-stimulus recognition, whole report, partial report, detection and search in a general Theory of Visual Attention (TVA). In TVA, both visual recognition and attentional selection of objects in the

visual field consist in making *visual categorizations*. A visual categorization has the form 'object x has feature i' or, equivalently, 'object x belongs to category i', where x is an object in the visual field, feature i is a visual feature, and category i is the class of all objects that have feature i. The categorization is *made* if and when it is encoded into VSTM. When this occurs, object x is said to be selected and object x is also said to be recognized as a member of category i. Thus, attentional selection is neither early (i.e. occurring before stimulus recognition) nor late (after recognition). Attentional selection and initial stimulus recognition occur at the same time (*simultaneous selection*, Logan, 2002; also see Bundesen & Harms, 1999).

When a visual categorization completes processing, the categorization enters VSTM if memory space is available there. The storage capacity of VSTM is limited to K different objects, but not to any particular number of features. In normal human subjects, K is about 4 (cf. Luck and Vogel, 1997; see also Klaver, Smid, & Heinze, 1999; Vogel et al., 2001).

When a subject prepares for sampling information from a new stimulus field, VSTM is assumed to be cleared so that memory space is available for encoding K new objects from the stimulus field. The objects that become encoded into VSTM are those objects that first complete processing with respect to some categorization. Thus the process of attentional selection is conceived as a parallel processing race among visual categorizations. The time course of the race is stochastically modelled in TVA.

Equations

Let processing of a stimulus display begin at time 0, and consider the event that a particular visual categorization, 'x belongs to i', completes processing at time t. The hazard function of this event is denoted $v(x, i)$. A v value can be thought of as the 'speed' of a particular visual categorization in the race for selection. It is assumed that

$$v(x, i) = \eta(x, i)\, \beta_i w_x / \sum\nolimits_{z \in S} w_z \qquad (4.2)$$

where $\eta(x, i)$ is the strength of the sensory evidence that supports the categorization that object x belongs to category i, β_i is the subject's bias for assigning objects to category i, S is the set of all objects in the visual field, and w_x and w_z are attentional weights of objects x and z, respectively.

Attentional weights are derived from *pertinence* values. The pertinence of a visual category is a measure of the current importance (priority) of attending to objects that belong to the category. The attentional weight of an object x in the visual field is given by

$$w_x = \sum\nolimits_{j \in R} \eta(x, j)\pi_j \qquad (4.3)$$

where R is the set of all visual categories, $\eta(x, j)$ is the strength of the sensory evidence that object x belongs to category j, and π_j is the pertinence value of category j.

In most applications of the theory to analysis of experimental data, v values are assumed to be constant during the presentation of a stimulus display. When v values (hazard functions) are constant, processing times are exponentially distributed with the v values as rate parameters.

Mechanisms

Equations (4.2) and (4.3) describe two mechanisms of selection: a mechanism for selection of objects (*filtering*) and a mechanism for selection of categories (*pigeonholing*; cf. Broadbent, 1970). The filtering mechanism is represented by pertinence values and attentional weights. As an example, if selection of red objects is wanted, the pertinence of *red* should be high. Equation (4.3) implies that when *red* has a high pertinence, red objects get high attentional weights. Accordingly, by equation (4.2), processing of red objects is fast, so (categorizations of) red objects are likely to win the processing race and be encoded into VSTM.

The pigeonholing mechanism is represented by perceptual bias parameters. Whereas pertinence values determine *which* objects are selected (e.g. red objects), perceptual bias parameters determine *how* objects are categorized (e.g. with respect to alphanumeric identity). If particular types of categorizations are desired, bias parameters of the relevant categories should be high. By equation (4.2), then, the desired types of categorizations are likely to win the race for selection.

Filtering and pigeonholing are complementary mechanisms of selection that can be controlled independently. This dual setting allows the attentional system to perform complex tasks such as noting the shapes of the red objects in a search display. A neural interpretation of filtering and pigeonholing is described below in the section on Neural TVA (p. 123).

Applications

TVA has been applied to findings from a broad range of paradigms concerned with single-stimulus recognition and selection from multielement displays in normal subjects (see Bundesen, 1990, 1991, 1993a, 1998a) and brain-damaged patients (Bundesen, 1998b; Duncan, Bundesen, Olson, Humphreys, Chavda, & Shibuya, 1999; Habekost & Bundesen, 2003) (also see critical discussions by Enns, DiLollo, & Rensink, 2000; van der Heijden, 1993, 2004; van der Velde & van der Heijden, 1993). For single-stimulus recognition, the theory provides a derivation of a successful model of effects of visual discriminability and bias: the biased-choice model of Luce (1963). For selection from multielement displays, the fixed-capacity independent race model (FIRM; Shibuya & Bundesen, 1988) can be derived as a special case of TVA. Independent channels behavior like that observed by C. W. Eriksen and Lappin (1967; cf. Figure 4.4) should be found only in conditions in which a fixed set of information sources is monitored for appearance of targets so that attention is allocated to the information sources before the targets are presented. Serial processing should be found when the time cost of shifting attention is outweighed by gain in speed of processing once attention has been shifted (Bundesen, 1990: 536–537). Typical data on slow feature and conjunction search are explained by attention shifting among groups of display items such that processing is parallel within groups but serial between groups.

Extensions

Logan (1996) combined TVA with a theory of perceptual grouping by proximity (the CODE theory; van Oeffelen & Vos, 1982, 1983). The resulting theory, CTVA, explains effects of perceptual grouping and spatial distance between items in multielement displays (also see Logan & Bundesen, 1996). More recently, Logan and Gordon (2001) have extended CTVA into a theory of executive control of visual attention in dual-task situations (ECTVA), and Logan (2002) has proposed an Instance Theory of Attention and Memory (ITAM), which combines ECTVA with theories of categorization (Nosofsky, 1986; Nosofsky & Palmeri, 1997) and automaticity (Logan, 1988). Such developments may be important steps towards a unified account of visual cognition.

FINDINGS ON ATTENTIONAL CAPTURE

Experimental research on attentional capture has blossomed during the past 15 years (for reviews, see Theeuwes, 1996; Yantis, 1996, 1998). Most studies have concerned the propensity of salient, preattentively processed feature discontinuities or abrupt onsets to attract attention. Theeuwes (1992, 1994, 1995) provided evidence that when the target of search is a featural *singleton* (e.g. a single red item among black ones), attention will be captured by the most salient singleton in the display, regardless of whether this singleton is relevant to the subject's task. Bacon and Egeth (1994) argued that when subjects are looking for a featural singleton in a given dimension, they adopt a strategy (*singleton-detection mode*) of directing attention to the locations with the highest feature contrast, regardless of the dimension in which the contrast is found. Thus attention should be guided by the output of a general feature-contrast detector.

Yantis has argued that when the subject's task does not require a deliberate attentional set for a featural singleton, then an abrupt-onset visual stimulus will capture attention (Jonides, 1981; Jonides & Yantis, 1988; Remington, Johnston, & Yantis, 1992; Yantis & Hillstrom, 1994; Yantis & Jonides, 1984), but other types of stimuli will not (Hillstrom & Yantis, 1994; Jonides & Yantis, 1988). However, even capture by abrupt onsets seems not completely automatic. Yantis and Jonides (1990) reported that when subjects had focused attention on a spatial location, then no stimuli appearing elsewhere captured attention. Folk, Remington, and Johnston (1992) and Folk, Remington, and Wright (1994) argued that all cases of attentional capture are contingent on *attentional control settings*: abrupt-onset stimuli may capture attention when subjects are looking for abrupt-onset targets, but not when

looking for color targets, and vice versa (for further discussion, see Folk, Remington, & Johnston, 1993; Yantis, 1993; but also see Theeuwes, 1994).

As noted by Folk et al. (1992: 1042), the attentional mechanisms of TVA may be used for setting attentional controls for salient features and abrupt onsets. For example, if a general feature-contrast detector is available, attention can be guided by the output (η values) of the general feature-contrast detector by letting the perceptual priority (π value) of feature contrast be high and letting perceptual priorities of other properties be low. When TVA is configured in this mode (singleton-detection mode), the attentional weight of an item primarily depends on the feature contrast of the item. Similarly, if separate detectors are available for static versus dynamic discontinuities (cf. Folk et al., 1992, 1994), then attention can be guided by the output (η values) of the detector for static discontinuities (e.g. color and shape singletons) by letting the perceptual priority (π value) of static discontinuity be high, and attention can be guided by the output (η values) of the detector for dynamic discontinuities (e.g. onset and motion singletons) by letting the perceptual priority (π value) of dynamic discontinuity be high.

CONNECTIONIST MODELS

Formal theories like TVA are highly abstract. Connectionist models are attempts to theorize at a level that is closer to neurobiology (cf. Lamberts, Chapter 18, this volume; McClelland & Rumelhart, 1986; Rumelhart & McClelland, 1986). In connectionist models, information processing consists in a flow of activation through a network of neuron-like units, which are linked together by facilitatory and inhibitory connections. Important examples of connectionist models of visual attention are the selective attention model (SLAM) of Phaf, van der Heijden, and Hudson (1990; see also van der Heijden, 1992, 2004), the multiple object recognition and attentional selection (MORSEL) model of Mozer (1991), the search via recursive rejection (SERR) model of Humphreys and Müller (1993), and the selective attention for identification model (SAIM) of Heinke and Humphreys (2003). Deco and Zihl's (2001) *neurodynamical* model of visual search is related to these models. It will be presented in some detail to illustrate the connectionist approach.

Neurodynamical model

In the model of Deco and Zihl (2001), the elementary units are *populations* of neurons. The mean firing activity of each population is governed by a set of differential equations (cf. Usher & Niebur, 1996).

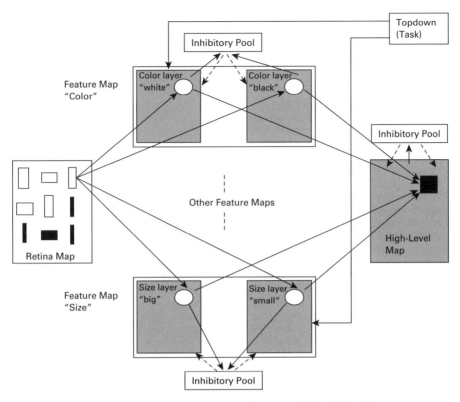

Figure 4.7 *Architecture of the neurodynamical model of Deco and Zihl (2001). Solid arrows represent excitatory connections between modules, dotted arrows represent inhibitory connections. (From 'Top-down selective visual attention: a neurodynamical approach', by G. Deco and J. Zihl, 2001, Visual Cognition, 8, p. 123. Copyright 2001 by Psychology Press.)*

The architecture of the model is as follows (see Figure 4.7). Input to the system is represented in a *retina map*. The retina map has excitatory connections to a set of *feature maps* (representing color, size, etc.), with separate layers for each value of the feature (e.g. white, big). The feature maps are organized retinotopically, and in every position of each layer the neuron population receives excitatory input from the corresponding position in the retina map. In this distributed way, activity in the feature maps encode values of features at specific locations on the retina. To each feature map a pool of inhibitory neurons is attached. Each layer of the feature map sends excitatory connections to this pool, which indirectly inhibits activity in other layers of the feature map. In this way, feature values compete for activation in a winner-take-all fashion. Conjunctions of features are represented in a *high-level map*. The high-level map is also retinotopic, and a unit representing a conjunction at a certain location in the map receives excitatory inputs from representations of the components of the conjunction at corresponding locations in feature maps. Like the feature maps, the high-level map is connected to a pool of inhibitory neurons, producing competition among conjunctions at different

locations. A *top-down module* provides memory information about the feature values of the target item (cf. Duncan & Humphreys, 1989). This information is transmitted by excitatory inputs to the relevant feature layers. For example, if the target is 'small' and 'white', all activations in these layers of the feature maps are enhanced.

Consider the model in function. In a visual search task the system is given sensory input and a specification of target attributes. The parallel competition mechanisms in the feature and conjunction maps eventually yield convergence of activity levels throughout the system: Only the neuron populations receiving both bottom-up and top-down excitatory inputs (i.e. units with sensory inputs matching the target features) will be able to develop and sustain high activity levels. This convergence of activity corresponds to focusing of attention at the target object. The variable of interest is the *latency* of the system; that is, how long time convergence takes to develop in a given search task. In simulations of human performance this corresponds to reaction time. Deco and Zihl demonstrated that the performance of the system is qualitatively similar to human performance in various feature and conjunction search tasks. Specifically, the 'serial' search pattern in conjunction search, with linear reaction time functions of display size, emerges from the parallel dynamics of the system without assuming an explicit saliency map or a serial scanning mechanism (cf. Wolfe, 1994).

NEUROPHYSIOLOGICAL FINDINGS AND MODELS

The study of attention is increasingly being influenced by findings and models of neuroscience. The neurological aspect of attention has been investigated by a wide range of methods including patient and brain imaging studies (for overviews, see Humphreys, Duncan, & Treisman, 1999; Parasuraman, 1998; also see Chapter 15, this volume, by Humphreys and Riddoch, pp. 341–364). In this section the emphasis is on single-cell studies, which seem particularly pertinent to the issues covered in the present chapter.

The *classical receptive fields* (RFs) of individual neurons (i.e. those parts of the visual field in which the neurons are responsive to stimuli) increase greatly in size along the pathways from low- to high-level visual areas in the brain. Whereas RFs in primary visual cortex typically subtend less than one degree by one degree of visual angle, neurons in inferior temporal cortex (IT) can be driven by stimuli from most of the visual field. To protect these high-level neurons from overload by concurrent stimuli, some sort of selective mechanism seems necessary.

In a classical study, Moran and Desimone (1985) used single-cell recordings to demonstrate attentional filtering of visual stimuli. In brain areas V4 and IT of macaque monkeys, Moran and Desimone observed what seemed to be a functional contraction of a neuron's RF around an attended stimulus. When both a target and a distractor were located within the recorded neuron's RF, the firing rate was nearly the same as when the target was presented alone. The distractor seemed to be 'filtered out'. In an influential series of experiments in the 1990s, Desimone and colleagues further investigated the neurophysiological correlates of attention (Chelazzi et al., 1993, 1998; Luck, Chelazzi, Hillyard, & Desimone, 1997), eventually replacing the notion of absolute filtering with a weighting-based model (Reynolds, Chelazzi, & Desimone, 1999).

Biased competition model

In an attempt to integrate this line of work with findings from other areas of cognitive neuroscience, Desimone and Duncan (1995) proposed a biased competition model of attention (see also Desimone, 1999; Duncan, 1996, 1999). In this account, multiple objects in the visual field initially activate many brain systems in parallel. The activations are competitive: throughout the visually responsive brain areas, activations representing features of the same object reinforce each other, while activations representing different objects are mutually suppressive. Eventually the brain tends to reach a relatively stable state in which activations of the same object dominate throughout (cf. Deco & Zihl, 2001; Phaf et al., 1990), making its different features available together for consciousness and control of behavior.

In the model of Desimone and Duncan, attentional selection is an emergent effect of competition between neural representations in multiple brain systems. Consistent with psychophysical findings on attentional dwell times, resolution of the competition is assumed to take hundreds of milliseconds. The competition is *biased* so that objects with particular features are more likely to win. Top-down priming of target-selective neurons gives a competitive advantage to currently relevant objects (cf. Chelazzi et al., 1998). Bottom-up mechanisms also influence the probability of selecting a certain object (cf. attentional capture). Unlike spotlight and zoom lens models, space is only one of many dimensions of selection, and biasing works on numerous attributes including color, shape and complex conjunctions of features.

The biased competition model has been criticized for underestimating the *binding problem*. Recall that in feature integration theory, focused attention is necessary for correct binding of features into objects. Treisman (1999) pointed out that in order for features of the same object to cooperate in a (biased) competition against other objects, the features must be bound in advance (i.e. preattentively). Duncan and Desimone attempted to explain the binding by preattentive grouping processes (cf. Grossberg, Mingolla, & Ross, 1994) and pointed out that many neurons respond to complex conjunctions of features (e.g. faces) irrespective of attention. Still, more work on binding seems needed.

Woodman and Luck (1999) criticized the notion of extended attentional dwell times on neurophysiological grounds. They performed EEG recordings under a visual search task. In one condition, subjects searched for a C in a particular orientation among a large number of C's in other orientations. In each display, one of the C's was red, another was green, and the red and the green C appeared in different hemifields (left vs. right). Subjects were informed that if a target was present in a display, it was three times more likely to be the red C than the green one. The results showed that on target-absent trials, the so-called 'N2pc' component of the event-related potential appeared first in the hemisphere contralateral to the red C and about 100 ms later in the hemisphere contralateral to the green C. Provided that the N2pc component reflects allocation of attentional resources (rather than, e.g., encoding into VSTM), the results suggest that attention can be reallocated at a rate of at least 10 times per second during visual search.

Neural TVA

Bundesen (2002) proposed a neural interpretation of TVA. In TVA, categorizations of the form 'object *x* has feature *i*' compete for entrance into visual short-term memory (VSTM), each with an exponential rate parameter of $v(x, i)$ (see equation (4.2)). In neural TVA, $v(x, i)$ is interpreted as the expected value of the *total rate of firing* of the population of neurons that represent the categorization 'object *x* has feature *i*' at the level of processing where objects compete for entrance into VSTM. At this level in the visual system, it is assumed that the classical RFs of neurons are so large that each RF covers the entire visual field. However, the *effective* RF of each neuron is thought to contract so that the neuron represents the properties of only one of the objects in the visual field (cf. Moran & Desimone, 1985). The probability that a given neuron selects object *x* is determined by the attentional weight of the object, w_x. Thus the expected number of neurons with RFs contracted around object *x* equals $w_x / \sum_{z \in S} w_z$ of all the neurons at this stage of processing (cf. equation (4.2)). In this way, *dynamic remapping* of RFs accounts for the filtering mechanism, which determines *which* objects are likely to be selected for VSTM entrance.

Pigeonholing, which determines *how* objects are categorized, is implemented by a different neural mechanism. Whereas filtering changes the number of neurons in which an object *x* is represented, pigeonholing changes the way in which the object is represented in each of those neurons that are allocated to the object. Specifically, pigeonholing is assumed to be done by a *feature-based* mechanism of attention, which scales the rates of firing in feature-*i* selective neurons by multiplication with a certain factor, β_i (cf. equation (4.2)). Suggestive evidence for a feature-based mechanism of attention that selects groups of neurons with similar stimulus preferences for a multiplicative change in response strength was recently provided by Treue and Trujillo (1999; also see McAdams & Maunsell, 1999a, 1999b). Neural TVA needs further development, but attention research seems to have reached a point at which integration of quantitative psychological and neurophysiological models has become feasible.

CONCLUSION

Modern research on attention sprung from the theoretical framework developed by Broadbent and other pioneers. Since the early work most research has concerned visual attention. Fundamental issues continue to arouse debate, most prominently the question of serial versus parallel processing. Although no consensus has been reached, progress is evident. Many empirical findings have emerged, and some convergence between theories is discernible. For example, contemporary parallel models allow for serial processing by reallocation of attentional resources, whereas serial models include an important component of (preattentive) parallel processing.

Two developments seem particularly promising for the future. The involvement of neuroscience has come to stay, and can be expected to shed further light on the basic issues in the study of attention. A second prospect for research concerns the theoretical wedding of attention to related functions such as memory, object recognition and executive control. General quantitative models have been proposed in several of these research areas, and attempts at theoretical integration should prove rewarding.

ACKNOWLEDGMENTS

The preparation of this chapter was supported by grants to Thomas Habekost from Aase og Ejnar Danielsens Fond, Fonden for Neurologisk Forskning, HjerneSagen, Ivan Nielsens Fond, and Lundbeckfonden. The Center for Visual Cognition is supported by the Danish Research Council for the Humanities.

REFERENCES

Allport, A. (1989). Visual attention. In M. I. Posner (ed.), *Foundations of cognitive science* (pp. 631–682). Cambridge, MA: MIT Press.

Allport, A. (1993). Attention and control: have we been asking the wrong questions? A critical review of twenty-five years. In D. E. Meyer & S. Kornblum (Eds.), *Attention and performance XIV: Synergies in experimental psychology, artificial intelligence, and cognitive neuroscience* (pp. 183–218). Cambridge, MA: MIT Press.

Atkinson, R. C., Holmgren, J. E., & Juola, J. F. (1969). Processing time as influenced by the number of elements in a visual display. *Perception and Psychophysics, 6,* 321–326.

Bacon, W. F., & Egeth, H. E. (1994). Overriding stimulus-driven attentional capture. *Perception and Psychophysics, 55,* 485–496.

Baylis, G. C., & Driver, J. (1992). Visual parsing and response competition: the effect of grouping factors. *Perception and Psychophysics, 51,* 145–162.

Brehaut, J. C., Enns, J. T., & DiLollo, V. (1999). Visual masking plays two roles in the attentional blink. *Perception and Psychophysics, 61,* 1436–1448.

Broadbent, D. E. (1958). *Perception and communication.* Oxford: Pergamon Press.

Broadbent, D. E. (1970). Stimulus set and response set: two kinds of selective attention. In D. I. Mostofsky (ed.), *Attention: contemporary theory and analysis* (pp. 51–60). New York: Appleton-Century-Crofts.

Broadbent, D. E., & Broadbent, M. H. P. (1987). From detection to identification: response to multiple targets in rapid serial visual presentation. *Perception and Psychophysics, 42*, 105–113.

Bundesen, C. (1987). Visual attention: race models for selection from multielement displays. *Psychological Research, 49*, 113–121.

Bundesen, C. (1990). A theory of visual attention. *Psychological Review, 97*, 523–547.

Bundesen, C. (1991). Visual selection of features and objects: is location special? A reinterpretation of Nissen's (1985) findings. *Perception and Psychophysics, 50*, 87–89.

Bundesen, C. (1993a). The notion of elements in the visual field in a theory of visual attention: a reply to van der Velde and van der Heijden (1993). *Perception and Psychophysics, 53*, 350–352.

Bundesen, C. (1993b). The relationship between independent race models and Luce's choice axiom. *Journal of Mathematical Psychology, 37*, 446–471.

Bundesen, C. (1998a). A computational theory of visual attention. *Philosophical Transactions of the Royal Society of London B, 353*, 1271–1281.

Bundesen, C. (1998b). Visual selective attention: outlines of a choice model, a race model, and a computational theory. *Visual Cognition, 5*, 287–309.

Bundesen, C. (2002). A general theory of visual attention. In L. Bäckman & C. von Hofsten (Eds.), *Psychology at the turn of the millennium: Vol. 1, Cognitive, biological, and health perspectives* (pp. 179–200). Hove, UK: Psychology Press.

Bundesen, C., & Harms, L. (1999). Single-letter recognition as a function of exposure duration. *Psychological Research/Psychologische Forschung, 62*, 275–279.

Bundesen, C., Shibuya, H., & Larsen, A. (1985). Visual selection from multielement displays: a model for partial report. In M. I. Posner & O. S. M. Marin (Eds.), *Attention and performance XI* (pp. 631–649). Hillsdale, NJ: Erlbaum.

Cave, K. R., & Bichot, N. P. (1999). Visuospatial attention: beyond a spotlight model. *Psychonomic Bulletin and Review, 6*, 204–223.

Cave, K. R., & Kosslyn, S. M. (1989). Varieties of size-specific visual selection. *Journal of Experimental Psychology: General, 118*, 148–164.

Cave, K. R., & Wolfe, J. M. (1990). Modeling the role of parallel processing in visual search. *Cognitive Psychology, 22*, 225–271.

Chelazzi, L., Duncan, J., Miller, E. K., & Desimone, R. (1998). Responses of neurons in inferior temporal cortex during memory guided visual search. *Journal of Neurophysiology, 80*, 2918–2940.

Chelazzi, L., Miller, E. K., Duncan, J., & Desimone, R. (1993). A neural basis for visual search in inferior temporal cortex. *Nature, 363*, 345–347.

Cherry, E. C. (1953). Some experiments on the recognition of speech, with one and with two ears. *Journal of the Acoustical Society of America, 25*, 975–979.

Chun, M. M., & Potter, M. C. (1995). A two-stage model for multiple target detection in rapid serial visual presentation. *Journal of Experimental Psychology: Human Perception and Performance, 21*, 109–127.

Colegate, R. L., Hoffman, J. E., & Eriksen, C. W. (1973). Selective encoding from multielement visual displays. *Perception and Psychophysics, 14*, 217–224.

Czerwinski, M., Lightfoot, N., & Shiffrin, R. M. (1992). Automatization and training in visual search. *American Journal of Psychology, 105*, 271–315.

Dalrymple-Alford, E. C., & Budayr, B. (1966). Examination of some aspects of the Stroop color-word test. *Perceptual and Motor Skills, 23*, 1211–1214.

Deco, G., & Zihl, J. (2001). Top-down selective visual attention: a neurodynamical approach. *Visual Cognition, 8*, 119–141.

Desimone, R. (1999). Visual attention mediated by biased competition in extrastriate visual cortex. In G. W. Humphreys, J. Duncan, & A. M. Treisman (Eds.), *Attention, space, and action* (pp. 13–30). Oxford: Oxford University Press.

Desimone, R., & Duncan, J. (1995). Neural mechanisms of selective visual attention. *Annual Review of Neuroscience, 18*, 193–222.

Deutsch, J. A., & Deutsch, D. (1963). Attention: some theoretical considerations. *Psychological Review, 70*, 80–90.

Driver, J., & Tipper, S. P. (1989). On the nonselectivity of 'selective' seeing: contrasts between interference and priming in selective attention. *Journal of Experimental Psychology: Human Perception and Performance, 15*, 304–314.

Duncan, J. (1984). Selective attention and the organization of visual information. *Journal of Experimental Psychology: General, 113*, 501–517.

Duncan, J. (1996). Cooperating brain systems in selective perception and action. In T. Inui & J. L. McClelland (Eds.), *Attention and performance XVI: Information integration in perception and communication* (pp. 549–578). Cambridge, MA: MIT Press.

Duncan, J. (1999). Converging levels of analysis in the cognitive neuroscience of visual attention. In G. W. Humphreys, J. Duncan, & A. M. Treisman (Eds.), *Attention, space, and action* (pp. 112–129). Oxford: Oxford University Press.

Duncan, J., Bundesen, C., Olson, A., Humphreys, G., Chavda, S., & Shibuya, H. (1999). Systematic analysis of deficits in visual attention. *Journal of Experimental Psychology: General, 128*, 450–478.

Duncan, J., & Humphreys, G. W. (1989). Visual search and stimulus similarity. *Psychological Review, 96*, 433–458.

Duncan, J., Ward, R., & Shapiro, K. (1994). Direct measurement of attentional dwell time in human vision. *Nature, 369*, 313–315.

Enns, J. T., DiLollo, V., & Rensink, R. A. (2000). Competition for consciousness among visual events: the psychophysics of reentrant visual processes. *Journal of Experimental Psychology: General, 129*, 481–507.

Eriksen, B. A., & Eriksen, C. W. (1974). Effects of noise letters upon the identification of a target letter in a non-search task. *Perception and Psychophysics, 16*, 143–149.

Eriksen, C. W. (1966). Independence of successive inputs and uncorrelated error in visual form perception. *Journal of Experimental Psychology, 72*, 26–35.

Eriksen, C. W., & Hoffman, J. E. (1973). The extent of processing of noise elements during selective encoding from visual displays. *Perception and Psychophysics, 14*, 155–160.

Eriksen, C. W., & Lappin, J. S. (1965). Internal perceptual system noise and redundancy in simultaneous inputs in form identification. *Psychonomic Science, 2*, 351–352.

Eriksen, C. W., & Lappin, J. S. (1967). Independence in the perception of simultaneously presented forms at brief durations. *Journal of Experimental Psychology, 73*, 468–472.

Eriksen, C. W., & Spencer, T. (1969). Rate of information processing in visual perception: some results and methodological considerations. *Journal of Experimental Psychology Monograph, 79* (2, Pt. 2).

Eriksen, C. W., & St James, J. D. (1986). Visual attention within and around the field of focal attention: a zoom lens model. *Perception and Psychophysics, 40*, 225–240.

Eriksen, C. W., & Webb, J. M. (1989). Shifting of attentional focus within and about a visual display. *Perception and Psychophysics, 45*, 175–183.

Eriksen, C. W., & Yeh, Y. (1985). Allocation of attention in the visual field. *Journal of Experimental Psychology: Human Perception and Performance, 11*, 583–597.

Feller, W. (1968). *An introduction to probability theory and its applications* (3rd ed., Vol. 1). New York: Wiley.

Folk, C. L., Remington, R. W., & Johnston, J. C. (1992). Involuntary covert orienting is contingent on attentional control settings. *Journal of Experimental Psychology: Human Perception and Performance, 18*, 1030–1044.

Folk, C. L., Remington, R. W., & Johnston, J. C. (1993). Contingent attentional capture: a reply to Yantis (1993). *Journal of Experimental Psychology: Human Perception and Performance, 19*, 682–685.

Folk, C. L., Remington, R. W., & Wright, J. H. (1994). The structure of attentional control: contingent attentional capture by apparent motion, abrupt onset, and color. *Journal of Experimental Psychology: Human Perception and Performance, 20*, 317–329.

Fox, E. (1995a). Negative priming from ignored distractors in visual selection: a review. *Psychonomic Bulletin and Review, 2*, 145–173.

Fox, E. (1995b). Pre-cuing target location reduces interference but not negative priming from visual distractors. *Quarterly Journal of Experimental Psychology, 48A*, 26–40.

Gibson, B. S., and Egeth, H. (1994). Inhibition of return to object-based and environment-based locations. *Perception and Psychophysics, 55*, 323–339.

Grossberg, S., Mingolla, E., & Ross, W. D. (1994). A neural theory of attentive visual search: interactions of boundary, surface, spatial, and object representations. *Psychological Review, 101*, 470–489.

Habekost, T., & Bundesen, C. (2003). Patient assessment based on a theory of visual attention (TVA): subtle deficits after a right frontal-subcortical lesion. *Neuropsychologia, 41*, 1171–1188.

Harms, L., & Bundesen, C. (1983). Color segregation and selective attention in a nonsearch task. *Perception and Psychophysics, 33*, 11–19.

Heinke, D., & Humphreys, G. W. (2003). Attention, spatial representation, and visual neglect: simulating emergent attention and spatial memory in the selective attention for identification model (SAIM). *Psychological Review, 110*, 29–87.

Hillstrom, A. P., & Yantis, S. (1994). Visual motion and attentional capture. *Perception and Psychophysics, 55*, 399–411.

Hillyard, S. A., Vogel, E. K., & Luck, S. J. (1999). Sensory gain control (amplification) as a mechanism of selective attention: electrophysiological and neuroimaging evidence. In G. W. Humphreys, J. Duncan, & A. M. Treisman (Eds.), *Attention, space, and action* (pp. 31–53). Oxford: Oxford University Press.

Hoffman, J. E. (1978). Search through a sequentially presented visual display. *Perception and Psychophysics, 23*, 1–11.

Hoffman, J. E. (1979). A two-stage model of visual search. *Perception and Psychophysics, 25*, 319–327.

Hoffman, J. E. (1998). Attention and eye movements. In H. Pashler (ed.), *Attention* (pp. 119–155). Hove, UK: Psychology Press.

Horowitz, T. S., & Wolfe, J. M. (1998). Visual search has no memory. *Nature, 394*, 575–577.

Humphreys, G. W. (1999). Neural representation of objects in space. In G. W. Humphreys, J. Duncan, & A. M. Treisman (Eds.), *Attention, space, and action* (pp. 165–182). Oxford: Oxford University Press.

Humphreys, G. W., Duncan, J., & Treisman, A. M. (Eds.) (1999). *Attention, space, and action.* Oxford: Oxford University Press.

Humphreys, G. W., & Müller, H. J. (1993). SEarch via Recursive Rejection (SERR): a connectionist model of visual search. *Cognitive Psychology, 25*, 43–110.

Isaak, M. I., Shapiro, K. L., & Martin, J. (1999). The attentional blink reflects retrieval competition among multiple rapid serial visual presentation items: tests of an interference model. *Journal of Experimental Psychology: Human Perception and Performance, 25*, 1774–1792.

Itti, L., Koch, C., & Niebur, E. (1999). A model of saliency-based visual attention for rapid scene analysis. *Pattern Analysis and Machine Intelligence, 20*, 1254–1260.

Jolicoeur, P. (1990). Orientation congruency effects on the identification of disoriented shapes. *Journal of Experimental Psychology: Human Perception and Performance, 16*, 351–364.

Jonides, J. (1981). Voluntary versus automatic control over the mind's eye's movement. In J. Long & A. Baddeley (Eds.), *Attention and performance IX* (pp. 187–203). Hillsdale, NJ: Erlbaum.

Jonides, J., & Yantis, S. (1988). Uniqueness of abrupt visual onset in capturing attention. *Perception and Psychophysics, 43*, 346–354.

Kahneman, D. (1973). *Attention and effort.* Englewood Cliffs, NJ: Prentice-Hall.

Klaver, P., Smid, H. G., & Heinze, H. J. (1999). Representations in human visual short-term memory: an event-related brain potential study. *Neuroscience Letters, 268*, 65–68.

Koch, C., & Ullman, S. (1985). Shifts in selective visual attention: towards the underlying neural circuitry. *Human Neurobiology, 4,* 219–227.

Kramer, A. F., & Jacobson, A. (1991). Perceptual organization and focused attention: the role of objects and proximity in visual processing. *Perception and Psychophysics, 50,* 267–284.

Kyllingsbæk, S., Schneider, W. X., & Bundesen, C. (2001). Automatic attraction of attention to former targets in visual displays of letters. *Perception and Psychophysics, 63,* 85–98.

Larsen, A., & Bundesen, C. (1978). Size scaling in visual pattern recognition. *Journal of Experimental Psychology: Human Perception and Performance, 4,* 1–20.

Lavie, N. (1995). Perceptual load as a necessary condition for selective attention. *Journal of Experimental Psychology: Human Perception and Performance, 21,* 451–468.

Lavie, N., & Fox, E. (2000). The role of perceptual load in negative priming. *Journal of Experimental Psychology: Human Perception and Performance, 26,* 1038–1052.

Logan, G. D. (1988). Toward an instance theory of automatization. *Psychological Review, 95,* 492–527.

Logan, G. D. (1996). The CODE theory of visual attention: an integration of space-based and object-based attention. *Psychological Review, 103,* 603–649.

Logan, G. D. (2002). An instance theory of attention and memory. *Psychological Review, 109,* 376–400.

Logan, G. D., & Bundesen, C. (1996). Spatial effects in the partial report paradigm: a challenge for theories of visual spatial attention. In D. L. Medin (ed.), *The psychology of learning and motivation* (Vol. 35, pp. 243–282). San Diego, CA: Academic Press.

Logan, G. D., & Gordon, R. D. (2001). Executive control of visual attention in dual-task situations. *Psychological Review, 108,* 393–434.

Lowe, D. G. (1979). Strategies, context, and the mechanisms of response inhibition. *Memory and Cognition, 7,* 382–389.

Luce, R. D. (1963). Detection and recognition. In R. D. Luce, R. R. Bush, & E. Galanter (Eds.), *Handbook of mathematical psychology* (Vol. 1, pp. 103–189). New York: Wiley.

Luck, S. J., Chelazzi, L., Hillyard, S. A., & Desimone, R. (1997). Neural mechanisms of spatial selective attention in areas V1, V2 and V4 of macaque visual cortex. *Journal of Neurophysiology, 77,* 24–42.

Luck, S. J., & Vogel, E. K. (1997). The capacity of visual working memory for features and conjunctions. *Nature, 390,* 279–281.

MacLeod, C. M. (1991). Half a century of research on the Stroop effect: an integrative review. *Psychological Bulletin, 109,* 163–203.

May, C. P., Kane, M. J., & Hasher, L. (1995). Determinants of negative priming. *Psychological Bulletin, 118,* 35–54.

McAdams, C. J., & Maunsell, J. H. R. (1999a). Effects of attention on orientation-tuning functions of single neurons in macaque cortical area V4. *Journal of Neuroscience, 19,* 431–441.

McAdams, C. J., & Maunsell, J. H. R. (1999b). Effects of attention on the reliability of individual neurons in monkey visual cortex. *Neuron, 23,* 765–773.

McClelland, J. L., & Rumelhart, D. E. (Eds.) (1986). *Parallel distributed processing* (Vol. 2). Cambridge, MA: MIT Press.

McLaughlin, E. N., Shore, D. I., & Klein, R. M. (2001). The attentional blink is immune to masking-induced data limits. *Quarterly Journal of Experimental Psychology, 54A,* 169–196.

Milliken, B., Joordens, S., Merikle, P. M., & Seiffert, A. E. (1998). Selective attention: a reevaluation of the implications of negative priming. *Psychological Review, 105,* 203–229.

Milliken, B., & Tipper, S. P. (1998). Attention and inhibition. In H. Pashler (ed.), *Attention* (pp. 13–75). Hove, UK: Psychology Press.

Moore, C. M. (1994). Negative priming depends on probe-trial conflict: where has all the inhibition gone? *Perception and Psychophysics, 56,* 133–147.

Moore, C. M., Egeth, H., Berglon, L. R., & Luck, S. J. (1996). Are attentional dwell times inconsistent with serial visual search? *Psychonomic Bulletin and Review, 3,* 360–365.

Moran, J., & Desimone, R. (1985). Selective attention gates visual processing in the extrastriate cortex. *Science, 229,* 782–784.

Moray, N. (1959). Attention in dichotic listening: affective cues and the influence of instructions. *Quarterly Journal of Experimental Psychology, 11,* 56–60.

Mozer, M. C. (1991). *The perception of multiple objects: a connectionist approach.* Cambridge, MA: MIT Press.

Nakayama, K., & Silverman, G. H. (1986). Serial and parallel processing of visual feature conjunctions. *Nature, 320,* 264–265.

Neill, W. T., Valdes, L. A., Terry, K. M., & Gorfein, D. S. (1992). The persistence of negative priming. II. Evidence for episodic trace retrieval. *Journal of Experimental Psychology: Learning, Memory, and Cognition, 18,* 993–1000.

Neisser, U. (1967). *Cognitive psychology.* New York: Appleton-Century-Crofts.

Nickerson, R. S. (1966). Response times with a memory-dependent decision task. *Journal of Experimental Psychology, 72,* 761–769.

Nosofsky, R. M. (1986). Attention, similarity, and the identification-categorization relationship. *Journal of Experimental Psychology: General, 115,* 39–57.

Nosofsky, R. M., & Palmeri, T. (1997). An exemplar-based random walk model of speeded classification. *Psychological Review, 104,* 266–300.

Palmer, J. (1995). Attention in visual search: distinguishing four causes of a set-size effect. *Current Directions in Psychological Science, 4,* 118–123.

Palmer, J., Verghese, P., & Pavel, M. (2000). The psychophysics of visual search. *Vision Research, 40,* 1227–1268.

Paquet, L., & Lortie, C. (1990). Evidence for early selection: precuing target location reduces interference from same-category distractors. *Perception and Psychophysics, 48,* 382–388.

Parasuraman, R. (ed.). (1998). *The attentive brain.* Cambridge, MA: MIT Press.

Parasuraman, R., Warm, J. S., & See, J. E. (1998). Brain systems of vigilance. In Parasuraman, R. (ed.), *The attentive brain* (pp. 221–256). Cambridge, MA: MIT Press.

Pashler, H. (1987). Detecting conjunctions of color and form: reassessing the serial search hypothesis. *Perception and Psychophysics, 41,* 191–201.

Pashler, H. (1998). *The psychology of attention.* Cambridge, MA: MIT Press.

Phaf, R. H., van der Heijden, A. H. C., & Hudson, P. T. W. (1990). SLAM: a connectionist model for attention in visual selection tasks. *Cognitive Psychology, 22,* 273–341.

Posner, M. I. (1980). Orienting of attention. *Quarterly Journal of Experimental Psychology, 32,* 3–25.

Posner, M. I., & Cohen, Y. (1984). Components of visual orienting. In H. Bouma & D. G. Bouwhuis (Eds.), *Attention and performance X: Control of language processes* (pp. 531–556). Hillsdale, NJ: Erlbaum.

Posner, M. I., Nissen, M. J., & Ogden, W. C. (1978). Attended and unattended processing modes: the role of set for spatial location. In H. L. Pick & I. J. Saltzman (Eds), *Modes of perceiving and processing information.* Hillsdale, NJ: Erlbaum.

Posner, M. I., Snyder, C. R. R., & Davidson, B. J. (1980). Attention and the detection of signals. *Journal of Experimental Psychology: General, 109,* 160–174.

Pratt, J., & Abrams, R. A. (1999). Inhibition of return in discrimination tasks. *Journal of Experimental Psychology: Human Perception and Performance, 25,* 229–242.

Raymond, J. E., Shapiro, K. L., & Arnell, K. M. (1992). Temporary suppression of visual processing in an RSVP task: an attentional blink? *Journal of Experimental Psychology: Human Perception and Performance, 18,* 849–860.

Remington, R. W., Johnston, J. C., & Yantis, S. (1992). Involuntary attention capture by abrupt onsets. *Perception and Psychophysics, 51,* 279–290.

Reynolds, J. H., Chelazzi, L., & Desimone, R. (1999). Competitive mechanisms subserve attention in macaque areas V2 and V4. *Journal of Neuroscience, 19,* 1736–1753.

Robertson, L., Treisman, A., Friedmann-Hill, S., & Grabowecky, M. (1997). The interaction of spatial and object pathways: evidence from Balint's syndrome. *Journal of Cognitive Neuroscience, 9,* 295–318.

Ross, S. M. (2000). *Introduction to probability and statistics for engineers and scientists* (2nd ed.). London: Academic Press.

Rumelhart, D. E., & McClelland, J. L. (Eds.) (1986). *Parallel distributed processing* (Vol. 1). Cambridge, MA: MIT Press.

Scharf, B. (1998). Auditory attention: the psychoacoustical approach. In H. Pashler (ed.), *Attention* (pp. 75–119). Hove, UK: Psychology Press.

Schneider, W., & Shiffrin, R. M. (1977). Controlled and automatic human information processing. I. Detection, search, and attention. *Psychological Review, 84,* 1–66.

Shapiro, K. L., Driver, J., Ward, R., & Sorensen, R. E. (1997). Priming from the attentional blink: a failure to extract visual tokens but not visual types. *Psychological Science, 8,* 95–100.

Shapiro, K. L., Raymond, J. E., & Arnell, K. M. (1994). Attention to visual pattern information produces the attentional blink in rapid serial visual presentation. *Journal of Experimental Psychology: Human Perception and Performance, 20,* 357–371.

Shaw, M. L. (1978). A capacity allocation model for reaction time. *Journal of Experimental Psychology: Human Perception and Performance, 4,* 586–598.

Shaw, M. L., & Shaw, P. (1977). Optimal allocation of cognitive resources to spatial locations. *Journal of Experimental Psychology: Human Perception and Performance, 3,* 201–211.

Shibuya, H. (1991). Comparison between stochastic models for visual selection. In J.-P. Doignon & J.-C. Falmagne (Eds.), *Mathematical psychology: current developments* (pp. 337–356). New York: Springer.

Shibuya, H. (1993). Efficiency of visual selection in duplex and conjunction conditions in partial report. *Perception and Psychophysics, 54,* 716–732.

Shibuya, H., & Bundesen, C. (1988). Visual selection from multielement displays: measuring and modeling effects of exposure duration. *Journal of Experimental Psychology: Human Perception and Performance, 14,* 591–600.

Shiffrin, R. M., & Schneider, W. (1977). Controlled and automatic human information processing. II. Perceptual learning, automatic attending, and a general theory. *Psychological Review, 84,* 127–190.

Sperling, G. (1960). The information available in brief visual presentations. *Psychological Monographs, 74* (11, Whole No. 498).

Sperling, G. (1963). A model for visual memory tasks. *Human Factors, 5,* 19–31.

Sperling, G. (1967). Successive approximations to a model for short-term memory. *Acta Psychologica, 27,* 285–292.

Sperling, G. (1984). A unified theory of attention and signal detection. In R. Parasuraman & D. R. Davies (Eds.), *Varieties of attention* (pp. 103–181). New York: Academic Press.

Sperling, G., Budiansky, J., Spivak, J. G., & Johnson, M. C. (1971). Extremely rapid visual search: the maximum rate of scanning letters for the presence of a numeral. *Science, 174,* 307–311.

Sternberg, S. (1966). High-speed scanning in human memory. *Science, 153,* 652–654.

Sternberg, S. (1967). Scanning a persisting visual image versus a memorized list. Paper presented at the Annual Meeting of the Eastern Psychological Association.

Sternberg, S. (1969a). Memory-scanning: mental processes revealed by reaction-time experiments. *American Scientist, 57,* 421–457.

Sternberg, S. (1969b). The discovery of processing stages: extensions of Donders' method. *Acta Psychologica, 30,* 276–315.

Sternberg, S. (1998). Discovering mental processing stages: the method of additive factors. In D. Scarborough & S. Sternberg (Eds.), *An invitation to cognitive science: Vol. 4. Methods, models, and conceptual issues* (pp. 365–454). Cambridge, MA: MIT Press.

Stroop, J. R. (1935). Studies of interference in serial verbal reactions. *Journal of Experimental Psychology, 18*, 643–662.

Theeuwes, J. (1992). Perceptual selectivity for color and form. *Perception and Psychophysics, 51*, 599–606.

Theeuwes, J. (1994). Stimulus-driven capture and attentional set: selective search for color and visual abrupt onsets. *Journal of Experimental Psychology: Human Perception and Performance, 20*, 799–806.

Theeuwes, J. (1995). Temporal and spatial characteristics of preattentive and attentive processing. *Visual Cognition, 2*, 221–233.

Theeuwes, J. (1996). Perceptual selectivity for color and form: on the nature of the interference effect. In A. F. Kramer, M. G. H. Coles, & G. D. Logan (Eds.), *Converging operations in the study of visual selective attention* (pp. 297–314). Washington, DC: American Psychological Association.

Tipper, S. P. (1985). The negative priming effect: inhibitory priming by ignored objects. *Quarterly Journal of Experimental Psychology, 37A*, 571–590.

Tipper, S. P. (2001). Does negative priming reflect inhibitory mechanisms? A review and integration of conflicting views. *Quarterly Journal of Experimental Psychology, 37A*, 321–343.

Tipper, S. P., & Cranston, M. (1985). Selective attention and priming: inhibitory and facilitatory effects of ignored primes. *Quarterly Journal of Experimental Psychology, 37A,* 591–611.

Townsend, J. T. (1969). Mock parallel and serial models and experimental detection of these. In *Purdue Centennial Symposium on Information Processing* (pp. 617–628). Purdue University.

Townsend, J. T., & Ashby, F. G. (1983). *The stochastic modeling of elementary psychological processes.* Cambridge: Cambridge University Press.

Treisman, A. M. (1964a). The effect of irrelevant material on the efficiency of selective listening. *American Journal of Psychology, 77*, 533–546.

Treisman, A. M. (1964b). Verbal cues, language, and meaning in selective attention. *American Journal of Psychology, 77*, 206–219.

Treisman, A. M. (1988). Features and objects: the fourteenth Bartlett memorial lecture. *Quarterly Journal of Experimental Psychology, 40A*, 201–237.

Treisman, A. M. (1999). Feature binding, attention and object perception. In G. W. Humphreys, J. Duncan, & A. M. Treisman (Eds.), *Attention, space, and action* (pp. 91–111). Oxford: Oxford University Press.

Treisman, A. M., & Gelade, G. (1980). A feature-integration theory of attention. *Cognitive Psychology, 12*, 97–136.

Treisman, A. M., & Gormican, S. (1988). Feature analysis in early vision: evidence from search asymmetries. *Psychological Review, 95*, 15–48.

Treisman, A. M., & Paterson, R. (1984). Emergent features, attention, and object perception. *Journal of Experimental Psychology: Human Perception and Performance, 10*, 12–31.

Treisman, A. M., & Sato, S. (1990). Conjunction search revisited. *Journal of Experimental Psychology: Human Perception and Performance, 16*, 459–478.

Treisman, A. M., & Schmidt, H. (1982). Illusory conjunctions in the perception of objects. *Cognitive Psychology, 14*, 107–141.

Treisman, A. M., Sykes, M., & Gelade, G. (1977). Selective attention and stimulus integration. In S. Dornic (ed.), *Attention and performance VI* (pp. 333–361). Hillsdale, NJ: Erlbaum.

Treue, S., & Trujillo, J. C. M. (1999). Feature-based attention influences motion processing gain in macaque visual cortex. *Nature, 399*, 575–579.

Tsal, Y., Meiran, N., & Lavie, N. (1994). The role of attention in illusory conjunctions. *Perception and Psychophysics, 55*, 350–358.

Usher, M., & Niebur, E. (1996). Modelling the temporal dynamics of IT neurons in visual search: a mechanism for top-down selective attention. *Journal of Cognitive Neuroscience, 8*, 311–327.

van der Heijden, A. H. C. (1992). *Selective attention in vision*. London: Routledge.

van der Heijden, A. H. C. (1993). The role of position in object selection in vision. *Psychological Research, 56*, 44–58.

van der Heijden, A. H. C. (2004). *Attention in vision: perception, communication and action*. Hove, UK: Psychology Press.

van der Velde, F., & van der Heijden, A. H. C. (1993). An element in the visual field is just a conjunction of attributes: a critique of Bundesen (1991). *Perception and Psychophysics, 53*, 345–349.

van Oeffelen, M. P., & Vos, P. G. (1982). Configurational effects on the enumeration of dots: counting by groups. *Memory and Cognition, 10*, 396–404.

van Oeffelen, M. P., & Vos, P. G. (1983). An algorithm for pattern description on the level of relative proximity. *Pattern Recognition, 16*, 341–348.

Vogel, E. K., Luck, S. J., & Shapiro, K. L. (1998). Electrophysiological evidence for a postperceptual locus of suppression during the attentional blink. *Journal of Experimental Psychology: Human Perception and Performance, 24*, 1656–1674.

Vogel, E. K., Woodman, G. F., & Luck, S. J. (2001). Storage of features, conjunctions, and objects in visual working memory. *Journal of Experimental Psychology: Human Perception and Performance, 27*, 92–114.

Ward, R., Duncan, J., & Shapiro, K. (1996). The slow time-course of visual attention. *Cognitive Psychology, 30*, 79–109.

Weichselgartner, E., & Sperling, G. (1987). Dynamics of automatic and controlled visual attention. *Science, 238*, 778–780.

Wolfe, J. M. (1994). Guided Search 2.0: a revised model of visual search. *Psychonomic Bulletin and Review, 1*, 202–238.

Wolfe, J. M. (1998a). Visual search. In H. Pashler (ed.), *Attention* (pp. 13–75). Hove, UK: Psychology Press.

Wolfe, J. M. (1998b). What can 1 million trials tell us about visual search? *Psychological Science, 9*, 33–39.

Wolfe, J. M., Cave, K. R., & Franzel, S. L. (1989). Guided search: an alternative to the feature integration model for visual search. *Journal of Experimental Psychology: Human Perception and Performance, 15*, 419–433.

Woodman, G. F., & Luck, S. J. (1999). Electrophysiological measurement of rapid shifts of attention during visual search. *Nature, 400*, 867–869.

Yantis, S. (1993). Stimulus-driven attentional capture and attentional control settings. *Journal of Experimental Psychology: Human Perception and Performance, 19*, 676–681.

Yantis, S. (1996). Attention capture in vision. In A. F. Kramer, M. G. H. Coles, & G. D. Logan (Eds.), *Converging operations in the study of visual selective attention* (pp. 45–76). Washington, DC: American Psychological Association.

Yantis, S. (1998). Control of visual attention. In H. Pashler (ed.), *Attention* (pp. 223–256). Hove, UK: Psychology Press.

Yantis, S., & Hillstrom, A. P. (1994). Stimulus-driven attentional capture: evidence from equiluminant visual objects. *Journal of Experimental Psychology: Human Perception and Performance, 20*, 95–107.

Yantis, S., & Jonides, J. (1984). Abrupt visual onsets and selective attention: evidence from visual search. *Journal of Experimental Psychology: Human Perception and Performance, 10*, 601–621.

Yantis, S., & Jonides, J. (1990). Abrupt visual onsets and selective attention: voluntary versus automatic allocation. *Journal of Experimental Psychology: Human Perception and Performance, 16*, 121–134.

Zeki, S. (1993). *A vision of the brain*. Oxford: Blackwell.

5

Action and Motor Skills: Adaptive Behaviour for Intended Goals

YVONNE DELEVOYE-TURRELL
AND ALAN M. WING

Compared to other areas of cognitive neuroscience, it might appear that the mechanisms controlling our actions should be readily understood, because the observation of the outcome of a motor action reveals its goal and gives access to its biological significance. However, adaptive control of movement involves much more than the contraction of a predefined sequence of muscles. Well-adjusted motor actions must be informed not only by the constraints of the environment in which the movement is performed, but also by knowledge of our own effector limits. This chapter will specifically address these issues and will focus primarily on two fundamental questions:

1 How do we react to unexpected events?
2 What is the nature of predictive control in a stable and well-known environment?

In each case, we consider how higher-order mechanisms – e.g. integration of perceptual information, memory-based object representations, action intentions, knowledge about the context stability, or even knowledge of what is to come – can penetrate lower levels of motor control, and hence significantly affect the selection, planning and execution of simple motor actions. Throughout, we examine the theoretical aspects of the questions and present clinical cases, when applicable, that pinpoint specific brain mechanisms that may be involved.

In the first section of this chapter, we consider some basic concepts and definitions that are commonly used in the field of motor control. Then, we address the topics of reactive (feedback) control of

movement and predictive (feedforward) control of movement. But before getting into detailed descriptions of relevant experimental data, consider the following illustrative scene.

It is five o'clock and a waiter is faced with the task of clearing a littered table, after a group of customers depart. On the palm of his left hand, he is balancing a tray. That is to say, the weight of the tray and its load are balanced by the upward force provided by his arm. With his right hand, he is taking things off the table. Here, palm-up support will not work and consequently, when lifting each object, he uses a grip in which fingers and thumb squeeze in on opposite sides of the object. Usually, people learn from experience to produce grip force levels that are adapted to the needs of commonly manipulated objects. For example, the waiter will apply lower grip force levels when lifting empty glasses than full ones. But what will happen if he reaches out to lift a bottle that he thought was empty, when in fact it is full? In such a case, the bottle is heavier than expected, and at first his hand may slide up the object as he tries to lift it with insufficient grip force. Luckily, reactive mechanisms will quickly intervene to increase grip force and, hence, restore stability of the object within grasp. Finally, we may note that more cognitive aspects related to the intention of the motor output can play a critical role in the selection, the sequencing and even the coordination of hand and finger movements. For example, reaching out for the bottle is unlikely to be carried out with the same degree of care he would use when picking up a delicate, long-stemmed wine glass. The goal of action, or intended outcome, is thus an important factor to bear in mind even when trying to understand the control of seemingly simple movements.

WHAT IS MOTOR CONTROL?

Research into motor control is fundamentally the study of transformations between sensory inputs and motor outputs. A fundamental issue is, for example, how those movements defined in terms of joint angles and muscle torques are related to the manipulation of an object represented in visual coordinates. Through the systematic observation and analysis of motor behaviour, we seek to understand how actions are controlled as a function of the environmental conditions.

For the motor system to move its effectors (e.g. hand, arm, body) to apply forces to objects, it must integrate a variety of sensory data, and coordinate them with movement elements. Sensorimotor transformations relate afferent/sensory and efferent/motor reference frames for effective interaction with the environment. In the following section, a few important concepts are reviewed to help us understand the nature of these transformations, e.g. the concepts of motor program (inverse model), feedback (corrective) and feedforward (predictive) control. Then, we note a few general terms that are frequently used in the study of motor control.

General concepts

The notion of a motor program comes from Lashley's (1951) classic view on serial order of behaviour. This states that the time delay in neural transmission between sensorimotor (proprioceptive, visual) afferences to the central nervous system (CNS), then back to the muscular effectors, is too long to permit feedback during rapid-movement sequences. Therefore, these sequences must be organized centrally (programmed) before their initiation. Hence, after defining desired outcome based on an intention (top left of Figure 5.1), a generative process determines the set of muscle commands (the motor program) required to reach the intended goal. This motor program generator must relate desired movement outcome to required motor commands. In that sense it must do the inverse of what the skeletomuscular system achieves, which is to convert motor commands into movement outcomes. Thus, the motor program generator may be considered as an inverse model (of the skeletomuscular system).

Two types of neural mechanisms are available to enable the CNS to verify that a performed motor action corresponds to the desired outcome, and to adjust the action if it does not. First, for slower movements, *feedback control* enables the adjustment of an ongoing motor action. A *feedback comparator* uses sensory afference to determine if the ongoing movement corresponds to the intended movement (loop 1 of Figure 5.1). In the motor tasks considered in the following sections, the most relevant form of afferent input is either visual, when moving the hand through space, or kinaesthetic, when manipulating an object.

Significant time delays are associated with sensory input and motor output in feedback control. For motor actions that are too short in duration to allow error corrections on the basis of afferent information, *feedforward control* operates. In this mode of control, a copy of the muscle commands (or efference copy) is sent to a *forward model* that enables the CNS to predict the dynamic consequences of an action before it is executed (loop 2 of Figure 5.1). By comparing this predicted (virtual) outcome with that intended, the muscle commands can be corrected early in the movement, or possibly even before the initiation of the movement itself. Consequently, feedforward control enables a movement of improved accuracy with little or no apparent correction. However, as it is based on information gained in anticipation of the execution of a movement, it is especially useful when acting in stable and predictable environments.

It is often the case that fine manipulative movements of the hand – e.g. reaching to grasp an object – are treated as distinct from gross movement involving larger segments of the body – e.g. when the arm might be used for balance. However, at both of these levels, feedback and feedforward mechanisms work together to support interaction with objects in the environment. Thus, hand/arm actions are linked to postural control in anticipatory (Wing, Flanagan, & Richardson, 1997) and reactive (Elger, Wing, & Gilles, 1999) maintenance of balance. In this chapter, the study of hand function (the control of grip force and hand trajectory) is used as a general model of the control of motor action.

Defining the terms

Moving through space

Moving the hand from point A to point B can involve muscle contractions that extend over single or multiple joints, depending on the desired trajectory. For example, movements around the single elbow joint involve the coordination of biceps and triceps muscles, and with the arm horizontal, these contractions take the hand closer to or further away from the body. Isolated shoulder movements can also do this, and in such cases the hand traces a larger arc. However, it is commonly recognized that the most natural type of movement involves taking

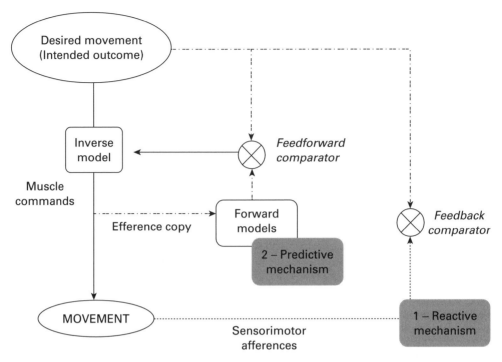

Figure 5.1 *Diagram of the internal models theory, which presents a schematic representation of how the predictive mechanisms may be implemented in the central nervous system of the human brain. This model, based on the internal control of the efference commands, has three internal states of representation: the general goal of the action (intended outcome), the predicted consequences of the action (issued by the forward model) and the true consequences of the action (sensorimotor afferences that are secondary to movement execution). For more details see text.*

the hand along a straight line, which requires simultaneous activation of muscles at both the shoulder and the elbow. When considering more complex movements like drinking or walking, it is evident that coordination of movement across joints within and between limbs is a key problem of movement control. The study of changes in position of the limbs, or in angular relations between limb segments, as a function of time, is central to the field of motor control, and is termed *kinematics.*

Controlling movements under the effects of force

From the time we are born, gravity is a force that acts upon our body. Keeping our feet on the ground, gravity also affects our every move, making us lose balance or drop manipulated objects. Hence, movement is not only about positions and displacements in space. It also involves forces and our understanding of them. For example, moving the hand up and down a certain distance looks very similar in terms

of position change. But while carrying out this simple movement, the effect of gravity is to assist the downward displacement whereas it resists the upward one. Hence, in terms of forces, these two movements are not simple opposites. The study of forces (and torques) that are involved in the control of movement is termed *kinetics.* It is sometimes also referred to as *dynamics.*

Manipulating objects

So far, we have considered moving the hand through the environment. However, in most situations, we tend to use the upper limb to reach for, lift and manipulate objects. We may then ask how properties of the to-be-grasped object affect the movement. The location in space of an object relative to the limb's initial position determines the hand path required to bring the hand precisely to the object. Visual information about the size of the object also affects the planning of the reach, in that a larger object will require the hand to open wider.

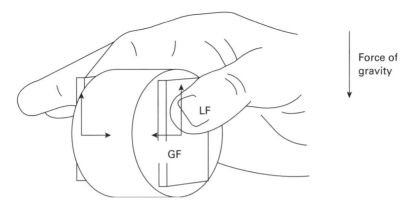

Force of gravity

Figure 5.2 *Schematic diagram of the forces acting upon an object during lift: grip force (GF), load force (LF) and the force of gravity are represented.*

Other aspects of the target, such as its shape or orientation, also affect the kinematics of the reach. At the same time, object properties like mass and compliance will affect upper limb kinetics. Thus, when picking up lighter or heavier objects, sufficient *grip force (GF)* normal to the surfaces must be applied to overcome *load forces (LF)* that act tangential to the surfaces of the object (see Figure 5.2). In most cases, visual information will enable to predict the weight of the object before hand–object contact, in order to squeeze the object with just enough GF to ensure a stable grip. One further constraint on the way an object is picked up is its intended use. For example, the tips of the thumb and index finger may be selected to lift a wine glass, whereas a large bowl piled high with fruit might prompt use of a two-hand grasp with the palms providing much larger areas of contact for greater stability.

Predictive versus reactive mechanisms

How is grasp shape adjusted to the task at hand? If the object is familiar, knowledge about the object may allow the predictive adjustment of GF. The third section of this chapter considers specifically the *predictive control of action* (for which the feedforward mode of control is predominant) and the knowledge base of this control. An important issue here is: what are the sources of information used and how are the different sources integrated in order to perform appropriate and efficient actions? One route is to estimate object characteristics such as size, using vision or touch, and then use size to infer weight from some rule-based mechanism that does not require recognition of the object. Another route is to retrieve information from memory specific to that object. This memory representation will have been elaborated through previous experience in manipulating the object. Monitoring previous

actions, whose successful outcome indicates adequacy of action, may allow update of certain attributes of such representations (see feedforward learning models, e.g. Kawato & Gomi, 1992). However, in some cases prediction is not possible. The object may be unknown, so that attributes relevant to manipulation are not available. Sometimes prediction of object properties fails as, for example, when the weight of an object is misjudged: a milk carton may be full whereas it was expected to be empty. In such cases *reactive feedback mechanisms* can intervene, in which mismatch between intended and observed outcome leads to the adjustment of movements during their execution. The following section addresses this problem of reacting to unpredictable events that perturb planned intentions. We shall see that feedback correction is not always effective because it requires time and, hence, may occur too late to avoid dropping the manipulated object. However, data will be presented that demonstrate that feedback-based behaviour can still be quite effective, for example in cases of neural dysfunction of the predictive mechanisms.

REACTING TO UNPREDICTABLE EVENTS

Reach, touch, grip, lift, move… All of these motor actions may be subject to unexpected events that result in a mismatch between intended action and outcome. In such a case, feedback corrections are required to achieve the desired goal. In the following, we address a postural problem – keeping an object steady in the hand – and the role of proprioceptive feedback for movement correction. Then, we consider the act of reaching for various types of objects. In this case, we shall see that vision is a more appropriate sense upon which to base corrections.

First, by way of setting the scene, we return to the example of the waiter, who is now talking to a colleague and is not being very careful with the task at hand. While stepping forward to reach for a bottle on the far side of the table, his foot catches one of the table legs. In trying to regain his balance, he misreaches for the bottle; and the tray begins to tilt dangerously. A rapid feedback correction is required if he is to avoid dropping everything. In this section we review experimental studies that capture this problem and illuminate the factors that determine reactions to unexpected environmental events that disrupt object-directed actions.

Maintaining stable posture

The experimental data presented in the following paragraphs deal with the problem that occurs when we handle objects under frictional and loading conditions that are unpredictable, as in washing dishes by hand and encountering one dish more soapy (and so more slippery) than the others, or restraining a child led by the hand who suddenly tries to run across the road to greet a friend.

Experimental paradigm

To investigate the nature of the grip force adjustments occurring during object manipulation in the laboratory, subjects were typically required to use opposed thumb and index finger forming a precision grip to lift and hold an experimental target object. A force transducer (or load cell) placed within the object allowed the precise measurement of the fluctuations in the grip force (GF), applied at right angles (normal) to the surfaces of the object. Depending on the experimental conditions, the transducer was subjected to unpredictable loading forces, for example by attachment to a robotic arm (Witney, Goodbody, & Wolpert, 2000). When the experimental goal was to investigate predictable variations in load force (LF), the manipulated object, or manipulandum, was in an inert 'passive' state and subjects were asked to actively move it. This situation will be considered in later sections. Here, we examine the case where the manipulandum was 'active' and produced sudden pulling or pushing LFs. Under these conditions, time of initiation and rate and amplitude of the LF changes were unpredictable. The subjects' task was to react to the sudden load in order to maintain the manipulandum steady within grip (see Johansson, 1996, for a review).

When restraining an active manipulandum, GF changes were triggered by the changes in LF following a neuromuscular delay of up to 150 ms (Johansson, Riso, Häger, & Bäckström, 1992). Because of this delay, GF responses to extended and unpredictable periods of imposed LF increases

consisted of an initial strong GF rate pulse followed by a period of slower, often stepwise, GF increase (Johansson et al., 1992). The first GF response was generally strong and stereotyped in nature, and was termed a catch-up response, acting to quickly compensate for the initial steep fall in the GF to LF ratio that occurred during the latent period, prior to the initiation of the GF response. For large and long-lasting LF increases, the catch-up response was not always sufficient to restore an adequate GF to LF ratio. Hence, GF could continue to increase after the catch-up response. In this case, the GF response tracked LF maintaining an approximately constant force ratio between GF and LF. This two-phase GF response (catch-up and then tracking) was generally successful in restoring an adequate force ratio within 200 ms of the start of the changes in LF (Johansson et al., 1992).

Unpredictable frictional and loading conditions

Friction changes with the mechanical surface characteristics of an object, i.e. the surface irregularities or texture. In the research literature on GF control, the most commonly used textures are sandpaper, suede leather and rayon-polyester, which are textures with increasing smoothness. When lifting passive objects with known textured surfaces, GF was adjusted to the friction between skin and object surfaces (Johansson & Westling, 1984a; Westling & Johansson, 1984). In restraining an active manipulandum, GF baseline (force level before the start of the LF increase) and the amplitude of the catch-up and tracking responses were scaled to the frictional conditions at each digit–surface interface. All subjects produced larger catch-up and tracking responses when holding more slippery surfaces.

When surface texture was changed unpredictably from trial to trial, GF baseline, catch-up and tracking responses were immediately affected by the new frictional condition (Cole & Johansson, 1993). Information about the new texture influenced GF as early as 100 ms after the initial touch (Johansson & Westling, 1987). Similar results were reported when the properties of the skin of the fingertips were modified (Johansson & Westling, 1984b). Subjects carried out a series of lifting trials before and after washing their hands with soap and water. During the washing procedure, sweat was removed from the skin, i.e. the skin was made less adhesive and the friction in relation to the object was temporarily decreased. In this case, GF was quickly readjusted to the new frictional conditions.

The *loading conditions* of a grasped object were manipulated by either varying the rate of LF application or the LF amplitude. When the amplitude of the LF fluctuations was manipulated in an unpredictable manner, a marked catch-up response was observed for all LF amplitudes and appeared 140 ± 30 ms after the onset of the LF increase (Johansson et al., 1992). The latency of these responses was not influenced either by the load amplitude or by the load amplitude of the previous trial. The catch-up response was apparently released as a unit, with the same appearance for the different load amplitudes (all applied at the constant rate of 4 N/s). Indeed, the shape, duration and size of these responses remained unaffected. If the catch-up response was not sufficient to restore a safe GF to LF ratio, a tracking response was then released.

To study the influence of the rate of loading, an experimental protocol was developed to deliver trapezoid LF profiles at various rates with plateau amplitudes of 2 N. In these experiments, the latency of the catch-up trials was found to be inversely correlated with the LF rate: the latency was twice as long for the LF rate of 2 N/s compared to that observed for the LF rate of 32 N/s. This effect may be explained by the fact that GF responses were elicited when a fixed LF amplitude threshold was exceeded (Johansson, Häger, & Riso, 1992a). Experimental data confirmed this hypothesis by showing that GF responses were triggered approximately 82 ms after a threshold LF of 0.2 N was reached. Two explanations have been proposed for this finding. First, there may be a threshold effect from the relevant digital mechanoreceptors, as they show amplitude thresholds to skin deformation (Johansson & Vallbo, 1979). Alternatively, catch-up responses may be triggered once a critical GF to LF ratio is reached (Johansson & Westling, 1987).

The catch-up response was scaled to the LF rate from the very start, which suggested that afferent information related to LF rate was being utilized to specify the force output level before the onset of the GF response (Johansson et al., 1992a). In another series of studies, Johansson and collaborators (1992a) observed that the duration of the LF ramp influenced the general profile of the catch-up response. A series of loading trials was run in which the loading phase (8 N/s) was terminated after various fixed ramp durations (25 to 500 ms). Results revealed that, for the longer ramp durations, catch-up responses were fully released. However, for the shorter durations (<120 ms), the peak GF rate was reduced and graded with the duration of the ramp. Moreover, the maximum GF rate occurred earlier for briefer ramps, which suggested that the termination of the LF ramps triggered the end of the GF response in as little as 45 ms (Johansson et al., 1992a). In summary, these observations indicate that triggered GF responses can be modified during the initial catch-up response to reflect changes in the duration and rate of LF changes. This suggests that afferent information, which signals the CNS about load profile changes, is continuously utilized for early updating of response parameters. In the following, the sensorimotor

receptors that contribute to this adaptive control of reactive GF responses are reviewed.

Sensorimotor receptors

GF adaptation to changes in friction and/or loading conditions is markedly impaired in patients suffering from total loss (Rothwell, Traub, Day, Obeso, Thomas, & Marsden, 1982) or moderate degradation of tactile signals, e.g. due to median nerve compression (Cole, 1994), nerve regeneration following laceration (Johansson & Westling, 1991) or age (Cole, 1991; Cole & Beck, 1994; Cole, Rotella, & Harper, 1999). These results suggest a strong involvement of tactile signals in the control of fine manipulative actions.

In the restraint of an active manipulandum, the reactive adjustments of GF responses during digital nerve blocks of the index and thumb were severely impaired, indicating that the normal regulation of GF to unpredictable loading depends on afferent information from the mechano receptors in the digits (Johansson, Häger, & Riso, 1992b). There were frequently no discernible GF responses triggered by LF changes and, when present, GF modulations were delayed and significantly smaller under digital block than normally observed. Appropriate GF adjustments to changes in surface texture were also lost (Westling & Johansson, 1984). For most subjects, GF levels were high enough to avoid object slippage only for rough-textured surfaces. A conscious increase in GF was necessary to successfully lift the objects with a smoother surface like silk. From these observations, it was concluded that sensory inputs from the mechanoreceptors of the glabrous skin of the digits are the dominant source of information in the sensory-driven control of GF response. However, afferent systems innervating tissues (skin and muscle) proximal to the digits may also be capable of mediating some control under favourable conditions (Häger-Ross, Cole, & Johansson, 1996).

Four different types of mechanoreceptors can be distinguished on the basis of their adaptation to sustained skin deformation (indentation, vibration and pressure) and on the structure of their cutaneous receptive field (Knibestöl & Vallbo, 1970; Johansson & Vallbo, 1979). Fast-adapting mechanoreceptors (FA) of class I (*Meissner corpuscles*) and II (*Pacinian corpuscles*) are excited by skin motion and code the velocity of movement as a frequency of discharge. If a ramp and plateau stimulus is given, they respond only during the movement and not when the skin is held constant at a new position. Slowly adapting mechanoreceptors (SA) of class I (*Merkel cells*) and II (*Ruffini endings*) respond not only during displacement of the skin, but in addition they sustain a discharge of impulses when the skin is held in a new position. Thus, in contrast to FA receptors, they can provide information about the long-term changes

TABLE 5.1   *Possible relation between afferent signals and the control of grip force (GF), during the simple act of lifting an object between index and thumb. FAI and FAII are the fast-adapting receptors; SAI and SAII are the slowly adapting receptors. See text for more detail.*

Events	Activated afferent units	Role of the afferent signal
First contact and loss of contact with an object	SAI & FAI	Triggers the following sequence of a multiphase action
Start of the vertical movement of an object	FAII	Informs CNS of erroneous programming of an anticipatory GF response May trigger reactive GF response
Initiation of unloading and loading phases	SAII	Codes an estimate of object's weight Codes the balance between normal and tangential forces
Frictional slips, i.e. local redistribution of strain/stress patterns in the skin contact area	FAI & SAI	Informs CNS of relative orientation of object and contact area Helps decrease the amount of GF used
Localised finger slip	FAI & FAII SAI	Codes the duration and magnitude of a finger slip May trigger reactive GF response

Based on Turrell (2000), from experimental results reported by Westling and Johansson (1987) and Johansson and Westling (1987).

in mechanical conditions in the skin. Table 5.1 summarizes the specific role that each of these mechanoreceptors is thought to play in the reactive control of GF levels, during the simple act of lifting an object between index and thumb.

Origin of sensory-driven grip force adjustments

When restraining an active manipulandum, the latencies of the reactive GF responses were approximately 82 ms (Johansson et al., 1992, 1992a). The latency between a slip and the onset of the force ratio change was on average 74 ms (Johansson & Westling, 1987). In both of these cases, the range of latencies was about twice the latency of the most rapid spinal reflex in intrinsic hand muscles (Darton, Lippold, Shahani, & Shahani, 1985: 35 ms) but less than half the voluntary reaction time for a GF response triggered by cutaneous input (Johansson & Westling, 1987: 180 ms). Interestingly, the latency of the reactive GF response was of the same order of magnitude as the latencies of the long-latency or long-loop reflex response to suddenly imposed finger or thumb movements (Marsden, Merton, & Morton, 1976; Loo & Mccloskey, 1985). Based on evidence suggesting that long-latency reflexes were supraspinally mediated (Darton et al., 1985) or modulated, Johansson and colleagues proposed that the automatic scaling of GF responses might involve supraspinal, possibly transcortical, pathways (Johansson & Westling, 1987).

The evidence in humans supporting the idea of transcortical reflexes in the automatic control of GF was obtained in studies correlating long-latency reflexes elicited by muscle stretch with electrical stimulation on the one hand, and cortical potentials on the other. In one such study, human subjects were required to maintain a stable grasp on an active manipulandum, while brisk increases in pulling forces were randomly delivered (Macefield & Johansson, 1994). The electroencephalographic (EEG) activity was recorded over the hand area of primary motor cortex (area 4) and the premotor cortex (area 6) of the frontal lobe. EMG of the first interosseous muscle was recorded along with GF and LF measurements. Results provided evidence that short-latency changes in cortical activity were indeed evoked by unpredictable changes in LF. The EMG latency of the interosseous muscle was of 61 ms, which was similar to that observed in response to stretch of that same muscle (Darton et al., 1985) or electrical stimulation of the digital nerves (Evans, Harrisson, & Stephens, 1989). The earliest changes in cortical activity evoked by the brisk loading was a negativity over the hand area appearing 32 ms after the loading, the peak of which represented presumably the arrival of the afferent volley at the cerebral cortex. Contrary to what was hypothesized, there was no evidence of an electrical sign representing an efferent corticospinal volley. Thus, Macefield and Johansson (1994) proposed that the cortex might not directly initiate the long-latency reflexes in grasping actions. Similar conclusions were reached in studies using transcranial magnetic brain stimulation (TMS; Lemon, Johansson, & Westling, 1995, 1996). These studies suggested that the role of the cerebral (premotor and primary motor) cortex may be to provide ongoing regulation of a motor response initiated from subcortical and more specifically cerebellar generators (Macefield & Johansson, 1994).

The *basal ganglia* may be involved in processing and integrating sensory information to guide the motor commands of precision grip. Indeed, patient studies demonstrated that Parkinsonian patients used smaller rates and ranges of GF in lifting tasks, consistent with the clinical observation of bradykinesia (Wing, 1988). This hypothesis was further supported by the observation that Parkinsonian patients have slower onset latencies in sequential tasks where sensory input was needed to trigger the next phase of the motor task (Müller & Abbs, 1991). In cerebellar patients (i.e. patients suffering degenerative lesions of the *cerebellum*) the latency between LF increase after finger–object contact was significantly longer and the level of GF at the start of LF rise was elevated compared to healthy subjects (Müller & Dichgans, 1994). This pattern of response was very similar to that observed in healthy subjects with digital nerve block (Johansson & Westling, 1984a). Hence, one of the roles of the cerebellum might be to integrate central motor commands with tactile signals arriving from the periphery for the release of serial motor commands (Müller & Dichgans, 1994).

In summary, both the basal ganglia and the cerebellum might directly influence neural activity in the hand area of the primary motor cortex via the ventrolateral thalamus (Holsapple, Preston, & Stick, 1991). Consequently, they could both play a role in determining the use of afferent signals for the sensor-driven control of dextrous manipulation, the cerebellum being the possible candidate for the initiation of triggered response in the case of unpredicted destabilizing forces. This hypothesis has been proposed following experimental data studying the initiation of conditioned reflex responses of eyelid to tone- and light-conditioned stimuli in rats (Buonomano & Mauk, 1994), as well as for GF control in man (Macefield & Johansson, 1994).

Reaching for an object

If our friend the waiter decides at some point to stop for a drink of water, he will need to reach for a glass and lift it to his lips. What does the reaching movement comprise? At the end of the initial, rapid, distance-covering phase of movement that brings the hand close to its target, thumb and finger will have opened sufficiently to allow the glass to be grasped. The second phase is made more slowly and leads up to contact of the hand with the glass. In this phase, coordination between transport of the hand by the arm (hand transport) and the distance between thumb and finger (hand aperture) becomes critical if the impact of the collision on contact is to be minimized – especially if the glass is full to the brim!

Since transport of the hand and grasp aperture are subserved by anatomically distinct elements that are capable of being moved separately under voluntary control, the nature of coordination in reaching is of some interest. How does the movement control architecture of the brain specify the linkage between hand transport and hand aperture? This question is considered in the following section. After describing the typical paradigm that is used to study the kinematics of reaching movements, empirical data are presented on the effects of unpredictable step changes in the extrinsic (position, orientation) and intrinsic (size) properties of the to-be-grasped object.

Experimental paradigm

Typically, the target object, for example a cylindrical wood dowel, is placed on end some distance in front of the subject. Starting with the hand close to the body, the subject is required to pick up the cylinder from the side. While keeping the cylinder upright, the subject's task is then to move it some distance before putting it down. Because the cylinders used are relatively lightweight and their diameters are much smaller than their height, these objects are easily knocked over. Consequently, errors in positioning the hand or in adjusting the hand's aperture when picking up the cylinders can have a dramatic effect on movement outcome. Good coordination of hand transport and hand aperture is therefore important, particularly if a degree of positional uncertainty is introduced by varying the location or the orientation of the cylinder from trial to trial. The task may be given a further dimension by using cylinders of various diameters. Indeed, with objects of varying size, the maximum aperture attained by the hand is adjusted in proportion to their size (Jeannerod, 1981).

With the advent of computerized motion analysis, it is now possible to record precise information about the trajectories, final precision of the movements, coordination of digit movements, reaction and movement time as well as their variability. The kinematics of hand transport are typically measured by following a marker placed upon the wrist. This approach usually enables the measurement of the hand movement without contamination by finger movements. The grasp component of the reaching movement can be characterized by the distance between the markers of the tips of the thumb and the index.

The kinematics of normal grasping were described in the basic observations of Jeannerod (1981, 1984, 1986). The transport component was characterized by an asymmetrical velocity profile with a single peak. When the target distance increased, the maximum velocity was higher (see also Chieffi, Fogassi, Gallese, & Gentilucci, 1992; Gentilucci, Chieffi, Scarpa, & Castiello, 1992). During the deceleration phase the velocity decreased rapidly up to a point (peak deceleration) and then decreased less rapidly or even increased again. Peak deceleration occurred at around 70–80% of movement time (Jeannerod, 1986). Typically, for the grasp size pattern, the fingers opened to a maximum aperture and then closed around the object. The maximum size of hand aperture was larger than the real size of the object. The peak aperture of the grasp occurred consistently after the velocity peak of the wrist with a delay of 100–120 ms; that is, around the time of peak deceleration.

Sudden changes

Location   Several experiments have been carried out on grasping stationary objects located at different distances or directions from the subjects' body midline (Chieffi et al., 1992; Gentilucci, Castiello, Corradini, Scarpa, Umiltà, & Rizzolatti, 1991; Gentilucci et al., 1992; Paulignan, MacKenzie, Marteniuk, & Jeannerod, 1991). In these studies, the maximum velocity increased with distance. Hence, the position of the object affected the kinematics of the reach. However, neither distance nor direction affected the size of grasp aperture. What would happen if the object location suddenly changed as subjects were initiating their reach? Would the sudden displacement of the object also affect the size of grasp aperture?

To investigate this question, Paulignan, MacKenzie, Marteniuk, and Jeannerod (1991) presented subjects with three identical objects (10 cm high, 1.5 cm in diameter) placed at 10°, 20° and 30° from the body midline. Subjects were required to reach, grasp and lift as accurately as possible one of the three dowels using a precision grip. The set-up enabled the illumination of one object at a time. On certain trials, upon movement initiation towards the middle dowel, the dowel was made to instantaneously change its location to one of the two other positions, requiring the subject to reorient the hand to the new dowel location. Changing the illumination instantneously from one object to another was perceived by the subject as a displacement of the object. Results consisted of comparing the movement characteristics of the transport and grasp components of these perturbed movements with those measured for non-perturbed control trials.

Analysis of the wrist kinematics (acceleration profile) showed that the motor system reacted to the perturbation as early as 100 ms after the object location had changed (Paulignan, MacKenzie, Marteniuk, & Jeannerod, 1991). The velocity profile of the wrist showed a double peak pattern. The second velocity peak, of lower amplitude than the first, corresponded to the observed reorientation of the hand to the next target location. These results demonstrate that the mechanism responsible for hand transport reacts within a short time when confronted with an unexpected visual error message about object position. Contrary to what was expected, the grasp component was also affected by the perturbation. The change in grasp size showed a double peak pattern in 80% of the perturbed movements

(Paulignan, MacKenzie, Marteniuk, & Jeannerod, 1991). This led the authors to suggest that both the transport and the grasp component might be governed by a single motor program. However, there was no significant correlation between the new velocity peak of the hand and the second peak in grasp aperture, whereas on control trials there was a correlation between velocity and the single peak in hand aperture. In addition, the percentage of movements with a double peak was only 80%. In the remaining 20% of the trials there was only an inflexion point, which implied that the fingers did not close but only stopped opening – reflecting a pause in the actual program. If the two components had been the expression of a single program, such variability would not have been expected. This observation led Jeannerod and colleagues (see, e.g., Jeannerod, Arbib, Rizzolatti, & Sakata, 1995) to suggest that when a perturbation occurs, the double peak pattern reflects coordination or interaction between two separate channels, a size channel for finger opening and a location channel for hand trajectory. We return later to the issue of a temporal coupling between reaching and grasping.

Orientation   What happens if the target object to be grasped remains at the same position but suddenly changes orientation? How does the brain cope with such an event? Does this require the reorientation of the distal segment (wrist), the proximal segment (forearm) or maybe both? Will this change in orientation affect grasp aperture? To investigate these questions, Desmurget, Prablanc, Arzi, Rossetti, Paulignan, and Urquizar (1996) had subjects reach and grasp cylindrical objects presented at a given location with different orientations. During the movements, object orientation was either kept constant (unperturbed trials) or modified at movement onset (perturbed trials).

Results showed that the perturbations in orientation had no effect on the endpoint mean accuracy: no trials were observed in which subjects failed to grasp the object. Hence, the CNS was able to quickly use visual information about the new orientation to reorient the hand. Further analysis of the kinematics revealed that these corrections occurred within 130 ms of the perturbation – approximately the time required for the arm to reach peak acceleration. The spatial parameters of the arm transport were all significantly affected by the change in object orientation (wrist path was significantly perturbed). However, the important point is that during the perturbed trials, the reorganization of the elbow position, forearm rotation and final hand orientation brought the wrist into the exact same final position as that observed when the object was initially presented along the final orientation, i.e. the one reached after perturbation. This indicated that, contrary to robots, humans use all redundant degrees of freedom to optimize movement outcome. Once more, these results highlight the fact that the CNS reacts to unpredictable changes in the environment by a total reorganization of the motor output.

In the study by Desmurget et al. (1996), the effect of a sudden change in object orientation on the size of grasp aperture was not investigated. However, in another study in which the orientation of the object was modified between trials (Mamassian, 1997), it was reported that subjects displayed size constancy from object orientation, i.e. peak hand aperture was linearly related to the physical size of the object without being affected by the orientation of the object. It is possible that similar results would have been observed when sudden changes in object orientation occurred. However, because of the unpredictability of the perturbation, the decrease in achievable accuracy in the transport phase of the reach may have led subjects to opt for a strategic compensation, i.e. to widen their grasp to minimize the risk of a misreach. This hypothesis is discussed in more detail at the end of this section. But before considering the effects of uncertainty, we consider the effects of a sudden change in the intrinsic properties of target objects, such as size.

Size In a study specifically designed to investigate the effect of a sudden change in object size on the kinematics of reaching (Paulignan, Jeannerod, MacKenzie, & Marteniuk, 1991), subjects reached to grasp cylindrical objects between thumb and index finger. The objects were two concentric dowels made of translucent material. The inner ('small') dowel was 10 cm high and 1.5 cm in diameter. The outer ('large') dowel was 6 cm high and 6 cm in diameter. In 20% of the trials a perturbation occurred: the light was unexpectedly shifted from the initial target to the other one. Due to the low level of ambient light, the appearance was that of an instantaneous change in dowel size. Results showed that the profile of change in grip size during the movement in perturbed trials (small to large objects) was marked by a discontinuity: grip size increased up to a first peak, then stopped increasing and finally increased again up to a second peak before decreasing until contact with the dowel. Kinematic analysis revealed that the first peak corresponded to the maximum grasp aperture observed in control trials directed to the small object. The second peak in grasp size occurred later in time and its amplitude corresponded to the size of grip observed in control trials for the large object. The double-peak pattern in grasp size was clearly visible on the curve of grasp velocity. The time of occurrence of the first grasp velocity peak had the same value as in small control trials, and this first peak was followed by a second one corresponding to the reopening of the hand. The point where the velocity of the grasp size was the lowest occurred 330 ms following movement onset. This represented in fact the earliest sign of motor program correction, in the event of the detection of a mismatch between predicted and actual object size. In this experiment, no significant change was found in the time values of the wrist kinematic landmarks with respect to their control trials. This suggests that the transport phase of the reach was not affected by the perturbation, at least in the first 300 ms following movement onset.

In another experiment investigating the effects of a sudden change in object size on the kinematics of reaching actions (Castiello, Bennett, & Stelmach, 1993), subjects used either a precision grip for small objects (2 cm high and 0.7 cm diameter) or a whole-hand grip for larger objects (8 cm high and 8 cm diameter). In this case, results showed that when subjects had to shift from the precision grip/small object to the whole-hand prehension/large object, the transport phase was affected, particularly the deceleration phase (being significantly longer than that observed in unperturbed trials). However, a problem that remained in this study was whether the effect was due to the change in object size or to the change in type of grasp. A study conducted by Bootsma, Marteniuk, MacKenzie, and Zaal (1994) precisely controlled both object size and width, and their results suggested that the critical parameter was neither the size nor the grasp type but rather the area available for placing the fingers upon the object. A significant change in the size of this contact area was indeed the factor affecting the kinematics of the transport phase of the hand.

In summary, these results demonstrate that both the extrinsic (position, orientation) and intrinsic (size, nature) properties of an object can affect not only one of the reaching components but usually both – hand transport and hand aperture – at various degrees. Hence, it seems logical to suggest that these different components are neither planned nor controlled independently. Indeed, whatever the mechanisms that are responsible for hand transport, orientation and grasp opening, they must have access to and use a common representation of the extrapersonal space to reach the intended goal.

Origins of fast visually evoked corrections

Day and Brown (2001) examined the kinematics of reaching movements towards objects that could suddenly change location, performed by a healthy subject with complete agenesis of the corpus callosum. This condition precludes direct communication between left and right cerebral cortices and so, in this subject, a purely cortical visuomotor process would be expected to produce longer latency responses to a target that appears in the visual hemifield contralateral to the responding limb (crossed) compared with ipsilateral hemifield (uncrossed). This acallosal subject showed a significant crossed–uncrossed latency difference (36 ms) that was not present in control subjects. This result is in agreement with data reported for subjects performing simple reaction-time tasks that involve lifting a finger or an arm in response to a visual stimulus presented in either hemifield. In contrast, when the acallosal subject reached for a target that unexpectedly jumped into either visual hemifield, the latencies of mid-flight adjustments were the same (120 ms) irrespective of either the target jump direction or which hand was used.

These results suggest that the mechanisms responsible for the fast corrections of reaching movements are organized at a subcortical level. The precise subcortical pathways involved in mid-flight reach adjustments remain to be established by future studies, possibly in patients with focal brain lesions. However, it is interesting to note that the primate superior colliculus receives direct retinal input (Kaas & Huerta, 1988) and also contains units that have firing patterns closely linked to upper-limb reaching movements (Werner, 1993). The cerebellum is also a structure of interest since it has been shown that ataxic patients with cerebellar damage have some motor abnormalities that are specifically related to the visual corrections of reaching (Day, Thompson, Harding, & Marsden, 1998).

Conclusion

The experimental results reviewed in this section have shown that the central nervous system is able to quickly use incoming information to readjust ongoing movements. Sensorimotor afferences intervene to quickly restore object stability within grasp; visual feedback on the other hand is especially useful to correct the direction and the orientation of a reaching movement. We have seen that various subcortical centres, and especially the cerebellum, are in constant interaction with the cortical regions to adjust and adapt the triggered responses to the context in which the perturbation is experienced, in order to reach the intended goal. The main drawback of reacting to a perturbation, however, is that all corrective mechanisms take time to implement the modification. Hence, in some cases, namely if the environment is stable, predicting changes before they occur may allow for a more efficient interaction with the environment (or at least a faster one). In the following, we consider what mechanisms are available in the human brain to allow an efficient control of goal-directed motor actions in stable environments.

ANTICIPATING DESTABILIZING EVENTS

Anticipatory mechanisms are used prior to movement initiation to prepare the motor apparatus for the destabilizing forces resulting from self-generated and externally imposed movements. This section is concerned specifically with this issue and presents an overview of experimental data obtained in studies where the task involved reaching for, lifting and moving mechanically predictable, passive objects whose relevant physical attributes were stable over time. Because the motor output is self-paced and the force fluctuations are self-generated, the coordinative programming of muscle commands can rely largely on stereotyped behaviour based on memory information from previous motor actions. In the following, we first consider the grip force and grip aperture patterns observed when reaching, lifting and holding well-known objects within precision grip. Then we examine the problems that the CNS must face when the goal of the motor action is to transport these objects through space.

Let us set the scene. Having cleared the table, our friend the waiter is now in the kitchen, preparing to wash the glasses. Picking up each glass in turn, he concentrates on the task at hand in order to minimize the risk of dropping the items as his hands and fingers are covered with soapy water. Transporting the fragile long-stemmed wine glass through the air before dipping it and moving it through the dishwater, the waiter suddenly realizes that his motions are different – slower? – when acting under water than in the air. He suddenly asks himself: how does my brain know in advance how to direct and adjust my actions appropriately when manipulating various objects, and moving them through different environments (air, water)?

Reaching and lifting well-known objects

When grasping an object, a particular type of grip must be selected. Once decided and the reaching movement initiated, the fingers are then required to shape and open wide before closing upon the object. Many behavioural studies have shown that the intrinsic properties of manipulated objects significantly influence both the selection of the type of grip and the grasp kinematics (Gentilucci et al., 1991; Goodale, Meenan, Bülthoff, Nicolle, Murphy, & Racicot, 1994; Jeannerod, 1988). Certain object properties (shape, size, position) may be considered as affordances, i.e. motor representations eliciting particular types of interaction with the object (Gibson, 1966). For example, a wine glass's shape and volume are usually related to affordances eliciting grasping its goblet or its stem. Hence, the question that is posed is which visual analysis occurs when an object is about to be grasped. A first hypothesis assumes that the visual analysis of the object extracts each affordance separately. As a consequence, it analyses the same object from different motor points of view in order to code multiple and independent representations of the same object. In the following, we consider object geometry, size and texture, respectively. Then we continue the discussion by showing that a more probable hypothesis is that the visual analysis extracts concurrently all the affordances from a given object and codes a single motor representation formed by all the types of possible interaction with that object. The formation of such a representation is very probably influenced by our knowledge about that object. A few examples highlighting the role of prior knowledge will thus be presented in a third section. Finally, we consider the brain areas, which may intervene to code the intrinsic properties of the to-be-manipulated objects.

Intrinsic attributes of target objects

When we reach for and grasp objects based on visual cues, we transport the hand towards the target object and orient the hand to position the digits on to the surfaces of the object first to promote grasp stability and also to facilitate the act of gripping (Desmurget et al., 1996) and, hence, to achieve further action goals. Visuomotor mechanisms are also involved in the anticipatory control of the forces applied to the object, once contacted. Indeed, the kinetics (development of GF) of grasping and lifting may be determined largely by the initial view of the object, by a process involving visual identification of the object and the retrieval of implicit memory information concerning its physical properties (Jackson, Jackson, & Rosicky, 1995; Gentilucci, Daprati, Gangitano, Saetti, & Toni, 1996). In the following, we consider three properties that have been experimentally examined: weight, friction and geometry.

Weight   The influence of object weight on the pattern of static GF responses was studied in serial lifting of an object with a constant surface structure (Westling & Johansson, 1984). The weight was varied in an ascending–descending order and results showed that the heavier the weight the larger the GF response, even if somatosensory information about the object's weight was unavailable before lift-off. Indeed, right from the beginning, GF development was adequately programmed for the current weight, with GF- and LF-rate trajectories mainly single-peaked, bell-shaped and roughly proportional to the final force level (Johansson & Westling, 1988). These results suggest that subjects made use of previously acquired and stored information about the object's weight to appropriately scale GF response before initiating the lift. This hypothesis was confirmed in a serial lifting study with unexpected weight changes between lifts. Indeed, in this experiment, results showed that the GF-rate profiles were

programmed on the basis of the weight experienced in the previous trial. Note at this point that the strategy to scale GF levels on the basis of previous trials is especially efficient when constantly lifting the same object, as expected in laboratory-based experiments (see also Witney, Vetter, & Wolpert, 2001). In real-life manipulations, however, the cost of dropping the object may be high and thus, in these situations, anticipatory GF responses may be scaled to the heaviest possible weight in order to minimize the risk of letting the object slip.

Size–weight relationship   To gain accurate information on weight, an object must be hefted in some way or another to get information about its dynamic characteristics. This can be achieved through, e.g., lifting or probing actions. However, at certain times, haptic exploration of an object is not possible. Because most manipulated objects are of similar density, visual information on size can be used, in many cases, to infer weight.

In a lifting task, results showed that when the size and the weight of an object were covaried, subjects used visual size information to adjust GF accordingly before finger–object contact (Gordon, Forssberg, Johansson, & Westling, 1991a). Larger GF magnitudes and force peaks were used when lifting large compared to small boxes. All objects reached similar peak acceleration, indicating an adequate parameterization of the arm movement for the various objects. When the size of the boxes only was varied (constant mass), the differentiation of the anticipatory GF patterns for large and small objects remained (Gordon et al., 1991a, 1991b, 1991c). Peak GF and LF rates as well as peak GF were bigger for the larger boxes. In addition, peaks of acceleration patterns for the large boxes were significantly bigger than for the small boxes (Gordon et al., 1991a), which suggested that subjects were programming GF levels and LF rates for objects of heavier weights when preparing to lift larger boxes. Over the course of the trials, subjects markedly altered their lifting strategies so that by the end of the series, the loading phase and the GF levels used were adequate for the weight of the manipulated boxes (i.e. no difference remained for the different-sized boxes). Hence, it was proposed that afferent information is not only used to correct the GF levels but that it is also useful to update the internal representations of the object attributes. Similar results were demonstrated in experiments where the density of objects was manipulated (Gordon, Westling, Cole, & Johansson, 1993).

Friction   When GF responses are sensory-driven, the GF adjustments are implemented on the basis of friction per se, whether this reflects surface texture or skin properties (see p. 135). However, predictive mechanisms set GF levels before the fingers contact the surface of an object. At this instant, tactile information about slipperiness is not available. Hence, anticipatory GF scaling can be considered to be based on the visual aspect of the texture of the to-be-manipulated object.

As previously described, the relationship between GF and the weight of an object is approximately linear: the heavier the object, the greater the GF peaks. Experimental results have shown that GF levels are also adjusted in anticipation of the texture of an object. In an experiment by Johansson and Westling (1984a), results showed that the balance between GF and LF was adapted to the friction between the skin and the object providing a relatively small safety margin to prevent slips: the more slippery the object, the higher the GF for any given load. The rate of change of GF was also affected by the texture of the object, which indicated that GF was increased faster when the object was covered with smoother surfaces. This strategy, which resembled the pulse height control policy, enabled subjects to reach peak GF within the same time period whatever its required magnitude.

Considering trials with sandpaper, the amount of excess GF employed was greater if the preceding trials were with suede or silk (i.e. more slippery materials) compared to previous trials with sandpaper. These results were interpreted as reflecting an after-effect or a memory trace of frictional characteristics of the manipulated object. Hence, parameter selection for the anticipatory scaling of GF responses appears to rely substantially on memory representations of the physical properties of the object (weight, density, frictional conditions) acquired during previous manipulations.

Geometry In lifting tasks, the shape of an object also must be taken into account, because the geometric relationship between the grasp surfaces imposes various constraints on the force coordination (Blake, 1992). First, for each grasp surface the direction of the applied fingertip force must be within the limits imposed by the frictional condition, i.e. within a certain angle relative to the normal of the grasp surface. Second, for equilibrium, all forces and moments applied to the object must sum to zero (Baud-Bovy & Soechting, 2001). Recently, Jenmalm and colleagues conducted a series of studies to examine the relative importance of visual versus digital afferent information for the adaptation of GF to object shape (Jenmalm & Johansson, 1997) and surface curvature (Jenmalm, Goodwin, & Johansson, 1998) while subjects lifted objects with precision grip.

To investigate the effect of the curvature of the grip surfaces, Jenmalm et al. (1998) asked subjects to lift and hold objects of various weights. The matching pairs of grasped surfaces were spherically curved with one of five different curvatures: concave with radius 20 or 40 mm; flat; convex with

radius 20 or 40 mm. Results showed that subjects adjusted GF to the weight of the object but that the motor responses were inconsistently and incompletely modified by the surface curvature. At first, one may think that subjects were not able to adjust GF levels to the geometry of the to-be-manipulated object. However, this behaviour may simply be a strategy used to minimize the chances of dropping an object with curved surfaces. Results revealed, for example, that subjects used larger safety margins for objects with higher curvatures.

In contrast to the situation with curvature, modifying the shape of an object drastically affected the GF used by the subjects. In their experiment, Jenmalm and Johansson (1997) had subjects lift a test object with interchangeable grip surfaces, of which the angle – in relation to the vertical plane – could be changed in 10° steps, from –40° to +30°. At 0°, the grip surfaces were parallel in two vertical planes; at positive and negative angles, the object tapered upward and downward, respectively. With these different surface properties, subjects adapted the balance between GF and LF in a very systematic fashion with respect to the object's shape. Hence, a rather constant safety margin was maintained against frictional slips. More detailed analyses of the results revealed that subjects used visual cues to adapt parametrically, and in anticipation, the GF level to the shape of the object. Indeed, in the absence of somatosensory information from the digits (with local anaesthesia of the index finger and thumb), sighted subjects still adjusted the GF levels to the object shape. However, with neither vision nor somatosensory inputs, the subjects' performance was severely impaired. With normal digital sensibility and in absence of visual feedback, shape cues were obtained after finger–object contact and modifications in the GF profiles were then implemented within 100 ms after first contact. Consequently, when the fingers first contacted the object, only memory information from the previous trial could control the GF level applied. Overall, these results strongly argue for the conjunction of both visual and somatosensory inputs with sensorimotor memories, for the fine adjustment of GF levels to the geometry of objects during manipulative tasks.

Internal representations of target objects for action planning

As we have just seen, an object possesses multiple features that need to be taken into account by the CNS in order to reach for and lift an object with success. One may then ask how grasping movements are guided. First, it is possible that a single motor representation of an object is available and used to plan motor actions. This single representation would code all the possible affordances enabled by that object. Alternatively, it is possible that motor actions are guided by multiple representations

(Salimi, Hollender, Frazize, & Gordon 2000), each of which would code a different motor act according to the physical properties of that item. In a recent study, Gentilluci (2002) ran a series of studies to test these two competing hypotheses.

Opposition space is the space surrounding the portion of the object with which the hand must interact. It is characterized by the axis along which the fingers approach and touch the object. If one considers the first hypothesis for which a single representation of an object is used to scale movement parameters, then the kinematics of a reaching–grasping action should be affected not only by the size and orientation of the object but also by other object affordances that do not have a direct relevance with the task at hand, e.g. the semantic family of the object (fruit vs. animal). If, however, the second hypothesis is true and multiple representations of the object are available, then the kinematics of a movement where the subject must reach and grasp for a complex object will be affected only by the affordance related to the opposition space of that object (Arbib, 1990). Gentilluci (2002) had subjects reach for different objects (items of fruit, bells, or cylindrical pegs) that varied in size and shape. In all experiments (8 in total), care was taken to maintain constant the surface where subjects' fingers grasped the object, i.e. the contact area on all objects had identical physical features. Results revealed that volume, shape and also familiarity of the object influenced the grasp kinematics. These data suggest that even if not relevant for the task at hand, multiple features of an object can influence the planning and scaling of the motor parameters. This is in agreement with the first hypothesis, which suggests that a single object motor representation, coding for all object affordances, is involved in the implementation of grasp kinematics, and also probably for grasp kinetics. Along these lines, it has recently been suggested (Glover, 2003) that when planning an action, the CNS may use a richer visual representation than does on-line control, in order to allow the latter to be faster and more adaptable. Further studies are, however, required in order to specify the fundamentals of such a dichotomy.

The role of prior knowledge and intention

Until now we have considered the intrinsic properties of the target object. However, what about the context in which the action is performed? One can imagine that the speed of the movement, the direction of the reach or even the position of the hand on the object will depend on what motivated the action in the first place. Indeed, when interacting with the environment, it is sometimes necessary to control and modulate intentionally the outcome of otherwise preplanned movement. How do our intentions or prior knowledge of what is to come modify the low-level, automatic control of action? Very little

work has investigated the role of these cognitive processes in the fine adjustment of motor actions, and consequently we briefly pinpoint a few relevant studies.

During natural lifting actions, many objects require careful movements because they are fragile or placed on unstable surfaces. Hence, in such a situation, the accuracy requirements of the reach are high. An early study by Marteniuk, MacKenzie, Jeamerod, Antènes, and Dugas (1987) revealed in fact that the fragility of an object could influence the transport component of a reach. Subjects' performance was contrasted in picking up a light bulb (with the metal base facing away from the subject) and a tennis ball. Even though both objects were, from the subjects' perspective, similar in shape and size, the deceleration phase of the reach was longer for the light bulb than for the tennis ball. This adjustment presumably served to reduce the impact on collision, to limit the risk of breaking the fragile light bulb. Although not documented, there may also have been widening of the hand aperture to reduce the possibility of bumping into the object during the approach.

Depending on the environmental conditions in which they must perform, subjects can voluntarily modify the parameters of the reach and grasp movement, in order to optimize the endpoint accuracy of the action. For example, when subjects are asked to grasp objects with a precision grip at two different speeds (normal and fast), Wing, Turton, and Fraser (1986) observed that the fingers opened wider for fast reaches than those performed at normal speed. Similar results were reported in later studies (Wallace & Weeks, 1988; Wallace, Weeks, & Kelso, 1990) but also in a study where subjects reached for objects with unpredictable visual conditions (Jakobson & Goodale, 1991). Without visual feedback, subjects moved more slowly and the hand aperture was wider. Under both of these conditions (vision and speed), it appeared that the increased width of hand opening served to compensate for the increase in transport variability. It is interesting to note that instruction and knowledge of what is to come can also affect the execution of reactive responses that are triggered by sudden changes in the environment. This was demonstrated, for example, in the 'sherry glass' experiment (Traub, Rothwell, & Marsden, 1980), in restraining an active manipulandum (Ohki, Edin, & Johansson, 2002) or in a situation of externally imposed collisions (Turrell, Li, & Wing, 1999).

Another good example of the effect of self-knowledge on coordination was provided by a case study of reaching by a girl fitted with a below-elbow artificial hand that provided no tactile feedback (Wing & Fraser, 1983). The girl was asked to pick up cylindrical pieces of wooden dowel balanced on end and to use either her natural left hand or her artificial right hand. In the later phases of reaching, as the target was neared, the trajectories of the artificial hand revealed a slower approach and a delayed closing relative to the trajectories of the natural hand. Whereas delayed closing gave greater clearance as the hand approached the target object, the slower approach was probably a strategy to allow more time to process visual feedback and, consequently, compensate for the lack of tactile feedback. Hence, the knowledge of our own limited capabilities can play a substantial role in the planning of motor parameters. This is the central idea of the theoretical model proposed by Rosenbaum and colleagues, for the control of grasping actions.

In the last ten years, Rosenbaum and colleagues have debated that a key issue in the cognitive control of movement is to determine how movements are chosen when many movements are possible. To address this issue in one of their studies, they had subjects reach for a bar that was to be moved as quickly as possible from a home location to a final location (Rosenbaum, Vaughan, Barnes, & Jorgensen, 1992). Subjects generally grabbed the bar in a way that would afford a comfortable posture once placed on the final location. In addition, the thumb was oriented towards the end of the bar that was to be aligned with the final target. From these data, they concluded that the CNS makes use of hand-grip positions by retrieving a selection of hand posture representations of previous reaches (Rosenbaum, Meulenbroek, Vaughan, & Janien, 1999). Action selection was not carried out by series of computations that treated each reach as a new behavioural event. In fact, the knowledge of subjects' own limited capabilities, the knowledge of the goal of their action and also of their specific intentions seemed to have guided the selection of the preferred movement and/or final hand posture.

The earlier version of this model proposed that when a spatial target is selected, stored postures are evaluated for the contributions they can make to the task (Rosenbaum, Engelbrecht, Bushe, & Loukopoulos, 1993; Rosenbaum, Loukopoulos, Meulenbroek, Vaughan, & Engelbrecht, 1995). A special weighted average (the Gaussian average) is taken of the postures to find a single target posture. Hence, movement to the target posture is achieved without explicit planning of the trajectory, but the reaching motion is driven by error correction (reducing the discrepancy between the current and target posture) shaped by inertia. Rosenbaum's model is now based on the idea that coordination of reaching and grasping movements capitalize on avoiding obstacle (Rosenbaum, Meulenbroek, & Vaughan, 1999; Vaughan, Rosenbaum, & Meulenbroek, 2001). According to this version of the model, movement is achieved by reducing the distance between the starting angle and target angle of each joint. In their view, one of the most important aspects of motion planning is establishing a constraint hierarchy – a set of prioritized requirements defining the task to be performed (Rosenbaum,

Meulenbroek, & Vaughan, 2001). For grasping, constraints would include avoiding collisions with the to-be-grasped objects and minimizing movement-related effort. The model explains compensation for reduced joint mobility, tool use, practice effects and performance errors as well as certain aspects of movement kinematics (Rosenbaum, Meulenbroek, Vaughan, & Janien, 2001).

Even if more work is needed in order to fully understand the relationship between the automatic and the more controlled processes involved in the fluid adjustment of motor actions (Delevoye-Turrell, Giersch, & Danion, 2002, 2003), the data reported here suggest that higher-order brain processes can affect and modulate the activity of the more automatic motor mechanisms that are involved in the predictive control of motor actions. In the following, we consider the brain mechanisms and the neural substrate that may be involved.

Neural substrate of internal representations

It has been proposed that there may exist neural sensorimotor memories that encode various features of the external world (Ito, 1994), such as the physical and dynamic properties of objects (weight, texture, density), the context in which an action is to be performed, or the consequences that the performed actions may have on whole body balance. The advantage of using updated internal memories is that reliable prediction of the consequences of an action is made possible and, consequently, the appropriate set of motor commands can be programmed and released. This process would optimize the chances of performing a task with success and, furthermore, it would minimize the need for corrective reactive responses. In addition, in manual exploratory tasks where independent finger movements are superimposed on the basic grasp component, a stable hand posture would be beneficial for the tactile exploration of the object (Johansson & Westling, 1984a).

The internal neural representation of the intrinsic (physical and dynamic) properties of a manipulated object includes information on weight and friction (Johansson & Westling, 1991), size (Gordon et al., 1991a, 1991b, 1991c), density and mass distribution (Gordon et al., 1993). The anatomical location of neural circuits involved in storage and retrieval of internal neuronal representations is still unclear, but both animal and human clinical data implicate the *posterior parietal* and *premotor cortical areas* in the control of object-oriented manual actions (Jeannerod, 1994; Sakata & Taira, 1994). The anticipatory control of GF adjustments related to visual identification of intrinsic physical properties of an object is thought to involve the dorsal stream projecting from the striate cortex to the primary somatosensory cortex (S1) of the posterior parietal lobe. Indeed, pharmacological inactivation of SI neurons in area 2 causes deficits in precision grasping (Hikosaka, Tanaka, Sakamoto, & Iwamura, 1985). Furthermore, the integration of proprioceptive, tactile and visual cues necessary for object-oriented manual actions would be made possible by the various egocentric and allocentric spatiotemporal maps which would register and integrate the different sources of information into a common frame of reference (Pause, Kunesch, Binkofski, & Freund, 1989), ready to use for the generation of motor programs. Evidence for this comes from a recent monkey study reported by Graziano, Cooke, and Taylor (2000). In a human patient, Wolpert, Goodbody, and Husain (1998) present an interesting case study that further demonstrates the possible role of the superior parietal lobe in the storage of internal representations.

To adequately generate motor programs to gently lift an object in precision grip, it is necessary to predict the intrinsic characteristics of the object as well as the state of one's own body, i.e. the configuration of the body (joint angles and limb position). Wolpert and colleagues (Wolpert, 1997; Wolpert, Goodbody, & Husain 1998) proposed that the estimates of the state of an object and limb are provided by combining sensory feedback and motor commands integrated throughout the duration of an action. The new state estimate would be made by recursively updating the current state estimate based on the incoming motor and sensory signals. In this framework, the state representation needs to be stored and updated as new information arrives (see Figure 5.3). Updating the state estimate and storing it between updates can be considered as two functionally and possibly anatomically distinct processes (Wolpert, Goodbody, & Husain, 1998). It has been shown that the intermediate cerebellum is specialized for the adaptive control of object-oriented manual actions (van Kan, Horn, & Gbson, 1994). Consequently, the updating of the state estimate could take place within the cerebellum (Wolpert, Ghahramani, & Jordan, 1995a, 1995b; Wolpert, Msall, & Kavato, 1998). A case study of impaired manipulation suggests that the parietal cortex is a potential candidate for storing the updated state estimate.

In their case study, Wolpert, Goodbody, and Husain (1998) report the performance of a patient (PJ) with a parietal lesion who had unusual sensory and motor deficits that became apparent only as the duration of a sensory stimulus or movement increased. When tactile stimuli were held still on her hand, with her eyes closed, PJ reported that the sensation faded over seconds until she could no longer detect the stimulus. The time to fade increased linearly with the mass of the object (for 10 g, the percept took 2.9 s; for 150 g, it took 10.5 s to fade). The motor consequence of this tactile fading was the incapacity to maintain a constant

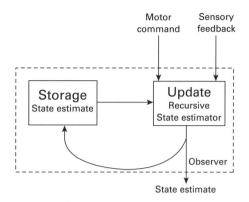

Figure 5.3 *Schematic diagram of the sensorimotor integration process: the observer monitors and integrates both the inputs and the outputs of the system (i.e. the sensory feedback and motor commands) by recursively updating the stored state estimate. The storing of the state estimate would be localized within the superior parietal lobe; the updating of the state estimate would be in micro zones of the intermediate cerebellum. (Adapted from Wolpert, Miall, & Kawato, 1998.)*

level of GF in absence of visual information about her hand: GF decayed to near zero over 10–15 s. When maintaining a constant arm posture (in absence of vision), PJ perceived her limb to start drifting after a latency of 18 s, following always the same trajectory, until it seemed to disappear. Corresponding to this proprioceptive drift, PJ had a deficit when making slow pointing movements to peripheral targets while fixating a central stimulus. Her results were similar to those obtained with patients with optic ataxia, who had lesions of the superior parietal lobe and adjacent intraparietal sulcus (Perenin & Vighetto, 1988). However, the interesting point was that these pointing inaccuracies were observed only for very slow movements (normal performance was observed for fast movements). These results suggested that the fading observed with constant stimuli was a process that continued when the sensory signal was changing, such as during movement, and was therefore manifested only when the time course of movement was prolonged to that of the temporal decay.

The explanation proposed by Wolpert, Goodbody, and Husain (1998) was that in PJ the storage mechanism for the state estimate was damaged so that the stored state estimate was continually decaying over time. Importantly, the observed deficits emerged on a similar time course for sensory and motor processes. It was hypothesized that, although the sensory and motor signals that were used to update the representation might have been normal, they were integrated into a representation that was continually decaying. The recursive state estimation process, which used this corrupted and inaccurate estimate to form the next estimate, would thus result in an accumulation of error over time. Consequently, it was suggested that the superior parietal lobe is the location for maintaining internal representations common to both the sensory and motor systems, which are necessary for both perception and action.

Transporting objects through various load force regimes

When accelerating and decelerating an object through space, appreciable inertial forces act upon the hand in addition to the effects of gravity acting upon the object. Consequently, to maintain a stable grasp on an object during transport, GF needs to overcome the LF fluctuations corresponding to the vectorial sum of gravitational force and inertial force, the latter being proportional to the acceleration of the hand. Thus, LF fluctuates with the acceleration pattern of the hand grasping an object. The question then arises as to how GF is modulated during movement: is GF adapted as a reflex response to LF changes or is there anticipation? If the latter is true, is GF modulated in parallel with LF fluctuations or do subjects opt for a simpler solution, i.e. use a constant but high level of GF throughout the movement?

Self-imposed movements through air

In point-to-point transport, the faster the movement, the bigger the acceleration and, consequently, the bigger the LF changes. In both vertical and horizontal movements, GF is modulated with and thus anticipates LF fluctuations (Flanagan, Tresilias, & Wing, 1995a; Flanagan & Wing, 1995). A significant correlation is found between both the timing (>0.9) and the relative magnitudes (0.6) of GF and LF peaks, indicating that GF responses are programmed to compensate for the predicted changes in LF (Flanagan & Wing, 1995). These findings are robust and have been observed while lifting objects at different rates (Kinoshita, Ikuta, Kawai, & Udo, 1993), making cyclic arm movements at different frequencies (Flanagan, Tresilian, & Wing, 1995b), during shaking actions (Kinoshita, Kawai, Ikuta, & Teraoka, 1996), maintaining a stable grip on an object while jumping up to or down from a chair (Flanagan & Tresilian, 1994) and using precision grip to maintain whole body postural stability (Wing et al., 1997).

The parallel changes observed in GF and LF suggested that modulations in GF are planned as opposed to being reactive in nature (Flanagan & Wing, 1995). Indeed, if changes in GF were reflex responses, then one would expect peak GF to lag behind peak LF by 30–90 ms (Johansson & Westling, 1987; Cole & Abbs, 1988), which is not the case. In addition, sensory-driven corrections (e.g. GF increases in response to slips) would have resulted in loss of grasp stability with rapid movements of a small object, since the hand could have slipped off the object in the time it took long-latency reflexes to have an effect. Hence, it has been hypothesized that the tight GF to LF scaling is anticipatory in nature. This implies that the CNS is able to predict detailed features of the movement kinematics (Flanagan & Wing, 1995, 1997; Flanagan et al., 1995a, 1995b).

Two mechanisms have been proposed to explain the anticipatory modulation of GF to LF changes. First, commands to hand and arm muscles might be issued in parallel by some high-level control system, which would specify both the arm movement and GF trajectories (Flanagan & Wing, 1995). An alternative hypothesis is that the commands resulting in arm movement are used to predict the load at the hand, and hence used to plan current needs for the hand. In this scheme, the arm commands are sent to a GF module that transforms them into GF commands. Hence, this module would be able to predict the LF changes resulting from arm movement on the basis of the planned arm kinematics (Flanagan & Wing, 1997). To optimize the process, the GF module would also receive inputs about the physical and dynamic properties of the object, the final goal of the action and even the environmental constraints in which the action is to be performed.

In summary, experimental results indicate that GF adjustments anticipate not only the environmental constraints imposed by the physical properties of the object but also the consequences of our own actions (timing and amplitude of the movement). The underlying reason for tightly scaling GF to LF fluctuations could be to economize effort (Johansson & Westling, 1984b) and render the manipulative action more efficient (Delevoye-Turrell, Li, & Wing, 2003). Another possibility is that GF responses are skilfully adjusted to improve the ability to sense changes in forces acting upon the hand. With lower GF levels, the finger pads are less compressed, which may allow greater sensitivity in the sensory apparatus of the hand (Flanagan et al., 1995a). Finally, lower GF levels afford a more compliant grasp, which can be useful to disengage a digit for a further use in tactile exploration (Flanagan, Burstedt, & Johansson, 1999) or essential to dampen collision-induced vibrations (Turrell et al., 1999). Very probably, the tight GF to LF scaling is the outcome of a combination of these three possibilities and more. Regardless, a striking feature of the coupling between GF and LF is that it is not easily over-ridden by voluntary control (Flanagan & Wing, 1995; Flanagan et al., 1995b). When asked to keep GF constant during the movement, subjects increased the overall level of GF but were unable to follow instructions: GF was still modulated in phase with LF, although the amplitude of the modulation was reduced. These empirical results indicate that the tight GF to LF scaling is not penetrable (i.e. can not be consciously disrupted) but that top-down control is possible to a certain degree.

Adapting to various micro-gravity environments

So far, the LF fluctuations that have been considered have been those experienced under normal conditions on Earth, i.e. gravitational (effect of mass) and inertial (effect of accelerating an object) under the effects of 1G force. In the following we review a selection of studies that were run to investigate if subjects are also able to predict LF changes following different physical laws.

Hyper-gravity and micro-gravity conditions

During parabolic flight manoeuvres, gravity changes are induced with two periods of hyper-gravity, associated with a doubling of normal terrestrial gravity and a 20 s period of zero gravity. Accordingly, the object's weight changes from being weightless to being twice as heavy as normally experienced.

Previous work has suggested that proprioceptive feedback is degraded in hyper-gravity conditions (Lackner & Graybiel, 1981), which is thought to explain the impairments observed during weight discrimination tasks (Darwood, Repperger, & Goodyear, 1991; Ross & Reschke, 1982), as well as in pointing and grasping tasks (Canfield, Comrey, & Wilson, 1953; Bock, Howard, Money, & Arnold, 1992). A more recent study also showed that the control of isometric forces is impaired under hyper-gravity condition. Subjects consistently underestimated the force they produced (Bock & Cheung, 1998). An interesting question is then: how will GF be controlled when subjects are asked (1) to maintain an object stationary or (2) to perform point-to-point movements? If proprioceptive information is required to perform such a task (because GF adjustments are based on feedback control mechanisms), then the fine adjustments of GF responses should be severely impaired in these tasks in hyper- and micro-gravity conditions.

During parabolic flights, GF recordings revealed that force control exerted against stationary held objects was seriously disturbed during the first experience of hyper- and micro-gravity, with GF being exceedingly high and yielding irregular fluctuations (Hermsdörfer et al., 1999). However, within a few test trials (i.e. very quickly), GF traces were found to

be smooth, the force level being scaled to the object's weight under normal and high-G conditions. Furthermore, the GF responses changed in parallel with the weight of the object during the transitions between hyper- and micro-gravity. These results suggest that GF control mechanisms are able to cope with both hyper- and micro-gravity, either by incorporating relevant receptor signals, such as those originating from cutaneous mechanoreceptors, or by adequately including perceived gravity signals into the motor programs. Overall these results strongly suggest that the adjustment of GF during object manipulation is primarily based on a predictive control of force which takes into account the force conditions of the environment in which the motor action is performed.

Previously, we have seen that during point-to-point movements under normal gravitational conditions, GF precisely anticipates both gravitational and inertial loads. During vertical movements performed under normal and hyper-gravity, a LF maximum occurs at the lower turning point and a minimum at the upper turning point; the LF pattern is, however, completely changed under micro-gravity. Indeed, in this latter case, the upper turning point is also associated with a LF maximum. Even if subjects are not fully aware of such gravity-dependent LF variations, recent results have shown that GF responses (in two healthy subjects) underwent the same characteristic changes as the LF (Hermsdörfer et al., 2000). Hence, the CNS is able to adjust GF in anticipation of arm movement-induced fluctuations in LF, under different and novel load conditions. Interestingly, the predictive coupling of GF and LF was observed even during the transitions between gravity levels, indicating very rapid adaptation to changing LF regimes. In agreement with these results, Nowak, Hermsdörfer, Philipp, Marquardt, Glausser, and Mai (2001) and Nowak, Glasauer, Meyer, Mai, and Hermsdörfer (2002) have recently reported similar results but further investigated the effects of anaesthetizing the thumb and index finger during the manipulation of the object. Under these conditions, results revealed that initially, i.e. on the first two trials, the object slipped within the subjects' fingers. Thereafter, subjects substantially increased the GF levels used, which resulted in elevated force ratios between maximum GF and LF. Interestingly, GF was still modulated with the movement-induced load changes. These results are similar to those reported by Flanagan et al. (1995b) during cyclic movements under normal gravity conditions, and imply that cutaneous afferent information from the grasping digits is important for the economic scaling of the GF magnitude according to the actual loading conditions. This information is also necessary for reactive grip force adjustments in response to sudden load perturbations. However, sensory feedback seems to play only a subordinate role for the precise anticipatory temporal coupling between grip and load forces (Nowak et al., 2002).

Artificial load force regimes

Flanagan and Wing (1997) conducted an experiment in which subjects rapidly moved a passive manipulandum that could be subjected to three contrasting LF regimes: a pure inertial condition (LF proportional to hand acceleration), a viscous condition (LF proportional to hand velocity) and a spring-like condition (LF proportional to the distance from the start position).

Under the inertial condition, GF had two peaks that corresponded in time and magnitude to the two peaks in LF produced as a consequence of accelerating and decelerating the object. Under the viscous condition, there was a single GF peak, which corresponded both in amplitude and in time to the peak LF. Finally, in the spring-like condition, LF primarily reflected changes in position and once more GF was modulated in parallel with LF fluctuations. The cross-correlation between GF rate and LF rate revealed that, in all three LF regimes, GF preceded and, thus, anticipated LF changes on average by 14 ms. In this study, LF was dependent on both the dynamics of the manipulandum (i.e. the load properties) and the kinematics of the arm movement. Consequently, as was suggested for hyper- and micro-gravity conditions, the CNS not only builds an internal representation of the physical properties of the external load but it also integrates its dynamics into an internal dynamic model of the motor apparatus and contextual environment as a whole (Flanagan & Wing, 1997). The concept and theoretical bases for the existence of internal dynamic models in the human brain is now considered.

Internal dynamic models for motor control

To achieve a given acceleration pattern and maintain a stable grasp of an object, the motor commands (sent to the arm and fingers, respectively) must take into account (1) the state of the arm (its joint angles and angular velocities); (2) the masses, the moments of inertia and the centre of masses of the upper arm and forearm; and finally (3) the intrinsic attributes of the grasped object (physical and dynamic properties). More global environmental conditions or contexts (e.g. the orientation of the body relative to gravity) will also contribute to arm dynamics. Hence, multiple factors can influence the limb dynamics and must be taken into account to generate adequate motor commands. The notion of internal models, a system that mimics the behaviour of a natural process, has emerged as an important theoretical concept in motor control to explain how the CNS adapts to produce

effective motor control in a variety of, and constantly changing, environments.

Internal forward and inverse models   There are two types of internal models relevant to the control of intended self-generated actions: *internal forward* and *internal inverse models*. Forward models capture the forward or causal relationship between the inputs to the motor system and the movement outputs (Kawato, Furwaka, & Suzuki, 1987). This internal process mimics the *motor-to-sensory transformations* that are achieved on a slower time scale by the physical receptors in the musculoskeletal system (Jordan, 1995). A forward dynamic model of the arm, for example, predicts the next state (position and velocity) given the current state and an efference copy of the descending motor command (Wolpert, 1997), i.e. given a motor command as input, it outputs the expected movement of the limb. To correct a movement on the basis of reafferences from the periphery takes time because of the inevitable delays in the control pathways (afferent delays from the receptors to the CNS; delays in processing the motor command; efferent axonal delays to send the motor commands down to the muscles; muscle latency and delays between acceleration and significant change in position). Consequently, internal forward models can be used to predict errors and, hence, to compute fast (internal) corrections, without the need to wait for delayed feedback about the outcome of the actual movement. Because they provide a rapid prediction of the sensory consequences of a movement, forward models can also be used to cancel the sensory effects of self-generated actions (Blakemore, Goodbody, & Wolpert, 1998; Blakemore, Wolpert, & Frith, 1998).

Inverse models, in contrast, invert the motor system in the sense of specifying the motor command that will achieve the desired change in state (e.g. make the hand reach a given position in space). Thus, this model provides the *sensory-to-motor transformations* and is a fundamental module in open-loop control systems:[1] such transformations allow the computation of appropriate motor commands without relying on feedback (Jordan, 1995). A simple example of an inverse model is the vestibulo-ocular reflex, which couples the movement of the eyes with the motion of the head, thereby allowing gaze fixation in space. In effect, the CNS computes an internal inverse model of the physical relationship between muscle contraction and eye motion. The generated motor command that is predicted to yield a particular eye velocity will be set to make the eyes move by an amplitude equal and opposite to the motion of the head (Robinson, 1981). In limb movements it has been proposed that, in a system made of pairs of forward and inverse models, internal inverse models could act as the *controllers*. In this case, forward models would act as the *predictors* to determine and select

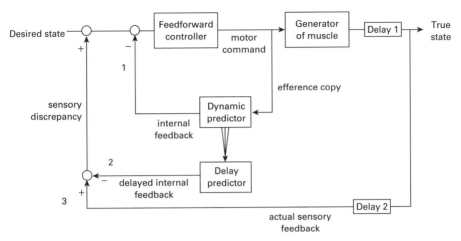

Figure 5.4 *The Smith predictor. The* desired output *is sent to a* feedforward controller *that generates a set of motor commands. This is then transformed into a set of muscle commands that reaches the peripheral effectors after a given efference delay. The* dynamic predictor, *which receives an* efference copy *of the muscle commands, is the centre that generates the internal feedback (loop 1). The* delay predictor *receives a copy of the* internal feedback *and delays it by an estimated time corresponding to the summation of the delays in the efference and afference pathways (loop 2). To ensure that the executed movement is equal to that desired, the* actual sensory feedback *(loop 3) is compared to the* delayed internal feedback. *(Adapted from Miall et al., 1993.)*

the most appropriate inverse model (Wolpert & Kawato, 1998).

The Smith predictor model We have just seen that an inverse model (or controller) transforms motor goals into motor commands allowing rapid actions. A forward model (or predictor) provides a rapid prediction of the outcome of the current movement. Because of the uncertainties associated with the execution of the movement (e.g. errors can be made in estimating the current state of the limb or the state of the environment), the motor control process can never be sure that the action that was produced was actually the intended one. Thus, for accuracy, the motor process needs at one point to compare the internal feedback (as provided by the forward model) and the actual sensory feedback signals from the receptors. The difficulty is then to detect a mismatch between a rapid prediction of the outcome of a movement and the real feedback that arrives later in time. At this point what is required is an estimate of the time delay before actual feedback is received (Miall, Weir, Wolpert, & Stein, 1993).

First suggested for factory processes with long transport delays (Smith, 1959), the *Smith predictor* has been shown to be applicable to biological systems (Miall et al., 1993). The Smith predictor controller operates on two separate models, which both lie on internal feedback loops. In Figure 5.4, the desired output is sent to an *inverse model* that generates a set of motor commands. This is then

transformed into a set of muscle commands that reaches the peripheral effectors (e.g. muscles of the arm and fingers) after a given efference delay (delay 1). To confirm that the executed movement is equal to the desired one, the *actual sensory feedback* needs to be compared to the predicted sensory feedback. The *dynamic predictor*, which receives a copy of the motor commands *(efference copy)*, is the centre that generates the predicted sensory feedback or *internal feedback*. This process is represented by loop 1. The *delay predictor* receives a copy of the *internal feedback* and delays it by an estimated time corresponding to the summation of the delays in the efference (delay 1) and efference pathways (delay 2). This process is represented by loop 2. By comparing the *actual sensory feedback* (loop 3) with the *delayed internal feedback*, an error signal or *sensory discrepancy* signal is computed.

Because the transport delays are excluded, loop 1 constitutes the internal negative-feedback loop. If it is accurate and the system performance is reliable, this loop can provide near-optimal control of the system. Because the control loop that includes the *delay predictor* takes into account an accurate representation of all temporal delays, its role is to delay the *internal feedback* to synchronize it with the *actual sensory feedback* from the periphery. Thereby, it is possible to compare the actual performance of the system (loop 3) with the predicted performance (loop 2). The two signals cancel out if the sensory feedback from the produced movement is equal to

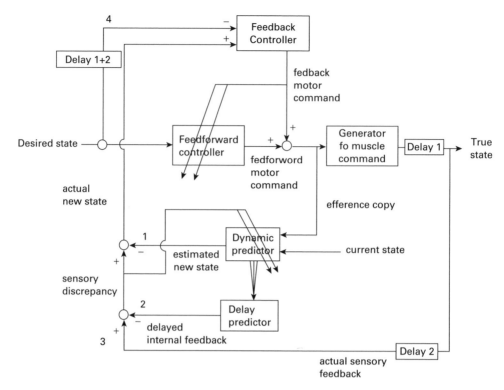

Figure 5.5 *Feedback error learning model. At the end of each movement, the actual* sensory feedback *(loop 3) is compared to the* delayed internal feedback *(loop 2) in order to compute a* sensory
discrepancy. *After integration with the new state estimate (computed by the dynamic predictor, loop 1)
the* new state *is known. This signal is used as input to a* feedback controller *that will compute an
error signal representing the discrepancy between the desired and actual state (loop 3). The feedback controller transforms the error signal into a set of* feedback motor commands *that is used both
to correct the* feedforward motor commands *and as a training signal to correct and refine the* feedforward controller. *(Adapted from Wolpert, Miall, & Kawato, 1998.)*

that predicted. Conversely, if these signals are
not equal, the *sensory discrepancy* can be used to
render the *dynamic predictor* more accurate and,
thus, improve the prediction of future similar
movements.

Adapting to new conditions Both forward and
inverse internal models depend on the dynamics of
the motor systems, which change greatly during
development or injury. In addition, motor actions
often involve interacting with the external world,
e.g. handling objects with unknown mechanical
properties or acting in unstable environments. Thus,
they must be adaptable (Wolpert & Kawato, 1998;
Jordan, 1995). Forward models can be learned relatively straightforwardly by supervised learning,
using the sensory feedback that results from the comparison between the predicted consequences of an
action (delayed internal feedback, loop 2 of Figure 5.4)
and the actual sensory feedback (loop 3). The
implementation of inverse models is, however,

more problematic. Hence, several approaches have
been proposed to solve the problem of motor learning, e.g. direct inverse modelling (Kuperstein,
1988), distal supervised learning (Jordan &
Rumelhart, 1992), reinforcement learning (Sutton,
1988) and bootstrap learning (Nowlan, 1991). The
focus of the next paragraph is on a direct approach
known as *feedback error learning* (Kawato et al.,
1987), for which the feedback error learning makes
use of a feedback controller to guide the learning of
the feedforward controller.

Figure 5.5 is a simplified diagram of the proposed model. At the end of each movement, the
actual sensory feedback (loop 3) is compared to the
delayed internal feedback (loop 2) in order to compute a *sensory discrepancy*. After integration with
the *new state estimate* (inferred from the efference
copy), the actual *new state* is known. This signal is
used as input to a *feedback controller*, who computes
an error signal representing the discrepancy
between the desired and actual state (loop 4). The

feedback controller transforms this error signal into a set of *feedback motor commands* that are used both to correct the *feedforward motor commands* and as a training signal to learn and refine the *inverse model*.

As we interact with multiple different objects and contexts, Wolpert and Kawato (1998) proposed three potential benefits in the use of multiple pairs of inverse and forward models. First, a modular approach would permit an efficient coding of the world as each pair of inverse and forward models could capture the motor commands necessary when acting with a particular object or within a particular environment. Second, the use of multimodular systems would allow individual modules to participate in motor learning without affecting the motor behaviours already learned by other modules. Finally, many situations are derived from combinations of previously experienced contexts. Hence, by modulating the contribution of the outputs of various inverse models to the final motor commands, an enormous repertoire of behaviour may be generated. The possibility of such modularity is supported by experimental work on adaptation to dynamic perturbation (Shadmehr & Mussa-Ivaldi, 1994), kinematic alteration (Flanagan, Nakano, Imamizu, Osu, Yoshioka, & Kawato, 1999) and to prismatic distortion (Ghahramani & Wolpert, 1997).

Internal models in the cerebellum Patient studies have pointed to the fact that patients with cerebellar deficits successfully scale GF responses to the weight of different objects lifted in precision grip (Müller & Dichgans, 1994) and also to changes in texture (Babin-Ratté, Sirigu, Gilles, & Wing, 1999). Hence, these results suggest that the cerebellum is not involved in the anticipatory scaling of GF responses pertaining to the intrinsic characteristics of an object. In contrast, Babin-Ratté et al. (1999) demonstrated that cerebellar patients do not adequately time GF adjustments to LF fluctuations when patients produced vertical upwards and downward movements. GF responses were increased before or at movement onset without differentiation between the patterns of inertial LF fluctuations arising from the arm kinematics. These findings suggest that cerebellar patients are impaired in predicting the dynamic consequences of self-generated actions. This would imply that the cerebellum could be the locus for internal dynamic models. This hypothesis has been put forward in the past by various research groups (e.g. Miall et al., 1993; Miall, 1997; Wolpert, Miall, & Kawato, 1998). Note that overall the clinical results raise the possibility that aspects of GF control related to object intrinsic characteristics and those related to limb dynamics are implemented by different neural structures (Babin-Ratté et al., 1999).

In their review, Wolpert, Miall, and Kawato (1998) summarized behavioural, anatomical and physiological data, which directly and indirectly support the existence of inverse and forward models within the cerebellum. The Smith predictor hypothesis sets certain constraints. First, there should be separate dynamic and time delay neural models. Second, the models need to receive as inputs an efferent copy of the motor commands being sent to the spinal mechanism and proprioceptive information from the periphery about the current state of the body. Third, there must be a neural learning mechanism to allow the model to be adaptable. Following these constraints, Miall et al. (1993) proposed that the lateral cerebellum could be the site for inverse models. Indeed, the lateral cerebellum receives inputs from the parietal posterior cortex via the pontine nuclei (Mower, Gibson, Robinson, Stein, & Glickstein, 1980), which is believed to be concerned with the localization of targets in egocentric coordinates (Stein, 1989). One of the outputs of the lateral cerebellum projects via the dentate nucleus to the ventrolateral thalamus, before reaching the premotor and motor cortices (Allen & Tsukahara, 1974). Thus, this cerebrocerebellar pathway could serve to transform a desired movement, specified by the posterior parietal cortex in visual egocentric coordinates (Stein, 1989), into a motor control signal that would then be sent to the motor cortex to generate the adequate set of muscle commands.

The modularity scheme presupposes that the cerebellum contains multiple pairs of forward and inverse modules, each instantiated within a micro zone (Wolpert & Kawato, 1998). Because of strong interconnections between the intermediate cerebellar cortex, red nucleus and the motor cortex (Allen & Tsukahara, 1974), a second Smith predictor model could be situated for example in the intermediate cerebellar cortex, operating on the outflow from the motor cortex (Miall et al., 1993). The loop would be formed by the corticobulbar fibres and collateral branches of corticospinal fibres reaching the intermediate cerebellum, via the pontine nuclei, en route to the spinal circuits. Predicting the consequences of descending motor commands in motor coordinates, this micro-system would predict the kinematic consequences of limb movement (Miall et al., 1993). If the forward dynamic model in the lateral cerebellum were to predict the dynamic state changes in the arm in response to the forthcoming movement, one could imagine that this signal coupled with a prediction of the kinematics of the movement could provide sufficient information for an accurate prediction of LF fluctuations acting upon a grasped object. In such a case, a feedforward controller of GF responses would use predictions about dynamic and kinematic state changes to scale the GF appropriately, and consequently to counter the predicted force changes arising as the consequence of self-generated actions.

Conclusion

In this section, we considered how the sensorimotor memories from previous manipulative experiences with an object allowed a finely modulated and efficient coordination of grip force with load force. We saw that these coordinative patterns were adjusted both to the physical properties of the object to be grasped but also to the gravitational constraints of the environment in which the manipulative action was to be performed. A key issue for predictive control is the nature of the supporting memory processes encompassing information about the object, the environment and the effector system. Hence, in the last part, we turned to the neural basis that allows the storage of related information to explicit knowledge. At this stage, experimental results reveal in fact that in many cases, sensory information about the progress of the action is used to update stored information. Hence, feedback mechanisms and the predictive control of motor action are not two separate entities but they often work together to optimize the performance of a motor action.

GENERAL CONCLUSION

This chapter has been about the control of movement in goal-directed actions. Although the focus has been on motor control, it will now be apparent that sensory input plays a key role in the way we interact through movement with our surroundings. Thus, the senses inform us about targets for action in terms of what and where. They allow us to determine the context for movement, including the state of our limbs and the forces acting upon them, so that we can determine, select and finally execute the appropriate motor behaviour. The senses also provide us with information about errors in attaining a predetermined target so that movement can be well adjusted. Vision plays an important role in allowing us to determine distant targets and to observe remote consequences of motor action as well as to assess at a glance the disposition of the hands in relation to a complex array of objects from which we might select any one as a target for action. However, blind people are clearly able to organize effective goal-directed action and so it is clear that the most important sensory input for the control of actions is touch, involving both tactile input from the skin and proprioceptive input from the muscles.

In this chapter, we extensively considered the example of hand–arm coordination in holding an object in a stable posture. We started with an analysis of the reactive mechanisms that intervene when it is sensed that a movement departs from the desired goal of stable grip. The more frequent reaction is to increase the overall grip force level to prevent the object from slipping from grasp. However, we also presented cases where various other possibilities were adopted by the system, such as decreasing the load force fluctuations, e.g. by halting the arm movement in mid-flight in order to give more time to the motor system to modify sufficiently the grasp formation. Yet another solution – not considered here, however – is to readjust the type of grasp, perhaps by bringing in another finger to help stabilize the object. Nevertheless, in all of these cases sufficient time is required to implement the reactive corrections. Consequently, we then turned to the predictive control of behaviour, where sensorimotor memories from previous experience with an object allow a control of action in anticipation of destabilizing events. In this way, grip–load force coordination remains within the physical constraints for stable grasp, even during major and sometimes impulsive fluctuations of the load force levels. We saw that a key issue for predictive control is the nature of the supporting memory processes that encompass information about the object, the environment and the effector system. Finally, a theoretical model of how these predictive mechanisms may be implemented in the central nervous system of the human brain was presented.

With a reasonably clear idea of how lower-level mechanisms intervene to adjust our every move both in prediction of and in reaction to changes in the environment, it is commonly agreed, at least in the field of motor control, that it is now time to address the possible role of higher cognitive functions, and incorporate for example the notions of attention, awareness and even consciousness in the control of action. Throughout this chapter, a few findings suggested that knowledge about what is to come, or what are the subjects' intentions, could affect movement selection and even execution. Much more work is, however, needed. A first issue may be for example to consider how explicit knowledge and desire can contribute (or interfere?) in reaching intended goals. By combining what is known about movement control with results obtained in the fields of cognitive psychology, neurology and psychiatry, it will be possible to propose theoretical models that truly reflect the role of cognition in the control of action.

NOTE

1 Note this use of 'open-loop' to contrast with 'closed-loop' feedback mechanisms. Sometimes the term 'feedforward' is also used for open-loop control.

REFERENCES

Allen, G. I., & Tsukahara, N. (1974). Cerebro-cerebellar communication systems. *Physiological Reviews, 54,* 957–1006.

Arbib, M. A. (1990). Programs, schemas and neural networks for control of hand movement: beyond the RS frameworks. In M. Jeannerod (ed.), *Attention and performance XIII: motor representation and control* (pp. 111–138). Hillsdale, NJ: Erlbaum.

Babin-Ratté, S., Sirigu, A., Gilles, M., & Wing, A. M. (1999). Impaired anticipatory finger grip-force adjustments in a case of cerebellar degeneration. *Experimental Brain Research, 128,* 81–85.

Baud-Bovy, G., & Soechting, F. (2001). Two virtual fingers in the control of the tripod grasp. *Journal of Neurophysiology, 86,* 604–615.

Blake, A. (1992). Computational modelling of hand-eye coordination. *Philosophical Transactions of the Royal Society of London B, 337,* 351–360.

Blakemore, S. J., Goodbody, S. J., & Wolpert, D. M. (1998b). Predicting the consequences of our own actions: the role of sensorimotor context estimation. *Journal of Neuroscience, 18,* 7511–7518.

Blakemore, S. J., Wolpert, D. M., & Frith, C. D. (1998a). Central cancellation of self-produced tickle sensation. *Nature Neuroscience, 1,* 635–640.

Bock, O., & Cheung, B. S. K. (1998). Control of isometric force in hypergravity. *Aviation Space Environment Medicine, 69,* 27–31.

Bock, O., Howard, I. P., Money, K. E., & Arnold, K. E. (1992). Accuracy of aimed arm movements in changed gravity. *Aviation Space Environment Medicine, 63,* 994–998.

Bootsma, R. J., Marteniuk, R. G., MacKenzie, C. L., & Zaal, F. T. (1994). The speed-accuracy trade-off in manual prehension: effect of movement amplitude, object size and object width on kinematic characteristics. *Experimental Brain Research, 98,* 535–541.

Buonomano, D. V., & Mauk, M. D. (1994). Neural network model of the cerebellum: temporal discrimination and the timing of motor responses. *Neural Computation, 6,* 38–55.

Canfield, A. A., Comrey, A. L., & Wilson, R. C. (1953). The influence of increased positive G on reaching movements. *Journal of Applied Psychology, 37,* 230.

Castiello, U., Bennett, K. M. B., & Stelmach, G. E. (1993). Reach to grasp: the natural response to perturbation of object size. *Experimental Brain Research, 94,* 163–178.

Chieffi, S., Fogassi, L., Gallese, V., & Gentilucci, M. (1992). Prehension movements directed to approaching objects: influence of stimulus velocity on the transport and the grasp components. *Neuropsychologia, 30,* 877–897.

Cole, K. J. (1991). Grasp force control in older adults. *Journal of Motor Behavior, 23,* 251–258.

Cole, K. J. (1994). The effects of graded tactile anaesthesia on the control of grip force. *Society for Neuroscience Abstract, 20,* 4906.

Cole, K. J., & Abbs, J. H. (1988). Grip force adjustments evoked by load force perturbations of a grasped object. *Journal of Neurophysiology, 60,* 1513–1522.

Cole, K. J., & Beck, C. L. (1994). The stability of precision grip force in older adults. *Journal of Motor Behavior, 26,* 171–177.

Cole, K. J., & Johansson, R. S. (1993). Friction at the digit-object interface scales the sensorimotor transformation for grip responses to pulling loads. *Experimental Brain Research, 95,* 523–532.

Cole, K. J., Rotella, D. L., & Harper, J. G. (1999). Mechanisms for age-related changes of fingertip forces during precision gripping and lifting in adults. *Journal of Neuroscience, 19,* 3238–3247.

Darton, K., Lippold, O. C. J., Shahani, M., & Shahani, U. (1985). Long-latency spinal reflexes in humans. *Journal of Neurophysiology, 53,* 1604–1618.

Darwood, J. J., Repperger, D. W., & Goodyear, C. D. (1991). Mass discrimination under G acceleration. *Aviation Space Environm Medicine, 62,* 319–324.

Day, B. L., & Brown, P. (2001). Evidence for subcortical involvement in the visual control of human reaching. *Brain, 124,* 1832–1840.

Day, B. L., Thompson, P. D., Harding, A. E., & Marsden, C. D. (1998). Influence of vision on upper limb reaching movements in patients with cerebellar ataxia. *Brain, 121,* 357–372.

Delevoye-Turrell, Y., Giersch, A., & Danion, J. M. (2002). A deficit in the adjustment of grip force responses in schizophrenia. *Neuro Report, 13,* 1537–1539.

Delevoye-Turrell, Y., Giersch, A., & Danion, J. M. (2003). Abnormal sequencing of motor actions in patients with schizophrenia: evidence from grip force adjustment during object manipulation. *American Journal of Psychiatry, 160,* 134–141.

Delevoye-Turrell, Y., Li, F. X., & Wing, A. M. (2003). Efficiency of grip force adjustment for impulsive loading. *Quarterly Journal of Experimental Psychology, 56A,* 1113–1128.

Desmurget, M., Prablanc, C., Arzi, M., Rossetti, Y., Paulignan, Y., & Urquizar, C. (1996). Integrated control of hand transport and orientation during prehension movements. *Experimental Brain Research, 110,* 265–278.

Elger, K., Wing, A. M., & Gilles, M. (1999). Integrating of the hand in postural reactions to sustained sideways force at the pelvis. *Experimental Brain Research, 128,* 52–60.

Evans, A. L., Harrisson, L. M., & Stephens, J. A. (1989). Task-dependent changes in cutaneous reflexes recorded from various muscles controlling finger movements in man. *Journal of Physiology (London), 418,* 1–12.

Flanagan, J. R., Burstedt, M. K. O., & Johansson, R. S. (1999). Control of fingertip forces in multi-digit manipulation. *Journal of Neurophysiology, 81,* 1706–1717.

Flanagan, J. R., Nakano, E., Imamizu, H., Osu, R., Yoshioka, J., & Kawato, M. (1999). Composition and decomposition of internal models in motor learning under altered kinematic and dynamic environments. *Journal of Neuroscience, 19,* RC34.

Flanagan, J. R., & Tresilian, J. R. (1994). Grip-load force coupling: a general control strategy for transporting objects. *Journal of Experimental Psychology: Human Perception and Performance, 20*, 944–957.

Flanagan, J. R., Tresilian, J. R., & Wing, A. M. (1995a). Coupling of grip force and load force during arm movements with grasped objects. *Neuroscience Letters, 152*, 53–56.

Flanagan, J. R., Tresilian, J. R., & Wing, A. M. (1995b). Grip force adjustments during rapid hand movements suggests that detailed movement kinematics are predicted. *Behavioral and Brain Sciences, 18*, 753–754.

Flanagan, J. R., & Wing, A. M. (1995). The stability of precision grip force during cyclic arm movements with a hand-held load. *Experimental Brain Research, 105*, 455–464.

Flanagan, J. R., & Wing, A. M. (1997). The role of internal models in motion planning and control: evidence from grip force adjustments during movements of hand-held loads. *Journal of Neuroscience, 17*, 1519–1528.

Gentilucci, M. (2002). Object motor representation and reaching-grasping control. *Neuropsychologia, 40*, 1139–1153.

Gentilucci, M., Castiello, U., Corradini, M. L., Scarpa, M., Umiltà, C., & Rizzolatti, G. (1991). Influence of different types of grasping on the transport components of prehension movements. *Neuropsychologia, 29*, 361–378.

Gentilucci, M., Chieffi, S., Scarpa, M., & Castiello, U. (1992). Temporal coupling between transport and grasp components during prehension movements: effects of visual perturbation. *Behavioural Brain Research, 47*, 71–82.

Gentilucci, M., Daprati, E., Gangitano, M., Saetti, M. C., & Toni, I. (1996). On orienting the hand to reach and grasp an object. *NeuroReport, 7*, 589–592.

Ghahramani, Z., & Wolpert, D. M. (1997). Modular decomposition in visuo-motor learning. *Nature, 386*, 392–395.

Gibson, J. J. (1966). *The senses considered as a perceptual system.* Boston: Houghton Mifflin.

Glover, S. (2003). Separate visual representations in the planning and control of action. *Behavioral and Brain Sciences, in press.*

Goodale, M. A., Meenan, J. P., Bülthoff, H. H., Nicolle, D. A., Murphy, K. J., & Racicot, C. I. (1994). Separate neural pathways for the visual analysis of object shape in perception and prehension. *Current Biology, 1*, 604–610.

Gordon, A. M., Forssberg, H., Johansson, R. S., & Westling, G. (1991a). Integration of haptically acquired size information in the programming of precision grip: comments on the contribution of size cues. *Experimental Brain Research, 85*, 226–229.

Gordon, A. M., Forssberg, H., Johansson, R. S., & Westling, G. (1991b). Visual size cues in the programming of manipulative forces during precision grip. *Experimental Brain Research, 83*, 477–482.

Gordon, A. M., Forssberg, H., Johansson, R. S., & Westling, G. (1991c). Integration of haptically acquired size information in the programming of precision grip. *Experimental Brain Research, 83*, 483–488.

Gordon, A. M., Westling, G., Cole, K. J., & Johansson, R. S. (1993). Memory representations underlying motor commands used during manipulation of common and novel objects. *Journal of Neurophysiology, 69*, 1789–1796.

Graziano, M. S., Cooke, D. F., & Taylor, C. S. (2000). Coding the location of the arm by sight. *Science, 290*, 1782–1786.

Häger-Ross, C., Cole, K., & Johansson, R. S. (1996). Grip force responses to unanticipated object loading: load direction reveals body- and gravity-referenced intrinsic task variables. *Experimental Brain Research, 110*, 142–150.

Hermsdörfer, J., Marquardt, C., Philipp, J., Zierdt, A., Nowak, D., Glasauer, S., & Mai, N. (1999). Grip force exerted against stationary held objects during gravity changes. *Experimental Brain Research, 126*, 205–214.

Hermsdörfer, J., Marquardt, C., Philipp, J., Zierdt, A., Nowak, D., Glasauer, S., & Mai, N. (2000). Moving weightless objects: grip force control during micro-gravity. *Experimental Brain Research, 132*, 52–64.

Hikosaka, O., Tanaka, M., Sakamoto, M., & Iwamura, Y. (1985). Deficits in manipulative behaviours induced by local injections of muscimol in the first somatosensory cortex of the conscious monkey. *Brain Research, 325*, 375–380.

Holsapple, J., Preston, J., & Strick, P. (1991). The origin of thalamic inputs to the hand representation in the primary motor cortex. *Journal of Neuroscience, 11*, 2644–2654.

Ito, M. (1994). Neurophysiological aspects of the cerebellar motor control system. *International Journal of Neurology, 7*, 162–176.

Jackson, S. R., Jackson, G. M., & Rosicky, J. (1995). Are non-relevant objects represented in working memory? The effects of nontarget objects on reach and grasp kinematics. *Experimental Brain Research, 102*, 519–530.

Jakobson, I. S., & Goodale, M. A. (1991). Factors affecting higher-order movement planning: a kinematic analysis of human prehension. *Experimental Brain Research, 86*, 199–208.

Jeannerod, M. (1981). Intersegmental coordination during reaching for natural objects. In J. Long and A. D. Baddeley (Eds.), *Attention and performance* (Vol. IX, pp. 135–169). Hillsdale, NJ: Erlbaum.

Jeannerod, M. (1984). The timing of natural prehension movements. *Journal of Motor Behavior, 16*, 235–254.

Jeannerod, M. (1986). The formation of finger grip during prehension: a cortically mediated visuomotor pattern. *Behavioural Brain Research, 19*, 99–116.

Jeannerod, M. (1988). *The neural and behavioural organisation of goal-directed movements.* Oxford: Oxford University Press.

Jeannerod, M. (1994). Object oriented action. In K. M. B. Bennett and U. Castiello (Eds.), *Insights into the reach to grasp movement* (pp. 3–15). Amsterdam: Elsevier/North-Holland.

Jeannerod, M., Arbib, M. A., Rizzolatti, G., & Sakata, H. (1995). Grasping objects: the cortical mechanisms of visuomotor transformations. *Trends in Neurosciences, 18*, 314–320.

Jenmalm, P., Goodwin, A. W., & Johansson, R. S. (1998). Control of grasp stability when humans lift objects with different surface curvatures. *Journal of Neurophysiology, 79*, 1643–1652.

Jenmalm, P., & Johansson, R. S. (1997). Visual and somatosensory information about object shape control manipulative fingertip forces. *Journal of Neuroscience, 17*, 4486–4499.

Johansson, R. S. (1996). Anticipatory control of grip force in rapid arm movements. In A. M. Wing, P. O. Haggard, & J. R. Flanagan (Eds.), *Hand and brain: the neurophysiology and psychology of hand movements* (pp. 301–324). San Diego: Academic Press.

Johansson, R. S., Häger, C., & Riso, R. (1992a). Somatosensory control of precision grip during unpredictable pulling loads. II. Changes in load force rate. *Experimental Brain Research, 89*, 181–191.

Johansson, R. S., Häger, C., & Riso, R. (1992b). Somatosensory control of precision grip during unpredictable pulling loads. III. Impairments during digital anaesthesia. *Experimental Brain Research, 89*, 204–213.

Johansson, R. S., Riso, R., Häger, C., & Bäckström, L. (1992). Somatosensory control of precision grip during unpredictable pulling loads. I. Changes in load force amplitude. *Experimental Brain Research, 89*, 181–191.

Johansson, R. S., & Vallbo, A. B. (1979). Tactile sensibility in the human hand: relative and absolute densities of four types of units in the glabrous skin. *Journal of Physiology (London), 186*, 283–300.

Johansson, R. S., & Westling, G. (1984a). Roles of glabrous skin receptors and sensorimotor memory in automatic control of precision grip when lifting rougher or more slippery objects. *Experimental Brain Research, 56*, 550–564.

Johansson, R. S., & Westling, G. (1984b). Influences of cutaneous sensory input on the motor coordination during precision manipulation. In C. Vonfulen, O. Franzen, U. Lundblom, & A. Ottoson (Eds.), *Somatosensory mechanisms* (pp. 249–260). London: Macmillan.

Johansson, R. S., & Westling, G. (1987). Signals in tactile afferents from the fingers eliciting adapting motor responses during precision grip. *Experimental Brain Research, 66*, 141–154.

Johansson, R. S., & Westling, G. (1988). Coordinated isometric muscle commands adequately and erroneously programmed for the weight during lifting task with precision grip. *Experimental Brain Research, 71*, 59–71.

Johansson, R. S., & Westling, G. (1991). Afferent signals during manipulative tasks in man. In O. Franzen, & J. Westman (Eds.), *Somatosensory mechanisms* (pp. 25–48). London: Macmillan.

Jordan, M. I. (1995). Computational motor control. In M. S. Gazzaniga (ed.), *The cognitive neurosciences* (pp. 597–609). Cambridge, MA: MIT Press.

Jordan, M. I., & Rumelhart, D. E. (1992). Forward models: supervised learning with a distal teacher. *Cognitive Science, 16*, 307–354.

Kaas, J. H., & Huerta, M. F. (1988). The subcortical visual system of primates. In H. D. Steklis & J. Erwin (Eds.), *Neurosciences: Vol. 4. Comparative primate biology* (pp. 327–391). New York: Alan R. Liss.

Kawato, M., Furwaka, K., & Suzuki, R. (1987). A hierarchical neural network model for the control and learning of voluntary movements. *Biological Cybernetics, 56*, 1–17.

Kawato, M., & Gomi, H. (1992). A computational model of four regions of the cerebellum based on feedback-error-learning. *Biological Cybernetics, 68*, 95–103.

Kinoshita, H., Ikuta, K., Kawai, S., & Udo, M. (1993). Effects of lifting speed and height on the regulation of forces during lifting tasks using a precision grip. *Human Movement Science, 25*, 151–175.

Kinoshita, H., Kawai, S., Ikuta, K., & Teraoka, T. (1996). Individual finger forces acting on a grasped object during shaking actions. *Ergonomics, 39*, 243–256.

Knibestöl, M., & Vallbo, A. B. (1970). Single unit analysis of mechanoreceptor activity from the human glabrous skin. *Acta Physiologica Scandinavica, 80*, 178–195.

Kuperstein, M. (1988). Neural model of adaptive hand-eye coordination for single postures. *Science, 239*, 1308–1311.

Lackner, J. R., & Graybiel, A. (1981). Illusion of visual, postural and aircraft motion elicited by deep knee bends in the increased gravito-inertial force phase of parabolic flight: evidence for dynamic calibration of sensory-motor control to earth-gravity force levels. *Experimental Brain Research, 44*, 312–316.

Lashley, K. S. (1951). The problem of serial order in behavior. In L. A. Jeffress (ed.), *Cerebral mechanisms in behavior* (pp. 112–136). New York: Wiley.

Lemon, R. N., Johansson, R. S., & Westling, G. (1995). Corticospinal control during reach, grasp and precision lift in man. *Journal of Neuroscience, 15*, 6145–6156.

Lemon, R. N., Johansson, R. S., & Westling, G. (1996). Modulation of corticospinal influence over hand muscles during gripping tasks in man and monkey. *Canadian Journal of Physiology and Pharmacology, 74*, 547–558.

Loo, C. K. C., & McCloskey, D. I. (1985). Effects of prior instruction and anaesthesia on long-latency responses to stretch in the long flexor of the human thumb. *Journal of Physiology (London), 365*, 285–296.

Macefield, V. G., & Johansson, R. S. (1994). Electrical signs of cortical involvements in the automatic control of grip force. *NeuroReport, 5*, 2229–2232.

Mamassian, P. (1997). Prehension of objects oriented in three-dimensional space. *Experimental Brain Research, 114*, 235–245.

Marsden, C. D., Merton, P. A., & Morton, H. B. (1976). Servo-action in the human thumb. *Journal of Physiology (London), 257*, 1–44.

Marteniuk, R. G., MacKenzie, C. L., Jeannerod, M., Ahtènes, S., & Dugas, C. (1987). Constraints on human arm movement trajectories. *Canadian Journal of Psychology, 41*, 365–378.

Miall, R. C. (1997). Sequences of sensory predictions. *Behavioral and Brain Sciences, 20*, 258.

Miall, R. C., Weir, D. J., Wolpert, D. M., & Stein, J. F. (1993). Is the cerebellum a Smith Predictor? *Journal of Motor Behavior, 25*, 203–216.

Mower, G., Gibson, A., Robinson, F., Stein, J., & Glickstein, M. (1980). Visual ponto-cerebellar projections in the cat. *Journal of Neurophysiology*, *43*, 355–365.

Müller, F., & Abbs, J. H. (1991). Precision grip in Parkinsonian patients. In M. B. Streifler, A. D. Korezyn, E. Melamed, & M. B. H. Youdim (Eds.), *Advances in neurology* (pp. 191–195). New York: Raven Press.

Müller, F., & Dichgans, J. (1994). Disco-ordination of pinch forces during grasp in patients with cerebellar lesions. *Experimental Brain Research*, *101*, 485–492.

Nowak, D. A., Glasauer, S., Meyer, L., Mai, N., & Hermsdörfer, J. (2002). The role of cutaneous feedback for anticipatory grip force adjustments during object movements and externally imposed variation of the direction of gravity. *Somatosensory and Motor Research*, *19*, 49–60.

Nowak, D. A., Hermsdörfer, J., Philipp, J., Marquardt, C., Glasauer, S., & Mai, N. (2001). Effect of changing gravity on anticipatory grip force control during point-to-point movements of a hand-held object. *Motor Control*, *5*, 231–253.

Nowlan, S. J. (1991). Soft competitive adaptation: neural network learning algorithms based on fitting statistical mixtures. Technical Report CMU-CS-91-126, Pittsburgh: Carnegie Mellon University.

Ohki, Y., Edin, B. B., & Johansson, R. S. (2002). Predictions specify reactive control of individual digits in manipulation. *Journal of Neuroscience*, *22*, 600–610.

Paulignan, Y., Jeannerod, M., MacKenzie, C. L., & Marteniuk, R. G. (1991). Selective perturbation of visual input during prehension movements. 2. The effects of changing object size. *Experimental Brain Research*, *83*, 502–512.

Paulignan, Y., MacKenzie, C. L., Marteniuk, R. G., & Jeannerod, M. (1991). Selective perturbation of visual input during prehension movements. 1. The effects of changing object position. *Experimental Brain Research*, *83*, 502–512.

Pause, M., Kunesch, E., Binkofski, F., & Freund, H. J. (1989). Sensorimotor disturbances in patients with lesions of the parietal cortex. *Brain*, *112*, 1599–1625.

Perenin, M. T., & Vighetto, A. (1988). Optic ataxia: a specific disruption in visuo-motor mechanisms. I. Different aspects of the deficit in reaching for objects. *Brain*, *111*, 643–674.

Robinson, D. A. (1981). The use of control system analysis in the neurophysiology of eye movements. *Annual Review of Neuroscience*, *4*, 463–503.

Rosenbaum, D. A., Engelbrecht, S. E., Bushe, M. M., & Loukopoulos, L. D. (1993). Knowledge model for selecting and producing reaching movements. *Journal of Motor Behavior*, *25*, 217–227.

Rosenbaum, D. A., Loukopoulos, L. D., Meulenbroek, R. G., Vaughan, J., & Engelbrecht, S. E. (1995). Planning reached by evaluating stored postures. *Psychological Review*, *102*, 28–67.

Rosenbaum, D. A., Meulenbroek, R. G., & Vaughan, J. (1999). Remembered positions: stored locations or stored postures? *Experimental Brain Research*, *124*, 503–512.

Rosenbaum, D. A., Meulenbroek, R. G., & Vaughan, J. (2001). Planning reaching and grasping movements: theoretical premises and practical implications. *Motor Control*, *5*, 99–115.

Rosenbaum, D. A., Meulenbroek, R. G., Vaughan, J., & Jansen, C. (1999). Coordination of reaching and grasping by capitalizing on obstacle avoidance and other constraints. *Experimental Brain Research*, *128*, 92–100.

Rosenbaum, D. A., Meulenbroek, R. G., Vaughan, J., & Jansen, C. (2001b). Posture-based motion planning: applications to grasping. *Psychological Review*, *108*, 709–734.

Rosenbaum, D. A., Vaughan, J., Barnes, H. J., & Jorgensen, M. J. (1992). Time course of movement planning: selection of handgrips for object manipulation. *Journal of Experimental Psychology: Learning, Memory, Cognition*, *18*, 1058–1073.

Ross, H. E., & Reschke, M. F. (1982). Mass estimation and discrimination during brief periods of zero gravity. *Perception and Psychophysics*, *31*, 429–436.

Rothwell, J. C., Traub, M. M., Day, B. L., Obeso, J. A., Thomas, P. K., & Marsden, C. D. (1982). Manual motor performance in a deafferented man. *Brain*, *105*, 515–542.

Sakata, H., & Taira, M. (1994). Parietal control of hand action. *Current Opinion in Neurobiology*, *4*, 847–856.

Salimi, I., Hollender, I., Frazize, W., & Gordon, A. M. (2000). Specificity of internal representations underlying grasping. *Journal of Neurophysiology*, *84*, 2390–2397.

Shadmehr, R., & Mussa-Ivaldi, F. (1994). Adaptive representation of dynamics during learning of a motor task. *Journal of Neuroscience*, *14*, 3208–3224.

Smith, O. J. M. (1959). A controller to overcome dead time. *ISA Journal*, *6*, 28–33.

Stein, J. F. (1989). Representation of egocentric space in the posterior parietal cortex. *Quarterly Journal of Experimental Psychology*, *74*, 583–606.

Sutton, R. S. (1988). Learning to predict by the methods of temporal differences. *Machine Learning*, *3*, 9–44.

Traub, M. M., Rothwell, J. C., & Marsden, C. D. (1980). A grab reflex in the human hand. *Brain*, *103*, 869–884.

Turrell, Y. (2000). Grip force adjustments in collisions. Doctoral thesis, University of Birmingham, UK.

Turrell, Y., Li, F. X., & Wing, A. M. (1999). Grip force dynamics in the approach to a collision. *Experimental Brain Research*, *128*, 86–91.

van Kan, P. L. E., Horn, K. M., & Gibson, A. R. (1994). The importance of hand use to discharge of interpositus neurons of the monkey. *Journal of Physiology (London)*, *480*, 171–190.

Vaughan, J., Rosenbaum, D. A., & Meulenbroek, R. G. (2001). Planning reaching and grasping movements: the problem of obstacle avoidance. *Motor Control*, *5*, 116–135.

Wallace, S. A., & Weeks, D. L. (1988). Temporal constraints in the control of prehensile movement. *Journal of Motor Behavior*, *20*, 81–105.

Wallace, S. A., Weeks, D. L., & Kelso, J. A. S. (1990). Temporal constraints in reaching and grasping behavior. *Human Movement Science*, *9*, 69–93.

Werner, W. (1993). Neurones in the primate superior colliculus are active before and during arm movements to visual targets. *European Journal of Neuroscience, 5*, 335–340.

Westling, G., & Johansson, R. S. (1984). Factors influencing the force control during precision grip. *Experimental Brain Research, 53*, 277–284.

Westling, G., & Johansson, R. S. (1987). Responses in glabrous skin mechanoreceptors during precision grip in humans. *Experimental Brain Research, 66*, 128–140.

Wing, A. M. (1988). A comparison of the rate of pinch grip force increases and decreases in Parkinsonian bradykinesia. *Neuropsychology, 26*, 479–482.

Wing, A. M., Flanagan, J. R., & Richardson, J. (1997). Anticipatory postural adjustments in stance and grip. *Experimental Brain Research, 116*, 122–130.

Wing, A. M., & Fraser, C. (1983). The contribution of the thumb to reaching movements. *Quarterly Journal of Experimental Psychology, 35A*, 297–309.

Wing, A. M., Turton, A., & Fraser, C. (1986). Grasp size and accuracy of approach in reaching. *Journal of Motor Behavior, 18*, 245–260.

Witney, A. G., Goodbody, S. J., & Wolpert, D. M. (2000). Learning and decay of prediction in object manipulation. *Journal of Neurophysiology, 84*, 334–343.

Witney, A. G., Vetter, P., & Wolpert, D. M. (2001). The influence of previous experience on predictive motor control. *NeuroReport, 12*, 649–653.

Wolpert, D. M. (1997). Computational approaches to motor control. *Trends in Cognitive Science, 1*, 209–216.

Wolpert, D. M., Ghahramani, Z., & Jordan, M. I. (1995a). Are arm trajectories planned in kinematics or dynamic coordinates: an adaptation study. *Experimental Brain Research 103*, 460–470.

Wolpert, D. M., Ghahramani, Z., & Jordan, M. I. (1995b). An internal model for sensorimotor integration. *Science, 103*, 1880–1882.

Wolpert, D. M., Goodbody, S. J., & Husain, M. (1998). Maintaining internal representations: the role of the human superior parietal lobe. *Nature Neuroscience, 1*, 529–533.

Wolpert, D. M., & Kawato, M. (1998). Multiple paired forward and inverse models for motor control. *Neural Networks, 11*, 1317–1329.

Wolpert, D. M., Miall, R. C., & Kawato, M. (1998). Internal models in the cerebellum. *Trends in Cognitive Science, 2*, 338–347.

PART TWO

Learning and Memory

6

Theories of Learning

MICHAEL E. YOUNG AND EDWARD
A. WASSERMAN

In the two fields of learning and of motivation will be worked out the basic theory that will eventually make the science of psychology a much more powerful instrument than it now is. When we are able to state the general principles which govern human learning we shall have the most important tool needed for the prediction and control of human behavior. (Guthrie, 1946: 3)

Our remarkable capacity for learning is arguably the single factor that elevates humanity to its commanding position in the animal kingdom. Our ability to learn appears limitless – people can learn languages, mathematics, music, electronics, world history and basketball to a degree that goes well beyond what any other species can achieve. Although our manual dexterity and voice box play important roles in some of these achievements, other species that possess similar dexterity (the chimpanzee) or strong vocalization skills (the African gray parrot) fall far short of human potential. The centrality of learning to human achievement is a large part of what has made it a core topic of study throughout the history of psychology as a science. This extensive history, however, makes the task of reviewing this work an especially daunting one.

Our goal is to examine certain oft-observed aspects of learning that shape contemporary theories of human learning in cognitive psychology and then to explore some of the most prominent of those theories and their origins. Although certain phenomena will necessarily be neglected for lack of space, we do not intend to diminish their importance. For example, we do not recapitulate the well-known principles of Pavlovian and Thorndikian conditioning. Thus, there will be no consideration of the relationship

between classical and instrumental conditioning, the effects of schedules of reinforcement, choice behavior, etc. Discussions of these topics can be obtained from numerous textbooks and reviews (e.g. Rescorla, 1988; Wasserman & Miller, 1997).

Throughout our presentation, we ground most of our outlook in the processes that affect the learning of *associations*. It is unfortunate that some contemporary cognitive psychologists resist associationist accounts of cognitive phenomena because of the historical influence of behaviorism. It is difficult, however, to develop theories of learning from the ground up without an appeal to the learning of associations. Even decidedly cognitive theories like Soar, in which knowledge is represented by a large collection of rules, rely on associative mechanisms to chunk together (i.e. associate) prior knowledge to establish new associations (Lehman, Laird, & Rosenbloom, 1996). At least to us, 'association' is not a dirty word.

The behaviorist baggage that associationist theories bear has been burdensome in recent discussions of the promise or peril of connectionist models of cognitive processes. Connectionist theories are sometimes dismissed as merely 'association machines' with the presumption that this label will remind us of the evil days of behaviorism and its empty promises. But the beauty of connectionist models is that they can produce remarkably complex, even rule-like behavior out of a large collection of simple associations. Given the impact that connectionism is having on modern psycholinguistics (Christiansen, Chater, & Seidenberg, 1999), it is becoming increasingly apparent that these association machines are not so glibly discounted and are, in fact, capable of acquiring and producing a wide range of elaborate behaviors. Recent years have, however, rightly tempered the initial fervor over connectionist models as researchers have come to realize that modeling complex behaviors may require equally complex, multistage models involving various learning algorithms and a level of sophistication in building these models that requires considerable expertise and dedication.

The advent of connectionist theorizing has helped psychologists recognize that associative learning is more than acquiring simple stimulus–response associations. A sophisticated cognitive machine must be able to learn associations between configurations of stimuli, associations between sequences, the precise temporal relations among events, hierarchical relationships, and how much attention to pay to the variety of features, dimensions and events extant in the environment. On occasion, our discussion of contemporary theories and their empirical bases will draw on the latest data and theories from researchers investigating non-human animal learning. Modern theories of animal learning have substantially changed since the early days of Pavlov, despite the contrary impression left by many introductory psychology texts. The study of human cognition can be enriched by an examination of animal learning to the same extent that the latest theories and experiments in animal cognition have been enriched by incorporating the designs and theories of human cognitive psychology (Wasserman, 1981).

Nevertheless, we do not claim that all learning is associative. Identifying stimulus features or dimensions appears to occur through processes like differentiation or unitization (Goldstone, 1996), and these processes may or may not be explainable in associative terms (Hall, 1991). People learn to differentially allocate their attention to task-relevant dimensions (Goldstone, 1996; Kruschke, 1992; Nosofsky, 1986) and they also learn to broaden or restrict the degree of generalization between concepts (Shepard, 1991). Our brains are equipped with a number of mechanisms for acquiring useful information about the world.

We begin our discussion of learning theories with a consideration of some of the major empirical results that theories of learning must explain. This recitation will clarify the interpretive challenge that we face and also provide the backdrop for the specific theories that we consider in the second part of the chapter. We hope that readers will begin to see the ubiquity of these learning processes and be motivated to study those processes that are common to the various and sundry domains of cognitive psychology.

BASIC FINDINGS

In our consideration of learning phenomena, we focus our discussion on: (a) the role of time,

(b) competition among predictors, (c) configural learning, (d) generalization and similarity and (e) unlearning.

The role of time

The importance of temporal contiguity (closeness of events in time) to the acquisition of an association between events has been recognized for centuries (Hume, 1739/1969; James, 1890; Mill, 1843). William James (1890) expressed the importance of contiguity clearly and to the point: 'When two elementary brain processes have been active together or in immediate succession, one of them, on re-occurring, tends to propagate its excitement to the other' (p. 566).

Early psychologists generally accepted that temporal contiguity between events (between the conditioned stimulus, or CS, and the unconditioned stimulus, or US, or between a response and a reinforcer) was the critical factor in learning. Pavlov (1927: 89) noted that at longer CS–US intervals, the conditioned response was 'difficult if not impossible' to establish. Grice's (1948) study of the effect of delay of reinforcement in operant conditioning further established that contiguity plays a critical role in learning the consequences of an action.

An early difficulty with the requirement that two events must be temporally contiguous centered around data demonstrating trace conditioning. In delay conditioning, CS onset precedes US onset, but the CS is still present at US onset (e.g. the tone is still on at the time the food is delivered). In trace conditioning, CS offset precedes US onset, thus creating an unfilled or 'trace' interval between the events. Despite the absence of direct temporal contiguity, animals still appear to learn and to retain the CS–US relationship (Pavlov, 1927). Pavlov and others salvaged the prominence of temporal contiguity by appealing to the presence of a neural or mental trace of the CS (analogous to a rapidly decaying short-term memory) that extends beyond its actual presence in the environment – it is this trace that is contiguous with the onset of the US.

Further difficulties for the centrality of contiguity arose in a study by Rescorla (1967) that suggested the importance of a *contingent* relationship between a CS and a US. When two animals received equal numbers of temporally contiguous pairings of a CS and a US, but the second animal also received a large number of non-contiguous presentations, the first animal demonstrated much better acquisition of a conditioned response to the CS. Rescorla proposed that this finding was due to the greater predictive power of the CS for the first subject. More formally, a CS should prompt a conditioned response (CR) if the probability of the US when the CS is present exceeds the probability of the US when the CS is absent [i.e. if $P(\text{US}|\text{CS})$ –

$P(US|\sim CS) > 0$]. A parallel analysis of operant conditioning suggests that the strength of the relationship between a response and an outcome is determined by $P(O|R) - P(O|\sim R)$ (Seligman, Maier, & Solomon, 1971). The detrimental effect of unsignaled outcomes has also been observed in human causal learning (Reed, 1992; Shanks, 1989). Thus, contingency seemed to be the critical variable, not contiguity.

Rescorla and Wagner (1972) later tempered this shift in emphasis by proposing a model of associative learning that relied solely on temporal contiguity (including contiguity of a US with contextual stimuli other than the CS) in order to account for the findings of Rescorla (1967). A stimulus is always contiguous with other stimuli, even if these stimuli are constant and in the background (e.g. the Skinner box, the color of the walls, the smell of the food). Normally, the context is considered to be of little consequence because it is omnipresent and will thus be associated with everything that occurs in its presence. But in the Rescorla–Wagner model, stimuli contiguous with the US compete with one another as predictors of the US. If the US is paired with the context alone more often than with the CS, then the context can become a better predictor than the CS and thus outcompete it for associative control. Thus, effects of contingency can emerge from a model that only incorporates contiguity. Note, however, that the parsing of an event stream into trials (as is necessary for the application of the Rescorla–Wagner model) produces further analytical problems to be resolved (Hammond & Paynter, 1983; Young, 1995).

The adequacy of the Rescorla–Wagner model as an account of contingency effects hinges on the proposed role of context. If there is no evidence that the context acquires independent, direct associations with the outcome, then the model's validity is undermined. There is, however, substantial evidence of contextual learning (Bouton, 1993, 1994). The deeper, and still unanswered, question is whether the context operates in the direct manner suggested by Rescorla and Wagner's (1972) model or if it plays the more indirect role of mediating responses between CSs and their outcomes (Bouton, 1993).

Temporal contiguity in human learning

The effect of temporal contiguity on associative learning in people is exemplified by studies involving causal learning, in which participants try to determine the causal relationships between one or more candidate causes and an effect of central interest. In one such study, Wasserman and Neunaber (1986) trained college students to press a telegraph key to earn points. In experiment 1, a point was awarded every t seconds regardless of the participants' keypresses; however, the time at which the point was awarded during the t-second interval was determined by when and whether they made a keypress. Wasserman and Neunaber reported that responses which decreased the temporal interval between response and point gain were produced more often and judged to be more causal, whereas those that increased the temporal interval were produced less often and judged to be less causal or even preventative. These changes occurred even though the absolute rate of point gain was held constant across conditions. Temporal contiguity between keypress and point delivery governed learning. Similarly, Siegler and Liebert (1974) asked children between the ages of 5 and 9 to judge the degree to which inserting a card into a machine caused onset of a light. Judgments were decidedly lower when there was a 5-second delay between card insertion and the light's onset than when there was no response-outcome delay.

Temporal contiguity, however, has many facets. Reed (1992, 1999) too reported that participants rated an action that produced an immediate outcome as more causally effective than an action that produced a delayed outcome. Moreover, his participants gave higher ratings of the causal effectiveness of an action that produced a delayed outcome when the delay was filled by a stimulus (different from the context) than when the delay was unfilled. Thus, an intervening event can help overcome the otherwise adverse effect of response–outcome delay (see also Bolles, Collier, Bouton, & Marlin, 1978; Kaplan & Hearst, 1982; Rescorla, 1982). The principle in operation seems to be that placing a stimulus in the delay makes the interstimulus interval (ISI) between the predictor and the outcome distinctly different from the intertrial interval (ITI); this distinction produces a situation in which the stimulus filling the ISI is both predicted by the cause and, in turn, predicts the outcome. When the ISI contains no distinctive external stimuli, the contextual stimuli that fill it are not particularly predictive of the outcome because they also occur during the ITI (cf. Reed, 1999).

The effect of the intertrial interval

Although temporal contiguity is most often discussed as holding between predictors and their outcomes (e.g. CSs and USs or responses and consequences), the time between trials (the ITI) also affects learning in important ways. The first researchers to systematically examine this issue were Gibbon and Balsam (1981). They found that the efficacy of a predictor decreased as the ITI decreased. They explained the effects of manipulating the ITI (and stimulus duration) by proposing their scalar expectancy theory (SET). According to SET, the learner develops an expectancy of when an outcome is due, both in the presence of the candidate predictors and in the presence of the contextual stimuli. The strength of association between the candidate predictor and the outcome is proposed to be directly related to the degree to which the expectancy evoked by the predictor exceeds that evoked by the contextual stimuli. Although Gibbon and Balsam originally assumed that expectancy is constant across the ITI, subsequent data have clearly shown that expectancy of the outcome waxes and wanes in accordance with the experienced outcome intervals in both humans and other animals (e.g. Allan, 1998; Kirkpatrick & Church, 2000; Staddon & Higa, 1991).

Think of it this way. One's ability to predict the occurrence of an outcome based only on contextual stimuli is much greater at shorter ITIs than at longer ones (assuming, of course, that there are no environmental cues like clocks or solar movements to chronicle the passage of time). If trials occur in rapid succession, then the outcomes to be predicted (e.g. the USs) are close together in time. The learner can anticipate when the outcome is going to occur by using time as a predictor. To the degree that time is a sufficient predictor, the CS is a superfluous predictor and thus commands less attention (recent evidence indicates that the passage of time can be more salient than a CS when both are available as predictors: Kirkpatrick & Church, 2000; Williams & LoLordo, 1995). If the ITI is long (or highly variable), however, then the learner will find the passage of time to be an inadequate predictor of the outcome, thus necessitating attention to the more proximal and informative CS.

In a recent study of predictive learning by people, Young, Johnson, and Wasserman (2000) examined the role of the ITI as part of a control group. They reported stronger learning of predictive relationships when the ITI was increased by a mere 6 s. The effect of ITI on learning, however, is multifaceted and may emerge for different reasons in the performance of different tasks. For example, the advantage of distributed over massed presentation for long-term learning has been documented across a range of species and tasks (for a review see Glenberg, 1979).

ISIs between multiple predictors

Thus far, we have considered the effect of temporal contiguity between predictors and an outcome, between responses and their consequences, and between presentations of the events to be predicted (e.g. the USs). Although not often studied, research has also revealed the effects of temporal contiguity between the predictors of an outcome. In most studies of predictive learning, the predictors are presented simultaneously (e.g. the multiple contemporary causes in causal learning, the stimulus features in category learning, and the multiple cues in multiple cue probability learning). There are, however, exceptions.

Studies of sequence learning involve the presentation of a series of stimuli, and it is the sequence of those stimuli that is learned. If making a correct prediction or a fast response to a stimulus requires learning a dependence between contiguous predictors, then people tend to learn quickly. If, however, that response requires one to learn a dependence that bridges a much longer time gap, then learning is retarded (e.g. Cleeremans & McClelland, 1991). Thus, the temporal relation among the predictors is an important determiner of the ease with which one can learn the relations among those events.

It was only recently that researchers studying causal learning began examining the effects of varying the temporal relations between multiple predictors of an outcome. In one such study (Young, Johnson, & Wasserman, 2000), when one predictor preceded a second, the latter produced the outcome; when the earlier predictor did not occur, the latter did not produce the outcome. People learned to use the first event to 'set the occasion' for the operability of the second. Importantly, Young, Johnson, and Wasserman (2000) documented that people behaved quite differently when the contingencies were maintained, but the temporal relationships were altered by presenting the predictors simultaneously rather than successively. This finding suggests that the temporal relation between the two predictors is central to the occasion-setting phenomenon (cf. Holland, 1983; Holland, Hamlin, & Parsons, 1997; Holland & Reeve, 1991).

Competition among predictors

The advantage of learning the temporal relations among environmental events is that it allows an observer to anticipate or control future events. Given the vast array of possibilities, encoding all of the potential relations seems a daunting task. One method for limiting the number of associations that must be acquired is to avoid redundancy; if two predictors are perfectly correlated, then only one must be encoded as a predictor of its consequence. To avoid redundancy, the cognitive system appears to set predictors in direct competition with one another.

Blocking

In forward blocking, one predictor, B, is paired with another predictor, A, which has received pretraining as a predictor of a third event, the outcome, O (i.e. A^+ training followed by AB^+ training; the + indicates the outcome occurred on those trials). In this design, B elicits significantly less anticipation of the outcome as compared to a control condition (e.g. AB^+ without prior A^+ training) as demonstrated in both non-human animal studies (e.g. Kamin, 1969; Kaye & Pearce, 1984; Miller &

Matute, 1996) and human studies (e.g. Arcediano, Matute, & Miller, 1997; Shanks, 1985; Williams, Sagness, & McPhee, 1994).

When the order of the training phases is reversed (AB⁺ followed by A⁺ training), some studies have revealed a *backward blocking* effect in which the learned anticipation of the outcome following event B (acquired during the AB⁺ training) decreases during the second phase of training (involving A⁺). Backward blocking has been readily observed in human studies (e.g. Chapman, 1991; Kruschke & Blair, 2000; Shanks, 1985; Wasserman & Berglan, 1998), but it was much harder to establish in non-human animals ostensibly because of the greater biological relevance of to-be-blocked cues in standard Pavlovian conditioning (Miller & Matute, 1996). The retrospective re-evaluation apparently at play in backward conditioning is problematic for many theories of the learning process (Van Hamme & Wasserman, 1994).

The explanations of this competition between predictors are quite varied and form the basis of fundamentally different theoretical accounts. Does this competition prevent one from learning the blocked association (e.g. Rescorla & Wagner, 1972; Van Hamme & Wasserman, 1994), from expressing a learned association (Miller & Matzel, 1988), or from attending to the blocked stimulus (Kruschke, 2001; Kruschke & Blair, 2000; Mackintosh, 1975)? We shall examine these issues more closely in the section on Supervised Learning (see p. 169).

Relative validity effect

Further evidence of competition between predictors has been revealed in observations of the relative validity effect. Studying rats and rabbits, Wagner, Logan, Haberlandt, and Price (1968) observed that responding to a stimulus, X, was lower after training that had involved AX⁺ and BX⁻ trials than when it had involved AX± and BX± trials. In both of these cases, X was paired with the outcome on 50% of the trials, so a simple contiguity account would predict equivalent learning in these two tasks. Therefore, the judged validity of the X cue was not solely a function of its own predictive efficacy, but also that of the other cues with which it had been paired. In the first condition, X was paired with two perfectly predictive cues (A was always followed by reinforcement but B never was), whereas in the second condition, X was paired with two unpredictive cues (A and B were each followed by reinforcement half of the time). Wasserman (1990a) replicated and extended the relative validity effect in investigating human judgments of causality.

The observation of competition among predictors provides evidence of the brain's tendency to focus the learning process on acquiring information that provides unique predictive power. In the short run,

it is inefficient to try to encode all of the observed relationships, including redundant ones; but in the long run, some redundancy is useful in a dynamic environment. A truly optimal learning system must learn to exploit the best predictors of future events while hedging its bets by storing some information that might be useful in the future because the best predictors might not always be available or circumstances might change. Configural learning, discussed next, provides one example of the human cognitive system encoding more than is absolutely necessary.

Configural learning

Configural learning involves the acquisition of information about entire sets of features, cues or events. Examples include context learning (Bouton, 1993), learning causal interactions (Young, Wasserman, Johnson, & Jones, 2000) and learning categories involving integral dimensions (Garner, 1970). In all of these situations, the stimulus is not subdivided into its component features, but is treated as a whole. This wholistic stimulus can be many things, including the context, a photograph, an auditory stream or any other multidimensional stimulus. Some features of a stimulus are easy to extract (e.g. its color, size or general shape), but others are more difficult either because they are not transparent to the human sensory system (e.g. lightness and saturation) or because of the vast number of features involved and the relations among those features (e.g. in the context).

Psychologists have also come to appreciate that feature identification can be difficult and dynamic (Schyns, Goldstone, & Thibaut, 1998; Schyns & Murphy, 1994). Thus, there are both mechanistic limitations in stimulus processing in that not all relevant features can be easily identified and extracted, plus there are practical advantages to treating a stimulus as a whole.

Cue interaction

Many of the empirical phenomena that we have considered so far presuppose that humans acquire simple associations between pairs of events (e.g. the CS and US, the response and its consequence, the context and an outcome). Reality is much more complex. Interactions between and among cues are vital to human (and animal) judgments and thus require us to learn these interactions.

The classic example of an interaction is found in the exclusive-OR (XOR) problem. In the XOR problem, the subject must make one response (R_1) when either of two features is present, but make a different response (R_2) when both features are absent or present. Learning to associate each feature with the desired response is insufficient because the presence of both features should make it twice as likely that R_1 is appropriate. A solution of the XOR problem requires special treatment of the combination of the two features.

When the two responses correspond to two different categories, the XOR problem is instantiated as the *biconditional rule* (e.g. Bourne, Ekstrand, & Montgomery, 1969); when the two responses correspond to the presence or absence of an event, the XOR problem is instantiated as the *negative patterning* problem.

Category learning studies (and the closely related non-metric multiple cue probability learning tasks: Castellan, 1977) have tended to show that tasks that require configural learning are more difficult to master than those that do not, although this finding is mediated by the number of relevant and irrelevant dimensions present in the task (Shepard, Hovland, & Jenkins, 1961). Causal learning studies involving negative patterning in non-human animals (e.g. Bellingham, Gillette-Bellingham, & Kehoe, 1985; Kehoe & Graham, 1988) and people (Young, Wasserman, Johnson, & Jones, 2000) have revealed that this form of the XOR problem is more difficult to learn than many non-configural discrimination problems.

There are many tasks, however, that may be solved configurally or elementally depending on the framing of the problem. For example, positive patterning, a causal learning task in which two events must occur together before the outcome will be produced, appears to require configural learning; the efficacy of the combination of the two events is greater than the sum of their individual efficacies. Yet a simple non-linear response rule (only predict the outcome when the sum of the event efficacies is greater than 70%) used in conjunction with a system that learns elementally can produce the correct behavior.

The conditional nature of occasion setting represents another form of configural learning requiring cue interaction (e.g. Holland, 1983, 1991; Young, Johnson, & Wasserman, 2000). In occasion setting, the outcome of one of the events is conditional on the (prior) occurrence of a second event (the occasion setter). As clearly documented by Rescorla (1985), many occasion-setting problems can be solved by summing the individual efficacies of the occasion setter and its targets, so long as a thresholding mechanism is included. The documentation of ambiguous occasion setting, in which the occasion setter both raises the efficacy of one event and lowers the efficacy of another, cannot be so easily explained by summation plus thresholding. Occasion setting does appear to require the learning of a cue interaction.

Holistic versus elemental/dimensional learning

Research has also documented that there is a developmental shift from classifying by overall similarity to classifying by specific dimensions (e.g.

Kemler, 1983; Smith, 1983). Thus, two stimuli that are very similar overall, but do not match one another on any particular dimension, are judged to be the most similar (e.g. in a grouping task) by very young children; however, two stimuli that match one another on a dimension (e.g. color or size) are judged to be the most similar by older children and adults (Evans & Smith, 1988). These results suggest that development produces a bias toward individuating dimensions rather than treating a stimulus as a whole entity. This research might lead us to believe that some fundamental changes are occurring in our neural hardware that drives this shift, but we now know that training after development (i.e. in adults) can produce similar shifts from configural to dimensional processing (or vice versa).

For example, Williams et al. (1994) found that pretraining people on a task that encouraged dimensional learning increased a dimensional analysis of stimuli during a second task (see also Williams & Braker, 1999). Also, the oft-used 'easy-to-hard' procedure (Mackintosh, 1974) leverages the notion that early exposure to large differences along the relevant dimension will make it easier for the observer to attend to the relevant dimension when it is necessary to make smaller distinctions along that dimension. Peron and Allen (1988) reported that experience with tasting beers improved later learning of the difference between them, and Burns and Shepp (1988) discovered that prior experience with color (e.g. in art students) affords better selective attention to individual color dimensions like chroma and hue that are normally configured (see also Foard & Kemler, 1984).

Nevertheless, some dimensions appear to be easier to separate than others. Garner (1970) classified stimulus dimensions into two general categories, *integral* and *separable*. The classic example of integral dimensions are those involved in color (e.g. lightness and saturation); our day-to-day experience does not appear to be sufficient to encourage differentiation of color into its component dimensions, perhaps because these dimensions are highly correlated in the real world (Shepard, 1991). In contrast, dimensions like size, color, orientation and texture appear to be readily separable (at least by older children and adults).

Generalization and similarity

Another fundamental aspect of learning involves similarity and generalization. We have all encountered situations in which we find it easy to learn a new concept because it is very similar to ones that we already know, but we struggle mightily when the new concept is dramatically different from familiar ones. Our ability to generalize prior knowledge to novel situations both leverages prior knowledge and eases new learning. This process of generalization is rooted in similarity, and similarity has proved to be a slippery phenomenon to pin down (Medin, Goldstone, & Gentner, 1993). Despite these difficulties, there are some fundamental laws that appear to be operating in studies of similarity.

Roger Shepard (1987) offered a 'universal law of generalization' that has been instrumental in providing a formalization of the similarity process. For Shepard, similarity is a function of the distance between psychological representations. Each representation to be compared can be conceptualized as a point in a multidimensional space (e.g. in a five-dimensional space, a point might be specified as {0.3, 0.8, −0.2, 0.9, −0.4} in which each value corresponds to the representation's score on that dimension). The distance between points h and a is measured by the Minkowski metric:

$$d = \left(\sum_i |h_i - a_i|^r \right)^{1/r} \qquad (6.1)$$

where r is a free parameter that determines the shape of the generalization function. The precise shape of the empirically observed generalization function for a set of stimuli varies as a function of the properties of the stimuli. For separable dimensions, the Minkowski metric best fits observed data when r is about 1, and for integral dimensions when r is about 2. But integrality and separability define a continuum rather than a dichotomy, thus allowing for r values between 1 and 2 (Garner, 1970; Shepard, 1991). Finally, Shepard proposed that similarity is an exponential function of the distance computed in equation (6.1) (i.e. $s = e^{-cd}$ where c is a free parameter that specifies the rate of exponential decay).

The effects of similarity are most often documented in studies of discrimination learning. In these studies, people learn to discriminate two or more stimuli by making different responses to different stimuli. The comparative ease of these learning tasks is a function of the similarity of the items to be discriminated. But similarity can be altered by the learning process itself.

Changes in perceived similarity can be produced by at least two processes: differential attention to dimensions and differential attention to values along a dimension. Examples of dimensional attention are ubiquitous in both humans (e.g. Ashby, Queller, & Berretty, 1999; Castellan, 1973; Gluck & Bower, 1988a; Nosofsky, 1986) and animals (Lubow, 1973; Mackintosh & Little, 1969; Pearce & Hall, 1980; Sutherland & Mackintosh, 1971) and shifting attention between dimensions is readily observed (e.g. Blough, 1969; Gottselig, Wasserman, & Young, 2001; Kruschke, 1992).

Examples of changes in value-specific attention are less prevalent (e.g. Goldstone, 1994; Kersten, Goldstone, & Schaffert, 1998; Lively, Logan, &

Pisoni, 1993), but these attentional shifts can change the perceived similarity of stimuli. For example, Goldstone (1994) trained people to categorize squares of varying size and brightness. Participants in the *size* condition learned to place the smaller squares into one category and the larger squares into a different category; participants in the *brightness* condition learned to place the darker squares into one category and the brighter squares into a different category. After extensive training, the participants performed a perceptual, same–different task involving the same squares. Goldstone found that participants' same–different judgments were not only sensitized to the dimension that was relevant during the training stage, but also were maximally sensitive to the dimensional values near the border between the trained categories.

Other species have also been found to show increased sensitivity near category borders in demonstrations of 'dimensional contrast' (Blough, 1975). Hinson and Tennison (1997) proposed a model of dimensional contrast that supplements standard measures of stimulus similarity with a graded attentional mechanism that extends over the pertinent region of the similarity space. The gradient is presumed to peak near the border between categories and to decline with distance from that border. The combined effect of the attentional gradient and stimulus similarity was shown to provide nice fits to a wide range of dimensional contrast phenomena (Hinson & Tennison, 1997).

Differential attention to specific dimension values is also revealed in a somewhat different context. Some features may be either present or absent (e.g. 'has tail' or 'lacks tail'). These two values, present and absent, have differential salience (the 'feature-positive effect': see Hearst, 1991, for a review). When a feature is present, it commands attention; when it is not, it does not command attention (except, perhaps, by its unexpected absence: cf. Tassoni, 1995; Van Hamme & Wasserman, 1994). This asymmetry in salience for specific dimensional values (feature presence commands more attention than feature absence) has been documented by others in various contexts (e.g. Goldstone, 1994; Hearst, 1991; Newman, Wolff, & Hearst, 1980; Tassoni, 1995; Van Hamme & Wasserman, 1994). Unfortunately, most general theories of learning do not account for the feature-positive effect.

Unlearning

Early notions (e.g. by the British associationists) deemed learning as strengthening the association between 'ideas'; unlearning, in which the two ideas were no longer paired, was expected to weaken that association. Pavlov (1927), however, demonstrated that extinction (a form of unlearning) did not succeed in eradicating the original association. When a conditioned stimulus was extinguished, pairing it with the unconditioned stimulus after extinction resulted in a rapid recovery of the conditioned response. This second phase of 'learning' – so-called relearning – was actually faster than that observed in the first phase, evidence that the original learning was never really obliterated. Pavlov posited that, during extinction, an inhibitory association was learned that counteracted the excitatory association that was originally acquired (Pavlov, 1927). In analogous studies involving paired associate learning by humans, Ebbinghaus (1885/1913) documented that an unexpressed association may still exist by showing savings in the learning of nonsense syllables.

The phenomena of savings and spontaneous recovery are known to every psychologist. Despite the ubiquity of this knowledge, many contemporary theories of learning fail to address the phenomena. As we shall see, most theories conveniently, but inaccurately, represent unlearning as the opposite of learning.

Synopsis

Our recitation of some important learning phenomena lays the groundwork for a discussion of theories that attempt to explain some or all of these phenomena. These principles can be revealed in the diverse domains of inquiry that involve learning processes: causal learning, Pavlovian and Thorndikian conditioning, implicit learning, category learning, language learning, *inter alia*. Thus, theories of basic learning processes provide a good foundation for theoretical development in these other investigative domains.

THEORIES OF LEARNING

Despite the skepticism of B.F. Skinner (1950), theories of learning can play many important and positive roles in the development of our understanding of the learning process. Theories summarize empirical data, ease the communication of general principles, guide the empirical process and, when instantiated computationally, allow us to play out the numerous implications of a theory; even the relatively simple Rescorla–Wagner mathematical model of learning (Rescorla & Wagner, 1972) has generated surprising predictions that were unanticipated by the theory's authors.

Learning, however, has been submitted to empirical investigation longer than nearly any other phenomenon in the field of psychology (with the exception of psycho-physics and, perhaps, memory).

This state of affairs means that there is an abundance of empirical phenomena that must be explained by a comprehensive theory of learning. To date, there is no single 'unified theory of learning' that has emerged. There are, however, many accounts of particular classes of learning.

Contemporary learning theories typically involve one of two forms of learning: supervised or unsupervised. In supervised learning, the learner is modeled as producing a response, comparing that response to the one that should have been produced (this information is provided by a 'teacher'), computing the error (the difference between the actual response and the correct response) and then altering its internal representations in order to reduce future error. The response does not have to be overt, but may be an internal mental state (e.g. the anticipation of a future stimulus configuration). Likewise, the teacher may be an instructor, the environment (e.g. the outcome of an action) or an internally generated signal from another brain system.

The purpose of supervised learning systems is to reduce the error between actual and correct responses. By this account, supervised learning faces a task analogous to that faced by statistical models like regression and ANOVA, which seek to minimize the error between the observed dependent variable value and its predicted value. Indeed, iterative instantiations of these statistical models (which converge on the optimal parameter weights during exposure to data elements over time) are isomorphic to some classes of connectionist models of supervised learning.

In unsupervised learning, the learner is a statistical regularity detector. There is no single correct response; the goal of the unsupervised learner is to encode the correlations between features, the boundaries between clusters of stimuli (analogous to cluster analysis and discriminant analysis) or the major axes of variation (analogous to principal component analysis). Unsupervised learning systems may serve to preprocess the environmental input before it is passed on to a supervised learning system (as represented explicitly by counterpropagation networks: Hertz, Krogh, & Palmer, 1991); but because unsupervised learning is not driven by the need to make a correct response, this preprocessing may not generate the most useful representation.

Both forms of learning involve the encoding of statistical regularities of the environment, but supervised learning tries to encode only those regularities that serve a purpose. There are many incidental correlations that have no immediate behavioral consequences and thus could be rightly ignored by a supervised learning system. The frequent observation that people's behavior is affected by irrelevant aspects of a task (Castellan, 1973; Edgell, Castellan, Roe, & Barnes, 1996; Goldstone, 1995; MacLeod, 1991) suggests that people do encode relationships that serve no immediate purpose.

This state of affairs nevertheless has some important benefits; the encoding of apparently irrelevant information serves to prepare a learner for unanticipated tasks. Historically, most theories of learning are of the supervised variety, so we consider this class of theories first.

Supervised learning

The Rescorla–Wagner model

One of the most influential theories of supervised learning in psychology was that proposed by Rescorla and Wagner (1972). According to their model, the learner's goal was to predict the occurrence or non-occurrence of an outcome given the presence or absence of various predictors. To the degree that the learner's expectation of the outcome and the actual occurrence of that outcome diverged, learning was deemed necessary to reduce this predictive error. Learning was conceptualized as occurring during discrete trials, in which each of the predictors and the outcome was either present or absent. The division of a learning session into discrete trials is problematic as a representation of real-time learning (Hammond & Paynter, 1983), but it serves as a good first approximation for many learning situations.

According to the Rescorla-Wagner model, an observer learns to associate predictors with the outcome in order to improve prediction. The strength of each predictor's association with the outcome changes as a function of the following equation:

$$\Delta V_x = \alpha_x \, \beta \, (\lambda - V_T) \qquad (6.2)$$

in which ΔV_x designates the change in the strength of the association between predictor X and the outcome, V_T designates the total associative strength for any predictors present on the trial and represents the anticipated outcome, λ designates the actual outcome of the trial (with a value that is usually modeled as 1 or 100 when the outcome occurs and 0 when the outcome does not occur), α_x is a parameter representing the salience of the predictor X, and β a learning rate particular to the outcome (β is sometimes modeled as having two different values, β_O on trials when the outcome occurs and β_{NO} on trials when the outcome does not occur).

The associative strength between every predictor present on a trial and the outcome is modified using equation (6.2); absent predictors do not change their associative strength because the α_x for an absent predictor is assumed to be 0. When there are multiple predictors present on any given trial, equation (6.2) produces competition among those predictors. Because V_T is the degree to which the US is anticipated by the constellation of predictors, a single strong predictor (e.g. $V_A = 90$) can block any learning involving

new predictors of that US that are coexistent with that predictor (i.e. the model shows forward blocking).

The Rescorla–Wagner model accounts for contingency-like learning by treating the context as just another stimulus. When an outcome occurs in the absence of any punctate predictors, thus decreasing contingency, the context gains associative strength. When the outcome occurs in the presence of a predictor, the associative values of those predictors and the context will sum to determine V_T. If the context acquires sufficient strength, then it will interfere with the acquisition of strength by punctate predictors during trials in which they occur because the context is omnipresent. So, according to the Rescorla–Wagner model, a decrease in 'contingency' is accompanied by an increase in context-outcome associative strength through a contiguity mechanism, ultimately producing a decrease in the strength of the relationship between punctate predictors and the outcome.

The Rescorla–Wagner model has been relatively successful at predicting the ordinal strength of causes and effects in human causal attribution (e.g. Allan, 1993; Shanks & Dickinson, 1987; Wasserman, 1990b; Young, 1995). It is a reasonable description of the acquisition of causality judgments (Shanks, 1987), and it successfully predicts how predictors interact when more than one is present (e.g. as observed in forward blocking and the relative validity effect). In general, its ordinal predictions of the effect of various contingency schedules are correct, although there are some exceptions (see Shanks & Dickinson, 1987).

The consequences of event absence One of the marked distinctions between causal learning and many category learning tasks is that the former involves predictors that are either present or absent, whereas the latter often, but not always, involves predictors that have a value that lies on a dimension (e.g. black vs. white, big vs. small, angle of orientation). There is a long history documenting that presence and absence are not two values along a single dimension, each of which has equal access to our cognitive machinery. Indeed, people often have much greater difficulty noting the importance of absence regardless of whether this involves the non-occurrence of an event, the absence of a feature or the deletion of an object (Hearst, 1991).

In the original Rescorla–Wagner theory, this asymmetry was incorporated by having present events or features modify their associative strengths, whereas absent ones did not. Although the non-learning of absence may be the rule, exceptions abound. In particular, observations of backward blocking (wherein absent cues change their associative strength) have inspired revisions of the model, and learning theorists have offered variations on the model in order to incorporate different degrees of absence.

Van Hamme and Wasserman (1994) suggested that a *notably* absent event could also change its associative strength in accordance with equation (6.2), but that it would be assigned a negative α_x and its absolute salience would be expected to be less than that for present events. The issue of *notable* absence is central to their proposal (see Tassoni, 1995, for a similar proposal); if all absent events or features could alter their associative strengths, then the computational overload might swamp any cognitive system as well as produce catastrophic retroactive interference. To forgo this possibility, these proposals distinguish between notable absence, for which learning occurs, and inconsequential absence, for which learning does not occur. Absence may be notable for many reasons: (a) a feature that has historically always accompanied another may no longer do so; (b) attention could be specifically directed to the absence of an event (e.g. through instructions or explicit signaling); or (c) an event's offset may be particularly salient (e.g. when the constant hum in the background suddenly stops). Dickinson and Burke (1996) provided an empirical demonstration that backward blocking – an effect that appears to rely on notable absence – is directly affected by the formation of within-compound associations (for further empirical substantiation see Wasserman & Berglan, 1998).

Although these variations of the Rescorla–Wagner model provided a considerable increase in the explanatory power of the model (e.g. Dickinson & Burke, 1996; Tassoni, 1995; Van Hamme & Wasserman, 1994), their full implications are not yet known. The interaction between notable absence and the representation of stimulus configurations is a thorny problem (are there notably absent configurations?), and changes in the notability of absence have not been confronted (how does learning change expectations of absence or presence?).

Representation of configurations   In their original formulation, Rescorla and Wagner (1972) represented a stimulus constellation as comprising a collection of independent features. As a result, this early version could not learn tasks that involve appreciating the interactions between and among features (e.g. as required in negative patterning), even though human and other animals could be shown to do so. In response, Wagner and Rescorla (1972) quickly offered a variation on their basic model in which configurations of features or stimuli could acquire their own, independent associative strengths. Thus, an AB compound would involve learning about the association between the outcome and A, B and X, with the latter representing a 'unique cue' peculiar to the AB configuration. This minor modification allowed the model to account for negative patterning and other tasks requiring configural learning.

Gluck and Bower (1988b) extended this approach by developing a connectionist model in which the input comprised individual element features, pairs of features or triplets of features. Their 'configural-cue' model used the delta rule (which is mathematically equivalent to the Rescorla–Wagner model: Sutton & Barto, 1981) to associate these individual features and their configurations with correct responses.

Although this model had many positive characteristics, it also highlighted one of the difficulties with the unique-cue approach to configural learning: the exponential growth in configural cues. For example, in a relatively simple environment involving 10 cues, there are $\binom{10}{2}$ or 45 possible pairs, $\binom{10}{3}$ or 120 possible triplets, $\binom{10}{4}$ or 210 possible quartets, etc. Tracking all of these possibilities quickly becomes impractical.

One alternative considered by Gluck and Bower and later implemented (Gluck, Bower, & Hee, 1989) was to use a multilayer connectionist model that ostensibly learned which configurations were necessary prerequisites to good classification performance. These configurations were represented by nodes at an intermediate stage of processing (the 'hidden layer' of a connectionist network). This modification certainly helped to minimize the explicit encoding of the multitude of possible configural representations, but it also had its undesirable side effects as a model of human learning, including catastrophic retroactive interference (e.g. McCloskey & Cohen, 1989; Ratcliff, 1990) and an oversensitivity to linear boundaries (Kruschke, 1993).

The Gluck and Bower (1988b) and Wagner and Rescorla (1972) models retained the original emphasis on elemental learning, but supplemented it with configural representations. In contrast, Pearce (1987, 1994) abandoned elemental learning altogether and proposed a purely configural model (see Kruschke, 1992, for a similar proposal that also incorporates attentional learning). For Pearce, every learning situation involves a collection of cues and learning involves encoding the entire set of cues as a predictor of a future outcome. Responding to novel situations thus involves generalization from already known situations.

According to Pearce's model, an organism encodes entire configurations of stimuli as it moves about its environment. Favorable outcomes may or may not occur in each situation. The organism learns to associate favorable outcomes with certain configurations of stimuli and to respond according to the developing expectations. In each new situation, the organism can compare the new configuration of stimuli to known configurations. It can then anticipate outcomes similar to those outcomes that were previously experienced in similar situations. In Pearce's model, similarity is judged by comparing the individual features of each configuration and integrating these elemental similarities (specifically, using the dot product of two vectors representing each configuration). The organism thus learns that red items are associated with reinforcement because red items (e.g. red circle, red square, red triangle) have historically been followed by reinforcement. Thus, learning is not elemental in the traditional, Rescorla–Wagner sense; the organism does not learn that the feature 'red' is associated with reinforcement.

This approach may appear to be as computationally imposing as the former approach except for two important theoretical proposals. First, each cue attracts different levels of attention. Thus, many cues of low salience or of known irrelevance (e.g. ambient noise) command few resources. Second, representations of all possible configurations are not assumed to pre-exist. If they did, then 10 cues (each involving their presence or absence) would require 2^{10} or 1024 configural representations. If configural representations are created only when needed, then considerably fewer resources would be required. Although Pearce does not offer a mechanism for this latter process, mechanisms in which configurations were created only when error could not be reduced to a sufficient degree (e.g. Fahlman & Lebiere, 1990; Kadirkamanathan & Niranjan, 1993) could be readily adopted. A similar modification to the configural-cue model might provide an analogous benefit: the system could add configurations as needed, starting with the simplest (pairs) first and adding higher-order configurations only when necessary.

Choosing between purely configural models and elemental plus configural models is made even more difficult by data indicating that the fit of these models differs across preparations (Myers, Vogel, Shin, & Wagner, 2001). Myers et al. suggest that the nature of the stimuli may be the primary determinant of whether the Pearce model or the configural Rescorla–Wagner model will best fit any given data set. More specifically, Pearce's model may provide the best fit for stimuli involving integral dimensions, whereas the configural Rescorla–Wagner model may provide the best fit for stimuli involving separable dimensions. Although Myers et al. suggest an extension of the Rescorla–Wagner model to provide better fits for experiments involving integral dimensions (see also Wagner & Brandon, 2001), it is important to consider ways in which extant configural models similar to Pearce's (e.g. Kruschke, 1992) might already provide a comprehensive theoretical perspective of the data.

Shortcomings The Rescorla–Wagner model and its variants have achieved considerable success as models of basic associative learning. In an assessment of the Rescorla–Wagner model, Miller, Barnet, and Grahame (1995) pointed out 18 distinct successes, providing a strong rationale for the theory's

continuing influence on the psychology of learning. Miller et al. (1995), however, then delineated 23 failures of the model (i.e. opportunities for improvement). Some of the recent variants discussed above attempt to address one or more of these shortcomings, but more work is clearly necessary. In their examination of the 23 failures, the authors identified several clusters of problems at the root of these failures. Some of these clusters warrant further discussion because they are problematic for a wide range of contemporary learning theories.

First, excitation and inhibition are viewed as symmetrical opposites in the Rescorla–Wagner model. This problem is endemic to nearly all theories of learning, including those not based on the Rescorla–Wagner model or the delta rule. Given that empirical observation suggests that this symmetry is not well founded, theoretical modification is needed, but no single alternative has yet emerged as a replacement.

Second, the Rescorla–Wagner model assumes fixed associability of a stimulus with reinforcing outcomes. This assumption is widely recognized as untenable, and models discussed below (Kruschke, 1992; Pearce & Hall, 1980) specifically address this problem by proposing that attention to stimulus features varies throughout the learning process. Be that as it may, many theorists avoid the additional complexity of attentional variation and still rely on the original formulation. In all fairness, the additional degrees of freedom offered by an attentional learning mechanism are not necessitated by all experimental paradigms.

Third, the Rescorla–Wagner model assumes that learners possess only the current associative value of a cue and retain no knowledge of its prior associative history (the *path independence* problem). This assumption prevents the model from accounting for spontaneous recovery of an extinguished response and related phenomena. The problem is at least partially addressed by connectionist models that incorporate representations that intervene between the input and the output of the learning system. Because of the large number of connections between a cue and the anticipated outcome, new associations can be acquired that overwhelm a residual of the original association. However, the catastrophic retroactive interference documented in some connectionist models (e.g. McCloskey & Cohen, 1989; Ratcliff, 1990) suggests that historical associations can still be easily lost.

Real-time adaptations? One of the major shortcomings of the Rescorla–Wagner model that was not addressed by Miller et al. (1995) is that it was designed for the trial level of analysis in which stimuli are either present or absent. It is possible, however, to incorporate temporal variables into the model by encoding event activation levels as a function of time (e.g. Sutton & Barto, 1981, 1991).

A straightforward proposal is to incorporate an exponential decay in the activation of a stimulus, a_x, so that a change in associative strength between X and the outcome is the joint function of the following equations:

$$\Delta V_x = \alpha_x \beta (\lambda - V_T) a_x \qquad (6.3)$$

$$a_x = a_0 \times e^{-kt} \qquad (6.4)$$

where a_0 is the salience of the stimulus independent of time, k is a decay rate parameter, and t is the amount of elapsed time since the offset of the stimulus, X. The activation of the stimulus thus represents its memory trace strength and this strength modulates learning. Consequently, a stimulus that had very recently occurred could experience a change in its associative strength that is nearly as large as when it was present (unless k was high, thus producing rapid trace strength decay), but a stimulus whose memory is fading would experience little if any change in its associative strength.

Given the observation of trace conditioning, ITI effects, ISI effects and temporal conditioning (in which time is a predictor), a non-temporal theory like the Rescorla–Wagner model is constrained in its ability to account for many phenomena. Although doing so greatly increases the complexity of theorizing (e.g. Broadbent, 1994; Gallistel & Gibbon, 2000; Sutton & Barto, 1991; Wagner, 1981; Wagner & Brandon, 1989), temporal extensions are necessary to provide adequate theories for many cognitive domains. The difficult task may be making these complex theories comprehensible by the larger body of psychologists interested in learning phenomena.

Comparator theories: indiscriminate learning

Comparator theories (e.g. Barnet, Arnold, & Miller, 1991; Matzel, Held, & Miller, 1988; Miller & Matzel, 1988) represent an alternative class of contiguity models. Comparator theories suggest that subjects learn about every stimulus relation that they experience; performance, however, is not a direct function of learning. In contrast to the Rescorla–Wagner model, CS–US contiguity is posited to produce learning regardless of the presence of other predictors of the US; but unless the CS is presented under conditions that are favorable for the behavioral expression of that learning, knowledge of the CS–US relation will not be evidenced. Conditioned performance is determined by the associative value of the CS relative to the value of its comparison context. When the value of the CS is greater than the value of its comparison context, the CS will produce a conditioned response; when it is lower in value, it will inhibit a conditioned response. Miller and Schactman (1985) suggested

that the comparison context comprises general background cues and other discrete stimuli that were prominent during training. The principal difference between comparator theories and most other associative theories is a difference in the relation between learning and performance.

Work in the field of causal learning has also faced the issue of whether failures to exhibit knowledge are due to failures to learn or to perform. Researchers advocating an associative view of causality (Chapman & Robbins, 1990; Shanks & Dickinson, 1987; Wasserman, 1990b) commonly assume that only some relations are learned, whereas those advocating a more normative, contingency-based view (Cheng, 1997; Cheng & Novick, 1992; Shaklee & Elek, 1988; Waldmann & Holyoak, 1992) suggest that most relations are encoded, but only some are exhibited. Cheng and Novick (1992) proposed a view of causal attribution that bears some resemblance to comparator theories. The production of a causal inference depends on the context in which the inference is required (they call this context a *focal set*). Unfortunately, the choice of a focal set is largely underdetermined, thus making it difficult to test this theory against alternative formulations (Shanks, 1993).

Attention-based learning theories

The principal difference between attention-based learning theories and the Rescorla–Wagner model is the additional consideration that the value of α (the learning rate parameter) might be determined not only by the intrinsic qualities of the stimulus (e.g. its salience) but also by the organism's past experience with that stimulus (see Mackintosh, 1975, for the basis of this proposal). Hence, some stimuli might be deemed to be less worthy of our attention than others.

Pearce and Hall (1980) presented a model of classical conditioning formalizing changes in α as a result of experience. They assumed that α initially tends to be high (a novel stimulus attracts great attention), but declines as the organism comes to predict the outcome. The associability of a stimulus, α_x, depends on how well the consequences of that stimulus are predicted. Animals (and that includes people) need to attend to and learn about a stimulus only when its implications for the future are uncertain. Thus, paradoxically, α decreases as the predictive efficacy of a stimulus increases. Note, however, that a stimulus can have low associability but high predictive efficacy; more formally, stimulus X can have a low α but a high V. This formulation thus attempts to capture the everyday idea that, once we have learned something well, it demands less of our attention in order to respond appropriately. This notion is evidenced in processes like reading, driving or responding to our name – they demand little of our attention once they are automatized.

According to Pearce and Hall (1980), α on trial n is a function of the amount of uncertainty that remains about the consequences of stimulus X on the prior trial $(n - 1)$:

$$\alpha_x^n = \left| \lambda^{n-1} - V_T^{n-1} \right| \qquad (6.5)$$

where λ is the actual consequence and V_T is determined in the same way as for the Rescorla–Wagner model. Hall (1991) clarified this equation by noting that associability does not change as rapidly as equation (6.5) would suggest. He offered an anchor-and-adjust version in which α was determined by a weighted average of its most recent value plus the application of equation (6.5):

$$\alpha_x^n = \gamma \left| \lambda^{n-1} - V_T^{n-1} \right| - (1 - \gamma)\alpha_x^{n-1} \quad (6.6)$$

where γ, which lies between 0 and 1, determines the responsiveness of α to recent events.

The proposal that α changes during learning does not directly map onto the original Rescorla–Wagner model to determine the associative strength of a stimulus. A comparison of the Rescorla–Wagner (1972) and Pearce and Hall (1980) equations for changing associative strength will clarify the distinction:

Rescorla–Wagner: $\Delta V_x = \alpha_x \beta(\lambda - V_T)$ (6.7)
Pearce–Hall: $\Delta V_x = \alpha_x S_X V_X$ (6.8)

Pearce and Hall introduced a parameter, S_X, that corresponds to the intensity of the stimulus. Whereas the Rescorla–Wagner model uses a single parameter, α, to capture the associability *and* intensity of the stimulus, Pearce and Hall consider these factors to have independent effects on learning; an intense stimulus (e.g. a bull horn) would prompt large changes in its predictive efficacy (due to a high S_X) even if its consequences are relatively certain (low α). Also note that the uncertainty of an outcome, λ, determines α in the Pearce–Hall formulation ($\lambda^{n-1} - V_T^{n-1}$), but it is independent of α in the Rescorla–Wagner model ($\lambda - V_T$).

It is now readily accepted that attention does change during the learning process (e.g. as documented by changes in orienting responses: Kaye & Pearce, 1984; Swan & Pearce, 1988; Wilson, Boumphrey, & Pearce, 1992). Although the Rescorla–Wagner model does not specify the mechanism of such change, it did allow attention to change under the direction of the modeler. Latent inhibition, the decreased learning after pre-exposure to a stimulus that signals no notable consequences (e.g. Lipp, Siddle, & Vaitl, 1992; Lubow, 1973; Mackintosh, 1973), provides concrete evidence of changes in associability.

These clear examples of attentional learning, however, belie the difficulty of disentangling attentional learning from associative learning in many preparations. The Rescorla–Wagner and Pearce–Hall models provide two very different accounts of blocking. Both models attribute the poor learning of B during AB$^+$ training that follows A$^+$ alone training to the unsurprising positive outcome on the AB trials. But the Pearce–Hall model assumes that the learner will pay little attention to B during the AB phase of a blocking experiment (*learned inattention*), whereas the Rescorla–Wagner model assumes that the learner fully attends to B but fails to learn the association between B and the outcome (*lack of learning*).

In an attempt to distinguish between the learned inattention and lack-of-learning accounts in a causal learning study involving humans, Kruschke and Blair (2000) performed experiments that provide initial evidence that both forward and backward blocking involve changes in attention. Further experimentation should reveal the robustness of this finding and its consequences for other learning phenomena.

Part of the failure of the Pearce–Hall model to eclipse the Rescorla–Wagner model as the basic theory of learning stems from a series of unanswered questions involving configural learning (e.g. Can there be differential attention to stimulus configurations and elements?) and the fact that the Pearce–Hall model still retains many of the shortcomings of the Rescorla–Wagner model (Miller et al., 1995). The continuing development of attentional learning mechanisms in models of category learning (Goldstone, Steyvers, Spencer-Smith, & Kersten, 2000; Kersten et al., 1998; Kruschke, 1992, 2001; Kruschke & Johansen, 1999) will help in testing these principles in other domains of learning.

Connectionist association models

During the past 15 years, learning processes have most often been instantiated in connectionist or neural network models (see Chapter 18 by Lamberts, this volume). This trend has produced adaptations of the early learning theories: Sutton and Barto (1981) showed that the Rescorla–Wagner equation is isomorphic to the delta rule, Pearce adapted his 1987 model to a connectionist architecture (Pearce, 1994), and Kruschke offered a connectionist generalization of Mackintosh's theory of attentional change (Kruschke, 2001).

One of the most promising directions for connectionist models of associative learning is the class of models based on radial basis functions (Moody & Darken, 1989). Radial basis function networks preprocess the environmental stimuli so as to develop more abstract classifications of experience that can then be associated with desired responses, expectations, motor sequences, etc. Recently, these models have had good success as the basis of models of predictive learning across a wide range of paradigms (DeLosh, Busemeyer, & McDaniel, 1997;

Kruschke & Blair, 2000; Kruschke & Johansen, 1999; Shanks, Charles, Darby, & Azmi, 1998; Shanks, Darby, & Charles, 1998; Young, Wasserman, Johnson, & Jones, 2000).

One of the reasons for the success of radial basis function models is that their principles are soundly rooted in historical learning theories. Their similarity metric is based on Shepard's (1964) use of the Minkowski metric, the acquisition of associations between the emerging environmental classification and desired outputs (responses, expectations, etc.) is accomplished using the delta rule, and the models are similar to configural models like Pearce's (1987, 1994). In Kruschke's (2001) adaptation of ALCOVE (a radial basis function model: Kruschke, 1992), he adopted an attentional learning mechanism that is a generalization of Mackintosh's (1975) attention learning mechanism, thus showing the adaptability of this framework. Radial basis function models further allow for the development of representations that are far less susceptible to the catastrophic retroactive interference evidenced by models based on backpropagation (cf. Kruschke, 1993, for descriptions of the problem and possible solutions; Lewandowsky & Li, 1995; McCloskey & Cohen, 1989; Ratcliff, 1990).

Although connectionist models frustrate many theorists because their complexity can make it seem like we are trading one black box (the brain) for another (the model), these models provide an opportunity to explore the consequences of an integration of various psychological principles based on historical theories. These consequences can indeed be unpredictable, but the greater accessibility of these networks to analysis (relative to the coarse and indelicate methods that are currently available for analyzing the brain *in vivo*) has provided insights into how the brain might implement cognitive processes.

Learning temporal relations

A major limitation to nearly all of the models discussed thus far is that they have not been designed to learn the temporal relations between environmental events. Yet environmental stimuli are encountered amidst a temporal stream (Zacks & Tversky, 2001). Learning the temporal order of these stimuli is vital to the survival of an organism. For example, the sequence of retinal images will indicate whether the cougar is approaching or departing, the order of words affects their interpretation ('She took only one test on Friday' vs. 'Only she took one test on Friday'), and the order of events determines their consequence (e.g. the two events (a) loading a gun and (b) pulling its trigger produce two very different results when presented as (a) before (b) vs. (b) before (a)).

Producing properly ordered responses to stimuli is also critical. For example, generating the correct order of spoken words is important to being understood (although some variation is tolerable, as demonstrated by the odd affectations of Yoda in *Star Wars*), closing one's hand before it actually reaches the coffee mug will not fetch you the desired caffeine, and playing the notes in any old order and at any pace is unlikely to produce pleasant music.

Methods for encoding temporal relationships fall into two general classes: those that encode the ordered relations among stimuli and those that encode a time-of-occurrence with each event. To encode the ordinal relations among events, the learner must appreciate which events are followed by which others through interitem associations. These associations are not constrained to be between adjacent events, but can include temporally remote associations as well (e.g. in compound chaining models: Slamecka, 1985). This idea is prominent in many contemporary theories of learning (e.g. Desmond & Moore, 1988; Elman, 1990).

To encode the time-of-occurrence of events, researchers have proposed an assortment of interpretive alternatives. The representation of an event may decay over time, thus making the *trace strength* of its memory a measure of how long ago it occurred (e.g. Desmond & Moore, 1991; Grossberg, 1978). Other theories propose that memory traces are not the basis of knowing when an event occurred, but rather each memory is *time-stamped* with its time-of-occurrence. This time stamp may be a decaying scalar (Hertz et al., 1991), the state of a series of oscillators (Brown, Preece, & Hulme, 2000), a position code (Burgess & Hitch, 1992; Sejnowski & Rosenberg, 1986) or an externally derived stamp (the events that surrounded its occurrence).

Unfortunately, there is little consensus as to how the brain actually encodes temporal relations; it is even possible that many if not all of these mechanisms may be in operation for different tasks, skills or situations. Be that as it may, temporal extensions of successful theories (e.g. radial basis functions) should provide a fertile area of exploration for many learning phenomena.

Unsupervised learning

Not all situations involve a teacher providing the correct response. Indeed, much of our learning occurs without explicit direction as to the correct response to make in any given situation (Clapper & Bower, 1991). In unsupervised learning algorithms, the system is assumed to have an implicit goal, and it strives to achieve this goal. These goals are usually very straightforward: learn the correlation between environmental features or events, develop an efficient representation of environmental stimuli, or maximize reinforcement. The utility of this knowledge may not be immediately apparent, but it can certainly prove useful for the solution of some future problem.

From a human learning perspective, unsupervised learning is often assumed to be one of the mechanisms that subserves perceptual learning. Perceptual learning involves relatively long-lasting changes to an organism's perceptual system (Gibson & Gibson, 1955; Goldstone, 1996). Thus, unsupervised learning is frequently conceptualized as a preprocessing mechanism; perceptual information is transformed (e.g. by identifying correlations or performing similarity-based classification) before being passed farther up the processing stream and entering a more supervised learning system (although not necessarily so). This stage-like approach is explicit in counterpropagation models (Hertz et al., 1991), of which radial basis function models are a subset.

Hebbian learning is based on a proposal first put forth by Donald Olding Hebb (1949): cell assemblies that are active at the same time become interconnected. Hebbian learning identifies the base rates of occurrence and co-occurrence of environmental events. The identification of environmental regularities can serve two important adaptive goals: the better prediction of missing information (e.g. where there is smoke, there is fire) and the effective reduction of redundancy in representation (e.g. highly correlated features can be represented by a single value). In contemporary statistical vernacular, Hebbian learning can be used to identify correlations and principal components. (For a detailed presentation of some Hebbian learning techniques, see Hertz et al., 1991.)

An alternative form of unsupervised learning is evidenced in connectionist models that use *competitive learning* (Grossberg, 1987; Rumelhart & Zipser, 1985). Competitive learning algorithms identify the naturally occurring clusters of stimuli in the environment; similar items are thus placed into the same category (similarity is determined using the Minkowski metric, the normalized dot product or a related measure). In effect, these algorithms summarize the environment by classifying similar stimuli together, with the hope that these stimuli can be treated similarly. This reduced representation increases storage efficiency, but this efficiency may come at a cost if the loss of finer distinctions between stimuli within a class proves to be detrimental.

Concerns about the loss of information has produced an emphasis on algorithms like backpropagation that supervise the creation of useful intermediate representations. But supervising this process is computationally expensive, thus retarding learning and undermining backpropagation as a good model of short-term learning processes (e.g. one-trial learning). Although completely unsupervised competitive learning algorithms have their limitations, perhaps a more constrained form of feedback may be sufficient to overcome their

drawbacks (de Sa & Ballard, 1998; Goldstone et al., 2000; Kohonen, 1989).

In addition to the many studies of perceptual learning, unsupervised learning of categories has been documented (e.g. Ashby et al., 1999; Billman & Knutson, 1996; Clapper & Bower, 1994; Pothos & Chater, 2002; Rosenthal, Fusi, & Hochstein, 2001; Wills & McLaren, 1998), but this line of research is still in its infancy. Theoretical models based on connectionist algorithms of unsupervised learning are providing the foundation of theories of these processes. Researchers are investigating both Hebbian (Rosenthal et al., 2001) and competitive learning algorithms (Goldstone et al., 2000) as the basis of theories of human unsupervised learning. This work has the potential to significantly extend prevailing theories in an attempt to provide a unified model of category learning.

Selection mechanisms

An intermediate form of supervised learning is captured by theories that posit various selection mechanisms (Palmer & Donahoe, 1992). Thorndike's (1911) trial-and-error learning (originally called 'selecting and connecting') conceived of the learner as trying various responses and learning from the consequences of those actions (e.g. the situation faced by a cat in one of his puzzle boxes). The environment serves to teach the learner, but much less directly than is the case in supervised learning algorithms.

There are many ways for a cat to escape from a Thorndike puzzle box and the teacher does not direct which method to use; instead, the teacher simply provides feedback as to the relative success of a series of actions. Skinner (1938) famously extended Thorndike's selection mechanism through his investigation of the reinforcement of operant behaviors (the repertoire of behaviors not elicited by a known stimulus, but spontaneously emitted by the organism).

An important prerequisite for a selection mechanism is a substrate of varied behaviors from which to select. Neuringer and his colleagues (e.g. Neuringer, Deiss, & Olson, 2000; Neuringer, Kornell, & Olufs, 2001) have been exploring the relationship between learning and response variability. Recently, Neuringer et al. (2001) reported that, when a previously reinforced behavior was no longer reinforced, rats increased the variability in their response repertoire by increasing their production of response sequences that had been relatively rare while they continued to produce the previously reinforced sequences. 'The rats' combination of generally doing what worked before but occasionally doing something very different may maximize the possibility of reinforcement from a previously bountiful source while providing necessary variations for new learning' (from the abstract, p. 79).

Bertenthal (1999) conducted studies of behavioral variability during childhood and documented that variability seems to increase at certain times of development (e.g. Woollacott & Sveistrup, 1994). These changes in variability are often driven by changes in the developing motor, perceptual and cognitive systems (e.g. changes in muscular strength or working memory capacity) as well as by interactions between these developing systems and the environment (e.g. the greater demands of balance while sitting or standing).

These demonstrations of the utility of selection mechanisms have renewed interest in reinforcement learning in the field of psychology. Reinforcement learning involves two distinct subsystems: a system that generates exploratory behavior and one that produces actions that tend to be associated with favorable mental or environmental states. Because a teacher does not need to tell the system which responses to make, but rather whether the current state of affairs is good or bad, the feedback is not as specific as that typically used in supervised learning. Another important distinction between reinforcement learning and traditional supervised learning algorithms is that supervised learning systems exclusively rely on exploitation of all current learning to minimize error, whereas reinforcement learning systems balance exploitation with exploration in order to improve the system's ability to identify previously unknown response sequences that lead to positive outcomes.

Although reinforcement learning is increasingly popular in developing artificial learning systems (e.g. in the field of robotics), it has had a smaller impact on recent psychological theories of learning. There is budding interest, however, in the utility of these algorithms as accounts of human learning and development (e.g. Berthier, 1996; Gullapalli, 1997; Schlesinger & Parisi, 2001); the maturation of this approach bears watching.

THE STATE OF AFFAIRS: FRAGMENTATION OR SPECIALIZATION?

During the heyday of behaviorism, basic learning processes reigned supreme. Much of this work was based on studies involving the conditioning of non-human animals, but researchers saw parallels to basic behavioral mechanisms in humans. Although there were no overarching theories that truly encompassed the myriad results being generated in laboratories, there was widespread recognition that parallels to these learning mechanisms were present across an impressive range of species and situations. These general phenomena included Thorndike's law of effect, the law of stimulus generalization, the role of contingency, the behavioral

consequences of reinforcement schedules and the detrimental effects of reinforcement delay. Although the cognitive revolution brought about many positive changes in the study of cognition, one of the unfortunate consequences has been the fragmentation of the study of learning: as an independent field of study at the core of psychology, learning has fallen by the wayside. Indeed, some departments no longer teach a psychology of learning course.

Although many of the basic mechanisms of learning can still be identified across species and situations, a decreasing number of students are aware of their long history. The modularization of the study of learning in cognitive psychology has resulted in the 'rediscovery' of well-established principles and the true discovery of new principles. There is a panoply of research domains in which learning is studied. All of these areas examine people's ability to learn the relationship between environmental events, but they vary in some important and some not so important ways. A relatively complete list includes: conditioning, category learning, causal learning, function learning, probability learning, implicit learning, perceptual learning, language learning, skill learning, machine learning, classroom learning and the encoding processes of memory.

Too much of the work in each of these fields is carried out in ignorance of the research being conducted in the others. This fragmented state of affairs is not surprising given that the burgeoning research traditions in these many specialized domains make it a daunting task to stay abreast of even the major findings in each one. However, several individuals have endeavored to bring together some of these fields by integrating theories and data across domains (e.g. DeLosh et al., 1997; Goldstone et al., 2000; Kruschke & Johansen, 1999; Schyns et al., 1998; Shanks, 1994; Wasserman, 1990b). Nevertheless, additional attempts to identify the common threads across these domains would certainly help all of those who study learning to avoid rediscovering established principles and to effectively leverage discoveries in other domains.

EPILOGUE

Despite the difficulties in doing so, developing good theories of learning can indeed 'make the science of psychology a much more powerful instrument than it now is' (Guthrie, 1946: 3). Organisms learn and the human organism appears to be one of the most adaptive of all organisms. The human brain is capable of acquiring vastly different languages, nearly limitless quantities of information from the trivial to the profound, and highly varied skills spanning an incredible range from reading, knitting and playing the piano to solving equations, writing poems and designing experiments. It is no wonder that roboticists and artificial intelligence researchers look to the human as the best example of how to design an artificial organism that is capable of learning about the world rather than being programmed by its designers. Our study of learning is not only helping us to improve human competence, but it may also be providing the basis for the development of new, artificially created species (Menzel & D'Alusio, 2000).

ACKNOWLEDGEMENT

We would like to thank Michelle Ellefson for her comments on earlier drafts of this chapter.

REFERENCES

Allan, L. G. (1993). Human contingency judgments: rule based or associative? *Psychological Bulletin*, *114*, 435–448.

Allan, L. G. (1998). The influence of the scalar timing model on human timing research. *Behavioural Processes*, *44*, 101–117.

Arcediano, F., Matute, H., & Miller, R. R. (1997). Blocking of Pavlovian conditioning in humans. *Learning and Motivation*, *28*, 188–199.

Ashby, F. G., Queller, S., & Berretty, P. M. (1999). On the dominance of unidimensional rules in unsupervised categorization. *Perception and Psychophysics*, *61*, 1178–1199.

Barnet, R. C., Arnold, H. M., & Miller, R. R. (1991). Simultaneous conditioning demonstrated in second-order conditioning: evidence for similar associative structure in forward and simultaneous conditioning. *Learning and Motivation*, *22*, 253–268.

Bellingham, W. P., Gillette-Bellingham, K., & Kehoe, E. J. (1985). Summation and configuration in patterning schedules with the rat and rabbit. *Animal Learning and Behavior*, *13*, 152–164.

Bertenthal, B. I. (1999). Variation and selection in the development of perception and action. In G. Savelsbergh, H. van der Maas, & P. van Geert (Eds.), *Nonlinear analyses of developmental processes* (pp. 105–124). Amsterdam: Elsevier Science.

Berthier, N. E. (1996). Learning to reach: a mathematical model. *Developmental Psychology*, *32*, 811–823.

Billman, D., & Knutson, J. (1996). Unsupervised concept learning and value systematicity: a complex whole aids learning the parts. *Journal of Experimental Psychology: Learning, Memory, and Cognition*, *22*, 458–475.

Blough, D. S. (1969). Attention shifts in a maintained discrimination. *Science*, *166*, 125–126.

Blough, D. S. (1975). Steady-state generalization and a quantitative model of operant generalization and discrimination. *Journal of Experimental Psychology: Animal Behavior Processes*, *104*, 3–21.

Bolles, R. C., Collier, A. C., Bouton, M. E., & Marlin, N. A. (1978). Some tricks for ameliorating the trace-conditioning deficit. *Bulletin of the Psychonomic Society*, *11*, 403–406.

Bourne, L. E. J., Ekstrand, B. R., & Montgomery, B. (1969). Concept learning as a function of the conceptual rule and the availability of positive and negative instances. *Journal of Experimental Psychology*, *82*, 538–544.

Bouton, M. E. (1993). Context, time, and memory retrieval in the interference paradigms of Pavlovian conditioning. *Psychological Bulletin*, *114*, 80–99.

Bouton, M. E. (1994). Conditioning, remembering, and forgetting. *Journal of Experimental Psychology: Animal Behavior Processes*, *20*, 219–231.

Broadbent, H. A. (1994). Periodic behavior in a random environment. *Journal of Experimental Psychology: Animal Behavior Processes*, *20*, 156–175.

Brown, G. D. A., Preece, T., & Hulme, C. (2000). Oscillator-based memory for serial order. *Psychological Review*, *107*, 127–181.

Burgess, N., & Hitch, G. (1992). Toward a network model of the articulatory loop. *Journal of Memory and Language*, *31*, 429–460.

Burns, B., & Shepp, B. E. (1988). Dimensional interactions and the structure of psychological space: the representation of hue, saturation, and brightness. *Perception and Psychophysics*, *43*, 494–507.

Castellan, N. J., Jr. (1973). Multiple-cue probability learning with irrelevant cues. *Organizational Behavior and Human Decision Processes*, *9*, 16–29.

Castellan, N. J., Jr. (1977). Decision making with multiple probabilistic cues. In N. J. Castellan, Jr., D. B. Pisoni, & G. R. Potts (Eds.), *Cognitive theory* (Vol. 2, pp. 117–147). Hillsdale, NJ: Lawrence Erlbaum.

Chapman, G. B. (1991). Trial order affects cue interaction in contingency judgment. *Journal of Experimental Psychology: Learning, Memory, and Cognition*, *17*, 837–854.

Chapman, G. B., & Robbins, S. J. (1990). Cue interaction in human contingency judgment. *Memory and Cognition*, *18*, 537–545.

Cheng, P. W. (1997). From covariation to causation: a causal power theory. *Psychological Review*, *104*, 367–405.

Cheng, P. W., & Novick, L. R. (1992). Covariation in natural causal induction. *Psychological Review*, *99*, 365–381.

Christiansen, M. H., Chater, N., & Seidenberg, M. S. (1999). Connectionist models of human language processing: progress and prospects. *Cognitive Science*, *23*, 415–634.

Clapper, J. P., & Bower, G. H. (1991). Learning and applying category knowledge in unsupervised domains. In G. H. Bower (ed.), *The psychology of learning and motivation* (Vol. 27, pp. 65–108). San Diego, CA: Academic Press.

Clapper, J. P., & Bower, G. H. (1994). Category invention in unsupervised learning. *Journal of Experimental Psychology: Learning, Memory, and Cognition, 20,* 443–460.

Cleeremans, A., & McClelland, J. L. (1991). Learning the structure of event sequences. *Journal of Experimental Psychology: General, 120,* 235–253.

DeLosh, E. L., Busemeyer, J. R., & McDaniel, M. A. (1997). Extrapolation: the sine qua non for abstraction in function learning. *Journal of Experimental Psychology: Learning, Memory, and Cognition, 23,* 968–986.

de Sa, V. R., & Ballard, D. H. (1998). Category learning through multimodality sensing. *Neural Computation, 10,* 1097–1117.

Desmond, J. E., & Moore, J. W. (1988). Adaptive timing in neural networks: the conditioned response. *Biological Cybernetics, 58,* 405–415.

Desmond, J. E., & Moore, J. W. (1991). Altering the synchrony of stimulus trace processes: tests of a neural-network model. *Biological Cybernetics, 65,* 161–169.

Dickinson, A., & Burke, J. (1996). Within-compound associations mediate the retrospective revaluation of causality judgements. *Quarterly Journal of Experimental Psychology, 49B,* 60–80.

Ebbinghaus, H. (1885/1913). *On memory* (H. A. Ruger & C. Bossinger, Trans.). New York: Teachers College Press.

Edgell, S. E., Castellan, N. J. Jr., Roe, R. M., & Barnes, J. M. (1996). Irrelevant information in probabilistic categorization. *Journal of Experimental Psychology: Learning, Memory, and Cognition, 22,* 1463–1481.

Elman, J. L. (1990). Finding structure in time. *Cognitive Science, 14,* 179–211.

Evans, P. M., & Smith, L. B. (1988). The development of identity as a privileged relation in classification: when very similar is just not similar enough. *Cognitive Development, 3,* 265–284.

Fahlman, S. E., & Lebiere, C. (1990). The Cascade-Correlation learning architecture. In D. S. Touretzky (ed.), *Advances in neural information processing systems* (Vol. 2, pp. 524–532). San Mateo, CA: Morgan Kaufman.

Foard, C. F., & Kemler, D. G. (1984). Holistic and analytic models of processing: the multiple determinants of perceptual analysis. *Journal of Experimental Psychology: General, 113,* 94–111.

Gallistel, C. R., & Gibbon, J. (2000). Time, rate, and conditioning. *Psychological Review, 107,* 289–344.

Garner, W. R. (1970). The stimulus in information processing. *American Psychologist, 25,* 350–358.

Gibbon, J., & Balsam, P. (1981). Spreading association in time. In C. M. Locurto, H. S. Terrace, & J. Gibbon (Eds.), *Autoshaping and conditioning theory* (pp. 219–253). New York: Academic Press.

Gibson, J. J., & Gibson, E. J. (1955). Perceptual learning: differentiation or enrichment? *Psychological Review, 62,* 32–41.

Glenberg, A. M. (1979). Component-levels theory of the effects of spacing of repetitions on recall and recognition. *Memory and Cognition, 7,* 95–112.

Gluck, M. A., & Bower, G. H. (1988a). Evaluating an adaptive network model of human learning. *Journal of Memory and Language, 27,* 166–195.

Gluck, M. A., & Bower, G. H. (1988b). From conditioning to category learning. *Journal of Experimental Psychology: General, 17,* 227–247.

Gluck, M. A., Bower, G. H., & Hee, M. R. (1989). A configural-cue network model of animal and human associative learning. *Proceedings of the Eleventh Annual Conference of the Cognitive Science Society* (pp. 323–332). Hillsdale, NJ: Lawrence Erlbaum.

Goldstone, R. L. (1994). Influences of categorization on perceptual discrimination. *Journal of Experimental Psychology: General, 123,* 178–200.

Goldstone, R. L. (1995). Effects of categorization on color-perception. *Psychological Science, 6,* 298–304.

Goldstone, R. L. (1996). Perceptual learning. *Annual Review of Psychology, 49,* 585–612.

Goldstone, R. L., Steyvers, M., Spencer-Smith, J., & Kersten, A. W. (2000). Interactions between perceptual and conceptual learning. In E. Diettrich & A. B. Markman (Eds.), *Cognitive dynamics: conceptual change in humans and machines* (pp. 119–228). Mahwah, NJ: Lawrence Erlbaum.

Gottselig, J. M., Wasserman, E. A., & Young, M. E. (2001). Attentional trade-offs in pigeons learning to discriminate newly relevant visual stimulus dimensions. *Learning and Motivation, 32,* 240–253.

Grice, G. R. (1948). The relation of secondary reinforcement to delayed reward in visual discrimination learning. *Journal of Experimental Psychology, 38,* 1–16.

Grossberg, S. (1978). Behavioral contrast in short-term memory: serial binary memory models or parallel continuous memory models? *Journal of Mathematical Psychology, 17,* 199–219.

Grossberg, S. (1987). Competitive learning: from interactive activation to adaptive resonance. *Cognitive Science, 11,* 23–63.

Gullapalli, V. (1997). Reinforcement learning of complex behavior through shaping. In J. W. Donahoe & V. P. Dorsel (Eds.), *Neural-network models of cognition: biobehavioral foundations* (Vol. 121, pp. 302–314). Amsterdam: North-Holland/Elsevier Science.

Guthrie, E. R. (1946). Psychological facts and psychological theory. *Psychological Bulletin, 43,* 1–20.

Hall, G. (1991). *Perceptual and associative learning.* Oxford: Clarendon Press.

Hammond, L. J., & Paynter, W. E. (1983). Probabilistic contingency theories of animal conditioning: a critical analysis. *Learning and Motivation, 14,* 527–550.

Hearst, E. (1991). Psychology and nothing. *American Scientist, 79,* 432–443.

Hebb, D. O. (1949). *The organization of behavior.* New York: Wiley.

Hertz, J., Krogh, A., & Palmer, R. G. (1991). *Introduction to the theory of neural computation.* Redwood City, CA: Addison-Wesley.

Hinson, J. M., & Tennison, L. R. (1997). An attentional model of dimensional contrast. *Journal of Experimental Psychology: Animal Behavior Processes, 23,* 295–311.

Holland, P. C. (1983). Occasion-setting in Pavlovian feature positive discriminations. In M. L. Commons, R. J. Herrnstein, & A. R. Wagner (Eds.), *Quantitative analyses of behavior: Discrimination processes* (Vol. 4, pp. 183–206). New York: Ballinger.

Holland, P. C. (1991). Transfer of control in ambiguous discriminations. *Journal of Experimental Psychology: Animal Behavior Processes, 17,* 231–248.

Holland, P. C., Hamlin, P. A., & Parsons, J. P. (1997). Temporal specificity in serial feature-positive discrimination learning. *Journal of Experimental Psychology: Animal Behavior Processes, 23,* 95–109.

Holland, P. C., & Reeve, C. E. (1991). Acquisition and transfer of control by an ambiguous cue. *Animal Learning and Behavior, 19,* 113–124.

Hume, D. (1739/1969). *A treatise of human nature.* New York: Penguin Books.

James, W. (1890). *Association* (Vol. 1). New York: Henry Holt.

Kadirkamanathan, V., & Niranjan, M. (1993). A function estimation approach to sequential learning with neural networks. *Neural Computation, 5,* 954–975.

Kamin, L. J. (1969). Selective association and conditioning. In N. J. Mackintosh & W. K. Honig (Eds.), *Fundamental issues in associative learning* (pp. 42–64). Halifax: Dalhousie University Press.

Kaplan, P. S., & Hearst, E. (1982). Bridging temporal gaps between CS and US in autoshaping: insertion of other stimuli before, during and after CS. *Journal of Experimental Psychology: Animal Behavior Processes, 8,* 187–203.

Kaye, H., & Pearce, J. M. (1984). The strength of the orienting response during blocking. *Quarterly Journal of Experimental Psychology, 36B,* 131–144.

Kehoe, E. J., & Graham, P. (1988). Summation and configuration: Stimulus compounding and negative patterning in the rabbit. *Journal of Experimental Psychology: Animal Behavior Processes, 14,* 320–333.

Kemler, D. G. (1983). Exploring and reexploring issues of integrality, perceptual sensitivity, and dimensional salience. *Journal of Experimental Child Psychology, 36,* 365–379.

Kersten, A. W., Goldstone, R. L., & Schaffert, A. (1998). Two competing attentional mechanisms in category learning. *Journal of Experimental Psychology: Learning, Memory, and Cognition, 24,* 1437–1458.

Kirkpatrick, K., & Church, R. M. (2000). Stimulus and temporal cues in classical conditioning. *Journal of Experimental Psychology: Animal Behavior Processes, 26,* 206–219.

Kohonen, T. (1989). *Self-organization and associative memory* (3rd ed.). Berlin: Springer.

Kruschke, J. K. (1992). ALCOVE: an exemplar-based connectionist model of category learning. *Psychological Review, 99,* 22–44.

Kruschke, J. K. (1993). Human category learning: implications for backpropagation models. *Connection Science, 5,* 3–36.

Kruschke, J. K. (2001). Toward a unified model of attention in associative learning. *Journal of Mathematical Psychology, 45,* 812–863.

Kruschke, J. K., & Blair, N. J. (2000). Blocking and backward blocking involve learned inattention. *Psychonomic Bulletin and Review, 7,* 636–645.

Kruschke, J. K., & Johansen, M. K. (1999). A model of probabilistic category learning. *Journal of Experimental Psychology: Learning, Memory, and Cognition, 25,* 1083–1119.

Lehman, J. F., Laird, J. E., & Rosenbloom, P. S. (1996). A gentle introduction to Soar, an architecture for human cognition. In S. Sternberg & D. Scarborough (Eds.), *Invitation to cognitive science* (Vol. 4). Cambridge, MA: MIT Press.

Lewandowsky, S., & Li, S. (1995). Catastrophic interference in neural networks: causes, solutions and data. In F. N. Dempster & C. J. Brainerd (Eds.), *Interference and inhibition in cognition* (pp. 330–362). San Diego, CA: Academic Press.

Lipp, O. V., Siddle, D. A. T., & Vaitl, D. (1992). Latent inhibition in humans: single-cue conditioning revisited. *Journal of Experimental Psychology: Animal Behavior Processes, 18,* 115–125.

Lively, S. E., Logan, J. S., & Pisoni, D. B. (1993). Training Japanese listeners to identify English /r/ and /l/. II. The role of phonetic environment and talker variability in learning new perceptual categories. *Journal of the Acoustical Society of America, 94,* 1242–1255.

Lubow, R. E. (1973). Latent inhibition. *Journal of Comparative and Physiological Psychology, 79,* 398–407.

Mackintosh, N. J. (1973). Stimulus selection: learning to ignore stimuli that predict no change in reinforcement. In R. A. Hinde & S. J. Hinde (Eds.), *Constraints on learning* (pp. 75–96). London: Academic Press.

Mackintosh, N. J. (1974). *The psychology of animal learning.* New York: Academic Press.

Mackintosh, N. J. (1975). A theory of attention: variations in the associability of stimuli with reinforcement. *Psychological Review, 82,* 276–298.

Mackintosh, N. J., & Little, L. (1969). Intradimensional and extradimensional shift learning by pigeons. *Psychonomic Science, 14,* 5–6.

MacLeod, C. M. (1991). Half a century of research on the Stroop effect: an integrative review. *Psychological Bulletin, 109,* 163–203.

Matzel, L. D., Held, F. P., & Miller, R. R. (1988). Information and expression of simultaneous and backward associations: implications for contiguity theory. *Learning and Motivation, 19,* 317–344.

McCloskey, M., & Cohen, N. J. (1989). Catastrophic interference in connectionist networks: the sequential learning problem. In G. H. Bower (ed.), *The psychology of learning and motivation* (Vol. 24). New York: Academic Press.

Medin, D. L., Goldstone, R. L., & Gentner, D. (1993). Respects for similarity. *Psychological Review, 100,* 254–278.

Menzel, P., & D'Alusio, F. (2000). *Evolution of a new species: Robo sapiens.* Cambridge, MA: MIT Press.

Mill, J. S. (1843). *A system of logic, ratiocinative and inductive.* London: J.W. Parker.

Miller, R. R., Barnet, R. C., & Grahame, N. J. (1995). Assessment of the Rescorla-Wagner model. *Psychological Bulletin, 117*, 363–386.

Miller, R. R., & Matute, H. (1996). Biological significance in forward and backward blocking: resolution of a discrepancy between animal conditioning and human causal judgment. *Journal of Experimental Psychology: General, 125*, 370–386.

Miller, R. R., & Matzel, L. D. (1988). The comparator hypothesis: a response rule for the expression of associations. In G. H. Bower (ed.), *Psychology of learning and motivation* (Vol. 22, pp. 51–92). San Diego, CA: Academic Press.

Miller, R. R., & Schactman, T. R. (1985). Conditioning context as an associative baseline: implications for response generation and the nature of conditioned inhibition. In P. D. Balsam & A. Tomie (Eds.), *Information processing in animals: conditioned inhibition* (pp. 51–88). Hillsdale, NJ: Lawrence Erlbaum.

Moody, J., & Darken, C. (1989). Fast learning in networks of locally-tuned processing units. *Neural Computation, 1*, 281–294.

Myers, K. M., Vogel, E. H., Shin, J., & Wagner, A. R. (2001). A comparison of the Rescorla–Wagner and Pearce models in a negative patterning and a summation problem. *Animal Learning and Behavior, 29*, 36–45.

Neuringer, A., Deiss, C., & Olson, G. (2000). Reinforced variability and operant learning. *Journal of Experimental Psychology: Animal Behavior Processes, 26*, 98–111.

Neuringer, A., Kornell, N., & Olufs, M. (2001). Stability and variability in extinction. *Journal of Experimental Psychology: Animal Behavior Processes, 27*, 79–94.

Newman, J. P., Wolff, W. T., & Hearst, E. (1980). The feature-positive effect in adult human subjects. *Journal of Experimental Psychology: Human Learning and Memory, 6*, 630–650.

Nosofsky, R. M. (1986). Attention, similarity, and the identification-categorization relationship. *Journal of Experiment Psychology: General, 115*, 39–57.

Palmer, D. C., & Donahoe, J. W. (1992). Essentialism and selectionism in cognitive science and behavior analysis. *American Psychologist, 47*, 1344–1358.

Pavlov, I. P. (1927). *Conditioned reflexes* (G. V. Anrep, Trans.). London: Oxford University Press.

Pearce, J. M. (1987). A model for stimulus generalization in Pavlovian conditioning. *Psychological Review, 94*, 61–73.

Pearce, J. M. (1994). Similarity and discrimination: a selective review and a connectionist model. *Psychological Review, 101*, 587–607.

Pearce, J. M., & Hall, G. (1980). A model for Pavlovian learning: variations in the effectiveness of conditioned but not of unconditioned stimuli. *Psychological Review, 87*, 532–552.

Peron, R. M., & Allen, G. L. (1988). Attempts to train novices for beer flavor discrimination: a matter of taste. *Journal of General Psychology, 115*, 403–418.

Pothos, E. M., & Chater, N. (2002). A simplicity principle in unsupervised human categorization. *Cognitive Science, 26*, 303–343.

Ratcliff, R. (1990). Connectionist models of recognition memory: constraints imposed by learning and forgetting functions. *Psychological Review, 97*, 285–308.

Reed, P. (1992). Effect of a signalled delay between an action and outcome on human judgement of causality. *Quarterly Journal of Experimental Psychology, 44B*, 81–100.

Reed, P. (1999). Role of a stimulus filling an action-outcome delay in human judgments of causal effectiveness. *Journal of Experimental Psychology: Animal Behavior Processes, 25*, 92–102.

Rescorla, R. A. (1967). Pavlovian conditioning and its proper control procedures. *Psychological Review, 74*, 71–80.

Rescorla, R. A. (1982). Effect of a stimulus intervening between CS and US in autoshaping. *Journal of Experimental Psychology: Animal Behavior Processes, 8*, 131–141.

Rescorla, R. A. (1985). Conditioned inhibition and facilitation. In R. R. Miller & N. E. Spear (Eds.), *Information processing in animals: conditioned inhibition* (pp. 299–326). Hillsdale, NJ: Lawrence Erlbaum.

Rescorla, R. A. (1988). Pavlovian conditioning: it's not what you think it is. *American Psychologist, 43*, 151–160.

Rescorla, R. A., & Wagner, A. R. (1972). A theory of Pavlovian conditioning: variations in the effectiveness of reinforcement and nonreinforcement. In A. H. Black & W. F. Prokasy (Eds.), *Classical conditioning II: current research and theory* (pp. 64–99). New York: Appleton-Century-Crofts.

Rosenthal, O., Fusi, S., & Hochstein, S. (2001). Forming classes by stimulus frequency: behavior and theory. *Proceedings of the National Academy of Sciences of the USA, 98*, 4265–4270.

Rumelhart, D. E., & Zipser, D. (1985). Feature discovery by competitive learning. *Cognitive Science, 9*, 75–112.

Schlesinger, M., & Parisi, D. (2001). The agent-based approach: a new direction for computational models of development. *Developmental Review, 21*, 121–146.

Schyns, P. G., Goldstone, R. L., & Thilbaut, J.-P. (1998). The development of features in object concepts. *Behavioral and Brain Sciences, 21*, 1–54.

Schyns, P. G., & Murphy, G. L. (1994). The ontogeny of part representation in object concepts. In D. L. Medin (ed.), *The psychology of learning and motivation: advances in research and theory* (Vol. 31, pp. 305–349). San Diego, CA: Academic Press.

Sejnowski, T. J., & Rosenberg, C. R. (1986). NETtalk: a parallel network that learns to read aloud. Johns Hopkins University Electrical Engineering and Computer Science Technical Report JHU/EECS-86/01.

Seligman, M. E. P., Maier, S. F., & Solomon, R. L. (1971). Unpredictable and uncontrollable aversive events. In F. R. Brush (ed.), *Aversive conditioning and learning* (pp. 347–400). New York: Academic Press.

Shaklee, H., & Elek, S. (1988). Cause and covariate: development of two related concepts. *Cognitive Development, 3*, 1–13.

Shanks, D. R. (1985). Forward and backward blocking in human contingency judgement. *Quarterly Journal of Experimental Psychology, 37B*, 1–21.

Shanks, D. R. (1987). Acquisition functions in contingency judgment. *Learning and Motivation, 18*, 147–166.

Shanks, D. R. (1989). Selectional processes in causality judgment. *Memory and Cognition, 17*, 27–34.

Shanks, D. R. (1993). Associative versus contingency accounts of category learning: reply to Melz, Cheng, Holyoak and Waldmann (1993). *Journal of Experimental Psychology: Learning, Memory, and Cognition, 19*, 1411–1423.

Shanks, D. R. (1994). Human associative learning. In N. J. Mackintosh (ed.), *Animal learning and cognition* (pp. 335–374). San Diego, CA: Academic Press.

Shanks, D. R., Charles, D., Darby, R. J., & Azmi, A. (1998). Configural processes in human associative learning. *Journal of Experimental Psychology: Learning, Memory, and Cognition, 24*, 1353–1378.

Shanks, D. R., Darby, R. J., & Charles, D. (1998). Resistance to interference in human associative learning: evidence of configural processing. *Journal of Experimental Psychology: Animal Behavior Processes, 24*, 136–150.

Shanks, D. R., & Dickinson, A. (1987). Associative accounts of causality judgment. In G. H. Bower (ed.), *The psychology of learning and motivation* (Vol. 21, pp. 229–261). San Diego, CA: Academic Press.

Shepard, R. N. (1964). Attention and the metric structure of the stimulus space. *Journal of Mathematical Psychology, 1*, 54–87.

Shepard, R. N. (1987). Toward a universal law of generalization for psychological science. *Science, 237*, 1317–1323.

Shepard, R. N. (1991). Integrality versus separability of stimulus dimensions: from an early convergence of evidence to a proposed theoretical basis. In G. R. Lockhead, & J. R. Pomerantz (Eds.), *The perception of structure: essays in honor of Wendell R. Garner* (pp. 53–71). Washington, DC: American Psychological Association.

Shepard, R. N., Hovland, C. L., & Jenkins, H. M. (1961). Learning and memorization of classifications. *Psychological Monographs, 75* (13, Whole No. 517).

Siegler, R. S., & Liebert, R. M. (1974). Effects of contiguity, regularity and age on children's causal inference. *Developmental Psychology, 10*, 574–579.

Skinner, B. F. (1938). *The behavior of organisms: an experimental analysis.* Englewood Cliffs, NJ: Prentice-Hall.

Skinner, B. F. (1950). Are theories of learning necessary? *Psychological Review, 57*, 193–216.

Slamecka, N. (1985). Ebbinghaus: some associations. *Journal of Experimental Psychology: Learning, Memory, and Cognition, 11*, 414–435.

Smith, L. B. (1983). Development of classification: the use of similarity and dimensional relations. *Journal of Experimental Child Psychology, 36*, 150–178.

Staddon, J. E. R., & Higa, J. J. (1991). Temporal learning. In G. H. Bower (ed.), *Psychology of learning and motivation* (Vol. 27, pp. 265–294). San Diego, CA: Academic Press.

Sutherland, N. S., & Mackintosh, N. J. (1971). *Mechanisms of animal discrimination learning.* New York: Academic Press.

Sutton, R. S., & Barto, A. G. (1981). Toward a modern theory of adaptive networks: expectation and prediction. *Psychological Review, 88*, 135–170.

Sutton, R. S., & Barto, A. G. (1991). Time-derivative models of Pavlovian reinforcement. In M. Gabriel & J. W. Moore (Eds.), *Learning and computational neuroscience* (pp. 497–537). Cambridge, MA: MIT Press.

Swan, J. A., & Pearce, J. M. (1988). The orienting response as an index of stimulus associability in rats. *Journal of Experimental Psychology: Animal Behavior Processes, 14*, 292–301.

Tassoni, C. J. (1995). The least mean squares network with information coding: a model of cue learning. *Journal of Experimental Psychology: Learning, Memory, and Cognition, 21*, 193–204.

Thorndike, E. L. (1911). *Animal intelligence.* New York: Macmillan.

Van Hamme, L. J., & Wasserman, E. A. (1994). Cue competition in causality judgments: the role of nonpresentation of compound stimulus elements. *Learning and Motivation, 25*, 127–151.

Wagner, A. R. (1981). SOP: a model of automatic memory processing in animal behavior. In N. S. Spear & R. R. Miller (Eds.), *Information processing in animals: memory mechanisms* (pp. 5–47). Hillsdale, NJ: Lawrence Erlbaum.

Wagner, A. R., & Brandon, S. E. (1989). Evolution of a structured connectionist model of Pavlovian conditioning (AESOP). In S. B. Klein & R. R. Mowrer (Eds.), *Contemporary learning theories: Pavlovian conditioning and the status of traditional learning theory* (pp. 149–189). Hillsdale, NJ: Lawrence Erlbaum.

Wagner, A. R., & Brandon, S. E. (2001). A componential theory of Pavlovian conditioning. In R. R. Mowrer & S. B. Klein (Eds.), *Handbook of contemporary learning theories* (pp. 23–64). Mahwah, NJ: Lawrence Erlbaum.

Wagner, A. R., Logan, F. A., Haberlandt, K., & Price, T. (1968). Stimulus selection in animal discrimination learning. *Journal of Experimental Psychology, 76*, 177–186.

Wagner, A. R., & Rescorla, R. A. (1972). Inhibition in Pavlovian conditioning: application of a theory. In R. A. Boakes, & M. S. Halliday (Eds.), *Inhibition and learning* (pp. 301–336). London: Academic Press.

Waldmann, M. R., & Holyoak, K. J. (1992). Predictive and diagnostic learning within causal models: asymmetries in cue competition. *Journal of Experimental Psychology: General, 121*, 222–236.

Wasserman, E. A. (1981). Comparative psychology returns: a review of Hulse, Fowler, and Honig's *Cognitive processes in animal behavior. Journal of the Experimental Analysis of Behavior, 35*, 243–257.

Wasserman, E. A. (1990a). Attribution of causality to common and distinctive elements of compound stimuli. *Psychological Science, 1*, 298–302.

Wasserman, E. A. (1990b). Detecting response-outcome relations: toward an understanding of the causal structure of the environment. In G. H. Bower (ed.), *The psychology of learning and motivation* (Vol. 26, pp. 27–82). San Diego, CA: Academic Press.

Wasserman, E. A., & Berglan, L. R. (1998). Backward blocking and recovery from overshadowing in human causal judgment: the role of within-compound associations. *Quarterly Journal of Experimental Psychology, 51B*, 121–138.

Wasserman, E. A., & Miller, R. R. (1997). What's elementary about associative learning? *Annual Review of Psychology, 48*, 573–607.

Wasserman, E. A., & Neunaber, D. J. (1986). College students' responding to and rating of contingency relations: the role of temporal contiguity. *Journal of the Experimental Analysis of Behavior, 46*, 15–35.

Williams, D. A., & Braker, D. S. (1999). Influence of past experience on the coding of compound stimuli. *Journal of Experimental Psychology: Animal Behavior Processes, 25*, 461–474.

Williams, D. A., & LoLordo, V. M. (1995). Time cues block the CS, but the CS does not block time cues. *Quarterly Journal of Experimental Psychology, 48B*, 97–116.

Williams, D. A., Sagness, K. E., & McPhee, J. E. (1994). Configural and elemental strategies in predictive learning.

Journal of Experimental Psychology: Learning, Memory, and Cognition, 20, 694–709.

Wills, A. J., & McLaren, I. P. L. (1998). Perceptual learning and free classification. *Quarterly Journal of Experimental Psychology, 51B*, 235–270.

Wilson, P. N., Boumphrey, P., & Pearce, J. M. (1992). Restoration of the orienting response to a light by a change in its predictive accuracy. *Quarterly Journal of Experimental Psychology, 44B*, 17–36.

Woollacott, M., & Sveistrup, H. (1994). The development of sensorimotor integration underlying posture control in infants during the transition to independent stance. In S. P. Swinnen, J. Massion, & H. Heuer (Eds.), *Interlimb coordination: neural, dynamical, and cognitive constraints* (pp. 371–389). San Diego, CA: Academic Press.

Young, M. E. (1995). On the origin of personal causal knowledge. *Psychonomic Bulletin and Review, 2*, 83–104.

Young, M. E., Johnson, J. L., & Wasserman, E. A. (2000). Serial causation: occasion setting in a causal induction task. *Memory and Cognition, 28*, 1213–1230.

Young, M. E., Wasserman, E. A., Johnson, J. L., & Jones, F. L. (2000). Positive and negative patterning in human causal learning. *Quarterly Journal of Experimental Psychology, 53B*, 121–138.

Zacks, J., & Tversky, B. (2001). Event structure in perception and cognition. *Psychological Bulletin, 127*, 3–21.

7

Category Learning

JOHN K. KRUSCHKE

What have we here? a man or a fish? dead
or alive? A fish: he smells like a fish; a very
ancient and fish-like smell; a kind of not of
the newest Poor-John. A strange fish!

Shakespeare, *The Tempest*, Act II, Scene
II, line 22; spoken by Trinculo

CATEGORIZATION IS CENTRAL TO COGNITION

Beachcombers categorize flotsam as man or fish.
Players of 20 questions categorize things as animal,
vegetable or mineral. Guards categorize approach-
ers as friend or foe. Bystanders categorize flying
objects: 'Look, up in the sky! It's a bird; it's a plane!
No, it's Superman!' Categorization permeates cognition in myriad protean variations. Our categorization
of an object we encounter determines what we do
with it. If it is an old dead fish, we walk away in dis-
gust, but if it is just an unkempt rascally scoundrel,
we ... Well, at least in *some* cases our categorization
of an object affects our reaction to it.

The overriding purpose of categorization is inference of unseen attributes, especially for novel stimuli. Thus, we classify a handwritten squiggle as the
letter 'A' because we then infer its sound and meaning in the context of other letters. The sound and
meaning are not visible in the squiggle itself. We
classify animals as tigers or zebras in order to infer
unseen attributes such as being threatening or
innocuous. The potential threat is not explicit in the
visible features of the animal. Classification takes
us from the information given in the stimulus to previously learned, associated information. The classification is itself an inference of an unseen attribute.

As anyone knows who has tried to read messy
handwriting, the classification of squiggles into letter
categories is often not at all obvious. Occasionally
also we encounter unusual animals, or flying objects,
or flotsam, that are difficult to identify. In principle,
any classification is a non-trivial inference of an
unseen attribute.

Induction of invisible features is called categorization when it applies to novel stimuli that are not
exact replicas of the stimuli experienced during
learning. That is, categorization depends on generalizing from particular learned instances to novel
situations. Categorization is sometimes defined
merely as dividing a set of items into subsets.
Typically, however, such a division is only of interest to the extent that novel items are inferred to be
in one subset or another. If learned knowledge consisted merely of isolated facts with no generalization, then the knowledge would be useless except
for the unlikely exact recurrence of the learned situation. For example, learning that a 4 cm tall,
round-capped, beige-colored mushroom is edible
would not generalize to 3 cm tall mushrooms. This
failure to generalize could result in a starved categorizer. On the other hand, if generalization is too
liberal, then complementary problems can arise. For
example, inferring that a flat-capped, 4 cm tall,
beige mushroom is edible might result in a poisoned
categorizer. Thus, generalization from learned cases
must be appropriately tuned, not too narrow and not
too broad.

Generalization is not the only goal when learning
categories. Just as important is retaining previously
learned knowledge while quickly acquiring new
knowledge. For example, after having learned about
edible mushrooms, it could prove catastrophic if
learning about poisonous mushrooms required

TABLE 7.1 *Examples of categorization models that instantiate various options for representation and matching processes*

Representation	Matching process	
	Graded Similarity	Strict Match/Mismatch
Content, piecemeal	(A) Context model (Medin & Schaffer, 1978); Generalized context model (Nosofsky, 1986); ALCOVE/RASHNL (Kruschke, 1992; Kruschke & Johansen, 1999); rational model (Anderson, 1991).	(B) Exemplar subsystem of Smith and Minda (2000); Sparse Distributed Memory (Kanerva, 1988); discrete dim. RULEX (Nosofsky, Palmeri, & McKinley, 1994); disjunctive featural rules (Bourne, 1970; Levine, 1975).
Content, global	(C) Modal features (Reed, 1972); central tendency (Smith & Minda, 2000); component-cue network (Gluck & Bower, 1988); ADIT/EXIT (Kruschke, 1996a, 2001a).	(D) Conjunctive featural rules (Bourne, 1970; Levine, 1975).
Boundary, piecemeal	(E) ATRIUM (Erickson & Kruschke, 1998, 2002).	(F) Continuous dim. RULEX (Nosofsky & Palmeri, 1998); COVIS (Ashby et al., 1998).
Boundary, global	(G) PRAS (Vandierendonck, 1995).	(H) Quadratic bound (Ashby, Waldron, Lee, & Berkman, 2001).

dozens of exposures. It could also be disastrous if the learning about poisonous mushrooms erased still-valid knowledge about edible mushrooms (French, 1999; Kruschke, 1993; McCloskey & Cohen, 1989; Mirman & Spivey, 2001; Ratcliff, 1990). Yet edible and poisonous mushrooms share many prominent features, so learning that they should be treated dramatically differently, while also generalizing appropriately to other mushrooms, could be very challenging.

Because classification, i.e. naming the category label of an object, is a paramount example of inference of an unseen attribute, many laboratory experiments in categorization examine people's ability to learn novel classification labels. In a typical experiment, a participant is shown a stimulus and asked to guess which of several category labels is correct. After his or her guess, the correct label is displayed, and the participant studies the stimulus and correct label for a few seconds before moving on to the next case. After many cases (typically but not always with repetition of individual cases), the participant learns the correct category labels of the stimuli. The experiment might then test the learner's generalization with novel stimuli, or his or her ability to learn new categorizations.

For the cognitive scientist, the key questions then are the following: What has the participant learned and how? What sort of representation best describes the learner's knowledge? What sort of processes best describe the learning and classifying activities? Answers to these questions can be constrained by data from the learned items, from generalization to novel items, from learning of new categories, from inference of features from category labels (e.g. Anderson, Ross, & Chin-Parker, 2002; Anderson & Fincham, 1996; Thomas, 1998; Yamauchi & Markman, 2000a, 2000b) and from other types of information.

Category learning is critically important because it underlies essentially all cognitive activities, yet it is very difficult because learned categories must generalize appropriately, learning must occur quickly, and new learning must not overwrite previous knowledge. Moreover, categorization occurs on different dimensions and at different levels of abstraction simultaneously. For example, a cardinal (i.e. the bird) can evoke the color category red or the part category feather or the object category animal, and so on. Within these dimensions there are levels of abstraction, such as scarlet, red or warm within the 'color' dimension, or cardinal, bird or animal within the 'object' dimension.

VARIETIES OF THEORIES OF CATEGORIZATION

Theories of categorization vary on three aspects. Table 7.1 shows theories that instantiate each of the combinations of the three dimensions. First, the theory specifies what is explicitly represented about the category. Some theories assert that the *contents* within each category are explicitly specified whereas other theories assert that the *boundaries* between categories are explicitly specified. For example, the category 'skyscraper' might be described by a boundary that separates it from 'low-rise', as follows: if the ratio of height to width is greater than 1.62 (the golden ratio), then the building is a skyscraper. The specific ratio of 1.62 determines the boundary in height/width space that separates skyscrapers from low-rises. Alternatively, the skyscraper and low-rise categories might be specified by their contents, e.g. if a building is more similar to Philip Johnson's AT&T Headquarters (now the Sony Building) than to Frank Lloyd Wright's Taliesin, then it is a skyscraper.[1]

Second, for either type of representation, the contents or boundary can be specified by a *global summary* or by *piecemeal components*. For example, the two descriptions of skyscrapers given above were global summaries, insofar as a single condition defined the boundary or the content of each category. By contrast, a piecemeal definition of a boundary might be the following: a building is a skyscraper if it is greater than 20 stories tall or if it is taller than 7 stories and less than 100 feet wide. A piecemeal definition of content might be the following: a building is a skyscraper if it is more like the Sears Tower *or* the John Hancock Building than the O'Hare Airport Terminal *or* Navy Pier.

Third, whatever type of representation is used for the categories, it must be compared with the incoming item that is to be categorized. This comparison process can yield a *strict match versus mismatch*, or a degree of *graded similarity*. For example, the height/width ratio to define skyscraper is strict, but the content definition ('it's like the Sears Tower') uses graded similarity.

In the remainder of this chapter, a few combinations of representation and matching process will be described in detail. Notice that the matching processes are distinct from *learning* processes. Learning is the process that actually generates the representations. Learning will also be discussed en route.

The three dimensions of categorization shown in Table 7.1 were described intuitively in the previous paragraphs. Upon further reflection, however, the dimensions are subtle and demand more careful clarification. Perhaps the clearest distinction is between content and boundary. A representation of content specifies what is in the category, but the extent of the category might be vague. A representation of boundary specifies exactly what the limit of the category is, and any item within that limit is a full member of the category. The only situation in which the distinction between content and boundary breaks down is when the stimulus attributes are nominal features. In this situation a specification of the category's features is tantamount to a specification of the boundary around the category, because the features themselves are assumed to be sharply bounded categories. For example, if we define a bachelor as a human who is male, unmarried and eligible, then we have specified a description of the content of the category. But because the attribute 'male' lies on a dichotomous dimension that has a sharp, genetically specified boundary between it and 'female', a specification of content is informationally equivalent to a specification of boundary.[2] Only when the stimulus dimensions vary continuously, rather than discretely, is there a difference between content and boundary representations.

The distinction between global and piecemeal specification is intuitively acceptable but needs rigorous definition for maximal usefulness. For example, a piecemeal specification of the category 'dog' could be this: a dog is something like Lassie or Rin-tin-tin or Benjie or Pongo. A global specification of dog might be this: a dog is an animal with four legs and a tail and fur and toenails (not claws or hooves) and a height between 0.5 and 1.0 meters and the ability to bark. (This is not an accurate specification of 'dog', but it illustrates the idea.) From these examples it appears that global specifications use a conjunction of properties, whereas piecemeal specifications use a disjunction of properties. The problem with this distinction is that conjunctions and disjunctions can be exchanged via negation: 'A or B' is equivalent to 'Not (Not A and Not B)'. For example, to say that 'a dog is like Lassie or like Benjie' is logically equivalent to saying that 'a dog is not both unlike Lassie and unlike Benjie'. Despite this subtlety in the distinction between global and piecemeal specifications, for the purposes of this chapter I shall define a piecemeal representation as one that involves disjunctions in stimulus characteristics that are natural or primitive in the theory. The disjunctions could be formally realized as logical or as other mathematical expressions.

Finally, there is the distinction between strict and graded matching of stimulus to category specification. All theories of categorization must account for the fact that human (and other species') categorization is probabilistic or graded. For example, a letter drawn as '/-\' could be interpreted as an 'H' or as an 'A', as in 'T/-\E C/-\T'. As another example of gradedness in category membership, a Labrador retriever is usually rated as a more typical dog than a Pekinese. Theories that use a graded matching process naturally account for gradedness in categorization. But theories that use strict matching cannot explain gradedness unless other mechanisms are included. Some strict-matching theories assume that the encoding of the stimulus is probabilistic (i.e. imperfect or distorted) or the specification of the category conditions is probabilistic or the generation of the categorical response is probabilistic. Some graded-matching theories also incorporate probabilistic mechanisms.

In summary, any theory of category learning must specify what information from the world is actually retained in the mind and the format in which that information is structured, how that information is used, and how that information is learned. Hopefully the theory also motivates why that particular learning procedure is useful. In this chapter these issues are addressed in turn, for a few different theories from Table 7.1. Each type of theory is initially described informally, to convey the basic motivating principles of the theory. Each theory is also described with formal, mathematical terms. By expressing a theory mathematically, the theory gains quantitative precision rather than merely vague verbal description. Mathematical formulation allows publicly derivable predictions rather than theorist-dependent intuitively derived predictions. Mathematical derivations permit stronger support when predictions are confirmed in quantitative detail. Formal models also engender greater explanatory power when the formal mechanisms in the model have clear psychological interpretation. Specification in formal terms sometimes permits clearer applicability because of precise specification of relevant factors.

EXEMPLAR THEORIES

One sure way to learn a category is merely to memorize its instances. For example, a learner's knowledge of the category bird might consist of knowing that the particular cases named Tweety, Woody and Polly are exemplars of birds. There is no derived representation of a prototypical bird, nor is there any abstracted set of necessary and sufficient features that define what a bird is. As new cases of birds are experienced, these cases are also stored in memory. Notice, however, that just because these exemplars of birds are in memory, the learner need not be able to distinctly recall every bird ever encountered. Retrieving a specific memory might be quite different than using it for categorization.

So how are these stored exemplars used to categorize novel items? A new stimulus is classified according to how similar it is to all the known instances of the various candidate categories. (Some exemplar models use only a subset of the stored exemplars, e.g. Sieck & Yates, 2001.) For example, a newly encountered animal is classified as a bird if it is more similar to known exemplars of birds than it is to known exemplars of squirrels or bats, etc. The notion of similarity, therefore, plays a critical role in exemplar theories.

This kind of exemplar theory falls in the top left cell (A) of Table 7.1. The category is specified by its contents, in this case by its exemplars. The specification of contents is not a global summary but is instead a collection of piecemeal information. The process for matching a stimulus to the category representation relies on graded similarity to exemplars, not on strict match or mismatch with exemplars.

Selective attention

Not all features are equally relevant for all category distinctions. For example, in deciding whether an animal is a duck or a rabbit (a potential confusion highlighted by Wittgenstein, 1953), it might be important to pay attention to whether it can fly, but to determine whether the animal is a crow or a bat, it might be important to pay attention to whether it has feathers (cf. Gelman & Markman, 1986). Selective attention plays an important role not only in exemplar theory but in many theories of categorization. Selective attention will be further discussed in a subsequent section.

Learning for error reduction

In principle, exemplar encoding can accurately learn any possible category structure, no matter how complicated, because the exemplars in memory directly correspond with the instances in the world. This potential computational power of exemplar models is one rationale for their use. But realizing this potential can be difficult, because exemplar encoding can retard learning if highly similar instances belong to different categories. One way around this problem is to associate exemplars with categories only to the extent that doing so will reduce errors in categorization. Analogously, various features or stimulus dimensions can be attended to only to the extent that doing so will reduce error. Thus, error reduction is one important rationale for theories of learning.

The formal model described next expresses the notion of error reduction in precise mathematical notation. Variants of this exemplar model have been shown to fit a wide range of phenomena in category learning and generalization (e.g. Choi, McDaniel, & Busemeyer, 1993; Estes, 1994; Kruschke & Johansen, 1999; Lamberts, 1998; Nosofsky & Kruschke, 1992; Nosofsky, Gluck, Palmeri, McKinley, & Glauthier, 1994; Nosofsky & Palmeri, 1997; Palmeri, 1999; Pearce, 1994), but it is not without challenges (e.g. Cohen, Nosofsky, & Zaki, 2001, and others cited later). Exemplar models have also been used to characterize individual differences in learning and attention (e.g. Treat, McFall, Viken, & Kruschke, 2001). Some exemplar models have been extended to involve dynamic processes that yield predictions of response latencies (e.g. Cohen & Nosofsky, 2000; Lamberts, 2000b).

Formal models of exemplar theory

A perceived stimulus can be formally represented by its values on various psychological dimensions. For example, among birds, an eagle might be represented by a large numerical value on the dimension of perceived size, and by another large numerical value on the dimension of ferocity, along with other values on other dimensions. The psychological value on the dth dimension is denoted Ψ_d^{stim}. These psychological scale values can be determined by methods of multidimensional scaling (e.g. Kruskal & Wish, 1978; Shepard, 1962).

In a prominent exemplar-based model (Kruschke, 1992; Kruschke & Johansen, 1999; Medin & Schaffer, 1978; Nosofsky, 1986), the mth exemplar in memory is formally represented by its psychological values on the various dimensions; the value on the dth dimension is denoted Ψ^{ex}_{md}. The similarity of the stimulus to a memory exemplar corresponds to their proximity in psychological space. The usual measure of distance between the stimulus, s, and the mth memory exemplar is given by $\text{dist}(s, m) = \sum_i \alpha_i |\Psi^{stim}_i - \Psi^{ex}_{mi}|$, where the sum is taken over the dimensions indexed by i, and $\alpha_i \geq 0$ is the attention allocated to the ith dimension. (This assumes, of course, that the psychological dimensions can be selectively attended to.) When attention on a dimension is large, then differences on that dimension have a large impact on the distance, but when attention on a dimension is zero, then differences on that dimension have no impact on distance. The distance is converted to similarity by an exponentially decaying function: $\text{sim}(s, m) = \exp(-\text{dist}(s, m))$. Therefore, when the stimulus exactly matches the memory exemplar so that the distance between them is zero, then the similarity is 1.0, and as the distance between the stimulus and the memory exemplar increases, the similarity drops off toward zero. Shepard (1987) provided a review of the exponential function as a model of human (and other animal) similarity gradients. Lee and Navarro (2002) describe a variation of the model in which the stimulus dimensions are nominally scaled instead of interval scaled.

The exemplars then influence the categorization of the stimulus by 'voting'. The strength of an exemplar's vote is its similarity to the stimulus, such that exemplars that are highly similar to the stimulus cast a strong vote, while exemplars that are remote from the stimulus cast only a weak vote. Each exemplar votes for candidate categories according to associative strengths from the exemplars to the categories. The associative strength from exemplar m to category k is denoted w_{km}, and the total 'voting' for category k is $v_k = \sum_m w_{kn} \, \text{sim}(s, m)$. The overall probability of classifying the stimulus into category k is the total vote for category k *relative* to the total votes cast overall. Formally, the probability of classifying stimulus s into category k is given by $p_k = v_k / \sum_c v_c$. Often this response rule is generalized by including a parameter to adjust the decisiveness of the choice probability; two such forms are $p_k = v_k^y / \sum_c v_c^y$ and $p_k = \exp(\gamma v_k) / \sum_c \exp(\gamma v_c)$, whereby high values of γ map small differences in voting to large differences in choice probability. Wills, Reimers, Stewart, Suret, and McLaren (2000) discuss problems with these response rules and propose an alternative.

Participants in laboratory learning experiments get corrective feedback on each learning trial. The same procedure applies to learning in the model: the model 'sees' the stimulus, votes for what it deems to be the best classification, and then is presented with the correct categorization. The model adjusts its associative weights and attention strengths to reduce the error between its vote and the correct answer. Error is defined as $E = \sum_k (t_k - v_k)^2$, where t_k is the 'teacher' value: $t_k = 1$ if k is the correct category, and $t_k = 0$ otherwise. There are many possible methods by which the associative weights and attention strengths could be adjusted to reduce this error, but one sensible method is *gradient descent* on error. According to this procedure, the changes that make the error decrease most rapidly are computed according to the derivative of the error with respect to the associative weights and attention strengths. The resulting formula for weight changes is $\Delta w_{km} = \lambda_w (t_k - v_k) \, \text{sim}(s, m)$, where λ_w is a constant of proportionality called the learning rate. This formula states that the associative weight between exemplar m and category k increases to the extent that the exemplar is similar to the current input and the category teacher is underpredicted. Notice that after the weight changes according to this formula, the predicted category will be closer to the correct category, i.e. the error will have been reduced. The analogous formula for attentional changes is a little more complicated, but it essentially combines information from all the exemplars to decide whether attention on a dimension should be increased or decreased (see Kruschke, 1992; Kruschke & Johansen, 1999).

PROTOTYPE THEORIES

It might seem inefficient or wasteful to remember every instance of a category. Perhaps some sort of summary could be abstracted during learning, and then the individual cases could be safely jettisoned. The summary, also called a prototype, should be representative of the various instances of the category. There are several possible forms of this prototype. One option is for the prototype to be the *central tendency*, or *average*, of all the known cases of the category. For example, the mental representation of dog might be a medium-sized mutt that blends the features of all the experienced instances of dog. The dog prototype need not necessarily correspond to any actually experienced individual dog.

Another option for the prototype could be an *idealized caricature* or extreme case that is maximally distinctive from other categories. For example, Lynch, Coley, and Medin (2000) reported that expert foresters thought of trees in terms of ideal extreme height, rather than in terms of typical medium height. Palmeri and Nosofsky (2001) report a similar finding with random dot patterns.

Alternatively, a prototype could be the most frequent, i.e. modal, *instance*; or a prototype might consist of a combination of the most frequent or modal *features* of the instances.

Whatever the specific nature of the prototypes, a new stimulus is classified according to how similar it is to the prototypes of the various candidate categories. A newly encountered animal is classified as a dog to the extent that it is more similar to the dog prototype than to other category prototypes.

This type of theory appears in the second row and left column of Table 7.1, cell C. The theory specifies a single global summary for the content of each category. The process of matching a stimulus to the category representation uses graded similarity, not strict match or mismatch.

One rationale for this approach to categorization is that it is efficient: an entire set of members in a category is represented by just the small amount of information in the prototype. The economy of representation does not eliminate the need for learning: as new instances appear, a prototype must be updated to reflect current information.

In several studies that compare prototype and exemplar models, it has been found that prototype models do not fit data better than exemplar models (e.g. Ashby & Maddox, 1993; Busemeyer, Dewey, & Medin, 1984; Busemeyer & Myung, 1988; Nosofsky, 1992; Reed, 1972). Other studies have found evidence that is difficult for basic exemplar models to address, but which can (or might) be better addressed by prototype models (e.g. Blair & Homa, 2001; Homa, Sterling, & Trepel, 1981; Minda & Smith, 2001; Smith & Minda, 1998). One conclusion is that human behavior is best described as using a combination of exemplar and prototype representations (e.g. Storms, DeBoeck, & Ruts, 2001), and also rule representations, which will be described later. The challenge for cognitive scientists is carefully discerning the conditions under which each type of representation is used and how they interact.

Formal models of prototype theory

Because a prototype has a value on every dimension of the stimulus, it can be formally represented much like an exemplar, although a prototype need not correspond with any actually experienced instance. The prototype for category k has psychological value on dimension i denoted by Ψ_{ki}^{proto}. For the particular prototype model defined here, this value represents the central tendency of the category instances on that dimension. Other prototype models might instead use the ideal value or modal value on each dimension. The model classifies a stimulus as category k in a manner directly analogous to the exemplar model, such that the probability of classifying stimulus s into category k is given by: $p_k = \mathrm{sim}(s, k)/\sum_m \mathrm{sim}(s, m)$. The sum in the denominator is over all category prototypes, instead of over all exemplars. In principle, the probability choice formula for prototype models could include a decisiveness parameter like the exemplar model, but in the prototype model such a decisiveness parameter trades off with the specificity parameter in the similarity computation so that it has no independent influence.

As new instances are experienced during learning, the prototypes are adjusted to reflect the instances. For the first experienced instance of a category, the prototype is created and set to match that instance. For subsequently experienced instances of the category, the prototype changes from its current values slightly toward the new case. By gradually moving toward the instances of the category as they are experienced, the prototype gradually progresses toward the central tendency of those instances.

The learning of central tendencies can be formalized in the following algorithm, closely related to so-called 'competitive learning' or 'clustering' methods. The idea is that a prototype should be adjusted so that it is as similar as possible to as many instances as possible; in this way the prototype is maximally representative of the stimuli in its category. Define the total similarity of the prototypes to the instances as $S = \sum_{k,s} \mathrm{sim}(s, k)$, where $\mathrm{sim}(s, k) = (-\exp(\sum_i \alpha_i[\Psi_i^{stim} - \Psi_{ki}^{proto}]^2))$. The question then is how best to adjust Ψ_{ki}^{proto} so that the total similarity increases. One way to do this is gradient ascent: the prototype values are adjusted to increase the total similarity as quickly as possible. The resulting formula, determined as the derivative of the total similarity with respect to the coordinates, yields $\Delta\Psi_{ki}^{proto} = \lambda\, \mathrm{sim}(s, k)\alpha_i(\Psi_i^{stim} - \Psi_{ki}^{proto})$. This formula causes each prototype's values to move toward the currently experienced stimulus, but only to the extent that the prototype is already similar to the stimulus, and only to the extent that the dimension is being attended to. In this way, prototypes that do not represent the stimulus very well are not much influenced by the stimulus.

An intermediate scheme between prototype representation and exemplar representation is the use of multiple prototypes per category, which can be useful to capture multimodal distributions (e.g. Rosseel, 2002). Alternative learning schemes have been used, such as methods derived from Bayesian statistics (Anderson, 1991). As the number of prototypes per category increases, there can eventually be one prototype per exemplar, and such models become equivalent to exemplar models (Nosofsky, 1991). In exemplar models, however, the coordinates of the exemplars typically do not get adjusted from one trial to the next.

RULE THEORIES

Other ways of representing categories are with *rules*. There are a variety of so-called rule-based models in the literature, so that it can be difficult to define exactly what a rule-based model is (e.g. Hahn & Chater, 1998; Smith & Sloman, 1994). One candidate rule that defines membership in the category of rule-based models is this: a rule-based model uses either a strict match/mismatch process or a boundary representation, i.e. a rule-based model does not use graded matching to content. In Table 7.1 this corresponds to cells in the right column or the bottom two rows (i.e. all cells except A and C). The usage of the term 'rule' is merely conventional, however. What really defines the nature of a categorization model is the type of representation and matching process (and learning process) it uses, as analyzed in Table 7.1.

An example of a rule-based model is one that uses *featural rules* that specify strict necessary and sufficient conditions that define category membership. For example, something is a member of the category 'bachelor' if it is human, male, unmarried and eligible. This type of featural rule theory falls in the second row and right column of Table 7.1, cell D. In this case, the category is specified by a global summary of its content, and the summary must be perfectly matched or else the stimulus is not in the category.

One subtlety of features in a rule is that each feature is itself a category. For example, for something to be a bachelor it must have the features of being human, male, unmarried and eligible. Each of these features is itself a category that must be defined in terms of content or boundary, globally or piecemeal, etc. This echoes a theme mentioned above, that categories occur at many levels of analysis simultaneously.

It is possible for strict rules of content to be specified piecemeal. This type of theory falls in the first row and right column of Table 7.1, cell B. For example, a pitch in baseball is a strike if it is swung at by the batter and missed, *or* it is in the strike zone but not hit.

Another example of such a piecemeal rule theory is a strictly matching exemplar model. In this type of theory, a category is represented by its instances, but a stimulus is classified as a member of the category if and only if it exactly matches one of the instances. The exemplar subsystem of Smith and Minda (2000) is one such example of this kind of theory. The Sparse Distributed Memory (SDM) model developed by Kanerva (1988) uses an internal representation that consists essentially of randomly distributed exemplars that have a strict threshold for matching: a stimulus 'matches' the exemplar if and only if it lies within a specific distance from the exemplar.

Instead of specifying content, rule theories can instead specify boundaries that separate categories. Rules for category definition are typically a single threshold on a single dimension, e.g. a building is a skyscraper if it is more than ten stories tall. In some rule-based theories, rules can be more complicated boundaries, e.g. a building is a skyscraper if its height divided by its width is greater than 1.62.

Rule models that use strict match/mismatch processes predict that human performance should be perfect, i.e. classification should be strictly all or nothing depending on whether the conditions (content or boundary) are perfectly matched or not. Yet human classification is imperfect. Rule models that use a strict match/mismatch process must accommodate the 'fuzziness' of human classification performance through mechanisms such as perceptual randomness or decisional randomness. Thus, the rule is strict, but the stimuli are imperfectly perceived or the classification dictated by the rule is imperfectly produced.

Some boundary-based (rule) models do not assume strict match/mismatch processes, and instead used graded similarity to the boundary. One example of this is the PRAS model of Vandierendonck (1995), which combines rectangular decision boundaries with exponentially decaying similarity gradients.

Rules are computationally attractive as category representations because they can be uniformly applied to all stimuli, regardless of the instances actually experienced. For example, the rule for 'bachelor' can be applied with equal facility to all stimuli, regardless of the specific bachelors we have previously encountered. This uniformity of applicability might not mimic human categorization (Allen & Brooks, 1991). Rules are also computationally attractive because they can describe feature combinations that are not tied to the specific featural realizations. For example, a rule could be that an item is a member of a category if the item has either one of two features but not both. This 'exclusive-or' rule can be applied to *any* two features, and is not tied to particular features such as color or shape. Shanks and Darby (1998) showed that people can indeed learn such abstract rules that are not tied to specific features. The hypothesis-testing model of Levine (1975) is one model that uses structural similarities of abstract rules to predict ease of shifting from one rule to another during learning.

Many natural categories are very difficult to specify in terms of content rules, however (e.g. Rosch & Mervis, 1975). For example, the category 'game' appears to have no necessary and sufficient features (Wittgenstein, 1953). Nevertheless, people are prone to look for features that define category distinctions, and people tend to believe that such defining features exist even if in fact they do not (Ashby, Queller, & Berretty, 1999; Brooks, 1978). The propensity to focus on single dimensions might depend on the context and content domain; for example, in social conditions people might be more prone to sum evidence across dimensions (Wattenmaker, 1995).

Formal models of rule theory

In the 1960s and 1970s, popular rule models included 'hypothesis testing' or 'concept learning' models (for a review, see Levine, 1975). The emphasis at the time was on how people learn logical combinations of features that define a category. The models therefore emphasized strict matching to content (features), and these models fall into the top two rows of the right column of Table 7.1, cells B and D. In these sorts of models, individual features are tested, one at a time, for the ability to account for the correct classifications of the stimuli. For example, the model might test the rule, 'If it's red it's in category K'. As long as the rule works, it is retained, but when an error is encountered, another rule is tested. As simple rules are excluded, more complicated rules are tried. A recent incarnation of this type of model also is able to learn exceptions to rules, by testing additional features of instances that violate an otherwise successful rule (Nosofsky, Palmeri, & McKinley, 1994). This model is also able to account for differences in behavior across people, because there can be different sets of rules and exceptions that equally well account for the classifications of the stimuli. A different rule-based model is presented by Miller and Laird (1996), for which typicality and similarity effects are addressed by probing discrete prediction rules in a series of steps.

When stimuli vary on continuous dimensions instead of discrete features, rule models can specify the boundary that separates the categories (cell H of Table 7.1). In one class of models, the decision boundary is assumed to be have a shape that can be described by a quadratic function, because a quadratic describes the optimal boundary between two multivariate normal distributions, and natural categories are sometimes assumed to be distributed normally (e.g. Ashby, 1992). In this approach, there are three basic postulates. First, the stimulus is represented as a point in multidimensional space, but the exact location of this point is variable because of perceptual noise. Second, a stimulus is classified according to which side of a quadratic decision boundary it falls on. Third, the decision boundary is also subject to variability because of noise in the decision process. Thus, although the classification rule is strict and there is no explicit role in the model for similarity gradients, the model as a whole produces a gradation of classification performance across the boundary because of noise in perception and decision. There are many variations on this scheme of models, involving different shapes of boundaries,

deterministic versus probabilistic decision rules, etc. (Ashby & Alfonso-Reese, 1995; Ashby & Maddox, 1993).

It is possible to combine multiple boundaries to specify a category distinction (cell F of Table 7.1). For example, a model by Ashby, Alfonso-Reese, Turken, and Waldron (1998) combines linear decision boundaries that involve single dimensions, corresponding to verbalizable rules, with linear decision boundaries that combine two or more dimensions, corresponding to implicitly learned rules. These decision boundaries are then weighted to generate an overall linear decision boundary. Thus, while several component boundaries are involved, the overall system behaves as if it had a single globally defined boundary.

HYBRID REPRESENTATION THEORIES

Is human category learning completely described by any one of the types of representation in Table 7.1? It is not likely. Recent theories combine different representations to account for complex patterns in human behavior. A variety of work has shown that neither rule-based nor prototype models can fully account for human categorization (e.g. Ashby & Waldron, 1999; Kalish & Kruschke, 1997). In particular, exemplar representation must be supplemented with rules to account for human learning and generalization (e.g., Erickson & Kruschke, 2002; Shanks & St John, 1994; Smith, Patalano, & Jonides, 1998). Some evidence apparently for multiple systems can, it turns out, be explained by single-representation systems (e.g. Lamberts, 2001; Nosofsky & Johansen, 2000; Nosofsky & Kruschke, 2002), but follow-up work continues to challenge the single-representation approach (e.g. Ashby & Ell, 2002; Erickson & Kruschke, 2002).

When multiple representations are combined into a single model, a significant challenge to the theorist is determining how the two representations interact or compete during learning and categorization. One approach to his problem is presented in a model by Erickson and Kruschke (1998, 2002; Kruschke & Erickson, 1994), which combines exemplars with single-dimension rules. The exemplar representation falls in the top left cell (A) of Table 7.1, and the rule representation falls within the third row and left column (cell E). What is important about this model is how it decides when to apply which representation. The model does this with a gating mechanism that learns which representation to pay attention to, depending on the exemplar. Thus, the attentional distribution (attend more to exemplars versus attend more to rules) is itself a categorization before the final categorization of the stimulus. When a stimulus appears, the model first classifies it as a rule-governed stimulus or an exemplar-governed stimulus, and then the model accordingly classifies the stimulus using the rule-based or exemplar-based subsystem.[3]

Hybrid representation models are proliferating (e.g. Anderson & Betz, 2001), and are sure to appear in creative new approaches in the future. There is also evidence for multiple learning processes, which might also interact with the types of representations being learned (e.g. Raijmakers, Dolan, & Molenaar, 2001; VanOsselaer & Janiszewski, 2001).

ROLE OF SIMILARITY

Exemplar models depend on the computation of similarity between stimuli and items in memory. Prototype models also rely on the determination of similarity between stimuli and memory representations (namely, the prototypes). Even some rule models compute similarity between stimuli and boundaries (e.g. Vandierendonck, 1995), or can be re-conceptualized as doing so.

Some researchers have criticized the notion of similarity as being internally incoherent, and some critics have argued that similarity does not always correlate with categorization. If similarity as a theoretical construct is decrepit and dilapidated, then category learning models founded on similarity are also in peril of collapse.

There have been a number of demonstrations that suggest that similarity is incoherent. In these situations, similarity seems to change depending on how it is measured. Psychological similarity can be empirically assessed by a number of methods. One method simply asks people to rate the similarity of two items on a scale from 1 to 10; another method measures discriminability or confusability of items. Usually these different assessments agree: items measured to be more similar than other items by one method are also measured to be more similar by a different method. But sometimes different assays do not agree (e.g. Tversky, 1977). Similarity can also be context-specific: in the context of hair, gray is more similar to white than to black, but in the context of clouds, gray is more similar to black than to white (Medin & Shoben, 1988). In general, models of psychological similarity presume which features or dimensions are used for comparing the objects, without any explanation of why those features or dimensions are selected. Models of similarity do have parameters for specifying the attention allocated to different features, but the models do not describe how these attentional values come about (Goodman, 1972; Murphy & Medin, 1985).

Other research suggests that similarity is not always an accurate predictor of categorization. Consider the category, *things to remove from a burning house*. The items *heirloom jewelry* and *children*

are both central members of this category, yet they have little similarity in terms of visual appearance (Barsalou, 1983). On the other hand, if attention is directed only to the features *valuable, irreplaceable* and *portable*, then children and heirloom jewelry bear a strong similarity. As another example, this one taken from personal experience, consider an actual label on a product: 'Great for sleeping, gun shooting, studying, aircraft.' What is the product? Earplugs. The applications of the product, i.e. the members of this category, are highly similar only when attention is directed to the critical feature of undesired noise. Once again the issue of what to attend to is a theoretical crux, not addressed by current theories of similarity.

Thus, similarity is itself a complex psychological phenomenon in need of theoretical explication. Despite the complexities, there are strong regularities in similarity and categorization data that should yield to formal treatment. Excellent reviews of these topics have been written by Goldstone (1994) and by Medin, Goldstone, and Gentner (1993). In particular, a comprehensive theory of similarity will need a theory of attention. The role of attention will be discussed again, below.

MORE COMPLEX REPRESENTATIONS

The previous discussion has assumed that items are represented by collections of features. These representations are 'flat' in the sense that no feature is a combination of other features, and every item within a category has the same universe of candidate features. But psychological representations of complex categories might involve structured representations, involving hierarchical combinations of features and dimensions that are present in some instances but not others. For example, the category *vehicle* has instances such as *car* that have windshields, but also has instances such as *bicycle* that have no windshields. Future models of category learning will need to address these non-flat representations (Lassaline & Murphy, 1998).

Palmeri (1999) showed that an exemplar-based model can account for some learning of hierarchically organized categories, structured by superordinate, basic and subordinate levels analogous to vehicle, car and Ford. But it is an open question as to whether any single-representation model can comprehensively account for learning of categories at multiple levels. Lagnado and Shanks (2002) discuss multiple levels of representation and suggest that a dual-component model is needed. Theories of category learning will eventually have to address other varieties of complex representation, e.g. Markman and Stilwell (2001) discuss the notion of a 'role'-governed category which specifies the relational role played by its members.

Whereas complex representations will eventually need to be addressed by category-learning models, at this time even the simplest types of cue combination are not fully understood. For example, there is active research in determining the conditions under which two features are processed as independently additive components in a representation or as a conjunctive compound that is distinct from the components (e.g. Shanks, Charles, Darby, & Azmi, 1998; Shanks, Darby, & Charles, 1998; Williams & Braker, 1999; Young, Wasserman, Johnson, & Jones, 2000). Lachnit, Reinhard, and Kimmel (2000) discuss the need for a representation of the abstract relational dimension of 'separate' versus 'together', distinct from the numerical quantification of one versus two.

OTHER FORMS OF INDUCTION

Until this point in the chapter, it has been emphasized that the function of categorization is to infer an unseen feature from given information. The inferred feature has been a nominal category or characteristic, and the process of inference has consisted of some kind of matching of a 'flat' stimulus vector to a stored vector or set of vectors. But the inferred information could be richer than a simple nominal category, and the inference process could use representations and processes more complicated than matching of flat vectors.

If the inferred information is a value on a continuous scale, then the mapping from stimuli to inferred values constitutes what is called a *function*. For example, a physician who must prescribe an appropriate amount of medication might know the functional relationship between (a) the observed values of body weight and blood pressure and (b) the inferred value of amount of medication. A baseball outfielder might know the functional relationship between (a) the observed values of distance to infielder and urgency and (b) the inferred values of amount of force and angle of throw.

The study of function learning is relatively nascent compared to category learning. A very useful review is provided by Busemeyer, Byun, Delosh, and McDaniel (1997). There are many analogous findings in the two areas, in terms of relative ease of learning different types of dimensional combinations. Theories of function learning can also be differentiated according to the dimensions in Table 7.1, but the most prominent difference among function-learning theories is whether the function is specified globally or piecemeal. Koh and Meyer (1991), for example, have proposed a function-learning model in which globally defined functions are gradually regressed onto the observed instances during learning, much like gradual tuning

of hidden nodes in backpropagation (Rumelhart, Hinton, & Williams, 1986; but cf. Kruschke, 1993). Delosh, Busemeyer, and McDaniel (1997) have described a model that learns exemplars, i.e. piecemeal input–output value combinations, analogous to the exemplar-based category-learning model ALCOVE (Kruschke, 1992), and then uses a linear extra-/interpolation response strategy between learned exemplars. Kalish, Lewandowsky, and Kruschke (in press) have described a sophisticated model that applies different globally defined functions to different specific regions of the input space, i.e. piecemeal application of global functions, analogous to the piecemeal application of global rules in the category-learning model ATRIUM (Kruschke & Erickson, 1994; Erickson & Kruschke, 1998, 2002).

The induction process might be based on representations more complicated than flat vectors. People have rich theoretical knowledge about many domains. For example, people know that birds are more than a collection of feathers, beak, wings, chirps, etc. People also know that wings enable flight, that flight has to do with air flow and air pressure; that some birds compete for territory with other birds of the same species, that bird songs can mark territory, etc. Rich knowledge such as this is packaged into *theories* of how behavior works and how the features are causally interrelated. This kind of knowledge might not be felicitously represented as a flat vector of features, and instead might need to be represented as a hierarchy of features in nested relations. Inference based on these complex representations must then also be more complex than feature–vector matching. Many interesting effects in inductive reasoning can be captured by simple feature–vector matching (Sloman, 1998), but more complex representations and processes are needed to account for other situations, such as those involving causal relations (e.g. Ahn, Kim, Lassaline, & Dennis, 2000). Nevertheless, just as categorization theorists debate exemplar versus rule-based models, inductive-reasoning theorists also debate exemplar versus rule-based models (Hahn & Chater, 1998; Heit, 2000; Sloman, 1996).

TOWARD A COMPREHENSIVE THEORY? THE ROLE OF ATTENTION

The many complexities of categorization and inference will not easily yield to a comprehensive theory, but it does seem that a crucial issue in the path of progress is *attention*. In its broadest definition, attention simply refers to the selectivity of information usage in inference. People learn that out of the plethora of available information, only some aspects should be attended to in certain situations. Attention refers to both enhanced or amplified processing of some information and diminished or suppressed processing of other information. What often poses the biggest challenges to theories of categorization is the fluidity and context specificity of information selection. Moreover, this selection can occur at multiple levels of information simultaneously, so that it is not only the input features that are selected, but the various higher-level re-representations as well. A variety of perplexing phenomena in category learning might be solved by appropriate theories of attention.

Why should there be attentional selection? One reason is that selection of relevant information can accelerate learning. This speed is engendered by the attentionally enhanced discriminability of information that requires different responses. For example, suppose that color is critical to discriminate edible from poisonous mushrooms, such that darker shades of brown are to be avoided. By attending to color, the discrimination between darker and lighter brown is improved, therefore accuracy and learning are improved.

Not only does the amplifying of relevant information benefit learning, so does the quashing of irrelevant information. This benefit occurs because learned associations will generalize across instances that differ on the irrelevant dimension if that dimension is ignored. For example, suppose that size is irrelevant for discriminating edible from poisonous mushrooms. If you learn that a certain 4 cm tall mushroom is edible, then when you see a 8 cm tall mushroom of the same color you will not starve. That is, by learning that size is irrelevant, learning about a 4 cm mushroom immediately benefits inference about an 8 cm mushroom.

A classic example of enhanced learning due to attentional quashing of irrelevant dimensions comes from the work of Shepard, Hovland, and Jenkins (1961). They studied the relative ease with which people learned different classifications of a set of objects. The objects varied on three binary-valued dimensions. For example, the objects could be simple geometric forms that vary on dimensions of shape (circle or triangle), size (large or small) and color (red or green). The so-called 'Type II' structure has *two* relevant dimensions; an example of such a structure can be described by this rule: a form is in category 1 if it is circular or large but not both, otherwise it is in category 2. A condition of that form, i.e. one feature or another but not both, is called an exclusive-or, also abbreviated as 'xor'. Notice in this example that shape and size are relevant, but not color. The so-called 'Type IV' structure, on the other hand, has *three* relevant dimensions; an example is as follows: a form is in category A if it has any two or more of circular, large and red. Shepard et al. (1961) found that the Type II structure, involving just two relevant dimensions, was easier to learn than the Type IV structure, involving three dimensions, despite the fact that instances in the Type IV structure are more compactly distributed in the three-dimensional stimulus space. Nosofsky and Palmeri (1996) found that this advantage for Type II occurs only for stimuli that have dimensions that can be selectively attended to. For the 'integral' dimensions of hue, saturation and brightness of colors, which are extremely difficult to selectively attend to, Type II is more difficult than Type IV. Nosofsky and colleagues (Nosofsky et al., 1994; Nosofsky & Palmeri, 1996) found that a model that incorporates learned selective attention (ALCOVE: Kruschke, 1992) accommodated the human learning data very well, but models without selective attention failed.

Attentional selection applies not only to the input end of information processing, but also to the output end. Of the many actions a person might take, typically only one action can be carried out at a time. Thus, cognition must ultimately be selective at its output, and this required selectivity might be enhanced by selectivity earlier in the processing stream. Moreover, action influences the input to cognition. Our eyes can be directed to only a limited part of the world, and our hands can feel only a limited extent of a surface. If the world imposes a cost for lingering too long on irrelevant information (e.g. by not detecting predators or competitors for limited resources before they strike), then it is adaptive to learn what to attend to. The selectivity imposed upon perceptions and actions by our effectors suggests that sources of information throughout the processing stream should *compete* for attention. Maddox (2002), for example, has tried to assess attention at different perceptual and decisional levels in the context of category learning. Thus, a third rationale for attentional learning is that perception and action have limited scope and the organism should therefore learn what to attend to when in a competitive environment.

Numerous studies have reported evidence that attention during learning is indeed of limited capacity, such that attending to one source of information detracts from utilizing another source (examples of recent relevant articles include Ashby & Ell, 2002; Gottselig, Wasserman, & Young, 2001; Kruschke & Johansen, 1999; Nosofsky & Kruschke, 2002; Waldron & Ashby, 2001). Many theories of learning include some attentional capacity constraint (e.g. Pearce, 1994) or cue competition (e.g. Rescorla & Wagner, 1972), but relatively few theories include mechanisms for attentional learning (Kruschke, 2001a). Evidence abounds for cue competition in associative or category learning, and some research has also found cue competition in function learning (e.g. Birnbaum, 1976; Busemeyer, Myung, & McDaniel, 1993; Mellers, 1986). If category learning and function learning share similar mechanisms, as discussed earlier, then attention learning should be robustly evident in function learning as well. In summary so far, attentional learning explains a number of phenomena in human learning because attention improves discrimination on relevant dimensions, improves generalization over irrelevant dimensions, and addresses the problem of limited capacity in perception and action.

Attentional shifting is assessed not only by its influence on learning in novel domains, but also by its influence on subsequent learning. Much research has examined transfer of learning when there are shifts in the relevance of information. The motivation for this type of assessment is straightforward: if a person has learned that some dimensions are relevant but others are irrelevant, then a subsequent categorization that retains the same relevant dimensions should be relatively easy to learn but a subsequent categorization that changes the relevance of dimensions should be relatively difficult. For example, if people initially learn that red indicates category 1 and green indicates category 2 whereas shape is irrelevant, then it should be easy subsequently to learn that blue indicates category 1 and yellow indicates category 2, but it should be difficult to learn that circle indicates category 1 and triangle indicates category 2. The former type of shift is called an 'intradimensional shift' (IDS) because the relevant values for the categorization remain within the same dimension. The latter type of shift is called an 'extradimensional shift' (EDS) because the relevant values change to a different dimension.

A useful notation for the structure of an IDS is $A(B) \rightarrow An(Bn)$, where the relevant dimension is denoted by a letter without parentheses, the irrelevant dimension is denoted by a letter with parentheses, the shift is denoted by the arrow, and the 'n' indicates novel values of the dimensions. An EDS is denoted by $A(B) \rightarrow Bn(An)$. It is interesting to ask whether the advantage of IDS over EDS is due to learned perseveration on the relevant dimension or to learned inhibition of the irrelevant dimension, or both. Owen, Roberts, Hodges, Summers, Polkey, and Robbins (1993) attempted to isolate those two influences with two shifts that eliminated one of the initial dimensions. One shift eliminated the initially irrelevant dimension so that it could no longer influence the learning of the shift stage. In abstract notation, the design was $A(B) \rightarrow Cn(An)$. This shift would be difficult only if people had learned to perseverate on dimension A. Another design was $A(B) \rightarrow Bn(Cn)$, which would be difficult only if people had learned to inhibit dimension B. Owen et al. (1993) found that both types of shift were difficult, indicating that people learn both perseveration on the relevant dimension and inhibition of the irrelevant dimension.

Kruschke (1996b) studied more complex designs so that relevance shifts could be conducted without introducing novel values of the dimensions. This allowed comparing relevance shifts with *reversal* shifts, wherein the mapping to categories is simply reversed without changing the stimuli. The initially learned structure was an xor on dimensions A and B, with dimension C irrelevant, denoted AxorB(C). The reversal shift, denoted $AxorB(C) \rightarrow AxorB(C)rev$, was extremely easy for people to learn. A shift that retained one of the relevant dimensions and was therefore a type of IDS, denoted $AxorB(C) \rightarrow A(B)(C)$, was next easiest, and a shift to the initially irrelevant dimension, a type of EDS denoted $AxorB(C) \rightarrow C(A)(B)$, was more difficult. Kruschke (1996b) found that the difficulty of shifting to a previous irrelevant dimension could be nicely captured by a model with learned attention, but the great facility of reversal shifting demanded an additional remapping mechanism. Neural evidence for the distinct processing of relevance and reversal shifts comes from Rogers, Andrews, Grasby, Brooks, and Robbins (2000). Further variations of IDS and EDS structures were studied by Oswald, Yee, Rawlins, Bannerman, Good, and Honey (2001), using rats as subjects. The researchers found that $AxorB(C) \rightarrow AxorBn(Cn)$, i.e. a type of IDS, was easier than $AxorB(C) \rightarrow AxorCn(Bn)$, a type of EDS. Not only was the structure more complex than the traditional IDS/EDS, but the dimensions were in three separate modalities (auditory, visual and tactile) and the A dimension was phasic (a brief tone) whereas the B and C dimensions were tonic (static patterns on the walls and floors). The robustness and generality of the advantage of IDS over EDS is generally interpreted as strong evidence for attentional learning in the initial phase of training, with perseveration of that learning into the subsequent phase.

Attentional learning does more than accelerate learning in completely novel domains. Attentional shifting also preserves previous learning for similar stimuli, whenever possible. Thus, when new stimuli appear that share some aspects with previously learned stimuli but also have some novel aspects, if the previously relevant aspects continue to correctly predict appropriate behavior, then the novel aspects will quickly be learned to be irrelevant. That is, the previously learned knowledge about the relevant aspects will be respected, to the extent that it continues to be successful. On the other hand, if the new stimuli demand different behavior, then attention will quickly shift to the novel aspects, thereby protecting the previously learned stimuli from being 'overwritten' by the new items. Thus, attention shifting protects previously learned categorizations by reducing interference when new items demand different categorizations. This is achieved by attentionally highlighting novel aspects of the stimuli, and associating these aspects with the new category.

An example of this attentional highlighting comes from the otherwise perplexing phenomenon known as the *inverse base-rate effect*, wherein a cue that indicates a rare category is apparently overweighted (Medin & Edelson, 1988). In this procedure, people initially learn that cues A and B indicate category 1, and subsequently learn that cues A and C indicate category 2. When tested with the new cue combination B and C, people tend to classify it as category 2, despite the facts that the cues are really equally predictive of the two categories and the first category was more frequent overall. The apparently irrational behavior is naturally explained by attentional shifting: when learning the second category, people shift attention away from cue A because they have already learned that it predicts category 1, and they shift attention to cue C because it does not conflict with previous learning. Therefore they learn a strong association from cue C to category 2, and, moreover, they learn that when cue C appears they should attend to it, especially in the context of cue A. The quantitative details of data from many such experiments are accurately accounted for by models that have rapid shifts of attention during learning (Dennis & Kruschke, 1998; Fagot, Kruschke, Depy, & Vauclair, 1998; Kalish, 2001; Kalish & Kruschke, 2000; Kruschke, 1996a, 2001b).

Another phenomenon, called apparent base-rate neglect (Gluck & Bower, 1988), can also be explained by attentional shifting of this nature (Kruschke, 1996a). The essential idea is that categories that occur more frequently (i.e. have higher base rates) are learned first. Subsequently the less frequent categories are learned, and attention highlights the distinctive features of the rare categories in order to protect the previous learning about the frequent categories. The highlighting of distinctive features of the rare categories is difficult for some popular exemplar-based models to account for (e.g. Lewandowsky, 1995), but it can be well accommodated by an exemplar-based model that has rapidly shifting, learned selective attention (Kruschke & Johansen, 1999). Another related phenomenon is the 'contrast effect' reported by Kersten, Goldstone, and Schaffert (1998). Essentially, the contrast effect occurs with an EDS using *novel* categories in the shift phase. Kersten et al. (1998) suggested that the ease of an EDS for novel categories was best explained by a distinct type of attention. Alternatively, it can be interpreted as a case of attentional highlighting. When the categories are novel, attention does not perseverate on previously relevant dimensions because doing so would contradict previously learned categories. Instead, attention highlights distinctive dimensions to rapidly accommodate the newly demanded outcomes. Thus, an EDS is relatively difficult when the categories are the same as the initial learning, but it is relatively easy when the categories are novel.

The attentional shift learned during the inverse base-rate effect is context-specific, i.e. attention shifts away from cue A to cue C especially in the context of those two cues and the corresponding responses. The theory of attention shifting propounded here asserts that attention shifts are context- and exemplar-specific, i.e. attentional redistributions are a learned response from particular cue combinations, with some degree of graded generalization from those learned cases. The context specificity of learned attention can address results of various other category-learning experiments. Macho (1997), for example, had people learn a prototype structure divided in two phases. In this structure, all dimensions had two values, denoted 1 and 2. If the stimuli had three dimensions (there were actually more dimensions in Macho's experiments), then the prototype of one category had values of 1 on all three dimensions, denoted 111. The prototype of the other category had the opposite values on all three dimensions, i.e. 222. Other instances were symmetrically distributed around the prototypes, e.g. the first category also included exemplars 112, 121 and 211, whereas the second category also included exemplars 221, 212 and 122. Training on the category instances was split across phases such that each phase made different dimensions more relevant than others despite the fact that when collapsed over the course of both phases the dimensions were equally relevant. Using our three-dimensional example, the first phase could have consisted of instances 111, 112, 221 and 212, for which only the first dimension is perfectly predictive of the correct categorization, and the second phase could have consisted of instances 121, 211, 122 and 222, for which only the third dimension is perfectly predictive of the correct categorization. Macho (1997) found that at least one exemplar-based model with attentional shifts (ALCOVE: Kruschke, 1992) could not accommodate the results. That model's problems were that it could not shift attention quickly enough, nor could it learn exemplar-specific attentional redistributions. It is likely that more recent models with rapid shifts of attention, and with exemplar-specific learned attention (e.g. Kruschke & Johansen, 1999; Kruschke, 2001a), could more accurately account for the results.

In another experiment demonstrating the context specificity of learned attention, Aha and Goldstone (1992) showed that people can learn that one dimension is relevant for categorization in one region of a stimulus space, but a different dimension is relevant in a different region of the space. Erickson and Kruschke (2001) extended their results by showing there are individual differences in which regions of the space are learned first, and that a model that shifts attention among rules, depending on the exemplar, fits the data well.

In general, the sequence of learning plays an important role in what is learned. The variety of experiments summarized above indicated that subsequent learning can be strongly influenced by previous learning. Base rates influence what is learned by influencing the sequence with which items and categories are learned. The order of learning influences what is learned in large part because attention will shift to those attributes that facilitate learning. Goldstone (1996) showed in several insightful experiments that people will learn more non-diagnostic features of a category if many instances of the category are presented consecutively than if the instances are interleaved with cases from a contrasting category. Spalding and Ross (1994) showed that the particular instances that people analyze early in learning have a strong influence on what is learned about the categories. In particular, attributes common to early-learned cases of a category will tend to dominate knowledge of those categories. Billman and Davila (2001) reported that it is easier for people to discriminate categories that contrast consistently on a few features.

These influences of training order are not merely laboratory curiosities, but apply also to real-life learning in clinical settings (Welk, 2002) and language acquisition (Smith, Jones, Landau, Gershkoff-Stowe, & Samuelson, 2002). Individual differences might also be usefully explained as differences in training history, or as individual differences in generalization gradients, attentional shifting rates or dimensional saliences (e.g. Dixon, Koehler, Schweizer, & Guylee, 2000; Niedenthal, Halberstadt, & Innes-Ker, 1999; Treat et al., 2001). The phenomena reviewed above are consonant with the general notions of attentional learning propounded here: attention focuses on features that consistently indicate a category because doing so facilitates learning of that category. When a contrasting category is presented, attention highlights the consistently distinctive (diagnostic) features of the new category, because doing so facilitates new learning and protects previous knowledge.

For attentional theories to have broad applicability to category learning, they must eventually address more complex representational structures. As an example of this need, Lassaline and Murphy (1998) showed that people learn categories differently depending on whether the features that differ across instances are 'alignable'. Alignable features are values from a common dimension, e.g. red vs. green, whereas non-alignable features are from different dimensions, e.g. wing vs. branch. (Alignability is itself a subtle psychological construct.) Current models of attentional learning do not address the alignability of dimensions. Even if this issue is sidestepped for now, there are still debated questions about how complex knowledge structures influence the distribution of attention over dimensions. Some researchers have argued that prior knowledge does more than simply reallocate attention across stimulus dimensions (e.g. Hayes & Taplin, 1995), whereas other investigators have concluded that background concepts and theories do influence new learning through redistribution of attentional weights (e.g. Vandierendonck & Rosseel, 2000). Whether or not attentional redistribution, combined with a variety of representational constructs, can comprehensively accommodate the wealth of phenomena in category learning, there is little doubt that sophisticated theories of attention shifting will play an important role in understanding category learning.

SUMMARY

Categorization in its broadest definition is simply the inference of unseen attributes from observable features. The unseen attribute could be a category label or some other characteristic of the item. Because inference of appropriate action is perhaps the fundamental goal of cognition, categorization and category learning can be viewed as a core research domain in cognitive science.

Different theories of categorization hypothesize different representations. Various theories also assume different processes for matching stimulus representations and memory representations. Some theories posit representations of content, such as exemplars or prototypes. Other theories posit representations of boundaries between categories. For either type of representation, the specification can be global or piecemeal. Once the representation is established, then the theories can assume that the matching of stimulus and memory representations is done with a graded degree of match, or with a strict match versus no match.

Research is moving toward the conclusion that no one type of representation can accommodate the full complexity of human category learning. The challenge facing researchers now is determining which representations are used in what situations and how the representations trade off in learning and inference. Theories are also moving away from simple 'flat' vector representations to more complex structured representations. Regardless of the representation, there is ample research showing the robust influence of attention in category learning. Theories will have to address how prior knowledge influences attention which influences subsequent learning which influences attention for future learning.

FURTHER READING

While writing this chapter, the author was frequently tempted to give up and simply point the reader to the many excellent previous summaries of research in categorization. Perhaps that would have been the better course of action! Here, then, are some pointers to previous summaries of the topic.

The book by Smith and Medin (1981) provides a highly readable introduction to the issues in categorization research. The collection of articles by Rosch and Lloyd (1978) are classic statements of fundamental results and theoretical perspectives. The book by Shanks (1995) is a lucid review of issues in associative learning in humans, and a summary of associative learning in animals has been written by Pearce and Bouton (2001). Estes (1994) presents a more mathematically oriented survey of theories of classification. An accessible collection of tutorials is presented by Lamberts and Shanks (1997), see also the review of concepts by Lamberts (2000a), and Goldstone and Kersten (2003) provide an excellent review of the field, all of which you should probably read instead of this chapter.

ACKNOWLEDGMENT

Supported in part by Grant BCS-9910720 from the National Science Foundation.

NOTES

1 'Wherever human life is concerned, the unnatural stricture of excessive verticality cannot stand against more natural horizontality' (Frank Lloyd Wright on skyscrapers).

2 'Male' and 'female' are clearly defined genetically in virtually all individuals. There are extremely rare exceptions for whom their chromosomes are neither XX (female) nor XY (male).

3 Mirman and Spivey (2001) described a mixture-of-experts model similar to Erickson and Kruschke's (1998, 2002; Kruschke & Erickson, 1994), in which the rule module is instead a standard backprop network (Rumelhart et al., 1986). The likely problem with Mirman and Spivey's approach is that the model will suffer the same problems as standard backprop, as pointed out by Kruschke (1993).

REFERENCES

Aha, D. W., & Goldstone, R. (1992). Concept learning and flexible weighting. In *Proceedings of the Fourteenth Annual Conference of the Cognitive Science Society* (pp. 534–539). Hillsdale, NJ: Erlbaum.

Ahn, W. K., Kim, N. S., Lassaline, M. E., & Dennis, M. J. (2000). Causal status as a determinant of feature centrality. *Cognitive Psychology, 41*, 361–416.

Allen, S. W., & Brooks, L. R. (1991). Specializing the operation of an explicit rule. *Journal of Experimental Psychology. General, 120*, 3–19.

Anderson, A. L., Ross, B. H., & Chin-Parker, S. (2002). A further investigation of category learning by inference. *Memory and Cognition, 30*, 119–128.

Anderson, J. R. (1991). The adaptive nature of human categorization. *Psychological Review, 98*, 409–429.

Anderson, J. R., & Betz, J. (2001). A hybrid model of categorization. *Psychonomic Bulletin and Review, 8*, 629–647.

Anderson, J. R., & Fincham, J. M. (1996). Categorization and sensitivity to correlation. *Journal of Experimental Psychology: Learning, Memory, and Cognition, 22*, 259–277.

Ashby, F. G. (1992). Multidimensional models of categorization. In F. G. Ashby (ed.), *Multidimensional models of perception and cognition* (pp. 449–483). Hillsdale, NJ: Erlbaum.

Ashby, F. G., & Alfonso-Reese, L. (1995). Categorization as probability density estimation. *Journal of Mathematical Psychology, 39*, 216–233.

Ashby, F. G., Alfonso-Reese, L. A., Turken, A. U., & Waldron, E. M. (1998). A neuropsychological theory of multiple systems in category learning. *Psychological Review, 105*, 442–481.

Ashby, F. G., & Ell, S. W. (2002). Single versus multiple systems of category learning. *Psychonomic Bulletin and Review, 9*, 175–180.

Ashby, F. G., & Maddox, W. T. (1993). Relations between prototype, exemplar and decision bound models of categorization. *Journal of Mathematical Psychology, 37*, 372–400.

Ashby, F. G., Queller, S., & Berretty, P. M. (1999). On the dominance of unidimensional rules in unsupervised categorization. *Perception and Psychophysics, 61*, 1178–1199.

Ashby, F. G., & Waldron, E. M. (1999). On the nature of implicit categorization. *Psychonomic Bulletin and Review, 6*, 363–378.

Ashby, F. G., Waldron, E. M., Lee, W. W., & Berkman, A. (2001). Suboptimality in human categorization and identification. *Journal of Experimental Psychology: General, 130*, 77–96.

Barsalou, L. (1983). Ad hoc categories. *Memory and Cognition, 11*, 211–227.

Billman, D., & Davila, D. (2001). Consistent contrast aids concept learning. *Memory and Cognition, 29*, 1022–1035.

Birnbaum, M. H. (1976). Intuitive numerical prediction. *American Journal of Psychology, 89*, 417–429.

Blair, M., & Homa, D. (2001). Expanding the search for a linear separability constraint on category learning. *Memory and Cognition, 29*, 1153–1164.

Bourne, L. E. (1970). Knowing and using concepts. *Psychological Review, 77*, 546–556.

Brooks, L. R. (1978). Nonanalytic concept formation and memory for instances. In E. Rosch & B. B. Lloyd (Eds.), *Cognition and categorization* (pp. 169–211). Hillsdale, NJ: Erlbaum.

Busemeyer, J. R., Byun, E., Delosh, E. L., & McDaniel, M. A. (1997). Learning functional relations based on experience with input-output pairs by humans and artificial neural networks. In K. Lamberts & D. Shanks (Eds.), *Knowledge, concepts and categories* (pp. 405–437). Cambridge, MA: MIT Press.

Busemeyer, J. R., Dewey, G. I., & Medin, D. L. (1984). Evaluation of exemplar-based generalization and the abstraction of categorical information. *Journal of Experimental Psychology: Learning, Memory, and Cognition, 10*, 638–648.

Busemeyer, J. R., & Myung, I. J. (1988). A new method for investigating prototype learning. *Journal of Experimental Psychology: Learning, Memory, and Cognition, 14*, 3–11.

Busemeyer, J. R., Myung, I. J., & McDaniel, M. A. (1993). Cue competition effects: empirical tests of adaptive network learning models. *Psychological Science, 4*, 190–195.

Choi, S., McDaniel, M. A., & Busemeyer, J. R. (1993). Incorporating prior biases in network models of conceptual rule learning. *Memory and Cognition, 21*, 413–423.

Cohen, A. L., & Nosofsky, R. M. (2000). An exemplar-retrieval model of speeded same-different judgments. *Journal of Experimental Psychology: Human Perception and Performance, 26*, 1549–1569.

Cohen, A. L., Nosofsky, R. M., & Zaki, S. R. (2001). Category variability, exemplar similarity, and perceptual classification. *Memory and Cognition, 29*, 1165–1175.

Delosh, E. L., Busemeyer, J. R., & McDaniel, M. A. (1997). Extrapolation: the sine qua non for abstraction in function learning. *Journal of Experimental Psychology: Learning, Memory, and Cognition, 23*, 968–986.

Dennis, S., & Kruschke, J. K. (1998). Shifting attention in cued recall. *Australian Journal of Psychology, 50*, 131–138.

Dixon, M. J., Koehler, D., Schweizer, T. A., & Guylee, M. J. (2000). Superior single dimension relative to 'exclusive or' categorization performance by a patient with category-specific visual agnosia: empirical data and an ALCOVE simulation. *Brain and Cognition, 43*, 152–158.

Erickson, M. A., & Kruschke, J. K. (1998). Rules and exemplars in category learning. *Journal of Experimental Psychology: General, 127*, 107–140.

Erickson, M. A., & Kruschke, J. K. (2001). Multiple representations in inductive category learning: evidence of stimulus- and time-dependent representation. Available from authors.

Erickson, M. A., & Kruschke, J. K. (2002). Rule-based extrapolation in perceptual categorization. *Psychonomic Bulletin and Review, 9*, 160–168.

Estes, W. K. (1994). *Classification and cognition.* New York: Oxford University Press.

Fagot, J., Kruschke, J. K., Depy, D., & Vauclair, J. (1998). Associative learning in baboons (*Papio papio*) and humans (*Homo sapiens*): species differences in learned attention to visual features. *Animal Cognition, 1*, 123–133.

French, R. M. (1999). Catastrophic forgetting in connectionist networks. *Trends in Cognitive Sciences, 3*, 128–135.

Gelman, S. A., & Markman, E. M. (1986). Categories and induction in young children. *Cognition, 23*, 183–209.

Gluck, M. A., & Bower, G. H. (1988). From conditioning to category learning: an adaptive network model. *Journal of Experimental Psychology: General, 117*, 227–247.

Goldstone, R. L. (1994). The role of similarity in categorization: providing a groundwork. *Cognition, 52*, 125–157.

Goldstone, R. L. (1996). Isolated and interrelated concepts. *Memory and Cognition, 24*, 608–628.

Goldstone, R. L., & Kersten, A. (2003). Concepts and categorization. In A. F. Healy & R. W. Proctor (Eds.), *Handbook of psychology: Vol. 4. experimental psychology* (pp. 599–621). New York: Wiley.

Goodman, N. (1972). Seven strictures on similarity. In N. Goodman (ed.), *Problems and projects* (pp. 437–447). New York: Bobbs-Merrill.

Gottselig, J. M., Wasserman, E. A., & Young, M. E. (2001). Attentional trade-offs in pigeons learning to discriminate newly relevant visual stimulus dimensions. *Learning and Motivation, 32*, 240–253.

Hahn, U., & Chater, N. (1998). Similarity and rules: distinct? exhaustive? empirically distinguishable? *Cognition, 65*, 197–230.

Hayes, B. K., & Taplin, J. E. (1995). Similarity-based and knowledge-based processes in category learning. *European Journal of Cognitive Psychology, 7*, 383–410.

Heit, E. (2000). Properties of inductive reasoning. *Psychonomic Bulletin and Review, 7*, 569–592.

Homa, D., Sterling, S., & Trepel, L. (1981). Limitations of exemplar-based generalization and the abstraction of categorical information. *Journal of Experimental Psychology: Human Learning and Memory, 7*, 418–439.

Kalish, M. L. (2001). An inverse base rate effect with continuously valued stimuli. *Memory and Cognition, 29*, 587–597.

Kalish, M. L., & Kruschke, J. K. (1997). Decision boundaries in one-dimensional categorization. *Journal of Experimental Psychology: Learning, Memory, and Cognition, 23*, 1362–1377.

Kalish, M. L., & Kruschke, J. K. (2000). The role of attention shifts in the categorization of continuous dimensioned stimuli. *Psychological Research (Psychologische Forschung), 64*, 105–116.

Kalish, M. L., Lewandowsky, S., & Kruschke, J. K. (in press). Population of linear experts: knowledge partitioning and function learning. *Psychological Review.*

Kanerva, P. (1988). *Sparse distributed memory.* Cambridge, MA: MIT Press.

Kersten, A. W., Goldstone, R. L., & Schaffert, A. (1998). Two competing attentional mechanisms in category learning. *Journal of Experimental Psychology: Learning, Memory, and Cognition, 24*, 1437–1458.

Koh, K., & Meyer, D. E. (1991). Function learning: induction of continuous stimulus-response relations. *Journal of Experimental Psychology: Learning, Memory, and Cognition, 17*, 811–816.

Kruschke, J. K. (1992). ALCOVE: an exemplar-based connectionist model of category learning. *Psychological Review, 99*, 22–44.

Kruschke, J. K. (1993). Human category learning: implications for backpropagation models. *Connection Science, 5*, 3–36.

Kruschke, J. K. (1996a). Base rates in category learning. *Journal of Experimental Psychology: Learning, Memory, and Cognition, 22*, 3–26.

Kruschke, J. K. (1996b). Dimensional relevance shifts in category learning. *Connection Science, 8*, 201–223.

Kruschke, J. K. (2001a). Toward a unified model of attention in associative learning. *Journal of Mathematical Psychology*, *45*, 812–863.

Kruschke, J. K. (2001b). The inverse base-rate effect is not explained by eliminative inference. *Journal of Experimental Psychology: Learning, Memory, and Cognition*, *27*, 1385–1400.

Kruschke, J. K., & Erickson, M. A. (1994). Learning of rules that have high-frequency exceptions: new empirical data and a hybrid connectionist model. In *Proceedings of the Sixteenth Annual Conference of the Cognitive Science Society* (pp. 514–519). Hillsdale, NJ: Erlbaum.

Kruschke, J. K., & Johansen, M. K. (1999). A model of probabilistic category learning. *Journal of Experimental Psychology: Learning, Memory, and Cognition*, *25*, 1083–1119.

Kruskal, J. B., & Wish, M. (1978). *Multidimensional scaling*. Beverly Hills, CA: Sage. (Sage University Paper series on Quantitative Applications in the Social Sciences, 07–011)

Lachnit, H., Reinhard, G., & Kimmel, H. D. (2000). Further investigations of stimulus coding in nonlinear discrimination problems. *Biological Psychology*, *55*, 57–73.

Lagnado, D. A., & Shanks, D. R. (2002). Probability judgment in hierarchical learning: a conflict between predictiveness and coherence. *Cognition*, *83*, 81–112.

Lamberts, K. (1998). The time course of categorization. *Journal of Experimental Psychology: Learning, Memory, and Cognition*, *24*, 695–711.

Lamberts, K. (2000a). Concepts: core readings. *American Journal of Psychology*, *113*, 663–667.

Lamberts, K. (2000b). Information-accumulation theory of speeded categorization. *Psychological Review*, *107*, 227–260.

Lamberts, K. (2001). Category-specific deficits and exemplar models. *Behavioral and Brain Sciences*, *24*, 484–485.

Lamberts, K., & Shanks, D. (Eds.) (1997). *Knowledge, concepts and categories*. Cambridge, MA: MIT Press.

Lassaline, M. E., & Murphy, G. L. (1998). Alignment and category learning. *Journal of Experimental Psychology: Learning, Memory, and Cognition*, *24*, 144–160.

Lee, M. D., & Navarro, D. J. (2002). Extending the ALCOVE model of category learning to featural stimulus domains. *Psychonomic Bulletin and Review*, *9*, 43–58.

Levine, M. (1975). *A cognitive theory of learning: research on hypothesis testing*. Hillsdale, NJ: Erlbaum.

Lewandowsky, S. (1995). Base-rate neglect in ALCOVE – a critical reevaluation. *Psychological Review*, *102*, 185–191.

Lynch, E. B., Coley, J. D., & Medin, D. L. (2000). Tall is typical: central tendency, ideal dimensions, and graded category structure among tree experts and novices. *Memory and Cognition*, *28*, 41–50.

Macho, S. (1997). Effect of relevance shifts in category acquisition: a test of neural networks. *Journal of Experimental Psychology: Learning, Memory, and Cognition*, *23*, 30–53.

Maddox, W. T. (2002). Learning and attention in multidimensional identification and categorization:

separating low-level perceptual processes and high-level decisional processes. *Journal of Experimental Psychology: Learning, Memory, and Cognition*, *28*, 99–115.

Markman, A. B., & Stilwell, C. H. (2001). Role-governed categories. *Journal of Experimental and Theoretical Artificial Intelligence*, *13*, 329–358.

McCloskey, M., & Cohen, N. J. (1989). Catastrophic interference in connectionist networks: the sequential learning problem. In G. Bower (ed.), *The psychology of learning and motivation, vol. 24* (pp. 109–165). New York: Academic Press.

Medin, D. L., & Edelson, S. M. (1988). Problem structure and the use of base-rate information from experience. *Journal of Experimental Psychology: General*, *117*, 68–85.

Medin, D. L., Goldstone, R. L., & Gentner, D. (1993). Respects for similarity. *Psychological Review*, *100*, 254–278.

Medin, D. L., & Schaffer, M. M. (1978). Context theory of classification learning. *Psychological Review*, *85*, 207–238.

Medin, D. L., & Shoben, E. J. (1988). Context and structure in conceptual combination. *Cognitive Psychology*, *20*, 158–190.

Mellers, B. A. (1986). Test of a distributional theory of intuitive numerical prediction. *Organizational Behavior and Human Decision Processes*, *38*, 279–294.

Miller, C. S., & Laird, J. E. (1996). Accounting for graded performance within a discrete search framework. *Cognitive Science*, *20*, 499–537.

Minda, J. P., & Smith, J. D. (2001). Prototypes in category learning: the effects of category size, category structure, and stimulus complexity. *Journal of Experimental Psychology: Learning, Memory, and Cognition*, *27*, 775–799.

Mirman, D., & Spivey, M. (2001). Retroactive interference in neural networks and in humans: the effect of pattern-based learning. *Connection Science*, *13*, 257–275.

Murphy, G. L., & Medin, D. L. (1985). The role of theories in conceptual coherence. *Psychological Review*, *92*, 289–316.

Niedenthal, P. M., Halberstadt, J. B., & Innes-Ker, A. H. (1999). Emotional response categorization. *Psychological Review*, *106*, 337–361.

Nosofsky, R. M. (1986). Attention, similarity and the identification-categorization relationship. *Journal of Experimental Psychology: General*, *115*, 39–57.

Nosofsky, R. M. (1991). Relation between the rational model and the context model of categorization. *Psychological Science*, *2*, 416–421.

Nosofsky, R. M. (1992). Exemplars, prototypes, and similarity rules. In A. F. Healy, S. M. Kosslyn, & R. M. Shiffrin (Eds.), *Essays in honor of William K. Estes, vol. 2. From learning processes to cognitive processes* (pp. 149–167). Hillsdale, NJ: Erlbaum.

Nosofsky, R. M., Gluck, M. A., Palmeri, T. J., McKinley, S. C., & Glauthier, P. (1994). Comparing models of rule-based classification learning: a replication of

Shepard, Hovland, and Jenkins (1961). *Memory and Cognition*, *22*, 352–369.

Nosofsky, R. M., & Johansen, M. K. (2000). Exemplar-based accounts of 'multiple-system' phenomena in perceptual categorization. *Psychonomic Bulletin and Review*, *7*, 375–402.

Nosofsky, R. M., & Kruschke, J. K. (1992). Investigations of an exemplar-based connectionist model of category learning. In D. L. Medin (ed.), *The psychology of learning and motivation* (Vol. 28, pp. 207–250). San Diego: Academic Press.

Nosofsky, R. M., & Kruschke, J. K. (2002). Single-system models and interference in category learning. *Psychonomic Bulletin and Review*, *9*, 169–174.

Nosofsky, R. M., & Palmeri, T. J. (1996). Learning to classify integral-dimension stimuli. *Psychonomic Bulletin and Review*, *3*, 222–226.

Nosofsky, R. M., & Palmeri, T. J. (1997). An exemplar-based random walk model of speeded classification. *Psychological Review*, *104*, 266–300.

Nosofsky, R. M., & Palmeri, T. J. (1998). A rule-plus-exception model for classifying objects in continuous-dimension spaces. *Psychonomic Bulletin and Review*, *5*, 345–369.

Nosofsky, R. M., Palmeri, T. J., & McKinley, S. C. (1994). Rule-plus-exception model of classification learning. *Psychological Review*, *101*, 53–79.

Oswald, C. J., Yee, B. K., Rawlins, J. N., Bannerman, D. B., Good, M., & Honey, R. C. (2001). Involvement of the entorhinal cortex in a process of attentional modulation: evidence from a novel variant of an ids/eds procedure. *Behavioral Neuroscience*, *115*, 841–849.

Owen, A. M., Roberts, A. C., Hodges, J. R., Summers, B. A., Polkey, C. E., & Robbins, T. W. (1993). Contrasting mechanisms of impaired attentional set-shifting in patients with frontal lobe damage or Parkinson's disease. *Brain*, *116*, 1159–1175.

Palmeri, T. J. (1999). Learning categories at different hierarchical levels: a comparison of category learning models. *Psychonomic Bulletin and Review*, *6*, 495–503.

Palmeri, T. J., & Nosofsky, R. M. (2001). Central tendencies, extreme points, and prototype enhancement effects in ill-defined perceptual categorization. *Quarterly Journal of Experimental Psychology*, *54A*, 197–235.

Pearce, J. M. (1994). Similarity and discrimination – a selective review and a connectionist model. *Psychological Review*, *101*, 587–607.

Pearce, J. M., & Bouton, M. E. (2001). Theories of associative learning in animals. *Annual Review of Psychology*, 111–139.

Raijmakers, M. E., Dolan, C. V., & Molenaar, P. C. (2001). Finite mixture distribution models of simple discrimination learning. *Memory and Cognition*, *29*, 659–677.

Ratcliff, R. (1990). Connectionist models of recognition memory: constraints imposed by learning and forgetting functions. *Psychological Review*, *97*, 285–308.

Reed, S. K. (1972). Pattern recognition and categorization. *Cognitive Psychology*, *3*, 382–407.

Rescorla, R. A., & Wagner, A. R. (1972). A theory of Pavlovian conditioning: variations in the effectiveness of reinforcement and non-reinforcement. In A. H. Black & W. F. Prokasy (Eds.), *Classical conditioning: Vol II. Current research and theory* (pp. 64–99). New York: Appleton-Century-Crofts.

Rogers, R. D., Andrews, T. C., Grasby, P. M., Brooks, D. J., & Robbins, T. W. (2000). Contrasting cortical and subcortical activations produced by attentional-set shifting and reversal learning in humans. *Journal of Cognitive Neuroscience*, *12*, 142–162.

Rosch, E., & Lloyd, B. B. (Eds.) (1978). *Cognition and categorization*. Hillsdale, NJ: Erlbaum.

Rosch, E. H., & Mervis, C. B. (1975). Family resemblances: studies in the internal structure of categories. *Cognitive Psychology*, *7*, 573–605.

Rosseel, Y. (2002). Mixture models of categorization. *Journal of Mathematical Psychology*, *46*, 178–210.

Rumelhart, D. E., Hinton, G. E., & Williams, R. J. (1986). Learning internal representations by error propagation. In J. L. McClelland & D. E. Rumelhart (Eds.), *Parallel distributed processing* (Vol. 1, pp. 318–362). Cambridge, MA: MIT Press.

Shanks, D. R. (1995). *The psychology of associative learning*. Cambridge: Cambridge University Press.

Shanks, D. R., Charles, D., Darby, R. J., & Azmi, A. (1998). Configural processes in human associative learning. *Journal of Experimental Psychology: Learning, Memory, and Cognition*, *24*, 1353–1378.

Shanks, D. R., & Darby, R. J. (1998). Feature- and rule-based generalization in human associative learning. *Journal of Experimental Psychology: Animal Behavior Processes*, *24*, 405–415.

Shanks, D. R., Darby, R. J., & Charles, D. (1998). Resistance to interference in human associative learning: evidence of configural processing. *Journal of Experimental Psychology: Animal Behavior Processes*, *24*, 136–150.

Shanks, D. R., & St John, M. F. (1994). Characteristics of dissociable human learning-systems. *Behavioral and Brain Sciences*, *17*, 367–395.

Shepard, R. N. (1962). The analysis of proximities: multidimensional scaling with an unknown distance function, I and II. *Psychometrika*, *27*, 125–140, 219–246.

Shepard, R. N. (1987). Toward a universal law of generalization for psychological science. *Science*, *237*, 1317–1323.

Shepard, R. N., Hovland, C. L., & Jenkins, H. M. (1961). Learning and memorization of classifications. *Psychological Monographs*, *75* (13) (Whole No. 517).

Sieck, W. R., & Yates, J. F. (2001). Overconfidence effects in category learning: a comparison of connectionist and exemplar memory models. *Journal of Experimental Psychology: Learning, Memory, and Cognition*, *27*, 1003–1021.

Sloman, S. A. (1996). The empirical case for two systems of reasoning. *Psychological Bulletin*, *119*, 3–22.

Sloman, S. A. (1998). Categorical inference is not a tree: the myth of inheritance hierarchies. *Cognitive Psychology*, *35*, 1–33.

Smith, E. E., & Medin, D. L. (1981). *Categories and concepts*. Cambridge, MA: Harvard University Press.

Smith, E. E., Patalano, A. L., & Jonides, J. (1998). Alternative strategies of categorization. *Cognition, 65*, 167–196.

Smith, E. E., & Sloman, S. A. (1994). Similarity- versus rule-based categorization. *Memory and Cognition, 22*, 377–386.

Smith, J. D., & Minda, J. P. (1998). Prototypes in the mist: The early epochs of category learning. *Journal of Experimental Psychology: Learning, Memory, and Cognition, 24*, 1411–1436.

Smith, J. D., & Minda, J. P. (2000). Thirty categorization results in search of a model. *Journal of Experimental Psychology: Learning, Memory, and Cognition, 26*, 3–27.

Smith, L. B., Jones, S. S., Landau, B., Gershkoff-Stowe, L., & Samuelson, L. (2002). Object name learning provides on-the-job training for attention. *Psychological Science, 13*, 13–19.

Spalding, T. L., & Ross, B. H. (1994). Comparison-based learning – effects of comparing instances during category learning. *Journal of Experimental Psychology: Learning, Memory, and Cognition, 20*, 1251–1263.

Storms, G., DeBoeck, P., & Ruts, W. (2001). Categorization of novel stimuli in well-known natural concepts: a case study. *Psychonomic Bulletin and Review, 8*, 377–384.

Thomas, R. D. (1998). Learning correlations in categorization tasks using large, ill-defined categories. *Journal of Experimental Psychology: Learning, Memory, and Cognition, 24*, 119–143.

Treat, T. A., McFall, R. M., Viken, R. J., & Kruschke, J. K. (2001). Using cognitive science methods to assess the role of social information processing in sexually coercive behavior. *Psychological Assessment, 13*, 549–565.

Tversky, A. (1977). Features of similarity. *Psychological Review, 84*, 327–352.

Vandierendonck, A. (1995). A parallel rule activation and rule synthesis model for generalization in category learning. *Psychonomic Bulletin and Review, 2*, 442–459.

Vandierendonck, A., & Rosseel, Y. (2000). Interaction of knowledge-driven and data-driven processing in category learning. *European Journal of Cognitive Psychology, 12*, 37–63.

VanOsselaer, S. M. J., & Janiszewski, C. (2001). Two ways of learning brand associations. *Journal of Consumer Research, 28*, 202–223.

Waldron, E. M., & Ashby, F. G. (2001). The effects of concurrent task interference on category learning: evidence for multiple category learning systems. *Psychonomic Bulletin and Review, 8*, 168–176.

Wattenmaker, W. D. (1995). Knowledge structures and linear separability – integrating information in object and social categorization. *Cognitive Psychology, 28*, 274–328.

Welk, D. S. (2002). Designing clinical examples to promote pattern recognition: nursing education-based research and practical applications. *Journal of Nursing Education, 41*, 53–60.

Williams, D. A., & Braker, D. S. (1999). Influence of past experience on the coding of compound stimuli. *Journal of Experimental Psychology: Animal Behavior Processes, 25*, 461–474.

Wills, A. J., Reimers, S., Stewart, N., Suret, M., & McLaren, I. P. (2000). Tests of the ratio rule in categorization. *Quarterly Journal of Experimental Psychology, 53A*, 983–1011.

Wittgenstein, L. (1953). *Philisophical investigations*. New York: Macmillan.

Yamauchi, T., & Markman, A. B. (2000a). Inference using categories. *Journal of Experimental Psychology: Learning, Memory, and Cognition, 26*, 776–795.

Yamauchi, T., & Markman, A. B. (2000b). Learning categories composed of varying instances: the effect of classification, inference, and structural alignment. *Memory and Cognition, 28*, 64–78.

Young, M. E., Wasserman, E. A., Johnson, J. L., & Jones, F. L. (2000). Positive and negative patterning in human causal learning. *Quarterly Journal of Experimental Psychology, 53B*, 121–138.

8

Implicit Learning

D A V I D   R .   S H A N K S

Implicit learning is generally characterized as learning that proceeds both unintentionally and unconsciously. Here are some examples:

1   Reber (1967), who coined the term 'implicit learning', asked participants to study a series of letter strings such as VXVS for a few seconds each. Then he told them that these strings were all constructed according to a particular set of rules (that is, a grammar; see Figure 8.1) and that in the test phase they would see some new strings and would have to decide which ones conformed to the same rules and which ones did not. Participants could make these decisions with better-than-chance accuracy but had little ability to describe the rules. For example, participants could not recall correctly which letters began and ended the strings. Reber described his results as a 'peculiar combination of highly efficient behavior with complex stimuli and almost complete lack of verbalizable knowledge about them' (p. 859).
2   In the 1950s, a number of studies asked people to generate words ad libitum and established that the probability with which they would produce, say, plural nouns was increased if each such word was reinforced by the experimenter saying 'umhmm' (e.g. Greenspoon, 1955). This result occurred in subjects apparently unable to report the reinforcement contingency.
3   Svartdal (1991) presented participants with brief trains of between 4 and 17 auditory clicks. Participants immediately had to press a response button exactly the same number of times and were instructed that feedback would be presented when the number of presses matched the number of clicks. In fact, though, feedback was contingent on speed of responding: for some

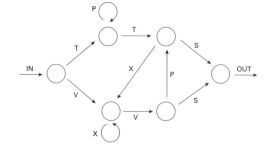

Figure 8.1   *The artificial grammar used by Reber (1967) to generate strings. Strings such as VXVS can be constructed by following a path through the grammar from the starting node at the left to the end note at the right picking up letters on the way. Other strings, such as TXSP, cannot be generated as there is no path that yields this sequence of letters.*

subjects, feedback was given when response speed was slower than in a baseline phase, while for others it was given when speed was faster. Svartdal obtained evidence of learning, in that speed adjusted appropriately to the reinforcement contingencies. But subjects seemed to be unaware that it was speed of responding that was important and believed instead that feedback depended, as the instructions had implied, on the number of responses. A structured questionnaire revealed no evidence of awareness of the contingency between response speed and feedback in subjects whose response rate had adjusted appropriately.

4 Clark and Squire (1998) reported that people can acquire conditioned eyeblink responses even when unaware of the relationship between the conditioned stimulus (CS) and the unconditioned stimulus (US). In their procedure one CS, say a tone, predicted a puff of air to the eye while another, say a white noise, did not. Participants watched a silent movie while the conditioning trials were presented. Conditioning was indexed as a relative increase in the likelihood of making a preparatory eyeblink response to the tone compared to the white noise. Clark and Squire reported equivalent conditioning under some circumstances in participants who could report the stimulus contingencies as in those who could not.

5 Karni (1996) describes experiments in which participants learned an extremely low-level texture discrimination skill. On each of many training trials a display was presented in which some lines were oriented differently from the rest and participants tried to judge whether these target lines were above or adjacent to each other. The display was masked after a varying, brief, interval. Initially, participants required the mask to be delayed by about 140 ms in order to make these judgments, but after several daily training sessions this was reduced to approximately 40 ms, a remarkable speed-up in a visual discrimination skill which, one might assume, is already massively overlearned. As Karni notes (p. 41), 'one would have expected that during the course of normal development, indeed as a result of everyday experience, this task would be perfected to the limit'. Another surprising finding is that this skill is highly specific: for instance, it was very local in a retinotopic sense. If the target appeared only a small distance away from a previously trained visual field location, little benefit of training was observed. Although Karni does not report his participants' insight into their learning, it seems extremely unlikely that they were aware of this specificity.

6 Nisbett and Wilson (1977) asked passers-by to examine four identical pairs of nylon stockings and to say which was the best quality and why. In Nisbett and Wilson's own words: 'There was a pronounced left-to-right position effect, such that the right-most object in the array was heavily over-chosen … with the right-most stockings being preferred over the left-most by a factor of almost four to one. When asked about the reasons for their choices, no subject ever mentioned spontaneously the position of the article in the array. And, when asked directly about a possible effect of the position of the article, virtually all subjects denied it, usually with a worried glance at the interviewer suggesting that they felt either that they had misunderstood the question or were dealing with a madman'

(pp. 243–4). They seem to have learned a position bias that affected their choice behavior unconsciously.

7 A densely amnesic individual, E.P., was asked to study a list of words for 3 seconds each (Hamann & Squire, 1997). Five minutes later a memory test was given in which E.P. was shown the words he had just seen randomly intermixed with some new words and he had to recognize the ones he had studied. He performed at chance (50% correct) on this test, which is characteristic of amnesic individuals: damage to the medial temporal lobe, especially the hippocampus, renders performance on standard memory tests such as recall and recognition very difficult. In another test, however, E.P.'s performance was entirely different and suggested perfectly normal memory. Again he first studied a list of words but in this case after 5 minutes he was given a perceptual identification test. On this task, words that were studied previously and new words were presented one at a time extremely briefly (i.e. for less than a tenth of a second) on the display and E.P.'s task was simply to identify them aloud. *Priming* is demonstrated if the percentage of studied words identified correctly is greater than the percentage of unstudied words identified correctly. E.P. showed completely normal priming. Thus it appears that he had learned the words presented in the study phase, but they were not represented in a form that allowed conscious access in the recognition test. They were in a form that did allow access on the priming test, however.

8 In a variant of Reber's artificial grammar learning experiment, Dienes and Altmann (1997) asked participants to study letter strings generated from a grammar and then asked them to judge whether new strings conformed or not to the same rules. The novel aspect of the task was that participants had to report how confident they were in each of these decisions using a scale from 'complete guess' to 'completely confident'. Dienes and Altmann found that participants performed with better-than-chance accuracy in judging the well-formedness of test strings even on those trials where they claimed to be purely guessing. They plainly had learned something about the rules governing stimulus structure but were unaware of their own ability to apply this knowledge to new cases.

9 In the serial reaction time (SRT) task, which, together with Reber's grammar, learning procedure has become a paradigmatic method of studying implicit learning, a target such as a dot appears in one of several possible locations on a computer display and the participant presses as fast as possible a response key assigned to that location. Instead of appearing at random across a series of trials, however, the target follows a

predictable or partially predictable sequence of locations. Learning is measured chronometrically by changing the sequence after a number of training blocks; an increase in reaction time (RT) on the transfer sequence is evidence that participants learned something about the training sequence and were using their knowledge to anticipate the target location on each trial, thus achieving rapid RTs. This learning, however, generally is not consciously available. For instance, Destrebecqz and Cleeremans (2001) asked participants to 'report' their conscious knowledge of the sequence by pressing keys in a way that reproduced the sequence and found that under some circumstances they were unable to do this.

What do these examples have in common? First, they involve situations in which the primary task the person engages in is something other than deliberately, explicitly, trying to learn about the contingencies programmed by the experimenter. For instance, in Reber's artificial grammar learning (AGL) task, all that participants are told in the learning phase is that they should try to memorize a series of letter strings. They are not told to try to work out the rules governing the structure of these strings. Hence any evidence that they have indeed learned these rules would suggest that learning was incidental or unintentional. This focus on unintentional learning has been quite important in the historical development of research on learning and memory as it came against a background in which research on explicit, deliberative learning was dominant. When Reber began his studies in the 1960s, most ideas about learning were rooted in notions of explicit hypothesis-testing (e.g. Bruner, Goodnow, & Austin, 1956; Hunt, Marin, & Stone, 1966).

Secondly, the examples have in common the implication that learning can be dissociated from awareness. Participants were shown in these situations to have learned something – to have their behavior controlled by a variable – of which they were apparently unaware. In most of the cases awareness is assumed to be synonymous with 'verbally reportable'. This is not the only method by which awareness might be gauged, though. In example 7, awareness was measured by means of a recognition test on the assumption that such a test requires conscious access to stored information.

Research on implicit learning has become a major topic in the landscape of experimental psychology in the last few years. For example, in the 1980s there were only 15 journal articles with this term in their title or abstract (according to the combined Science and Social Sciences Citation Indexes), but this number jumped to 253 during the 1990s. Moreover, the implicit/explicit learning distinction is largely synonymous with other terms such as procedural/declarative (Cohen & Squire, 1980),

which have themselves generated sizable research literatures. The procedural/declarative distinction has been especially influential in neuroscience and is discussed in more depth by Knowlton in the present volume (see Chapter 16). Implicit learning has been extensively reviewed in books by Reber (1993), Berry and Dienes (1993), Cleeremans (1993), Stadler and Frensch (1998), and French and Cleeremans (2002).

In this chapter I consider whether examples such as these do genuinely establish the existence of a form of learning that is both unintentional and unconscious. A variety of issues, both conceptual and methodological, have emerged in the evaluation of this area and have led to some debate about the conclusions that are licensed by demonstrations such as those given above. Another issue I consider is whether implicit and explicit learning should be thought of as separate and independent mechanisms or as different manifestations of a common underlying learning system. I also briefly consider some of the computational mechanisms that have been explored as accounts of the basic processes underlying implicit learning.

UNINTENTIONAL AND AUTOMATIC LEARNING

There can be little dispute that learning is possible even under conditions of reduced attention. Numerous studies demonstrate that people can become sensitive to informational structure even when they are not deliberately trying to learn that structure and when they are engaging in other simultaneous mental activities. For example, Shanks and Johnstone (1999) required a group of participants to perform the SRT task described above (example 9) in combination with a tone-counting task for 14 blocks of trials each comprising 8 cycles of a 12-location repeating sequence. For the secondary tone-counting task, the computer generated a tone after each correct target location response that was randomly determined to be either low or high and participants were instructed to count the number of high tones emitted during each block of trials. At the end of each block, participants were asked to provide their count and feedback presented at the end of the block encouraged them to count the tones accurately (participants were excluded from the analysis if they made more than 10% errors on average). When the underlying sequence was changed on block 15, RTs increased significantly, suggesting that the sequential structure had been learned in the preceding blocks. This seems to be a good case of unintentional learning in that (a) participants were not told anything about possible sequential regularities in the target movements and (b) they were occupied with a demanding secondary task.

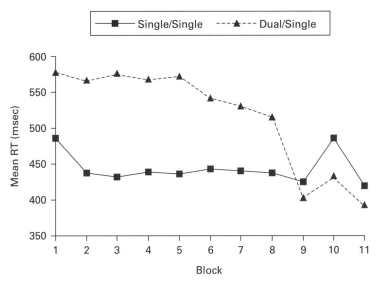

Figure 8.2 *Mean reaction times across blocks of trials in Shanks and Channon's (2002)
experiment 2. Group Single/Single performed an SRT speeded target-detection task under
single-task conditions in blocks 1–8 while group Dual/Single performed under dual-task conditions
on these blocks. On blocks 9–11 both groups performed under single-task conditions. It can be seen
that on block 9 RTs in group Dual/Single fell to those of group Single/Single with the removal of the
secondary task. On block 10, the transfer block, the sequence was changed. This led to an increase
in RTs in both groups but the effect was much bigger in group Single/Single suggesting they had
learned the original sequence better than participants trained with a concurrent secondary task.
On block 11 the original sequence was reinstated and RTs fell to their level on block 9.*

However, the finding that reductions in attention to an environment do not abolish learning does not tell us about two slightly different but perhaps more pertinent questions: (1) are there learning tasks in which reductions in attentional allocation have *no* detectable impact on learning? and (2) are there situations in which completely unattended information can still induce learning? The answers to these questions are somewhat less clear. Data obtained by Shanks and Channon (2002) reveal that divided attention does have a detrimental effect on sequence learning even if it does not abolish it. The disruption caused by introducing a transfer sequence was not as great in a dual-task group as in one that had performed the SRT task without the secondary tone-counting task (see Figure 8.2). Moreover, the fact that learning occurred in the dual-task group in Shanks and Johnstone's study does not answer the second question as we cannot be sure (and it is rather unlikely) that the tone-counting task was so taxing as to leave no attentional capacity for sequence learning. Thus the data do not answer these central questions.

I shall not attempt to review all of the relevant literature here (Goschke, 1997, provides an extensive review), but shall instead present a few examples of representative findings.[1] With regard to the first question, many studies have asked whether sequence learning in the SRT task (see example 9 above) is affected by concurrent secondary tasks that can be assumed to reduce participants' ability to intentionally learn the relevant sequence. Although tone-counting does appear to have an effect, other tasks do not. For example, Heuer and Schmidtke (1996) pointed out that the tone-counting task has two components, memorizing the current number of tones and classifying each tone as high or low. They therefore tried to tease these components apart. They found that sequence learning in the SRT task was completely unaffected by two secondary tasks (the verbal and visuo-spatial tasks of Brooks, 1967) that impose a memory load without additional stimulus processing, whereas it was affected by a task (pressing a foot pedal in response to a high-pitched but not a low-pitched tone) requiring stimulus processing without a memory load. On the assumption that the Brooks secondary tasks were to some degree attention-demanding, Heuer and Schmidtke's data represent quite strong evidence that sequence learning in the SRT task does not require central attentional resources: so long as an appropriate secondary task is used (i.e. one that does not require stimulus processing in the response–stimulus interval of the main task), no interference of sequence learning will be observed.

Pointing to the same conclusion, Jiménez and Méndez (1999) used a probabilistic sequence learning task in which the target stimulus could be one of four symbols; as well as reacting to the location of each target, dual-task participants had to count the frequency of two of the symbols. This secondary task had no detectable effect on sequence learning. Jiménez and Méndez speculated that the use of a probabilistic sequence was critical in their study for revealing a form of learning that is independent of attention. It is interesting that this secondary task did require stimulus processing to identify each symbol and therefore, on Heuer and Schmidtke's account, would have been expected to be disruptive. However, the obvious difference is that a task like tone-counting requires processing of stimuli that are irrelevant and additional to the primary task, whereas in Jiménez and Méndez's procedure the processing required by the secondary task (symbol counting) concerned stimuli that had to be processed anyway in the service of the primary target-detection task.

There is, hence, some evidence to support the claim that reductions in attentional capacity can be incurred without detectable cost on implicit learning and this plainly supports the idea that the latter is, to some extent, unintentional and automatic.

Another way to address the question of whether implicit learning is genuinely unintentional is to arrange a situation in which the experimental instructions require an individual to behave in a certain way but where implicitly acquired knowledge might cause them to behave in precisely the opposite way. For instance, my golf coach might explain to me how I should swing my golf club in a particular way and I might fully intend to do this but nevertheless find myself swinging in my old habitual manner instead. An ingrained habit seems to be able, in situations like this, to control my behavior even when it runs counter to my conscious intentions. A recent laboratory study by Destrebecqz and Cleeremans (2001) provides a nice example. These authors trained participants on a 4-choice SRT task in which the target again moved according to a repeating 12-element sequence. The learning phase consisted of 15 blocks of 96 trials for a total of 1440 trials. For half the participants there was a response–stimulus interval (RSI) of 250 ms between the execution of one response and the appearance of the next target while for the remainder the RSI was 0 ms. RTs reduced somewhat across blocks 1–12 in both groups. Then on block 13 the sequence was changed with the original sequence being reintroduced on blocks 14 and 15. Destrebecqz and Cleeremans found that RTs were significantly greater in the transfer block (block 13) and concluded that their participants had learned something about the sequence.

To ascertain whether this sequence knowledge was dependent or independent of intention, Destrebecqz and Cleeremans presented two tests following block 15. First, they informed participants that there had been a repeating sequence and asked them to generate a sequence of keypresses under both 'inclusion' and 'exclusion' conditions following the logic of opposition developed in the process dissociation procedure (Jacoby, Toth, & Yonelinas, 1993). In the inclusion test participants were to try to reproduce the sequence they saw in training while in the exclusion test they were to *avoid* reproducing the training sequence or any of its parts. The key finding was that, at least for participants in the RSI = 0 ms group, the sequence generated under exclusion conditions contained more chunks from the training sequence than would be expected by chance. Thus participants' sequence knowledge, Destrebecqz and Cleeremans argued, was divorced from intention in the sense that they could not exert voluntary control over it when explicitly required to exclude it in generating a sequence.

What about the second question above, whether completely unattended information can still induce learning? This issue raises some tricky methodological problems. For instance, it is hard to arrange for a stream of information to be unattended for any sustained period. This has become apparent in re-evaluations of two apparently clear examples of implicit learning. Miller (1987) used the famous 'flanker' task to argue that unattended information can influence performance. In Miller's version of this task, participants saw a brief display of three letters, a central target and two flankers that were to be ignored. A display thus might be [V J V]. The participant's task was to identify the target and make an appropriate keypress. Miller arranged for the identity of the flankers to be correlated with the target such that specific flankers co-occurred regularly with targets requiring a specific response. For example, on 80% of occasions (valid trials) on which the flankers were the letter V, the target was one (such as J) that required a right-finger response. On the remaining 20% of trials (invalid), V was paired with a target requiring a left-finger response. Although the flankers were supposedly ignored, Miller found that RTs were reliably shorter on valid than invalid trials and interpreted this as evidence of automatic and inattentional processing of the flankers combined with implicit learning of the flanker–target correlations. Miller's evidence that the flankers were not attended was supported by the finding that participants could not subsequently recall the flankers, but this result was later questioned by Schmidt and Dark (1998), who were unable to replicate the chance-level recall reported by Miller. Instead, they found very high levels of flanker recall and concluded that there was a failure of selective attention at some point during processing such that the flankers did receive attentional processing which in turn led to the formation of recallable memory traces.

In another much-cited study, Eich (1984) reported that participants picked up information about words presented in an unattended stream in a dichotic listening task. While shadowing a prose stream in the attended ear, word pairs that included a descriptor and a homophone, such as TAXI–FARE, were presented to the non-attended ear. Subsequently, participants (who performed at chance in a recognition test for the unattended words) were given a spelling test that included the homophones and were found to be more likely to spell them in their low-frequency form (i.e. FARE rather than FAIR) than would otherwise be expected. Eich concluded that unattended word pairs had been implicitly encoded and caused subsequent priming in the spelling test. This conclusion was challenged by Wood, Stadler, and Cowan (1997), however, who pointed out that the prose passage in the attended channel was presented by Eich at a very slow rate that would have made shadowing rather easy and hence might have allowed occasional shifts of attention to the unattended steam. To test this, Wood et al. replicated Eich's experiment but varied the presentation rate of the attended information. Under faster rates, which would be expected to reduce or eliminate shifts of attention, the critical homophone spelling bias was eliminated.

Overall, research on the possibility of unintended learning for unattended information is rather contradictory, with some well-studied lines of research, such as those on flanker effects and dichotic listening, being rather negative and others, for instance on the serial reaction time task (Destrebecqz & Cleeremans, 2001; Heuer & Schmidtke, 1996; Jiménez & Méndez, 1999), being rather more encouraging. Plainly, further research is needed to reconcile these conflicting findings and to delineate precisely the conditions (if any) in which learning can be divorced from intention and attention.

AWARENESS AND IMPLICIT LEARNING

The case for implicit learning being unconscious depends crucially on the validity of the tests used to index awareness. A common distinction is drawn between 'subjective' and 'objective' tests, where the former ask the participant to report his or her state of awareness while the latter demand some forced-choice discrimination.

Verbalization

With regard to the former, there is absolutely no doubt that participants' verbal reports in implicit learning experiments often fail to incorporate all of the information that can otherwise be detected in their behavior, as many of the examples given at the beginning of the chapter illustrate. However, although such results establish that in at least one sense learning can be implicit, they may have a rather mundane explanation. Researchers who have considered the properties of tests of awareness (e.g. Reingold & Merikle, 1990; Shanks & St John, 1994) have pointed out (at least) two criteria that an adequate test of awareness must satisfy. First, it must be 'exhaustive', which means that the test must be sensitive to all of the conscious knowledge the participant is in possession of. Secondly, it must measure the same stored knowledge that is actually controlling behavior in the implicit measure (Shanks & St John called this the 'information' criterion; much earlier, Dulany, 1961, made the same point under the label 'correlated hypotheses'). The exhaustiveness criterion is a problem for subjective tests of awareness because there is little to guarantee in such tests that the participant has indeed reported all available knowledge. For example, he or she may simply choose to withhold conscious knowledge held with low confidence. If that happens, then an implicit behavioral measure may dissociate from a subjective measure such as verbal report simply because the former is more sensitive to conscious knowledge. To avoid this problem, it would be necessary for the experimenter to induce and motivate the participant to report all relevant knowledge, including hunches and so on. This has not often been attempted. One way of achieving it is to force the participant to report a given number of pieces of information, a procedure that, when compared to unforced recall, can significantly improve performance (e.g. Schmidt & Dark, 1998). Moreover, some studies that have probed quite thoroughly for all available verbalizable knowledge have even ended up finding that *all* knowledge is accessible for report (e.g. Marescaux, 1997).

Tests of verbal awareness may be unsatisfactory not only because participants are insufficiently motivated to report low-confidence knowledge. There are many other ways in which they might lead to biased results. In case 4 above I described research that appears to demonstrate that classical conditioning may occur in the absence of awareness of the CS–US contingency. Although there has been a huge amount of research pointing to the same conclusion, a recent review (Lovibond & Shanks, 2002) questioned this claim. One of Lovibond and Shanks' main points was that the awareness tests used in studies like that of Clark and Squire (1998) often do not provide fair measures of CS–US contingency awareness. Clark and Squire's method of assessing awareness can be questioned on several grounds. First, the critical questions concerning CS–US contingencies (e.g. tone predicts shock, white noise predicts no shock) did not occur until after 28 other questions concerning other parts of the procedure, such as the silent movie participants watched during the experiment. Clearly this procedure may lead to underclassification of awareness due to forgetting and interference. Secondly, 17 true/false questions were used to classify awareness of the rather simple differential contingency. These questions were highly redundant and confusable, and participants were not able to change earlier answers. Five of the questions referred to the ordering of the two CSs (e.g. 'I believe the static noise and tone were always closely related in time'), which are of questionable relevance to ascertaining participants' knowledge of the CS–US relationships. Finally, the nominally correct answer was 'true' for only 4 of the 17 questions, further encouraging false positive responses. A participant who answered correctly to these four questions would need to resist answering yes to a large number of decoy questions to be classified as aware.

Thus tests of verbally reportable knowledge need to be scrutinized quite carefully to ensure that they do not introduce potential biasing factors. Lovibond and Shanks discuss many additional issues concerned with the measurement of subjective states of awareness. Results from conditioning experiments, although often not considered in the implicit learning literature, are quite striking. Bearing in mind that conditioning represents one of the simplest learning preparations imaginable, Lovibond and Shanks' conclusion – that conditioning does not occur without awareness – would seem to place a very major question mark over the possibility of learning without awareness. Further discussion of this controversial issue can be found in Wiens and Öhman (2002), Manns, Clark, and Squire (2002), and Shanks and Lovibond (2002).

The information criterion

The information criterion is even more problematic for implicit learning studies. To see why this might be the case, consider Reber's artificial grammar learning experiment described in example 1 above. After studying letter strings generated from a grammar, participants performed with better-than-chance accuracy in judging the well-formedness of novel test strings. Figure 8.1 presents an example of a grammar used to generate letter strings. Reber found, and many subsequent studies have confirmed (e.g. Dienes, Broadbent, & Berry, 1991), that participants have great difficulty reporting the rules used to generate the strings (e.g. 'an initial T can be followed by any number of consecutive P's'). Let us assume that the elicitation of verbally reportable rules is exhaustive. Even so, the result only demonstrates unconscious learning if participants' ability to judge well-formedness is based on (implicit) knowledge of those rules. It might indeed be the case that abstract rules can be learned unconsciously – Reber has been quite persistent and forceful in

defending this claim. For instance, Manza and Reber (1997: 75) wrote that

This position is based on the argument that the complex knowledge acquired during an AG learning task is represented in a general, abstract form. The representation is assumed to contain little, if any, information pertaining to specific stimulus features; the emphasis is on structural relationships among stimuli. The key here is the notion that the mental content consists, not of the representation of specific physical forms, but of abstract representations of those forms.

However, it might equally be the case that well-formedness decisions are based on processes that have nothing to do with rule knowledge. There is now abundant evidence that the latter provides a more perspicuous way of understanding behavior in this task. The first compelling evidence for this (though see Dulany, Carlson, & Dewey, 1984) came from a study by Perruchet and Pacteau (1990), who suggested that the only thing participants needed to learn in order to be able to make grammaticality decisions was the set of acceptable letter *pairs* (bigrams) that the grammar allows. They found that test performance was just as good in a group of participants who had only been trained on grammatical pairs of letters (e.g. TP) in the study phase as in participants who had seen complete strings. But if it is only knowledge of letter *pairs* that is responsible for performance, then it is mistaken to ask participants to report more complex rules. In fact, if participants are asked which bigrams are familiar, they are very accurate at doing this. In a further experiment, Perruchet and Pacteau trained participants on whole strings and then presented letter pairs in the test phase and asked participants to judge on a scale from 1 to 6 whether or not each pair had appeared in the training strings. The overall correlation between these judgments and the actual frequency of each letter pair was 0.61.

Thus the alternative to the rule-induction view of Reber is that participants merely focus on and learn about small letter chunks. In the test stage they endorse (i.e. call grammatical) any item composed mainly of familiar letter pairs. Two predictions that follow from this have been confirmed. First, if grammaticality and bigram familiarity are unconfounded in the test stage, it is familiarity rather than grammaticality that should control performance. Several experiments have tested this claim. Kinder and Assmann (2000) and Johnstone and Shanks (2001) examined it in artificial grammar experiments in which test items were either grammatical or ungrammatical, and orthogonally were made either of familiar or unfamiliar bigrams. Under these conditions, participants showed no tendency to endorse grammatical items more than ungrammatical ones; instead, they tended to call items grammatical if they were composed of familiar

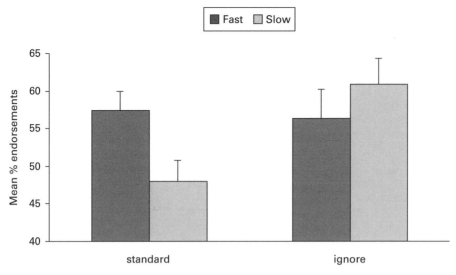

Figure 8.3   *Data from an AGL experiment by Kinder et al. (2003). Participants studied strings of letters generated from a grammar. In the test phase, they judged whether new strings were grammatical or ungrammatical. The test strings were initially masked by visual noise but gradually clarified with 'fast' strings coming into view slightly more rapidly than 'slow' ones. The data on the left reveal that speed affected the probability of calling a string 'grammatical', consistent with a fluency account. The data on the right reveal that the effect was eliminated in participants instructed to ignore differences in speed of clarification.*

bigrams, regardless of their grammaticality. These results suggest that Reber's initial results were an artifact caused by the fact that his grammatical test items tended to be made of familiar bigrams while his ungrammatical items tended to be made of unfamiliar ones.

The second prediction is that it should be possible to trick participants into calling strings grammatical by making them feel more familiar. Kinder, Shanks, Cock, and Tunney (2003) succeeded in doing this via a small modification of the standard procedure. Participants initially studied strings of letters generated from a grammar. In the test phase, letter strings appeared (they were in fact all new grammatical strings) and participants decided whether each string was grammatical or ungrammatical. The strings were presented in a slightly unusual way on the computer display whereby they were initially masked by visual noise but gradually clarified (this is called 'perceptual clarification') over a period of a few seconds. Critically, some strings came into view slightly faster than others. After the string had clarified, the participant judged whether or not it was grammatical. The prediction was that the strings that clarified faster would be read slightly more fluently than the others. This should then have tricked the participants into increasing the likelihood of calling these strings grammatical, regardless of whether they were or not.

The results (see the left-hand side of Figure 8.3) confirmed this prediction: a small but reliable increase in the probability of calling a string 'grammatical' occurred for the faster-clarifying strings, consistent with the view that fluency is an important cue to grammaticality decisions. Moreover, this 'fluency' effect was intentional in the sense that participants instructed to ignore differences in speed of clarification did not show the effect (see the right-hand side of Figure 8.3).

In summary, there is now a good deal of support for the idea that grammaticality decisions in these experiments are based on a mechanism that simply accumulates information about small-scale chunks and that uses this information to generate a feeling of familiarity; if this feeling is sufficiently strong, the string is called 'grammatical'. A number of connectionist models of grammar learning (Dienes, 1992; Kinder & Shanks, 2001) flesh out this approach in much greater deal.

Transfer

To be fair to Reber, there is another piece of evidence that seems to support his claim that rule knowledge governs performance in grammar learning experiments. This is the finding from 'transfer' tests that when participants memorize items from one letter-set or modality, they can successfully classify test items presented in a different letter-set or modality (e.g. Altmann, Dienes, & Goode, 1995). The only common factor between training and test items is their underlying abstract structure. For example, Altmann et al. (1995) trained one group of participants on standard letter strings and a second group on sequences of tones, with both the letter strings and tone sequences conforming to the same rule structure. Thus each letter string had an equivalent tone sequence in which, for instance, the letter M was translated into a tone at the frequency of middle C. In the test phase, participants classified strings presented in the same modality as their training strings (letters/letters or tones/tones) or in the opposite modality (letters/tones or tones/letters). There were two types of control groups who either received no training or who were trained on randomly generated sequences. The results suggested that prior exposure to the grammar led to accurate classification performance (same modality 56% correct, changed modality 54% correct), whereas control groups performed at chance (50%).

Although this experiment appears to provide evidence that changed modality groups used general, abstract, rule knowledge that goes beyond perceptual features, Redington and Chater (1996) demonstrated that participants could have used surface fragments of two or three letters to perform abstraction at test. Moreover, Gomez (1997) and Tunney and Shanks (2003) have presented strong evidence that such transfer is always accompanied by explicit knowledge: participants who achieved above-chance transfer scores also scored above-chance on tests of awareness in these experiments. Thus there is little evidence at present that transfer is mediated by implicit, abstract knowledge.

On the other hand, Marcus, Vijayan, Bandi Rao, and Vishton (1999) observed transfer in seven-month-old infants and it seems unlikely that they were aware of the rule structure of the materials presented to them. In this study, the infants were familiarized for 2 minutes to sequences of syllables (e.g. 'de-de-li') generated by a grammar and were then found to be able to discriminate in a habituation test between grammatical and ungrammatical syllable sequences even when they used different syllables. Thus if the grammar generated AAB sequences like the one above, the infants listened less to another AAB item like 'ba-ba-po' than to a more surprising sequence like ABB ('ba-po-po'). Marcus et al. (1999: 79) drew the following conclusion, very similar to Manza and Reber's:

We propose that a system that could account for our results is one in which infants extract abstract algebra-like rules that represent relationships between placeholders (variables), such as 'the first item X is the same as the third item Y', or more generally, that 'item I is the same as item J'.

Marcus et al. drew the intuitive conclusion that discriminating between test sequences that bear no surface similarity to the study sequences must rely on knowledge of 'deep' structure and assumed that only 'algebra'-like rules could allow this to be achieved. The study, however, provoked an avalanche of criticism from researchers proposing ways – generally based on connectionist networks – in which the infants' behavior could be explained without reference to structured rules but rather in terms of statistical learning (Altmann, 2002; Altmann & Dienes, 1999; Christiansen, Conway, & Curtin, 2000; Christiansen & Curtin, 1999; McClelland & Plaut, 1999; Seidenberg & Elman, 1999; Sirois, Buckingham, & Shultz, 2000) (many of these are published alongside responses from Marcus). If Marcus et al. had presented compelling evidence for rule-learning in infants, then it would surely follow that adults too can acquire rules under similar conditions (e.g. in the artificial grammar learning task). And if adult learning in AGL experiments is partly dependent on rules, then the pervasive inability to articulate such rules would constitute powerful evidence for implicit learning. It would be rash to say that this debate has been settled one way or the other, but it is clear that the results of Marcus et al. are nothing like as convincing as originally thought, and hence have less clear implications for the implicit learning debate.

In a nutshell, performance in AGL experiments appears to be fully explained without the need to impute unconscious rule-learning; that being the case, participants' inability to verbally report the rules of the grammar is neither here nor there and certainly does not establish that learning was implicit or unconscious. By generalization, this problem with the information criterion undermines quite a few apparent examples of implicit learning. Consider Greenspoon's (case 2 above) demonstration that people can be shaped to produce plural nouns if each such word is reinforced by the experimenter saying 'umhmm'. In an elegant deconstruction of this study, Dulany (1961) proved that subjects were hypothesizing that reinforcement was contingent on generating a word in the same semantic category as the previous word. Although incorrect, this hypothesis was 'correlated' with the true one, in that if the person said 'emeralds' and was reinforced, then staying in the same semantic category meant they were more likely to produce another plural noun ('rubies') than if they shifted categories. Thus Dulany conjectured that participants (including Greenspoon) in this experimental setting are perfectly aware of the contingency controlling their behavior, namely the contingency between staying in the same semantic category and reinforcement. They only appear to be unaware because the experimenter is looking for the wrong sort of belief.

Despite these caveats about the relationship between verbalization and learning, the belief that knowledge cannot always be verbally accessed has very powerful intuitive appeal. Probably the most persuasive evidence comes not from published research but from introspection, as there is nothing so powerful than our intuitions about our own cognitive processes. For instance, my own behavior in an SRT task is, introspectively, accompanied by almost no ability to verbalize my knowledge. In one version of this task that I perform frequently in the course of preparing experimental software, I react to a target across several blocks of trials in which a noisy sequence is used. Again there is a 12-element repeating sequence governing target locations. Instead of following a fixed sequence, each target appears according to the sequence with a probability of only 0.85. With probability 0.15, it appears in a location that violates the sequence (the precise details of the method can be found in Schvaneveldt & Gomez, 1998). Because of this noise in the sequence, it is particularly difficult to verbally describe the sequence. However, my RTs are much faster to predictable targets than to unpredictable ones, implying that I 'know' the sequence. But trying to articulate my knowledge, even only moments after performing the task, seems to require a Herculean effort of mental will that yields only the sketchiest useful information. This cannot be attributed to a problem meeting the information criterion as there is no dispute that it is knowledge of the sequential dependences between the target locations that controls my RTs and that I am tying to access for verbalization.

But is such a finding really that surprising? I believe not. As long ago as the 1960s, memory researchers were aware of the possibility that information might be stored in explicit memory but not accessible in a given test. Tulving's distinction between accessibility and availability, with the latter referring to the potential for information to be retrieved under suitable retrieval conditions, precisely captures this idea, and considerable evidence was accumulated showing that information inaccessible in free recall can become available in appropriately cued recall (Tulving, 1983: 201–5; Tulving & Pearlstone, 1966). Thus implicit knowledge may not be any different from explicit knowledge in this regard. Perhaps it is a property of all knowledge – explicit, implicit, motor skills, and so on – that it can be inaccessible without being unavailable, and perhaps the retrieval cues provided by an implicit test serve exactly the same function as the sorts of cues used by Tulving in his classic explicit memory experiments. For instance, in performing the SRT task, sequence knowledge is accessed in the context of a dynamic task presenting certain visual (boxes on the display) as well as temporal cues (the immediately preceding target and response) for eliciting sequence knowledge, none of which is present in a later test of verbal sequence recall.

In this rather weak sense at least, no one can doubt the reality of implicit learning: knowledge can be inaccessible to free verbal recall. It could, of course, be argued that the cuing effect is due to a contribution of implicit processes in cued recall over and above those that contribute to free recall (Jacoby et al., 1993). However, logic requires that the improvement of access with retrieval cues cannot both be *explained* by implicit influences and be used to *justify* the existence of such influences, nor can inaccessibility to verbal introspection and access be taken as evidence for implicit learning if such inaccessibility is also a property of explicit learning. To obtain independent evidence of implicit learning, we therefore need to look elsewhere.

Objective tests

As a reaction to these problems with evaluating the outcomes of subjective tests of awareness, attention has turned to objective tests and it has been widely accepted that such tests avoid some of the problems with subjective tests and possibly provide the best measures of awareness. An example of such a test was given in case 7 above, where awareness was assessed via a recognition test. That example concerns an individual with brain damage leading to amnesia, but there now exist a good number of cases where normal individuals can be shown to have acquired some information that influences their behavior in a certain context but where that information is insufficient to support recognition, cued recall or some other objective test. If we do not accept the implicit/explicit distinction, if in our experiments we avoid problems associated with the information criterion, and if we interpret all failures of verbalization as problems of accessibility, then we would predict that sensitive tests such as recognition would not produce results that dissociate from implicit measures. Therefore the existence of such dissociations should provide particularly strong evidence for implicit learning.

A striking example of the way in which knowledge may be inaccessible on a recognition test but accessible on an almost identical implicit test is seen in studies of the 'mere-exposure effect'. In this procedure, stimuli such as geometrical figures are initially presented briefly (e.g. for 1 second). In a later test a pair of figures is shown side by side for an unlimited period, one being a previously seen one and the other being novel. Participants are either asked to select the old stimulus (i.e. recognition) or to make some judgment that does not refer to the previous exposure stage. For instance, in Kunst-Wilson and Zajonc's (1980) classic study participants made liking judgments. The striking result is that while objective recognition was almost impossible (participants were at chance), they were much more likely to choose the old than the new stimulus if making a liking judgment. This suggests that information can be available on an implicit test but not on a matched objective test of awareness. Presumably the old stimuli were processed slightly more fluently than the new ones as a result of priming, and under implicit test instructions participants inadvertently attributed this fluency to the pleasantness of the stimuli.

It has to be said that experimental reports of chance-level recognition in implicit learning experiments have not always proved easy to replicate. For example, Reed and Johnson (1994) reported chance-level recognition in an SRT experiment, but Shanks and Johnstone (1999), in a replication, found very high levels of recognition under identical circumstances. It is not difficult to imagine, for example, that a participant might find a recognition memory test quite difficult and hence resort to guessing on each trial, thus generating performance no better than chance. Good experimental practice is to reward participants according to their performance in such tests to motivate them to perform at their best. The only reason Shanks and Johnstone were able to offer for the different results they obtained was that they provided performance-related payoffs whereas Reed and Johnson did not.

Nevertheless, it seems unlikely that this would account for all examples of null recognition (indeed the Kunst-Wilson and Zajonc finding has been replicated many times, e.g. Seamon et al., 1995). Do such findings unequivocally point to the existence of an implicit learning mechanism? It is probably too early to say, but there are possible ways in which such a result might be explained without the need to posit a mechanism of this sort. Whittlesea and Price (2001) have suggested that a better account is that participants adopt different strategies for using the same memory representations in the two tests. This account proposes that a fluency-attribution heuristic is only one of a pair of strategies that participants can adopt whereby past experience is deployed in the service of current decisions. This heuristic, which might be used to explain participants' greater liking for the old member of each pair, is 'non-analytic' in the sense that participants are assumed to process a stimulus as a whole rather than analyzing it by its parts. If the whole item engenders a feeling of fluent or coherent processing, then an attribution process is recruited to find a suitable dimension in the environment (e.g. pleasantness) to which that fluent processing can be attributed. The other strategy, by contrast, is 'analytic' and involves examining the parts of which a stimulus is composed to see whether any of them acts as a cue for recalling details of the context in which the item was previously encountered. The assumption is that participants may shift the balance between these strategies and that in so doing the influence of processing fluency on current decisions may change. Critically, however, this distinction cuts across the implicit/explicit distinction. Participants may adopt analytic processing in one version of a test and non-analytic processing in another but without the

task changing in terms of its demands on implicit or explicit memory.

What reason is there to believe that participants may shift their decision strategies in implicit and explicit memory tests? Whittlesea and Price provide one compelling example within the context of the mere-exposure effect. Participants saw a continuous stream of pictures each presented for about 40 ms and in a subsequent test stage were shown pairs of pictures, one being from the study set (i.e. old) and the other being novel. Whittlesea and Price replicated the finding that participants under such circumstances tend to pick the old item when asked to make a preference rating (see Figure 8.4). They also found that when asked instead explicitly to select the old stimulus (i.e. recognition), participants were unable to do so, hence replicating the classic dissociation result of Kunst-Wilson and Zajonc. Whittlesea and Price proposed that participants normally adopted a non-analytic strategy under preference conditions but an analytic strategy under recognition conditions. In the former, participants would choose the item at test that evoked the greatest global feeling of 'goodness' and this would tend to be the true old item whose processing would be subtly more fluent than that of the novel item. In contrast, under recognition conditions participants would study each test item analytically in an attempt to find some discriminating detail diagnostic of a prior encounter with that item. Because the study items were presented so briefly and the test items were so similar to one another, this analytic strategy was doomed to failure.

To test this account, Whittlesea and Price attempted to reverse the mere-exposure effect, observing a tendency for the old stimulus now to be selected under recognition but not preference conditions. They achieved this by implementing two changes: first, in the preference condition participants were required to justify their decisions, which Whittlesea and Price assumed would evoke an analytic strategy; and secondly, in the recognition condition participants were asked to select the stimulus that was globally most similar to a study item, a change of instructions that Whittlesea and Price assumed would encourage non-analytic processing. The results, shown in Figure 8.4, were consistent with these assumptions: old stimuli were now selected with higher probability under recognition than under preference conditions. It is hard to see how an account that proposes that recognition decisions are based on an explicit memory system and preference decisions on an implicit system would explain this crossover effect as the modified instructions did not change the implicit or explicit nature of the tests.

It is far too early to judge whether this account is adequate to explain cases of dissociation between implicit and explicit measures such as those used in the studies described above. Kinder et al. (2003) have obtained some further supporting evidence from

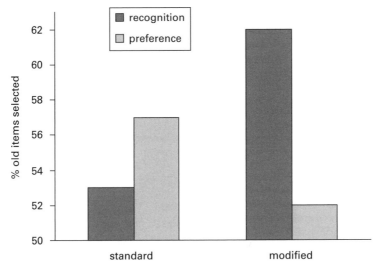

Figure 8.4   *Results from Whittlesea and Price's (2001) experiments. Participants chose between a pair of test pictures according to which one they preferred or which one they recognized. In the standard case the classic result of Kunst-Wilson and Zajonc (1980) was replicated: old items were only selected under (implicit) preference conditions. Chance performance is 50% of old items selected. However, under modified conditions the reverse pattern was obtained, consistent with the analytic/non-analytic account. In the modified recognition condition, participants selected the picture they thought was globally similar to a study picture (a non-analytic decision) and in the modified preference condition they had to justify each choice by pointing to the quadrant of the picture they felt made it pleasant (an analytic decision).*

artificial grammar learning experiments, demonstrating again that participants can apparently be shifted from one strategy to the other, but just as it is important to seek independent evidence for an implicit learning process, so equally is it critical to obtain independent evidence for analytic and non-analytic processes. As yet the major evidence is circumstantial.

DISSOCIATIONS – AN INVENTION OF THE DEVIL

A very common practice in implicit learning research is to administer an implicit learning task followed by a test of explicit knowledge and then to select participants who performed at chance on the explicit test and study their performance on the implicit one (e.g. Baeyens, Eelen, & Van den Bergh, 1990; Burke & Roodenrys, 2000; Clark & Squire, 1998; Frensch, Lin, & Buchner, 1998; Gomez, 1997; Higham, 1997; Rugg et al., 1998; Seger, 1997; Willingham, Greeley, & Bardone, 1993; Willingham, Nissen, & Bullemer, 1989). If implicit test performance is better than chance, then the researcher usually concludes that learning was genuinely implicit, as (at least for this subsample) there was no accompanying explicit knowledge. Putting aside all the previous caveats about suitable indices of awareness, I want in the present section

to highlight some of the extreme dangers of relying on such dissociation results. Many previous papers critical of dissociations have been published (Dunn & Kirsner, 1988; Ostergaard, 1992; Perruchet & Gallego, 1993; Plaut, 1995; Poldrack, 1996; Poldrack, Selco, Field, & Cohen, 1999). The present section aims to add to this largely theoretical literature by providing an extremely simple but concrete illustration of how such dissociations can arise without needing to posit a separate implicit system.

The top panel of Figure 8.5 plots from a study by Shanks and Johnstone (1999; see also Shanks & Perruchet, 2002) and the precise details of the experiment can be found there. For present purposes, it suffices to know that in this experiment we obtained concurrent implicit and explicit measures of sequence knowledge in 79 participants who undertook an SRT experiment. After 17 training blocks of 100 trials of a 4-choice target detection task in which a repeating 12-element sequence was used, a test was administered. Here, there were 12 short old sequences (i.e. from the training sequence) and 12 short new sequences (not from the training sequence), which were randomly intermixed. Each of these items comprised 6 targets and participants executed each of these sequences prior to giving a recognition judgment on a six-point scale from *certain new* (1) to *certain old* (6). We expected, and

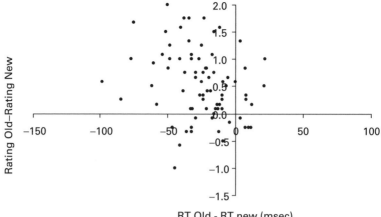

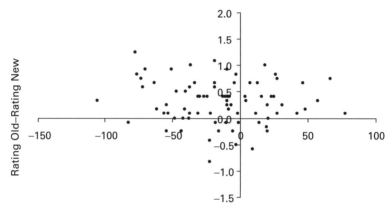

Figure 8.5   *(Top) Each point represents an individual participant in Shanks and Johnstone's (1999) experiment. After training in an SRT task a test was administered that yielded concurrent measures of (implicit) priming on the abscissa and (explicit) recognition on the ordinate. Old and new sequences of 6 targets were presented in a random order. Recognition results are based on the mean difference between ratings to old and new sequences with scores greater than zero reflecting above-chance recognition. Priming results are based on the mean speed of responding to old sequences versus new ones with negative scores reflecting priming (i.e. faster responding to old than new sequences). Both recognition and priming are overall significantly above chance (i.e. the mean across participants lies in the upper left quadrant). However, some participants (lower left quadrant) scored at or below chance in recognition while still showing priming. (Bottom) Results from the model described in the text. As in the experimental data, both recognition and priming are above chance and some simulated participants score at or below chance in recognition while still showing priming.*

found, that old sequences were executed faster than new ones (i.e. priming) to the tune of about 20 ms per target. We also found that participants could to some extent recognize the old sequences: recognition judgments were significantly greater for old than for new sequences (Shanks & Perruchet, 2002).

The important result, though, is that the priming and recognition measures can be dissociated, and Figure 8.5 reveals such a dissociation (Shanks &

Perruchet, 2002, present another one). Participants who performed at or below chance in the recognition test (all points below the horizontal diagonal) nonetheless showed priming. Points to the bottom left of the figure represent individual participants who showed priming but whose average recognition score was zero or less. This group as a whole shows significant priming (most points below the horizontal axis are also to the left of the vertical axis) without being able to recognize chunks of the training sequence.

What can we conclude from such results? I shall argue that any temptation to take these results as evidence for implicit learning is mistaken as they can be reproduced by a simple model that does not incorporate an implicit/explicit distinction.

A model of priming and recognition

The model (Shanks & Perruchet, 2002; Shanks, Wilkinson, & Channon, 2003), which is conceptually very similar to standard signal detection theory models for recognition judgments and their latencies (Pike, 1973; Ratcliff & Murdock, 1976), starts with the simple assumption that new and old test items are associated with a memory strength variable which we will call familiarity f. Greater degrees of familiarity lead to higher recognition judgments and faster RTs, and familiarity can be thought of as some composite but unidimensional function of the perceptual familiarity of the stimulus sequence and the motor fluency of the executed response sequence. In the model, f is a uniformly distributed random variable in the interval [0,0.8] for new items and in the interval [0.2,1] for old items. Thus the mean familiarity of old items, f_{old}, is slightly higher (by 0.2) than the mean for new items, f_{new}. For each participant a single value of familiarity is independently sampled for new and old items from these distributions. Next, we assume that RT is a decreasing function of f but with the addition of some random error:

$$RT_{old} = 200 + 100(1 - f_{old}) + 300e \qquad (8.1)$$
$$RT_{new} = 200 + 100(1 - f_{new}) + 300e \qquad (8.2)$$

where e is uniformly distributed random error in the interval [0,1]. The numbers in these equations are simply chosen to ensure that RTs are generated between a maximum of 600 ms when the familiarity of the test item is zero and a minimum of 200 ms when familiarity is 1. These correspond roughly to observed response times.

Recognition judgments (J) are also based on familiarity, but include another (independent) source of error:

$$J_{old} = 2f_{old} + 3e + 1 \qquad (8.3)$$
$$J_{new} = 2f_{new} + 3e + 1 \qquad (8.4)$$

where e is again uniformly distributed random error in the interval [0,1]. J is rounded to the nearest integer value. These equations generate recognition ratings between a maximum of 6 when the familiarity of the test item approaches 1 and a minimum of 1 when familiarity is 0.

Despite the fact that RTs and recognition judgments depend on the same variable (f) in this model, and depend on nothing else apart from noise, the model nevertheless generates a pattern of data strikingly similar to that shown in the top panel of Figure 8.5. The bottom panel of the figure presents the mean priming and recognition scores based on 79 simulated participants. For each simulated participant, I generated 12 values of f_{old} and 12 values of f_{new} which were then used to produce RTs and ratings according to the above equations. These old and new values were then averaged to yield a single priming/recognition data point for each simulated participant.

On average RTs are faster overall to old than new items (i.e. priming scores tend to be negative) and recognition ratings are generally positive, just as in the experimental data. Overall the pattern of the simulation results, while not perfectly reproducing the experimental data, is fairly similar (Shanks & Perruchet, 2002, describe how this model captures another dissociation evident in this data set). More significantly, though, the model yields a number of data points in which recognition is at or below chance combined with a sizable degree of priming (in the lower left quadrant of the figure). But this is simply an automatic by-product of the fact that in the model the two measures are assumed to be affected by the random variation and measurement error that plague any experimental measure (i.e. the term e in the equations). More specifically, for old and new sequences to be rated equally in recognition, a larger value of e in equation (8.4) compared to equation (8.3) is necessary, on average, to offset the larger average value of f_{old} compared to f_{new}. However, when these same f values are used to determine RTs in equations (8.1) and (8.2), they will be combined with independently generated values of e. Since the latter are uncorrelated with the e values incorporated in the recognition judgments, on average they will not differ for old and new items. Hence, as f_{old} is on average greater than f_{new}, simulated participants in whom recognition ratings for old items are the same as or lower than those for new items will tend to generate RT_{old} values that are lower than RT_{new} values, as observed empirically in the behavior of the selected subset of participants.

There have been many criticisms of conclusions that rely for their support on dissociation evidence. The example I have presented here extends this body of critical work simply by demonstrating how the incorporation of noise into a model can yield dissociations even though a common memory base underlies performance on both the explicit (recognition) and implicit (priming) tests. Noise and measurement error are facts of life and it is important that researchers begin to explore their implications in performance models, especially when concerned with behavioral dissociations and their potential conceptual significance.

Computational Models

In this chapter I have concentrated on behavioral evidence concerning the relationship between implicit learning and attention and awareness and have said relatively little about formal models of implicit learning. However, the discussion in the last section should make it clear that models can play a very important role in helping us to understand learning processes, and indeed there has been a great deal of work trying to develop models for standard implicit learning tasks such as grammar learning and the SRT task. In much of this work issues of awareness and attention are often left to one side, the principal question being simply to try to account for fine-grained aspects of performance.

I shall not review progress in this area (examples and further references are contained in Cleeremans, 1993; Dienes, Altmann, & Gao, 1999; Kinder & Shanks, 2001) but shall merely emphasize one point that has some relevance to the issue of awareness. If it were the case that the most successful models of implicit learning were symbol-processing ones in which performance is explained in terms of the acquisition and usage of structured rules, then this would provide quite strong evidence for the implicit/explicit dichotomy for the following reason (see O'Brien & Opie, 1999; Shanks, 1997, for a much more detailed exposition). It cannot be the case that the contents of consciousness are coextensive with information coded symbolically in rules as the brain would need to represent far more information in this way than would be available to consciousness. For example, a huge symbol-processing machinery comprising an endless number of rules would need to be employed in understanding language, and of course we have no conscious awareness of such machinery operating. Therefore it would have to be assumed that only certain privileged symbolic representations gain access to consciousness. The implicit/explicit distinction would then provide an appropriate characterization of these two distinct representational states.

The empirical force of this argument, however, is weak because by far the most successful models of implicit learning are ones based on distributed rather than symbolic representations (Cleeremans, 1993; O'Brien & Opie, 1999). For example, recurrent connectionist network models of artificial grammar learning (Dienes et al., 1999; Kinder & Shanks, 2001) assume that knowledge is represented not via grammatical rules but in a large network of connections coding the statistical relationships between letters in different positions. In this case, it is no longer quite so obvious that a separation between implicit and explicit mental representations is necessary; instead it is possible to argue that there is only a single type of representation (i.e. distributed ones) and that what makes some representations conscious is not a special property but merely, for instance, their achieving some level of stability. A good deal of recent work on classic philosophical topics such as mental representation has taken consideration of the implicit/explicit distinction (e.g. Dienes & Perner, 1999; O'Brien & Opie, 1999).

Concluding Remarks

Research on implicit learning has provided a rich seam of new information concerning the processes that control learning and the relationships between learning, attention and awareness. In my view it has yet to be proved beyond reasonable doubt that there exists a form of learning that proceeds both unintentionally and unconsciously, yet it cannot be disputed that the examples described at the beginning of the chapter all possess a common 'essence' that marks them out from the more traditional varieties of (explicit) learning studied by psychologists. In attempting to understand this essence, much has been discovered: for example, that learning can be exquisitely tied to the processing systems that carry out a specific task (Karni, 1996), that examples of abstract learning can often be understood in terms of very elementary processes (McClelland & Plaut, 1999), and that even quite simple models can generate complex patterns of behavior. Whatever the final conclusion about the status of implicit learning, these discoveries will have enduring value.

In the Appendix I provide some brief comments on each of the examples I presented at the outset of this chapter. In some cases I argue that closer examination might lead to a re-evaluation of conclusions. In other cases the evidence for implicit learning appears stronger.

Acknowledgements

The writing of this chapter was supported by grants from the Leverhulme Trust, the Economic and Social Research Council, and the Biotechnology and Biological Sciences Research Council. The work is part of the programme of the ESRC Centre for Economic Learning and Social Evolution, University College London.

Note

1 Here I am using the terms 'attention' and 'intention' as almost synonymous, which of course they are not. In a fuller treatment it would be necessary to distinguish between situations in which a person is not intending via a voluntary act of will to learn about some domain from those in which that person is not attending to a particular source of information.

REFERENCES

Altmann, G. T. M. (2002). Learning and development in neural networks: the importance of prior experience. *Cognition, 85*, B43–B50.

Altmann, G. T. M., & Dienes, Z. (1999). Rule learning by seven-month-old infants and neural networks. *Science, 284*, 875.

Altmann, G. T. M., Dienes, Z., & Goode, A. (1995). Modality independence of implicitly learned grammatical knowledge. *Journal of Experimental Psychology: Learning, Memory, and Cognition, 21*, 899–912.

Baeyens, F., Eelen, P., & Van den Bergh, O. (1990). Contingency awareness in evaluative conditioning: a case for unaware affective-evaluative learning. *Cognition and Emotion, 4*, 3–18.

Berry, D. C., & Dienes, Z. (1993). *Implicit learning: theoretical and empirical issues.* Hove, UK: Lawrence Erlbaum.

Brooks, L. R. (1967). The suppression of visualization by reading. *Quarterly Journal of Experimental Psychology, 19*, 289–299.

Bruner, J. S., Goodnow, J. J., & Austin, G. A. (1956). *A study of thinking.* New York: Wiley.

Burke, D., & Roodenrys, S. (2000). Implicit learning in a simple cued reaction-time task. *Learning and Motivation, 31*, 364–380.

Christiansen, M. H., Conway, C. M., & Curtin, S. (2000). A connectionist single-mechanism account of rule-like behavior in infancy. In L. R. Gleitman & A. K. Joshi (Eds.), *Proceedings of the 22nd Annual Conference of the Cognitive Science Society* (pp. 83–88). Mahwah, NJ: Lawrence Erlbaum.

Christiansen, M. H., & Curtin, S. (1999). Transfer of learning: rule acquisition or statistical learning? *Trends in Cognitive Sciences, 3*, 289–290.

Clark, R. E., & Squire, L. R. (1998). Classical conditioning and brain systems: the role of awareness. *Science, 280*, 77–81.

Cleeremans, A. (1993). *Mechanisms of implicit learning.* Cambridge, MA: MIT Press.

Cohen, N. J., & Squire, L. R. (1980). Preserved learning and retention of pattern-analyzing skill in amnesia: dissociation of knowing how and knowing that. *Science, 210*, 207–210.

Destrebecqz, A., & Cleeremans, A. (2001). Can sequence learning be implicit? New evidence with the process dissociation procedure. *Psychonomic Bulletin and Review, 8*, 343–350.

Dienes, Z. (1992). Connectionist and memory-array models of artificial grammar learning. *Cognitive Science, 16*, 41–79.

Dienes, Z., & Altmann, G. (1997). Transfer of implicit knowledge across domains: how implicit and how abstract? In D. C. Berry (Ed.), *How implicit is implicit learning?* (pp. 107–123). Oxford: Oxford University Press.

Dienes, Z., Altmann, G. T. M., & Gao, S.-J. (1999). Mapping across domains without feedback: a neural network model of transfer of implicit knowledge. *Cognitive Science, 23*, 53–82.

Dienes, Z., Broadbent, D. E., & Berry, D. (1991). Implicit and explicit knowledge bases in artificial grammar learning. *Journal of Experimental Psychology: Learning, Memory, and Cognition, 17*, 875–887.

Dienes, Z., & Perner, J. (1999). A theory of implicit and explicit knowledge. *Behavioral and Brain Sciences, 22*, 735–808.

Dulany, D. E. (1961). Hypotheses and habits in verbal 'operant conditioning'. *Journal of Abnormal and Social Psychology, 63*, 251–263.

Dulany, D. E., Carlson, R. A., & Dewey, G. I. (1984). A case of syntactical learning and judgment: how conscious and how abstract? *Journal of Experimental Psychology: General, 113*, 541–555.

Dunn, J. C., & Kirsner, K. (1988). Discovering functionally independent mental processes: the principle of reversed association. *Psychological Review, 95*, 91–101.

Eich, E. (1984). Memory for unattended events: remembering with and without awareness. *Memory and Cognition, 12*, 105–111.

French, R. M., & Cleeremans, A. (2002). *Implicit learning: an empirical, philosophical and computational consensus in the making.* Hove, UK: Psychology Press.

Frensch, P. A., Lin, J., & Buchner, A. (1998). Learning versus behavioral expression of the learned: the effects of a secondary tone-counting task on implicit learning in the serial reaction task. *Psychological Research, 61*, 83–98.

Gomez, R. L. (1997). Transfer and complexity in artificial grammar learning. *Cognitive Psychology, 33*, 154–207.

Goschke, T. (1997). Implicit learning and unconscious knowledge: mental representation, computational mechanisms, and brain structures. In K. Lamberts & D. Shanks (Eds.), *Knowledge, concepts and categories* (pp. 247–333). Hove, UK: Psychology Press.

Greenspoon, J. (1955). The reinforcing effect of two spoken sounds on the frequency of two responses. *American Journal of Psychology, 68*, 409–416.

Hamann, S. B., & Squire, L. R. (1997). Intact perceptual memory in the absence of conscious memory. *Behavioral Neuroscience, 111*, 850–854.

Heuer, H., & Schmidtke, V. (1996). Secondary-task effects on sequence learning. *Psychological Research, 59*, 119–133.

Higham, P. A. (1997). Dissociations of grammaticality and specific similarity effects in artificial grammar learning. *Journal of Experimental Psychology: Learning, Memory, and Cognition, 23*, 1029–1045.

Higham, P. A., Vokey, J. R., & Pritchard, J. L. (2000). Beyond dissociation logic: evidence for controlled and automatic influences in artificial grammar learning. *Journal of Experimental Psychology: General, 129*, 457–470.

Hunt, E. B., Marin, J., & Stone, P. J. (1966). *Experiments in induction.* San Diego: Academic Press.

Jacoby, L. L., Toth, J. P., & Yonelinas, A. P. (1993). Separating conscious and unconscious influences of memory: measuring recollection. *Journal of Experimental Psychology: General, 122*, 139–154.

Jiménez, L., & Méndez, C. (1999). Which attention is needed for implicit sequence learning? *Journal of Experimental Psychology: Learning, Memory, and Cognition, 25*, 236–259.

Johnstone, T., & Shanks, D. R. (2001). Abstractionist and processing accounts of implicit learning. *Cognitive Psychology, 42,* 61–112.

Juslin, P., Olsson, H., & Björkman, M. (1997). Brunswikian and Thurstonian origins of bias in probability assessment: on the interpretation of stochastic components of judgment. *Journal of Behavioral Decision Making, 10,* 189–209.

Karni, A. (1996). The acquisition of perceptual and motor skills: a memory system in the adult human cortex. *Cognitive Brain Research, 5,* 39–48.

Kinder, A., & Assmann, A. (2000). Learning artificial grammars: no evidence for the acquisition of rules. *Memory and Cognition, 28,* 1321–1332.

Kinder, A., & Shanks, D. R. (2001). Amnesia and the declarative/nondeclarative distinction: a recurrent network model of classification, recognition, and repetition priming. *Journal of Cognitive Neuroscience, 13,* 648–669.

Kinder, A., & Shanks, D. R. (2003). Neuropsychological dissociations between priming and recognition: a single-system connectionist account. *Psychological Review, 110,* 728–744.

Kinder, A., Shanks, D. R., Cock, J., & Tunney, R. J. (2003). Recollection, fluency, and the explicit/implicit distinction in artificial grammar learning. *Journal of Experimental Psychology: General, 132,* 551–565.

Kunst-Wilson, W. R., & Zajonc, R. B. (1980). Affective discrimination of stimuli that cannot be recognized. *Science, 207,* 557–558.

Lovibond, P. F., & Shanks, D. R. (2002). The role of awareness in Pavlovian conditioning: empirical evidence and theoretical implications. *Journal of Experimental Psychology: Animal Behavior Processes, 28,* 3–26.

Manns, J. R., Clark, R. E., & Squire, L. R. (2002). Standard delay eyeblink classical conditioning is independent of awareness. *Journal of Experimental Psychology: Animal Behavior Processes, 28,* 32–37.

Manza, L., & Reber, A. S. (1997). Representing artificial grammars: transfer across stimulus forms and modalities. In D. C. Berry (Ed.), *How implicit is implicit learning?* (pp. 73–106). Oxford: Oxford University Press.

Marcus, G. F., Vijayan, S., Bandi Rao, S., & Vishton, P. M. (1999). Rule learning by seven-month-old infants. *Science, 283,* 77–80.

Marescaux, P.-J. (1997). Can dynamic control task knowledge be communicated? *Psychologica Belgica, 37,* 51–68.

McClelland, J. L., & Plaut, D. C. (1999). Does generalization in infant learning implicate abstract algebra-like rules? *Trends in Cognitive Sciences, 3,* 166–168.

Meulemans, T., & Van der Linden, M. (2002). Artificial grammar learning in amnesia. In R. M. French & A. Cleeremans (Eds.), *Implicit learning: an empirical, philosophical and computational consensus in the making* (pp. 144–163). Hove, UK: Psychology Press.

Miller, J. (1987). Priming is not necessary for selective-attention failures: semantic effects of unattended, unprimed letters. *Perception and Psychophysics, 41,* 419–434.

Nisbett, R. E., & Wilson, T. D. (1977). Telling more than we can know: verbal reports on mental processes. *Psychological Review, 84,* 231–259.

Nosofsky, R. M., & Zaki, S. R. (1998). Dissociations between categorization and recognition in amnesic and normal individuals: an exemplar-based interpretation. *Psychological Science, 9,* 247–255.

O'Brien, G., & Opie, J. (1999). A connectionist theory of phenomenal experience. *Behavioral and Brain Sciences, 22,* 127–196.

Ostergaard, A. L. (1992). A method for judging measures of stochastic dependence: further comments on the current controversy. *Journal of Experimental Psychology: Learning, Memory, and Cognition, 18,* 413–420.

Peirce, C. S., & Jastrow, J. (1884). On small differences of sensation. *Memoirs of the National Academy of Sciences, 3,* 75–83.

Perruchet, P., & Gallego, J. (1993). Association between conscious knowledge and performance in normal subjects: reply to Cohen and Curran (1993) and Willingham, Greeley, and Bardone (1993). *Journal of Experimental Psychology: Learning, Memory, and Cognition, 19,* 1438–1444.

Perruchet, P., & Pacteau, C. (1990). Synthetic grammar learning: implicit rule abstraction or explicit fragmentary knowledge? *Journal of Experimental Psychology: General, 119,* 264–275.

Pike, R. (1973). Response latency models for signal detection. *Psychological Review, 80,* 53–68.

Plaut, D. C. (1995). Double dissociation without modularity: evidence from connectionist neuropsychology. *Journal of Clinical and Experimental Neuropsychology, 17,* 291–321.

Poldrack, R. A. (1996). On testing for stochastic dissociations. *Psychonomic Bulletin and Review, 3,* 434–448.

Poldrack, R. A., Selco, S. L., Field, J. E., & Cohen, N. J. (1999). The relationship between skill learning and repetition priming: experimental and computational analyses. *Journal of Experimental Psychology: Learning, Memory, and Cognition, 25,* 208–235.

Ratcliff, R., & Murdock, B. B. (1976). Retrieval processes in recognition memory. *Psychological Review, 83,* 190–214.

Reber, A. S. (1967). Implicit learning of artificial grammars. *Journal of Verbal Learning and Verbal Behavior, 6,* 855–863.

Reber, A. S. (1993). *Implicit learning and tacit knowledge: an essay on the cognitive unconscious.* Oxford: Oxford University Press.

Redington, M., & Chater, N. (1996). Transfer in artificial grammar learning: a reevaluation. *Journal of Experimental Psychology: General, 125,* 123–138.

Reed, J., & Johnson, P. (1994). Assessing implicit learning with indirect tests: determining what is learned about sequence structure. *Journal of Experimental Psychology: Learning, Memory, and Cognition, 20,* 585–594.

Reingold, E. M., & Merikle, P. M. (1990). On the interrelatedness of theory and measurement in the study of unconscious processes. *Mind and Language, 5,* 9–28.

Rosenfeld, H. M., & Baer, D. M. (1969a). Unbiased and unnoticed verbal conditioning: the double agent robot procedure. *Journal of the Experimental Analysis of Behavior, 14,* 99–105.

Rosenfeld, H. M., & Baer, D. M. (1969b). Unnoticed verbal conditioning of an aware experimenter by a more aware subject: the double-agent effect. *Psychological Review, 76,* 425–432.

Rugg, M. D., Mark, R. E., Walla, P., Schloerscheidt, A. M., Birch, C. S., & Allan, K. (1998). Dissociation of the neural correlates of implicit and explicit memory. *Nature, 392,* 595–598.

Schmidt, P. A., & Dark, V. J. (1998). Attentional processing of 'unattended' flankers: evidence for a failure of selective attention. *Perception and Psychophysics, 60,* 227–238.

Schvaneveldt, R. W., & Gomez, R. L. (1998). Attention and probabilistic sequence learning. *Psychological Research, 61,* 175–190.

Seamon, J. G., Williams, P. C., Crowley, M. J., Kim, I. J., Langer, S. A., Orne, P. J., et al. (1995). The mere exposure effect is based on implicit memory: effects of stimulus type, encoding conditions, and number of exposures on recognition and affect judgments. *Journal of Experimental Psychology: Learning, Memory, and Cognition, 21,* 711–721.

Seger, C. A. (1997). Two forms of sequential implicit learning. *Consciousness and Cognition, 6,* 108–131.

Seidenberg, M. S., & Elman, J. L. (1999). Networks are not 'hidden rules'. *Trends in Cognitive Sciences, 3,* 288–289.

Shanks, D. R. (1997). Distributed representations and implicit knowledge: a brief introduction. In K. Lamberts & D. Shanks (Eds.), *Knowledge, concepts and categories* (pp. 197–214). Hove, UK: Psychology Press.

Shanks, D. R., & Channon, S. (2002). Effects of a secondary task on 'implicit' sequence learning: learning or performance? *Psychological Research, 66,* 99–109.

Shanks, D. R., & Johnstone, T. (1999). Evaluating the relationship between explicit and implicit knowledge in a sequential reaction time task. *Journal of Experimental Psychology: Learning, Memory, and Cognition, 25,* 1435–1451.

Shanks, D. R., & Lovibond, P. F. (2002). Autonomic and eyeblink conditioning are closely related to contingency awareness: reply to Wiens and Öhman (2002) and Manns et al. (2002). *Journal of Experimental Psychology: Animal Behavior Processes, 28,* 38–42.

Shanks, D. R., & Perruchet, P. (2002). Dissociation between priming and recognition in the expression of sequential knowledge. *Psychonomic Bulletin and Review, 9,* 362–367.

Shanks, D. R., & St John, M. F. (1994). Characteristics of dissociable human learning systems. *Behavioral and Brain Sciences, 17,* 367–447.

Shanks, D. R., Wilkinson, L., & Channon, S. (2003). Relationship between priming and recognition in deterministic and probabilistic sequence learning. *Journal of Experimental Psychology: Learning, Memory, and Cognition, 29,* 248–261.

Sirois, S., Buckingham, D., & Shultz, T. R. (2000). Artificial grammar learning by infants: an auto-associator perspective. *Developmental Science, 3,* 442–456.

Stadler, M. A., & Frensch, P. A. (1998). *Handbook of implicit learning.* Thousand Oaks, CA: Sage.

Svartdal, F. (1991). Operant modulation of low-level attributes of rule-governed behavior by nonverbal contingencies. *Learning and Motivation, 22,* 406–420.

Tulving, E. (1983). *Elements of episodic memory.* Oxford: Oxford University Press.

Tulving, E., & Pearlstone, Z. (1966). Availability versus accessibility of information in memory for words. *Journal of Verbal Learning and Verbal Behavior, 5,* 381–391.

Tunney, R. J., & Shanks, D. R. (2003). Subjective measures of awareness and implicit cognition. *Memory and Cognition, 31,* 1060–1071.

Whittlesea, B. W. A., & Price, J. R. (2001). Implicit/explicit memory versus analytic/nonanalytic processing: rethinking the mere exposure effect. *Memory and Cognition, 29,* 234–246.

Wiens, S., & Öhman, A. (2002). Unawareness is more than a chance event: commentary on Lovibond and Shanks (2002). *Journal of Experimental Psychology: Animal Behavior Processes, 28,* 27–31.

Willingham, D. B., Greeley, T., & Bardone, A. M. (1993). Dissociation in a serial response time task using a recognition measure: comment on Perruchet and Amorim (1992). *Journal of Experimental Psychology: Learning, Memory, and Cognition, 19,* 1424–1430.

Willingham, D. B., Nissen, M. J., & Bullemer, P. (1989). On the development of procedural knowledge. *Journal of Experimental Psychology: Learning, Memory, and Cognition, 15,* 1047–1060.

Wood, N. L., Stadler, M. A., & Cowan, N. (1997). Is there implicit memory without attention? A reexamination of task demands in Eich's (1984) procedure. *Memory and Cognition, 25,* 772–779.

APPENDIX

Here I briefly return to each of the nine examples described at the beginning of the chapter with re-evaluation on the basis of the methodological and theoretical points made in the chapter.

1   The case for implicit learning in the artificial grammar learning task is quite weak. Much of the evidence relies on participants' inability to verbalize the rules of the grammar, but this is problematic for reasons discussed in the chapter. More intriguing evidence, not relying on verbal reports, has been presented by Higham, Vokey, and Pritchard (2000) and Meulemans and Van der Linden (2002).

2   Dulany's challenge to Greenspoon's data is described in the chapter. A beautiful extension of this type of study was reported by Rosenfeld

and Baer (1969b) under the label of a 'double agent' effect. In their study a participant was led to believe that he was fulfilling the role of experimenter (E) in a conditioning experiment while another participant was told to pretend to be the subject (S) in this experiment but in fact functioned as the real experimenter (hence 'double agent'). E attempted to condition S's responses while at the same time S tried to condition E's. Thus E reinforced with a nod all occasions on which S rubbed his chin, while at the same time S reinforced E by rubbing his chin every time E said 'yeah'. Rosenfeld and Baer observed that the number of 'yeah's' emitted by E increased under this schedule despite his being oblivious to the fact that it was his behavior rather than S's that was the focus of the study. Of course the possibility of contamination by a correlated hypothesis remains, but the use of such a powerful technique to direct attention away from the critical contingency should be exploited in further research (ethical considerations permitting). Rosenfeld and Baer (1969a) replicated this effect under better experimental control where the double agent actually became a robot, but to the best of my knowledge these studies have never been followed up.

3 Svartdal's findings appear superficially to be quite compelling, especially as the contingency to be learned is such a simple one. However, it is unclear that the information criterion is met in these and similar studies, because it is very difficult to rule out the possibility that subjects acquire correlated hypotheses about the reinforcement contingency that are incorrect from the experimenter's point of view but happen to produce response profiles that are correlated with those generated by the correct hypothesis. For example, suppose that subjects learn that resting their hand in a certain position increases reinforcement rate. This could be a true experienced contingency if that hand position was conducive to a fast or slow response rate. Such an 'incorrect' hypothesis would generate behavior that is very similar to what would be produced by the correct hypothesis, yet a subject who reported hand position as the crucial variable would be regarded by the experimenter as 'unaware' of the reinforcement contingency.

4 Problems with interpreting Clark and Squire's data are discussed in the chapter. For further discussion of the relationship between conditioning and awareness see Lovibond and Shanks (2002), Wiens and Öhman (2002), Manns et al. (2002), and Shanks and Lovibond (2002).

5 The nature of learning in Karni's procedure seems to be at such a low level (e.g. in primary visual cortex) that it could not possibly be affected by such high-level cognitive functions as awareness and attention. However, Karni did find that learning was abolished if the target was irrelevant for task performance, consistent with a top-down attentional influence. Moreover, arguments appealing to the low physiological level at which a particular form of learning may occur are weakened by the fact that eyeblink conditioning, which also might be characterized as low-level (for instance, there is a major involvement of the cerebellum, and it is specific to the trained eye), is invariably accompanied by awareness, at least according to Lovibond and Shanks' (2002) review. Nevertheless, Karni's demonstration is striking and studies specifically exploring awareness in this sort of task would be very useful.

6 Nisbett and Wilson's classic and compelling demonstration, like that of Dienes and Altmann (see below), suggests that people's behavior can be influenced by a factor without them being aware of this influence.

7 There have been attempts to simulate dissociations in amnesia between performance on implicit and explicit tests such as those given to E.P. using single-process models that do not incorporate any distinction between implicit and explicit knowledge. See Kinder and Shanks (2001, 2003) and Nosofsky and Zaki (1998).

8 Dienes and Altmann's finding provides compelling evidence of one conception of implicit learning: specifically, a learning process that yields information that can be applied in a certain set of contexts without the person being aware that he or she possesses this knowledge or that it is being applied. Actually, the existence of this type of phenomenon has been known for over a century (Peirce & Jastrow, 1884). There have also been some impressive recent attempts to model the relationship between confidence and performance (e.g. Juslin, Olsson, & Björkman, 1997). However, some evidence that casts doubt on the idea that grammar learning induces knowledge that is subjectively unavailable is presented by Tunney and Shanks (2003).

9 The SRT task has spawned a small industry and much controversy surrounds the issue of whether sequence knowledge is consciously accessible in this procedure. Destrebecqz and Cleeremans' finding that participants are unable to 'report' their knowledge of a sequence via keypresses is impressive. The claim that sequence knowledge can be accessed implicitly but not in explicit recognition is questioned by Shanks and Perruchet (2002) and Shanks et al. (2003).

9

Mechanisms of Memory

IAN NEATH AND AIMÉE M. SURPRENANT

Memory research in the 1990s often focused on the question of whether memory is best characterized as a set of independent systems or as a set of inter-related processes (see, e.g., Foster & Jelicic, 1999). In this chapter we provide a functional analysis of memory mechanisms that allows the specification of general principles of memory. These principles, we argue, apply to all memory, regardless of the type of information, the type of processing, the hypothetical system supporting the memory, or the time scale. We critique both the multiple systems and the processing views, showing how each misses something fundamental about the psychology of memory. We end by briefly describing three models of memory that are based on the functional principles identified.

THE ENCODING/RETRIEVAL INTERACTION

Memory is usually conceived as having three stages: encoding, storage and retrieval. Encoding refers to the acquisition and initial processing of information; storage refers to the maintenance of the encoded information over time; and retrieval refers to the processes by which the stored information is accessed and used. Historically, the scientific study of human memory can be seen as focusing on each of these stages in turn before coming to the realization that a dynamic interaction between the encoding and retrieval phases critically determines memory performance (Neath, 2000a).

An appreciation of the importance of the encoding/retrieval interaction came about as the result of studies that examined the potency of various cues to elicit items from memory. A *strong cue* is a word that elicits a particular target word most of the time. For example, when most people hear the word BLOOM, the first word that pops into their head is FLOWER. A *weak cue* is a word that only rarely elicits a particular target. When people hear FRUIT, they respond with FLOWER only about 1% of the time. A reasonable prediction seems to be that strong cues should be better than weak cues at eliciting the correct item. However, this inference is not valid because it fails to take into account the relationship between the encoding and retrieval conditions. For example, Thomson and Tulving (1970) reported an experiment in which they manipulated what cues were present at study and test. Some target words were presented alone at study and some were presented along with a weak cue. At test, there were three cue conditions: no cue, a weak cue or a strong cue. The results, shown as the probability of recalling the correct target word, are displayed in Table 9.1. When there was no cue present at study, a strong cue at test led to better performance (0.68) than either a weak cue (0.43) or no cue (0.49). However, when there was a weak cue present at study, the weak cue at test led to better performance (0.82) than a strong cue (0.23). The important aspect of this result is that the effectiveness of even a long-standing strong cue depends crucially on the processes that occurred at study.

As Tulving (1983: 239) noted, the dynamic interaction between encoding and retrieval conditions prohibits any statements that take the following forms:

Items (events) of class X are easier to remember than items (events) of class Y.
Encoding operations of class X are more effective than encoding operations of class Y.
Retrieval cues of class X are more effective than retrieval cues of class Y.

TABLE 9.1   *The proportion of items correctly recalled as a function of the presence or absence of various types of cues at study and retrieval*

Study cue	Retrieval cue		
	None	Weak	Strong
None	0.49	0.43	0.68
Weak	0.30	0.82	0.23

Data from Thomson & Tulving (1970).

One cannot say, for example, that pictures are remembered better than words, that deep processing leads to better memory performance than shallow processing, or that highly associated cues are better than weakly associated cues. What is missing from each of these statements is a description of the learning and retrieval conditions.[1] Variations at either of these stages, as detailed below, can reverse each of these phenomena.

Pictures are remembered better than words

As Tulving (1983) suggested, one should not state that one kind of item is easier to remember than another. As its name suggests, the picture superiority effect refers to the finding that pictures of objects are usually remembered more accurately than names of those objects (Paivio, Rogers, & Smythe, 1968). The label is misleading, however, as this effect depends on the type of test. When a recognition test is used and the measure of memory is the number of items correctly recognized as being on the list, pictures are indeed remembered better than words. However, the picture superiority effect reverses if the test is word fragment completion and the measure is the amount of priming (Weldon & Roediger, 1988). In this kind of task, there are two phases. In phase 1, the subjects are exposed to the items, both words and pictures. Phase 2 is the actual test, and it requires two groups: an experimental group who were in phase 1 and a control group who were not in phase 1. The test consists of word fragments and the subjects are asked to complete the fragment with the first word that pops into their head. For example, if they saw the word fragment T_B_GG_N, a solution would be TOBOGGAN. The measure of memory, priming, is the difference between the mean proportion of fragments completed by the experimental group and the mean proportion completed by the control group. Weldon and Roediger found that word fragments that could be completed to form a word that had been shown in phase 1 were more likely to be completed than those fragments that could be completed to form the name of a picture that had been shown in phase 1. Using word fragment completion as the task and

priming as the measure, words are remembered better than pictures. As a result, one cannot make the statement 'pictures are remembered better than words' or, more generally, that one type of item is easier to remember than another.

Deep processing is better than shallow processing

Just as with items, one cannot make absolute statements about the mnemonic properties of various types of processes. The levels of processing framework (Craik & Lockhart, 1972) proposed that deeper types of processing, such as semantic or meaning-based processing, will lead to better memory performance than more shallow types of processing, such as processing items based on how they look or sound. Thus, if you rate words for pleasantness – a deep task because you need to think about what the word means and consider the word's various connotations – you will recall more items on a free recall test than if you judged whether the words contained a particular letter (Hyde & Jenkins, 1973). However, if the test is changed, shallow processing can lead to better performance than deep processing.

For example, Morris, Bransford, and Franks (1977) presented sentences in which a word was missing. In one condition, subjects judged whether a target word made semantic sense if inserted in the blank. For example, the sentence might be 'The (blank) had a silver engine' and the target word might be TRAIN. In a different condition, subjects judged whether the target word rhymed with another. In this case, the sentence might be '(Blank) rhymes with legal' and the target word might be EAGLE. Two different tests were used. One test was a standard recognition test, where a target word was presented and subjects were asked whether it had been seen previously. The second test was a rhyming recognition test, where subjects were asked whether a word rhymed with one of the target words. With a standard recognition test, the deeper encoding process (whether the word fit in the sentence) led to better performance than did the more shallow encoding process (whether the word rhymed). However, with the rhyme recognition test, the shallow processing led to better performance than did the deep processing. As a result, one cannot say, 'deep processing is better than shallow processing' or, more generally, that one type of processing is better than another.

The best cue is the item itself

Just as with items and processes, one cannot make absolute statements about the mnemonic properties of retrieval cues. It might seem reasonable that the best memory cue for an item is the item itself, a so-called copy cue. That is, if we wanted to find out whether you remembered seeing the word CHAIR on a list, we would use a cue that included a copy of the item in which we were interested. If this were true, then the phenomenon known as 'recognition failure of recallable words' would not exist. In this paradigm (e.g. Watkins & Tulving, 1975), the subject studies a list of word pairs in which the first word in the pair is a weak cue of the second word; for example, GLUE might be paired with CHAIR. Then, a word that is a strong cue is given, such as TABLE, and subjects are asked to write down as many words as they can that are associated with TABLE. A recognition test is then given, in which a copy cue (the word CHAIR itself) is used and subjects often fail to recognize this item as one of the words on the original list. The final test is cued recall, where GLUE is the cue. Now, subjects are quite likely to recall the word they earlier failed to recognize. CHAIR is not always an effective cue when trying to remember CHAIR. As a result, one cannt say that copy cues are the most effective cue or, more generally, that one type of cue is better than another.

The three examples above illustrate that whether a particular item or event is remembered depends on the interaction between the particular study and test conditions. Our first functional principle of memory can now be stated:

(1) Remembering depends on the interaction between the conditions at encoding and the conditions at retrieval.

This principle, essentially Tulving's (1983) encoding specificity principle, means that all statements about the mnemonic properties of items, processes and cues need to specify completely the encoding and retrieval conditions. The next three functional principles of memory, then, are just as Tulving (1983: 239) proposed:

(2) Items do not have intrinsic mnemonic properties.
(3) Processes do not have intrinsic mnemonic properties.
(4) Cues do not have intrinsic mnemonic properties.

TASK PURITY

There are numerous ways of assessing memory. Typically, some event or set of items is presented to the subject, followed by a series of questions. The encoding can be either *intentional*, in which the subject knows there is a memory test that will follow and intends to remember the material, or *incidental*, in which the subject is unaware that there will be a later memory test and does not intentionally try to remember the material. Similarly, at test, the subject can try to relate the cues back to the learning episode, a *direct test* of memory, or the subject may be unaware that the test is related to the encoding episode, an *indirect test* of memory.

In addition to these distinctions, Craik (1983) suggested that many commonly used tests can also be classified with respect to how much environmental support they provide or how much self-initiated activity they require. Two related variables at work are whether the test requires identification of a particular encoding context and whether the test includes a more specific cue or a more general cue.

A free recall test provides little environmental support and requires a lot of self-initiated activity. A list of items is presented, and the subject is asked to recall which items were on the list. Say the list included the words GREYHOUND, TABLE and BROCCOLI. The subject knows all of these words prior to the presentation of the list, and will know these words after the experiment is over. The experimenter simply says 'recall the words that were on the list' and it is up to the subject to identify which list and to discriminate the items that were on this particular list from those that were not. This is memory for an item in context. Typical recognition and cued-recall tests provide more specific cues, but still require the subject to discriminate which items were on the list. Did 'GREYHOUND' appear on the list or not? In this case, specific items are queried (recognition) or specific cues are provided (cued recall), which can reduce the need for self-initiated retrieval processes.

Immediate memory tests (e.g. digit span) seem to require contextual information, but on further review this may not be necessary. A person is given six or seven digits in random order, and is then asked to recall the digits in the same order. Because so little time has elapsed from the end of list presentation to the beginning of the retrieval attempt, the episodic context is unlikely to have changed and so the subject is likely to be still in the original encoding state. Thus, contextual reinstatement may not be necessary. If the same test is delayed, however, then the test is removed in time from the learning episode, the context will have changed, and the test will require more self-initiated activity.

Some tests, such as word fragment completion and general knowledge questions, provide far more targeted cues and, because neither of these tests requires the reinstatement of a particular context, little, if any, self-initiated activity is required. For both tests, it does not really matter to the subject whether a specific encoding context is remembered or not. For example, if you are given a word fragment and asked to complete it with the first word that pops into your head, you are free to try a variety of strategies. You might just try random words, or you might think back to the first part of the experiment you were in and see if any of those words fit the fragment. In one case, you are ignoring a particular learning episode, in the other you are not, and different results might obtain (e.g. Bowers & Schacter, 1990). Similarly, you might just know that Hannibal Hamlin was Abraham Lincoln's first vice president, or you might actually remember sitting in a class and hearing the instructor use Hamlin as an example of an obscure person. Very different types of processing can be used by subjects even when given the same type of test or cue. People will use any and all processes to help them answer a question. This leads to the next principle:

(5) Tasks are not pure.

'Task' is meant quite generally, and can be any type of test or other cognitive functioning performed in the service of memory. As Jacoby (1991) noted, many researchers act as if they are making the assumption that tasks or certain tests are 'process pure'; that is, they act as if a particular test taps a particular memory system or that a particular task requires only one type of process. As the examples above illustrate, this assumption is likely to be false: one cannot make the assumption that a particular test taps only one particular system or process.

FORGETTING

One of the most salient features of memory is that it often appears to fail. What causes these failures? Given the prohibition on statements of the form 'Items of class X are easier to remember than items of class Y', we must also prohibit the complementary statement about what types of items are harder to recall or, to put it another way, more likely to be forgotten. In more general terms, if items do not have intrinsic mnemonic properties, then it seems unlikely that forgetting is due to an intrinsic mnemonic property of the items. Given that remembering depends on the interaction of the encoding and retrieval conditions, forgetting must depend on this also. This conclusion accords nicely with one of the most influential analyses of forgetting, that forgetting is due to interference.

John McGeoch (1932) argued that forgetting is caused by interference rather than by the passage of time. His analogy was to how an iron bar might rust over time: it is not time per se that causes rust but rather oxidation. Similarly, although memory often can get worse over time, time does not cause forgetting; rather, interference does.[2] Evidence consistent with this analysis includes the numerous instances where memory performance *improves* over time even in the absence of opportunities to rehearse or relearn the material (e.g. Bjork, 2001; Knoedler, Hellwig, & Neath, 1999; Neath & Knoedler, 1994; Wright, Santiago, Sands, Kendrick, & Cook, 1985). In particular, reminiscence (Payne, 1987) and spontaneous recovery (Wheeler, 1995) are exactly this type of memory phenomenon: better memory after more time has elapsed when there is no opportunity for further study. McGeoch's arguments (see also Osgood, 1953) were such that it is hard to find a memory researcher who invokes decay or any other time-based forgetting process in all of memory, except for transient or short-term memories. We argue later that time-based forgetting is not appropriate in those situations either.

There are two types of interference: *proactive interference*, in which previous information affects your ability to remember more recent information, and *retroactive interference*, in which information you have recently learned affects your ability to remember older information. The difference between them is conveniently illustrated by using paired associate terminology, which has the benefit of being extremely general. In a paired associate task, two items are associated, for example A and B. At test, A is given as the cue, and B is the correct response. You might be asked to respond with CHOCOLATE when you see the cue MAGAZINE. To measure interference, one must have an experimental condition in which interfering items are present, and a control condition in which there is no interfering material.

Table 9.2 illustrates when retroactive and proactive interference will occur. In all conditions, people learn A-B and are tested on their memory for A-B. In the Control 1 condition, the subjects are asked to learn C-D after learning A-B and before they are tested on A-B. The term C-D represents non-interfering items; there is no overlap between items A, B, C and D. The term A-D represents interfering items, because item A now acts as a cue for two different responses, B and D. The Experimental 1 group will perform more poorly than the Control 1 group due to retroactive interference. The bottom part of the table shows how proactive interference occurs. Again, C-D will not interfere with A-B, but learning A-D prior to learning A-B will cause interference. The Experimental 2 group will perform more poorly than the Control 2 group when trying to recall B due to proactive interference.[3]

TABLE 9.2 *A schematic illustration of when retroactive and proactive interference will occur*

	Time 1	Time 2	Test	Interference Type
Control 1	A-B	C-D	A-B	
Experimental 1	A-B	A-D	A-B	Retroactive
Control 2	C-D	A-B	A-B	
Experimental 2	A-D	A-B	A-B	Proactive

This schematic also illustrates why the term *forget* should be taken to mean only a failure to remember rather than a loss of information. Consider the Experimental 1 group. When cued with A at test, there are at least three options: the subject could recall B, the correct item; D, an interfering item; or the subject might not be able to recall anything. What can be assumed about the memory for B if the subject recalls D or recalls nothing? Nothing can be assumed: one cannot assume a loss of information from a lack of performance. It is always possible that a different cue could lead to successful remembering. For example, the cue A might be 'Recall the items that you were just shown' and the subject may recall only one or two items. The cue might then be modified by adding the phrase 'some of which were names of indoor games.' Recall is likely to be facilitated (Gardiner, Craik, & Birtwistle, 1972). A control group can always establish that the added cue is not sufficient to produce the word if it had not been experienced earlier.

Forgetting is a memory failure at a particular time using a particular set of retrieval cues and processes, where failure means no information was recalled or incorrect information was recalled. It does not imply that the information is lost or otherwise permanently unavailable. Indeed, the literature is replete with studies that demonstrate that a failure to remember in a particular task under one set of conditions can be readily alleviated under a different set of retrieval conditions (see Capaldi & Neath, 1995, for a review). To the extent that the different set of conditions reduces interference, performance will be enhanced. The sixth functional principle, then, can be stated as:

(6) Forgetting is due to extrinsic factors.

Forgetting in sensory memory

Decay is posited as the forgetting mechanism in only two areas of research, sensory memory and short-term/working memory. A detailed critique of these areas is beyond the scope of the current chapter; rather, the reader is referred to a recent review by Nairne (2003; see also Crowder & Surprenant, 2000; Neath & Surprenant, 2003). In short, the evidence for sensory memory is not nearly as strong or compelling as it used to appear.

Most researchers now distinguish between two different forms of persistence, *stimulus persistence* and *information persistence* (see Coltheart, 1980). A typical visible persistence task might involve a synchrony judgment: a stimulus is presented, followed by an interval of variable duration, and then followed by a signal, such as a tone. The subject is asked to adjust the signal so that its appearance coincides with the disappearance of the stimulus. If the subject adjusts the signal such that it appears 150 ms after the true offset of the stimulus, then one can infer that the original stimulus persisted for 150 ms. In contrast, a typical information persistence task would involve trying to extract some information from the original stimulus. The partial report task involves presenting a matrix of stimuli (usually letters) for a brief period (around 50 ms). After a variable delay, a signal is presented that indicates which part of the matrix should be recalled. Performance in this partial report condition is compared to performance in a whole report condition, in which all the information in the matrix is recalled. When the matrix is shown for 50 ms, the partial report advantage lasts approximately 500 ms. Recent experimental work suggests, contrary to claims of most conceptions of sensory memory, that visible persistence tasks and information persistence tasks are *not* measuring the same thing (Loftus & Irwin, 1998).

Most likely, stimulus persistence is not part of memory, as most people would define that term. Rather, there is an emerging consensus that it is the result of a particular continuing pattern of neural activity set up by the original stimulus. One key finding that argues against decay here is the inverse duration effect: stimulus persistence *decreases* with increases in stimulus duration (e.g. Bowen, Pola, & Matin, 1974). It is hard to conceive of a form of forgetting where the longer you are exposed to a stimulus, the faster the forgetting. Whereas stimulus persistence is best thought of as not memory, information persistence is now increasingly viewed as the same type of memory as short-term/working memory (Nairne, 2003; Neath & Surprenant, 2003). There is thus only one type of memory in which decay is proposed as a mechanism for forgetting, and we examine this next.

Forgetting in short-term/working memory

One reason why time-based forgetting, such as decay, is often invoked is the common belief that short-term/working memory is immune to interference, especially proactive interference (e.g. Cowan, 2001). This is simply not so. The suffix effect (Crowder, 1967; Dallett, 1965) is a retroactive interference effect. Recall of the last item in a list of auditorily presented items is impaired if the list is followed by a stimulus suffix, an irrelevant item that is the same on every trial and that does not need to be recalled or processed by the subject. The phonological similarity effect (Conrad, 1964), the finding that lists of similar-sounding items are harder to recall than lists of dissimilar-sounding items, is an example of both proactive and retroactive interference in short-term/working memory. As a third example, Tehan and his colleagues (e.g. Tehan & Humphreys, 1996, 1998; Tolan & Tehan, 1999) have developed a task in which proactive interference (PI) can be observed in short-term memory settings. Subjects are asked if an instance of a particular category was seen on the immediately preceding list of four items. They are to ignore any instances prior to the most recent list. However, if there are either semantically similar or phonologically similar items in the preceding list, PI can be observed. Thus, interference effects are readily observed in the short term.

The idea of a separate short-term memory has been challenged (e.g. Melton, 1963) almost since it was first proposed and has continued to be challenged (e.g. Crowder, 1982). Most recently, Nairne (2002a) provides a critical evaluation of the current 'standard model' of short-term/working memory (e.g. Baddeley, 1986; Burgess & Hitch, 1999; Cowan, 1995; Shiffrin, 1999). In this version, permanent knowledge is activated and the collective set of activated items is defined as short-term memory. The activation decays over time and can be offset by refreshing the decaying items through rehearsal. The key finding supporting this idea is that words that take less time to pronounce are recalled better than otherwise equivalent words that take more time to pronounce (Baddeley, Thomson, & Buchanan, 1975). This basic finding, however, has recently been challenged: Lovatt, Avons, and Masterson (2000) have shown that this result holds only for one particular set of words. When other sets of words are used, the time-based word length effect is not observed (see also Neath, Bireta, & Surprenant, 2003). The other finding historically used to support time-based decay comes from the Brown–Peterson paradigm. However, these findings are better conceived as supporting an interference rather than decay explanation (see Nairne, 2002a; Neath & Surprenant, 2003: 125–35).

Forgetting, then, is best accounted for not by time-based decay but rather by interference. The only two areas of memory research in which decay was seriously considered no longer offer good empirical support for the idea. An additional benefit of viewing memory as due to forgetting is that it provides a natural way of examining the importance of cues.

CUES

One thing all tests of memory have in common is that they are cue-driven; that is, all memory retrieval requires and depends on a retrieval cue. The cue can be explicit, in the case of 'Did you see this word on the list?' or 'What is the capital of Assyria?', or it can be less obvious, such as 'Do you have turkey for Christmas?' or 'Complete this fragment with the first word that pops into your head'. With no cue, there can be no memory. This may be obvious for most memory research, and so we will not belabor the point here. For now we simply state this as the next principle:

(7) All memory is cue-driven.

Providing one cue rather than another can change performance on a memory test from failure to success (and from success to failure!). We have already argued (above) that cues do not have intrinsic mnemonic properties; rather, the effectiveness of a cue will depend on the interaction between the encoding and retrieval conditions. One can, however, turn this latter qualification into a general principle, based on the idea of cue overload (Watkins & Watkins, 1975; Watkins, 1979).

Cue overload refers to the idea that a cue will become less and less effective the more stimuli it subsumes.[4] For example, the cue could be a particular list in a particular context. If the list contains one item, the cue is very effective. As list length increases, the probability of recalling any particular item decreases due to cue overload (Watkins, 2001). As another example, lists made up of the digits 1 to 9 in random order do not afford many cues for their successful recollection, particularly when multiple trials are presented one after the other. This is why digit span for English speakers is around 7 to 8 items (e.g. Schweickert & Boruff, 1986). On the other hand, if cues are created that are particularly well suited to discriminate the desired item from other items, digit span can increase to over 100 or more (Ericsson & Staszewski, 1989).

Cue overload, we suggest, is better expressed as its complement: the more specific (less overloaded) a cue, the more likely it is to elicit the appropriate memory. Two examples from the implicit memory literature illustrate such cue hyperspecificity. Given a specific enough cue, memory should last a very long time and there should be little or no correlation between two hyperspecific cues even when they refer to the same nominal target (i.e. there should be stochastic independence).

Sloman, Hayman, Ohta, Law, and Tulving (1988) conducted a repetition priming experiment in which a list of words was presented. In the test phase, they used a word fragment completion task. Of importance, the fragments were created such that only one English word could be made. Subjects who had previously read the word AARDVARK were more likely to complete the fragment A_D_RK than those who did not. Of more interest for current purposes, this priming was still seen on a test conducted 16 months after the initial exposure. That is, seeing a word 16 months earlier facilitated completing the unique fragment.

Two hyperspecific cues should show stochastic independence: performance on task 1 should be uncorrelated with performance on task 2 even though both tasks have the same nominal target and are, apart from the cue, identical. Hayman and Tulving (1989) conducted a series of studies in which subjects first read a series of words during which they were instructed to think about the word's meaning. The key tests involved word fragment completion. The first test might use A_D_RK as the word fragment for AARD-VARK, whereas the second test, which followed 3 minutes later, would use a different fragment, such as _AR_VA_. Note that the fragments are complementary: blanks in the first fragment are replaced with letters in the second fragment, and letters in the first fragment are replaced with blanks in the second fragment. Performance on the second test was essentially independent of performance on the first test.

The more specific the cue, the more effective it will be in eliciting the appropriate memory. Thus,

(8) Cues are subject to overload.

Overload, in this sense, is a result of the interaction between the processes performed at study and the processes performed at test.

CONSTRUCTIVE AND RECONSTRUCTIVE PROCESSES

Memory, like other cognitive processes, is inherently constructive. Information from encoding and cues from retrieval, as well as generic information, are all exploited to construct a response. Work in several areas has long established that people will use whatever information is available to them to help them reconstruct or build up a memory (e.g. Bartlett, 1932). The processes that can lead to

successful and accurate remembering are the same ones that can lead to distortion (Estes, 1997). The reconstructive nature of memory is most obvious when conditions are set up so that errors can be observed. As the three examples below illustrate, providing a particular cue can change how an item or event is remembered, even if the item or event never occurred.

One classic example concerns the ability to reproduce a simple line drawing. Carmichael, Hogan, and Walter (1932) presented simple line drawings to subjects and told half of the subjects the drawing looked like one particular object and told the other half of the subjects that the drawing looked like a second, different, object. For example, one group of subjects might be told that the drawing resembled a pair of eyeglasses whereas the other group was told the drawing looked like a set of dumbbells. At a later test, the subjects were asked to draw the original figure as accurately as possible. Most subjects changed the figure so that it looked more like the verbal label. The idea is that adding a verbal label provided another cue that was available at test, but the label was only partially helpful (i.e. it said only what the object was *like*, not what the object *was*). At test, the cue misled the subjects into reconstructing a drawing that made sense given the cue, but differed from the original drawing (see also Moore, 1910).

A second example involves eyewitness memory. Loftus and Palmer (1974) asked subjects to watch a film that included a car accident. After seeing the film, the subjects were asked: 'How fast were the cars going when they _____ each other?' The researchers varied the intensity of the verb that described the collision, using *smashed*, *collided*, *bumped*, *hit* and *contacted*. When the verb was *smashed*, the estimates averaged 41 mph; when the verb was *contacted*, the estimates averaged 32 mph. A follow-up question asked whether there was broken glass. Nearly one-third of the subjects who had the verb *smashed* said 'yes', but only one-tenth of those who had the verb *contacted* said there was broken glass. There was actually no broken glass. Clearly, the verb used led to the subjects' reconstructing their memory to be consistent with the implied speed of the verb. Many other studies show similar findings. For example, subjects will say 'yes' more often to a question like 'Did you see *the* broken headlight?' than 'Did you see *a* broken headlight?' (Loftus & Zanni, 1975).

Another example involves recalling items that were not presented. Based on a series of studies by Deese (1959a, 1959b), Roediger and McDermott (1995) presented lists of words, such as THREAD, PIN, EYE, SEWING, SHARP, POINT, PRICKED, THIMBLE, HAYSTACK, PAIN, HURT and INJECTION. All these words are related to NEEDLE, which does not appear on the list, but which was recalled approximately 40% of the time. Following recall, the subjects were given a recognition test and were asked to indicate on a scale of 1 to 4 whether each item was from one of the lists. A rating of 4 meant they were sure the word was on the list, a rating of 3 meant they thought the word was probably on the list, a rating of 2 meant the word was probably not on the list, and a rating of 1 meant the word was definitely not on the list. On average, the words that were on the list were given a rating of 3.6, whereas words that were neither on the list nor related to words in the list were given a rating of 1.2. The critical words, which were related but were not on the list, received a mean rating of 3.3, not significantly different from words that were actually on the list. In a subsequent experiment, the subjects were asked to make a remember–know judgment (Tulving, 1985). In this procedure, subjects are given a recognition test and are asked to indicate whether they actually remember the information (have a conscious recollection of the information's occurrence on the study list) or just somehow know the answer (know that the item was on the list but have no conscious recollection of its actual occurrence). Surprisingly, the proportion of studied items that received a remember judgment (0.79) was almost identical to the proportion of critical lures that received a remember judgment (0.73).

These three examples illustrate the dynamic nature of memory and how people reconstruct a memory based on a combination of information available both at encoding and retrieval. The name given to a drawing can alter how it is subsequently reproduced, the words used in questions can affect what is recalled, and events can be recalled that were not present at encoding. As the Loftus and Palmer (1974) verb study shows, once a particular memory has been constructed, it can affect subsequent recollections: people who thought *smashed* implied fast also thought they saw broken glass; people who thought *contacted* implied slow also thought they did not see broken glass.

(9)   All memories are reconstructed.

FALSE MEMORY

Given that memory is a reconstructive process, it should not be surprising to find that there is a large literature showing that people have difficulty distinguishing between memories of events that happened and memories of events that did not happen (see, e.g., Conway, 1997). In a typical reality monitoring experiment (cf. Johnson & Raye, 1981), subjects are shown pictures of common objects. Every so often, instead of a picture, the subjects are shown the name of an object and are asked to create a mental image of the object. The test involves presenting a list of object names, and the subject is asked to judge whether they saw the item (i.e. judge the memory as 'real') or whether they saw the name of the object

and only imagined seeing it (i.e. judge the memory as 'imagined'). People are more likely to judge imagined events as real than real events as imagined.

People can remember entire episodes that did not happen (Ceci, 1995; Hyman & Pentland, 1996). This can be demonstrated in the laboratory by picking an episode (such as getting lost at a shopping mall) and ensuring that it did not happen to the subject. Then, a confederate, usually a relative or close friend, starts reminiscing about events that did occur. After a couple of these, the confederate reminisces about an event that did *not* occur. Although the subjects might not recall the event at first, they will usually begin to supply their own details very soon, and within a few days will have a memory that is rated as vivid and as accurate as a genuine memory (Loftus, 1993).

Even if most of a memory is accurate, making a mistake about one small piece of information can render it inaccurate. Baddeley (1990) relates one such case. Donald Thomson, an Australian psychologist, was picked up by police and identified by a woman as the man who had raped her. His alibi was that he had been on a television talk show at the time and that he had an assistant police commissioner as a witness. The police interrogator reportedly responded with 'Yes, and I suppose you've got Jesus Christ and the Queen of England too!' (Baddeley, 1990: 27). Later released and exonerated, Thomson found out that the television had been on when the woman was raped. Her memory was accurate enough to identify Thomson, but she made an attribution error: she attributed the face she remembered to her attacker rather than to the person on television.

Unfortunately, memories of events that did not happen have been termed *false* memories. There are two problems with this term. First, it suggests a dichotomy between those memories that are true and those that are false. The problem is that all memories are a combination of details recalled about the event supplemented by information unrelated to the actual event. For example, you might really remember seeing a particular movie and can recreate for yourself what it was like sitting there, who you were with, and so on. But your memory of eating popcorn while viewing the film might come from your general knowledge that you often eat popcorn while watching films. Thus, at least part of every memory is likely to be 'false' because at least some details are not of the original event but are drawn from generic memory or other sources. To divide memory up as either true or false masks the fact that all memories are constructed and that the construction process draws on a lot of different types of information. If one has to label memories as either true or false, then all memories must be false, in the sense that memories are rarely, if ever, veridical to the actual event.

The second problem with the term *false memory* is that it suggests that the memory system *stored* false information. This obscures the important point that the memory system is not like a library where the books (memories) are stored on shelves and just sit there. When retrieved, the books may be a little dusty but are otherwise the same as when they were stored. In contrast, memory is dynamic and continuously changing, as the examples above demonstrate. As Wechsler (1963: 151) phrased it: 'Memories are not like filed letters stored in cabinets or unhung paintings in the basement of a museum. Rather, they are like melodies realized by striking the keys on a piano.' Each time the piano is played, the melody is slightly different: the pianist might occasionally strike the wrong key, might speed up or slow down, might press a key slightly harder or more softly, might misread a note, might press the foot pedal slightly earlier or later, or the piano itself might be slightly out of tune or have a slightly different timbre. Each time an event is recalled, the memory is slightly different. Because of the interaction between encoding and retrieval, and because of the variations that occur between two different retrieval attempts, the resulting memories will always differ, even if only slightly.

MEMORY: SYSTEM, PROCESS, OR FUNCTION?

There are three basic conceptions of memory. The multiple systems view emphasizes the structure of memory, fractionating it into separate but related systems. The processing view focuses on the cognitive processes that are used, both at encoding and at retrieval. The functional view stresses the role of memory, addressing the question of how memory works and what its fundamental characteristics are.

The systems view

Advocates of the systems approach (e.g. Schacter & Tulving, 1994; Schacter, Wagner, & Buckner, 2000) identify five major memory systems: working memory, semantic memory, episodic memory, procedural memory and the perceptual representation system. *Working memory* (Baddeley, 1994) is a system for the temporary maintenance and storage of internal information and can be thought of as the place where cognitive 'work' is performed. It has multiple subsystems, most notably one for the processing of verbal or speech-like stimuli (e.g. the phonological store and articulatory control process) and another for the processing of visuo-spatial information (e.g. the visuo-spatial sketchpad and the visual scribe). *Semantic memory* refers to memory for general knowledge and includes facts, concepts and vocabulary (Tulving, 1983). A better term is *generic memory* (Hintzman, 1984) because 'semantic memory' implies storage of only semantic information, which is not the case. Rather, the distinguishing feature of this system is the lack of conscious awareness of the learning episode. In contrast, *episodic memory* is the system that does provide this awareness of the learning episode and enables the individual to mentally 'travel back' into his or her personal past (Tulving, 1998). All of these systems are together part of *declarative memory*, which is contrasted with *procedural memory*, the fourth proposed major memory system. Declarative memory is concerned with knowing 'that' rather than with knowing 'how'. For example, if you know that two plus two equals four, the information is said to be in declarative memory. In contrast, if you know how to ride a bicycle, that information is said to be in procedural memory. Finally, the *perceptual representation system* is a collection of non-declarative domain-specific modules that operate on perceptual information about the form and structure of words and objects (Schacter et al., 2000).

There are many current descriptions of the systems approach; the interested reader is referred especially to the various chapters in Tulving and Craik (2000), Foster and Jelicic (1999), and Schacter and Tulving (1994). Here we focus on what we think are the major weaknesses of this approach for the psychology of memory.

One major weakness with the systems approach is the lack of consensus on what the systems are and even on what the criteria should be. One set of criteria are those of Sherry and Schacter (1987):

1 Functional dissociations: an independent variable that has one effect on a task thought to tap system A either has no effect or a different effect on a task thought to tap system B.
2 Different neural substrates: system A must depend on different brain regions than system B.
3 Stochastic independence: performance on a task that taps system A should be uncorrelated with performance on a task that taps system B.
4 Functional incompatibility: a function carried out by system A cannot be performed by system B.

Roediger, Buckner, and McDermott (1999) show how recall and recognition meet the first three of these criteria: the variable word frequency produces functional dissociations between recall and recognition (Gregg, 1976); neuropsychological dissociations between recall and recognition are observable in amnesic subjects (Hirst, Johnson, Phelps, & Volpe, 1988); and numerous studies have found essentially no correlation between performance on the two tests (Nilsson & Gardiner, 1993). A Gedänken experiment suggests that recall and recognition might also demonstrate functional incompatibility: memory for taste or odors is a function that is well supported by recognition (consider the case of Marcel Proust) but not very well supported by recall. Of course, no memory researcher proposes that recall and recognition are separate memory systems, but this is precisely the problem with the criteria. A slightly different set of criteria have been proposed by Schacter and Tulving (1994). Essentially, they propose that memory systems should be defined in terms of their brain systems, the particular kind of information they process, and their principles of operation (but see the original for a detailed discussion). Neither set of criteria results in producing just the five systems mentioned above.

A second major problem with the multiple systems account is the reliance on dissociations. Although there exist numerous dissociations between episodic and semantic memory, for example, there also exist dissociations between two tasks thought to tap the semantic memory system (Balota & Neely, 1980) and between two tasks thought to tap the episodic memory system (Balota & Chumbley, 1984). Even some of the dissociations between episodic and semantic memory are questionable. As Parkin (1999) notes, many studies show that retrieval in episodic tasks involves right prefrontal activation whereas retrieval of semantic information involves left prefrontal activation. This neuropsychological dissociation, however, reverses when the two tasks are equated for difficulty: retrieval of semantic information produces larger amounts of right frontal activation than the episodic task. In one sense, then, semantic memory under one set of conditions has a different neural substrate than semantic memory under a second set of conditions.

Another problem related to dissociations is the inability of the systems view to predict which way a particular dissociation will turn out (Hintzman, 1984; McKoon, Ratcliff, & Dell, 1986). Thus, variables are found that have one effect on semantic memory and a different effect on episodic memory, but there is nothing in the systems view that predicts a priori which way around the dissociation should occur. Had results come out exactly the reverse of what was seen, these completely opposite findings would still have been taken as evidence for the proposed distinction.

The multiple systems view, then, lacks a principled and consistent set of criteria for delineating memory systems. Given the current state of affairs, it is not unthinkable to postulate ten or twenty or even more different memory systems (Roediger et al., 1999). Even for a particular system, there seem as many opportunities for dissociations within it as dissociations between it and other systems. It is always possible that as knowledge of underlying brain anatomy increases, researchers will specify an increasingly precise and principled set of criteria and will develop a consistent and useful taxonomy of systems. Until that time, however, many researchers have adopted a different approach, one that emphasizes processing rather than structure.

The processing view

The processing or proceduralist view (e.g. Bain, 1855; Crowder, 1993; Kolers & Roediger, 1984) emphasizes the encoding and retrieval processes rather than the system or location in which the memory might be stored. Rather than saying that performance on a memory test depends on the memory system that supports the information, processing theorists propose that what is important is the type of processing that the person used. The original idea was that memory is a by-product of a successive series of analyses, from the perceptual to the conceptual (Craik & Lockhart, 1972). The idea was refined to become *transfer appropriate processing*: a given type of processing at study will lead to better memory performance if it is appropriate for the particular test (see Morris et al., 1977; Tulving & Thomson, 1973).

The basic idea of transfer appropriate processing, as Nairne (2001, 2002b) documents, is often misrepresented as saying that memory depends on the *similarity* of the processes performed at study and those required at test or, to put it another way, on the match between the cue and target. There are two things wrong with this 'transfer similar processing' account. First, it is not transfer appropriate processing. Transfer appropriate processing requires only that the processes be appropriate, not that they be similar. It allows for the processes to be similar, but it also allows them to be dissimilar. Second, transfer similar processing is empirically wrong. There are numerous examples in the memory literature of cases where a copy cue – a cue that is identical to the target – does not elicit the target, such as in recognition failure of recallable words (Watkins & Tulving, 1975). Another example is part-set cueing (Slamecka, 1968): cueing you with part of a set of items (which presumably provides a better overall match between cue and target) can lead to worse performance than cueing you with none of the items in the set (which presumably has a worse match between cue and target).

One problem with transfer appropriate processing is in identifying the processes used. One popular approach has been to focus on two different types of processing (or, more accurately, the endpoints on a continuum): data-driven and conceptually driven processing (Jacoby, 1983). Data-driven processing emphasizes more perceptual or low-level aspects of an item (e.g. whether upper or lower case, whether male or female voice, whether it rhymes with ORANGE) whereas conceptually driven processing emphasizes more semantic or high-level aspects of an item (e.g. whether it is an antonym or synonym of another item, whether it has pleasant or unpleasant associations).

A second problem with this approach has been the almost exclusive focus on data-driven versus conceptually driven processing. Dividing all possible cognitive processing into just two types is most likely oversimplified. Clearly, there are more than just two basic types of processing, and evidence supporting this comes from studies in which dissociations have been found between two conceptually driven tasks (McDermott & Roediger, 1996). Until a more reasoned and complete account of the varieties of processing is provided, the processing view will remain vulnerable to the charge that it is vague in its predictions and certainly incomplete.

Three functional views

There currently is no model of memory that encompasses all of the principles we have presented above and that addresses all of the main research areas. However, there are three models, which are all clearly functional in approach, that do address much of the more heavily researched areas: short-term/working memory, episodic memory and semantic memory.

The feature model

Rather than invoking separate sensory and short-term or working memory systems, the feature model (Nairne, 1988, 1990; Neath & Nairne, 1995; Neath, 2000b) proposes that sensory and short-term memory phenomena can be accounted for within a single framework. Items are represented as vectors of features. Modality-dependent features represent information that is dependent upon the presentation modality (e.g. male or female voice, upper or lower case) whereas modality-independent features represent information that is the same regardless of the modality of presentation (e.g. that the word was 'dog'). There are no capacity limits and there is no decay. Rather, features from one item can retroactively interfere with features from an earlier item. At test, a cue samples all the items and the one with the best relative match is selected. The model can account for suffix effects, modality effects, word length effects, phonological similarity effects, grouping effects, and the effects of articulatory suppression and irrelevant speech. It predicts not only which items will be recalled, but also the error patterns (Neath, 2000b; Surprenant, Kelley, Farley, & Neath, in press). Perhaps its most impressive accomplishment is the prediction of complex interactions among these variables. For example, it predicts the correct pattern of results when word length, phonological similarity, presentation modality and presence or absence of articulatory suppression are factorially manipulated. Although it does not account for all short-term/working memory data, it does suggest that concepts such as separate systems and time-based forgetting may not be necessary.

Compound cue theory

We have argued that items do not have intrinsic mnemonic properties, but spreading activation theory, one very popular account of association priming, posits just such a property (Collins & Loftus,

1975; Anderson, 1983). Association priming is the finding that processing of a word such as NURSE is facilitated if the word DOCTOR has been seen immediately before. The basic idea is that when a concept is processed, it becomes activated and that activation spreads to all related concepts. Because the concept NURSE is partially activated, it can be processed more accurately and quickly when it is encountered. An alternative account avoids attributing specific mnemonic properties to items and instead accounts for the facilitation of primed items by invoking cueing. According to compound cue theory (Dosher & Rosedale, 1989; Ratcliff & McKoon, 1988, 1994), semantic memory functions in the same way as any other form of memory. Rather than having just one item serve as a cue, multiple items can enter into a compound cue. Thus, when NURSE is presented, but DOCTOR is shown just prior, the compound cue of DOCTOR and NURSE is what enhances processing (see Neath & Surprenant, 2003, for details).

Simple

SIMPLE (Brown, Neath, & Chater, 2002) stands for Scale Invariant Memory, Perception, and Learning. It proposes that items are represented internally on a log-transformed scale of the relevant physical dimension. All retrieval is cue-driven and there is no decay or time-based forgetting. Items do not have intrinsic mnemonic properties; rather, a particular item will be retrieved if it has the most local relative distinctiveness given a particular cue. This account explains many memory phenomena, but of particular note here is that the model claims scale invariance (see below). It explains data when the time scale is a few seconds, a few minutes, several hours or several weeks. Thus, it accounts for data from three separate memory systems: short-term/working memory, episodic memory and semantic memory.

Summary of functional models

Although all three functional models of memory above have as their focus different areas of memory research, the models are similar in that they reflect functional principles. All posit that memory is cue-driven, that there can be cue overload, and that neither items nor cues nor processes have intrinsic mnemonic properties. Forgetting is not due to time-based decay but rather is due to interference or discrimination problems. All predict that an item that might not be retrieved under one set of circumstances might be retrievable under a different set. A final similarity is that none requires that the principles it proposes change as a function of time scale, type of processing or type of structure; they propose principles that are invariant.

INVARIANCE

All of the principles noted in this chapter should apply widely; they should be invariant. Invariance has several components, most notably scale invariance. It is a characteristic of natural laws to apply or to hold over a wide range of temporal, spatial or physical scales (see Chater & Brown, 1999). For example, physical laws apply whether the unit of measurement is 1 milligram, 1 gram, 1 kilogram or 1 tonne. Thus, from 1 mg to 1,000,000,000 mg, the laws all hold or, to put it another way, demonstrate scale invariance.

The claim that memory principles are scale invariant is more controversial and is rarely made (although see Gallistel & Gibbon, 2000, for a notable exception). For example, it has long been common practice (e.g. Izawa, 1999) to divide memory into one system that operates from 0 to 500 ms (sensory memory), a second system that operates until approximately 20 or 30 s (short-term or working memory) and a third system that operates on all temporal durations beyond that (long-term memory).[5] Not only does this view propose that the natural laws of memory fundamentally change over a range as small as 200 ms to 20,000 ms, but it proposes they change twice! In contrast, scale invariance means that the fundamental principles of memory apply regardless of the scale, whether remembering immediately after an event or several years after an event. Brown et al. (2002) review much of the evidence for the argument that principles of memory do not change as a function of time scale involved. Here we focus on just three examples.

In a free recall task, subjects are given a list of items and are asked to recall as many of them as they can in any order they like. With free recall, people usually recall the first few items well, which is known as the primacy effect, and the last few items well, which is known as the recency effect. The inter-item presentation interval (or IPI) is the time between items and the retention interval (or RI) is the time between the offset of the final item and the beginning of recall. The ratio rule (Glenberg, Bradley, Kraus, & Renzagila, 1983; see also Bjork & Whitten, 1974) relates the size of the recency effect to the ratio of the IPI to the RI. For example, if items are presented with a 1 s IPI and 1 s RI, the ratio is 1:1. If the items are presented with a 1 week IPI and a 1 week RI, the ratio is still 1:1. The size of the recency effect (defined as the slope of the best-fitting line over the last three points) is predicted to be the same for both situations. The results of an experiment reported by Nairne, Neath, Serra, and Byun (1997) are shown in Figure 9.1: the linear relationship holds quite well for ratios varying between 12:1 and 1:12![6]

One hallmark of short-term/working memory is its limited capacity and one of the most common measures of this limit is memory span (e.g. Schweickert & Boruff, 1986). The subject is shown a series of items and immediately after presentation,

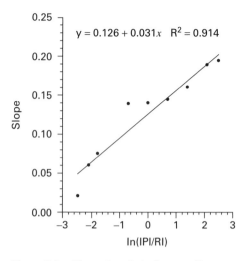

Figure 9.1 *The ratio rule in free recall. The size of the recency effect (measured as the slope of the best-fitting line over the last three points) is proportional to the log of the ratio of the inter-item presentation interval (IPI) and the retention interval (RI).*

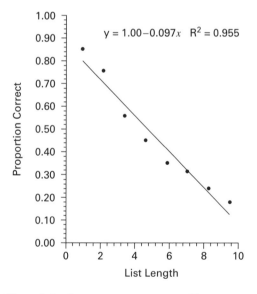

Figure 9.2 *Long-term memory span. The proportion of items correctly placed in order as a function of list length.*

the subject is asked to recall the items in order. There are a variety of ways of measuring span, one of which is the identification of the list length at which performance is 50%. Nairne and Neath (2001) conducted an experiment based on the memory span technique but delayed recall for 5 minutes. The results are shown in Figure 9.2: long-term memory span for two-syllable words is approximately

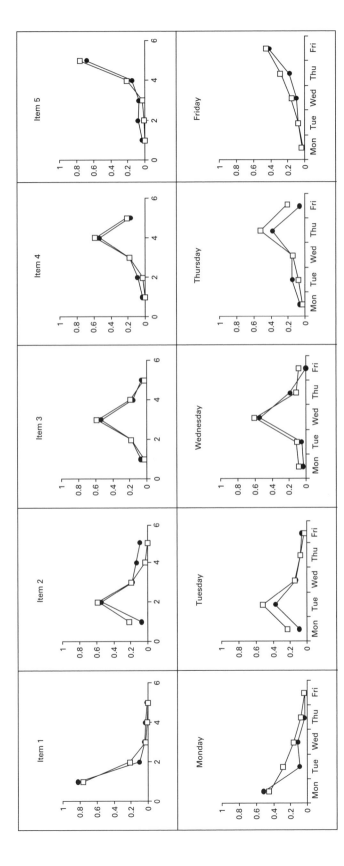

Figure 9.3   The positional uncertainty gradients after retention intervals of 30 seconds (top row, data from Nairne, 1992) and after 1–5 weeks (bottom row, data from Huttenlocher et al., 1992). Each plot shows the proportion of times a particular item or day of the week was recalled in each possible position or day of the week. (Figure adapted from Neath & Surprenant, 2003.)

the same as short-term memory span for two syllable words: about 4–5 items.

A final example of scale invariance concerns the type of errors observed when people are asked when a particular item or event occurred. When an error is made, the item is most likely to be recalled in an adjacent position. Nairne (1992) asked subjects to reconstruct the order in which they had seen a list of five items 30 seconds earlier. Huttenlocher, Hedges, and Prohaska (1992) asked subjects to recall the day on which they had participated in a telephone survey that had taken place between 1 and 5 weeks earlier. Figure 9.3 shows these data (adapted as described by Neath & Surprenant, 2003: 303) as black circles. Similar patterns are seen when subjects are tested immediately (Healy, 1974) or after 24 hours (Nairne, 1992). The white squares are a fit of a one-parameter model of memory for order, perturbation theory (Estes, 1972). Consistent with the claim of scale invariance, one would not be able to tell the duration of the retention interval just by looking at the figures; one needs additional information.

These three examples all demonstrate that certain memory phenomena are scale invariant, that the principles that govern them do not change solely as a function of the time scale. Our final principle, then, may be stated as

(10) Memory principles are invariant.

By this, we mean to imply not just time-scale invariance, but that all of the previous nine principles apply to all of memory, regardless of the hypothetical underlying memory system, the time scale or the processing.

Summary and Conclusions

Tulving (1983: 265) proposed that the encoding specificity principle (which is represented as Principle 1 in our accounting) 'holds for all phenomena of episodic memory … [and] probably also holds for semantic memory … The postulated generality implies that such interactions could be demonstrated with all kinds of rememberers, to-be-remembered events, encoding operations, and retrieval information, in appropriately controlled and sufficiently sensitive experiments.' The encoding specificity principle has been attacked as untestable (see Tulving, 1983, for a review) and, indeed, all the principles noted above are subject to similar attacks. In response, Tulving makes the point that although a principle might be 'untestable' in the sense that one could never test all possible experiments, this is unrelated to whether the principle has empirical support. We have presented only a fraction of the studies that support the principles in the current chapter. However, we too want to claim that the principles identified above apply to all of memory. They are not restricted by time scale,

by type of processing or by type of structure. These principles are, we claim, invariant.

Acknowledgements

We are indebted to Gordon D. A. Brown and James S. Nairne for many insightful discussions and valuable comments.

Notes

1 For simplicity and due to space constraints, we omit consideration of factors that occur after encoding but before retrieval. Such factors can and do affect memory performance (e.g. Proctor & Fagnani, 1978).

2 McGeoch's (1932) three-factor theory of forgetting focused on response competition, set, and altered stimulating conditions. All three can be seen as forms of interference.

3 The paired associate terminology is a useful schematic for comprehending retroactive and proactive interference, but it is oversimplified in that it assumes the cue A will be processed in exactly the same way at both study and test, which is rarely the case.

4 Note that Luce's (1963) choice rule predicts a form of cue overload in a way that does not attribute an intrinsic mnemonic property to a cue.

5 Within the working memory framework (e.g. Baddeley, 1986), the proposed temporal divisions differ. The articulatory control process and the phonological store are no longer factors after as few as 2 to 4 s. It has recently been proposed that an episodic buffer handles memories in situations that require longer storage than this, but shorter than long-term memory (Baddeley, 2000). This view still requires fundamental changes in principles over a very small time scale, but whether one or two or three changes are required depends on the particular version of the theory.

6 There is one apparent departure from the ratio rule. Cowan, Saults, and Nugent (1997) presented data that suggested that the absolute amount of time that has passed before a memory test takes place does have an effect on subsequent performance even when the temporal information is held constant (i.e. the ratios remain constant). However, Cowan, Saults, and Nugent (2001: 326) performed further analyses and concluded that 'we have failed to find clear evidence of decay in a situation that has often been viewed as one of the simplest paradigm cases for decay, namely in two-tone comparisons.'

References

Anderson, J. R. (1983). A spreading activation theory of memory. *Journal of Verbal Learning and Verbal Behavior*, 22, 261–295.

Baddeley, A. D. (1986). *Working memory*. New York: Oxford University Press.

Baddeley, A. D. (1990). *Human memory*. Boston: Allyn & Bacon.

Baddeley, A. D. (1994). Working memory: the interface between memory and cognition. In D. L. Schacter & E. Tulving (Eds.), *Memory systems 1994* (pp. 351–367). Cambridge, MA: MIT Press.

Baddeley, A. D. (2000). The episodic buffer: a new component of working memory? *Trends in Cognitive Sciences*, *4*, 417–423.

Baddeley, A. D., Thomson, N., & Buchanan, M. (1975). Word length and the structure of short-term memory. *Journal of Verbal Learning and Verbal Behavior*, *14*, 575–589.

Bain, A. (1855). *The senses and the intellect*. London: John W. Parker & Son.

Balota, D. A., & Chumbley, J. I. (1984). Are lexical decisions a good measure of lexical access: the role of word frequency in the neglected decision stage. *Journal of Experimental Psychology: Human Perception and Performance*, *10*, 340–357.

Balota, D. A., & Neely, J. H. (1980). Test-expectancy and word-frequency effects in recall and recognition. *Journal of Experimental Psychology: Human Learning and Memory*, *6*, 576–587.

Bartlett, F. C. (1932). *Remembering: a study in experimental and social psychology*. Cambridge: Cambridge University Press.

Bjork, R. A. (2001). Recency and recovery in human memory. In H. L. Roediger III, J. S. Nairne, I. Neath, & A. M. Surprenant (Eds.), *The nature of remembering: essays in honor of Robert G. Crowder* (pp. 211–232). Washington, DC: American Psychological Association.

Bjork, R. A., & Whitten, W. B. II (1974). Recency sensitive retrieval processes in long-term free recall. *Cognitive Psychology*, *6*, 173–189.

Bowen, R., Pola, J., & Matin, L. (1974). Visual persistence: effects of flash luminance, duration and energy. *Vision Research*, *14*, 295–303.

Bowers, J. S., & Schacter, D. L. (1990). Implicit memory and test awareness. *Journal of Experimental Psychology: Learning, Memory, and Cognition*, *16*, 404–416.

Brown, G. D. A., Neath, I., & Chater, N. (2002). SIMPLE: a local distinctiveness model of scale invariant memory and perceptual identification. Manuscript submitted for publication.

Burgess, N., & Hitch, G. (1999). Memory for serial order: a network model of the phonological loop and its timing. *Psychological Review*, *106*, 551–581.

Capaldi, E. J., & Neath, I. (1995). Remembering and forgetting as context discrimination. *Learning and Memory*, *2*, 107–132.

Carmichael, L., Hogan, H. P., & Walter, A. A. (1932). An experimental study of the effect of language on the reproductions of visually perceived forms. *Journal of Experimental Psychology*, *15*, 73–86.

Ceci, S. J. (1995). False beliefs: some developmental and clinical considerations. In D. L. Schacter (ed.), *Memory distortions* (pp. 91–125). Cambridge, MA: Harvard University Press.

Chater, N., & Brown, G. D. A. (1999). Scale invariance as a unifying psychological principle. *Cognition*, *69*, 17–24.

Collins, A. M., & Loftus, E. F. (1975). A spreading-activation theory of semantic processing. *Psychological Review*, *82*, 407–428.

Coltheart, M. (1980). Iconic memory and visible persistence. *Perception and Psychophysics*, *27*, 183–228.

Conrad, R. (1964). Acoustic confusions in immediate memory. *British Journal of Psychology*, *55*, 75–84.

Conway, M. A. (ed.) (1997). *Recovered memories and false memories*. New York: Oxford University Press.

Cowan, N. (1995). *Attention and memory: an integrative framework*. New York: Cambridge University Press.

Cowan, N. (2001). The magical number 4 in short-term memory: a reconsideration of mental storage capacity. *Behavioral and Brain Sciences*, *24*, 87–114.

Cowan, N., Saults, J. S., & Nugent, L. D. (1997). The role of absolute and relative amounts of time in forgetting within immediate memory: the case of tone pitch comparisons. *Psychonomic Bulletin and Review*, 4, 393–397.

Cowan, N., Saults, J. S., & Nugent, L. D. (2001). The ravages of absolute and relative amounts of time on memory. In H. L. Roediger III, J. S. Nairne, I. Neath, & A. M. Surprenant (Eds.), *The nature of remembering: essays in honor of Robert G. Crowder* (pp. 315–330). Washington, DC: American Psychological Association.

Craik, F. I. M. (1983). On the transfer of information from temporary to permanent memory. *Philosophical Transactions of the Royal Society of London B*, *302*, 341–359.

Craik, F. I. M., & Lockhart, R. S. (1972). Levels of processing: a framework for memory research. *Journal of Verbal Learning and Verbal Behavior*, *11*, 671–684.

Crowder, R. G. (1967). Prefix effects in immediate memory. *Canadian Journal of Psychology*, *21*, 450–461.

Crowder, R. G. (1982). The demise of short-term memory. *Acta Psychologica*, *5*, 291–323.

Crowder, R. G. (1993). Systems and principles in memory theory: another critique of pure memory. In A. F. Collins, S. E. Gathercole, M. A. Conway, & P. E. Morris (Eds.), *Theories of memory* (pp. 139–161). Hove, UK: Erlbaum.

Crowder, R. G., & Surprenant, A. M. (2000). Sensory memory. In A. E. Kazdin (ed.), *Encyclopedia of psychology* (pp. 227–229). New York: Oxford University Press and American Psychological Association.

Dallett, K. (1965). 'Primary memory': the effects of redundancy upon digit repetition. *Psychonomic Science*, *3*, 237–238.

Deese, J. (1959a). Influence of inter-item associative strength upon immediate free recall. *Psychological Reports*, *5*, 305–312.

Deese, J. (1959b). On the prediction of occurrence of particular verbal intrusions in immediate recall. *Journal of Experimental Psychology*, *58*, 17–22.

Dosher, B. A., & Rosedale, G. (1989). Integrated retrieval cues as a mechanism for priming in retrieval from memory. *Journal of Experimental Psychology: General*, *118*, 191–211.

Ericsson, K. A., & Staszewski, J. (1989). Skilled memory and expertise: mechanisms of exceptional performance. In D. Klahr & K. Kotovsky (Eds.), *Complex information* processing: the impact of Herbert A. Simon (pp. 235–267). Hillsdale, NJ: Erlbaum.

Estes, W. K. (1972). An associative basis for coding and organization in memory. In A. W. Melton & E. Martin (Eds.), *Coding processes in human memory* (pp. 161–190). Washington, DC: Winston.

Estes, W. K. (1997). Processes of memory loss, recovery, and distortion. *Psychological Review, 104,* 148–169.

Foster, J. K., & Jelicic, M. (Eds.) (1999). *Memory: systems, process, or function?* New York: Oxford University Press.

Gallistel, C. R., & Gibbon, J. (2000). Time, rate, and conditioning. *Psychological Review, 107,* 219–275.

Gardiner, J. M., Craik, F. I. M., & Birtwistle, J. (1972). Retrieval cues and release from proactive inhibition. *Journal of Verbal Learning and Verbal Behavior, 11,* 778–783.

Glenberg, A. M., Bradley, M. M., Kraus, T. A., & Renzaglia, G. J. (1983). Studies of the long-term recency effect: support for the contextually guided retrieval hypothesis. *Journal of Experimental Psychology: Learning, Memory, and Cognition, 9,* 231–255.

Gregg, V. H. (1976). Word frequency, recognition, and recall. In J. Brown (ed.), *Recall and recognition* (pp. 183–216). New York: Wiley.

Hayman, C. A. G., & Tulving, E. (1989). Is priming in fragment completion based on a 'traceless' memory system? *Journal of Experimental Psychology: Learning, Memory, and Cognition, 15,* 941–956.

Healy, A. F. (1974). Separating item from order information in short-term memory. *Journal of Verbal Learning and Verbal Behavior, 13,* 644–655.

Hintzman, D. L. (1984). Episodic versus semantic memory: a distinction whose time has come – and gone? *Behavioral and Brain Sciences, 7,* 240–241.

Hirst, W., Johnson, M. K., Phelps, E. A., & Volpe, B. T. (1988). More on recognition and recall in amnesics. *Journal of Experimental Psychology: Learning, Memory, and Cognition, 14,* 758–763.

Huttenlocher, J., Hedges, L. V., & Prohaska, V. (1992). Memory for day of the week: a 5 ± 2 day cycle. *Journal of Experimental Psychology: General, 121,* 313–326.

Hyde, T. S., & Jenkins, J. J. (1973). Recall of words as a function of semantic, graphic, and syntactic orienting tasks. *Journal of Verbal Learning and Verbal Behavior, 12,* 471–480.

Hyman, I. E., & Pentland, J. (1996). The role of mental imagery in the creation of false childhood memories. *Journal of Memory and Language, 35,* 101–117.

Izawa, C. (ed.) (1999). *On human memory: evolution, progress, and reflections of the 30th anniversary of the Atkinson-Shiffrin model.* Mahwah, NJ: Erlbaum.

Jacoby, L. L. (1983). Remembering the data: analyzing interactive processes in reading. *Journal of Verbal Learning and Verbal Behavior, 22,* 485–508.

Jacoby, L. L. (1991). A process dissociation framework: separating automatic from intentional uses of memory. *Journal of Memory and Language, 30,* 513–541.

Johnson, M. K., & Raye, C. L. (1981). Reality monitoring. *Psychological Review, 88,* 67–85.

Knoedler, A. J., Hellwig, K. A., & Neath, I. (1999). The shift from recency to primacy with increasing delay. *Journal of Experimental Psychology: Learning, Memory, and Cognition, 25,* 474–487.

Kolers, P. A., & Roediger, H. L. III (1984). Procedures of mind. *Journal of Verbal Learning and Verbal Behavior, 23,* 425–449.

Loftus, E. F. (1993). The reality of repressed memories. *American Psychologist, 48,* 518–537.

Loftus, E. F., & Palmer, J. C. (1974). Reconstruction of automobile destruction: an example of the interaction between language and memory. *Journal of Verbal Learning and Verbal Behavior, 13,* 585–589.

Loftus, E. F., & Zanni, G. (1975). Eyewitness testimony: the influence of the wording of a question. *Bulletin of the Psychonomic Society, 5,* 86–88.

Loftus, G. R., & Irwin, D. E. (1998). On the relations among different measures of visible and informational persistence. *Cognitive Psychology, 35,* 135–199.

Lovatt, P., Avons, S. E., & Masterson, J. (2000). The word-length effect and disyllabic words. *Quarterly Journal of Experimental Psychology, 53A,* 1–22.

Luce, R. D. (1963). Detection and recognition. In R. D. Luce, R. R. Bush, & E. Galanter (Eds.), *Handbook of mathematical psychology* (pp. 103–189). New York: Wiley.

McDermott, K. B., & Roediger, H. L. III (1996). Exact and conceptual repetition dissociate conceptual memory tests: problems for transfer appropriate processing theory. *Canadian Journal of Psychology, 50,* 57–71.

McGeoch, J. A. (1932). Forgetting and the law of disuse. *Psychological Review, 39,* 352–370.

McKoon, G., Ratcliff, R., & Dell, G. S. (1986). A critical evaluation of the semantic/episodic distinction. *Journal of Experimental Psychology: Learning, Memory, and Cognition, 12,* 295–306.

Melton, A. W. (1963). Implications of short-term memory for a general theory of memory. *Journal of Verbal Learning and Verbal Behavior, 2,* 1–21.

Moore, T. V. (1910). The process of abstraction: an experimental study. *California University Publications in Psychology, 1,* 73–197.

Morris, C. D., Bransford, J. D., & Franks, J. J. (1977). Levels of processing versus transfer appropriate processing. *Journal of Verbal Learning and Verbal Behavior, 16,* 519–533.

Nairne, J. S. (1988). A framework for interpreting recency effects in immediate serial recall. *Memory and Cognition, 16,* 343–352.

Nairne, J. S. (1990). A feature model of immediate memory. *Memory and Cognition, 18,* 251–269.

Nairne, J. S. (1992). The loss of positional certainty in long-term memory. *Psychological Science, 3,* 199–202.

Nairne, J. S. (2001). A functional analysis of memory. In H. L. Roediger III, J. S. Nairne, I. Neath, & A. M. Surprenant (Eds.), *The nature of remembering: essays in honor of Robert G. Crowder* (pp. 283–296). Washington, DC: American Psychological Association.

Nairne, J. S. (2002a). Remembering over the short-term: the case against the standard model. *Annual Review of Psychology, 53,* 53–81.

Nairne, J. S. (2002b). The myth of the encoding-retrieval match. *Memory, 10,* 389–395.

Nairne, J. S. (2003). Sensory and working memory. In A. H. Healy & R. W. Proctor (Eds.), *Comprehensive handbook of psychology: Vol. 4. Experimental psychology* (pp. 423–446). New York: Wiley.

Nairne, J. S., & Neath, I. (2001). Long-term memory span. *Behavioral and Brain Sciences, 24,* 134–135.

Nairne, J. S., Neath, I., Serra, M., & Byun, E. (1997). Positional distinctiveness and the ratio rule in free recall. *Journal of Memory and Language, 37,* 155–166.

Neath, I. (2000a). Learning and memory: human. In A. E. Kazdin (ed.), *Encyclopedia of psychology* (pp. 16–19). New York: Oxford University Press and American Psychological Association.

Neath, I. (2000b). Modeling the effects of irrelevant speech on memory. *Psychonomic Bulletin and Review, 7,* 403–423.

Neath, I., Bireta, T. J., & Surprenant, A. M. (2003). The time-based word length effect and stimulus set specificity. *Psychonomic Bulletin and Review, 10,* 430–434.

Neath, I., & Knoedler, A. J. (1994). Distinctiveness and serial position effects in recognition and sentence processing. *Journal of Memory and Language, 33,* 776–795.

Neath, I., & Nairne, J. S. (1995). Word-length effects in immediate memory: overwriting trace-decay theory. *Psychonomic Bulletin and Review, 2,* 429–441.

Neath, I., & Surprenant, A. M. (2003). *Human memory: an introduction to research, data, and theory* (2nd ed). Belmont, CA: Wadsworth.

Nilsson, L.-G., & Gardiner, J. (1993). Identifying exceptions in a database of recognition failure studies from 1973 to 1992. *Memory and Cognition, 21,* 397–410.

Osgood, C. E. (1953). *Method and theory in experimental psychology.* New York: Oxford University Press.

Paivio, A., Rogers, T. B., & Smythe, P. C. (1968). Why are pictures easier to recall than words? *Psychonomic Science, 11,* 137–138.

Parkin, A. J. (1999). Component processes versus systems: is there really an important difference? In J. K. Foster & M. Jelicic (Eds.), *Memory: systems, process, or function?* (pp. 273–287). Oxford: Oxford University Press.

Payne, D. G. (1987). Hypermnesia and reminiscence in recall: a historical and empirical review. *Psychological Bulletin, 101,* 5–27.

Proctor, R. W., & Fagnani, C. A. (1978). Effects of distractor-stimulus modality in the Brown-Peterson distractor task. *Journal of Experimental Psychology: Human Learning and Memory, 4,* 676–684.

Ratcliff, R., & McKoon, G. (1988). A retrieval theory of priming in memory. *Psychological Review, 95,* 385–408.

Ratcliff, R., & McKoon, G. (1994). Retrieving information from memory: spreading-activation theories versus compound-cue theories. *Psychological Review, 101,* 177–184.

Roediger, H. L. III, & McDermott, K. B. (1995). Creating false memories: remembering words not presented in lists. *Journal of Experimental Psychology: Learning, Memory, and Cognition, 21,* 803–814.

Roediger, H. L. III, Buckner, R. L., & McDermott, K. B. (1999). Components of processing. In J. K. Foster & M. Jelicic (Eds.), *Memory: systems, process, or function?* (pp. 32–65). Oxford: Oxford University Press.

Schacter, D. L. & Tulving, E. (1994). What are the memory systems of 1994? In D. L. Schacter & E. Tulving (Eds.), *Memory systems 1994* (pp. 1–38). Cambridge, MA: MIT Press.

Schacter, D. L., Wagner, A. D., & Buckner, R. L. (2000). Memory systems of 1999. In E. Tulving and F. I. M. Craik (Eds.), *The Oxford handbook of memory* (pp. 627–643). New York: Oxford University Press.

Schweickert, R., & Boruff, B. (1986). Short-term memory capacity: magic number or magic spell? *Journal of Experimental Psychology: Learning, Memory, and Cognition, 12,* 419–425.

Sherry, D. F., & Schacter, D. L. (1987). The evolution of multiple memory systems. *Psychological Review, 94,* 439–454.

Shiffrin, R. M. (1999). 30 years of memory. In C. Izawa (ed.), *On human memory: evolution, progress, and reflections of the 30th anniversary of the Atkinson-Shiffrin model* (pp. 17–33). Mahwah, NJ: Erlbaum.

Slamecka, N. J. (1968). An examination of trace storage in free recall. *Journal of Experimental Psychology, 76,* 504–513.

Sloman, S. A., Hayman, C. A. G., Ohta, N., Law, J., & Tulving, E. (1988). Forgetting in primed fragment completion. *Journal of Experimental Psychology: Learning, Memory, and Cognition, 14,* 223–239.

Surprenant, A. M., Kelley, M. R., Farley, L. A., & Neath, I. (in press). Fill-in and infill errors in order memory. *Memory.*

Tehan, G., & Humphreys, M. S. (1996). Cueing effects in short-term recall. *Memory and Cognition, 24,* 719–732.

Tehan, G., & Humphreys, M. S. (1998). Creating proactive interference in immediate recall: building a DOG from a DART, a MOP, and a FIG. *Memory and Cognition, 26,* 477–489.

Thomson, D. M., & Tulving, E. (1970). Associative encoding and retrieval: weak and strong cues. *Journal of Experimental Psychology, 86,* 255–262.

Tolan, G. A., & Tehan, G. (1999). Determinants of short-term forgetting: decay, retroactive interference, or proactive interference? *International Journal of Psychology, 34,* 285–292.

Tulving, E. (1983). *Elements of episodic memory.* New York: Oxford University Press.

Tulving, E. (1985). Memory and consciousness. *Canadian Psychology, 26,* 1–12.

Tulving, E. (1998). Neurocognitive processes of human memory. In C. von Euler, I. Lundberg, & R. Llinas (Eds.), *Basic mechanisms in cognition and language* (pp. 261–281). Amsterdam: Elsevier.

Tulving, E., & Craik, F. I. M. (Eds.) (2000). *The Oxford handbook of memory.* New York: Oxford University Press.

Tulving, E., & Thomson, D. M. (1973). Encoding specificity and retrieval processes in episodic memory. *Psychological Review, 80,* 352–373.

Watkins, M. J. (1979). Engrams as cuegrams and forgetting as cue overload: a cueing approach to the structure of memory. In C. R. Puff (ed.), *Memory organization and structure* (pp. 347–372). New York: Academic Press.

Watkins, M. J. (2001). The modality effect and the gentle law of speech ascendancy. In H. L. Roediger III, J. S. Nairne, I. Neath, & A. M. Surprenant (Eds.), *The nature of remembering: essays in honor of Robert G. Crowder* (pp. 189–209). Washington, DC: American Psychological Association.

Watkins, M. J., & Tulving, E. (1975). Episodic memory: when recognition fails. *Journal of Experimental Psychology: General, 104,* 5–29.

Watkins, O. C., & Watkins, M. J. (1975). Buildup of proactive inhibition as a cue-overload effect. *Journal of Experimental Psychology: Human Learning and Memory, 1,* 442–452.

Wechsler, D. B. (1963). Engrams, memory storage, and mnemonic coding. *American Psychologist, 18,* 149–153.

Weldon, M. S., & Roediger, H. L. III (1988). Altering retrieval demands reverses the picture superiority effect. *Memory and Cognition, 15,* 269–280.

Wheeler, M. A. (1995). Improvement in recall over time without repeated testing: spontaneous recovery revisited. *Journal of Experimental Psychology: Learning, Memory, and Cognition, 21,* 173–184.

Wright, A. A., Santiago, H. C., Sands, S. F., Kendrick, D. F., & Cook, R. G. (1985). Memory processing of serial lists by pigeons, monkeys, and people. *Science, 229,* 287–289.

PART THREE

Language

10

Language Comprehension

ALAN GARNHAM

Language permeates our lives. For most people, on most days, language comprehension and language production are central activities, not only because of the time they occupy, but also because of the role they play in people's lives. For the most part we take our linguistic abilities for granted, though they may come to our attention when we encounter a word whose meaning we do not know or, more seriously, when we hear, or attempt to learn, a language with which we are not familiar. Indeed, people often show a remarkable lack of curiosity about the mental representations, mechanisms and processes that underlie their linguistic abilities. This chapter details some of the mental capacities on which the ability to understand language is based. For more detailed information about specific aspects of comprehension, see the following chapters by McQueen and by Pollatsek and Rayner.

For ordinary language users, comprehension is either listening or reading. Listening is the more basic form of comprehension. It is both phylogenetically and ontogenetically prior to reading, and it does not have to be taught. There are many special questions about reading, which are addressed in Chapter 12 by Pollatsek and Rayner. However, many of the processes of comprehension are assumed to be common to listening and reading, and much of the work reported in this chapter has used visual materials.

Comprehension is a process that unfolds in time. Speech is inherently temporal. Written and printed material is read in a sequential manner (see Pollatsek & Rayner, Chapter 12, this volume). Not only that, but as we shall see, there is no simple single process of comprehension that is applied to each part of a text or discourse, but rather a series of processes that themselves unfold through time and become less specifically tied to individual parts of the text.

Traditionally (e.g. Forster, 1979) these processes are divided into three groups: lexical, syntactic and discourse (message) level. The listener or reader has to identify the words being heard or read, to group them into phrases and clauses, and to use those groupings, together with other information, to determine their meaning. These processes are not necessarily wholly sequential, when we consider the processing of a single stretch of a discourse. Indeed the temporal (and indeed the logical) connections between these different processes is an empirical and unresolved question.

WORD IDENTIFICATION

In order to characterize the process of language comprehension, we first need to consider the nature of the incoming stimulus. McQueen's Chapter 11 deals with this problem for the case of speech. Important obstacles to identifying individual words in speech are the largely continuous nature of the speech signal (there are no breaks between most words) and the non-canonical pronunciation of words in context (e.g. 'green' might be pronounced 'greem' in a context such as 'green mitten'). Printed materials do not present such problems, typos excepted. Spaces between words are clear, and canonical spelling is the norm. Handwriting is more complex, but the identification of handwritten words has been the subject of comparatively little research. Manso de Zuniga, Humphreys, and Evett (1991) suggest that the differences in the recognition of handwriting and printed text lie primarily in very early processes that 'normalize' the representation of handwritten letters, by eliminating differences from one occurrence of a letter to the next.

The identification of what words are present in a particular utterance or written sentence depends on the use of a mental store of knowledge about the words in the language one knows – *the mental lexicon*. This knowledge, as well as more general knowledge about the sound structure of words in the language, is also used to segment the continuous speech signal into words, as McQueen's Chapter 11 explains. At a broad level, the mental lexicon contains the same kinds of information as an ordinary (printed) lexicon or dictionary: information about how a word is spelled, about its canonical pronunciation, about its part of speech and about its meaning. Exactly how this information is represented, and what the overall organization of the mental lexicon is, are, however, matters of debate. Is the pronunciation of a word encoded as a sequence of phonemes, for example? Or, what corresponds to the alphabetic principle of organization of entries in printed lexicons, which allows for the systematic location of entries?

Finding words in printed dictionaries is usually a case of systematic search in a small part of the dictionary, found by using knowledge of the general principles of alphabetic organization, and page headers. Broadly similar search mechanisms have been proposed for locating items in the mental lexicon (Forster, 1976). However, they have generally been rejected in favour of detector models, in which detectors for individual words accrue evidence that their word has been presented until one is deemed to have won the 'race' among them: the detection of the word. Morton's (1969) logogen model was an early model of this kind, in which the detectors were independent of each other, and were effectively watched over by a device that noted which one reported first that its word had been detected. More recently, interactive activation models (McClelland & Rumelhart, 1981) have been influential. In such models, detectors are linked together, with detectors of the same type (e.g. word detectors) inhibiting each other. The logic behind this mechanism is that any evidence that a particular word is such-and-such (say, 'table') can be thought of as indirect evidence that it is not any other word.

Interactive activation models are typically localist in their representations. They retain discrete detectors for individual words. Connectionist models with distributed representations became popular when learning procedures, such as 'back propagation', were developed for them (see Lamberts, Chapter 18, this volume). They have been proposed for word identification (e.g. Seidenberg & McClelland, 1989). However, after learning has taken place, the operation of such models can be difficult to understand, and it has been argued that, for this reason, they are unsatisfactory as models of

cognitive processes (see, e.g., Grainger & Jacobs, 1998, for the particular case of word recognition).

Over the last thirty years a very large number of experiments on the recognition of individual words, and in particular individual printed words, has been reported. Early findings included the effects of length, frequency, degradation and context on identification. Short words are easier to recognize, as are common ones, and ones that are easy to see. Words are recognized more quickly in lexical semantic contexts (e.g. the word 'butter' is recognized faster if it is preceded by the related word 'bread' than if it is preceded by the unrelated word 'brake': Meyer & Schvaneveldt, 1971) and in discourse contexts (Schuberth & Eimas, 1977). Different models made different predictions about how these basic effects might interact with one another (Garnham, 1985). In the late 1970s and early 1980s, before the interactive activation model became dominant, findings related to these effects led to a series of proposals that were variants on or hybrids of search and (logogen-type) detector models (e.g. Becker, 1980; Norris, 1986).

English orthography bears a complex relation to sound, and another early discovery was that regular words (i.e. ones that follow the most common spelling-to-sound patterns) are easier to recognize than irregular words, other things being equal. A further finding (Glushko, 1979) was that consistency also has an effect. A regular spelling-to-sound pattern may also be consistent, if all words with that pattern are pronounced in the same way. Alternatively it may be inconsistent, if there is a minority of words with a different pronunciation (e.g. the ending '-int' is regularly pronounced with a short 'i' as in 'mint', 'hint', 'dint', etc., but is not consistently pronounced that way, because of the inconsistent 'pint'). This finding led to a more general consideration of the kind of neighbourhood in which a word found itself (orthographic and/or phonological) and of how that affected its recognition (e.g. Grainger, 1990). (See Pollatsek & Rayner, Chapter 12, this volume, for a more detailed discussion of the role of sound in the recognition of printed words.)

As findings on word identification became ever more complex, attention began to focus on the tasks used to study this process, and how they were related to it. Perhaps the most important, and at the same time the most controversial, task is the lexical decision task. In this task, subjects have to decide whether a letter string is a word of the language they know. Logically, the task can be performed simply by detecting whether the string has an entry in the mental lexicon. Whether this is actually how the task is performed is another question, and a cause of much of the controversy about the interpretation of results from lexical decision tasks. In particular, it is thought that the results of lexical decision experiments might be contaminated by factors that affect decision-making rather than lexical access.

Other important issues in word identification are the role of morphology and the processing of ambiguous words. Many English words have prefixes and suffixes and the question is whether they are identified as wholes or by decomposing them and using the parts to identify them. A further complication is that some affixes, such as plural endings on nouns and endings on verbs indicating person or tense, have no effect or entirely predictable effects on meaning. They are referred to as *inflexional*. Others (e.g. '-er', '-ness', 'un-') have only partly systematic effects, and are referred to as *derivational*. Inflexional endings are best treated as part of the grammar, but derivational endings, being idiosyncratic, are lexical. Taft and Forster (1975) provided evidence for morphological decomposition by showing that pseudo-prefixes (like re- in rejuvenate) can affect word recognition. However, later research has suggested a more complex picture, with results depending on the semantic and phonological transparency of the complex words (Marslen-Wilson, Tyler, Waksler, & Older, 1994). Definite research remains to be carried out in this area.

The question about ambiguous words is what happens when an ambiguous word form (such as 'bank', which can mean a riverside or a financial institution) is identified. Intuitively, since people typically do not notice ambiguity, it might be thought that only the intended meaning is accessed. However, it is not clear in general how such *selective access* could occur. An alternative view is that all meanings are initially accessed and the one that fits with the context is retained (Swinney, 1979). A third idea is that the most frequent meaning is considered first, and only if it does not fit with the context are other meanings considered (Hogaboam & Perfetti, 1975). More recent accounts focus on context occurring before the ambiguous word and look at its effects on access of dominant and non-dominant meanings. Rayner, Pacht, and Duffy's (1994) reordered access model and Vu, Kellas, and Paul's (1998) context-sensitive model take different views of the nature of the interaction between context and dominance. However, it is difficult to decide between these models, because it is difficult to distinguish empirically between a meaning being very weakly activated (reordered access model) and not being activated at all (context-sensitive model).

SYNTACTIC PROCESSING

As words are identified, they have to be linked to other words that have just been identified. The dominant Chomskian approach to linguistics of the past forty years claims that words within sentences are grouped into phrases and clauses (and then sentences) according to rules that can be specified independently of what the groups mean, but which are then important in determining their meaning (syntactic rules). On this view, once words have been recognized, they have to be grouped syntactically with what has just gone before.

The psycholinguistic study of this aspect of language comprehension has a rather strange history. Early versions of Chomsky's syntactic theory (1957, 1965) held that the surface syntactic structure of a sentence was derived (in an analytic sense) from an underlying structure or structures by a series of operations called transformations. These operations, for example, created questions from assertions, or passive sentences from actives (and, in early versions of the theory, complex sentences from simple sentences). The derivational theory of complexity, formulated by George Miller, claimed that the difficulty of understanding a sentence depended on the complexity of the derivation of its surface structure from its underlying structure, but did not deal directly with how its surface structure was computed. In fact, in comprehension, the transformations would have to be reversed, so that the underlying structure could be computed from the surface structure. By 1965, Chomsky had explicitly proposed a version of his theory in which all the information relevant to determining the meaning of a sentence was contained, in a simple form, in its underlying structure. This idea lent support to the notion that to understand a sentence was to derive its underlying structure.

Purported arguments against the derivational theory of complexity (see Fodor, Bever, & Garrett, 1974, for a summary, but see Garnham, 1983) led to the suggestion that meaning had to be computed more directly from surface structure. For example, Bever (1970) suggested the use of heuristics such as that the first noun...verb...noun sequence in a sentence introduced the actor, the main action, and the person or object acted upon.

The first clear proposal for how detailed information about surface structure might be computed was put forward by Kimball (1973). This account and most subsequent accounts have the following basic form. They assume that the syntactic category (part of speech), or the set of possible syntactic categories, of a word is retrieved from the mental lexicon and used together with information about possible surface structure configurations for the language to determine the surface structure of the current sentence. As Kimball realized, such information alone is not enough, and additional parsing principles are required. Such principles may be syntactic in nature or, as we shall see later, may be semantically based.

Kimball's piecemeal proposal for seven principles was replaced by the more systematic proposals of Frazier and Fodor's (1978) sausage machine, which later transformed itself (Frazier, 1979) into the hugely influential *garden path theory* with its two main syntactic principles of minimal attachment and late closure. Empirical research focused on preferences between two structures at points of ambiguity in the analysis of sentences. The garden path theory claimed: (1) that such ambiguities would always be resolved, at least initially, in the same way; and (2) that the way the ambiguities were resolved could be explained by the two principles, along with the general claim that structures were built using information about syntactic categories and syntactic rules.

For example, the word 'that' can, among other things, introduce both complement clauses and relative clauses. A *that*-complement to the verb 'tell', for example, presents the content of what was told, as in (1).

(1) The fireman told the woman that he had rescued many people in similar fires.

A relative clause, on the other hand, provides further information, maybe identifying information, about a person or thing, as in (2).

(2) The fireman told the woman that he was worried about to install a smoke detector.

The garden path theory's first principle, minimal attachment, favours simpler structures over more complex ones. It predicts that the complement clause analysis will be favoured over the relative clause analysis at the point at which 'that' is analysed and incorporated into the structure constructed so far. Thus, at the point at which the two sentences above diverge ('many people' versus 'to install'), readers should have difficulty in the 'to install' version. This result is indeed found (Frazier & Rayner, 1982; Altmann, Garnham, & Dennis, 1992).

The second principle, late closure, favours incorporation of the current word into the local phrase, and operates when minimal attachment fails to establish a preference. For example, it explains why 'yesterday' in (3) is taken to qualify 'left' and not 'said'.

(3) John said Bill left yesterday.

The garden path theory was highly influential for about fifteen years, but it came under increasing attack on two fronts. First, there were claims that parsing preferences could be overridden by non-syntactic information, in a way that the theory did not allow. Second, there were claims that the principle of late closure was not universal, but that although some languages, including English, favour late closure, others including Spanish favour the opposite: early closure. Crain and Steedman (1985) suggested that the preference for complement clause over relative clause readings of 'that' clauses might arise because, with no context, the relative clause was

unexpected – no additional information was required about the woman, so why not just say (4)?

(4) The fireman told the woman to install a smoke detector.

However, in a context in which there were two women, one of whom the fireman was worried about and one whom he was not, the relative clause is justified. A series of studies suggested that, given the right context, the difficulty of the relative clause reading could be completely eliminated (see especially Altmann et al., 1992). This finding suggests that referential information influences parsing decisions directly.

Another type of information that appears to have an early effect on parsing decisions incompatible with the garden path theory is information associated with verbs and the sentence frames in which they prefer to occur. Many verbs can appear in more than one type of construction. The most common alternation in English is probably that between transitive and intransitive uses of the same verb ('John is eating his breakfast' vs. 'John is eating'). Some verbs that show this alternation are more commonly used transitively and others are more commonly used intransitively. This kind of frequency information has been shown to influence parsing decisions (e.g. Clifton, Frazier, & Connine, 1984).

A generalization from the results just discussed would be that many types of information (e.g. syntactic, referential, lexical) could work together to produce a syntactic analysis of a sentence. Such a view leads to so-called *constraint-satisfaction* theories (e.g. MacDonald, Pearlmutter, & Seidenberg, 1994; McRae, Spivey-Knowlton, & Tanenhaus, 1998), which claim that different types of information can act as concurrent constraints on the final analysis.

The second line of evidence against the garden path theory began with a study by Cuetos and Mitchell (1988) in which they examined the interpretation of Spanish sentences such as (5).

(5) Someone shot the servant of the actress who was on the balcony

Late closure suggests that the relative clause should be taken as qualifying 'actress'. However, Spanish speakers took it to qualify 'servant'.

This result, and a whole series on a variety of languages that followed from it (for a summary, see Mitchell, Brysbaert, Grondelaers, & Swanpoel, 2000: 494–6), led the principal proponents of the garden path theory to formulate a new account of syntactic analysis called construal (Frazier & Clifton, 1996). On this account, the attachment of so-called non-primary phrases, such as relative clauses, can be determined by a variety of considerations, which need not be purely syntactic.

Mitchell, on the other hand, suggested that parsing decisions were affected by previous knowledge of which structures were more common in a particular language, the so-called *tuning* hypothesis (e.g. Mitchell, 1994), another generalization of the results on verb preferences. Mitchell argued that different languages might show different statistical patterns with respect to, say, early versus late closure. The precise predictions of this hypothesis depend on the level of detail (or 'grain') at which statistical information is accumulated. For example, Mitchell concluded that the hypothesis is not supported for Dutch (Mitchell & Brysbaert, 1998), but a more recent analysis with a finer grain size has questioned this conclusion (Desmet, Brysbaert, & De Baecke, 2002).

We have already seen that information associated with particular verbs and the structures in which they occur can influence parsing decisions. Related views (e.g. Abney, 1989) suggest that, once a verb has been encountered, the parser tries to fill thematic roles (such as theme or instrument) associated with it, and that it prefers analyses in which these roles are filled. 'Put' has three roles. So, 'the table' in 'put the block in the basket on the table' is preferentially interpreted as the place where the block is put, not the original location of the block (as in 'put the block in the basket on the table into the box on the floor').

A somewhat neglected issue in syntactic processing (but see papers in Fodor & Ferreira, 1998) is the type of reanalysis that must take place if the initial analysis is found to be incorrect, as it will reasonably often be, according to the garden path theory and other accounts. However, Pickering and colleagues have recently proposed a model, the *unrestricted race model*, in which reanalysis is the principal determinant of parsing difficulty (van Gompel, Pickering, & Traxler, 2000).

Finally, it should be mentioned that readers and listeners might not always perform a full syntactic analysis of what they are hearing or reading (see Ferreira, Ferraro, & Bailey, 2002, for a recent version of this view). Caramazza and Zurif (1976) argued that agrammatic aphasics could understand many sentences simply by identifying the main content words in them and constructing a plausible message. Such processes probably also occur in comprehension by normal subjects. The misunderstanding of phrases such as 'fills a much needed gap' and of questions such as 'After an air crash on the border between France and Spain, where should the survivors be buried?' (Barton & Sanford, 1993) may be at least partly explained by the lack of a complete syntactic analysis. It seems unlikely, however, that such obvious constituents as simple noun phrases (e.g. 'the red book') are not recognized in normal comprehension. Thus, a notion of minimal commitment to syntactic structure, or underspecification of syntactic structure,

has often been suggested (e.g. Weinberg, 1994). Unfortunately, it is difficult to provide a principled and empirically satisfactory account of the conditions under which underspecification occurs.

DISCOURSE-LEVEL PROCESSING

The notions of word identification and syntactic processing in language comprehension are relatively constrained. The notion of discourse-level processing is much less clearly defined. Syntax is generally regarded as a sentence-level phenomenon. Thus, syntactic analysis groups together words within sentences ready for interpretation. Interpretation is a much more complex phenomenon and is not restricted to processes operating on single sentences.

Some basic aspects of meaning are determined by within-sentence syntactic structure. Each clause in a sentence usually presents one *eventuality* (event, action, state or process). The finite verb in the clause specifies what kind of eventuality and the other parts of the clause present the participants in the eventuality, so that the clause as a whole conveys local 'who did what to whom' information. One view, popular among formal semanticists, is that this kind of information follows from syntactic structure, with each rule of syntactic combination paired with a rule of syntactic interpretation (the so-called rule-to-rule hypothesis of Bach, 1976). So, a very simple sentence might be formed by having a subject noun phrase (itself comprising a proper name) followed by an intransitive verb (e.g. 'John walks'). The interpretation is that the person denoted by the proper name performs the action described by the verb. Note that the syntactic and semantic rules, though paired, are very different in content: one is about structure, the other about meaning conveyed by structure.

The rule-to-rule hypothesis implies compositionality of semantics. However, it deals only with the literal meaning of sentences, and not with other aspects of their meaning, those that depend on context, for example, or non-literal aspects of meaning. Some cross-sentence aspects of interpretation have been analysed in the same kind of formal semantics framework as within-clause interpretation, in theories such as discourse representation theory (Kamp, 1981; Kamp & Reyle, 1993). In particular, this approach has been applied to the interpretation of anaphoric expressions (e.g. pronouns and ellipses, which take their meaning from a previous part of the text).

Formal, compositional, semantics characterizes both word meanings and combinatorial operations in a highly abstract way. Because of its roots in philosophical logic it recognizes the distinction between sense (roughly speaking, meaning as provided by definitions) and denotation (the thing or things in the world that a word stands for). Hence, it indirectly recognizes what has been called in cognitive science the *grounding problem* (Harnad, 1990). The grounding problem is the problem of explaining how language links with the world and hence how understanding language is understanding information about the world. This problem is particularly acute for certain types of approach to both language and language understanding, those that treat language as merely a formal symbolic system and model language understanding as the manipulation of symbols. In formal semantics, the denotation of a common noun, such as 'table', might be modelled as a set of tables, or rather as a function from possible words to sets of tables. Thus, 'table' means (in the sense of denotes) all those things that are tables in every possible state of affairs. However, formal semanticists are not primarily concerned with word meaning, so that the abstractness of this definition is not a problem for them. Also, since sets of tables are sets of things in the world, this type of analysis does link language and the world, and 'solves' the grounding problem, at least in principle.

However, a growing number of researchers feel that a more concrete solution to the grounding problem is needed. They suggest that the meaning of 'table', for example, has to be spelled out in terms of the way human bodies interact with parts of the world to perform certain functions, relatively formal acts of eating, for example (see, e.g., Glenberg, 1997). This approach takes a very specific view of what concepts are. However, it is not necessarily incompatible with a formal semantic approach. A table still has to be something that can be sat at, for example, and the meaning of 'sat at the table' must derive in some way from the meanings of, among other things, 'sit' (which will also be characterized in terms of human bodies and how they interact with objects for specific functions) and 'table'. Proponents of this view, which is part of the embodied cognition movement, often extend these ideas from the interpretation of individual concepts (such as table) to the interpretation of constructions such as TRANSITIVE VERB + OBJECT. However, it is not clear what all examples of such structures have in common from the embodied cognition perspective, and hence what corresponds in this framework to the formal semanticists' claim that there is a uniform account of the semantics of those structures.

We have already seen that there have been attempts to formalize intersentential relations, such as the relations of coreference indicated by certain anaphoric expressions, in particular definite pronouns (in English, 'he', 'she', 'it', 'they' and their variants, such as 'him'). There is also a long-standing tradition of identifying discourse relations as holding between the propositions (or similar parts) of a text (e.g. Hobbs, 1983; Mann & Thompson, 1986).

Unfortunately there is no precise agreement about the set of discourse relations that exist, how they are to be identified and how they are to be interpreted. It is, however, clear that texts depict temporal and causal relations between events, they elaborate on previous descriptions and they present arguments whose parts bear various relations to one another, and that these are among the kinds of relation that must be described by a theory of discourse relations.

A Theoretical Framework for Studying Discourse Processing: Mental Models Theory

Discourse and text play many roles in our lives. Conversation, in particular, has many social functions. These social functions are studied primarily, though not exclusively, by social psychologists rather than cognitive scientists. Whether this division of labour is a sensible one is a moot point. Cognitive scientists who study discourse processing think of language primarily as a system for conveying information. The information that is conveyed is primarily about some aspect of a world, whether it be the real world (as in newscasts), a fictional world (as in novels) or an abstract world (as in many academic texts – those describing theories of text comprehension, for example). This information is conveyed using a complex systems of signs (a language), which itself has a structure that can be described (e.g. in academic texts about linguistics). Early psycholinguistic theories of comprehension failed to make a clear distinction between information being conveyed by language and information about the linguistic structure conveying that information. In the 1960s, Chomsky's ideas about language were beginning to have a major impact, and psychologists such as George Miller correctly recognized that Chomsky's ideas were of crucial importance for theories of language processing. However, the proposal, implicit in many of the early psycholinguistic theories, that comprehension was basically the extraction of syntactic deep structure, failed to recognize the difference between the linguistic structures and the information conveyed.

Chomsky's ideas, as imported into psychology by Miller and others, were developed and modified by Fodor et al. (1974) and their colleagues. However, by 1970 a number of authors, most influentially John Bransford, were suggesting a different perspective on language comprehension, one that was eventually to develop into modern theories based on the notion of situation models or *mental models*.

Bransford (Bransford, Barclay, & Franks, 1972; Bransford & Franks, 1971) made three main claims about language comprehension. The first is based on the distinction between information conveyed and structures in the system used to convey it. This claim is that the mental representation of the content of a text (what a person had in their mind when they had understood the text) is not a representation of any of the text's linguistic structures. Rather, it is a representation of the situation in the world that the text is about. Bransford illustrated this idea in an experiment (Bransford et al., 1972) in which people confused two sentences (6) and (7), which probably describe the same situation.

(6) Three turtles sat on a floating log and a fish swam beneath it.
(7) Three turtles sat on a floating log and a fish swam beneath them.

However, they did not confuse two other sentences, (8) and (9), which differ linguistically in exactly the same way, but which probably do not describe the same situation.

(8) Three turtles sat beside a floating log and a fish swam beneath it.
(9) Three turtles sat beside a floating log and a fish swam beneath them.

Bransford's other two ideas were also put forward to contrast with theories of comprehension based on the idea of extraction of syntactic deep structure. They were that comprehension is (a) an *integrative* process and (b) a *constructive* process. By saying that comprehension is an integrative process, Bransford was stressing that comprehension requires the combination (or integration) of pieces of information from different parts of a text. Because syntax has typically been assumed to be a sentence-level phenomenon, theories of comprehension based on syntax tend to focus on the comprehension of individual sentences, and thus fail to give consideration to the complexities of how mental representations of different sentences might be combined.

By saying that comprehension is a constructive process, Bransford was pointing out that comprehension requires the combination of explicitly presented information with relevant background information. This idea is illustrated in the turtles, logs and fish sentences above. It is only by using our mundane knowledge that we can work out what situations are probably being described. And it is this mundane knowledge, about the likely (relative) sizes of logs and turtles and about how logs float on water, for example, that allows us to come to the conclusion that the first two sentences probably describe much the same situation.

Construction and integration often work hand in hand. That is to say, links between different parts of a text are often made, or at least made concrete, by background knowledge. Consider, for example, a very brief text such as (10a) followed by (10b):

(10a) John's car left the road at high speed and hit a tree.
(10b) The nearside front tyre had burst.

The use of a definite noun phrase ('the nearside front tyre') in the second sentence suggests a reference to an object whose existence is already established in some way. In other words the linguistic form of the text suggests one way in which information in the two sentences of the text might be integrated. However, the first sentence does not mention a tyre (but rather John, a car, a road and a tree). It is our background knowledge that cars have tyres, or more specifically that each car usually has one nearside front tyre, that allows us to make specific the link between the information in the two sentences. The full understanding of this text also further illustrates the use of mundane knowledge (about the link between tyres bursting and drivers losing control of cars) to compute a full interpretation of a text.

Although construction and integration often work hand in hand in this way, they do not always do so. In some cases integration is based only on linguistic information. For example in (11), the link between the first sentence and the second is established by the fact that the English pronoun 'he' refers to a single male person. The previous sentence, which is the only other sentence of the discourse, introduced one male person (a man), one object (a room) and a relation between them (entering). Thus 'he' in the second sentence must refer to the man in the first sentence:

(11) The man entered the room. He sat down.

Conversely, if we are told that a delicate glass pitcher fell on to a hard floor (Johnson, Bransford, & Solomon, 1973), we can infer, using our background knowledge, that the pitcher (most probably) broke. However, that inference is not needed, at the point when the pitcher is described as falling, to link bits of information in different sentences of the text. At that point it merely elaborates or expands on one piece of information that is explicit in the text.

A crucial question about text comprehension is, therefore, how much integration and construction occurs and when. Obviously if we do not integrate all the information in a text we will not be able to create a fully coherent interpretation of the text. It does not follow that such integration does occur – discourse and text is not always fully understood. However, such integration should occur if comprehension is to be achieved, and integration, whether based on purely textual features (as in the '... the man ... he ...' example) or on constructive processes as well (as in the '... the car ... the nearside front tyre ...' example), is likely to be demonstrated experimentally. Indeed, many experimental studies, from Haviland and Clark (1974) onwards, have provided evidence that is consistent with this conclusion, at least for cases where the integration is of information in adjacent sentences or clauses. A strong view is that inferences necessary to establish a coherent interpretation of a text (*necessary inferences* for short) are always made (e.g. Garnham, 1989). However, it is possible that such inferences are not made, or are less likely to be made, if they link distant pieces of information in a text (McKoon & Ratcliff, 1992).

A related issue is whether inferences that are not necessary for integration, sometimes called *merely elaborative* inferences, are made in the normal course of comprehension. Bransford claimed that many of them were. For example, when people heard about a delicate glass pitcher falling on a hard floor, they later responded positively when asked if a sentence about the pitcher breaking had appeared in the text. However, such responses to later questions do not necessarily show that the inference was made during reading. And indeed, the way these questions were asked effectively made them leading questions.

A strong view (e.g. Thorndyke, 1976) is that no merely elaborative inferences are made as texts are understood. Two main ideas underlie this claim. The first is that any text supports many possible inferences. Since most inferences of this kind are not certain (maybe the pitcher did not break) and it is difficult to set a threshold for how likely the conclusion of the inference must be, given the information in the text, it is hard to justify making them. Second, inferences presumably require cognitive effort, and that effort should only be expended if it has a payoff. The payoff for a necessary inference is a coherent interpretation of a text. But the payoff for a merely elaborative inference may never come. Maybe it is better to wait and see if the inference is needed. What would be an elaborative inference at one point in a text could become a necessary inference later on. For example, when reading (12), it could be inferred, elaboratively, that the car had a nearside front tyre.

(12) John's car left the road at high speed and hit a tree.

Indeed, it could be inferred that the car had any of the very many normal parts of an automobile. The same inference becomes necessary when the passage continues as it did when this example was previously discussed in (13):

(13) The nearside front tyre had burst.

Are no elaborative inferences made, then? Perhaps some require so little effort or have such certain conclusions that it is worth making them. McKoon and Ratcliff (1992) have made a claim of this kind. They suggest that inferences based on readily available knowledge are made in the normal course of comprehension (automatically, in their terms,

although there are problems with the use of this term: see, e.g., Graesser, Singer, & Trabasso, 1994). If this claim is to have scientific content, there has to be an independent way of defining what knowledge is readily available, one that is independent of any test for whether an inference has been made. Intuition is not a good guide here. For example, it might seem that information about typical instruments for everyday actions would be readily available. Everyone knows that coffee is usually stirred with a spoon, so that if a text merely mentions coffee being stirred, it could be inferred that a spoon was (in all probability) used. However, there is evidence that instrument inferences are not routinely made in comprehension (Corbett & Dosher, 1978; Singer, 1979). It may nevertheless be true that inferences based on readily available information are made, but we do not yet have a good definition of readily available information.

A different suggestion for a class of inferences that might be made when they are not necessary to integrate information in different parts of a text is: inferences based on the presence of a single word in the text. So, if a text mentions dressing, it can be inferred that there are clothes, or if a text mentions a nurse it can be inferred that that person is (probably) female. The reason why such inferences might be made is that in constructing a mental model of the information in a text, information about the meanings, in the broadest sense, of the words in the text must be used. That information is accessed from long-term memory (mental lexicon/ semantic memory) in the course of comprehension. To the extent that lexical entries are complex, information may be included from those entries in the mental model (the mental representation of the content of the text), and that information may be inferential.

The two examples given above appear to be different in kind. The fact that 'to dress' means 'to put clothes on' implies that 'clothes' is part of the definition of 'dress', in the strict sense. However, it is not part of the definition of 'nurse' that a nurse has to be, or is likely to be, female. That is a fact about how our society is organized. Nevertheless, there is evidence that both kinds of inference are made. Garrod and Sanford (1981) showed that a sentence such as (14) was no more difficult to understand following (15) than following (16).

(14) The clothes were made of pink wool.
(15) Mary dressed the baby.
(16) Mary put the clothes on the baby.

This result contrasted with the standard Haviland and Clark (1974) result that (17) did take longer to read after (18) than after (19).

(17) The beer was warm.
(18) We checked the picnic supplies.
(19) We got some beer out of the trunk.

Similarly, in a variety of published and unpublished studies we have provided a range of evidence to suggest that inferences from stereotyped role names to the genders of the people they refer to are made as the role names are read (see Garnham, 2001: chap. 10 for a summary).

However, it cannot be assumed that because some classes of inference based on the presence of single words in a text are made, they all are. One class for which we could not find any evidence is that based on the implicit causality of verbs. For some verbs, such as 'confess to', a simple sentence such as (20) suggests an action that tells us something about the subject of the sentence, John. He in all probability instigated the confession, perhaps because he was feeling guilty.

(20) John confessed to Bill.

For other verbs, such as 'blame', the object is implicated. In (21) it is likely (but not necessary) that Bill has done something wrong.

(21) John blamed Bill.

This implicit indication of causality may either be supported, as in (22), or countered, as in (23), by the explicit statement of a cause, so that the explicit cause may be congruent with the implicit cause or incongruent.

(22) John confessed to Bill because he wanted a reduced sentence. (congruent)
(23) John confessed to Bill because he offered a reduced sentence. (incongruent)

Incongruent endings are typically understood more slowly than congruent endings (e.g. Garnham & Oakhill, 1985), but this finding in itself does not show what happens when the verb is read. It could arise as part of the process of integrating the information in the two clauses. Garnham, Traxler, Oakhill, and Gernsbacher (1996) suggested that if a causality inference was made as the verb was read, it should place the implicit cause in focus and hence speed responding to the name (presented as a probe immediately after the first clause) of that cause. However, in a series of probe word recognition studies they found no evidence for this idea. Instead the effect was confined to the processing of the subordinate clause.

Although Bransford stressed the role of integration in text comprehension, he did not consider in detail the ways in which the need for integration is signalled in a text and the ways in which it is achieved. Indeed, his best-known demonstration of integration is the somewhat bizarre 'ants in the kitchen' experiment (Bransford & Franks, 1971), which gave rise to the much-studied Bransford and Franks *linear effect*. Bransford and Franks constructed a set of complex sentences each expressing four 'ideas', for example (24), which expresses the four ideas stated in (25)–(28).

(24) The ants in the kitchen ate the sweet jelly that was on the table.
(25) The ants were in the kitchen.
(26) The ants ate the jelly.
(27) The jelly was sweet.
(28) The jelly was on the table.

In addition, they constructed sentences containing two or three ideas from each set, for example (29) and (30).

(29) The ants ate the sweet jelly.   (TWO)
(30) The ants in the kitchen ate the jelly (THREE) that was on the table.

They then presented a mixed-up collection of sentences expressing either one, two or three (but never four) ideas from many sets and later asked people whether they remembered sentences containing one, two, three or four ideas. The results were that people were most confident that they had seen sentences with all four ideas from a set, even though they never had. Furthermore, both the probability of recognizing a sentence and the confidence with which it was recognized increased in a roughly linear manner with the number of ideas. Thus, Bransford and Franks claimed, the four ideas in a set were integrated in memory, even though they were never presented together.

In normal text comprehension, integration does not usually comprise the reassembling of sets of ideas that are randomly interspersed with other sets of ideas. Rather, it requires the use of textual cues, and often (as we have seen) relevant background knowledge, to link the different parts of a text. At a local, or fairly local, level, a very important set of links are those signalled by anaphoric expressions, such as pronouns and verbal ellipses of various kinds. Anaphoric expressions themselves have little, or in the case of some ellipses, no semantic content, which makes it somewhat surprising that they succeed in referring to specific people, things and eventualities. For example, the semantic content of the English pronoun 'she' specifies merely that it should refer to a single female entity. However, in the context of a text or a discourse it will usually refer to one specific person. Bransford did not consider this aspect of integration, but it is addressed in detail in mental models theory. According to that theory, the model that has been constructed when the anaphoric expression is encountered must be structured in such a way that there is either only one relevant item for the interpretation of the anaphor, or a very few items, among which a choice can readily be made. For example, in (31) there is only one appropriate referent for 'he', whereas in (32) there are two.

(31) The man entered the room. He sat down.
(32) John confessed to Bill because he wanted a reduced sentence.

However, background knowledge about confessing and about whether someone who is confessing is likely to be given a prison sentence or in a position to sentence someone else allows a choice between John and Bill to be made in favour of Bill.

The typically local link that an anaphoric device creates is just one of the ways in which integration occurs. Another type of link has been studied under the head of *coherence relations*. The pieces of information in (again usually adjacent) parts of a text bear various relations to one another, such as event and sub-event, cause and effect, premise of argument and conclusion. For example, Mann and Thompson (1986), who used the term relational predicates in their *rhetorical structure theory*, to mean coherence relations, identified the following types of relation that could hold: solutionhood, evidence, justification, motivation, reason, sequence, enablement, elaboration, restatement, condition, circumstance, cause, concession, background, thesis–antithesis. One notable aspect of this list is that, despite the tendency of psycholinguists to focus on narrative texts, comparatively few of the relations are narrative relations, and many more are relations between parts of arguments.

The kinds of relations that hold between parts of a text are signalled by, among other things, the order in which information is presented, the tense and aspects of finite verbs, and explicit connectives, such as 'and', 'and then', 'but', 'so' and 'however'. For example, two adjacent past tense sentences, as in (33), often describe two events in sequence, whereas an imperfect followed by a past, as in (34), describes a state that holds while an event takes place (Kamp, 1979; Kamp & Rohrer, 1983).

(33) The man came into the room. He sat down.
(34) The man was feeling exhausted. He sat down.

However, past–past can have other interpretations, such as event and sub-event, in (35).

(35) John drove to London. His car broke down.

It may be that background knowledge plays a role in determining the particular relation that holds (Caenepeel, 1989).

Where explicit markers or other properties of text indicate relations, it is relatively easy to see how they are extracted. One complication is that the details of the relation may be underpinned by knowledge about the world, and that knowledge may or may not be available. For example, 'because' often signals a causal relation, but in an unfamiliar domain the basis of the cause may be unknown. So, someone reading (36) can compute that there is a causal relation between there being little wind and using Kevlar sails, but may not know what property of Kevlar makes it appropriate for conditions in which there is little wind.

(36) Connors used Kevlar sails because he expected little wind.

Noordman and Vonk (1992) showed that people typically do not compute these relations while reading. Providing explicit information about the relation between wind and Kevlar sails had no effect on the time taken to read the 'because' clause, but it did affect subsequent verification of this relation.

Texts are also structured at a more global level and this structure should be an aid to comprehension. However, how this structure is computed and how it contributes to comprehension is not well understood. Some types of text have highly regimented structures, which may be explicitly flagged. Reports of experiments in cognitive psychology journals would be a typical example. Other texts have less systematic shifts from topic to topic or subtopic. Sometimes these shifts can be explicitly flagged, by phrases such as 'another aspect of …' or by paragraph structure. Sometimes detecting the change in topic may depend on background knowledge.

As the topic of a text shifts, the reader or listener must follow those shifts and use them to aid comprehension. It is usual to distinguish between local and global focusing effects in text. Global focus changes from one 'discourse segment' to another (Grosz & Sidner, 1986), and the relations between these segments are determined by the intentions of the person producing the discourse. These relations could be those listed in Mann and Thompson's rhetorical structure theory (see above), though Grosz and Sidner themselves resist any attempt to provide a definite list of relations. Local focusing effects operate within discourse segments and determine which of the people or things just mentioned is likely to be mentioned again. Thus, even more than having a mental model for a particular text, local focusing effects further narrow the range of possible referents for referring expressions with little semantic content, such as simple noun phrases (e.g. 'the tree') and pronouns (e.g. 'it'). The main account of local focus for about fifteen years has been *centering theory* (see Grosz, Joshi, & Weinstein, 1995, for a recent version). Centering theory recognizes a set of forward-looking 'centers' for each utterance, primarily the things actually mentioned in that utterance. These centers are ranked according to various criteria, such as subjecthood, and the highest ranked is the most likely to be mentioned again and is the primary candidate for pronominal reference in a subsequent utterance. The single backward-looking center of each utterance must be identified with one of the forward-looking centers of the previous utterance. Backward-looking centers sometimes remain the same from one utterance to the next, though shifting is permitted so that the topic can move on.

A recent alternative to centering theory is Almor's (1999) informational load hypothesis, which is more closely grounded in such psychological concepts as short-term memory. According to this hypothesis, the conceptual distance between words such as 'robin' and 'bird' or 'robin' and 'it' determines how difficult it is to establish that they refer to the same thing. However, this hypothesis is, if anything, even less precise than centering theory in its account of how focusing actually works.

ALTERNATIVES TO MENTAL MODELS THEORY?

The basic principles of mental models theory appear incontrovertible, and Garnham (1996) has argued that they arise from a logical ('task') analysis of comprehension and are, therefore, part of the computational theory of comprehension, in the sense of Marr (1982; see Hayward & Tarr, Chapter 2, this volume). However, partly for this reason, they do not specify in detail the psychological processes that underlie comprehension. Thus, some theories that might at first appear to be alternatives to mental models might be better interpreted as addressing somewhat different issues. For example, Kintsch's (1988) construction–integration theory postulates two main stages to the process of comprehension. In the first stage, construction, information from the text and from relevant background knowledge is extracted and linked into a network. This stage is largely 'bottom-up': any apparently relevant information is used (e.g. all meanings of an ambiguous word) without much in the way of a 'top-down' attempt to limit interpretation. In the second stage, integration, related pieces of information support each other in the overall interpretation, whereas isolated bits of information (e.g. the unintended meaning of an ambiguous word, which is unlikely to be related to much else in the text) are suppressed. This account does not address directly the questions that are central to the mental models theory, such as how coreference relations are established, but it does address legitimate processing questions about which the mental models theory itself is agnostic.

Much the same can be said about the recently proposed 'memory-based' theories of comprehension (see papers in O'Brien, Lorch, & Myers, 1998). These theories claim that the integrative aspects of comprehension depend on the incoming piece of text sending a passive signal to all of memory, including text memory, which will resonate with relevant information that is needed to understand the text. Again, such an account does not deal with processes such as reference resolution, but it does begin to address the difficult problem of how stored knowledge is used rapidly (and usually correctly) to interpret text.

PRAGMATIC INTERPRETATION

Mental models theory tends to focus on the literal meaning of text. It emphasizes the construction of mental representations of the information conveyed by the text. However, there are other aspects to text and discourse meaning. One aspect of language use that is easy to overlook within this perspective is that language is used to do things (e.g. ask questions, make promises, tie [marital] knots), not just to describe them. The ordinary language philosopher J.L. Austin emphasized this idea in his book *How to do things with words* (1962), and it was elaborated into the notion of *speech acts* by another philosopher, John Searle (1969). Some speech acts are direct ('I bet you $5 that the Yankees will win the World Series') but some are indirect. Understanding that someone who says 'I feel cold' actually wants you to close the window is an important aspect of comprehension.

One idea about how conversations are understood is that people follow a general principle of co-operation (Grice, 1975). Apparent deviations from this principle are resolved by conversational implicatures, which are a kind of inference. Thus, it should be obvious that a window is open, and it cannot be useful to mention that fact to someone who already knows it. So, the other person looks for a different interpretation of the description – as an indirect request to close the window. However, other researchers, in particular Sperber and Wilson (1986), argue that an assumption of co-operation is not necessary and that people will determine the most relevant interpretation of an utterance without any necessary presumption of co-operation.

SUMMARY

Language comprehension depends on the interplay of processes at three main levels: lexical, syntactic and message. Lexical processes identify individual words in the speech stream or on the printed page and determine their meanings. They use a store of knowledge about words called the mental lexicon and information about how complex words are built up from simpler words (strictly, morphemes) and affixes. Syntactic processes group the words into larger units. These units are based on recurrent patterns of word types, and can therefore be recognized before the meaning of a particular pattern has been determined. If they could not be, comprehension would not be possible unless the message had already been understood! Message-level processes not only compute the meanings of these groups of words, but determine other, broader, aspects of meaning that depend on, among other things, relations to context and background knowledge and conventions about how language is used to achieve things in the world.

Despite great progress in the last thirty or forty years, none of these processes is fully understood. Indeed, many fundamental issues about the overall structure of the language comprehension system and that of its parts remain to be definitively answered.

ACKNOWLEDGEMENTS

I would like to thank Koen Lamberts, Marc Brysbaert and Sandy Pollatsek for helpful comments on an earlier version of this chapter.

REFERENCES

Abney, S. P. (1989). A computational model of human parsing. *Journal of Psycholinguistic Research*, *18*, 129–144.

Almor, A. (1999). Noun-phrase anaphora and focus: the informational load hypothesis. *Psychological Review*, *106*, 748–765.

Altmann, G. T. M., Garnham, A., & Dennis, Y. (1992). Avoiding the garden path: eye movements in context. *Journal of Memory and Language*, *31*, 685–712.

Austin, J. L. (1962). *How to do things with words*. Oxford: Oxford University Press.

Bach, E. (1976). An extension of classical transformational grammar. *Problems in linguistic metatheory. Proceedings of the 1976 Conference at Michigan State University* (pp. 183–224).

Barton, S., & Sanford, A. J. (1993). A case study of pragmatic anomaly detection. *Memory and Cognition*, *21*, 477–487.

Becker, C. A. (1980). Semantic context effects in visual word recognition: an analysis of semantic strategies. *Memory and Cognition*, *8*, 493–512.

Bever, T. G. (1970). The cognitive basis for linguistic structures. In J. R. Hayes (ed.), *Cognition and the development of language* (pp. 272–362). New York: Wiley.

Bransford, J. D., Barclay, J. R., & Franks, J. J. (1972). Sentence memory: a constructive vs interpretive approach. *Cognitive Psychology*, *3*, 193–209.

Bransford, J. D., & Franks, J. J. (1971). The abstraction of linguistic ideas. *Cognitive Psychology*, *2*, 331–350.

Caenepeel, M. (1989). Aspect, temporal ordering and perspective in narrative fiction. Unpublished PhD thesis, University of Edinburgh.

Caramazza, A., & Zurif, E. B. (1976). Dissociation of algorithmic and heuristic processes in language comprehension: evidence from aphasia. *Brain and Language*, *3*, 572–582.

Chomsky, N. (1957). *Syntactic structures*. The Hague: Mouton.

Chomsky, N. (1965). *Aspects of the theory of syntax*. Cambridge, MA: MIT Press.

Clifton, C., Frazier, L., & Connine, C. (1984). Lexical expectations in sentence comprehension. *Journal of Verbal Learning and Verbal Behavior*, *23*, 696–708.

Corbett, A. T., & Dosher, B. A. (1978). Instrument inferences in sentence encoding. *Journal of Verbal Learning and Verbal Behavior*, *17*, 479–491.

Crain, S., & Steedman, M. J. (1985). On not being led up the garden path: the use of context by the psychological parser. In D. R. Dowty, L. Karttunen, & A. M. Zwicky (Eds.), *Natural language parsing: psychological, computational and theoretical perspectives* (pp. 320–358). Cambridge: Cambridge University Press.

Cuetos, F., & Mitchell, D. C. (1988). Cross-linguistic differences in parsing: restrictions on the use of the late closure strategy in Spanish. *Cognition*, *30*, 73–105.

Desmet, T., Brysbaert, M., & De Baecke, C. (2002). The correspondence between sentence production and corpus frequencies in modifier attachment. *Quarterly Journal of Experimental Psychology*, *53A*, 879–896.

Ferreira, F., Ferraro, V., & Bailey, K. G. D. (2002). Good-enough representations in language comprehension. *Current Directions in Psychological Science*, *11*, 11–15.

Fodor, J. A., Bever, T. G., & Garrett, M. F. (1974). *The psychology of language: an introduction to psycholinguistics and generative grammar*. New York: McGraw-Hill.

Fodor, J. D., & Ferreira, F. (Eds.) (1998). *Reanalysis in sentence processing*. Dordrecht: Kluwer.

Forster, K. I. (1976). Accessing the mental lexicon. In R. J. Wales & E. C. T. Walker (Eds.), *New approaches to language mechanisms* (pp. 257–287). Amsterdam: North Holland.

Forster, K. I. (1979). Levels of processing and the structure of the language processor. In W. E. Cooper & E. C. T. Walker (Eds.), *Sentence processing: studies presented to Merrill Garrett* (pp. 27–85). Hillsdale, NJ: Lawrence Erlbaum.

Frazier, L. (1979). *On comprehending sentences: syntactic parsing strategies*. Bloomington: Indiana University Linguistics Club.

Frazier, L., & Clifton, C. (1996). *Construal*. Cambridge, MA: MIT Press.

Frazier, L., & Fodor, J. D. (1978). The sausage machine: a new two-stage parsing model. *Cognition*, *6*, 291–325.

Frazier, L., & Rayner, K. (1982). Making and correcting errors during sentence comprehension: eye movements in the analysis of structurally ambiguous sentences. *Cognitive Psychology*, *14*, 178–210.

Garnham, A. (1983). Why psycholinguists don't care about DTC: a reply to Berwick and Weinberg. *Cognition*, *15*, 263–269.

Garnham, A. (1985). *Psycholinguistics: central topics*. London: Methuen.

Garnham, A. (1989). Inference in language understanding: what, when, why and how. In R. Dietrich & C. F. Graumann (Eds.), *Language processing in social context* (pp. 153–172). Amsterdam: North Holland.

Garnham, A. (1996). The other side of mental models: theories of language comprehension. In J. V. Oakhill & A. Garnham (Eds.), *Mental models in cognitive science: essays in honour of Phil Johnson-Laird* (pp. 35–52). Hove, UK: Psychology Press.

Garnham, A. (2001). *Mental models and the interpretation of anaphora*. Hove, UK: Psychology Press.

Garnham, A., & Oakhill, J. V. (1985). On-line resolution of anaphoric pronouns: effects of inference making and verb semantics. *British Journal of Psychology*, *76*, 385–393.

Garnham, A., Traxler, M., Oakhill, J. V., & Gernsbacher, M. A. (1996). The locus of implicit causality effects in comprehension. *Journal of Memory and Language*, *35*, 517–543.

Garrod, S. C., & Sanford, A. J. (1981). Bridging inferences and the extended domain of reference. In J. Long & A. Baddeley (Eds.), *Attention and performance IX* (pp. 331–346). Hillsdale, NJ: Lawrence Erlbaum.

Glushko, R. J. (1979). The organization and activation of orthographic knowledge in reading aloud. *Journal of Experimental Psychology: Human Perception and Performance*, *5*, 674–691.

Glenberg, A. M. (1997). What memory is for. *Behavioral and Brain Sciences*, *20*, 1–55.

Graesser, A. C., Singer, M., & Trabasso, T. (1994). Constructing inferences during narrative text comprehension. *Psychological Review*, *101*, 371–395.

Grainger, J. (1990). Word frequency and neighborhood frequency effects in lexical decision and naming. *Journal of Memory and Language*, *29*, 228–244.

Grainger, J., & Jacobs, A. M. (1998). On localist connectionism and psychological science. In J. Grainger & A. M. Jacobs (Eds.), *Localist connectionist approaches to human cognition* (pp. 1–38). Mahwah, NJ: Lawrence Erlbaum.

Grice, H. P. (1975). Logic and conversation. In P. Cole & J. Morgan (Eds.), *Syntax and Semantics: Vol. 3. Speech acts* (pp. 41–48). New York: Academic Press.

Grosz, B., Joshi, A., & Weinstein, S. (1995). Centering: a framework for modelling the local coherence of discourse. *Computational Linguistics*, *21*, 203–226.

Grosz, B., & Sidner, C. L. (1986). Attentions, intentions and the structure of discourse. *Computational Linguistics*, *12*, 175–204.

Harnad, S. (1990). The symbol grounding problem. *Physica D*, *42*, 335–346.

Haviland, S. E., & Clark, H. H. (1974). What's new? Acquiring new information as a process in comprehension. *Journal of Verbal Learning and Verbal Behaviour*, *13*, 512–521.

Hobbs, J. R. (1983). Why is discourse coherent? In F. Neubauer (ed.), *Coherence in natural language texts* (Papers in Text Linguistics, Vol. 38). Hamburg: Helmut Buske.

Hogaboam, T. W., & Perfetti, C. A. (1975). Lexical ambiguity and sentence comprehension: the common sense effect. *Journal of Verbal Learning and Verbal Behavior*, *14*, 265–275.

Johnson, M. K., Bransford, J. D., & Solomon, S. (1973). Memory for tacit implications of sentences. *Journal of Experimental Psychology*, *98*, 203–205.

Kamp, H. (1979). Events, instants and temporal reference. In R. Bauerle, U. Egli, & A. von Stechow (Eds.), *Semantics from different points of view* (pp. 376–417). Berlin: Springer.

Kamp, H. (1981). A theory of truth and semantic representation. In J. A. G. Groenendijk, T. M. V. Janssen, & M. B. J. Stockhof (Eds.), *Formal methods in the study of language* (pp. 227–322). Amsterdam: Mathematic Centre Tracts.

Kamp, H., & Reyle, U. (1993). *From discourse to logic: introduction to modeltheoretic semantics of natural language, formal logic and discourse representation theory*. Dordrecht: Kluwer.

Kamp, H., & Rohrer, C. (1983). Tense in texts. In R. Bauerle, C. Schwarze, & A. von Stechow (Eds.), *Meaning, use, and interpretation of language* (pp. 250–269). Berlin: Walter de Gruyter.

Kimball, J. (1973). Seven principles of surface structure parsing in natural language. *Cognition*, *2*, 15–47.

Kintsch, W. (1988). The role of knowledge in discourse comprehension: a construction-integration model. *Psychological Review*, *65*, 163–182.

MacDonald, M. C., Pearlmutter, N. J., & Seidenberg, M. S. (1994). The lexical nature of syntactic ambiguity resolution. *Psychological Review*, *101*, 676–703.

Mann, W. C., & Thompson, S. A. (1986). Relational propositions in discourse. *Discourse Processes*, *9*, 57–90.

Manso de Zuniga, C., Humphreys, G. W., & Evett, L. J. (1991). Additive and interactive effects of repetition, degradation, and word frequency in the reading of handwriting. In D. Besner & G. W. Humphreys (Eds.), *Basic processes in reading: visual word recognition* (pp. 10–33). Hillsdale, NJ: Lawrence Erlbaum.

Marr, D. (1982). *Vision: a computational investigation into the human representation and processing of visual information*. San Francisco: Freeman.

Marslen-Wilson, W. D., Tyler, L. K., Waksler, R., & Older, R. (1994). Morphology and meaning in the English mental lexicon. *Psychological Review*, *101*, 653–675.

McClelland, J. L., & Rumelhart, D. E. (1981). An interactive model of context effects in letter perception. Part 1: An account of basic findings. *Psychological Review*, *88*, 375–407.

McKoon, G., & Ratcliff, R. (1992). Inference during reading. *Psychological Review*, *99*, 440–466.

McRae, K., Spivey-Knowlton, M. J., & Tanenhaus, M. K. (1998). Modeling the influence of thematic fit (and other constraints) in on-line sentence comprehension. *Journal of Memory and Language*, *38*, 283–312.

Meyer, D. E., & Schvaneveldt, R. W. (1971). Facilitation in recognizing pairs of words: evidence of a dependence between retrieval operations. *Journal of Experimental Psychology*, *90*, 227–235.

Mitchell, D. C. (1994). Sentence parsing. In M. A. Gernsbacher (Ed.), *Handbook of psycholinguistics* (pp. 375–409). San Diego: Academic Press.

Mitchell, D. C., & Brysbaert, M. (1998). Challenges to recent theories of crosslinguistic variation in parsing: evidence from Dutch. *Syntax and Semantics*, *31*, 313–335.

Mitchell, D. C., Brysbaert, M., Grondelaers, S., & Swanpoel, P. (2000). Modifier attachment in Dutch: testing aspects of construal theory. In A. Kennedy, R. Radach, D. Heller, & J. Pynte (Eds.), *Reading as a perceptual process* (pp. 493–516). Amsterdam: North Holland.

Morton, J. (1969). Interaction of information in word recognition. *Psychological Review*, *76*, 165–178.

Noordman, L. G. M., & Vonk, W. (1992). Readers' knowledge and the control of inferences in reading. *Language and Cognitive Processes*, *7*, 373–391.

Norris, D. (1986). Word recognition – context effects without priming. *Cognition*, *22*, 93–136.

O'Brien, E. J., Lorch, R. F. Jr., & Myers, J. L. (Eds.) (1998). *Memory-based text processing*. Special issue of *Discourse Processes*.

Rayner, K., Pacht, J. M., & Duffy, S. A. (1994). Effects of prior encounter and global discourse bias on the processing of lexically ambiguous words. *Journal of Memory and Language*, *33*, 527–544.

Schuberth, R. E., & Eimas, P. D. (1977). Effects of context on the classification of words and non-words. *Journal of Experimental Psychology: Human Perception and Performance*, *2*, 243–256.

Searle, J. R. (1969) *Speech acts*. Cambridge: Cambridge University Press.

Seidenberg, M. S., & McClelland, J. L. (1989). A distributed, developmental model of word recognition and naming. *Psychological Review*, *96*, 523–568.

Singer, M. (1979). Temporal locus of inference in the comprehension of brief passages: recognizing and verifying implications about instruments. *Perceptual and Motor Skills*, *49*, 539–550.

Sperber, D., & Wilson, D. (1986). *Relevance: communication and cognition*. Oxford: Blackwell.

Swinney, D. A. (1979). Lexical access during sentence comprehension: (re)considerations of context effects. *Journal of Verbal Learning and Verbal Behavior*, *18*, 645–659.

Taft, M., & Forster, K. I. (1975). Lexical storage and retrieval of prefixed words. *Journal of Verbal Learning and Verbal Behavior*, *14*, 638–647.

Thorndyke, P. W. (1976). The role of inferences in discourse comprehension. *Journal of Verbal Learning and Verbal Behavior*, *15*, 437–446.

van Gompel, R. P. G., Pickering, M. J., & Traxler, M. J. (2000). Unrestricted race: a new model of syntactic ambiguity resolution. In A. Kennedy, R. Radach, D. Heller, & J. Pynte (Eds.), *Reading as a perceptual process* (pp. 621–648). Amsterdam: North Holland.

Vu, H., Kellas, G., & Paul, S. T. (1998). Sources of sentence constraint on lexical ambiguity resolution. *Memory and Cognition*, *26*, 979–1001.

Weinberg, A. (1994). Parameters in the theory of sentence processing: minimal commitment theory goes east. *Journal of Psycholinguistic Research*, *22*, 339–364.

11

Speech Perception

JAMES M. MCQUEEN

The core process in speech perception is word recognition. If someone tells you *'Jim chose cucumber-green paper to wrap the present in'*, the only way you can come to understand this utterance is to map the auditory information in the speech signal onto your stored knowledge about the sound forms of the words of your language. Given that you usually do not know in advance what someone is going to say, and that every talker has an infinity of possible utterances to choose from, the only way you can decode any particular message is to recognize each of the words in that message (since the words do come from a finite set). This may sound trivial and, indeed, spoken word recognition seems to be pretty effortless. If someone says *'Jim chose cucumber-green paper to wrap the present in'*, no matter how unlikely that utterance may be, those are the words that you will perceive, and you will probably do so without any apparent difficulty.

But this is no mean feat. Spoken word recognition entails a complex decoding problem. The physical speech signal is a quasi-continuous stream of acoustic energy, varying over time in amplitude and spectral shape (i.e. consisting of different components at different frequencies). As shown in the spectrogram in Figure 11.1, for example, the first consonant [dʒ] is an affricate which consists of an abrupt onset of energy, followed by turbulent noise (aspiration and frication noise caused as air passes the partial constriction of the tongue on the roof of the mouth). This noise is spread mainly over relatively high-frequency bands above 1500 Hz. The first vowel [ɪ] consists of periodic energy (voicing due to vibration of the vocal folds), with energy concentrated in a number of frequency bands called formants (the resonant frequencies of the vocal tract). Each vowel has a characteristic formant pattern,

depending on the shape of the vocal tract as that vowel is spoken (e.g. the position of the tongue, jaw and lips). The first three formants for this token of the vowel [ɪ] are centered roughly at 500, 1800 and 2300 Hz. This is the merest sketch of the acoustic parameters that code [dʒ] and [ɪ]. Ladefoged and Maddieson (1996) and Stevens (1998) provide detailed accounts of the acoustic structure of these and many other sounds of the world's languages, and of how the articulatory system generates those sounds.

To add to the complexity of the decoding problem, speech sounds (and therefore spoken words) are not invariant. As can be seen in Figure 11.1, for example, the acoustic realization of the [p] at the beginning of *paper* is not the same as the [p] at the end of *wrap*, nor the [p] in the middle of *paper*, nor the [p] at the beginning of *present*. This variability is due in part to the phonological context. Thus, syllable-initial and syllable-final stops are not the same (the initial [p] in *paper* has a release burst and has high-frequency aspiration energy; syllable-final stops do not have aspiration and may indeed not have a burst, as in the [p] of *wrap*). Furthermore, the two [p]'s in *paper* differ because of the stress pattern and syllabification of the word (the first [p] is syllable-initial in a stressed syllable; the second is ambisyllabic, at the boundary between a full and a reduced vowel). Similarly, the first [k] of *cucumber* is in a stressed syllable, and is therefore different from (e.g. longer than) the second [k], which is in an unstressed syllable.

Furthermore, speech is coarticulated: the shape of the vocal tract at any moment in time is usually determined by motor commands not only for the current speech sound, but also in part by those for preceding and following sounds. This means that

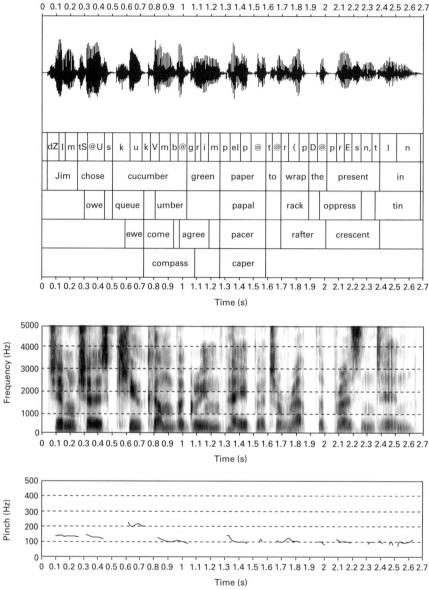

Figure 11.1   *A waveform, spectrogram and pitch track representing the sentence* 'Jim chose cucumber-green paper to wrap the present in', *spoken by a male native speaker of British English. The waveform (top panel) shows the waveform as it varies in amplitude (on the vertical axis) over time (on the horizontal axis). Each sound in the utterance is transcribed using the Speech Assessment Methods Phonetic Alphabet (SAMPA, Wells, 1987; see Ladefoged, 2001, for an introduction to phonetic transcription and the International Phonetic Alphabet, IPA, which is used in the main text). Each sound is roughly aligned with the center of the information for that sound in the utterance. A selection of the words that are consistent with the different parts of the utterance is given under the phonetic transcription. The spectrogram (middle panel) shows how the different components of the speech signal are arrayed over a range of frequencies (on the vertical axis); these components change continuously over time. The relative darkness of the different components indicates their relative amplitude. The pitch track (bottom panel) shows how the speaker's fundamental frequency changes over the course of the utterance.*

each sound in the acoustic signal is influenced by its neighboring sounds, and thus that the realization of any given word is dependent, at least in part, on the sounds in neighboring words (e.g. the [ə] preceding the [p] and the following [r] in *the present* have consequences for the realization of the [p], thus making it different from the first [p] *in green paper*, which in turn is influenced by its neighboring sounds). Similarly, coarticulation has consequences on the realization of vowels, in particular their formant structure (i.e. as the mouth changes shape to create different consonantal constrictions the resonant frequencies of the vocal tract change; e.g. compare the slightly rising formants of the [ə] at the end of *paper*, before a [t], with the strongly falling formants of the [ə] of *to*, before a [r]).

The position of words and sounds in the prosodic structure of an utterance also has a strong effect on the way they are produced. Thus, for example, the production of *cucumber*, which the speaker accented, is marked by the lengthening of its segments, increased amplitude and pitch movement. The placement of this accent also has consequences for the realization of the rest of the utterance, as do the location of intonational boundaries (e.g. the [ɪ] of utterance-initial *Jim* is approximately 45 ms long, and thus much shorter than the [ɪ] of utterance-final *in*, which is approximately 124 ms long) and the type of utterance (e.g. whether it is a declarative or interrogative sentence).

To make matters even worse, the speech signal varies as a function of many other factors: the talker's sex, age and dialect; the idiosyncrasies of his or her vocal tract; his or her speaking rate and speaking style (e.g. formal, careful speech versus casual, colloquial speech); and the nature of any background noise. The utterance in Figure 11.1 would obviously look very different if it had been spoken by a female speaker of American English in a crowded restaurant to her partner, instead of by a male speaker of British English as a psycholinguistic example in a recording booth.

The listener is faced with yet other problems. The phonological space of possible words in a given language can be quite dense: many words share the same sequences of sounds, either because they begin in the same way (e.g. *wrap*, *rack*, *rafter*, *ramekin*, etc.), or because they rhyme (e.g. *present*, *crescent*), or because longer words often have shorter words embedded within them (e.g. *cucumber* contains *queue*, *ewe*, *come* and *umber*). It is therefore not easy to distinguish one word from all other words. The continuous nature of the speech signal (e.g. in Figure 11.1, the lack of a break in the signal between *to* and *wrap* in spite of the word boundary) adds to this problem: there is no way of knowing, in advance, how many words are in a given utterance, nor where they begin and end.

The task faced by the cognitive psychologist seeking to understand speech perception, then, is to derive a theory of the mental processes and representations that are used by listeners as they map complex acoustic speech signals onto their knowledge of spoken words. In this chapter, I argue that spoken word perception involves the simultaneous evaluation of multiple lexical hypotheses and a process of inter-word competition among those hypotheses. I also argue that listeners perform a detailed phonetic analysis of the speech signal prior to lexical access, at a prelexical stage of processing. That is, they first derive an abstract representation of the sounds in the speech signal before lexical access, rather than try to map the speech signal directly onto the mental lexicon. However, information appears to flow in cascade from the signal to the prelexical level, and from there in cascade up to the lexical level. A controversial question has been whether information also flows from the lexical to the prelexical level. I shall argue that there is no benefit to be had from on-line feedback of information from the lexicon to lower levels of processing, and no evidence that requires this type of feedback. Thus, for example, the knowledge that *wrap* is a word does not interfere with the prelexical analysis of its component sounds [r], [æ] and [p].

The chapter concludes with a brief discussion of several models of speech perception. The focus will again be on models of the perception of words rather than on models of the perception of speech sounds. Although an understanding of how the individual sounds of speech are decoded is critical in any account of speech perception, as indeed is an understanding of how the prosodic structure of utterances is decoded, I suggest that these components must be viewed in the context of a theory about how we perceive spoken words. This is because word forms are the primary perceptual representations of spoken language. That is, when we listen to speech, the perceptual level of analysis on which we focus our attention is the lexical level, not the level of individual sounds. Furthermore, as I have already argued, word forms provide the key to unlocking the speech code: speech comprehension is only possible if speech sounds are linked up to meaning representations via the phonological knowledge stored in the mental lexicon.

PERCEPTION OF SPOKEN WORDS

Multiple activation of lexical hypotheses

Word recognition involves the simultaneous evaluation of many candidate words. As an utterance like our example sentence unfolds over time, words like *cucumber*, *queue*, *cute*, *cube*, *come* and *umber* will be considered in parallel as *cucumber* is heard. A common way to describe this process is in terms of lexical activation: each word that is being considered is assumed to be activated (e.g. like a node in a connectionist network). Evidence for multiple activation comes from cross-modal semantic priming experiments, where participants decide whether visually presented letter strings are real words or not, as they hear spoken words or sentences.[1] Facilitation (i.e. speeding up) of responses to semantic associates of particular words is taken to reflect activation of those words. Cross-modal semantic priming has shown that competitors beginning at the same time are activated (e.g. in Dutch, listeners responded more rapidly to associates of both *kapitaal*, capital, and *kapitein*, captain, when they heard [kæpɪt] than when they heard the beginning of an unrelated word: Zwitserlood, 1989; see also Moss, McCormick, & Tyler, 1997; Zwitserlood & Schriefers, 1995). Other evidence for multiple activation of words that begin in the same way comes from recognition memory experiments. Participants make false positive errors on words that have not been presented earlier in the experiment but that begin in the same way as words that have appeared earlier (Wallace, Stewart, & Malone, 1995; Wallace, Stewart, Shaffer, & Wilson, 1998; Wallace, Stewart, Sherman, & Mellor, 1995).

Words beginning at different points in the signal can also be activated. For example, in English, faster responses to an associate of *bone* were found when listeners heard *trombone* than when they heard an unrelated word (Shillcock, 1990; but see also Vroomen & de Gelder, 1997). Other evidence that words beginning at different points in the signal can be simultaneously activated comes from Italian and English. In Italian, responses to an associate of *visite*, visits, for example, were faster when listeners heard *visi tediati*, bored faces, than in a control condition (Tabossi, Burani, & Scott, 1995). In English, faster responses to associates of both *lips* and *tulips*, for example, were found when listeners heard *two lips* than in a control condition (Gow & Gordon, 1995). These latter two studies show that candidate words can be activated even if they span word boundaries in the input.

Words that end in the same way as the input speech material are also activated. Connine, Blasko, and Titone (1993), for example, found evidence in cross-modal semantic priming when nonword primes differed from the base words in only one or two articulatory features (*zervice* primed responses to *tennis*, presumably due to activation of *service*). Similar results have also been observed with intramodal (auditory-auditory) priming in Dutch (Marslen-Wilson, Moss, & van Halen, 1996). Connine et al. found no reliable priming effect, however, when the primes differed from the base words on more than two features (e.g. *gervice*; the [g] differs from the [s] of *service* on more featural dimensions than the [z] of *zervice* does; see, e.g., Jakobson, Fant, & Halle, 1952, for a feature-based analysis of speech sounds).

The importance of the degree of mismatch between the material in the speech signal and stored lexical knowledge has also been observed using the phoneme monitoring task. Connine, Titone, Deelman, and Blasko (1997) asked listeners to detect the phoneme /t/, for example, in *cabinet, gabinet* (one feature change on the initial phoneme), *mabinet* (many features changed) and *shuffinet* (control). Phoneme monitoring latencies were fastest for targets in the base words (*cabinet*), slower for targets in the minimally mismatching nonwords (*gabinet*), even slower for targets in the nonwords with greater mismatch (*mabinet*) and slowest for targets in control nonwords (*shuffinet*). As will be discussed in more detail later, phoneme monitoring latency reflects degree of lexical activation. These results thus suggest that the lexical representation for *cabinet* is more strongly activated when *gabinet* is heard than when *mabinet* is heard. Likewise, in another phoneme monitoring study, Frauenfelder, Scholten, and Content (2001) found evidence of lexical activation of French words when the initial phonemes of those words were distorted by a single feature (e.g. *vocabulaire*, vocabulary, produced as *focabulaire*). Monitoring latencies on target phonemes in these words were faster than on targets in control items, but only when the target phonemes were word-final. Frauenfelder et al. suggest that the lexical effect only emerged when enough time had elapsed for the matching information later in the word to overcome the effects of the initial mismatch.

It therefore appears that the word recognition process is relatively intolerant of mismatch between the speech signal and stored phonological knowledge. This is true for initial mismatch, as in the studies just cited, and for mismatch occurring later in the input. Zwitserlood (1989), for example, found evidence of activation of both *kapitaal* and *kapitein* when listeners had heard [kæpɪt], but of only the correct word when disambiguating information (the final vowel and consonant) had been heard. There is thus rapid selection of the intended word and rapid rejection of other candidates as soon as the signal mismatches with the incorrect candidates.

Results from phoneme monitoring support this suggestion. Frauenfelder et al. (2001) found no evidence of activation of, for example, *vocabulaire* given *vocabunaire* (i.e. responses to the final /r/ were no faster than in control nonwords). Soto-Faraco, Sebastián-Gallés, and Cutler (2001) carried out a series of cross-modal fragment-priming experiments (in Spanish) to examine the effects of non-initial mismatch. Lexical decision responses to visually presented words like *abandono*, abandonment, were faster, relative to a control condition, if listeners had just heard the matching fragment *aban*, and slower if they had just heard the mismatching fragment *abun*, the onset of *abundancia*, abundance. Again, it appears that incorrect candidate words are rapidly rejected as soon as they mismatch with the signal.

In general, however, words that begin in the same way as the input and then diverge from it will tend to be activated earlier and more strongly than those that have initial mismatches but end in the same way as the input. This is because candidates with initial overlap will at least initially be as strongly supported by the input as the actual word in the input, while those with final overlap will never be as good a match to the input as the actual word. The difference due to overlap position has been observed in eye-tracking experiments, where participants' fixations to pictures on a computer screen are collected while they are auditorily instructed to click on one of those pictures. As the name of the target picture unfolds over time, participants tend to make more fixations to pictures with names that are compatible with the available spoken information than to unrelated pictures (e.g. looks to a picture of a beetle when the initial sounds of *beaker* are heard: Allopenna, Magnuson, & Tanenhaus, 1998). Somewhat later in time, and to a lesser extent, listeners tend to look at pictures with names that rhyme with the input (e.g. listeners look at a picture of a speaker when they hear *beaker*: Allopenna et al., 1998).

Modulation of lexical activation by fine-grained information

The activation of lexical hypotheses therefore varies continuously over time, in response to the goodness of match of each hypothesis to the current input. As *paper* is heard, for example, *papal* and *pacer* and *caper* (among others) will be activated to differing degrees at different moments in time (*papal* will be more active than *pacer*, and for longer, and will be as good a hypothesis as *paper* itself until evidence that there is no /l/ heard; the activation of *caper* will increase as that for *pacer* drops, and so on). The results of Connine et al. (1993, 1997) suggest in addition that lexical activation is graded not only with respect to the number of matching and mismatching phonemes, but also in response to more fine-grained differences in the input: words that mismatch with the signal on fewer features are more strongly activated than those that mismatch on more features.

Many other studies have also shown that lexical activation varies in response to fine-grained differences in the speech signal (see, e.g., Warren & Marslen-Wilson, 1987, 1988). A series of studies on the effect of subphonemic mismatch in cross-spliced words and nonwords has examined this issue in detail (Dahan, Magnuson, Tanenhaus, & Hogan, 2001; Marslen-Wilson & Warren, 1994;

McQueen, Norris, & Cutler, 1999; Streeter & Nigro, 1979; Warren & Marslen-Wilson, 1987; Whalen 1984, 1991). In these experiments, cross-spliced versions of monosyllabic words and nonwords were constructed by concatenating their initial portions (up to the vowel) with the final consonants of other tokens. For example, the word *job* could be made with the [dʒɒ] of *jog* and the [b] of *job*. The vocalic portion would thus contain formant-transition information consistent with a velar [g] (coarticulation, as described in the Introduction, results in changes in the formant structure of the vowel before the [g], relative to the same vowel before a [b]). The cues to an upcoming [g] would thus mismatch with the final bilabial stop release burst of the [b]. These experiments showed that the strength of the interference due to this kind of mismatch depends on lexical factors (whether the portions used for cross-splicing come from words or nonwords, and whether the resulting sequence is a word or a nonword). They thus show that subphonemic details filter through to the lexical level to influence lexical activation.

Studies by Andruski, Blumstein, and Burton (1994) and by Utman, Blumstein, and Burton (2000) also show that lexical activation varies as a function of subphonemic differences in the speech signal. Andruski et al., for example, present evidence that the degree of activation of words beginning with unvoiced stop consonants varies with the Voice Onset Time (VOT) of those stops (VOT is the time from the release burst to the onset of voicing, approximately 90 ms for the initial [k] of *cucumber* and approximately 16 ms for the [g] of *green* in Figure 11.1; VOT is one acoustic cue to the distinction between unvoiced and voiced stops, such as [k] and [g], or [p] and [b]). The [p] of *pear*, for example, was presented by Andruski et al. in unedited form, or with the VOT reduced by either one-third or two-thirds. All three forms primed responses to an associate word (*fruit*), but responses were faster after the unedited prime than after the less extremely edited prime, which in turn were faster than responses after the more extremely edited prime.

Information about the syllabic structure of utterances also influences the activation levels of words. Tabossi, Collina, Mazzetti, and Zoppello (2000) have shown in a fragment-priming study in Italian that words that match the syllabic structure of the fragments are more strongly activated than words that mismatch the fragments. For example, *si.lenzio*, silence, appeared to receive more support than *sil.vestre*, silvan, when the input was the fragment [si.l], taken from *si.lenzio*. The opposite was true when the fragment was [sil] from *sil.vestre*. Small durational differences between the vowels in these fragments appear to have signaled the difference in syllabic structure. Spinelli, McQueen, & Cutler (2003) have recently shown in a cross-modal identity-priming experiment that, even though French sequences such as *dernier oignon* (last onion) and *dernier rognon* (last kidney) are phonemically identical, French speakers signal the difference between these two sequences to listeners. Only responses to the words that the speaker intended were significantly primed. The duration of the medial [ʁ] in *dernier oignon*, for example (where it was the final sound of *dernier*, and was produced because of the phonological process of liaison), was slightly shorter than the equivalent [ʁ] in *dernier rognon* (where it was the first sound of *rognon*), and this difference influenced the degree of activation of these words.

Gow and Gordon (1995) also found that fine-grained durational differences in the speech signal influence lexical activation. They found evidence of activation of, for example, both *tulips* and *lips* when listeners heard *two lips* (where the medial [l] was longer) but of only *tulips* when listeners heard *tulips* (where the [l] was shorter). Likewise, subtle durational differences between productions of an ambiguous sequence (e.g. [kæp]), which can either be a monosyllabic word (*cap*) or as the onset of a longer word (*captain*), bias lexical activation in favor of the speaker's intentions (Davis, Marslen-Wilson, & Gaskell, 2002; Salverda, Dahan, & McQueen, 2003).

The picture that therefore emerges is that lexical activation is fine-tuned to the acoustic-phonetic detail in the speech signal. Small differences in the duration of segments can influence the amount of support for particular candidate words. Two other sources of variation in the signal also influence lexical activation. First, the phonological context can determine the effect of mismatching information. Spoken in isolation, the sequence [grim] is not a good match to the word *green*. But this is how this word was produced in the utterance shown in Figure 11.1, where the following word (*paper*) begins with the bilabial stop [p]. In English, word-final coronal consonants (like [n]) can take on the place of articulation of the following consonant ([n] can thus become the bilabial [m]). Research on this assimilation process has shown that a form such as [grim] can be recognized as a token of the word *green*, but only if the change is contextually appropriate (Coenen, Zwitserlood, & Boelte 2001; Gaskell & Marslen-Wilson, 1996, 1998, 2001; Gow, 2001; Marslen-Wilson, Nix, & Gaskell, 1995). Gow (2002) has recently shown that there are also subphonemic cues to assimilation (e.g. the [raɪp] in *right berries*, where the final /t/ of *right* is assimilated to a [p], is not identical to the [raɪp] in *ripe berries*), and that this information, like the other subphonemic cues mentioned above, appears to influence lexical activation.

Second, lexical stress information appears to influence the degree of activation of words (Cooper, Cutler, & Wales, 2002; Cutler & van Donselaar, 2001;

Soto-Faraco et al., 2001; see also the review in Cutler, Dahan, & van Donselaar, 1997). For example, Soto-Faraco et al. showed that mismatching stress information inhibits responses in Spanish cross-modal fragment priming: responses to the visual target *principio* (beginning), which is stressed on the second syllable, were slower after listeners heard the fragment *PRINci-*, the beginning of *príncipe* (prince), which is stressed on the first syllable, than after they heard a control fragment. The use of stress information appears to be limited to languages where this information is useful for lexical disambiguation. In French, for example, where words do not contrast in stress, this information does not appear to influence lexical activation (Dupoux, Pallier, Sebastián-Gallés, & Mehler, 1997).

At any one moment in the unfolding of a speech signal, therefore, multiple lexical hypotheses are being considered. The activation process is fairly intolerant of mismatching information, such that, as soon as one word has sufficient support, the system settles on that candidate and the other words will drop out of the running. Furthermore, lexical representations are activated in a graded fashion, in response to their goodness of fit to the available input. Even very subtle acoustic details in the speech signal have an impact on lexical activation levels.

Competition between lexical hypotheses

How then is a choice made from among the set of activated lexical hypotheses? When *paper* is heard, how is *paper* selected and how are *papal*, *caper* and so on rejected? One possibility is that the selection is made purely on the basis of bottom-up goodness of fit. The word that best matches the input is selected, and all other words are then rejected. Another possibility, however, is that, in addition, the lexical hypotheses compete with each other. Competition between candidate words would act to sharpen the distinctions in activation levels made on the basis of goodness of match.

There are many different sources of evidence suggesting that there is inter-word competition between candidate words. Listeners in a word-spotting task find it harder to spot words embedded at the beginning of longer words (like *sack* in [sækrəf], the beginning of *sacrifice*) than in matched sequences that are not word onsets (like [sækrəf]: McQueen, Norris, & Cutler, 1994). This effect presumably reflects competition between the shorter and the longer word. Competition also occurs in word spotting when the shorter and the longer word begin at different points (e.g. spotting *mess* in [dəmɛs], the beginning of *domestic*, is harder than in the nonword onset [nəmɛs]: McQueen et al., 1994). Furthermore, the number of competitors beginning at a different point in the signal from the target word influences how easy it is to recognize that target. Recognizing a word embedded in a longer nonsense word is harder when the nonsense word contains a sequence consistent with many other words than when it contains a sequence consistent with fewer other words (Norris, McQueen, & Cutler, 1995; Vroomen & de Gelder, 1995).

A comparison between the studies of Soto-Faraco et al. (2001) and Cutler and van Donselaar (2001) offers further support for lexical competition. As mentioned earlier, Soto-Faraco et al. showed that responses to the Spanish target word *principio* (stressed on the second syllable, *prinCIpio*) were slower after listeners heard the mismatching fragment *PRINci-*, the beginning of *príncipe* (stressed on the first syllable, *PRINcipe*), than after they heard a control fragment. In a similar fragment-priming study in Dutch, however, no such inhibition was observed (e.g. the prime *MUzee*, a fragment mismatching with the target *museum*, which, as in English, is stressed on the second syllable, *muSEum*, did not inhibit responses to the target: Cutler & van Donselaar, 2001). The difference between the two studies is that the mismatching fragments in Spanish were consistent with other words (e.g. *príncipe*, prince) while those in Dutch were not (e.g. *MUzee* is not the beginning of any Dutch word). The inhibitory effect in Spanish thus appears to be due to the conjoint effects of bottom-up mismatch and lexical competition.

Lexical competition can also be inferred from the effects of manipulating the lexical neighborhood density of words (the number and frequency of similar-sounding words). It should be harder to recognize a word in a dense neighborhood than in a sparse neighborhood because of stronger inter-word competition in the denser neighborhood. Inhibitory effects of high neighborhood density have indeed been found (Cluff & Luce, 1990; Luce, 1986; Luce & Large, 2001; Vitevitch, 2002; Vitevitch & Luce, 1998, 1999). In priming paradigms, responses to target words tend to be slower when they are preceded by phonologically related prime words than when they are preceded by unrelated words, suggesting that the target words were activated when the related primes were heard, and that they then lost the competition process, making them harder to recognize (Goldinger, Luce, Pisoni, & Marcario, 1992; Luce, Goldinger, Auer, & Vitevitch, 2000; Monsell & Hirsh, 1998; Slowiaczek & Hamburger, 1992).

Yet another source of evidence for lexical competition comes from experiments examining the effects of subphonemic mismatch on the activation of monosyllabic words. A number of studies (Andruski et al., 1994; Gow, 2001; Marslen-Wilson et al., 1996; Marslen-Wilson & Warren, 1994; McQueen et al., 1999) have all shown that degree of activation of short mismatching words depends on the lexical competitor environment. Monosyllabic

words that mismatch with the input tend to be activated more strongly when there are no other phonologically close candidate words (i.e. when their activation is not reduced because of strong lexical competition).

Segmentation of continuous speech into words

Speech decoding thus involves the multiple graded activation of candidate words, and competition between those words. Lexical competition acts to exaggerate the differences in activation of candidate words as signaled by the (sometimes very fine-grained) acoustic detail in the speech signal, and thus makes word recognition more efficient. Lexical competition can also help in segmenting the continuous signal into individual words (McClelland & Elman, 1986; McQueen, Cutler, Briscoe, & Norris, 1995; McQueen et al., 1994; Norris, 1994). As the evidence reviewed earlier suggests, candidate words compete with each other when they begin at the same point in the signal (e.g. *cucumber* and *queue*) and when they begin at different points (e.g. *cucumber* and *agree*, which, though their onsets are well separated, are still fighting over one vowel in the input, see Figure 11.1; note that this is true in Standard Southern British English, but not in American English). This competition process will thus help to select the best-matching sequence of words for the entire utterance. That is, not only will competition help in the selection of, for example, *cucumber*, but it will also help in segmenting the signal at word boundaries (e.g. as *cucumber* and *green* win, candidates spanning the boundary between these words, such as *agree*, will lose). The correct segmentation will thus emerge out of the competition process, even when no word boundary is marked in the signal at that point.

There is, however, more to segmentation than competition. Although the speech signal is continuous, with coarticulation of sounds both within and between words, and there are no fully reliable cues to word boundaries (Lehiste, 1972; Nakatani & Dukes, 1977), there are nonetheless a variety of cues to likely word boundaries in the speech signal. When those cues are available, listeners appear to use them (Norris, McQueen, Cutler, & Butterfield, 1997). For example, some sequences of speech sounds do not co-occur within syllables (e.g. [mr] in English); such sequences signal the location of a likely word boundary (e.g. between the [m] and the [r]). Listeners use such phonotactic constraints for lexical segmentation (Dumay, Frauenfelder, & Content, 2002; McQueen, 1998; Weber, 2001). Likewise, sound sequence constraints that are probabilistic rather than absolute (some sound sequences are more likely to be associated with a word boundary than other sequences) are also used by listeners for segmentation (van der Lugt, 2001).

The rhythmic structure of speech is also used by listeners for lexical segmentation. English and Dutch listeners use metrical information based on stress (Cutler & Butterfield, 1992; Cutler & Norris, 1988; Norris et al., 1995; Vroomen & de Gelder, 1995; Vroomen, van Zon, & de Gelder, 1996). French, Catalan and Spanish listeners use metrical information based on the syllable (Cutler, Mehler, Norris, & Seguí, 1986; Pallier, Sebastián-Gallés, Felguera, Christophe, & Mehler, 1993; Sebastián-Gallés, Dupoux, Seguí, & Mehler, 1992; but see also Content, Meunier, Kearns, & Frauenfelder, 2001). Japanese listeners use metrical information based on a sub-syllabic structure, called the mora (Cutler & Otake, 1994; McQueen, Otake, & Cutler, 2001; Otake, Hatano, Cutler, & Mehler, 1993). The differences between the results of these studies reflect differences in the rhythmic structures of the languages that were tested. In each case, however, the edge of a rhythmic unit (a strong syllable in English, a syllable in French, a mora in Japanese) can be considered to be a likely word boundary in the speech signal (see Norris et al., 1997, for further discussion).

In addition to phonotactic and metrical cues to word boundaries, other sources of evidence in the speech signal indicate where words are likely to begin and end. Allophonic cues such as the aspiration of word-initial stops (such as the first [k] of *cucumber* in Figure 11.1) could be used in segmentation (Church, 1987; Lehiste, 1960; Nakatani & Dukes, 1977). In addition to allophonic cues, other acoustic differences (such as in the duration of segments) signal the correct segmentation of ambiguous sequences such as *night rate/nitrate* or *two lips/tulips*, and appear to be used by listeners for this purpose (Christie, 1974; Gow & Gordon, 1995; Lehiste, 1972; Nakatani & Dukes, 1977; Oller, 1973; Quené, 1992, 1993; Turk & Shattuck-Hufnagel, 2000).

How then can all of these cues influence the activation of candidate words, the competition among them, and hence the segmentation of an utterance? Norris et al. (1997) have proposed that a penalty is applied to the activation levels of candidate words that are misaligned with likely word boundaries (irrespective of how any particular boundary might be cued). They argued that a candidate word would count as misaligned if the stretch of speech between that word and the likely word boundary did not contain a vowel. Such stretches of speech (single consonants, or consonant sequences) are themselves not possible words, so any segmentation of an utterance into a potential sequence of words (a 'lexical parse') involving these consonantal chunks is highly implausible. For example, the lexical parse *queue come b agree m paper* is not going to be what the speaker of the utterance in Figure 11.1 intended.

The Possible Word Constraint (PWC: Norris et al., 1997) thus penalizes *agree*, for example, because the [m] between the end of *agree* and the boundary at the onset of *paper* (cued in this case by the fact that the first syllable of this word is strong [Cutler & Norris, 1988] and/or by the fact that the [p] is aspirated [Church, 1987]) is not a possible English word. Penalization of misaligned words will help the correct words to win the competition process.

Norris et al. (1997) provided empirical support for the PWC. English listeners found it harder to spot words like *apple* in nonsense sequences like *fapple* (the [f] between the onset of *apple* and the preceding silence, a very likely word boundary, is not a possible English word) than in sequences like *vuffapple* (*vuff* is not an English word, but could be). Further support for the PWC has since been found in English (Norris, McQueen, Cutler, Butterfield, & Kearns, 2001) and a number of other languages (Dutch: McQueen, 1998, McQueen & Cutler, 1998a; Japanese: McQueen, Otake, & Cutler, 2001; and Sesotho: Cutler, Demuth & McQueen, 2002). In spite of differences between these languages in what constitutes a well-formed word (how long or complex a sequence of sounds has to be to form a word in a particular language), this research suggests that the PWC operates according to a simple, and possibly language-universal, principle: namely, that a stretch of speech without a vowel is not a viable chunk in the lexical parse of an utterance.

The PWC is thus an important mechanism that enriches the competition process. It acts to rule out spurious candidate words, and thus helps in the segmentation of continuous speech into the sequence of words that the speaker of that utterance intended. While the PWC may be the means by which many cues to word boundaries modulate the activation and competition process, it may not be the only mechanism. In some cases, the activation of candidate words appears to be influenced by cues to word-boundary locations even when those words are not misaligned with those locations. As was discussed earlier, subtle durational differences in the input can influence lexical activation (Davis et al., 2002; Gow & Gordon, 1995; Salverda et al., 2003). Salverda et al., for instance, found in a study in Dutch that the word *ham* (id.) was more strongly activated when listeners heard a token of *hamster* (id.) in which the first syllable [hæm] had been taken from an utterance where the speaker intended the word *ham* (and was longer in duration), than when it had been taken from another token of the word *hamster* (and was shorter).

One way to interpret findings such as this is to assume that the durational information signals a word boundary (e.g. a longer [hæm] indicates that there is a boundary after the [m]). Many authors have indeed argued that segmental lengthening signals the edges of prosodic domains (e.g. utterance and phrase boundaries, but also word boundaries: Beckman & Edwards, 1990; Cho & Keating, 2001; Fougeron, 2001; Fougeron & Keating, 1997; Turk & Shattuck-Hufnagel, 2000). While the PWC could penalize candidate words that are misaligned with boundaries that have been cued by segmental lengthening, it will not penalize an aligned word such as *hamster*. The results of Davis et al. (2002) and Salverda et al. (2003) thus suggest that, in addition to the PWC, there may be another segmentation process, one that would boost the activation of words that are aligned with prosodic boundaries. It will be important in future research to establish whether a single mechanism can account for the modulation of competition-based segmentation by word-boundary cues, and, if not, to establish the relative roles of processes that boost the activation of words that are aligned with possible word boundaries and processes that penalize misaligned words.

Summary

Spoken word perception emerges from competition among candidate lexical hypotheses. The activation of any given word is modulated by three crucial factors: its own goodness of fit to the current signal; the number of other words that are currently active; and their goodness of fit. The quality of match between any candidate and the signal is in turn determined by a number of factors: how well the signal and the stored lexical knowledge match in terms of segmental material (individual speech sounds); how well they match in terms of suprasegmental material (e.g. stress pattern); the appropriateness of the word's form in the phonological context (e.g. as in the case of place assimilation); and its (mis)alignment with likely word boundaries in the signal. We have seen that lexical activation is finely tuned to the signal, such that even very subtle acoustic details in the input can influence the pattern of activation at the lexical level. We have also seen that the segmentation of a continuous utterance into individual words is a product of this activation and competition process.

There is of course much more to speech comprehension than this. Word perception is not language understanding. The listener has much more to do than recognize the words of an utterance if he or she wants to comprehend the speaker's message. An interpretation must be built on the basis of the meanings of the words, the syntactic structure of the utterance, and the discourse and situational context of the utterance. It is beyond the scope of this chapter to review the evidence on these higher levels of speech comprehension. A review of research on the morphological structure of words (inflectional structures like *leap* + *ing*; derivational structures like *sweet* + *ly*; compounds like *tree* + *stump*)

and the role of morphology in speech processing can be found in McQueen and Cutler (1998b). A recent discussion of the representation of word semantics is provided by Rodd, Gaskell, and Marslen-Wilson (2002). In speech comprehension (as opposed to reading), the prosodic and intonational structure of sentences plays a key role in syntactic and discourse processing. Reviews on these issues are to be found in Cutler et al. (1997) and in Cutler and Clifton (1999).

The next part of the chapter will instead focus on the way in which the speech signal is mapped onto the mental lexicon, and on the perception of speech sounds. It is important to note, however, that this perceptual process appears to be uninfluenced by higher-level factors. That is, sentential context does not affect the early stages of the perceptual analysis of speech (van Alphen & McQueen, 2001; Connine, 1987; Connine, Blasko, & Hall, 1991; Miller, Green, & Schermer, 1984; Samuel, 1981). With respect to the effects of context on lexical activation, it appears that context does not influence which words are activated, but does influence the process of word selection (Marslen-Wilson, 1987; Zwitserlood, 1989). Recent evidence suggests that context can start to influence lexical interpretation very early; that is, before information in the signal is available to distinguish the intended word from its competitors (van den Brink, Brown, & Hagoort, 2001; Van Petten, Coulson, Rubin, Plante, & Parks, 1999). But it has not yet been determined whether context influences the activation of form representations of words, or meaning representations, or the integration of lexical information into the interpretation of the utterance. What is clear, however, is that the core perceptual process – that is, the generation of lexical hypotheses – is driven by the speech signal alone.

PERCEPTION OF SPEECH SOUNDS

Intermediate representations

One possible account of speech perception is that acoustic-phonetic information is mapped directly onto the mental lexicon, with no intermediate stage of processing. On this view, the output of the peripheral auditory system would be the input to the lexicon, and knowledge about the sound-form of words would have to be stored in each lexical representation in the form of auditory primitives (Klatt, 1979). The alternative is that there is a prelexical level of representation (or indeed, more than one such level), which mediates between the output of the auditory system and the lexicon. There are several arguments that can be made in support of a prelexical level of processing.

First, intermediate representations could remove considerable redundancy that otherwise would have to exist at the lexical level. If knowledge about the acoustic form of a particular speech sound, [p] for example, can be stored prelexically, then it does not need to be stored multiple times at the lexical level, in the representations of every word with one or more [p]'s. Instead, only the symbolic phonological information would need to be stored lexically. Recoding the acoustic signal in terms of a relatively small number of speech sounds (most languages have fewer than 50 phonemes: Maddieson, 1984), or in terms of other abstract phonological representations (e.g. syllables: Mehler, 1981), would achieve considerable information reduction and would thus make word recognition much more efficient.

Clearly, given the variability and complexity of the speech signal, as sketched in the Introduction (e.g. the different [p] sounds in the utterance in Figure 11.1 are all different), it is far from trivial to recode the signal in terms of abstract phonological representations. The variability problem raises many issues about the nature of prelexical representation (e.g. should there be position-specific, 'allophonic' units that code the major differences within phoneme categories, such as those for syllable-initial versus syllable-final [p]?). Nevertheless, variability does not invalidate the benefits of abstract prelexical recoding. Word recognition would benefit if at least part of the speech code could be cracked prelexically.

Speech-sound perception entails the integration of many different acoustic cues (Diehl & Kluender, 1987; Fitch, Halwes, Erickson, & Liberman, 1980; Liberman, Cooper, Shankweiler, & Studdert-Kennedy, 1967; Repp, 1982; Repp & Liberman, 1987; Repp, Liberman, Eccardt, & Pesetsky, 1978). The prelexical level provides a stage of processing at which this integration can take place. The prelexical level also provides a way of coding how those speech sounds are contextually conditioned. Indeed, coarticulation and other connected speech phenomena make it clear that speech sounds must always be interpreted in their phonetic context (Fowler, 1984). As Repp and Liberman (1987) point out, different acoustic signals need to be interpretable, depending on context, as the same sound, and it must also be possible to interpret the same acoustic signal in different contexts as different sounds. One kind of context is that provided by neighboring speech sounds. The identity of fricative sounds like [s] and [ʃ], for example, is dependent in large part on the frication noise itself, but also on neighboring vowels (Mann & Repp, 1980; Nearey, 1992; Smits, 2001a, 2001b; Whalen, 1981). Similarly, fricative sounds affect the perception of following stop consonants (Mann & Repp, 1981). It is usually assumed that the mechanisms that are responsible for these perceptual compensations for coarticulation have a prelexical locus (Elman & McClelland, 1986, 1988). One source of evidence in support of this assumption is

that compensatory effects can dissociate from lexical effects on phonetic perception (Pitt & McQueen, 1998; see below). If the mechanism responsible for compensation for coarticulation acted at the lexical level, compensatory and lexical effects should not dissociate.

Another kind of contextual influence on speech sound perception is that due to speech rate (Miller, 1981). Miller and Liberman (1979) showed that the duration of the formant transitions from the consonants to the vowels in [ba] and [wa] is a cue to the distinction between [b] and [w], but also that this durational cue depended on the speaking rate. Changes in the duration of the steady-state vowel (as a cue to speaking rate) modified the interpretation of the formant transition duration. As with the adjustments for coarticulation, those responsible for rate normalization appear to dissociate from higher-level biases in phonetic perception (Miller et al., 1984; Miller & Dexter, 1988). It is therefore reasonable to assume that the mechanisms responsible for speaking rate normalization should also have a prelexical rather than a lexical locus.

There are thus good grounds to assume that there is an intermediate level of processing in the speech perception system, between auditory processing and lexical processing. This stage of processing (or perhaps separate sub-stages) acts to normalize the signal and to abstract some kind of phonetic code that can then be used for lexical access. One line of research that is potentially problematic for the view that speech perception involves abstract prelexical representations is that on talker variability. This research has shown, for example, that listeners cannot ignore talker variability, that the processing of talker information and phonetic information are not entirely independent, and that talker-specific knowledge is stored in long-term memory (Church & Schacter, 1994; Goldinger, 1996; Mullennix & Pisoni, 1990; Mullennix, Pisoni, & Martin, 1989; Palmeri, Goldinger, & Pisoni, 1993; Schacter & Church, 1992). Such data have been taken as evidence for episodic theories of spoken word recognition, in which the lexicon consists of detailed episodic traces of the words that the listener has heard (Goldinger, 1998), and in which there are no abstract prelexical representations. These results certainly challenge pure abstractionist accounts, in which all speaker-specific information is thrown away at a prelexical normalization stage. But there is considerable scope for hybrid models in which talker-specific information (and other indexical information) is preserved, but in which there are also abstract, symbolic representations (Schacter & Church, 1992). Such models could account for the evidence on memory for talker details and at the same time could account for the evidence supporting abstract intermediate representations.

Even among theories that include a prelexical level, however, there is no consensus on the size of the representational units. Many possibilities have been proposed, including phonemes (Foss & Blank, 1980; Nearey, 2001; Norris, 1994), syllables (Massaro, 1987; Mehler, 1981), acoustic-phonetic features (Lahiri & Marslen-Wilson, 1991; Marslen-Wilson & Warren, 1994; Stevens, 2002), a combination of a featural level followed by a phonemic level (McClelland & Elman, 1986), articulatory gestures (Liberman & Mattingly, 1985) and context-sensitive allophones (Luce et al., 2000; Wickelgren, 1969). Space limits preclude a detailed review of the arguments for and against each of these representational alternatives. The short version of the story is this: the issue has not been resolved. One recurring issue in this debate has been whether the objects of speech perception are fundamentally acoustic in nature (Kluender, 1994), or are gestural in nature (Fowler, 1986, 1996; Liberman & Mattingly, 1985), or are the product of pattern-recognition processes (Massaro, 1987; Nearey, 1997). Another, related issue has been whether speech perception calls on special processes (Liberman & Mattingly, 1985), or depends on general auditory processes that are also used in the perception of other complex sounds (Pastore, 1981; see, e.g., the debate between Fowler, Brown, & Mann, 2000, and Lotto & Kluender, 1998, and Lotto, Kluender, & Holt, 1997).

One reason why an answer to the 'unit of perception' question has eluded speech scientists is that such units are mental representations to which, during normal communicative speech processing, the listener does not attend (instead, as I suggested earlier, the listener focuses on words and on building an interpretation of the current utterance). There is thus no direct way to examine the contents of the prelexical level. Representations at the prelexical level of processing must be inferred from experiments that probe lexical-level processing, or from experiments that require decisions about speech sounds (e.g. the classification of a sound as one of two phonetic categories, or the detection of target sounds or sound sequences). Either way, it is possible that such experiments may call not only on the processes and representations that are used in normal speech comprehension, but also on processes that are required for the experimental task but that are not part of normal processing. It is thus possible that results that might be taken as support for a particular form of prelexical representation instead reflect lexical-level representations (if the task involves word responses) or decision-level representations (if the task involves phonological decision-making). Another reason for the stalemate in the 'unit of perception' debate is that results are often consistent with a number of representational alternatives (see, e.g., McQueen et al., 1999).

While it remains very difficult to tie down the size of the prelexical 'unit of perception', one aspect about the way the prelexical level operates

does now seem to be very clear. This is that it operates in cascade. Activation flows through this level of processing in a continuous fashion. The evidence showing subphonemic effects on lexical activation reviewed earlier in this chapter supports this claim. Since fine-grained information in the speech signal modulates the activation of words, it cannot be the case that the prelexical level acts in a serial and categorical way. If phonemic units, for example, reached some threshold of activation and then only passed on discrete signals to the lexicon that particular phonemes had been detected, then subphonemic variation would be unable to influence lexical activation. Instead, prelexical representations must be activated in proportion to their match with the speech signal, and in turn pass activation continuously to word representations. Units larger than the phoneme (e.g. syllabic representations) or smaller (e.g. featural representations) could also pass fine-grained information on to the lexical level in cascade, just like phonemic representations.

Note that cascaded processing in speech perception is not limited to the interface between the prelexical and lexical stages. The evidence that was presented earlier on the activation of word meanings before the acoustic offset of those words (e.g. Allopenna et al., 1998; van den Brink et al., 2001; Zwitserlood, 1989) suggests that activation also cascades from word-form representations to meaning representations. Thus, for example, it is not the case that categorical decisions about each of the sounds of *cucumber* are made before the lexical representation of *cucumber* is activated. Instead, as soon as some degree of support has accumulated at the prelexical level for [k], for example, this information cascades up to the lexical level, influencing the activation of words beginning with [k], and the activation of their meanings.

Flow of information in the recognition system

Information must flow from the prelexical level to the lexical level, but need not flow from the lexicon back to the lower level. There is in fact no benefit for word recognition to be had from lexical–prelexical feedback (Norris, McQueen, & Cutler, 2000a). The best that the lexical level can do is select the words that best match the information in the current utterance. Feedback offers no improvement on this performance, since all it does is cause the prelexical level to agree with the decision that has already been reached at the lexical level.

There is, however, a considerable body of evidence suggesting that listeners use lexical knowledge in tasks that require explicit phonemic judgments. For example, in phonetic categorization tasks, where listeners have to identify ambiguous phonemes, there are lexical biases: listeners are more likely to identify a sound between [b] and [p] as [b] in a *beef–peef* context than in a *beace–peace* context (Ganong, 1980). Although such effects are variable (i.e. are sometimes present and sometimes absent), they have now been replicated many times under a variety of different conditions (Burton, Baum, & Blumstein, 1989; Connine, 1990; Connine & Clifton, 1987; Fox, 1984; McQueen, 1991; Miller & Dexter, 1988; Pitt, 1995; Pitt & Samuel, 1993). The phonemic restoration illusion (Warren, 1970) also shows lexical biases (it is harder to distinguish between a sound that has had noise added to it and a sound that has been replaced with a noise when the sound is in a real word than when it is in a nonsense word: Samuel, 1981, 1987). These lexical biases are also variable (Samuel, 1996). Furthermore, target phonemes can be identified faster in real words than in nonwords, but these effects again come and go (Cutler, Mehler, Norris, & Seguí, 1987; Eimas, Marcovitz Hornstein, & Payton, 1990; Eimas & Nygaard, 1992; Frauenfelder, Seguí, & Dijkstra, 1990; Pitt & Samuel, 1995; Rubin, Turvey, & Van Gelder, 1976; Wurm & Samuel, 1997). Lexical biases in phonemic tasks can also be found in nonwords (Connine et al., 1997; Frauenfelder et al., 2001; Marslen-Wilson & Warren, 1994; McQueen et al., 1999; Newman, Sawusch, & Luce, 1997). As was mentioned earlier in the chapter, for example, Connine et al. found that phoneme monitoring latencies were fastest for targets in real words (e.g. /t/ in *cabinet*), slower for targets in the nonwords that were very similar to the real words (*gabinet*), and slower still for targets in nonwords with greater mismatch (*mabinet*).

One way to explain these results is to postulate feedback from the lexicon to the prelexical level (McClelland & Elman, 1986). On an interactive account such as this, decisions about speech sounds are based on the activation of prelexical representations. Feedback from the lexicon would boost the activation of lexically consistent sounds in words, thus speeding responses to those sounds relative to sounds in nonwords. The other lexical effects in phonemic decision-making could be explained in the same way, including the lexical biases in word-like nonwords (where partially activated word representations feed activation back to prelexical representations). An alternative account, however, is that phoneme decisions are based on the activation of decision units, which receive input from both the prelexical and lexical levels (Norris et al., 2000a). According to this modular account, there is no feedback: information flows forward from the prelexical level to the lexical level and forward to the decision level, and from the lexical level forward to the decision level. The activation of units at the decision level would nonetheless be biased by lexical activation when words or word-like nonwords are heard, in much the same way as in the interactive account, but without feedback.

It is difficult to distinguish between these two alternative accounts (see Norris et al., 2000a, 2000b, and accompanying commentaries for extended discussion). Nevertheless, there are several reasons to prefer the feedforward account. The first reason has already been mentioned: feedback offers no benefit to spoken word recognition. Feedback would therefore be postulated simply to explain the data on lexical involvement in phonemic decision-making. But since these data can be explained without feedback, there is no need to include feedback in an account of speech perception. One might want to argue, however, that since phoneme decision units are not a necessary part of spoken word recognition, their addition is also only motivated by a need to explain the data on lexical effects. In other words, is the postulation of decision units any more parsimonious than the postulation of feedback? But, since listeners can make explicit phonemic judgments, the machinery for this ability must be included in any model of speech perception, whether it has feedback or not. As Norris et al. (2000b) argued, a model with feedback requires all of the components for phonemic decision-making that a model without feedback has, with the addition of the feedback connections themselves. A model without feedback, especially since feedback has no benefit to offer in normal word recognition, should therefore be preferred.

There is also empirical evidence that challenges the feedback account. In the earlier discussion of compensation for coarticulation, I pointed out that Pitt and McQueen (1998) have shown that lexical and compensatory effects can dissociate. Listeners tend to label more sounds on a [t]–[k] stop continuum as [t] when the sounds are presented after a word ending with the fricative [ʃ], such as *foolish*, than after a [s]-final word such as *christmas* (Elman & McClelland, 1988; Mann & Repp, 1981; Pitt & McQueen 1998). As argued above, this compensation for coarticulation process has a prelexical locus. Demonstrations of this compensation effect when word-final fricatives were replaced with an ambiguous sound (e.g. *foolish* becoming [fulɪʔ]; *christmas* becoming [krɪsmə?]) have thus been taken as evidence for feedback (the lexicon providing the missing fricative information, and thus inducing the prelexical compensation process: Elman & McClelland, 1988).

Pitt and McQueen (1998) have shown, however, that there was a confound in the Elman and McClelland (1988) study between lexical bias and the phoneme transition probability from the final vowels in the context words to the final fricatives. When these transition probabilities were controlled, lexical biases still determined decisions about the ambiguous fricatives, but those decisions had no further consequences for the processing of the following stops. The dissociation between the lexical effect and the compensation for coarticulation effect suggests that they have different loci. If the lexical bias were due to feedback, it should have caused a compensation effect (a shift in the identification of the following stop). As mentioned above, dissociations between lexical biases and another low-level adjustment process, that of speech rate normalization, have also been observed (Miller & Dexter, 1988; Miller et al., 1984). These dissociations challenge the feedback account, and support the feedforward account, where the perceptual effects have a prelexical locus, and the lexical effects are due to biases acting at the decision stage.

It would be misleading to suggest that the debate on feedback in speech perception is resolved. Recent papers have presented evidence that appears to challenge the feedforward account of lexical effects (Samuel, 1997, 2001). Interestingly, however, these experiments involved a learning component (i.e. selective adaptation effects, in which listeners' perception of speech sounds was changed over time as a result of repeated exposure to particular sounds: Eimas & Corbit, 1973; Samuel, 1986). It is possible that lexical knowledge could influence perceptual learning over time, without having any effect on the on-line processing of any particular utterance. It has in fact recently been shown that listeners do use their lexical knowledge to adjust their perceptual categories over time as they listen to unfamiliar speech sounds (McQueen, Norris, & Cutler, 2001; Norris, McQueen, & Cutler, 2003). The lexicon may thus influence perceptual learning at the prelexical level but not on-line prelexical processing.

Summary

Speech-sound perception is in many ways more controversial than spoken word perception. While there is considerable consensus on many aspects of the word recognition process, there is considerable disagreement about how speech sounds are perceived. Thus, while I have argued that there is an intermediate level of processing between the output of the auditory system and the mental lexicon, I have also had to point out that there is no agreement about the nature of the representations at this level of processing, nor indeed agreement that such a level of processing must exist. It is clear, however, that if there is a prelexical stage of processing, activation must cascade continuously through this stage, from the auditory level to the lexicon. I have also argued that there is no feedback of information from the lexicon to the prelexical stage, except perhaps where feedback acts as an error-correcting signal in perceptual learning. The claim that there is no on-line feedback in the perceptual system comes, however, with an important additional claim: that listeners' judgments about speech sounds are not based directly on the output of the prelexical processing stage, but instead on separate decision units.

MODELS OF SPEECH DECODING

In conclusion, I turn to models of speech decoding. Table 11.1 lists a number of these models, together with their major features. Note, however, that there may be important differences even between models that appear to share a particular assumption. For example, although both TRACE and ARTWORD have both featural and phonemic representations that mediate between the speech signal and the lexicon, the nature of processing in these two models is radically different. The table thus omits a large number of fundamental differences between the models. I make no attempt to provide full descriptions of the models (many, but not all, of which have computational implementations). The references on each model provide those details. Nor do I offer a detailed evaluation of each model. Instead, my aim is to provide a recapitulation of the major themes of this chapter in the context of these models.

In the listing of word-form representations, the term 'logogen' is used. This term derives from Morton's (1969) seminal logogen model of word recognition. A logogen is a mental representation that accrues evidence, coded in terms of an activation value, for a particular word. All of the models, with the exception of the Lexical Access From Spectra (LAFS) model, MINERVA 2, the Distributed Cohort Model (DCM) and the Lexical Access From Features (LAFF) model, could thus be said to have logogens of one kind or another, since they all have abstract localist word representations with activation levels that code support for candidate words. The lexical representations in the Cohort and Shortlist models are not listed as logogens, however, since additional claims have been made about the phonological content of word representations in these two models.

As can be seen from Table 11.1, all the models assume that multiple words are simultaneously activated when a speech signal is heard, but only four assume that there is direct competition between those candidate words. In each of these four models, there are inhibitory connections between word representations, and thus direct competition between words. In two of the other models, however, competition is included as a decision-level process (i.e. in the Cohort model and the Neighborhood Activation Model, NAM). In these models, decisions about which word has been heard are based on computations of the degree of support for a given word relative to the degree of support for other candidates. Thus, while there is no inter-word competition in these two models, the number of alternative candidate words, and their degree of support, influences lexical identification. Furthermore, although there are no inter-word connections in the DCM (note that there can be no such connections in a network with fully distributed

TABLE 11.1 *Models of spoken word perception*

Model	Primary references	Prelexical representations	Word-form representations	Multiple activation of lexical hypotheses	Direct inter-word competition	Feedforward prelexical–lexical cascade	On-line lexical–prelexical feedback
Lexical Access From Spectra (LAFS)	Klatt (1979, 1989)	None	Spectral templates	Yes	No	Not applicable	Not applicable
MINERVA 2	Hintzman (1986); Goldinger (1998)	None	Episodic traces	Yes	No	Not applicable	Not applicable
Lexical Access From Features (LAFF)	Stevens (2002)	Features and segments	Features and segments	Yes	No	No	No
Cohort	Marslen-Wilson & Welsh (1978); Marslen-Wilson (1987, 1993); Lahiri & Marslen-Wilson (1991)	Features	Underspecified phonological structures	Yes	No	Yes	No
Distributed Cohort Model (DCM)	Gaskell & Marslen-Wilson (1997, 1999)	Features	Fully distributed vectors in a recurrent network	Yes	No	Yes	No
Neighborhood Activation Model (NAM)	Luce (1986); Luce & Pisoni (1998)	Acoustic-phonetic patterns	Logogens	Yes	No	Yes	No
PARSYN	Luce, Goldinger, Auer, & Vitevitch (2000)	Allophones	Logogens	Yes	Yes	Yes	Yes
TRACE	Elman & McClelland (1986); McClelland & Elman (1986); McClelland (1991)	Features and phonemes	Logogens	Yes	Yes	Yes	Yes
Shortlist	Norris (1994); Norris, McQueen, Cutler, & Butterfield (1997)	Phonemes	Phoneme strings	Yes	Yes	No	No
ARTWORD	Grossberg, Boardman, & Cohen (1997); Grossberg & Myers (2000)	Features and phonemes	Logogens	Yes	Yes	Yes	Yes

representations), there is nonetheless a form of competition between candidate words as the network settles into a stable state (i.e. the performance of the model is sensitive to the number of words activated by a particular input, and the similarities among those words). Although lexical competition has not been addressed directly in the remaining models (LAFS, MINERVA 2, LAFF), the lexical selection processes in these models are also likely to be affected by the number and similarity of activated lexical hypotheses.

Thus, while only some models have direct interword competition, all models have some form of competitive process. Direct inter-word competition may be preferred because it provides an efficient means by which continuous speech can be segmented into words (Grossberg & Myers, 2000; McQueen et al., 1995). Note also that, of these ten models, only Shortlist includes a mechanism that uses cues to likely word boundaries in continuous speech to modulate the competition process and thus improve lexical segmentation (Norris et al., 1997).

Of the eight models with prelexical representations, only the LAFF model and Shortlist have no cascaded processing from the prelexical level to the lexical level. Little has been said about the temporal dynamics of lexical access in the LAFF model (Stevens, 2002); whether the model can account for subphonemic effects on lexical activation will depend on specification of the time course of the spread of information from the prelexical featural representations to the lexicon. In the Norris (1994) implementation of Shortlist, processing evolves on a phoneme-by-phoneme basis, with categorical phonemic representations at the prelexical level acting as the input to lexical processing. It is important to note, however, that this implementation was considered to be an approximation of a continuous lexical access process (Norris, 1994). Indeed, more recent simulations of lexical access in Shortlist involve cascaded processing (Norris et al., 2000a). Shortlist, like the other models with prelexical–lexical cascade, may therefore be able to account for the evidence of continuous lexical access, including at least some of the recent results showing the influence of fine-grained acoustic detail on lexical activation.

Three models (TRACE, PARSYN and ARTWORD) have on-line feedback from the lexicon to prior stages of processing. The challenge posed by Norris et al. (2000a) to theorists postulating this kind of feedback was that the value of feedback for speech perception needs to be shown. As far as I am aware, this challenge has not yet been met. It is possible, however, that lexical feedback could be required for perceptual learning (Grossberg, 2000; Norris, 1993; Norris et al., 2000b, 2003). This kind of feedback would act off-line, to alter prelexical representations over time, but would in principle not influence on-line perception of a particular utterance. It is possible, however, that feedback for perceptual learning could produce effects that might appear to be the result of on-line feedback. It will be important to establish (not only in this domain but also in other areas of speech perception) the extent to which particular effects reflect learning (the dynamic adjustments of the perceptual system over time) and the extent to which effects reflect the steady-state operation of the system.

This review has provided a brief introduction to models of spoken word perception by setting them in the context of the issues that were raised in the main part of this chapter. A more thorough evaluation of these models would require a much more detailed analysis of the detailed assumptions of each model. Nevertheless, it should be clear that while there is considerable agreement on several of the major assumptions of the models, there are also many fundamental disagreements. There is therefore still plenty work to be done. Progress will be made in this field, as in other fields of cognitive science, through the continuing interplay between the development of computationally explicit models and simulation results on the one hand, and the results of experimental investigations with human listeners on the other.

One final point is that Table 11.1 is incomplete. The models listed in the table have all explicitly addressed spoken word perception. There are many other theories of speech perception, which have been concerned primarily with speech-sound perception. Such accounts include: the motor theory of speech perception (Liberman & Mattingly, 1985); a direct-realist theory of speech perception (Fowler, 1986, 1996); pattern-classification models (Nearey, 1992, 1997; Smits, 2001b); the Merge model of phonemic decision-making (Norris et al., 2000a); and the Fuzzy Logical Model of Perception (FLMP: Massaro, 1987, 1989, 1997). Lexical factors do play a role in some of these models (e.g. Merge is explicitly linked to the Shortlist account of word recognition; FLMP has been used to examine lexical effects in phonemic decision-making: Massaro & Oden, 1995), but even in these cases the emphasis has been on the perception of speech sounds. In most of these theories, no account of word perception is provided.

These accounts of speech-sound perception have been, and will continue to be, critical to the development of our understanding of speech decoding (e.g. in the debate on 'units of perception', or in specifying how the acoustic-phonetic information that specifies particular sounds is integrated). In my view, however, such accounts will be incomplete until they specify how spoken words are perceived. In particular, it will be necessary to make explicit the extent to which the processes that are postulated for speech-sound perception and those for word perception are shared or distinct, and, if distinct, how they are related. This complaint can of course also apply to models of word perception, where the details of prelexical processing and speech-sound perception have often been evaded. The ideal, of course, is a model that accounts for the perception of both the words and the individual sounds of speech (and indeed the prosodic and intonational structure of spoken utterances). I believe that word perception will nevertheless remain as the central element in such a model of speech decoding, both because words are the primary objects of speech perception and because words are the key to the speech code.

ACKNOWLEDGEMENTS

I thank my colleagues Anne Cutler, Delphine Dahan, Dennis Norris and Roel Smits for comments on a previous version of this chapter, and Tau van Dijck for assistance with Figure 11.1.

NOTE

1 Many experimental tasks used in speech perception and spoken word recognition are described in a special issue of the journal *Language and Cognitive Processes, 11* (1996), which also appears as Grosjean and Frauenfelder (1996). Please see those descriptions for details on the tasks described in this chapter.

REFERENCES

Allopenna, P. D., Magnuson, J. S., & Tanenhaus, M. K. (1998). Tracking the time course of spoken word recognition using eye movements: evidence for continuous mapping models. *Journal of Memory and Language, 38*, 419–439.

Andruski, J. E., Blumstein, S. E., & Burton, M. (1994). The effect of subphonetic differences on lexical access. *Cognition, 52*, 163–187.

Beckman, M. E., & Edwards, J. (1990). Lengthenings and shortenings and the nature of prosodic constituency. In J. Kingston & M. E. Beckman (Eds.), *Papers in laboratory phonology I: Between the grammar and physics of speech* (pp. 152–178). Cambridge: Cambridge University Press.

Burton, M. W., Baum, S. R., & Blumstein, S. E. (1989). Lexical effects on the phonetic categorization of speech: the role of acoustic structure. *Journal of Experimental Psychology: Human Perception and Performance, 15*, 567–575.

Cho, T., & Keating, P. A. (2001). Articulatory and acoustic studies on domain-initial strengthening in Korean. *Journal of Phonetics, 29*, 155–190.

Christie, W. M. (1974). Some cues for syllable juncture perception in English. *Journal of the Acoustical Society of America, 55*, 819–821.

Church, B. A., & Schacter, D. L. (1994). Perceptual specificity of auditory priming: implicit memory for voice intonation and fundamental frequency. *Journal of Experimental Psychology: Learning, Memory, and Cognition, 20*, 521–533.

Church, K. W. (1987). Phonological parsing and lexical retrieval. *Cognition, 25*, 53–69.

Cluff, M. S., & Luce, P. A. (1990). Similarity neighborhoods of spoken two-syllable words: retroactive effects on multiple activation. *Journal of Experimental Psychology: Human Perception and Performance, 16*, 551–563.

Coenen, E., Zwitserlood, P., & Boelte, J. (2001). Variation and assimilation in German: consequences for lexical access and representation. *Language and Cognitive Processes, 16*, 535–564.

Connine, C. M. (1987). Constraints on interactive processes in auditory word recognition: the role of sentence context. *Journal of Memory and Language, 26*, 527–538.

Connine, C. M. (1990). Effects of sentence context and lexical knowledge during speech processing. In G. T. M. Altmann (ed.), *Cognitive models of speech processing: psycholinguistic and computational perspectives* (pp. 281–294). Cambridge, MA: MIT Press.

Connine, C. M., Blasko, D., & Hall, M. (1991). Effects of subsequent sentence context in auditory word recognition: temporal and linguistic constraints. *Journal of Memory and Language, 30*, 234–250.

Connine, C. M., Blasko, D. G., & Titone, D. (1993). Do the beginnings of spoken words have a special status in auditory word recognition? *Journal of Memory and Language, 32*, 193–210.

Connine, C. M., & Clifton, C. (1987). Interactive use of lexical information in speech perception. *Journal of Experimental Psychology: Human Perception and Performance, 13*, 291–299.

Connine, C. M., Titone, D., Deelman, T., & Blasko, D. (1997). Similarity mapping in spoken word recognition. *Journal of Memory and Language, 37*, 463–480.

Content, A., Meunier, C., Kearns, R. K., & Frauenfelder, U. H. (2001). Sequence detection in pseudowords in French: where is the syllable effect? *Language and Cognitive Processes, 16*, 609–636.

Cooper, N., Cutler, A., & Wales, R. (2002). Constraints of lexical stress on lexical access in English: evidence from native and nonnative listeners. *Language and Speech, 45*, 207–228.

Cutler, A., & Butterfield, S. (1992). Rhythmic cues to speech segmentation: evidence from juncture misperception. *Journal of Memory and Language, 31*, 218–236.

Cutler, A., & Clifton, C. (1999). Comprehending spoken language: a blueprint of the listener. In C. M. Brown & P. Hagoort (Eds.), *The neurocognition of language* (pp. 123–166). Oxford: Oxford University Press.

Cutler, A., Dahan, D., & van Donselaar, W. (1997). Prosody in the comprehension of spoken language: a literature review. *Language and Speech, 40*, 141–201.

Cutler, A., Demuth, K., & McQueen, J. M. (2002). Universality versus language-specificity in listening to running speech. *Psychological Science, 13,* 258–262.

Cutler, A., & van Donselaar, W. (2001). Voornaam is not a homophone: lexical prosody and lexical access in Dutch. *Language and Speech, 44,* 171–195.

Cutler, A., Mehler, J., Norris, D., & Seguí, J. (1986). The syllable's differing role in the segmentation of French and English. *Journal of Memory and Language, 25,* 385–400.

Cutler, A., Mehler, J., Norris, D., & Seguí, J. (1987). Phoneme identification and the lexicon. *Cognitive Psychology, 19,* 141–177.

Cutler, A., & Norris, D. (1988). The role of strong syllables in segmentation for lexical access. *Journal of Experimental Psychology: Human Perception and Performance, 14,* 113–121.

Cutler, A., & Otake, T. (1994). Mora or phoneme? Further evidence for language-specific listening. *Journal of Memory and Language, 33,* 824–844.

Dahan, D., Magnuson, J. S., Tanenhaus, M. K., & Hogan, E. M. (2001). Subcategorical mismatches and the time course of lexical access: evidence for lexical competition. *Language and Cognitive Processes, 16,* 507–534.

Davis, M. H., Marslen-Wilson, W. D., & Gaskell, M. G. (2002). Leading up the lexical garden-path: segmentation and ambiguity in spoken word recognition. *Journal of Experimental Psychology: Human Perception and Performance, 28,* 218–244.

Diehl, R. L., & Kluender, K. R. (1987). On the categorization of speech sounds. In S. R. Harnad (ed.), *Categorical perception* (pp. 226–253). Cambridge: Cambridge University Press.

Dumay, N., Frauenfelder, U. H., & Content, A. (2002). The role of the syllable in lexical segmentation in French: word-spotting data. *Brain and Language, 81,* 144–161.

Dupoux, E., Pallier, C., Sebastián-Gallés, N., & Mehler, J. (1997). A destressing deafness in French. *Journal of Memory and Language, 36,* 399–421.

Eimas, P. D., & Corbit, J. D. (1973). Selective adaptation of linguistic feature detectors. *Cognitive Psychology, 4,* 99–109.

Eimas, P. D., Marcovitz Hornstein, S. B., & Payton, P. (1990). Attention and the role of dual codes in phoneme monitoring. *Journal of Memory and Language, 29,* 160–180.

Eimas, P. D., & Nygaard, L. C. (1992). Contextual coherence and attention in phoneme monitoring. *Journal of Memory and Language, 31,* 375–395.

Elman, J. L., & McClelland, J. L. (1986). Exploiting lawful variability in the speech wave. In J. S. Perkell & D. H. Klatt (Eds.), *Invariance and variability of speech processes* (pp. 360–380). Hillsdale, NJ: Erlbaum.

Elman, J. L., & McClelland, J. L. (1988). Cognitive penetration of the mechanisms of perception: compensation for coarticulation of lexically restored phonemes. *Journal of Memory and Language, 27,* 143–165.

Fitch, H. L., Halwes, T., Erickson, D. M., & Liberman, A. M. (1980). Perceptual equivalence of two acoustic cues for stop-consonant manner. *Perception and Psychophysics, 27,* 343–350.

Foss, D. J., & Blank, M. A. (1980). Identifying the speech codes. *Cognitive Psychology, 12,* 1–31.

Fougeron, C. (2001). Articulatory properties of initial segments in several prosodic constituents in French. *Journal of Phonetics, 29,* 109–135.

Fougeron, C., & Keating, P. A. (1997). Articulatory strengthening at edges of prosodic domains. *Journal of the Acoustical Society of America, 101,* 3728–3740.

Fowler, C. A. (1984). Segmentation of coarticulated speech in perception. *Perception and Psychophysics, 36,* 359–368.

Fowler, C. A. (1986). An event approach to the study of speech perception from a direct-realist perspective. *Journal of Phonetics, 14,* 3–28.

Fowler, C. A. (1996). Listeners do hear sounds, not tongues. *Journal of the Acoustical Society of America, 99,* 1730–1741.

Fowler, C. A., Brown, J. M., & Mann, V. A. (2000). Contrast effects do not underlie effects of preceding liquids on stop-consonant identification by humans. *Journal of Experimental Psychology: Human Perception and Performance, 26,* 877–888.

Fox, R. A. (1984). Effect of lexical status on phonetic categorization. *Journal of Experimental Psychology: Human Perception and Performance, 10,* 526–540.

Frauenfelder, U. H., Scholten, M., & Content, A. (2001). Bottom-up inhibition in lexical selection: phonological mismatch effects in spoken word recognition. *Language and Cognitive Processes, 16,* 583–607.

Frauenfelder, U. H., Seguí, J., & Dijkstra, T. (1990). Lexical effects in phonemic processing: facilitatory or inhibitory? *Journal of Experimental Psychology: Human Perception and Performance, 16,* 77–91.

Ganong, W. F. (1980). Phonetic categorization in auditory word perception. *Journal of Experimental Psychology: Human Perception and Performance, 6,* 110–125.

Gaskell, M. G., & Marslen-Wilson, W. D. (1996). Phonological variation and inference in lexical access. *Journal of Experimental Psychology: Human Perception and Performance, 22,* 144–158.

Gaskell, M. G., & Marslen-Wilson, W. D. (1997). Integrating form and meaning: a distributed model of speech perception. *Language and Cognitive Processes, 12,* 613–656.

Gaskell, M. G., & Marslen-Wilson, W. D. (1998). Mechanisms of phonological inference in speech perception. *Journal of Experimental Psychology: Human Perception and Performance, 24,* 380–396.

Gaskell, M. G., & Marslen-Wilson, W. D. (1999). Ambiguity, competition, and blending in spoken word recognition. *Cognitive Science, 23,* 439–462.

Gaskell, M. G., & Marslen-Wilson, W. D. (2001). Lexical ambiguity resolution and spoken word recognition: bridging the gap. *Journal of Memory and Language, 44,* 325–349.

Goldinger, S. D. (1996). Words and voices: episodic traces in spoken word identification and recognition memory. *Journal of Experimental Psychology: Learning, Memory, and Cognition, 22,* 1166–1183.

Goldinger, S. D. (1998). Echoes of echoes? An episodic theory of lexical access. *Psychological Review, 105*, 251–279.

Goldinger, S. D., Luce, P. A., Pisoni, D. B., & Marcario, J. K. (1992). Form-based priming in spoken word recognition: the roles of competition and bias. *Journal of Experimental Psychology: Learning, Memory, and Cognition, 18*, 1211–1238.

Gow, D. W. (2001). Assimilation and anticipation in continuous spoken word recognition. *Journal of Memory and Language, 45*, 133–159.

Gow, D. W. (2002). Does English coronal place assimilation create lexical ambiguity? *Journal of Experimental Psychology: Human Perception and Performance, 28*, 163–179.

Gow, D. W., & Gordon, P. C. (1995). Lexical and prelexical influences on word segmentation: evidence from priming. *Journal of Experimental Psychology: Human Perception and Performance, 21*, 344–359.

Grosjean, F., & Frauenfelder, U. H. (Eds.) (1996). *A guide to spoken word recognition paradigms.* Hove, UK: Psychology Press.

Grossberg, S. (2000). Brain feedback and adaptive resonance in speech perception. *Behavioral and Brain Sciences, 23*, 332–333.

Grossberg, S., Boardman, I., & Cohen, M. (1997). Neural dynamics of variable-rate speech categorization. *Journal of Experimental Psychology: Human Perception and Performance, 23*, 481–503.

Grossberg, S., & Myers, C. W. (2000). The resonant dynamics of speech perception: interword integration and duration-dependent backward effects. *Psychological Review, 107*, 735–767.

Hintzman, D. L. (1986). 'Schema abstraction' in a multiple-trace memory model. *Psychological Review, 93*, 411–428.

Jakobson, R., Fant, C. G. M., & Halle, M. (1952). *Preliminaries to speech analysis: the distinctive features and their correlates.* Cambridge, MA: MIT Press.

Klatt, D. H. (1979). Speech perception: a model of acoustic-phonetic analysis and lexical access. *Journal of Phonetics, 7*, 279–312.

Klatt, D. H. (1989). Review of selected models of speech perception. In W. D. Marslen-Wilson (ed.), *Lexical representation and process* (pp. 169–226). Cambridge, MA: MIT Press.

Kluender, K. (1994). Speech perception as a tractable problem in cognitive science. In M. A. Gernsbacher (ed.), *Handbook of psycholinguistics* (pp. 173–214). San Diego: Academic Press.

Ladefoged, P. (2001). *A course in phonetics* (4th ed.). New York: Harcourt Brace Jovanovich.

Ladefoged, P., & Maddieson, I. (1996). *The sounds of the world's languages.* Oxford: Blackwell.

Lahiri, A., & Marslen-Wilson, W. (1991). The mental representation of lexical form: a phonological approach to the recognition lexicon. *Cognition, 38*, 245–294.

Lehiste, I. (1960). An acoustic-phonetic study of internal open juncture. *Phonetica, 5* (Suppl. 5), 1–54.

Lehiste, I. (1972). The timing of utterances and linguistic boundaries. *Journal of the Acoustical Society of America, 51*, 2018–2024.

Liberman, A. M., Cooper, F. S., Shankweiler, D. P., & Studdert-Kennedy, M. (1967). Perception of the speech code. *Psychological Review, 74*, 431–461.

Liberman, A. M., & Mattingly, I. G. (1985). The motor theory of speech perception revised. *Cognition, 21*, 1–36.

Lotto, A., & Kluender, K. (1998). General contrast effects in speech perception: effect of preceding liquid on stop consonant identification. *Perception and Psychophysics, 60*, 602–619.

Lotto, A., Kluender, K., & Holt, L. (1997). Perceptual compensation for coarticulation by Japanese quail (*Coturnix coturnix japonica*). *Journal of the Acoustical Society of America, 102*, 1134–1140.

Luce, P. A. (1986). Neighborhoods of words in the mental lexicon (PhD dissertation, Indiana University). In *Research on Speech Perception, Technical Report No. 6*, Speech Research Laboratory, Department of Psychology, Indiana University.

Luce, P. A., Goldinger, S. D., Auer, E. T., & Vitevitch, M. S. (2000). Phonetic priming, neighborhood activation, and PARSYN. *Perception and Psychophysics, 62*, 615–625.

Luce, P. A., & Large, N. R. (2001). Phonotactics, density, and entropy in spoken word recognition. *Language and Cognitive Processes, 16*, 565–581.

Luce, P. A., & Pisoni, D. B. (1998). Recognizing spoken words: the Neighborhood Activation Model. *Ear and Hearing, 19*, 1–36.

Maddieson, I. (1984). *Patterns of sounds.* Cambridge: Cambridge University Press.

Mann, V. A., & Repp, B. H. (1980). Influence of vocalic context on perception of the [S]-[s] distinction. *Perception and Psychophysics, 28*, 213–228.

Mann, V. A., & Repp, B. H. (1981). Influence of preceding fricative on stop consonant perception. *Journal of the Acoustical Society of America, 69*, 548–558.

Marslen-Wilson, W. D. (1987). Functional parallelism in spoken word-recognition. *Cognition, 25*, 71–102.

Marslen-Wilson, W. D. (1993). Issues of process and representation in lexical access. In G. T. M. Altmann & R. Shillcock (Eds.), *Cognitive models of speech processing: The Second Sperlonga Meeting* (pp. 187–210). Hillsdale, NJ: Erlbaum.

Marslen-Wilson, W., Moss, H. E., & van Halen, S. (1996). Perceptual distance and competition in lexical access. *Journal of Experimental Psychology: Human Perception and Performance, 22*, 1376–1392.

Marslen-Wilson, W. D., Nix, A., & Gaskell, M. G. (1995). Phonological variation in lexical access: abstractness, inference and English place assimilation. *Language and Cognitive Processes, 10*, 285–308.

Marslen-Wilson, W., & Warren, P. (1994). Levels of perceptual representation and process in lexical access: words, phonemes, and features. *Psychological Review, 101*, 653–675.

Marslen-Wilson, W. D., & Welsh, A. (1978). Processing interactions and lexical access during word recognition in continuous speech. *Cognitive Psychology, 10*, 29–63.

Massaro, D. W. (1987). *Speech perception by ear and eye: a paradigm for psychological inquiry*. Hillsdale, NJ: Erlbaum.

Massaro, D. W. (1989). Testing between the TRACE model and the Fuzzy Logical Model of Speech Perception. *Cognitive Psychology, 21*, 398–421.

Massaro, D. W. (1997). *Perceiving talking faces: from speech perception to a behavioral principle*. Cambridge, MA: MIT Press.

Massaro, D. W., & Oden, G. C. (1995). Independence of lexical context and phonological information in speech perception. *Journal of Experimental Psychology: Learning, Memory, and Cognition, 21*, 1053–1064.

McClelland, J. L. (1991). Stochastic interactive processes and the effect of context on perception. *Cognitive Psychology, 23*, 1–44.

McClelland, J. L., & Elman, J. L. (1986). The TRACE model of speech perception. *Cognitive Psychology, 10*, 1–86.

McQueen, J. M. (1991). The influence of the lexicon on phonetic categorization: stimulus quality in word-final ambiguity. *Journal of Experimental Psychology: Human Perception and Performance, 17*, 433–443.

McQueen, J. M. (1998). Segmentation of continuous speech using phonotactics. *Journal of Memory and Language, 39*, 21–46.

McQueen, J. M., & Cutler, A. (1998a). Spotting (different types of) words in (different types of) context. *Proceedings of the 5th International Conference on Spoken Language Processing* (Vol. 6, pp. 2791–2794). Sydney: Australian Speech Science and Technology Association.

McQueen, J. M., & Cutler, A. (1998b). Morphology in word recognition. In A. Spencer & A. M. Zwicky (Eds.), *The handbook of morphology* (pp. 406–427). Oxford: Blackwell.

McQueen, J. M., Cutler, A., Briscoe, T., & Norris, D. (1995). Models of continuous speech recognition and the contents of the vocabulary. *Language and Cognitive Processes, 10*, 309–331.

McQueen, J. M., Norris, D., & Cutler, A. (1994). Competition in spoken word recognition: spotting words in other words. *Journal of Experimental Psychology: Learning, Memory, and Cognition, 20*, 621–638.

McQueen, J. M., Norris, D., & Cutler, A. (1999). Lexical influence in phonetic decision making: evidence from subcategorical mismatches. *Journal of Experimental Psychology: Human Perception and Performance, 25*, 1363–1389.

McQueen, J. M., Norris, D., & Cutler, A. (2001). Can lexical knowledge modulate prelexical representations over time? In R. Smits, J. Kingston, T. M. Nearey, & R. Zondervan (Eds.), *Proceedings of the SPRAAC Workshop* (pp. 9–14). Nijmegen: MPI for Psycholinguistics.

McQueen, J. M., Otake, T., & Cutler, A. (2001). Rhythmic cues and possible-word constraints in Japanese speech segmentation. *Journal of Memory and Language, 45*, 103–132.

Mehler, J. (1981). The role of syllables in speech processing: infant and adult data. *Philosophical Transactions of the Royal Society of London B, 295*, 333–352.

Miller, J. L. (1981). Effects of speaking rate on segmental distinctions. In P. D. Eimas & J. L. Miller (Eds.), *Perspectives on the study of speech* (pp. 39–74). Hillsdale, NJ: Erlbaum.

Miller, J. L., & Dexter, E. R. (1988). Effects of speaking rate and lexical status on phonetic perception. *Journal of Experimental Psychology: Human Perception and Performance, 14*, 369–378.

Miller, J. L., Green, K., & Schermer, T. (1984). On the distinction between the effects of sentential speaking rate and semantic congruity on word identification. *Perception and Psychophysics, 36*, 329–337.

Miller, J. L., & Liberman, A. M. (1979). Some effects of later-occurring information on the perception of stop consonant and semivowel. *Perception and Psychophysics, 25*, 457–465.

Monsell, S., & Hirsh, K. W. (1998). Competitor priming in spoken word recognition. *Journal of Experimental Psychology: Learning, Memory, and Cognition, 24*, 1495–1520.

Morton, J. (1969). The interaction of information in word recognition. *Psychological Review, 76*, 165–178.

Moss, H. E., McCormick, S. F., & Tyler, L. K. (1997). The time course of activation of semantic information during spoken word recognition. *Language and Cognitive Processes, 10*, 121–136.

Mullennix, J. W., & Pisoni, D. B. (1990). Stimulus variability and processing dependencies in speech perception. *Perception and Psychophysics, 47*, 379–390.

Mullennix, J. W., Pisoni, D. B., & Martin, C. S. (1989). Some effects of talker variability on spoken word recognition. *Journal of the Acoustical Society of America, 85*, 365–378.

Nakatani, L. H., & Dukes, K. D. (1977). Locus of segmental cues for word juncture. *Journal of the Acoustical Society of America, 62*, 714–719.

Nearey, T. M. (1992). Context effects in a double-weak theory of speech perception. *Language and Speech, 35*, 153–171.

Nearey, T. M. (1997). Speech perception as pattern classification. *Journal of the Acoustical Society of America, 101*, 3241–3254.

Nearey, T. M. (2001). Phoneme-like units and speech perception. *Language and Cognitive Processes, 16*, 673–681.

Newman, R. S., Sawusch, J. R., & Luce, P. A. (1997). Lexical neighborhood effects in phonetic processing. *Journal of Experimental Psychology: Human Perception and Performance, 23*, 873–889.

Norris, D. (1993). Bottom-up connectionist models of 'interaction'. In G. T. M. Altmann & R. Shillcock (Eds.), *Cognitive models of speech processing: The Second Sperlonga Meeting* (pp. 211–234). Hillsdale, NJ: Erlbaum.

Norris, D. (1994). Shortlist: a connectionist model of continuous speech recognition. *Cognition, 52*, 189–234.

Norris, D., McQueen, J. M., & Cutler, A. (1995). Competition and segmentation in spoken-word recognition. *Journal of Experimental Psychology: Learning, Memory, and Cognition, 21*, 1209–1228.

Norris, D., McQueen, J. M., & Cutler, A. (2000a). Merging information in speech recognition: feedback is never necessary. *Behavioral and Brain Sciences*, 23, 299–325.

Norris, D., McQueen, J. M., & Cutler, A. (2000b). Feedback on feedback on feedback: it's feedforward. *Behavioral and Brain Sciences*, 23, 352–370.

Norris, D., McQueen, J. M., & Cutler, A. (2003). Perceptual learning in speech. *Cognitive Psychology*, 47, 204–238.

Norris, D., McQueen, J. M., Cutler, A., & Butterfield, S. (1997). The possible-word constraint in the segmentation of continuous speech. *Cognitive Psychology*, 34, 191–243.

Norris, D., McQueen, J. M., Cutler, A., Butterfield, S., & Kearns, R. (2001). Language-universal constraints on speech segmentation. *Language and Cognitive Processes*, 16, 637–660.

Oller, D. K. (1973). The effect of position in utterance on speech segment duration in English. *Journal of the Acoustical Society of America*, 54, 1235–1247.

Otake, T., Hatano, G., Cutler, A., & Mehler, J. (1993). Mora or syllable? Speech segmentation in Japanese. *Journal of Memory and Language*, 32, 358–378.

Pallier, C., Sebastián-Gallés, N., Felguera, T., Christophe, A., & Mehler, J. (1993). Attentional allocation within the syllable structure of spoken words. *Journal of Memory and Language*, 32, 373–389.

Palmeri, T. J., Goldinger, S. D., & Pisoni, D. B. (1993). Episodic encoding of voice attributes and recognition memory for spoken words. *Journal of Experimental Psychology: Learning, Memory, and Cognition*, 19, 309–328.

Pastore, R. E. (1981). Possible acoustic factors in speech perception. In P. D. Eimas & J. L. Miller (Eds.), *Perspectives on the study of speech* (pp. 165–205). Hillsdale, NJ: Erlbaum.

Pitt, M. A. (1995). The locus of the lexical shift in phoneme identification. *Journal of Experimental Psychology: Learning, Memory, and Cognition*, 21, 1037–1052.

Pitt, M. A., & McQueen, J. M. (1998). Is compensation for coarticulation mediated by the lexicon? *Journal of Memory and Language*, 39, 347–370.

Pitt, M. A., & Samuel, A. G. (1993). An empirical and meta-analytic evaluation of the phoneme identification task. *Journal of Experimental Psychology: Human Perception and Performance*, 19, 699–725.

Pitt, M. A., & Samuel, A. G. (1995). Lexical and sublexical feedback in auditory word recognition. *Cognitive Psychology*, 29, 149–188.

Quené, H. (1992). Durational cues for word segmentation in Dutch. *Journal of Phonetics*, 20, 331–350.

Quené, H. (1993). Segment durations and accent as cues to word segmentation in Dutch. *Journal of the Acoustical Society of America*, 94, 2027–2035.

Repp, B. H. (1982). Phonetic trading relations and context effects: new evidence for a phonetic mode of perception. *Psychological Bulletin*, 92, 81–110.

Repp, B. H., & Liberman, A. M. (1987). Phonetic category boundaries are flexible. In S. R. Harnad (ed.),

Categorical perception (pp. 89–112). Cambridge: Cambridge University Press.

Repp, B. H., Liberman, A. M., Eccardt, T., & Pesetsky, D. (1978). Perceptual integration of acoustic cues for stop, fricative and affricate manner. *Journal of Experimental Psychology: Human Perception and Performance*, 4, 621–637.

Rodd, J., Gaskell, G., & Marslen-Wilson, W. (2002). Making sense of semantic ambiguity: semantic competition in lexical access. *Journal of Memory and Language*, 46, 245–266.

Rubin, P., Turvey, M. T., & Van Gelder, P. (1976). Initial phonemes are detected faster in spoken words than in non-words. *Perception and Psychophysics*, 19, 394–398.

Salverda, A. P., Dahan, D., & McQueen, J. M. (2003). The role of prosodic boundaries in the resolution of lexical embedding in speech comprehension. *Cognition*, 90, 51–89.

Samuel, A. G. (1981). Phonemic restoration: insights from a new methodology. *Journal of Experimental Psychology: General*, 110, 474–494.

Samuel, A. G. (1986). Red herring detectors and speech perception: in defense of selective adaptation. *Cognitive Psychology*, 18, 452–499.

Samuel, A. G. (1987). Lexical uniqueness effects on phonemic restoration. *Journal of Memory and Language*, 26, 36–56.

Samuel, A. G. (1996). Does lexical information influence the perceptual restoration of phonemes? *Journal of Experimental Psychology: General*, 125, 28–51.

Samuel, A. G. (1997). Lexical activation produces potent phonemic percepts. *Cognitive Psychology*, 32, 97–127.

Samuel, A. G. (2001). Knowing a word affects the fundamental perception of the sounds within it. *Psychological Science*, 12, 348–351.

Schacter, D. L., & Church, B. A. (1992). Auditory priming: implicit and explicit memory for words and voices. *Journal of Experimental Psychology: Learning, Memory, and Cognition*, 18, 521–533.

Sebastián-Gallés, N., Dupoux, E., Seguí, J., & Mehler, J. (1992). Contrasting syllabic effects in Catalan and Spanish. *Journal of Memory and Language*, 31, 18–32.

Shillcock, R. C. (1990). Lexical hypotheses in continuous speech. In G. T. M. Altmann (ed.), *Cognitive models of speech processing: psycholinguistic and computational perspectives* (pp. 24–49). Cambridge, MA: MIT Press.

Slowiaczek, L. M., & Hamburger, M. B. (1992). Prelexical facilitation and lexical interference in auditory word recognition. *Journal of Experimental Psychology: Learning, Memory, and Cognition*, 18, 1239–1250.

Smits, R. (2001a). Evidence for hierarchical categorization of coarticulated phonemes. *Journal of Experimental Psychology: Human Perception and Performance*, 27, 1145–1162.

Smits, R. (2001b). Hierarchical categorization of coarticulated phonemes: a theoretical analysis. *Perception and Psychophysics*, 63, 1109–1139.

Soto-Faraco, S., Sebastián-Gallés, N., & Cutler, A. (2001). Segmental and suprasegmental mismatch in lexical access. *Journal of Memory and Language, 45,* 412–432.

Spinelli, E., McQueen, J. M., & Cutler, A. (2003). Processing resyllabified words in French. *Journal of Memory and Language, 48,* 233–254.

Stevens, K. N. (1998). *Acoustic phonetics.* Cambridge, MA: MIT Press.

Stevens, K. N. (2002). Toward a model for lexical access based on acoustic landmarks and distinctive features. *Journal of the Acoustical Society of America, 111,* 1872–1891.

Streeter, L. A., & Nigro, G. N. (1979). The role of medial consonant transitions in word perception. *Journal of the Acoustical Society of America, 65,* 1533–1541.

Tabossi, P., Burani, C., & Scott, D. (1995). Word identification in fluent speech. *Journal of Memory and Language, 34,* 440–467.

Tabossi, P., Collina, S., Mazzetti, M., & Zoppello, M. (2000). Syllables in the processing of spoken Italian. *Journal of Experimental Psychology: Human Perception and Performance, 26,* 758–775.

Turk, A. E., & Shattuck-Hufnagel, S. (2000). Word-boundary-related duration patterns in English. *Journal of Phonetics, 28,* 397–440.

Utman, J. A., Blumstein, S. E., & Burton, M. W. (2000). Effects of subphonetic and syllable structure variation on word recognition. *Perception and Psychophysics, 62,* 1297–1311.

van Alphen, P., & McQueen, J. M. (2001). The time-limited influence of sentential context on function word identification. *Journal of Experimental Psychology: Human Perception and Performance, 27,* 1057–1071.

van den Brink, D., Brown, C. M., & Hagoort, P. (2001). Electrophysiological evidence for early contextual influences during spoken-word recognition: N200 versus N400 effects. *Journal of Cognitive Neuroscience, 13,* 967–985.

van der Lugt, A. H. (2001). The use of sequential probabilities in the segmentation of speech. *Perception and Psychophysics, 63,* 811–823.

Van Petten, C., Coulson, S., Rubin, S., Plante, E., & Parks, M. (1999). Time course of word identification and semantic integration in spoken language. *Journal of Experimental Psychology: Learning, Memory, and Cognition, 25,* 394–417.

Vitevitch, M. S. (2002). Influence of onset density on spoken-word recognition. *Journal of Experimental Psychology: Human Perception and Performance, 28,* 270–278.

Vitevitch, M. S., & Luce, P. A. (1998). When words compete: levels of processing in spoken word recognition. *Psychological Science, 9,* 325–329.

Vitevitch, M. S., & Luce, P. A. (1999). Probabilistic phonotactics and neighborhood activation in spoken word recognition. *Journal of Memory and Language, 40,* 374–408.

Vroomen, J., & de Gelder, B. (1995). Metrical segmentation and lexical inhibition in spoken word recognition. *Journal of Experimental Psychology: Human Perception and Performance, 21,* 98–108.

Vroomen, J., & de Gelder, B. (1997). Activation of embedded words in spoken word recognition. *Journal of Experimental Psychology: Human Perception and Performance, 23,* 710–720.

Vroomen, J., van Zon, M., & de Gelder, B. (1996). Cues to speech segmentation: evidence from juncture misperceptions and word spotting. *Memory and Cognition, 24,* 744–755.

Wallace, W. P., Stewart, M. T., & Malone, C. P. (1995). Recognition memory errors produced by implicit activation of word candidates during the processing of spoken words. *Journal of Memory and Language, 34,* 417–439.

Wallace, W. P., Stewart, M. T., Shaffer, T. R., & Wilson, J. A. (1998). Are false recognitions influenced by prerecognition processing? *Journal of Experimental Psychology: Learning, Memory, and Cognition, 24,* 299–315.

Wallace, W. P., Stewart, M. T., Sherman, H. L., & Mellor, M. (1995). False positives in recognition memory produced by cohort activation. *Cognition, 55,* 85–113.

Warren, P., & Marslen-Wilson, W. (1987). Continuous uptake of acoustic cues in spoken word recognition. *Perception and Psychophysics, 41,* 262–275.

Warren, P., & Marslen-Wilson, W. (1988). Cues to lexical choice: discriminating place and voice. *Perception and Psychophysics, 43,* 21–30.

Warren, R. M. (1970). Perceptual restoration of missing speech sounds. *Science, 167,* 392–393.

Weber, A. (2001). Language-specific listening: the case of phonetic sequences. Doctoral dissertation, University of Nijmegen (MPI Series in Psycholinguistics, 16).

Wells, J. C. (1987). Computer-aided phonetic transcription. *Journal of the International Phonetic Association, 17,* 94–114.

Whalen, D. H. (1981). Effects of vocalic formant transitions and vowel quality on the English [s]-[š] boundary. *Journal of the Acoustical Society of America, 69,* 275–282.

Whalen, D. H. (1984). Subcategorical phonetic mismatches slow phonetic judgments. *Perception and Psychophysics, 35,* 49–64.

Whalen, D. H. (1991). Subcategorical phonetic mismatches and lexical access. *Perception and Psychophysics, 50,* 351–360.

Wickelgren, W. A. (1969). Context-sensitive coding, associative memory, and serial order in (speech) behavior. *Psychological Review, 76,* 1–15.

Wurm, L. H., & Samuel, A. G. (1997). Lexical inhibition and attentional allocation during speech perception: evidence from phoneme monitoring. *Journal of Memory and Language, 36,* 165–187.

Zwitserlood, P. (1989). The locus of the effects of sentential-semantic context in spoken-word processing. *Cognition, 32,* 25–64.

Zwitserlood, P., & Schriefers, H. (1995). Effects of sensory information and processing time in spoken-word recognition. *Language and Cognitive Processes, 10,* 121–136.

12

Reading

ALEXANDER POLLATSEK AND
KEITH RAYNER

It is clearly impossible to cover reading fully in a chapter of this length, as there are entire textbooks (Crowder & Wagner, 1992; Just & Carpenter, 1987; Rayner & Pollatsek, 1989) devoted to reading. The focus in this chapter is on the processes by which the visual information on the printed page is extracted by the visual system and turned into language, which is largely the study of how printed words are identified. Chapter 10 by Garnham in this volume fills in much of the rest of the story, as it is devoted to the more 'global' aspects of reading comprehension. In the process of discussing how words are identified in the context of reading, we shall also discuss, in some detail, how the eyes move and are controlled during the reading process, the role of 'sound coding' in the word identification process, and how sentence context influences word identification. Although we shall briefly touch on comparisons across languages, most of our discussion will be about reading English. However, the existing data indicate that the process of skilled reading is not radically different across languages.[1]

METHODS FOR STUDYING READING

Having a chapter focused on the topic of word identification tacitly assumes both that this is an important topic and that one can study it sensibly without having to understand reading and language at all levels. With respect to the first assumption, we do feel that word identification is indeed an important topic in reading. Indeed, the skill needed in learning to read is largely the skill of word identification. That is, the 5–6 year old learning to read

has already mastered most of the higher-order skills of processing language, so that becoming a skilled reader is largely a process of mastering visual word identification and blending this skill with the existing skills of understanding spoken language (Rayner, Foorman, Perfetti, Pesetsky, & Seidenberg, 2001). With respect to the second assumption, there is a large body of data indicating that the process of visual word identification is a relatively independent process. Two of the clearest lines of evidence for that assumption are: (a) people can easily and rapidly identify words in isolation; and (b) although context can speed word identification, its effects are relatively minor.

The prior paragraph presupposes, and we shall continue to assume, that there is a well-defined process of word identification. However, it should be clear that the process is not likely to be unitary. That is, if we ask the question 'When is a word identified?', what do we mean by that? When all the letters are identified? When the sound of the word is identified? When the meaning or meanings of a word are identified? When we are assuming that there is a well-defined process of word identification, we are tacitly assuming that the information on the printed page is leading to the access of all of these types of information connected with a word (i.e. orthographic, phonological and semantic) – and possibly others. However, we do not presuppose that all of these types of information are accessed at once, nor whether there is a fixed order in which the types of information are extracted. In fact, one of the major questions in word identification is how the extraction of these types of information relate to each other and whether there is a fixed order in which the types of information are extracted. We should also note that, unless we specify otherwise, we are talking about how *skilled* readers extract information from the printed page.[2]

Three methods used to study word identification

Dozens of methods have been invented to study the process of word identification. However, most are varieties of three basic methodologies. Two of them usually (but not always) involve presenting a word in isolation: (1) briefly exposing a word and seeing how accurately it can be identified; (2) presenting a word and seeing how quickly it can be named or identified as a word. The third method involves having people read text and examining the pattern of eye movements on the text.[3]

Brief presentation

Use of the brief presentation method dates back to well over a hundred years and originally involved complex optical devices called *tachistoscopes* (i.e. machines with shutters, lenses and prisms that could present things briefly and could control the exposure duration precisely). Today, however, most tachistoscopic presentation work is done using computer screens, which are much cheaper and easier to use. Although the control of the timing and the visual properties of the stimuli is not quite as exact on the computer screen as in a tachistoscope, the results using the two methodologies have been quite similar. Two questions that have been central in this literature are: (a) How briefly can a word be presented such that one can identify it? (b) Which aspects of a word (e.g. its frequency in the language) influence the ease with which it can be identified? Typically, in these brief exposure experiments, words are presented on the order of 10–60 ms followed by a 'backward masking' pattern. A typical backward masking pattern is something like a series of number signs (i.e. ######) that appear in the same spatial location in which the word appeared. Most of the data indicate that such patterned masks do prevent a visual afterimage of the word from persisting. Nonetheless, if a word is presented for something like 60 ms, it can usually be fully identified! This indicates that early stages of word processing occur very quickly.

Speeded identification

Getting people to make speeded identification responses to words also goes back at least a hundred years. The two most commonly used 'identification' tasks used now are *naming* and *lexical decision*. In the naming task, a word appears on the screen, and the participant says the word aloud as quickly as possible, and the time when the vocal response starts (or at least the first burst of sound is picked up by the microphone) is used as the response measure. (Hence, the measure is really naming onset latency.) In the lexical decision task, a string of letters is presented on the screen, and the participant judges whether the string of letters is a word or not (usually by manually pressing a response key). Although the latencies of all responses are recorded, typically the response times to the words are usually of most interest. However, the times recorded in such a task are a function of the types of nonwords used in the task; times to judge a stimulus to be a word will be faster, the less 'wordlike' the nonwords are. For most of the experiments of interest (and virtually all we shall discuss), the nonwords used are 'pseudowords' – strings of letters like *WARK* that are orthographically legal and pronounceable, but happen not to be English words (but there is no reason why they could not become words at some time in the future). A third type of speeded classification task that is often used is *categorization*. In a common version of the task, a category label is presented, such as *FURNITURE*, followed by a target word, such as *chair*. The participant's task is to judge whether the target word is an exemplar of the category.

Eye movements

In order to be able to talk sensibly about how eye movements are used to study reading, we need to discuss the basic characteristics of eye movements in reading (Rayner, 1998). First, in reading, as in any visual task involving a static display, the eye-movement pattern is a sequence of rapid, ballistic, eye-movements (called *saccades*) that move from one location where the eyes are essentially still to another location. (The periods where the eyes are still are called *fixations*.) Second, no useful information gets in during the saccades, so that reading, like the viewing of any static visual display, is essentially getting a series of snapshots. Fixations in reading typically last 200–300 ms and the duration of a fixation is influenced by text characteristics (e.g. fixations are shorter on words that are common in the language). Not infrequently, a word is fixated more than once before the reader moves on. A common measurement used in reading research is the *gaze duration*, which is the sum of the durations of fixations on a word before the reader moves forward in the text.[4] Another common measure of processing time on a word is the duration of the first fixation on a word. The length and direction of saccades is also of interest in reading research. However, as the duration of a saccade is essentially determined by its length (longer saccades take longer to execute), it is of little interest in studying reading. The length of saccades is not constant and is influenced by text characteristics. For example, a word is more likely to be skipped (causing a longer saccade) if it is very frequent in the language and/or highly predictable from the prior context. In addition, about 10% of the saccades in normal reading are *regressions* (i.e. move backward through the text). This does not include *return sweeps* (large saccades taking the reader from the end of one line to the beginning of the next line).[5]

There are two types of experiments that use eye movements to study reading. In the first, text is presented on the screen and the person simply reads the text and pushes a button when he or she has finished reading a sentence or some larger unit of text. (Sometimes the material is unrelated single sentences and sometimes it is more extended passages of text.) In these studies, what is often manipulated is some aspect of a single target word (such as its frequency in the language), and the effects of this manipulation on various 'on-line' eye-movement measures of reading, such as the gaze duration on the target word, are examined. We shall return to these studies below.

In the second type of study, changes in the text are manipulated contingent on where a reader is fixating. For example, in the *moving window* technique, *a window* of normal text is presented around where the reader is fixating and all the letters outside the window are changed to 'garbage' (e.g. random letters). As the reader moves from fixation to fixation, he or she always sees a 'window' of normal text around the current fixation point. A major question in these studies is how much information is actually extracted by the reader from the printed page on a fixation. The surprising answer is that the area on the page from which useful information is extracted is quite limited. In the original studies employing the moving window technique (McConkie & Rayner, 1975), it was found that no useful information was available to readers that was further than 14–15 characters from fixation. The above limitation is imposed by acuity; this is roughly the region on the line from which useful letter information *can be* extracted. As we shall see below in a fuller discussion of these experiments, there are further limitations on where readers *are* actually extracting letter information from the page.

THE RELATION BETWEEN THE ENCODING OF LETTERS AND THE ENCODING OF WORDS

One of the key issues in reading print is the relationship between the encoding of individual letters and the encoding of a word. Naïvely, it may seem that one has to first encode the constituent letters and then put them together (in sequence) to identify a word. However, this is not logically necessary, as, for example, the stimulus *DOG* may just be recognized

Fixation Point	*	*	*
Stimulus	work	orwk	k
Mask and forced choice	d XXXX K	d XXXX K	d XXXX K

Figure 12.1   *Example of the Reicher–Wheeler paradigm. In all three conditions the sequence is the same: a fixation marker is first followed by the target stimulus, which is followed by a masking pattern flanked by the two forced choice alternatives in the same location as the letter in the target being probed. In the condition on the left, the target stimulus is a word; in the condition in the center, the target stimulus is a (non-pronounceable) nonword; and in the condition on the right, the target stimulus is a single letter. Note that the position of the target letter and the position of the probes is the same for all three targets in the figure. (However, for other triples of stimuli, the other three letter locations would be probed.)*

as a whole visual pattern (i.e. a *template*) and the fact that it is composed of three letters may be irrelevant to the visual system. Thus, one possibility is that words (or at least some common short words) are recognized as unitary visual patterns or templates. Another possibility is that the letters are all recognized in parallel (i.e. at the same time) and these letter detectors send excitation to word detectors. (Of course, the serial position of the letters has to be encoded somehow so that the reader can distinguish *DOG* from *GOD*.) A third possibility is that the letters are encoded in series (presumably from left to right) and that the identification of a word follows this serial identification of the letters.

A series of experiments (Reicher, 1969; Wheeler, 1970) using tachistoscopic techniques came up with a surprising finding, called the *word superiority effect*, which supported the second view (i.e. that letters in words are processed in parallel). However, the findings also indicated that the relationship between letter and word detection is not a simple 'bottom-up' process (i.e. letter identification feeding into word identification), but that there is also excitation flowing back the other way – from word identification to letter identification. The basic task in these studies is relatively simple (see Figure 12.1). A target stimulus is shown for something like 30–40 ms and then masked. (The exposure duration is set so that people perform at about 75% correct – about halfway between perfect performance and chance.) Simultaneous with the mask, two alternatives are presented and the participant must choose one of them as the stimulus just seen. As in the illustration, the stimulus presented was either a (four-letter) word (e.g. *WORK*), a *nonword* (e.g. *ORWK*, a scrambled version of a target word that was orthographically illegal), or a single letter (e.g. *K*). A key feature of the task was that the two letters presented in the forced choice – above and below one of the letters of the word – could each spell a word (e.g. *WORK* and *WORD*). Thus, better performance in the word condition could not be due to merely guessing that the stimulus was a word.

The findings are quite surprising. Not only was performance in the word condition better than in the nonword condition, it was also better than in the single-letter condition! In fact, in many of these studies, performance in the nonword condition and the single-letter condition are about equal. So how does one explain these findings? Clearly, the hypothesis that letters are processed one at a time cannot be viable. However, can one tell whether words are visual templates or whether the letters are processed in parallel and then sent up to the word processor? One hint is that performance is often as good in the nonword condition as in the single-letter condition. This indicates that letters, even in short nonwords, can be processed in parallel. There are several other pieces of data that are also in favor of the parallel processing of letters and against the hypothesis that a word is a visual template. First, the words in these 'word superiority' experiments were typically presented in all upper case, and we rarely see words in this format. Thus, it is hard to believe that people have pre-stored *visual* templates for many stimuli that they may never have seen in that particular form. Second, there are several experiments in reading and word identification in which the case of the letters is varied and it does not affect the speed or accuracy of performance very much. For example, Smith, Lott, and Cronnell (1969) presented text in mixed case LiKe ThIs and found it only had a moderate effect on reading speed and comprehension after a little bit of practice (see also Besner, Coltheart, & Davelaar, 1984; Evett & Humphreys, 1981; McConkie & Zola, 1979; Rayner, McConkie, & Zola, 1980). Third, in other experiments (Baron & Thurston, 1973), one gets similar, but slightly smaller, 'superiority effects' (over letters) from pronounceable *pseudo-words* such as *WARK*.[6]

Thus, it does not appear that an often repeated *visual* stimulus is needed to produce the effect. Instead, something that has the correct sequence of letters will do, and a sequence of letters that is orthographically wordlike (and pronounceable) gives you almost as big a 'superiority effect' as an actual word. So how does one explain this effect?

There are now many computational models of this effect, but most are variations of the initial two models (McClelland & Rumelhart, 1981; Paap, Newsome, McDonald, & Schvaneveldt, 1982). Some look different on the surface, but most have the following key features. First, these models posit two processing 'boxes', one of which contains the equivalent of letter detectors and the other contains the equivalent of word detectors. Moreover, these two boxes interact, so that not only does the letter information feed into the word detectors, but the information from the word detectors feeds back and constrains the excitation of the letter detectors.[7] Many of these models have indeed successfully accounted for the word superiority effect data both qualitatively and quantitatively. However, the fact that seeing words in unfamiliar visual forms (e.g. in mixed case) does not make much difference indicates that the letter detectors discussed in these models are 'abstract letter detectors' at a remove from the visual form. That is, if *DaY* is easy to process, the letter detectors feeding into the word detector are detectors that respond approximately equally to upper- and lower-case letters and are also relatively insensitive to other surface features of the letters such as the font.

The word superiority effect, together with a lot of other data on reading, indicates that (abstract) letters are an important component of word identification, but that the relationship between letters and words is complex. That is, it is not merely that letters are feeding into word detection; words are also feeding into letter detection. We mentioned that virtually all of the word superiority experiments were run using four-letter words (or other short words). This raises the possibility that letters in longer words may not all be processed at the same time. The issue of how longer words are processed has still not been settled; however, it appears to be a good guess that readers are trying to process the letters for all reasonable length words in parallel, although acuity problems may cause some of the letters to be encoded fairly poorly. We shall return to this issue when we discuss eye movements in more detail.

THE ROLE OF AUDITORY CODING IN WORD IDENTIFICATION

One of the most contentious issues in the literature on word encoding is the role of auditory or 'sound' coding in the process of word identification. There are several reasons why the issue is contentious. One is that people often mean different things by 'sound coding'. On one level, someone might mean that in order to identify a printed word, one has to consciously say the word to oneself. Certainly, children who are learning to read often sound words out aloud as they read, and it is logically possible that skilled readers do so, but somewhat more quietly. This is the 'subvocal speech' hypothesis. Another possibility is that the sounds of printed words (i.e. auditory images) are produced during reading without any use of the speech apparatus. (To convince yourself that this is plausible, try counting out loud from one to ten over and over while thinking of the sound of the word *dog*. You will see that it is easy to generate and maintain this auditory image while your speech apparatus is fully engaged.) Moreover, although we have tried to explain auditory images using situations where one is conscious of them (to make clear that you can generate them without speech), there is no necessity that auditory images accessed in reading by skilled readers are conscious. That is, one could be using auditory imagery all the time in reading but only rarely be aware of it.

One series of experiments that strongly implicates auditory coding in identifying words employs homophones (Van Orden, 1987; Van Orden, Johnston, & Hale, 1988). These experiments typically use the category judgment task mentioned earlier. On a trial, a participant is given a category label, such as *TREE*, then sees a target word, and then judges whether the target word is a member of the category or not. The key trials in the experiment are those on which a homophone of a category member is presented (e.g. *BEACH*). The surprising finding in these studies is that people make quite a few errors on these trials (often 10–15% more errors than from control words such as *BENCH*) and are slow in rejecting these homophones of category members even when they are correct. (This finding has been replicated many times in many laboratories, so is not merely due to a particular group of students having deficient spelling abilities.) Interestingly, a reduced interference effect is often obtained with pseudo-word homophones, such as deciding whether *CHARE* is an item of furniture (Van Orden et al., 1988). There is also a reduced interference effect with words that could be homophones but are not (Lesch & Pollatsek, 1998). That is, when people are asked to judge whether two words are semantically related, they find it harder to judge that *PILLOW* and *BEAD* are unrelated than *PILLOW* and *BEND*. (*BEAD* could be a homophone of *BED* but it isn't – it could rhyme with *DEAD* and *HEAD*.)

These experiments (and others we discuss in a later section) indicate that sound codes are being used in the access of the meaning of words. However, it is far from clear exactly how they are involved. That is, it is not clear how the sound code is activated from the letters. The *PILLOW–BEAD* and pseudoword results mentioned above indicate that it cannot simply be that the letters activate the meaning of the written word, which then, in turn, activates the sound code. Thus, the activation of the sound code must be part of the activity involved in the early stages of identification of a word.

The issue of *how* sound codes are activated from the printed text is far from agreed upon. As a result, we shall merely try to raise a few issues, define a few terms, and try to indicate why this is such a difficult issue (especially in English). This issue is often framed in terms of *dual routes* to a sound code: *addressed phonology* versus *assembled phonology* (Coltheart, 1978; Coltheart, Rastle, Perry, Langdon, & Ziegler, 2001). These models posit that one can arrive at the sound of a printed letter string in two different ways: (a) access the sound from a pre-stored memory 'address' of how that letter string sounds (if it is a word); or (b) compute the sound from some rules or procedures for sounding out letter strings. One reason why this way of framing the issue was appealing was that there was evidence from *acquired dyslexics* (i.e. adults who could once read normally but, due to brain injury, no longer can) that indicated there were two separable systems for computing sounds from printed words such that brain injuries left one or the other relatively intact (Coltheart, 1981; Coltheart, Masterson, Byng, Prior, & Riddoch, 1983; Coltheart, Patterson, & Marshall, 1980). First, there were two clinical syndromes, *deep dyslexia* and *phonological dyslexia*, in which it looked as though the addressed phonology system was relatively intact, but the assembled one has been damaged severely. These people could read all words relatively well, but were largely unable to sound out pronounceable nonwords (*pseudowords*) such as *mard*. (Often, they would fail to come up with any pronunciation for them.) In contrast, the *surface dyslexics* would be able to come up with a pronunciation for nonwords, but would often make errors in pronouncing *irregular words*. They would often *regularize* them (e.g. pronouncing *island* as /is-land/). That is, it appeared that these patients had a relatively intact assembled phonology system but a severely damaged addressed phonology system.

The data from normal skilled readers also appears to support a *dual-route* model that assumes separate pathways for addressed and assembled phonology. A reliable finding (Baron & Strawson, 1976; Perfetti & Hogaboam, 1975) is that irregular words are named more slowly than regular words (this is often called the *regularity effect*), and that the difference between irregular and regular words is most pronounced for words that are less frequent in the language. That is, for regular words like *seed*, the two systems would presumably come up with the same pronunciation. However, for irregular words like *island*, the two systems would come up with different answers, and hence one might expect some interference. However, for high-frequency words, one would expect that their sound would be accessed by the addressed (direct look-up) system much more rapidly than the assembly system could construct a pronunciation; thus one would expect there might be little interference effect for high-frequency words if they were irregular. In contrast, for low-frequency words, the addressed system may not be any faster than the assembled system. As a result, for irregular low-frequency words, one would expect competition between the two different pronunciations (e.g. /I-land/ vs. /is-land/) that would slow the naming process. The process of getting the the sound of a word appears to be more than a simple 'race' between the two systems (with the fastest system producing the response, however, as people make few errors in this task, even for low-frequency words). Instead, it appears to be a process in which the systems interact or 'cooperate' (Carr & Pollatsek, 1985) to produce a sound code.

We need to mention, however, that there is an interesting theoretical alternative to the dual-route models. In these *parallel distributed processing* (PDP) models of visual word recognition, the memory codes of past experience with printed words are not in the form of individual units that code for letters or words; rather the coding is *distributed*. That is, when a printed word is seen, it engages a large number of memory units, none of which responds selectively for anything like a word or letter; instead the memory of a word or letter is represented by a particular pattern of activation across these memory units (e.g. Plaut, McClelland, Seidenberg, & Patterson, 1996; Seidenberg & McClelland, 1989). An important feature of these models is that processes in the model that look like assembled phonology enter into processing both regular and irregular words (as well as nonwords) and that processes that look like addressed phonology enter into processing nonwords. Currently there is controversy about whether dual-route or PDP models handle the data on sound coding of words better (see Besner, Twilley, McCann, & Seergobin, 1990; Coltheart et al., 2001; Seidenberg & McClelland, 1990). However, at a deeper level, it is not clear whether these models are fundamentally different from the current versions of dual-route models, or whether the difference is in the level of explanation.

To briefly summarize this section, the last part indicates that we are far from certain how the sound codes of printed words are activated. However, the first part indicates quite clearly that skilled readers do activate them and this activation is an integral part of accessing the meaning of a word.[8]

The Speed and Automaticity of Identifying Words in and out of Context

The word superiority experiments described above (and many others using brief presentation techniques) indicate that words can be identified even when presented very briefly (for 30 ms or less). Of course, that brief duration may not necessarily reflect the time to identify a word; it may merely be the time that the visual information gets transferred to a more permanent type of storage (e.g. case-independent forms of letters). Nonetheless, it is clear that word identification is quite rapid, as a typical skilled reader reads about 300–350 words per minute, which means that the average word in reading is identified in something like a fifth of a second or 200 ms. Even if one grants that processing words in context may speed things up a bit, one is doing a lot of work in reading besides word identification (e.g. constructing the syntax and meaning of sentences), so that the speed of skilled reading is a fairly amazing phenomenon.

What may be more amazing about word identification than its speed is its automaticity. 'Automaticity' can mean several things. One common meaning associated with an automatic process is that it cannot be turned off. This appears to be true for words. There is a phenomenon called the 'Stroop effect' which demonstrates this quite dramatically (Stroop, 1935; see MacLeod, 1991, for a comprehensive review). In the classic version of the task one sees words (one at a time) written in various colored inks (e.g. *RED* written in green ink, *GREEN* written in yellow ink, etc.) and one's task is to name the color of the ink – and thus try to ignore the written word. The finding, replicated many times, is that people cannot ignore the word. They are much slower in saying 'green' to *RED* written in green ink than to a green color patch (and make many errors as well). Moreover, even days of practice cannot eliminate this interference effect. Similar interference effects have been observed (Rayner & Posnansky, 1978; Rosinski, Golinkoff, & Kukish, 1975) when people try to name line drawings of objects with words superimposed on them (e.g. trying to name a line drawing of a dog with *CHAIR* superimposed on it). The boundaries of this phenomenon, however, are a little unclear, as there is some recent evidence indicating that there may be some situations in which people can avoid processing a word when they are trying to ignore it (Besner, Stolz, & Boutilier, 1997). However, there are many situations where, even after repeated practice and effort, people are processing a word when they are trying their best to ignore it.

A second finding indicates that word encoding is automatic (in a different sense). That is, the meaning of a word can be processed without one being aware of having seen the word. One way this phenomenon has been demonstrated is using the technique of *semantic priming*. In semantic priming, a prime word (e.g. *dog*, or *chair*) is presented on the screen followed by a target word (e.g. *cat*) and the participant has to make a lexical decision on the target word (i.e. judge whether it is a word or not).

The finding (Meyer & Schvaneveldt, 1971) is that responses to the target word are faster when the prime is semantically related to it (e.g. *cat* preceded by *dog*) than when the prime is an unrelated word or a meaningless stimulus (e.g. ###). This may not seem surprising, but what is quite amazing is that one can obtain semantic priming even when people cannot identify the prime or even be aware that there was a prime. The techniques (Balota, 1983; Carr, McCauley, Sperber, & Parmelee, 1982; Marcel, 1983) that demonstrated this varied somewhat, but the basic idea was as follows. A prime word is presented even more briefly than in the word superiority effect (about 10–15 ms) followed by a mask. The duration is adjusted for each participant so that they are chance at identifying the prime word (or in some experiments, are even at chance at being able to distinguish between whether the mask is preceded by a prime word or whether only the mask appeared). However, in spite of being unaware of the prime, these experiments still observed semantic priming – sometimes obtaining as big an effect as when the prime is visible! Thus, the meaning of the prime must have been processed even though people were unaware of it.

The above discussion indicates that words are processed rapidly and automatically, but is the time to process all words the same? This seems unlikely, and indeed it is false. One of the most reliable findings in the word identification literature is that the time to identify a word depends on its frequency in the printed language (e.g. Broadbent, 1967; Perfetti, Goldman, & Hogaboam, 1979; Schilling, Rayner, & Chumbley, 1998). The frequency of a printed word in the language is usually assessed through the use of databases containing printed text. In English, one of the most widely used is the Kučera and Francis database, in which frequencies of words are reported in terms of how often they appear per million words. Needless to say, there is a confounding with length: high-frequency (common) words tend to be short and low-frequency (rare) words tend to be long. However, the typical experiment studying the effects of word frequency control for length (i.e. they use a set of higher-frequency and lower-frequency words that have the same average length)[9]. There are a large number of experiments using lexical decision or naming indicating that response time to the word is faster, the higher the frequency of the word.

Moreover, there are a large number of experiments in reading that have demonstrated that word frequency also affects the speed of identification in reading. In reading, the most common measure of processing used to assess word identification is the *gaze duration* measure we discussed earlier (the sum of all fixation durations on a word on the first encounter with it). If one simply does an analysis of a large corpus of text (Just & Carpenter, 1980), there is a large effect of word frequency on gaze

(a)   Moving Window Paradigm

Xhis is an example of x xxxxxx xxxxx xxxxxxx.
    *

Xxxx xx xn example of a movixx xxxxx xxxxxxx.
       *

Xxxx xx xx xxxxxxx xx a moving window parxxxxx.
                   *

(b)   Moving Mask paradigm

Thxx xx xx xxxxxxx xx x xxxxxx mask paradigm.
            *

Figure 12.2   *Panel (a) illustrates the moving window paradigm. The asterisks below the lines indicate where the reader is fixating. Around each fixation point, 4 characters are visible to the left of fixation and 14 characters are visible to the right. In this condition, reading proceeds at a normal rate; however, if the window is more restricted, people read more slowly. Panel (b) illustrates one fixation of a moving mask experiment. You can get a good feeling for this experiment by fixating on the letter indicated by the asterisk and seeing how much of the text you can process.*

duration, with lower-frequency words being looked at longer than higher-frequency words. However, as noted above, there is a confounding here, as high-frequency words tend to be shorter and low-frequency words tend to be longer. As a result, there is a more controlled type of experiment that assesses word frequency effects eliminating problems like the above. In this type of experiment, there is a single sentence frame in which two target words, equated on length but differing in frequency (such as *steward* or *student*, or *waltz* or *music*), are inserted. Typically, other participants would rate the sentences for how 'natural' they seem and the sentences for high- and low-frequency words would be equally natural. The finding in these experiments (Inhoff & Rayner, 1986; Rayner & Duffy, 1986) is also that fixation times (i.e. gaze durations) on high-frequency words are shorter than on low-frequency words, even when the length of the word and the influences of the surrounding text are controlled.

We should note that the findings in the above paragraph document two things. First, as noted above, they document that the frequency of the word in the language influences the time to process it.[10] However, they document something else important: the immediacy of the effects of linguistic processing on the behavior of the eyes. That is, it is logically possible that words are processed rapidly, and the time to process them differs for low- and high-frequency words, but that it would take a second or two for this to influence the eye-movement system (i.e. when the eyes were a word or two past the target word). However, the fact that word frequency (also, several other variables we shall discuss below) has such immediate effects on eye movements indicates that there is a close and fascinating interrelationship between cognitive processing in reading and eye-movement control. In fact, to intelligently continue our discussion of how words are processed in context, we need to explain more about what is known about the uptake of visual information during reading text and the role of eye movements in modulating that flow of information.

Eye Movements in Reading: The 'Perceptual Span' and Parafoveal Preview

Earlier, we covered some basics of eye movements on reading and indicated that the pattern of eye movements could be used to study cognitive processes in reading 'on-line' (e.g. both the fixation time on a word and the probability that a word is fixated are influenced by the difficulty of processing that word). We now return to flesh out the details.

First, we claimed that the area on the page that people can extract meaningful information from the text is fairly small and briefly gave evidence for that using the *moving window* technique (McConkie & Rayner, 1975; Rayner & Bertera, 1979). We shall now make this story more precise. Again, the idea of the moving window technique is to present the reader a 'window' of text around his or her current fixation point, and when a saccade is executed, present a new window (usually of the same size and shape) around the new fixation point (see Figure 12.2a). Previously, we noted that when this window extended 14–15 characters to either side of fixation, readers could read at normal speed and with normal comprehension.[11] Thus, readers are extracting no useful information outside this region.

This limitation is one imposed by visual acuity as readers can extract no useful visual information outside this region even when it is the only text information present. The experiments demonstrating this used the *moving mask* technique (Rayner & Bertera, 1979), which is the inverse of the moving window technique. In one version of this technique, readers would see nothing but *x*'s between 14 characters to the left and right of fixation and normal text outside of this mask (see Figure 12.2b). The basic finding in these experiments was that reading was virtually impossible under these conditions: people extracted useful letter information on only a very small fraction of the fixations (occasionally a short word or a letter sequence of a longer word). Thus, readers not

only *don't* extract useful letter information outside of this region, they *can't*. Thus, claims of some speed-reading advocates that one can read entire lines of text in a single glance are science fiction.

The window that readers are using to extract useful information during reading, however, is even more limited than this – largely due to attention. First, some of the original moving window experiments (McConkie & Rayner, 1976; Rayner, Well, & Pollatsek, 1980) demonstrated that reading rate and comprehension were unaffected even when the window was reduced to 4 characters to the left of fixation and 14 characters to the right of fixation. In addition, another experiment (Pollatsek, Raney, LaGasse, & Rayner, 1993) showed that when all the lines of a paragraph of text below the one currently being read were replaced with random letters, reading was totally unaffected.

Thus, visual information that is close enough to fixation to be processed (e.g. the words immediately to the left of and immediately below the fixated word) is often not processed. This asymmetry of the window has two potential causes. The first is that English is read from left to right and thus, when you are fixating on a word, you have already processed the material to the left of it and are concentrating on the fixated word and at least some of the material to come, which is to the right of fixation. The second possibility for the asymmetry of the window on the line of text is that the right part of the visual field feeds more directly into the left hemisphere of the brain, which, for most people, is the hemisphere that controls language processing.

Several experiments have indicated that the attentional explanation is the correct one. For example, Pollatsek, Bolozky, Well, and Rayner (1981) used the moving window technique with Hebrew readers. (Hebrew is written from right to left.) For Hebrew readers, the asymmetry observed was the opposite from that with readers of English. That is, for the Hebrew readers, windows that extended 4 characters to the left and 14 to the right interfered markedly with reading, whereas windows that extended 14 characters to the left and 4 to the right did not interfere at all. Interestingly, when these same readers (who were also fluent in English) read English, their pattern was the same as other readers of English. Thus, the shape of the window is not 'hard-wired' in any way, but instead is determined by the task at hand.

Thus, readers are using information from the word they are fixating and at least some information from the word or two coming up (which are to the right of it in English). Can we tell anything more about what information is processed on a given fixation, and more generally, what the actual flow of information in reading is? Presumably, readers are almost always processing the word that is being fixated and are processing some information from the next word or two. But are they always processing

(a) Boundary Paradigm in Reading

|
This is an example of the bouclqad paradigm
                          *

|
This is an example of the boundary paradigm
                               *

(b) Boundary Paradigm in Naming

|
(Fixation 1)   chovt
                    *

|
(Fixation 2)   chart
                                        *

Figure 12.3   *Panel (a) illustrates the boundary paradigm used when people read text. As in Figure 12.2, the asterisks below the line indicate where the reader is fixating and the bar over the line indicates an (invisible) boundary such that the preview will be visible until the eyes cross the boundary for the first time. The target then remains visible for the rest of the trial. The preview may be a nonword, as in this illustration, or it could be a word. Panel (b) illustrates the boundary technique used for single words. The person initially fixates on a cross in the center of the screen and a string of letters appears at about 5 to 10 character spaces from the fixation point. The person then fixates the position of the string of letters and a word appears. (The typical task is for the person to name the word.) Surprisingly, people are rarely aware of the display change.*

information from this region? And is all the information from these words about to be fixated important? One experiment that attempted to answer this question was by Rayner, Well, Pollatsek, and Bertera (1982) in which the window was manipulated in terms of words rather than letters. In one condition (*one-word window*), only the fixated word was normal (visible), whereas in a second (*two-word window*), only the fixated word and the word to the right were normal, and in a third (*three-word window*), the fixated word and the two to the right were normal. One interesting finding was that reading was still fairly fluent even in the *one-word window* condition (when readers can only process one word per fixation); people read with normal comprehension and at about 60% of their normal speed. When the window was expanded to two words, reading speed went up to about 90% of normal, and when it was

expanded to three words, reading speed was the same as when there was no window. Thus, although people are (at least some of the time) extracting information from two words to the right of fixation, the main agenda in reading appears to be to process the word you are fixating and get at least some information about the word to the right.

A technique that was devised to study the details of the acquisition of information to the right of the fixated word is called the *boundary technique* (Rayner, 1975). In essence, this technique is a miniaturization of the moving window technique, as there is only one display change, rather than a display change on each eye movement. In these experiments there is an invisible boundary, and crossing it from left to right triggers the display change. (In contrast, crossing back to the left over the boundary does not undo the change.) The key idea of these experiments is to make well-controlled changes in a *target word* by presenting a *preview* in the target word location that has a precise relation to the target word. (The preview and the target word are always the same length.) Moreover, there are two versions of the technique. In one, a sentence is presented on the screen containing the preview, and when the reader crosses the boundary (usually set to be just to the left of the target word region), the target word replaces the preview (see Figure 12.3a). As with the studies described above, participants merely read a sentence and press a key when they are done. Of primary interest are measures such as fixation times on the target word. The second form of the boundary technique involves presenting a preview that is a single letter string (which may or may not be a word) a degree or two from fixation and have participants move their eyes to fixate the target word location and name the target. As with the other version of the boundary technique, the preview changes to the target when the eye movement is made to the target word region and, in the experiments we present here, the preview is in the same location as the target. (It is worth emphasizing that the reader never fixates the preview.) In these experiments, the time to name the target word is the critical measure of processing (see Figure 12.3b).

We should point out that one remarkable feature of all of these boundary experiments is that participants are rarely, if ever, aware of what the previews are or that there are display changes. A second important (and somewhat surprising) feature of these experiments is that the effects of the previews are quite similar in the reading experiments and in the single-word naming experiments. This provides good converging validity for what is being measured. That is, naming latency is a more controlled measure of processing time, but naming is a more artificial task than reading. The similarity of the results in the two paradigms also provides strong support for our assertion that word processing in context works remarkably similarly to word processing in isolation.

The original experiments using this technique (Rayner, 1978; Rayner, McConkie, & Ehrlich, 1978) investigated whether partial letter information seen before a word is fixated would aid the identification of the target word (e.g. whether a preview of *chest* or *chovt* would facilitate processing of the target word *chart*). In fact, previews that shared the first two or three letters of the target word facilitated processing almost as much as when the target itself was the preview (i.e. when there was no display change). Moreover, the facilitation effects were approximately the same when the case of the letters changed as when they stayed the same (Rayner, McConkie, & Zola, 1980). These findings were obtained with both the sentence-reading version and the naming version of the boundary technique. (In the interest of brevity, it can be assumed that the results discussed below were obtained with both versions unless mentioned otherwise.)

A second important finding using the boundary technique is that phonological information about a word is obtained even before a reader fixates it. In these experiments (Pollatsek, Lesch, Morris, & Rayner, 1992; Henderson, Dixon, Petersen, Twilley, & Ferreira, 1995), a homophone as a preview was compared to an orthographic control (e.g. *beech* as a preview of *beach* compared to *bench* as a preview of *beach*), and the finding was that the facilitation from the homophone preview was larger than that from the orthographic control. Moreover, the beneficial effect of the homophone preview in reading is quite immediate: it shortens the first fixation on the target word. Perhaps somewhat surprisingly, a similar finding has been obtained in Chinese. In one experiment using the naming version of the boundary technique (Pollatsek, Tan, & Rayner, 2000), a Chinese character[12] that was a homophone provided more facilitation than an orthographic control. An analogous manipulation using the sentence-reading version of the boundary technique (Liu, Inhoff, Ye, & Wu, 2002) also found that a homophone preview benefited reading more than the control. However, there is some suggestion that the beneficial effect of the homophone in Chinese might come in a bit later than in English (possibly only on the second fixation after crossing the boundary).

Perhaps the most surprising finding emerging from these boundary experiments is that when the preview is related to the target in meaning, there is no benefit other than what could be predicted from the common letter and phonological information in the preview. Several experiments have shown that preview words related in meaning produce no benefit above and beyond what could be explained by orthographic similarity. In one (Rayner, Balota, & Pollatsek, 1986), words that were similar in meaning

(e.g. *song* and *tune*) did not facilitate each other in a sentence-reading version of the boundary technique, but did facilitate each other in a more standard *semantic priming* paradigm.[13] Moreover, Altarriba, Kambe, Pollatsek, and Rayner (2001) have shown, for Spanish-English bilinguals, that presenting a preview that is a translation of the target also provides no benefit over an orthographically matched preview that has no relation in meaning to the target.

The above experiments thus indicate that information about abstract letters and about the sounds of a word are extracted from a word before it is fixated. They also indicate either that the meaning of a word that is about to be fixated is not extracted or that, for some reason, people are not able to use this information when they later fixate the word. A variety of data indicates that the latter explanation is the correct one. The most obvious is that words to the right of fixation are often skipped, and the probability of skipping them is a function both of their frequency in the language and their predictability from the prior text (Ehrlich & Rayner, 1981; Rayner, Sereno, & Raney, 1996). Thus, words that have not yet been fixated are skipped due to their meaning; therefore, more about these words than their component letters and sounds must have been processed. Moreover, this skipping is not merely due to guessing. For example, Balota, Pollatsek, and Rayner (1985; see also Binder, Pollatsek, & Rayner, 1999) presented sentences which, in one version, had a word (e.g. *cake*) that was quite predictable from sentence context and, in another version, had a word in the same place (e.g. *pies*) that was acceptable but less predictable (e.g. *Since the wedding was today, the baker rushed the wedding cake/pies to the reception*). The finding was that people skipped the predictable word more than they skipped the unpredictable word. Thus, they skipped *cake* not only because they expected it, but because it actually was in the text and had been processed.

This, and other phenomena of skipping, indicate that the meaning of words not yet fixated can be processed (Rayner, 1998). However, it is an open question how often the extraction of the meaning of words not yet fixated occurs. Certainly, *function words* (prepositions, conjunctions and pronouns), which are both short and frequent, are typically skipped most of the time, suggesting that their meaning is often processed on the prior fixation. *Content words* (the others: nouns, verbs, adjectives, adverbs) are typically skipped much less frequently, so that their meaning may only occasionally be processed before they are fixated. We should also indicate that skipping a word does not necessarily mean that its meaning has been processed. Some of the time, its meaning could be guessed. Moreover, there could be errors of eye-movement programming, where the reader intends to fixate a word, but accidentally makes too long an eye movement. We shall see that such errors may be reasonably common.

Let us close here repeating the strangeness of these findings. On the one hand, the skipping data indicate clearly that the meaning of a word not yet fixated is extracted and controls the immediate behavior of the eyes. Yet the preview data indicate that partial extraction of this meaning serves little or no function in aiding processing of the word if it is later fixated. Why this is true is still a mystery that is worth investigating.

WORD IDENTIFICATION: THE ENGINE THAT DRIVES THE EYES FORWARD IN READING

Let us briefly recap what we have learned about the reading process and the role of word identification in it. First, we have seen that word identification is fairly rapid and automatic, although we have not quantified exactly how long word identification takes. Second, we have seen that the process of word identification goes through its component letters, but that the identification of a word and its component letters is an interactive process. Third, we have seen that word identification is not merely a process where one goes from print directly to meaning; instead, access of the sound of a word appears to be a significant part of the process of identifying printed words. In fact, we have seen that getting to the sound of a printed word occurs even before a word is fixated and that this extraction appears to involve both 'direct look-up processes' and 'constructive processes' (although it is far from clear how these constructive processes work or how the two processes interrelate). Fourth, it appears that people are often processing more than a single word on a fixation, although typically not more than two words, and possibly fewer. Moreover, we have seen that people often process a word on more than one fixation: they get a preview of the word before they fixate it and later complete the processing of the word when they fixate it.

Thus, it is clear that reading is a very complex process, and we have only discussed word encoding; we have not touched on how words are put together into phrases, clauses, sentences and narratives (see Garnham, Chapter 10, this volume, and Rayner & Clifton, 2002, for excellent treatments of these issues).[14] Is there some way to make sense out of this? We think that there is a reasonably simple model for how word encoding occurs in reading and causes the eyes to move. However, before embarking on explaining this model, we need to talk about a part of word encoding that we have just touched on that may complicate the picture somewhat. That is, we have been so far tacitly assuming that the meanings of words are unitary, and that once one encodes the letters and sounds of a word, a unitary whole, the 'meaning of a word', is accessed. Language, however, is not so simple, and the meanings of many words are not unitary. That is, there are smaller linguistic units of meaning, called *morphemes*. We touched on morphemes when discussing Chinese, but now we need to develop this topic more fully.

In most Western languages, there are four ways in which words can have more than one morpheme. First, there are *inflections* (i.e. *conjugations* and *declensions*). Conjugations of verbs indicate tense and they involve either using two words (e.g. *did walk*) or adding a suffix (e.g. *walked*). Thus, *walked* has two morphemes, the *root* morpheme *walk* and the suffix *-ed*. Declensions indicate the *person* and *number*, but English has a relatively 'impoverished' marking system, where, with the exception of pronouns, there is only pluralization and marking of possessives. Second, there are *derivational suffixes* that have many functions, but often the part of speech is changed (e.g. adding *-ly* to change adjectives to adverbs). Obviously, there are often specific meanings indicated, such as the *-er* in *worker* which signifies 'one who'. Closely related are *prefixes*, which can have similar functions to suffixes (e.g. *bedevil* changes the noun root to a verb). However, there are other functions for prefixes, such as negation (e.g. *dis-*, *un-*, *mis-*). In general, though, prefixes and derivational suffixes are less rule-bound than declensions. The last category of polymorphism is *compound words* (e.g. *cowboy*). Compounds in English need not be written as one word – the components may also be hyphenated or written as separate words such as *kitchen table*. (In some other languages, such as German or Finnish, however, compounds must be written as a single word without spaces.)[15] Needless to say, a word can have more than one type of complexity, such as *redoubling*, *untidily* or *cowboys*.

An obvious question about words with more than one morpheme is whether they are processed merely by mentally 'looking up' the entire word in a *lexicon* or 'mental dictionary' or whether a more analytic process is involved – where the components are accessed and the meaning of the compound then constructed from the parts. One way this issue has been addressed is to examine the role of the frequency of the components in the speed of word identification when the frequency of the whole word has been controlled for. There have been many studies that have examined this issue employing words in isolation, using either lexical decision time or naming time as indices of the speed of word identification (Baayen, Dijkstra, & Schreuder, 1997; Cole, Beauvillain, & Segui, 1989; Taft, 1979). However, we shall confine ourselves to studies that have examined the issue while people were reading text.

Perhaps the first studies in this line were done with two-component Finnish compound words (Hyönä & Pollatsek, 1998; Pollatsek, Hyönä, & Bertram, 2000). In these studies, the frequency of the compound word was held constant and the frequency of either the first or second component word was varied and matched compound words were inserted in the same place in a sentence.[16] In fact, varying the component frequencies produced large effects (over 70 ms) on the gaze durations on the target word. However, the frequency of the whole word was also shown to affect processing time even when the frequencies of the components were controlled. Hence, it appears that both the whole word and the word parts are active components of the process of identifying compound words.[17]

A similar picture has emerged in experiments with inflected words, words with derivational suffixes, and prefixed words. That is, both the frequency of the whole word and the frequency of the root morpheme have an influence on how long it takes to process a word in text (Niswander, Pollatsek, & Rayner, 2000). On some level, this may not be surprising for compound words, as even if one knows the meaning of the components, one does not necessarily know the meaning of the whole word. (For example, knowing what the words *cow* and *boy* mean tells you that a *cowboy* has some male characteristics and has something to do with *cows*, but knowing this you could think it meant a *calf* if you had never encountered the word.) In contrast, obtaining a word frequency effect for inflected words when the frequency of the root is held constant might seem a bit surprising, because the meaning of the word is completely determined by the meaning of the components (e.g. *boys* means more than one *boy*). However, the data indicate that word frequency effects for inflected words are at least as reliable as root frequency effects (Niswander et al., 2000).

Below, we shall sketch a possible model of how people read, or at least of an important component of the reading process. Before we do, however, we shall briefly summarize what we have discussed about eye movements in reading. First, it appears that encoding words is an important factor in moving the eyes forward. That is, because the frequency of a word (and/or its meaningful components) influences the amount of time spent on a word, it appears that, in some sense, the eyes are waiting for a word to be identified in order to move on (at least some of the time). Second, the frequency and predictability of a word influence the probability of skipping a word. This indicates that word encoding is somehow influencing where the eyes are going next. In contrast, many effects of 'higher-order' processing, such as processing syntactically difficult sentence constructions, are often delayed at least a fixation from the point at which the difficulty should be

apparent to the reader (if the difficulty were apprehended immediately).

These findings suggest that word encoding may be the 'engine' that drives the eyes forward in skilled reading and that the 'higher-order processes' discussed by Garnham in Chapter 10, such as constructing a syntactic parse of the sentence or constructing the meaning of the sentence, are likely to be lagging behind the word-encoding process by a fixation or more (i.e. at least about one-quarter of a second). Thus, we think that it is plausible that these higher-order processes do not affect the forward progress of the eyes through the text unless these processes are not running smoothly. Instead, they may largely intervene only when a comprehension difficulty arises either (a) by programming a backward saccade (a *regression*) back to where the difficulty was likely to be or (b) telling the eyes to stay where they are until the difficulty is resolved.

A SKETCH OF A SIMPLE MODEL OF EYE MOVEMENTS IN READING

Below, we shall sketch a computational model that we have implemented to explain how the eyes move in reading (Reichle, Pollatsek, Fisher, & Rayner, 1998) which has provided good quantitative predictions for both fixation durations and where the eyes land in a substantial corpus of text. We hope that this sketch will help to put together some of the pieces we have discussed into a coherent whole. Our discussion immediately above indicates, however, that we do not see our modeling work so far as explaining the whole reading process. That is, to the extent it is successful, it will explain this 'normal engine' of identifying word and word components driving the eyes forward and leaves open the question of how syntactic and higher-order semantic processing in text influence progress through the text (as undoubtedly they do).[18] (As we shall see below, it is a challenge to even explain how word identification can be fast enough to influence eye movements 'on line'). Here is a plausibility argument for why these higher-order processes rarely influence the normal progress of the eyes in reading. It takes on the order of a quarter of a second to encode a word (possibly a bit longer). It would seem that it would take at least another quarter of a second to do additional processing of syntax and constructing sentence meaning. This would imply that, if the eyes were waiting for those events to occur before moving on, reading would be slowed at least by a factor of two. Thus, perhaps the only way the typical skilled reader can read 300–350 words per minute is to plow ahead on the basis of word encoding and hope that the rest of the processing (which lags behind a bit) does not run into trouble very often. In well-written prose, trouble (and regressions backward more than a word or two) might not in fact occur very often.

Our model of how the eyes are driven in reading is the following. One basic process we assume is that when the word that is being fixated is processed to a certain level (more about the details of that below), a signal goes out to program an eye movement to the next word. A second basic process we assume is that when a word is processed to a deeper level, attention moves from that word and attentional processing of the next word in the text begins. A second part of our model (inspired by an earlier model of Morrison, 1984) is that eye movements can be programmed in parallel (i.e. there can be more than one active at a given time) and that a later eye-movement program can cancel an earlier one. In particular, this cancelation can occur if the second program occurs within about 100–150 ms of the first one. The last assumption is that when the eyes land on a word, at least some of the time, an automatic program to refixate the word goes out immediately. With these relatively simple assumptions, one can explain a lot of the eye-movement data in reading.

First, it should be clear that the assumption that encoding a word to some level of understanding is the signal to move the eyes to the next word explains why fixations on lower-frequency words are longer than those on higher-frequency words (the signal goes out later for the lower-frequency word). What may be less clear is whether this process can occur in real time. That is, as we indicated earlier, it is likely to take on the order of 200–250 ms to encode many words, and furthermore, eye movements take on the order of 175–200 ms to execute once they are programmed (Becker & Jürgens, 1979; Rayner, Slowiaczek, Clifton, & Bertera, 1983). As a result, it is not trivial to explain why fixation times on words are often 250–350 ms. A key ingredient in our being able to explain this is that people are usually attending to words on the fixation prior to when they fixate them and thus are extracting significant information prior to when they fixate a word. (In fact, as we indicated earlier, when people are denied this preview in a moving window experiment, reading slows down about 40%.)

The other key part of the model, that a later eye movement can cancel an earlier one, allows an explanation of word skipping. For example, if one is reading ... *closed the door* ... and is fixating *closed*, then during that fixation, one may program a saccade to *the* and then program a saccade to *door*. Moreover, because *the* is very high frequency (the highest-frequency word in the English language), the time between these two programs is quite short (i.e. the time to encode *the*) and thus the second saccade program to *door* will be likely to cancel the

saccade program to *the* and *the* will be skipped. We have given an extreme case with *the* here, but our model successfully predicts skipping of words, in general, using this mechanism.[19]

Space does not permit us to go into greater detail or into extensions of the basic model (e.g. to explain how complex words are processed in reading), but we hope that the basic idea of the model is clear and that we have made plausible the idea that there might be a relatively simple process that can explain a lot about how we move our eyes in reading. It might be worth mentioning that a key idea of the model is that attentional processing of words is sequential. We think that is quite reasonable as encoding word order is an important part of understanding the meaning of a sentence.[20] In contrast, our model assumes complex interactions between eye movements and we think there is quite a bit of data supporting the idea that these interactions exist (e.g. Becker & Jürgens, 1979).

SUMMARY

Reading is a complex process. This chapter has concentrated on the first stage of reading: identifying printed words. Besides the fact that this is a necessary ingredient to being able to read, word identification appears to be a 'separable' process. That is, the process does not seem to differ very much when identifying words in isolation and when identifying them while reading text, although when a word is predictable from the preceding text, the identification process is speeded. Word identification is quite rapid, probably taking no more than about 200 ms per word, on average, and one reason for this is that letters (in short to medium-length words, at least) are processed in parallel and information at the word level facilitates the identification of letters. However, the identification of words is a complex process involving activating the sound of the letters and subunits of meaning (morphemes). Exactly how the activation of the sound components and the meaning components relate to the activation of a word's meaning, however, is still not clear.

NOTES

1 Unfortunately, space limitations do not allow a reasonable discussion of *dyslexia* (that is, the issue of why some people, who are otherwise intellectually unimpaired, have difficulty in reading). Most of the evidence, however, indicates that the problems for most of these people involve getting to the sounds of words from print rather than to purely visual problems (see, e.g., Fowler, 1991; Murphy & Pollatsek, 1994).

2 We should also note that we shall only discuss how *printed* words are processed. Although *written* language, especially cursive writing, may be processed somewhat differently, there is little enough data on the subject to draw much in the way of firm conclusions. Moreover, in our electronic age, the vast majority of reading is of printed text.

3 There is also a growing literature using physiological methods, such as *evoked potentials* or looking at brain activity with *functional magnetic resonance imaging* (*fMRI*); however, discussing these methods would take us too far afield for this chapter.

4 Both mean gaze duration measures and mean individual fixation duration measures are typically averaged only over instances when the word is not skipped the first time it is encountered. Thus, those trials on which the word is skipped are essentially considered a missing data point rather than a zero, and the measures should be viewed as fixation durations conditional on the word being fixated.

5 Return sweeps are actually fairly complex as large saccades are rarely made accurately. That is, the initial saccade that is presumably aimed at the first word on the next line often lands on the second or third word; there are then one or two short saccades to get a fixation on the first word, or sometimes the first word is never fixated. Because of these complexities, researchers often do not include data from the first and last words of a line of text in careful analyses of word processing.

6 We shall use the term *pseudoword* to refer to an orthographically legal and pronounceable nonword and, for simplicity, reserve the use of the term *nonword* for illegal and unpronounceable nonwords.

7 The models we have described use *discrete* representations for words and letters. Some of the newer variants (called PDP or parallel distributed processing models) use *distributed* representations for words and letters (e.g. McClelland, Rumelhart, & the PDP Research Group, 1986). That is, in these PDP models, there is no single representation for a word or a letter. Instead, there are a large number of processors at each level, and the representation of a letter or word is a distinct pattern of excitation among the processors at each level. However, at the level we are discussing the issues in this chapter, one can look at this as a different (micro) level of processing, rather than being contradictory to the models that view letters and words as discrete entities.

8 Some people have used the logical difficulty of computing the sound code of a word as an argument that skilled readers do not use sound codes when they read silently. However, as indicated in note 1, there is not only evidence that skilled readers use sound codes when they are reading silently, but that children who have difficulty either accessing sound codes or constructing them have difficulty in learning to read.

9 To save space, we shall avoid repeating that aspects of the target words are controlled for. In all the experiments that follow, the length of the target words is controlled for, as are many other variables that could be confounding. For example, in naming experiments, it is necessary to control for the initial phoneme in the word, as certain spoken initial consonants are just harder to initiate than others.

10 Due to space limitations, we have used *written word frequency* as a shorthand for all aspects of a word that would make its representation in memory more accessible due to past experience. Two other variables that are likely to be important (and would be reasonably highly correlated) are the frequency in the spoken language and the age at which a word is first learned. There is currently interest in trying to tease apart these factors. However, a problem in this research is that all the indices are flawed to some extent. For example, the written word frequencies that people usually use are both out of date and from a corpus of text that is unlikely to be representative of what most people usually read. Thus, a comparison of how well two measures predict reading speed may be a better reflection of how well the measure is indexing what it is supposed to than how important the underlying construct is in determining reading speed.

11 In most of the moving window experiments we discuss (and in the other related display-change experiments), the reader is positioned so that three characters subtends 1 degree of visual angle. Thus, the window from which useful letter information is extracted in these experiments could be characterized as being 5 degrees from fixation. However, within limits, characterizing distance from the fixation point in terms of letters is the right metric. That is, if one were closer to the text (so that each character subtended more than one-third of a degree horizontally), the window gets bigger in terms of visual angle because the letters are bigger and hence easier to see. (The opposite would be true if one moved the reader further from the text.) Within a reasonably large range, there is a pretty close trade-off between size of letters and visual angle, so that number of letters (or more generally, characters) is a good general metric. You can get a feeling for this by moving this book nearer and further from your eyes and, within a fairly wide range, the distance will not make a big difference – assuming you are not having problems focusing.

12 A Chinese character represents a *morpheme* (a unit of meaning that we shall define presently) rather than a word (although many Chinese characters are words). It is also a single syllable in the spoken language. Most characters are also not unitary, but are composed of two *radicals*, one which gives a hint to the meaning of the character and the other a hint to the pronunciation of the character.

13 The standard *semantic priming* paradigm involves showing a person two words in sequence foveally, the *prime* and the *target*. Typically, either the time to name the target word or the time to judge whether the target stimulus is a word or not (*lexical decision*) is used as the dependent variable. Hundreds of experiments have shown that a semantically related prime speeds the time to name or judge the target word by 15–30 ms. In fact, priming has been obtained in conditions where the prime is briefly presented and followed by a mask, so that people cannot identify the prime!

14 Another issue we can only touch on briefly is how lexically ambiguous words are processed during reading. A number of experiments (see Duffy, Morris, & Rayner, 1988; Rayner & Frazier, 1989) have demonstrated that when an ambiguous word with two equally likely meanings (such as straw) is encountered in a relatively neutral context, readers look at it longer than at an unambiguous control word (matched on length and frequency). However, when prior context disambiguates the appropriate meaning, readers no longer look at the ambiguous word longer than the control word. On the other hand, if the ambiguous word has a highly dominant meaning (such as bank), readers do not look at the ambiguous word any longer than a control word in a neutral context. Apparently, in this case they simply select the dominant meaning. However, if the prior context instantiates the subordinate meaning, readers look longer at the ambiguous word than the control word. These phenomena suggest that the prior context boosts the strength of one of the meanings. In the case of the word with equally frequent meanings, the context boosts one of the two meanings to be 'dominant'. In the case where the context is consistent with the less frequent meaning, its strength is boosted so that it is in competition with the more frequent meaning.

15 A full discussion of complex words is clearly beyond the scope of this chapter. A good introduction can be found in Selkirk (1982). One way to tell that something like 'kitchen table' is a compound rather than just two separate words is to note that, in this context, 'kitchen' is *not* an adjective. That is, it is still a noun, and the only sensible way to analyze its function is that 'kitchen table' is a noun-noun compound word (a very common type of compound).

16 In these studies, unless otherwise noted, a (counterbalanced) design is employed where half the subjects see the sentence frame with one of the target words in it and the other half of the subjects see the sentence frame with the other, matched, target word. In addition, care is taken to ensure that the two words fit equally naturally in the sentence (ratings are obtained from other subjects to ensure this).

17 We earlier indicated that there was no evidence that partial meanings of words could be extracted before a word is fixated that would aid in processing the word when it is subsequently fixated. In fact, in English (Inhoff, 1989; Lima, 1987), this extends to prefixes and compound words, as there is no bigger benefit from a true morpheme (e.g. cowxxx for *cowboy*) than from a pseudomorpheme (carxxx for carpet). However, in Hebrew (Deutsch, Frost, Pollatsek, & Rayner, 2000; Deutsch, Frost, Peleg, Pollatsek, & Rayner, 2003), the preview of a root morpheme does facilitate later processing of the word. (In Hebrew, the root is rarely represented by contiguous letters.) Whether this reflects a true cross-language difference in how morphemes are processed is still not clear, as the types of morphemic previews across the two languages were somewhat different.

18 We should hasten to point out that, consistent with our model not attempting to deal with 'higher-order' processes, our corpus of data is people reading individual sentences. In addition, as 'higher-order' processes often produce regressive fixations in the text when something is not clear, we did not attempt to fit the eye-movement pattern in a sentence in which the reader had made a regression back to a prior word.

19 A similar mechanism predicts the probability of refixating a word. That is, as we indicated above, often an automatic refixation is programmed to a word when it is initially fixated. When the word is relatively frequent (and thus rapidly processed), however, the saccade program to fixate the next word will occur quickly and cancel this refixation program, and the word will be fixated only once. In contrast, if encoding the word takes a long time, it could receive two or more fixations.

20 We are not claiming that words are necessarily processed sequentially in all contexts. For example, if one sees two words outside of sentence context and is asked to judge whether they are synonyms, they may not be processed one at a time.

REFERENCES

Altarriba, J., Kambe, G., Pollatsek, A., & Rayner, K. (2001). Semantic codes are not used in integrating information across eye fixations: evidence from fluent Spanish-English bilinguals. *Perception and Psychophysics, 63*, 875–891.

Baayen, R. H., Dijkstra, T., & Schreuder, R. (1997). Singulars and plurals in Dutch: evidence for a parallel dual route model. *Journal of Memory and Language, 36*, 94–117.

Balota, D. A. (1983). Automatic semantic activation and episodic memory encoding. *Journal of Verbal Learning and Verbal Behavior, 22*, 88–104.

Balota, D. A., Pollatsek, A., & Rayner, K. (1985). The interaction of contextual constraints and parafoveal visual information in reading. *Cognitive Psychology, 17*, 364–390.

Baron, J., & Strawson, C. (1976). Use of orthographic and word-specific knowledge in reading words aloud. *Journal of Experimental Psychology: Human Perception and Performance, 2*, 386–393.

Baron, J., & Thurston, I. (1973). An analysis of the word superiority effect. *Cognitive Psychology, 4*, 207–228.

Becker, W., & Jürgens, R. (1979). An analysis of the saccadic system by means of double step stimuli. *Vision Research, 19*, 967–983.

Besner, D., Coltheart, M., & Davelaar, E. (1984). Basic processes in reading: computation of abstract letter identities. *Canadian Journal of Psychology, 38*, 126–134.

Besner, D., Stolz, J. A., & Boutilier, C. (1997). The Stroop effect and the myth of automaticity. *Psychonomic Bulletin and Review, 4*, 221–225.

Besner, D., Twilley, L., McCann, R. S., & Seergobin, K. (1990). On the association between connectionism and data: are a few words necessary? *Psychological Review, 97*, 432–446.

Binder, K. S., Pollatsek, A., & Rayner, K. (1999). Extraction of information to the left of the fixated word in reading. *Journal of Experimental Psychology: Human Perception and Performance, 25*, 1142–1158.

Broadbent, D. E. (1967). Word-frequency effect and response bias. *Psychological Review, 74*, 1–15.

Carr, T. H., McCauley, C., Sperber, R. D., & Parmelee, C. M. (1982). Words, pictures, and priming: on semantic activation, conscious identification, and the automaticity of information processing. *Journal of Experimental Psychology: Human Perception and Performance, 8*, 757–777.

Carr, T. H., & Pollatsek, A. (1985). Recognizing printed words: a look at current models. In D. Besner, T. G. Waller, & G. E. MacKinnon (Eds.), *Reading research: advances in theory and practice* (Vol. 5, pp. 2–76). Orlando, FL: Academic Press.

Cole, P., Beauvillain, C., & Segui, J. (1989). On the representation and processing of prefixed and suffixed derived words: a differential frequency effect. *Journal of Memory and Language, 28*, 1–13.

Coltheart, M. (1978). Lexical access in simple reading tasks. In G. Underwood (ed.), *Strategies of information processing* (pp. 151–216). London: Academic Press.

Coltheart, M. (1981). Disorders of reading and their implications for models of normal reading. *Visible Language, 15*, 245–286.

Coltheart, M., Masterson, J., Byng, S., Prior, M., & Riddoch, J. (1983). Surface dyslexia. *Quarterly Journal of Experimental Psychology, 35A*, 469–495.

Coltheart, M., Patterson, K., & Marshall, J. (1980). *Deep dyslexia*. London: Routledge & Kegan Paul.

Coltheart, M., Rastle, K., Perry, C., Langdon, R., & Ziegler, J. (2001). DRC: a dual route cascaded model of visual word recognition and reading aloud. *Psychological Review, 108*, 204–256.

Crowder, R. G., & Wagner, R. K. (1992). *The psychology of reading*. New York: Oxford University Press.

Deutsch, A., Frost, R., Peleg, S., Pollatsek, A., & Rayner, K. (2003). Early morphological effects in reading: evidence from parafoveal preview benefit in Hebrew. *Psychonomic Bulletin and Review, 10*, 415–422.

Deutsch, A., Frost, R., Pollatsek, A., & Rayner, K. (2000). Early morphological effects in word recognition in Hebrew: evidence from parafoveal preview benefit. *Language and Cognitive Processes, 15*, 487–506.

Duffy, S. A., Morris, R. K., & Rayner, K. (1988). Lexical ambiguity and fixation times in reading. *Journal of Memory and Language, 27*, 429–446.

Ehrlich, S. F., & Rayner, K. (1981). Contextual effects on word perception and eye movements during reading. *Journal of Verbal Learning and Verbal Behavior, 20*, 641–655.

Evett, L. J., & Humphreys, G. W. (1981). The use of abstract graphemic information in lexical access. *Quarterly Journal of Experimental Psychology, 33A*, 325–350.

Fowler, A. (1991). How early phonological development might set the stage for phoneme awareness. In S. A. Brady & D. Shankweiler (Eds.), *Phonological processes in literacy: a tribute to Isabelle Y. Liberman*. Hillsdale, NJ: Erlbaum.

Henderson, J. M., Dixon, P., Petersen, A., Twilley, L. C., & Ferreira, F. (1995). Evidence for the use of phonological representations during transsaccadic word recognition. *Journal of Experimental Psychology: Human Perception and Performance, 21*, 82–97.

Hyönä, J. & Pollatsek, A. (1998). Reading Finnish compound words: eye fixations are affected by component morphemes. *Journal of Experimental Psychology: Human Perception and Performance, 24*, 1612–1627.

Inhoff, A. W. (1989). Parafoveal processing of words and saccade computation during eye fixations in reading. *Journal of Experimental Psychology: Human Perception and Performance, 15*, 544–555.

Inhoff, A. W., & Rayner, K. (1986). Parafoveal word processing during eye fixations in reading: effects of word frequency. *Perception and Psychophysics, 40*, 431–439.

Just, M. A., & Carpenter, P. A. (1980). A theory of reading: from eye fixations to comprehension. *Psychological Review, 87*, 329–354.

Just, M. A., & Carpenter, P. A. (1987). *The psychology of reading and language comprehension*. Newton, MA: Allyn & Bacon.

Lesch, M. F., & Pollatsek, A. (1998). Evidence for the use of assembled phonology in accessing the meaning of printed words. *Journal of Experimental Psychology: Learning, Memory and Cognition, 24*, 573–592.

Lima, S. D. (1987). Morphological analysis in sentence reading. *Journal of Memory and Language, 26*, 84–99.

Liu, W., Inhoff, A. W., Ye, Y., & Wu, C. (2002). Use of parafoveal visible characters during the reading of Chinese sentences. *Journal of Experimental Psychology: Human Perception and Performance, 28*, 1213–1227.

MacLeod, C. (1991). Half a century of research on the Stroop effect: an integrative review. *Psychological Bulletin, 109*, 163–203.

Marcel, A. J. (1983). Conscious and unconscious perception: experiments on visual masking. *Cognitive Psychology, 15*, 197–237.

McClelland, J. L., & Rumelhart, D. E. (1981). An interactive activation model of context effects in letter perception: Part 1. An account of basic findings. *Psychological Review, 88*, 375–407.

McClelland, J. L., Rumelhart, D. E., & the PDP Research Group (1986). *Parallel distributed: explorations in the microstructure of cognition: Vol. 2. Psychological and biological models*. Cambridge, MA: MIT Press.

McConkie, G. W., & Rayner, K. (1975). The span of the effective stimulus during a fixation in reading. *Perception and Psychophysics, 17*, 578–586.

McConkie, G. W., & Rayner, K. (1976). Asymmetry of the perceptual span in reading. *Bulletin of the Psychonomic Society, 8*, 365–368.

McConkie, G. W., & Zola, D. (1979). Is visual information integrated across successive fixations in reading? *Perception and Psychophysics, 25*, 221–224.

Meyer, D. E., & Schvaneveldt, R. W. (1971). Facilitation in recognizing pairs of words: evidence of a dependence between retrieval operations. *Journal of Experimental Psychology*, *90*, 227–234.

Morrison, R. E. (1984). Manipulation of stimulus onset delay in reading: evidence for parallel programming of saccades. *Journal of Experimental Psychology: Human Perception and Performance*, *10*, 667–682.

Murphy, L., & Pollatsek, A. (1994). Developmental dyslexia: heterogeneity without discrete subgroups. *Annals of Dyslexia*, *44*, 120–146.

Niswander, E., Pollatsek, A., & Rayner, K. (2000). The processing of derived and inflected suffixed words during reading. *Language and Cognitive Processes*, *15*, 389–420.

Paap, K. R., Newsome, S. L., McDonald, J. E., & Schvaneveldt, R. W. (1982). An activation-verification model for letter and word recognition: the word superiority effect. *Psychological Review*, *89*, 573–594.

Perfetti, C. A., Goldman, S. R., & Hogaboam, T. W. (1979). Reading skill and the identification of words in discourse context. *Memory and Cognition*, *7*, 273–282.

Perfetti, C. A., & Hogaboam, T. W. (1975). The relationship between single word decoding and reading comprehension skill. *Journal of Educational Psychology*, *67*, 461–469.

Plaut, D. C., McClelland, J. L., Seidenberg, M. S., & Patterson, K. (1996). Understanding normal and impaired word reading: computational principles in quasi-regular domains. *Psychological Review*, *103*, 56–115.

Pollatsek, A., Bolozky, S., Well, A. D., & Rayner, K. (1981). Asymmetries in the perceptual span for Israeli readers. *Brain and Language*, *14*, 174–180.

Pollatsek, A., Hyönä, J., & Bertram, R. (2000). The role of morphological constituents in reading Finnish compound words. *Journal of Experimental Psychology: Human Perception and Performance*, *26*, 820–833.

Pollatsek, A., Lesch, M., Morris, R. K., & Rayner, K. (1992). Phonological codes are used in integrating information across saccades in word identification and reading. *Journal of Experimental Psychology: Human Perception and Performance*, *18*, 148–162.

Pollatsek, A., Raney, G. E., LaGasse, L., & Rayner, K. (1993). The use of information below fixation in reading and in visual search. *Canadian Journal of Psychology*, *47*, 179–200.

Pollatsek, A., Tan, L.-H., & Rayner, K. (2000). The role of phonological codes in integrating information across saccadic eye movements in Chinese character identification. *Journal of Experimental Psychology: Human Perception and Performance*, *26*, 607–633.

Rayner, K. (1975). The perceptual span and peripheral cues in reading. *Cognitive Psychology*, *7*, 65–81.

Rayner, K. (1978). Foveal and parafoveal cues in reading. In J. Requin (ed.), *Attention and performance* (Vol. 7, pp. 149–162). Hillsdale, NJ: Erlbaum.

Rayner, K. (1998). Eye movements in reading and information processing: 20 years of research. *Psychological Bulletin*, *124*, 372–422.

Rayner, K., Balota, D. A., & Pollatsek, A. (1986). Against parafoveal semantic preprocessing during eye fixations in reading. *Canadian Journal of Psychology*, *40*, 473–483.

Rayner, K., & Bertera, J. H. (1979). Reading without a fovea. *Science*, *206*, 468–469.

Rayner, K., & Clifton, C., Jr. (2002). Language comprehension. In D. L. Medin (Vol. ed.), *Stevens' handbook of experimental psychology* (Vol. X, pp. 261–316). New York: Wiley.

Rayner, K., & Duffy, S. A. (1986). Lexical complexity and fixation times in reading: effects of word frequency, verb complexity, and lexical ambiguity. *Memory and Cognition*, *14*, 191–201.

Rayner, K., Foorman, B. R., Perfetti, C. A., Pesetsky, D., & Seidenberg, M. S. (2001). How psychological science informs the teaching of reading. *Psychological Science in the Public Interest*, *2*, 31–74.

Rayner, K., & Frazier, L. (1989). Selection mechanisms in reading lexically ambiguous words. *Journal of Experimental Psychology: Learning, Memory, and Cognition*, *15*, 779–790.

Rayner, K., McConkie, G. W., & Ehrlich, S. F. (1978). Eye movements and integrating information across fixations. *Journal of Experimental Psychology: Human Perception and Performance*, *4*, 529–544.

Rayner, K., McConkie, G. W., & Zola, D. (1980). Integrating information across eye movements. *Cognitive Psychology*, *12*, 206–226.

Rayner, K., & Pollatsek, A. (1989). *The psychology of reading.* Englewood Cliffs, NJ: Prentice-Hall.

Rayner, K., & Posnansky, C. (1978). Stages of processing in word identification. *Journal of Experimental Psychology: General*, *107*, 64–80.

Rayner, K., Sereno, S. C., & Raney, G. E. (1996). Eye movement control in reading: a comparison of two types of models. *Journal of Experimental Psychology: Human Perception and Performance*, *22*, 1188–1200.

Rayner, K., Slowiaczek, M. L., Clifton, C., & Bertera, J. H. (1983). Latency of sequential eye movements: implications for reading. *Journal of Experimental Psychology: Human Perception and Performance*, *9*, 912–922.

Rayner, K., Well, A. D., & Pollatsek, A. (1980). Asymmetry of the effective visual field in reading. *Perception and Psychophysics*, *27*, 537–544.

Rayner, K., Well, A. D., Pollatsek, A. & Bertera, J. H. (1982). The availability of useful information to the right of fixation in reading. *Perception and Psychophysics*, *31*, 537–550.

Reicher, G. M. (1969). Perceptual recognition as a function of meaningfulness of stimulus material. *Journal of Experimental Psychology*, *81*, 275–280.

Reichle, E. D., Pollatsek, A., Fisher, D. L., & Rayner, K. (1998). Towards a model of eye movement control in reading. *Psychological Review*, *105*, 125–157.

Rosinski, R. R., Golinkoff, R. M., & Kukish, K. (1975). Automatic semantic processing in a picture-word interference task. *Child Development*, *46*, 243–253.

Schilling, H. E. H., Rayner, K., & Chumbley, J. I. (1998). Comparing naming, lexical decision, and eye fixation times: word frequency effects and individual differences. *Memory and Cognition*, *26*, 1270–1281.

Seidenberg, M. S., & McClelland, J. L. (1989). A distributed, developmental model of word recognition and naming. *Psychological Review, 96*, 523–568.

Seidenberg, M. S., & McClelland, J. L. (1990). More words but still no lexicon: reply to Besner et al. (1990). *Psychological Review, 97*, 432–446.

Selkirk, L. (1982). *The syntax of words*. Cambridge, MA: MIT Press.

Smith, F., Lott, D., & Cronnell, B. (1969). The effect of type size and case alternation on word identification. *American Journal of Psychology, 82*, 248–253.

Stroop, J. R. (1935). Studies of interference in serial verbal reactions. *Journal of Experimental Psychology, 18*, 643–662.

Taft, M. (1979). Recognition of affixed words and the word frequency effect. *Memory and Cognition, 7*, 263–272.

Van Orden, G. (1987). A rows is a rose: spelling, sound, and reading. *Memory and Cognition, 15*, 181–198.

Van Orden, G. C., Johnston, J. C., & Hale, B. L. (1988). Word identification in reading proceeds from spelling to sound to meaning. *Journal of Experimental Psychology: Learning, Memory, and Cognition, 14*, 371–386.

Wheeler, D. D. (1970). Processes in word recognition. *Cognitive Psychology, 1*, 59–85.

PART FOUR

Reasoning and Decision Making

13

Reasoning

NICK CHATER, EVAN HEIT AND
MIKE OAKSFORD

The cognitive science perspective on the mind views thought as information processing. More specifically, this information processing is not merely arbitrary computation; it typically involves deriving new information from existing information. For example, visual perceptual analysis and categorization are viewed as taking low-level information about the pattern of light incident at the retina, and creating a representation of information about objects in the environment, their movements, interrelationships and causal powers. Speech production involves mapping from representations of an intention (the message to be conveyed), to a detailed set of information providing instructions to the tongue, lips and voice box. To take a final example, problem solving involves taking the information given in a problem, and mapping on to a representation of the solution to that problem.

We can call the process of using existing information to generate new information *inference*. The given pieces of information on which the inference is based are the premises, and the resulting information derived in the inference is the *conclusion*. The view that at least much of cognition is inference is therefore influential in many areas of cognitive science. Indeed, it turns out that this viewpoint may sometimes be more prevalent than might be thought at first sight. For example, connectionist models may seem to postulate that information processing involves mere propagation of activation through a neuron-like network, rather than involving any processes of inference. Nonetheless, many connectionist systems, and their learning algorithms, can be

viewed, in a rigorous way, as embodying probabilistic inference (e.g. Chater, 1995; McClelland, 1998).

So inference appears a fairly ubiquitous concept in cognitive science; inferences are routinely postulated in perception, motor control, language processing, commonsense reasoning and social cognition. But this chapter focuses on a much narrower domain: reasoning. Although 'inferential processes' and 'reasoning processes' might sound interchangeable, in reality the cognitive science of reasoning has taken a narrow focus. Specifically, it typically focuses on inferences that are based on premises and conclusions that are stated verbally. Typically, moreover, the reasoner's task is primarily to acquire knowledge from the premises – whereas in, for example, problem solving or decision making, this new knowledge is typically used for a purpose, such as checkmating the opponent, or getting the missionaries and cannibals across the river.

The boundaries of the domain of reasoning are, like most areas of inquiry, somewhat vague. But research on reasoning typically focuses on verbal problems that attempt to directly tap into the inferential machinery that people use, rather than, for example, probing their vocabulary or general knowledge. In an optimistic mood, a psychologist of reasoning might say: the idea is to study the inferential processes of the mind, as uncontaminated as possible by odd bits and pieces of knowledge that people have, that we do not know about, and that will be incredibly variable from one person to the next. The cognitive science of reasoning seeks to cut through to the essence of inference, and hence has potentially wide implications for the whole of cognitive science.

Note, though, that the very idea of such a separation, between probing inferential ability and assessing general knowledge, presupposes that it is possible to make a separation between inferences that depend on *form* and those that depend on *content*. Contrast the following three verbal arguments:

Premises: All swans are white
               All white things are large
Conclusion: All swans are large

Premises: All swans are white
               Fred believes that some swans are
               large
Conclusion: Fred believes that some white
               things are large

Premises: All swans are white
               Some swans are large
Conclusion: Some swans should be easy to see
               with binoculars

The first argument seems unequivocally to be a matter of 'form'. The point is that we can tell that the argument is valid, even if we have no idea what swans are, or what it means to be white or large. Any argument of the form

Premises: All X's are Y
               All Y's are Z
Conclusion: All X's are Z

will be valid. It is just the form of the argument that matters, not what it is about. This specific argument is a kind of syllogism, of which more later. Syllogisms were the first formal arguments to be identified and codified, by Aristotle, and until the eighteenth century were widely viewed as pretty much exhausting all formally valid inferences. The last 130 years have, however, seen a spectacular expansion in the domain of arguments that have been viewed as valid in virtue of their form – we shall see some examples later.

The third example argument may be reasonably convincing, and is the kind of argument that we provide to each other everyday. But it is not convincing just in virtue of its form. The content of the premises is of critical importance. A formally identical argument:

Premises: All fish are transparent
               Some fish are small
Conclusion: Some fish should be easy to see
               with blindfolds

where only vocabulary items have been modified is clearly completely unconvincing! The point is that general knowledge (about swans, size, whiteness, human vision, the purpose of binoculars, blindfolds, and so on) is critical to deciding whether these arguments are valid or not, and clearly which bits of general knowledge are relevant depends on the content of the things that the argument is about, not just the form of the argument. Here, we are in the territory of the general problem of how to update beliefs, where the content of those beliefs, not merely their form, appears to be important (Harman, 1989).

Finally, consider the intermediate argument in our set of examples above. Does this hold in virtue of its form or not? It might seem that the argument is clearly valid, like the first argument. If Fred believes that swans are large, then there are some things, which are swans, and which he believes are large. And if it is also true that all swans are white, then does it not follow that these same things are things that are both white and things that Fred thinks are large? And does this then not imply that Fred believes that some large things are white?

But things are not so straightforward. For example, what if Fred believes that all swans are blue. Then he may happily accept that some swans are large, but might consistently deny that there are any white things that are large – to Fred the swans, as blue things, are simply irrelevant.

So what might appear to be a fairly clear-cut case of a valid argument appears to sink into a mire of complexity. And this appearance is correct! Arguments involving belief, desire, and other so called propositional attitudes, are remarkably resistant to any formal analysis. And, equally, arguments concerning what might have happened (counterfactuals), arguments concerning what is plausibly, but not necessarily, going to happen, and many others, have proved inordinately difficult to analyse in terms of their form. Indeed, there are very few arguments that people use in everyday life that appear to be clearly comprehensible in formal terms.

Note that we have treated these issues lightly and informally here – but the question of which arguments can be made formal is a serious one. Indeed, the intimately related project of providing 'logical' forms for natural language statements was one of the central concerns of analytic philosophy throughout the twentieth century. Thus, we have been skating over issues that relate to deep and unresolved questions in the philosophy of language, philosophical and formal logic, and formal semantics. Here and elsewhere, the empirical study of reasoning rests on theoretical foundations of great subtlety and importance – an attractive, but somewhat precarious, location for what aims to be a primarily empirical investigation.

We noted above that the psychology of reasoning is largely (though, as we shall see, by no means exclusively) concerned with how people reason with arguments that are primarily a matter of 'form'. But it seems that this might be a rather narrow range of arguments. What are the implications of this? Is there a danger that the psychology of reasoning might turn out to be irrelevant to cognition at large?

One viewpoint is that formal arguments are actually more inclusive than one might think. One line of justification for this viewpoint is that many arguments appear to depend on content simply because they have not fully been stated, i.e. because crucial pieces of background knowledge have been left out. If the relevant background knowledge were also encoded as additional premises, then perhaps the resulting argument would depend only on form after all. So perhaps the rather constrained reasoning tasks studied in the psychology of reasoning (such as syllogisms) might be a microcosm of human reasoning after all. One attraction of this viewpoint is that if reasoning can be reduced to form, we can explain the cognitive processes involved in inference in computational terms – because computation involves the manipulation of the formal properties of representations. It is not so clear how the content of a representation can affect its computations (and indeed it has even been argued that this is incoherent in principle: Fodor, 1980). A difficulty with the viewpoint that, with enough effort, many or all arguments can be expressed in formal terms is that research in artificial intelligence has shown that there seems to be no natural limit to the amount of background knowledge that must be codified as additional premises, before intuitively reasonable arguments become formally justified (McDermott, 1987; Oaksford & Chater, 1991).

An alternative viewpoint is that formal reasoning tasks may be uninteresting as illustrations of general principles of inference in cognition, precisely because they eliminate the application of rich general knowledge that is fundamental to cognition. This viewpoint might suggest that studying reasoning that works by virtue of form, rather than content, is a bit like studying object recognition by having people look at uniform blank visual fields.

An intermediate viewpoint, which we explore in this chapter, is that the cognitive science of reasoning does, indeed, abstract away from some critical aspects of routine inference in the cognitive system. Indeed, by focusing on form it not only abstracts away from content and general knowledge, it also attempts to abstract away from the pragmatic communicative intent that underlies everyday use of language. The premises are to be understood as 'pure' information-bearing states; nothing is presupposed or implied by their use. Real communication is not like this; in choosing to make some utterance, we reveal a great deal about our thoughts and intentions, much of this deliberately (the study of such effects is called *pragmatics*: Levinson, 1983). But the intermediate viewpoint also suggests that even simple verbal reasoning problems may prove usefully illustrative of broader cognitive processes, not by sealing off those processes, but in the way that world knowledge and pragmatic

factors 'leak back in' to affect performance on these precisely defined tasks.

The focus on reasoning that depends on the formal properties of arguments, whatever its utility as a general window on inferential processes in cognition, has a further valuable spin-off. This is that we have a *normative theory*, or standard of correct performance, against which people's actual behaviour can be compared. Without such a normative standard, studying reasoning is rather like studying how people do mental arithmetic, without oneself knowing anything about arithmetic. If there are norms of 'good' performance, then we can compare people's performance against these norms, and systematic departures from these norms can be taken as evidence for particular features of human reasoning processes. Moreover, as we have mentioned, formal reasoning can be computationally automated. This means that it is possible, at least in principle, to put forward mathematical and computational models of reasoning processes, or at least proposals concerning how such models should look. For reasoning based on pragmatics and/or general knowledge, the computational challenge is vastly more difficult.

We have seen that reasoning researchers have focused on verbal problems that appear formal in character, i.e. that do not depend on the specific content of the items being described, or on unspecified background knowledge. In practice, the literature is large, and here we shall concentrate on two key domains, which are traditionally known as 'deductive' and 'inductive' reasoning; we shall leave aside the large and important literature on how people reason with probabilities (Gigerenzer & Hoffrage, 1995; Tversky & Kahneman, 1974), which is more closely allied to the field of judgement and decision-making research (e.g. Connolly, Arkes, & Hammond, 2000; Goldstein & Hogarth, 1997), which focuses on the degree to which people fit with the 'rational choice' models of 'correct' behaviour (e.g. Elster, 1986) that are prevalent in economics and some other areas of social science.

Instead, we focus on the traditions of research on deductive and inductive inference. As we shall see, the labels are not uncontroversial – indeed, some theorists view most research that has been aimed to explore deductive inference as actually concerning a kind of probabilistic inference. But these labels reflect the historical development of the field well enough. Roughly, research on deductive reasoning seeks to study reasoning in which conclusions follow with inexorable logic from the formal structure of the premises. The normative theory that is presumed to capture the formal structure of such inferences is deductive logic (Boolos & Jeffrey, 1989). Inductive reasoning, by contrast, does not have a clear candidate normative theory – and indeed, it has even been argued that inductive inference is not 'rational' at all (Popper, 1959), as we shall see below; whether induction can be justified at all has

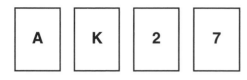

Figure 13.1   *The four cards in the abstract version of Wason's selection task.*

been a fundamental issue in epistemology and the philosophy of science for at least two and a half centuries (e.g. Hume, 1739/1986; Howson, 2000). Deep philosophical issues are again moving to the fore, but in this chapter we shall focus instead on the empirical methods that cognitive scientists have used to study human reasoning.

The structure of this chapter is as follows. First, we describe Wason's initial research into reasoning that threw human rationality into question, and started modern reasoning research. We then describe in turn five approaches to explaining reasoning data, using mental rules, mental models, biases, domain-specific theories and probability. We then turn to consider a parallel stream of research on inductive reasoning, before closing with remarks on future challenges for the field.

THE PSYCHOLOGY OF REASONING:
EXPERIMENTAL BEGINNINGS

The usual scattering of precursors aside, the programme of experimental research in the human reasoning processes, with which we are concerned in this chapter, was initiated in the 1960s by Wason. His experimental work was astonishingly innovative, fruitful and broad (see, e.g., the essays in Newstead & Evans, 1995). We focus here on his most celebrated experimental task, the selection task (Wason, 1966, 1968), which has remained probably the most intensively studied task in the field.

In the selection task, people must assess whether some evidence is relevant to the truth or falsity of a conditional rule of the form *if p then q*, where by convention '*p*' stands for the antecedent clause of the conditional and '*q*' for the consequent clause. In the standard abstract version of the task, the rule concerns cards, which have a number on one side and a letter on the other. A typical rule is *if there is a vowel on one side (p), then there is an even number on the other side (q)*. Four cards are placed before the participant, so that just one side is visible; the visible faces show an 'A' (*p* card), a 'K' (*not-p* card), a '2' (*q* card) and a '7' (*not-q* card) (see Figure 13.1). Participants then select those cards they must turn over to determine whether the rule is true or false. Typical results are: *p* and *q* cards (46%), *p*

card only (33%), *p*, *q* and *not-q* cards (7%), *p* and *not-q* cards (4%) (Johnson-Laird & Wason, 1970a).

The task participants confront is analogous to a central problem of experimental science: the problem of which experiment to perform. The scientist has a hypothesis (or a set of hypotheses) that must be assessed (for the participant, the hypothesis is the conditional rule) and must choose which experiment (card) will be likely to provide data (i.e. what is on the reverse of the card) that bears on the truth of the hypothesis.

The selection task has traditionally been viewed as a deductive task. This is because psychologists of reasoning have tacitly accepted Popper's hypothetico-deductive philosophy of science as an appropriate normative standard, against which people's performance can be judged. Popper (1959/1935) assumes that evidence can falsify but not confirm scientific theories. Falsification occurs when predictions that follow deductively from the theory do not accord with observation. This leads to a recommendation for the choice of experiments: to only conduct experiments that have the potential to falsify the hypothesis under test.

Applying the hypothetico-deductive account to the selection task, the recommendation is that participants should only turn cards that are potentially logically incompatible with the conditional rule. When viewed in these terms, the selection task has a deductive component, in that the participant must deduce which cards would be logically incompatible with the conditional rule. According to the rendition of the conditional as material implication (which is standard in elementary logic: see Haack, 1978), the only observation that is incompatible with the conditional rule *if p then q* is a card with *p* on one side and *not-q* on the other. Hence the participant should select only cards that could potentially yield such an instance. That is, they should turn the *p* card, since it might have a *not-q* on the back, and the *not-q* card, since it might have a *p* on the back.

These selections are rarely observed in the experimental results outlined above. Participants typically select cards that could *confirm* the rule, i.e. the *p* and *q* cards. However, according to falsificationism, the choice of the *q* card is irrational, and is an example of so-called 'confirmation bias' (Evans & Lynch, 1973; Wason & Johnson-Laird, 1972). The rejection of confirmation as a rational strategy follows directly from the hypothetico-deductive perspective.

The dissonance between this normative standard and observed behaviour appears to cast human rationality into severe doubt (e.g. Cohen, 1981; Stein, 1996; Stich, 1985, 1990; Sutherland, 1992). Moreover, a range of other experimental tasks studied by Wason and his co-workers (see Newstead & Evans, 1995, for a review) appeared to suggest that human reasoning is consistently faulty.

There are, though, circumstances under which it appears that 'logical' behaviour does occur. These are apparent effects of content on what is assumed to be logical reasoning performance, i.e. effects of content on reasoning where content is typically presumed to be irrelevant. But as we shall see, this interpretation is not uncontroversial.

Content effects first came to prominence when it was discovered that logic-like performance was observed when real-world content was used. People seemed to make more logical, *p* and *not-q* card selections for rules like (Wason & Johnson-Laird, 1972; Wason & Shapiro, 1971):

(1) If Johnny travels to Manchester, he takes the train.
(2) If you use a second class stamp, you must leave the envelope unsealed.

However, this seems at odds with the idea that people use *formal* logic that applies independent of content, i.e. it applies regardless of what the symbols mean. Moreover, not all contents facilitate the logical response. Rules like (1) only sometimes lead to logical responses whereas rules like (2) and (3) reliably produce logic-like performance (Griggs & Cox, 1982):

(3) If you are drinking beer, you must be over 21 years of age.

Moreover, the reason why rules like (2) and (3) reliably facilitate reasoning, but (1) does not, appears to have little to do with logic.

Rules like (2) and (3) are 'prescriptions' for how people should and should not behave, they are not descriptions of the world or of how someone behaves in the world. Although finding out that Johnny has travelled to Manchester by car may question the truth of (1), finding someone who is drinking beer underage does not question the truth of (3). (3) is in force regardless of the number of people found to be violating it. (1) is called an 'indicative' conditional, whereas (2) and (3) are 'deontic' conditionals. Only these deontic conditionals appear to reliably produce logic-like performance (Manktelow & Over, 1987). However, this is only because the task is no longer one for which standard logic provides the solution.

Put in these terms, the term 'content effects' is misleading. What is really driving 'logical' or 'non-logical' reasoning performance is a difference in the logical *form* of the conditionals being reasoned about: whether they are standard indicative or deontic conditionals. We shall discuss a related viewpoint below, in relation to probabilistic views of reasoning, where it is argued that neither of these problems involves logical deductive reasoning.

RULE-BASED THEORIES

When we attempt to describe how things should be done, we often specify sets of rules that must be obeyed. The core of the rule-based approach to reasoning is that the cognitive system uses the same general approach: reasoning is governed by sets of rules that specify which inferences are allowed and which are not. The idea that rules are central to thought goes far beyond the psychology of reasoning. It is fundamental, for example, to many of the most influential computational architectures for the cognitive system (e.g. Anderson, 1983, 1993; Newell, 1991), as well as being central to generative theories of grammar (e.g. Chomsky, 1965; Marcus, 2001) that dominate linguistics.

The idea of a 'rule' is one of the most central, if controversial, explanatory notions in cognitive science (Hahn & Chater, 1998; Sloman, 1996). To the degree that inferences depend only on form, then it seems appropriate to hypothesize that the relevant rules are logical rules: this approach is known as *mental logic*. To the degree that inferences appear to depend on content, though, such as in the 'content' effects that we have described in Wason's selection task, a different approach seems required: an approach that builds in rules that convey domain-specific knowledge. We begin by outlining the mental logic viewpoint.

Mental logic

The idea that human reasoning involves the application of logical rules has a long history in philosophy. The philosopher and logician Boole (1854) most clearly articulated the approach in his '*An Investigation of the Laws of Thought*', in which he both made important technical developments in logic and, at the same time, argued that logic may be part of the machinery of the mind. Piaget (Inhelder & Piaget, 1958) assumed that cognitive development could be viewed in terms of successive stages of increasingly sophisticated internal logical machinery.

Recent research in this tradition (Braine, 1978; Braine, Reiser, & Rumain, 1984; Henle, 1962; Rips, 1983, 1994; and the collection by Braine & O'Brien, 1998) has attempted to develop specific psychological proposals that capture empirical data on human reasoning. These proposals typically have two parts. First, they must specify the particular inferential rules to which reasoners are presumed to have access. Second, they appeal to the distinction between a logic and the control procedure that decides which logical rules to apply and when. Normally a person makes these decisions; for example, in constructing a proof, it is up to the mathematician. Applied in one order, a proof may be shorter and more elegant than when the rules are applied in another order. A computational model of human reasoning must also model this flow of control. These control procedures do not have to be as rigid as the logical rules themselves.

They might include *heuristics*, i.e. rules of thumb that often work, that suggest applying certain rules at certain stages of a proof.

These distinctions provide mental logic theories with more room for manoeuvre in explaining people's reasoning behaviour. So, in the Wason selection task, people try to apply logical inference rules to the card sides that they can see to predict what logically should be on the other, unseen side. If people possessed the logical inference rules *modus ponens* (MP: *if p, then q, p, therefore q*) and *modus tollens* (MT: *if p, then q, not-q, therefore not-p*), then they would turn the *p* card (A) expecting to see a *q* (2) by MP, and they would turn the *not-q* card (7) expecting to see a *not-p* (K) by MT. However, if people do not possess the MT rule, then they would only select the *p* card, as do about 33% of participants. People often interpret conditionals as 'bi-conditionals'. For example, they may perhaps interpret the rule *if you have the keys you can drive a car* as also entailing the truth of:

(4)   If you drive a car then you must have the keys.

The logical rules MP and MT then can also be applied to this conditional. This amounts to testing two rules: *if p then q* and *if q then p*. With only the MP rule available, this means that participants will now select the *p* and the *q* cards, as do about 46% of participants. Consequently, abstract rule theories would appear to be able to explain the main pattern of responses in the selection task.

Abstract rule theories appear to be less able to deal with content effects and everyday reasoning. However, this is not necessarily the case. Logicians have formulated abstract rule theories that deal with the 'modal' terms, e.g. *must*, that feature in deontic conditionals (Blackburn, de Rijke, & Venema, 2001). Thus there is no reason to assume that a mental modal logic cannot be formulated.

But scaling up to deal with everyday inference, on the other hand, appears more problematic because it seems to rely on an ability to draw inferences using large amounts of world knowledge stored in long-term memory. Logically this means that very large numbers of premises may be involved. However, algorithms for reasoning with logic are typically unable to cope with large numbers of premises: as the number of premises increases, the computational cost in terms of number of operations performed increases astronomically. Abstract rule theories avoid these problems by suggesting that everyday inference is really a form of 'inductive' inference, to do with changing one's beliefs about the world, rather than 'deductive' inference, which is dealt with by logic.

MENTAL MODELS

A different viewpoint on content effects, and reasoning in general, arises from the mental models

theory of reasoning, developed by Johnson-Laird (1983). Working closely with Wason, Johnson-Laird's early work built on the Gestalt problem-solving literature (Wertheimer, 1959), explaining patterns of performance on the selection task in terms of various levels of insight (Wason & Johnson-Laird, 1972; see also Johnson-Laird & Wason, 1970a, 1970b). People were capable of reasoning logically but required insight into the fact that logic applied to the task. This pattern of explanation also seemed to account for some new and surprising results that using certain contentful materials in the selection task appeared to cause people to switch to apparently logically correct performance (Johnson-Laird, Legrenzi, & Legrenzi, 1972; Wason & Shapiro, 1971). So, for example, using rules such as 'If I travel to Manchester, I take the train', and cards representing train journeys with destination and mode of transport on either side, seemed to facilitate selection of the logical *p* (Manchester) and *not-q* (car) cards. According to insight models, contentful materials improved insight into the relevance of logic to the task. Thus, it appeared that perhaps people are rational after all – but this rationality is somehow suppressed when reasoning about unnatural, abstract materials. However, the finding that content affects reasoning appears to fundamentally undercut 'formal' views of reasoning, because the logical *form* appears to be the same, independent of the change of content.

Mental models: the theory

During the late 1970s, Johnson-Laird began to develop a radically new theoretical perspective on reasoning, culminating in his celebrated book *Mental Models* (Johnson-Laird, 1983). In mental models theory, rationality does have a central place: specifically, standard deductive logic gives the *competence* theory for reasoning, specifying which inferences are valid and which are not. Moreover, the reasoning system is viewed as adapted to drawing valid inferences, at least in principle. What is distinctive about the mental models approach is that reasoning is assumed to involve not the direct application of logical rules in the mind, as had been assumed by Piaget (e.g. Inhelder & Piaget, 1958) and mental logic theorists (e.g. Braine, 1978; Rips, 1983, 1994), but by creating 'models' of the circumstances described in the premises. Reasoning involves constructing such models, one at a time, reading off conclusions that appear to hold in a model, and then searching for 'counterexample' models and checking whether the conclusion also follows in these models. If a counterexample model is not found, then the conclusion is assumed to be valid (this procedure follows the 'negation as failure' pattern used in logic programming in computer science: Clark, 1978). Mental model theory assumes that errors arise in practice because this process goes awry, most notably when people fail to construct relevant counterexample models.

There are constraints on the states of affairs that mental models can represent, which are not captured by traditional 'propositional' ways of representing information. This means that some sets of statements cannot be represented by a single mental model, but rather by a set of mental models. According to mental models theory, the number of models that must be entertained in order to make a valid inference is a key determinant of reasoning difficulty. To see how the theory works, we consider the difference between two apparently similar syllogisms. First, we consider the syllogism:

Some A's are B's
All B's are C's
———————————
∴ Some A's are C's

which can be represented by the mental model:

```
A    [B]    C
     [B]    C
...
```

Here, rows correspond to objects: an object corresponding to the second line of the mental model has properties A, B and C. Square brackets indicate that the item is exhaustively represented in the mental model. Hence in the above mental model there are no additional B's that are not represented in the model, but there might be additional A's or C's. The fact that there may be additional items not explicitly represented in the model is indicated by the '...' symbol below the model. (This notation is informally described in more detail in Johnson-Laird & Byrne, 1991.) A single model suffices to represent the premises above, so that the reasoner can draw a conclusion simply by reading off that 'Some A's are C's'. Because only a single model need be considered, mental models theory predicts that this is an easy syllogism, which indeed is confirmed empirically.

By contrast, consider the syllogism:

Some B's are A's
No B's are C's
———————————
∴ Some A's are not C's

which is compatible with three different models:

```
A [B]        A [B]          A [B]
A [B]        A [B]          A [B]
   [C]       A    [C]       A    [C]
   [C]          [C]         A    [C]
...          ...            ...
```

The crucial difference between the first and the second model is that in the second model there are A's that are also C's, whereas this is not the case in the first model. If a person constructs only the first model, then they are likely to conclude that No A's are C's – and indeed, this is a frequently produced conclusion (e.g. Johnson-Laird & Byrne, 1991). To realize that this conclusion does not follow requires that the person also consider the second model. The second model may erroneously lead to the conclusion that Some C's are not A's. However, this is ruled out by the third model, where All the C's are A's. All these models are consistent with the premises. The correct conclusion, that Some A's are not C's, holds in all models. Hence, reaching this conclusion should be substantially more difficult than in the one-model syllogism above, and this is observed experimentally. Quite generally, the number of models associated with representing a syllogism is a good predictor of syllogism difficulty. This is an advantage of mental models theory over the competing theory, mental logic, according to which reasoning involves the application of logical rules (Braine, 1978; Rips, 1983, 1994). The two syllogisms above are associated with very similar logical proofs and hence mental logic does not predict the difference in difficulty that mental models captures.

Explanatory breadth

The mental models theory has been very influential, with many researchers applying and extending the theory to many different domains of reasoning.[1] Across these domains, the number of mental models required to solve a reasoning problem is used to provide a measure of the difficulty of reasoning problems, and reasoning errors are predicted on the assumption that people do not always correctly entertain all models. Aside from syllogistic reasoning (Johnson-Laird & Bara, 1984; Johnson-Laird & Byrne, 1989; Johnson-Laird & Steedman, 1978), mental models theory has been applied to reasoning with multiply quantified statements (Johnson-Laird, Byrne, & Tabossi, 1990), meta-logical reasoning about truth and falsity (Johnson-Laird, & Byrne, 1990), modal reasoning (Johnson-Laird & Byrne, 1992; Bell & Johnson-Laird, 1998), counterfactual reasoning (Byrne & Tasso, 1999; Byrne, Segura, Culhane, Tasso, & Berrocal, 2000), spatial reasoning (Byrne & Johnson-Laird, 1989; Mani & Johnson-Laird, 1982), temporal reasoning (Schaeken, Johnson-Laird, & d'Ydewalle, 1996), propositional reasoning (Johnson-Laird, Byrne, & Schaeken, 1992, 1995), conditional reasoning (Byrne, 1989), the selection task (Johnson-Laird & Byrne, 1991), and to a limited class of reasoning about probability (Johnson-Laird, Legrenzi, Girotto, Legrenzi, & Caverni, 1999; Johnson-Laird & Savary, 1996). The extension to probabilistic reasoning is particularly important because a variety of probabilistic effects have been observed in, for example, conditional inference (Stevenson & Over, 1995, but see Byrne, Espino, & Santamaria, 1999).

Aside from its explanatory breadth in the area of human reasoning, a further attractive feature of the mental models account of reasoning is that it can be applied in other areas of cognition. Most notably it has been applied to theories of language understanding; constructing mental models is assumed to be an intrinsic part of normal language processing, rather than part of a separate 'reasoning system'. The notion that we reason by constructing concrete internal representations of situations making the premises true also has considerable introspective and intuitive plausibility. This plausibility is strengthened by recent work carried out by Stenning (Stenning & Oaksford, 1993; Stenning & Oberlander, 1995; Stenning & Yule, 1997), showing an equivalence between the mental models view of syllogistic reasoning and a mode of 'graphical' reasoning using Euler circles. Such graphical reasoning might be part of a general visual or imagistic reasoning capacity.

Effects of content on reasoning performance might appear problematic for the mental models view, to the degree that it is based on logic, because logical inference is independent of the content of the materials being reasoned about. However, research at around this time indicated that content effects in Wason's selection task were specific to particular kinds of content (Cheng & Holyoak, 1985). The contents that seemed to produce logical performance involved 'deontic regulations' concerning what preconditions one is obliged to satisfy to perform some action, for example 'if you want to enter the country you must be inoculated against cholera'. As Manktelow and Over (1987) pointed out, this move to deontic regulations changes the logical structure of the task, as discussed above. Deontic regulations cannot be falsified, for example it makes no sense to argue that someone attempting to enter the country without an inoculation falsifies the regulation that he should be inoculated. Such an individual *violates* the law but does not *falsify* it.[2] Consequently, performance is not 'facilitated' from an initially irrational baseline by the use of these materials. Rather the whole problem confronting participants has changed from a problem in inductive inference to a problem of how to enforce regulations. Johnson-Laird and Byrne (1992) argue that this change in the problem structure can readily be explained by mental models theory and consequently so-called content effects can be explained within this framework (although this is disputed by Manktelow & Over, 1992).

Recent developments

Perhaps the most distinctive feature of mental models theory is the claim that people search for counterexamples. However, recent work in this tradition seems to show that although people may be able to construct such alternative interpretations, they tend not to do so spontaneously (Bucciarelli & Johnson-Laird, 1999; Evans, Handley, Harper, & Johnson-Laird, 1999; Newstead, Handly, & Buck, 1999). That is, in the main the experimental results are consistent with people only constructing a single model from which a conclusion is read off. This possibility has always been important in mental models theory in explaining apparent errors in reasoning: if more than one model is required to reach the valid conclusion, people may balk and simply state a conclusion that is true in their initial model. However, this strategy places a heavy explanatory burden on the processes by which initial models are constructed. The way this is achieved has not changed much between the original formulations of mental models theory (e.g. Johnson-Laird & Steedman, 1978) and more recent computer programs for syllogistic reasoning (Johnson-Laird, 1992). The surface form of each premise is parsed into its mental model representation and then the two models are combined. This process of interpretation makes no reference to prior beliefs in long-term memory.

In their work on belief bias effects, where people tend to endorse erroneous but believable conclusions, Klauer, Musch, and Naumer (2000) have, however, argued that people consider just one mental model of the premises, and that beliefs can bias the process of model construction rather than affecting the search for alternative models (see also Newstead & Evans, 1993; Newstead, Pollard, & Evans, 1993). This position is also consistent with Evans, Handley, Harper, and Johnson-Laird's (1999) conclusions about how people draw syllogistic arguments (see also Evans & Over, 1996a). That is, prior beliefs can be expected to have a strong influence on the processes of comprehension and hence of initial model construction. As we observed above, according to recent research, it is these processes that appear to bear the main explanatory burden in mental models theory. However, advocates of mental models theory have concentrated on developing the core of mental model theory per se, rather than spelling out the mechanisms operating in language comprehension (Schroyens, Schaeken, Fias, & d'Ydewalle, 2000). Consequently the future for mental models would appear to be in the direction of outlining how prior beliefs about the world influence how initial models are constructed.

It could be argued that although this must be the case for contentful materials used in belief bias experiments, prior beliefs will play no role in interpreting the abstract materials used in the majority of reasoning experiments. There are two points to make. First, as with any theory of reasoning, mental models is not intended to be a theory of abstract laboratory tasks but of everyday human inference about the real world (Chater & Oaksford, 1993; Oaksford & Chater, 1993, 1995a). Thus any theory of reasoning must cope with content and prior knowledge. Second, even when abstract materials are used, people use their prior knowledge to interpret the claims that are made. For example, the work of Schroyens et al. (2000) on the mental models approach to conditional inference has shown that, 'even in the most abstract contexts probabilistic, knowledge-based processes are called upon'. They showed that the probability of counterexamples using letters and numbers was influenced by prior knowledge of set-sizes (see also Oaksford & Stenning, 1992; Oaksford & Chater, 1994).

In summary, it is becoming increasingly clear in research carried out in the mental models framework that the influence of prior knowledge on initial model construction is a key issue.

HEURISTICS, BIASES AND DUAL PROCESS THEORIES

A different viewpoint has been developed by Evans and his collaborators. In the selection task, for example, Evans has pointed out that participants may not be reasoning at all. In an ingenious experiment he introduced what has become known as the Evans' Negations Paradigm, where the task rules have negations systematically inserted into the antecedent and consequent producing three more rule forms: if *p* then *not-q*; if *not-p* then *q*; if *not-p* then *not-q* (Evans, 1972; Evans & Lynch, 1973). Evans argued that people could just be matching the items named in the rule rather than reasoning. If this were the case, then participants should continue to select the *p* and the *q* cards even for the rules containing negations. He therefore argued that people were prone to a matching bias in this task and were not reasoning at all (Evans & Lynch, 1973; see also Evans, 1998; Evans, Legrenzi, & Girotto, 1999).

Evans aims to explain these phenomena by postulating various relevance heuristics that the reasoning system follows (e.g. Evans, 1983, 1984, 1989, 1991). One such heuristic comes from an account of language processing (Wason, 1965) which suggests that the topic of a negated constituent is still that constituent, so the topic of the sentence 'The train is not late' is still the lateness of trains (this is called the *not*-heuristic). That is, this is still the relevant information to which the reasoner should attend. Despite these motivations, these heuristics are tied quite closely to the empirical data, and hence the explanation is quite direct, rather than arising from an overarching theory. Evans and colleagues have, however, also employed Johnson-Laird's mental

models theory as an explanatory framework, especially in the area of conditional inference (e.g. Evans, 1993; Evans, Clibbens, & Rood, 1995; Evans & Handley, 1999). They have also stressed a 'two process' view of human deductive reasoning: one, analytic, process is based on logic and may be implemented via mental models; the other, more dominant, process concerns the heuristics for linguistic interpretation, as in the example we have sketched above. The overarching goal of these heuristics is to direct attention to the most relevant information, which connects Evans' work to recent work in Europe by Sperber and colleagues (Sperber, Cara, & Girotto, 1995) and to probabilistic approaches to reasoning, described below (Oaksford & Chater, 1994, 1995b).

Two kinds of reasoning and rationality

Evans' account suggests that normative theories of good reasoning, such as logic and probability theory, may not play a major role in psychological accounts, whereas Johnson-Laird assumes that logic provides at least a competence theory for inference. Indeed, Evans and his collaborators have recently distinguished two notions of rationality (Evans & Over, 1996a, 1997; Evans, Over, & Manktelow, 1994):

Rationality$_1$: Thinking, speaking, reasoning, making a decision, or acting in a way that is generally reliable and efficient for achieving one's goals.

Rationality$_2$: Thinking, speaking, reasoning, making a decision, or acting when one has a reason for what one does sanctioned by a normative theory. (Evans & Over, 1997: 2)

They argue that 'people are largely rational in the sense of achieving their goals (rationality$_1$) but have only a limited ability to reason or act for good reasons sanctioned by a normative theory (rationality$_2$)' (Evans & Over, 1997: 1). If this is right, then achieving one's goals can be achieved without in any sense following a formal normative theory. This viewpoint fundamentally challenges the core assumption in the psychology of reasoning that we mentioned above: that human reasoning performance should be compared against the dictates of theories such as logic and probability. But it leaves a crucial question unanswered: why is human reasoning so successful in everyday life? After all, human intelligence vastly exceeds that of any artificial computer system, and generally deals effectively with an immensely complex and partially understood physical and social environment. If human reasoning is somehow tied to normative standards, then the justification of those standards as providing methods of good reasoning carries over to explain why human reasoning succeeds. But if this tie is broken, then the remarkable effectiveness of human reasoning remains unexplained.

Evans' work provides a bridge between approaches that concentrate on analytic reasoning and those that concentrate mainly on how people achieve their goals (see below). Evans assumes that the analytic component is based on mental models, and much of his work is in this framework. However, Evans, in collaboration with Over, has also concentrated his efforts on understanding human reasoning behaviour as resulting from processes adapted to achieving people's goals in the environment (Evans & Over, 1996a), i.e. from a rationality₁ perspective. This has involved a two-pronged approach. First, as we saw above, certain heuristics are suggested that are motivated by the pragmatic goals of successful communication, e.g. the *not*-heuristic that focuses attention on named items regardless of the negation because they are still the topic of the discourse. Such heuristics are influenced by prior knowledge. For example, assumed knowledge of the purpose of the utterance, 'the train is not late', can completely alter its topic. Said ironically to a fellow traveller on the platform, the topic is still the lateness of trains, but said urgently to the ticket seller, the topic is the train being on time. The interpretation of communicative speech depends crucially on prior knowledge.

Newstead has suggested that errors may occur in reasoning because people take account of these pragmatic communicative factors (Newstead, 1989, 1995) and prior knowledge (Newstead & Evans, 1993; Newstead et al., 1993). However, the evidence for pragmatic influences seem equivocal. Some data support the view (Newstead, 1989) while other data seem to show less influence (Newstead, 1995). Newstead's work on the belief bias effect (briefly discussed above) also supports the view that people only construct one model (Newstead & Evans, 1993; Newstead et al., 1993). More recently, Newstead, Handley, and Buck (1999) have also shown that there is little evidence that people search for alternative models in syllogistic reasoning (but see Bucciarelli & Johnson-Laird, 1999). This finding again suggests that the main explanatory burden lies with the processes that construct initial models and not on the search for counterexamples.

Individual differences and dual processes

A recent development that bears directly on the issue of whether more than one notion of rationality may be required is work looking at individual differences in reasoning. Until the work of Stanovich and West (1998a, 1998b, 2000; Stanovich, 1999), little research on individual

differences in human reasoning had been carried out. One very striking result is that some people do reason logically some of the time and they tend to have higher IQs. For example, there is a small group of participants who get the correct answer for both the deontic selection task and the indicative selection task and they have higher IQs (as measured by the scholastic aptitude test, or SAT, scores). Stanovich interprets these results as supporting a dual process view of reasoning (see also Sloman, 1996). Specifically, he proposes a distinction between what he calls System-1 and System-2 reasoning processes. System-1 processes are automatic, unconscious and based on implicitly acquired world knowledge. System-2 processes are controlled, analytic and based on explicitly acquired formal rules. This distinction is closely allied to Evans and Over's (1996a) rationality₁ and rationality₂ distinction that we have already discussed. The critical question is the balance of System-1 versus System-2 processes in human reasoning. Most contemporary theorizing is about System-2 processes; for example, both the mental logic and mental models theories are System-2 theories. However, Stanovich's results from the selection task suggest that at most 10% of University students (at an Ivy League North American university) are capable of engaging System-2 processes when reasoning. If, as this result suggests, most reasoning only invokes System-1 processes, then this is where reasoning researchers should be looking. Indeed, as we shall see, there are accounts that suggest that most human reasoning invokes only System-1 (see the section on *The Probabilistic Approach*, below).

DOMAIN-SPECIFIC THEORIES

Domain-specific theories (Cheng & Holyoak, 1985; Cosmides, 1989) have largely been inspired by the observation of content effects: the idea is that people must have domain-specific rules or schemas that underpin such effects, because logical rules are inevitably insensitive to context. The fact that reasoning seems to be better using deontic conditionals, which has been discussed above, is taken to suggest that people possess special-purpose reasoning mechanisms that apply only to particular domains.

There are two varieties of this type of theory. *Social contract theory* (Cosmides, 1989) and related approaches (e.g. Gigerenzer & Hug, 1992) take their lead from evolutionary psychology (e.g. Barkow, Cosmides, & Tooby, 1992). To be part of a social group requires conforming to rules of behaviour as in (4) and (5). According to social contract theory, because reasoning about social contracts was so important in early human evolution, an innate module has evolved to deal with this type of reasoning. One source of evidence for this view is the early emergence of correct deontic reasoning in children (Cummins, 1996; though see Chater & Oaksford, 1996).

According to *pragmatic reasoning schema theory* (Cheng & Holyoak, 1985; Cheng, Holyoak, Nisbett, & Oliver, 1986), people possess specific schemas for reasoning in many domains. These schemas contain rules that operate only in that particular domain. For example, rules (2) and (3) both have the same underlying form, they relate a *precondition* for performing an *action*: if someone is carrying out the action, then they must satisfy the precondition. A pragmatic reasoning schema for deontic reasoning contains rules concerning how to draw inferences about preconditions and actions. Such a schema is only triggered if the antecedent and consequent of a conditional can be interpreted as an action or as a precondition. Pragmatic reasoning schemas are typically viewed as learned rather than as innate.

Neither theory has much to say about the standard Wason selection task using indicative conditionals or about everyday reasoning. However, this may be because they have been derived from theoretical frameworks whose primary concerns lay elsewhere. Social contract theory (Cosmides, 1989) is seen mainly as a contribution to evolutionary psychology and researchers in this area are not primarily concerned with creating general theories of reasoning. Pragmatic reasoning schemas were originally a part of a more general theory of inductive reasoning. In the future these theories may be extended to deal with more of the phenomena in human reasoning than at present. However, one problem is that they do not adopt a theory of the inferences people should make, which is provided by logic in abstract rule theories and in mental models. Rather, since participants' responses and the experimenter's intuitions agree, these responses are assumed uncritically to be correct. However, they are not shown to be correct according to some theory of the domain, like logic, so it is difficult to see how they can be generalized to other contexts of reasoning.

THE PROBABILISTIC APPROACH

The second prong of Evans and Over's approach to reasoning is an appeal to Bayesian decision theory to characterize the way that prior knowledge can influence reasoning. Although such an approach was described in Evans and Over (1996b), they have not pursued it in detail for particular tasks (although see Green & Over 1997, 1998; Green, Over, & Pyne, 1997; Over & Green, 2001). But this kind of probabilistic approach has been explicitly formulated for a number of reasoning tasks, by two

TABLE 13.1 *The contingency table for a conditional rule, if p then q, where there is a dependency between the p and q that may admit exceptions (ε). $a = P(p)$, $b = P(q)$ and $\varepsilon = P(not\text{-}q|p)$.*

	q	not-q
p	$a\,(1-\varepsilon)$	$a\varepsilon$
not-p	$b - a\,(1-\varepsilon)$	$(1-b) - a\varepsilon$

of the present authors (Chater & Oaksford, 1999a, 1999b, 1999c, 2000; Oaksford & Chater, 1994, 1995a, 1995b, 1996, 1998a, 1998b, 1998c; Oaksford, Chater, Grainger, & Larkin, 1997; Oaksford, Chater, & Grainger, 1999; Oaksford, Chater, & Larkin, 2000).

The idea of the probabilistic approach to reasoning can be contrasted with the other two approaches we have reviewed by concentrating on how each accounts for human rationality. According to the mental models view, we are rational in principle but err in practice. That is, we have sound procedures for deductive reasoning, but the algorithms that we use to conduct such reasoning can fail to produce the right answers because of cognitive limitations such as working memory capacity. Such an approach seems hard to reconcile with two facts. First, these faulty algorithms can lead to error rates as high as 96% (in Wason's selection task) compared to the standard provided by formal logic. Second, our everyday rationality in guiding our thoughts and actions seems in general to be highly successful. How is this success to be understood if the reasoning system people use is prone to so much error? The distinction between rationality$_1$ and rationality$_2$ seems to resolve this problem. Our everyday rationality (rationality$_1$) does not depend on formal systems like logic and it is only our formal rationality (rationality$_2$) that is highly constrained and error-prone. This line of reasoning follows the old philosophical adage: if you reach a contradiction, draw a distinction. However, we then confront the problem of explaining the success of everyday inference. The problem here is that there are no obvious alternative explanations, aside from arguing that everyday rationality is also somehow based on normative formal reasoning principles, for which good justifications can be given. But this seems to bring us full circle.

One attempt to resolve this problem is by arguing that people's everyday reasoning can be understood from the perspective of probability theory and that people make errors in so-called deductive tasks because they generalize their everyday strategies to these laboratory tasks. This approach has been much influenced by Anderson's (1990, 1991) account of rational analysis. Any laboratory task will recruit some set of cognitive mechanisms that determine the participant's behaviour. But it is not obvious what problem these mechanisms are adapted to solving. This adaptive problem is not likely to be directly related to the problem given to the participant by the experimenter, precisely because adaptation is to the everyday world, not to laboratory tasks. In particular, this means that participants may fail with respect to the task that the experimenter thinks they have set. But this may be because this task is unnatural with respect to the participant's normal environment. Consequently people may assimilate the task that they are given to a more natural task, recruiting adaptively appropriate mechanisms that solve this, more natural, task successfully.

The psychology of deductive reasoning involves giving people problems that the experimenters conceive of as requiring logical inference. But people consistently respond in a non-logical way, thus calling human rationality into question (Stein, 1996; Stich, 1985, 1990). On the probabilistic view, everyday rationality is founded on uncertain rather than certain reasoning (Oaksford & Chater, 1991, 1998b) and so probability provides a better starting point for an account of human reasoning than logic. It also resolves the problem of explaining the success of everyday reasoning: it is successful to the extent that it approximates a probabilistic theory of the task. Second, we suggest that a probabilistic analysis of classic 'deductive' reasoning tasks provides an excellent empirical fit with observed performance. The upshot is that much of the experimental research in the 'psychology of deductive reasoning' does not engage people in deductive reasoning at all but rather engages strategies suitable for probabilistic reasoning. According to this viewpoint, the field of research appears to be crucially misnamed!

We illustrate the probabilistic approach in the three main tasks that have been the focus of research into human reasoning: conditional inference, Wason's selection task and syllogistic inference.

Conditional inference

Conditional inference is perhaps the simplest inference form investigated in the psychology of reasoning. It involves presenting participants with a conditional premise, *if p then q*, and then one of four categorical premises, *p*, *not-p*, *q*, or *not-q*. Logically, given the categorical premise *p* participants should draw the conclusion *q*, and given the categorical premise *not-q* they should draw the conclusion *not-p*. These are the logically valid inferences of modus ponens ('MP') and modus tollens ('MT') respectively. Moreover, given the categorical premise *not-p* participants should *not* draw the conclusion *not-q*, and given the categorical premise *q* they should *not* draw the conclusion *p*. These are the logical fallacies

of denying the antecedent ('DA') and affirming the consequent ('AC') respectively. So logically participants should endorse MP and MT in equal proportion and they should refuse to endorse DA or AC. However, they endorse MP significantly more than MT and they endorse DA and AC at levels significantly above zero.

Following a wide range of researchers in this area (Anderson, 1995; Chan & Chua, 1994; George, 1997; Liu, Lo, & Wu, 1996; Stevenson & Over, 1995), Oaksford, Chater, and Larkin (2000) proposed a model of conditional reasoning based on conditional probability. The greater the conditional probability of an inference, the more it should be endorsed. On their account the meaning of a conditional statement can be defined using a 2 by 2 contingency table as in Table 13.1 (see Oaksford & Chater, 1998c). This table represents a conditional rule, if *p* then *q*, where there is a dependence between the *p* and *q* that may admit exceptions (ε) and where *a* is the probability of the antecedent, $P(p)$, *b* is the probability of the consequent, $P(q)$, and ε is the probability of exceptions, i.e. the probability that *q* does not occur even though *p* has, $P(not\text{-}q|p)$. It is straightforward to then derive conditional probabilities for each inference. For example, the conditional probability associated with MP, i.e. $P(q|p) = 1 - \varepsilon$, only depends on the probability of exceptions. If there are few exceptions, the probability of drawing the MP inference will be high. However, the conditional probability associated with MT, i.e. $P(not\text{-}p|not\text{-}q) = \frac{1-b-a\varepsilon}{1-b}$, depends on the probability of the antecedent, $P(p)$, and the probability of the consequent, $P(q)$, as well the probability of exceptions. As long as there are exceptions ($\varepsilon > 0$) and the probability of the antecedent is greater than the probability of the consequent not occurring ($P[p] > 1 - P[q]$), then the probability of MT is less than MP ($P[not\text{-}p| not\text{-}q] < P[q|p]$). For example, if $P(p) = 0.5$, $P(q) = 0.8$ and $\varepsilon = 0.1$, then $P(q|p) = 0.9$ and $P(not\text{-}p|not\text{-}q) = 0.75$. This behaviour of the model accounts for the preference for MP over MT in the empirical data. In the model, conditional probabilities associated with DA and AC also depend on these parameters, and will typically be non-zero. Consequently the model also predicts that the fallacies should be endorsed to some degree.

Oaksford, Chater, and Larkin (2000) argue that this simple model can also account for other effects in conditional inference. For example, using Evans' Negations Paradigm (see above p. 305) in the conditional inference task leads to a bias towards negated conclusions. Oaksford and Stenning (1992; see also Oaksford & Chater, 1994) proposed that negations define higher probability categories than their affirmative counterparts; for example, the probability that an animal is not a frog is much higher than the probability that it is. Oaksford,

Chater, and Larkin (2000) show that according to their model the conditional probability of an inference increases with the probability of the conclusion. Consequently the observed bias towards negated conclusions may actually be a rational preference for high probability conclusions. If this is right, then when given rules containing high and low probability categories people should show a preference to draw conclusions that have a high probability analogous to negative conclusion bias. Oaksford, Chater, and Larkin (2000) confirmed this prediction in a series of three experiments (although see Schroyens & Schaeken, 2003, for a critique of this approach; and Oaksford & Chater, 2003, for a response).

Wason's selection task

The probabilistic approach was originally applied to Wason's selection task, which we introduced above (Oaksford & Chater, 1994, 1995b, 1996, 1998a, 1998b; Oaksford, Chater, Grainger, & Larkin, 1997; Oaksford, Chater, & Grainger, 1999). According to Oaksford and Chater's (1994) optimal data selection model, people select evidence (i.e. turn cards) to determine whether q depends on p, as in Table 13.1, or whether p and q are statistically independent (i.e. the cell values in Table 13.1 are simply the products of the marginal probabilities). The idea is that what participants are looking for, in the selection task, is evidence that gives the greatest probability of discriminating between these two possibilities. Initially participants are assumed to be maximally uncertain about which possibility is true, i.e. a prior probability of 0.5 is assigned to both the possibility of a dependence (the dependence hypothesis, H_D) and to the possibility of independence (the independence hypothesis, H_I). The participants' goal is to select evidence (turn cards) that would be expected to produce the greatest reduction in this uncertainty. This involves calculating the posterior probabilities of the hypotheses, H_D or H_I, being true given some evidence. These probabilities are calculated using Bayes' theorem, which requires information about prior probabilities ($P(H_D) = P(H_I) = 0.5$) and the likelihoods of evidence given a hypothesis, for example the probability of finding an A when turning the 2 card assuming H_D, $P(A|2, H_D)$. These likelihoods can be calculated directly from the contingency tables for each hypothesis: for H_D, Table 13.1, and for H_I, the independence model. With these values it is possible to calculate the reduction in uncertainty that can be expected by turning any of the four cards in the selection task. Oaksford and Chater (1994) observed that, assuming that the marginal probabilities $P(p)$ and $P(q)$ were small (their 'rarity

assumption'), the p and the q cards would be expected to provide the greatest reduction in uncertainty about which hypothesis was true. Consequently, the selection of cards that has been argued to demonstrate human irrationality may actually reflect a highly rational data selection strategy. Indeed this strategy may be optimal in an environment where most properties are rare; for example, most things are not black, not ravens, and not apples (but see Klauer, 1999, and Chater & Oaksford, 1999b, for a reply).

Oaksford and Chater (1994) argued that this model can account for most of the evidence on the selection task and defended the model against a variety of objections (Oaksford & Chater, 1996). For example, Evans and Over (Evans & Over, 1996b) criticized the notion of information used in the optimal data selection model and proposed their own probabilistic model. This model made some predictions that diverged from Oaksford and Chater's model and these have been experimentally tested by Oaksford et al. (1999). Although the results seem to support the optimal data selection model, there is still much room for further experimental work in this area. There has been interesting work exploring probabilistic effects in deontic selection tasks (Manktelow, Sutherland, & Over, 1995) and the standard selection task (Green et al., 1997; see also Green & Over, 1998). They have also extended this approach to what they refer to as 'causal selection tasks' (Green & Over, 1997, 1998; Over & Green, 2001). This is important because their work develops the link between research on causal estimation (e.g. Anderson & Sheu, 1995; Cheng, 1997) and research on the selection task.

Syllogistic reasoning

Chater and Oaksford (1999c) also apply the probabilistic approach to the more complex inferences involved in syllogistic reasoning, which we discussed above, in looking at mental models. In their probability heuristics model (PHM), they extend their probabilistic interpretation of conditionals to quantified claims, such as All, Some, None, and Some ... not. In Table 13.1, if there are no exceptions, then the probability of the consequent given the antecedent, ($P[q|p]$), is 1. The conditional and the universal quantifier 'All' have the same underlying logical form: $\forall x(P(x) \Rightarrow Q(x))$. Consequently Chater and Oaksford interpreted universal claims such as All P's are Q's as asserting that the probability of the predicate term (Q) given the subject term (P) is 1, i.e. $P(Q|P) = 1$. Probabilistic meanings for the other quantifiers are then easily defined: None, $P(Q|P) = 0$; Some, $P(Q|P) > 0$; Some ... not, $P(Q|P) < 1$. Given these probabilistic interpretations, it is possible to prove what conclusions follow probabilistically for all 64 syllogisms (i.e. which syllogisms are *p*-valid). Moreover, given these interpretations and again making the rarity assumption (see the above discussion of the selection task), the quantifiers can be ordered in terms of how informative they are: All > Some > None > Some … not. It turns out that a simple set of heuristics defined over the informativeness of the premises can successfully predict the *p*-valid conclusion if there is one. The most important of these heuristics is the *min*-heuristic, which states that the conclusion will have the form of the least informative premise. So, for example, a *p*-valid syllogism such as *All B are A, Some B are not C*, yields the conclusion *Some A are not C*. Note that the conclusion has the same form as the least informative premise. This simple heuristic captures the form of the conclusion for most *p*-valid syllogisms. Moreover, if over-generalized to the invalid syllogisms, the conclusions it suggests match the empirical data very well. Other heuristics determine the confidence that people have in their conclusions and the order of terms in the conclusion.[3]

Perhaps the most important feature of PHM is that it can generalize to syllogisms containing quantifiers such as Most and Few that have no straightforward logical interpretation. In terms of Table 13.1, the suggestion is that these terms are used instead of All when there are some (Most) or many (Few) exceptions. So the meaning of Most is: $1 - \Delta < P(Q|P) < 1$, and the meaning of Few is: $0 < P(Q|P) < \Delta$, where Δ is small. These interpretations lead to the following order of informativeness: All > Most > Few > Some > None > Some … not. Consequently, PHM uniquely makes predictions for the 144 syllogisms that are produced when Most and Few are combined with the standard logical quantifiers. Chater and Oaksford (1999c) show that (i) their heuristics pick out the *p*-valid conclusions for these new syllogisms, and (ii) they report experiments confirming the predictions of PHM when Most and Few are used in syllogistic arguments.

There has already been some work on syllogistic reasoning consistent with PHM. Newstead et al. (1999) found that the conclusions participants drew in their experiments were mainly as predicted by the *min*-heuristic, although they found little evidence of the search for counterexamples predicted by mental models theory for multiple model syllogisms. Evans, Handley, Harper, and Johnson-Laird (1999) also found evidence consistent with PHM. Indeed they found that an important novel distinction between different types of conclusions could be captured as well by the *min*-heuristic as by mental models theory. A conclusion is necessarily true if it is true in all models of the premises, a conclusion is possibly true if it is true in at least one model of the premises, and a conclusion is impossible if it is not true in any model of the premises. Evans et al. (1999) found that some possible conclusions were endorsed by as many participants as necessary conclusions, and that some were endorsed by a few participants as impossible conclusions. According to mental models theory, this happens because strong possible conclusions are those that are true in the initial model constructed but not in subsequent models. Moreover, weak possible conclusions are those that are only true in non-initial models.[4] Possible strong conclusions all conform to the *min*-heuristic, i.e. they either match the *min*-premise or are less informative than the *min*-premise. Possible weak conclusions all violate the *min*-heuristic (bar one), i.e. they have conclusions that are more informative than the *min*-premise. In sum, PHM appears to be gaining some empirical support.

Summary

The probabilistic approach contrasts with Evans and Over (1996a, 1996b) in that we see probability theory as a wholesale replacement for logic as a computational level theory of what inferences people should draw. According to Oaksford and Chater's viewpoint, logical inference is not a part of the basic architecture of cognition (this does not mean, of course, that people may learn a facility with logical reasoning, through extended training). Evans and Over, on the other hand, view some facility for logical thought, however limited, as part of our innate cognitive endowment. However, this difference is superficial compared to the major points of agreement. The one problem for all probabilistic approaches is that they are largely formulated at the computational level, i.e. they concern *what* gets computed, not *how*. However, if such an approach is to be viable at the algorithmic level, then there is a tacit assumption that the mind/brain is capable of working out how probable various events are.[5] This means that the probabilistic approach faces similar problems to mental models and Evans' relevance approach. The key to human reasoning appears to lie in how world knowledge provides only the most plausible model of some premises, or accesses only the most relevant information, or permits an assessment of the probabilities of events. This problem provides reasoning research, and the field of cognitive science as a whole, with an enormously difficult challenge, as we suggest in the final section of this chapter. First, though, we consider perhaps the most challenging area of reasoning research that has so far been extensively studied: inductive reasoning.

INDUCTIVE REASONING: LEARNING FROM EXAMPLES

Inductive reasoning, in its broadest sense, concerns inference from specific premises to general statements or to other non-logically related specific statements. So, for example, we might be given observations that robins have anatomical feature X, and be asked how likely it is that all birds have anatomical feature X. Or, more usually in experimental tasks, people are asked about the likelihood that eagles or sparrows also have that anatomical feature.

An immediate point about inductive inference is that, unlike the tasks that we have considered so far, everyone agrees that inductive inferences are not logically valid. It is clearly not a matter of logic that robins, eagles and sparrows have certain properties in common. On the other hand, it might be a matter of probability theory – and this possibility is taken up in some of the research described below. Indeed, the existence of a probabilistic viewpoint on non-inductive reasoning tasks, as we have discussed above, raises the possibility that a unified approach across these diverse reasoning tasks might be achievable. Nonetheless, as we shall see, historically, inductive reasoning has typically been studied separately from the reasoning tasks that we have described so far, by separate groups of researchers using different theoretical frameworks.

Inductive reasoning involves drawing conclusions that are probably true, given a set of premises. Inductive reasoning can thus be contrasted with deductive reasoning, in which the conclusion must necessarily follow from a set of premises. For example, the following two arguments (5) and (6) each have some degree of inductive strength.

Cows have sesamoid bones.   (5)
_____
All mammals have sesamoid bones.

Ferrets have sesamoid bones.   (6)
_____
All mammals have sesamoid bones.

Whereas all valid deductive arguments are perfectly strong, inductive arguments can differ in their perceived inductive strength. In the examples above, the conclusion in argument (5) may seem stronger, or more probable given the evidence, than the conclusion in (6).

Inductive reasoning is sometimes characterized as drawing inferences from specific statements to more general statements (as in arguments (5) and (6)), in contrast to deductive reasoning which would run from general statements to specifics. Although there is a grain of truth in this characterization, there is actually a broader variety of deductive as well as inductive arguments (Skyrms, 1977). For example, the following deductively valid argument (7) does not draw a more specific inference from general statements:

Gorillas are apes.   (7)
Apes are mammals.
_____
Gorillas are mammals.

Likewise it would be possible to draw inductive inferences that involve reasoning from one fairly specific statement to another, as in argument (8):

Ferrets have sesamoid bones.   (8)
_____
Squirrels have sesamoid bones.

Despite the probabilistic nature of induction, there is now a well-documented set of empirical regularities in this area of research. In what follows, we shall give an introduction to these empirical regularities, then describe theoretical accounts of inductive reasoning (see Heit, 2000, for a more extensive review).

Key results in inductive reasoning

One of the early experimental studies of inductive reasoning, by Rips (1975), looked at how people project properties of one category of animals to another. Subjects were told to assume that, on a small island, it has been discovered that all members of a particular species have a new type of contagious disease. Then subjects judged for various other species what proportion would also have the disease. For example, if all rabbits have this disease, what proportion of dogs have the disease? Rips used a variety of animal categories in the premise and conclusion roles. It was found that two factors consistently promoted inferences from a premise category to a conclusion category. First, similarity between premises and conclusions promoted strong inferences. For example, subjects made stronger inferences from rabbits to dogs than from rabbits to bears. Second, the typicality of the premise, with respect to its superordinate category, was critical in promoting inferences. The result was that more typical premise categories led to stronger inferences than atypical premise categories. For example, with the bird stimuli, having *bluejay* as a premise category led to stronger inferences overall compared to having *goose* as a premise category. Using multiple regression analyses, Rips found distinct contributions of premise–conclusion similarity and premise typicality. Interestingly, there was no evidence for a role of conclusion typicality. For example, all other things being equal, people would be as willing to draw a conclusion about a bluejay or about a goose, despite the difference in typicality of these two categories (see Osherson, Smith, Wilkie, Lopez, & Shafir, 1990, for further investigations of similarity and typicality effects).

The next major study of induction was by Nisbett, Krantz, Jepson, and Kunda (1983), who also asked subjects to draw inferences about items (animals, people and objects) found on a remote island. For example, subjects were told to imagine that one member of the Barratos tribe is observed to be obese, and they estimated the proportion of all members of this group that would be obese. Likewise, subjects were told that one sample of the substance 'floridium' was observed to conduct electricity, and they estimated the proportion of all members of this set that would conduct electricity. One key finding was that subjects were very sensitive to perceived variability of the conclusion category. For a variable category such as Barratos people (and their potential obesity), subjects were rather unwilling to make strong inferences about other Barratos, after just one case. But for a nonvariable category such as floridium samples, subjects were willing to generalize the observation of electrical conductance to most or all of the population. This result, that subjects are more willing to draw inferences about less variable conclusion categories, makes a striking contrast to the results of Rips (1975). Whereas Rips found that typicality of the conclusion did not affect inductive strength, Nisbett et al. showed that conclusion categories do matter, at least in terms of their variability.

The preceding results show how people reason based on a single premise. However, when people try to make an inference about some object or event, they are typically faced with a great deal of information. Rather than just one past case being available or relevant, in many realistic situations there will be an extensive set of cases or premises that could be relied on. What makes a set of premises seem strong, or useful for promoting inferences? One factor is numerosity. In their study involving inferences about people and objects on an island, Nisbett et al. (1983) systematically varied the given number of observations. For example, subjects were told that 1, 3 or 20 obese members of the Barratos group had been observed, and asked what proportion of all Barratos are obese. In general, inferences were stronger with increased sample size (see also Osherson et al., 1990).

Although sheer numerosity of cases does have some effect on induction, there is also substantial evidence that variability or diversity of cases affects inductive strength. Intuitively, repeating the same evidence, or highly similar pieces of evidence, again and again should not be much more convincing than just giving the evidence once. Consider the following arguments (adapted from Osherson et al., 1990):

Cows require vitamin K for the liver
to function.   (9)

Horses require vitamin K for the liver to function.

All mammals require vitamin K for the liver to function.

Cows require vitamin K for the liver
to function.   (10)

Ferrets require vitamin K for the liver to function.

All mammals require vitamin K for the liver to function.

Although both arguments seem to have some argument strength, most people find argument (10) to be stronger than argument (9), due to the greater diversity of premise information. Again, there is an interesting comparison to Nisbett et al. (1983), who found that variable conclusions led to weaker inductive inferences. In contrast, it has been found that diverse premise categories lead to stronger inductive inferences. Another fascinating aspect of the diversity effect is that it runs in the opposite direction to the typicality effect: whereas a typical premise category leads to a fairly strong inductive argument (5), an argument with two typical premise categories (9) is actually weaker than an argument with a typical premise and an atypical premise (10).

Effects of knowledge on inductive reasoning

Unlike deductive reasoning, where it should be possible to determine just from the form of an argument whether the conclusion must necessarily follow, inductive reasoning is uncertain by nature. Hence it should be rational to go beyond the information given, seeking other knowledge that could reduce this uncertainty and make inductive inferences more accurate. Indeed, all of the examples of inductive reasoning in this section rely on some use of world knowledge that is not explicitly stated in the inductive arguments, such as that cows and horses are more similar than are cows and ferrets. However, in other ways researchers have aimed to study the 'essence' of inductive reasoning by discouraging the use of outside knowledge. For example, Rips (1975) used fictional diseases that people would not have strong prior beliefs about, and Osherson et al. (1990) used 'blank' properties such as 'has sesamoid bones' which sounded somewhat biological but were fairly unfamiliar. These decisions by these researchers were helpful indeed in uncovering the various empirical regularities such as similarity, typicality and diversity effects.

Still other researchers have studied the role of knowledge in induction more directly. For example, Medin, Lynch, Coley, and Atran (1997) looked at inductive reasoning about categories of plants, by various kinds of tree experts, such as taxonomists and tree maintenance workers. Here the main interest was effects of similarity, for groups that differed in their notions of similarity. For example, in a sorting task, maintenance workers tended to organize tree species in terms of their shape or purpose for various landscaping tasks. Medin et al. devised questions on a test of inductive reasoning that pitted scientific matches against alternative, functional category structures. For example, two tree species might be distant in terms of the scientific taxonomy but they could both be useful for providing shade. It was found that taxonomists (not surprisingly) sorted trees on the basis of scientific taxonomy and likewise favoured inductive arguments between categories that were close in the scientific taxonomy. Maintenance workers seemed to favour a more functional category organization for both sorting and reasoning. In sum, the groups of experts generally showed the similarity effects that had been documented in other studies of induction, but their knowledge about trees mediated these similarity effects.

Other evidence for knowledge effects has highlighted the effects of the property that is being inferred. The Nisbett et al. (1983) study is a good illustration of how knowledge about the scope of a property affects inductive inference. As already reviewed, seeing that just one member of the Barratos group is obese does not seem to promote the inference that other people in this group will be obese. Obesity seems to be more of an individual characteristic rather than a group characteristic. On the other hand, Nisbett et al. found that people make stronger inferences for the same category but another property, skin colour. Here, seeing the skin colour of just one Barratos promotes inferences about other members of this group, on the assumption that members of the same ethnic group will likely have some shared physical characteristics. (See Goodman, 1955, for a further discussion of how properties differ in their tendency to promote induction.)

Although it might seem from the previous section that some properties have a wider scope for inference than others, the picture is actually more complicated. Depending on the categories in an inductive argument, a particular property may lead to strong inferences or weak inferences or something in between. Consider the following example, from Heit and Rubinstein (1994). For an anatomical property, such as 'has a liver with two chambers', people will make stronger inferences from chickens to hawks than from tigers to hawks. Because chickens and hawks are from the same biological category, and share many internal properties, people are quite willing to project a novel anatomical property from one bird to another. But since tigers and hawks differ in terms of many known internal biological properties, it seems less likely that a novel anatomical property will project from one to the other. However, now consider the behavioural property 'prefers to feed at night'. Heit and Rubinstein (1994) found that inferences for behavioural properties concerning feeding and predation were weaker between the categories *chicken* and *hawk* than between the categories *tiger* and *hawk* – the opposite of the result

for anatomical properties. Here, it seems that despite the major biological differences between tigers and hawks, people were influenced by the known similarities between these two animals in terms of predatory behaviour, thus making strong inferences about a novel behavioural property.

Theoretical accounts of inductive reasoning

So far, we have described several empirical regularities in inductive reasoning, including similarity effects, typicality effects, diversity effects, and effects based on knowledge about the property being inferred. Together, these results pose a challenge for psychological accounts of induction. Although there have been a number of proposals (see, in particular, Osherson et al., 1990, and Sloman, 1993), we shall focus on a model of inductive reasoning by Heit (1998) that has been applied to all of these results. Like Oaksford and Chater's model of deductive reasoning, this is a model derived from Bayesian statistics, influenced by Anderson's (1990, 1991) account of rational analysis.

According to the Bayesian model, evaluating an inductive argument is conceived of as learning about a property, in particular learning for which categories the property is true or false. For example, in argument (5) above, the goal would be to learn which animals have sesamoid bones and which animals do not. The model assumes that for a novel property such as in this example, people would rely on prior knowledge about familiar properties, to derive a set of hypotheses about what the novel property may be like. For example, people know some facts that are true of all mammals (including cows), but they also know some facts that are true of cows but not some other mammals. The question is: which of these known kinds of properties does the novel property, 'has sesamoid bones', resemble most? Is it an all-mammal property, or a cow-only property? What is crucial is that people assume that novel properties follow the same distribution as known properties. Because many known properties of cows are also true of other mammals, argument (5) regarding a novel property seems fairly strong.

The Bayesian model addresses many of the key results in inductive reasoning. For example, the model can predict similarity effects as in Rips (1975). Given that rabbits have some kind of disease, it seems more plausible to infer that dogs have the same disease rather than bears, because rabbits and dogs are more alike in terms of known properties than are rabbits and bears. The Bayesian model also addresses typicality effects, under the assumption that according to prior beliefs, atypical categories, such as *geese*, would have a number of idiosyncratic features. Hence a premise asserting a novel property about geese would suggest that this property is likewise idiosyncratic and not to be widely projected. In contrast, prior beliefs about typical categories, such as *bluejays*, would indicate that they have many properties in common with other categories, hence a novel property of a typical category should generalize well to other categories.

The Bayesian model also addresses diversity effects, with a rationale similar to that for typicality effects. An argument with two similar premise categories, such as cows and horses in (9), could bring to mind a lot of idiosyncratic properties that are true just of large farm animals. Therefore a novel property of cows and horses might seem idiosyncratic to farm animals, and not applicable to other mammals. In contrast, an argument with two diverse premise categories, such as cows and ferrets in (10), could not bring to mind familiar idiosyncratic properties that are true of just these two animals. Instead, the prior hypotheses would be derived from known properties that are true of all mammals or all animals. Hence a novel property of cows and ferrets should generalize fairly broadly.

To give a final illustration of the Bayesian approach, when reasoning about the anatomical and behavioural properties in Heit and Rubinstein (1994), people could draw on prior knowledge about different known properties for the two kinds of properties. Reasoning about anatomical properties could cause people to rely on prior knowledge about familiar anatomical properties. In contrast, when reasoning about a behavioural property such as 'prefers to feed at night', the prior hypotheses could be drawn from knowledge about familiar behavioural properties. These two different sources of prior knowledge would lead to different patterns of inductive inferences for the two kinds of properties.

To conclude, the Bayesian model does address a fairly broad set of phenomena (see Heit, 1998, 2000, for further applications, in greater detail). There are other models, such as those proposed by Osherson et al. (1990) and Sloman (1993), that can address many of the same results; however, we see a big advantage of the Bayesian model in that it derives from the same principles, probability theory and Anderson's (1990, 1991) rational analysis, as does Oaksford and Chater's model of deduction. Given that the same kind of model can address these two usually separate areas of reasoning research, perhaps it is not necessary after all to study deduction and induction in isolation from each other.

PROSPECTS FOR THE COGNITIVE
SCIENCE OF HUMAN REASONING

Despite the intensive research effort outlined above, human reasoning remains largely mysterious. While there is increased understanding of laboratory performance as we have discussed above, deep puzzles over the nature of everyday human reasoning processes remain. We suggest that three key issues may usefully frame the agenda for future research: (1) establishing the relation between reasoning and other cognitive processes; (2) developing formal theories that capture the full richness of everyday reasoning; and (3) explaining how such theories can be implemented in real time in the brain.

Reasoning and cognition

As we noted in the introduction to this chapter, from an abstract perspective, almost every aspect of cognition can be viewed as involving inference. Perception involves inferring the structure of the environment from perceptual input; motor control involves inferring appropriate motor commands from proprioceptive and perceptual input, together with demands of the motor task to be performed; learning from experience, in any domain, involves inferring general principles from specific examples; understanding a text or utterance typically requires inferences relating the linguistic input to an almost unlimited amount of general background knowledge. Is there a separate cognitive system for the kind of verbal *reasoning* that we have discussed in this chapter, or are the processes studied by reasoning researchers simply continuous with the whole of cognition? A key sub-question concerns the modularity of the cognitive system. If the cognitive system is non-modular, then reasoning would seem, of necessity, to be difficult to differentiate from other aspects of cognition. If the cognitive system is highly modular, then different principles may apply in different cognitive domains. Nonetheless, it might still turn out that even if modules are informationally sealed off from each other (e.g. Fodor, 1983; Pylyshyn, 1984), the inferential principles that they use might be the same; the same underlying principles and mechanisms might simply be re-used in different domains. Even if the mind is modular, it seems unlikely that there could be a module for *reasoning* in anything like the sense studied in psychology. This is because everyday reasoning (in contrast to some artificial laboratory tasks) requires engaging arbitrary world knowledge. Consequently, understanding reasoning would appear to be part of the broader project of understanding central cognitive processes and the knowledge they embody in full generality.

This is an alarming prospect for reasoning researchers because current formal research is unable to provide adequate tools for capturing even limited amounts of general knowledge, let alone reasoning with it effectively and in real time, as we shall discuss below. Reasoning researchers often attempt to seal off their theoretical accounts from the deep waters of general knowledge by assuming that these problems are solved by other processes (e.g. processes constraining how mental models are 'fleshed out' [Johnson-Laird & Byrne, 1991] or when particular premises can be used in inference [Politzer & Braine, 1991], what information is relevant [Evans, 1989; Sperber, Cara, & Girotto, 1995] or how certain probabilities are determined [Oaksford & Chater, 1994]). Whether or not this strategy is methodologically appropriate in the short term, substantial progress in understanding everyday reasoning will require theories that address, rather than duck, these crucial issues, i.e. that explicate, rather than presuppose, our judgements concerning what is plausible, probable or relevant. Moreover, as we have seen, the recent empirical work seems to strongly suggest that progress in understanding human reasoning even in the laboratory requires the issue of general knowledge to be addressed rather than ducked.

Formal theories of everyday reasoning

Explaining the cognitive processes involved in everyday reasoning requires developing a formal theory that can capture everyday inferences. Unfortunately, however, this is far from straightforward, because everyday inferences are *global*: whether a conclusion follows typically depends not just on a few circumscribed 'premises' but on arbitrarily large amounts of general world knowledge (see, e.g., Fodor, 1983; Oaksford & Chater, 1991, 1995a, 1998b). From a statement such as *While John was away, Peter changed all the locks in the house*, we can provisionally infer, for example, that Peter did not want John to be able to enter the house; that John possesses a key; that Peter and John have had a disagreement, and so on. But such inferences draw on background information, such as that the old key will not open the new lock, that locks secure doors, that houses can usually only be entered through doors, and a host of further information about the function of houses, the nature of human relationships, and the law concerning breaking and entering. Moreover, deploying each piece of information requires an inference that is just as complex as the original one. Thus, even to infer that John's key will not open the new lock requires background information concerning the way in which locks and keys are paired together, the convention that when locks are replaced they will not fit the old key, that John's key will not itself be changed when the locks are changed, that the match between lock and key is stable over time, and so on. This is what we call the 'fractal' character of everyday reasoning: just as, in geometry, each part of a fractal is as complex as the whole, each part of an everyday inference is as complex as the whole piece of reasoning.

How can such inferences be captured formally? Deductive logic is inappropriate, because everyday arguments are not deductively valid, but can be overturned when more information is learned.[6] The essential problem is that these methods fail to capture the global character of everyday inference successfully (Oaksford & Chater, 1991, 1992, 1993, 1995a, 1998b). In artificial intelligence, this has led to a switch to using probability theory, the calculus of *un*certain reasoning, to capture patterns of everyday inference (e.g. Pearl, 1988). This is an important advance, but only a beginning. Probabilistic inference can only be used effectively if it is possible to separate knowledge into discrete chunks – with a relatively sparse network of probabilistic dependences between the chunks. Unfortunately, this just does not seem to be possible for everyday knowledge. The large variety of labels for the current impasse (the 'frame' problem [McCarthy & Hayes, 1969; Pylyshyn, 1987], the 'world knowledge' problem or the problem of knowledge representation [Ginsberg, 1987], the problem of non-monotonic reasoning [Paris, 1994] and the criterion of completeness* [Oaksford & Chater, 1991, 1998b]) is testimony to its fundamental importance and profound difficulty. The problem of providing a formal calculus of everyday inference presents a huge intellectual challenge, not just in psychology, but in the study of logic, probability theory, artificial intelligence and philosophy.

Everyday reasoning and real-time neural computation

Suppose that a calculus that captured everyday knowledge and inference could be developed. If this calculus underlies thought, then it must be implemented (probably to an approximation) in real time in the human brain. Current calculi for reasoning, including standard and non-standard logics, probability theory, decision theory and game theory, are computationally intractable (Garey & Johnson, 1979; Paris, 1994). That is, as the amount of information with which they have to deal increases, the amount of computational resources (in memory and time) required to derive conclusions explodes very rapidly (or, in some cases, inferences are not computable at all, even given limitless time and memory). Typically, attempts to extend standard calculi to mimic everyday reasoning more effectively make problems of tractability *worse* (e.g. this is true of 'non-monotonic logics' developed in artificial intelligence). Somehow, a formal calculus of everyday reasoning must be developed that, instead, eases problems of tractability.

This piles difficulty upon difficulty for the problem of explaining human reasoning computationally. Nonetheless, there are interesting directions to explore. For example, modern 'graphical' approaches to probabilistic inference in artificial intelligence and statistics (e.g. Pearl, 1988) are very directly related to connectionist computation; and more generally, connectionist networks can be viewed as probabilistic inference machines (Chater, 1995; MacKay, 1992; McClelland, 1998). To the extent that the parallel, distributed style of computation in connectionist networks can be related to parallel, distributed computation in the brain, this suggests that the brain may be understood, in some sense, as directly implementing rational calculations. Nonetheless, there is presently little conception either of how such probabilistic models can capture the 'global' quality of everyday reasoning, or how these probabilistic calculations can be carried out in real time to support fluent and rapid inference, drawing on large amounts of general knowledge, in a brain consisting of notoriously slow and noisy neural components (Feldman & Ballard, 1982).

CONCLUSION

Early research in the psychology of reasoning appeared to bring human rationality into question – a conclusion that is both conceptually puzzling, and apparently at variance with the manifest practical effectiveness of human intelligence. Recent work has painted human rationality in a better light; for example, the probabilistic approach attempts to reconcile experimental data with human rationality – by allowing that the rational theory of the task is not specified a priori, but is part of an empirical scientific explanation. But the psychology of reasoning faces vast challenges, in developing theoretical accounts that are rich enough to capture the 'global' character of human everyday reasoning, and that can be implemented in real time in the human brain. This is probably a challenge not merely for the remainder of this century, but for the rest of the millennium.

NOTES

1 A useful source is the Mental Models website maintained by Ruth Byrne at Trinity College, Dublin (http://www2.tcd.ie/Psychology/Ruth_Byrne/mental_models/index.html).

2 There is potentially a question of truth or falsity regarding which norms are in force in a particular society or culture, e.g. what the law is in Britain concerning drinking ages. But this is a claim *about* the norm; there is no question of the norm *itself* being true or false.

3 In our example, the *min*-heuristic only dictates that the conclusion should be *Some ... not*, but this is consistent

with either *Some A are not C* or *Some C are not A*; however, only *Some A are not C* is *p*-valid.

4 This again shows that the main burden of explanation lies with the processes that construct initial models.

5 Of course, such information need not be represented as a number over which the probability calculus operates (e.g. it could be the activation level of a node of a neural network).

6 Technically, these inferences are non-monotonic, and extensions to logic to capture everyday inference, though numerous, have been uniformly unsuccessful: they just do not capture inferences that people routinely make, or they fall into paradox (Ginsberg, 1987; Hanks & McDermott, 1985; Oaksford & Chater, 1991).

REFERENCES

Anderson, J. R. (1983). *The architecture of cognition.* Cambridge, MA: Harvard University Press.

Anderson, J. R. (1990). *The adaptive character of thought.* Hillsdale, NJ: Erlbaum.

Anderson, J. R. (1991). Is human cognition adaptive? *Behavioral and Brain Sciences*, *14*, 471–517.

Anderson, J. R. (1993). *Rules of the mind.* Hillsdale, NJ: Erlbaum.

Anderson, J. R. (1995). *Cognitive psychology and its implications.* New York: W. H. Freeman.

Anderson, J. R., & Sheu, C.-F. (1995). Causal inferences as perceptual judgments. *Memory and Cognition*, *23*, 510–524.

Barkow, J., Cosmides, L., & Tooby, J. (1992). *The adapted mind: evolutionary psychology and the generation of culture.* New York: Oxford University Press.

Bell, V. A., & Johnson-Laird, P. N. (1998). A model theory of modal reasoning. *Cognitive Science*, *22*, 25–51.

Blackburn, P., de Rijke, M., & Venema, Y. (2001). *Modal logic.* Cambridge: Cambridge University Press.

Boole, G. (1854). *An investigation of the laws of thought.* London: Walton & Maberly.

Boolos, G., & Jeffrey, R. (1989). *Computability and logic* (3rd edn.). Cambridge: Cambridge University Press.

Braine, M. D. S. (1978). On the relation between the natural logic of reasoning and standard logic. *Psychological Review*, *85*, 1–21.

Braine, M. D. S., & O'Brien, D. P. (1998). *Mental logic.* Mahwah, NJ: Erlbaum.

Braine, M. D. S., Reiser, B. J., & Rumain, B. (1984). Some empirical evidence for a theory of natural propositional logic. In G. H. Bower (ed.), *The psychology of learning and motivation: advances in research and thinking* (Vol. 18, pp. 317–371). New York: Academic Press.

Bucciarelli, M., & Johnson-Laird, P. N. (1999). Strategies in syllogistic reasoning. *Cognitive Science*, *23*, 247–303.

Byrne, R. M. J. (1989). Suppressing valid inferences with conditionals. *Cognition*, *31*, 1–21.

Byrne, R. M. J., Espino, O., & Santamaria, C. (1999). Counterexamples and the suppression of inferences. *Journal of Memory and Language*, *40*, 347–373.

Byrne, R. M. J., & Johnson-Laird, P. N. (1989). Spatial reasoning. *Journal of Memory and Language, 28,* 564–575.

Byrne, R. M. J., Segura, S., Culhane, R., Tasso, A., & Berrocal, P. (2000). The temporality effect in counterfactual thinking about what might have been. *Memory and Cognition, 28,* 264–281.

Byrne, R. M. J., & Tasso, A. (1999). Deductive reasoning with factual, possible, and counterfactual conditionals. *Memory and Cognition, 27,* 726–740.

Chan, D., & Chua, F. (1994). Suppression of valid inferences: syntactic views, mental models, and relative salience. *Cognition, 53,* 217–238.

Chater, N. (1995). Neural networks: the new statistical models of mind. In J. P. Levy, D. Bairaktaris, J. A. Bullinaria, & P. Cairns (Eds.), *Connectionist models of memory and language* (pp. 207–227). London: UCL Press.

Chater, N., & Oaksford, M. (1993). Logicism, mental models and everyday reasoning: reply to Garnham. *Mind and Language, 8,* 72–89.

Chater, N., & Oaksford, M. (1996). Deontic reasoning, modules and innateness: a second look. *Mind and Language, 11,* 191–202.

Chater, N., & Oaksford, M. (1999a). Ten years of the rational analysis of cognition. *Trends in Cognitive Sciences, 3,* 57–65.

Chater, N., & Oaksford, M. (1999b). Information gain vs. decision-theoretic approaches to data selection: response to Klauer. *Psychological Review, 106,* 223–227.

Chater, N., & Oaksford, M. (1999c). The probability heuristics model of syllogistic reasoning. *Cognitive Psychology, 38,* 191–258.

Chater, N., & Oaksford, M. (2000). The rational analysis of mind and behaviour. *Synthese, 122,* 93–131.

Cheng, P. W. (1997). From covariation to causation: a causal power theory. *Psychological Review, 104,* 367–405.

Cheng, P. W., & Holyoak, K. J. (1985). Pragmatic reasoning schemas. *Cognitive Psychology, 17,* 391–416.

Cheng, P. W., Holyoak, K. J., Nisbett, R. E. & Oliver, L. M. (1986). Pragmatic versus syntactic approaches to training deductive reasoning. *Cognitive Psychology, 18,* 293–328.

Chomsky, N. (1965). *Aspects of the theory of syntax.* Cambridge, MA: MIT Press.

Clark, K. L. (1978). Negation as failure. In *Logic and databases* (pp. 293–322). New York: Plenum Press.

Cohen, L. J. (1981). Can human irrationality be experimentally demonstrated? *Behavioral and Brain Sciences, 4,* 317–370.

Connolly, C., Arkes, H. R., & Hammond, K. R. (2000). *Judgment and decision making: an interdisciplinary reader.* New York: Cambridge University Press.

Cosmides, L. (1989). The logic of social exchange: has natural selection shaped how humans reason? Studies with the Wason selection task. *Cognition, 31,* 187–276.

Cummins, D. D. (1996). Evidence for the innateness of deontic reasoning. *Mind and Language, 11,* 160–190.

Elster, J. (ed.) (1986). *Rational choice.* Oxford: Basil Blackwell.

Evans, J. St B. T. (1972). Interpretation and 'matching bias' in a reasoning task. *Quarterly Journal of Experimental Psychology, 24,* 193–199.

Evans, J. St B. T. (1983). Selective processes in reasoning. In J. St B. T. Evans (ed.), *Thinking and reasoning: psychological approaches.* London: Routledge & Kegan Paul.

Evans, J. St B. T. (1984). Heuristic and analytic processes in reasoning. *British Journal of Psychology, 75,* 451–468.

Evans, J. St B. T. (1989). *Bias in human reasoning: causes and consequences.* Hove, UK: Erlbaum.

Evans, J. St B. T. (1991). Theories of human reasoning: the fragmented state of the art. *Theory & Psychology, 1,* 83–105.

Evans, J. St B. T. (1993). The mental model theory of conditional reasoning: critical appraisal and revision. *Cognition, 48,* 1–20.

Evans, J. St B. T. (1998). Matching bias in conditional reasoning: do we understand it after 25 years? *Thinking and Reasoning, 4,* 45–82.

Evans, J. St B. T., Clibbens, J., & Rood, B. (1995). Bias in conditional inference: implications for mental models and mental logic. *Quarterly Journal of Experimental Psychology, 48A,* 644–670.

Evans, J. St B. T., & Handley, S. J. (1999). The role of negation in conditional inference. *Quarterly Journal of Experimental Psychology, 52A,* 739–770.

Evans, J. St B. T., Handley, S. J., Harper, C. N. J., & Johnson-Laird, P. N. (1999). Reasoning about necessity and possibility: a test of the mental model theory of deduction. *Journal of Experimental Psychology: Learning, Memory, and Cognition, 25,* 1495–1513.

Evans, J. St B. T., Legrenzi, P., & Girotto, V. (1999). The influence of linguistic form on reasoning: the case of matching bias. *Quarterly Journal of Experimental Psychology, 52A,* 185–216.

Evans, J. St B. T., & Lynch, J. S. (1973). Matching bias in the selection task. *British Journal of Psychology, 64,* 391–397.

Evans, J. St B. T., & Over, D. (1996a). *Rationality and reasoning.* Hove, UK: Psychology Press.

Evans, J. St B. T. & Over, D. (1996b). Rationality in the selection task: epistemic utility vs. uncertainty reduction. *Psychological Review, 103,* 356–363.

Evans, J. St B. T., & Over, D. (1997). Rationality in reasoning: the problem of deductive competence. *Cahiers de Psychologie Cognitive, 16,* 1–35.

Evans, J. St B. T., Over, D., & Manktelow, K. I. (1994). Reasoning, decision making and rationality. *Cognition, 49,* 165–187.

Feldman, J., & Ballard, D. (1982). Connectionist models and their properties. *Cognitive Science, 6,* 205–254.

Fodor, J. A. (1980). Methodological solipsism considered as a research strategy in cognitive psychology. *Behavioral and Brain Sciences, 3,* 63–73.

Fodor, J. A. (1983). *Modularity of mind.* Cambridge, MA: MIT Press.

Garey, M. R., & Johnson, D. S. (1979). *Computers and intractability: a guide to the theory of NP-completeness.* San Francisco: W. H. Freeman.

George, C. (1997). Reasoning from uncertain premises. *Thinking and Reasoning*, *3*, 161–190.

Gigerenzer, G., & Hoffrage, U. (1995). How to improve Bayesian reasoning without instruction: frequency formats. *Psychological Review*, *102*, 684–704.

Gigerenzer, G., & Hug, K. (1992). Domain-specific reasoning: social contracts, cheating, and perspective change. *Cognition*, *43*, 127–171.

Ginsberg, M. L. (Ed.) (1987). *Readings in Nonmonotonic Reasoning*. Los Altos, CA: Morgan Kaufman.

Goldstein, W. M., & Hogarth, R. M. (1997). *Research on judgment and decision making: currents, connections, controversies*. New York: Cambridge University Press.

Goodman, N. (1955). *Fact, fiction, and forecast*. Cambridge, MA: Harvard University Press.

Green, D. W., & Over, D. E. (1997). Causal inference, contingency tables and the selection task. *Current Psychology of Cognition*, *16*, 459–487.

Green, D. W., & Over, D. E. (1998). Reaching a decision: a reply to Oaksford. *Thinking and Reasoning*, *4*, 231–248.

Green, D. W., Over, D. E., & Pyne, R. A. (1997). Probability and choice in the selection task. *Thinking and Reasoning*, *3*, 209–235.

Griggs, R. A., & Cox, J. R. (1982). The elusive thematic-material effect in Wason's selection task. *British Journal of Psychology*, *73*, 407–420.

Haack, S. (1978). *Philosophy of logics*. Cambridge: Cambridge University Press.

Hahn, U., & Chater, N. (1998). Similarity and rules: Distinct? Exhaustive? Empirically distinguishable? *Cognition*, *65*, 197–230.

Hanks, S., & McDermott, D. (1985). Default reasoning, nonmonotonic logics, and the frame problem. *Proceedings of the American Association for Artificial Intelligence* (pp. 328–333). Philadelphia, PA.

Harman, G. (1989). *Change in view*. Cambridge, MA: MIT Press.

Heit, E. (1998). A Bayesian analysis of some forms of inductive reasoning. In M. Oaksford & N. Chater (Eds.), *Rational models of cognition* (pp. 248–274). Oxford: Oxford University Press.

Heit, E. (2000). Properties of inductive reasoning. *Psychonomic Bulletin and Review*, *7*, 569–592.

Heit, E., & Rubinstein, J. (1994). Similarity and property effects in inductive reasoning. *Journal of Experimental Psychology: Learning, Memory, and Cognition*, *20*, 411–422.

Henle, M. (1962). On the relation between logic and thinking. *Psychological Review*, *69*, 366–378.

Howson, C. (2000). *Hume's problem: induction and the justification of belief*. Oxford: Oxford University Press.

Hume, D. (1986). A treatise of human nature (E. C. Mossner, ed.). New York: Viking. (Original work published 1739.)

Inhelder, B., & Piaget, J. (1958). *The growth of logical reasoning*. New York: Basic Books.

Johnson-Laird, P. N. (1983). *Mental models*. Cambridge: Cambridge University Press.

Johnson-Laird, P. N. (1992). Syllogs [computer programme]. World Wide Web: http://www.cogsci.princeton.edu/~phil/syl.txt.

Johnson-Laird, P. N., & Bara, B. G. (1984). Syllogistic inference. *Cognition*, *16*, 1–62.

Johnson-Laird, P. N., & Byrne, R. M. J. (1989). Only reasoning. *Memory and Language*, *28*, 313–330.

Johnson-Laird, P. N., & Byrne, R. M. J. (1990). Meta-logical reasoning: knights, knaves and Rips. *Cognition*, *36*, 173–182.

Johnson-Laird, P. N., & Byrne, R. M. J. (1991). *Deduction*. Hillsdale, NJ: Erlbaum.

Johnson-Laird, P. N., & Byrne, R. M. J. (1992). Modal reasoning, models, and Manktelow and Over. *Cognition*, *43*, 173–182.

Johnson-Laird, P. N., Byrne, R. M. J., & Schaeken, W. (1992). Propositional reasoning by model. *Psychological Review*, *99*, 418–439.

Johnson-Laird, P. N., Byrne, R. M. J., & Schaeken, W. (1995). Why models rather than rules give a better account of propositional reasoning: a reply to Bonatti and to O'Brien, Braine, and Yang. *Psychological Review*, *101*, 734–739.

Johnson-Laird, P. N., Byrne, R. M. J., & Tabossi, P. (1990). Reasoning by model: the case of multiple quantification. *Psychological Review*, *96*, 658–673.

Johnson-Laird, P. N., Legrenzi, P., Girotto, V., Legrenzi, M. S., & Caverni, J.-P. (1999). Naïve probability: a mental model theory of extensional reasoning. *Psychological Review*, *106*, 62–88.

Johnson-Laird, P. N., Legrenzi, P., & Legrenzi, M. S. (1972). Reasoning and a sense of reality. *British Journal of Psychology*, *63*, 395–400.

Johnson-Laird, P. N., & Savary, F. (1996). Illusory inferences about probabilities. *Acta Psychologica*, *93*, 69–90.

Johnson-Laird, P. N., & Steedman, M. (1978). The psychology of syllogisms. *Cognitive Psychology*, *10*, 64–99.

Johnson-Laird, P. N., & Wason, P. C. (1970a). A theoretical analysis of insight into a reasoning task. *Cognitive Psychology*, *1*, 134–148.

Johnson-Laird, P. N., & Wason, P. C. (1970b). Insight into a logical relation. *Quarterly Journal of Experimental Psychology*, *22*, 49–61.

Klauer, K. C. (1999). On the normative justification for information gain in Wason's selection task. *Psychological Review*, *106*, 215–222.

Klauer, K. C., Musch, J., & Naumer, B. (2000). On belief bias in syllogistic reasoning. *Psychological Review*, *107*, 852–884.

Levinson, S. (1983). *Pragmatics*. Cambridge: Cambridge University Press.

Liu, I., Lo, K., & Wu, J. (1996). A probabilistic interpretation of 'If-then'. *Quarterly Journal of Experimental Psychology*, *49A*, 828–844.

MacKay, D. J. C. (1992). Information-based objective functions for active data selection. *Neural Computation*, *4*, 590–604.

Mani, K., & Johnson-Laird, P. N. (1982). The mental representation of spatial descriptions. *Memory and Cognition, 10*, 181–187.

Manktelow, K. I., & Over, D. E. (1987). Reasoning and rationality. *Mind and Language, 2*, 199–219.

Manktelow, K. I., & Over, D. E. (1992). Utility and deontic reasoning: some comments on Johnson-Laird and Byrne. *Cognition, 43*, 183–188.

Manktelow, K. I., Sutherland, E. J., & Over, D. E. (1995). Probabilistic factors in deontic reasoning. *Thinking and Reasoning, 1*, 201–220.

Marcus, G. (2001). *The algebraic mind*. Cambridge, MA: MIT Press.

McCarthy, J. M., & Hayes, P. (1969). Some philosophical problems from the standpoint of artificial intelligence. In B. Meltzer & D. Michie (Eds.), *Machine intelligence* (Vol. 4, pp. 463–502). Edinburgh: Edinburgh University Press.

McClelland, J. L. (1998). Connectionist models and Bayesian inference. In M. Oaksford & N. Chater (Eds.), Rational models of cognition (pp. 21–53). Oxford: Oxford University Press.

McDermott, D. (1987). A critique of pure reason. *Computational Intelligence, 3*, 151–160.

Medin, D. L., Lynch, E. B., Coley, J. D., & Atran, S. (1997). Categorization and reasoning among tree experts: do all roads lead to Rome? *Cognitive Psychology, 32*, 49–96.

Newell, A. (1991). *Unified theories of cognition*. Cambridge: Cambridge University Press.

Newstead, S. E. (1989). Interpretational errors in syllogistic reasoning. *Journal of Memory and Language, 28*, 78–91.

Newstead, S. E. (1995). Gricean implicatures and syllogistic reasoning. *Journal of Memory and Language, 34*, 644–664.

Newstead, S. E., & Evans, J. St B. T. (1993). Mental models as an explanation of belief bias effects in syllogistic reasoning. *Cognition, 46*, 93–97.

Newstead, S. E., & Evans, J. St. B. T. (Eds.) (1995). *Perspectives in thinking and reasoning: essays in honour of Peter Wason*. Hove, UK: Erlbaum.

Newstead, S. E., Handley, S. J., & Buck, E. (1999). Falsifying mental models: testing the predictions of theories of syllogistic reasoning. *Memory and Cognition, 27*, 344–354.

Newstead, S. E., Pollard, P., & Evans, J. St B. T. (1993). The source of belief bias effects in syllogistic reasoning. *Cognition, 45*, 257–284.

Nisbett, R. E., Krantz, D. H., Jepson, C., & Kunda, Z. (1983). The use of statistical heuristics in everyday inductive reasoning. *Psychological Review, 90*, 339–363.

Oaksford, M., & Chater, N. (1991). Against logicist cognitive science. *Mind and Language, 6*, 1–38.

Oaksford, M., & Chater, N. (1992). Bounded rationality in taking risks and drawing inferences. *Theory and Psychology, 2*, 225–230.

Oaksford, M., & Chater, N. (1993). Reasoning theories and bounded rationality. In K. I. Manktelow & D. E. Over (Eds.), *Rationality* (pp. 31–60). London: Routledge.

Oaksford, M., & Chater, N. (1994). A rational analysis of the selection task as optimal data selection. *Psychological Review, 101*, 608–631.

Oaksford, M., & Chater, N. (1995a). Theories of reasoning and the computational explanation of everyday inference. *Thinking and Reasoning, 1*, 121–152.

Oaksford, M., & Chater, N. (1995b). Information gain explains relevance which explains the selection task. *Cognition, 57*, 97–108.

Oaksford, M., & Chater, N. (1996). Rational explanation of the selection task. *Psychological Review, 103*, 381–391.

Oaksford, M., & Chater, N. (Eds.) (1998a). *Rational models of cognition*. Oxford: Oxford University Press.

Oaksford, M., & Chater, N. (1998b). *Rationality in an uncertain world*. Hove, UK: Psychology Press.

Oaksford, M., & Chater, N. (1998c). A revised rational analysis of the selection task: exceptions and sequential sampling. In M. Oaksford & N. Chater (Eds.), *Rational models of cognition* (pp. 372–398). Oxford: Oxford University Press.

Oaksford, M., & Chater, N. (2003). Computational levels and conditional inference: reply to Schroyens and Schaeken (2003). *Journal of Experimental Psychology: Learning, Memory and Cognition, 29*, 150–156.

Oaksford, M., Chater, N., & Grainger, B. (1999). Probabilistic effects in data selection. *Thinking and Reasoning, 5*, 193–243.

Oaksford, M., Chater, N., Grainger, B., & Larkin, J. (1997). Optimal data selection in the reduced array selection task (RAST). *Journal of Experimental Psychology: Learning, Memory, and Cognition, 23*, 441–458.

Oaksford, M., Chater, N., & Larkin, J. (2000). Probabilities and polarity biases in conditional inference. *Journal of Experimental Psychology: Learning, Memory, and Cognition, 26*, 883–899.

Oaksford, M., & Stenning, K. (1992). Reasoning with conditionals containing negated constituents. *Journal of Experimental Psychology: Learning, Memory, and Cognition, 18*, 835–854.

Osherson, D. N., Smith, E. E., Wilkie, O., Lopez, A., & Shafir, E. (1990). Category-based induction. *Psychological Review, 97*, 185–200.

Over, D. E., & Green, D. W. (2001). Contingency, causation, and adaptive heuristics. *Psychological Review, 108*, 682–684.

Paris, J. (1994). *The uncertain reasoner's companion*. Cambridge: Cambridge University Press.

Pearl, J. (1988). *Probabilistic reasoning in intelligent systems: networks of plausible inference*. San Mateo, CA: Morgan Kaufman.

Politzer, G., & Braine, M. D. S. (1991). Responses to inconsistent premises cannot count as suppression of valid inferences. *Cognition, 38*, 103–108.

Popper, K. R. (1959). *The logic of scientific discovery*. London: Hutchinson. (Originally published in 1935.)

Pylyshyn, Z. W. (1984). *Computation and cognition: toward a foundation for cognitive science*. Montgomery, VT: Bradford.

Pylyshyn, Z. W. (ed.) (1987). *The robot's dilemma: the frame problem in artificial intelligence.* Norwood, NJ: Ablex.

Rips, L. J. (1975). Inductive judgments about natural categories. *Journal of Verbal Learning and Verbal Behavior, 14,* 665–681.

Rips, L. J. (1983). Cognitive processes in propositional reasoning. *Psychological Review, 90,* 38–71.

Rips, L. J. (1994). *The psychology of proof.* Cambridge, MA: MIT Press.

Schaeken, W., Johnson-Laird, P. N., & d'Ydewalle, G. (1996). Mental models and temporal reasoning. *Cognition, 60,* 205–234.

Schroyens, W., & Schaeken, W. (2003). A critique of Oaksford, Chater, and Larkin's (2000) conditional probability model of conditional reasoning. *Journal of Experimental Psychology: Learning, Memory, and Cognition, 29,* 140–149.

Schroyens, W., Schaeken, W., Fias, W., & d'Ydewalle, G. (2000). Heuristic and analytic processes in propositional reasoning with negatives. *Journal of Experimental Psychology: Learning, Memory, and Cognition, 26,* 1713–1734.

Skyrms, B. (1977). *Choice and chance.* Belmont, CA: Wadsworth.

Sloman, S. A. (1993). Feature-based induction. *Cognitive Psychology, 25,* 231–280.

Sloman, S. A. (1996). The empirical case for two systems of reasoning. *Psychological Bulletin, 119,* 3–22.

Sperber, D., Cara, F., & Girotto, V. (1995). Relevance theory explains the selection task. *Cognition, 57,* 31–95.

Stanovich, K. E. (1999). *Who is rational? Studies of individual differences in reasoning.* Hillsdale, NJ: Erlbaum.

Stanovich, K. E., & West, R. F. (1998a). Cognitive ability and variation in selection task performance. *Thinking and Reasoning, 4,* 193–230.

Stanovich, K. E., & West, R. F. (1998b). Individual differences in rational thought. *Journal of Experimental Psychology: General, 127,* 161–188.

Stanovich, K. E., & West, R. F. (2000). Individual differences in reasoning: implications for the rationality debate. *Behavioral and Brain Sciences, 23,* 645–726.

Stein, E. (1996). *Without good reason.* Oxford: Oxford University Press.

Stenning, K., & Oaksford, M. (1993). Rational reasoning and human implementations of logics. In K. I. Manktelow & D. E. Over (Eds.), *Rationality* (pp. 136–177). London: Routledge.

Stenning, K., & Oberlander, J. (1995). A cognitive theory of graphical and linguistic reasoning: logic and implementation. *Cognitive Science, 19,* 97–140.

Stenning, K., & Yule, P. (1997). Image and language in human reasoning: a syllogistic illustration. *Cognitive Psychology, 34,* 109–159.

Stevenson, R. J., & Over, D. E. (1995). Deduction from uncertain premises. *Quarterly Journal of Experimental Psychology, 48A,* 613–643.

Stich, S. (1985). Could man be an irrational animal? *Synthese, 64,* 115–135.

Stich, S. (1990). *The fragmentation of reason.* Cambridge, MA: MIT Press.

Sutherland, N. S. (1992). *Irrationality: the enemy within.* London: Constable.

Tversky, A., & Kahneman, D. (1974). Judgments under uncertainty: heuristics and biases. *Science, 185,* 1124–1131.

Wason, P. C. (1965). The contexts of plausible denial. *Journal of Verbal Learning and Verbal Behavior, 4,* 7–11.

Wason, P. C. (1966). Reasoning. In B. Foss (ed.), *New horizons in psychology* (pp. 135–157). Harmondsworth, UK: Penguin.

Wason, P. C. (1968). Reasoning about a rule. *Quarterly Journal of Experimental Psychology, 20,* 273–281.

Wason, P. C., & Johnson-Laird, P. N. (1972). *The psychology of reasoning: structure and content.* Cambridge, MA: Harvard University Press.

Wason, P. C., & Shapiro, D. (1971). Natural and contrived experience in a reasoning problem. *Quarterly Journal of Experimental Psychology, 23,* 63–71.

Wertheimer, M. (1959). *Productive thinking.* New York: Harper & Row.

14

Judgment and Decision Making

CRAIG R. M. MCKENZIE

A habit of basing convictions upon evidence, and of giving to them only that degree of certainty which the evidence warrants, would, if it became general, cure most of the ills from which the world is suffering.

Bertrand Russell

The above quotation suggests that our ability to properly evaluate evidence is crucial to our well-being. It has been noted elsewhere that only a very small number of things in life are certain, implying that assessing 'degree of certainty' is not only important, but common. Lacking omniscience, we constantly experience uncertainty, not only with respect to the future (will it rain tomorrow?), but also the present (is my colleague honest?) and the past (did the defendant commit the crime?).

Understanding what determines degree of belief is important and interesting in its own right, but it also has direct implications for decision making under uncertainty, a topic that encompasses a wide variety of behavior. The traditional view of making decisions in the face of uncertain outcomes is that people seek (or at least should seek) to maximize expected utility (or pleasure, broadly construed). 'Expected' is key here. Expectations refer to degrees of belief on the part of the decision maker. For example, imagine having to decide now between two jobs, A and B. The jobs are currently equally good in your opinion, but their value will be affected by the outcome of an upcoming presidential election. If the Republican candidate wins the election, job A's value to you will double (B's will remain the same), and if the Democratic candidate wins, job B's value to you will double (and A's will

remain the same). Your decision as to which job to accept now should depend on who you think is more likely to win the upcoming election. Hence, your ability to increase future happiness hinges on your ability to assess which candidate is more likely to win. According to this view of decision making under uncertainty, life is a gamble, and the better you understand the odds, the more likely you are to prosper.

Always lurking in the background in research on judgment and decision making are normative models, which dictate how one ought to behave. For example, Bayes' theorem tells us what our degree of belief in an event should be, given (a) how informative (or diagnostic) a new piece of evidence is, and (b) how confident we were in the event before receiving the new piece of evidence. Normative models provide convenient benchmarks against which to compare human behavior, and such comparisons are routinely made in research on inference and choice.

Given that assessing uncertainty is an important aspect of life, and that normative models are routinely used as benchmarks, a natural question is, 'So, are we good at making inferences?' This turns out to be a difficult question, one that will be a focus of this chapter. Just how we compare to normative benchmarks – indeed, what the benchmark even should be in a given situation – is often disputed. The degree of optimism regarding people's inferential abilities has varied considerably over the past four decades, and this chapter provides a brief review of the reasons for this variability.

Readers should keep in mind that the judgment and decision making literature is very large, and this overview is necessarily limited in terms of the research covered. In particular, the emphasis is on important ideas of the past forty years of research on inference and uncertainty. (For a recent broad overview of the judgment and decision making literature, see Hastie & Dawes, 2001.) Much of the current chapter is devoted to a theme that has come into sharper focus since about 1990, namely the role of environment in understanding inferential and choice behavior. In particular, it will be argued that many behavioral phenomena considered to be non-normative turn out be *adaptive* when the usual environmental context in which such behavior occurs is taken into account. It is further argued that many of these adaptive behaviors are also *adaptable* in the sense that, when it is clear that the environmental context is different from what would normally be expected, behavior changes in predictable ways. Placing the 'adaptive and adaptable' theme in its proper context requires appreciation of earlier research and, accordingly, the chapter begins by describing important views prior to 1990. The chapter concludes with an overview of where the field has been, and where it might be headed.

THE 1960s: STATISTICAL MAN

An article by Peterson and Beach (1967), entitled 'Man as an Intuitive Statistician', is generally considered to exemplify the view of human inference held in the 1960s. The authors reviewed a large number of studies that examined human performance in a variety of tasks resembling problems that might be encountered in a textbook on probability theory and statistics: estimating proportions, means and variances of samples; estimating correlations between variables; and updating confidence after receiving new evidence in ball-and-urn-type problems. For each task, there was an associated normative model (i.e. correct answer) prescribed by probability theory and statistics. Although these tasks tended to be highly abstract and unfamiliar to participants, Peterson and Beach (1967: 42–3) concluded that participants performed quite well: 'Experiments that have compared human inferences with those of statistical man [i.e. normative models] show that the normative model provides a good first approximation for a psychological theory of inference. Inferences made by participants are influenced by appropriate variables and in appropriate directions.' The authors did note some discrepancies between participants' behavior and normative models, but the upshot was that normative models found in probability theory and statistics provided a good framework for building psychological models. Some simple adjustments to the normative models matched participants' responses well. (Not all researchers agreed with this conclusion, however;

see Pitz, Downing, & Reinhold, 1967; Slovic & Lichtenstein, 1971.)

Two examples serve to illustrate this viewpoint. First, consider tasks in which participants estimated variance. The mathematical variance of a distribution is the average of the *squared* deviations from the mean of the distribution, but participants' responses (perhaps unsurprisingly) did not correspond exactly to this benchmark. Peterson and Beach (1967) described research that sought to estimate the power to which the average deviation of a distribution needed to be raised in order to match participants' judgments of variance. The exponent that led to the best match often differed from 2. Arguably, this is not concerning. What one might like to see, though, is consistency in the exponent, whatever the particular value turns out to be. Researchers found, however, that sometimes the best-fitting exponent was larger than 2 (indicating that participants were influenced more by large deviations from the mean of the distribution, relative to the normative model) and sometimes the exponent was smaller than 2 (indicating that participants were less influenced by large deviations). In either case, the modified normative model served as a psychological model of variance judgments.

A second example comes from tasks in which participants updated their beliefs in light of new evidence. As mentioned, the model usually considered normative in this context is Bayes' theorem, which multiplies the prior odds (representing strength of belief before receiving the new evidence) by the likelihood ratio (which captures how informative the new evidence is) to produce the posterior odds (representing strength of belief after the new evidence). Again, it was found that participants' responses were not in accord with the normative ones. Edwards (1968) reported that when the exponent of the likelihood ratio, which is implicitly 1 in Bayes' theorem, was allowed to vary, this modified model matched participants' responses well. Sometimes the exponent that matched responses best was smaller than 1 (when responses were too close to 50%, or conservative, relative to the normative model) and sometimes the exponent was greater than 1 (when responses were too close to 0% or 100%). Once again, the starting point for the psychological model was the normative one, which was then modified to account for participants' behavior. The general idea was that, though normative models might need some adjustment, they nonetheless captured human behavior in a fundamental way.

It is worth noting that human inference was not the only area of psychology during this period that considered behavior largely normative. Although propositional logic was falling out of favor as a good description of lay deductive reasoning (Wason, 1966, 1968; Wason & Johnson-Laird, 1972), the dominant model of risky choice was subjective expected utility theory, and psychophysics was heavily influenced by signal detection theory (see, e.g., Coombs, Dawes, & Tversky, 1970). These two latter theories often assume optimal behavior on the part of participants.

THE 1970S: HEURISTICS AND BIASES

The view that normative models provide the framework for psychological models of judgment under uncertainty was changed dramatically by a series of papers published in the early 1970s by Daniel Kahneman and Amos Tversky (summarized in Tversky & Kahneman, 1974; see also Kahneman, Slovic, & Tversky, 1982). These authors proposed that people use simple rules of thumb, or heuristics, for judging probabilities or frequencies. Furthermore, these heuristics lead to systematic errors, or biases, relative to normative models. One of the important changes relative to the earlier research was an emphasis on *how* people perform these tasks. For instance, researchers in the 1960s did not claim that people reached their estimates of variance by actually calculating the average squared (or approximately squared) deviation from the mean, but only that the outputs of such a model matched people's responses well. Kahneman and Tversky argued that the *psychological processes* underlying judgment bore little or no resemblance to normative models.

In their widely cited *Science* article, Tversky & Kahneman (1974) discussed three heuristics that people use to simplify the task of estimating probabilities and frequencies. One such heuristic was 'representativeness' (Kahneman & Tversky, 1972, 1973; Tversky & Kahneman, 1971), which involves using similarity to make judgments. When asked to estimate the probability that object A belongs to class B, that event A originated from process B, or that process B will generate event A, people rely on the degree to which A is representative of, or resembles, B. For example, the more representative A is of B, the higher the judged probability that A originated from B.

Because similarity is not affected by some factors that should influence probability judgments, Tversky and Kahneman (1974) claimed that the representativeness heuristic led to a long list of biases, but just two will be mentioned here. The first is base-rate neglect. One well-known task that led to base-rate neglect was the 'lawyer–engineer' problem (Kahneman & Tversky, 1973), in which participants were presented with personality sketches of individuals said to be randomly drawn from a pool of 100 lawyers and engineers. One group was told that the pool consisted of 70 lawyers and 30 engineers, while another group was told that there were 30 lawyers and 70 engineers. Participants assessed the probability that a given personality sketch belonged to an engineer rather than a lawyer. According to Bayes' theorem, the base rates of lawyers and engineers should have a large influence on reported probabilities, but Kahneman and Tversky (1973) found that the base rates had little influence. Instead, they argued, participants were basing their probabilities on the similarity between the personality sketch and stereotypes of lawyer and engineers. To the extent that the personality sketch seemed to describe a lawyer, participants reported a high probability that the person was a lawyer, largely independent of the base rates and in violation of Bayes' theorem.

Another bias said to result from the representativeness heuristic is insensitivity to sample size. The law of large numbers states that larger samples are more likely than smaller samples to accurately reflect the populations from which they were drawn. Kahneman and Tversky (1972) asked participants which of two hospitals would have more days of delivering more than 60% boys. One hospital delivered about 45 babies a day, and the other delivered about 15. Although the small hospital would be more likely to deliver more than 60% boys on a given day (due to greater sampling variation), participants tended to respond that the two hospitals were equally likely to do so. Kahneman and Tversky (1972) argued that representativeness accounted for the finding: participants were assessing the similarity between the sample and the expected sample from the 50/50 generating process, which is equivalent for the two hospitals.

A second heuristic that Kahneman and Tversky argued people use is 'availability' (Tversky & Kahneman, 1973), according to which people estimate probability or frequency based on the ease with which instances can be brought to mind. This appears to be a reasonable strategy insofar as it is usually easier to think of instances of larger classes than smaller ones. However, there are other factors, such as salience, that can make instances more available independently of class size. For example, Tversky and Kahneman (1973) read a list of names to participants. For one group of participants, there were more male names than female names, whereas the opposite was true for another group. The smaller class always consisted of relatively famous names, however. When asked whether there were more male or female names, most participants mistakenly thought the smaller class was larger. The idea was that the relatively famous names were easier to recall (which was verified independently) and participants used ease of recall – or availability – to judge class size.

Another example of availability is found when people are asked to estimate the frequency of various causes of death. Which is a more common cause of death, homicide or diabetes? Many people report incorrectly that the former is more common (Lichtenstein, Slovic, Fischhoff, Layman, & Combs, 1978). Generally, causes of death that are more sensational (e.g. fire, flood, tornado) tend to be overestimated, while causes that are less dramatic (diabetes, stroke, asthma) tend to be underestimated. Availability provides a natural explanation: it is easier to think of instances of homicide than instances of death from diabetes because we hear about the former more often than the latter. Indeed, Combs and Slovic (1979) showed that newspapers are much more likely to report more dramatic causes of death. For example, there were 3 times more newspaper articles on homicide than there were on deaths caused by disease, even though disease deaths occur 100 times more often. (The articles on homicide were also more than twice as long.)

The third and final heuristic described by Tversky and Kahneman (1974) is anchoring-and-adjustment, whereby people estimate an uncertain value by starting from some obvious value (or anchor) and adjusting in the desired direction. The bias is that the anchor exerts too much influence, and resulting estimates stay too close to the anchor. For example, participants were asked to assess uncertain values such as the percentage of African nations that were members of the United Nations. Before providing a best guess, participants were to state whether they thought the true value was above or below a particular value, determined by spinning a wheel of fortune in view of the participants. Tversky and Kahneman (1974) found that the median best guess was 25 when the random value was 10, and the median best guess was 45 when the random value was 65. Their explanation was that the random value served as an anchor, which then influenced subsequent best guesses.

Another demonstration of anchoring and adjustment comes from asking participants for the product of either $1 \times 2 \times 3 \times 4 \times 5 \times 6 \times 7 \times 8$ or $8 \times 7 \times 6 \times 5 \times 4 \times 3 \times 2 \times 1$ within 5 seconds. Most people cannot compute the value in that amount of time and must therefore base their estimate on the partially computed product. Because the partial product is presumably smaller for the ascending series than the descending series (assuming people start on the left), the resulting estimates should also be smaller, which is what Tversky and Kahneman (1974) found. Median estimates of the ascending and descending series were 512 and 2250, respectively. Furthermore, because both groups are using a low anchor, both underestimated the actual product, which is 40,320.

Note the sharp contrast between the heuristics-and-biases view and the 1960s view that people, by and large, behave in accord with normative models. For example, in contrast to Edwards' (1968) conclusion that a simple adjustment to Bayes' theorem captured people's judgments, Kahneman and Tversky (1972: 450) concluded that 'In his evaluation of evidence, man is apparently not a conservative Bayesian; he is not Bayesian at all.' The heuristics-and-biases research suggested that

people were not as good as they might otherwise think they were when assessing uncertainty – and that researchers could offer help. The impact of the program was fast and widespread, leaving none of the social sciences untouched. Indeed, it did not take long for the heuristics-and-biases movement to make significant headway outside of the social sciences and into applied areas such as law (Saks & Kidd, 1980), medicine (Elstein, Shulman, & Sprafka, 1978) and business (Bazerman & Neale, 1983; Bettman, 1979).

THE 1980s: DEFENDING AND EXTENDING THE HEURISTICS-AND-BIASES PARADIGM

Despite the huge success of the heuristics-and-biases paradigm, it began receiving a significant amount of criticism around 1980. Some authors criticized the vagueness of the heuristics and the lack of specificity regarding when a given heuristic would be used (Gigerenzer & Murray, 1987; Wallsten, 1980), while many others considered misleading the negative view of human performance implied by the research (Cohen, 1981; Edwards, 1975; Einhorn & Hogarth, 1981; Hogarth, 1981; Jungermann, 1983; Lopes, 1982; Phillips, 1983). Note that the methodology of the heuristics-and-biases program is to devise experiments in which the purported heuristic makes one prediction and a normative model makes a different prediction. Such experiments are designed to reveal errors. Situations in which the heuristic and the normative model make the same prediction are not of interest. The rise of the heuristics-and-biases paradigm was accompanied by a predictable rise in results purportedly showing participants violating normative rules. (Also of interest is that articles demonstrating poor performance were cited more often than articles demonstrating good performance; Christensen-Szalanski & Beach, 1984.) In the concluding paragraph of their 1974 *Science* article, Tversky and Kahneman wrote, 'These heuristics are highly economical and usually effective, but they lead to systematic and predictable errors.' However, the authors provided numerous examples illustrating the second half of the sentence, and none illustrating the first half (Lopes, 1991).

L. J. Cohen, a philosopher, launched the first systematic attack on the heuristics-and-biases paradigm (Cohen, 1977, 1979, 1981). One of the major points in his 1981 article was that, in the final analysis, a normative theory receives our stamp of approval only if it is consistent with our intuition. How, then, can people, who are the arbiters of rationality, be deemed irrational? Cohen concluded that they cannot, and that experiments purportedly demonstrating irrationality are actually demonstrating, for instance, the participants' ignorance (e.g. that they have not been trained in probability theory) or the experimenters' ignorance (because they are applying the wrong normative rule). There is, in fact, a long history of rethinking normative models when their implications are inconsistent with intuition, dating back to at least 1713, when the St Petersburg paradox led to the rejection of the maximization of expected value as a normative theory of choice under uncertainty. (For more modern discussions on the interplay between behavior and normative models, see Larrick, Nisbett, & Morgan, 1993; March, 1978; Slovic & Tversky, 1974; Stanovich, 1999.) Nonetheless, the subsequent replies to Cohen's article (which were published over a course of years) indicate that most psychologists were not persuaded by his arguments, and his attack appears to have had little impact.

Einhorn and Hogarth (1981) provided more moderate – and influential – criticism. Rather than dismissing the entire empirical literature on human rationality, Einhorn and Hogarth urged caution in interpreting experimental results given the *conditional nature* of normative models. Because the real world is complex, simplifying assumptions need to be made in order for a given normative model to apply. This creates ambiguity when behavior departs from the predictions of normative models. Is the discrepancy due to inappropriate behavior or due to applying an overly simplified normative model? Arguably, many researchers at the time were quick to reach the first conclusion without giving much thought to the second possibility. As Einhorn and Hogarth (1981: 56) noted, 'To consider human judgment as suboptimal without discussion of the limitations of optimal models is naïve.' The authors also pointed out that the problem becomes even more complicated when there are competing normative models for a given situation. The existence of multiple normative responses raises doubts about claims of the proponents of the heuristics-and-biases paradigm. What if purported normative errors – which provided the evidence for the use of heuristics – were consistent with an alternative normative perspective?

To illustrate the complexity of interpreting behavior in an inference task, consider base-rate neglect, discussed earlier. The following is the well-known 'cab problem' (from Tversky & Kahneman, 1982a):

A cab was involved in a hit and run accident at night. Two cab companies, the Green and the Blue, operate in the city. You are given the following data:

(a) 85% of the cabs in the city are Green and 15% are Blue.
(b) A witness identified the cab as Blue. The court tested the reliability of the witness

under the same circumstances that existed on the night of the accident and concluded that the witness correctly identified each one of the two colors 80% of the time and failed 20% of the time.

What is the probability that the cab involved in the accident was Blue rather than Green?

Participants' median response was 80%, indicating a reliance on the witness's reliability and a neglect of the base rates of cabs in the city. This was considered a normative error by Tversky and Kahneman (1982a), who argued that 41% was the normative (Bayesian) response. However, Birnbaum (1983) pointed out an implicit assumption in their normative analysis that may not be realistic: the witness is assumed to respond the same way when tested by the court, where there were equal numbers of Green and Blue cabs, and when in the city, where there are far more Green than Blue cabs. It is conceivable that the witness took into account the fact that there are more Green cabs when identifying the cab color on the night of the accident. Indeed, if the witness were an 'ideal observer' (in the signal detection theory sense) who maximizes the number of correct identifications, then the probability that the cab was Blue, given that the witness said it was Blue, is 0.82, which nearly coincides with participants' median response. Birnbaum's (1983) point was not that participants (necessarily) assume that the witness is an ideal observer, but that the normative solution is more complicated than it first appears and, furthermore, that evidence purportedly indicating a normative error might show nothing of the sort. A wide variety of normative responses are appropriate, depending on the participants' theory of the witness. Tversky and Kahneman's (1982a) normative analysis is a reasonable one, but it is not the only one.

Base rates themselves can be controversial. A given object or event belongs to indefinitely many reference classes, so how does one decide which reference class should be used for determining the base rate? The cab problem uses cabs that 'operate in the city' as the reference class, but one could use 'operate at night', 'operate in the state', 'operate in the city at night', or any number of other reference classes, and the base rates might differ considerably between them. Furthermore, Einhorn and Hogarth (1981) point out that 'There is no generally accepted normative way of defining the appropriate population' (p. 65; see also McKenzie & Soll, 1996). Again, the point is not that the normative analysis offered by researchers arguing that participants underweight base rates is untenable, but that the normative issues are often trickier than is implied by such research. The complexity of the normative issues makes it difficult to draw strong conclusions regarding normative errors. (The controversy surrounding base-rate neglect continues to this day; see Cosmides & Tooby, 1996; Gigerenzer, 1991a, 1996; Gigerenzer, Hell, & Blank, 1988; Gigerenzer & Hoffrage, 1995; Kahneman & Tversky, 1996; Koehler, 1996.)

Responding to the accusation that they were portraying human inference in an overly negative light, Kahneman and Tversky (1982) defended their reliance on errors by pointing out that studying errors is a common way of understanding normal behavior. For example, perceptual illusions reveal how normal perception works. (Some authors have taken exception to the analogy between perceptual errors and inferential errors; see Funder, 1987; Gigerenzer, 1991b; Jungermann, 1983; Lopes, 1991.) Nonetheless, they conceded that 'Although errors of judgment are but a method by which some cognitive processes are studied, the method has become a significant part of the message' (p. 124). However, despite other authors' concerns (Cohen, 1977, 1979, 1981; Einhorn & Hogarth, 1981), Kahneman and Tversky (1982) appeared to remain steadfast that there exist straightforward normative answers to inferential problems: '[S]ystematic errors and inferential biases ... expose some of our intellectual limitations and suggest ways of improving the quality of our thinking' (p. 124). Drawing such a conclusion assumes uncontroversial normative solutions to problems presented to participants.

Despite mounting criticism, the heuristics-and-biases approach remained the dominant paradigm, and its status was boosted even further when another major article in that tradition was subsequently published (Tversky & Kahneman, 1983). This article showed that people violate another fundamental principle of probability theory, the conjunction rule, because of the representativeness and availability heuristics. The conjunction rule states that the probability of the conjunction of two events cannot exceed the probability of either event individually, or $p(A\&B) \leq p(A)$. In certain contexts, the rule is transparent. For example, probably everyone would agree that the probability of going skiing this weekend *and* breaking a leg is lower than the probability of going skiing this weekend (and lower than the probability of breaking a leg this weekend). However, Tversky and Kahneman (1982b, 1983) demonstrated violations of this rule. Consider the following description presented to participants:

Linda is 31 years old, single, outspoken, and very bright. She majored in philosophy. As a student, she was deeply concerned with issues of discrimination and social justice, and also participated in anti-nuclear demonstrations.

Some participants were asked which was more probable: (a) Linda is a bank teller, or (b) Linda is a bank teller and is active in the feminist movement. Most selected (b), thereby violating the conjunction rule. The reason for this, according to Tversky and Kahneman (1982b, 1983), is that creating the conjunction by adding the 'feminist' component increased similarity between the conjunction and the description of Linda. That is, Linda is more similar to a 'feminist bank teller' than to a 'bank teller' and hence the former is judged more probable. Tversky and Kahneman interpreted this finding as yet another fundamental violation of rational thinking resulting from the use of heuristics. (This conclusion has been controversial; see, e.g., Gigerenzer, 1991a, 1996; Kahneman & Tversky, 1996; Mellers, Hertwig, & Kahneman, 2001.)

SINCE 1990: THE ROLE OF ENVIRONMENT

There is no question that the heuristics-and-biases paradigm is historically important and that it continues to be an active research program (e.g. Gilovich, Griffin, & Kahneman, 2002). But its impact, in psychology at least, appears to be waning. There are several reasons for this (Gigerenzer, 1991a, 1996; Lopes, 1991), but here we shall focus on one in particular: the traditional heuristics-and-biases approach ignores the crucial role that the environment plays in shaping human behavior. Focusing on environmental structure as a means to understanding behavior is certainly not new (e.g. Brunswik, 1956; Gibson, 1979; Hammond, 1955; Marr, 1982; Simon, 1955, 1956; Toda, 1962; Tolman & Brunswik, 1935), but the idea is now mainstream in the area of judgment and decision making and is no longer tied to individuals or small camps. One can view the heuristics-and-biases approach as studying cognition in a vacuum, whereas an important recent theme is that the key lies in understanding how cognition and environment interact, even mesh. Studying cognition independently of environmental considerations can lead to highly misleading conclusions. The current section will illustrate this point with several examples.

The examples are sorted into two categories, one indicating adapt*ive* behavior, and the other indicating adapt*able* behavior (Klayman & Brown, 1993; McKenzie & Mikkelsen, 2000). Examples in the 'adaptive' category show that participants' apparently irrational strategies in the laboratory can often be explained by the fact that the strategies work well in the natural environment. Participants appear to harbor strong (usually tacit) assumptions when performing laboratory tasks that reflect the structure of the environment in which they normally operate. When these assumptions do not match the laboratory task, adaptive behavior can appear maladaptive. Examples in the 'adaptable' category show that, when it is made clear to participants that their usual assumptions are inappropriate, then their behavior changes in predictable and sensible ways.

Both categories of examples show that consideration of real-world environmental structure can lead to different views not only of why people behave as they do, but even of what is rational in a given task.

Adaptive behavior

Hypothesis testing

In 1960, Peter Wason published a study that received (and continues to receive) lots of attention. Participants were to imagine that the experimenter had a rule in mind that generates triples of numbers. An example of a triple that conforms to the rule is 2–4–6. The task was to generate triples of numbers in order to figure out the experimenter's rule. After announcing each triple, participants were told whether or not it conformed to the experimenter's rule. They could test as many triples as they wished and were to state what they thought was the correct rule only after they were highly confident they had found it. The results were interesting because few participants discovered the correct rule (with their first 'highly confident' announcement), which was 'numbers in increasing order of magnitude'.

How could most participants be so confident in a wrong rule after being allowed to test it as much as they wished? The 2–4–6 example naturally suggests a tentative hypothesis such as 'increasing intervals of two' (which was the most commonly stated incorrect rule). They would then test their hypothesis by stating triples such as 8–10–12, 14–16–18, 20–22–24 and 1–3–5 – triples that were consistent with their hypothesized rule. Of course, each of these triples is consistent with the correct rule as well, and hence participants received a positive response from the experimenter ('Yes, it conforms to the rule'), leading them to believe incorrectly that they had discovered the correct rule. Wason (1960) claimed that participants appeared unwilling to test their hypotheses in a manner that would lead to disconfirmation (which is what Popper, 1959, claimed was the normative way to test hypotheses). The only way to falsify the 'increasing intervals of two' hypothesis is to test triples that are not expected to conform to the hypothesis, such as 2–4–7 or 1–2–3. Instead, Wason argued, participants tested their hypotheses in a way that would lead them to be confirmed. This came to be known as 'confirmation bias' (Wason, 1962) and made quite a splash because of the apparent dire implications: we gather information in a manner that leads us to believe whatever hypothesis we happen to start with, regardless of its correctness. This view of lay hypothesis testing became common in psychology (Mynatt, Doherty, & Tweney, 1977, 1978), but it was especially popular in social psychology (Nisbett & Ross, 1980; Snyder, 1981; Snyder & Campbell, 1980; Snyder & Swann, 1978).

This view persisted until 1987 – almost three decades after Wason's original findings were published – when Klayman and Ha set things straight. They first pointed out that Popper (1959) had prescribed testing hypotheses so that they are most likely to be disconfirmed; he did not say that the way to achieve this is by looking for examples that your theory or hypothesis predicts will fail to occur. In other words, Klayman and Ha (1987) distinguished between disconfirmation as a goal (as prescribed by Popper) and disconfirmation as a search strategy. Wason (1960) confounded these two notions: because the true rule is more general than the tentative 'increasing intervals of two' hypothesis, the only way to disconfirm the latter is by testing a triple that is hypothesized not to work. But notice that the situation could easily be reversed: one could entertain a hypothesis that is more general than the true rule, in which case the only way to disconfirm the hypothesis is by testing cases hypothesized to work (and finding they do not work) – exactly opposite from the situation in Wason's task. In this situation, testing only cases hypothesized not to work could lead to incorrectly believing the hypothesis (because all the cases that the hypothesis predicts will not work will, in fact, not work).

Thus, whether the strategy of testing cases you expect to work ('positive testing') is a good one depends on the structure of the task – in this case the relationship between the hypothesized and the true rule. Furthermore, positive testing is more likely than negative testing (testing cases you expect will not work) to lead to disconfirmation when (a) you are trying to predict a minority phenomenon and (b) your hypothesized rule includes about as many cases as the true rule (i.e. it is about the right size). These two conditions, Klayman and Ha (1987) argue, are commonly met in real-world hypothesis-testing situations. In short, positive testing appears to be a highly adaptive strategy for testing hypotheses. This virtual reversal of the perceived status of testing cases expected to work is primarily due to Klayman and Ha's *analysis of task structure*. Seen independently of the environmental context in which it is usually used, positive testing can look foolish (as in Wason's task). Seen in its usual environmental context, it makes good normative sense. Klayman and Ha's work underscores the point that understanding inferential behavior requires understanding the context in which it usually occurs. In their own words (p. 211), 'The appropriateness of human hypothesis-testing strategies and prescriptions about optimal strategies must be understood in terms of the interaction between the strategy and the task at hand.'

The selection task

Anderson (1990, 1991) has taken the environmental structure approach to its logical conclusion: rather than looking to the mind to explain behavior, we need only look to the structure of the environment. He calls this approach 'rational analysis', which 'is an explanation of an aspect of human behavior based on the assumption that it is optimized somehow to the structure of the environment' (Anderson, 1991: 471). His approach has led to interesting accounts of memory, categorization, causal inference and problem solving (Anderson, 1990, 1991; Anderson & Milson, 1989; Anderson & Sheu, 1995).

Oaksford and Chater (1994) have provided a rational analysis of the 'selection task' (Wason, 1966, 1968). Behavior in this task has long been considered a classic example of human irrationality. In the selection task, participants test a rule of the form 'If P, then Q' and are shown four cards, each with P or ~P on one side and Q or ~Q on the other, and they must select which cards to turn over to see if the rule is true or false. For example, Wason (1966) asked participants to test the rule 'If there is a vowel on one side, then there is an even number on the other side'. Each of the four cards had a number on one side and a letter on the other. Imagine that one card shows an A, one K, one 2 and one 7. Which of these cards needs to be turned over to see if the rule is true or false? According to one logical interpretation of the rule ('material implication'), standard logic dictates that the A and 7 (P and ~Q) cards should be turned over because only these potentially reveal the falsifying vowel/odd number combination. It does not matter what is on the other side of the K and 2 cards, so there is no point in turning them over. Typically, fewer than 10% of participants select only the logically correct cards (Wason, 1966, 1968); instead, they prefer the A and 2 (P and Q) cards (i.e. those mentioned in the rule). (An alternative logical interpretation of the rule, 'material equivalence', dictates that all four cards should be turned over, but this is also a rare response.)

However, Oaksford and Chater (1994, 1996; see also Nickerson, 1996) have argued that selecting the P and Q cards may not be foolish at all. They showed that, from an inductive, Bayesian perspective (rather than the standard deductive perspective), the P and Q cards are the most informative with respect to determining if the rule is true or not – if one assumes that P and Q, the events mentioned in the rule, are rare relative to ~P and ~Q. Oaksford and Chater argue further that this 'rarity assumption' is adaptive because rules, or hypotheses, are likely to mention rare events (see also Einhorn & Hogarth, 1986; Mackie, 1974). Thus, Oaksford and Chater (1994) make two assumptions that they consider to mirror real-world inference: it is usually probabilistic rather than deterministic, and hypotheses usually regard rare events. These considerations lead not only to a different view of participants' behavior, but also to a different view of what is rational. Under the above two conditions, it is normatively defensible to turn over the P and Q cards.

Note that Oaksford and Chater's 'rarity assumption' is similar to Klayman and Ha's (1987) 'minority phenomenon' assumption. Because rarity will play a role in several studies discussed in this chapter, it is worthwhile to illustrate its importance in inference with an example. Imagine that you live in a desert and are trying to determine if the new local weather forecaster can accurately predict the weather. Assume that the forecaster rarely predicts rain and usually predicts sunshine. On the first day, the forecaster predicts sunshine and is correct. On the second day, the forecaster predicts rain and is correct. Which of these two correct predictions would leave you more convinced that the forecaster can accurately predict the weather and is not merely guessing? The more informative of the two observations is the correct prediction of rain, the rare event, at least according to Bayesian statistics (Horwich, 1982; Howson & Urbach, 1989; see also Alexander, 1958; Good, 1960; Hosiasson-Lindenbaum, 1940; Mackie, 1963). Qualitatively, the reason for this is that it would not be surprising to correctly predict a sunny day by chance in the desert because almost every day is sunny. That is, even if the forecaster knew only that the desert is sunny, you would expect him or her to make lots of correct predictions of sunshine just by chance alone. Thus, such an observation does not help much in distinguishing between a knowledgeable forecaster and one who is merely guessing. In contrast, because rainy days are rare, a correct prediction of rain is unlikely to occur by chance alone and therefore provides relatively strong evidence that the forecaster is doing better than merely guessing. Rarity is extremely useful for determining the informativeness of data.

Evidence for the rarity assumption

Thus far we have relied rather heavily on the rarity assumption to argue that behavior in the selection task and in hypothesis testing is adaptive. Is the rarity assumption empirically accurate? That is, do people tend to phrase conditional hypotheses in terms of rare events? It appears that they do. Recently, McKenzie, Ferreira, Mikkelsen, McDermott, and Skrable (2001) found that participants often had a strong tendency to phrase conditional hypotheses in terms of rare, rather than common, events. Thus, people might consider mentioned confirming observations most informative, or consider turning over the mentioned cards most informative, because they usually *are* most informative, at least from a Bayesian perspective.

Covariation assessment

Relatedly, Anderson (1990, 1991; Anderson & Sheu, 1995) has argued that 'biases' exhibited in assessing the covariation between two binary variables are justified by the structure of the natural environment. In a typical covariation task, the two variables are either present or absent. For example, participants might be asked to assess the relationship between a medical treatment and recovery from an illness given that 15 people received the treatment and recovered (cell A); 5 people received the treatment and did not recover (cell B); 9 people did not receive the treatment and recovered (cell C); and 3 people did not receive the treatment and did not recover (cell D). Assessing covariation underlies such fundamental behavior as learning (Hilgard & Bower, 1975), categorization (Smith & Medin, 1981) and judging causation (Cheng, 1997; Cheng & Novick, 1990, 1992; Einhorn & Hogarth, 1986), to name just a few. It is hard to imagine a more important cognitive activity and, accordingly, much research has been devoted to this topic since the groundbreaking studies of Inhelder and Piaget (1958) and Smedslund (1963) (for reviews, see Allan, 1993; Alloy & Tabachnik, 1984; Crocker, 1981; McKenzie, 1994; Nisbett & Ross, 1980; Shaklee, 1983). The traditional normative models (delta-p or the phi coefficient) consider the four cells equally important. However, decades of research have revealed that participants' judgments are influenced most by the number of cell A observations and are influenced least by the number of cell D observations (Levin, Wasserman, & Kao, 1993; Lipe, 1990; McKenzie, 1994; Schustack & Sternberg, 1981; Wasserman, Dorner, & Kao, 1990). These differences in cell impact have traditionally been seen as irrational. For example, Kao and Wasserman (1993: 1365) state that 'It is important to recognize that unequal utilization of cell information implies that nonnormative processes are at work', and Mandel and Lehman (1998) attempted to explain differential cell impact in terms of a combination of two reasoning biases.

Anderson has noted, however, that (for essentially the same reasons noted earlier) being influenced more by joint presence makes normative sense from a Bayesian perspective if it is assumed that the presence of variables is rare ($p < 0.5$) and their absence is common ($p > 0.5$). Rather than approaching the task as one of statistical summary (the traditional view), it is assumed that participants approach it as one of induction, treating the cell frequencies as a sample from a larger population. Participants are presumably trying to determine the likelihood that there is (rather than is not) a relationship between the variables based on the sample information. The assumption that presence is rare (outside of the laboratory at least) seems reasonable: most things are not red, most people do not have a fever, and so on (McKenzie & Mikkelsen, 2000, in press; Oaksford & Chater, 1994, 1996). (Note that this is somewhat different from the rarity assumption, which regards how hypotheses are phrased.) When trying to determine if two binary variables are dependent vs. independent, a rare cell A observation is more informative than a

common cell D observation. Furthermore, this is consistent with the usual finding that cells B and C fall in between A and D in terms of their impact on behavior: if the presence of both variables is equally rare, then the ordering of the cells in terms of informativeness from the Bayesian perspective is $A > B = C > D$. Thus, once again, 'biases' in the laboratory might reflect deeply rooted tendencies that are highly adaptive outside the laboratory.

One aspect of the Bayesian approach to covariation assessment that Anderson did not exploit, however, concerns the role of participants' beliefs that the variables are related before being presented with any cell information (McKenzie & Mikkelsen, in press). Alloy and Tabachnik (1984) reviewed a large number of covariation studies (that used both humans and non-human animals as participants) showing that prior beliefs about the relationship to be assessed had large effects on judgments of covariation. The influence of prior beliefs on covariation assessment has been traditionally interpreted as an error because only the four cell frequencies presented in the experiment are considered relevant in the traditional normative models. However, taking into account prior beliefs is the hallmark of Bayesian inference and not taking them into account would be considered an error. Thus, the large number of studies reviewed by Alloy and Tabachnik provide additional evidence that participants make use of information beyond the four cell frequencies presented to them in the experiment, and that they do so in a way that makes normative sense from a Bayesian perspective.

Note that the Bayesian view of covariation assessment – combined with reasonable assumptions about which events are rare in the natural environment – not only explains why participants behave as they do, but it also provides a new normative perspective of the task. There is more than one normatively defensible way to approach the task.

Overconfidence

Environmental factors also play a role in interpreting findings of overconfidence. Studies of calibration examine whether people report degrees of confidence that match their rates of being correct. A person is well calibrated if, when reporting $x\%$ confidence, he or she is correct $x\%$ of the time. A common finding is that people are not well calibrated. In particular, people tend to be overconfident: they report confidence that is too high relative to their hit rate. For example, participants are right about 85% of the time when reporting 100% confidence (e.g. Fischhoff, Slovic, & Lichtenstein, 1977; Lichtenstein, Fischhoff, & Phillips, 1982). Probably the most common means of assessing calibration is through the use of general knowledge questions. For example, participants might be asked whether 'Absinthe is (a) a precious stone, or (b) a liqueur'. They then select the answer they think is most likely correct and report their confidence that they have selected the correct answer (on a scale of 50–100% in this example). Participants would typically be asked dozens of such questions.

Gigerenzer, Hoffrage, and Kleinbölting (1991; see also Juslin, 1994) argued that at least part of the reason for the finding of overconfidence is that general knowledge questions are not selected randomly. In particular, they tend to be selected for difficulty. For example, participants are more likely to be asked, 'Which is further north, New York or Rome?' (most participants incorrectly select New York) than 'Which is further north, New York or Miami?' This is a natural way to test the limits of someone's knowledge, but it is inappropriate for testing calibration. Gigerenzer et al. (1991) created a representative sample from their German participants' natural environment by randomly sampling a subset of German cities with populations greater than 100,000. Participants were then presented with all the pairs of cities, chose the city they thought had more inhabitants, and reported confidence in their choice. The results indicated quite good calibration (see also Juslin, 1994; but see Brenner, Koehler, Liberman, & Tversky, 1996; Griffin & Tversky, 1992).

Though the overconfidence phenomenon is probably due to multiple factors, one of them is whether the structure of the task is representative of the structure of participants' real-world environment. Furthermore, it has been shown that 'noise' in reported confidence (e.g. random error in mapping internal feelings of uncertainty onto the scale used in the experiment) can lead to overconfidence (Erev, Wallsten, & Budescu, 1994; Soll, 1996). Both the ecological account and the 'noise' account can explain the usual finding of overconfidence in the laboratory without positing motivational or cognitive biases.

A related area of research has examined subjective confidence intervals. For example, Alpert and Raiffa (1982) asked participants to provide 98% confidence intervals for a variety of uncertain quantities, such as 'the total egg production in millions in the U.S. in 1965' (the study was originally reported in 1969). When reporting such interval estimates, the participants should be 98% confident that the true value lies within the interval, and they would therefore be well calibrated if the true value really did fall inside their intervals 98% of the time. However, Alpert and Raiffa (1982) found a hit rate of only 59%. Corrective procedures for improving calibration increased the hit rate to 77%, but this was still far from the goal of 98%.

Yaniv and Foster (1995, 1997) have argued that, when speakers usually report interval estimates, and when listeners 'consume' them, *informativeness* as well as accuracy is valued. An extremely wide interval is likely to contain the true value, but it is not going to be very useful. When you ask a friend what time the mail will be picked up, you would probably not appreciate a response of 'between 6 a.m. and midnight'. Your friend is likely to be accurate, but not very informative. Yaniv and Foster (1997) found that the average participant's reported intervals would have to be *17 times wider* to contain the true value 95% of the time. Presumably, in a typical situation most people would feel silly reporting such wide intervals and, relatedly, the recipients of the intervals would find them utterly useless. Also of interest is that participants reported essentially the same interval estimates when asked for 95% confidence intervals and when asked to report intervals they 'felt most comfortable with' (Yaniv & Foster, 1997), suggesting that instructions have little effect on participants' usual strategy for generating interval estimates.

To illustrate that accuracy is not the only consideration when evaluating (and hence producing) interval estimates, imagine that two judges are asked to estimate the amount of money spent on education by the U.S. federal government in 1987. Judge A responds '$20 billion to $40 billion' and Judge B responds '$18 billion to $20 billion'. The true value is $22.5 billion. Which judge is better? Yaniv and Foster (1995) found that 80% of their participants chose Judge B, even though the true value falls outside B's interval and inside A's. The authors describe, and provide empirical evidence for, a descriptive model that trades off accuracy and informativeness. (For a normative Bayesian interpretation of these findings, see McKenzie & Amin, 2002.)

The upshot is that understanding the interval estimates that people generate requires understanding their usual context and purpose. The reasons underlying participants' inability to be well calibrated when asked to produce (for example) 98% confidence intervals reveal much about what is adaptive under typical circumstances. The lesson about cognition does not come from the finding *that* people have difficulty reporting wide interval estimates, but *why*. To regard such findings as indicating human cognition as 'error-prone' is to miss the important point.

Framing effects

Framing effects, which are said to occur when 'equivalent' redescriptions of objects or outcomes lead to different preferences or judgments, are also best understood when the usual context is taken into account. The best-known examples of framing effects involve choosing between a risky and a riskless option that are described in terms of either gains or losses (Kahneman & Tversky, 1979, 1984; Tversky & Kahneman, 1981, 1986), but the effects also occur with simpler tasks that describe a single option in terms of an attribute in one of two ways (for reviews, see Kühberger, 1998; Levin, Schneider, & Gaeth, 1998). As an example of the latter type of framing effect (an 'attribute framing effect': Levin et al., 1998), a medical treatment described as resulting in '75% survival' will be seen more favorably than if it is described as resulting in '25% mortality'. Because framing effects are robust and violate the basic normative principle of 'description invariance', they are widely considered to provide clear-cut evidence of irrationality. However, researchers have not been clear about what it means for two descriptions to be equivalent. Some researchers simply appeal to intuition, but more careful demonstrations involve logically equivalent descriptions (as in 75% survival vs. 25% mortality). A crucial assumption is that these purportedly equivalent descriptions are not conveying different, normatively relevant, information. Clearly, if two frames conveyed different information that was relevant to the decision or judgment, then any resulting framing effect would not be a normative error. That is, different frames need to satisfy *information equivalence* if it is to be claimed that responding differently to them is irrational (Sher & McKenzie, 2003).

However, recent research has shown that even logically equivalent frames can convey choice-relevant information (McKenzie & Nelson, 2003; Sher & McKenzie, 2003). In particular, a speaker's *choice of frame* can be informative to the listener. Using the above medical example, for instance, it was shown that speakers are more likely to select the '75% survival' frame to describe a new treatment outcome if, relative to an old treatment, it led to a higher survival rate than if it led to a lower survival rate (McKenzie & Nelson, 2003). That is, treatment outcomes were more likely to be described in terms of their survival rate if they led to relatively high survival rates. Generally, speakers prefer to use the label (e.g. percent survival vs. percent mortality) that has increased, rather than decreased, relative to their reference point. To take a more intuitive example, people are more likely to describe a glass as 'half empty' (rather than 'half full') if it used to be full than if it used to be empty (McKenzie & Nelson, 2003). When the glass was full and is now at the halfway mark, its 'emptiness' has increased, making it more likely that the glass will be described in terms of how empty it is. Thus, information can be 'leaked' by the speaker's choice among logically equivalent frames. Furthermore, the medical example illustrates that this leaked information can be normatively relevant: describing the treatment in terms of percent survival signals that the speaker considers the treatment relatively successful, whereas describing it in terms of percent mortality signals that the speaker considers the treatment relatively unsuccessful. Should a listener not take this information into account? It is hard to deny the normative relevance of this information. Moreover, research has shown that listeners 'absorb' this leaked information. For example, participants were more likely to infer that, relative

to an old treatment, the new treatment led to a higher survival rate when it was described in terms of percent survival than when it was described in terms of percent mortality (McKenzie & Nelson, 2003; see also Sher & McKenzie, 2003).

Thus, rather than indicating deep irrationality, framing effects (or at least attribute framing effects) appear to be the result of both speakers and listeners exploiting regularities in language in an adaptive way. (For more general discussions of the role of conversational norms in interpreting 'irrational' responses, see Hilton, 1995; Schwarz, 1996.) In this case, systematic frame selection by speakers provides the environmental context for listeners, who respond accordingly.

Adaptable behavior

The above studies indicate that many purportedly irrational behaviors are adaptive in the sense that they reflect the structure of our environment. However, a different question is whether behavior is *adaptable*; that is, whether it changes in appropriate ways when it is clear that the current environment, or task structure, is atypical or changing in important ways. Perhaps our cognitive system is shaped to perform in the usual environmental structure, but we are incapable of changing behavior when the environment changes. Recent evidence, however, indicates that behavior is at least sometimes adaptable as well as adaptive.

Hypothesis testing

Recall that people's apparent default strategy of testing hypotheses – positive testing (Klayman & Ha, 1987) – is generally adaptive in part because hypotheses tend to be phrased in terms of rare events (McKenzie et al., 2001). McKenzie and Mikkelsen (2000) had participants test hypotheses of the form 'If X1, then Y1' and asked them whether an X1&Y1 observation or an X2&Y2 observation – both of which support the hypothesis – provided stronger support. For example, some participants were told that everyone has either genotype A or genotype B, and everyone has either personality type X or personality type Y. Some then tested the hypothesis, 'If a person has genotype A, then he or she has personality type X', and chose which person provided stronger support for the hypothesis: a person with genotype A and personality type X, or a person with genotype B and personality type Y. Just as many other studies have shown (e.g. Evans, 1989; Fischhoff & Beyth-Marom, 1983; Johnson-Laird & Tagart, 1969; Klayman & Ha, 1987; McKenzie, 1994), the authors found that when testing 'If X1, then Y1', participants overwhelmingly preferred confirming observations named in the hypothesis, or X1&Y1 observations.

However, McKenzie and Mikkelsen (2000) found this preference for the mentioned observation only when the hypothesis regarded unfamiliar variables and there was no information regarding the rarity of the observations (as in the above example). When participants were told that X1 and Y1 were common relative to X2 and Y2, or when they had prior knowledge of this fact because familiar, concrete variables were used, they were more likely to correctly select the unmentioned X2&Y2 observation as more supportive. The combination of familiar variables and a 'reminder' that X1 and Y1 were common led participants to correctly select the X2&Y2 observation more often than the X1&Y1 observation, even though they were testing 'If X1, then Y1'. These results suggest that when presented with abstract, unfamiliar variables to test – the norm in the laboratory – participants fall back on their (adaptive) default assumption that mentioned observations are rare. However, when the context makes it clear that the mentioned observation is common, participants are more likely to choose the more informative *un*mentioned observation.

The selection task

In the selection task, in which participants must select which cards to turn over in order to test whether an 'If P, then Q' rule is true, Oaksford and Chater (1994, 1996) argued that turning over the P and Q cards is adaptive if one adopts an inductive (Bayesian) approach to the task and it is assumed that P and Q are rare. An interesting question, though, is to what extent participants are sensitive to changes in how common P and Q are. Studies have revealed that participants' card selections do change in qualitatively appropriate ways when the rarity assumption is violated. For example, when it is clear that Q is common rather than rare, participants are more likely to select the not-Q card, as the Bayesian account predicts (Oaksford, Chater, & Grainger, 1999; Oaksford, Chater, Grainger, & Larkin, 1997; but see Evans & Over, 1996; Oberauer, Wilhelm, & Diaz, 1999).

Covariation assessment

Recall also that it was argued that being influenced most by cell A (joint presence observations) when assessing covariation is rational from a Bayesian perspective if it is assumed that the presence of variables is rare. This account predicts that, if it is clear that the *absence* of the variables to be assessed is rare, participants will be more likely to find cell D (joint absence) more informative than cell A. That is exactly what McKenzie and Mikkelsen (*in press*) found. Furthermore, much like the hypothesis-testing results of McKenzie and Mikkelsen (2000), these effects were only found when variables were used that participants were familiar with. When abstract,

unfamiliar variables were used, participants fell back on their (adaptive) default strategy of considering cell A more informative than cell D. When it was clear that the default assumption was inappropriate, participants' behavior changed in a qualitatively Bayesian manner. Indeed, the behavior of all the groups in McKenzie and Mikkelsen's (*in press*) experiment could be explained by participants' sensitivity to rarity: when presented with familiar variables, participants exploited their real-world knowledge about which observations were rare, and when presented with unfamiliar variables, they exploited their knowledge about how labeling (presence vs. absence) indicates what is (usually) rare.

All of the above findings regarding adaptability with respect to rarity are important because they show that the claims regarding adaptiveness (discussed in the previous subsection) are not mere post hoc rationalizations of irrational behavior. That is, it is no coincidence that the rarity assumption provides a rational explanation of hypothesis-testing and selection-task findings, and that the assumption that presence is rare provides a rational account of covariation findings. Participants are indeed sensitive to the rarity of data (see also McKenzie & Amin, 2002).

Choice behavior

Interestingly, choice-strategy behavior appears especially adaptable. In a typical choice task, participants are presented with various alternatives (e.g. apartments) that vary along several dimensions, or attributes (e.g. rent, distance to work/school, size). A robust finding is that participants' strategies for choosing are affected by task properties. For example, participants are more likely to trade off factors (e.g. rent vs. size) when there are two or three alternatives rather than four or more (for reviews, see Payne, 1982; Payne, Bettman, & Johnson, 1993). Participants are also more likely to process the information by attribute (e.g. compare apartments in terms of rent) rather than by alternative (evaluate each apartment separately in terms of its attributes). These findings are perplexing from the traditional normative perspective because factors such as the number of alternatives should have no effect on behavior. The typically presumed normative rule remains the same regardless of the task structure: evaluate each alternative on each attribute, assign each alternative an overall score, and choose the one with the highest score.

Payne, Bettman, and Johnson (1993) have provided an illuminating analysis of why such seemingly irrational changes in strategy occur: the changes represent an intelligent trade-off between effort and accuracy (see also Beach & Mitchell, 1978). Using computer simulation, the authors examined the accuracy of several heuristic (non-normative) choice strategies in a wide variety of task environments. One finding was that, at least in some environments, heuristics can be about as accurate as the normative strategy with substantial savings in effort (see also Thorngate, 1980, on efficient decision strategies, and McKenzie, 1994, on efficient inference strategies). For example, one task environment allowed one heuristic to achieve an accuracy score of 90% while requiring only 40% of the effort of the normative strategy. A second finding was that no single heuristic performed well in all decision environments. The interesting implication is that, if people strive to reach reasonably accurate decisions with simple strategies, then they should switch strategies in predictable ways depending on task structure. Such changes in strategy were just what were found in subsequent empirical work that allowed participants to search for information however they wished in a variety of decision environments (Payne, Bettman, & Johnson, 1988, 1990, 1993). Clearly, knowledge about the decision environment is crucial for *understanding* (not just predicting) choice-strategy behavior.

Summary of post-1990 research

When studied independently of the environment, behavior can appear maladaptive and irrational. Often, though, seemingly irrational behavior makes normative sense when the usual environmental context is taken into account. Not only is seemingly foolish behavior sometimes revealed to be adaptive, it is often found to be adaptable, changing in qualitatively appropriate ways when it is clear that the usual assumptions about the environment are being violated. The findings regarding adaptable behavior are important because they show that claims about adaptiveness are not mere post hoc rationalizations of irrational behavior.

The claim is not that the above research shows that cognition is optimal, only that 'errors' are often normatively defensible. For example, though I believe that covariation assessment behavior is best understood from a Bayesian perspective, I do not believe that people are optimal Bayesians (McKenzie & Mikkelsen, *in press*; see also McKenzie, 1994; McKenzie & Amin, 2002). Instead, I claim that people are sensitive to two factors when assessing covariation, which probably goes a long way toward behaving in a Bayes-like fashion: people take into account their prior beliefs about whether the variables are related, and they take into account the rarity of the different observations. There is clear evidence of both phenomena, and both are justified from a Bayesian perspective, which in turn has formidable normative status. In a nutshell: taking into account the environmental conditions under which people typically operate – together with normative principles that make sense given these conditions – can help explain why people behave as they do.

WHERE THE FIELD MIGHT BE HEADED

Given that (a) the 1960s view was that people do quite well in inference tasks, (b) the subsequent heuristics-and-biases message was that people make systematic and sometimes large errors, and (c) the more recent message is that people do well in inference tasks, it is tempting to reach the conclusion that the pendulum is simply swinging back and forth in the field of judgment and decision making, with no real progress being made (cf. Davis, 1971). The pendulum is moving forward, however, not just back and forth. First, the emphasis in the heuristics-and-biases program on studying the cognitive processes underlying judgment and decision making behavior represents important progress. Second, comparing the two optimistic views, the 1960s perspective and the research post-1990 described earlier, there are clear and important differences. The latter stresses the importance of environment in determining what is normative and why people behave as they do. Content and context matter, both normatively and descriptively. The realization (by psychologists) that a given task might have multiple reasonable normative responses opens the door to better understanding of behavior (Birnbaum, 1983; Einhorn & Hogarth, 1981; Gigerenzer, 1991a; Hogarth, 1981; McKenzie & Mikkelsen, *in press*; Oaksford & Chater, 1994). The focus shifts from whether or not responses are 'correct' to what is the best explanation of the behavior. Questions emerge such as, 'Under what conditions would such behavior make sense?' and 'What are the conditions under which people normally operate?' The answers can be interesting and highly informative – especially when the answers to the two questions are the same.

Assuming, then, that progress is being made, what lies ahead for the field of judgment and decision making? First, a safe bet: emphasizing the role of environment in understanding laboratory behavior will become even more commonplace. Now for a long shot: the current conception of what it means to be rational will change.

Let me explain. It should first be kept in mind that behaving rationally – that is, following normative rules – and being accurate in the real world are not the same thing (e.g. Funder, 1987; Gigerenzer & Goldstein, 1996; Gigerenzer, Todd, & the ABC Research Group, 1999; Hammond, 1996). The heuristics-and-biases literature has amassed a large collection of purported errors in human thinking (e.g. Gilovich et al., 2002; Kahneman et al., 1982). It has been argued here that some, perhaps most, of these purported errors have explanations that indicate strengths, not weaknesses, of human cognition.

Nonetheless, at the very least, the possibility that people do routinely violate some basic normative rules has not been ruled out. Note that the heuristics-and-biases approach is largely concerned with studying the processes underlying cognition in the laboratory. In particular, it examines whether people follow normative rules. An important, often tacit, assumption is that failing to follow these rules will lead to decreased real-world performance. However, somewhat paradoxically, research examining real-world performance has concluded that people are surprisingly accurate (e.g. Ambady, Bernieri, & Richeson, 2000; Brehmer & Joyce, 1988; Funder, 1987; Wright & Drinkwater, 1997), even though these judgments are often based on very little information and the judges have little or no insight into how they made them (Ambady et al., 2000; see also Hogarth, 2001).

Could it be that following normative rules is not the key to real-world accuracy? Of interest is that research on artificial intelligence (AI), which implements rules in the form of computer programs in an attempt to perform real-world tasks, has been plagued by failure (Dreyfus, 1992). Despite early claims that machines would be able to rival – even exceed – human performance, this has not turned out to be the case, except in highly constrained, well-defined environments, such as playing chess (and even in this domain, a staggering amount of computing power is required to outperform experts). Interestingly, the benchmark in AI is human behavior – and this benchmark is essentially never reached. Given that computers are 'logic machines', it is interesting that it is so difficult to get them to do tasks that we perform routinely, such as understand a story, produce and understand speech, and recognize scenes.

Thus, not only might rule-following behavior fail to guarantee real-world accuracy, the two might not even be compatible. In fact, scholars outside of psychology have reached the same conclusion: depending on a purely logical analysis will not get you very far in the real world, where context, meaning and relevance, rather than pure structure, are crucial (Damasio, 1994; Devlin, 1997; Dreyfus, 1992). Functioning in the real world requires *common sense*, which might be impossible, in principle, to capture formally (Dreyfus, 1992). It is generally understood in cognitive psychology (outside of the areas of reasoning and judgment and decision making, at least) that the cognitive system's most fascinating quality is its ability to solve apparently intractable problems with such apparent ease (e.g. Medin, Ross, & Markman, 2001). How it does so largely remains a mystery, but the failings of AI suggest that following rules is not the key. To the extent that normative rule-following behavior does not entail real-world accuracy, we are comparing human behavior to the wrong benchmark, and the field of judgment and decision making will need to undergo a radical change.

So what is a researcher to do if he or she wants to know whether, to use Russell's (1957) words, a person's degree of certainty is warranted by the evidence? With perhaps the exception of ball-and-urn-type problems, there simply are no simple answers. Given that there is often uncertainty about what constitutes the normative response to a given situation, and that following normative rules might not even lead us to where we want to go, I can only offer the following: treat normative models as *theories* of behavior, not as *standards* of behavior. This is the best bet for researchers in judgment and decision making – and for the field itself.

I'm *certain* of it.

ACKNOWLEDGMENTS

The preparation of this chapter was supported by National Science Foundation Grant SES-0079615. For their critical comments, the author thanks Gerd Gigerenzer, Robin Hogarth, Gideon Keren, Luis Pinto, Shlomi Sher and Jack Soll (probably none of whom agrees with everything in the chapter).

REFERENCES

Alexander, H. G. (1958). The paradoxes of confirmation. *British Journal for the Philosophy of Science, 9*, 227–233.

Allan, L. G. (1993). Human contingency judgments: rule based or associative? *Psychological Bulletin, 114*, 435–448.

Alloy, L. B., & Tabachnik, N. (1984). Assessment of covariation by humans and animals: the joint influence of prior expectations and current situational information. *Psychological Review, 91*, 112–149.

Alpert, M., & Raiffa, H. (1982). A progress report on the training of probability assessors. In D. Kahneman, P. Slovic, & A. Tversky (Eds.), *Judgment under uncertainty: heuristics and biases* (pp. 294–305). New York: Cambridge University Press.

Ambady, N., Bernieri, F. J., & Richeson, J. A. (2000). Toward a histology of social judgment behavior: judgmental accuracy from thin slices of the behavioral stream. In M. P. Zanna (ed.), *Advances in experimental social psychology* (pp. 201–271). San Diego: Academic Press.

Anderson, J. R. (1990). *The adaptive character of thought*. Hillsdale, NJ: Erlbaum.

Anderson, J. R. (1991). Is human cognition adaptive? *Behavioral and Brain Sciences, 14*, 471–517.

Anderson, J. R., & Milson, R. (1989). Human memory: an adaptive perspective. *Psychological Review, 96*, 703–719.

Anderson, J. R., & Sheu, C.-F. (1995). Causal inferences as perceptual judgments. *Memory and Cognition, 23*, 510–524.

Bazerman, M. H., & Neale, M. A. (1983). Heuristics in negotiation: limitations to dispute resolution effectiveness. In M. H. Bazerman & R. J. Lewicki (Eds.), *Negotiating in organizations* (pp. 51–67). Beverly Hills, CA: Sage.

Beach, L. R., & Mitchell, T. R. (1978). A contingency model for the selection of decision strategies. *Academy of Management Review, 3*, 439–449.

Bettman, J. R. (1979). *An information processing theory of consumer choice.* Reading, MA: Addison-Wesley.

Birnbaum, M. H. (1983). Base rates in Bayesian inference: signal detection analysis of the cab problem. *American Journal of Psychology, 96*, 85–94.

Brehmer, B., & Joyce, C. R. B. (Eds.) (1988). *Human judgment: the SJT view.* Amsterdam: Elsevier.

Brenner, L. A., Koehler, D. J., Liberman, V., & Tversky, A. (1996). Overconfidence in probability and frequency judgments: a critical examination. *Organizational Behavior and Human Decision Processes, 65*, 212–219.

Brunswik, E. (1956). *Perception and the representative design of psychological experiments* (2nd ed.). Berkeley: University of California Press.

Cheng, P. W. (1997). From covariation to causation: a causal power theory. *Psychological Review, 104*, 367–405.

Cheng, P. W., & Novick, L. R. (1990). A probabilistic contrast model of causal induction. *Journal of Personality and Social Psychology, 58*, 545–567.

Cheng, P. W., & Novick, L. R. (1992). Covariation in natural causal induction. *Psychological Review, 99*, 365–382.

Christensen-Szalanski, J. J. J., & Beach, L. R. (1984). The citation bias: fad and fashion in the judgment and decision literature. *American Psychologist, 39*, 75–78.

Cohen, L. J. (1977). *The probable and the provable.* Oxford: Oxford University Press.

Cohen, L. J. (1979). On the psychology of prediction: whose is the fallacy? *Cognition, 7*, 385–407.

Cohen, L. J. (1981). Can human irrationality be experimentally demonstrated? *Behavioral and Brain Sciences, 4*, 317–370.

Combs, B., & Slovic, P. (1979). Causes of death: biased newspaper coverage and biased judgments. *Journalism Quarterly, 56*, 837–843, 849.

Coombs, C. H., Dawes, R. M., & Tversky, A. (1970). *Mathematical psychology: an introduction.* Englewood Cliffs, NJ: Prentice-Hall.

Cosmides, L., & Tooby, J. (1996). Are humans good intuitive statisticians after all? Rethinking some conclusions from the literature on judgment under uncertainty. *Cognition, 58*, 1–73.

Crocker, J. (1981). Judgment of covariation by social perceivers. *Psychological Bulletin, 90*, 272–292.

Damasio, A. R. (1994). *Descartes' error: emotion, reason, and the human brain.* New York: Avon.

Davis, M. S. (1971). That's interesting! Towards a phenomenology of sociology and a sociology of phenomenology. *Philosophy of the Social Sciences, 1*, 309–344.

Devlin, K. (1997). *Goodbye, Descartes: the end of logic and the search for a new cosmology of the mind.* New York: Wiley.

Dreyfus, H. L. (1992). *What computers still can't do: a critique of artificial reason.* Cambridge, MA: MIT Press.

Edwards, W. (1968). Conservatism in human information processing. In B. Kleinmuntz (ed.), *Formal representations of human judgment* (pp. 17–52). New York: Wiley.

Edwards, W. (1975). Comment. *Journal of the American Statistical Association, 70*, 291–293.

Einhorn, H. J., & Hogarth, R. M. (1981). Behavioral decision theory: processes of judgment and choice. *Annual Review of Psychology, 32*, 53–88.

Einhorn, H. J., & Hogarth, R. M. (1986). Judging probable cause. *Psychological Bulletin, 99*, 3–19.

Elstein, A. S., Shulman, L. S., & Sprafka, S. A. (1978). *Medical problem solving: an analysis of clinical reasoning.* Cambridge, MA: Harvard University Press.

Erev, I., Wallsten, T. S., & Budescu, D. V. (1994). Simultaneous over- and underconfidence: the role of error in judgment processes. *Psychological Review, 101*, 519–527.

Evans, J. St B. T. (1989). *Bias in human reasoning: causes and consequences.* Hillsdale, NJ: Erlbaum.

Evans, J. St B. T., & Over, D. E. (1996). Rationality in the selection task: epistemic uncertainty versus uncertainty reduction. *Psychological Review, 103*, 356–363.

Fischhoff, B., & Beyth-Marom, R. (1983). Hypothesis testing from a Bayesian perspective. *Psychological Review, 90*, 239–260.

Fischhoff, B., Slovic, P., & Lichtenstein, S. (1977). Knowing with certainty: the appropriateness of extreme confidence. *Journal of Experimental Psychology: Human Perception and Performance, 3*, 552–564.

Funder, D. C. (1987). Errors and mistakes: evaluating the accuracy of social judgment. *Psychological Bulletin, 101*, 75–90.

Gibson, J. J. (1979). *The ecological approach to visual perception.* Boston: Houghton Mifflin.

Gigerenzer, G. (1991a). How to make cognitive illusions disappear: beyond 'heuristics and biases'. *European Review of Social Psychology, 2*, 83–115.

Gigerenzer, G. (1991b). On cognitive illusions and rationality. *Poznan Studies in the Philosophy of the Sciences and the Humanities, 21*, 225–249.

Gigerenzer, G. (1996). On narrow norms and vague heuristics: a reply to Kahneman and Tversky. *Psychological Review, 103*, 592–596.

Gigerenzer, G., & Goldstein, D. G. (1996). Reasoning the fast and frugal way: models of bounded rationality. *Psychological Review, 103*, 650–669.

Gigerenzer, G., Hell, W., & Blank, H. (1988). Presentation and content: the use of base rates as a continuous variable. *Journal of Experimental Psychology: Human Perception and Performance, 14*, 513–525.

Gigerenzer, G., & Hoffrage, U. (1995). How to improve Bayesian reasoning without instruction: frequency formats. *Psychological Review, 102*, 684–704.

Gigerenzer, G., Hoffrage, U., & Kleinbölting, H. (1991). Probabilistic mental models: a Brunswikian theory of confidence. *Psychological Review, 98*, 506–528.

Gigerenzer, G., & Murray, D. J. (1987). *Cognition as intuitive statistics*. Hillsdale, NJ: Erlbaum.

Gigerenzer, G., Todd, P. M., & the ABC Research Group (1999). *Simple heuristics that make us smart*. Oxford: Oxford University Press.

Gilovich, T., Griffin, D., & Kahneman, D. (2002). *Heuristics and biases: the psychology of intuitive judgment*. Cambridge: Cambridge University Press.

Good, I. J. (1960). The paradox of confirmation. *British Journal for the Philosophy of Science, 11*, 145–149.

Griffin, D., & Tversky, A. (1992). The weighing of evidence and the determinants of confidence. *Cognitive Psychology, 24*, 411–435.

Hammond, K. R. (1955). Probabilistic functioning and the clinical method. *Psychological Review, 62*, 255–262.

Hammond, K. R. (ed.) (1996). *Human judgment and social policy*. New York: Oxford University Press.

Hastie, R., & Dawes, R. M. (2001). *Rational choice in an uncertain world: the psychology of judgment and decision making*. Thousand Oaks, CA: Sage.

Hilgard, E. R., & Bower, G. H. (1975). *Theories of learning* (4th ed.). Englewood Cliffs, NJ: Prentice-Hall.

Hilton, D. J. (1995). The social context of reasoning: conversational inference and rational judgment. *Psychological Bulletin, 118*, 248–271.

Hogarth, R. M. (1981). Beyond discrete biases: functional and dysfunctional aspects of judgmental heuristics. *Psychological Bulletin, 47*, 116–131.

Hogarth, R. M. (2001). *Educating intuition*. Chicago: University of Chicago Press.

Horwich, P. (1982). *Probability and evidence*. Cambridge: Cambridge University Press.

Hosiasson-Lindenbaum, J. (1940). On confirmation. *Journal of Symbolic Logic, 5*, 133–148.

Howson, C., & Urbach, P. (1989). *Scientific reasoning: the Bayesian approach*. La Salle, IL: Open Court.

Inhelder, B., & Piaget, J. (1958). *The growth of logical thinking: from childhood to adolescence*. New York: Basic Books.

Johnson-Laird, P. N., & Tagart, J. (1969). How implication is understood. *American Journal of Psychology, 82*, 367–373.

Jungermann, H. (1983). The two camps on rationality. In R. W. Scholz (ed.), *Decision making under uncertainty* (pp. 63–86). Amsterdam: Elsevier.

Juslin, P. (1994). The overconfidence phenomenon as a consequence of informal experimenter-guided selection of almanac items. *Organizational Behavior and Human Decision Processes, 57*, 226–246.

Kahneman, D., Slovic, P., & Tversky, A. (Eds.) (1982). *Judgment under uncertainty: heuristics and biases*. Cambridge: Cambridge University Press.

Kahneman, D., & Tversky, A. (1972). Subjective probability: a judgment of representativeness. *Cognitive Psychology, 3*, 430–454.

Kahneman, D., & Tversky, A. (1973). On the psychology of prediction. *Psychological Review, 80*, 237–251.

Kahneman, D., & Tversky, A. (1979). Prospect theory: an analysis of decision under risk. *Econometrica, 47*, 263–291.

Kahneman, D., & Tversky, A. (1982). On the study of statistical intuitions. *Cognition, 11*, 123–141.

Kahneman, D., & Tversky, A. (1984). Choices, values, and frames. *American Psychologist, 39*, 341–350.

Kahneman, D., & Tversky, A. (1996). On the reality of cognitive illusions: a reply to Gigerenzer's critique. *Psychological Review, 103*, 582–591.

Kao, S.-F., & Wasserman, E. A. (1993). Assessment of an information integration account of contingency judgment with examination of subjective cell importance and method of information presentation. *Journal of Experimental Psychology: Learning, Memory, and Cognition, 19*, 1363–1386.

Klayman, J., & Brown, K. (1993). Debias the environment instead of the judge: an alternative approach to reducing error in diagnostic (and other) judgment. *Cognition, 49*, 97–122.

Klayman, J., & Ha, Y.-W. (1987). Confirmation, disconfirmation, and information in hypothesis testing. *Psychological Review, 94*, 211–228.

Koehler, J. J. (1996). The base rate fallacy reconsidered: descriptive, normative, and methodological challenges. *Behavioral and Brain Sciences, 19*, 1–53.

Kühberger, A. (1998). The influence of framing on risky decisions: a meta-analysis. *Organizational Behavior and Human Decision Processes, 75*, 23–55.

Larrick, R. P., Nisbett, R. E., & Morgan, J. N. (1993). Who uses the cost-benefit rules of choice? Implications for the normative status of microeconomic theory. *Organizational Behavior and Human Decision Processes, 56*, 331–347.

Levin, I. P., Schneider, S. L., & Gaeth, G. J. (1998). All frames are not created equal: a typology and critical analysis of framing effects. *Organizational Behavior and Human Decision Processes, 76*, 149–188.

Levin, I. P., Wasserman, E. A., & Kao, S.-F. (1993). Multiple methods for examining biased information use in contingency judgments. *Organizational Behavior and Human Decision Processes, 55*, 228–250.

Lichtenstein, S., Fischhoff, B., & Phillips, L. D. (1982). Calibration of probabilities: the state of the art to 1980. In D. Kahneman, P. Slovic, & A. Tversky (Eds.), *Judgment under uncertainty: heuristics and biases* (pp. 306–334). Cambridge: Cambridge University Press.

Lichtenstein, S., Slovic, P., Fischhoff, B., Layman, M., & Combs, B. (1978). Judged frequency of lethal events. *Journal of Experimental Psychology: Human Learning and Memory, 4*, 551–578.

Lipe, M. G. (1990). A lens-model analysis of covariation research. *Journal of Behavioral Decision Making, 3*, 47–59.

Lopes, L. L. (1982). Doing the impossible: a note on induction and the experience of randomness. *Journal of Experimental Psychology: Learning, Memory, and Cognition, 8*, 626–636.

Lopes, L. L. (1991). The rhetoric of irrationality. *Theory and Psychology, 1*, 65–82.

Mackie, J. L. (1963). The paradox of confirmation. *British Journal for the Philosophy of Science, 13*, 265–277.

Mackie, J. L. (1974). *The cement of the universe: a study of causation*. Oxford: Clarendon.

Mandel, D. R., & Lehman, D. R. (1998). Integration of contingency information in judgments of cause, covariation, and probability. *Journal of Experimental Psychology: General*, *127*, 269–285.

March, J. G. (1978). Bounded rationality, ambiguity, and the engineering of choice. *Bell Journal of Economics*, *9*, 587–608.

Marr, D. (1982). *Vision*. San Francisco: W. H. Freeman.

McKenzie, C. R. M. (1994). The accuracy of intuitive judgment strategies: covariation assessment and Bayesian inference. *Cognitive Psychology*, *26*, 209–239.

McKenzie, C. R. M., & Amin, M. B. (2002). When wrong predictions provide more support than right ones. *Psychonomic Bulletin and Review*, *9*, 821–828.

McKenzie, C. R. M., Ferreira, V. S., Mikkelsen, L. A., McDermott, K. J., & Skrable, R. P. (2001). Do conditional hypotheses target rare events? *Organizational Behavior and Human Decision Processes*, *85*, 291–309.

McKenzie, C. R. M., & Mikkelsen, L. A. (2000). The psychological side of Hempel's paradox of confirmation. *Psychonomic Bulletin and Review*, *7*, 360–366.

McKenzie, C. R. M., & Mikkelsen, L. A. (in press). A Bayesian view of covariation assessment. *Cognitive Psychology*.

McKenzie, C. R. M., & Nelson, J. D. (2003). What a speaker's choice of frame reveals: reference points, frame selection, and framing effects. *Psychonomic Bulletin and Review*, *10*, 596–602.

McKenzie, C. R. M., & Soll, J. B. (1996). Which reference class is evoked? *Behavioral and Brain Sciences*, *19*, 34–35.

Medin, D. L., Ross, B. H., & Markman, A. B. (2001). *Cognitive psychology* (3rd ed.). Fort Worth, TX: Harcourt.

Mellers, B., Hertwig, R., & Kahneman, D. (2001). Do frequency representations eliminate conjunction effects? An exercise in adversarial collaboration. *Psychological Science*, *12*, 269–275.

Mynatt, C. R., Doherty, M. E., & Tweney, R. D. (1977). Confirmation bias in a simulated research environment: an experimental study of scientific inference. *Quarterly Journal of Experimental Psychology*, *29*, 85–95.

Mynatt, C. R., Doherty, M. E., & Tweney, R. D. (1978). Consequences of confirmation and disconfirmation in a simulated research environment. *Quarterly Journal of Experimental Psychology*, *30*, 395–406.

Nickerson, R. S. (1996). Hempel's paradox and Wason's selection task: logical and psychological puzzles of confirmation. *Thinking and Reasoning*, *2*, 1–31.

Nisbett, R., & Ross, L. (1980). *Human inference: strategies and shortcomings of social judgment*. Englewood Cliffs, NJ: Prentice-Hall.

Oaksford, M., & Chater, N. (1994). A rational analysis of the selection task as optimal data selection. *Psychological Review*, *101*, 608–631.

Oaksford, M., & Chater, N. (1996). Rational explanation of the selection task. *Psychological Review*, *103*, 381–391.

Oaksford, M., Chater, N., & Grainger, B. (1999). Probabilistic effects in data selection. *Thinking and Reasoning*, *5*, 193–243.

Oaksford, M., Chater, N., Grainger, B., & Larkin, J. (1997). Optimal data selection in the reduced array selection task (RAST). *Journal of Experimental Psychology: Learning, Memory, and Cognition*, *23*, 441–458.

Oberauer, K., Wilhelm, O., & Diaz, R. R. (1999). Bayesian rationality for the Wason selection task? A test of optimal data selection theory. *Thinking and Reasoning*, *5*, 115–144.

Payne, J. W. (1982). Contingent decision behavior. *Psychological Bulletin*, *92*, 382–402.

Payne, J. W., Bettman, J. R., & Johnson, E. J. (1988). Adaptive strategy selection in decision making. *Journal of Experimental Psychology: Learning, Memory, and Cognition*, *14*, 534–552.

Payne, J. W., Bettman, J. R., & Johnson, E. J. (1990). The adaptive decision maker. In R. M. Hogarth (ed.), *Insights in decision making: a tribute to Hillel J. Einhorn* (pp. 129–153). Chicago: University of Chicago Press.

Payne, J. W., Bettman, J. R., & Johnson, E. J. (1993). *The adaptive decision maker*. Cambridge: Cambridge University Press.

Peterson, C. R., & Beach, L. R. (1967). Man as an intuitive statistician. *Psychological Bulletin*, *68*, 29–46.

Phillips, L. D. (1983). A theoretical perspective on heuristics and biases in probabilistic thinking. In P. C. Humphreys, O. Svenson, & A. Vari (Eds.), *Analysing and aiding decision processes* (pp. 525–543). Amsterdam: North Holland.

Pitz, G. F., Downing, L., & Reinhold, H. (1967). Sequential effects in the revision of subjective probabilities. *Canadian Journal of Psychology*, *21*, 381–393.

Popper, K. R. (1959). *The logic of scientific discovery*. New York: Harper & Row.

Russell, B. (1957). Preface. In P. Edwards (ed.), *Why I am not a Christian (and other essays on religion and related subjects)* (pp. v–vii). New York: Simon & Schuster.

Saks, M. J., & Kidd, R. F. (1980). Human information processing and adjudication: trial by heuristics. *Law and Society Review*, *15*, 123–160.

Schustack, M. W., & Sternberg, R. J. (1981). Evaluation of evidence in causal inference. *Journal of Experimental Psychology: General*, *110*, 101–120.

Schwarz, N. (1996). *Cognition and communication: judgmental biases, research methods, and the logic of conversation*. Mahwah, NJ: Erlbaum.

Shaklee, H. (1983). Human covariation judgment: accuracy and strategy. *Learning and Motivation*, *14*, 433–448.

Sher, S., & McKenzie, C. R. M. (2003). Information leakage from logically equivalent frames. Unpublished manuscript.

Simon, H. A. (1955). A behavioral model of rational choice. *Quarterly Journal of Economics*, *69*, 99–118.

Simon, H. A. (1956). Rational choice and the structure of the environment. *Psychological Review*, *63*, 129–138.

Slovic, P., & Lichtenstein, S. (1971). Comparison of Bayesian and regression approaches to the study of information processing in judgment. *Organizational Behavior and Human Performance, 6,* 649–744.

Slovic, P., & Tversky, A. (1974). Who accepts Savage's axiom? *Behavioral Science, 19,* 368–373.

Smedslund, J. (1963). The concept of correlation in adults. *Scandinavian Journal of Psychology, 4,* 165–173.

Smith, E. E., & Medin, D. L. (1981). *Categories and concepts.* Cambridge, MA: Harvard University Press.

Snyder, M. (1981). Seek and ye shall find: testing hypotheses about other people. In E. T. Higgins, C. P. Heiman, & M. P. Zanna (Eds.), *Social cognition: the Ontario symposium on personality and social psychology* (pp. 277–303). Hillsdale, NJ: Erlbaum.

Snyder, M., & Campbell, B. H. (1980). Testing hypotheses about other people: the role of the hypothesis. *Personality and Social Psychology Bulletin, 6,* 421–426.

Snyder, M., & Swann, W. B., Jr. (1978). Hypothesis-testing in social interaction. *Journal of Personality and Social Psychology, 36,* 1202–1212.

Soll, J. B. (1996). Determinants of overconfidence and miscalibration: the roles of random error and ecological structure. *Organizational Behavior and Human Decision Processes, 65,* 117–137.

Stanovich, K. E. (1999). *Who is rational? Studies of individual differences in reasoning.* Mahwah, NJ: Erlbaum.

Thorngate, W. (1980). Efficient decision heuristics. *Behavioral Science, 25,* 219–225.

Toda, M. (1962). The design of a fungus-eater: a model of human behavior in an unsophisticated environment. *Behavioral Science, 7,* 164–183.

Tolman, E. C., & Brunswik, E. (1935). The organism and the causal structure of the environment. *Psychological Review, 42,* 43–77.

Tversky, A., & Kahneman, D. (1971). The belief in the 'law of small numbers'. *Psychological Bulletin, 76,* 105–110.

Tversky, A., & Kahneman, D. (1973). Availability: a heuristic for judging frequency and probability. *Cognitive Psychology, 4,* 207–232.

Tversky, A., & Kahneman, D. (1974). Judgment under uncertainty: heuristics and biases. *Science, 185,* 1124–1131.

Tversky, A., & Kahneman, D. (1981). The framing of decisions and the psychology of choice. *Science, 211,* 453–458.

Tversky, A., & Kahneman, D. (1982a). Evidential impact of base rates. In D. Kahneman, P. Slovic, & A. Tversky (Eds.), *Judgment under uncertainty: heuristics and biases* (pp. 153–160). Cambridge: Cambridge University Press.

Tversky, A., & Kahneman, D. (1982b). Judgments of and by representativeness. In D. Kahneman, P. Slovic, & A. Tversky (Eds.), *Judgment under uncertainty: heuristics and biases* (pp. 84–98). Cambridge: Cambridge University Press.

Tversky, A., & Kahneman, D. (1983). Extensional versus intuitive reasoning: the conjunction fallacy in probability judgment. *Psychological Review, 90,* 293–315.

Tversky, A., & Kahneman, D. (1986). Rational choice and the framing of decisions. *Journal of Business, 59,* S251–S278.

Wallsten, T. S. (1980). Processes and models to describe choice and inference behavior. In T. S. Wallsten (ed.), *Cognitive processes in choice and decision behavior* (pp. 215–237). Hillsdale, NJ: Erlbaum.

Wason, P. C. (1960). On the failure to eliminate hypotheses in a conceptual task. *Quarterly Journal of Experimental Psychology, 12,* 129–140.

Wason, P. C. (1962). Reply to Wetherick. *Quarterly Journal of Experimental Psychology, 14,* 250.

Wason, P. C. (1966). Reasoning. In B. M. Foss (ed.), *New horizons in psychology* (pp. 135–151). Harmondsworth, UK: Penguin.

Wason, P. C. (1968). Reasoning about a rule. *Quarterly Journal of Experimental Psychology, 20,* 273–281.

Wason, P. C., & Johnson-Laird, P. N. (1972). *Psychology of reasoning: structure and content.* Cambridge, MA: Harvard University Press.

Wasserman, E. A., Dorner, W. W., & Kao, S.-F. (1990). Contributions of specific cell information to judgments of interevent contingency. *Journal of Experimental Psychology: Learning, Memory, and Cognition, 16,* 509–521.

Wright, J. C., & Drinkwater, M. (1997). Rationality vs. accuracy of social judgment. *Social Cognition, 15,* 245–273.

Yaniv, I., & Foster, D. P. (1995). Graininess of judgment under uncertainty: an accuracy-informativeness trade-off. *Journal of Experimental Psychology: General, 124,* 424–432.

Yaniv, I., & Foster, D. P. (1997). Precision and accuracy of judgmental estimation. *Journal of Behavioral Decision Making, 10,* 21–32.

PART FIVE

Cognitive Neuropsychology

15

The Cognitive Neuropsychology of Object Recognition and Action

GLYN W. HUMPHREYS AND M. JANE RIDDOCH

Visual object recognition operates with truly amazing efficiency in normal observers, well beyond the capabilities of even the most powerful artificial (computational) vision systems. For example, even within 100 ms or so we are able to recognize objects drawn from wide sets of classes (Thorpe, Fize, & Marlot, 1996). Recognition is also difficult to suppress. To take but one example, the time taken to match objects according to whether they have the same global shape or orientation is affected by whether the objects are semantically related to one another (Boucart & Humphreys, 1992). Thus the semantic relations between objects can influence performance on tasks where judgements are only required to the physical properties of stimuli. The efficiency and automaticity of object recognition can make it difficult to explain the complexity of the underlying processes. If human object recognition is fast and automatic, it seems as if there is hardly anything to explain.

Cognitive neuropsychology, however, teaches us that there is indeed something to explain. Through the study of patients with selective disturbances of a cognitive ability, cognitive neuropsychology aims to throw light on the processes that normally support human performance. The role of a particular cognitive process may be gleaned by analysing how performance is affected when the process goes wrong. In addition, our understanding of the patients can be boosted by using theories of normal processing as frameworks against which to conceptualize any deficits (see Coltheart, 1984). Consider then a patient who, after a particular brain lesion, is unable to recognize an object from vision, and, moreover, is unable even to make perceptual judgements about apparently the most basic properties of the object – for instance, its size or orientation. One might think that such a patient should be functionally blind.

Yet this is not necessarily the case. Milner and colleagues (Milner et al., 1991) were the first to document a patient who, despite showing such poor perceptual judgements, was nevertheless able to make appropriate reach-and-grasp actions to objects. In one striking example, this patient (patient DF) was able to take a letter and post it without hesitation through a slot that could be at different orientations. Despite this, DF was unable to orientate her hand to an orientation matching the slot, when asked to indicate the orientation that she perceived. Similar results were found when DF had to indicate the perceived size of an object (when performance was poor) in contrast to when she was asked to reach and pick up objects of different sizes (when her grip was accurately scaled to the size of the object; see Goodale, Milner, Jakobson, & Carey, 1991). This striking dissociation, between impaired perceptual judgements and spared reaching-and-grasp actions to stimuli, is counter-intuitive. Rather than object recognition and the guidance of action to objects being 'all of a whole', it appears that the visual information used for object recognition can be separated from the visual information used to guide action. DF has an impairment in using vision for object recognition, but not in the use of vision for reaching and grasping. Here cognitive neuropsychology reveals the existence of distinct visual processes (for perceptual judgements and for action) that can be difficult to prise apart in normal observers. In this chapter, we shall review work on the cognitive neuropsychology of object recognition and action. We shall argue that, even if object processing is normally efficient and recognition automatic, there are numerous component operations that support recognition and action. These operations can be selectively affected by brain damage, which in turn throws light on their organization in normal observers.

PROCESSING AND INTEGRATING BASIC PERCEPTUAL DIMENSIONS

Patients such as DF have severely impaired form perception, and seem unable to discriminate even basic dimensions of shapes, such as their orientation and size (at least in perceptual judgement tasks). Nevertheless, such patients often can name colours and they can judge the speed and direction of motion (see also Benson & Greenberg, 1969; Efron, 1968, for earlier descriptions of similar cases). There is a dissociation between the perception of shape information and the perception of other basic visual properties of the world, such as colour and motion. There have also been cases reported with the opposite pattern of impairment. For example, patients can manifest impaired colour perception whilst processing of the basic dimensions of form is relatively preserved (Heywood, Cowey, & Newcombe, 1991; Humphreys & Riddoch, 1987; see Heywood & Cowey, 1999, for a review), whilst other patients can have impaired motion perception but relatively spared colour and form perception (Zihl, Von Cramon, & Mai, 1983; see Heywood & Zihl, 1999, for a review). In some instances, patients have even been documented with a relatively good ability to perceive shape from contour but not from texture (with both static and dynamic images; see Battelli, Casco, & Sartori, 1997). The dissociations in processing these basic properties of stimuli suggest that the properties are coded in separable neural pathways – for form from contour, form from texture, colour and motion. This argument, for some degree of modularity in the processing of the basic dimensions of visual stimuli, is supported by work on functional brain imaging in normal observers, where distinct neural areas respond to at least some of these basic dimensions (e.g. area V4 for colour, MT for motion, and so forth; see Zeki, 1993). Selective damage to these areas can produce discrete deficits in patients.

If there is some independence in the processing of basic dimensions of visual stimuli, how is it that we are able to perceive a coherent world in which colours and textures are bound to objects? One answer to this question is that, having decomposed stimuli into their basic dimensions, the brain then recombines them to produce integrated percepts.[1] Two main accounts have been offered for how this integration process takes place. One proposal is that the brain uses information about the temporal firing of cells in order to bind the properties of objects together (e.g. Singer & Gray, 1995). If neurons responding to properties of one object fire in synchrony, whilst those responding to properties of different objects fire asynchronously, then the brain has a temporal signal for binding together properties represented by those cells firing in synchrony. There is neurophysiological evidence for cells firing synchronously to properties of a stimulus that group together (Eckhorn, 1999; Singer & Gray, 1995), and also psychophysical evidence from normal observers that temporal synchronization of inputs provides an important cue for binding (Elliott & Müller, 1998; Fahle, 1993).

Neuropsychological evidence for this notion comes from Humphreys, Riddoch, Nys, and Heinke (2002). These investigators were studying the factors that improved the report of a stimulus presented in the impaired (contralesional, left) field of a patient GK, with lateralized damage to the parietal lobe (GK actually had bilateral parietal lesions, but the lesion on the right side was larger). The finding of poor identification of stimuli on the side of space contralateral to the lesion site is quite common after posterior brain damage, reflecting the retinotopic organization of cells in that neural area. Humphreys et al., however, reported an unusual finding, which was that GK was better able to report a left-side stimulus if it appeared simultaneously with an item on the right side, relative to when the left item was presented alone. This 'boost' for identifying the contralesional item was greater when the two stimuli appeared as onsets against previously empty regions of field, compared to when they were created by 'offsetting' contours from pre-masks. It may be that the boost is produced by temporal binding between the ipsi- and contralesional stimuli, which enables the contralesional item to be recovered as part of a single group. However, an alternative proposal is that the boost is caused by the simultaneous onsets cueing attention to the region covered by both stimuli. There is a stronger cue to attention from two stimuli than from the contralesional item alone, and hence identification of the left-side item improves.

To test this, Humphreys et al. employed displays such as those shown in Figure 15.1a. GK was presented with 1, 2 or 3 letters on a trial, with the central letter created by offsetting contours from a central pre-mask and two flanker letters created by two new onsets. The task was for GK to identify as many letters as he could. If the onset letters cue his attention to the region of field covered by the flankers, then GK should have been relatively good

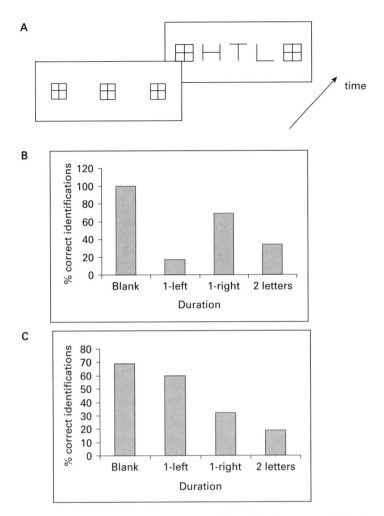

Figure 15.1 *(a) Example displays from Humphreys et al. (2002), with a central 'offset' letter as well as 'onset' flanker letters. The task was to report as many letters as possible. (b) Percentage correct identification of the onset letters. Note that report on 2 letter trials was better than on trials with 1 left letter – the 'anti-extinction' effect. (c) Percentage correct identification of the central offset letter, as a function of whether 0, 1-left, 1-right or 2 onset letters were presented. Note that there was relatively poor report of the central letter when both onset letters were reported.*

at identifying the central letter when both flankers appeared. This was not what was found. When report of the flankers alone was considered, then report of the left item was better in the '2 letter' condition (left and right flankers onsetting together) than when a single left letter appeared. This is the 'boost' for the contralesional letter (see Figure 15.1b). However, when both flankers appeared, report of the central (offset) letter was then relatively poor (Figure 15.1c). Indeed, on many trials GK identified the two flankers but not the central

(offset) item he was then looking at (e.g. given the example in Figure 15.1a, GK reported L and H, but not the central T). This result is hard to understand in terms of attentional cueing, since the central item should be attended whenever GK reports the left, onset letter. On the other hand, the finding is consistent with a temporal grouping account. Grouping of the flanking letters, by their common onset, enables the left-hand letter to be identified. The central offset letter is not part of this group, and so suffers in report.

Humphreys et al. (2002) also observed that GK was quite unconscious of the temporal signal leading to binding between the contra- and ipsilesional elements. For example, when asked to judge whether contra- and ipsilesional stimuli appeared simultaneously or not, GK reported that the right stimulus preceded the left one when they appeared together. In fact, the left (contralesional letter) had to precede the right letter by about 750 ms before GK judged that the letters appeared simultaneously. This phenomenon, in which an ipsilesional item is perceived as occurring prior to a contralesional one, is known as 'prior entry', and has been reported on several occasions in patients with parietal lesions (Rorden, Mattingley, Karnath, & Driver, 1997). For GK, the prior entry effect on temporal order judgements dissociated from the effect of time on actual stimulus identification. Stimulus identification was better when the ipsi- and contralesional stimuli were presented at the same time than when the left letter led the right. Thus temporal synchrony between the stimuli boosted identification, but the signal was not available for conscious judgements of synchronicity.

The second major account of how binding operates in vision is that it is contingent on attention to the spatial location occupied by an object. Treisman, in particular, has argued that spatial attention is required to 'filter out' properties of irrelevant stimuli, so that only attended properties are available for binding (e.g. Treisman, 1998; Treisman & Gelade, 1980). Again there is physiological evidence for this view, from single-cell recordings in monkeys trained to attend to a given spatial location (e.g. Moran & Desimone, 1985). Neuropsychological data again come from patients with lesions of the parietal lobe, who seem to be impaired at spatial attention. The problems are most striking in patients with bilateral parietal damage, who present with deficits known as Balint's syndrome (Balint, 1909). In this syndrome, patients appear limited to perceiving a single object at a time and they show poor reaching to stimuli under visual guidance ('optic ataxia'). This poor reaching is associated also with poor spatial localization; patients can be severely impaired not only at acting but also at judging where a stimulus falls in the world (see, e.g., Humphreys, Romani, Olson, Riddoch, & Duncan, 1994). Friedman-Hill, Robertson, and Treisman (1995) and Robertson, Treisman, Friedman-Hill, and Grabowecky (1997) reported that their patient with Balint's syndrome not only had impoverished spatial localization, but also made abnormally high numbers of 'illusory conjunction' errors, in which he incorrectly combined features from different stimuli. For example, given a red O and a green X, he was quite likely to respond that there was a green O and a red X, even when he could look at the items for an unlimited

duration. These investigators proposed that the parietal lesions suffered by their patient affected the ability to fix spatial attention upon each stimulus, which would normally filter out the attributes of the other item. The result was that features from both items were available and could be incorrectly bound together.

Similar results to this have been reported by Humphreys, Cinel, Wolfe, Olson, and Klempen (2000) in patient GK (see above), who also shows aspects of Balint's syndrome due to his bilateral parietal lesions. However, Humphreys et al. noted an interesting contrast between GK's tendency to mis-combine features from separate visual dimensions (e.g. colour and shape) and his ability to group visual information within the form dimension. GK's ability to report visual forms was affected by grouping: if an element on the left (his worse side) grouped with an item on the (better) right side, then report of the left item was better than if the two elements did not group (see also Humphreys, 1998; Mattingley, Davis, & Driver, 1997; Ward, Goodrich, & Driver, 1994, for similar evidence). Thus GK was influenced by correct grouping in the form domain, but he then often incorrectly grouped the form information with the surface details belonging to a different object. Humphreys et al. propose that grouping operates early on in the visual coding of form, but that a parietal system concerned either with precise spatial registration of different features, or with allocating attention to space, is then needed in order to integrate across visual dimensions (in particular, to integrate form with surface detail). Thus we may need to distinguish between different types of binding process. The binding of form elements in particular may be distinct from the binding of form and surface detail. Such an argument would be consistent with computational theories of vision, such as that put forward by Grossberg and colleagues (e.g. Grossberg & Mingolla, 1985; Grossberg & Pessoa, 1998). Grossberg makes a distinction between a 'Boundary Contour System' (BCS), which first binds oriented edges from luminance discontinuities in the image, and a 'Feature Contour System' (FCS), which fills in the surface of an object within the boundaries formed by the BCS. On this account, a patient such as GK has a relatively intact BCS but then is impaired at integrating between the BCS and the FCS.

A final point to note here is that Robertson et al. (1997) also found that their patient with Balint's syndrome showed what may be termed 'implicit' binding between visual elements, even when he could not explicitly report the relations between the elements present. For example, he was faster to respond to the word TOP when it appeared within the top region of a rectangle than when it appeared within the bottom region (and vice versa for the

Figure 15.2 *Example of stimuli used in the Efron shape discrimination task. The task requires a patient to discriminate whether a shape is a square or a rectangle.*

word BOTTOM). However, he was at chance at deciding whether the word fell at the top or bottom of the shape (see also Wojciulik & Kanwisher, 1998). We have also observed a similar phenomenon in patient GK (Cinel, 2002). At present, however, it is unclear how these implicit binding effects relate to the poor binding demonstrated when visual attributes have explicitly to be reported by patients with Balint's syndrome. It may be that imprecise integration of visual elements can nevertheless be sufficient to produce evidence of implicit binding in tasks requiring speeded responses to stimuli; or it may be that explicit perceptual report depends on either precise co-registration of attributes or on attention to the locations of stimuli, moderated by the parietal lobe. Either way, explicit binding of attributes from different visual dimensions can be impaired after damage to the parietal lobe.

IMPAIRMENTS OF OBJECT RECOGNITION

Patients with Balint's syndrome can be impaired at integrating the shapes and surface details of visual stimuli, but their basic object recognition can be relatively spared. This suggests that, whilst the parietal role plays a part in binding surfaces and forms, it is not vital to the identification of single objects. We now consider patients who have impaired object recognition, a problem associated with damage to more ventral areas of cortex, linking primary visual areas in occipital cortex to areas of temporal cortex that likely mediate higher-level recognition processes. Again we shall show how such cases illustrate the complexity of the underlying processes, which can fractionate in a variety of ways after different brain lesions.

The pioneering studies of disorders of object recognition were conducted by the German neurologist Lissauer. He first distinguished two types of visual recognition problem that can occur after brain damage, which he labelled *apperceptive* and *associative* agnosia (Lissauer, 1890). Nowadays the term apperceptive agnosia is used to describe patients whose recognition problem seems contingent on poor perception of object form, whilst the term associative agnosia is applied to patients

without a deficit in form perception but who have difficulty in matching ('associating') form information to memory (see Farah, 1990; Humphreys & Riddoch, 1987, 1993; Warrington, 1985, for reviews). We start out with this historical framework, though we shall also elaborate differences between patients within each subtype, and we shall review whether the distinction, between apperceptive and associative processes, is a useful way to conceptualize object recognition.

The apperceptive agnosias

Processing elementary form information

One clinical test used to assess form perception is known as the Efron shape-matching task, in which the patient is asked to discriminate between squares and rectangles of the same area and brightness (see Figure 15.2). Patients can be impaired at this task, though, as we have noted, perceptual judgements based on 'surface' properties of objects (colour, brightness, texture) may still be made. Patient DF (Milner et al., 1991) would provide one example. A common aetiology across such patients is carbon monoxide poisoning, which can produce multiple, disseminated lesions throughout the cortex (Garland & Pearce, 1967). Campion and Latto (1985) argued that, owing to these disseminated lesions, patients see the world through a kind of 'peppery' mask, with the result that they lose detail about the global shape of objects. However, on this account we might expect patients to adapt over time, 'filling in' the 'holes' in their visual field (see Grossberg & Mingolla, 1985, for a discussion of perceptual filling-in across the blind spot and retinal veins). Also it should be possible to integrate objects that move across the peppery mask. There is no evidence for this in such patients.

An alternative argument is that such patients have deficits in some basic aspects of early form processing, such as the grouping of form elements into larger perceptual wholes. There is physiological evidence that grouping of features into larger wholes takes place even in the very earliest stages of cortical vision (see Gilbert, Ito, Kapadia, & Westheimer, 2000; Von der Heydt & Peterhans, 1989). Hence damage to early cortical areas may prevent patients from grouping parts into coherent perceptual structures, leading to problems even in simple shape-matching tasks. Vecera and Gilds (1998) attempted to pit the 'peppery mask' and grouping accounts of apperceptive agnosia against one another. They had normal subjects respond to a spatially cued target under two viewing conditions: either a peppery mask was present, or stimuli were degraded to mimic impaired grouping (the stimuli were rectangles that could have corners removed). The targets were small squares that could appear in the same rectangle as the cue or in another object the same distance away from the cued position. When the rectangles are not degraded, reaction times are usually faster when targets fall in the cued relative to the uncued object. Vecera and Gilds found that the object-cueing advantage was disrupted when the corners of the cued objects were removed, whilst the effects of object cueing combined additively with the slowing of processing produced by the peppery mask. They suggest that the object-cueing effect reflects processes involved in grouping visual elements into shape representations. Although a peppery mask can slow processing, it does not selectively disrupt the shape coding that gives rise to the object-cueing effect.

More direct evidence from patients, which goes against a 'peppery mask' account, comes from the contrast between perceptual judgements and action, which we have already discussed in the case of patient DF (Milner et al., 1991). Given that DF can show normal reaching and grasping responses to visual stimuli, it is hard to attribute her problem to simple visual masking of images. If this were the case, why would prehensile actions be unaffected?

Milner and Goodale (1995) use the neurological distinction between the ventral (occipital-temporal) and dorsal (occipital-parietal) streams of the visual cortex to explain the difference between impaired perception and spared action. They propose that DF's lesion affected the ventral visual system, which supports object recognition. As a consequence, perceptual judgements about even the basic dimensions of form were disrupted. In contrast, DF's intact dorsal visual stream not only codes stimulus location but also provides visual information for prehensile actions. On this account, the ventral stream (for object recognition) and the dorsal system (for location coding and action) are separated even from the early stages of cortical coding.

Interestingly, DF's ability to code orientation has been shown not only in action but also in perceptual judgement tasks, provided orientation information does not have to be consciously appreciated. The McCollough effect is a long-lasting negative after-effect that is contingent on the relative orientations of 'adapting' and 'test' patterns (McCollough, 1965). For example, after looking for a prolonged period at a vertical pattern with green and black stripes (the 'adaptation stimulus'), a test pattern

with white and black vertical stripes will be seen with the white areas replaced by pink (a negative after-effect). However, if the test pattern has horizontal stripes, then the negative colour after-effect does not occur. Thus the effect is contingent on the coding of orientation as well as colour. Humphrey, Goodale, and Gurnsey (1991) showed that DF manifested a positive McCollough effect. This can be interpreted in various ways. It could be that orientation is processed jointly with colour in a colour-sensitive pathway in the brain, which remains intact in DF. Provided her judgements are based on outputs from that pathway, she shows sensitivity to orientation. Her deficits become apparent only when she attempts to use orientation within the form-processing module. Alternatively, the contrast may reflect a difference between the use of orientation information for implicit or explicit judgements. DF may be able to use orientation information implicitly but not explicitly for perceptual judgements (thus she may not be conscious of orientation information even when it affects her perceptual judgements, as in the McCollough after-effect). On this view, her lesion disrupts the explicit representation of orientation information, and this is required for conscious perceptual judgements (but perhaps not for action).

Other studies with DF suggest that there are some limitations on her ability to use visual information for action, so that it is not the case that a dorsal 'vision for action' system is duplicating the same coding as the ventral system that leads to object recognition. Goodale, Jakobson, Milner, Perrett, Benson, and Hietanen (1994) demonstrated that DF was impaired at posting a T-shaped object into a matching aperture. Dijkerman, Milner, and Carey (1998) further showed that she could not position her fingers correctly when asked to place them into three holes in a Plexiglass disk (similar to the three holes in a ball used for ten-pin bowling). Apparently forms of relational coding between visual elements require the involvement of the ventral stream, which for her is impaired.

Integrating parts to wholes

In contrast to cases such as DF, other patients are able to demonstrate the coding of basic features of visual forms in perceptual judgement tasks, and this may even extend to forms of elementary grouping of these features. Nevertheless, they can still be impaired at binding of features into more wholistic shapes. Problems in binding features into wholes can be demonstrated most clearly when multiple items are present, perhaps because there is then more competition in assigning elements to shapes. This can be illustrated by studies conducted with the visual agnosic patient HJA (see Riddoch & Humphreys, 1987a; Riddoch, Humphreys, Gannon, Blott, & Jones, 1999). HJA suffered bilateral damage

Exemplars   **HJA's copies**

Figure 15.3   *Examples of HJA's copies, with the exemplars on the left (guitar and owl).*

to the ventral visual cortex (including the lingual and fusiform gyri and posterior regions of the inferior temporal gyri), which left him with a profound visual agnosia. He was typically only able to identify about one-third of the line drawings shown to him, though the recognition of photographs and real objects was somewhat better (see below). Unlike DF, HJA could perform the Efron shape-matching task (Figure 15.2; see Humphreys, Riddoch, Quinlan, Donnelly, & Price, 1992). He was also generally able to produce identifiable copies of objects that he failed to recognize (see Figure 15.3). At first sight then, HJA might be thought to have an *associative* rather than an *apperceptive* deficit (cf. Lissauer, 1890), but a closer analysis reveals that this is not correct. For example, his copying was often rather slow. Furthermore, when given sets of overlapping figures and asked to copy each different figure in a different coloured pen, HJA showed evidence of mis-segmentation – assigning parts of different shapes the same colour and parts of the same shape different colours (Figure 15.4a). He made particularly interesting errors with occluded shapes, where he sometimes drew in the occluded contour that would lie between visible parts of a background shape (Figure 15.4b). We return to consider this result in more detail shortly. HJA's object recognition

was also strongly affected by varying the quality of the perceptual information available. Overlapping forms were not only difficult to copy but also to identify; his identification levels decreased at a greater rate than normal when stimulus presentation times were reduced and, unlike control participants, line drawings tended to be harder to identify than silhouettes (Riddoch & Humphreys, 1987a; Riddoch et al., 1999). All of these last results are consistent with there being a perceptual origin to his deficits.

The perceptual deficit in HJA's case seems to stem from poor integration of local form elements into more wholistic shapes. Evidence for this comes from experiments on visual search and on shape matching. Humphreys et al. (1992) contrasted HJA's visual search for a target that differed in terms of a salient local feature from distractors (its orientation), relative to search for a target that differed in terms of how its features are combined (e.g. an inverted T amongst upright T's, all of which contain horizontal and vertical line elements). For normal observers, search for a target defined by a combination of features is typically more difficult than search for a target defined by a single feature from distractors, but search for feature-combination targets can be made efficient if the distractors form a homogeneous set. When distractors are

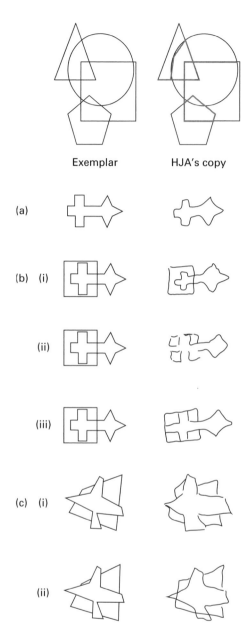

Exemplar   HJA's copy

(a)

(b) (i)

(ii)

(iii)

(c) (i)

(ii)

Figure 15.4 *(a) Example of overlapping figures and HJA's copying response (different textures signify the use of different coloured pens, to indicate when he thought a new shape began). (b) Example of HJA's copies of non-occluding (a) and occluding shapes ((b) and (c)). In examples such as b(i) and c(i) HJA includes the occluded contour in his drawing.*

homogeneous they can form a group distinct from the target, enabling the target to be selected efficiently (Duncan & Humphreys, 1989; Humphreys,

Quinlan, & Riddoch, 1989). HJA performed well on the single-feature search tasks. He was also as good as normal observers in searching for a combined-feature target when the distractors did not group. In contrast, he was markedly impaired in searching for a combined-feature target amongst homogeneous distractors, which normal subjects group and reject efficiently. This suggests that HJA was impaired specifically under conditions in which normal participants benefit from grouping taking place in parallel across the display. HJA is impaired at this type of parallel grouping of form.

Now consider data taken from a shape-matching task. Giersch, Humphreys, Boucart, and Kovacs (2000) presented HJA with line drawings of three geometric shapes that could be spatially separated, superimposed or occluding (see Figure 15.5). In addition, sets of occluding silhouettes were also presented. After a brief interval, the target was exposed again along with a distractor in which the positions of the shapes were rearranged. The task was to discriminate which of the second two stimuli matched the first. HJA found this task difficult with occluding shapes, and the problem was most evident when the length of the occluded edge was small (i.e. there was only a small gap between the visible parts that had to be completed). This is interesting because it should be easiest to compute the occluded edge in the small gap condition, based on collinearity between the visible edges of the object in the background. This suggests that HJA did compute the occluded edge, but the edge, once computed, produced problems in HJA coding the occluding shapes – which was in front, which behind, and so on. This was not an across-the-board loss of depth perception, since other aspects of HJA's depth perception were good (e.g. the ability to see depth from stereo images; see Humphreys & Riddoch, 1987). Rather, it reflects poor integration of line elements when complex relations between whole shapes have also to be coded.

This last finding, of poor matching of occluded shapes when an occluded contour could be computed, can be linked to the evidence from HJA's copying, where he sometimes draws in an occluded contour on to the front (occluding) surface of a shape (see Figure 15.4). Again this indicates that HJA computes occluded contours, but then shows impaired use of this information in perception (e.g. responding as if the contours were actually present, rather than being occluded). There is intact initial coding (and filling-in of missing contours) but impaired higher-level perceptual organization. The result also has implications for understanding normal vision. In particular it shows that occluded contours are computed at some early processing stage, prior to the assignment of figure–ground relations between shapes. The occluded contour is presumably computed locally from the presence of collinearity between edge elements, whereas figure–ground

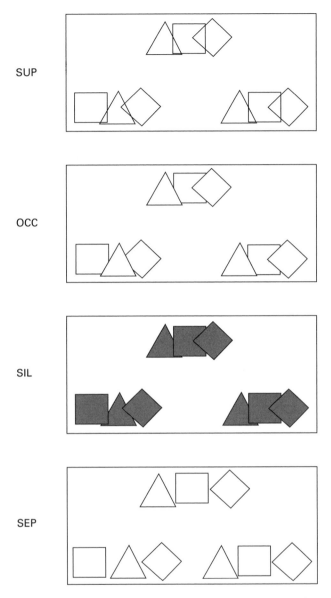

Figure 15.5   *Example stimuli used by Giersch et al. (2000). SUP = superimposed shapes; OCC = occluding shapes; SIL = silhouettes; SEP = spatially separated shapes. The task was to decide, as quickly as possible, which of the two lower triplets of shapes matched the upper triplet. Giersch et al. found that the agnosic patient, HJA, was particularly impaired with the occluding shapes.*

representations are derived from more wholistic coding between the shapes present. HJA can code local oriented elements into edges, but he is impaired at integrating the edges into shapes and in coding the figure–ground relations between shapes.

In a further study, Giersch et al. (2000) tested HJA's performance on a task designed to 'tap' this initial processing stage of linking oriented elements.

HJA was presented with displays such as those shown in Figure 15.6, with the task being to find the circular pattern. The numbers of background 'distractors' were increased until the target became impossible to find. HJA's threshold on this task was entirely normal! We conclude that there is a first stage of grouping oriented elements in form perception, followed by a subsequent stage in which the

Figure 15.6   *Example stimuli from Giersch et al. (2000), used to test whether HJA had intact computation of edge elements. The task was to detect the presence of the circular shape against the background elements (here it is mid-way down the figure on the left). The number of background elements was varied in order to determine the threshold at which the circular target could just be discriminated.*

edge elements are integrated into shapes. HJA's deficit is at this second stage. This fits with neuro-physiological data indicating that horizontal connections between cells even within primary visual areas (striate cortex) may play a role in grouping oriented edge elements (Gilbert et al., 2000). HJA's damage is confined to extra-striate areas that seem to support higher-level perceptual organization.

The impairment to perceptual organization in HJA seems to generate particular problems in dealing with line drawings, where there is minimal visual information from other sources (surface texture, depth, motion) to constrain identification. For example, with line drawings HJA tended to segment parts as if they belonged to separate objects, once describing a paintbrush as being two distinct things (Humphreys & Riddoch, 1987). A similar tendency has been noted in other patients. For example, Butter and Trobe (1994) reported that their agnosic patient thought that there were several distinct objects present within line drawings of single stimuli. For such patients, the internal edges within line drawings may be used as segmentation cues, breaking up the stimulus into separate objects for their perceptual system. Indeed, one reason why silhouettes may be relatively easy (despite having

reduced detail) is that there are fewer internal segmentation cues in such stimuli (see Butter & Trobe, 1994; Lawson & Humphreys, 1999; Riddoch & Humphreys, 1987a, for evidence). Also, as we pointed out above, HJA, like many agnosic patients, was better at identifying photographs and real objects than line drawings. With photographs and real objects, other visual cues may be used to help overcome the problems in the perceptual organization of line drawings.

Chainay and Humphreys (2001) compared HJA's identification of black and white line drawings, correctly coloured line drawings and drawings filled with incorrect colours. They found an advantage for the coloured drawings over black and white drawings, but this held whether the colours were correct or wrong. Apparently the identity of the colour per se was relatively unimportant but it mattered whether the colours divided the object up into appropriate parts. With real objects, further cues may also come into play. Chainay and Humphreys evaluated this. HJA was asked to identify real objects seen (i) from within arm's length or at a distance out of arm's reach, (ii) binocularly or monocularly, and (iii) with or without free head movements. Binocular cues are particularly useful

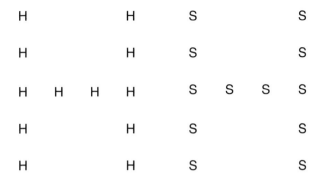

Figure 15.7 *Example of compound letters used in tests of hierarchical (local–global) shape processing (after Navon, 1977). Here the same response (H) would be made to the global letter but different responses (H or S) would be made to the local letters.*

for depth when objects fall close to the body, and depth from disparity drops rapidly as distance increases (see Bruce, Green, & Georgeson, 1996). When objects fall at a distance, depth information may nevertheless be derived by motion disparity, for example due to head movements relative to an object. Chainay and Humphreys found advantages for real objects viewed binocularly from a close distance, and for objects seen at a distance provided that small head movements were allowed. However, when compared with line drawings, HJA showed no advantage for identifying real objects viewed at a distance. This indicates that depth information can contribute to the 'real object advantage' in agnosia and, hence, that depth information can contribute to object recognition. We also note that, when depth cues were minimized (with objects seen at a distance, with no head movements), HJA made copying errors in which he segmented and omitted some parts of objects. For a patient such as this, depth and surface texture information can help to 'glue' the parts of objects together when integration by form information alone is impaired.

Interestingly, although agnosics seem to 'weight' individual parts strongly in object identification, they typically do not report the whole object as if it were just the part (e.g. describing a bicycle as a wheel). This suggests that agnosic patients can have some information about 'whole' objects, but do not assign this information a large role in recognition. In an additional test of this idea with HJA, Humphreys, Riddoch, and Quinlan (1985) examined responses to compound letter stimuli (see Figure 15.7). Subjects can be asked to respond to either the local letters or the global letter, and (depending on the precise presentation conditions) there can be an advantage for identifying the global letter and interference from the global letter on identification of the local part (see Navon, 1977). Humphreys et al. found that HJA responded normally

to the global form but, unlike normal subjects, the global form did not interfere with response latencies to the local parts (see also Lamb, Robertson, & Knight, 1990, for a similar result with patients with unilateral lesions to the superior temporal gyrus). Why should a global advantage arise but not global interference? The global form of an object may be conveyed by low spatial frequency components, which are derived rapidly from an image. This could generate a global advantage on RTs, but low spatial frequencies will not specify local parts in sufficient detail to enable their accurate identification. Hence the patient may need to focus attention on local elements to identify them, reducing any interference from the global shape. In contrast, normal observers may have a global shape representation embellished by information about the local parts of objects, and so respond to the local parts using a relatively broad 'attentional window'. The consequence of this is that some information about the global letter is also computed, causing an interference effect. In patients such as HJA, it is this integration of wholistic shape with local parts that seems to break down.

Recognition across viewpoints

The neuropsychological evidence indicates that there are at least two separable stages in the early part of the object recognition process: elements are coded into oriented edges and primitive shapes, and these edge-representations are integrated to form more complex shape representations. Theories differ on how object recognition subsequently takes place following these early stages. One critical issue is whether object recognition proceeds directly from the image as coded or whether there is a form of 'normalization' which, for example, abstracts the shape of the object away from the particular view that the object is seen from. Warrington and colleagues

Figure 15.8   *Example stimuli used in tests of matching across viewpoints (after Humphreys & Riddoch, 1984).*

(e.g. Warrington & James, 1986; Warrington & Taylor, 1973, 1978) first noted that patients with damage to the right hemisphere were poor at tasks where they had to match prototypical views of objects with 'unusual' views, where often parts of the object might be obscured. Warrington and James (1986) suggested that patients had difficulty in extracting critical features that would enable objects to be matched across viewpoints. Humphreys and Riddoch (1984) further documented a double dissociation between patients who were affected by changing some critical local features across the viewpoints and patients affected by changing the principal axis of the object across the views.

Figure 15.8 gives an example from the study. Three stimuli were presented on each trial, two different views of the same target, and a third, different, distractor object. The task was to point to the distractor. In Figure 15.8, a target has its principal axis foreshortened in one view; in another condition the principal axis of the object remained salient but an important critical feature was obscured. They found that one patient was impaired in the minimal feature condition but not the foreshortened condition; in contrast, four other patients (all with right parietal damage) had poor matching of foreshortened but not minimal feature images. This suggests that objects can be matched across views either by detecting some critical feature or by computing the principal axis and coding the object in relation to that. After a brain lesion, there can be selective impairment of either strategy. Humphreys and Riddoch (1984) provided additional converging evidence for the use of the principal axis in recognizing the objects, since they found that the difficulty

with foreshortened images was reduced when foreshortened objects were depicted against a background with strong linear perspective cues to depth. These depth cues appeared to help the patients code the main axis of the objects more easily, benefiting object identification.

These neuropsychological data are consistent with the idea that recognition can be based on abstracted representations of objects, coded across viewpoints. For example, Marr (1982) proposed that recognition depends on a 3-D model representation in which the parts of objects are coded in relation to the principal axis. Humphreys and Riddoch's evidence suggests that some patients find it more difficult than normal to derive such representations when the principal axis of the object is foreshortened. However, is this 'normalization' process *necessary* for object recognition? For instance, a deficit in matching 'unusual views' in patients could follow if there were generally impaired procedures for dealing with degraded objects, but this would not be important when objects are not degraded and/or appear in more usual views. It is interesting to note, then, that many patients with deficits on 'unusual views' are able to recognize objects in prototypical views (see also Davidoff & De Bleser, 1994; Davidoff & Warrington, 1999), and they are not classically agnosic. Thus, evidence from such patients does not necessarily tell us how objects are recognized in familiar viewpoints.

Turnbull and colleagues (Turnbull, 1997; Turnbull, Breschin, & Della Sala, 1997; Turnbull, Laws, & McCarthy, 1995) have also provided evidence that damage to the right parietal lobe can

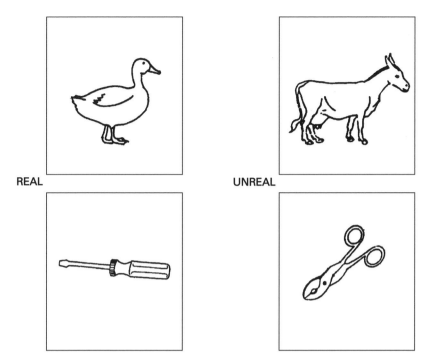

REAL   **UNREAL**

Figure 15.9   *Examples of non-objects used for object decision tasks (after Riddoch &*
Humphreys, 1987b).

impair judgements of whether objects are in an upright orientation or not. In some cases, patients believe that objects rotated in the plane are upright; and, in simple copying tasks, rotated versions of the objects can be depicted as upright. This 'orientation agnosia' can be understood if damage to the parietal lobes impairs the ability to encode object orientation, making performance reliant on a ventral visual system that is insensitive to orientation. For example, the ventral object recognition system may be relatively viewpoint-invariant, with rotated versions of objects being mapped on to these viewpoint-invariant representations by having matching features (see Humphreys & Quinlan, 1987). In the absence of parietal information specifying the retinal and/or environmental orientation of the object, judgements about whether objects are really upright may be difficult.

If the parietal lobes are indeed sensitive to object orientation, then this may also help to explain why they are important for identifying objects depicted from unusual viewpoints. For example, the parietal lobe may help in deriving a principal axis for an object (coding its primary orientation), in encoding features across the orientation change, and in mental rotation conducted as an explicit problem-solving strategy when objects are in an unusual view.

The associative agnosias

Impairments of stored perceptual knowledge

Object recognition requires more than high-level perceptual processing, it also requires that objects are matched to memory, for recognition to occur. This is the 'association process' discussed by Lissauer (1890). Neuropsychology again provides evidence here indicating that the association process (like 'apperception') can be decomposed into a set of dissociable procedures. This is illustrated by patterns of sparing and deficits on 'object decision' tasks. In these tasks, patients are typically given pictures of real objects along with pictures of 'non-objects', which can be formed by combining the parts of different objects. The task is to decide whether a stimulus is a real object or a non-object. Non-objects created by interchanging the parts of real objects can be 'perceptually good' stimuli (see Figure 15.9), so that the discrimination cannot be based on simple perceptual properties; rather it requires access to stored knowledge about the stimulus (e.g. sufficient to tell us that the stimulus is familiar, even if we do not know what it is!).

Interestingly, there are now several reports of patients capable of normal performance on difficult

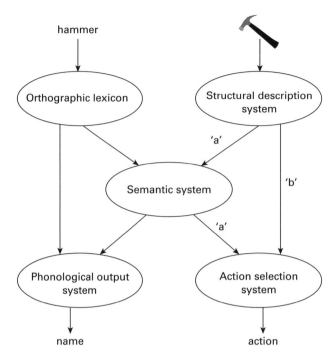

Figure 15.10   *A framework for object recognition that can account for dissociations between object recognition and access to learned actions to objects; 'a' indicates a semantically mediated route to action, 'b' a direct route based on access to stored perceptual knowledge about objects (here represented in a 'structural description system' (after Riddoch et al., 1989).*

object decision tasks but who remain unable to recognize objects (Hillis & Caramazza, 1995; Riddoch & Humphreys, 1987b; Sheridan & Humphreys, 1993; Stewart, Parkin, & Hunkin, 1992). An example here is patient JB (Riddoch & Humphreys, 1987b), who performed object decisions at a normal level but who was impaired at judging from vision which two of three objects would be used together (e.g. hammer, nail, spanner). A judgement about which objects are used together may require access to semantic information about the object's function and associations. The good object decision, along with impaired 'function' matches, suggests that access to stored perceptual knowledge about objects (assessed by the object decision task) is distinct from access to semantic knowledge (assessed by the function-matching task). In JB's case, access to perceptual knowledge was preserved whilst access to semantic knowledge was not. In fact, this problem was modality-specific; when given the name of the objects, JB carried out the function-matching task with ease. Thus JB did not have a general loss of semantic knowledge, but a modality-specific access problem. Note that, within the terms introduced by Lissauer (1890), access to stored perceptual knowledge and access to semantic knowledge would both be termed part of the

'association' process. We suggest, however, that this process is composed of separable stages, in which access to stored perceptual knowledge precedes access to semantic knowledge. A framework illustrating this proposed framework for object identification is given in Figure 15.10. In this figure, the process of accessing stored perceptual knowledge would involve an object activating the 'structural description' system, but this would not necessarily result in access to associative or functional knowledge about objects, represented in the semantic system (e.g. where semantic knowledge is damaged).

Cases such as JB contrast with other patients who are impaired at object decision but who remain able to accomplish tests stressing earlier perceptual processes (such as unusual view matching) (Forde, Francis, Riddoch, Rumiati, & Humphreys, 1997; Humphreys & Rumiati, 1998; Rumiati, Humphreys, Riddoch, & Bateman, 1994; Sartori & Job, 1988). In these cases, we might presume that there has been damage to the patient's stored perceptual knowledge about objects. It is interesting then that, in addition to having poor visual object recognition, these patients are also typically impaired at answering verbal questions about the visual properties of objects (e.g. does an elephant have a long tail relative to its body?). This suggests that stored perceptual knowledge is called upon not only in order to recognize objects visually but also when we must retrieve visual knowledge when the input is non-visual.

Category effects and stored perceptual knowledge

In some patients, disorders of perceptual knowledge about objects seem to impact on the recognition of particular categories of object more than others. For example, the patients reported by Forde et al. (1997) and by Sartori and Job (1988) had more difficulty in recognizing living things (animals, fruit, vegetables) than in recognizing non-living things (tools, vehicles, clothing). This co-occurrence of problems in stored perceptual knowledge and a category-specific deficit for living things may arise because living things, in general, often have similar perceptual structures (see Gaffan & Heywood, 1993; Humphreys, Riddoch, & Quinlan, 1988). One can think here of their representations being quite closely clustered within a perceptual knowledge store (cf. Gale, Done, & Frank, 2001). Damage to the perceptual knowledge store may then create special problems for retrieving information about these items.

Arguin, Bub and colleagues (Arguin, Bub, & Dudek, 1996; Dixon, Bub, & Arguin, 1997) have made similar arguments. They had an agnosic patient learn relationships between names and shapes that varied along either one or two dimensions (e.g. elongation and bending, to describe a banana-like shape). The patient found it difficult to learn names for the shapes when (i) the stimuli varied along two dimensions rather than one dimension, and (ii) the names paired with the shapes came from a semantically close set. Semantic proximity alone had little effect provided the stimuli varied along a single dimension. Similarly, having stimuli vary along two dimensions had little effect when the names belonged to semantically dissimilar items. From this we conclude that the patient had difficulty when complex visual information (varying along two dimensions rather than one dimension) had to be related to semantic representations that were themselves quite close.

Outside the laboratory this combination of visually complex representations and semantically similar stimuli may hold particularly for living things; living things thus are vulnerable to deficits affecting stored perceptual (and perhaps also semantic) knowledge. We do not have the space here to review the extensive literature on category-specific deficits in detail, and there is further discussion of this topic by Martin and Wu (Chapter 17, this volume) (see also Forde & Humphreys, 1999; Humphreys &

Forde, 2001, for recent reviews). Our view is that category-specific problems can emerge for a variety of reasons in different patients, and no one functional deficit is sufficient to account for all cases. Nevertheless we suggest that one contributory factor can be a loss of perceptual knowledge about stimuli. This is further supported by evidence on the longer-term impact of perceptual deficits on patients' stored knowledge about stimuli, which we consider below.

The interaction between perceptual impairments and stored perceptual knowledge

Some agnosic patients do not appear to have deficient stored knowledge about objects. For example, HJA, whom we have already discussed extensively, initially showed a very impressive ability both to describe objects and to draw them from memory – despite his marked deficit in visual object recognition. His verbal descriptions were rich in content and expressed knowledge about the shape and size of objects (see Riddoch & Humphreys, 1987a). His drawings were detailed and captured aspects of individual objects (see Figure 15.11). Similarly impressive stored knowledge about stimuli has been documented in other cases too (e.g. Behrmann, Winocur, & Moscovitch, 1992). This pattern is consistent with patients having a form of apperceptive deficit that disrupts access to intact stored knowledge representations (including perceptual as well as semantic knowledge about stimuli). However, what is the longer-term impact of the perceptual problem on stored knowledge? Longer-term follow-ups of agnosic patients have been conducted on a few occasions (e.g. Sparr, Jay, Drislane, & Venna, 1991; Wilson & Davidoff, 1993), but these cases are complicated by some indications of damage to stored knowledge in the first place.

Riddoch et al. (1999) conducted a 16-year follow-up with HJA, where they re-assessed both his perceptual abilities and his long-term knowledge about objects. They found that, whilst his perceptual abilities had remained relatively stable, his stored perceptual knowledge about objects had deteriorated. In particular, his definitions no longer contained precise details about the shape and size of objects, though they tended to contain more information about where the objects came from, what was done with them, and so forth. Also, when asked to draw objects from memory, HJA's depictions became less representative of individual stimuli (see Figure 15.11). This suggests that there is some interaction between ongoing perception and stored perceptual memories for objects. Stored perceptual memories need to be updated by intact perceptual descriptions in order to be well maintained. Interestingly, the effect of the deterioration of perceptual knowledge was most pronounced on living

1985   **1995**

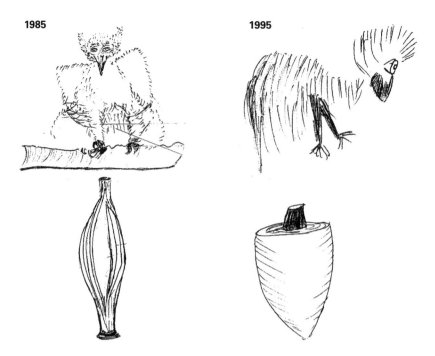

Figure 15.11   *Examples of HJA's drawings from memory (from Riddoch & Humphreys, 1987a).*
At the top: renditions of an eagle; at the bottom: renditions of celery. The drawings on the left were
produced in 1985 and those on the right in 1995, after HJA had been agnosic respectively for 4 and
14 years. Note that the later drawings fail to depict some of the individuating features of the objects
present in the earlier drawings.

things. This is consistent with living things tending to have similar perceptual structures, so that these items suffer most when perceptual knowledge degenerates. Similar results, on the longer-term impact of agnosia on long-term perceptual memory for objects, have been reported by Thomas, Forde, Humphreys, and Graham (2002).

Deficits in semantic knowledge

In patients such as JB (Riddoch & Humphreys, 1987b), there seems to be a selective problem in mapping from visual knowledge to semantic information about object association and function; semantic knowledge, accessed via other modalities, seemed relatively intact (see above). In other patients, though, recognition problems can be caused by a semantic deficit. Such patients may be unable to demonstrate knowledge of functional and associative properties of objects whether tested visually (from the object) or verbally (from names). Nevertheless, access to stored structural descriptions, assessed via object decision tasks, can be preserved (see Sheridan & Humphreys, 1993; Stewart et al., 1992). Patients with impaired access to

semantic knowledge, and patients with impaired semantic knowledge, appear to constitute two different subcategories of associative agnosia.

OBJECTS, FACES AND WORDS

Our visual system processes many different perceptual forms – including faces and words as well as objects such as cats, carrots and cups. One question, then, is whether visual recognition operates in much the same way for all these stimuli or whether there is some degree of specialized development, of different routines for different stimuli; alternatively it may be that the same routines are involved but that stimuli differ in the specificity with which any routines must be applied (e.g. face recognition requires the identification of a specific exemplar within a visually homogeneous category, whilst objects are generally only categorized at a 'base' level – 'cat' but not 'Siamese'; see Henke, Schweinberger, Grigo, Klos, & Sommer, 1998). This question is particularly relevant for understanding the nature of visual agnosia, as we elaborate below.

Farah (1990) argued that the perceptual processes leading to object, word and face recognition differed to some degree. She proposed that recognition could broadly be characterized in terms of two independent processes: 'non-decomposed', wholistic pattern recognition and parts-based recognition (where the whole object is recognized by the parts present and their interrelations). Faces stress wholistic recognition processes. Words stress parts-based recognition processes (e.g. letter identification as a precursor to word identification). Other objects may stress either wholistic or parts-based processing, depending on their structure. As a consequence of this, a disorder affecting wholistic pattern processing should disrupt faces and perhaps also the recognition of some objects, but not word recognition. The opposite pattern may be expected after damage to parts-based processes (word recognition should be affected, and perhaps also object recognition to some degree; however, face recognition should be spared). This account predicts that there should be patients solely with problems in visual word recognition ('pure' alexia) and patients with problems solely in face recognition ('pure' prosopagnosia), but not patients with problems only with objects (but with both word and face recognition being preserved). There is indeed reasonable evidence for 'pure' deficits in word and face recognition (e.g. Warrington & Shallice, 1980; De Renzi, 1986). It is also true that many patients with agnosia have ancillary problems with words and faces (Humphreys & Riddoch, 1987), as would be expected from Farah's account. On the other hand, there are some patients who present with a relatively 'pure' agnosia, affecting object recognition but not face or word recognition. For example, Rumiati, Humphreys and colleagues (Humphreys & Rumiati, 1998; Rumiati et al., 1994) have reported two patients like this. Both patients suffered degenerative changes to the temporal cortex and had problems in retrieving semantic information about stimuli; nevertheless, the problems were more serious with objects than when the material was presented verbally. Both patients were also impaired at object decision tasks, which we have suggested 'tap' access to structural knowledge about objects (see above), and one patient primarily made visual errors (Humphreys & Rumiati, 1998). This pattern, with objects being harder than words, with poor object decision and visual naming errors, is consistent with the patients losing stored visual memories for objects. It may be that stored memory representations differ for objects, words and faces, so that there can be selective loss of memories for objects but not for the other classes of stimulus.

One other prediction made by Farah's account is that only some (but not all) patterns of associated deficits in object, word and face recognition should be evident depending upon whether damage affects more than just the parts-based or just the wholistic recognition process. For example, agnosia and

alexia should arise from damage to parts-based processing; agnosia and prosopagnosia from damage to wholistic processing; and agnosia, alexia and prosopagnosia after damage to both parts-based and wholistic processing. However, alexia and prosopagnosia should not co-occur without there being some form of agnosia, because damage to both parts-based processing (generating alexia) and to wholistic processing (generating prosopagnosia) should also affect object processing. Again, however, this prediction is problematic. Both Buxbaum, Glosser, and Coslett (1999) and De Renzi and Di Pellegrino (1998) have reported patients with alexia and prosopagnosia along with relatively preserved object recognition. This contradicts the view that recognition disorders can be understood simply in terms of damage to either parts-based or wholistic perceptual processes. Patients with alexia and prosopagnosia without agnosia may suffer damage to stored knowledge specific to each type of stimulus affected (words and faces, but not objects).

FROM OBJECTS TO ACTION

As we noted at the outset of this chapter, with our discussion of patient DF, there is neuropsychological evidence that the visual information that leads normally to conscious perceptual reports about stimuli can be dissociated from the visual information that can be used to direct prehensile actions, such as reaching and grasping an object (see Milner & Goodale, 1995, for an extensive discussion of this). In agnosia, vision for object recognition can be impaired whilst vision for prehensile action is spared. There is also evidence that suggests the opposite dissociation, so that visual object recognition is intact but visual information is used inaccurately to direct action. In the syndrome of optic ataxia, patients can make accurate perceptual judgements but be impaired at placing their fingers in the correct position and orientation when reaching to pick up an object (Perenin & Vighetto, 1988). This kind of double dissociation provides a strong argument favouring the idea of visual information being coded for different purposes in different brain areas.

Of course we are not limited to making prehensile actions to objects. After reaching and grasping an object, we can make what we shall term a 'categorical action' in which we use the object in a particular way – for example, guiding a cup to our lips to drink rather than to our ear to hear. On many traditional accounts of cognition, this ability to select the appropriate categorical action to make to an object is thought to depend on access to semantic information, linking the object to abstract conceptual knowledge about the functional and associative properties of objects.

Again, however, neuropsychological data indicates that this is not necessarily the case. Visual information may be directly associated with categorical actions, independently of access to semantic knowledge about the particular items involved. We shall now consider some of this evidence, for direct relations between vision and categorical action.

Critical disorders

Optic aphasia

The term optic aphasia is applied to patients with a modality-specific naming disorder for visually presented stimuli (e.g. Beauvois, 1982; Coslett & Saffran, 1992; Hillis & Caramazza, 1995; Lhermitte & Beauvois, 1973; Manning & Campbell, 1992; Riddoch & Humphreys, 1987b). The defining symptoms of the disorder are that (1) a patient has problems in naming visually presented objects, but (2) is better at generating the same names when given a verbal definition for the stimuli. In addition, (3) such patients may make relatively good gestures to the items that they cannot name. Such good gestures have traditionally been taken to indicate that the patients can access conceptual knowledge about objects, so that their failure arises at the stage of name retrieval (Lhermitte & Beauvois, 1973). However, when detailed conceptual knowledge about the stimuli has been tested using visual matching tasks, a modality deficit has again been apparent suggesting a problem in gaining full access to semantic knowledge from vision. As we have noted, our patient, JB (Riddoch & Humphreys, 1987b), was impaired at function matching, relative to when he was given the names and performed the task verbally. Thus he did have conceptual knowledge about which objects were associated together, but access to this knowledge from vision was impaired. Despite this, JB made many precise gestures to visually presented objects, including hand-specific responses to knives and forks (using with his right hand when shown a knife and his left hand with a fork). Similar results were reported by Hillis and Caramazza (1995).

To explain how patients such as JB can make accurate actions to objects, when he had problems making function matches, we proposed the existence of a direct route from stored perceptual knowledge about the stimulus to associated actions, which by-passed stored conceptual knowledge (Riddoch & Humphreys, 1987b). This pathway is labelled 'b' in Figure 15.10. Consistent with this proposal, we also found that JB performed well on difficult object decision tasks, which appear to require access to stored perceptual knowledge to be achieved. Alternatively, optic aphasic patients may make gestures based on incomplete access to conceptual knowledge along with inferences concerning action derived from the shape of the object (see Hillis & Caramazza, 1995). In either case, the evidence indicates that actions can be formed even when conceptual knowledge about stimuli is deficient (see also Martin & Wu, Chapter 17, this volume).

Semantic dementia

The term semantic dementia is applied to patients with progressive, degenerative loss of tissue in the medial and anterior temporal lobes, who show gradual problems in retrieving knowledge about facts, objects and the meanings of words. In contrast to Alzheimer's disease, short-term (working) memory and episodic memory can be good (Snowden, Goulding, & Neary, 1989).

Group studies of semantic dementia patients indicate that the patients often have problems in using objects correctly, in addition to performing poorly on tests of conceptual knowledge (Hodges, Bozeat, Lambon Ralph, Patterson, & Spatt, 2000). However, associated deficits of this type could be generated by neural damage that affects both semantically mediated access to knowledge and a direct route to action. Studies of single cases, in contrast, indicate that semantic knowledge deficits can be dissociated from correct object use. Hodges, Spatt, and Patterson (1999), for example, report data from individual patients able to make judgements about how novel objects might be used, despite poor conceptual knowledge. Riddoch, Humphreys, Heslop, and Castermans (2002) report an even more striking dissociation. They document a dementia patient, MC, who was impaired at categorizing and providing definitions to pictures relative to words, indicating an impairment in visual access to conceptual knowledge. Nevertheless, MC performed well at everyday life tasks with the same objects (see also Lauro-Grotto, Piccini, and Shallice, 1997). She also made more correct sequential actions when using the objects in the tasks than when she was asked to sequence cards on which the action steps were written (though she was able to read the words aloud). Thus, MC showed the opposite pattern when asked to perform actions with objects (objects > words) than she did on tests of conceptual knowledge (categorizing and providing verbal definitions, when words > objects). Again it appears that patients may still use objects appropriately even when access to conceptual knowledge is impaired. Everyday tasks, when objects are used in sequence, may be supported by a direct visual route to action, which can be relatively spared in some dementing patients.

Visual apraxia

Visual apraxia presents the opposite picture to optic aphasia and semantic dementia. Visual apraxic patients can be impaired at using visually presented objects even though access to conceptual knowledge is intact. Patients are labelled as apraxic if they have difficulty in performing skilled, learned movements that are not attributable to either a motor deficit, to general intellectual deterioration or to defective comprehension (Liepmann, 1905; Rothi & Heilman, 1997). In visual apraxia, as the term suggests, the deficit in action is greater when stimuli are presented visually than when they are presented verbally (using written or spoken words). The disorder was first reported in a group study by De Renzi, Faglioni, and Sorgato (1982), and single cases have been described by Pilgrim and Humphreys (1991) and Riddoch, Humphreys, and Price (1989). The last patients could perform semantic matching tasks, and even named objects correctly. Despite this, the patients were impaired at gesturing the appropriate action. Thus while optic aphasics and semantic dementia patients can show good object use with impaired access to conceptual knowledge, visual apraxic patients can access conceptual knowledge but are impaired at retrieving actions to visually presented objects. Moreover, as the label implies, this is a modality-specific deficit. Thus visual apraxics can make an appropriate gesture when just given the object's name; however, when the objects are presented in front of them, then the actions seemed to be blocked. Riddoch et al. (1989) proposed that, in such patients, there was damage to a visual route to action, which interfered with the retrieval of actions from conceptual knowledge. Interestingly, this disruptive effect of vision in visual apraxia indicates that any direct link between vision and categorical action is not based just on inference and visual problem-solving, but rather it operates in an automatic fashion, even when it harms task performance. Next we discuss a more formal account of why this and other patterns of disorder arise.

Towards computational cognitive neuropsychology

The convergent route model

We have discussed data indicating that categorical actions are retrieved through object recognition and the activation of semantic knowledge, and through a more direct (non-semantic) route from vision. Consider now the relationship between these routes. Within cognitive psychology, several 'dual route' accounts of performance have been offered – perhaps the best-known being the dual-route model of reading (e.g. Coltheart, 1978). These accounts typically assume that, following damage to one route, the spared route should continue to operate; if this route is sufficient for a task, then no deficit should be observable. However, there are clear difficulties for this approach in explaining a disorder such as visual apraxia. For example, visual apraxics have a relatively preserved conceptual/semantic route to action (e.g. when tested verbally), and yet they fail when presented with objects visually (Riddoch et al., 1989). How can this come about?

Yoon, Heinke, and Humphreys (2002) rejected the idea of a horse-race model for action retrieval and instead suggested a 'convergent route' account. In this account, activation from the direct and indirect (conceptual/semantic) routes to action converges to guide selection of the appropriate action to an object, enabling selection to be influenced by both the visual properties of objects and by more abstract semantic (functional and contextual) knowledge. Co-operative interaction between the direct and indirect routes pushes activation within an action selection system into 'basins of attraction' – states associated with particular categorical actions ('raise the cup to the lips'). The cost of this convergent route approach is that, when processing along one route is damaged, it can affect whether outputs from the other route push the system into the correct basin of attraction. Thus damage to a visual route may push activation within the action selection system away from the appropriate basin of attraction, so that the correct action cannot be selected.

This very pattern was simulated by Yoon et al. (2002), using a formal model of this convergent route account, termed NAM (for Naming and Action Model). Objects activated a 'structural description system' sensitive to the presence of component parts in the appropriate spatial locations relative to one another, whilst words activated a visual lexicon sensitive to the presence of letter strokes in the correct relative positions. Activation in each of these input systems was passed through to a conceptual/semantic system where processing units corresponded to particular objects and to their superordinate categories. Conceptual/semantic knowledge in this model serves as a form of 'convergence zone', pooling activation from different input modalities and relaying it on to different output systems (see Damasio, 1990, for a discussion of conceptual/semantic knowledge in terms of convergence zones). In NAM two output systems were simulated – one for action selection and one for name selection (again including names for superordinate terms) – with a 'winner takes all' competitive process implemented in each case so that one action or name was eventually selected. Input into the name selection system came from the visual lexicon and the conceptual/semantic system. Input came into the action selection system from the structural description system and the conceptual/semantic system (see Figure 15.10).

Yoon et al. modelled visual apraxia by adding noise to the route connecting the structural description system to the action selection system. Because of this, noisy activation from visually presented objects tended to push the excitation within the action selection system away from appropriate basins of attraction, even though the semantic input to action selection was intact. As a consequence of the noisy direct route, performance was worse with visually presented objects relative to when words were presented alone (when the action selection system received no input from the structural description system). Optic aphasia was simulated by adding noise to the 'other' route to action, through the conceptual/semantic system. This disrupted name retrieval more than action selection, because action selection was still supported to some extent by direct activation from the structural description system.

SUMMARY

We have reviewed studies demonstrating that, even though object recognition is both fast and automatic, there are nevertheless a substantial number of distinct processes that take place. These processes lead to objects being identified and named, to our being able to direct prehensile reaching and grasping responses to these stimuli, and to our selecting the appropriate categorical action to perform. We propose that cognitive neuropsychological studies of patients with damage to object recognition and action provide an invaluable source of insight into the different component processes involved. We have also tried to show how studies combining a cognitive neuropsychological analysis of a disorder with a detailed computational model, illustrated here in the convergent route model of action retrieval, can further advance our understanding. Such models not only provide a framework into which the different disorders of recognition and action retrieval can be 'slotted', they also indicate how dynamic interactions between different processing routes can determine some of the details of neuropsychological performance. Formal modelling is helpful here, since interactive effects are typically difficult to capture within models that are only described verbally or in 'box and arrow' form. To provide a full account of both normal and abnormal performance, we may thus need to move from 'pure' cognitive neuropsychology to what we might term computational cognitive neuropsychology. At present there are no similar formal accounts to explain some of the complex interactions that take place in the different forms of agnosia we have described (e.g. between global object representations and parts-based coding), but we look forward to such models emerging.

ACKNOWLEDGEMENTS

This work was supported by grants from the Medical Research Council (UK) and the Wellcome Trust.

NOTE

1 This in turn throws open the question of why processing may be decomposed along certain dimensions in the first place. There are various reasons why this might be, but one possibility is that this enables interactions to take place within a given dimension using short connections within a given neural area. Interactions between features within a dimension may be important for perceptual coding (e.g. enhancing a signal through lateral inhibition), whilst short connections may be both faster and spatially more accurate (see Jacobs & Jordan, 1992).

REFERENCES

Arguin, M., Bub, D. N., & Dudek, G. (1996). Shape integration for visual object recognition and its implication in category-specific visual agnosia. *Visual Cognition, 3*, 221–275.

Balint, R. (1909). Seelenlähmung des Schauens, optische Ataxie, räumliche Störung der Aufmerksamkeit. *Monatschrift für Psychiatrie und Neurologie, 25*, 51–81.

Battelli, L., Casco, C., & Sartori, G. (1997). Dissociation between contour-based and texture-based shape perception: a single case study. *Visual Cognition, 4*, 275–310.

Beauvois, M.-F. (1982). Optic aphasia: a process of interaction between vision and language. *Philosophical Transactions of the Royal Society of London B, 289*, 35–47.

Behrmann, M., Winocur, G., & Moscovitch, M. (1992). Dissociation between mental imagery and object recognition in a brain damaged patient. *Nature, 359*, 636–637.

Benson, D. F., & Greenberg, J. P. (1969). Visual form agnosia: a specific deficit in visual discrimination. *Archives of Neurology, 20*, 82–89.

Boucart, M., & Humphreys, G. W. (1992). The computation of perceptual structure from collinearity and closure: normality and pathology. *Neuropsychologia, 30*, 527–546.

Bruce, V., Green, P., & Georgeson, M. A. (1996). *Visual perception.* London: Psychology Press.

Butter, C. M., & Trobe, J. D. (1994). Integrative agnosia following progressive multifocal leukoencephalopathy. *Cortex*, *30*, 145–158.

Buxbaum, L. J., Glosser, G., & Coslett, H. B. (1999). Impaired face and word recognition with object agnosia. *Neuropsychologia*, *37*, 41–50.

Campion, J., & Latto, R. (1985). Apperceptive agnosia due to carbon monoxide poisoning: an interpretation based on critical band masking from disseminated lesions. *Behavioural Brain Research*, *15*, 227–240.

Chainay, H., & Humphreys, G. W. (2001). The effects of surface and depth information on object recognition: the real object advantage in agnosia. *Cognitive Neuropsychology*, *18*, 175–191.

Cinel, C. (2002). Feature binding in visual and cross-modal perception. PhD thesis, University of Birmingham.

Coltheart, M. (1978). Lexical access in simple reading tasks. In G. Underwood (ed.), *Strategies of information processing* (pp. 151–216). London: Academic Press.

Coltheart, M. (1984). Editorial. *Cognitive Neuropsychology*, *1*, 1–8.

Coslett, H. M., & Saffran, E. M. (1992). Optic aphasia and the right hemisphere: a replication and extension. *Brain and Language*, *43*, 148–161.

Damasio, A. R. (1990). Category-related recognition defects as a clue to the neural substrates of knowledge. *Trends in Neuroscience*, *13*, 95–98.

Davidoff, J., & De Bleser, R. (1994). A case study of photographic anomia: impaired picture naming with preserved object naming and reading. *Brain and Cognition*, *24*, 1–23.

Davidoff, J., & Warrington, E. K. (1999). The bare bones of object recognition: implications from a case of object recognition impairment. *Neuropsychologia*, *37*, 279–292.

De Renzi, E. (1986). Current issues in prosopagnosia. In H. D. Ellis, M. A. Jeeves, F. Newcombe, & A. W. Young (Eds.), *Aspects of face processing* (pp. 243–252). Dordrecht: Martinus Nijhoff.

De Renzi, E., & De Pellegrino, D. (1998). Prosopagnosia and alexia without object agnosia. *Cortex*, *34*, 41–50.

De Renzi, E., Faglioni, P., & Sorgato, P. (1982). Modality-specific and supramodal mechanisms of apraxia. *Brain*, *105*, 301–312.

Dijkerman, H. C., Milner, A. D., & Carey, D. P. (1998). Grasping spatial relationships: failure to demonstrate allocentric coding in a patient with visual form agnosia. *Consciousness and Cognition*, *7*, 424–437.

Dixon, M., Bub, D. N., & Arguin, M. (1997). The interaction of object form and object meaning in the identification performance of a patient with a category-specific visual agnosia. *Cognitive Neuropsychology*, *14*, 1085–1130.

Duncan, J., & Humphreys, G. W. (1989). Visual search and visual similarity. *Psychological Review*, *96*, 433–458.

Eckhorn, R. (1999). Neural mechanisms of visual feature binding investigated with microelectrodes and models. *Visual Cognition*, *6*, 231–266.

Efron, R. (1968). What is perception? *Boston Studies in Philosophy of Science*, *4*, 137–173.

Elliott, M. A., & Müller, H. M. (1998). Synchronous information presented in 40 Hz flicker enhances visual feature binding. *Psychological Science*, *9*, 277–283.

Fahle, M. (1993). Figure-ground discrimination from temporal information. *Proceedings of the Royal Society of London B*, *254*, 199–203.

Farah, M. J. (1990). *Visual agnosia*. Cambridge, MA: MIT Press.

Forde, E. M. E., Francis, D., Riddoch, M. J., Rumiati, R. I., & Humphreys, G. W. (1997). On the links between visual knowledge and naming: a single case study of a patient with a category-specific impairment for living things. *Cognitive Neuropsychology*, *14*, 403–458.

Forde, E., & Humphreys, G. W. (1999). Category-specific recognition impairments: a review of important case studies and influential theories. *Aphasiology*, *13*, 169–193.

Friedman-Hill, S., Robertson, L. C., & Treisman, A. (1995). Parietal contributions to visual feature binding: evidence from a patient with bilateral lesions. *Science*, *269*, 853–855.

Gaffan, D., & Heywood, C. A. (1993). A spurious category-specific agnosia for living things in normal human and nonhuman primates. *Journal of Cognitive Neuroscience*, *5*, 118–128.

Gale, T. M., Done, D. J., & Frank, R. J. (2001). Visual crowding and category specific deficits for pictorial stimuli: a neural network model. *Cognitive Neuropsychology*, *18*, 509–550.

Garland, H., & Pearce, J. (1967). Neurological complications of carbon monoxide poisoning. *Quarterly Journal of Medicine*, *144*, 445–455.

Giersch, A., Humphreys, G. W., Boucart, M., & Kovacs, I. (2000). The computation of occluded contours in visual agnosia: evidence for early computation prior to shape binding and figure-ground coding. *Cognitive Neuropsychology*, *17*, 731–760.

Gilbert, C., Ito, M., Kapadia, M., & Westheimer, G. (2000). Interactions between attention, context and learning in primary visual cortex. *Vision Research*, *40*, 1217–1226.

Goodale, M. A., Jakobson, L. S., Milner, A. D., Perrett, D. I., Benson, P. J., & Hietanen, J. K. (1994). The nature and limits of orientation and pattern processing supporting visuomotor control in a visual form agnosic. *Journal of Cognitive Neuroscience*, *6*, 46–56.

Goodale, M. A., Milner, A. D., Jakobson, L. S., & Carey, D. P. (1991). A neurological dissociation between perceiving objects and grasping them. *Nature*, *349*, 154–156.

Grossberg, S., & Mingolla, E. (1985). Neural dynamics of form perception: boundary completion, illusory figures, and neon color spreading. *Psychological Review*, *92*, 173–211.

Grossberg, S., & Pessoa, L. (1998). Texture segregation, surface representation and figure-ground separation. *Vision Research*, *38*, 2657–2684.

Henke, K., Schweinberger, S. R., Grigo, A., Klos, T., & Sommer, W. (1998). Specificity of face recognition:

recognition of exemplars of non-face objects in prosopagnosia. *Cortex*, *34*, 289–296.

Heywood, C. A., & Cowey, A. (1999). Cerebral achromatopsia. In G. W. Humphreys (ed.), *Case studies in the neuropsychology of vision* (pp. 17–40). Hove, UK: Psychology Press.

Heywood, C. A., Cowey, A., & Newcombe, F. (1991). Chromatic discrimination in a cortically blind observer. *European Journal of Neuroscience*, *3*, 802–812.

Heywood, C. A., & Zihl, J. (1999). Motion blindness. In G. W. Humphreys (ed.), *Case studies in the neuropsychology of vision* (pp. 1–16). Hove, UK: Psychology Press.

Hillis, A. E., & Caramazza, A. (1995). Cognitive and neural mechanisms underlying visual and semantic processing: implications from 'optic aphasia'. *Journal of Cognitive Neuroscience*, *7*, 457–478.

Hodges, J. R., Bozeat, S., Lambon Ralph, M. A., Patterson, K., & Spatt, J. (2000). The role of conceptual knowledge in object use: evidence from semantic dementia. *Brain*, *123*, 1913–1925.

Hodges, J. R., Spatt, J., & Patterson, K. E. (1999). 'What' and 'how': evidence for the dissociation of object knowledge and mechanical problem-solving skills in the human brain. *Proceedings of the National Academy of Sciences of the USA 96*, 9444–9448.

Humphrey, G. K., Goodale, M. A., & Gurnsey, R. (1991). Orientation discrimination in a visual form agnosia: evidence from the McCollough effect. *Psychological Science*, *2*, 331–335.

Humphreys, G. W. (1998). Neural representation of objects in space: a dual coding account. *Philosophical Transactions of the Royal Society of London B*, *353*, 1341–1352.

Humphreys, G. W., Cinel, C., Wolfe, J., Olson, A., & Klempen, N. (2000). Fractionating the binding process: neuropsychological evidence distinguishing binding of form from binding of surface features. *Vision Research*, *40*, 1569–1596.

Humphreys, G. W., & Forde, E. M. E. (2001). Hierarchies, similarity and interactivity in object recognition: on the multiplicity of 'category-specific' deficits in neuropsychological populations. *Behavioural and Brain Sciences*, *24*, 453–509.

Humphreys, G. W., & Quinlan, P. T. (1987). Normal and pathological processes in visual object constancy. In G. W. Humphreys & M. J. Riddoch (Eds.), *Visual object processing: a cognitive neuropsychological approach* (pp. 43–106). London: Lawrence Erlbaum.

Humphreys, G. W., Quinlan, P. T., & Riddoch, M. J. (1989). Grouping effects in visual search: effects with single- and combined-feature targets. *Journal of Experimental Psychology: General*, *118*, 258–279.

Humphreys, G. W., & Riddoch, M. J. (1984). Routes to object constancy: implications from neurological impairments of object constancy. *Quarterly Journal of Experimental Psychology*, *36A*, 385–415.

Humphreys, G. W., & Riddoch, M. J. (1987). *To see but not to see: a case of visual agnosia*. London: Erlbaum.

Humphreys, G. W., & Riddoch, M. J. (1993). Object agnosias. In C. Kennard (ed.), *Baillière's clinical neurology* (pp. 173–198). London: Baillière Tindall.

Humphreys, G. W., Riddoch, M. J., Nys, G., & Heinke, D. (2002). Unconscious transient binding by time: neuropsychological evidence from anti-extinction. *Cognitive Neuropsychology*, *19*, 361–380.

Humphreys, G. W., Riddoch, M. J., & Quinlan, P. T. (1985). Interactive processes in perceptual organisation: evidence from visual agnosia. In M. I. Posner & O. S. M. Marin (Eds.), *Attention and performance XI* (pp. 301–318). Hillsdale, NJ: Erlbaum.

Humphreys, G. W., Riddoch, M. J., & Quinlan, P. T. (1988). Cascade processes in picture identification. *Cognitive Neuropsychology*, *5*, 67–103.

Humphreys, G. W., Riddoch, M. J., Quinlan, P. T., Donnelly, N., & Price, C. A. (1992). Parallel pattern processing and visual agnosia. *Canadian Journal of Psychology*, *46*, 377–416.

Humphreys, G. W., Romani, C., Olson, A., Riddoch, M. J., & Duncan, J. (1994). Non-spatial extinction following lensions of the parietal lobe in humans. *Nature*, *372*, 357–359.

Humphreys, G. W., & Rumiati, R. I. (1998). When joys come not in single spies but in battalions: within-category and within-modality identification increases the accessibility of degraded store knowledge. *Neurocase*, *4*, 111–126.

Jacobs, R. A., & Jordan, M. I. (1992). Computational consequences of a bias towards short connections. *Journal of cognitive Neuroscience*, *4*, 323–336.

Lamb, M. R., Robertson, L. C., & Knight, R. T. (1990). Component mechanisms underlying the processing of hierarchically organised patterns – inferences from patients with unilateral cortical lesions. *Journal of Experimental Psychology: Learning, Memory, and Cognition*, *16*, 471–483.

Lauro-Grotto, R., Piccini, C., & Shallice, T. (1997). Modality-specific operations in semantic dementia. *Cortex*, *33*, 593–622.

Lawson, R., & Humphreys, G. W. (1999). The effects of view in depth on the identification of line drawings and silhouettes of familiar objects: normality and pathology. *Visual Cognition*.

Lhermitte, F., & Beauvois, M. F. (1973). A visual-speech disconnection syndrome: report of a case with optic aphasia. *Brain*, *96*, 695–714.

Liepmann, H. (1905) *The left hemisphere and action*. (Doreen Kimura, 1980, Trans.). London, Ontario: University of Western Ontario.

Lissauer, H. (1890). Ein Fall von Seelenblindheit nebst einem Beitrage zur Theorie derselben. *Archiv für Psychiatrie und Nervenkrankheiten*, *21*, 222–270.

Manning, L., & Campbell, R. (1992). Optic aphasia with spared action naming: a case of pathological verbal dominance. *Cortex*, *11*, 83–89.

Marr, D. (1982). *Vision*. San Francisco: W. H. Freeman.

Mattingley, J. B., Davis, G., & Driver, J. (1997). Pre-attentive filling in of visual surfaces in parietal extinction. *Science*, *275*, 671–674.

McCollough, C. (1965). Colour adapation of edge-detectors in the human visual system. *Science*, *149*, 1115–1116.

Milner, A. D., & Goodale, M. A. (1995). *The visual brain in action*. Oxford: Oxford University Press.

Milner, A. D., Perrett, D. I., Johnston, R. S., Benson, P. J., Jordan, T. R., Heeley, D. W., Bettucci, D., Mortara, F., Mutani, R., Terazzi, E., & Davidson, D. L. W. (1991). Perception and action in 'visual form agnosia'. *Brain*, *114*, 405–428.

Moran, J., & Desimone, R. (1985). Selective attention gates visual processing in the extra-striate cortex. *Science*, *229*, 782–784.

Navon, D. (1977). Forest before trees: the precedence of global features in visual perception. *Cognitive Psychology*, *9*, 353–383.

Perenin, M. T., & Vighetto, A. (1988). Optic ataxia: a specific disruption in visuomotor mechanisms. *Brain*, *111*, 643–674.

Pilgrim, E., & Humphreys, G. W. (1991). Impairment of action to visual objects in a case of ideomotor apraxia. *Cognitive Neuropsychology*, *8*, 459–473.

Riddoch, M. J., & Humphreys, G. W. (1987a). A case of integrative agnosia. *Brain*, *110*, 1431–1462.

Riddoch, M. J., & Humphreys, G. W. (1987b). Visual object processing in optic aphasia: a case of semantic access agnosia. *Cognitive Neuropsychology*, *4*, 131–185.

Riddoch, M. J., Humphreys, G. W., Gannon, T., Blott, W., & Jones, V. (1999). Memories are made of this: the effects of time on stored visual knowledge in a case of visual agnosia. *Brain*, *122*, 537–559.

Riddoch, M. J., Humphreys, G. W., Heslop, J., & Castermans, E. (2002). Dissociations between object knowledge and everyday action. *Neurocase*, *8*, 100–110.

Riddoch, M. J., Humphreys, G. W., & Price, C. J. (1989). Routes to action: evidence from apraxia. *Cognitive Neuropsychology*, *6*, 437–454.

Robertson, L. C., Treisman, A., Friedman-Hill, S., & Grabowecky, M. (1997). A possible connection between spatial deficits and feature binding in a patient with parietal damage. *Journal of Cognitive Neuroscience*, *9*, 295–317.

Rorden, C., Mattingley, J. B., Karnath, H. O., & Driver, J. (1997). Visual extinction and prior entry: impaired perception of temporal order with intact motion perception after parietal injury. *Neuropsychologia*, *35*, 421–433.

Rothi, L. J. G., & Heilman, K. M. (1997). *Apraxia: the neuropsychology of action*. London: Psychology Press.

Rumiati, R. I., Humphreys, G. W., Riddoch, M. J., & Bateman, A. (1994). Visual object agnosia without prosopagnosia or alexia: evidence for hierarchical theories of object recognition. *Visual Cognition*, *1*, 181–225.

Sartori, B., & Job, R. (1988). The oyster with four legs: a neuropsychological study on the interaction of visual and semantic information. *Cognitive Neuropsychology*, *5*, 677–709.

Sheridan, J., & Humphreys, G. W. (1993). A verbal-semantic category-specific recognition impairment. *Cognitive Neuropsychology*, *10*, 143–184.

Singer, W., & Gray, C. M. (1995). Visual feature integration and the temporal correlation hypothesis. *Annual Review of Neuroscience*, *18*, 555–586.

Snowden, J. S., Goulding, P. J., & Neary, D. (1989). Semantic dementia: a form of circumscribed cerebral atrophy. *Behavioral Neurology*, *2*, 167–182.

Sparr, S. A., Jay, M., Drislane, F. W., Venna, N. (1991). A historic case of visual agnosia revisited after 40 years. *Brain*, *114*, 789–800.

Stewart, F., Parkin, A. J., & Hunkin, H. N. (1992). Naming impairments following recovery from herpes simplex encephalitis. *Quarterly Journal of Experimental Psychology*, *44A*, 261–284.

Thomas, R. M., Forde, E. M. E., Humphreys, G. W., & Graham, K. S. (2002). The effects of passage of time on a patient with category-specific agnosia. *Neurocase*, *8*, 101–115.

Thorpe, S., Fize, D., & Marlot, C. (1996). Speed of processing in the human visual system. *Nature*, *381*, 520–521.

Treisman, A. (1998). Feature binding, attention and object perception. *Philosophical Transactions of the Royal Society of London B*, *353*, 1295–1306.

Treisman, A., & Gelade, G. (1980). A feature-integration theory of attention. *Cognitive Psychology*, *12*, 97–136.

Turnbull, O. H. (1997). A double dissociation between knowledge of object identity and object orientation. *Neuropsychologia*, *35*, 567–570.

Turnbull, O. H., Breschin, N., & Della Sala, S. (1997). Agnosia for object orientation: implication for theories of object recognition. *Neuropsychologia*, *35*, 153–163.

Turnbull, O. H., Laws, K. R., & McCarthy, R. A. (1995). Object recognition without knowledge of object orientation. *Cortex*, *31*, 387–395.

Vecera, S. P., & Gilds, K. S. (1998). What processing is impaired in apperceptive agnosia? Evidence from normal subjects. *Journal of Cognitive Neuroscience*, *10*, 568–580.

Von der Heydt, R., & Peterhans, E. (1989). Mechanisms of contour perception in monkey visual cortex. 1. Lines of pattern discontinuities. *Journal of Neuroscience*, *9*, 1731–1748.

Ward, R., Goodrich, S., & Driver, J. (1994). Grouping reduces visual extinction: neuropsychological evidence for weight-linkage in visual selection. *Visual Cognition*, *1*, 101–130.

Warrington, E. K. (1985). Agnosia: the impairment of object recognition. In P. J. Vinken, G. W. Bruyn, & H. L. Klawans (Eds.), *Handbook of Clinical Neurology* (Vol. 45, pp. 333–349). Amsterdam: Elsevier Science.

Warrington, E. K., & James, M. (1986). Visual object recognition in patients with right hemisphere lesions: axes or features? *Perception*, *15*, 355–356.

Warrington, E. K., & Shallice, T. (1980). Word form dyslexia. *Brain*, *103*, 99–112.

Warrington, E. K., & Taylor, A. (1973). The contribution of the right parietal lobe to object recognition. *Cortex*, *9*, 152–164.

Warrington, E. K., & Taylor, A. (1978). Two categorical stages of object recognition. *Perception*, *9*, 152–164.

Wilson, B. A., & Davidoff, J. (1993). Partial recovery from visual object agnosia: a 10-year follow-up study. *Cortex*, *29*, 529–542.

Wojciulik, E., & Kanwisher, N. (1998). Implicit but not explicit feature binding in a Balint's patient. *Visual Cognition*, *5*, 157–182.

Yoon, E. Y., Heinke, D., & Humphreys, G. W. (2002). Modelling direct perceptual constraints on action selection: the Naming and Action Model (NAM). *Visual Cognition*, *9*, 615–661.

Zeki, S. (1993). *A vision of the brain*. Oxford: Blackwells.

Zihl, J., Von Cramon, D., & Mai, N. (1983). Selective disturbance of movement vision after bilateral brain damage. *Brain*, *106*, 313–340.

16

Cognitive Neuropsychology of Learning and Memory

BARBARA J. KNOWLTON

The study of learning and memory is an area of high convergence between neuroscience and cognitive science. How the brain acquires, stores and later retrieves information are among the most fundamental questions in neuroscience. Learning is ubiquitous in the animal kingdom, and we have gained a great deal of knowledge about brain learning mechanisms through the study of animal models (see Squire, 1992, for a review). These studies have provided information about the neural substrates of learning and memory, and it appears that the circuitry devoted to learning and memory in monkeys, rats and mice is quite similar to that found in the human brain. The extensive study of human learning and memory in the past century has allowed researchers to begin to understand the psychological processes that arise from this circuitry.

The basic logic of cognitive neuropsychology is to examine the performance of patients with brain injury, and to infer the structure of cognition through the pattern of impaired and intact performance. This discipline relies on the development of clever tests that can isolate specific components of cognition. If a particular process is impaired in a patient against a background of relatively normal function in other areas, it may be taken as evidence for this particular process as a distinct psychological entity. A similar logic exists in the field of cognitive development. If young children of a particular age have trouble with a specific cognitive task but not with other similar tasks, it would support the idea that this task requires a specific cognitive process that only emerges later in development. Both developmental psychology and cognitive neuropsychology are aimed at discovering the structure of human cognition, but the neuropsychological approach can offer additional information about the brain structures underlying these processes.

THE STUDY OF AMNESIA

Nearly every lecture or chapter on the human amnesic syndrome begins with the discussion of the case of patient HM. This patient underwent surgical removal of most of the medial temporal lobe on both sides of the brain for the treatment of epilepsy that was intractable to drug treatment. Although this surgical procedure apparently removed the epileptic foci, it was quickly noted that HM suffered a profound memory impairment as an unexpected result (Scoville & Milner, 1957). HM was no longer able to remember specific events that occurred post-surgery, and he was effectively unable to learn new facts, such as the names of new people. Despite his profound amnesia, HM's other cognitive abilities, such as perception, language and reasoning, were relatively spared. Thus, the primary lesson to be taken from the case of HM is that memory is a mental faculty with distinct underlying brain circuitry. Although this seems quite self-evident today, at that time there was a strong feeling that brain systems were equipotential when it came to higher cognitive functions (e.g. Lashley, 1929). The case of HM focused attention on the medial temporal lobes as playing a specific role in learning and memory.

The case of HM was not only informative regarding the neural substrates of learning and memory, but it also helped to shape psychological theory. The fact that HM was able to retain information for several seconds, and could maintain information indefinitely if not distracted, supported the idea that short-term memory is a stage of processing distinct from long-term memory. Another important feature of HM's condition is that it was not specific to a particular modality. His memory was impaired for words, faces, melodies, pictures, etc. Memory processing thus appears to be general across materials, at least in part. In addition, the fact that HM retained information acquired before surgery indicated that the retrieval of memories does not rely on the structures required for forming new memories. Thus, HM could remember events occurring throughout his childhood and retained vocabulary and semantic knowledge that was learned before the surgery (Milner, Corkin, & Teuber, 1968).

Perhaps the most important insight gained from the study of HM was that memory is not unitary. Although HM's memory deficit was extremely profound, it appeared that he was able to show some new kinds of learning. For example, HM was apparently able to learn perceptuo-motor skills like rotor pursuit normally. In this task, the subject must learn to maintain contact with a rotating disk using a stylus. HM showed improvement across trials as he practiced the skill, despite an inability to recall previous training episodes or to recognize the testing apparatus (Corkin, 1968). Thus, it appeared that the learning that occurs in perceptuo-motor skill tasks is accomplished using brain circuitry that is independent of the circuitry required for learning about facts and events. We may therefore infer that these types of learning differ in terms of behavioral properties as well.

The intensive interest in the case of HM has led to numerous further studies of the cognitive abilities of amnesic patients. Although the study of HM has been of utmost importance to the field of neuropsychology, one could argue that his severe childhood epilepsy limits the generalizability of these findings to our understanding of how cognition is organized in the normal brain. However, the results of studies of additional amnesic patients have corroborated the results from HM. Most of these patients have become amnesic not through surgical resection of the medial temporal lobes but through various incidents that have resulted in damage to medial temporal lobe structures or damage to structures in the diencephalon that are interconnected with medial temporal lobe structures. Examples of the various etiologies of amnesia are anoxic episodes, encephalitis, Korsakoff's disease and thalamic infarcts (Damasio, Tranel, & Damasio, 1991; Guberman & Stuss, 1983; Oscar-Berman, 1980). Although amnesia can arise in many ways, studies of these patients have supported the finding that there are forms of memory that are spared. In addition to the learning of perceptuo-motor skills, amnesic patients have been shown to exhibit intact priming (Cermak, Talbot, Chandler, & Wolbarst, 1985; Schacter, 1985). Priming refers to

the fact that people are able to process a stimulus a little more quickly and accurately if they have been presented with it before. For example, subjects are able to identify a word or picture at a shorter duration if they have seen that word or picture recently. Subjects are also better able to identify a stimulus in noise if they had been presented with the stimulus recently. Amnesic patients exhibit priming to the same extent as normal subjects, although their memory for the presentation of the items to be primed is impaired, or even at chance.

The finding that learning on some tasks is spared and on some tasks it is impaired leads one to attempt to find the defining characteristics for the two types of learning. Performance is impaired in amnesia when subjects are aware of learning in a task. That is, when subjects have conscious knowledge of the information learned, amnesic patients are severely impaired relative to controls. For example, when one experiences an event, one is aware of learning about and of using this knowledge when later asked about the event. When a certain face looks familiar, one is aware that the face is evoking a past encounter. When we retrieve facts we are also aware that we have this information stored in memory. This type of memory has been referred to as explicit, or declarative, in that one is able to 'declare' the information stored as memory (Squire & Cohen, 1984). Explicit memory is characterized by its flexibility (Eichenbaum, Mathews, & Cohen, 1989). Many different cues can be used to retrieve explicit memories, and explicit memories can be used to guide behavior in new situations. The declarative nature of explicit memories allows this information to be transmitted across individuals. Explicit memory is what people mean when they casually refer to memory.

In contrast to the information stored in explicit memory, people are not necessarily aware of the information stored in implicit memory. For example, people may be able to recognize that they are showing improvement in a motor skill with practice, but they are not aware of what the particular changes in movement were that afforded improved performance. Likewise, participants are not aware that a primed stimulus will be processed more readily in a future encounter; priming only emerges during this future encounter.

The psychological difference between explicit and implicit memory is further supported by the dissociation seen in the performance of amnesic patients. The fact that amnesic patients exhibit normal skill learning and priming has led researchers to better define the role of the medial temporal lobe in terms of its specific role in conscious memory for facts and events. It has also led to extensive study of the learning capabilities of amnesic patients to investigate whether implicit learning can support performance in other tasks. Studies of amnesic patients have been useful in studying mechanisms of priming, sequence learning, preference learning, habit learning and category learning. The impact of neuropsychological work in each of the areas will be discussed in turn.

Priming

As described above, priming can lead to an item being perceived more fluently. The fact that amnesic patients show normal levels of this ability demonstrates that the mental representations that give rise to priming are formed independently of the neural circuitry that supports the formation of explicit recognition memory for the items. Behavioral evidence also indicates that recognition and priming are supported by different representations. Unlike recognition, priming is not influenced by depth of processing at study. Thinking about the meaning of words and counting the vowels in words leads to similar levels of priming on a visual identification task, while semantic processing is clearly superior for later recognition (Roediger, Weldon, Stadler, & Riegler, 1992). Priming and recognition also differ in terms of the effects of stimulus change between study and test. Seeing pictures results in less priming for words than if the words themselves had been studied (Weldon & Jackson-Barrett, 1993). This is particularly true if the subject does not have much time to think about the verbal label of the picture. However, the opposite is true for recognition: viewing pictures sometimes leads to better recognition of the corresponding words than if the words themselves had been studied (Snodgrass & Asiaghi, 1977)! Interestingly, it is not the case that the representation supporting recognition is less specific than the representation supporting priming, since subjects are often able to explicitly recognize if the word was presented in the same form or modality as it was during study. The explicit memory representation may contain a great deal of information about the study episode that can be accessed flexibly depending on the task demands (Cooper, Schacter, Ballesteros, & Moore, 1992).

Priming can also exist for conceptual, or semantic, representations. Prior presentation of a semantically related item will allow for more fluent processing of a stimulus (e.g. reading 'doctor' will cause one to read or identify 'nurse' as a word faster than if 'window' had been read; e.g. den Heyer, Briand, & Dannenbring, 1983). Semantic priming can also be shown in a category exemplar generation task. If the word 'pineapple' had been presented to you recently, you would be more likely to give the response 'pineapple' when asked to name four fruits that come to mind than if you had heard another word (Graf, Shimamura, & Squire, 1985). In these cases, what is primed is not a perceptual, but rather a conceptual, representation. When 'doctor' is read, knowledge associated with this term is activated, and then comes

to mind more readily than if it had not been primed. Similarly, if the concept of 'pineapple' is activated, it will come to mind readily when one considers fruits. Importantly, amnesic patients show intact conceptual priming, demonstrating that this activation can occur independently of explicit memory. Indeed, even in neurologically intact subjects, neither perceptual nor conceptual priming seems to require that subjects explicitly remember that the primed items had been presented.

One curious aspect of the intact priming ability of amnesic patients is that they appear unable to use the fluency that they presumably experience when they see old items to help them in recognizing these items. If amnesic patients were readily able to use perceptual fluency as a cue that an item was old, one would expect their recognition memory to be reliably better relative to their recall. In fact, the recall and recognition abilities of amnesic patients seem impaired to the same degree (Haist, Shimamura, & Squire, 1992). Thus, these data appear to argue against a substantial contribution of perceptual fluency to recognition memory.

Sequence learning

Evidence from the serial reaction time task (SRT) indicates that subjects are able to implicitly learn sequences. In this task, subjects see a stimulus such as an asterisk that appears in different locations on a computer screen and are asked to respond by pressing a key below the location where the asterisk appears. As the asterisk jumps from location to location, the subject continues to press the key beneath the asterisk as fast as he or she can. Unbeknownst to the subject, the asterisks are not appearing in random locations, but rather are appearing according to a complex sequence. It can be shown that subjects are learning this sequence, because when the asterisk locations are surreptitiously switched to random, their reaction time increases significantly. Subjects need not be aware of the sequence, or even that there was a sequence at all, to show this effect. Amnesic patients also show normal sequence learning in this task even though they may have no recognition of the sequence and little memory for the testing episode (Nissen, Willingham, & Hartman, 1989; Reber & Squire, 1998).

Rather than a series of motor movements, it appears that subjects are learning a series of locations. They are thus able to implicitly anticipate where the asterisk will appear and can shift their attention more rapidly than when the asterisk is appearing in random locations. Subjects do not show much of a decrement in performance when they transfer to using a new set of motor effectors if the sequence of locations is the same. However, if a new set of locations is remapped to the old ones, performance suffers substantially, even if the motor responses do not change (Willingham, Wells, Farrell, & Stemwedel, 2000).

Another task that measures the learning of sequential dependences is the artificial grammar task (Reber, 1967). In this task, the subject views a series of letter strings formed according to a rule system that allows only certain letters to follow each letter. Subjects are not told that the letter strings are formed according to any rules until after viewing the letter strings. At that point, subjects are told that their task will be to decide for a new set of letter strings whether each one does or does not follow the rules. Subjects are understandably perplexed at these instructions because they generally feel that they did not notice any rules. Nevertheless, they are reliably able to classify new letter strings at a level significantly above chance. Amnesic patients also show normal artificial grammar learning despite having extremely poor memory for the letter strings that were shown during training (Knowlton, Ramus, & Squire, 1992).

A great deal of research has focused on exactly what subjects are learning in the artificial grammar learning task. In making their classification judgments, subjects appear to be very sensitive to the frequency with which letter bigrams and trigrams had been presented among the training strings. Subjects are likely to endorse test items that include letter combinations that had been frequently repeated during training, and will tend not to endorse items that are comprised of letter combinations that had not been repeated frequently during training. The endorsement of items containing high-frequency bigrams and trigrams may be similar to what happens during priming (Knowlton & Squire, 1994). Those test strings with components that had been repeatedly presented during training might be processed more readily than those containing mostly low-frequency or novel components. Subjects may be using this processing fluency in their classification decisions. As is the case with priming, amnesic patients seem to be using this bigram and trigram frequency information to the same extent as controls, so it appears that this type of learning is not dependent on explicit memory for training strings.

There is evidence that subjects are learning more abstract information about the rules of the artificial grammar as well. If subjects are trained using one letter set, and then are tested using strings formed with a new letter set that maps to the first, subjects are able to classify these 'translated' letter strings at a level significantly above chance (Knowlton & Squire, 1996). Amnesic patients also exhibit normal letter-set transfer. There have even been demonstrations of transfer across stimulus domains in which symbols are mapped onto tones (Altmann, Dienes, & Goode, 1995). Subjects seem particularly sensitive to the repetition structure of training items. Test items that contain a pattern of repetitions that was seen frequently during training are more likely to be endorsed (Gomez, Gerken, & Schvaneveldt, 2000). The artificial grammar learning data suggest that both exemplar-based and abstract information about the stimuli can be learned implicitly, and that this information can influence judgments.

Preference learning

The idea that 'familiarity breeds contempt' is generally not supported in studies of preference learning. In fact, subjects generally will express preferences for items presented before as compared to novel items. This 'mere exposure' effect has been demonstrated with a wide variety of stimuli, including geometric shapes, faces and melodies (see Zajonc, 2001, for a review). Subjects do not need to be aware that the preferred stimuli were shown previously. Subjects simply feel that they are expressing a preference, not that they are recognizing items. In fact, the mere exposure effect can sometimes be stronger for subliminally presented stimuli (Bornstein & D'Agostino, 1992). It is as if explicitly remembering that an item had been seen before gives one a reason for whatever enhanced processing normally gives rise to the preference effect, and thus the apparent preference can be discounted. If processing is enhanced in the absence of explicit memory, then this enhanced processing can be attributed to a preference.

Two studies with amnesic patients have demonstrated that attitude change can occur without explicit memory for previous experience with items. The mere exposure effect has been shown in amnesic patients for Korean melodies that were novel for the subjects (Johnson, Kim, & Risse, 1985). In another experiment, Lieberman, Ochsner, Gilbert, and Schacter (2001) showed that amnesic patients changed their preferences for art prints as a result of having ranked them. In this study, subjects ranked a series of prints in order of preference. Later, they were given a series of pairs of prints two at a time, and they were asked to choose which pair they preferred. Among these pairs were the subject's 4th and 10th ranked prints and 6th and 12th ranked prints. When subjects subsequently ranked the initial set of prints again, both amnesic patients and control subjects tended to rank the prints in the selected pair higher than previously and the items in the rejected pair lower than previously. Amnesic patients, however, were very poor at remembering which pairs of prints they had chosen between. These results suggest that attitude change resulting from one's previous behavior does not require explicit memory for that behavior.

Habit learning

The term 'habit' has traditionally been used in the field of animal learning to refer to a gradually acquired stimulus–response (S–R) association. Examples of this type of learning in rats include certain visual discrimination tasks in which the animal must make a response (e.g. pressing a bar) when a cue is present to receive a reward (Reading, Dunnett, & Robbins, 1991). Another habit-learning task is the win–stay task in which a rat learns to run down lit alleys of a maze to receive food (Packard, Hirsh, & White, 1989). It appears that in both of these cases, the rat is learning to associate a cue (e.g. a light) with a response (e.g. pressing a bar or running down an alley). The role of the reward in these tasks is to 'stamp in' the S–R association. Studies with experimental animals indicate that habit learning can proceed normally if the hippocampal system is damaged. These data raise the question of whether this type of learning occurs in humans, and whether it also is independent of the hippocampus. If so, one might expect that these S–R associations would be formed without awareness of what has been learned. Also, because the learned associations are between cues and responses, the reward would not be necessarily accessed when the cue is present – the response would simply be elicited. Such a situation may occur in everyday learning when a particular response is overlearned, such as the route to your university. The stimuli that you encounter along the way (such as the site of a particular intersection) will elicit particular responses (e.g. turn left). The fact that driving an overlearned route can be based on S–R associations is demonstrated by the phenomenon of finding yourself halfway to your university when in fact you know it is a holiday and you had intended to go elsewhere. You had been relying on S–R habits!

Can we measure human habit learning in a laboratory setting, and examine whether it is independent of the brain system that gives rise to explicit memory? One difficulty with this endeavor is that the tasks used to measure habit learning in rats would be approached quite differently by humans. It is unlikely that a human subject would need several sessions of training to learn that pressing a bar when a light is on will deliver food. A human subject would probably explicitly test the hypothesis that something will happen when the bar is pressed, and after a single reinforcement, the relationship between the light, the bar press and the food would be induced by the subject. In order to circumvent the ability of subjects to use their memory for explicit trials, we used a task in which the association between stimuli and outcomes was probabilistic (Knowlton, Squire, & Gluck, 1994). Memory for individual trials would not be nearly as useful as knowledge gleaned across many trials. We designed a computer game in which a set of cues were probabilistically associated with two outcomes (rainy or sunny weather). The association probabilities ranged from about 80% to about 60%.

Subjects saw a combination of the cues on each trial, and decided whether the outcome would be sun or rain. They were given feedback on each trial as to whether their choice was correct, although because of the probabilistic nature of the task there were many trials in which they actually picked the most associated outcome but were given error feedback. Although subjects generally felt that they were not doing very well, they nevertheless generally exhibited learning across 50 trials of the task in that they gradually tended to select the most associated outcome for each cue combination. Amnesic patients showed the same degree of learning as control subjects, although the patients had poor memory for facts about the testing episode, such as the appearance of the cards and the computer screen. Thus, it appears that this task may be an analog of the type of habit-learning tasks that have been used in studies of experimental animals.

Category learning

One of the most important cognitive abilities is the capacity to classify new items based on experience. Category learning is nearly ubiquitous and thus cannot be explained by a single mechanism. People are able to classify based on the similarity of new items to previous items stored as explicit memories. People may also use rules to classify new items. These rules may have been acquired by direct hypothesis testing, or they may be implicitly acquired through exposure to exemplars, as in the case of artificial grammar learning. Implicit rule learning has also been demonstrated using intersecting-line stimuli in which a complex (non-linear) rule determines the relationship between the lengths of two lines. Amnesic patients have been shown to learn this classification task normally (Filoteo, Maddox, & Davis, 2001).

For most categories in the real world, however, it appears that we use similarity to a central tendency, or prototype, or a category to make classification judgments. People are much faster at classifying a robin as a bird than a chicken, even though both of these adhere to the rules of what defines a bird. The robin, however, is closer to the prototype of a bird that has presumably been formed across the multiple exposure to birds across one's lifetime (see Posner & Keele, 1968; Rosch, 1988). Prototype formation has some of the defining characteristics of implicit learning: people are not aware that they are forming a prototype during exemplar exposure, they may not necessarily be able to tell you what their prototype is for a particular category (knowledge is non-declarative), and knowledge of the prototype only emerges through the pattern of classification of new items.

The idea that prototype formation can occur implicitly and independently of explicit memory of exemplars is supported by findings from amnesic patients (Knowlton & Squire, 1993). In a series of experiments, amnesic patients and control subjects were shown a set of dot patterns that had been generated by making large random distortions of a 'prototype' dot pattern that had been randomly selected. Subjects were not told that the training patterns were generated from a single dot pattern. Later at test, subjects viewed new dot patterns generated by the prototype, some dot patterns that were generated from other prototypes, and some examples of the prototype itself. Control subjects demonstrated evidence of a prototype abstraction effect, in that they endorsed the prototype as being in the category the most often of any trial type, even though the training stimuli were actually high distortions of this prototype, and it was not seen during training. The low distortions were endorsed the next most frequently, followed by the high distortions. Amnesic patients exhibited this same pattern of responses, and endorsed the items in the category as accurately as control subjects did. These results support the notion that general knowledge categories may have a distinct status in the brain, separate from knowledge of specific exemplars.

THE LOGIC OF THE DOUBLE DISSOCIATION

Intact learning in amnesic patients is taken as compelling evidence that the system engaged is independent of the system that is required for explicit learning. However, it is possible that such dissociations could be obtained if there was only one learning system, with different tasks drawing on it differentially. For example, if the weather prediction task described above requires only weak, fuzzy declarative memory for the cue–outcome relationships, it is possible that amnesic patients could exhibit nearly normal learning on this task, even though they would exhibit severe impairments on tasks that draw heavily on explicit memory, like recognition tests. One approach to address this issue is to look for double dissociations, in which there is a second group of patients with different brain pathology who are intact on an ability impaired in the first group, but impaired on an ability intact in the first group. If a double dissociation is demonstrated, it is unlikely that intact learning performance by amnesic patients on a task is simply due to low explicit memory demands on that task. Rather, it would suggest that learning is dependent on a different system that is specifically affected in the second patient group. The logic of the double dissociation in neuropsychology has been attributed to Hans-Lukas Teuber (1950), who advocated its use in assigning functions to specific brain systems.

A concrete example of a double dissociation exists for perceptual priming. There have been a few case studies of patients with diffuse occipital lobe damage who exhibit impaired perceptual priming, even though they appear to recognize stimuli normally (Fleischman, Vaidya, Lange, & Gabrieli, 1997; Keane, Gabrieli, Mapstone, Johnson, & Corkin, 1995; Samuelsson, Bogges, & Karlsson, 2000). Thus, the normal performance of amnesic patients on priming tasks cannot be explained by assuming it is a more sensitive measure of residual declarative memory, since patients with damage elsewhere in the brain find priming to be the more difficult task. The fact that patients with occipital lobe damage exhibit impaired perceptual priming is consistent with neuroimaging studies showing a decrease in activation in occipital regions for primed items (e.g. Koutstaal, Wagner, Rotte, Maril, Buckner, & Schacter, 2001). This decrease in activation, typically measured as blood flow in functional magnetic resonance imaging paradigms, could be seen as the neural substrate of perceptual fluency. Those items previously presented require fewer neural resources for subsequent processing.

Another example of a double dissociation in memory exists for habit learning and explicit memory. Patients with Parkinson's disease, which affects the basal ganglia system of the brain, are impaired on the weather prediction task described above. Despite this impairment in habit learning, patients with Parkinson's disease can exhibit completely normal recognition memory for the stimuli used to train the habit (Knowlton, Mangels, & Squire, 1996). This is the exact opposite of the pattern seen in amnesic patients. This double dissociation argues against the idea that habit learning is simply an easy explicit memory test. Rather, it suggests that habit learning depends on a different brain system than explicit memory, namely the basal ganglia. As is the case with priming, neuroimaging data support this idea. Activation in the basal ganglia is seen when subjects perform the weather prediction task (Poldrack, Prabhakaran, Seger, & Gabrieli, 1999). It appears that activity in the medial temporal lobe actually decreases when subjects perform this task (Poldrack et al., 2001).

RETROGRADE AMNESIA

In addition to difficulties in forming new memories, patients with the amnesic syndrome typically exhibit some impairment in remembering information that was acquired before the onset of amnesia. Typically, retrograde amnesia occurs for a period just preceding the event that precipitated amnesia, while memory for more remote time periods remains intact (see Squire & Zola-Morgan, 1996, for a review). The duration of this period varies substantially across amnesic patients. For some, retrograde amnesia may only extend for months or a few years before the onset of amnesia. For other patients, retrograde amnesia can last for decades with only childhood memories spared. The extent of retrograde amnesia is typically related to the severity of anterograde amnesia, although many exceptions have been reported in which retrograde amnesia is more or less severe than the severity of anterograde amnesia (Kopelman & Kapur, 2001).

The existence of retrograde amnesia demonstrates that the brain structures damaged in amnesia are not only involved in the storage of new memories, but also may play a role in the retrieval of memories for some period of time after learning. The temporally graded nature of retrograde amnesia is consistent with the idea that the medial temporal lobe contributes to a consolidation process whereby memory traces gradually undergo a transformation such that they can ultimately be retrieved independently of medial temporal lobe structures. This process would appear to be a slow one, lasting years.

The idea that memories gradually 'consolidate' is puzzling in a sense. Why should memories that are perfectly retrievable at one time undergo such a transformation? One possible reason why memories should consolidate may arise from the fact that medial temporal lobe structures including the hippocampus have limited storage capacity that makes them inadequate to hold the vast amount of memories that one gains across one's lifetime. Rather, the vast expanse of the cerebral cortex is more likely to provide such space. It is generally thought that the hippocampus has the capacity for plasticity that affords extremely rapid learning. In contrast, the formation of permanent memory traces in cortex may take considerably more time. Although some types of cortical plasticity may occur rapidly (e.g. priming), the formation of long-lasting declarative memory traces that involve multiple semantic interconnections and can be accessed flexibly is likely to occur more gradually. According to one view, it is the role of the hippocampal system to acquire memories and then 'train' the cortex until the memory is fully instantiated there (McClelland, McNaughton, & O'Reilly, 1995). This process of reinstantiation of memories is hypothesized to be gradual: the interleaving of reinstated memories in the cortex fosters the formation of robust, integrated representations that are less susceptible to interference than if memories were stored in cortex successively.

Patients who have retrograde amnesia that extends for several decades have usually sustained extensive damage to cortical regions in the temporal lobes (Cermak & O'Connor, 1983; Reed & Squire, 2000). This finding is consistent with the notion that cortical regions are the ultimate storage site for memories, since these patients are likely to have sustained damage to these sites. Only childhood memories exist in these patients, which perhaps are represented in a very distributed manner because they were acquired while the cortex was maturing. There have been a few case studies of patients who lose all memories for events, including those occurring during childhood (Damasio, Eslinger, Damasio, Van Hoesen, & Cornell, 1985; Tulving, Schacter, McLachlan, & Moscovitch, 1988). In these patients, there is likely to be damage to both frontal and temporal lobes, which might broadly affect the strategic ability to recall as well as memory storage sites. Interestingly, much semantic knowledge is generally intact in these patients, such as their language abilities and knowledge of game rules. It appears that well-learned semantic knowledge may be a particularly robust form of memory.

The finding that retrograde episodic memories are particularly affected in some cases of brain damage has led to the view that these memories may be stored differently than semantic memories. Patients with retrograde amnesia are particularly poor at recounting autobiographical memories; that is, memories of events that have happened to them. These patients are much better at personal semantics. For example, they may be able to remember the date of their wedding but not have a first-person recollection of the event. It is unfortunately difficult to definitively separate true episodic memories from semantic memories. Many of our childhood memories are in the form of stories that we have told many times, and thus may lack the episodic character of memories where we can feel that we can travel back to another place and time. As time passes, an episodic memory for an event becomes a memory for the fact that the event happened. Soon after a lecture, a student may remember the episode when a professor mentions a particular experimental finding. Much later, knowledge of the finding may persist without remembering the exact moment when the information was learned. It may be that structures in the medial temporal lobes play a persistent role in supporting true episodic retrieval for memories throughout the lifespan, while older memories become 'semantisized' and thus independent of this system (Rosenbaum, Winocur, & Moscovitch, 2001). However, it is also possible that the difference between episodic and semantic memories is one of degree and not kind. By definition, episodic memories occur only once, whereas memories for facts can occur across multiple study occasions. Also, memories for episodes tend to include many multimodal components. Thus, these memories may be more fragile by their nature and could be more susceptible to damage to storage sites in cortex than would semantic memories.

ALZHEIMER'S DISEASE AND DEMENTIA

The study of amnesia receives the greatest attention in the neuropsychology of memory because of its theoretical importance to the study of mnemonic processes and their neural substrates. However, the majority of patients who exhibit memory impairments as a consequence of a neurological disorder suffer from Alzheimer's disease and not the amnesic syndrome. Alzheimer's disease is a degenerative disease that strikes older adults. A memory deficit is the most commonly associated symptom of Alzheimer's disease. However, Alzheimer's disease can only be diagnosed if there is at least one additional cognitive deficit present. This is often a problem with naming objects (Price, Gurvit, Weintrub, Geula, Leimkuhler, & Mesulam, 1993). Visuospatial problems, difficulties with executive function and attention deficits are also common in Alzheimer's disease. Patients with Alzheimer's disease may also exhibit psychiatric symptoms such as apathy or agitation, which can be particularly difficult for caregivers to manage (Mega, Cummings, Fiorello, & Gombein, 1996). At the very earliest stages of the disease, however, the memory impairment may be the only significant deficit.

Another primary characteristic of Alzheimer's disease is that cognitive abilities decline as the disease progresses. The non-selective and progressive nature of Alzheimer's disease makes it less well suited than the amnesic syndrome for the study of the brain areas involved in memory processing. However, the study of Alzheimer's disease has enormous clinical significance given that people are living longer into old age.

Alzheimer's disease is associated with neuronal loss and characteristic neuropathology in the brain. Plaques composed of amyloid protein and neurofibrillary tangles are readily visible through a microscope in the post-mortem brains of patients with Alzheimer's disease, especially in medial temporal lobe regions (Arnold, Hyman, Flory, Damasio, & Van Hoesen, 1991). It is not known whether these pathological changes directly cause the cell loss, or if they are only markers of a disease process that is killing cells. The vast majority of cases of Alzheimer's disease are not linked to the inheritance of a particular gene. However, there are genetic risk factors associated with Alzheimer's disease (see Holmes, 2002, for a review). For example, people with the gene that codes for a particular form of apolipoprotein E have a greater risk than those who have genes that code for other forms of this protein. This risk is even greater when this gene is present on both alleles. Apolipoprotein E is involved in the transport of lipoproteins into cells. Thus, it may be important in order for neurons to maintain health and normal synaptic contacts (see Poirier, 2000, for a review). Particular forms of apolipoprotein E may not be quite as efficient at these tasks as other forms, and this may hasten the disease process. Other risk factors that have been suggested include head trauma and low education level (Lye & Shores, 2000; Small, 1998). Both of these factors relate to the idea that there is a certain amount of 'cognitive reserve'. If individuals become symptomatic at the point at which cognitive abilities decline beyond the level at which daily life activities are affected, then confronting old age with a higher level of cognitive reserve would delay the onset of Alzheimer's disease, perhaps past the point of the end of life. Head trauma may induce brain damage that may not have a functional effect until the brain is further challenged by aging and the Alzheimer's disease process. Education appears to have a protective effect such that patients with higher education levels receive the diagnosis of Alzheimer's disease later (although the mortality rate does not appear to be affected: Qui, Backman, Winblad, Aguero-Torres, & Fratiglioni, 2001). Higher educational achievement is likely to be associated with continued intellectual stimulation throughout life. It may not be the case that such intellectual stimulation prevents the Alzheimer's disease process, but rather it might prolong the capacity to function within a normal range.

The cognitive reserve idea is particularly relevant if one accepts the view that Alzheimer's disease is an inevitable consequence of aging in the nervous system. By this view, if we each lived long enough, we all would develop Alzheimer's disease eventually. The strategy for developing treatments is not necessarily one of finding a way to prevent the disease, but of putting it off sufficiently.

The memory deficits in Alzheimer's disease patients are similar to those of amnesic patients. Patients with Alzheimer's disease exhibit declarative memory deficits accompanied by normal motor skill learning and perceptual priming (see Gabrieli, 1998, for a review). This is consistent with the anatomical findings that the basal ganglia and primary motor and sensory cortical regions are relatively spared in Alzheimer's disease. Patients with Alzheimer's disease differ from amnesic patients in that they exhibit deficits in forms of priming that depend on more complex representations. For example, patients with Alzheimer's disease have been reported to exhibit poor semantic priming, as in category exemplar generation tasks. These deficits may be due to a breakdown in the semantic networks that support such priming (Vaidya, Gabrieli, Monti, Tinklenberg, & Yesavage, 1999). Because semantic deficits are somewhat variable in Alzheimer's disease, deficits in semantic priming do not seem to be as consistent as the declarative memory deficits. Patients with Alzheimer's disease also often have deficits with word stem and fragment completion tasks that are performed normally by amnesic patients (Russo & Spinnler, 1994). These deficits point to disruption in lexical-level representations in Alzheimer's disease.

Patients with Alzheimer's disease exhibit retrograde amnesia that becomes increasingly dense as the disease progresses. More remote memories are generally preserved (Beatty, Salmon, Butters,

Heindel, & Granholm, 1988). It is common for patients in later stages of Alzheimer's disease to eventually forget such pertinent information as the names of their children or their spouse. This loss is not confined to episodic memories. As mentioned above, patients also lose semantic knowledge as the disease progresses. The loss of past memories is likely related to involvement of cortical regions that are the sites of memory storage.

FRONTOTEMPORAL DEMENTIA

Although Alzheimer's disease is the most common form of dementia, other progressive dementia disorders have been described. One of these disorders, frontotemporal dementia, is particularly interesting to neuropsychologists because the constellation of symptoms can be fairly selective early in the disease, and the symptom pattern can be contrasted with that of Alzheimer's disease. Frontotemporal dementia appears to exist in at least two subtypes (see Hodges & Miller, 2001, for a review). In the frontal variant, personality changes, social disinhibition and problems with executive function are the earliest signs, and degeneration of prefrontal cortex is present, especially in cell layers involved in communication between cortical areas. In the temporal variant, there are differences between patients depending on whether the left or right temporal lobe is affected. Patients with left temporal lobe degeneration exhibit a decline in semantic knowledge (also called semantic dementia). This would manifest itself as problems in answering general knowledge questions about the world (e.g. What continent is Egypt located in?), defining vocabulary words, or naming pictures (Hodges, Patterson, Oxbury, & Funnell, 1992). The deficit is not specific to language output, since these patients also have difficulty in displaying semantic knowledge nonverbally. For example, they have difficulty in recognizing incompatibilities in the pyramid and palm trees test, such that they may not identify that a palm tree, and not a pine tree, belongs in a desert pyramid scene. Degeneration in the left temporal lobe appears to disrupt semantic networks that had been built up across the lifespan. Patients with severe semantic dementia may be able to identify only simple familiar items learned early in life (like 'dog' or 'cup': Lambon Ralph, Graham, Ellis, & Hodges, 1998). Right-sided temporal lobe degeneration results in problems with empathy and social cognition (Perry, Rosen, Kramer, Beer, Levenson, & Miller, 2001). It may be that the right temporal lobe has a similar function to the left in storing semantic knowledge, but specific to social interaction.

The profile of frontotemporal dementia is somewhat different from that of Alzheimer's disease. Frontotemporal dementia typically begins in late middle age, while Alzheimer's disease affects older adults with risk increasing with age. Many patients with the frontal variant are diagnosed initially with a psychiatric condition. There is a much stronger genetic component to frontotemporal dementia than there is to Alzheimer's disease. In frontotemporal dementia, deficits in declarative memory are not as pronounced as they are in Alzheimer's disease. Patients with semantic dementia may have difficulty with memory tasks when control subjects are able to benefit from deep (semantic) encoding. Semantic dementia patients can perform normally on recognition memory tasks using meaningless stimuli or simple objects that do not benefit much by elaborative encoding. Likewise, patients with the frontal variant may have difficulty with memory tasks that require strategic processing (see section below on frontal lobe contributions to memory). Finally, the plaques and tangles that are characteristic of the neuropathology in Alzheimer's disease are not present in frontotemporal dementia. In Alzheimer's disease, medial temporal lobe structures are in general affected earliest, while in frontotemporal dementia frontal lobes or polar and temporal cortex is affected at the onset. Structures in the medial temporal lobe tend to be spared initially. In both of these disorders, degeneration is progressive and eventually includes extensive regions of cortex.

A comparison of the performance of patients with semantic dementia and Alzheimer's disease on retrograde memory tests yields an interesting double dissociation. Patients with Alzheimer's disease have greatest difficulty recalling more recent events, while the opposite is true for semantic dementia patients. These patients generally have more difficulty relative to control subject in recalling old memories than new memories (Graham & Hodges, 1997). These results support the view that medial temporal lobe structures are important for the acquisition of information into declarative memory, but that the eventual storage site of these memories is in networks in the temporal cortex. In the semantic dementia patients, new memories could be stored in remaining neocortex, but cortical degeneration had impaired access to older memories.

FRONTAL LOBES AND MEMORY

Damage to prefrontal cortex is relatively common, and can result from strokes, removal of tumors or head injury. Because of their position on the head, the frontal lobes are particularly susceptible to damage during vehicular accidents. Although medial temporal lobe structures are firmly identified with declarative memory processing, the frontal lobes are clearly part of the circuit that contributes to this cognitive ability. While subjects are performing declarative memory tasks, activation is typically seen in regions of prefrontal cortex using neuroimaging techniques (for reviews see Cabeza & Nyberg, 2000; Maguire, 2001; Yancey & Phelps, 2001). In fact, these prefrontal activations are often more pronounced than activations in the medial temporal lobe. Patients with frontal lobe damage do not exhibit an amnesic syndrome, in that they are not globally impaired on all recall and recognition tasks. However, deficits in memory function are readily apparent in patients with prefrontal damage, and these deficits have an impact on their daily life activities.

Activation in left inferior prefrontal cortex is present while subjects are asked to encode information for a later memory test, and this activation is correlated with the ability of subjects to later remember words and pictures. It seems that this region is involved in semantic processing of items, and those items that are deeply processed are remembered better later (see Gabrieli, Poldrack, & Desmond, 1998, for a review). Although patients with prefrontal damage are not necessarily impaired on semantic tasks, such as tests of vocabulary, they do seem to have trouble using this information to benefit memory encoding. Patients with prefrontal cortical damage do not benefit from the inclusion of semantically similar items in the study list (Hirst & Volpe, 1988; Incisa della Rocchetta & Milner, 1993). For example, if control subjects are given a list of fruits (apple, pear, orange), they will recall the list better than a list of unrelated words. Patients with prefrontal damage do not show this benefit. It is as if they are not able to actively form the inter-list associations that are required in order to benefit from the semantic relatedness of the words.

This is also shown by differences in the recall output of controls and patients with prefrontal damage. If given a list with multiple intermixed categories, control subjects will tend to cluster items within a category when they are recalling the list. Patients with prefrontal damage show this clustering to a lesser extent, suggesting that they are not making use of semantic relatedness at encoding (Gershberg & Shimamura, 1995). Patients with prefrontal damage who also have memory problems have been reported to show a lack of release from proactive interference (Freedman & Cermak, 1986). For example, if control subjects learn successive lists of items from the same semantic category (e.g. animals), their performance will decline due to proactive interference from successive lists. When a new list of items from a different semantic category is given (e.g. cities), there is a release from this proactive interference, and performance improves. Patients with prefrontal cortical damage show proactive interference even for non-related lists because they have general difficulty with interfering stimuli (Shimamura, Jurica, Mangels, Gershberg, & Knight, 1995; Smith, Crane, & Milner, 1995). Frontal lobe patients may have particular difficulty benefiting from a category switch across lists when memory traces are weak.

The deficits in semantic encoding in prefrontal patients can be attenuated to some extent by providing encoding support (Gershberg & Shimamura, 1995; Incisa della Rocchetta & Milner, 1993; Vogel, Markowitsch, Hempel, & Hackenberg, 1987). For example, giving a category label or clustering items in a mixed list seems to help these patients encode semantic information. These manipulations also benefit control subjects to some extent, although in most cases control subjects already use semantic encoding well enough for them not to receive additional benefit from making semantic relatedness more transparent. The fact that prefrontal patients can use semantic encoding underscores the idea that their semantic networks are largely intact, but are not employed effectively in memory encoding.

Patients with prefrontal damage also have difficulty with memory retrieval. Their recall performance is typically much poorer than their recognition performance (Dimitrov, Granetz, Peterson, Hollnagel, Alexander, & Grafman, 1999; Jetter, Poser, Freeman, & Markowitsch, 1986; Wheeler, Stuss, & Tulving, 1995). This contrasts with the performance of amnesic patients, in which recall and recognition are impaired to the same extent. The fact that prefrontal patients can perform normally on recognition tasks suggests that they may be able to encode new information, but they may not be able to effectively use strategies to retrieve information. The less support given to recall, the greater the deficit in prefrontal patients. For example, these patients fare the most poorly with tasks of free recall and exhibit relatively smaller deficits with cued recall. Recognition memory can be quite normal, especially forced choice recognition in which the subject must choose between a novel and a familiar item. With free recall, the subject must essentially form a retrieval 'plan' in which items are strategically retrieved that will aid in retrieving the desired information. Thus, to recall the name of one's third-grade teacher, one might attempt to retrieve memories of one's third-grade playmates and important events that happened that year in order to activate the memory of the teacher. Deficits in the ability to form this plan would impair effective recall but would leave recognition intact. Patients with prefrontal damage have particular difficulty with assessing the source of memories or the temporal order with which memories occurred (Janowsky, Shimamura, & Squire, 1989; Mangels, 1997; McAndrews & Milner, 1991). Even for items that are correctly recognized, prefrontal patients have difficulty with discriminating where and when the memory was acquired. This stands in contrast to the performance of amnesic patients, who generally exhibit proportionate impairments in item and source memory.

Source memory and temporal order judgments require the recall of specific information that requires a great deal of self-generated cueing. Thus, prefrontal patients may find it particularly hard to access the specific context in which learning took place.

The role of the prefrontal cortex in memory is also supported by neuroimaging evidence. Prefrontal activation is commonly seen when subjects retrieve items (Cadoret, Pike, & Petrides, 2001; Henson, Rugg, Shallice, & Dolan, 2000; McDermott et al., 1999). It is not known whether this activation is related to the search of memory contents, the evaluation of the products of the retrieval process (such as whether a retrieved item actually exceeds threshold for being in the study phase) or some other retrieval-related process. Given the fact that the prefrontal cortex is a large, heterogeneous region in humans, it is likely that it is involved in multiple retrieval-related subprocesses.

The idea that prefrontal patients have trouble with monitoring the products of retrieval has been suggested in order to explain the phenomenon of confabulation in these patients. Prefrontal patients, particularly those with memory disorders, have been reported to answer questions with impossible, inconsistent answers (Fischer, Alexander, D'Esposito, & Otto, 1995; Stuss, Alexander, Lieberman, & Levine, 1978). For example, a man might claim that he is a newly-wed despite the fact that he had been married for several decades. These confabulations appear to be distinct from deliberate untruths, in that patients do not seem to have any motivation to lie. Also, it does not seem that the confabulations are simply due to poor memory for facts and events in the past. Amnesic patients who have profound retrograde memory deficits do not typically confabulate. It may be that prefrontal patients have a deficit in their ability to judge whether what has been retrieved is appropriate and to inhibit retrieved information that is inappropriate. According to this view, a query into memory would result in the retrieval of several different pieces of information that were activated. For example, when asked to recount a recent vacation, one might initially broadly retrieve memories about the recent vacation as well as previous vacations, and even vacations imagined or described in recent television programs. The products of retrieval are immediately filtered for credibility. Also, as specific temporal information for the memories is retrieved, memories of older vacations can be eliminated from contention. In this way, memory for the recent vacation can emerge as the correct memory in this context. Even in control subjects, many recounted memories are blended with elements of related memories. Prefrontal patients may not be able to effectively inhibit inappropriately retrieved memories and thus they may come up with odd confabulations that are really blends of various bits of retrieved information. A

similar difficulty in retrieval monitoring may contribute to the finding that prefrontal patients make numerous intrusion errors from previous lists when given successive lists to remember.

All of the memory processes that are disrupted by frontal lobe damage appear to draw heavily on working memory resources. Because neuroimaging and neuropsychological studies have linked working memory to the function of cortical loops that include prefrontal cortex (for a review see Baddeley & Della Sala, 1996; Carpenter, Just, & Reichle, 2000), it is possible that long-term memory deficits are a direct consequence of working memory impairment in these patients. For example, deficits in semantic encoding could result if subjects were unable to hold and manipulate information in working memory. It would be difficult to form inter-list associations or extract common semantic content across items if working memory capacity or the ability to manipulate or update items in working memory were impaired. Providing prefrontal patients with some semantic structure during learning may help to overcome working memory limitations.

Working memory deficits would also have a major impact on strategic abilities such as planning and problem solving. Patients with prefrontal cortical damage are notoriously poor at planning (see Owen, 1997, for a review). Planning requires the generation and simultaneous consideration of multiple subgoals that should be followed in order to execute a plan. For example, in order to plan a meal one must form subgoals, such as shopping for food and preparing the various dishes. Each of these subgoals can be further broken down into additional subgoals. Multiple subgoals must be integrated in order to form an efficient plan. One must start cooking the planned dishes at different times, and one must make sure that if two dishes require the same ingredient that there is enough for both. Prefrontal patients often perform tasks like shopping inefficiently because of their difficulty in forming and/or using goal hierarchies.

This strategic deficit could also extend to the formation and execution of retrieval plans. The generation of effective retrieval cues requires the simultaneous consideration of the ultimate retrieval goal as well as retrieval subgoals for relevant information. For example, if I want to remember what I had for breakfast last Tuesday, I would keep this main goal in mind while I tried to recall last Tuesday's date, which might help me remember if I had given a lecture that day. If I could remember the lecture, I could remember if I was in a hurry that day, and thus I could remember if I ate at home or not. If I did, remembering when I had gone shopping would give me cues as to what I might have had in the house at the time. Performing a difficult recall task such as this requires several pieces of information to be held in mind at once, and thus requires substantial working memory. Such tasks may be difficult for prefrontal patients because of working memory deficits. Retrieval based on familiarity, as in many recognition tasks, does not require such strategic processing, and is relatively intact after prefrontal damage.

The concept of working memory does not merely refer to a passive buffer of information held in mind, but also to the manipulation of the information in the service of cognition. The delineation of the processes that comprise working memory is currently a 'hot' topic in cognitive science. Patients with prefrontal damage may have limitations in working memory capacity, or they may have problems with inserting items into working memory, integrating multiple propositions in working memory, or inhibiting irrelevant items from flooding working memory. If the inhibition of irrelevant information is considered as part of working memory, one could also interpret intrusion errors and confabulations as stemming from working memory dysfunction. Recent neuroimaging studies have suggested that different components of working memory may be subserved by different regions within the prefrontal cortex. It is thus likely that working memory is affected differently in different prefrontal patients depending on the locus of damage. Because the prefrontal cortex represents almost one-third of the human brain, it is likely to support multiple cognitive operations that contribute to complex thought.

MEMORY AND NORMAL AGING

Neuropsychology has traditionally focused on the effects of brain injury, but it is clear that even normal, healthy, aging results in brain changes that affect cognition. Older adults, on average, exhibit a number of deficits compared to young adults. One of the most striking differences is in reaction time, suggesting that processing is slowed with age (see Salthouse, 1996, for a review). Older subjects also exhibit poorer declarative memory than young adults. Non-declarative memory appears to be relatively spared, although mild deficits are also reported. Working memory deficits have also been reported, which appears to have a negative impact on executive function in aging (Li, Lindenberger, & Sikstrom, 2001). Many brain systems are affected by aging, and thus it follows that many cognitive systems are affected as well. However, it is not the case that aging involves an across the board decline in cognitive function. Semantic knowledge such as vocabulary and fact knowledge seem to be spared, or even superior in older adults (Eustache et al., 1995; Horn & Donaldson, 1976). Older subjects have had more time to acquire semantic knowledge over the course of their lifetime. Thus, older subjects can perform very well on tasks that require knowledge of the world, but have relatively more

trouble when participants must quickly generate solutions to novel problems.

Memory problems are a typical complaint among older adults. Older adults seem to have particular difficulty with source memory, with relatively fewer problems with recognition memory (Schacter, Osowiecki, Kaszniak, Kihlstrom, & Valdiserri, 1994). This pattern supports the idea that the deterioration of memory with aging has much to do with prefrontal involvement. The working memory problems seen in aging are also consistent with prefrontal degeneration. There is also neuropathological evidence that the frontal lobes are particularly affected in aging. The frontal lobes continue to develop late into childhood, and this late development is mirrored at the opposite end of the developmental spectrum by relatively early degeneration in old age (Scheibel, Lindsay, Tomiyasu, & Scheibel, 1975; Thatcher, 1991).

Although aging is associated with cognitive deficits on average, equally striking is the increase in variability in performance that accompanies aging (Christensen, Mackinnon, Jorm, Henderson, Scott, & Korten, 1994). A significant number of older adults perform well into the range of younger subjects on declarative memory tasks. There are probably several reasons for this variability. First, older adults are likely to differ in the extent of age-related neuropathology. Second, some older adults may be able to use alternative strategies to solve problems, such as relying on well-developed semantic knowledge to enhance encoding. A third factor may be the extent to which older subjects have continued to develop their cognitive capabilities. It appears that individuals who continue social and physical activities into old age maintain cognitive function longer (Laurin, Verreault, Lindsay, MacPherson, & Rockwood, 2001; Stuck, Walthert, Nikolaus, Bijla, Hohmann, & Beck, 1999). Increased activity may protect against neurodegeneration, or it may allow more efficient use of remaining neural substrate. Social and physical activities are likely to convey specific benefits, and these activities generally involve cognitive stimulation as well (e.g. joining a bridge club, or noticing new things along a daily walk). Maintaining an active lifestyle into advanced age appears to have many interactive health benefits. As medical advances prolong the lifespan, it is becoming increasingly important to find ways to enhance the quality of life of older adults. Enhancing opportunities for cognitive, social and physical activity among the aged may be an effective means toward this goal.

NEUROPSYCHOLOGY AND FUNCTIONAL NEUROIMAGING

The most fundamental discoveries in neuropsychology were made before the development of modern brain-imaging techniques. Studies of brain-injured patients provided key support to concepts such as cerebral lateralization, executive function and levels of representation in visual perception. Neuropsychology relied on the careful study of patients in whom the site of brain damage was only generally known. Even when a post-mortem analysis of the brain revealed the extent of damage, it was difficult to pinpoint which of the multiple regions that were damaged were truly responsible for the behavioral deficit. In some sense, this was not critical since the goal of neuropsychology was to understand the components of cognition and not necessarily link structure and function. More recently, magnetic resonance imaging of the brain has allowed neuropsychologists to identify the extent of brain damage with excellent resolution in a non-invasive manner, allowing more information about the specific structures damaged. However, the problem remains that the brain damage that occurs in patients often encompasses more than one neuroanatomical region. For example, in the case of patient HM described above, several structures were removed so it was not clear which of these structures were critical for declarative memory.

Functional neuroimaging techniques can avoid some of the ambiguity that arises in the study of patients in whom damage is typically non-specific. Techniques such as positron emission tomography (PET) and functional magnetic resonance imaging (fMRI) allow one to examine brain regions that are activated during performance of a cognitive task. Rather than inferring structure–function relationships by examining functional losses when a structure is damaged, a direct link can potentially be made between a structure and its function. PET and fMRI do not directly measure the medium of communication in the brain (neuronal action potentials), but rather cerebral metabolism (PET) and blood oxygenation level (fMRI), which are thought to be reasonable proxies for neural activity. The resolution of PET is about 5 mm, while that of fMRI is much better (as low as 1 mm) which can allow, for example, the differentiation of hippocampus from surrounding medial temporal lobe cortices.

Functional neuroimaging also offers a degree of temporal resolution not possible in neuropsychological studies. For example, in patients with amnesia, damage is present during the encoding, consolidation and retrieval phases. Thus, it is not known how the medial temporal lobe structures damaged in amnesia may play different roles in these processes. Unlike studies with PET, in which brain activation over blocks of several minutes is measured, fMRI allows the measurement of activation associated with specific single events, such as correct recollection of stimuli or the study of stimuli that will be later remembered. Such event-related fMRI allows us to assess brain activation associated

with different hypothesized stages of cognitive processes.

Another difficulty with inferring structure–function relationships from neuropsychological studies is the possibility of functional recovery. Plasticity in the nervous system is well documented. It is quite possible that a given structure may typically contribute to a cognitive ability, but other structures may be able to take over after damage, leading to no loss of function. Thus, the study of brain-injured patients may underestimate the contribution various structures make to cognitive function.

Despite these advantages of the neuroimaging approach, neuropsychology arguably offers some complementary advantages. For example, there are many constraints one must make in the design of neuroimaging experiments. In PET, blocks of one trial type must last several minutes, and thus it is impossible to intermix stimuli in different conditions. For example, if brain activation to recognized words was compared to brain activation to unrecognized words, one would need to block old and new words separately at test. In event-related fMRI, one can measure activation on intermixed trials, but one must design the experiment so that there are many trials of each type to measure reliable activation. In addition, subjects are very constrained in terms of the response they can make (generally button presses), since subjects are confined to the scanning apparatus and movement must be minimized.

Another issue in the interpretation of neuroimaging data is the fact that these techniques are contrastive. Thus, activation is always measured relative to some other condition. Often this condition is rest or the performance of a cognitively undemanding task. However, such contrasts may lead to misinterpretation (Newman, Tweig, & Carpenter, 2001; Stark & Squire, 2001). For example, comparing the activation associated with the recall of a list of words with the activation during 'rest' might not reveal structures truly involved in recall if those are also actively involved in recalling the subject's shopping list during the 'rest' condition!

Finally, neuropsychological studies can help answer the question of whether or not a region of the brain is necessary for a function or simply active during performance. For example, neuroimaging studies of declarative memory have in the past shown much more robust activation in prefrontal structures than in the medial temporal lobe. Medial temporal lobe activation may simply be more difficult to see because of its position in the brain, its vascularization, or because it may be constantly active even during baseline conditions. The frontal lobe is clearly active in strategic aspects of encoding and recall as can be seen in the performance of prefrontal patients on memory tasks. However, the findings from the case of patient HM endure as to the primary and critical role of medial temporal lobe structures in declarative memory.

REFERENCES

Altmann, G. T. M., Dienes, Z., & Goode, A. (1995). Modality independence of implicitly learned grammatical knowledge. *Journal of Experimental Psychology: Learning, Memory, and Cognition, 21,* 899–912.

Arnold, S. E., Hyman, B. T., Flory, J., Damasio, A. R., & Van Hoesen, G. W. (1991). The topographical and neuroanatomical distribution of neurofibrillary tangles and neuritic plaques in the cerebral cortex of patients with Alzheimer's disease. *Cerebral Cortex, 1,* 103–106.

Baddeley, A., & Della Sala, S. (1996). Working memory and executive control. *Philosphical Transactions of the Royal Society of London B, 351,* 1397–1403.

Beatty, W. W., Salmon, D. P., Butters, N., Heindel, W. C., & Granholm, E. L. (1988). Retrograde amnesia in patients with Alzheimer's disease or Huntington's disease. *Neurobiology of Aging, 9,* 181–186.

Bornstein, R. F., & D'Agostino, P. R. (1992). Stimulus recognition and the mere exposure effect. *Journal of Personality and Social Psychology, 63,* 545–552.

Cabeza, R., & Nyberg, L. (2000). Neural bases of learning and memory: functional neuroimaging evidence. *Current Opinion in Neurology, 13,* 415–421.

Cadoret, G., Pike, G. B., & Petrides, M. (2001). Selective activation of the ventrolateral prefrontal cortex in the human brain during active retrieval processing. *European Journal of Neuroscience, 14,* 1164–1170.

Carpenter, P. A., Just, M. A., & Reichle, E. D. (2000). Working memory and executive function: evidence from neuroimaging. *Current Opinion in Neurobiology, 10,* 195–199.

Cermak, L. S., & O'Connor, M. (1983). The anterograde and retrograde retrieval ability of a patient with amnesia due to encephalitis. *Neuropsychologia, 21,* 213–234.

Cermak, L. S., Talbot, N., Chandler, K., & Wolbarst, L. R. (1985). The perceptual priming phenomenon in amnesia. *Neuropsychologia, 23,* 615–622.

Christensen, H., Mackinnon, A., Jorm, A. F., Henderson, A. S., Scott, L. R., & Korten, A. E. (1994). Age differences and interindividual variation in cognition in community-dwelling elderly. *Psychological Aging, 9,* 381–390.

Cooper, L. A., Schacter, D. L., Ballesteros, S., & Moore, C. (1992). Priming and recognition of transformed three-dimensional objects: effects of size and reflection. *Journal of Experimental Psychology: Learning, Memory, and Cognition, 18,* 43–57.

Corkin, S. (1968). Acquisition of motor skill after bilateral medial temporal lobe excision. *Neuropsychologia, 6,* 255–265.

Damsio, A. R., Eslinger, P. J., Damasio, H., Van Hoesen, G. W., & Cornell, S. (1985). Multimodal amnesic syndrome following bilateral temporal and basal forebrain damage. *Archives of Neurology, 42,* 252–259.

Damasio, A. R., Tranel, D., & Damasio, H. (1991). Amnesia caused by herpes simplex encephalitis, infarctions in basal forebrain, Alzheimer's disease, and anoxia/ischemia. In L. R. Squire & G. Gainotti (Eds.),

Handbook of neuropsychology (Vol. 3, pp. 149–166). Amsterdam: Elsevier.

den Heyer, K., Briand, K., & Dannenbring, G. L. (1983). Strategic factors in a lexical-decision task: evidence for automatic and attention-driven processes. *Memory and Cognition, 11,* 374–381.

Dimitrov, M., Granetz, J., Peterson, M., Hollnagel, C., Alexander, G., & Grafman, J. (1999). Associative learning impairments in patients with frontal lobe damage. *Brain and Cognition, 41,* 213–230.

Eichenbaum, H., Mathews, P., & Cohen, N. J. (1989). Further studies of hippocampal representation during odor discrimination learning. *Behavioral Neuroscience, 103,* 1207–1216.

Eustache, F., Rioux, P., Desgranges, B., Marchal, G., Petit-Taboue, M. C., Dary, M., Lechavalier, B., & Baron, J. C. (1995). Healthy aging, memory subsystems, and regional cerebral oxygen consumption. *Neuropsychologia, 33,* 867–887.

Filoteo, J. V., Maddox, W. T., & Davis, J. D. (2001). Quantitative modeling of category learning in amnesic patients. *Journal of the International Neuropsychological Society, 7,* 1–19.

Fischer, R. S., Alexander, M. P., D'Esposito, M., & Otto, R. (1995). Neuropsychological and neuroanatomical correlates of confabulation. *Journal of Clinical and Experimental Neuropsychology, 17,* 20–28.

Fleischman, D. A., Vaidya, C. J., Lange, K. L., & Gabrieli, J. D. (1997). A dissociation between perceptual explicit and implicit memory processes. *Brain and Cognition, 35,* 42–57.

Freedman, M., & Cermak, L. S. (1986). Semantic encoding deficits in frontal lobe disease and amnesia. *Brain and Cognition, 5,* 108–114.

Gabrieli, J. D. E. (1998). Cognitive neuroscience of human memory. *Annual Review of Psychology, 49,* 87–115.

Gabrieli, J. D., Poldrack, R. A., & Desmond, J. E. (1998). The role of left prefontal cortex in language and memory. *Proceedings of the National Academy of Sciences of the USA, 95,* 906–913.

Gershberg, F. B., & Shimamura, A. P. (1995). Impaired use of organizational strategies in free recall following frontal lobe damage. *Neuropsychologia, 33,* 1305–1333.

Gomez, R. L., Gerken, L., & Schvaneveldt, R. W. (2000). The basis of transfer in artificial grammar learning. *Memory and Cognition, 28,* 253–263.

Graf, P., Shimamura, A. P., & Squire, L. R. (1985). Priming across modalities and priming across category levels: extending the domain of preserved function in amnesia. *Journal of Experimental Psychology: Learning, Memory, and Cognition, 11,* 386–396.

Graham, K. S., & Hodges, J. R. (1997). Differentiating the roles of the hippocampal complex and the neocortex in long-term memory storage: evidence from the study of semantic dementia and Alzheimer's disease. *Neuropsychology, 11,* 77–89.

Guberman, A., & Stuss, D. (1983). The syndrome of bilateral paramedian thalamic infarction. *Neurology, 33,* 540–546.

Haist, F., Shimamura, A. P., & Squire, L. R. (1992). On the relationship between recall and recognition memory. *Journal of Experimental Psychology: Learning, Memory, and Cognition, 18*, 691–702.

Henson, R. N., Rugg, M. D., Shallice, T., & Dolan, R. J. (2000). Confidence in recognition memory for words: dissociating right prefrontal roles in episodic retrieval. *Journal of Cognitive Neuroscience, 12*, 913–923.

Hirst, W., & Volpe, B. T. (1988). Memory strategies with brain damage. *Brain and Cognition, 8*, 379–408.

Hodges, J. R., & Miller, B. (2001). The neuropsychology of frontal variant frontotemporal dementia and semantic dementia. Introduction to the special topic papers: Part 2. *Neurocase, 7*, 113–121.

Hodges, J. R., Patterson, K., Oxbury, S., & Funnell, E. (1992). Semantic dementia: progressive fluent aphasia with temporal lobe atrophy. *Brain, 115*, 1783–1806.

Holmes, C. (2002). Genotype and phenotype on Alzheimer's disease. *British Journal of Psychiatry, 180*, 131–134.

Horn, J. L., & Donaldson, G. (1976). On the myth of intellectual decline in adulthood. *American Psychologist, 31*, 701–719.

Incisa della Rocchetta, A., & Milner, B. (1993). Strategic search and retrieval inhibition: the role of the frontal lobes. *Neuropsychologia, 31*, 503–524.

Janowsky, J. S., Shimamura, A. P., & Squire, L. R. (1989). Source memory impairment in patients with frontal lobe lesions. *Neuropsychologia, 27*, 1043–1056.

Jetter, W., Poser, U., Freeman, R. B., Jr., & Markowitsch, H. J. (1986). A verbal long term memory deficit in frontal lobe damaged patients. *Cortex, 22*, 229–242.

Johnson, M. K., Kim, J. K., & Risse, G. (1985). Do alcoholic Korsakoff's syndrome patients acquire affective reactions? *Journal of Experimental Psychology: Learning, Memory, and Cognition, 11*, 22–36.

Keane, M. M., Gabrieli, J. D., Mapstone, H. C., Johnson, K. A., & Corkin, S. (1995). Double dissociation of memory capacities after bilateral occipital lobe or medial temporal lobe lesions. *Brain, 118*, 1129–1148.

Knowlton, B. J., Mangels, J. A., & Squire, L. R. (1996). A neostriatal habit learning system in humans. *Science, 273*, 1353–1354.

Knowlton, B. J., Ramus, S. J., & Squire, L. R. (1992). Intact artificial grammar learning in amnesia: dissociation of classification learning and explicit memory for specific instances. *Psychological Science, 3*, 172–179.

Knowlton, B. J., & Squire, L. R. (1993). The learning of categories: parallel brain systems for item memory and category knowledge. *Science, 262*, 1747–1749.

Knowlton, B. J., & Squire, L. R. (1994). The information acquired during artificial grammar learning. *Journal of Experimental Psychology: Learning, Memory, and Cognition, 20*, 79–91.

Knowlton, B. J., & Squire, L. R. (1996). Artificial grammar learning depends on implicit acquisition of both abstract and exemplar-specific information. *Journal of Experimental Psychology: Learning, Memory, and Cognition, 22*, 169–181.

Knowlton, B. J., Squire, L. R., & Gluck, M. A. (1994). Probabilistic classification learning in amnesia. *Learning and Memory, 1*, 106–120.

Kopelman, M. D., & Kapur, N. (2001). The loss of episodic memories in amnesia: single case and group studies. *Philosophical Transactions of the Royal Society of London B, 356*, 1409–1421.

Koutstaal, W., Wagner, A. D., Rotte, M., Maril, A., Buckner, R. L., & Schacter, D. L. (2001). Perceptual specificity in visual object priming: functional magnetic resonance imaging evidence for a laterality difference in fusiform cortex. *Neuropsychologia, 39*, 184–199.

Lambon Ralph, M. A., Graham, K. S., Ellis, A. W., & Hodges, J. R. (1998). Naming in semantic dementia: what matters? *Neuropsychologia, 36*, 775–784.

Lashley, K. S. (1929). *Brain mechanisms and intelligence.* Chicago: University of Chicago Press.

Laurin, D., Verreault, R., Lindsay, J., MacPherson, K., & Rockwood, K. (2001). Physical activity and risk of cognitive impairment and dementia in elderly persons. *Archives of Neurology, 58*, 498–504.

Li, S. C., Lindenberger, U., & Sikstrom, S. (2001). Aging cognition: from neuromodulation to representation. *Trends in Cognitive Science, 5*, 479–486.

Lieberman, M. D., Ochsner, K. N., Gilbert, D. T., & Schacter, D. L. (2001). Do amnesics exhibit cognitive dissonance reduction? The role of explicit memory and attention in attitude change. *Psychological Science, 121*, 135–140.

Lye, T. C., & Shores, E. A. (2000). Traumatic brain injury as a risk factor for Alzheimer's disease: a review. *Neuropsychology Review, 10*, 115–129.

Maguire, E. A. (2001). Neuroimaging studies of autobiographical event memory. *Philosophical Transactions of the Royal Society of London B, 356*, 1441–1451.

Mangels, J. A. (1997). Strategic processing and memory for temporal order in patients with frontal lobe lesions. *Neuropsychology, 11*, 207–221.

McAndrews, M. P., & Milner, B. (1991). The frontal cortex and memory for temporal order. *Neuropsychologia, 29*, 849–859.

McClelland, J. L., McNaughton, B. L., & O'Reilly, R. C. (1995). Why there are complementary learning systems in the hippocampus and neocortex: insights from the success and failures of connectionist models of learning and memory. *Psychological Review, 102*, 419–457.

McDermott, K. B., Ojemann, J. G., Petersen, S. E., Ollinger, J. M., Snyder, A. Z., Akbudak, E., Conturo, T. E., & Raichle, M. E. (1999). Direct comparison of episodic encoding and retrieval of words: an event-related fMRI study. *Memory, 7*, 661–678.

Mega, M. S., Cummings, J. L., Fiorello, T., & Gornbein, J. (1996). The spectrum of behavioral changes in Alzheimer's disease. *Neurology, 46*, 130–135.

Milner, B., Corkin, S., & Teuber, H.-L. (1968). Further analysis of the hippocampal amnesic syndrome: 14 year follow up study of H. M. *Neuropsychologia, 6*, 215–234.

Newman, S. D., Tweig, D. B., & Carpenter, P. A. (2001). Baseline conditions and subtractive logic in neuroimaging. *Human Brain Mapping, 14*, 228–235.

Nissen, M. J., Willingham, D., & Hartman, M. (1989). Explicit and implicit remembering: when is learning preserved in amnesia? *Neuropsychologia, 27*, 341–352.

Oscar-Berman, M. (1980). Neuropsychological consequences of long-term chronic alcoholism. *American Scientist, 68*, 410–419.

Owen, A. M. (1997). Cognitive planning in humans: neuropsychological, neuroanatomical, and neuropharmacological perspectives. *Progress in Neurobiology, 53*, 431–450.

Packard, M. G., Hirsh, R., & White, N. M. (1989). Differential effects of fornix and caudate nucleus lesions on two radial maze tasks: evidence for multiple memory systems. *Journal of Neuroscience, 9*, 1465–1472.

Perry, R. J., Rosen, H. R., Kramer, J. H., Beer, J. S., Levenson, R. L., & Miller, B. L. (2001). Hemispheric dominance for emotions, empathy and social behaviour: evidence from right and left handers with frontotemporal dementia. *Neurocase, 7*, 145–160.

Poirier, J. (2000). Apolipoprotein E and Alzheimer's disease: a role in amyloid catabolism. *Annals of the New York Academy of Sciences, 824*, 81–90.

Poldrack, R. A., Prabhakaran, V., Seger, C. A., & Gabrieli, J. D. (1999). Striatal activation during acquisition of a cognitive skill. *Neuropsychology, 13*, 564–574.

Poldrack, R. A., Clark, J., Pare-Blagoev, E. J., Shohamy, D., Creso-Moyano, J., Myers, C., & Gluck, M.A. (2001). Interactive memory systems in the human brain. *Nature, 414*, 546–550.

Posner, M. I., & Keele, S. W. (1968). On the genesis of abstract ideas. *Journal of Experimental Psychology, 77*, 353–363.

Price, B. H., Gurvit, H., Weintrub, S., Geula, C., Leimkuhler, E., & Mesulam, M. (1993). Neuropsychological patterns and language deficits in 20 consecutive cases of autopsy confirmed Alzheimer's disease. *Archives of Neurology, 50*, 931–937.

Qui, C., Backman, L., Winblad, B., Aguero-Torres, H., & Fratiglioni, L. (2001). The influence of education on clinically diagnosed dementia incidence and mortality: data from the Kungsholm project. *Archives of Neurology, 58*, 2034–2039.

Reading, P. J., Dunnett, S. B., & Robbins, T. W. (1991). Dissociable roles of the ventral, medial and lateral striatum on the acquisition and performance of a complex visual stimulus-response habit. *Behavioural Brain Research, 45*, 147–161.

Reber, A. S. (1967). Implicit learning of artificial grammars. *Journal of Verbal Learning and Verbal Behavior, 6*, 855–863.

Reber, P. J., & Squire, L. R. (1998). Encapsulation of implicit and explicit memory in sequence learning. *Journal of Cognitive Neuroscience, 10*, 248–263.

Reed, J. M., & Squire, L. R. (2000). Retrograde amnesia for facts and events: findings from four new cases. *Journal of Neuroscience, 18*, 3943–3954.

Roediger, H. L., Weldon, M. S., Stadler, M. L., & Riegler, G. L. (1992). Direct comparison of two implicit memory tests: word fragment and word stem completion. *Journal of Experimental Psychology: Learning, Memory, and Cognition, 18*, 1251–1269.

Rosch, E. (1988). Principles of categorization. In A. M. Collins & E. E. Smith (Eds.), *Readings in cognitive science: a perspective from psychology and artificial intelligence* (pp. 312–322). San Mateo, CA: Morgan Kaufman.

Rosenbaum, R. S., Winocur, G., & Moscovitch, M. (2001). New views on old memories: re-evaluating the role of the hippocampal complex. *Behavioural Brain Research, 127*, 183–189.

Russo, R., & Spinnler, H. (1994). Implicit verbal memory in Alzheimer's disease. *Cortex, 30*, 359–375.

Salthouse, T. A. (1996). The processing-speed theory of adult age differences in cognition. *Psychological Review, 103*, 403–428.

Samuelsson, S., Bogges, T. R., & Karlsson, T. (2000). Visual implicit memory deficit and developmental surface dyslexia: a case of early occipital damage. *Cortex, 36*, 365–376.

Schacter, D. L. (1985). Priming of old and new knowledge in amnesic patients and normal subjects. *Annals of the New York Academy of Sciences, 444*, 41–53.

Schacter, D. L., Osowiecki, D., Kaszniak, A. W., Kihlstrom, J. F., & Valdiserri, M. (1994). Source memory: extending the boundaries of age-related deficits. *Psychological Aging, 9*, 81–89.

Scheibel, M. E., Lindsay, R. D., Tomiyasu, U., & Scheibel, A. B. (1975). Progressive dendritic changes in aging human cortex. *Experimental Neurology, 47*, 392–403.

Scoville, W. B., & Milner, B. (1957). Loss of recent memory after bilateral hippocampal lesions. *Journal of Neurology, Neurosurgery, and Psychiatry, 20*, 11.

Shimamura, A. P., Jurica, P. J., Mangels, J. A., Gershberg, F. B., & Knight, R. T. (1995). Susceptibility to memory interference effects following frontal lobe damage: findings from tests of paired-associate learning. *Journal of Cognitive Neuroscience, 7*, 144–152.

Small, G. W. (1998). The pathogenesis of Alzheimer's disease. *Journal of Clinical Psychiatry, 59* (Suppl. 9), 7–14.

Smith, M. L., Crane, L. G., & Milner, B. (1995). The effects of frontal- or temporal-lobe lesions on susceptibility to interference in spatial memory. *Neuropsychologia, 33*, 275–285.

Snodgrass, J. G., & Asiaghi, A. (1977). The pictorial superiority effect in recognition memory. *Bulletin of the Psychonomic Society, 10*, 1–4.

Squire, L. R. (1992). Memory and the hippocampus: a synthesis from findings with rats, monkeys, and humans. *Psychological Review, 99*, 195–231.

Squire, L. R., & Cohen, N. J. (1984). Human memory and amnesia. In G. Lynch, J. L. McGaugh, & N. M. Weinberger (Eds.), *Neurobiology of learning and memory* (pp. 3–64). New York: Guilford Press.

Squire, L. R., & Zola-Morgan, S. M. (1996). Structure and function of declarative and nondeclarative memory systems. *Proceedings of the National Academy of Sciences of the USA, 93*, 13515–13522.

Stark, C. E., & Squire, L. R. (2001). When zero is not zero: the problem of ambiguous baseline conditions in fMRI. *Proceedings of the National Academy of Sciences of the USA 98*, 12760–12766.

Stuck, A. E., Walthert, J. M., Nikolaus, T., Bijla, C. J., Hohmann, C., & Beck, J. C. (1999). Risk factors for functional status decline in community-living elderly people: a systematic literature review. *Social Science and Medicine, 48*, 445–469.

Stuss, D. T., Alexander, M. P., Lieberman, A., & Levine, H. (1978). An extraordinary form of confabulation. *Neurology, 28*, 1166–1172.

Teuber, H.-L. (1950). Neuropsychology. In M. R. Harrower (ed.), *Recent advances in psychological testing* (pp. 30–52). Springfield, IL: Charles C. Thomas.

Thatcher, R. W. (1991). Maturation of the human frontal lobes: physiological evidence for staging. *Developmental Neuropsychology, 7*, 397–419.

Tulving, E., Schacter, D. L., McLachlan, D. R., & Moscovitch, M. (1988). Priming of semantic autobiographical knowledge: a case of retrograde amnesia. *Brain and Cognition, 8*, 3–20.

Vaidya, C. J., Gabrieli, J. D., Monti, L. A., Tinklenberg, J. R., & Yesavage, J. A. (1999). Dissociation between two forms of conceptual priming in Alzheimer's disease. *Neuropsychology, 13*, 516–524.

Vogel, C. C., Markowitsch, H. J., Hempel, U., & Hackenberg, P. (1987). Verbal memory in brain damaged patients under different conditions of retrieval aids: a study of frontal, temporal, and diencephalic damaged subjects. *International Journal of Neuroscience, 33*, 237–256.

Weldon, M. S., & Jackson-Barrett, J. L. (1993). Why do pictures produce priming on the word-fragment completion test? A study of encoding and retrieval factors. *Memory and Cognition, 21*, 519–528.

Wheeler, M. A., Stuss, D. T., & Tulving, E. (1995). Frontal lobe damage produces episodic memory impairment. *Journal of the International Neuropsychological Society, 1*, 525–536.

Willingham, D. B., Wells, L. A., Farrell, J. M., & Stemwedel, M. E. (2000). Implicit motor sequence learning is represented in response locations. *Memory and Cognition, 28*, 366–375.

Yancey, S. W., & Phelps, E. A. (2001). Functional neuroimaging and episodic memory: a perspective. *Journal of Clinical and Experimental Neuropsychology, 23*, 32–48.

Zajonc, R. B. (2001). Mere exposure: a gateway to the subliminal. *Current Directions in Psychological Science, 10*, 224–228.

17

The Cognitive Neuropsychology of Language

RANDI C. MARTIN AND DENISE H. WU

The best-known model in the cognitive neuropsychology of language is no doubt the Wernicke–Lichtheim model (Wernicke, 1874; Lichtheim, 1885). According to this model, auditory word representations that are essential to language comprehension are represented in a posterior left hemisphere brain region termed Wernicke's area, whereas the motor word representations that are essential to language production are represented in an anterior left hemisphere brain region termed Broca's area. Both areas connect to a more distributed, less localized concept center, which contains the semantic representations for words. Damage to Broca's area spares comprehension but disrupts speech production, resulting in slow, labored articulation. Damage to Wernicke's area disrupts comprehension but spares production in terms of fluency. Speech output is disordered, however, containing phonological, grammatical and semantic errors. Wernicke accounted for this speech disruption on the grounds that both concepts and sensory word representations are needed in selecting appropriate motor representations for output. In addition to being linked through the concept center, Wernicke's and Broca's areas are assumed to be directly connected through a fiber tract (the arcuate fasciculus). This connection allows for repetition and the ability to learn new pronunciations without knowing semantics (i.e. for nonwords and foreign words). Damage to this connection results in conduction aphasia, characterized by poor repetition but relatively preserved language comprehension and production.

The traditional theory seems to provide a ready account for the striking differences in speech fluency between aphasic patients who have anterior lesions and those who have posterior lesions. Close examination of these two groups of patients, however, reveals inadequacies of the model. First, Broca's aphasics tend to produce speech that is agrammatic; that is, producing simplified grammatical form and omitting function words (i.e. grammatical words like determiners, prepositions and auxiliary verbs) and grammatical markers (e.g. noun and verb inflections). The agrammatic quality of Broca's aphasics' speech seems to present a strong challenge to the traditional approach as it is unclear why motor representations for content words should be better preserved than motor representations for function words and grammatical markers, given that the latter are highly frequent in the language and thus might be expected to be more rather than less immune to brain damage. (Attempts along these lines have been made, however; see Lenneberg, 1973.) Second, one would need to postulate some mechanism by which the lack of input from Wernicke's area to Broca's area sometimes results in semantic errors (e.g. 'day' for 'night') and sometimes in neologistic utterances (e.g. 'fold the britty') to explain the characteristics of Wernicke's aphasics. Third, the written expression of aphasic patients is no better than the spoken, and tends to show a similar pattern to the speech production. That is, Broca's aphasics usually have agrammatic written output, and Wernicke's aphasics make phonological, grammatical and semantic errors in writing. To explain the similar difficulties in written expression, one would have to argue that the sensory and motor representations that are crucial in oral language are also crucial in written language.

Research findings from the 1970s and 1980s on sentence comprehension also caused great difficulty for this traditional model. Although patients classified as Broca's aphasics seem to have good comprehension on clinical assessment, they were found to show poor comprehension when comprehension depended on understanding the syntactic information in a sentence (e.g. Caramazza & Zurif, 1976; Schwartz, Saffran, & Marin, 1980). For example, these patients had difficulty choosing between a correct picture and one that reversed the roles of 'agent' and 'theme' (that is, the thing acted upon) when given a sentence such as 'the lion that the tiger chased was yellow' (Caramazza & Zurif, 1976). They did not have difficulty, however, if the incorrect picture included a lexical substitution (i.e. a different noun or verb). Subsequent studies showed that these difficulties with syntactic comprehension could be demonstrated on sentence–picture matching with simpler sentences, such as 'The dog was chased by the cat', or 'The circle is above the square' (Schwartz et al., 1980). Although Wernicke's aphasics had the same problem comprehending the trials with incorrect pictures depicting role reversals, they also demonstrated difficulty with the trials depicting lexical substitutions. Consequently, their difficulty could be attributed to a failure to understand the meaning of the individual lexical items.

Based on the aforementioned results, Berndt and Caramazza (1980) argued for a revision of the traditional theory to one in which Broca's aphasia was defined by a disruption of syntax. This central deficit was the source of their agrammatic spoken and written output as well as their syntactic comprehension deficit. The labored articulation of the Broca's aphasics was thought to be a co-occurring deficit resulting from damage to motor areas for speech that were adjacent to Broca's area. As for the function of Wernicke's area, Caramazza and Berndt (1978) argued that a number of findings indicated that aphasic patients with posterior damage had a disruption of semantic representations, which affected both their comprehension and production. They cited findings from Blumstein, Baker, and Goodglass (1977) as indicating that these patients' word comprehension deficits could not be attributed to difficulty in perceiving phonological information.

In the last twenty years, many findings have caused difficulties for this more modern synthesis as well as for the traditional approach. Neuroanatomical findings have called into question the claim that Broca's area serves either as the locus for the motor representations for words or for syntactic knowledge. Mohr, Pessin, Finkelstein, Funkenstein, Duncan, and Davis (1978) concluded that a circumscribed lesion to Broca's area gave rise to disruptions of motor speech and other language functions, but these were of short duration, lasting only a few

days to a few months. Agrammatism was not a feature of the acute or chronic state for these patients. Mohr et al. argued for functional overlap between the insula and other areas of the frontal and parietal opercula, with the result that damage to one region could be compensated for by the activity of another region. As a result, a larger lesion covering more than Broca's area was required in order for permanent disruptions of language output and agrammatism to occur. Such reasoning implies that Broca's area is involved in speech production, but that it is not the sole necessary component.

Another line of evidence against the claim about a general syntactic deficit in Broca's aphasics is from the co-occurrence of agrammatic speech and preserved syntactic comprehension (Berndt, Mitchum, & Haendiges, 1996). In addition, other studies have shown that different aspects of syntactic comprehension can be selectively impaired (e.g. Linebarger, Schwartz, & Saffran, 1983), which led some researchers to argue that Broca's aphasics have a more restrictive comprehension deficit involving the mapping of grammatical to thematic roles (e.g. object to patient) rather than a global syntactic deficit (Linebarger et al., 1983; Linebarger, 1990).

The proposed functional role of Wernicke's area on speech comprehension is also challenged by empirical data. Anatomically, the location of Wernicke's area is less agreed upon than Broca's area (Wise, Scott, Blank, Mummery, Murphy, & Warburton, 2001). Using the most common definition – the posterior third of superior temporal gyrus (Damasio, 1998) – there is evidence that a lesion restricted to this area does not give rise to the long-lasting symptoms termed Wernicke's aphasia and that a much wider lesion is needed (Selnes, Knopman, Niccum, Rubens, & Larson, 1983). Also, patients have been reported who have lesions outside of Wernicke's area, yet who show the symptoms of Wernicke's aphasia (e.g. Dronkers, Redfern, & Knight, 2000).

As described above, both the traditional Wernicke–Lichtheim model and the more recent syndrome-based approach (e.g. Berndt & Caramazza, 1980) suffer from the heterogeneity of the deficits exhibited by patients falling into one of the clinical classifications. For example, the poor comprehension of some patients classified as Wernicke's aphasics might arise from a disruption of phoneme identification; for other Wernicke's aphasics, a disruption of phonological word forms; and yet for other Wernicke's aphasics, a disruption of semantics. Among the patients producing agrammatic speech, not all show syntactic comprehension deficits (Berndt et al., 1996). Group studies that average results across members of the group and contrast these averages across clinical groups or with normal subjects are thus unlikely to provide a solid basis for determining the functional components of language and their organization in the brain. What is needed is a more fine-grained,

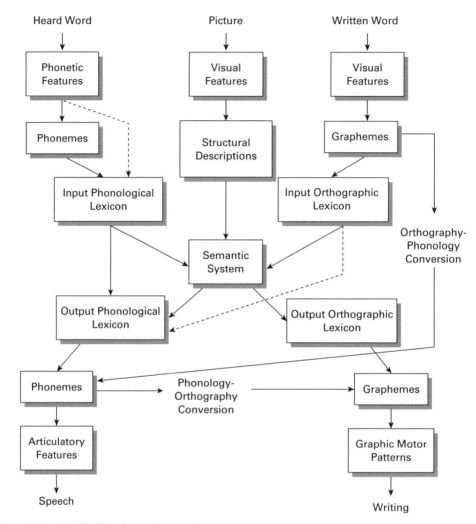

Figure 17.1   *Model of single word processing.*

theory-based analysis of the nature of the language deficits in individual cases.

Consequently, the discussion of neuropsychological data in this chapter will focus on individual case studies in which the precise nature of the patients' deficit has been identified. The discussion will be organized in terms of theoretical issues with regard to single word and sentence processing, for which comprehension and production will be discussed in turn. Reading and spelling of single words, and the interaction between syntactic and semantic processing, will be examined in light of neuropsychological data as well. As there are relatively few studies in which lesion overlap has been examined for a series of cases showing the same functional deficit, precise information concerning the relation between language function and brain areas is often unavailable from patient studies for many functional components of interest. In the present

chapter we shall focus only on the functional components of language processing. For an overview of lesion data and functional neuroimaging data on the localization of these components in the brain, see Martin (2003) for a recent review.

SINGLE WORD PROCESSING

Neuropsychological data provide evidence concerning the independence and functional organization of the different components involved in language processing. An overall model has been put forward to account for single word processing, based on data from normal subjects and brain-damaged patients (Figure 17.1). In this section, we shall first review the data supporting the independence of lexical, semantic and grammatical representations.

Then we shall turn to subdivisions within these levels. Specifically, the independence between phonological and orthographic representations will be established, and the possible independence of input (comprehension) and output (production) processing for these two kinds of representations will be examined. The organization of the semantic and the grammatical systems will be discussed as well. Finally, the mechanisms for reading words aloud will be discussed in the framework of the overall model and in light of patient studies.

Independence of different language representations

Dissociation of lexical and semantic representations

Numerous studies have shown that meaning and the phonological or orthographic forms of words are dissociable, as they can be selectively affected by brain damage (e.g. Hillis, Boatman, Hart, & Gordon, 1999; Howard & Franklin, 1988; N. Martin & Saffran, 1992). When speech recognition is considered, the independence between phonological representations and semantics is evident as some patients with word meaning deafness demonstrate a selectively disrupted access from the phonological lexicon to the semantic system (e.g. Franklin, Howard, & Patterson, 1994; Franklin, Turner, Lambon Ralph, Morris, & Bailey, 1996; Hall & Riddoch, 1997; Kohn & Friedman, 1986). Hall and Riddoch (1997) reported a patient KW, who was a particularly striking example of this pattern. KW performed well on auditory and written lexical decision. On semantic tasks, he performed very poorly with auditory presentation but was within the normal range with written presentation.

When speech production is considered, anomic patients whose impaired naming is not associated with impaired comprehension provide strong evidence for the independence of phonological and semantic representations. Anomic aphasia is characterized by pervasive word finding impairments in spontaneous speech and naming in conjunction with intact repetition and fluent, grammatically correct speech. Martin, Lesch, and Bartha (1999) presented such a patient MS, whose naming difficulty was not caused by a semantic deficit per se, since he performed normally on various comprehension tasks, such as spoken word/picture verification tasks and semantic attributes judgment tasks. MS's deficit is not caused by some lower-level output deficit, either, since he repeated two- and three-word lists perfectly. Rapp and Caramazza (1997) also reported a patient PW who showed a similar pattern to MS.

To obtain a double dissociation between semantic representations and lexical representations on the output side to contrast with MS and PW, a case with intact phonological representations but disrupted semantics is needed. However, it would be difficult to observe such a pattern in a task such as picture naming since access to the lexical form representations in production tasks may well depend on accessing the semantic representations first. One means to demonstrate such a pattern is to show that some patients can read words aloud that are spelled irregularly but for which they have lost the meaning. Specifically, as proposed in a dual-route model for reading (e.g. Coltheart, Rastle, Perry, Langdon, & Ziegler, 2001), a word can be read aloud through orthography-to-phonology conversion rules, an orthography–semantics–phonology pathway, or an (input) orthography–(output) phonology pathway (Figure 17.1). If the semantic pathway is disrupted, an irregularly spelled word can only be read correctly via the direct lexical route, since the conversion rules do not apply. Such cases will be discussed further in the reading section, p. 392 below.

An alternative means to approach this issue is to demonstrate that the naming difficulty in production can be fully explained by the impairment in the semantic system without postulating additional deficit in the lexicons. Hillis, Rapp, Romani, and Caramazza (1990) reported a patient KE who provides such evidence. KE made semantically related errors in written and oral naming to pictures and tactually presented objects, oral and written word/picture verification tasks, oral reading, and writing to dictation. More importantly, when the same set of items was used, his error rate was nearly identical in all lexical tasks across all input and output modalities, and the performance in one task predicted the performance in other tasks. Since the semantic system is the only cognitive component that is required by all these tasks, KE's deficit is attributed to the semantics, and the similar error rates in different tasks suggests that no deficit in other lexical representations is needed to account for his impairment.

Dissociation of lexical and grammatical representations

Besides lexical and semantic information, words contain grammatical information (e.g. word class, case, count/mass distinction, etc.) as well. Some findings indicate that word-specific syntactic information is separate from phonological information about words. For example, patients who, in picture naming, were unable to retrieve any of the phonemes in the target word could correctly judge the grammatical gender of the target word (Badecker, Miozzo, & Zanuttini, 1995) or whether it fits into count or mass phrasal contexts (Vigliocco, Vinson, Martin, & Garrett, 1999). These findings have generated considerable debate concerning whether they imply two lexical representations for words: a semantic/syntactic representation (termed the lemma) and a phonological representation (termed the lexeme). Garrett (1993) and Levelt, Roelofs, and Meyer (1999) have argued for the existence of the two levels whereas others have argued for a single lexical representation that is phonological and that connects to general syntactic properties for words (Caramazza & Miozzo, 1997). At present, the two positions appear difficult to distinguish on the basis of currently available data (Nickels, 2001).

Lexical representations

Dissociation of phonological and orthographic representations

As depicted in the model in Figure 17.1, separate phonological and orthographic lexicons have been proposed to process spoken and written words, respectively. Some cases of word meaning deafness discussed above also provide evidence for the dissociation between phonological and orthographic representations, as they show impaired comprehension of spoken words but preserved comprehension of written words (Franklin et al., 1994, 1996; Hall & Riddoch, 1997; Kohn & Friedman, 1986). Since these patients could understand written words, semantics must be preserved. The intact ability to perform auditory lexical decision also indicates that the disruption is not localized at some lower level of phonological processing. Based on these findings, it is argued that these patients suffer from a complete or partial disconnection between the (input) phonological lexicon and the semantic system, while the mechanisms/representations for orthographic processing on the input side are preserved.

The selective impairment from phonology to meaning with intact comprehension of written materials also provides strong evidence against the phonological mediation hypothesis of reading, which assumes that meaning can be recovered from print only if the written stimulus is first recorded in phonological form (e.g. Lukatela & Turvey, 1994a, 1994b; Van Orden, 1987). If the phonological mediation hypothesis were correct, impaired access to semantics from phonological representations should prevent the patients from understanding written materials. Instead, their intact comprehension of written sentences, despite the disrupted input from phonological representations, supports a position of direct access to meaning from orthography.

The independence of phonological and orthographic representations is also supported by patients who show a selective deficit in one domain on the output side. For example, Bub and Kertesz (1982a) reported a patient MH who had difficulties naming objects and making judgments on whether the names of objects rhymed. The disruption was at the output phonological lexicon rather than the semantic system or some peripheral aspect of phonological processing because MH's comprehension and nonword repetition were intact. In contrast to her severe deficit on picture naming, MH was able to correctly write most of the names for objects she could not name orally. Rapp, Benzing, and Caramazza (1997) reported a patient PW who showed a similar pattern to MH. For example, when shown a picture of an owl, PW incorrectly named it as a turtle but correctly wrote down the word 'owl'.

Phonological representations

One important question concerning phonological processes is whether they are unique to linguistic input, or whether they deal with other auditory signals as well. Patients labeled as 'pure word deaf' are particularly relevant to the issue as they have difficulty perceiving speech but do better on the perception of other auditory stimuli such as music or environmental sounds (see Griffiths, Rees, & Green, 1999; Poeppel, 2001, for recent reviews). Some of these cases have preserved written word processing abilities and preserved speech output (e.g. Auerbach, Allard, Naeser, Alexander, & Albert, 1982), which rule out a deficit at the semantic level. The impairment does not appear to result from disruption specific to lexical phonology, either, as the patients show deficits in phoneme discrimination (Auerbach et al., 1982). Specifically, it has been demonstrated that these patients have difficulty perceiving rapid changes in complex pitch patterns, which affects the perception of speech more than other sounds. Evidence consistent with this view is that these patients show better discrimination of vowels than consonants, which can be attributed to the longer duration of the acoustic cues signaling vowel identity (Denes & Semenza, 1975; Wang, Peach, Xu, Schneck, & Manry, 2000). Also, these patients have been shown to have difficulty discriminating nonspeech sounds that depend on perceiving rapid temporal changes (e.g. Albert & Bear, 1957; Auerbach et al., 1982; Tanaka, Yamadoi, & Mori, 1987; Wang et al., 2000).

Another important question regarding phonological representations is whether there are separate input and output lexicons for speech recognition and production respectively, as depicted in Figure 17.1. Although the disrupted spoken input and intact spoken output demonstrated by pure word deaf patients seem to support such a dissociation, their deficit appears to be caused by a lower-level, prelexical impairment. Clearer evidence has been presented by patients termed 'deep dysphasics' who make semantic errors in single word repetition (e.g. repeating 'woman' as 'lady') (see Shallice, 1988, for discussion). These semantic errors indicate that the word has been understood, so the difficulty cannot be in accessing a lexical phonological form on the input side. This phonological form should serve as the basis of repetition if there is only one form that is the same for speech perception and production. However, the semantic error indicates that the patient has used the semantic information to access a different phonological form from the input. According to the two lexicons view, the direct connection between input and output lexicons has been disrupted and the patient has to repeat via access to semantics. One means of accounting for this deep dysphasic pattern in terms of a single lexicon model is to assume that even though the correct phonological form is initially activated, the activation dies very rapidly, and the patient has to use whatever semantic information has been activated to reconstruct the output (N. Martin & Saffran, 1992). Hence, the opportunity for semantic errors arises. However, at least one patient who made semantic errors in repetition did quite well on an auditory matching span task that required him to indicate whether two four-item word or nonword lists were the same or different (Howard & Franklin, 1990). These results argue against a rapid loss of phonological information as the source of the patient's semantic errors.

Another means of addressing the independence between input and output is to examine the relation between error rates on input tasks, such as auditory lexical decision with close phonological distractors as nonwords, and phonological errors on output tasks, such as picture naming. Mixed results have been obtained – with no correlation reported (Nickels & Howard, 1995a) or moderate but significant correlations reported (N. Martin & Saffran, 2002). As Hillis (2001) pointed out, however, a correlation could result because areas subserving input and output are anatomically close.

Orthographic representations

We have discussed the dissociation between phonological and orthographic representations. The same evidence also supports the direct connection between the orthographic lexicon and the semantic system without the mediation of phonological representations (Bub & Kertesz, 1982a; Ellis, 1984; Shelton & Weinrich, 1997). Another important question regarding orthographic representations, as for phonological representations, is whether there are separate input and output lexicons for recognizing and producing the spelling for words (Figure 17.1).

Several cases have been presented who provide evidence for one single orthographic lexicon (e.g. Behrmann & Bub, 1992; Coltheart & Funnell, 1987; Friedman & Hadley, 1992). For example, a patient HG was reported who was characterized as having surface dyslexia and surface dysgraphia as he read *quay* as /kwe/, *chaos* as /tʃoz/, and *borough* as /baraf/, and spelled, when provided with a disambiguating phrase, *mane* as main (Coltheart & Funnell, 1987). HG's performance indicated a failure to use lexical knowledge and the reliance on a sublexical mechanism for both reading and spelling. After establishing the fact that HG's deficit originated from orthographic knowledge rather than the semantics or other peripheral levels, it was demonstrated that there was a good correspondence between his reading and spelling even when word frequency was taken into account. Based on these findings, Coltheart and Funnell (1987) argued that there is only one orthographic lexicon subserving reading and spelling. When the lexicon is disrupted, both tasks are impaired to the same degree.

The theory of a single orthographic lexicon cannot account for some other patients' performance, however. Beauvois and Derouesne (1981) reported a patient RG who showed a deficit on spelling irregular words (36% correct) but not on reading them (above 95% correct). RG's impairment could not be due to a peripheral problem relevant to spelling to dictation since her accuracy was 93% on spelling words with low ambiguity and 100% with nonwords. Therefore, one intact input orthographic lexicon and one partially impaired output orthographic lexicon seem to be needed to account for such a dissociation. In the face of such evidence, however, Allport and Funnell (1981) proposed an alternative interpretation. They argued that there might still be only one orthographic lexicon with separate connections to and from semantics. The selective deficit of either reading or spelling while the other ability is intact might be the result of the well-preserved orthographic knowledge and the selective disruption of one of the connections.

To test the theory of one common orthographic lexicon with separate connections for reading and spelling, Park and Martin (2001) reported a patient ML whose lexical reading was normal whereas spelling was impaired. ML's spelling deficit included a severely damaged sublexical mechanism together with partially damaged orthographic knowledge. More critically, ML performed differently in a delayed copying task with words that he could spell and words that he could not spell. That is, with a 3-second delay after seeing a word, ML correctly copied 93% of those words that he could spell correctly, but only 73% of the words that he could not spell. If there were only one orthographic lexicon, the disrupted connection from semantics to the orthographic lexicon should have no influence on the copying task, and ML should be able to copy the two sets of words equally well, since the lexical-orthographic form was presented to him and he simply had to maintain this information in the intact orthographic lexicon until being asked to write the word. ML's differential copying performance thus supports the existence of separate input and output orthographic representations.

Semantic representations

Single or multiple semantic systems?

Some patients who demonstrate difficulty with the same items across different tasks, such as patient KE discussed above (Hillis et al., 1990), provide evidence for a single semantic system. Some other patients, however, show semantic impairment only with input from a specific modality. For example, Lhermitte and Beauvois (1973) presented a case of optic aphasia, who named a picture of comb as 'toothbrush' but correctly gestured combing the hair. The naming difficulty cannot be explained by some visual deficit at the input side, since the patient made a correct gesture to the same item. The naming difficulty did not result from defective lexical representations at the output side, either, because the patient named objects to verbal definitions correctly. Other cases have been reported who showed naming errors restricted to the tactile modality (Beauvois, Saillant, Meininger, & Lhermitte, 1978) or to the auditory modality (Denes & Semenza, 1975). Based on these findings, some researchers have argued that there are multiple semantic systems (e.g. Beauvois, 1982; Shallice, 1987), and optic aphasia emerges from a disrupted visual semantic system and an intact verbal semantic system.

The evidence given in support of the hypothesis of modality-specific semantic systems has received criticism, however. Methodological problems with regard to the relative difficulty of producing gestures versus names and the means by which gestures versus names are scored have been discussed. In addition, selective naming difficulty in a particular modality can still be adequately explained in terms of a single, amodal semantic system. For example, Hillis and Caramazza (1995) pointed out that optic aphasics may have partial semantic knowledge that can support gesturing but is insufficient to generate correct naming. The same position has been taken by other researchers (e.g. Riddoch, Humphreys, Coltheart, & Funnell, 1988; Caramazza, Hillis, Rapp, & Romani, 1990).

Category-specific deficits and the organization of the semantic system

Many patients have been reported who have semantic deficits with only certain semantic categories (e.g. animals, plants, man-made objects, etc.) (Allport, 1985; Farah & McClelland, 1991; Warrington & McCarthy, 1987; Warrington & Shallice, 1984; for recent reviews, see Forde & Humphreys, 1999; Shelton & Caramazza, 1999, 2001). Within a model assuming amodal semantic representations, some theories have been proposed that argue for separate clusters of perceptual and functional information, although these clusters can

be accessed by any modality of input. According to this approach, the brain segregates different types of information, and selective damage to different parts of the brain gives rise to specific problems with certain semantic categories (e.g. animals, plants, man-made objects, etc.) (Allport, 1985; Farah & McClelland, 1991; Warrington & McCarthy, 1987; Warrington & Shallice, 1984; for recent reviews, see Shelton & Caramazza, 1999, 2001). Some patients show these category-specific effects on semantic tasks even after familiarity, visual complexity and processing difficulty of items in different categories have been controlled (e.g. Caramazza & Shelton, 1998). Moreover, although it is more common to find patients who have greater difficulty with living things than artifacts, a few cases have been reported who show the reverse pattern (e.g. Hillis & Caramazza, 1991; Warrington & McCarthy, 1987).

Warrington and Shallice (1984) presented two patients who showed relatively impaired performance on living things. Since these patients also demonstrated deficits in other semantic categories (e.g. foods, musical instruments, gemstones, fabric and metals), the researchers argued that the semantic knowledge is organized in terms of perceptual and functional information, and the apparent category-specific deficit is caused by the disruption of perceptual information, which is more important for living things and other impaired categories. Several cases who show a selective deficit with living things and are more impaired with visual than non-visual information in this category have been reported to support this theory (e.g. Sartori & Job, 1988; Silveri & Gainotti, 1988). But it should be noted that, although the hypothesized disruption to visual information should be general across different categories, there was no difference observed in these patients regarding visual and non-visual information in other categories.

The category-specific organization of the semantic system based on perceptual/functional information has been challenged by some recent cases. First, some patients have shown a deficit with only a subset of the living-thing category (i.e. animals) while other categories for which visual information is important (e.g. musical instruments and foods) are intact (e.g. Caramazza & Shelton, 1998; Hillis & Caramazza, 1991). Other patients have also been reported to have difficulties with only fruits and vegetables (e.g. Farah & Wallace, 1992; Hart, Berndt, & Caramazza, 1985) or only body parts (e.g. Goodglass, Klein, Carey, & Jones, 1966). Second, a few cases have been presented who have difficulties processing visual information, but they do not exhibit any category-specific deficits (Coltheart, Inglis, Cupples, Michie, Bates, & Budd, 1998; Lambon Ralph, Howard, Nightingale, & Ellis, 1998).

If semantic knowledge is not organized in terms of category-specific information, is it organized by intercorrelations among features? A model that argues for this position is the Organized Unitary Content Hypothesis (OUCH; Caramazza et al., 1990). According to this model, members of a semantic category tend to share attributes, and core semantic properties of objects in the same category tend to be highly intercorrelated. That is, members of semantic categories would cluster closely together in the space of semantic features. As a result, brain damage to a clustered region in semantic space would result in category-specific deficits. Different from the category-specific hypothesis, OUCH does not make a distinction between perceptual and functional features, and it accounts for the more fine-grained semantic categories (e.g. animals, fruits and vegetables in the category of living things) naturally. The weakness of this model, however, it that it is too unconstrained. Since any tightly correlated set of features can form a category and is a candidate for a category-specific deficit, it is very difficult to falsify this model. More recently, Caramazza and Shelton (1998; Shelton & Caramazza, 1999) have proposed a domain-specific knowledge hypothesis, in which they argue that semantic knowledge is organized in domains/ categories that are evolutionarily important (e.g. animals and plants). The virtue of this approach is that it can account for the fact that deficits to living things are the most commonly observed category-specific deficit, which would not be anticipated from the OUCH hypothesis. However, there is no specific claim regarding how the knowledge within each domain is organized according to this position, and the perceptual/functional-specific hypothesis and OUCH, among other principles, are possible candidates for the organization within each domain. The domain-specific knowledge hypothesis suffers the same weakness as OUCH, namely almost any kind of category-specific deficit can be explained since it may result from the clustered features within one of the domains. For example, although there is not a domain for vehicles, the clustered features relevant to vehicles (e.g. moving, carrying passengers) in the domain of artifacts can be selectively impaired, and hence the deficit.

In addition to the theories discussed above, a connectionist network has been used to explain the selective deficit with different semantic categories as well (e.g. Devlin, Gonnerman, Andersen, & Seidenberg, 1998; Tyler, Moss, Durrant-Peatfield, & Levy, 2000). The core idea behind this approach is that there is only one unitary semantic system in which concepts of different categories are structured in different ways. The critical difference between this account and other theories is that the observed selective deficits with living things and artifacts are actually caused by the overall impairment to the semantic system, and emerge as a function of severity of this overall damage. Moss and Tyler (2000) reported a longitudinal study of a patient, ES, who suffered from a progressive degenerative disorder. When first tested, ES performed better with non-living things than living things on picture naming, and performed about the same with these two categories on other tasks. As her disorder progressed, ES performed worse with non-living things than living things in all the tasks administered.

The crossover effect of different categories on picture naming cannot be easily accommodated by any of the accounts we discussed earlier. On the other hand, the connectionist model offers an explanation of this phenomenon by hypothesizing different structures of semantic attributes among different categories. Specifically, the biological functions and perceptual properties of living things (e.g. can see > has eyes) are strongly connected and widely shared by other members in the same category, whereas their distinctive features are weakly correlated (e.g. has mane) and therefore vulnerable to damage. As a result, the distinctive features of living things are more susceptible to even mild impairment. In contrast, the individual, distinctive features of non-living things (e.g. has a serrated edge > used for sawing) are strongly connected whereas the shared properties are fewer and weakly correlated than those of living things (Moss & Tyler, 2000). Even though the more robust distinctive features of non-living things protect this category from mild damage, when the impairment progresses to the level that the model can only operate on the shared features of items, non-living things are more vulnerable now since they share fewer (thus less learned) features with other members in the same category.

It should be noted that an opposite prediction could be derived from another connectionist network (e.g. Devlin et al., 1998). Whether the model can reproduce the disrupted performance similar to particular patients seems to be largely dependent on how the network is structured and how the deficit is implemented. Moreover, large-scale studies of patients with degenerative diseases affecting semantic representations have failed to find any evidence of a crossover between living and non-living things as the disease progresses (Garrard, Patterson, Watson, & Hodges, 1998; Garrard, Lambon Ralph, Watson, Powis, Patterson, & Hodges, 2001). Consequently, these connectionist accounts do not provide a means of accounting for the course of category-specific semantic deficits for the majority of cases. Garrard and colleagues (Garrard et al., 2001) instead argue for anatomical specificity in the representation of particular semantic categories.

Grammatical representations

Word class effects

Deficits specific to certain grammatical categories have been reported in many studies. Some patients have selective difficulties in the production of function words (i.e. prepositions, pronouns and auxiliary verbs that play primarily a grammatical role in a sentence) compared to content words whereas others show the reverse patterns (Goodglass, 1993). Another often-reported dissociation is between nouns and verbs, again with some patients having more difficulty with verbs and others having more difficulty with nouns (e.g. Miceli, Silveri, Villa, & Caramazza, 1984; Zingeser & Berndt, 1988, 1990; see Druks, 2002, for a review). In some cases, these apparent grammatical class effects have a semantic basis. For example, better production of nouns than verbs and better production of verbs than grammatical words may be observed because the patient is better able to produce more concrete words (e.g. Bird, Franklin, & Howard, 2002). However, for some patients, it appears that grammatical class effects cannot be reduced to a semantic basis, and consequently, these deficits suggest that at some level in the production system words are distinguished neurally with regard to the grammatical role that they play in a sentence (Berndt, Haendiges, Burton, & Mitchum, 2002; Rapp & Caramazza, 2002).

Morphological processing

Many words are morphologically complex, containing either an inflectional morpheme (e.g. 'worked', 'books') or a derivational morpheme (e.g. 'teacher', 'similarly') or both ('undecided'). One issue is whether these morphologically complex words are broken down into their separate morphemes in language production and comprehension (e.g. Allen & Badecker, 1999) or whether they are treated as unitary words (e.g. Bybee, 1988). Many aphasic patients produce what appear to be inflectional errors in language production and oral reading (e.g. producing 'welds' for 'welding' or 'teaching' for 'teacher'), which would appear to support a decompositional view. That is, these errors could be explained on the grounds that the patients have decomposed a complex word into stem plus affix and have produced the stem correctly but made an error on retrieving the appropriate affix. However, because many patients make errors that consist of words that are either semantically or phonologically related to a target word, such apparently inflectional errors could be attributed to whole word confusions based on phonological and semantic similarity rather than to a deficit in morphological processing (see Funnell, 1987).

Several patients have been reported, however, whose morphological difficulties cannot be attributed to such factors. For instance, Badecker and Caramazza (1991) reported a patient who made affix errors on reading regularly inflected words (e.g. bowled and links) but did not make similar word ending errors on monomorphemic homophones (e.g. bold and lynx) or on irregularly inflected words (e.g. knew, spent). Other patients have been reported who made morphological errors only on words of one word class – that is, either nouns (Shapiro, Shelton, & Caramazza, 2000) or verbs (Tsapkini, Jarema, & Kehayia, 2002). Restriction to a particular word class would not be expected if the errors were due solely to semantic and phonological similarity of the incorrectly produced word to the inflected word.

An issue that has recently attracted a great deal of debate is whether different processes are involved in computing past tense forms for regular versus irregular verbs. According to standard linguistic formulations, regular past tense forms in English (e.g. talked, gazed, needed) are computed by a rule which adds a past tense marker /d/ to verbs, with the pronunciation varying depending on the final consonant of the verb. On the other hand, irregular past tense forms must be memorized as the pronunciations are not predictable from the present tense forms (e.g. 'is/was', 'run/ran', 'catch/caught', 'go/went'). Since novel words (i.e. nonsense words such as 'plag' or 'spuff') have no representation in memory, the regular rule should apply to these as well. In support of the dual systems view, Ullman et al. (1997) presented evidence that patient groups with posterior damage (Wernicke's aphasia, Alzheimer's disease) had difficulty producing irregular but not regular past tense forms for real words or novel forms whereas patients with frontal or basal ganglia damage (i.e. Broca's aphasics or Parkinson's patients) showed the reverse pattern. They argued that this was due to general properties of posterior versus frontal systems in which posterior regions support declarative memory-based representations, whereas frontal/basal ganglia regions support procedural or rule-based knowledge.

In opposition to the dual systems view, other researchers have argued that a single connectionist system supports retrieval of the past tense for both regular and irregular forms (e.g. Rumelhart & McClelland, 1986). Joanisse and Seidenberg (1999) and Patterson, Lambon Ralph, Hodges, and McClelland (2001) have provided computational and empirical evidence for a single system approach. They argue that the observed double dissociation derives from other factors, specifically semantic deficits in patients with posterior brain injury and phonological deficits in patients with frontal brain injury. Patterson et al. (2001) provide evidence for lexical damage for semantic dementia cases, in the form of semantic loss for verbs, and show that the degree of semantic loss for irregular verbs predicts degree of difficulty in generating past tense forms for these verbs. With regard to the other side of the dissociation, Patterson (2002) argued that regular past tenses tend to be more phonologically complex in that they often end in a consonant cluster (e.g. 'walked', 'banged'), and computing the past tense of a novel form may involve more complex phonological

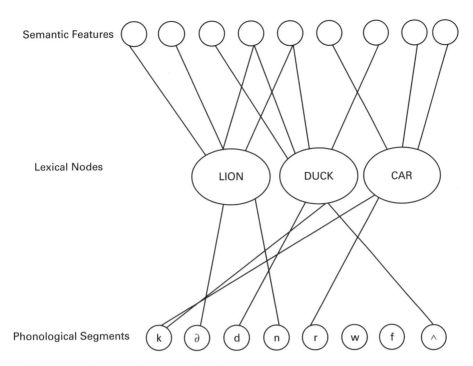

Figure 17.2 *Interactive activation model of word production.*

processes as well. Since patients suffering from frontal deficits may have difficulty on phonological processing, their performance on producing regular past tense forms for real and novel words is thus more affected. Consistent with this view, Patterson (2002) presented evidence that when irregular and regular forms closely matched in phonological complexity are used, the difference between them disappears for patients with anterior damage.

Tyler, Randall, and Marslen-Wilson (2002) argued, however, that a phonological deficit cannot account for anterior aphasics' difficulty with regular forms as their patients who showed worse performance on regular than irregular verb inflection performed quite well on various phoneme discrimination tasks. It was the case, though, that all of their anterior aphasics had difficulty with tasks tapping phoneme segmentation, a phonological process that may be specifically related to output phonology that is subserved by inferior frontal regions.

It should be noted that the plausibility of the claim that frontal brain regions support rule-based grammatical processing hinges in part on claims that anterior aphasics have difficulty with such processes in comprehension as well as production. Given the current evidence in the literature, it is far from clear that this is the case. Several studies have documented that such patients do well on grammaticality judgments, even when such judgments depend on detecting errors in verb inflections (Linebarger et al., 1983).

Spoken word production

Deficits in spoken word production can arise from several sources, including the output phonological representations and the semantic system discussed above. Certainly, a disruption of semantic abilities will lead to errors in word production, with the patient producing predominantly semantically related errors ('parsley' for 'carrot', for example) (e.g. Caramazza & Hillis, 1990; Cuetos, Aguado, & Caramazza, 2000; Howard & Orchard-Lisle, 1984; Hillis et al., 1990; Hodges, Patterson, Oxbury, & Funnell, 1992). Beyond the semantic level, a disruption in the phonological or articulatory processing can be identified, since many patients have been reported who show excellent semantic abilities as evidenced by tests of comprehension, but who show difficulty in retrieving the phonological forms of words in production (e.g. Caramazza & Hillis, 1990; Martin, Lesch, & Bartha, 1999; Nickels & Howard, 1995a). For some of these patients, their responses are overwhelmingly circumlocutions; that is, descriptions of the object. For example, patient MS (Martin et al., 1999) said for 'cane': 'This is something you use to walk with if you have trouble walking, if you have, if you broke your leg or something, and you need something to help you walk.' For other patients, the responses may be primarily phonologically related words (e.g. 'golf' for 'glove') (e.g. Blanken, 1990) or phonologically related nonwords (e.g. 'brend' for 'bread') (e.g. Caplan, Vanier, & Baker, 1986; Caramazza, Papagno, & Ruml, 2000).

These different error patterns suggest disruptions to different stages in the production process. It is the case, however, that most patients do not produce only one type of error, but produce a mixture of error types – those described above plus errors that are both phonologically and semantically related to the target (e.g. 'cat' for 'rat'), unrelated words, and failures to respond. Dell, Schwartz, Martin, Saffran, and Gagnon (1997) attempted to account for the different relative proportions of error types across different fluent aphasic patients in terms of global disruptions to all levels of an interactive activation model of word production initially derived to account for normal production. As shown in Figure 17.2, the model includes semantic, lexical and phonological levels, and feedforward and feedback connections between levels. In the first version of the model to be applied to patient data, 'lesions' to the model consisted of reducing connection strengths between all levels or in increasing the decay rate at all levels. Although this approach provided a relatively good fit to the error patterns of the patients they tested, it has difficulty accounting for patients who produce virtually all semantic errors (Caramazza & Hillis, 1990; Cuetos et al., 2000) and others who produce virtually all phonological errors (Caplan et al., 1986; Caramazza et al., 2000).

A revised model was proposed by Foygel and Dell (2000) in which the globality assumption was abandoned and lesions were made separately to the connections between the semantic and lexical and between the lexical and phonemic levels. Although this approach provided a better fit to the predominantly semantic or phonological errors produced by some patients, the model still has difficulty accounting for some aspects of performance; for example, the interactivity in the model results in an overprediction of the proportion of phonologically related word errors for some patients who produce many phonologically related nonword errors (Caramazza et al., 2000; Rapp & Goldrick, 2000). Thus, the data strongly suggest that selective deficits can occur to different levels in the production process, but the details of models to account for such errors are debated with regard to the degree of interactivity between levels (Rapp & Goldrick, 2000; Ruml, Caramazza, Shelton, & Chialant, 2000).

Reading: from print to sound

To account for people's ability to read words and nonwords aloud, a general dual-route approach has been proposed (Coltheart, 1978; Coltheart, Curtis, Atkins, & Haller, 1993), in which the conversion from print to sound is achieved via either the lexical-semantic route or the sublexical route. As discussed above, there is evidence that input orthographic representations connect to the semantic system which in turn connects to output phonological representations. Thus, reading can be accomplished through this lexical-semantic route. On the other hand, sublexical letter units (e.g. graphemes, syllables) can be mapped onto sounds through the other route without consulting the lexicon. Some people refer to this sublexical route as the grapheme–phoneme conversion route (GPC route), although there is considerable evidence indicating that units larger than the single grapheme are involved (Lesch & Martin, 1998; Treiman & Zukowski, 1988). Functionally, the lexical-semantic route is necessary for irregular words (e.g. pint) and readily available for familiar words (regardless of regularity), whereas the sublexical route is necessary for nonwords (e.g. plif).

Strong evidence for the existence of the lexical-semantic route comes from deep dyslexia. The characteristic symptoms of this deficit are semantic errors in reading aloud (e.g. 'bush' read as 'tree'), visual errors (e.g. 'sword' read as 'words'), morphological errors (e.g. 'standing' read as 'stand'), particular difficulties in reading abstract words and function words, and a complete inability to read nonwords (Coltheart, 1980; Marshall & Newcombe, 1973; Kremin, 1982). Although the explanation for deep dyslexia remains controversial, and it is probably not a homogeneous syndrome (see Ellis & Young, 1988; Shallice, 1988), the severely impaired nonword reading ability and semantic errors on word reading are taken as evidence for reading words through the semantic system (but see Coltheart, 2000, for an alternative account).

The existence of the sublexical route is also well accepted since normal readers can easily produce the sound of a pseudoword (a pronounceable nonword) that does not have a representation in the lexicon. Additional evidence for the sublexical (GPC) route comes from surface dyslexia. The characteristic of this impairment is that the ability to read nonwords and regular words aloud is selectively preserved relative to the reading of irregular words. Moreover, exception words are often read as the GPC rules specify (e.g. reading 'one' as 'own'). For example, patient KT (McCarthy & Warrington, 1986) achieved an accuracy of 100% with nonword reading and 81% with regular word reading whereas his accuracy was only 41% with irregular words. Among his errors on irregular words, KT committed regularization errors – that is, he incorrectly pronounced the word according to the GPC rules – for at least 71% of them.

In addition to the two routes postulated in the dual-route model, a third direct lexical route has been proposed to account for the performance of some acquired dyslexics (e.g. Coltheart & Funnell, 1987; Coslett, 1991; Ellis & Young, 1988; Funnell, 1983;

Lambon Ralph, Ellis, & Franklin, 1995; Wu, Martin, & Damian, 2002). Phonological dyslexia is a form of acquired dyslexia in which the reading aloud of nonwords is selectively impaired relative to the reading aloud of words. Some of these patients showed fluent and accurate reading of at least some irregular words, despite having very impaired comprehension of these words. For example, Coltheart, Masterson, Byng, Prior, and Riddoch (1983) reported a patient who read 'steak' aloud correctly but defined it as 'fencing post'. Since sublexical rules cannot be applied to derive the correct pronunciation of the irregular word, and the poor comprehension also makes it unlikely that the correct word reading is achieved via the lexical-semantic route, a direct route is needed to explain the correct word reading without accessing the semantic information. It is argued that this third route directly connects the input orthographic lexicon and the output phonological lexicon without going through the semantic system.

Although several other cases also support the existence of the third route for reading, Hillis and Caramazza (1991, 1995) provided a dual-route account of these findings termed the summation hypothesis, in which they argued that these patients achieve correct word reading via the cooperation between a partially preserved lexical-semantic route and a partially preserved sublexical route. That is, although the impaired lexical-semantic route results in disrupted comprehension and the impaired sublexical route results in disrupted nonword reading, these two routes can work together to support correct word reading. In support of their argument, Hillis and Caramazza (1991, 1995) reported several patients whose performance was consistent with the predictions derived from the summation hypothesis. For example, a patient JJ demonstrated very good correspondence between his word-reading ability and his semantic knowledge for different words. Specifically, JJ never made a word-reading error on a word for which he showed some semantic knowledge. He correctly read words for which he showed no comprehension only if those words had a regular spelling.

According to the summation hypothesis, it is possible to account for patients' performance by the lexical-semantic and the sublexical routes instead of positing a third mechanism. A problem with this approach, however, is that it seems very difficult to falsify because there is usually no objective evidence from accuracy data for the preserved processing in either route. That is, if the patient demonstrates very poor written word comprehension and nonword reading, it is still possible to claim that there is some preserved ability in the lexical-semantic and the sublexical routes respectively, and thus enable the summation hypothesis to work. One attempt to examine the summation hypothesis empirically has been made using reaction time in addition to accuracy data for word reading and picture naming from a phonological dyslexic patient ML (Wu et al., 2002). ML's sublexical processing was severely impaired, as evident in his poor nonword reading ability (38% correct). With regard to the lexical-semantic route, ML exhibited difficulty naming the pictures of some body parts (e.g. knuckle, eyelashes, shin). This difficulty could not be attributed to disrupted visual processing specific to pictures, since he showed the same deficit on naming to definitions. Evidence also indicated that the naming deficit was not due to the impairment of the semantic representations of body parts per se, since ML performed normally on a picture–word matching task, which included semantic-related distractors. Rather, his selective impairment is due to a disruption in the connections between semantics and output phonology for body parts – connections that should also be used in the lexical-semantic route for reading.

If the summation hypothesis were correct, ML should have problems in terms of accuracy and/or reaction time in reading the words that he had difficulty producing in picture naming and naming to definition, because the lexical-semantic route for these items was evidently impaired. This prediction was confirmed by computational modeling of a dual-route model (Wu et al., 2002). Contrary to the predictions derived from the summation hypothesis and the computational modeling, ML's word reading was preserved in terms of both accuracy and reaction time, even for items he could not name (i.e. some body parts). These findings, together with other cases reported previously (e.g. Coltheart & Funnell, 1987; Coslett, 1991; Funnell, 1983; Lambon Ralph et al., 1995), argue against the summation hypothesis, and can only be adequately accounted for by postulating the third route for reading.

Computational models have been implemented to account for reading performance of normal subjects as well as brain-damaged patients. Despite the strong evidence for two (or even three) reading routes from patient studies, a connectionist approach in which only one mechanism is postulated to account for reading of exception words and nonwords has been taken by Seidenberg and McClelland (1989) and Plaut, McClelland, Seidenberg, and Patterson (1996). In these models, it is argued that both irregular words and nonwords are read through the same trained orthography-to-phonology attractor network, and the disruption of this route would result in phonological dyslexia, in which words are primarily read through the (not-implemented) orthography–semantic–phonology pathway. Presumably, a severely impaired orthography-to-phonology pathway with a relatively preserved but not perfect semantic pathway would lead to deep dyslexia, although this prediction is not simulated empirically, either. (See Plaut & Shallice, 1993, for computational modeling work simulating deep dyslexia.)

The greatest challenge to the single-route models for reading comes from surface dyslexia. Plaut et al. (1996) first tried to simulate this deficit by inducing 'lesions' to the trained orthography-to-phonology attractor network. Although they were able to simulate the accuracy data of reading both regular and irregular words from one surface dyslexic MP (reported by Bub, Cancelliere, & Kertesz, 1985), they could not simulate the performance of the more severe surface dyslexic KT mentioned above. To account for such cases, Plaut et al. (1996) resorted to the unimplemented, indirect semantic pathway, and proposed a division-of-labor hypothesis. According to this hypothesis, the orthography-to-phonology pathway may be more responsible for reading high-frequency and high-consistency words, whereas the indirect semantic pathway may be more responsible for low-frequency, irregular words. Since the division of labor between these two pathways may be different for individual readers, surface dyslexia can arise from people whose orthography-to-phonology pathway is only able to read regular words while their semantic pathway is disrupted.

Even though the implementation of the semantic pathway provides a possible means to account for surface dyslexia in the model of Plaut et al. (1996), it still cannot readily explain some patients' performance reviewed above. Specifically, for patients whose reading on irregular words is relatively preserved compared to impaired sublexical and semantic processing (e.g. Coltheart & Funnell, 1987; Coslett, 1991; Funnell, 1983; Lambon Ralph et al., 1995), their reading is unlikely to have been achieved through either the orthography-to-phonology or the indirect semantic pathway. In order for the model of Plaut et al. (1996) to be reconciled with the data presented by these patients and surface dyslexics, it is necessary to suppose that individual differences in the division of labor between the two pathways is so great premorbidly that the orthography-to-phonology pathway can read all irregular words for some people, whereas it can mainly read regular words only for some other people.

Some computational models take a different approach from the single-route models, and implement separate routes for reading irregular words and nonwords (e.g. Coltheart et al., 1993, 2001). Although these dual-route models also assume a direct orthography-to-phonology (lexical–lexical) pathway and an orthography–semantics–phonology pathway, they differ from the model of Plaut et al. (1996) in that there is an additional sublexical route. According to Coltheart et al. (2001), the sublexical and lexical-semantic routes are interactive, and both would contribute to the resulting pronunciation of a letter string. The simulation of this dual-route (or 'three-route', to be more precise) model not only fits the accuracy and reaction time data from normal subjects, it also provides a natural account for deep dyslexia, surface dyslexia and phonological dyslexia (Coltheart et al., 2001).

The spelling process

Similar to the mechanisms of reading, different routes have been proposed to account for the normal and impaired spelling process. As evident in our ability to spell nonwords based on the rules between phonemes and graphemes, the spelling process can be achieved sublexically. The existence of this sublexical spelling process is also supported by the performance of surface dysgraphic patients, whose nonword spelling is intact while their accuracy of word spelling depends on the number of phonemes in the word with an ambiguous or irregular correspondence (e.g. Beauvois & Derouesne, 1981; Behrmann & Bub, 1992; Hatfield & Patterson, 1983). For example, a surface dysgraphic TP spelled 'flood' as 'flud' and 'laugh' as 'laf' (Hatfield & Patterson, 1983). To account for these patients' performance, it is argued that the sublexical rules of phoneme-to-grapheme correspondence are used to spell all words and nonwords.

In contrast to surface dysgraphia, some other patients show an opposite pattern, namely phonological dysgraphia. Shallice (1981) presented such a patient PR who wrote most real words correctly (94%), whereas his nonword spelling was extremely poor (18%). PR's difficulty with nonword spelling could not be attributed to a deficit in processing nonwords auditorily since he could repeat most of them (94% correct). Another patient MH, reported by Bub and Kertesz (1982a), demonstrated a similar pattern to PR.

In addition to a disruption of the sublexical spelling process, some other dysgraphic patients have been reported to have impairment in the lexical-semantic route for spelling as well, as evident in semantic errors in spelling. Bub & Kertesz (1982b) reported a deep dysgraphic patient JC who had great difficulty writing nonwords, even though she could repeat all these words, which again ruled out the possibility of a deficit on auditory processing of nonwords. Importantly, JC's spelling ability was better on concrete than abstract words, and poor on function words, which indicated the influence of semantic features. Moreover, many of JC's writing errors were semantic errors (e.g. 'clock' for 'time', 'chair' for 'desk'). These results argue for a semantic route for spelling. Also, interestingly, JC was not deep dyslexic in reading; in fact, her reading and understanding of single words was very good.

Sentence comprehension

Independence of semantic and syntactic representations

As discussed in the introduction, agrammatic speakers do not provide unequivocal evidence for a dissociation between syntax and semantics. However, some patients do show a selective deficit in syntactic processing with intact semantics, while other patients show the opposite pattern. Ostrin and Tyler (1995) reported a patient (JG) who performed poorly on sentence–picture matching when the distractor picture depicted a reversal of role relations but performed well when the distractor included a lexical substitution. This patient also performed poorly on grammaticality judgment tasks and showed no sensitivity to violations of grammatical structure in a word detection task. In contrast to his disrupted syntactic processing, JG performed well on comprehension tests for single words and showed normal semantic priming.

Whereas JG demonstrated a selective deficit in syntactic processing, other patients show impaired semantic knowledge but preserved grammatical knowledge. Some patients with Alzheimer's dementia demonstrate very impaired knowledge of word meanings yet show preserved grammatical knowledge. For example, they might be unable to realize that a phrase such as 'The jeeps walked' is nonsensical but yet be able to detect the grammatical error in a phrase like 'The jeeps goes' (Hodges, Patterson, & Tyler, 1994). Two semantic dementia cases have been reported who show a remarkable ability to understand grammatical structure and appropriately assign thematic roles such as agent or theme (i.e. the entity being acted upon) to complex constructions like 'It was the tiger that the lion bit' even though they cannot distinguish the meaning of the nouns in the sentence (Breedin & Saffran, 1999; Schwartz & Chawluk, 1990).

Interactions between syntax and semantics

Although syntax and semantics involve independent representations, they do not operate in isolation. Some neuropsychological data support the contention that sentence comprehension is accomplished via the interaction between syntactic and semantic processing. For example, patients may use the grammatical structure of sentences when there are weak semantic constraints (e.g. understanding that 'girl' is the agent of 'pushed' in 'The boy that the girl pushed...'), but fail to use the grammatical structure when there are strong semantic constraints

(e.g. mistakenly interpreting the 'woman' as the agent of 'spanked' in 'The woman that the child spanked...') (Saffran, Schwartz, & Linebarger, 1998).

An agrammatic aphasic patient DE reported in Tyler's (1989) word-monitoring studies also provides evidence for an interaction between semantic and syntactic influences. It had been shown in a previous study that DE had difficulty in structuring prose materials syntactically (Tyler, 1985). In a later study, DE was shown to be sensitive to local syntactic violations (e.g. 'slow very kitchen') in sentences that were otherwise well formed syntactically, but semantically anomalous (Tyler, 1989). Interestingly, for meaningful prose sentences, DE's sensitivity to the local syntactic violations disappeared. Tyler concluded that for meaningful materials, the patient's analysis focused on the use of word meaning and pragmatic inference to construct an interpretation of the sentence, and made little use of at least some aspects of syntactic structure. These findings support the view that information from both semantic and syntactic sources typically combines during comprehension, but when one of these systems is weakened due to brain damage, the other system may override its influence.

Working memory and sentence comprehension

Theories of sentence comprehension often assume a short-term or working memory system that holds the partial results of comprehension processes while the rest of a sentence is processed and integrated with earlier parts (e.g. Just & Carpenter, 1992). Given the fact that aphasic patients often have very restricted short-term memory spans, as indicated by a list span of only one or two words compared to normal subjects' ability to recall five or six words (De Renzi & Nichelli, 1975), it seems plausible that comprehension would be impeded by the restricted short-term memory capacity. Contrary to this intuition, however, a number of studies have shown that patients with very restricted memory spans may show excellent sentence comprehension even for sentences with complex syntactic structures (Butterworth, Campbell, & Howard, 1986; Caplan & Waters, 1999; Hanten & Martin, 2001). Such findings are actually consistent with the results from sentence comprehension with normal subjects supporting immediacy of processing, i.e. findings indicating that syntactic analysis and semantic interpretation are carried out on a word-by-word basis, to the extent possible (e.g. Boland, 1997). Since many of the patients with short-term memory impairment appear to have a deficit specifically in the ability to retain phonological information (Martin, 1993; Waters, Caplan, & Hildebrandt, 1991), they will still be able to understand complex sentence structures as

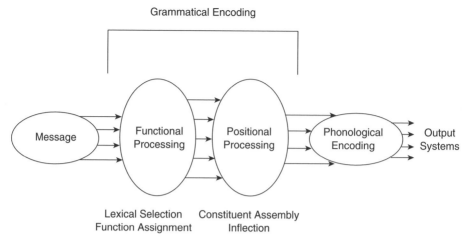

Figure 17.3   *Bock and Levelt's (1994) model of language production.*

long as they can retain the syntactic structure and the semantic information that is built up as each word is processed, despite the loss of phonological information. Phonological information is needed only in cases when verbatim information is needed – as in sentence repetition, or the learning of new phonological forms (i.e. new words) (Martin, 1993; Baddeley, Gathercole, & Papagno, 1998).

To account for the co-occurrence of restricted memory span and intact sentence comprehension, Caplan and Waters (1999) (see also Caplan & Hildebrandt, 1988) divide the procedures involved in sentence processing into interpretive and post-interpretive processes. Interpretive processes include all on-line syntactic and semantic processes, including those involved in semantic interpretation based on the ongoing discourse. This processing draws on the capacity specific to sentence processing. Post-interpretive processes involve using the products of interpretive processing to carry out some task, such as sentence–picture matching or enactment of the action in the sentence. This processing draws on the capacity tapped by span tasks. The disrupted post-interpretive processing with an intact interpretive processing would result in the selective disruption in short-term memory span but not in sentence comprehension.

While agreeing that syntactic processing draws on capacities separate from those involved in phonological retention, Martin and colleagues (Martin & Romani, 1994; Martin, Shelton, & Yaffee, 1994) argued that traditional span tasks also tap a capacity for the retention of semantic information (see also N. Martin & Saffran, 1997), and this capacity does play a role in initial sentence interpretation. The restricted ability to retain semantic information does impede comprehension

for certain sentence types; that is, those that put a strain on the capacity to retain individual word meanings. Specifically, Martin and colleagues found that patients with a semantic retention deficit, but not a patient with a phonological retention deficit, had difficulty comprehending sentences if the structure of the sentence delayed the integration of word meanings into larger semantic units (Martin & Romani, 1994; Martin & He, 2004). One sentence type causing difficulty was sentences with several prenominal adjectives, such as 'The rusty old red wagon was taken to the beach'. In this example, the meaning of 'rusty' cannot be integrated with the noun it modifies until two intervening words have been processed. The patients with a semantic retention deficit did not have difficulty comprehending similar sentences where word meanings could be integrated immediately. For example, these patients could understand sentences in which several adjectives follow the noun (e.g. 'The wagon was old, red, and rusty, but she took it along anyway'), as these sentences allow for the immediate integration of each adjective with the preceding noun. Thus, these results indicate that semantic but not phonological retention capacity is crucial to some aspects of sentence comprehension.

Sentence production

Bock and Levelt (1994) presented a model of language production (see Figure 17.3), that represents a modified version of a theory initially proposed by Garrett (1980). The starting point of speech production is a non-linguistic representation of the message to be expressed at the top level. At the next level, lexical-semantic forms are accessed and the functional relations among them are spelled out (e.g. grammatical roles of nouns with respect to verbs, modification relations between adjectives and nouns). Then syntactic frames are chosen to express the functional relations and lexical phonological forms are inserted into the frame at the next level. At this point a linear ordering of the words is developed and function words and grammatical markers are inserted at appropriate points. Finally, the phonetic representation of the utterance is specified.

According to the model outlined above, there are two levels of grammatical representations; that is, the functional and positional levels. As a result, one might hypothesize that patients with grammatical deficits in production could have selective damage to one of these two components. Moreover, since there are various representations and processes at each of these levels, different types of deficits are expected from damage to the same level. At the functional level, one major component involves mapping of relations between the verbs and nouns that play thematic roles with respect to the verb (Bock & Levelt, 1994). The specific verb to be used dictates what grammatical role a noun with a specific thematic role will play. For example, the recipient will be the subject of an active sentence using the verb 'receive' but the indirect object of an active sentence using 'give'. A disruption on this component could potentially lead to an incomplete specification at the functional level and a reduction in sentence structure, such as the failure to produce a required indirect object (Saffran, Schwartz, & Marin, 1980). Berndt, Haendiges, Mitchum, and Sandson (1997) found some support for this notion in a study of ten patients who varied in their relative ability to produce nouns and verbs in single word tasks. They found a strong relation between greater difficulty with verbs than nouns and impairments on structural measures of spontaneous speech such as mean sentence length, sentence elaboration with content words, and proportion of words in sentences. Two of the five verb-impaired patients showed a much greater proportion of grammatically acceptable sentences and greater production of the object noun when asked to generate a sentence using an experimenter-provided verb compared to a noun.

Another type of deficit that would emerge from a disruption to the functional level does not involve difficulty on verb lexicalization in sentences. Rather, the patients might reverse the roles of the nouns with respect to the verb. Martin and Blossom-Stach (1986) and Caramazza and Miceli (1991) both reported such cases. They argued that these patients had difficulty with the mapping between thematic roles and grammatical roles at the functional level (i.e. they had a mapping deficit on the production side), resulting in a misordering of nouns with respect to the verb (e.g. saying 'The boy was pushed by the girl' for a picture of a boy pushing a girl).

Interestingly, these patients produced appropriate nouns, verbs and otherwise grammatically correct utterances, indicating that the other stages in the production process ran off appropriately. Also, both patients showed similar mapping deficits in comprehension, suggesting that a central process subserves the mapping between grammatical and thematic roles in both production and comprehension.

A disruption at the positional level could also take different forms. Difficulty with accessing syntactic frames could be another possible locus of reduced structural complexity (Goodglass, Christiansen, & Gallagher, 1994), as patients might be able to access only the simplest, most frequent structural frames (Stemberger, 1984). Also, given that function words and inflections are specified at the positional level, a disruption at this level could be postulated to account for patients with selectively impaired production of such elements relative to content words. Caramazza and Hillis (1989) reported a patient who omitted a large proportion of function words and omitted a smaller, yet substantial, proportion of inflections in oral and written sentence production, sentence reading and sentence repetition. Her single word reading and repetition was preserved for function words, however, and she showed excellent comprehension of syntax. Thus, her deficit was specific to sentence-level production.

Garrett (1980) claimed that function words and inflectional markers are part of the syntactic frame. If so, then difficulty with accessing frames would lead to errors involving such elements. Caramazza and Hillis (1989) endorsed such an account of their patient's deficit. They pointed out, however, that Garrett's model is underspecified with regard to accounting for aspects of their patient's behavior (i.e. the greater difficulty with function words than inflections) and patterns observed in other patients (e.g. varying degrees of omission vs. substitution of grammatical morphemes and selectively greater difficulty with certain types of function words or inflections: Miceli, Silveri, Romani, & Caramazza, 1989; Thompson, Fix, & Gitelman, 2002).

In contrast to Garrett's model, other theorists have argued that grammatical elements are retrieved in the same fashion as content words (Bock, 1989). For this approach to explain the selective disorders of function words and inflectional markers, various hypotheses have been proposed. First, it is argued that function words and grammatical markers constitute a specialized word class, and it is subject to selective impairment (Bradley, Garrett, & Zurif, 1980). Second, it may be caused by a syntactic deficit that prevents determination of the correct function word or inflection to express grammatical relations (Thompson et al., 2002). Third, this deficit may result from disrupted accessing to all low imageability words, which include functional words (Bird et al., 2002). Fourth, a phonological disturbance that affects late stages of the production process where the phonological forms of function words and inflections are determined may give rise to this deficit (Saffran et al., 1980). It may be true that these hypotheses are not mutually exclusive, and they are correct with respect to different patients.

Working memory deficits in production

According to the model depicted in Figure 17.3, working memory capacities of various types are involved in sentence production, as the representations for several words would have to be maintained simultaneously at different stages in the process. Also, this maintenance would have to persist long enough for the processes at the next stage to be carried out. Consistent with this logic, Kolk (1995) has hypothesized that aphasic language production patterns derive from a disruption of temporal coordination during syntactic planning. Specifically, he proposes that both content words and function words are inserted into a syntactic frame at the positional level, and difficulties would arise due to slow activation or overly rapid decay of some elements that should be expressed in the same syntactic unit. This impairment would be more evident with more complex syntactic structures, since they have more elements to be realized, and it is more likely that some temporal mismatch would occur between elements. Patients can adapt to this deficit either by using simpler structures or by sticking with more complex structures but omitting some elements. In support of this view, he and his colleagues have shown that patients' production patterns can appear quite different under different task demands (Hofstede & Kolk, 1994; Kolk & Heeschen, 1992).

Recent findings by Linebarger, Schwartz, Romania, Kohn, and Stephens (2000) also support a capacity limitation as a factor in at least the structural limitations of agrammatic speech. They trained six agrammatic speakers on a computerized augmentative communication system and examined their ability to describe videos with and without use of this system. Their system allowed patients to record segments of speech and then each segment was associated with a symbol on the computer screen. The patients moved these symbols to a staging area where they could assemble the segments into a narrative about the video. Use of the system resulted in substantially more words in sentences, longer mean length of sentences, and greater realization of arguments of the verb in their utterances. Morphological characteristics of their speech were not, however, improved significantly by use of the system.

Martin and Freedman (2001) presented evidence that a specific type of short-term memory limitation can affect patients' productions. Patients with a lexical-semantic retention deficit (but not those with a phonological retention deficit) had difficulty producing adjective noun phrases (e.g. 'small leaf' or 'short dark hair'), although they were able to produce the individual adjectives and nouns in isolation. To account for the production deficit, Martin and Freedman (2001) argued that subjects plan speech in a phrase-by-phrase fashion, planning the head noun and all the preceding content words in the phrase at a lexical-semantic level prior to initiating phonological retrieval. These patients' lexical-semantic retention deficits prevented them from being able to simultaneously maintain such representations for several words. In support of this argument, they showed that these patients did better at producing the same content in a sentence form (e.g. 'The leaf is small' or 'The hair is short and dark') as these sentence forms allowed them to produce fewer content words in an individual phrase.

CONCLUSIONS

This overview of cognitive neuropsychological findings indicates that our understanding of the functional organization of language has progressed considerably since the Wernicke–Lichtheim model was proposed. Particularly during the last twenty years or so, considerable knowledge has accumulated concerning the organization of the systems involved in single word processing for both speech and writing. The data that have been collected have had important implications for various issues that have been greatly debated in the normal literature (e.g. the commonality vs. dissociation between input and output phonological/orthographic representations, different mechanisms for reading aloud, the separation of semantic, syntactic and phonological processing in speech production). Progress has also been made in terms of understanding the nature of sentence-level processing, but here the representations and processes are very complex, and only some relatively global aspects of processing have been delineated. Clearly much more work is needed to spell out the various components involved. The cognitive neuropsychological work at the single word level, particularly in the domain of reading, has been informed by (and has informed) relatively explicit models of processing. At the sentence level, more precise theoretical accounts are needed that could guide further work. There already exists a substantial database of findings on neuropsychological disorders of sentence processing, and these should contribute to such theory development.

ACKNOWLEDGEMENTS

Preparation of this chapter was supported in part by NIH Grant DC-00218 to Rice University. The authors would like to thank Frank Tamborello for his assistance with technical aspects of the manuscript.

REFERENCES

Albert, M. L., & Bear, D. (1957). Time to understand: a case study of word deafness with reference to the role of time in auditory comprehension. *Brain*, *97*, 373–384.

Allen, M., & Badecker, W. (1999). Stem homograph and stem allomorphy: representing and processing inflected forms in a multilevel lexical system. *Journal of Memory and Language*, *41*, 105–123.

Allport, D. A. (1985). Distributed memory, modular subsystems and dysphasia. In S. K. Newman & R. Epstein (Eds.), *Current perspectives in dysphasia* (pp. 207–244). Edinburgh: Churchill Livingstone.

Allport, D. A., & Funnell, E. (1981). Components of the mental lexicon. *Philosophical Transactions of the Royal Society of London B*, *295*, 397–401.

Auerbach, S. H., Allard, T., Naeser, M., Alexander, M. P., & Albert, M. L. (1982). Pure word deafness: analysis of a case with bilateral lesions and a defect at the prephonemic level. *Brain*, *105*, 271–300.

Baddeley, A., Gathercole, S., & Papagno, C. (1998). The phonological loop as a language learning device. *Psychological Review*, *105*, 158–173.

Badecker, W., & Caramazza, A. (1991). Morphological composition in the lexical output system. *Cognitive Neuropsychology*, *8*, 335–367.

Badecker, W., Miozzo, M., & Zanuttini, R. (1995). The two-stage model of lexical retrieval: evidence from a case of anomia with selective preservation of grammatical gender. *Cognition*, *57*, 193–216.

Beauvois, M.-F. (1982). Optic aphasia: a process of interaction between vision and language. *Proceedings of the Royal Society of London B*, *298*, 35–47.

Beauvois, M.-F., & Derouesne, J. (1981). Lexical or orthographic agraphia. *Brain*, *104*, 21–49.

Beauvois, M.-F., Saillant, B., Meininger, V., & Lhermitte, F. (1978). Bilateral tactile aphasia: a tacto-verbal dysfunction. *Brain*, *101*, 381–401.

Behrmann, M., & Bub, D. (1992). Surface dyslexia and dysgraphia: dual routes, single lexicon. *Cognitive Neuropsychology*, *9*, 209–251.

Berndt, R. S., & Caramazza, A. (1980). A redefinition of the syndrome of Broca's aphasia: implications for a neuropsychological model of language. *Applied Linguistics*, *1*, 225–278.

Berndt, R. S., Haendiges, A. N., Burton, M. W., & Mitchum, C. C. (2002). Grammatical class and imageability in aphasic word production: their effects are independent. *Journal of Neurolinguistics*, *15*, 353–371.

Berndt, R. S., Haendiges, A. N., Mitchum, C. C., & Sandson, J. (1997). Verb retrieval in aphasia: 2. Relationship to sentence processing. *Brain and Language*, *56*, 107–137.

Berndt, R. S., Mitchum, C., & Haendiges, A. (1996). Comprehension of reversible sentences in 'agrammatism': a meta-analysis. *Cognition*, *58*, 289–308.

Bird, H., Franklin, S., & Howard, D. (2002). 'Little words' – not really: function and content words in normal and aphasic speech. *Journal of Neurolinguistics*, *15*, 209–237.

Blanken, G. (1990). Formal paraphasias: a single case study. *Brain and Language*, *38*, 534–554.

Blumstein, S. E., Baker, E., & Goodglass, H. (1977). Phonological factors in auditory comprehension in aphasia. *Neuropsychologia*, *15*, 19–30.

Bock, K. (1989). Closed-class immanence in sentence production. *Cognition*, *31*, 163–186.

Bock, K., & Levelt, W. (1994). Language production: grammatical encoding. In M. A. Gernsbacher (ed.), *Handbook of psycholinguistics* (pp. 945–984). San Diego, CA: Academic Press.

Boland, J. (1997). The relationship between syntactic and semantic processes in sentence comprehension. *Language and Cognitive Processes*, *12*, 423–484.

Bradley, D. C., Garrett, M. F., & Zurif, E. B. (1980). Syntactic deficits in Broca's aphasia. In D. Caplan (ed.), *Biological studies of mental processes* (pp. 269–286). Cambridge, MA: MIT Press.

Breedin, S., & Saffran, E. (1999). Sentence processing in the face of semantic loss: a case study. *Journal of Experimental Psychology: General*, *128*, 547–562.

Bub, D., Cancelliere, A., & Kertesz, A. (1985). Wholeword and analytic translation of spelling-to-sound in a non-semantic reader. In K. E. Patterson, M. Coltheart, & J. C. Marshall (Eds.), *Surface dyslexia* (pp. 15–34). London: Erlbaum.

Bub, D., & Kertesz, A. (1982a). Evidence for lexicographic processing in a patient with preserved written over oral single word naming. *Brain*, *105*, 687–717.

Bub, D., & Kertesz, A. (1982b). Deep agraphia. *Brain and Language*, *17*, 146–165.

Butterworth, B., Campbell, R., & Howard, D. (1986). The uses of short-term memory: a case study. *Quarterly Journal of Experimental Psychology*, *38A*, 705–737.

Bybee, J. L. (1988). Morphology as lexical organization. In M. Hammond & M. Noonan (Eds.), *Theoretical morphology: approaches in modern linguistics* (pp. 119–141). San Diego, CA: Academic Press.

Caplan, D., & Hildebrandt, N. (1988). *Disorders of syntactic comprehension*. Cambridge, MA: MIT Press.

Caplan, D., Vanier, M., & Baker, C. (1986). A case study of reproduction conduction aphasia: 1. Word production. *Cognitive Neuropsychology*, *3*, 99–128.

Caplan, D., & Waters, G. (1999). Verbal working memory and sentence comprehension. *Behavioral Brain Sciences*, *22*, 77–126.

Caramazza, A., & Berndt, R. S. (1978). Semantic and syntactic processes in aphasia: a review of the literature. *Psychological Bulletin*, *85*, 898–918.

Caramazza, A., & Hillis, A. E. (1989). The disruption of sentence production: some dissociations. *Brain and Language*, *36*, 625–650.

Caramazza, A., & Hillis, A. E. (1990). Where do semantic errors come from? *Cortex*, *26*, 95–122.

Caramazza, A., Hillis, A. E., Rapp, B. C., & Romani, C. (1990). The multiple semantic hypothesis: multiple confusions? *Cognitive Neuropsychology*, *7*, 161–189.

Caramazza, A., & Miceli, G. (1991). Selective impairment of thematic role assignment in sentence processing. *Brain and Language*, *41*, 402–436.

Caramazza, A., & Miozzo, M. (1997). The relation between syntactic and phonological knowledge in lexical access: evidence from the 'tip-of-the-tongue' phenomenon. *Cognition*, *64*, 309–343.

Caramazza, A., Papagno, C., & Ruml, W. (2000). The selective impairment of phonological processing in speech production. *Brain and Language*, *75*, 428–450.

Caramazza, A., & Shelton, J. R. (1998). Domain specific knowledge systems in the brain: the animate-inanimate distinction. *Journal of Cognitive Neuroscience*, *10*, 1–34.

Caramazza, A., & Zurif, E. B. (1976). Dissociation of algorithmic and heuristic processes in language comprehension: evidence from aphasia. *Brain and Language*, *3*, 572–582.

Coltheart, M. (1978). Lexical access in simple reading tasks. In G. Underwood (ed.), *Strategies of information processing* (pp. 151–216). San Diego, CA: Academic Press.

Coltheart, M. (1980). Deep dyslexia: a review of the syndrome. In M. Coltheart, K. E. Patterson, & J. C. Marshall (Eds.), *Deep dyslexia* (pp. 22–47). London: Routledge & Kegan Paul.

Coltheart, M. (2000). Deep dyslexia is right-hemisphere reading. *Brain and Language*, *71*, 299–309.

Colheart, M., Curtis, B., Atkins, P., & Haller, M. (1993). Models of reading aloud: dual-route and parallel-distributed-processing approaches. *Psychological Review*, *100*, 589–608.

Coltheart, M., & Funnell, E. (1987). Reading and writing: one lexicon or two? In D. A. Allport, D. G. Mackay, W. Prinz, & E. Scheerer (Eds.), *Language perception and production: relationships among listening, speaking, reading, and writing* (pp. 313–339). London: Academic Press.

Coltheart, M., Inglis, L., Cupples, L., Michie, P., Bates, A., & Budd, B. (1998). A semantic subsystem of visual attributes. *Neurocase*, *4*, 353–370.

Coltheart, M., Masterson, J., Byng, S., Prior, M., & Riddoch, J. (1983). Surface dyslexia. *Quarterly Journal of Experimental Psychology*, *35A*, 469–495.

Coltheart, M., Rastle, K., Perry, C., Langdon, R., & Ziegler, J. (2001). DRC: a dual route cascaded model of visual word recognition. *Psychological Review*, *108*, 204–256.

Coslett, H. B. (1991). Read but not write 'idea': evidence for a third reading mechanism. *Brain and Language*, *40*, 425–443.

Cuetos, F., Aguado, G., & Caramazza, A. (2000). Dissociation of semantic and phonological errors in naming. *Brain and Language*, *75*, 451–460.

Damasio, H. (1998). Neuroanatomical correlates of the aphasias. In M. T. Sarno (ed.), *Acquired aphasia* (3rd ed., pp. 43–70). San Diego, CA: Academic Press.

Dell, G., Schwartz, M., Martin, N., Saffran, E., & Gagnon, D. (1997). Lexical access in aphasic and nonaphasic speakers. *Psychological Review*, *104*, 801–838.

Denes, G., & Semenza, C. (1975). Auditory modality-specific anomia: evidence from a case study of pure word deafness. *Cortex*, *11*, 401–411.

De Renzi, E., & Nichelli, P. (1975). Verbal and non-verbal short-term memory impairment following hemispheric damage. *Cortex*, *11*, 341–354.

Devlin, J. T., Gonnerman, L. M., Andersen, E. S., & Seidenberg, M. S. (1998). Category-specific semantic deficits in focal and widespread brain damage: a computational account. *Journal of Cognitive Neuroscience*, *10*, 77–94.

Dronkers, N. F., Redfern, B. B., & Knight, R. T. (2000). The neural architecture of language disorders. In M. S. Gazzaniga (ed.), *The New Cognitive Neurosciences* (2nd ed., pp. 949–958). Cambridge, MA: MIT Press.

Druks, J. (2002). Verbs and nouns: a review of the literature. *Journal of Neurolinguistics*, *15*, 289–319.

Ellis, A. W. (1984). Introduction to Bramwell's (1897) case of word meaning deafness. *Cognitive Neuropsychology*, *1*, 245–258.

Ellis, A. W., & Young, A. W. (1988). *Human cognitive neuropsychology*. Hove, UK: Erlbaum.

Farah, M. J., & McClelland, J. L. (1991). A computational model of semantic memory impairment: modality specificity and emergent category specificity. *Journal of Experimental Psychology: General*, *120*, 339–357.

Farah, M. J., & Wallace, M. A. (1992). Semantically-bounded anomia: implications for the neural implementation of naming. *Neuropsychologia*, *30*, 609–621.

Forde, E. M. E., & Humphreys, G. W. (1999). Category-specific recognition impairments: a review of important case studies and influential theories. *Aphasiology*, *13*, 169–193.

Foygel, D., & Dell, G. S. (2000). Models of impaired lexical access in speech production. *Journal of Memory and Language*, *43*, 182–216.

Franklin, S., Howard, D., & Patterson, K. (1994). Abstract word meaning deafness. *Cognitive Neuropsycholinguistics*, *11*, 1–34.

Franklin, S., Turner, J., Lambon Ralph, M. A., Morris, J., & Bailey, P. J. (1996). A distinctive case of word meaning deafness? *Neuropsychology*, *13*, 1139–1162.

Friedman, R. B., & Hadley, J. A. (1992). Letter-by-letter surface alexia. *Cognitive Neuropsychology*, *9*, 185–208.

Funnell, E. (1983). Phonological processes in reading: new evidence from acquired dyslexia. *British Journal of Psychology*, *74*, 159–180.

Funnell, E. (1987). Morphological errors in acquired dyslexia: a case of mistaken identity. *Quarterly Journal of Experimental Psychology*, *39*, 497–539.

Garrard, P., Lambon Ralph, M. A., Watson, P. C., Powis, J., Patterson, K., & Hodges, J. R. (2001). Longitudinal profiles of semantic impairment for living and non-living concepts in dementia of Alzheimer's type. *Journal of Cognitive Neuroscience*, *13*, 892–909.

Garrard, P., Patterson, K., Watson, P. C., & Hodges, J. R. (1998). Category specific semantic loss in dementia of Alzheimer's type: functional-anatomical correlations from cross-sectional analyses. *Brain*, *121*, 633–646.

Garrett, M. F. (1980). Levels of processing in sentence production. In B. Butterworth (ed.), *Language production* (Vol. 1, pp. 177–220). London: Academic Press.

Garrett, M. F. (1993). Errors and their relevance for models of language production. In G. Blanken, J. Dittman, H. Grim, J. Marshall, & C. Wallesch (Eds.), *Linguistic disorders and pathologies* (pp. 69–96). Berlin: de Gruyter.

Goodglass, H. (1993). *Understanding aphasia*. San Diego, CA: Academic Press.

Goodglass, H., Christiansen, J. A., & Gallagher, R. E. (1994). Syntactic constructions used by agrammatic speakers: comparison with conduction aphasics and normals. *Neuropsychology, 8*, 598–613.

Goodglass, H., Klein, B., Carey, P., & Jones, K. (1966). Specific semantic word categories in aphasia. *Cortex, 2*, 74–89.

Griffiths, T. D., Rees, A., & Green, G. G. R. (1999). Disorders of human complex sound processing. *Neurocase, 5*, 365–378.

Hall, D. A., & Riddoch, M. J. (1997). Word meaning deafness: spelling words that are not understood. *Cognitive Neuropsychology, 14*, 1131–1164.

Hanten, G., & Martin, R. C. (2001). A developmental phonological short-term memory deficit: a case study. *Brain and Cognition, 45*, 164–188.

Hart, J., Berndt, R. S., & Caramazza, A. (1985). Category-specific naming deficit following cerebral infarction. *Nature, 316*, 439–440.

Hatfield, F. M., & Patterson, K. E. (1983). Phonological spelling. *Quarterly Journal of Experimental Psychology, 35A*, 451–468.

Hillis, A. E. (2001). The organization of the lexical system. In B. Rapp (ed.), *The handbook of cognitive neuropsychology: what deficits reveal about the human mind* (pp. 291–320). Philadelphia, PA: Psychology Press/Taylor & Francis.

Hillis, A. E., Boatman, D., Hart, J., & Gordon, B. (1999). Making sense out of jargon: a neurolinguistic and computational account of jargon aphasia. *Neurology, 53*, 1813–1824.

Hillis, A. E., & Caramazza, A. (1991). Mechanisms for accessing lexical representations for output: evidence from a category-specific semantic deficit. *Brain and Language, 40*, 106–144.

Hillis, A. E., & Caramazza, A. (1995). Converging evidence for the interaction of semantic and sublexical phonological information in accessing lexical representations for spoken output. *Cognitive Neuropsychology, 12*, 187–227.

Hillis, A. E., Rapp, B. C., Romani, C., & Caramazza, A. (1990). Selective impairment of semantics in lexical processing. *Cognitive Neuropsychology, 7*, 191–243.

Hodges, J. R., Patterson, K., Oxbury, S., & Funnell, E. (1992). Semantic dementia: progressive fluent aphasia with temporal lobe atrophy. *Brain, 115*, 1783–1786.

Hodges, J., Patterson, K., & Tyler, L. (1994). Loss of semantic memory: implications for the modularity of mind. *Cognitive Neuropsychology, 11*, 505–542.

Hofstede, B., & Kolk, H. (1994). The effects of task variation on the production of grammatical morphology in Broca's aphasia: a multiple case study. *Brain and Language, 46*, 278–328.

Howard, D., & Franklin, S. (1988). *Missing the meaning: a cognitive neuropsychological study of processing of words by an aphasic patient*. Cambridge, MA: MIT Press.

Howard, D., & Franklin, S. (1990). Memory without rehearsal. In G. Vallar & T. Shallice (Eds.), *Neuropsychological impairments of short-term memory* (pp. 287–318). Cambridge, UK: Cambridge University Press.

Howard, D., & Orchard-Lisle, V. (1984). On the origin of semantic errors in naming: evidence from the case of a global aphasic. *Cognitive Neuropsychology, 1*, 163–190.

Joanisse, M. F., & Seidenberg, M. S. (1999). Impairments in verb morphology after brain injury: a connectionist model. *Proceedings of the National Academy of Sciences of the USA, 96*, 7592–7597.

Just, M., & Carpenter, P. (1992). A capacity theory of comprehension: individual differences in working memory. *Psychological Review, 99*, 122–149.

Kohn, S. E., & Friedman, R. B. (1986). Word-meaning deafness: a phonological-semantic dissociation. *Cognitive Neuropsychology, 3*, 291–308.

Kolk, H. (1995). A time-based approach to agrammatic production. *Brain and Language, 50*, 282–303.

Kolk, H., & Heeschen, C. (1992). Agrammatism, paragrammatism, and the management of language. *Language and Cognitive Processes, 7*, 89–129.

Kremin, H. (1982). Alexia: theory and research. In R. N. Malatesha & P. G. Aaron (Eds.), *Reading disorders: varieties and treatments* (pp. 341–367). New York: Academic Press.

Lambon Ralph, M. A., Ellis, A. W., & Franklin, S. (1995). Semantic loss without surface dyslexia. *Neurocase, 1*, 363–369.

Lambon Ralph, M. A., Howard, D., Nightingale, G., & Ellis, A. (1998). Are living and nonliving category-specific deficits causally linked to impaired perceptual or associative knowledge? Evidence from a category-specific double dissociation. *Neurocase, 4*, 311–338.

Lenneberg, E. H. (1973). The neurology of language. *Daedalus, 102*, 115–133.

Lesch, M. F., & Martin, R. C. (1998). The representation of sublexical orthographic-phonologic correspondences: evidence from phonological dyslexia. *Quarterly Journal of Experimental Psychology, 51A*, 905–938.

Levelt, W. J. M., Roelofs, A., & Meyer, A. S. (1999). A theory of lexical access in speech production. *Behavioral Brain Sciences, 22*, 1–75.

Lhermitte, F., & Beauvois, M.-F. (1973). A visual-speech disconnexion syndrome: report of a case with optic aphasia, agnosic alexia and colour agnosia. *Brain, 97*, 695–714.

Lichtheim, L. (1885). On aphasia. *Brain, 7*, 433–484.

Linebarger, M. (1990). Neuropsychology of sentence parsing. In A. Caramazza (ed.), *Cognitive neuropsychology and neurolinguistics: advances in models of cognitive function and impairment* (pp. 55–122). Hillsdale, NJ: Erlbaum.

Linebarger, M. C., Schwartz, M. F., Romania, J. R., Kohn, S. E., & Stephens, D. L. (2000). Grammatical encoding in aphasia: evidence from a 'processing prosthesis'. *Brain and Language, 75*, 416–427.

Linebarger, M., Schwartz, M., & Saffran, E. (1983). Sensitivity to grammatical structure in so-called agrammatic aphasics. *Cognition, 13*, 361–392.

Lukatela, G., & Turvey, M. T. (1994a). Visual lexical access is initially phonological: 1. Evidence from associative priming by words, homophones, and pseudohomophones. *Journal of Experimental Psychology: General, 123*, 107–128.

Lukatela, G., & Turvey, M. T. (1994b). Visual lexical access is initially phonological: 2. Evidence from phonological priming by homophones and pseudohomophones. *Journal of Experimental Psychology: General, 123*, 331–353.

Marshall, J. C., & Newcombe, F. (1973). Patterns of paralexia: a psycholinguistic approach. *Journal of Psycholinguistic Research, 2*, 175–199.

Martin, N., & Saffran, E. M. (1992). A computational account of deep dysphasia: evidence from a single case study. *Brain and Language, 43*, 240–274.

Martin, N., & Saffran, E. M. (1997). Language and auditory-verbal short-term memory impairments: evidence for common underlying processes. *Cognitive Neuropsychology, 14*, 641–682.

Martin, N., & Saffran, E. M. (2002). The relationship of input and output phonological processing: an evaluation of models and evidence to support them. *Aphasiology, 16*, 107–150.

Martin, R. C. (1993). Short-term memory and sentence processing: evidence from neuropsychology. *Memory and Cognition, 21*, 176–183.

Martin, R. C. (2003). Language processing: functional organization and neuroanatomical basis. In S. Fiske, D. Schacter, & C. Zahn-Waxler (Eds.), *Annual review of psychology* (pp. 55–89). Palo Alto, CA: Annual Reviews.

Martin, R. C., & Blossom-Stach, C. (1986). Evidence of syntactic deficits in a fluent aphasic. *Brain and Language, 28*, 196–234.

Martin, R. C., & Freedman, M. L. (2001). Short-term retention of lexical-semantic representations: implications for speech production. *Memory, 9*, 261–280.

Martin, R. C. & He, T. (2004). Semantic short-term memory and its role in sentence processing: a replication. *Brain and Language, 89*, 76–82.

Martin, R. C., Lesch, M. F., & Bartha, M. C. (1999). Independence of input and output phonology in word processing and short-term memory. *Journal of Memory and Language, 41*, 3–29.

Martin, R. C., & Romani, C. (1994). Verbal working memory and sentence comprehension: a multiple-components view. *Neuropsychology, 8*, 506–523.

Martin, R. C., Shelton, J. R., & Yaffee, L. S. (1994). Language processing and working memory: neuropsychological evidence for separate phonological and semantic capacities. *Journal of Memory and Language, 33*, 83–111.

McCarthy, R., & Warrington, E. K. (1986). Phonological reading: phenomena and paradoxes. *Cortex, 22*, 359–380.

Miceli, G., Silveri, M. C., Romani, C., & Caramazza, A. (1989). Variation in the pattern of omissions and substitutions of grammatical morphemes in the spontaneous speech of so-called agrammatic patients. *Brain and Language, 36*, 447–492.

Miceli, G., Silveri, M. C., Villa, G., & Caramazza, A. (1984). On the basis for the agrammatics' difficulty in producing main verbs. *Cortex, 20*, 207–220.

Mohr, J. P., Pessin, M. S., Finkelstein, S., Funkenstein, H. H., Duncan, G. W., & Davis, K. R. (1978). Broca aphasia: pathologic and clinical. *Neurology, 28*, 311–324.

Moss, H. E., & Tyler, L. K. (2000). A progressive category-specific semantic deficit for non-living things. *Neuropsychologia, 38*, 60–82.

Nickels, L. (2001). Spoken word production. In B. Rapp (ed.), *The handbook of cognitive neuropsychology: what deficits reveal about the human mind* (pp. 291–320). Philadelphia, PA: Psychology Press/ Taylor & Francis.

Nickels, L. A., & Howard, D. (1995a). Phonological errors in aphasic naming: comprehension, monitoring and lexicality. *Cortex, 31*, 209–237.

Nickels, L. A., & Howard, D. (1995b). Aphasic naming: what matters? *Neuropsychologia, 33*, 1281–1303.

Ostrin, R., & Tyler, L. (1995). Dissociations of lexical function: semantics, syntax, and morphology. *Cognitive Neuropsychology, 12*, 345–389.

Park, N., & Martin, R. C. (2001). Reading versus writing: evidence for the dissociation of input and output graphemic lexicons. Poster presented at Cognitive Neuroscience Society Eighth Annual Meeting, New York.

Patterson, K. (2002). A double dissociation but a single mechanism? Further neuropsychological evidence on the past-tense debate. Presented at Cognitive Neuroscience Society Ninth Annual Meeting, San Francisco.

Patterson, K., Lambon Ralph, M. A., Hodges, J. R., & McClelland, J. L. (2001). Deficits in irregular past-tense verb morphology associated with degraded semantic knowledge. *Neuropsychologia, 39*, 709–724.

Plaut, D. C., McClelland, J. L., Seidenberg, M. S., & Patterson, K. (1996). Understanding normal and impaired word reading: computational principles in quasi-regular domains. *Psychological Review, 103*, 56–115.

Plaut, D. C., & Shallice, T. (1993). Deep dyslexia: a case study of connectionist neuropsychology. *Cognitive Neuropsychology, 10*, 377–500.

Poeppel, D. (2001). Pure word deafness and the bilateral processing of the speech code. *Cognitive Science, 25*, 679–693.

Rapp, B. C., Benzing, L., & Caramazza, A. (1997). The autonomy of lexical orthographic representations. *Cognitive Neuropsychology, 14*, 71–104.

Rapp, B. C., & Caramazza, A. (1997). The modality specific organization of lexical categories: evidence from impaired spoken and written sentence production. *Brain and Language*, *56*, 248–286.

Rapp, B., & Caramazza, A. (2002). Selective difficulties with spoken nouns and written verbs: a single case study. *Journal of Neurolinguistics*, *15*, 373–402.

Rapp, B., & Goldrick, M. (2000). Discreteness and inter-activity in spoken word production. *Psychological Review*, *107*, 460–499.

Riddoch, M. J., Humphreys, G. W., Coltheart, M., & Funnell, E. (1988). Semantic systems or system? Neuropsychological evidence re-examined. *Cognitive Neuropsychology*, *5*, 3–25.

Rumelhart, D. E., & McClelland, J. L. (1986). On learning the past tenses of English verbs. In J. McClelland & D. Rumelhart (Eds.), *Parallel distributed processing: explorations in the microstructure of cognition* (Vol. 2, pp. 216–271). Cambridge, MA: MIT Press.

Ruml, W., Caramazza, A., Shelton, J., & Chialant, D. (2000). Testing assumptions in computational theories of aphasia. *Journal of Memory and Language*, *43*, 217–248.

Saffran, E., Schwartz, M., & Linebarger, M. (1998). Semantic influences on thematic role assignments: evidence from normals and aphasics. *Brain and Language*, *62*, 255–297.

Saffran, E. M., Schwartz, M. F., & Martin, O. S. (1980). The word order problem in agrammatism: II. Production. *Brain and Language*, *10*, 263–280.

Sartori, G., & Job, R. (1988). The oyster with four legs: a neuropsychological study on the interaction of visual and semantic information. *Cognitive Neuropsychology*, *5*, 105–132.

Schwartz, M., & Chawluk, J. (1990). Deterioration of language in progressive aphasia: a case study. In M. Schwartz (ed.), *Modular deficits in Alzheimer-type dementia* (pp. 245–296). Cambridge, MA: MIT Press.

Schwartz, M. F., Saffran, E. M., & Marin, O. S. (1980). The word order problem in agrammatism: I. Comprehension. *Brain and Language*, *10*, 249–262.

Seidenberg, M. S., & McClelland, J. L. (1989). A distributed, developmental model of word recognition and naming. *Psychological Review*, *96*, 523–568.

Selnes, O. A., Knopman, D. S., Niccum, N., Rubens, A. B., & Larson, D. (1983). Computed tomographic scan correlates of auditory comprehension deficits in aphasia: a prospective recovery study. *Annals of Neurology*, *13*, 558–566.

Shallice, T. (1981). Phonological agraphia and the lexical route in writing. *Brain*, *104*, 413–429.

Shallice, T. (1987). Impairments of semantic processing: multiple dissociations. In M. Coltheart, G. Sartori, & R. Job (Eds.), *The Cognitive neuropsychology of language* (pp. 111–127). London: Erlbaum.

Shallice, T. (1988). *From neuropsychology to mental structure*. New York: Cambridge University Press.

Shapiro, K., Shelton, J., & Caramazza, A. (2000). Grammatical class in lexical production and morphological processing: evidence from a case of fluent aphasia. *Cognitive Neuropsychology*, *17*, 665–682.

Shelton, J. R., & Caramazza, A. (1999). Deficits in lexical and semantic processing: implications for models of normal language. *Psychonomic Bulletin and Review*, *6*, 5–27.

Shelton, J. R., & Caramazza, A. (2001). The organization of semantic memory. In B. Rapp (ed.), *The handbook of cognitive neuropsychology: what deficits reveal about the human mind* (pp. 423–443). Philadelphia, PA: Psychology Press/Taylor & Francis.

Shelton, J. R., & Weinrich, M. (1997). Further evidence of a dissociation between output phonological and orthographic lexicons: a case study. *Cognitive Neuropsychology*, *14*, 105–129.

Silveri, M. C., & Gainotti, G. (1988). Interaction between vision and language in category-specific impairment. *Cognitive Neuropsychology*, *5*, 677–709.

Stemberger, J. P. (1984). Structural errors in normal and agrammatic speech. *Cognitive Neuropsychology*, *1*, 281–313.

Tanaka, Y., Yamadori, A., & Mori, E. (1987). Pure word deafness following bilateral lesions: a psychophysical analysis. *Brain*, *110*, 381–403.

Thompson, C. K., Fix, S., & Gitelman, D. (2002). Selective impairment of morphosyntactic production in a neurological patient. *Journal of Neurolinguistics*, *15*, 189–207.

Treiman, R., & Zukowski, A. (1988). Units in reading and spelling. *Journal of Memory and Language*, *27*, 466–477.

Tsapkini, K., Jarema, G., & Kehayia, E. (2002). A morphological processing deficit in verbs but not in nouns: a case study in a highly inflected language. *Journal of Neurolinguistics*, *15*, 265–288.

Tyler, L. (1985). Real-time comprehension problems in agrammatism: a case study. *Brain and Language*, *26*, 259–275.

Tyler, L. (1989). Syntactic deficits and the construction of local phrases in spoken language comprehension. *Cognitive Neuropsychology*, *6*, 333–355.

Tyler, L. K., Moss, H. E., Durrant-Peatfield, M. R., & Levy, J. P. (2000). Conceptual structure and the structure of concepts: a distributed account of category-specific deficits. *Brain and Language*, *75*, 195–231.

Tyler, L. K., Randall, B., & Marslen-Wilson, W. D. (2002). Phonology and neuropsychology of the English past tense. *Neuropsychologia*, *40*, 1154–1166.

Ullman, M. T., Corkin, S., Coppola, M., Hickok, G., Growdon, J. H., et al. (1997). A neural dissociation within language: evidence that the mental dictionary is part of declarative memory, and that grammatical rules are processed by the procedural system. *Journal of Cognitive Neuroscience*, *9*, 266–276.

Van Orden, G. C. (1987). A ROWS is a ROSE: spelling, sound, and reading. *Memory and Cognition*, *15*, 181–198.

Vigliocco, G., Vinson, D. P., Martin, R. C., & Garrett, M. F. (1999). Is 'count' and 'mass' information available when the noun is not? An investigation of tip of the tongue states and anomia. *Journal of Memory and Language*, *40*, 534–558.

Wang, E., Peach, R. K., Xu, Y., Schneck, M., & Manry, C. (2000). Perception of dynamic acoustic patterns by an individual with unilateral verbal auditory agnosia. *Brain and Language, 73*, 442–455.

Warrington, E. K., & McCarthy, R. (1987). Categories of knowledge: further fractionation and an attempted integration. *Brain, 100*, 1273–1296.

Warrington, E. K., & Shallice, T. (1984). Category-specific semantic impairments. *Brain, 107*, 829–853.

Waters, G., Caplan, D., & Hildebrandt, N. (1991). On the structure of verbal short-term memory and its functional role in sentence comprehension: evidence from neuropsychology. *Cognitive Neuropsychology, 8*, 81–126.

Wernicke, C. (1874). *Der aphasische Symptomenkomplex*. Breslau: Cohn Weigert. (Translated in Eggert, G. 1977. *Wernicke's works on aphasia*. The Hague: Mouton.)

Wise, R. J. S., Scott, S. K., Blank, S. C., Mummery, C. J., Murphy, K., & Warburton, E. A. (2001). Separate neural subsystems within 'Wernicke's area'. *Brain, 124*, 83–95.

Wu, D. H., Martin, R. C., & Damian, M. F. (2002). A third route for reading? Implications from a case of phonological dyslexia. *Neurocase, 8*, 274–293.

Zingeser, L. B., & Berndt, R. S. (1988). Grammatical class and context effects in a case of pure anomia: implications for models of language production. *Cognitive Neuropsychology, 5*, 473–516.

Zingeser, L. B., & Berndt, R. S. (1990). Retrieval of nouns and verbs in agrammatism and anomia. *Brain and Language, 39*, 14–32.

PART SIX

Modelling Cognition

18

Mathematical Modelling of Cognition

KOEN LAMBERTS

Mathematical models are essential in many scientific disciplines. Physicists, engineers, economists and biologists make extensive use of mathematical and formal techniques to express, develop and test scientific theories. In psychology, mathematical models have a long tradition too. From the earliest days of experimental psychology, theorists have attempted to construct formal models that capture the regularities of behaviour and cognition (see Luce, Bush, & Galanter, 1963, 1965).

There are many reasons why mathematical models can be superior to other kinds of models (such as informal verbal theories). First, mathematical models must be precise and consistent. A mathematical or computational model that contains elements that are ill-defined or that contradict each other will simply not work. Second, this definitional and conceptual precision implies that mathematically formulated theories are easily communicated. This can be an important advantage, especially for theories that are highly complex or that contain a large number of components. Third, mathematical models have an important role as analytical tools. They can be used to test hypotheses about cognition that would be difficult to test in any other way.

In this chapter, I attempt to give an introduction to some of the basic principles of mathematical modelling in psychology. The chapter should be read in conjunction with the chapter by Myung, Pitt, and Kim (Chapter 19, this volume). First, I present the principles of formal model construction and some important distinctions that can be made between different types of cognitive modelling. Next, I discuss the role of parameters and parameter estimation in cognitive modelling. Finally, I show how formal models can be used as tools for testing hypotheses about cognitive processes.

CONSTRUCTING MODELS OF COGNITION

The construction of mathematical models is not fundamentally different from the construction of other kinds of theories. Typically, a formal model of cognition is formulated in an attempt to describe and explain a collection of data, and to generate predictions about new data sets. A good mathematical model can reveal patterns in data that may not be immediately obvious, and can form the basis of new (and perhaps surprising) predictions. To achieve this, formal models should not merely restate the main distinctions in the data. Instead, they should reveal underlying patterns and regularities, and provide descriptions that generalize to other data sets (see Myung, Pitt, & Kim, Chapter 19, this volume, for a detailed discussion of this issue).

Before a formal model can be constructed, a decision has to be made about the formalism that will be used and the type of model that will be developed. Although it is difficult to provide a principled taxonomy of formal models of cognition, there are some useful distinctions that can be made. An important distinction is that between 'black box' or behavioural models on the one hand, and information-processing models on the other hand (see Luce, 1999; Myung & Pitt, 2001). In a black-box model, the purpose is to formulate properties of observable behaviour, without making assumptions about unobservable internal processes. A simple example of such a model is Fechner's logarithmic model of the relation between physical stimulus magnitude or intensity and psychological (perceived) magnitude or intensity:

$$\Psi(x) = k \ln(x) \qquad (18.1)$$

in which $\Psi(x)$ is the (measurable) psychological magnitude or intensity of a stimulus with physical magnitude or intensity x, and k is a constant. Although this model relates a psychological variable to a physical variable, it does not say anything about the internal processes that give rise to the logarithmic relation between the two variables, and it is therefore a true black-box model.

Black-box models have a number of advantages (Luce, 1999). Because they contain observable variables, they are transparent and usually easy to test empirically (at least in principle). Of course, it may be difficult in practice to measure the variables with the necessary precision, but normally it should be possible to define very clearly what the model's predictions are and under which conditions these predictions can be verified. A second advantage of black-box models is that they tend to make few, if any, unverifiable assumptions. This also means that they often have few free parameters and limited flexibility (which is an advantage when it comes to model testing).

In modern psychology, black-box models are quite rare. The main reason for this seems to be that it is very difficult to find regularities of behaviour that lend themselves to a description in terms of a functional relation between observable variables, without recourse to assumptions about internal processing. In fact, much of the cognitive revolution that took place forty years ago was motivated by the failure to find black-box models of a wide range of complex behaviours that seemed to exhibit interesting regularities. These regularities could only be captured if assumptions about internal processes were incorporated in the models.

Information-processing models describe the nature of the processes that are assumed to occur between stimulus and response. They often take the form of flow diagrams, which specify the component stages of information transformation through the cognitive system. Information-processing models can be informal, if they only contain verbal descriptions of the component stages of information processing. Other information-processing models do specify the component stages of processing in a formal (usually mathematical) manner. Formal processing models can further be divided into two broad categories, *simulation models* and *algebraic models*.

Simulation models are usually expressed in terms of an effective procedure or algorithm, which indicates how input information is transformed into output information. For this reason, simulation models are also generally known as computational models. Usually, the processes that occur in simulation models are too complex to be specified as closed-form expressions (i.e. as functions that permit direct computation of outputs through assignment of values to variables; the formula for Fechner's law is an example of a closed-form expression). This implies that the model's procedures must be carried out explicitly (usually on a computer) in order to derive predictions from the model. In this sense, the model simulates cognitive processing. The computations that are carried out mimic those that underlie the cognitive processes that are modelled. The simulation program is thus assumed to be functionally equivalent to some aspect of the cognitive system.

Simulation models can take many different forms. Some models, such as production systems (e.g. Anderson, 1983; Klahr, Langley, & Neches, 1987; Newell, 1973, 1990), describe information processing as rule-based manipulation of structured symbolic expressions. Rule-based models have been used mainly to explain high-level cognitive processing, such as language comprehension and problem solving. Connectionist or neural-network models simulate cognitive processes by passing activation between relatively simple, neuron-like processing units or nodes (see Quinlan, 1991; Rumelhart & McClelland, 1986). Each node has an activation value (which can be discrete or continuous, depending on the type of model). The nodes are linked by connections that have a weight value. The weight of a connection determines how activation passes between the connected nodes. Connectionist models thus mimic essential properties of real networks of neurons in the brain. However, the analogy is often superficial. Single nodes in connectionist models of cognition rarely have the functional properties of real neurons. Often, a node in a connectionist model of cognition does not correspond to a single neuron in the brain. Instead, nodes can represent assemblies of neurons, entire brain regions, or (if little is known about the neural mechanisms that underlie a cognitive process) purely abstract cognitive entities such as a concept, a letter or a word. In the latter case, the connectionist model is purely functional, and a physiological or neural interpretation is not appropriate.

Another type of simulation model that is popular in cognitive psychology is the random-walk model (e.g. Nosofsky & Palmeri, 1997; Ratcliff, 1978; Van Zandt, Colonius, & Proctor, 2000). Random-walk models are sequential-sampling models, in which it is assumed that information (which can be perceptual or retrieved from memory) gradually accumulates in the course of processing. As an illustration, suppose that we want to model the process that underlies a binary decision, such as whether a letter on a computer display is an 'O' or a 'Q'. Figure 18.1 shows how this process can be represented as a random walk in a two-dimensional space.

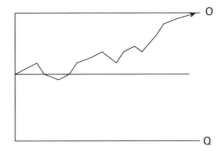

Figure 18.1 *Example of a random-walk process.*

The space is bounded by two response barriers, which represent an 'O' and a 'Q' response, respectively. A random-walk counter starts off on the midline between the response barriers. Information about the stimulus is sampled repeatedly. The sampling process is assumed to be noisy, so it does not always produce the same outcome. If the sampling process suggests that the stimulus is an 'O', the random-walk counter moves towards the 'O' barrier. If the sampling process indicates that a 'Q' is present, the counter moves in the opposite direction. Sampling is repeated until the counter reaches one of the two barriers, after which the corresponding response is produced. Random-walk models have been very successful in accounting for accuracy and response times in a wide range of tasks. They have the additional benefit that they are well understood, and that closed-form expressions can be found for many aspects of their behaviour (such as the expected termination time of the random walk; see Feller, 1968; Ratcliff, 1978). There are many other types of sequential-sampling models, such as race models (Logan, 1988, 1992; Pike, 1973; Townsend & Ashby, 1983), accumulator models (Smith & Vickers, 1988; Vickers, 1970, 1979), feature-sampling models (Lamberts, 2000), and so forth. All these models share the assumption that the time course of information processing somehow involves gradual accumulation of information.

Simulation models are widely used in cognitive psychology and cognitive science. Their popularity probably has several reasons, not all of which are entirely positive. One advantage of simulation models is that they are relatively easy to construct and modify, which often means that they can be adapted to accommodate new data without too much effort. However, this flexibility also has the drawback that it can make falsification of simulation models difficult. A second advantage of simulation models is that their complexity is of little practical concern. As long as the model can be translated into a working computer program, it is possible to generate predictions, no matter how complex the model might be. Although this can be of great benefit (cognitive processes tend to be very complex, after all), it can also remove

the incentive to do the hard conceptual work that produces simpler models that have more explanatory power (see Myung, Pitt, & Kim, Chapter 19, this volume, for a discussion of the role of simplicity in model evaluation).

Loftus (1985) discusses an interesting thought experiment that is highly relevant in this context. He asked what would have happened if Johannes Kepler, the sixteenth-century astronomer, had had a computer. In Kepler's days, the dominant Copernican view was that planetary motion was based on circular trajectories. To account for irregularities in planetary orbits, a system of interlocking epicycles was designed that could handle the discrepancies in the observational data, at the cost of increased theoretical complexity. It is likely that Kepler was driven to find an alternative account because the ever-increasing complexity of epicycle models (to account for increasingly accurate observational data) made them computationally impractical. The result was that Kepler discovered his famous theory of elliptical trajectories, and thereby laid the foundations of modern dynamical astronomy. It is quite possible that Kepler would never have made his fundamental discovery if he had been able to use a computer simulation of planetary motion. To explain new data, he would only have had to add a few more epicycle subroutines to the simulation program.

Algebraic processing models generate predictions about behaviour without simulation. They typically consist of a set of equations and rules for the application of these equations. The equations describe the component stages of information processing in detail, indicating the inputs and outputs of each stage. A good example of an algebraic processing model is Nosofsky's (1986, 1987, 1989, 1991) Generalized Context Model (GCM). The GCM is an exemplar model of categorization. It relies on the assumption that exemplars are stored in memory during category learning. If an object is presented for categorization, the GCM assumes that the category decision depends on the similarity of the object to the exemplars stored in memory. In the GCM, it is assumed that stimuli correspond to points in a space defined by the stimulus dimensions. Similarity is assumed to be a decreasing function of the distance between stimuli in the multidimensional stimulus space. Distance in the stimulus space is given by a weighted power model:

$$d_{ij} = c \left[\sum_{k=1}^{N} w_k \left| x_{ik} - x_{jk} \right|^r \right]^{1/r} \qquad (18.2)$$

in which $c > 0$, $0 \le w_k \le 1$, and $\sum w_k = 1$. In the equation, x_{ik} is the value of stimulus i on dimension k, N is the number of stimulus dimensions, c is a discriminability parameter, and w_k is the weight of dimension k in computing overall distance. The weight parameters serve to stretch or shrink the stimulus space along its coordinate axes. The value of r defines the type of distance metric. If $r = 1$, distance corresponds to a city-block metric, which is usually assumed to be appropriate for separable-dimension stimuli (Nosofsky, 1986). If $r = 2$, distances are Euclidean, which is usually optimal for integral dimension stimuli. Distance is then converted into similarity by an exponential transformation:

$$\eta_{ij} = \exp(-d_{ij}) \qquad (18.3)$$

The information about the similarity of a test stimulus to all the exemplars in memory enters the next component process, in which a category decision is made. Specifically, the probability that stimulus S_i is assigned to category R_J is given by the following choice rule:

$$P(R_J \mid S_i) = \frac{b_J \sum\limits_{j \epsilon C_J} \eta_{ij}}{\sum\limits_{K=1}^{m} (b_K \sum\limits_{k \epsilon C_K} \eta_{ik})} \qquad (18.4)$$

in which η_{ij} is the similarity between stimulus i and stored exemplar j, m is the number of categories, b_J represents the bias for making response J ($\sum b = 1$), and the index $j \epsilon C_J$ refers to all stored exemplars that belong to category J. The probability that a particular category is chosen is thus a function of the summed similarity of the stimulus to all exemplars from that category, divided by its similarity to all exemplars in memory.

The GCM is a proper algebraic model, because it can be used to predict categorization probabilities without the need for simulation. If all the free parameters in the model (c, r, the dimension weights and the bias parameters) are given a value (and the next section describes how this can be done), it is sufficient to enter the values of each training exemplar on each stimulus dimension into the equations, as well as the values of the test stimulus. The equations will then generate the probability that the test stimulus is classified in a given category, and this probability can be compared directly to the relative classification frequency in an actual experiment.

Algebraic models have considerable advantages over simulation models. Algebraic models tend to be more transparent and easier to understand, because the role of each parameter, variable and constant in the model is defined directly by the model equations. This often makes it much easier to understand the psychological meaning of the different model components. To assess the impact of a parameter on model predictions, for instance, analytical work can sometimes be sufficient. In a simulation model, the same assessment would be more elaborate.

There are other distinctions that can be made between formal models. Some models are deterministic, which means that they always generate the same predictions under the same conditions and assumptions. Other models are probabilistic, which means that their predictions depend on a stochastic process. Models can be linear or nonlinear, and static or dynamic. A good discussion of these distinctions and of the advantages and disadvantages of the different types of models can be found in Luce (1999).

PARAMETERS

Almost all formal models in cognitive psychology have free parameters. Why do we need them? The answer lies in the kinds of regularities about cognition and behaviour that we can hope to discover. It would be ideal if we were able to find laws of cognition that applied in the same way to everybody in all circumstances, and that contained only directly measurable quantities and universal constants. Although we cannot rule out that such parameter-free laws of cognition may be found eventually, there are good reasons to assume that this is highly unlikely. First, the cognitive system is incredibly complex. Even the simplest cognitive tasks (such as comparing the identity of two visually presented objects) involve a staggering range of sub-processes. It is unrealistic to expect that a single model can describe all these sub-processes in great detail, and yet that may be exactly what would be required in order to obtain a strong, parameter-free account. In practice, formal models of cognition tend to focus on a very small subset of processes, and make simplifying assumptions about the other processes that are inevitably involved.

A second factor concerns individual differences. Genetic and situational variables determine the cognitive make-up of an individual, and although we do not understand these influences and cannot measure them, somehow we still have to allow for their effects in the cognitive models that we develop. The importance of individual differences seems to depend on the processes that are studied. For instance, the processes that underlie low-level vision probably exhibit far less inter-individual variation than the processes involved in problem solving or reasoning. A third relevant factor is the intrinsic non-stationarity of the cognitive system (see Luce, 1997, 1999). People's cognitive processes are subject to constant change and fluctuation, as a result of learning, maturation, and so forth. These changes tend to be irreversible, which poses serious challenges for cognitive modelling, and for model testing in particular (Luce, 1999).

So, the cognitive modeller is faced with a highly complex system that differs between individuals and that changes over time. Yet the aim is to explain the regularities of this system. The only way to achieve this aim is to accept the uncertainty that will be intrinsic to any workable account, and to build parametric models. The parameters can express uncertainty that stems from individual differences and previous experience, or uncertainty about processes that are not part of the model. Inevitably, this weakens the model's ability to make unique predictions, because the predictions depend on the values of the model parameters. This is one of the reasons why some researchers in cognitive psychology are somewhat suspicious about models that contain free parameters (e.g. Roberts & Pashler, 2000). Often, such models give the impression that they are too flexible to be useful, because they can be made to fit many different data patterns, and they may therefore appear difficult to falsify. However, although models with free parameters may not make unique predictions, they usually do not predict just anything. Predictions vary across the parameter space, but the prediction space is usually bounded. If data are observed that lie outside the prediction space (i.e. if there is no combination of parameter values that produces predictions that match the data), a model can still be rejected.

The testability of a model not only depends on the number of parameters, but also on the functional form of the model (Bamber & Van Santen, 1985; Myung & Pitt, 2001). It is premature to dismiss models without analysing flexibility in relation to functional form. Recent techniques for model evaluation explicitly incorporate these ideas (see Myung, 2000; Myung & Pitt, 1997; Pitt, Myung, & Zhang, 2002; Myung, Pitt, & Kim, Chapter 19, this volume).

It is important to note that model parameters are not always independent. For instance, in the GCM, one dimension weight is estimated for each stimulus dimension. However, the sum of these weights must be 1. This implies that the value of one weight is completely determined by the sum of the other weights, so the number of independent weight parameters in the model is effectively 1 less than the number of stimulus dimensions (see Bamber & Van Santen, 1985, for a formal definition of parameter independence).

GOODNESS-OF-FIT

Before a model can be applied, values must be assigned to its parameters. If a model is correct, then its parameters have true values. Sometimes it is possible to assign parameter values beforehand, based on analysis or on previous applications of the model. For instance, if we are applying a mathematical model of learning to a new data set, we may be able to set the value of a learning-rate parameter

in the model on the basis of estimates obtained from previous experiments. However, we usually do not know what the true parameter values are before we can apply a model, and in those circumstances parameter estimation becomes important.

The idea behind parameter estimation is quite simple. Given that we do not know the true values of the parameters in a model, we can at least guess what these values are, on the basis of the data that we have available. The main objective of parameter estimation is to find a set of parameter values that maximizes the correspondence between the observed values and the values predicted by the model. This process is sometimes also called *model optimization*. The correspondence between observed and predicted values is usually defined by a measure of *goodness-of-fit*. Optimization involves a search for the combination of parameter values that produces predictions that maximize the goodness-of-fit function.

Which measure of goodness-of-fit is appropriate in a given situation depends on different factors, such as whether the data are discrete or continuous, which assumptions can be made about the distribution of noise in the data, and so forth. Model parameters are almost always chosen on the basis of some form of *maximum-likelihood* criterion. The idea behind such a criterion is that parameter values should be chosen that maximize the likelihood that the observed data occurred if the model were true.

Let us consider discrete data first. Discrete data represent the frequency of observations in each of a number of categories. A model for discrete data predicts the frequency in each category, and a useful measure of goodness-of-fit for such data measures the discrepancy between observed counts and predicted counts. Sometimes it is possible to compute exact likelihood values, and use the likelihood function as a goodness-of-fit function in model optimization. Suppose that there are J categories in some data set, and that $\mathbf{F} = (F_1, F_2, ..., F_J)$ is a vector of observed frequencies within each category. It is assumed that the frequencies arise from N independent observations or trials, such that each trial generates an observation that is assigned to a single category. A model for these data predicts the probability that observations are assigned to each category, and these probabilities form the vector $\mathbf{P} = (P_1, P_2, ..., P_J)$. The probabilities depend on the model's parameter values. Using these probabilities, the likelihood of the data set can be worked out, because the response frequencies will have a multinomial distribution (see, e.g., Hays, 1988):

$$L(\mathbf{X}, \mathbf{P}) = N! \prod_{j=1}^{J} P_j^{F_j} / F_j! \qquad (18.5)$$

Because likelihood values computed in this way can become very small, causing undesirable underflow and round-off errors in the computation, it is often more convenient to compute the logarithm of the likelihood (called the *log-likelihood*) and use that in parameter estimation. The logarithm is a monotone transformation, which implies that the parameter values that maximize log-likelihood also maximize likelihood. The multinomial log-likelihood function is

$$\ln L(\mathbf{X}, \mathbf{P}) = \ln N! - \sum_{j=1}^{J} \ln F_j!$$
$$+ \sum_{j=1}^{J} F_j \cdot \ln P_j \qquad (18.6)$$

The product in the likelihood function is replaced in the log-likelihood function by a sum, which can be computed more easily.

In many discrete data sets, there is more than one category system. This is the case for data from categorization or identification experiments, for instance, where people have to assign a label to each of a number of different stimuli (e.g. Nosofsky, 1989). The data take the form of a confusion matrix, which lists the frequency of each response for each stimulus. The data for each stimulus are multinomially distributed, and these distributions are assumed to be independent. A model for the entire data set is called a joint multinomial model (Riefer & Batchelder, 1988), and the likelihood for such a model is given by the product of the separate multinomial likelihoods (see also Wickens, 1982: 119). The log-likelihood for a joint multinomial model is simply the sum of the separate multinomial log-likelihoods.

Another approach to goodness-of-fit for discrete data uses statistics from the so-called power divergence family (Cressie & Read, 1984; Read & Cressie, 1988). This approach is useful when it is not practical to compute exact likelihood values. Two of the best-known examples from this family are Pearson's X^2:

$$X^2 = \sum_{j=1}^{J} \frac{(F_j - N \cdot P_j)^2}{N \cdot P_j} \qquad (18.7)$$

and the log-likelihood ratio G^2:

$$G^2 = 2 \sum_{j=1}^{J} F_j \ln [F_j / (N \cdot P_j)] \qquad (18.8)$$

Both statistics apply directly to multinomially distributed data, and both can be extended to data that have a joint multinomial distribution. Note that X^2 and G^2 are actually measures of lack of fit, with larger values indicating worse correspondence between predictions and observations. Model parameters can be estimated that minimize the value of X^2 or G^2. One advantage of this approach is that it immediately offers a test of goodness-of-fit of the model (see Wickens, 1982), because both X^2 and G^2

have an asymptotic chi-square distribution, with degrees of freedom equal to $J - T - 1$, where T is the number of estimated model parameters.

The goodness-of-fit measures discussed so far apply only to discrete data (such as choice frequencies). When data are continuous, other indices of goodness-of-fit must be used. One commonly used measure is the residual sum of squares (RSS), which is defined as follows:

$$\text{RSS} = \sum_{j=1}^{n} (obs_j - pred_j)^2 \qquad (18.9)$$

in which n is the number of observations, obs_j is the observed value j, and $pred_j$ is the corresponding value predicted by the model. Large values of RSS indicate that the model predictions do not correspond well to the observed values. When RSS is used in model optimization, parameter values are chosen such that RSS becomes as small as possible. Parameter estimates obtained in this way are maximum-likelihood estimates, if each observed data point corresponds to the sum of a value predicted by the model, and an error value, drawn at random from an independent normal distribution with mean zero and fixed variance (see, e.g., Borowiak, 1989, for a proof).

Another popular measure of goodness-of-fit is the coefficient of variation, commonly called R^2:

$$R^2 = 1 - \frac{\text{RSS}}{\text{TSS}} \qquad (18.10)$$

in which the total sum of squares, TSS, is given by

$$\text{TSS} = \sum_{j=1}^{n} (obs_j - \overline{obs})^2 \qquad (18.11)$$

R^2, which is of course closely related to RSS, can have values between 0 (indicating very poor fit) and 1 (when predicted values correspond exactly to observed values). There are many other measures of goodness-of-fit for discrete and continuous data (see Myung, Pitt, & Kim, Chapter 19, this volume, and Read & Cressie, 1988, for further discussion). Their correct use depends on a careful consideration of their properties and assumptions.

An issue that merits some further discussion concerns the definition of goodness-of-fit statistics for *distributions* of continuous variables. A typical example is the distribution of response times (RTs) in an experiment. A model of these data could either specify an explicit probability density function for the response times, or it could simulate a large number of trials to generate distribution predictions. In both cases, a number of different techniques can be used to establish the correspondence between the observed and predicted distributions (see Van Zandt, 2000, for an excellent overview). One approach to fitting RT distributions uses the

Pearson X^2 statistic, or the G^2 statistic. In this approach, the observed data are sorted and placed in bins. For instance, the first bin would contain all trials with response times between 100 and 150 ms, the second bin all trials with response times between 151 and 200 ms, and so forth. The model is used to obtain predicted frequencies in each bin (either analytically, if an explicit density function is specified, or through simulation of a large number of trials). The observed and predicted frequencies are entered into the standard equation for X^2 or G^2, providing a measure of goodness-of-fit. The goodness-of-fit measure can then be used to estimate model parameter values (by minimizing X^2 or G^2 in the normal way). Alternative methods involve the computation of exact likelihood values or residual sums of squares.

Whenever a formal model is applied to data, one needs to be absolutely clear about the level of aggregation at which the model applies. Because behaviour is noisy and subject to uncontrollable variation between and within individuals, it is almost always necessary in psychology to replicate the data collection process. This usually involves testing a number of subjects in the same conditions, and repeating the experimental procedure many times for each subject. Averaging data across subjects and trials can then be used to cancel out noise in the data, and to produce more reliable and stable parameter estimates.

Unfortunately, when it comes to formal modelling, averaging is not without risks. If the model aims to account for an individual's behaviour (which is usually the case), data obtained by averaging across groups of subjects can provide misleading information about the model's validity. In the worst possible scenario, average data can support a model that does not apply to any of the individuals in the group. Averaging can therefore make an incorrect model appear correct – it can produce spurious regularity (Estes, 1956; Newell, 1973). Generally, averaging is not acceptable in conditions where it affects the underlying structure of the data (Ashby, Maddox, & Lee, 1994; Luce, 1997; Maddox, 1999; Myung, Kim, & Pitt, 2000). If the data were generated by a nonlinear process, and if there are large individual differences in the characteristics of this process, averaging is likely to distort the data and to cause difficulties for model evaluation. In those cases, averaging should be avoided altogether, or a special, model-preserving averaging function should be used, the form of which depends on the model that is being evaluated (Myung et al., 2000).

A particularly compelling example of the dangers of averaging can be found in studies that purported to support the power law of practice. For a long time, it had been assumed that a power function provides an accurate description of the relation between practice and response times in a wide range of tasks (e.g. Anderson, 1982; Logan, 1992; Newell &

Rosenbloom, 1981). However, almost all the evidence favouring this law was obtained by averaging performance across subjects (Heathcote, Brown, & Mewhort, 2000). In a careful analysis of previous studies, Heathcote et al. (2000) demonstrated that an exponential function (which belongs to an entirely different family of functions than the power function and behaves differently) tended to perform much better when data from individual subjects were used as the unit of analysis. Averaging across subjects appears to have produced data that favoured a power function (see also Anderson & Tweney, 1997; Myung et al., 2000), although this function was not appropriate for most subjects.

Aggregating data across subjects poses special difficulties if one is interested in modelling distributions (of response times, or some other continuous dependent variable). Although the distributions from each subject can have roughly the same shape, they may differ in mean and variance. If the data are aggregated, the resulting distribution has a shape that may be very different from that of the individual distributions. One solution to this problem is called Vincent averaging (Ratcliff, 1979). This technique produces a group distribution, by arranging the data from each subject in ascending order, and computing quantiles for each subject. The quantiles are then averaged across subjects to obtain a group distribution. Ratcliff (1979) has shown that Vincent averaging preserves the shape of individual distributions of response times, although Van Zandt (2000) subsequently demonstrated that other techniques (such as Gaussian kernel estimation) may produce better results.

Parameter Estimation

Once a goodness-of-fit measure has been defined, parameter values can be estimated. Sometimes, parameter estimation can be done analytically. This is the case for many linear models, such as linear regression models. Analytical estimation is achieved by taking the partial derivatives of the goodness-of-fit function with respect to each parameter, setting the partial derivatives equal to zero, and solving the resulting set of equations. Illustrations of this method can be found in any textbook of mathematical statistics (see also Riefer & Batchelder, 1988; Wickens, 1982). However, for most nonlinear models, analytical parameter estimation is impossible, either because the goodness-of-fit function cannot be differentiated, or because the resulting set of equations cannot be solved. For those models, parameters have to be estimated using numerical techniques. These techniques usually involve a search through the parameter space, in an attempt to discover the parameter values that maximize the goodness-of-fit of the model.

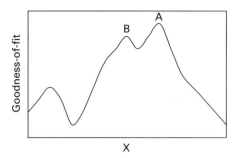

Figure 18.2 *Example of a goodness-of-fit function.* X *is a parameter,* A *is a global maximum, and* B *is a local maximum.*

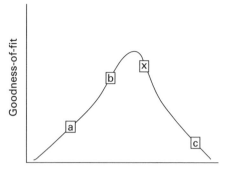

Figure 18.3 *Example of a bracketing triplet in golden section search. The points* a, b *and* c *form the bracketing triplet.* x *is a new point.*

Numerical parameter estimation can be done using a wide range of different techniques. In many commercial software packages (such as spreadsheets or packages for data analysis), built-in algorithms for optimization are provided. Although these algorithms tend to be versatile and sophisticated, they can have practical limitations. For some modelling problems, the general-purpose algorithms in such packages tend to be too slow or unwieldy, and in those cases alternative solutions should be considered. In this chapter, I can only provide a very limited overview of some of the most common optimization algorithms, but I shall attempt to provide some insight into their main features.

The simplest optimization problem occurs when there is only one free parameter. In that case, the goodness-of-fit function can be represented by a simple graph, such as the one shown in Figure 18.2. The graph shows how goodness-of-fit varies as a function of the value of X, the model parameter. The point labelled 'A' represents the global maximum of the function, and this is the point that we wish to find using our optimization routine. Point 'B' represents a local maximum, which is the highest point in a defined region of the parameter space, but not the highest point overall. The main risk in numerical optimization is that a local maximum can be mistaken for a global maximum. Especially with models that have many parameters and in which the goodness-of-fit function is highly irregular, there is a real risk that the optimization procedure will fail to find a truly global maximum. There are several ways to reduce this risk, but unfortunately it can never be ruled out completely without exhaustive mapping of the goodness-of-fit function for the entire parameter space (which is usually not feasible – see below). The best we can hope for is that the goodness-of-fit function is sufficiently well behaved and the optimization procedure sufficiently sophisticated to minimize the risk associated with local maxima.

Returning to the single-parameter optimization problem, how can we locate a maximum such as the one shown in Figure 18.2? The simplest method

would be to evaluate the goodness-of-fit function for a very large number of parameter values (going from a small parameter value to a high parameter value in small steps), and to simply pick the parameter value that produced the highest goodness-of-fit. Although this grid search procedure can work in practice, it is not very satisfactory. Depending on the required precision of the parameter estimate, the number of parameter values that must be evaluated can be very high. And although the procedure might just work in the single-parameter case, it quickly becomes unusable if there are more model parameters. Suppose there are four parameters, and we want to evaluate 1000 different values of each parameter – that leaves us with 1,000,000,000,000 evaluations of the goodness-of-fit function.

More sophisticated numerical methods for parameter estimation exploit the fact that goodness-of-fit functions are usually not entirely haphazard, but exhibit at least some regularity. In many models, parameter values that are close together tend to produce goodness-of-fit values that are close together, and this property can be used to make parameter estimation easier. Of course, there are models that generate highly irregular goodness-of-fit functions, such as models of chaotic phenomena. In such models, even a tiny change in a parameter can produce a dramatic difference in the predictions. Traditional parameter estimation techniques will not work very well with such models. Fortunately, this is hardly ever a concern in formal models of cognition.

An effective method for solving the single-parameter optimization problem is the *golden section search method*. This method starts with three points (i.e. three parameter values), a, b and c, that are chosen such that $a < b < c$, $GOF(b) > GOF(a)$, and $GOF(b) > GOF(c)$ (GOF stands for goodness-of-fit). If these conditions are met, the three points a, b and c are called a bracketing triplet (see Figure 18.3).

The goodness-of-fit function must have a maximum somewhere between a and c. The aim of golden section search is to make the bracketing interval sufficiently small to obtain an estimate of the maximum with the desired precision. This is done initially by choosing a new point x in the interval (a, b) or in the interval (b, c). The goodness-of-fit function is evaluated for this new point. Suppose first that x was chosen somewhere in the interval (a, b). If $GOF(x)$ is better than $GOF(b)$, then the new bracketing triplet contains x as the middle point, and a and b as outer points, so the new bracketing triplet becomes (a, x, b). If, on the contrary, $GOF(x)$ is worse than $GOF(b)$, the new bracketing triplet is (x, b, c). If x was initially chosen from the interval (b, c), then the new triplet becomes (b, x, c) if $GOF(x) > GOF(b)$ (see Figure 18.3), or (a, b, x) if $GOF(x) < GOF(b)$. In other words, the procedure works by choosing a new point x in the original interval. If the GOF of x is better than the best estimate at the moment (which is b), then x becomes the new best estimate (i.e. the middle point of the bracketing interval) and b becomes an outer boundary of the bracketing interval. If the GOF of x is not better than the best estimate thus far (b), then b remains as the best estimate, but x now becomes an outer boundary of the bracketing interval. In either case, the bracketing interval shrinks, and this procedure is repeated until the bracketing interval is sufficiently small (according to some predetermined precision setting). When the bracketing interval is small enough, the middle point is retained as the estimated parameter value.

Although the new points x can be chosen in any way as long as they are within the current bracketing interval, the efficiency of the procedure depends very much on the choice of x at each iteration. It turns out that there is an optimal way of choosing the new point x at every step (see Press, Flannery, Teukolsky, & Vetterling, 1989, for a simple proof). If, in the current bracketing triplet, $(c - b) > (b - a)$, then the best choice of x equals $b + 0.382 (c - b)$. If, on the other hand, $(c - b) < (b - a)$, then the best choice of x is $b - 0.382 (b - a)$. So, the best choice for x is always a fraction of 0.328 into the larger of the two intervals (a, b) and (b, c), measured from the point b. This fraction, 0.328, is the smaller part of the traditional golden section (which divides a length such that the smaller part is to the greater as the greater is to the whole), from which the optimization method derives its name.

There are many other methods for single-parameter optimization. Some, such as Brent's (1973) method, use parabolic interpolation. If a function looks somewhat like a parabola near its maximum (which is the case for many well-behaved functions), fitting a parabola through three points with known function values can be used to approach the maximum very rapidly. Other methods use information about derivatives to make the search more efficient (see Acton, 1970; Press et al., 1989). However, the derivatives of goodness-of-fit

functions of psychological models are often not available, so these methods are of limited practical use in cognitive modelling. For most purposes, golden section search is the most practical and reliable single-parameter search method.

If a model has more than one parameter, searching for the parameter values that yield the best GOF becomes much more difficult. Depending on the form of the model, the goodness-of-fit function can be very complex, with a large number of local maxima. It is not surprising, therefore, that considerable effort has been devoted to the design of optimization procedures that attempt to make the search process as efficient as possible (Brent, 1973; Jacobs, 1977). Still, no procedure is guaranteed to work with any model and any data set. With complex models, it is usually a good idea to carry out the parameter estimation process several times, from different starting points in the parameter space. If all these trials converge on the same set of optimal values, one can be reasonably confident that a truly global maximum has been found. Sometimes, careful formal analysis of the model's behaviour can reveal useful information about the shape of the goodness-of-fit function in different regions of the parameter space, and this information can further bolster confidence in the optimality of the solution that has been found.

To illustrate some of the difficulties that have to be overcome in multiple parameter estimation, consider what can happen if an unsophisticated, but intuitively appealing, method is applied. Suppose that we have a model with two parameters, and that we try to find a maximum of the goodness-of-fit function by applying the golden section search method that was explained above. We could do this by choosing a starting point in the two-dimensional parameter space (based on our best guess about where the maximum of the goodness-of-fit function might be located). We could then keep the value of the second parameter fixed at its chosen starting value, and apply golden section search to find the best-fitting value of the first parameter (given the fixed value of the second parameter, of course). When that value has been found, we keep the first parameter fixed at its new value, and apply golden section search to the second parameter. We then fix the second parameter at its new value, and repeat the search procedure with the first parameter. We then fix the first parameter, and return to the second parameter, and so forth. If this alternating optimization procedure is repeated many times, there is every chance that the best-fitting simultaneous values of both parameters will be found.

There is nothing fundamentally wrong with this technique. The technique might even work with models that have many free parameters. By repeatedly cycling through the set of parameters, optimizing one at a time, an (at least locally) optimal set of

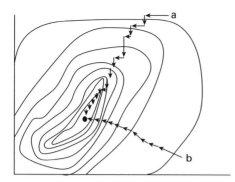

Figure 18.4   *Contour plot of the goodness-of-fit function of a two-parameter model. The black dot represents the global maximum.* a *represents the search path generated by a successive single-parameter optimization method.* b *is the search path that moves along the gradient.*

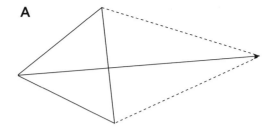

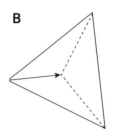

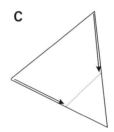

Figure 18.5   *Possible steps in simplex optimization: (a) reflection; (b) unidimensional contraction; (c) multidimensional contraction. The solid triangle represents the original simplex, and the dashed lines represent the new simplex.*

values will eventually be found. However, the procedure has the drawback that it can be incredibly inefficient. Consider the goodness-of-fit function shown in the contour plot in Figure 18.4. This plot represents the goodness-of-fit values for a model with two parameters, x and y. The global maximum of the function is marked with a black dot. Suppose we start our search at the point labelled a. Because the optimization procedure only permits moves along the direction of the axes (as only one parameter is changed at each step), the approach along the narrow ridge close to the maximum takes a very large number of small steps. The situation is similar to climbing a mountain that has a summit to the south-west, while only being allowed to travel either to the south or to the west, which is not very efficient.

A more efficient search path is the one shown from starting point b in Figure 18.4. This path always moves in the steepest uphill direction or *gradient*. To determine the gradient, one needs to be able to calculate not only the value of the GOF function, but also the partial derivatives of the function with respect to each of the parameters. This is often not possible analytically. There are methods that attempt to determine the gradient numerically, but they are quite complex and beyond the scope of this chapter (see Press et al., 1989).

An interesting and robust method for optimization of models with multiple parameters is Nelder and Mead's (1965) simplex method. Although this method is not particularly efficient, it has the advantage that it can be applied almost everywhere, and that it does not require any knowledge about derivatives of the goodness-of-fit function. The method uses the concept of a *simplex*. A simplex is a geometrical

figure that consists of a number of interconnected points. In Nelder and Mead's (1965) method, a simplex is defined in a space with the same number of dimensions as there are model parameters. The simplex has one point more than there are parameters. So, if there are two parameters in a model, the simplex has three interconnected points (and thus corresponds to a triangle in a two-dimensional space; see Figure 18.5). Each point of the simplex represents one set of parameter values. The method starts with an initial simplex (preferably based on a good guess of where the maximum of the GOF function might be located). The GOF at each point of the simplex is evaluated. The method then takes one of three possible steps (the choice of step depends on a test that determines what will produce the best result):

1   A reflection from the worst point to a better point through the opposite face of the simplex. This reflection may also involve an expansion away from the worst point.
2   A one-dimensional contraction away from the worst point.
3   A multidimensional contraction towards the best point.

Figure 18.5 illustrates these three possibilities, for a simplex with three points. The method iterates until the simplex becomes sufficiently small, and the best point of that small simplex is returned as the estimated parameter vector.

The optimization techniques that I have discussed so far all assume that parameters are continuous, and that the goodness-of-fit function is at least somewhat well behaved (i.e. reasonably smooth and continuous). This is not always the case – the goodness-of-fit function may not be continuous. This can happen in models with discrete (e.g. integer) parameters, or in models that contain threshold functions, for instance. The goodness-of-fit function of such a model can be entirely flat in a region of the parameter space, but suddenly jump to a different value when a boundary in the parameter space is crossed. The optimization methods that I discussed can run into difficulties with such models, because they will tend to wander around aimlessly along the featureless plains of the parameter space, and may fail to cross the ridge that would suddenly take them to the summit of the goodness-of-fit function.

Optimization of discrete models (or of models that combine discrete and continuous elements) is not impossible, but it requires different techniques from those that I have sketched. Two techniques are worth mentioning here. *Genetic algorithms* (see Goldberg, 1989; Holland, 1975; Vose, 1999) use a biological analogy to the solution of optimization problems. A genetic algorithm operates on a set of individuals, each of which represents a possible solution (not necessarily a *good* solution!) of an optimization problem (in the case of cognitive modelling, each individual would represent a particular set of parameter values). Typically, the individuals are represented as binary strings, and one can think of these strings as the genetic material or genome of the individuals. Each individual has a fitness value (which, in cognitive modelling, corresponds to the goodness-of-fit of the model that uses the parameter values represented by the individual). The genetic algorithm operates by selecting individuals on the basis of their fitness (in such a way that fitter individuals have a higher selection probability), and allowing them to reproduce. The offspring that is the result of reproduction is not identical to the parents. Changes that can occur in reproduction include mutations (in which random changes are made to the individuals), cross-overs (in which

individuals exchange parts of their material, and pass this new combination on to the offspring), inversions (in which sections of material are reversed), insertions and deletions. Other operations are possible as well – the nature of the optimization problem will determine what works best. The offspring then replaces the weakest individuals in the pool, and the process of selection and reproduction starts again. This cycle continues until there are no further increases in the fitness of the fittest individual in the pool within some predetermined number of reproductive cycles.

Despite their simplicity and apparent lack of sophistication, genetic algorithms are very useful. They work very well with discrete models and with mixed discrete–continuous models. Their main drawback is that they can be slow and computationally expensive. Still, they can provide solutions to optimization problems that would be intractable by other means.

A second technique that can be used with discrete models is called *simulated annealing* (Kirkpatrick, Gellatt, & Vecchi, 1983). In thermodynamics, annealing refers to the process of heating and slowly cooling a substance. If the cooling process is slow, a strong crystalline structure will be obtained. In simulated annealing for model optimization, an initial set of parameter values is chosen. These values are then modified at random, and the goodness-of-fit of the new set is evaluated. If the goodness-of-fit is better than the goodness-of-fit of the initial set, the changes are accepted and the new set becomes the current best set. However, if the goodness-of-fit of the new set is worse than that of the initial set, there are two possible courses of action. The first is to reject the new set, and to try a new random distortion of the original set. The second possibility is that the new set is accepted anyway. The choice between these two courses is probabilistic – normally, the first option is more probable than the second. The result is a system that normally moves consistently towards higher goodness-of-fit values, but that sometimes deliberately takes a downward step. This allows the system to jump out of local minima, which makes the method extremely useful for optimization problems that have complex goodness-of-fit functions with many local minima.

The techniques that I have discussed so far will only work well if the goodness-of-fit function is deterministically related to the model parameters. This means that the model will always produce exactly the same predictions for a given set of parameter values. The GCM is an example of a deterministic model. The GCM predicts a choice probability, and a given set of parameter values will always produce the same prediction. In many models, however, the relation between parameters and predictions is probabilistic.

This is the case in stochastic simulation models, for example. In these simulation models, a random-number generator is used to simulate the stochastic elements of cognitive processes. Examples of this class of models are random-walk models and some connectionist simulation models. Because of its random nature, each run of the simulation model can produce different predictions, even without changing the values of the model parameters. For instance, a random-walk model of binary decision-making may terminate after 11 random steps on one run, and after 7 random steps on another run, with the same parameter values. This trial-by-trial variability will cause great difficulties for standard optimization methods. Most techniques designed for deterministic models will simply fail to converge with stochastic simulation models. One solution to this problem involves replicating the simulation many times on each function evaluation step of the optimization process, and computing mean predictions across all these replications. If the number of replications is large enough, the means will be sufficiently stable to permit the application of a standard optimization algorithm. How many replications are needed to achieve stability depends entirely on the nature of the model and the required precision of the parameter estimates (see Kleijnen, 1987). This technique has the obvious drawback that it may require a large number of replications of the simulation procedure, which could prove impractical. Sometimes it is possible to start the optimization process with a relatively small number of replications to obtain an initial estimate of the model parameters. This estimate can then be refined by increasing the number of replications in subsequent optimization, using the estimates from the first round as starting values.

Another approach to parameter estimation in stochastic simulation models uses an optimization algorithm that has been designed specifically for noisy models. Examples of such algorithms are Subplex (Rowan, 1990), which is based on the Simplex algorithm, and implicit filtering (Kelley, 1999).

MODEL-BASED DATA ANALYSIS

Formal modelling of cognition can have several different purposes. It can be used to test a theory about some cognitive process. By translating the theory into a formal model and evaluating the model, the value of the theory can be assessed. Myung, Pitt, and Kim (Chapter 19, this volume) provide a detailed discussion of the complex issues surrounding model evaluation, and I shall therefore not pursue this topic further. Instead, I shall focus on another purpose of cognitive modelling, which concerns the use of formal modelling to incorporate theoretical assumptions in data analysis (e.g. Riefer and Batchelder, 1988). Formal models can be used to test hypotheses, in a number of different ways.

In one approach, the estimated parameter values of a formal model are treated as data in their own right, and analysed using standard statistical techniques. In this approach, the model is essentially used as a descriptive or measurement tool, and testing the model's validity is not of primary concern – in fact, the model's validity is a precondition of the analysis.

As an example, suppose that we are interested in the difference in learning rate in a classification task between a group of subjects who receive immediate feedback, and a group who receive delayed feedback. All subjects take part in a learning task that consists of 200 trials. On each trial, a response is required. Subjects in one condition receive feedback immediately after each response, whereas subjects in the delayed condition receive feedback after a short interval. The data for each subject consist of an ordered sequence of 200 numbers (0's and 1's), where 0 indicates an error and 1 indicates a correct response. We want to find out whether the subjects in one group learned to do the task faster than the subjects in the other group.

Finding the answer to this question can be surprisingly difficult. One method that could be used consists of a straightforward analysis of the number of errors made by each subject in each condition (see, e.g., Medin & Schwanenflugel, 1981). This method relies on the assumption that the proportion of errors accurately reflects the learning rate. That may not be the case, however. The meaning of an error with respect to learning rate depends on the trial on which the error occurred. A subject who makes 100 errors on the first 150 trials, and makes no more errors thereafter, has clearly learned more than a subject who makes 100 errors that are evenly spread across the 200 trials. Another method involves counting the number of trials needed by a subject to reach a performance criterion. For instance, a typical criterion could be an uninterrupted run of 10 or 15 correct responses. Although this method is better than the first, it has the problem that criterion choice is largely arbitrary. If the criterion is too strict or too lenient, it will not differentiate properly between high and low learning rates. The results of this analysis can be manipulated by modifying the criterion, and that is obviously not desirable. Yet another method consists of grouping the data in blocks of trials (say, 10 blocks of 20 trials), computing mean accuracy scores in each block for each subject, and then analysing the means (using an ANOVA or another statistical technique). Inferences can then be based on a joint consideration of the main effects of feedback condition and block, and of their interaction. This method is not bad at all, but it still requires informal interpretation of the results to draw any conclusions about learning rates. A significant interaction between trial block and feedback condition can have many different causes, and the significance tests themselves will not reveal much about these. Another problem with this approach is that block size is arbitrary, although it can determine the outcome of the analysis.

The difficulties with the three analyses that were mentioned ultimately stem from their vagueness about the meaning of 'learning rate'. For the reasons that were mentioned, it is not very satisfactory to equate learning rate with total number of errors or number of trials needed to reach a criterion. In a situation like this, a model-based analysis can help. The function of the model is to provide an unambiguous definition of learning rate, and to provide a tool for measuring it. Suppose that we know from previous research that accuracy in categorization tasks increases exponentially with practice. We use this finding to define the following model of accuracy in our experiment:

$$P(\text{correct}, t) = 1 - \frac{\exp[-\lambda(t-1)]}{2} \quad (18.12)$$

The model has one parameter, λ, which corresponds to the learning rate (t is the trial number). On the first trial, when no learning has occurred, the predicted probability of a correct response is 0.5. This probability will increase with trial number, at a rate that depends entirely on λ.

This model can be applied to the data from each subject individually. Using one of the optimization methods described previously (golden section search is a good candidate), we try to find the best-fitting value of λ for each subject. Maximum likelihood can be used as the criterion for goodness-of-fit. As a result, we obtain an estimated learning rate for each subject. Of course, it is necessary to verify that the exponential model provides a reasonable account of the data for each subject. If the model is inadequate, the estimates may be meaningless. If the model is generally acceptable, then the estimated learning rates can be treated as data, and the difference between the feedback conditions can be tested (using a t-test, for instance, or a nonparametric equivalent). The exponential model thus served primarily as an analytical tool that facilitated measurement and hypothesis testing.

Another widely used technique for model-based analysis involves comparisons between nested models. Two models are nested if one of them is a restricted version of the other. A restricted version can be created by fixing one or more model parameters at certain values (so that they become constants in the model), by imposing constraints on parameter values (for instance, by imposing some restrictive relation between the values of different parameters), or by removing components from the general model. To be considered a restricted version

of a general model, a necessary (but not sufficient) condition is that the restricted model's predictions must also be obtainable from the general model. By choosing the appropriate restriction of a model and comparing the goodness-of-fit of the restricted model with that of the general model, specific hypotheses about the data can be tested.

If we return to our example about the effects of feedback on learning rate, we could test the hypothesis that learning rate differs between the groups by fitting two exponential learning models to the aggregated group data (which is risky, of course, but we shall ignore the perils of aggregation for the moment). The first model is the general model, which has two free parameters. One parameter is the learning rate in the immediate feedback group, and the other parameter is the learning rate in the delayed feedback group. The second model is a restricted version of the first. The restricted model has only one learning-rate parameter, which applies to both groups of subjects. The restricted model will fit the data worse than the general model (even if the restricted model is actually correct), because the general model is more flexible and can pick up some random variability in the data. Therefore, if we force λ to have the same value for both groups (as we do in the restricted model), we can expect to find a log-likelihood value that is smaller than that from the general model version. The crucial question is whether the difference between the model versions is greater than expected, if the restricted model is correct. If the difference in goodness-of-fit between the restricted and the general version is relatively small, this indicates that the additional flexibility of the general model is not necessary to explain the data. If the general model fits the data considerably better than the restricted version, the conclusion is that the restriction was not justified, and that the restricted model version is therefore not appropriate. Applied to the example, this would mean that the learning rates in the two groups differ reliably.

If log-likelihood is used as a measure of goodness-of-fit, a test of the reliability of a difference in goodness-of-fit between a restricted and a general model version is based on the likelihood-ratio statistic (and therefore called a likelihood-ratio test):

$$\chi^2 = -2[\ln L(\text{restricted}) - \ln L(\text{general})] \quad (18.13)$$

In this equation, $\ln L(\text{restricted})$ is the log-likelihood value of the restricted version, and $\ln L(\text{general})$ is the log-likelihood of the general version. If the restricted model version is correct, χ^2 has an approximate chi-squared distribution if sample size is sufficiently large. The degrees of freedom of this chi-squared distribution correspond to the number of parameters that were eliminated in the restricted model version, compared to the general version.

If χ^2 exceeds the critical value that corresponds to the conventional 95th or 99th percentile under the chi-squared distribution, the null hypothesis that the restricted model is correct is rejected.

If RSS is used as a measure of goodness-of-fit, the likelihood-ratio test has a slightly different form (although the underlying principle is exactly the same). Instead of the previous definition, χ^2 is defined as (Borowiak, 1989):

$$\chi^2 = -2 \ln \left[\frac{\text{RSS (general)}}{\text{RSS (restricted)}} \right]^{n/2} \qquad (18.14)$$

in which n is the number of data points. Again, χ^2 has an asymptotic chi-square distribution, with degrees of freedom equal to the number of restricted parameters.

Conclusions

Mathematical modelling is an essential tool in the study of cognition. Algebraic and simulation techniques can be used to create, explore and test complex models of cognitive processing. Formal models can also be used to test hypotheses about data that would otherwise be difficult to test. In this chapter, I have reviewed some elementary techniques that are used in mathematical modelling of cognition. Inevitably, I could provide little more than a basic introduction, but I hope I have been able to give some insight into the issues that need to be addressed in any attempt to build and test a mathematical model of cognition. In Myung, Pitt, and Kim's chapter (Chapter 19, this volume), many of the issues that I introduced are discussed in greater depth. Readers who want to explore the principles of mathematical modelling in psychology further should also find a wealth of useful material in Myung and Pitt (2001), Wickens (1982), Townsend and Ashby (1983), Luce (1986) and Myung et al. (2000).

References

Acton, F. S. (1970). *Numerical methods that work.* New York: Harper & Row.

Anderson, J. R. (1982). Acquisition of cognitive skills. *Psychological Review, 89,* 369–406.

Anderson, J. R. (1983). *The architecture of cognition.* Cambridge, MA: Harvard University Press.

Anderson, R. B., & Tweney, R. D. (1997). Artifactual power curves in forgetting. *Memory and Cognition, 25,* 724–730.

Ashby, F. G., Maddox, W. T., & Lee, W. W. (1994). On the dangers of averaging across subjects when using multidimensional scaling or the similarity-choice model. *Psychological Science, 5,* 144–151.

Bamber, D., & Van Santen, J. P. H. (1985). How many parameters can a model have and still be testable? *Journal of Mathematical Psychology, 29,* 443–473.

Borowiak, D. S. (1989). *Model discrimination for nonlinear regression models.* New York: Marcel Dekker.

Brent, R. P. (1973). *Algorithms for minimization without derivatives.* Englewood Cliffs, NJ: Prentice-Hall.

Cressie, N., & Read, T. R. C. (1984). Multinomial goodness-of-fit tests. *Journal of the Royal Statistical Society, Series B, 46,* 440–464.

Estes, W. K. (1956). The problem of inference from curves based on group data. *Psychological Review, 53,* 134–140.

Feller, W. (1968). *An introduction to probability theory and its applications* (Vol. 1). New York: Wiley.

Goldberg, D. F. (1989). *Genetic algorithms.* Leading, MA: Addison-Wesley.

Hays, W. L. (1988). *Statistics.* New York: Holt, Rinehart, & Winston.

Heathcote, A., Brown, S., & Mewhort, D. J. K. (2000). The power law repealed: the case for an exponential law of practice. *Psychonomic Bulletin and Review, 7,* 185–207.

Holland, J. H. (1975). *Adaptation in natural and artificial systems.* Ann Arbor: University of Michigan Press.

Jacobs, D. A. H. (ed.) (1977). *The state of the art in numerical analysis.* London: Academic Press.

Kelley, C. T. (1999). *Iterative methods for optimization.* SIAM Frontiers in Applied Mathematics, Vol. 18. Philadelphia: Society for Industrial and Applied Mathematics.

Kirkpatrick, S., Gelatt, C. D., & Vecchi, M. P. (1983). Optimization by simulated annealing. *Science, 220,* 671–680.

Klahr, D., Langley, P., & Neches, R. (Eds.) (1987). *Production system models of learning and development.* Cambridge, MA: MIT Press.

Kleijnen, J. (1987). *Statistical tools for simulation practitioners.* New York: Marcel Dekker.

Lamberts, K. (2000). Information-accumulation theory of speeded categorization. *Psychological Review, 107,* 227–260.

Loftus, G. (1985). Johannes Kepler's computer simulation of the universe: some remarks about theory in psychology. *Behavioral Research Methods, Instruments, and Computers, 17,* 149–156.

Logan, G. D. (1988). Toward an instance theory of automatization. *Psychological Review, 95,* 492–527.

Logan, G. D. (1992). Shapes of reaction time distributions and shapes of learning curves: a test of the instance theory of automaticity. *Journal of Experimental Psychology: Learning, Memory, and Cognition, 18,* 883–914.

Luce, R. D. (1986). *Response times: their role in inferring elementary mental organization.* New York: Oxford University Press.

Luce, R. D. (1997). Several unresolved conceptual problems of mathematical psychology. *Journal of Mathematical Psychology, 47,* 79–87.

Luce, R. D. (1999). Where is mathematical modelling in psychology headed? *Theory and Psychology, 9,* 723–737.

Luce, R. D., Bush, R. R., & Galanter, E. (1963). *Readings in mathematical psychology* (Vol. 1). New York: Wiley.

Luce, R. D., Bush, R. R., & Galanter, E. (1965). *Readings in mathematical psychology* (Vol. 2). New York: Wiley.

Maddox, W. T. (1999). On the dangers of averaging across observers when comparing decision bound models and generalized context models of categorization. *Perception and Psychophysics, 61*, 354–374.

Medin, D. L., and Schwanenflugel, P. J. (1981). Linear separability in classification learning. *Journal of Experimental Psychology: Human Learning and Memory, 7*, 355–368.

Myung, I. J. (2000). The importance of complexity in model selection. *Journal of Mathematical Psychology, 44*, 190–204.

Myung, I. J., Kim, C., & Pitt, M. A. (2000). Toward an explanation of the power law artifact: insights from response surface analysis. *Memory and Cognition, 28*, 832–840.

Myung, I. J., and Pitt, M. A. (1997). Applying Occam's razor in modeling cognition: a Bayesian approach. *Psychonomic Bulletin and Review, 4*, 79–95.

Myung, I. J., & Pitt, M. A. (2001). Mathematical modeling. In J. Wixted (ed.), *Stevens' handbook of experimental psychology: Vol. IV. Methodology* (3rd ed., pp. 429–459). New York: Wiley.

Nelder, J. A., & Mead, R. (1965). A simplex method for function minimization. *Computer Journal, 7*, 308–313.

Newell, A. (1973). Production systems: models of control structure. In W. G. Chase (ed.), *Visual information processing* (pp. 463–526). New York: Academic Press.

Newell, A. (1990). *Unified theories of cognition.* Cambridge, MA: Harvard University Press.

Newell, A., & Rosenbloom, P. S. (1981). Mechanisms of skill acquisition and the power law of practice. In J. R. Anderson (ed.), *Cognitive skills and their acquisition* (pp. 1–55). Hillsdale, NJ: Erlbaum.

Nosofsky, R. M. (1986). Attention, similarity, and the identification-categorization relationship. *Journal of Experimental Psychology: General, 115*, 39–57.

Nosofsky, R. M. (1987). Attention and learning processes in the identification and categorization of integral stimuli. *Journal of Experimental Psychology: Learning, Memory, and Cognition, 13*, 87–108.

Nosofsky, R. M. (1989). Further test of an exemplar-similarity approach to relating identification and categorization. *Perception and Psychophysics, 45*, 279–290.

Nosofsky, R. M. (1991). Stimulus bias, asymmetric similarity, and classification. *Cognitive Psychology, 23*, 94–140.

Nosofsky, R. M., & Palmeri, T. J. (1997). An exemplar-based random walk model of speeded classification. *Psychological Review, 104*, 266–300.

Pike, R. (1973). Response latency models for signal detection. *Psychological Review, 80*, 53–68.

Pitt, M. A., Myung, I. J., & Zhang, S. (2002). Toward a method of selecting among computational models of cognition. *Psychological Review, 109*, 472–491.

Press, W. H., Flannery, B. P., Teukolsky, S. A., & Vetterling, W. T. (1989). *Numerical recipes in Pascal: the art of scientific computing.* Cambridge: Cambridge University Press.

Quinlan, P. T. (1991). *Connectionism and psychology: a psychological perspective on new connectionist research.* London: Harvester Wheatsheaf.

Ratcliff, R. (1978). A theory of memory retrieval. *Psychological Review, 85*, 59–108.

Ratcliff, R. (1979). Group reaction time distributions and an analysis of distribution statistics. *Psychological Bulletin, 86*, 446–461.

Read, T. R. C., & Cressie, N. A. C. (1988). *Goodness-of-fit statistics for discrete multivariate data.* New York: Springer.

Riefer, D. M., & Batchelder, W. H. (1988). Multinomial modeling and the measurement of cognitive processes. *Psychological Review, 95*, 318–339.

Roberts, S., & Pashler, H. (2000). How persuasive is a good fit? A comment on theory testing in psychology. *Psychological Review, 107*, 358–367.

Rowan, T. (1990). Functional stability analysis of numerical algorithms. PhD thesis, University of Texas, Austin.

Rumelhart, D. E., & McClelland, J. L. (1986). *Parallel distributed processing: explorations in the microstructure of cognition* (Vols. 1–2). Cambridge, MA: MIT Press.

Smith, P. L., & Vickers, D. (1988). The accumulator model of two-choice discrimination. *Journal of Mathematical Psychology, 32*, 135–168.

Townsend, J. T., & Ashby, F. G. (1983). *Stochastic modeling of elementary psychological processes.* New York: Cambridge University Press.

Van Zandt, T. (2000). How to fit a response time distribution. *Psychonomic Bulletin and Review, 7*, 424–465.

Van Zandt, T., Colonius, H., & Proctor, R. W. (2000). A comparison of two response-time models applied to perceptual matching. *Psychonomic Bulletin and Review, 7*, 208–256.

Vickers, D. (1970). Evidence for an accumulator model of psychophysical discrimination. *Ergonomics, 13*, 37–58.

Vickers, D. (1979). *Decision processes in visual perception.* New York: Academic Press.

Vose, M. D. (1999). *The simple genetic algorithm: foundations and theory.* Cambridge, MA: MIT Press.

Wickens, T. D. (1982). *Models for behavior: stochastic processes in psychology.* San Francisco: Freeman.

19

Model Evaluation, Testing and Selection

JAE I. MYUNG, MARK A. PITT
AND WOOJAE KIM

INTRODUCTION

As mathematical modeling increases in popularity in cognitive psychology, it is important for there to be tools to evaluate models in an effort to make modeling as productive as possible. Our aim in this chapter is to introduce some of these tools in the context of the problems they were meant to address. After a brief introduction to building models, the chapter focuses on their testing and selection. Before doing so, however, we raise a few questions about modeling that are meant to serve as a backdrop for the subsequent material.

Why mathematical modeling?

The study of cognition is concerned with uncovering the architecture of the mind. We want answers to questions such as how decisions are made, how verbal and written modes of communication are performed, and how people navigate through the environment. The source of information for addressing these questions are the data collected in experiments. Data are the sole link to the cognitive process of interest, and models of cognition evolve from researchers inferring the characteristics of the processes from these data. Most models are specified verbally when first proposed, and constitute a set of assumptions about the structure and function of the processing system.

A verbal form of a model serves a number of important roles in the research enterprise, such as providing a good conceptual starting point for experimentation. When specified in sufficient detail, a verbal model can stimulate a great deal of research, as its predictions are tested and evaluated. Even when the model is found to be incorrect (which will always be the case), the mere existence of the model will have served an important purpose in advancing our understanding and pushing the field forward. When little is known about the process of interest (i.e. data are scarce), verbal modeling is a sensible approach to studying cognition.

However, simply by virtue of being verbally specified, there is a limit to how much can be learned about the process. When this point is reached, one must turn from a verbal description to a mathematical description to make progress. In this regard, mathematical modeling takes the scientific enterprise a step further to gain new insights into the underlying process and derive quantitative predictions, which are rarely possible with verbal models. In the remainder of this section, we highlight some points to consider when making this transition.

What is a mathematical model of cognition?

Although there is no single answer to this question, thinking about it can be quite instructive when evaluating one's goals. For instance, functional equation modeling focuses on developing the most accurate description of a phenomenon. Models of forgetting (Wixted & Ebbesen, 1991) describe how retention changes over time. Similarly, 'laws' of psychophysics (Gesheider, 1985) describe the relationship between a physical stimulus and its psychological counterpart (e.g. amplitude vs. loudness). Models such as these are merely quantitative redescriptions of the input–output relationship between a stimulus and a response. There is little in the function itself that represents characteristics of the underlying process responsible for the mapping (e.g. memory). Put another way, there is no content in the 'black box' (i.e. the model) to which one can appeal to understand how the input was processed to lead to a particular response. Artificial neural networks that are trained to do nothing more than learn a stimulus–response relationship fall into this category as well (e.g. Gluck, 1991).[1]

Often this type of modeling can be quite informative. For example, there have been many demonstrations in recent years showing the sufficiency of a statistical associator (i.e. artificial neural network) in learning properties of language (e.g. verb morphology, segment co-occurrences) that were previously assumed to require explicit rules (Brent, 1999; Elman, Bates, Johnson, Karmiloff-Smith, Parisi, & Plunkett, 1996; Joanisse & Seidenberg, 1999). However, this approach differs in important ways from a process-oriented approach to modeling, wherein a verbal model is instantiated mathematically. In processing models, theoretical constructs in the verbal model (e.g. memory, attention, activation, levels of representation) are represented in the quantitative model. There are direct ties between the two types of models. The parameters of the quantitative model are linked to mental constructs and the functional form (i.e. the mathematical equation) integrates them in a meaningful way. The quantitative model replaces, even supersedes, the verbal model, becoming a closer approximation of the cognitive process of interest.

Processing models differ widely in the extent to which they are linked to their verbal form. In general, this link may be stronger for algebraic models (Nosofsky, 1986; Shiffrin & Steyvers, 1997) than localist networks (Grainger & Jacobs, 1998), in large part because of the additional parameters needed to implement a network. Both types of models not only strive to reproduce behavior, but they attempt to do so in a way that provides an explanation for the *cause* of the behavior. This is what makes a cognitive model cognitive.

Virtues and vices of modeling

As mentioned above, the allure of modeling is in the potential it holds for learning more about the cognitive process of interest. Precise predictions can be tested about how variables should interact or the time course of processing. In essence, cognitive modeling allows one to extract more information from the data than just ordinal mean differences between conditions. The magnitude of effects and the shape of distributions can be useful information in deciding between equally plausible alternatives.

Another virtue of cognitive modeling is that it provides a framework for understanding what can be complex interactions between parts of the model. This is especially true when the model has many parameters and the parameters are combined nonlinearly. Simulations can help assess how model behavior changes when parameters are combined in different ways (e.g. additively vs. multiplicatively) or what type of distribution (e.g. normal, exponential) best approximates a response-time distribution. Work such as this will not only lead to a better understanding of the model as it was designed, but it can also lead to new insights. One example of this is when a model displays unexpected behavior, which is later found in experimental data, thereby extending the explanatory reach of the model. They are sometimes referred to as emergent properties, particularly in the context of connectionist models. Frequently they are compelling demonstrations of the power of models (and modeling), and of the necessity of such demonstrations prior to settling on a theoretical interpretation of an experimental finding. One example is provided here to illustrate this point.

A central question in the field of memory has been whether memory is composed of multiple subsystems. Dissociations in performance across tasks and populations offer some of the most irrefutable evidence in favor of separate systems. In one such study, Knowlton and Squire (1993) argued that classification and recognition are mediated by independent memory systems on the basis of data showing a dissociation between the two in normal adults and amnesic individuals. Amnesiacs performed as well as normals in pattern classification, but significantly worse in old/new recognition of those same patterns. Knowlton and Squire postulated that an implicit memory system underlies category acquisition (which is intact in amnesiacs) whereas a separate declarative knowledge system (damaged in amnesiacs) is used for recognition.

As compelling as this conclusion may be, Nosofsky and Zaki (1998) performed a couple of equally convincing simulations that demonstrate a single (exemplar) memory system could account for the findings. Although an exemplar model may not account for all such findings in the literature (see Knowlton, 1999; Nosofsky & Zaki, 1998), its success offers an instructive lesson: modeling can be a means of overcoming a limitation in our own ability to understand how alternative conceptualizations can account for what seems like strong evidence against them. (See Ratcliff, Spieler, & McKoon, 2000, for a similar example in the field of cognitive aging.)

Despite the virtues of cognitive modeling, it is not risk-free. Indeed, it can be quite hazardous. It is far too easy for one to unknowingly create a behemoth of a model that will perform well for reasons that have nothing to do with being a good approximation of the cognitive process. How can this situation be identified and avoided? More fundamentally, how should a model be evaluated? Model testing is most often post-dictive, carried out after the data were collected. Although necessary, it is a weak test of the model's adequacy because the model may well have been developed with those very data. Far more impressive, yet much rarer, are tests in which the model's predictions are substantiated or invalidated in future experimentation. In the absence of such work, how might tests of one or more models be carried out most productively? After a brief overview of parameter estimation, the remainder of this chapter provides some preliminary answers to these questions.

MODEL SPECIFICATION AND PARAMETER ESTIMATION

Model as a parametric family of probability distributions

From a statistical standpoint, observed data is a random sample from an unknown population, which represents the underlying cognitive process of interest. Ideally, the goal of modeling is to deduce the population that generated the observed data. A model is in some sense a collection of populations. In statistics, associated with each population is a probability distribution indexed by the model's parameters. Formally, a model is defined as a parametric family of probability distributions.

Let us use $f(y|w)$ to denote the probability density function that gives the probability of observing data $y = (y_1, ..., y_m)$ given the model's parameter vector $w = (w_1, ..., w_k)$. Under the assumption that individual observations, y_i's, are independent of one another, $f(y|w)$ can be rewritten as a product of individual probability density functions:

$$f(y = (y_1, ..., y_m)|w) = f(y_1|w)f(y_2|w)...f(y_m|w).$$

As an illustrative example, consider the Generalized Context Model (GCMcv) of categorization that describes the probability (p_{aj}) of category C_j response given stimulus X_a by the following equation (Nosofsky, 1986):

$$\text{GCMcv: } p_{aj} = \frac{\sum_{b \varepsilon C_j} S_{ab}}{\sum_{j'} \sum_{c \varepsilon C_{j'}} S_{ac}}$$

$$\text{Where } S_{ab} = \exp\left(-c\left(\sum_{k=1}^{q} v_k |x_{ak} - x_{bk}|^r\right)^{1/r}\right)$$

In the equation, S_{ab} denotes a similarity measure between two multidimensional stimuli $X_a = (x_{a1}, ..., x_{aq})$ and $X_b = (x_{b1}, ..., x_{bq})$, q is the number of stimulus dimensions, c (> 0) is a sensitivity parameter, v_k (> 0) is an attention weight satisfying $\sum v_k = 1$, and finally, r is the Minkowski metric parameter. Typically, the model is specified in terms of the city-block distance metric of $r = 1$ or the Euclidean metric of $r = 2$, with the rest of the parameters being estimated from data. The model therefore has q free parameters; that is, $w = (c, v_1, v_2, ..., v_{q-1})$. Note that the last attention weight, v_q, is determined from the normalization constraint, $\sum v_k = 1$ based on the first $(q - 1)$ weights.

In a categorization experiment with J categories, each y_i itself, obtained under condition i ($i = 1, ..., m$), becomes a vector of J elements, $y_i = (y_{i1}, ..., y_{iJ})$, $0 < y_{ij} < 1$, where y_{ij} represents the response proportion for category C_j. Each y_{ij} is obtained by dividing the number of category responses (x_{ij}) by the number of independent trials (n) as $y_{ij} = x_{ij}/n$ where $x_{ij} = 0, 1, 2, ..., n$. Note that the vector $x_i = (x_{i1}, ..., x_{iJ})$ itself is distributed according to a multinomial probability distribution. For instance, suppose that in condition i, the task was to categorize stimulus X_a into one of three categories, C_1 to C_3 (i.e. $J = 3$). Then the probability distribution function of x_i is given by

$$f(x_i = (x_{i1}, x_{i2}, x_{i3})|w) = \frac{n!}{x_{i1}! x_{i2}! x_{i3}!} p_{a1}^{x_{i1}} p_{a2}^{x_{i2}} p_{a3}^{x_{i3}}$$

In the equation, p_{aj} is defined earlier as a function of the parameter vector w such that $p_{a1} + p_{a2} + p_{a3} = 1$, and note also that $x_{i1} + x_{i2} + x_{i3} = n$. The desired probability distribution function $f(y_i|w)$ in terms of $y_i = (y_{i1}, y_{i2}, y_{i3})$ is obtained simply by substituting $n \times y_{ij}$ for x_{ij} in the above equation. Finally, the probability distribution function $f(y|w)$ for the entire set of data $y = (y_1, ..., y_m)$ is given as a product of individual $f(y_i|w)$'s over m conditions.

Parameter estimation

Once a model is specified with its parameters and data have been collected, the model's ability to fit the data can be assessed. Model fit is measured by finding parameter values of the model that provide the 'best' fit to the data in some defined sense – a procedure called parameter estimation in statistics. For more in-depth treatment of the topic, the reader is advised to consult Casella and Berger (2002).

There are two generally accepted methods of parameter estimation: least-squares estimation (LSE) and maximum likelihood estimation (MLE). In LSE, we seek the parameter values that minimize the sum of squares error (SSE) between observed data and a model's predictions:

$$SSE(w) = \sum_{i=1}^{m}(y_i - y_{i,\,prd}(w))^2$$

where $y_{i,\,prd}(w)$ denotes the model's prediction for observation y_i. Note that SSE(w) is a function of the parameter w. In MLE, we seek the parameter values that are most likely to have produced the data. This is obtained by maximizing the log-likelihood of the observed data:

$$loglik(w) = \sum_{i=1}^{m} \ln f(y_i|w)$$

where ln denotes the natural logarithm of base e, the natural number. Note that by maximizing either the likelihood or the log-likelihood, the same solution is obtained because the two are monotonically related to each other. In practice, the log-likelihood is preferred for computational ease. The parameters that minimize the sum of squares error or the log-likelihood are called the LSE or MLE estimates, respectively.

For normally distributed data with constant variance, LSE and MLE are equivalent in the sense that both methods yield the same parameter estimates. For nonnormal data such as proportions and response times, however, LSE estimates tend to differ from MLE estimates. Although LSE is often the de facto method of estimation in cognitive psychology, MLE is preferable, especially for nonnormal data. In particular, MLE is well suited for statistical inference in hypothesis testing and model selection. LSE implicitly assumes normally distributed error, and hence, will work as well as MLE to the extent that the assumption is reasonable.

Finding LSE or MLE estimates generally requires use of a numerical optimization procedure on computer, as it is usually not possible to obtain an analytic form solution. In essence, the idea of numerical optimization is to find optimal parameter values by making use of a search routine that applies heuristic criteria in a trial-and-error fashion iteratively until stopping criteria are satisfied (see Lamberts, Chapter 18, this volume).

MODEL EVALUATION AND TESTING

Once a model is specified and its best-fitting parameters are found, one is in a position to assess the viability of the model. Researchers have proposed a number of criteria that were thought to be important for model evaluation (e.g. Jacobs & Grainger, 1994). These include three qualitative criteria (explanatory adequacy, interpretability, faithfulness) and four quantitative criteria (falsifiability, goodness-of-fit,

simplicity/complexity, generalizability). Below we discuss these criteria one at a time.

Qualitative criteria

A model satisfies the *explanatory adequacy* criterion if its assumptions are plausible and consistent with established findings, and importantly, the theoretical account is reasonable for the cognitive process of interest. In other words, the model must be able to do more than redescribe observed data. The model must also be *interpretable* in the sense that the model makes sense and is understandable. Importantly, the components of the model, especially its parameters, must be linked to psychological processes and constructs. Finally, the model is said to be *faithful* to the extent that the model's ability to capture the underlying mental process originates from the theoretical principles embodied in the model, rather than from the choices made in its computational instantiation.

Although we cannot overemphasize the importance of these qualitative criteria in model evaluation, they have yet to be quantified. Accordingly, we must rely on our subjective assessment of the model on each. In contrast, the four criteria discussed next are quantifiable.

Quantitative criteria

Falsifiability

This is a necessary condition for testing a model or theory, and refers to whether there exist potential observations that a model cannot describe (Popper, 1959). If so, then the model is said to be falsifiable. An unfalsifiable model is one that can describe unerringly all possible data patterns in a given experimental situation. Obviously, there is no point in testing an unfalsifiable model.

A heuristic rule for determining a model's falsifiability is already familiar to us: the model is falsifiable if and only if the number of its free parameters is less than the number of data observations. This counting rule, however, turns out to be imperfect, in particular for certain nonlinear models (Bamber & van Santen, 1985). For example, they showed that Luce's (1959) choice model is falsifiable even if its number of parameters exceeds the number of observations! To remedy limitations of the counting rule, Bamber and van Santen (1985) provide a formal rule for assessing a model's falsifiability, which yields the counting rule as a special case. The rule states that a model is falsifiable if the rank of its Jacobian matrix is less than the number of data observations for all values of the parameters. The Jacobian matrix is defined in terms of partial derivatives as: $J_{ij}(w) = \partial E(y_i)/\partial w_i$ ($i = 1, ..., k; j = 1, ..., m$) where $E(x)$ stands for the expectation of a random variable x.

Goodness-of-fit

A model should also provide a good description of the observed data. *Goodness-of-fit* refers to the model's ability to fit the particular set of observed data. Examples of goodness-of-fit measures are the minimized sum of squares error (SSE), the mean squared error (MSE), the root mean squared error (RMSE), the percent variance accounted for (PVAF) and the maximum likelihood (ML). The first four of these, defined below, are related to one another in a way that one can be written in terms of another:

$$MSE = SSE\,(w^*_{LSE})/m$$
$$RMSE = \sqrt{SSE\,(w^*_{LSE})/m}$$
$$PVAF = 100(1 - SSE\,(w^*_{LSE})/SST$$
$$ML = f(y\,|\,w^*_{MLE})$$

In the equation, w^*_{LSE} is the parameter that minimizes $SSE(w)$ – that is, an LSE estimate – and SST stands for the sum of squares total defined as $SST = \sum_i (y_i - y_{mean})^2$. ML is the probability density function maximized with respect to the model's parameters, evaluated at w^*_{MLE}, which is obtained through MLE.

Complexity

Not only should a model describe the data in hand well, but it should also do so in the least complex (i.e. simplest) way. Intuitively, *complexity* has to do with a model's inherent flexibility that enables it to fit a wide range of data patterns. There seem to be at least two dimensions of model complexity: the number of parameters and the model's functional form. The latter refers to the way the parameters are combined in the model equation. The more parameters a model has, the more complex it is. Importantly also, two models with the same number of parameters but different functional forms can differ significantly in their complexity. For example, it seems unlikely that two one-parameter models, $y = x + w$ and $y = e^{wx}$, are equally complex. The latter is probably much better at fitting data than the former.

It turns out that one can devise a quantitative measure of model complexity that takes into account both dimensions of complexity and at the same time is theoretically justified as well as intuitive. One example is the *geometric complexity* (GC) of a model (Pitt, Myung, & Zhang, 2002; Rissanen, 1996), defined as:

$$GC = \frac{k}{2} \ln \frac{n}{2\pi} + \ln \int dw \sqrt{\det I(w)}$$

where k is the number of parameters, n is the sample size, $I(w)$ is the Fisher information matrix defined as

$I_{ij}(w) = -E[\partial^2 \ln f(y\,|\,w)/\partial w_i \partial w_j]$, $i, j = 1, \ldots, k$, and det denotes the determinant of $I(w)$. Functional form effects of complexity are reflected in the second term of GC through $I(w)$. How do we interpret geometric complexity? The meaning of geometric complexity is related to the number of 'different' (i.e. distinguishable) probability distributions that a model can account for. The more distinguishable distributions that the model can describe by finely tuning its parameter values, the more complex it is (Myung, Balasubramanian, & Pitt, 2000). For example, when geometric complexity is calculated for the following two-parameter psychophysical models, Stevens' law ($y = w_1 x^{w_2}$) and Fechner's logarithmic law ($y = w_1 \ln(x + w_2)$), the former turns out to be more complex than the latter (Pitt et al., 2002). For another measure of model complexity called the *effective number of parameters*, which takes into account the model's functional form as well as the number of parameters, see Murata, Yoshizawa, and Amari (1994; Moody, 1992).

Generalizability

The fourth quantitative criterion for model evaluation is *generalizability*. This criterion is defined as a model's ability to fit not only the observed data in hand, but also new, as yet unseen data samples from the same probability distribution. In other words, model evaluation should not be focused solely on how well a model fits observed data, but how well it fits future data samples generated by the cognitive process underlying the data. This goal will be achieved best when generalizability is considered.

To summarize, these four quantitative criteria work together to assist in model evaluation and guide (even constrain) model development and selection. The model must be sufficiently complex, but not too complex, to capture the regularity in the data. Both a good fit to the data *and* good generalizability will ensure an appropriate degree of complexity, so that the model captures the regularity in the data. In addition, because of its broad focus, generalizability will constrain the power of the model, thus making it falsifiable. Although all four criteria are interrelated, generalizability may be the most important. It should be the guiding principle in model evaluation and selection.

Why generalizability?

On the face of it, goodness-of-fit might seem as though it should be the main criterion in model evaluation. After all, it measures a model's ability to fit observed data, which is our only window into cognition. So why not evaluate a model on the basis of its fit? This might be all right if the data reflected only the underlying regularity. However, data are corrupted by uncontrollable, random variation (noise)

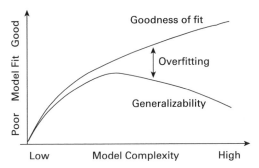

Figure 19.1 *Goodness-of-fit and generalizability as a function of model complexity. (Adapted from Figure 11.4 of Myung and Pitt, 2001.)*

due to the inherently stochastic nature of cognitive processes and the unreliable tools used to measure cognition. An implication of noise-contaminated data is that a model's goodness-of-fit reflects not only its ability to capture the underlying process, but also its ability to fit random noise. This relationship is depicted conceptually in the following equation:

$$\text{Goodness of fit} = \text{Fit to regularity}$$
$$\text{(Generalizability)} + \text{Fit to noise(overfitting)}$$

We are interested only in the first term on the right-hand side of the above equation. This is the quantity that renders generalizability and therefore ties in with the goal of cognitive modeling. The problem is that fitting a data set gives only the overall value of goodness-of-fit, not the value of the first or second terms on the right-hand side of the equation. The problem is further complicated by the fact that the magnitude of the second term is not fixed but depends upon the complexity of the model under consideration. That is, a complex model with many parameters and a highly nonlinear model equation absorbs random noise easily, thereby improving its fit, independent of the model's ability to capture the underlying process. Consequently, an overly complex model can fit data better than a simpler model even if the latter generated the data. It is well established in statistics that goodness-of-fit can *always* be improved by increasing model complexity, such as adding extra parameters. This intricate relationship among goodness-of-fit, generalizability and complexity is summarized in Figure 19.1. Note that the model must possess enough complexity to capture the trends in the data, and thus provide a good fit. After a certain point, additional complexity reduces generalizability because data are overfitted, capturing random variability.

An example of overfitting is illustrated in Table 19.1 using artificial data from known models. The data were generated from M_2, which is the true model with one parameter.[2] As can be seen in the first row

of the table, M_2 provided a better fit than M_1, which has the same number of parameters as M_2 but is an incorrect model. On the other hand, M_3 and M_4, with their two extra parameters, provided a better fit than the true model. In fact, M_2 never fitted better than either of these models. The improvement in fit of M_3 and M_4 over M_2 represents the extent of overfitting. The overfitting must be the work of the two extra parameters in these models, which enabled them to absorb random noise above and beyond the underlying regularity. Note also that M_4 provided an even better fit more often than M_3, although both have the same number of parameters (3). The difference in fit between these two models is due to their differences in functional form. This example should make it clear that model testing based solely on goodness-of-fit can result in choosing the wrong (i.e. overly complex) model.

To reiterate, the good fit of a model does not directly translate into a measure of the model's fidelity. As shown in Table 19.1, a good fit can be achieved for reasons that have nothing to do with the model's exactness. A good fit is only a necessary but not a sufficient condition for capturing the underlying process. Rather, a good fit merely qualifies the model as one of the candidate models for further consideration (see Roberts & Pashler, 2000).

This drawback of goodness-of-fit is one reason why generalizability is preferable as a method of model selection. Generalizability should be considered the 'gold standard' of model evaluation because it provides a more accurate measure of the model's approximation of the underlying process. Quantitatively, this refers to the model with the smallest generalization error, which is defined as the average prediction error that the model makes over all possible data coming from the same source. At a more conceptual level, it is important to emphasize that the form of generalizability that we advocate involves finding the model that makes good predictions of future data (Grunwald, 2002), not necessarily to find the 'true' model that generated the data. Ideally, the latter should be the goal of modeling, but this is unrealistic, even unachievable in practice, for the following reasons. First, the task of identifying a model with a data sample of finite size is inherently an ill-posed problem, in the sense that finding a unique solution is not generally possible. This is because there may be multiple models that give equally good descriptions of the data. There is rarely enough information in the data to discriminate between them. This is known as the *curse of dimensionality* problem, which states that the sample size required to accurately estimate a model grows exponentially with the dimensionality (i.e. number of parameters) of the model (Bellman, 1961). Second, even if there is enough data available to identify the true model, that model may be missing from the models under consideration. In the rather unlikely scenario that the true model just so happens to be a

TABLE 19.1   *Goodness-of-fit and generalizability of models differing in complexity*

Model:	M_1	M_2 (true)	M_3	M_4
Goodness of fit	2.14 (0%)	1.85 (0%)	1.71 (12%)	1.62 (88%)
Generalizability	2.29 (17%)	2.05 (75%)	6.48 (5%)	3.44 (3%)

Note: Root mean squared error (RMSE) of the fit of each model to the data and the percentage of samples in which the particular model fitted the data best (in parentheses). The four models are as follows: M_1: $y = w_1x + e$; M_2: $y = \ln(x + w_1) + e$; M_3: $y = w_1 \ln(x + w_2) + w_3 + e$; M_4: $y = w_1x + w_2x^2 + w_3 + e$. The error e was normally distributed with a mean of zero and a standard deviation of 2. A thousand pairs of samples were generated from M_2 (true model) using $w_1 = 10$ on the same 10 points for x, which ranged from 1 to 10 in increments of 1.

member of this set, it would be the one that minimizes generalization error and is thus selected.

MODEL SELECTION

Since a model's generalizability is not directly observable, it must be estimated using observed data. The measure developed for this purpose trades off a model's fit to the data with its complexity, the aim being to select the model that is complex enough to capture the regularity in the data, but not overly complex to capture the ever-present random variation. Looked at in this way, generalizability formalizes the principle of Occam's razor.

Model selection methods

In this section, we describe specific measures of generalizability and discuss their application in cognitive psychology. Four representative generalizability criteria are introduced. They are the Akaike Information Criterion (AIC: Akaike, 1973), the Bayesian Information Criterion (BIC: Schwarz, 1978), cross-validation (CV: Stone, 1974; Browne, 2000) and minimum description length (MDL: Rissanen, 1983, 1989, 1996; Grunwald, 2000, 2002). In all four methods, the maximized log-likelihood is used as a goodness-of-fit measure, but they differ in how model complexity is conceptualized and measured. For a fuller discussion of these and other selection methods, the reader should consult a special *Journal of Mathematical Psychology* issue on model selection (Myung, Forster, & Browne, 2000; see also Linhart & Zucchini, 1986; Burnham & Anderson, 1998; Pitt et al., 2002).

AIC and BIC

AIC and BIC for a given model are defined as follows:

$$\text{AIC} = -2 \ln f(y|w^*) + 2k$$
$$\text{BIC} = -2 \ln f(y|w^*) + k \ln n$$

where w^* is a MLE estimate, ln is the natural logarithm of base e, k is the number of parameters and n is the sample size. For normally distributed errors with constant variance, the first term of both criteria, $-2 \ln f(y|w^*)$, is reduced to $(n \ln(\text{SSE}(w^*)) + c_o)$, where c_o is a constant that does not depend upon the model. In each criterion, the first term represents a lack of fit measure, the second term represents a complexity measure, and together they represent a lack of generalizability measure. A lower value of the criterion means better generalizability. Accordingly, the model that minimizes a given criterion should be chosen.

Complexity in AIC and BIC is a function of only the number of parameters. Functional form, another important dimension of model complexity, is not considered. For this reason, these methods are not recommended for comparing models with the same number of parameters but different functional forms. The other two selection methods, CV and MDL, described next, are sensitive to functional form as well as the number of parameters.

Cross-validation

In CV, a model's generalizability is estimated without defining an explicit measure of complexity. Instead, models with more complexity than necessary to capture the regularity in the data are penalized through a resampling procedure, which is performed as follows. The observed data sample is divided into two subsamples, calibration and validation. The calibration sample is then used to find the best-fitting values of a model's parameters by MLE or LSE. These values, denoted by w^*_{cal}, are then fixed and fitted, without any further tuning of the parameters, to the validation sample, denoted by y_{val}. The resulting fit to y_{val} by w^*_{cal} is called the model's CV index and is taken as the model's generalizability estimate. If desired, this single-division-based CV index may be replaced by the average CV index calculated from multiple divisions of calibration and validation samples. The latter is a more accurate estimate of the model's generalizability, though it is also more computationally demanding.

The main attraction of cross-validation is its ease of use. All that is needed is a simple resampling routine that can easily be programmed on any desktop computer. The second attraction is that unlike AIC and BIC, CV is sensitive to the functional form dimension of model complexity, though how it works is unclear because of the implicit nature of the method. For these reasons, the method can be used in all modeling situations, including the case of comparing among models that differ in functional form but have the same number of parameters. The price that is paid for its ease of use is performance, which is measured by the accuracy of its generalizability estimate. Our own experience with CV has been disappointing, with CV quite often performing worse than AIC and BIC.

It is important to mention another type of generalizability that is similar to cross-validation but differs in important ways from CV and other selection criteria discussed in this chapter. It is called the generalization criterion methodology (GNCM: Busemeyer & Wang, 2000). The primary difference between CV and GNCM is the way that the data set is divided into calibration and validation samples. In CV, the sample data set is *randomly* divided into two subsamples, both from the *same* experimental design. In contrast, in GNCM, the data are *systematically* divided into two subsamples from *different* experimental designs. That is, the calibration data are sampled from specific experimental conditions and the generalization data are sampled from new experimental conditions. Consequently, model comparison for the second stage using the generalization data set is based on a priori predictions concerning new experimental conditions. In essence, GNCM tests the model's ability to extrapolate accurately beyond the current experimental set-up, whereas CV and other generalizability criteria such as AIC and BIC test the model's ability to predict new, as yet unseen, samples within the same experimental set-up.

Minimum description length

MDL is a selection method that has its origin in algorithmic coding theory in computer science. According to MDL, both models and data are viewed as codes that can be compressed. The basic idea of this approach is that regularities in data necessarily imply the existence of statistical redundancy and that the redundancy can be used to compress the data (Grunwald, 2000). Put another way, the amount of regularity in data is directly related to the data description length. The shorter the description of the data by the model, the better the approximation of the underlying regularity, and thus, the higher the model's generalizability is. Formally, MDL is defined as:

$$MDL = -\ln f(y \mid w^*) + \frac{k}{2} \ln \frac{n}{2\pi} + \ln \int dw \sqrt{\det I(w)}$$

The first term is the same lack of fit measure as in AIC and BIC. The second and third terms together represent a complexity measure, which is the geometric complexity measure defined earlier in the chapter. In coding theory, MDL is interpreted as the length in 'ebits' of the shortest possible code that describes the data unambiguously with the help of a model.[3] The model with the minimum value of MDL encodes the most regularity in the data, and therefore should be preferred.

Note that the second term in the MDL equation, which captures the effects of model complexity due to the number of parameter (k), is a logarithmic function of sample size n. In contrast, the third term, which captures functional form effects, is not sensitive to sample size. This means that as sample size increases, the relative contribution of the effects due to functional form to those due to the number of parameters will be gradually reduced. Therefore, functional form effects can be ignored for sufficiently large n, in which case the MDL value becomes approximately equal to one-half of the BIC value.

Probably the most desirable property of MDL over other selection methods is that its complexity measure takes into account the effects of both dimensions of model complexity, the number of parameters and functional form. The MDL complexity measure, unlike CV, shows explicitly how both factors contribute to model complexity. In short, MDL is a *sharper* and more accurate method than these three competitors. The price that is paid for MDL's superior performance is its computational cost. MDL can be laborious to calculate. First, the Fisher information matrix must be obtained by calculating the second derivatives of the log-likelihood function, $\ln f(y \mid w)$. This calculation can be nontrivial, though not impossible. Second, the square root of the determinant of the Fisher information matrix must be integrated over parameter space. This generally requires use of a numerical integration method such as Markov chain Monte Carlo (e.g. Gilks, Richardson, & Spiegelhalter, 1996).

Application example of the four selection methods

In this section we present an application example of the four selection methods (AIC, BIC, CV, MDL). Maximum likelihood (ML), a purely goodness-of-fit measure, is included as well for comparison.

Five categorization models that differ in the number of parameters and functional form were compared. They were the prototype model (PRTcv: Reed, 1972) and four versions of the generalized context model (GCMcv, GCMc, GCMv: Nosofsky & Palmeri, 1997; GCMcvg: Ashby & Maddox, 1993; McKinley & Nosofsky, 1995). GCMcv is the categorization model defined in the Model Specification and Parameter Estimation section (p. 425 above) and has six free parameters. They are the sensitivity parameter (c) and five attention weights ($0 < v_k < 1$, $k = 1, ..., 5$), with the sixth weight being determined from the first five as $v_6 = 1 - \Sigma v_k$. GCMc is a one-parameter version of GCMcv obtained by fixing the six attention weights to $v_k = 1/6$ for all k. GCMv is a five-parameter version of GCMcv obtained by fixing the sensitivity parameter to $c = 2$. GCMcvg is the same as GCMcv except that it has one extra parameter g ($g > 0$):

$$\text{GCMcvg: } p_{aj} = \left(\sum_{b \in Cj} S_{ab} \right)^g \Big/ \sum_{j'} \left(\sum_{c \in Cj} S_{ac} \right)^g$$

PRTcv is defined as

$$\text{PRTcv: } p_{aj} = \frac{S_{ab}(j)}{\sum_k S_{ab}(j)}$$

$$\text{where } S_{ab(j)} = \exp\left(-c \left(\sum_{k=1}^{q} vk \, |x_{ak} - x_{b(j)k}|^r \right)^{1/r} \right)$$

where $S_{ab(j)}$ is a similarity measure between a test stimulus X_a and the prototype stimulus $X_{b(j)}$ of category C_j. PRTcv has the same number of parameters as GCMcv. The Euclidean distance metric of $r = 2$ was assumed for all five models.

Note that the four generalized context models are nested within one another, meaning that one model can be obtained as a special case of another by fixing the values of one or more parameters. Both GCMc and GCMv are nested within GCMcv, which is in turn nested within GCMcvg. On the other hand, PRTcv and GCMcvg are not nested. When a model is nested within another model, the former is called the reduced model and the latter is called the full model. The standard hypothesis-testing procedure that is based on the generalized likelihood ratio statistic (e.g. Johnson & Wichern, 1998) is often employed to compare nested models. It is important to note that this procedure does not estimate generalizability – the paramount goal of model selection. Instead, the likelihood ratio test tests the null hypothesis that the reduced model is correct, in the sense that it offers a sufficiently good description of the data, thereby making unnecessary the extra parameters of the full model to account for the observed data pattern. On the other hand, the model selection criteria discussed in this chapter are designed to compare among models, nested or non-nested, based on their generalizability.

Artificial data were generated from GCMv using the six-dimensional scaling solution from experiment 1 of Shin and Nosofsky (1992) with the Euclidean distance metric. The experimental task was to categorize nine new stimuli into one of three pre-specified categories after having learned six exemplars with feedback. Data were created from predetermined values of the parameters, $v = (0.3, 0.3, 0.2, 0.1, 0.05, 0.05)$. From these, 27 trinomial response probabilities (p_{aj}, $a = 1, ..., 9, j = 1, 2, 3$) were computed using the model equation. For each probability, a series of independent ternary outcomes of a given sample size ($n = 20$ or 100) were generated from the corresponding trinomial probability distribution. The number of outcomes of each type in the series was summed and divided by n to obtain an observed proportion. This way, each sample consisted of 27 observed proportions. Next, each of the five models was fitted to the sample data separately, and the model that generalized best under a given selection criterion was determined. This procedure was repeated for each of a thousand replication samples and for each sample size.

The simulation results are shown in Table 19.2. Looking across rows, the values in the cells represent the percentage of tests that each model was chosen for the particular selection criterion. With ML as the selection criterion, the over-parameterized model GCMcvg was almost always chosen ($> 90\%$), while the true model, GCMv, was never selected. The result is not surprising given that ML is a goodness-of-fit measure that does not adjust for model complexity. When model complexity is incorporated into the selection process, the recovery rate of the true model was markedly improved, though it varied considerably depending upon the selection method used. For AIC and BIC, model recovery rate was modest at 50% and 29%, respectively, for the small sample size of $n = 20$, but climbed to the 80–90% range when sample size increased to $n = 100$. Model recovery performance of CV trailed rather distantly behind that of AIC and BIC for both sample sizes.

MDL was the most impressive of all. Recovery of the true model was already at 89% for the small sample size, and virtually perfect (99%) for the large sample size. The sizable gap in performance between MDL and the other three methods (AIC, BIC, CV) shows that there are aspects of model complexity that are not picked up fully by the latter three methods. Calculation of geometric complexity confirmed this conjecture.

Geometric complexity measures of the five models are shown in Table 19.3 for each sample size. First, note that the geometric complexity of GCMcv is greater than that of PRTcv (7.56 vs. 6.16, 12.39 vs. 10.98). These differences must be due to the functional form dimension of model complexity because both models have the same number of parameters. Second, the complexity difference between GCMcv and GCMcvg, which differ by one parameter (g), was greater than or about equal to that between GCMc and GCMv, which differ by four parameters (3.53 vs. 1.94 for $n = 20$ and 4.33 vs. 5.16 for $n = 100$). Upon first encounter, this might seem odd. One might have expected that differences in complexity would increase as the number of parameters between models increased. This relationship

TABLE 19.2 *Model recovery performance (%) of the five selection methods to the simulated data*

Model Fitted:	PRT cv	GCMc	GCMv (true)	GCMcv	GCMcvg
Sample size $n = 20$					
ML	10	0	0	0	93
AIC	4	34	50	10	2
BIC	2	66	29	2	1
CV	11	25	37	10	17
MDL	2	9	89	0	0
Sample size $n = 100$					
ML	0	0	0	0	100
AIC	0	0	85	15	0
BIC	0	4	92	4	0
CV	1	1	58	13	27
MDL	0	1	99	0	0

Note: For each row and each model fitted, the percentage of samples in which the particular model was selected under the given method is shown. For each sample size, a thousand samples were generated from GCMv.

TABLE 19.3 *Geometric complexity measures of the five categorization models*

Model:	PRTcv	GCMc	GCMv	GCMcv	GCMcvg
No. of parameters:	6	1	5	6	7
$n = 20$	6.16	1.72	3.66	7.56	11.09
$n = 100$	10.98	2.53	7.69	12.39	16.72

Note: In calculating geometric complexity measures, the range of each parameter was restricted to the following: $0 < v_k < 1$, $k = 1, ..., 6$, satisfying $\sum v_k = 1$, and $0 < c, g < 5$.

holds for AIC and BIC, which make the simplifying assumption that all parameters contribute equally to model complexity. MDL, in contrast, makes no such assumption. Each parameter contributes to the model's geometric complexity in relation to the function it performs in the model (e.g. the extent to which it aids in fitting data).

In summary, the above simulation results demonstrate the importance of using a generalizability measure in model selection to avoid choosing an unnecessarily complex model. MDL's superiority over the other selection methods was not only demonstrated, but shown to be due to its superior measure of complexity. Finally, the ability to calculate independently the complexity of a model enables one to learn how much the models under consideration differ in complexity, not just which model should be preferred.

Selecting among qualitative models

Application of any of the preceding selection methods requires that the models are quantitative models, each defined as a parametric family of probability distributions. Yet many theories of cognition have not been formalized to this degree. In this final section of this chapter, we introduce some new work

that extends MDL to select among these so-called qualitative models, which make only ordinal prediction among conditions. We sketch out the basic idea, and then provide an application example.

An example of a qualitative model would be a model of word recognition that states that lexical decision response times will be faster to high-frequency than low-frequency words, but these models make few statements about the magnitude of the time difference between frequency conditions, how frequency is related to response latency (e.g. linearly or logarithmically), or the shape of the response-time distribution. The axiomatic theory of judgment and decision-making is another example of qualitative modeling (e.g. Fishburn, 1982). The theory is formulated in rigorous mathematical language and makes precise predictions about choice behavior given a set of hypothetical gambles, but lacks an error theory. Without one, it is not possible to express the axiomatic theory as a parametric family of probability distributions.

Pseudo-probabilistic MDL approach

The 'pseudo-probabilistic' approach (Grunwald, 1999) for selecting among qualitative models derives a selection criterion that is similar to the

MDL criterion for quantitative models, but it is a formulation that is closer to the original spirit of the MDL principle (Li & Vitanyi, 1997), which states:

> Given a data set D and a model M, the description length of the data, $DL_M(D)$, is given by the sum of (a) the description length of the data when encoded with help of the model, $DL(D|M)$, and (b) the description length of the model itself, $DL(M)$: $DL_M(D) = DL(D|M) + DL(M)$. Among a set of competing models, the best model is the one that minimizes $DL_M(D)$.

The above MDL principle is broad enough to include the MDL criterion for quantitative models as a specific instantiation. The first lack-of-fit term of the quantitative criterion $(-\ln f(y|w^*))$ can be seen as $DL(D|M)$, whereas the second and third terms

$$\left(\frac{k}{2} \ln \frac{n}{2\pi} + \int dw \sqrt{\det I(w)}\right)$$

represent geometric complexity as $DL(M)$. Likewise, a computable criterion that implements the above principle can be obtained with the pseudo-probabilistic approach. It is derived from the Kraft-inequality theorem in coding theory (Li & Vitanyi, 1997: 74). The theorem proves that one can always associate arbitrary models with their 'equivalent' probability distributions in a procedure called *entropification* (Grunwald, 1999).

MDL criterion for qualitative models

Entropification proceeds as follows. We first 'construct' a parametric family of probability distributions for a given qualitative model in the following form:

$$p(y = (y_1, ..., y_m) | w) = \exp\left(-w\sum_{i=1}^{m} \text{Err}\right.$$
$$\left.(y_i - y_{i,\text{prd}})\right) \Big/ Z(w)$$

In the equation, $\text{Err}(x)$ is an error function that measures performance of the model's prediction, $y_{i,\text{prd}}$, such as $\text{Err}(x) = |x|$ or x^2, w is a scalar parameter, and $Z(w)$ is the normalizing factor defined as

$$z(w) = \sum_{yi} ... \sum_{ym} \exp\left(-w\sum_{i=1}^{m} \text{Err}(y_i - y_{i,\text{prd}})\right).$$

The above formulation requires that each observation y_i be represented by a discrete variable that takes on a finite number of possible values representing the model's qualitative (e.g. ordinal) predictions.

Once a suitable error function, $\text{Err}(x)$, is chosen, the above probability distribution function is then used to fit observed data, and the best-fitting parameter w^* is sought by MLE. The description length of the data encoded with the help of the model is

then obtained by taking the minus logarithm of the maximum likelihood (ML):

$$DL(DIM) = -\ln p(y|w^*)$$

The second term, $DL(M)$, the description length of the model itself, is obtained simply by counting the number of different data patterns the model can account for and then taking the logarithm of the resulting number. Putting these together, the desired MDL criterion for a qualitative model is given by

$$MDL_{\text{qual}} = w^* \sum_{i=1}^{m} \text{Err}(y_{i,\text{obs}} - y_{i,\text{pro}}(w^*))$$
$$+ \ln Z(w^*) + \ln N$$

where N is the number of all possible data patterns or data sets that the model predicts and ln is the logarithm of base e.

Application example

Suppose we wish to compare two fictitious models of word recognition. The models make ordinal predictions about lexical decision times (faster or slower) depending on the values of particular factors. Model M_1 assumes that there are two factors that determine response time: word frequency (high or low) and lexical neighborhood (sparse or dense). Further, this model predicts that the second factor matters only when the word is high in frequency. The model can be represented as a decision tree and is shown in the left panel of Figure 19.2. Note in the figure that the model makes its predictions in terms of three types of outcomes, Y1 to Y3, each of which takes a binary value of S (slow response) or F (fast response). The number of all possible data patterns that are consistent with the model is then eight $(= 2^3)$. Accordingly, the complexity of this model is $DL(M_1) = \ln(8) = 2.08$ ebits.

Model M_2 is a three-factor model that is identical to model M_1 except that it presupposes an additional factor will influence response time: word length (short or long). Predictions of M_2 are somewhat more elaborate, as shown in the right panel of Figure 19.2. Intuitively this model is more complex than M_1. This is indeed the case: $DL(M_2) = \ln(2^5) = 3.47$ ebits.

Artificial data were generated from each of the two models in an experiment that crossed all three factors, thereby yielding a set of eight binary strings, $y = (y_1, ..., y_8)$, where $y_i = $ 'S' or 'F'. The number of all possible data patterns that can be observed in this design is therefore $2^8 = 256$, only a small portion of which is consistent with either model, 8 for M_1 and 32 for M_2. It turns out that four of the eight patterns of M_1 were also consistent with M_2. A data set of eight binary strings was generated from each model, and random noise was added to

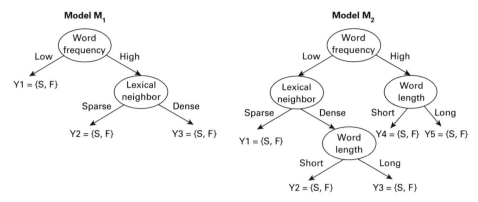

Figure 19.2 *Two qualitative models of semantic priming make ordinal predictions on lexical decision times (faster or slower) based on two factors (M_1) or three factors (M_2).*

TABLE 19.4 *Model recovery rates (%) for two qualitative models*

		Selection criterion			
		DL(D|M)		MDL_{qual}	
P(random flip)	Data from:	M_1	M_2	M_1	M_2
	Model fitted:				
0.0	M_1	100	0	100	0
	M_2	0	100	0	100
0.1	M_1	66	2	93	10
	M_2	34	98	7	90
0.2	M_1	39	5	84	31
	M_2	61	95	16	69
0.5	M_1	12	10	62	60
	M_2	88	90	38	40

Note: For each row and each model fitted, the percentage of samples in which the particular model was selected under the given selection criterion is shown. A thousand samples were generated from each model by adding random noise to each binary string of a given population vector, $y = (y_1, ..., y_8)$ where $y_i =$ 'S' or 'F'. The probability of random flip is indicated on the leftmost column. The population vectors used were $y = $ (S, S, S, S, F, S, S) for M_1 and $y = $ (S, S, S, F, F, S, F, S) for M_2.

the data by flipping the value (S → F or F → S) of each of the eight binary strings with a pre-specified probability of 0, 0.1, 0.2, or 0.5. One thousand samples were generated from each model at each of the noise levels. The two models were then fitted to each simulated sample separately, and the parameter w^* that minimizes DL(D|M) (i.e. first two terms of MDL_{qual}) was sought, under the error function of Err$(x) = 0$ if no prediction error and 1 otherwise. The model's MDL_{qual} was then obtained by combining this result with its complexity measure, 2.08 or 3.47. The model that minimizes the criterion was selected.

The simulation results are summarized in Table 19.4. The table shows the model recovery rate of MDL_{qual} across the four noise levels. For comparison, results under DL(D|M), solely a goodness-of-fit measure, are also shown. Of interest is the ability of each selection method to recover the model that generated the data. A good selection method should discern which model generated the data, and not exhibit a bias for simpler or more complex models. Errors are evidence of such a bias, and reveal the direction in which the method overgeneralizes (e.g. to more or less complex models).

As expected, in the absence of random noise, both models were recovered perfectly 100% of the time under DL(D|M) and also under MDL_{qual}. As the level of noise increased, however, selection under DL(D|M) exhibited a typical pattern of overfitting, selecting the more complex model (M_2) when the data were in fact generated by the simpler model (M_1). For example, at P(random flip) $= 0.2$, when the data were generated from M_1 (true model),

M_1 was selected only 39% of the time. In contrast, when MDL_{qual} was used, M_1 was selected 84% of the time. The superior model recovery of MDL_{qual} is also evident at the 0.1 noise level. Note that when the data were nothing but random noise (P(random flip) = 0.5), MDL_{qual} preferred the simple model (M_1) to the complex one (M_2), in accord with the principle of Occam's razor.

In short, the preliminary investigation presented here suggests that the MDL-based, pseudo-probabilistic approach is suitable for comparing qualitative models, thereby extending MDL (see Karabatsos, 2001, for a Bayesian approach to selecting qualitative models). Obviously, much more work is needed before the approach becomes fully functional. For instance, the approach should be able to deal with non-binary decision-tree models and also non-binary data, even models that cannot be expressed in decision trees, and finally, large data sets.

CONCLUSION

If there is one thing that the reader should take away from this chapter, it is that models should be judged on their generalizability, not how well they fit one particular data sample, or even a set of data samples when the parameters are adjusted for each fit. The vexing problem of how to choose among competing quantitative models is not unique to psychology. It has been studied in depth in related fields, such as statistics, engineering and computer science, and in each field generalizability has emerged as a guiding principle. Model selection tools such as MDL were developed with this goal in mind. Details on how to use it can be found elsewhere (Hansen & Yu, 2001). Our purpose here was to introduce the rationale behind generalizability and demonstrate how it is implemented in MDL. This method of model evaluation and selection, especially when it is combined with a skillful application of various model development strategies (Shiffrin & Nobel, 1997), should aid in advancing the field of cognitive modeling.

ACKNOWLEDGEMENTS

This chapter draws on prior publications by the authors, especially Myung and Pitt (2001) and Pitt et al. (2002). Preliminary results of the simulation dealing with qualitative models were presented at the 2001 Annual Mathematical Psychology Meeting held in Providence, RI, and at the Third International Conference on Cognitive Science (ICCS2001) held in Beijing, China, and were published in the Proceedings of the latter conference.

The authors were supported by NIMH Grant MH57472.

NOTES

1 An exception is the type of network models in which specific psychological principles are formalized explicitly in the network architecture. An example of this type is localist connectionist networks (Grainger & Jacobs, 1998) such as ALCOVE (Kruschke, 1992) and TRACE (McClelland & Elman, 1986).

2 Defining what a true model is can be a tricky business. For example, suppose that artificial data are generated from a model equation, $y = \ln(x + 10)$, there are multiple models that are consistent with the data: (a) $y = \ln(x + w_1)$ (M_1: $w_1 = 10$); (b) $y = w_1 \ln(x + w_2)$ (M_2: $w_1 = 1, w_2 = 10$); (c) $y = w_1 \ln(w_2 x + w_3) + w_4 x + w_5$ (M_3: $w_1 = 1, w_2 = 1, w_3 = 10, w_4 = 0, w_5 = 0$), etc. A true model is defined as the one, among all the models that are consistent with the data, that has the fewest number of parameters. In the above example, M_1 should be the true model.

3 One 'ebit' is defined in this chapter as the coding capacity of a system that can transmit e (= 2.781828..., the natural number) distinct messages in an unambiguous manner.

REFERENCES

Akaike, H. (1973). Information theory and an extension of the maximum likelihood principle. In B. N. Petrox & F. Caski (Eds.), *Second International Symposium on Information Theory* (pp. 267–281). Budapest: Akademiai Kiado.

Ashby, F. G., & Maddox, W. T. (1993). Relations between prototype, exemplar and decision bound models of categorization. *Journal of Mathematical Psychology, 37*, 372–400.

Bamber, D., & van Santen, J. P. H. (1985). How many parameters can a model have and still be testable? *Journal of Mathematical Psychology, 29*, 443–473.

Bellman, R. (1961). *Adaptive control processes: a guided tour*. Princeton, NJ: Princeton University Press.

Brent, M. (1999). Speech segmentation and word discovery: a computational perspective. *Trends in Cognitive Science, 3*, 294–301.

Browne, M. W. (2000). Cross-validation methods. *Journal of Mathematical Psychology, 44*, 108–132.

Burnham, K. P., & Anderson, D. R. (1998). *Model selection and inference: a practical information-theoretic approach*. New York: Springer.

Busemeyer, J. R., & Wang, Y.-M. (2000). Model comparisons and model selections based on generalization criterion methodology. *Journal of Mathematical Psychology, 44*, 171–189.

Casella, G., & Berger, R. (2002). *Statistical inference* (2nd ed., Chap. 7). Pacific Grove, CA: Duxberry.

Elman, J. L., Bates, E. A., Johnson, M. H., Karmiloff-Smith, A., Parisi, D., & Plunkett, K. (1996). Rethinking innateness: *a connectionist perspective on development*. Cambridge, MA: MIT Press.

Fishburn, P. C. (1982). *The foundations of expected utility*. Dordrecht: Reidel.

Gescheider, G. A. (1985). *Psychophysics: method, theory, and application*. Mahwah, NJ: Erlbaum.

Gilks, W. R., Richardson, S., & Spiegelhalter, D. J. (1996). *Markov chain Monte Carlo in Practice*. London: Chapman & Hall.

Gluck, M. A. (1991). Stimulus generalization and representation in adaptive network models of category learning. *Psychological Science*, 2, 50–55.

Grainger, J., & Jacobs, A. M. (1998). *Localist connectionist approaches to human cognition*. Mahwah, NJ: Erlbaum.

Grunwald, P. (1999). Viewing all models as 'probabilistic'. *Proceedings of the Twelfth Annual Conference on Computational Learning Theory (COLT' 99)*, Santa Cruz, CA.

Grunwald, P. (2000). The minimum description length principle. *Journal of Mathematical Psychology*, 44, 133–152.

Grunwald, P. (2002). *Minimum description length and maximum probability*. Boston, MA: Kluwer.

Hansen, M. H., & Yu, B. (2001). Model selection and the principle of minimum description length. *Journal of the American Statistical Association*, 96, 746–774.

Jacobs, A. M., & Grainger, J. (1994). Models of visual word recognition – sampling the state of the art. *Journal of Experimental Psychology: Human Perception and Performance*, 29, 1311–1334.

Joanisse, M. F., & Seidenberg, M. S. (1999). Impairments in verb morphology after brain injury: a connectionist model. *Proceedings of the National Academy of Sciences of the USA*, 96, 7592–7597.

Johnson, R. A., & Wichern, D. W. (1998). Applied *multivariate statistical analysis* (pp. 234–235). Upper Saddle River, NJ: Prentice-Hall.

Karabatsos, G. (2001). The Rasch model, additive conjoint measurement and new models of probabilistic measurement theory. *Journal of Applied Measurement*, 2, 389–423.

Knowlton, B. J. (1999). What can neuropsychology tell us about category learning? *Trends in Cognitive Science*, 3, 123–124.

Knowlton, B. J., & Squire, L. R. (1993). The learning of categories: parallel brain systems for item memory and category knowledge. *Science*, 262, 1747–1749.

Kruschke, J. K. (1992). ALCOVE: an exemplar-based connectionist model of category learning. *Psychological Review*, 99, 22–44.

Li, M., & Vitanyi, P. (1997). *An introduction to Kolmogorov complexity and its applications*. New York: Springer.

Linhart, H., & Zucchini, W. (1986). *Model selection*. New York: Wiley.

Luce, R. D. (1959). *Individual choice behavior*. New York: Wiley.

McClelland, J. L., & Elman, J. L. (1986). The TRACE model of speech perception. *Cognitive Psychology*, 18, 1–86.

McKinley, S. C., & Nosofsky, R. M. (1995). Investigations of exemplar and decision bound models in large, ill-defined category structures. *Journal of Experimental Psychology: Human Perception and Performance*, 21, 128–148.

Moody, J. E. (1992). The effective number of parameters: an analysis of generalization and regularization in nonlinear modeling. In J. E. Moody, S. J. Hanson, & R. P. Lippmann (Eds.), *Advances in neural information processing systems* (Vol. 4, pp. 847–854). Cambridge, MA: MIT Press.

Murata, N., Yoshizawa, S., & Amari, S.-I. (1994). Network information criterion: determining the number of hidden units for an artificial neural network model. *IEEE Transactions on Neural Networks*, 5, 865–872.

Myung, I. J., Balasubramanian, V., & Pitt, M. A. (2000). Counting probability distributions: differential geometry and model selection. *Proceedings of the National Academy of Sciences of the USA*, 97, 11170–11175.

Myung, I. J., Forster, M., & Browne, M. W. (2000). Special issue on model selection. *Journal of Mathematical Psychology*, 44, 1–2.

Myung, I. J., & Pitt, M. A. (2001). Mathematical modeling. In J. Wixted (ed.), *Stevens' handbook of experimental psychology: Vol. IV. Methodology* (3rd ed., pp. 429–459). New York: Wiley.

Nosofsky, R. M. (1986). Attention, similarity and the identification-categorization relationship. *Journal of Experimental Psychology: General*, 115, 39–57.

Nosofsky, R. M., & Palmeri, T. J. (1997). An exemplar-based random walk model of speeded classification. *Psychological Review*, 104, 266–300.

Nosofsky, R. M., & Zaki, S. (1998). Dissociation between categorization and recognition in amnesic and normal individuals: an exemplar-based interpretation. *Psychological Science*, 9, 247–255.

Pitt, M. A., Myung, I. J., & Zhang, S. (2002). Toward a method of selecting among computational models of cognition. *Psychological Review*, 109, 472–491.

Popper, K. R. (1959). *The logic of scientific discovery*. New York: Basic Books.

Ratcliff, R., Spieler, D., & McKoon, G. (2000). Explicitly modeling the effects of aging on response time. *Psychonomic Bulletin and Review*, 7, 1–25.

Reed, S. K. (1972). Pattern recognition and categorization. *Cognitive Psychology*, 3, 382–407.

Rissanen, J. (1983). A universal prior for integers and estimation by minimum description length. *Annals of Statistics*, 11, 416–431.

Rissanen, J. (1989). *Stochastic complexity in statistical inquiries*. Singapore: World Scientific.

Rissanen, J. (1996). Fisher information and stochastic complexity. *IEEE Transactions on Information Theory*, 42, 40–47.

Roberts, S., & Pashler, H. (2000). How persuasive is a good fit? A comment on theory testing in psychology. *Psychological Review*, 107, 358–367.

Schwarz, G. (1978). Estimating the dimension of a model. *Annals of Statistics*, 6, 461–464.

Shiffrin, R. M., & Nobel, P. A. (1997). The art of model development and testing. *Behavioral Research Methods, Instruments and Computers*, 29, 6–14.

Shiffrin, R. M., & Steyvers, M. (1997). A model for recognition memory: REM – retrieving effectively from memory. *Psychonomic Bulletin and Review, 4,* 145–166.

Shin, H. J., & Nosofsky, R. M. (1992). Similarity-scaling studies of dot-pattern classification and recognition. *Journal of Experimental Psychology: General, 121,* 278–304.

Stone, M. (1974). Cross-validatory choice and assessment of statistical predictions (with discussion). *Journal of Royal Statistical Society, Series B, 36,* 111–147.

Wixted, J. T., & Ebbesen, E. B. (1991). On the form of forgetting. *Psychological Science, 2,* 409–415.

Index